# EVALUATION STUDIES REVIEW ANNUAL
## Volume 3

# Evaluation Studies

## EDITORIAL ADVISORY BOARD

# Review Annual

# Evaluation Studies

# Review Annual

Volume 3                    1978

Edited by

# Thomas D. Cook
# Marlyn L. Del Rosario
# Karen M. Hennigan
# Melvin M. Mark
# William M.K. Trochim

SAGE PUBLICATIONS  /  BEVERLY HILLS  /  LONDON

## DEDICATION

*To Philip Brickman and Donald T. Campbell, two outstanding scholars and human beings, whose concern for excellence and growth made the Social Psychology Program at Northwestern so exciting and humane.*

H
/
E77
vol. 3
1978

*For information address:*

BT 4072-79    12-22-78

**SAGE** PUBLICATIONS, INC.
275 South Beverly Drive
Beverly Hills, California 90212

**SAGE** PUBLICATIONS LTD
28 Banner Street
London EC1Y 8QE, England

Printed in the United States of America

International Standard Book Number 0-8039-1075-4

Library of Congress Catalog Card No. 76-15865

FIRST PRINTING

# CONTENTS

# ABOUT THE EDITORS

THOMAS D. COOK is currently Professor of Psychology at Northwestern University. A member of the American Psychological Association, the Society for the Psychological Study of Social Issues, and the Society of Experimental Social Psychologists, Dr. Cook has published over 25 articles in various publications. He is also the author of *"Sesame Street" Revisited*, and the forthcoming book, *The Design and Analysis of Quasi-Experiments for Field Settings*. Dr. Cook also serves on the editorial boards of seven journals, including *Evaluation Quarterly*, *Evaluation* (Magazine), *Journal of Personality and Social Psychology*, and *Law and Politics Review*, and is a consultant to over 15 government agencies, corporations and foundations. Dr. Cook received his B.A. degree from Oxford University and his Ph.D. from Stanford University.

MARLYN L. DEL ROSARIO is a doctoral candidate in Social Psychology at Northwestern University. She received her B.A. in Psychology from the University of the Philippines, and has an M.A. in Social Psychology from the Ateneo de Manila University (Philippines). She has done evaluation research in the areas of education, population, and criminal justice. Her current research interests include organizational commitment, the effects of television, and social science methodology particularly in relation to policy-oriented research. Ms. Del Rosario has written for population publications such as *Initiatives in Population*, and *Options for Policy and Practice*.

KAREN M. HENNIGAN is an Assistant Professor at the University of Southern California. She recently received a Ph.D. in Social Psychology from Northwestern University and spent a post-doctoral year doing policy and evaluation research there. She has worked on evaluations in the areas of health, criminal justice, and communications. Her research interests include methods for planning and conducting utilizable evaluations, and the social psychology of distributive justice.

MELVIN M. MARK is a doctoral candidate in Social Psychology at Northwestern University. He received his B.A. from the University of Nebraska—Lincoln. Mr. Mark's research interests include social science methodology, the social effects of economic shifts, and evaluation research, especially in the areas of education and communications. His publications include a chapter on design issues in evaluation research.

WILLIAM M.K. TROCHIM is a doctoral candidate in the Methodology and Evaluation Research program of the Department of Psychology, Northwestern University. He has a background in social psychology and in the evaluation of therapeutic interventions in mental health settings. Currently, he is active in human services and mental health evaluation and in the development of evaluation strategies, especially time-series analysis. Mr. Trochim received a B.A. from Mundelein College and an M.A. in Psychology from Southern Connecticut State College.

# Introduction

*Thomas D. Cook*

## UTILIZATION, KNOWLEDGE-BUILDING, AND INSTITUTIONALIZATION: THREE CRITERIA BY WHICH EVALUATION RESEARCH CAN BE EVALUATED

When Judgment Day arrives for evaluation research, by which criteria might it be evaluated? Two come most readily to mind. First, the Lord may enquire about the extent to which evaluation research produced findings which were profitably used in debates about policy actions; and second, He may ask whether evaluation research advanced our knowledge of methodological or substantive matters in different areas of the social sciences. A third criterion also comes to mind, but one which is perhaps oriented to postponing Judgment Day rather than to giving a reckoning on that day. In any event this criterion concerns the extent to which evaluation research has become institutionalized. Though many other criteria can be advanced, it seems that the degree of success in utilization, knowledge-building, and institutionalization should be considered among the criteria by which evaluation research is evaluated.

How these criteria should be weighted is a different issue. And as we nearly always see as practitioners of evaluation, different constituencies may implicitly or explicitly assign different weights to the subset of criteria on which they agree. Our guess is that most officials of the legislative and executive branches assign utilization the greatest weight; that many employees of contract research firms and university research centers assign more weight than others to institutionalization; and that many scholars give knowledge-building a higher priority than do either government officials or persons whose salary or professional reputation depends on evaluation research. Of course, there are many exceptions to the above generalization; and many persons from each of the constituencies we have identified are interested in all three criteria. Moreover, some persons have links to more than one constituency. Our statements about the different priorities of different constituencies are therefore somewhat crude and subject to empirical tests. Nonetheless, we believe them to be warranted, and if they are true we shall later see that they might have important implications.

## UTILIZATION

Utilization would probably be most widely accepted as the single most important criterion of the success of evaluation research. Defining utilization is difficult, but it is clear that in a political democracy like ours utilization should include a role for evaluation results in the debates from which changes in policy or procedure are decided on. The nature of this role is not clear, and might vary from being uncited background information in pre-debate deliberations by one of the parties through to being cited in formal debates as one of the crucial issues on which a decision rests. The absence of some simple "unit of utilization" makes all utilization research difficult and the results particularly dependent on the assumptions implied by particular definitions of utilization.

Within the utilization research of our day, most effort seems to have been devoted to identifying sources of resistance to the utilization of evaluation findings. Some of the more important of these sources include: poorly designed evaluations that are not addressed to specific policy issues; policy issues that change during an evaluation; evaluation results that are not considered credible, perhaps because they were generated by "outsiders" or institutions without a sterling reputation; public officials' unwillingness to understand or use evaluations that they did not really want to see conducted; results which appear to threaten the interests of operating agencies at all levels; results which are not disseminated in comprehensible form to potential users, etc. Perhaps the explanatory concept that has gained most visibility is Nathan Caplan's concept of two cultures: A knowledge-generating culture interested in truth, validity, and goal-oriented rationality; and a potential knowledge-utilization culture interested in turf, pragmatic action, and a process-oriented rationality which stresses the feasible over the desirable, the timely over the accurate, and the self-protective over the true. Being two cultures with different needs, the reasoning goes, communication between them is difficult and the products of the knowledge-generating culture are at best marginally relevant to the perceived needs of the presumed knowledge-using culture.

The literature on utilization is in general not very impressive in either its form or its findings. On the one hand, the frequent references to low utilization incline us to believe that, even if the utilization researchers are perennial Cassandras, there must be some reason for their pessimistic belief that much more useful knowledge is being generated than used. On the other hand, the quality and imaginativeness of most (but not all) utilization studies leaves something to be desired. This makes it more difficult to gain a well-founded estimate of the magnitude of underutilization than it is to gain a less precise sense that there is some underutilization.

Since utilization issues will play a crucial role in evaluating evaluation research, and since utilization studies will be one major determinant of impressions about the frequency of utilization, it is worth pondering how utilization studies might be improved. Definitional concerns are clearly of paramount importance, and I would like to cite two recent cases that would not be coded as utilization though they clearly seem to be. The first is a case where the formal evaluation was very positive in tone, but an analysis of the evaluation by a panel of outside experts concluded that the program was less successful than the evaluator claimed and that feasible alternatives could be generated for meeting the same goals more efficiently. The decision-makers were swayed by the recommendations of the outside panel, and cut off their financial support of the program. However, the decision-makers deliberately decided not to use the evaluation results or the comments upon them in their justification for cutting off funding for fear of being engaged in a debate about how effective the program was. Instead, they cited that the program did not fit new agency priorities hoping to avoid all issues of effectiveness. To look at the formal record in this case would not give much indication of utilization, and it would appear as though the original positive evaluation results were deliberately overlooked or flaunted. However, it is clear to us that the recommendations of the expert panel of evaluators who checked over the initial evaluation played an important role in the decision that was eventually made.

Many definitions of utilization are excessively decision-dependent, as though the only valid way evaluation research information should be used is in making decisions about the level of funding for programs and projects or about the distribution of resources within a program or project. Such definitions would not include as utilization such instances as the following which we have witnessed: a past and long-forgotten evaluation being invoked by persons designing a project in the same substantive area but not for the same program; an evaluation that was not used in policy making since the relevant issues changed before it became available but which has nonetheless been widely used for teaching purposes; or an evaluation that lay gathering dust on a shelf until it was later used by a scholar in a creative synthesizing analysis of several separate evaluations of the same program.

It is important, even within the context of a decision-oriented definition of evaluation, not to adopt too narrow a time perspective. If the evaluation of, say, a local magnet school is not used to modify practices within that school next year, this does not mean that the results will not be a part of the total evidence, including further evaluations, that will be used in the future, or that the evaluation of this magnet school will not form part of the later corpus of evaluations of magnet schools in general that is used in decision-making. Moreover, it is not starry-eyed, we think, to wonder where the ideas for new projects and programs come from, and to suggest that the weight of scientific evidence accumulated during one generation is taught as the conventional wisdom to persons who will later become decision-makers and will inadvertently carry into their jobs this wisdom and any personal reactions they may have to it. This may affect their decisions about what to fund. Our guess is that anyone educated in a social science at a graduate school in the 1970s will carry out—largely because of evaluation results—a sense of the difficulty of implementing social change that cohorts in the 1950s and 1960s did not have. In particular, they are likely to have a sense of the limitations of psychotherapy and of many types of compensatory eduction programs or forms of police surveillance, and they will be mindful of the intractability of poverty.

However, the most difficult problem with the research on utilization is the paucity (but not absence) of bold alternatives to a model of utilization which stresses having a utilization plan in the contract proposal and disseminating an abbreviated form of the results to identified interested parties to whom the evaluators are available for clarification. While we heartily endorse studies of particularly successful and unsuccessful cases of utilization, nonutilization, and the sorely lacking instances of misutilization, tests of new models of utilization seem to us to be needed more than case studies which describe and analyze current utilization. We shall outline one alternative later, but the need to identify and test many alternatives is more important than the testing of this particular one. For like it or not, utilization will probably be the most important single criterion for evaluating evaluation research, and innovative research on utilization is badly needed to test ways to increase utilization, however defined, and to decrease misutilization.

All the articles in the first section of this paper deal with utilization, some using this term in the title and others not. Those that do not place evaluation in a policy and political context out of which decisions about utilization derive. The articles on evaluation in the health field deal with utilization in a different way since most were chosen to deal with factors that have been predicted to become more salient once we have a national health insurance program. Here the presumption is that evaluations are more likely to be used because they deal with sectors of society that are likely to expand once a major political decision is taken—e.g., ambulatory hospital care, hospital cost-containment strategies, the expanded use of non-MDs in health service delivery, the expansion of preventive public health campaigns, and issues of long-term care. Utilization is also implicitly addressed in our stress throughout this volume of reviews and re-analyses of multiple evaluations of the same program rather than single evaluations. Presumably reviews, which are becoming increasingly more used as evaluations accumulate, have fewer problems of credibility than single studies, and so cannot be dismissed for particular lacunae as single studies invariably can.

## KNOWLEDGE-BUILDING

The knowledge generated by evaluation research is in many ways impressive. It is likely, for instance, that evaluation has provided an impetus to developing new methodological insights, for it has been the laboratory for testing out new ideas about field research methods that would still be available for other research purposes if there were no organized field called evaluation. The advances have been most noteworthy, we think, in areas concerned with the implementation of randomized experiments, the design of quasi-experiments, the analysis of nonequivalent control group designs, path analysis, systems for monitoring field operations including the delivery of a treatment, and systems for increasing the validity (and reliability) of data collection. Gains in qualitative methods have, in general, been less pronounced, but nonetheless they have been enough for qualitative methodologists to join with quantitative methodologists in claiming that they may have been the major beneficiaries of evaluation research, as well as the major contributors to it.

It would be wrong to believe that substantive gains in knowledge-building have not been made from evaluation research. For instance, in the mental health area, reviews of evaluations tend to suggest that short-term focused therapies are superior to more analytic therapies in alleviating certain kinds of symptoms; in early childhood education, focused projects with explicit cognitive goals based on repetition tend to be more effective than other types of projects in increasing achievement; at present, the labor force response of men to a guaranteed income seems to be less elastic than that of women; and public information campaigns do not, in general, seem to have much aggregate impact unless personal contact of some sort is added to media contact. At a more theoretical level, it is clear from the evaluations of school desegregation and integration that the contact hypothesis is, in its simplest form, incorrect and that prolonged contact does not invariably reduce stereotyping and prejudice. It is also the case that theories of labor force participation that stressed financial incentive as the major cause of participation are too simple. Finally, evaluations have suggested that theories of deterrence are not complete unless they incorporate notions relating to the salience of the deterrence and the public enforcement of sanctions against offenders.

We are not claiming that these findings were not available before evaluation, and we would not deny that the major (but not sole) substantive impact of evaluations has been to add to evidence that was already available, thereby fixing the conventional wisdom better or shifting the weight of evidence onto one side or the other in substantive debates. These are not trivial contributions, however, since the knowledge we need to have about social events and particular causal connections among events needs to be a knowledge built on multiple replication. (Whether evaluation is the most efficient means of replicating and extending theoretical propositions in field tests is another issue. While it is one means, it is not necessarily the most efficient one.)

An important corollary of the knowledge-building aspect of evaluation research is that its effectiveness in this domain cannot be ascertained after a period of systematic research as short as, say, a decade. Persons interested in knowledge-building do not focus on the next decision that an administrator has to make. Instead, they aim to *accumulate* a set of replicated findings that can be subsumed into some form of pattern. This pattern is continually being modified, and is judged in terms of truth value, parsimony, and usefulness to those who later choose to use it in their more practical work. Often, a considerable time lapses between when a pattern is first discerned, then rigorously tested, and finally comes to enter the conventional social science wisdom where it is used by whoever desires to do so. To evaluation researchers who value knowledge-building the slogan "We are working for 20 years from now, and not today" is no idle slogan.

This volume stresses knowledge-building in several ways. First, in the section devoted to methodology; second, in the stress we have placed on integrative reviews of the evaluation literature in a particular substantive area, for these often finish with theory-like statements of the form: These are the conditions under which a given effect of policy relevance comes about; and third, knowledge-building is stressed by the inclusion of modified replications that provide a cumulative record (the Negative Income Tax Experiments), debates between protagonists (on accepting the null hypothesis or the effects of Follow Through), and by one reanalysis of the conventional wisdom (on psychotherapy). Modified replications, public debates, and reinterpretations of the past record characterize progress in knowledge-building in most theoretical disciplinary contexts as well as evaluation.

## INSTITUTIONALIZATION

The success of social movements is sometimes measured by the number of their adherents and the degree to which the movement becomes institutionalized. For a research effort, institutionalization implies being integrated into the social structure of the science establishment, gaining a generally unquestioned acceptance as legitimate in the eyes of funders and scholars, and being taken seriously whenever issues arise that seem to affect the interests of persons who characterize themselves as belonging to the institution—in this case, "evaluators."

Being institutionalized means that a movement is relatively immune to criticism and attack from establishment sources because the movement is part of the establishment and not a contender to join the establishment or a perennial outsider to it. Being institutionalized also reduces the degree to which one is held accountable, for one's existence is accepted and not questioned. If this brief characterization is correct, it clearly illustrates why institutionalization is an important criterion for evaluating evaluation research: from one perspective, a movement is presumably most likely to be institutionalized if it is useful in some way—an indicator of goal efficacy; from another (more cynical?) perspective, institutionalization is an indicator of success since it protects against critics and postpones Judgment Day, whatever the verdict might be on that day.

The signs that evaluation research has become increasingly institutionalized over the last decade are impressive. There is the obvious fact that in some agencies a given percentage of program funds has to be spent for evaluation purposes; there are new professional organizations like the Evaluation Research Society and the Council for Applied Social Research; there are ever more professional journals devoted to evaluation as well as monograph series; there are calls for setting standards for evaluators and hence for licensing; funds are allocated for training programs in evaluation and centers for evaluation have sprung up; managers in federal, state, and local government agencies call themselves evaluators or evaluation specialists as do employees of contract companies specializing in social science contract research; bureaus with evaluation in the title occur increasingly frequently at all levels of government; managers whose mandate is not explicitly evaluation relate the concept more and more to the programs they fund, for they have been told that evaluation is a priority; given their interests in oversight, Congressional aides debate evaluation issues and seem increasingly aware of the need to request and evaluate evaluation reports; finally, the General Accounting Office also seems to be more mindful of evaluation than it was, for it is obvious that the functions of evaluation overlap with the functions of the GAO.

This flurry of institutionalization should not be overestimated. In many government agencies there are individuals and offices that only pay lip service to the concept, largely because the persons involved have seen managerial fads come and go and they see evaluation as just another fad. Moreover, the term is used very loosely, and many of the activities which would have gone on anyway are now called "evaluation." In contract research firms, the primary commitment is usually to bringing in the funds rather than to evaluation per se, and were applied research priorities to change we suspect that the proposals reflecting these new priorities would come from many of the same persons who now write power over interdisciplinary endeavors like evaluation, and it is still unwise for an untenured faculty member to devote all of his or her research time to evaluation.

Perhaps the best test of the extent to which evaluation research is institutionalized will come if federal outlays decline in the future in real money terms, perhaps because of increasing voter concerns with taxation. Then the issue will be: Is evaluation one of those marginal luxuries which can be cut out to preserve the programs and projects deemed to be of most value; or is evaluation one of the key tools by which decisions are made about what gets trimmed to accommodate shrinking dollars. As long as Congress mandated more and more programs; as long as the size of the Federal bureaucracy was a political issue, preventing its growth and its own ability to monitor programs; as long as inflation and deficit spending kept the Federal coffers filled, evaluation could be afforded and was constrained to occur in an organizational environment where the bureaucracy proposed and the contract research firms and the universities disposed. Changes in the past formula may well lead to less funds, and we might see whether evaluation is cut on the presumption that it is only marginally "useful" or is retained or even increased as one of the tools to perform the cutting, pruning, or fostering of some programs.

Several aspects of using institutionalization as a measure of the success of evaluation need stressing. First, it is not an outcome-oriented measure, for the rational objective of evaluation has never been its own institutionalization. Rather, it is a pragmatic indicator of success, and even in a sense a "biological" indicator insofar as institutionalization is a viable survival-oriented response to the ever-present uncertainties associated with government-funded research. Second, the growing institutionalization of evaluation is associated with increasing elasticity in the definition of the term, and we were recently struck in one agency by the bizarre context in which the concept was deliberately and cynically used in order to justify activities of no obvious evaluative importance. The more broadly the concept is used, the more inclusive it is and the greater we suspect the chances are of institutionalization. But conversely, the more broadly it is used, the harder it may be to dissociate those evaluative activities that are useful from those that are not, and all evaluation activities may be tarred with the same brush. Third, the ever more vocal calls for setting educational or achievement standards for evaluators is worrysome. Though licensing is regularly used by professions to maintain standards, it is also used to control the supply of persons providing services. Thus, it is not always clear that licensing serves the "public interest" better than the financial interests of the licensed. And finally, the institutionalization of a service like evaluation at a certain level implies that a need for evaluation will continue to exist at about that level or more. One does not have to be Ivan Illich, or one of his disciples, to note that institutions sometimes deliberately or inadvertently create the needs to which their services are relevant. A fully institutionalized evaluation industry might be an industry producing too much evaluation.

We were not able to find many good papers on the institutionalization of evaluation research for inclusion in this volume. However, the section on "Evaluations in the 'Public Interest' " deals with issues that go beyond the scope of most government agencies and with examples and methods used by nonprofessional evaluators, such as journalists and members of public interest groups. Such studies are in many ways technically impressive, and are clearly linked to action implications.

## INTERRELATING UTILIZATION, KNOWLEDGE-BUILDING, AND INSTITUTIONALIZATION

No rigorous evaluation can be carried out at present of the extent to which evaluation research is institutionalized and leads to acceptable utilization rates and acceptable gains in abstract knowledge. However, it is reasonable to state that there has been more evidence of success in institutionalization and knowledge-building than there has been in the utilization of evaluation findings.

If this conclusion is correct, it has very important implications. One is that utilization is the most widely accepted single indicator of success, and high rates of underutilization are not hopeful signs that evaluation is accomplishing its major explicit objective. Another is that utilization is probably ever more important as a criterion to members of the legislative and executive branches of government than it is to evaluators or evaluation users from other constituencies. The members of the legislative and executive will probably also be the most influential persons in determining the resources that will be devoted to evaluation in the future. Consequently, evaluation is potentially vulnerable to charges of low utilization that come from the persons who are most responsible for the welfare of evaluation. The issue of institutionalization is important here, for a more fully institutionalized evaluation industry would be less vulnerable to the attack of underutilization though it would be far from invulnerable. If evaluation cannot be justified in terms of knowledge-building, then it has to institutionalize more and/or improve utilization.

It is not clear how utilization can be significantly increased with the current model of utilization that is implicitly followed—that is, a utilization plan is included in the evaluation proposal, and a brief summary of the evaluation results is later disseminated to potential users either by mail or in special dissemination meetings. This is not the place to explicate and critique the model. Suffice it to say here that it does not seem in most cases to be very successful. We need alternatives, many of them, and soon. We also need alternatives to the current model of research on utilization, with its apparently near-exclusive emphasis on case studies and with only sporadic integrative or innovative papers.

One striking alternative model of utilization has been suggested by Caplan and was presented to us orally in modified form by Cronbach. Briefly, the idea is to convene panels of experts in a given substantive area, persons who are sensitive to the methodological, substantive, and organizational constraints and opportunities that affect the interpretation and utilization of applied social science findings, including evaluation findings. The functions of such a body are open to specification, but they might include some of the following: analyzing completed evaluations to assess their validity both in terms of what is in the report and the way the findings fit in with other related findings in the particular substantive area—this should also give credibility to strong findings; calling completed evaluations and integrative analyses of related evaluations to the attention of very senior officials in operating agencies who can disseminate them within their own organization; calling evaluation results to the attention of interested constituencies who might want to use the evaluation results in public debates; analyzing evaluation plans to assess their technical feasibility and desirability as well as to test whether the questions seem policy-relevant and are not restricted to the parochial perspective of only one or two constituencies that might be affected by the research results. The important functions, in a nutshell, would be to improve the quality of research plans, to give credibility to some results and cast doubt on others, and to control the dissemination of results, even pressing for utilization where necessary. Such a body would obviously need to be independent, especially of operating agencies, and it would have to have its own staff for handling day-to-day operations. It could also serve other functions, perhaps even commissioning its own evaluations under some circumstances or commissioning reviews of several evaluations of similar programs or projects.

One advantage of a body of experts who assess the credibility of results and push for utilization is that the responsibility for utilization is taken out of the hands of the evaluators themselves and also partly out of the hands of the operating agencies. Most evaluators are reluctant to advocate the utilization of their results for fear that their advocacy is seen as self-serving or will prejudice their future relationship with the agency that commissioned the evaluation. Such reluctance is not shared by all evaluators, of course, as is evidenced by Martinson's behavior when he was refused permission to disseminate his conclusions about the effects of prison rehabilitation projects. And such reluctance is not shared by journalists or public interest groups that evaluate the effectiveness of local government services. In this last case, the researchers, disseminators, and advocates of utilization are the same persons, or at least members of the same organization. A second model of utilization would, of course be to make future evaluation contracts contingent on the use of evaluation results, thereby cutting away the major restraint that now prevents the generator of evaluation results from being the advocate-like disseminator of results. However, this second model is in many ways less feasible than the first, largely because it does not fit in well with the current structure and rewards in the evaluation field.

The point we want to stress is not that one or another of the models we have so briefly sketched is worth pursuing. Rather, the point is that we need more fresh models of utilization, and we need to set up experiments to test these models. As evaluations continue to increase in technical quality, underutilization becomes more problematic than it was at an earlier date when some scholars blessed low utilization rates out of a fear that higher rates would entail an unacceptable level of utilizing incorrect findings, particularly incorrect findings about the direction of causal relationships. Now, though misutilization needs more study than it has yet had, the issue is even more one of underutilization, and our gains in knowledge about how to prompt responsible utilization do not seem as impressive as our gains in substantive and methodological knowledge or our gains in institutionalization. Yet utilization is probably the key issue for evaluating evaluation research, particularly in the eyes of the persons who are most responsible for the future of evaluation research.

# PART I
# THE POLICY AND POLITICAL CONTEXT
# OF EVALUATION

Evaluations have to fit into a policy context. Rationally, they are supposed to be one important input into making decisions about the form of programs and projects or about the level of funding that particular programs and projects deserve. A crucial issue is how widely evaluation results are used in policy decisions, for this is more likely than any other issue to determine the fate of systematic evaluation research in the future. The first three articles in this section deal with the utilization issue in different ways. Rein and White ask the very broadest question about whether social science data can help at all in policy formulation; Cohen and Weiss take a particular case study from education and trace how the evaluation issues were formulated and related to policy concerns; while Patton et al. discusses how evaluations might be designed ab initio to facilitate utilization of the results.

The next three articles overlap with the others but place major stress on how political factors influence evaluations. Wildavsky presents a provocative analysis of whether it is possible, or even desirable, to have organizations evaluate themselves or the activities they perform. Brickell presents an extremely frank portrayal of the pressures to which he was subjected in order to have him write an evaluation report that would please his sponsors, and he also candidly reveals the reasons why he sometimes gave into these pressures. The paper by Wright adds an illuminating commentary to Brickell's report.

# 1

# Can Policy Research Help Policy?

## *Martin Rein and Sheldon H. White*

Oₙₑ of the most striking developments of the new and expanded age of social policy, which dates roughly from the Johnson years, has been the great expansion in policy research to guide policy makers. In 1974, the General Accounting Office (G. A. O.), on behalf of the Joint Committee on Congressional Operations, conducted a telephone survey of Federally funded program evaluations. This survey was based on only a narrow definition of policy research, because it excluded studies designed to assess the scope and trends of phenomena, as well as many planning activities. Nevertheless, the G.A.O. study found a 500-percent increase in expenditures from 1969 to 1974. About 60 percent of the 1974 outlays of $146 million, or close to $88 million, went for contract research, with the rest going for grants or in-house studies. About half of the contract-research funds went to profit-making organizations, 30 percent to nonprofit organizations, and 20 percent to universities.

In addition, both G.A.O. and the Office of Management and Budget (O.M.B.) have been expanding their role of carrying out evaluations for the Executive and for Congress. The amounts spent by both these key agencies were not included in the G.A.O. study. But by its own estimate, over the past five years about 30 percent of the professional staff of G.A.O. has become involved in conduct-

From Martin Rein and Sheldon H. White, "Can Policy Research Help Policy?" 49 *The Public Interest* 119-136 (Fall 1977). Copyright 1977 by National Affairs Inc.

ing evaluations of Federal programs under the authority granted
by the Legislative Reorganization Act of 1970. In its 1974 survey,
G.A.O. found 40 legislative acts—dealing with health, education,
transportation, law enforcement, housing, the environment, economic opportunity, and agriculture—that called for evaluation. Six
of these acts specifically authorized funds and mandated that a
fixed percentage be set aside for evaluations. Another eight acts
specified methods of data collection.

Finally, in all the large domestic agencies there are now centers
for policy planning, management, and evaluation—some small, some
large, some influential, some not, some closely tied to budgetary
planning, some less closely tied. The resources that these centers
command make their thinking and their needs a force in bureaucratic politics.

But along with the growth of research, which is often mandated
by the legislation that institutes new social policies, there has grown
a chronic sense of frustration, among both those who carry out the
research and those who commission it. The feeling is that research
does not really serve to guide policy, or is misused, or lies on a shelf
unused. Has the contribution of research to action been oversold?
One administrator reports, "We might as well be candid: Federal
program evaluations so far have been largely ineffective." O.M.B.
officials also report that evaluations, by and large, have not been
timely, relevant, accurate, or accessible. Up to now, little systematic
investigation has been conducted on the extent to which policy
research enters the policy process. Recently, however, Nathan Caplan and his colleagues at the Institute for Social Research at the
University of Michigan conducted an empirical study addressed to
this very issue. They asked 204 persons in the executive branch who
were in a position to make decisions whether and how they made
use of social-science findings.

The respondents did believe in research: "One of the most striking findings is the very positive attitude of respondents toward the
social sciences in general, and more specifically, to the use of social-
science knowledge in the formation of policy." But Caplan did not
think they used research much: 13 percent of the respondents could
cite 5 to 10 instances of use with good supporting evidence; another
61 percent reported 2 to 4 instances of use with good documentation. On the other hand, 44 percent reported instances in which
they purposely disregarded or rejected relevant social-science information in reaching policy decisions. Both "information" and
"use" can mean different things: Information can be data-based

("hard") or nonempirical ("soft"); its use can be conceptual or directed toward reaching a specific decision. Caplan concluded that there were 350 examples of the conceptual use of soft information. (In all, 575 examples of utilization were reported.) But it is difficult to determine how this use of information actually influenced the policy makers. For the most part, the respondents integrated the information with their own values and experiences "to form a frame of reference or perspective within which the social implications of alternative policies ... are evaluated."

Caplan also found that social scientists and policy makers live in different worlds, characterized by conflicting values, rewards, and language. He concluded that lack of contact and lack of trust are the major explanations for variations in information use.

Yet the belief persists that rational intelligence *should* guide policy, at least to some extent. One approach to understanding the role of social science in decision making is to see how policy research is actually used: Perhaps our expectations and understanding of what it can do, and should be expected to do, have been misguided.

### Proposals for reform

Most discussions of the utility of social science envision policy formation and research usage in a special way. There have been many proposals for improving the level of use of research findings, and such proposals suggest the nature of the prevailing conception.

1. *Improve the research according to accepted canons of scientific quality.* Unfortunately, many evaluations are simply not scientifically sound. Ilene N. Bernstein and Howard Freeman have reviewed all the evaluation studies receiving support from the Federal government in 1970 and having a research budget of over $10,000. The primary purpose of their study (published in 1975 by the Russell Sage Foundation as *Academic and Entrepreneurial Research*) was to measure the quality of evaluation. They defined quality in methodological terms—the adequacy of the sampling procedure, the data analysis, the statistical procedures, the design of the study, etc. The main finding was that fewer than 20 percent of the evaluation studies "consistently follow generally accepted procedures with respect to design, data collection, and data analysis." And what determines quality? It seems that academic research yields high-quality work, whereas entrepreneurial research, performed in the profit and nonprofit sector, does not. In academic

research, funds are obtained for a relatively long period of time in the form of a grant and are awarded to academics who design and study in consultation with the staff administering the program.

Would the statistical and methodological purification of evaluation research make it more useful to policy makers? Probably not. Policy makers complain not only about the soundness of the research but also about its lack of timeliness. Improving the quality of research would only reduce its likelihood of arriving on time for a decision. The main problem, however, is out of the hands of researchers: Some programs are simply hard to evaluate, either because their objectives are not well specified or because their stipulated objectives are difficult to translate into research questions.

2. *Restrict the use of evaluation research to selected instances where the conditions necessary for effective research are available.* Political realities do not always permit establishing the conditions for good research design. It may not be possible to create control groups through random assignment, or to construct a sound study given the available time, resources, and managerial capability. It may not always be possible to devise indices that are reasonably representative of the issues at stake. Joseph Wholey has noted:

> The typical Federal program cannot be managed to achieve its stated objectives (as implied, for example, in the authorizing legislation) because: a) the program lacks specific, measurable objectives related to program goals, or b) the program lacks plausible, testable assumptions linking program activities to the achievement of program objectives, or c) managers lack the motivation, ability, or authority to manage.

Sheldon White and his colleagues made an extended examination of the possibilities for evaluating Federal preschool-education, day-care, family-intervention, health-care, housing, and income programs. It seems reasonably clear that virtually no program in these areas can be evaluated—at least not in the sense in which policy makers use the term "evaluation" and legislate for it. Interesting measures of some aspects of program performance do exist. But there do not seem to be measures definitive enough and credible enough to define the total value of programs. And if evaluations were made selectively, we would have very few evaluation studies.

3. *Require policy makers to define their objectives clearly.* The G.A.O. has developed a model statute, suggesting to Congress how objectives might be spelled out in reasonably precise terms. But how realistic is this? Legislation does not generally, or even occa-

sionally, arise out of a conception of a single objective or purpose. Head Start, for example, appears to have been created for several quite different reasons: 1) to stimulate the development of poor children; 2) to stimulate community action; 3) to coordinate services for poor children and their families; and 4) to provide a basis for experiments in school reform. Is it politically expedient, or possible, to rank the multiple purposes involved in creating a program? Is the vagueness of the goals expressed in legislation the result of fuzzy thinking by politicians or rather an attempt to find a general formula acceptable to all parties to the agreement? Can the political process lead very often to direct statements of an intended goal? The stated purpose of the Elementary and Secondary Education Act of 1964, for example, was to improve the school achievement of disadvantaged children. The program has repeatedly been evaluated in terms of that goal through the use of achievement tests. But the legislation was also intended to allow for a Federal subsidy to education. If that was, in fact, the primary purpose of the legislation, then the mere transfer of funds has provided its own indication of success.

We have a political process precisely because people have multiple goals that somehow must be reconciled into a single course of governmental action. This resultant course of action may be called a "policy," but that term is misleading if it is regarded as implying one mind, one will, and one theory. Legislation requires ambiguity in the statement of goals so that coalitions can be formed in support of it, and each group can believe that the legislation serves its own special purposes. As Charles Schultze has explained, "The first rule of a successful political process is, 'don't force a specification of goals or ends' . . . necessary agreement on particular policies can often be secured among the individuals or groups who hold quite divergent ends." Insisting that the government's purposes be clear may reduce the scope of legislation and thus limit government involvement in social programs.

4. *Centralize decision making.* Finally, the argument is sometimes made that the decision-making process in government is too decentralized and too "noisy" to permit the effective utilization of policy research. This argument is directed not so much at the multiple purposes involved in legislation but at the multiple administrative and decision-making responsibilities distributed in the bureaucracy. Moreover, this argument for centralization is reinforced by the fact that those who commission studies are often no longer in government to accept what they requested, and those

who are now empowered to act have formed a new agenda and are not interested in using the findings of studies they did not request.

This argument rests on the assumption that the dispersal of authority inhibits the capacity to act. In the halcyon days when the RAND Corporation enjoyed a close relationship with the Air Force, research produced by RAND was put to good use because the Air Force staff was empowered to act, and its short-term decisions were not subject to review. But such centralized decision-making power seldom prevails in the governmental bureaucracies concerned with social programs. (Indeed, the directness of the RAND/ Air Force relationship has probably been idealized.)

However, the argument for centralization demands changing the political process to accommodate policy research—in this case, concentrating even more authority in the bureaucracy. Needless to say, this is a rather unlikely prospect.

## The Westinghouse study

The four preceding proposals for bringing research and policy making together represent what might be called the problem-solving model. According to this model, the role of policy research is 1) to provide data to clarify a problem, 2) to conduct pilot projects or experiments to estimate whether proposed courses of action approach their goals, and 3) to evaluate implemented programs to determine if, and under what conditions, they are achieving their goals. The results of such policy research, transmitted to the policy maker or decision maker, permit changing or modifying targets or actions.

If this is why policy makers commission research, they will often be disappointed. But government continues to support policy research—and for good reasons.

Consider the Westinghouse evaluation of Head Start, conducted in 1968-1969. That study has been widely discussed, concerning both its scientific validity and its political effect. It has been argued, for example, that the evaluation was premature. Head Start was designed and implemented very quickly between November 1964 and the summer of 1965. The Westinghouse evaluation thus included third graders whose first summer of work occurred when start-up problems were severe. It is quite possible, then, that the entire sample was unrepresentative of what a fully-formed Head Start program might have achieved.

A second argument was that the very design of the study made it inconclusive. There were several technical problems that might have suppressed evidence of the program's effectiveness.

A third criticism was that the study neglected important goals of Head Start. The Westinghouse evaluation addressed one goal that was important to some proponents of the program: the effects of the Head Start on school achievement. But many of those involved in writing the guidelines for the program were not persuaded that direct intervention was possible in childhood development and felt, nonetheless, that Head Start could act as a catalyst for such things as community action.

Given these uncertainties, the Westinghouse study should not have had a definitively negative effect on the program; in a sense, it did not, for Head Start lives today. But when we examine the scope of the program since the study was conducted, we can see that the evaluation did have one significant effect: It was an important factor, among others, leading to a *containment* of the program. Immediately after the Westinghouse evaluation and in a fairly explicit response to it, Head Start began and completed the phasing out of its summer programs. (The Westinghouse evaluation had found no effect on cognitive development from the summer programs, but marginal effects from full-year programs.) And for some years after the Westinghouse study, the budget allocated to Head Start remained steady at about $350 million a year; some high officials in the Department of Health, Education, and Welfare took to characterizing it as an "experimental" program. Some of the staying power of the program flowed from its sentimental appeal and its small but belligerent constituency, which sustained the program even during the latter years of the Nixon Administration, when a serious effort was made to dismantle almost all of the other poverty programs. Such support would normally have caused some enlargement of Head Start; the Westinghouse study was probably responsible for keeping program funding at about the same level.

Finally, the dramatic impact of the Westinghouse findings helped support the contention that "nothing works," which has led much of the policy community, over the years, to switch from a faith in service programs to a belief in a strategy of income redistribution. The Westinghouse evaluation cast a shadow not simply on Head Start, but on the understanding of the problem Head Start was intended to address. In a similar vein, David Cohen and Michael Garret have argued that the cumulative effect of a whole variety of studies may have been to alter the context in which policy is shaped:

> Taken together, the Coleman report, its progeny, and the stream of negative Title-I evaluations have gradually eroded the assumptions underlying compensatory policy. The changing climate of opinion has made it more difficult to maintain or expand compensatory projects and has weakened support for categorical educational programs.

Recent research has thus had a serious influence on the ideas and ideological commitments at the basis of educational policy in the United States. So although research may not influence any specific policy, it can help shape the climate of opinion and contribute to the interchange of ideas.

### The power of knowledge

It is widely accepted that knowledge is power, and producing knowledge can play a role in the bid for power. A clear example of this political role of research occurred over the last few years in connection with the development of day-care legislation. It was uncertain which of several day-care bills would ultimately be administered by the bureaucracy. In the period before the passing of the first Mondale-Brademas bill, several rival agencies—the Office of Economic Opportunity, the Office of Child Development, the Department of Labor, and the Office of Education—were all actively sponsoring research on day care. There were, of course, the usual substantive reasons for commissioning such research— to provide information about demand, about the trade-offs between costs and quality, about the effects of child development, etc. But at the same time, those who dealt with the day-to-day management of contract research in Washington were aware that the rival agencies were "establishing a position" in day care, trying to build up information, staff competence, and visibility to deal with the upcoming legislation.

Research is thus commissioned not only out of the need for information but in the service of political positioning. Individuals, research offices, and agencies periodically find it necessary to make visible commitments toward significant issues and constituencies. Moreover, a symbolic gesture can substitute for definite, but risky, political action. Systematic research buys time for political leaders, while maintaining the commitment to action. Commissions, national surveys, task forces, experiments, and demonstrations all provide concrete and symbolic benefits to interested parties.

The political use of research to postpone decisions and win political leverage need not detract from the substantive value of the work, however. In the majority of cases, cynicism is not warranted. Moreover, in the research-producing agencies, there are always a few individuals who are passionately committed to the value of either general or specific activities. So an agency can have a mixed commitment to research as a means to gain knowledge and as an end in itself.

The role and interests of researchers and research administrators must also be considered. It is in their interest to have a "portfolio" of grants and contracts that promise help with critical problems or groups, to enlarge their budget and staff, and to move research into positions of leverage in the bureaucracy—for example, into the areas of budgeting and planning.

It is important not to regard the instrumental use of research for career advancement as utterly cold-blooded calculation. Many administrators, in fact, have a more complete faith in the genuine value of research than most social scientists do. But good bureaucrats must inevitably be good survivors. They use their research activities for power and positioning because they have to: The rules of the game require it.

### The demand for accountability

Evaluation research also serves now as a management device to insure that agencies do what is expected of them. Evaluation is thus linked to monitoring and auditing. The most prominent expression of this responsibility is in the current demand for "accountability." There is an increased unwillingness to take it for granted that benefits will follow from new legislation or that judgment and testimony should be exclusively limited to professionals and administrators. Ideally, the value of a program should be expressed in hard numbers.

Pressures for accountability have been building over the years at all levels of government; without doubt, such pressures are behind much of the recent Congressional interest in evaluations of social programs. Conservatives who are skeptical about a program may insist upon a legislative provision for evaluation, and liberals may accept the provision begrudgingly or willingly. Yet all the puzzles remain about what is involved in a cost-benefit analysis of housing, or of income distribution, or of community action. To be sure, government does have more pieces of fragmentary information today concerning the costs and benefits of the programs it manages than ever before.

Guerrilla groups functioning outside the Federal establishment have also made use of research. For example, Title-I funds of the 1964 Elementary and Secondary Education Act were expected to add to the resources available to schools serving the poor, so that the poor would receive more resources than the well-to-do. Local communities theoretically had to satisfy the condition of equal expenditure across income classes before funds could be allocated. In the early days of Title I, however, there was a widespread failure to satisfy this condition—and there were, as well, a number of cases in which a more serious misallocation of funds occurred. So a number of black-militant groups filed suits against local Title-I programs, using monitoring and evaluation information made available under the statutory requirements of the program.

Such outside policing has been stimulated by the frequent inclusion in legislation of a requirement that local, parent, or community advisory groups be associated with new social programs. There may also be requirements that information about the local programs be made available to such groups in a regular and convenient form. Such groups can and will demand the production of information relevant to their interests. Thus a different kind of demand for research in the interest of accountability arises.

At times there is a close relationship between the formal and the grass-roots auditors. Bureaucrats may feel that the case for reform is stronger when outside pressure groups present it. They may leak the information that supports reforms to such groups. Some observers have suggested that just such a cooperative strategy was followed by bureaucratic reformers and outside activists in the case of Title I.

## Research as social reform

Research can also be used as a weapon in the efforts to reform government. In the early days of the poverty program, for example, the Federal administration tried to use research and evaluation as a means of wresting control away from local voluntary agencies that had preempted the social-welfare field. Similarly, David Tyack has argued in *The One Best System: A History of American Urban Education* (Cambridge, Harvard University Press, 1974) that there was a movement in the late 19th and early 20th centuries toward the professionalization of educational management, in order to shift control of the schools away from the local level. A coalition of the social elite and distinguished academics succeeded in bringing about this change. The ostensible basis for the reform was the desirability of making education and educational management more scientific. Superintendents were to become members of a "learned profession." Schooling was to be taken out of the realm of politics and placed on the higher plane of scientific administration, based on the best research evidence at hand:

> Nicholas Murray Butler could confidently assert, to the applause of the Merchant's Club of Chicago, that he should "as soon think of talking about the democratization of the treatment of appendicitis" as to speak of "the democratization of the schools." "The fundamental confusion is this: Democracy is a principle of government; the schools belong to the administration; and a democracy is as much entitled as a monarchy to have its business well done." A common school run for the people but not by the people. . . .

At the turn of the century, the reform movement tried to move away from a pluralistic system of local control. Now we are taking some pains to try to reinstitute it—the Democrats under slogans like "community action," the Republicans under revenue-sharing and slogans like "the new Federalism."

A further example of research as reform comes from the bureaucratic history behind the idea of the negative income tax (NIT) in the Office of Economic Opportunity. NIT was first introduced in government circles and most staunchly defended by a federal agency whose legislative mandate embraced the idea of "opportunity," but rejected the principle of transfers. The story of OEO's involvement with NIT suggests that it is often social scientists acting as reformers, rather than as social scientists per se, who contribute to the development of policy. Joseph Kershaw, the first director of OEO's Office of Research, Plans, Programs, and Evaluation, and latter assistant director of OEO, lucidly described the rationale underlying the activities of his office—and illustrated the political use of social theory:

> The Economic Opportunity Act was seen by its supporters . . . as being new and different . . . it was thought to be aimed at the correction of the causes of poverty rather than at the alleviation of symptoms. "Opportunity is our middle name," the poverty warriors were fond of saying. "We don't give handouts," Director Sargent Shriver said on many occasions. . . . Training programs, the teaching of adult literacy, family planning, and most things OEO does or did are directed at making it possible for people to pull themselves out of poverty, whereas most welfare expenditures can only be regarded as relief in one form or another. . . .

But within OEO's Office of Research, Plans, Programs, and Evaluation were a group of economists acting, at least to some extent, as bureaucratic insurgents struggling against the agency that employed them. As economists, they accepted as self-evident the idea that the poor needed money as well as jobs, services, and community power. They believed that cash transfers in the form of a negative income tax, which would preserve work incentives and expand personal choice, would provide one of the decisive strategies in any war against poverty. And they pushed their idea by means of research, not only in OEO but also in H.E.W., the agency officially responsible for welfare policy.

### What is the problem?

If policy formation is just problem solving, it should not involve the kinds of functions described above: containment, policing, power, and reform. But policy formation is more than merely problem solving, and social-science research enters into all stages of the process. Some deep differences between research and politics, however, seem to insure that as an individual achieves legitimacy in one area he loses it in the other. The research-policy alliance is thus quite painful to all participants, both researchers and policy makers.

The long-standing problem-solving model is in large part a myth: Research may solve problems, but it also has three other important functions: 1) identifying problems as a step toward putting issues on the agenda, 2) mobilizing government action, and 3) confronting and settling dilemmas and trade-offs.

According to the problem-solving model, policy making begins with articulated and self-evident problems, about which it is possible to hypothesize different courses of action and develop goals. But there is actually an earlier stage, often quite extended, during which various indications of stress emerge. It is not clear problems but diffuse worries that appear. Political pressure groups become unusually active, or their activities become more obvious. Formal and informal social indicators give signs of trends that are unfavorable or can be interpreted as unfavorable. There are indications that a problem exists, but as yet no one knows what it is. In the development of most governmental activities there is an important period during which troublesome elements have to be interpreted before even the statement of a problem is possible.

Problem setting is a form of pattern recognition; it involves finding or imposing an order or structure on incipient events. It is an integral part of the work of the scientist, perhaps the most crucial part, but it has traditionally been the least well codified aspect of research in the canons of methodology and "normal science." There is, in fact, no orderly and prescribed way of problem setting. In politics, the activity is no less fundamental and no more orderly. Different interest groups compete to impose a pattern on current events. Labor uses selected social indicators to suggest a crisis in worker satisfaction; business uses other indicators to proclaim a crisis in productivity. Rival groups thus implicitly bid for a mandate for action, selectively using data.

The search for "an issue" is the lifeblood of politics. It is increasingly the social scientist who locates and reports events, who probes for patterns, and who tries to confirm or deny patterns asserted by others. The social scientist is thus a significant participant in the business of defining and raising issues. Moreover, he has undeniable credentials and competence for the activity of problem setting.

The special relevance of the social-science researcher to the questions of politics rests on his understanding of generalized, average, modal human beings. No layman—no social worker, teacher, physician, or politician—has ever met an average child, a median unemployed factory worker in the Northeast, a modal big-city superintendent of schools. The layman generalizes from a limited series of personal encounters. To be sure, this mode of understanding should not be underestimated. Much can be learned from projecting from a few particulars to the general case; in politics much is done in this manner. But sometimes it is necessary to have aggregate estimates that go beyond the precision and the detail of private and casual encounters. The social-science researcher has tools—sampling and other techniques of statistical methodology—that permit detailed inferences concerning what the average child knows at the end of the first grade, what the distribution of disease by ethnic group is in the Southwest, what the recidivism rate is for juvenile reformatories, what the average voter thinks about fluoridation, etc. Public policy ministers to the generalized human being and so the social scientist is almost inevitably involved.

The activity of problem setting, in and of itself, is not deeply problematical. The only technical difficulty for social scientists is that they are curiously awkward in articulating their activities. In the political arena, however, problem setting is only one facet of the broader activity of issue setting, which raises a more fundamental concern: To assert an issue is to assert a mixture of facts and values. Contending political groups vie with one another not in the spirit of rival scientific theorists, but with the intention of mobilizing support leading to action. The next step in research for policy involves creating an effective coalition for action at the appropriate legislative or administrative level.

## Policy choices

The problem-solving model presupposes that a policy issue is simultaneously and automatically made evident to all members of the policy community. Government is thus regarded as monolithic: The assumption is that many individuals in government often and easily think as one. Important questions of the sociology of knowledge and action aside, governments do not think, nor do individuals joined by an organizational structure think in unison. In a public bureaucracy, there is a community of actors, whose actions are to some extent interwoven by the system that provides for the division of labor, lines of responsibility, and the ultimate integration of their efforts. However, the bureaucratic integration of the actions of individuals is, at best, limited. Cooperative action is only grossly structured, and there is much room for individuals to work at cross-purposes, thus cancelling out one another's actions. Each actor faces his own set of decisions, defined by the position he occupies in the institutional structure. He chooses among courses of action, but his set of possible actions is different from that of others in different positions. Policy research can almost never dictate precisely what decision each actor is to make.

But policy research can lead individuals within the bureaucratic web to share a conception of the problems that are important, thus insuring that each will emphasize similar concerns when approaching his unique set of decisions. Patterns imposed on data can ultimately lead to evocative slogans—for example, "the need for a sense of community," "the weakening of the family," "equality of educational opportunity," "advocacy," "the need for income redistribution." Such slogans, and the metaphors that underlie them, can provide a basis for harmonious action. Individuals influenced by such conceptions will emphasize them within the sphere of their discretionary power—by favoring a service or research project that seems in line with the conception, adopting it as a criterion of quality for personnel selection, or allowing it to influence budget allocations. Even though there is no overt plan of cooperation, individuals distributed throughout the bureaucracy can nevertheless transform a way of looking at a problem into a force determining the actions of the system. Individual actions and accommodations are then reinforced by more formal but secondary institutional organizations—committees, interagency task forces, societies, coordinating newsletters.

Research and theory can also help to provide an ideology that helps create coalitions. In politics, of course, it is hardly news that ideology springs from assertions about the state of society—assertions that rest on the authority of the social scientist, who is an expert at viewing large things like a society, but that seem at times to have been selected, exaggerated, and distorted so much that the social scientist will wonder whether they exceed and even jeopardize his authority. Contending political claimants may use social scientists in much the same way that contending court claimants often use psychiatrists: Each side, pro and con, has its experts who speak for it. Thus the seemingly paradoxical situation arises in which objective scientific evidence is used to support different, and at times radically opposed, courses of political action. Science seems to speak out of both sides of its mouth about the course that policy should take. Perhaps the answer to this apparent paradox is that political choices can be brought to light but never resolved by scientific information.

### Managing dilemmas and trade-offs

Finally, the problem-solving model overlooks the essential presence of dilemmas and trade-offs. Charles De Gaulle reportedly said, "I have lived a long life and I have never seen a single problem solved." Larger policy questions involve dilemmas and trade-offs virtually by definition: If a problem is clear and uncontested, it does not ordinarily emerge at high levels of political debate. It is merely a technical problem. Its solution will be debated and resolved through technical and bureaucratic institutions, away from the central policy-making arenas of government.

Genuine social-policy dilemmas, on the other hand, can arise (for example) from the effort to preserve work incentives and simultaneously to provide adequate income support for those who cannot be gainfully employed; or from the effort to design programs that will reach only those for whom they were intended, since administrative screening devices that focus on weeding out the ineligible also reduce the likelihood of reaching the eligible. Dilemmas can also arise in education from the tension between the notion of equality of educational opportunity on the one hand, and pluralism and cultural democracy on the other. In the recurrent efforts to establish Federal day-care standards that benefit both the mother and the child, minimal standards and low expenditures are essential to lower welfare costs by encouraging women to work, but high standards—according to much professional testimony—are necessary for the benefit of children.

Genuine social-policy dilemmas such as these involve a conflict of values—two ideals directing action in diametrically opposite directions. In practice, we can only act along a continuum of trade-offs, where more of one ideal is purchased at the expense of less of the other. The manifold dilemmas that exist in the political arena are not the kinds of problems that are envisaged in the problem-solving model, and they cannot be resolved in its terms. What research can do is articulate and clarify the range of practical choices and elucidate in concrete terms the practical consequences of each choice. But it cannot arbitrate the underlying value choices and thereby solve the problems.

Research is, or is supposed to be, value-free. Yet research that is brought into policy decisions is used to negotiate for the supremacy of some particular value position. The researcher may be chagrined by this political use of his work, in which case he will stoutly assert the irrelevance of his work to policy; or he may cooperate in the political exploitation of his findings, in which case he runs a real risk of having himself or his work discounted by the scientific community that provides the basis for his credibility.

But in another sense science is never value-free. Scientists function in a community that stresses the observance of rules and does not transmit values or adjudicate among competing values. Within the community, members engage in common routines of analytic operations—pattern recognition, induction, inference—which are largely value-neutral. (Or, at least, individual values are "washed out" for the most part in the process of trading back and forth.) But the community is composed of individuals, and the individual's work is always an expression of his personal values—not only through his choice of area and problem but through the way he imposes patterns on phenomena and assigns meaning to relationships. Part of the work of the scientific community, however, is to guard against this, to "keep him honest," by insisting that findings offered by an individual with one bias be confirmed by the observations of individuals with other biases. This is ideally how value-neutral knowledge should be produced out of the collective work of the community. Reality falls far short of this ideal, of course.

Politics, by contrast, depends upon the identification and expression of contending values. The basic intent of political action is thus not to "wash out" values but to arrive at courses of action that satisfy as much as possible all the contending interests. But the proposals for reforming the research-policy alliance that are based on the problem-solving model would generally have the effect of taking research farther away from policy making, or else changing the basic nature of political processes.

### The problem-solving myth

Policy research is increasingly receiving support, both in resources and from institutions, because it plays a genuine role in the American political process. But the policy-research alliance is an uneasy marriage, with dilemmas for both sides. These dilemmas go rather deep; participation in the alliance involves potential erosions of responsibility and credibility for both the researcher and the policy maker.

Science seeks to establish patterns of experience that all may share. They are value-neutral, in the sense that they are deliberately designed to filter out the values of individual participants and arrive at the "unbiased truth": Findings must be accepted by individuals whether they find them palatable or unpalatable. The scientist should be restrained, dispassionate, conservative,.and willing to suspend belief, pending more evidence.

Politics is quite different from science: The intent is to find one purpose, or course of action, acceptable to individuals espousing diverse purposes, values, and courses of action. Politics is value-expressive; facts are subordinate to and sustaining of values, and only contribute to the delineation of an issue. The politician seeks to maximize the satisfaction of his interests: He must be bold, persistent, opportunistic, and capable of mobilizing and sustaining belief and commitment.

It is extremely difficult for an individual to retain his credibility in these two very different areas. The scientist who is too action-oriented loses his credibility in the same way that the politician who is too theory-oriented loses his. But the basic problem is not the ability or inability of an individual to wear two hats, but rather the incompatibility of science and politics: One trades in facts and the other in values.

Researchers are now regularly asked to evaluate programs in education, housing, law enforcement, community development, etc. They are never concretely told what values or value-derived goals to pursue—because, virtually by definition, the political body setting forth such programs cannot make up its own mind, much less specify a goal with precision. So as the researcher pursues his supposedly technical function, he must make decisions about what constitutes good child development, good education, good housing, a good family, a good community. The political community has effectively passed on to the scientific community the problem of achieving a consensus regarding social values and goals. But this transfer of authority exceeds the professional competence of the researcher; by usurping some of the genuine political responsibility of the policy maker, it is improper as well.

Can research help policy? It can. Sometimes findings are so decisive that a new understanding of a problem or a new approach to dealing with it emerges and begins to affect the public, the politicians, and the policy makers. But more often, research affects policy in ways that are rather far removed from this problem-solving model—and indeed, are not even recognized by researchers or policy makers. But even though policy makers will be dissatisfied with the researchers they commission, and researchers will be unhappy over the inability of policy makers to provide them with the kind of tasks that fulfill the canons of their profession, policy research will probably grow and expand. For whether it solves problems or not, research helps those involved in the making of policy to decide what the problems are. Moreover, policy research is by now incorporated as a full partner in the art of politics.

# 2

## Social Science and Social Policy: Schools and Race

### David K. Cohen and Janet A. Weiss

The last twenty years were palmy ones for research on education and race. National racial policy advanced after *Brown*, and as efforts to eliminate segregation and discrimination multiplied, research on the problems prospered. What was a trickle of studies in the few years before 1954 became something of an academic torrent; as efforts to eliminate segregation moved closer to center stage, research on the problem multiplied. In part this was the result of government efforts to promote studies of current policy, and in part it was due to the fact the researchers' priorities are influenced by what they read in the papers.

In any event, the contacts between race research and policy increased. Researchers regularly found themselves testifying in courtrooms, evaluating government programs, or consulting with educational agencies. Sometimes they even found themselves in the newspapers and more often in the various magazines that publish popular science. Through all this period, research on education and race improved in all the usual ways researchers recognize. Methodology is now more sophisticated than it was twenty years ago. Basic concepts have been overhauled and refined, and new distinctions have been hatched. Various central scientific hypotheses have been weighed; some, perhaps, have even been tested. Evidence has accumulated at a startling pace, and some of it has been analyzed. Certainly, a much broader variety of analytic skills have been devised and used. And finally efforts to connect research and policy have multiplied, motivated by government, by private foundations, and by many researchers' desires for relevance.

But while research has improved and its contacts with policy have multiplied, it has only produced new arguments and complications. As a result, research has not become more helpful for particular policy decisions. Research has proliferated, but so have arguments among researchers. Methods of study have improved, but the results are less accessible: How many of the people who could read the Social Science Brief filed in *Brown*, for example, could also read the Coleman Report's sections on integration and school effects? Research projects have multiplied, but so have competing ways of defining problems and

The research for this chapter was supported partly by grants from the Carnegie Corporation of New York to the Center for Educational Policy Research, Harvard University, and by the American Jewish Committee to the Huron Institute.

interpreting results. In our view, this situation is not the fault of bad research, nor do we think it could be remedied by better research. The prosperity of research quite naturally contributes to a sense of growing complexity and to confusions over policy advice.

That, indeed, is the theme of this chapter: For the most part, the improvement of research on social policy does not lead to greater clarity about what to think or what to do; instead, it usually tends to produce a greater sense of complexity. This result is endemic to the research process. For what researchers understand by improvement in their craft leads not to greater consensus about research problems, methods, and interpretation of results, but to more variety in the ways problems are seen, more divergence in the way studies are carried out, and more controversy in the ways results are interpreted. It leads also to a more complicated view of problems and solutions, for the progress of research tends to reveal the inadequacy of accepted ideas about solving problems.

The ensuing complexity and confusion are naturally a terrific frustration both to researchers who think they should matter and to officials who think they need help. They expect direct policy guidance from social research and assume that knowledge in the social sciences ought to be convergent. As knowledge improves, more scientific agreement about the issues in question is expected, but knowledge in the social sciences generally is not convergent. Rather than picture the research process as scouts converging on a target, it might make more sense to picture the process as outriders offering different visions of what passes them by. Multiplying the outriders tends to multiply the visions—up to a point, of course—and sharpening their sight tends to refine their differences.

Thus, if the result of scientific improvement in some aspects of physical science is convergence—at least for a time, within important conceptual limits[1]— the result of improvement in the social sciences is a richer, more diverse picture of things. Naturally enough, if one expects the first and gets the second, one is bound to be disappointed, even angry. But it may make sense to locate the trouble in the expectation of convergence rather than in the science.

Our point in this chapter is to explore this view of social policy research and to suggest the criteria of research quality that we think it implies. We will do so by showing how the research process works in the case of schools and race. We have three main points in mind. The first is that as research on social policy matures, it tends to help redefine social problems. Research is often critical and questioning, and it reveals inadequacies in accepted views of a social problem. As practical experience in problem solving turns up unexpected and puzzling results, research excellently reports, amplifies, and embellishes them.

A second point is that the improvement of research method tends to increase divergence in the treatment of evidence and to multiply mystification in the interpretation of findings. Methodological sophistication is a cardinal academic virtue, but it does not increase consensus on research issues. Rather, it clarifies differences, reveals previously unsuspected problems in data and analysis, and progressively removes research from the everyday world in which most judges, legislators, and bureaucrats walk and think.

A final point is that as research on a social problem matures, the angles of vision multiply. Social problems typically are framed initially in terms of a particular discipline, profession, or research tradition, but as research on a problem prospers, other traditions and disciplines are drawn in. Each involves a different angle on social reality or different assumptions about how social investigations should be carried out. The result is a richer and more diverse vision of the problem and its possible remedies.

### Shifting Social Problems

In the beginning, the problem was lawful school segregation. The years immediately surrounding the *Brown* decision saw little ambiguity on this point, even though there was enormous controversy over the issues. According to the research centering on that decision, the legally mandated system of racially dual schools was a problem because it damaged the persons and impaired the opportunities of black Americans. The discussion of remedy was cast in similar terms—that is, eliminating the socially stigmatized black institutions and mixing blacks into the population of white schools.[2]

There was not a great deal of evidence underlying these points: The research was often thin, and the ratio of speculation to empirical findings was sometimes remarkably high. But for all this, there was not much diversity of opinion. The main division lay between those researchers who thought segregation was the problem and those who thought it was the solution. Most arguments in early desegregation research lay between the exponents of racial inferiority[3] and everyone else.

Today most researchers continue to oppose the doctrine of inherited inferiority among blacks. But they can't agree on much else. The desegregation of Southern schools brought the country closer to compliance with the Constitution, but it didn't produce the other results that earlier law and social science had suggested. In particular, desegregation didn't have the expected effects on school performance. The news on this point accumulated slowly throughout the early 1960s in a modest number of reports on desegregated districts. In some cases desegregation seemed to be associated with gains in achievement (and in some cases it didn't), but in no cases were the gains substantial.[4]

In the summer of 1966, the *Equality of Education Opportunity Survey*[5] (the so-called Coleman Report) was dropped—rather like a long-acting, repeating bomb—into this moderately confused scene. The survey reported that racial segregation had no independent impact on Negro school achievement although schools' social-class composition did seem to affect achievement. How this finding might be related to earlier research or legal ideas about racial segregation was not clear. And finally, the *EEO Survey* found no consistent relationship between school desegregation and racial attitudes. The net effect was to call into question several accepted ideas about race and schools.

The next major study didn't help. The U.S. Civil Rights Commission undertook a presidentially commissioned analysis of northern school segregation,[6] and the results were a little curious. The Commission accepted Coleman's findings about the noneffects of schools' racial composition, but found, in further analysis of the *EEOS* data, that racially integrated classrooms had a positive effect on achievement—in high school. The report also explored the relation between desegregation and racial attitudes in more detail, but it found no consistent "improvement" in racial attitudes associated with desegregation. Desegregated schools seemed as likely to produce tension and conflict as understanding and interracial harmony.

There ensued many smaller studies of particular districts as desegregation accelerated, but these accumulated the same small and inconsistent differences.[7] The questions thus multiplied. If desegregation didn't consistently or appreciably improve things for black students, what about earlier assertions that segregation damaged the hearts, minds, and future opportunities of black youth? These queries might have lain mercifully quiet in academic groves and bureaucratic files had it not been for the fact that research only reflected experience. Desegregated schools turned out to be more uncomfortable than anyone had expected, and often they were downright dangerous. This finding stimulated second thoughts all round and thus invited blacks to reflect on the comforts and advantages of separate institutions.[8]

If research helped to redefine the problem of segregation, the process was reinforced by social and political trends. Population shifts produced an increasing number of central cities with heavy black majorities in the public schools. Some social scientists interpreted this as evidence that racial balance was impossible within central-city schools. They maintained that desegregation would therefore have to occur on a metropolitan scale. They tried to support this conclusion with evidence that the academic effects of integration disappeared in majority-black settings and with research on the success of small-scale, city-suburban busing programs.[9]

But the notion was not warmly received. Black politicians in the central cities, especially those with an interest in the mayors' offices, quickly developed an allergy to metropolitan school desegregation. And some social scientists took exception to the idea that desegregation required the dilution of black student bodies in mostly white settings. By the 1970s that approach struck many as a sort of *raffine* racism.[10]

These reservations were reinforced by the movement for black community control. Somehow the conjunction of black demands for self-government with white proposals for metropolitan dispersal of black students seemed odd, if not downright embarrassing. Increasingly, social scientists held that the central problem in matters of education and race was no longer segregation; rather they argued that the racism that had engendered segregation also made desegregation as much a problem as segregation.

This brief account hardly captures all of the ways in which ideas about the problems of schools and race have changed. But the central point is that early and relatively clear definitions of the problem tended to blur under the pressure of experience. Once upon a time the problem was legally mandated dual schools, but by 1970—not to mention the later years of Boston and Detroit—that issue seemed almost quaint.

This phenomenon occurred in several ways. For one thing, segregation turned out to be more complex than had been expected. In 1954 no one really thought school desegregation suits would reach school flagpoles, teachers' rooms, and student clubs. For another, at the beginning of efforts to solve social problems, there is almost always a preferred solution—a social device that is appealing precisely because it offers a simplified view of how things can be improved. "Disestablishing the racially dual school system" was precisely such a device, but it turned out to hide a swamp of complexities.

And last but not least, the segregation problem became less clear because social reality changed in several ways. First, population shifts in central cities gradually frustrated efforts to desegregate schools. As a result, what had been a complex problem involving single jurisdictions became a supercomplicated problem crossing jurisdictional lines within metropolitan areas. Second, events beginning with *Brown* tended to legitimize black grievances, to encourage their expression, and to focus attention on them. As a result of school desegregation, blacks developed a much more refined sense of racial injustice in schools, a much decreased willingness to stand the pain, and a sharply reduced appetite for white people's solutions. All of this worked a change in social reality: What would have been an entirely acceptable integrated high school in 1954 would have seemed an outrageous insult in 1974.

So, trying to solve this social problem changed the way the problem was seen; it complicated and diversified views of the problem; it made once-appealing solutions seem limited; and it suggested alternative solutions. The result was not just that the problem came to seem more complex, but also that in some ways it came to seem different. The current view that desegregation is a major social problem is at cross-purposes with many ideas surrounding the *Brown* decision.

Research played several roles in all this complexity. For one thing, research on social policy is part of the intelligence apparatus by which society learns what seems to be happening. Research and evaluation taught Americans about the ambiguous impact of integration on achievement, about its contradictory effect on attitudes, and about the problems of the desegregation process. What is reported to society profoundly influences what society learns.

Second, social problem research played a critical role by picking apart earlier ideas and assumptions. The *EEO Survey*, for example, used powerful statistical techniques to blow apart many established ideas about schools and race. The intent was not critical, but the effect was to raise basic questions about the effects of desegregation. And third, research and social commentary by researchers often turns out to be a way of expressing new social tendencies and intellectual currents. Much of the "research" associated with the movement for community control partook of this quality and thus legitimized new ideas by introducing them in scientific garb.

Thus, research sometimes reports a complicating reality, and sometimes it complicates our picture of reality through criticism and the introduction of new ideas. In both ways, it helps to make our understanding of social problems more complex, and because formal inquiry is somewhat less absent-minded than the daily media, it provides a historical record of these changes for researchers and their consumers. This only heightens the sense of complexity and change. Research usually is not the primary moving force in all this, but because of the growing importance of formal studies in social reportage, it is rarely unimportant. In one way or another, it is a significant force in redefining and complicating our views of social problems.

## Research Methods and Frameworks

One might think from the account so far that social problems, not research, are to blame: The problems sneak up on the unwary investigator slowly, seductively let down their veils, and reveal their alluring complexity. The hopeful analyst is captivated but befuddled. That research contributes its share to befuddlement, though, is evident in considering the improved methodology.

Two improvements were central. For one thing, computer technology and the avalanche of money for large-scale studies made it possible for researchers to collect evidence on many factors in any social situation. Methodologists and data analysts adapted and developed statistical techniques that permit analysis of many such factors at one time, and so social scientists can now attack social phenomena with much more finesse than was possible three decades ago. These advances encouraged the collection of much more diverse and representative data. Investigators not only can report findings that are statistically more credible for national policy, but they can consider all sorts of interesting subgroups. All of this has helped research to become more self-conscious. There is heightened awareness of problems of analysis, methodology, and design. They are now a central interest in the social sciences and a focus in most debates over policy research.

A second improvement was the diversification of desegregation research since the early 1950s. At the outset most investigations were psychological, but gradually economists, sociologists, and anthropologists were drawn in—as were researchers from education and law. The relative importance of psychology has diminished, and research has flowered under the influence of several different disciplinary and professional orientations.

These advances are good for research, but one reward for the better studies has been a clearer idea of just how muddy the waters really are. Research on the effects of segregation and desegregation reveals this nicely. Early work on racial awareness and self-esteem[11]—the research summarized in the Social Science Brief—supported the idea that segregation caused psychological damage to black children. This broadly psychological emphasis was given specific focus by research that maintained that desegregation would never improve the achievement of black students because of their inherited intellectual inferiority.[12] In the political atmosphere of massive resistance, some social scientists felt that answering these racist studies was essential. They tried to show that desegregation did raise black students' achievement and IQ test scores.[13] This tendency was given added force by the post-Sputnik pressure for better achievement and by the growing fashion of programs to improve the academic performance of "culturally deprived" students.

The result was to ensconce achievement test scores as the variable of chief interest in research on race and schools. At the outset, these studies were few in number and straightforward in design: The relation between schools' racial composition and test scores would be presented in simple one- or two-way tables. In some cases it seemed as though black students were better off in desegregated schools, while in some cases it didn't. But the results were easy to read, and they dealt in a currency everyone thought they understood.

The *EEO Survey*, published in July of 1966, changed all that, for it brought a formidable array of methodological refinements to bear on the question. The *EEO Survey* was based on a nationally representative sample of schools and was designed to permit complex multiple regression analysis of the relative impact of racial composition, school resources, student background, and school social-class composition on achievement and attitudes. In these analyses, schools' racial composition was found to have no significant independent association with student achievement. In addition, there seemed to be little relation between school resources and school achievement. The two issues tended to merge after the report's publication, and Coleman's report was attacked almost as soon as it hit the streets. Henry Levin and Sam Bowles took Coleman to task for a series of high methodological crimes.[14] The *EEO Survey*, they argued, had used the wrong regression statistics; it was flawed by problems of nonresponse; it used analytic techniques that understated the impact of school resources; it was therefore useless for policy guidance.

The episode certainly undermined the report's credibility, but it also nicely illustrates disciplinary differences in the use of analytic techniques. Coleman is a sociologist, and he used the regression statistic dearest to that discipline (the standardized beta coefficient, which reflects the relative importance of several forces in a complex system of relationships). Bowles and Levin are economists, and they held out for the regression statistic most familiar to economists, which reflects the unique impact of one variable in an input-output system (the unstandardized beta coefficient). Adding disciplines to the scientific fray sharpened issues and created new arguments.[15]

In the aftermath, the Civil Rights Commission produced its reanalysis of the *EEO Survey* data. These results further complicated things because of the *EEO Survey*'s nationally representative character. The findings about classroom integration in *Racial Isolation* were based on data from high schools in the northeastern urban United States. There did seem to be an effect of integration in this region, but the Commission also published an appendix volume wherein lay parallel analyses of classroom integration from other regions. Sometimes these results showed no positive impact of integrated classrooms, and sometimes they showed a negative impact. Often they were inconclusive. Having nationally representative data did not produce more definitive conclusions.

Later in the decade, reanalyses of the *EEO Survey* data became a growth industry supported by government grants, public-spirited foundations, and scholarly animosity. One group at Harvard, under the scientific leadership of Daniel P. Moynihan, produced a raft of refinements and further qualifications.[16] David Armor, for example, found that school integration helped black students, but only if they were in more than token-integrated, but less than majority, black schools. Whites, it seemed, were good for blacks if taken in medium doses, rather than in very small or very large ones. Economic contributors in Moynihan's volume continued to moan over the *EEO Survey* and attack its results, while Jencks and other sociologists upheld the statistical virtue of Coleman's original findings with new and better analytic techniques. Another reanalysis group at the U.S. Office of Education attacked Coleman's and Jencks' findings on school effects while simultaneously repelling the advances of Levin, Bowles, Kain, and Hanushek on the *EEO Survey*'s methodology.[17] As one would expect from an agency that spends most of its time giving away money to public schools, the Office of Education group found that school resources did make a difference.

The reanalyses continued for years and produced more questions, more qualifications, and more occasions to exercise new analytic muscles. Some researchers thought Coleman had overstated the impact of social-class integration.[18] Others, reanalyzing the Civil Rights Commission's work, found that the effects of classroom integration seemed to hold at the ninth grade but not at the twelfth grade.[19] Jencks and company, in *Inequality*, thought there might be a small effect of school racial mixing in elementary schools, but they emphasized the modesty of the effect and the uncertainty of the evidence.[20] Shortly thereafter, the Civil Rights Commission reentered the picture—this time by denouncing the inadequacy of previous research on the subject and proclaiming its unreliability for policy guidance. The Commission commissioned a more comprehensive, complex, longitudinal study to resolve the issues.[21] The reanalyses, then, produced a swarm of contrary ideas, a host of refined analytic techniques, and a growing despair over the prospects for clear conclusions on the issues.

The controversies continue. They have moved on from what now seem old-hat, simple multiple regression techniques to more complex analytic methods such as path analysis and multistage regression. They also have moved to new and more complex analytic issues—the effects of schooling on adult success, rather than just achievement—and they have moved on to new bodies of data, the *EEOS* having been rubbed raw in various scientific embraces. The effect of schools' racial composition occasionally appears in these supersophisticated combats in mathematical sociology and econometrics, but the issue seems to have been dwarfed by larger questions about whether schooling itself makes a difference and obscured by the proliferation of complex analytic techniques. The only conclusion on which most researchers now seem to agree is that the data collected in the 1960s are inadequate and more studies are needed. Science marches on.

Our story of the improvement in desegregation research doesn't end here. As research on test scores accumulated, so did questions about that approach to assessing school integration. One reason was that some researchers became uneasy about reporting the persistent black-white gap in achievement scores—a gap that seemed unresponsive to any intervention. Another reason was that by the middle and late 1960s, sociology and economics had entered research on education and race in force, and they contemplated other outcomes of desegregation. Finally, the more test scores were used, the more psychologists questioned their meaning.

Some researchers questioned the technical basis of the tests; and others questioned their cultural foundations. On both counts, the tests' credibility suffered. The more research that was done, the less clear it seemed that test scores were a sensible way to assess the impact of integration. This discovery encouraged studies on other outcomes of desegregation. Researchers recalled that desegregation was supposed to have something to do with hearts as well as minds—with interracial attitudes and behavior as well as test scores. They cautioned that excessive reliance on tests would produce a distorted picture. The sophistication of studies on the social-psychological impact of desegregation increased appreciably as a result, but these improvements did nothing to offer clear policy advice.

Early research on racial attitudes had seemed to show that racial attitudes would benefit from interracial contact in equal status situations.[22] These studies viewed racial attitudes as a self-evidently important outcome of biracial settings, partly because social psychologists assumed that there were those links between attitudes and behavior. But in a period when bigoted attitudes were openly expressed, liberal social scientists understandably regarded the reduction of such expression as a good in itself.

As research on desegregation's effect on interracial attitudes flowered in the middle and late 1960s, dissatisfaction with the older attitude measures increased. They were few in number; they needed technical improvement; and as desegregation spread, the available sorts of interracial situations grew and demanded new measures appropriate to the circumstances. By the late 1960s, the result was a rich growth: forced-choice questionnaire items, social-distance scales, measures of racial stereotyping, doll-choice measures, sociometric preferences, simple Likert scales, and semantic differentials.[23]

The improvement here is plain: Attitudes are not simple, and it makes perfect sense to pursue them in a variety of ways. But one problem was the lack of comparability. Studies seldom repeated measures, let alone replicated study conditions. The issues were a little different, the populations were varied, and the measures were different. The variation did not seem to be a serious problem until researchers began to notice the tendency of attitude measures to be weakly related. Even within studies, there were almost always low correlations between scales measuring interracial attitudes.[24] If different ways of measuring the same conceptual variable did not lead to the same conclusions, then the proliferation of measures raised questions of generalizability. Most studies stood as socially scientific islands; each was more or less gleaming, but most were somewhat incomparable to the others.

A second problem arose partly from evidence about the weak relationships among measures. This problem increased uncertainty about the validity of any single measure and made using more measures seem even more sensible. But the focus of most work of this sort was demonstrating and explaining the effects of interracial schools on racial attitudes, and the weak connections among measures meant that explaining the causal connection for one measure of racial attitudes need not necessarily hold for another. Interracial schools that seemed to produce a good racial climate based on a self-administered questionnaire seemed to produce a bigoted climate based on observers' reports.[25] These findings confused interpretations of both reality and the research. Researchers learned that the way they measured attitudes seemed to influence the sort of attitudes they "found." Such self-consciousness is a good thing, but it doesn't produce much clarity about the policy implications of research findings, nor does it build confidence in the solidarity of research results.

A third problem was the relation between attitudes and behavior. Social psychologists who had focused research on attitudes had, of course, assumed that a change in attitudes would lead to a change in behavior. But by the mid 1960s, social psychology had changed its tune. One reviewer concluded:

Most socially significant questions involve overt behavior rather than peoples' feelings, and the assumption that feelings are directly translated into action has not been demonstrated.[26]

In the case of integration, research showed that the attitude-behavior link was fragile. In one study of biracial groups, white students from integrated schools were more likely to dominate blacks than whites from all white schools.[27] In another study, white college students who expressed more prejudice actually took more suggestions from blacks in group tasks than did white students who expressed less prejudice.[28] It is easy to conjure up after-the-fact explanations for such findings, but that is a little off the point. The advance of research on racial attitudes has revealed no strong or consistent connection between attitudes and behavior. This result is an interesting and important research development, but it rather weakened the ground under an entire line of policy-relevant studies based exclusively on attitude research.

Partly as a consequence of these findings, measures or reports of behavior came to be included routinely in research on desegregated schools. This research created a whole new set of outcomes to explain and greatly complicated the job of understanding the effect of school factors on student outcomes. And substituting behavioral for attitudinal variables—as many researchers did—made later studies increasingly incompatible with earlier ones.

In an effort to sort out the hodge-podge of findings, social scientists turned their attention to the social circumstances that might mediate the effects of interracial situations on attitudes and behavior. They turned up a formidable list. In some studies they weighed the impact of teachers' and principals' racial attitudes. In others, they probed whether students' social and economic class backgrounds affected student reaction to desegregation. Other studies explored other influences: segregation of classrooms, length of students' experience in interracial schools, the extent of minority students' participation in extracurricular activities, the age or grade level of students, community attitudes, and the degree of internal tracking and grouping.[29]

For each one of these influences, at least one study claimed that the factor in question did mediate the relationship between interracial settings and racial attitudes or behavior. But factors that seemed important in some studies seemed unimportant in others. Ordinarily, it was not possible to know just why this was so. As a result, the findings seemed unstable, and little was learned about the relative salience of the situational influences on racial climate. One study did try to quantify and compare the relative importance of many of these factors, but Crain and his colleagues found that most situational influences had no impact on the racial attitudes measured.[30] Some had very weak effects, and in some cases the effects varied between different measures. Complicated multivariate analyses of situational factors that mediate the impact of racial composition of schools on student attitudes and behavior did little to clear up the contradictions of earlier studies or to offer much guidance for policy.

Thus, social-psychological research was a useful balance to the heavy reliance on test scores, but it didn't exactly clarify matters. By adding another disciplinary perspective on desegregation, it complicated the picture. This phenomenon became widespread in the late 1960s and early 1970s, as sociologists and economists entered the field, but it was most striking in the work of some anthropologically oriented social scientists. They rejected all forms of quantitative and survey research and undertook direct observational studies of desegregated schools. These ethnographies offered a different disciplinary approach to the study of schools and race, and they presented rather a different picture of desegregation. They found social segregation within schools, insensitivity and racial stereotyping on the part of teachers, defensiveness and denial by teachers and administrators, and a mixed and often unhappy experience for black children. The most recent effort reported on a desegregation program carried out in a way that most communities would probably regard as either quite acceptable or ideal.[31] But the integration experience seemed a demeaning and unhappy one for most of the black children involved, though none of the school staff appear to have known about their feelings. This finding was rather a different portrait than emerged from the various quantitative evaluations of desegregation, and it resulted in rather more astringent conclusions. The author, an integrationist, held that desegregation simply ought not to occur under such conditions.

In summary, then, the improvement of research has had paradoxical results. On one hand, we have a less simple-minded and more plausible account of social reality. Artifacts are reduced, distortions due to faulty method are often eliminated, overblown interpretations are corrected, and more careful analyses are presented. The technical sophistication of recent research on desegregation is such as to inspire more confidence than twenty years ago that the results of any given study are valid. But these changes have led to more studies that disagree, to more qualified conclusions, more arguments, and more arcane reports and unintelligible results. If any given study is more valid, the inferences to policy from the lot seem much more uncertain.

One reason for this uncertainty, as we have pointed out, is that methodological refinement in social research often is not convergent but rather tends to sharpen differences. The research has grown, and grown more sophisticated, but the findings have not been cumulative. A good part of the reason is that no strong theory suggested what influences should be observed or what outcome variables are most important. Given this situation, social science tends to proliferate under the influence of empirical ideas, weak theories, intuitions from practical experience, suggestions from other fields, or the analytic possibilities suggested by new methodologies. The fruit of such scientific developments is sometimes rich and always varied, but not necessarily very coherent. Another reason is that the progress of research on a social problem tends to draw in diverse research traditions, and the consequence is more differences in approach and interpretation. Still another reason is that research on social problems tends to move backward, from relatively simple ideas about problems and their solutions to ever more basic questions about both. The net result is a more varied picture of reality, but such results don't lend themselves to straightforward policy guidance.

## Conclusion

One thing is clear from this story. The more research on a social problem prospers, the harder it is for policymakers and courts to get the sort of guidance they often say they want: clear recommendations about what to do, or at least clear alternatives. Predictably, the result is frustration. In both the race and school finance cases, for example, one can see the judges becoming more exasperated with the complexities and contradictions of research.[32]

But while we expect continued frustration in this connection, we don't think that social science is irrelevant to social policy, nor do we think it should be. At its best, social research provides a reasonable sense of the various ways a problem can be understood and a reasonable account of how solutions might be approached. Such general advice about controversial and problematic issues is a useful contribution to social knowledge, even if it is not crisply relevant to particular decisions.

But this view doesn't explain exactly how we should think about research and its relation to policy. One alternative is to think of policy formation as a process of competition for values and social goods and to think of research as ammunition for the various parties at interest. The growing diversity of approaches and findings may frustrate any given user of research, but the net satisfaction of all users will increase as more of them find studies that suit their special purposes. It goes almost without saying that this view will seem satisfying in proportion to the fairness of the competition.

But if this view is plausible, it isn't complete. Our account also suggests that the improvement of research has not simply been a matter of sharper argumentation. In addition, we know more. Research has helped provide a better picture of the desegregation process; it has taught us something about how desegregation does and doesn't work, and why; and it has helped broaden our picture of whom desegregation affects. Typically, however, these improvements do not offer a handy solution. Indeed, among the things we can learn from the accumulated studies of the last few decades are cautions about easy solutions, simple formulations, and social science findings. On this view, then, research on a social problem might be portrayed as a contribution to social wisdom. As more is learned through experience and investigation, simpler and appealing ideas give way to more qualified advice.

Finally, the studies cited in this chapter suggest that research is part and parcel of social enthusiasms. When whipping up the brains of America's youth was in fashion in the late 1950s and early 1960s, research on race and schools stepped to the tune of test scores. When desegregation was "out" and community control was "in," fate-control studies were all the rage. And when school desegregation came North early in the seventies, many liberal and moderate northern politicians who had supported this reform in the South suddenly developed cramps. Research on race and schools has suffered a similar affliction, which is evident in the recent work of Armor and Coleman, among others.[33]

On this view, research and policy might be pictured as the subjects of sea changes in social thought. Research contributes something to these changing climates of opinion, but it also responds to them. Research and policy affect each other, but both seem to bob along on larger waves.

These three pictures of the relation between research and policy imply rather different criteria for evaluating the contribution of research. If we think of social science as political ammunition, we would evaluate the quality of desegregation research at least partly in terms of fairness in its distribution. If, alternatively, we think of research as an incremental growth in social wisdom, then we would evaluate it in terms of its contribution to such general guidance. And if we imagine policy and research to be both swept away on waves of social enthusiasms, we might retreat, puzzled at the difficulty of devising any evaluative criterion.

Regardless of which picture is most appealing, our account suggests that on the evaluative criterion advanced by most advocates of policy research—does the research contribute more precise guidance for particular decisions?—most research would fail miserably. We think the problem here lies not so much with the quality of research as with a misconception of the research process. To expect more precise guidance for particular decisions is in most cases a dream hopelessly at variance with the divergent and pluralistic character of social policy research. Rather than helping, the dream generally seems to distract research workers from a clear view of their work and its role.

Instead, we think it is useful to picture the research process as a dialogue about social reality—that is, as a historical conversation about social problems and how they might be solved. A dialogue is good to the extent that the various relevant views are present and to the extent that points of difference are clarified. A dialogue is good to the extent that the whole represents a satisfying, if necessarily diverse, account of the ways in which an issue can be framed, explored, and resolved. We have tried to show how, as research prospers, the conversation is enriched.

This is not to suggest that the progress of research on race and schools has been entirely satisfying, for some parties have been better represented at the social science smorgasbord than others, nor is it to suggest that truth will complaisantly out, for dialogues are subject to fashion changes. While they can produce what we think of as wisdom, it is often only a passing fancy that later loses its appeal. But our chief point is simply that it is helpful to see social research this way. To those who ply the trade, it offers a more sensible view of their work. Among those who would like guidance, it presents a basis for more reasonable expectations. It also helps explain why improved knowledge doesn't always lead to more effective action.

Notes

1. For a discussion of these points, see Thomas Kuhn, *The Structure of Scientific Revolutions* (Chicago: University of Chicago Press, 1962).

2. Social Science Brief (Appendix to Appellant's Briefs: The Effects of Segregation and the Consequences of Desegregation: A Social Science Statement), reprinted in Kenneth B. Clark, *Prejudice and Your Child* (Boston: Beacon Press, 1963, 2nd ed.), pp. 166-84.

3. Henry E. Garrett, "A Note of the Intelligence Scores of Negroes and Whites in 1918," *Journal of Abnormal and Social Psychology* 40 (1945); Henry E. Garrett, "The Equalitarian Dogma," *Mankind Quarterly* 1 (1961); Audrey Shuey, *The Testing of Negro Intelligence* (Lynchburg, Va.: Bell, 1958).

4. See the extensive reviews in Nancy M. St. John, *School Desegregation* (New York: Wiley, 1975), and in Meyer Weinberg, "The Relationship between School Desegregation and Academic Achievement: A Review of the Research," *Law and Contemporary Problems* 39, no. 2 (Spring 1975), pp. 240-70.

5. James S. Coleman et al., *Equality of Educational Opportunity* (Washington, D.C.: U.S. Government Printing Office, 1966).

6. U.S. Commission on Civil Rights, *Racial Isolation in the Public Schools* (Washington, D.C.: U.S. Government Printing Office, 1967), vols. 1 and 2.

7. St. John, *School Desegregation*, p. 80.

8. See, for example, Charles V. Hamilton, "Race and Education: A Search for Legitimacy," *Harvard Educational Review* 38, no. 4 (Fall 1968).

9. The USCCR report, *Racial Isolation*, was the first in this line of thought.

10. Derrick A. Bell, Jr., "Waiting on the Promise of Brown," *Law and Contemporary Problems*, no. 1 (Winter 1975), pp. 341-73.

11. Kenneth and Mamie Clark, "Racial Identification and Preference in Negro Children," in T. Newcomb and E. Hartley (eds.), *Readings in Social Psychology* (New York: Holt, 1974, 1st ed.).

12. Garrett, "The Equalitarian Dogma," and Shuey, *The Testing*.

13. For example, Thomas Pettigrew writes about the desegregation of the Washington, D.C., schools: "Though Negro students, swelled by migrants now comprised three-fourths of the student body, achievement test scores had risen significantly for each grade level sampled and each subject area tested approached or equalled national norms. Furthermore, both Negro and White students shared in these increments." See T.F. Pettigrew, *A Profile of the Negro American* (Princeton, N.J.: Van Nostrand, 1964), p. 128.

14. Samuel Bowles and Henry M. Levin, "The Determinants of Scholastic Achievements—An Appraisal of Some Recent Evidence," *Journal of Human Resources* 3 (Winter 1968), pp. 3-24.

15. For fuller treatments of this phenomenon, see David K. Cohen and Michael S. Garet, "Reforming Educational Policy with Applied Social Research," *Harvard Educational Review* 45, no. 1 (February 1975).

16. Christopher Jencks et al., *Inequality* (New York: Harper & Row, 1972); Marshall S. Smith, "Equality of Educational Opportunity: The Basic Finds Reconsidered," in Frederick Mosteller and Daniel P. Moynihan (eds.), *On*

*Equality of Educational Opportunity* (New York: Random House, 1972); D.J. Armor, "The Evidence on Busing," *The Public Interest* (Summer 1972); Pettigrew, *A Profile*; and Coleman et al., *Equality*.

17. George Mayeske et al., *A Study of Our Nation's Schools* (Washington, D.C.: DHEW, 1972).

18. Smith, "Equality of Educational Opportunity."

19. D.K. Cohen, T.F. Pettigrew, and R.T. Riley, "Race and the Outcomes of Schooling," in Mosteller and Moynihan (eds.), *On Equality of Educational Opportunity*.

20. See, for example, the citations in St. John, *School Desegregation*.

21. *Design for a National Longitudinal Study of School Desegregation* (Santa Monica, Calif.: Rand Corp., 1974).

22. Gordon W. Allport, *The Nature of Prejudice* (Garden City, N.Y.: Doubleday Anchor Books, 1954), and Samual A. Stouffer et al., *The American Soldier* (Princeton, N.J.: Princeton University Press, 1949).

23. See St. John, *School Desegregation*, chapter 4.

24. James M. Jones, *Prejudice and Racism* (Reading, Mass.: Addison-Wesley, 1972); also St. John, *School Desegregation*.

25. See, for example, R. Hope (1967) cited in St. John, *School Desegregation*, and Judith Porter, *Black Child, White Child* (Cambridge, Mass.: Harvard University Press, 1971).

26. Allan Wicker, "Attitudes versus Actions: The Relationship of Verbal and Overt Behavioral Responses to Attitude Objects," *Journal of Social Issues* 25 (1969), p. 75.

27. J. Seidner (1971) described in Elizabeth G. Cohen, "The Effects of Desegregation on Race Relations," *Law and Contemporary Problems* 39 (Spring 1975), pp. 271-99.

28. I. Katz and L. Benjamin, "Effects of White Authoritarianism in Biracial Work Groups," *Journal of Abnormal and Social Psychology* 61 (1960), pp. 448-56.

29. Examples of this kind of research include Appendix C1, USCCR, *Racial Isolation*; J.E. Teele and C. Mayo, "School Racial Integration: Tumult and Shame," *Journal of Social Issues* 25 (1969), pp. 137-56; E. Useem, "White Students and Token Desegregation," *Integrated Education* (1972), pp. 44-56; and C. Willie and J. Baker, *Race Mixing in the Public Schools*, 1973.

30. Armor, "The Evidence on Busing," pp. 90-126; T.F. Pettigrew, E.L. Useem, C. Normand, and M.S. Smith, "Busing: A Review of the Evidence," *The Public Interest* (Winter 1973), pp. 88-118; D.J. Armor, "The Double Double Standard: A Reply," *The Public Interest* (Winter 1973), pp. 119-31.

31. Raymond Rist, *The Invisible Children: School Integration in American Society* (Cambridge, Mass.: Harvard University Press, forthcoming 1976).

32. See *Hart* v. *Community School Board*, 383 F. Supp. 699, 744 (E.D.N.Y. 1974), and *Hobson* v. *Hansen*, 327 F. Supp. 844, 859 (D.D.C. 1971).

33. Armor, "The Evidence on Busing," and J.S. Coleman et al., *Trends In School Segregation* (Washington, D.C.: The Urban Institute, 1975).

# 3

## In Search of Impact: An Analysis of the Utilization of Federal Health Evaluation Research

*Michael Q. Patton, Patricia Smith Grimes, Kathryn M. Guthrie, Nancy J. Brennan, Barbara Dickey French, and Dale A. Blyth*

### The Issue of Nonutilization

The problem of the nonutilization or the underutilization of evaluation research has been discussed frequently in the evaluation literature. There seems to be a consensus that the impact of evaluative research on program decision making has been less than substantial. Carol Weiss (1972) lists underutilization as one of the foremost problems in evaluation research:

Evaluation research is meant for immediate and direct use in improving the quality of social programming. Yet a review of evaluation experience suggests that evaluation results have not exerted significant influence on program decisions [pp. 10, 11].

Other prominent reviewers have reached a similar conclusion. Ernest House (1972, p. 412) put it this way: "Producing data is one thing! Getting it used is quite another." Williams and Evans (1969, p. 453) write that ". . . in the final analysis, the test of the effectiveness of outcome data is its impact on implemented policy. By this standard, there is a dearth of successful evaluation studies." Wholey (1971, p. 46) concluded that ". . . the recent literature is unanimous in announcing the general failure of evaluation to affect decision-making in a significant way." He goes on to note that his own study ". . . found the same absence of successful evaluations noted by other authors" (p. 48). David Cohen (1975, p. 19) finds that ". . . there is little evidence to indicate that government planning offices have succeeded in linking social research and decisionmaking." Alkin (1974) found that Title VII evaluations were useful to project directors but were not useful at the federal level because the results were not timely in terms of funding decisions. Weidman et al. (1973, p. 15) concluded that on those rare occasions when evaluation studies have been used, ". . . the little use that has occurred [has been] fortuitous rather than planned."

This research was conducted as part of an NIMH-supported training program in evaluation methodology at the University of Minnesota. Trainees worked through the Minnesota Center for Social Research, University of Minnesota. The following trainees, in addition to the authors, participated in the project: James Cleary, Joan Dreyer, James Fitzsimmons, Steve Froman, Kathy Gilder, David Jones, Leah Harvey, Gary Miller, Gail Nordheim, Julia Nutter, Darla Sandhofer, Jerome Segal, and John Townsend. In addition, the following Minnesota faculty made helpful comments on an earlier draft of this chapter: John Brandl, Director, School of Public Affairs; Martha Burt, Tom Dewar, and Ron Geizer. Neala Yount transcribed over one hundred hours of interviews with unusual diligence and care.

Decisionmakers continue to lament the disappointing results of evaluation research, complaining that the findings don't tell them what they need to know. And evaluators continue to complain about many things, "... but their most common complaint is that their findings are ignored" (Weiss, 1972, p. 319).

The issue at this time is not the search for a single formula of utilization success, nor the generation of ever-longer lists of possible factors affecting utilization. *The task for the present is to identify and refine a few key variables that may make a major difference in a significant number of evaluation cases* (cf. Weiss, 1972, p. 325). The research on utilization of evaluations described in this chapter is a modest effort to move a bit further along that path of refinement.

This chapter is based on a follow-up of twenty federal health evaluations. We attempted to assess the degree to which these evaluations had been used and to identify the factors that affected varying degrees of utilization. Given the pessimistic nature of most writings on utilization, we began our study fully expecting our major problem would be to find even one evaluation that had had a significant impact on program decisions. What we found was considerably more complex and less dismal than our original impressions led us to expect. Evaluation research is used but not in the ways we had anticipated. Moreover, we found that the factors we had expected would be important in explaining variations in utilization were less important than a new factor that emerged from our analysis. After reviewing our sample and methodology, we shall report these findings and discuss their implications.

## The Sample

The twenty case studies that constitute the sample in this study are national health program evaluations. They were selected from among 170 evaluations on file in the Office of Health Evaluation, HEW.[1] We excluded policy pieces, think pieces, and arm-chair reflections from our analysis. We also eliminated studies that did not examine national programs and any studies completed before 1971 or after 1973. We did this to enable a follow-up of evaluations that were recent enough to be remembered and at the same time had been completed far enough in the past to allow time for utilization to occur. These control variables reduced the number of abstracts from 170 to 76 and gave us a more homogeneous group of abstracts consisting of (1) program evaluation studies of (2) national scope where (3) some systematic data collection was done and (4) where the study was completed no earlier than 1971 and no later than 1973.

A stratified random sample of twenty studies was then drawn from among the remaining seventy-six abstracts. They consist of four evaluations of various community mental health center program activities, four health training programs, two national assessments of laboratory proficiency, two evaluations of neighborhood health center programs, studies of two health services delivery system programs, a training program on alcoholism, a health regulatory program, a federal loan forgiveness program, a training workshop evaluation, and two evaluations of specialized health facilities.

Since it is impossible to specify the universe of evaluation research studies, it is not possible to specify the degree to which this sample of twenty cases is representative of evaluation research in general. The sample is diverse in its inclusion of a broad range of evaluations. We feel that this heterogeneity increases the meaningfulness of those patterns of utilization that actually emerged in our follow-up interviews because those patterns were not systematically related to specific types of evaluations.

### Data on Utilization: The Interviews

The first purpose of this study is to examine the nature and degree of *utilization* of federal evaluation research. Very limited resources allowed for interviewing only three key informants about the utilization of each of the twenty cases in the final sample. These key informants were (1) the project officer[2] for the study, (2) the person *identified by the project officer* as being either the decisionmaker for the program evaluated or the person most knowledgeable about the study's impact.[3] and (3) the evaluator who had major responsibility for the study.

The project officer interviews were conducted primarily to identify informants, decisionmakers, and evaluators who would be interviewed. This snowball sampling technique resulted in considerable variation in whom we interviewed as the "decisionmakers" in each case. Most of the government informants had been or now are office directors (and deputy directors), division heads, or bureau chiefs. Overall, these decisionmakers each represent an average of over fourteen years' experience in the federal government. Evaluators in our sample each represent an average of nearly fourteen years' experience in conducting evaluative research.

Two forms of the interview were developed: one for government decisionmakers and one for evaluators. Both interviews were open-ended and ranged in length from one to six hours, with an average of about two hours.[4]

### Impact of Evaluation Research

The conceptualization and operationalization of the notion of *research impact* or *evaluation utilization* is no easy task. We began with an ideal-typical construct of utilization as *immediate and concrete effect on specific decisions and program activities resulting directly from evaluative research findings.* Yet, as noted earlier, the consensus in the evaluation literature is that instances of such impact are relatively rare. Because we expected little evidence of impact and because of our inability to agree on an operational definition of utilization, we adopted an open-ended strategy in our interviewing that allowed respondents to define utilization in terms meaningful to them. Our question was as follows:

Now we'd like to focus on the *actual* impact of this evaluation study. We'd like to get at *any* ways in which the study may have had an impact—an impact on program operations, on planning, on funding, on policy, on decisions, on thinking about the program, and so forth. From your point of view, what was the impact of this evaluation study on the program we've been discussing?

Following a set of probes and additional questions, depending upon the respondents' initial answers, we asked a question about the nonprogram impacts of the evaluation:

We've been focusing mainly on the study's impact on the program itself. Sometimes studies have a broader impact on things beyond an immediate program, things like *general thinking on issues that arise from a study*, or *position papers*, or *legislation. . . .* Did this evaluation have an impact on any of these kinds of things?

What we found in response to these questions on impact was considerably more complex and less dismal than our original thinking had led us to expect. We found that evaluation research *is used* by decisionmakers but not in the clear-cut and organization-shaking ways that social scientists sometimes believe research should be used. The problem we have come to feel may well lie more in many social scientists' overly grand expectations about their own importance to policy decisions than in the intransience of federal bureaucrats. The results of our interviews suggest that what is typically characterized as underutilization or nonutilization of evaluation research can be attributed in substantial degrees to a definition of utilization that is too narrow and fails to take into consideration the nature of actual decision-making processes in most programs.

*The Findings on Impact*

In response to the first question on impact, fourteen of eighteen responding decisionmakers and thirteen of fourteen responding evaluators felt that the evaluation had had an impact on the program. (Two of the decisionmakers and six of the evaluators felt that they had too little direct knowledge of actual use to comment.) Moreover, thirteen of sixteen responding decisionmakers and nine of thirteen responding evaluators felt these specific evaluation studies had had identifiable nonprogram impacts.

The number of positive responses to the questions on impact are quite striking when one considers the predominance of the theme of nonutilization in the evaluation literature. The main difference here, however, may be that the actual participants in each specific evaluation process were asked to define impact in terms that were meaningful to them and their situations. Thus, none of the impacts described was of the type where new findings from an evaluation led directly and immediately to the making of major, concrete program decisions. *The more typical impact was one where the evaluation findings provided additional pieces of information in the difficult puzzle of program action, thereby permitting some reduction in the uncertainty within which any federal decisionmaker inevitably operates.*

The most dramatic example of utilization reported in our sample was the case of an evaluation of a pilot program. The program administrator had been favorable to the program in principle, was uncertain what the results would be, but was "hoping the results would be positive." The evaluation proved to be negative. The administrator was "surprised, but not alarmingly so. . . . We had expected a more positive finding or we would not have engaged in the pilot studies" (DM367:13).[5] The program was subsequently ended with the evaluation carrying "about a third of the weight of the total decision" (DM367:8).

This relatively dramatic impact stood out as a clear exception to the more typical pattern where evaluation findings constitute an additional input into an ongoing, evolutionary process of program action. One decisionmaker with twenty-nine years' experience in the federal government, much of that time directing research, gave the following report on the impact of the evaluation study about which he was interviewed:

It served two purposes. One is that it resolved a lot of doubts and confusions and misunderstandings that the advisory committee had. . . . And the second one was that it gave me additional knowledge to support facts that I already knew, and, as I say, broadened the scope more than I realized. In other words, the perceptions of where the organization was going and what it was accomplishing were a lot worse than I had anticipated . . . , but I was somewhat startled to find out that they were worse, yet it wasn't very hard because it was partly confirming things that I was observing [DM232:17].

He goes on to say that following the evaluation:

. . . we changed our whole functional approach to looking at the identification of what we should be working on. But again I have a hard time because these things, *none of these things occurred overnight, and in an evolutionary process it's hard to say, you know, at what point it made a significant difference or what point did it merely verify and strengthen the resolve that you already had"* [DM232:17].

His overall assessment of the actual impact of the evaluation was quite constrained: "It filled in the gaps and pieces that various ones really had in their orientation to the program" (DM232:12), and "It verified my suspicions" (DM232:24).

Respondents frequently had difficulty assessing the degree to which an evaluation study actually affected decisions. This was t ue, for example, in the case of a large-scale evaluation effort that had been extremely expensive and had taken place over several years' time. The evaluation found some deficiencies in the program, but the overall findings were quite positive. Changes corresponding to those recommended in the study occurred when the report was published, but those changes could not be directly and simply attributed to the evaluation:

The staff was aware that the activities in the centers were deficient from other studies that we had done, and they were beefing up these budgets and providing technical assistance to some of the projects and improving health activities. Now I can't link this finding and that activity. Again that confirms that finding and you say, eureka, I have found _____ deficient, therefore I will [change] the program. That didn't happen. [The] deficiency was previously noted. A lot of studies like this confirmed what close-by people know and they were already taking actions before the findings. *So you can't link the finding to the action, that's just confirmation. . . . The direct link between the finding and the program decision is very diffuse.* [Its major impact was] confirming our setting, a credibility, a tone of additional credibility to the program [DM361:12,13].

Moreover, this decisionmaker felt that additional credibility for the program became one part of an overall process of information flow that helped to some degree reduce the uncertainty faced by decisionmakers responsible for the program: "People in the budget channels at OMB were, I guess, eager for and interested in any data that would help them make decisions, and this was certainly one useful bit of data" (DM361:13).

The kind of impact we found, then, was that evaluation research provides some additional information that is judged and used in the context of other available information to help reduce the unknowns in the making of difficult decisions. The impact ranges from "it sort of confirmed our impressions . . . , confirming some other anecdotal or impression that we had" (DM209:7,1) to providing a new awareness that can carry over into other programs:

Some of our subsequent decisions on some of our other programs were probably based on information that came out of this study. . . . The most significant information from this study that we really had not realized . . . made an impact on future decisions with regard to other programs that we carry on [DM209:7].

And why did it have this impact?

Well I guess I'll go back to the points I've already made, that it confirmed some impressionistic feelings and anecdotal information that we had about certain kinds of things. At least it gave us some hard data on which to base some future programming decisions. It may not have been the only data, but it was confirming data, and I think that's important. . . . And you know at the time this study was conceived, and even by the time it was reported to us, we really had very little data, and you know, probably *when you don't have any data, every little bit helps* [DM209:15].

This reduction of uncertainty emerged as highly important to decision-makers. In some cases it simply made them more confident and determined. On the other hand, where the need for change is indicated, an evaluation study can help speed up the process of change or provide an impetus for finally getting things rolling:

Well I think that all we did was probably speed up the process. I think that they were getting there anyhow. They knew that their performance was being criticized by various parts of the government and the private sector. As I said earlier, we didn't enter this study thinking that we were going to break any new ground, and when we got finished, we knew that we hadn't. All we did was document what the people have been saying for a long time—that _____ are doing a lousy job, so what else is new? But we were able to show just how poor a job they were doing [EV268:12].

Reducing uncertainty, speeding things up, and getting things finally started are real impacts—not revolutionary, organization-shaking impacts—but important impacts in the opinion of the people we interviewed. One administrator summarized this view both on the specific evaluation in question and about evaluation in general as follows:

Myself I have a favorable view toward evaluating. If nothing else it precipitates activity many times that could not be precipitated without someone taking a hard look at an organization. It did precipitate activity in [this program]. Some of it was not positive. Some of it was negative. *At least something occurred that wouldn't have occurred if the evaluation hadn't taken place* [DM312:21].

Another evaluator made it quite clear that simply reducing the enormous uncertainty facing many program administrators is a major purpose of evaluative research:

One of the things I think often is that the government itself gets scared . . . of whatever kinds of new venture that they want to go into, and they're quite uncertain as to what steps they want to take next. So then they say, okay, let's have some outside person do this for us, or maybe an inside person do this, so at least we have some "data" to base some of our policies on [EV283:34].

The image that emerges in our interviews is that there are few major, direction-changing decisions in most programming and that evaluation research is used as one piece of information that feeds into a slow, evolutionary process of program development. Program development is a process of "muddling through" (Lindblom, 1959; Allison, 1971; Steinbruner, 1974) and evaluation research is part of the muddling.

Further, we did not find much expectation that government decision making could be or should be otherwise. One person with thirty-five years' experience in the federal government (twenty of those years in evaluation) put it like this: "I don't think an evaluation's ever totally used. That was true whether I was using them as an administrator or doing them myself" (EV346:11). Later in the interview he said:

I don't think the government should go out and use every evaluation it gets. I think sometimes just the insights of the evaluation feed over to the next administrative reiteration, maybe just the right way to do it. That is, [decisions aren't] clearly the result of evaluation. There's a feedback in some way . . . , upgrading or a shifting of direction because of it. [Change] it is, you know, small and slow . . . [EV346:16].

An evaluator expressed a similar view:

I think it's just like everything else in life, if you're at the right place at the right time, it can be useful, but it's obviously only probably one ingredient in the information process. It's rather naive and presumptuous on the part of the evaluation community [to think otherwise] and also it presumes a rationality that in no way fits [EV264:18].

Our findings, then, suggest that the predominant image of nonutilization that characterizes much of the commentary on evaluation research can be attributed in substantial degree to a definition of utilization that is too narrow in its emphasis on seeing immediate, direct, and concrete impact on program decisions. Such a narrow definition fails to take into account the nature of most actual program development processes.

The impact of most basic research seems quite similar. Researchers in any field of specialization can count the studies of major impact on one hand. Most science falls into that great amorphous activity called "normal science." Changes come slowly. Individual researchers contribute a bit here and a bit there and thus reduce uncertainty gradually over time. Scientific revolutions are infrequent and slow in coming (Kuhn, 1972).

The situation is the same in applied research. Evaluation research is one part of the "normal science" of government decision making. Research impacts in ripples not in waves. Occasionally a major study emerges with great impact. But most applied research can be expected to have no more than a small and momentary effect on the operations of a given program. The epitaph for most studies will read something like this:

[We expected that it would be used] but in a way of providing background information around the consequences of certain kinds of federal decision-making options. But not necessarily in and of itself determining those decisions. In other words you might have some idea of what the consequences of the decision are, but there might be a lot of other factors you'd take into account in how you would decide . . . [DM264:8].

[It had a particular impact in that] it contributed to the general information context of what was going on at the time, rather than in itself. . . . It contributes to that background of understanding one of the policy issues, rather than resulting in one option versus another of policy being adopted [DM264:11].

## Factors Affecting Utilization

We took a dual approach to the problem of identifying the factors that affect utilization. Once the respondents had discussed their perceptions about the nature and degree of utilization of the specific evaluation study under investigation, we asked the following open-ended question:

Okay, you've described the impact of the study. Now we'd like you to think about *why* this study was used in the ways you've just described. . . . What do you feel were the important reasons why this study had the level of impact it did?

Following a set of probes and follow-up questions, we asked respondents to comment on the relevance and importance of eleven factors extracted from the literature on utilization: methodological quality, methodological appropriateness, timeliness, lateness of report, positive-negative findings, surprise of findings, central-peripheral program objectives evaluated, presence-absence of related studies, political factors, government-evaluator interactions, and resources available for the study. Finally, we asked respondents to "pick out the single factor you feel had the greatest effect on how this study was used."

Two related factors emerged as important in our interview: (1) a political considerations factor and (2) a factor we have called the personal factor. This latter factor was unexpected and its clear importance to our respondents has, we believe, substantial implications for the utilization of evaluation research. *None of the other specific literature factors about which we asked questions emerged as important with any consistency.* Moreover, when these specific factors were important in explaining the utilization or nonutilization of a particular study, it was virtually always in the context of a larger set of circumstances related to the issues and decisions at hand.

*Lateness of Study Completion*

We wanted to examine the allegation that much evaluation research is under-utilized because studies are completed too late to be used for making a specific decision, particularly budgetary decisions. This problem is based to a large extent on the notion that the purpose of evaluation research is to serve as the basis for the making of specific, identifiable, and concrete decisions. Inasmuch as we have already argued that most evaluation research does not serve such a narrow function and is not intended to serve such a narrow function, it is not surprising that lateness in the completion of studies was not an important factor in explaining utilization of the studies in our sample.

In four of our twenty cases, decisionmakers indicated that the final research reports were completed late, but in all four cases preliminary information was available to a sufficient extent to be used at the time the study should have been completed. In no case was lateness considered the critical factor in explaining the limited utilization of the studies. Rather, the information was viewed as feeding into a longer-term process of program development and decision making. Several decisionmakers commented that it was helpful to have the information on time, but had the final report been late the impact of the study would not likely have been different, partly because few issues become one-time decisions. As one decisionmaker put it:

[The] study was too late for the immediate budget that it was supposed to impact on, but it wasn't too late in terms of the fact that the same issue was occurring every year after that anyway [DM264:16].

*Methodological Quality and Appropriateness*

A major factor often identified as the reason for nonutilization is the poor quality of much evaluation research. Of the fifteen decisionmakers who rated methodological quality of the study about which they were interviewed, five rated the methodological quality as "high," eight said it was "medium," and only two gave the study a "low" rating. Of seventeen responding evaluators, seven gave "high" ratings, six "medium" responses, and four "low" ratings. No decisionmaker and only one evaluator felt that the methodology used was inappropriate for researching the question at issue.

More to the point, only four decisionmakers felt that methodological quality was "very important" in explaining the study's utilization. Further probing, however, revealed that "methodological quality" meant different things to different decisionmakers. For some, it meant the reputation of the evaluators; for others it meant asking the right question. In no case was methodological quality identified as the most important factor explaining either utilization or nonutilization.

The relevance of methodological quality must be understood in the full context of a study, the political environment, the degree of uncertainty with which the decisionmaker is faced and thus his/her relative need for any and all clarifying information. If information is scarce, then new information of even dubious quality may be somewhat helpful. For example, one administrator admitted that the evaluation's methodological rigor could be seriously questioned, but the study was highly useful in policy discussions:

The quality and the methodology were not even considered. All that was considered was that management didn't know what was going on, the terms, the procedures, the program was foreign to their background. And they did not have expertise in it, so they were relying on somebody else who had the expertise to translate to them what was going on in terms that they would understand and what the problems were [DM312:17].

Social scientists may lament this situation and may well feel that the methodology of evaluation research *ought* to be of high quality for value reasons—that is, because *poor quality studies ought not be used. But there is little in our data to suggest that improving methodological quality in and of itself will have much effect on increasing the utilization of evaluation research.*

Again, the importance of methodological quality as a factor explaining utilization is tempered by the nature of the utilization we found. Were evaluations being used as the major piece of information in making critical one-time decisions, methodological rigor might be paramount. But where evaluation research is one part, often a small part, in a larger whole, decisionmakers displayed less than burning interest in methodological quality. One highly experienced administrator viewed methodology as part of the political process of utilization:

Well, let me put it in another context. If it were negative findings programmatically we would have hit very hard on the methodology and tried to discredit it. You know, from the program standpoint. But since it was kind of positive findings, we said, "Okay, here it is." If anybody asked us about the methodological deficiencies we were never reluctant to tell them what we thought they were. *Not many people asked* [DM361:13].

## Political Factors

This last quote on methodological quality makes it clear that methodology, like everything else in evaluation research, can become partly a political question. The political nature of evaluation research has been well documented. The decisionmakers and evaluators in our sample demonstrated an acute awareness of the fact that social science research rarely produces clear-cut findings. Findings must be interpreted, and interpretation is partly a political process—a value-laden process where truth is partially a matter of whose priorities are being reviewed.

Of the eleven specific factors about which we asked respondents to comment, political considerations were identified more often than any of the others as important in explaining how study findings were used. In fifteen of the twenty cases, at least one person felt that politics had entered into the utilization process. Nine decisionmakers and seven evaluators felt that political considerations had been "very important" as a factor explaining utilization. On the other hand, nine decisionmakers and five evaluators reported that political considerations played no part in the utilization process.

The political factors mentioned include intra- and interagency rivalries; budgetary fights with OMB, the administration, and Congress; power struggles between Washington administrators and local program personnel; and internal debates about the purpose and/or accomplishments of pet programs. Budgetary battles seemed to be the most political.

We did not find, however, that political factors suddenly and unexpectedly surfaced once a study was completed. In almost every case, both the decision-makers and evaluators were well aware of the political context at the outset. Moreover, our respondents seemed to feel that political awareness on the part of everyone involved was the best one could expect. Social scientists will not change the political nature of the world, and while several respondents were quite cynical on this point, the more predominant view seemed to be that government would not be government without politics. One particularly articulate decisionmaker expressed this view quite explicitly:

This is not a cynical statement. . . . A substantial number of people have an improper concept of how politics works and what its mission is. And its mission is not to make logical decisions, unfortunately for those of us who think program considerations are important. Its mission is to detect the will of the governed group and express that will in some type of legislation or government action. And that will is very rarely, when it's pooled nationally, a rational will. It will have moral and ethical overtones, or have all kinds of emotional loads. . . .
*It's not rational in the sense that a good scientific study would allow you to sit down and plan everybody's life, and I'm glad it's not, by the way. Because I would be very tired very early of something that ran only by the numbers. Somebody'd forget part of the numbers, so I'm not fighting the system, but I am saying that you have to be careful of what you expect from a rational study when you insert it into the system. It has a tremendous impact. . . . It is a political, not a rational process. . . . Life is not a very simple thing* [DM328:18-19].

The importance of political considerations in much (though clearly not all) evaluation research can be partly understood in terms of our emphasis on the role of evaluation in reducing uncertainty for decisionmakers. Several organizational theorists (e.g., Thompson, 1967; Crozier, 1964) have come to view power and relationships within and between organizations as a matter of gaining control through the reduction of uncertainty.

More directly, James Thompson (1967) describes evaluation research as one major organizational mechanism for reducing internal as well as environmental uncertainty. He argues that the methodological design of much evaluation research can be predicted directly from the political function that assessment plays. We believe that our data directly support this viewpoint. Evaluations are undertaken as a mechanism for helping decisionmakers cope with the complexity of the programs for which they have responsibility. As one weapon or tool in the struggle to gain control over organizational and program processes evaluation research can fully be expected to take on a political character. Indeed, as Thompson argues, it is completely *rational* for decisionmakers to use evaluations in a political fashion for control and reduction of uncertainty.

*It would appear to us that it behooves social scientists to inform themselves fully about the political context of the evaluations on which they work. It is precisely through such a heightened awareness of the political implications and consequences of their research that social scientists can reduce their own uncertainty about the uses to which their work is put without impairing their ability to state their "truth" as they see it.*

## Other Factors Affecting Utilization

None of the other factors about which we asked specific questions emerged as consistently important in explaining utilization. When these other factors were important, their importance stemmed directly from the particular circumstances surrounding that evaluation and its purpose, particularly its political purpose. For example, the amount of resources devoted to a study might add to the credibility and clout of a study, but more costly evaluations did not show any discernible patterns of utilization different from less costly evaluation. The resources available for the study were judged inadequate for the task at hand by only two decisionmakers and five evaluators.

Whether or not findings were positive or negative had no demonstrable effect on utilization. We had studies in our sample in which the findings were rated by respondents as predominantly negative; other studies were predominantly positive in their conclusions; and still others had mixed findings. This variation was evenly distributed in our sample. Interestingly enough, the decisionmaker and evaluator on the same study often differed on whether findings were "positive" or "negative," but despite such disagreements, neither rated the positive or negative nature of the findings as particularly important in explaining either utilization or nonutilization of the evaluation.

Furthermore, the negative or positive nature of an evaluation report was unimportant as a factor explaining utilization partially because such findings, in either direction, were virtually never surprising. Only four decisionmakers expressed surprise at the findings of the study. Only one decisionmaker felt this surprise had an important effect on utilization. There was considerable consensus that surprises are not well received. Surprises are more likely to increase uncertainty rather than reduce uncertainty.

One decisionmaker took this notion a step further and made the point that a "good" evaluation process should build-in feedback mechanisms that guarantee the relative predictability of the content of the final report:

> If you're a good evaluator you don't want surprises. The last thing in the world you want to do is surprise people, because the . . . chances are surprises are not going to be well received. . . . Now you could come up with findings contrary to the conventional wisdom, but you ought to be sharing those ideas, if you will, with the people being evaluated during the evaluation process . . . , but if you present a surprise, it will tend to get rejected. See, we don't want surprises. We don't like surprises around here [DM346:30-31].

The evaluator for this project expressed the same opinion: "If there's a surprising finding it should be rare. I mean, *everybody's missed this insight except this great evaluator? Nonsense!"* (EV346:13).

It is sometimes suggested that evaluations aren't used because they concentrate on minor issues. But only two decisionmakers and one evaluator felt that the evaluation in question dealt with peripheral program objectives. On the other hand nine decisionmakers and eight evaluators felt that a major factor in utilization was whether or not the evaluation examined central program objectives. The most useful evaluations were those that focused on central objectives, but these were also precisely the kinds of evaluations that would not produce information that in and of itself could change a major policy direction. The reason may have been because by focusing on major objectives the studies in our sample became one part in the larger policy process; an evaluation aimed at some peripheral, easily-changed policy component might have had more potential for immediate, concrete impact. We lacked sufficient cases of the latter type, however, to explore this possibility more fully.

Another factor of interest to us concerned the point in the life of the program when the evaluation took place. Our sample contained studies that were done at all stages in the lives of programs. The key point that emerged with regard to this factor was that different questions emerge at different points in the life of a program. Early in the program the most useful information concerns procedures and implementation. Outcomes become important only after the program has been operating for a reasonable period. Budget and cost issues become central late in the program's life. Our respondents generally felt that in each case the questions examined had been appropriate to the point in the life of the program when the evaluation had taken place. The point in the program's history when the evaluation occurred was not a factor in explaining utilization in our data.

A factor that did emerge as somewhat important was the presence or absence of other studies on the same issue. Studies that broke new ground were particularly helpful because their potential for reducing uncertainty was greater. Nevertheless, such studies were viewed with some caution because our decision-makers clearly favored the accumulation of as much information from as many sources as possible. Thus, those studies that could be related to other studies had a clearly cumulative impact. On the whole, however, studies that broke new ground appeared to have somewhat greater identifiable impact. About half of the studies in our sample were of this latter type.

Finally, we asked our respondents about evaluator-government interactions. Interactions were almost universally described as cooperative, helpful, and frequent. Many respondents could offer horror stories about poor interactions on other studies, but with regard to the specific study on which we were conducting the follow-up, there appeared to be few problems. There was no indication that utilization would have been increased by greater government-evaluator interaction than that which actually occurred, though the degree of interaction that did occur was considered quite important.

We have reviewed eleven factors frequently identified in the evaluation literature as affecting utilization. The descriptions of the importance of these factors that emerged in the interviews clearly reinforced the definition of utilization as that of information feeding into an evolutionary process of program development—that is, information used in conjunction with other information to reduce uncertainty in decision making. None of these factors, at least as we were able to explore them, helped us a great deal in explaining variations in utilization. Nevertheless, there was one other factor that did consistently arise in the comments of decisionmakers, evaluators, and project officers—a factor so crucial that respondents repeatedly pointed to it as the single most important element in the utilization process.

## The Personal Factor

For lack of a better term, we have simply called this new variable the personal factor. It is made up of equal parts of leadership, interest, enthusiasm, determination, commitment, aggressiveness, and caring. Where the personal factor emerges, evaluations have an impact; where it is absent, there is a marked absence of impact.

The personal factor emerged most dramatically in our interviews when, having asked respondents to comment on the importance of each of our eleven utilization factors, we asked them to identify the single factor that was most important in explaining the impact or lack of impact of that particular study. Time after time, the factor they identified was not on our list. Rather, they responded in terms of the importance of individual people:

I would rank as the most important factor this division director's interest, [his] interest in evaluation. Not all managers are that motivated toward evaluation [DM353:17].

[The single most important factor that had the greatest effect on how the study got used was] the principal investigator. . . . If I have to pick a single factor, I'll pick people any time [DM328:20].

That it came from the Office of the Director—that's the most important factor. . . . The proposal came from the Office of the Director. It had had his attention and he was interested in it, and he implemented many of the things [DM312:21].

[The single most important factor was that] the people at the same level of decision making in [the new office] were not interested in making decisions of the kind that the people [in the old office] were, I think that probably had the greatest impact. The fact that there was no one at [the new office] after the transfer who was making programmatic decisions [EV361:27].

Probably the single factor that had the greatest effect on how it was used was the insistence of the person responsible for the initiating the study that the Director of _____ become familiar with its findings and arrive at a judgment on it [DM369:25].

[The most important factor was] the real involvement of the top decision-makers in the conceptualization and design of the study, and their commitment to the study [DM268:9].

While these comments concern the importance of interested and committed persons in studies that were actually used, studies that were *not* used stand out in that there was often a clear absence of the personal factor. One evaluator, who was not sure about how his study was used but suspected it had not been used, remarked: "I think that since the client wasn't terribly interested . . . and the whole issue had shifted to other topics, and since we weren't interested in doing it from a research point of view . . . , nobody was interested" (EV264:14).

Another evaluator was particularly adamant and articulate on the theory that the major factor affecting utilization is the personal energy, interests, abilities, and contacts of specific individuals. This person had had thirty-five years' experience in government, with twenty of those years spent directly involved in research and evaluation. Throughout his responses to our questions on the importance of various specific factors in affecting utilization, he returned to the theme of individual actions. When asked to identify the one factor that is most important in whether a study gets used he summarized his viewpoint:

The most important factor is desire on the part of the managers, both the central federal managers and the site managers. I don't think there's [any doubt], you know, that evaluation should be responsive to their needs, and if they have a real desire to get on with whatever it is they're supposed to do, they'll apply it. And if the evaluations don't meet their needs they won't. About as simple as you can get it. *I think the whole process is far more dependent on the skills of the people who use it than it is on the sort of peripheral issues of politics, resources. . . . Institutions are tough as hell to change. You can't change an institution by coming and doing an evaluation with a halo. Institutions are changed by people, in time, with a constant plugging away at the purpose you want to accomplish. And if you don't watch out, it slides back* [EV346:15-16].

He did not view this emphasis on the individual as meaning evaluation was simply a political tool. When asked how political considerations affected evaluations, he replied:

I don't think it's political at all. Oh, there's some pressures every once in a while to try and get more efficient, more money attributes, but I don't think that's the main course. The basic thing is how the administrators of the program view themselves, their responsibilities. That's the controlling factor. I don't think it's political in any way [EV346:8].

Later he commented:

It always falls back to the view of the administrator and his view of where his prerogatives are, his responsibilities. A good manager can manage with or without evaluations and a poor one can't, with or without evaluations. It just gives him some insights into what he should or shouldn't be doing, if he's a good manager. If they're poor managers, well . . . [EV346:11].

Earlier we described one project where the impact of the evaluation was unusually direct and concrete. After the evaluation had been completed, program funding was ended with the evaluation carrying "about a third of the weight of the total decision" [DM367:8]. The question then becomes why this study had such significant utilization. The answer from the decisionmaker was brief and to the point:

Well, [the evaluation had an impact] because we designed the project with an evaluation component in it, so we were expected to use it and we did. . . . Not just the fact that [evaluation] was built in, but the fact that *we* built it in on purpose. This is, *the agency head and myself had broad responsibilities for this, wanted the evaluation study results and we expected to use them. Therefore they were used. That's my point.* If someone else had built it in because they thought it was needed, and we didn't care, I'm sure the use of the study results would have been different [DM367:12].

The evaluator, (an external agent selected through an open RFP process), completely agreed that:

*The principal reason [for utilization] was because the decisionmaker was the guy who requested the evaluation and who used its results. That is, the organizational distance between the policy maker and the evaluator was almost zero in this instance.* That's the most important reason it had an impact [EV367:12]

What emerges here is a picture of a decisionmaker who knew what information he wanted, an evaluator committed to answering the decisionmaker's question, and a decisionmaker committed to using that information. The result was a high level of utilization in making a decision contrary to the decisionmaker's initial personal hopes.

This point was made often in the interviews. One highly placed and highly experienced administrator from yet a different project offered the following advice at the end of a four hour interview:

Win over the program people. Make sure you're hooked into the person who's going to make the decision in six months from the time you're doing the study, and make sure that he feels it's his study, that these are his ideas, and that it's focused on his values.... I'm sure it enters into personality things ... [DM283:40].

The personal factor applied not just to utilization but to the whole evaluation process. Several of the studies in our sample were initiated completely by a single person because of his personal interests and information needs. One study in particular stands out because it was initiated by a new office director with no support internally and considerable opposition from other affected agencies. The director found an interested and committed evaluator. The two worked closely together. The findings were initially ignored because there was no political heat at the time, but over the ensuing four years the director and evaluator worked personally to get the attention of key congressmen. They were finally successful in using personal contacts. The evaluation contributed to the eventual passing of significant legislation in a new area of federal control. From beginning to end, the story was one of personal human effort to get evaluation results used.

*The specifics vary from study to study but the pattern is markedly clear: Where the personal factor emerges, where some person takes direct, personal responsibility for getting the information to the right people, evaluations have an impact. Where the personal factor is absent, there is a marked absence of impact. Utilization is not simply determined by some configuration of abstract factors; it is determined in large part by real, live, caring human beings.*

*Implications of the Personal Factor in Evaluation*

If, indeed, utilization is to a large extent dependent upon the interests, capabilities, and initiative of individuals, then there are some profound implications for evaluators. First, evaluators who care about seeing their results utilized must take more seriously *their* responsibility for identifying *relevant* decisionmakers. Relevance in the context of the personal factor means finding decisionmakers who have a genuine interest in evaluation information—that is, persons who know what questions they want answered and who know how they can use evaluation information once findings are available. Such people are willing to take the time and effort to interact with evaluators about their information needs and interests.

Secondly, formal position and authority are only partial guides in identifying relevant decisionmakers. Evaluators must find a strategically located person (or persons) who is enthusiastic, committed, competent, interested, and aggressive. Our data suggest that more may be accomplished by working with a lower-level person displaying these characteristics than in working with a passive, disinterested person in a higher position.

Third, regardless of what an RFP calls for, the most valuable information with the highest potential for utilization is that information that directly answers the questions of the person(s) identified as the relevant decisionmaker(s). Requests for proposals (RFPs) may be written by individuals other than the decisionmakers who really need and want the evaluation information. It behooves evaluators to clarify the degree to which an RFP fully reflects the information needs of interested government officials.

Fourth, attention to the personal factor may assist not only evaluators in their efforts to increase the utilization of their research, but attention to the personal factor can also aid decisionmakers in their effort to find evaluators who will provide them with relevant and useful information. Evaluators who are interested in and knowledgeable about what they're doing, and evaluators who are committed to seeing their findings utilized in answering decisionmaker's questions will provide the most useful information to decisionmakers.

Fifth, there are political implications for both evaluators and decisionmakers in explicitly recognizing and acting on the importance of the personal factor. To do so is also to accept the assumption that decision making in government is likely to continue to be a largely personal and political process rather than a rationalized and scientific process. This assumption means that neither the decisionmaker nor the evaluator is merely a technician at any stage in the evaluation process. The personal factor is important from initiation of the study through design and data collection stages as well as in the final report and dissemination parts of the process. If decisionmakers have shown little interest in the study in its earlier stages, our data suggest that they are not likely to suddenly show an interest in using the findings at the end of the study. Utilization considerations are important throughout a study not just at the stage where study findings are disseminated.

Finally, the importance of the personal factor suggests that one of the major contributing reasons for underutilization of evaluation research is the high degree of instability in federal program operations. This instability, based on our data, is of three kinds: (1) high turnover rates among senior government staff so that the person initially interested in an evaluation may be in an entirely different office before the study is completed; (2) reorganization of government offices so that decision-making patterns are unstable, personnel are frequently rearranged, and responsibilities are almost constantly changing; and (3) program mobility as programs move from office to office (e.g., OEO to HEW) even if no formal, structural reorganization occurs.

We found the instability of federal organizational charts and the turnover among staff to be substantial. In trying to retrace the history of evaluations we frequently got a response like the following: "I've had so many changes in organizational assignments since then, I don't remember" (EV201:6). Asked about utilization of evaluation, the same person responded:

> Well since you're not going to identify me and my name, I'll tell you what I really think, and that is, I think these plans go up to the planning office and the rotation of personnel up there in the ____'s office is so fast and so furious, that they never get a chance to react to them. [It] just sits. We know that happens sometimes, because the guy who asked for it is gone by the time it gets up there [EV201:8].

The problem of instability appears to be particularly critical in actually implementing recommended changes:

> It was easier to get recommendations through with senior management approval. I mean, they read it and they could easily implement some of the areas, and they, I mean, at least they could implement them in theory anyhow. But still the problem, in any study or anything of this caliber, it's up to the people in the operating unit to make the change. And there's no way for senior management to measure that change. There's no way to see that it was even done. You know it's the old thing, of, you know, they tell people to do things, but in areas that require technical expertise there's no way to see that the change was done. *And so people in the operating area many times would just wait out the person, you know, some of these people have been through three directors, five associate directors, you know, and, they don't want to do something. They have tenure, and they know that if they sit long enough that that person will pass and someone else will come in with brand new ideas and . . .* [DM312:15].

Evaluators commented that it was common experience to go through several project officers on an evaluation.

Our own experience in trying to locate the respondents in the sample gave us a clear indication of this instability. Few of our interviewees were still in the same office at the time of the interview that they had been in at the time of the evaluation two to three years earlier. We still haven't been able to construct a meaningful organizational chart of HEW locating the various office changes and agency recommendations we encountered.

These structural conditions of mobility and instability make application of the personal factor in locating relevant decisionmakers or evaluators a risky business. That key person you locate may be gone by the time the study is completed. *Yet, these same structural conditions of mobility and instability may well be the underlying reasons why the decision-making process in the federal government has been and continues to be a highly personal and political process.*

## Conclusion

Two major themes emerge from this study of the utilization of evaluation research. First, we found that much of the evaluation literature has focused on an overly narrow definition of evaluation research impacts and has thereby underestimated the actual utilization of evaluative research. Second, the importance of the personal factor in evaluation research, particularly the utilization process, has been considerably underestimated.

The two themes are directly linked. The impact of evaluation research is most often experienced as a reduction in the uncertainty faced by individual decisionmakers as they attempt to deal with the complexity of programming reality. Evaluation information is one piece of data available to decisionmakers. It must be assimilated and fitted into a contextual whole: "The results are never self-explanatory" (EV209:9). The translation, the interpretation, the meaning, the relevance are established through the interactions over time of individuals who care enough to take the time to make the contextual fit, and then are interested enough to act on the basis of that contextual fit.

It is an energy-consuming process. Energetic and interested people in government can and do use evaluation research, not for the making of grand decisions with immediate, concrete, and visible impacts, but in a more subtle, clarifying, reinforcing, and reorienting way. Evaluators, then, might do well to spend less time lamenting their lack of visible impact on major decisions and more of their time providing relevant information to those key persons of energy and vision whose thoughts and actions, to a substantial extent, determine the general direction in the evolutionary process of program development. It is in consciously working with such decisionmakers to answer their questions that the utilization of evaluation research can be enhanced.

## Notes

1. The Office of Health Evaluation coordinates most evaluation research in the health division of HEW. In 1971 this office designed a new recordkeeping system that collected abstracts of all evaluations coming through that office. The 170 evaluations that were collected during the period 1971-73 became the population of evaluations from which we chose our final sample. We wish to

express our thanks to HEW officials for their assistance throughout this research project, particularly Harry Cain, Director, Office of Policy Development and Planning, Office of the Assistant Secretary for Health, and Isadore Seeman, Director, Office of Health Evaluation, Office of the Assistant Secretary for Planning and Evaluation, DHEW.

2. The term *project officer* refers to the person in the federal government who was identified as having primary responsibility for administering the evaluation. For studies that were done by organizations that are not a part of the federal government, the project officer was the person who administered the federal government's contract with that organization.

3. We identified decisionmakers by asking the project officers to name a person who would serve as an informant "about how the study was used in the government or elsewhere," and who "might be called a 'decisionmaker' vis-à-vis the study and its findings; who could tell us what decisions, if any, were made on the basis of information contained in the study."

4. This chapter represents the initial and general results of our analysis. A more extensive and detailed description of the sample, methodology, and analysis is presented in Nancy J. Brennan, "Variation in the Utilization of Evaluation Research in Decision Making," unpublished Ph.D. dissertation, University of Minnesota, 1976.

5. Citations for quotes taken from the interview transcripts will use the following format: (DM367;13) refers to the transcript of an interview with a decisionmaker about evaluation study number 367. The quote is taken from p. 13 of the transcript. Thus (EV201:10) and (PO201:6) refer to interviews about the same study; the former was an interview with the evaluator, the latter was an interview with the project officer.

### References

Alkin, Marvin C., Jacqueline Kosecoff, Carol Fitz, Gibbon and Richard Seligman. 1974. *Evaluation and Decision-Making: The Title VII Experience.* Los Angeles: Center for the Study of Evaluation, University of California.

Brennan, Nancy J. 1976. "Variation in the Utilization of Evaluation Research in Decision-Making." School of Social Work, University of Montana, Unpublished thesis.

Cohen, David K., and Michael S. Garet. 1975. "Reforming Educational Policy with Applied Social Research." *Harvard Educational Review* 45, no. 1 (February), pp. 17-41.

Coleman, James S. 1972. "Policy Research in the Social Sciences." Morristown, N.J.: General Learning Press.

Crozier, Michael. 1974. *The Bureaucratic Phenomenon*. Chicago: University of Chicago Press.

Grimes, Patricia Smith. 1976. "Descriptive Analysis of 170 Health Evaluations." School of Public Affairs, University of Minnesota, Unpublished thesis.

House, Ernest R. 1972. "The Conscience of Educational Evaluation." *Teachers College Record* 73, no. 3, pp. 405-414.

Kuhn, Thomas. 1970. *Structure of Scientific Revolutions*. Chicago: University of Chicago Press.

Patton, Michael Quinn. 1975. *Alternative Evaluation Research Paradigm*. North Dakota Study Group on Evaluation Monograph, Center for Teaching and Learning, University of North Dakota, Grand Forks, North Dakota.

Thompson, James D. 1967. *Organizations in Action*. New York: McGraw Hill.

Weidman, Donald R., Pamela Horst, Grace M. Taher, and Joseph S. Wholey. 1973. "Design of an Evaluation System for NIMH." *Contract Report 962-7*, January 15. Washington, D.C.: The Urban Institute.

Weiss, Carol H. 1972. *Evaluation Research: Methods of Assessing Program Effectiveness*. Englewood Cliffs, N.J.: Prentice-Hall.

Wholey, Joseph S., John W. Scanlon, Hugh G. Duffy, James S. Fikumoto, and Leona M. Vogt. 1971. *Federal Evaluation Policy*. Washington, D.C.: The Urban Institute.

Williams, Walter, and John W. Evans. 1969. "The Politics of Evaluation: The Case of Headstart." *Annals of the American Academy of Political and Social Science* (September).

# 4

# The Self-Evaluating Organization

## Aaron Wildavsky

W hy don't organizations evaluate their own activities? Why do they not appear to manifest rudimentary self-awareness? How long can people work in organizations without discovering their objectives or determining the extent to which they have been carried out? I started out thinking it was bad for organizations not to evaluate, and I ended up wondering why they ever do it. Evaluation and organization, it turns out, are to some extent contradictory terms. Failing to understand that evaluation is sometimes incompatible with organization, we are tempted to believe in absurdities much in the manner of mindless bureaucrats who never wonder whether they are doing useful work. If we asked more intelligent questions instead, we would neither look so foolish nor be so surprised.

Who will evaluate and who will administer? How will power be divided among these functionaries? Which ones will bear the costs of change? Can evaluators create sufficient stability to carry on their own work in the midst of a turbulent environment? Can authority be allocated to evaluators and blame apportioned among administrators? How to convince administrators to collect

*Author's Note* Presented at the National Conference of the American Society for Public Administration, New York City, March 24, 1972, as part of the first chapter of a book by Jeanne Nienaber and Aaron Wildavsky, *Buying Recreation Budgeting and Evaluation in Federal Outdoor Recreation Policy* (New York: Basic Books, forthcoming), this article stems from reflections on what at first glance may appear to be an entirely different problem. I had begun the study of line-item and program budgeting as they coexisted uneasily in several agencies concerned with outdoor recreation. The traditional budget was sensitive to politics but did not produce fundamental reexamination of activities; the program budget was insensitive to politics and also did not result in serious evaluation of current activities. Instead of asking which form of budgeting was superior, therefore, I turned my attention to the more fundamental question of why organizations ordinarily do not evaluate their own activities.

• This paper is the first chapter of a book on U.S. federal resource allocation in the field of outdoor recreation. Line-item budgeting turned out to be sensitive politically but did not lead to analysis of agency activities. Program budgeting was politically insensitive but did not lead to evaluation either. This turned attention to the question of why organizations resist evaluation. The thesis of the article is that evaluation is primarily an organizational problem. The needs of the organization and the people within it conflict with the desire to continuously monitor activities and change policies when they are found wanting. By considering how an organization wholeheartedly devoted to evaluation might function, and how people might survive whose major purpose was to maintain resources and objectives in a creative tension, the article suggests that it will be difficult to marry evaluation and organization. The article includes suggestions for bringing together substantive evaluation of policy and the imperatives of organizational life. But the degree of trust among social groups is seen as a critical regulator facilitating or depressing evaluation and conditioning the uses to which it is put.

information that might help others but can only harm them? How can support be obtained on behalf of recommendations that anger sponsors? Would the political problem be solved by creating a special organization — Evaluation Incorporated — devoted wholly to performing the analytic function? Could it obtain necessary support without abandoning its analytic mission? Can knowledge and power be joined?

### Evaluation

The ideal organization would be self-evaluating. It would continuously monitor its own activities so as to determine whether it was meeting its goals or even whether these goals should continue to prevail. When evaluation suggested that a change in goals or programs to achieve them was desirable, these proposals would be taken seriously by top

---

decision makers. They would institute the necessary changes; they would have no vested interest in continuation of current activities. Instead they would steadily pursue new alternatives to better serve the latest desired outcomes.

The ideal member of the self-evaluating organization is best conceived as a person committed to certain modes of problem solving. He believes in clarifying goals, relating them to different mechanisms of achievement, creating models (sometimes quantitative) of the relationships between inputs and outputs, seeking the best available combination. His concern is not that the organization should survive or that any specific objective be enthroned or that any particular clientele be served. Evaluative man cares that interesting problems are selected and that maximum intelligence be applied toward their solution.

To evaluative man the organization doesn't matter unless it meets social needs. Procedures don't matter unless they facilitate the accomplishment of objectives encompassing these needs. Efficiency is beside the point if the objective being achieved at lowest cost is inappropriate. Getting political support doesn't mean that the programs devised to fulfill objectives are good; it just means they had more votes than the others. Both objectives and resources, says evaluative man, must be continuously modified to achieve the optimal response to social need.

Evaluation should not only lead to the discovery of better policy programs to accomplish existing objectives but to alteration of the objectives themselves. Analysis of the effectiveness of existing policies leads to consideration of alternatives that juxtapose means and ends embodied in alternative policies. The objectives as well as the means for attaining them may be deemed inappropriate. But men who have become socialized to accept certain objectives may be reluctant to change. Resistance to innovation then takes the form of preserving social objectives. The difficulties are magnified once we realize that objectives may be attached to the clientele – the poor, outdoor men, lumbermen – with whom organizational members identify. The objectives of the organization may have attracted them precisely because they see it as a means of service to people they value. They may view changes in objectives, therefore, as proposals for "selling out" the clients they wish to serve. In their eyes evaluation becomes an enemy of the people.

Evaluative man must learn to live with contradictions. He must reduce his commitments to the organizations in which he works, the programs he carries out, and the clientele he serves. Evaluators must become agents of change acting in favor of programs as yet unborn and clienteles that are unknown. Prepared to impose change on others, evaluators must have sufficient stability to carry out their own work. They must maintain their own organization while simultaneously preparing to abandon it. They must obtain the support of existing bureaucracies while pursuing antibureaucratic policies. They must combine political feasibility with analytical purity. Only a brave man would predict that these combinations of qualities can be found in one and the same person and organization.

Evaluation and organization may be contradictory terms. Organizational structure implies stability while the process of evaluation suggests change. Organization generates commitment while evaluation inculcates skepticism. Evaluation speaks to the relationship between action and objectives while organization relates its activities to programs and clientele. No one can say for certain that self-evaluating organizations can exist, let alone become the prevailing form of administration. We can learn a good deal about the production and use of evaluation in government, nonetheless, by considering the requirements of obtaining so extraordinary a state of affairs – a self-evaluating organization.

### The Policy-Administration Dichotomy Revisited

Organization requires the division of labor. Not everyone can do everything. Who, then, will carry out the evaluative activity and who will administer the programs for which the organization is responsible?

Practically every organization has a program staff, by whatever name called, that advises top officials about policy problems. They are small in numbers and conduct whatever formal evaluation goes on in the organization. They may exert considerable power in the organization through their persuasiveness and access to the top men, or they may be merely a benign growth that can be seen but has little effect on the body of the organization. Insofar as one is interested in furthering analytical activities, one must be concerned with strengthening them in regard to other elements. The idea of the self-evaluating organization, however, must mean more than this: a few men trying to force evaluation on an organization hundreds or thousands of times larger than they are. The spirit of the self-evaluating organization suggests that, in some meaningful way, the entire organization is infused with the evaluative ethic.

Immediately we are faced with the chain of command. How far down must the spirit of evaluation go in order to ensure the responsiveness of the organization as a whole? If all personnel are involved there would appear to be insuperable difficulties in finding messengers, mail clerks, and secretaries to meet the criteria. If we move up one step to those who deal with the public and carry out the more complex kind of activity, the numbers involved may still be staggering. These tens of thousands of people certainly do not have the qualifications necessary to conduct evaluative activities, and it would be idle to pretend that they would. The forest ranger and the national park officer may be splendid people, but they are not trained in evaluation and they are not likely to be. Yet evaluational activity appropriate to each level must be found if evaluation is to permeate the organization.

There has long been talk in the management circles of combining accountability with decentralization. Organizational subunits are given autonomy within circumscribed limits for which they are held strictly accountable to their hierarchical superiors. Central power is masked but it is still there. Dividing the task so that each subunit has genuine autonomy would mean giving them a share in central decisions affecting the entire organization. Decentralization is known to exist only to the extent that field units follow inconsistent and contradictory policies. One can expect the usual headquarters–field rivalries to develop—the one stressing appreciation of local problems and interests, the other fearing dissolution as the mere sum of its clashing units. Presumably the tension will be manifested in terms of rival analyses. The center should win out because of its greater expertise, but the local units will always be the specialists on their own problems. They will have to be put in their place. We are back, it seems, to hierarchy. How can the center get what it wants out of the periphery without over-formalizing their relationship?

One model, the internalized gyroscope, is recorded in Herbert Kaufman's classic on *The Forest Ranger*. By recruitment and training, the forest rangers are socialized into central values that they carry with them wherever they go and apply to specific circumstances. Central control is achieved without apparent effort or innumerable detailed instructions, because the rangers have internalized

the major premises from which appropriate actions may generally be deduced. The problem of the self-evaluating organization is more difficult because it demands problem solving divorced from commitments to specific policies and organizational structures. The level of skill required is considerably higher and the locus of identification much more diffuse. The Israeli Army has had considerable success in inculcating problem-solving skills (rather than carrying out predetermined instructions) among its officers.[1] But their organizational identification is far more intense than can be expected elsewhere.

Suppose that most organizational personnel are too unskilled to permit them to engage in evaluation. Suppose it is too costly to move around hundreds of thousands of government officials who carry out most of the work of government. The next alternative is to make the entire central administration into an evaluative unit that directs the self-evaluating organization. Several real-world models are available. What used to be called the administration class in Great Britain illustrates one type of central direction. They move frequently among the great departments and seek (with the political ministers involved) to direct the activities of the vast bureaucracy around them. They are chosen for qualities of intellect that enable them to understand policy and for qualities of behavior that enable them to get along with their fellows. At the apex stands the Treasury, an organization with few operating commitments, whose task it is to monitor the activities of the bureaucracy and to introduce changes when necessary. Economic policy, which is the special preserve of the Treasury, is supposed to undergo rapid movement, and its personnel are used to changing tasks and objectives at short notice. Though divorced in a way from the organizations in which they share responsibility with the political ministers, top civil servants are also part of them by virtue of their direct administrative concerns. Complaints are increasingly heard that these men are too conservative in defense of departmental interests, too preoccupied with immediate matters, or too bound by organizational tradition to conduct serious evaluation. Hence, the Fulton Report claimed, they adapt too slowly, if at all, to changing circumstances. Tentative steps have been taken, therefore, to establish a Central Policy Review Staff to do policy analysis for the cabinet and to otherwise encourage evaluative activity.

Germany and Sweden have proceeded considerably further in the same direction. Departments in

Sweden are relatively small groups of men concerned with policy questions, while administration is delegated to large public corporations set up for the purpose.[2] The state governments in Germany (the *Lander*) do over 90 per cent of the administrative work, with the central government departments presumably engaged with larger questions of policy. The student of public administration in America will at once realize where he is at. The policy-administration dichotomy, so beloved of early American administrative theorists, which was thoroughly demolished, it seemed, in the decades of the '40's and '50's, has suddenly reappeared with new vitality.

The policy-administration dichotomy originated with Frank Goodnow and others in their effort to legitimate the rise of the civil service and with it the norm of neutral-competence in government. They sought to save good government from the evils of the spoils system by insulating it from partisan politics. Congress made policy, and the task of the administrative apparatus was to find the appropriate technical means to carry it out. Administrative actions were thought to be less general and more technical so that well-motivated administrators would be able to enact the will of the people as received from Congress or the President. Civil servants could then be chosen on the basis of their technical merits rather than their partisan or policy politics. An avalanche of criticism, begun in earnest by Paul Appleby's *Policy and Administration*, overwhelmed these arguments on every side. Observation of congressional statutes showed that they were often vague, ambiguous, and contradictory. There simply were not clear objectives to which the administrators could subordinate themselves. Observation of administrative behavior showed that conflicts over the policy to be adopted continued unabated in the bureaus and departments. Important decisions were made by administrators that vitally affected the lives of poeple. Choice abounded and administrators seized on it. Indeed, they were often themselves divided on how to interpret statutes or how generally to frame policies under them. Interest groups were observed to make strenuous efforts to get favorable administrative enactments. Moreover, sufficiently precise knowledge did not exist to determine the best way to carry out a general objective in many areas. Given the large areas of uncertainty and ignorance, the values and choices of administrators counted a great deal. Taken at this level there was not too much that could be

said for maintaining the distinction between policy and administration. Nevertheless, nagging doubts remained.

Were politics and administration identical? If they were, then it was difficult to understand how we were able to talk about them separately. Or was politics simply a cover term for all the things that different organs of the government did? If politics and administration could be separated in some way, then a division of labor might be based on them. No doubt the legislative will, if there was one, could be undermined by a series of administrative enactments. But were not these administrative decisions of a smaller and less encompassing kind than those usually made by Congress? Were there not ways in which the enactments of Congress were (or could be) made more authoritative than the acts of administrators? Overwhelming administrative discretion did violence to democratic theory.

As the world moves into the 1970's, we will undoubtedly see significant efforts to rehabilitate the policy-administration dichotomy. The dissatisfactions of modern industrial life are being poured on the bureaucracy. It seems to grow larger daily while human satisfaction does not increase commensurately. It has become identified with red tape and resistance to change. Yet no one can quite imagine doing away with it in view of the ever-increasing demand for services. So politicians who feel that the bureaucracy has become a liability,[3] clientele who think they might be better served under other arrangements, taxpayers who resent the sheer costs, policy analysts who regard existing organizations as barriers to the application of intelligence, will join together in seeking ways to make bureaucracy more responsive. How better do this than by isolating its innovative functions from the mass of officialdom? Instead of preventing administration from being contaminated by politics, however, the purpose of the new dichotomy will be to insulate policy from the stultifying influences of the bureaucracy.

## Who Will Pay the Costs of Change?

While most organizations evaluate some of their policies periodically, the self-evaluating organization would do so continuously. These evaluative activities would be inefficient, that is, they would cost more than they are worth, unless they led to change. Indeed the self-evaluating organization is purposefully set up to encourage change.

The self-evaluating organization will have to convince its own members to live with constant change. They may think they love constant upset when they first join the organization, but experience is likely to teach them otherwise. Man's appetite for rapid change is strictly limited. People cannot bear to have their cherished beliefs challenged or their lives altered on a continuing basis. The routines of yesterday are swept away, to be replaced by new ones. Anxiety is induced because they cannot get their bearings. They have trouble knowing exactly what they should be doing. The ensuing confusion may lead to inefficiencies in the form of hesitation or random behavior designed to cover as many bases as possible. Cynicism may grow as the wisdom of the day before yesterday gives way to new truth, which is in turn replaced by a still more radiant one. The leaders of the self-evaluating organization will have to counter this criticism.

Building support for policies within an organization requires internal selling. Leaders must convince the members of the organization that what they are doing is worthwhile. Within the self-evaluating organization the task may initially be more difficult than in more traditional bureaucracies. Its personnel are accustomed to question policy proposals and to demand persuasive arguments in their support. Once the initial campaign is proven successful, however, enthusiasm can be expected to reach a high pitch after all existing policies have been evaluated, new alternatives have been analyzed, and evidence has been induced in favor of a particular alternative. The danger here is overselling. Convinced that "science" is in their favor, persuaded that their paper calculations are in tune with the world, the evaluators believe a little too much in their own ideas. They are set up for more disappointment from those who expect less. How much greater the difficulty, then, when continuous evaluation suggests the need for another change in policy. Now two internal campaigns are necessary: the first involves unselling the old policy and the second involves selling the new one. All virtues become unsuspected vices and last year's goods are now seen to be hopelessly shoddy. Perpetual change has its costs.

Maintenance of higher rates of change depend critically on the ability of those who produce it to make others pay the associated costs. If the change makers are themselves forced to bear the brunt of their actions, they will predictably seek to stabilize their environment. That is the burden of virtually the entire sociological literature on organizations from Weber to Crozier. The needs of the members displace the goals of the organization. The public purposes that the organization was supposed to serve give way to its private acts. Its own hidden agendas dominate the organization.

Rather than succumb to the diseases of bureaucracy, the self-evaluating organization will be tempted to pass them on to others. The self-evaluating organization can split itself off into "evaluating" and "administering" parts, thus making lower levels pay the costs of change, or it can seek to impose them on other organizations in its environment. We shall deal first with difficulties encountered in trying to stabilize the evaluative top of the organization while the bottom is in a continuous state of flux.

Let us suppose that an organization separates its evaluative head from its administrative body. The people at the top do not have operating functions. They are, in administrative jargon, all staff rather than line. Their task is to appraise the consequences of existing policies, work out better alternatives, and have the new policies they recommend carried out by the administrative unit.

Who would bear the cost of change? One can imagine evaluators running around merrily suggesting changes to and fro without having to implement them. The anxiety would be absorbed by the administrators. They would have to be the ones to change gears and to smooth out the difficulties. But they will not stand still for this. Their belief about what is administratively feasible and organizationally attainable must be part of the policy that is adopted. So the administrators will bargain with the evaluators.

Administrators have significant resources to bring to this struggle. They deal with the public. They collect the basic information that is sent upward in one form or another. They can drag their feet, mobilize clientele, hold back information, or otherwise make cooperation difficult. The evaluators have their own advantages. They have greater authority to issue rules and regulations. They are experts in manipulating data and models to justify existing policies or denigrate them.

Held responsible for policy but prohibited from administering it directly, the evaluators have an incentive to seek antibureaucratic delivery systems. They will, for example, prefer an income to a service strategy.[4] The evaluators can be pretty certain that clients will receive checks mailed from the central computer, whereas they cannot be sure that the services they envisage will be delivered by hordes of bureaucrats in the manner they would like. Providing people with income to buy better living quarters has the great advantage of not requiring a corps of officials to supervise public housing. Evaluators do not have the field personnel to supervise innumerable small undertakings; they, therefore, will prefer large investment projects over smaller ones. They can also make better use of their small number of people on projects that are expensive and justify devotion of large amounts of analytical time. Contrarywise, administrators will emphasize far-flung operations providing services requiring large numbers of people that only they can perform. In a house of many mansions they will be the masters.

There are circumstances, of course, in which administrators and evaluators reverse their normal roles. If the evaluators feel that there is not enough government employment, for example, they may seek labor-intensive operations. Should the administrators feel they are already overburdened, they may welcome policies that are easily centralized and directed by machines performing rote operations. The more likely tendency, however, is for administrators and evaluators to expand into each other's domain. Each one can reduce the bargaining powers of the other by taking unto himself some of his competitors' advantages. Thus the administrators may recruit their own policy analysts to compete with the evaluators who, in turn, will seek their own contacts within the administrative apparatus in order to ensure a steady and reliable flow of information. If this feuding goes far enough, the result will be two organizations acting in much the same way as the single one they replaced but with additional problems of coordination.

### Evaluation Incorporated

It is but a short step from separating evaluation from administration to the idea of rival teams of evaluators. A rough equivalent of a competitive market can be introduced by allowing teams of evaluators to compete for direction of policy in a given area. The competition would take place in terms of price (we can accomplish a specified objective at a lower cost), quality (better policies for the same money), quantity (we can produce more at the same cost), maintenance (we can fix things when they go wrong), experience (we have a proven record), values (our policies will embody

your preferences) and talent (when it comes down to it, you are buying our cleverness and we are superior). The team that won the competition would be placed in charge until it left to go elsewhere or another team challenged it. The government might raise its price to keep a talented team or it might lower it to get rid of an incompetent one. The incentives for evaluation would be enormous, restrained, of course, by ability to perform lest the evaluators go bankrupt when they run out of funds or lose business to competitors.

The first task of the new enterprise would be to establish its own form of organization. What organizational arrangements are necessary to make competition among evaluators feasible?

Evaluators must either be assured of employment somewhere or engage in other dispensible occupations from which they can be recruited at short notice. A handful of evaluators could always be recruited by ad hoc methods from wherever they are found. But teams of evaluators sufficient to direct major areas of policy would be difficult to assemble at short notice. They would all be doing different things instead of working together, which is part of the experience they need to be successful. Nor can they form a team unless they can all promise to be on the job at a certain time if their bid is successful, yet at the same time have other jobs to fall back on if they are turned down.

In the previous model, where the evaluators generate new policies and the administrators carry them out, these bureaucrats carried the major burden of uncertainty. Under the new model this imbalance is redressed because the evaluators have to worry about security of employment. Few people like to shift jobs all the time; even fewer like the idea of periodic unemployment alternating with the anxiety of bidding to get jobs and performing to keep them. Mechanisms will be found, we can be certain, to reduce their level of uncertainty to tolerable dimensions.

Evaluators may choose to work within existing administrative organizations, accepting a lower status, learning to live with disappointment, in return for job stability. This is one pattern that already exists. Evaluators may go to private industry and universities on the understanding they will be able to make occasional forays into government as part of a tiny group of advisors to leading officials. This is also done now. Both alternatives do away with the idea of competition; they merely graft a small element of evaluation onto existing organizations on a catch-as-catch-can basis.

In order to preserve evaluators who are in a position to compete for the direction of policy, it will be necessary for them to form stable organizations of their own. Like the existing firms of management consultants they resemble, these evaluators would bid on numerous projects; the difference would be that they would do the actual policy work as part of the public apparatus rather than making recommendations and then disappearing. Evaluation, Incorporated, as we shall call it, would contain numerous possible teams, some of whom would be working and others who would be preparing to go to work. The firm would have to demand considerable overhead to provide services for the evaluators, to draw up proposals, and to compensate those of its members who are (hopefully) temporarily out of work. Keeping Evaluation, Incorporated, solvent by maintaining a high level of employment will become a major organizational goal.

Evaluation, Incorporated, is an organization. It has managers who are concerned with survival. It has members who must be induced to remain. It has clients who must be served. So it will constitute itself a lobby for evaluation. When the demand for its services is high, it will be able to insist on the evaluative ethic; it will take its services to those who are prepared to appreciate (by paying for) them. But when demands are low, Evaluation, Incorporated, must trim its sails. It has a payroll to meet. Rather than leave a job when nonanalytical criteria prevail, it may have to swallow its pride and stay on. Its managers can easily convince themselves that survival is not only good for them but for society, which will benefit from the good they will be able to do in better times.

If their defects stem from their insecurities, the remedy will be apparent: increase the stability of evaluators by guaranteeing them tenure of employment. Too close identification with party or policy proved, in any event, to be a mixed blessing. They feasted while they were in favor and famished when they were out. Apparently they require civil service status, a government corporation, say, devoted to evaluation.

Perhaps the General Accounting Office (GAO), which is beginning to do analytic studies, will provide a model of an independent governmental organization devoted to evaluation. Since it has a steady source of income from its auditing work, so

to speak, it can afford to form, break up, and recreate teams of evaluators. Its independence from the Executive Branch (the Accountant General is responsible to Congress and serves a 15-year term) might facilitate objective analysis. But the independence of GAO has been maintained because it eschews involvement in controversial matters. If the new General Evaluation Office (GEO) were to issue reports that increased conflict, there would undoubtedly be a strong impulse to bring it under regular political control. The old auditing function might be compromised because objectivity is difficult to maintain about a program one has sponsored, or because public disputes lower confidence in its operations. Opponents of its policy positions might begin to question its impartiality in determining the legality of government expenditures. Yet protection would be difficult to arrange because the new GEO did not have a political client.

By attending to the problems of an organization that supplies evaluation to others, we hope to illuminate the dilemmas of any organization that wishes to seriously engage in continuous analyses of its own activities.

Evaluation, which criticizes certain programs and proposes to replace them with others, is manifestly a political activity. If evaluation is not political in the sense of party partisanship, it is political in the sense of policy advocacy. Without a steady source of political support, without that essential manifestation of affection from somebody out there in society, it will suffer the fate of abandoned children: the self-evaluating organization is unlikely to prosper in an orphanage.

### Adjusting to the Environment

The self-evaluating organization is one that uses its own analysis of its own programs in order to alter or abolish them. Its ability to make changes when its analysis suggests they are desirable is an essential part of its capacity to make self-evaluation a living reality. Yet the ability of any single organization to make self-generated changes is limited by the necessity of receiving support from its environment.

The leaders of a self-evaluating organization cannot afford to leave the results of their labors up to the fates. If their "batting average" goes way down, they will be in trouble. Members of the organization will lose faith in evaluation because it does not lead to changes in actual policy. Those who are attracted to the organization by the prospect of being powerful as well as analytical will leave to join more promising ventures, or old clients will become dissatisfied without new ones to take their place. As the true believers depart, personnel who are least motivated by the evaluative ethic will move into higher positions. Revitalization of the organization via the promotion and recruitment of professing evaluators will become impossible.

In order to avoid the deadly cycle – failure, hopelessness, abandonment – leaders of the self-evaluating organization must seek some proportion of success. They must select the organization's activities, not only with an eye toward their analytical justification, but with a view toward receiving essential support from their environment. Hence they become selective evaluators. They must prohibit the massive use of organizational resources in areas where they see little chance of success. They must seek out problems that are easy to solve and changes that are easy to make because they do not involve radical departures from the past. They must be prepared to hold back the results of evaluation when they believe the times are not propitious; they must be ready to seize the time for change whether or not the evaluations are fully prepared or wholly justified. Little by little, it seems, the behavior of the leaders will become similar to those of other organization officials who also seek to adapt to their environment.

The growing conservatism of the self-evaluating organization is bound to cause internal strains. There are certain to be disagreements about whether the organization is being too cautious. No one can say for sure whether the leaders have correctly appraised the opportunities in a rapidly shifting environment. If they try to do too much, they risk failure in the political world. If they try to do too little, they risk abandoning their own beliefs and losing the support of their most dedicated members. Maintaining a balance between efficacy and commitment is not easy.

Now the self-evaluating organization need not be a passive bystander negotiating its environment. It can seek to mobilize interests in favor of the programs it wishes to adopt. It can attempt to neutralize opposition. It can try to persuade its present clientele that they will be better off, or instill a wish to be served on behalf of new beneficiaries. One fears that its reputation among clientele groups may not be the best, however,

because, as a self-evaluating organization, it must be prepared to abandon (or drastically modify) programs and with them the clientele they serve. The clients will know that theirs is only a marriage of convenience, that the self-evaluating organization is eager to consider more advantageous alliances, and that they must always be careful to measure their affection according to the exact degree of services rendered. The self-evaluating organization cannot expect to receive more love than it gives. In fact, it must receive less.

Evaluation can never be fully rewarded. There must, in the nature of things, be other considerations that prevail over evaluation, even where the powers that be would like to follow its dictates. The policies preferred by the self-evaluating organization are never the only ones being contemplated by the government; there are always multitudes of policies in being or about to be born. Some of these are bound to be inconsistent with following the dictates of evaluation. Consider the impact of fiscal policy upon analysis. Suppose the time has come for financial stringency; the government has decided that expenditures must be reduced. Proposals for increases may not be allowed no matter how good the justification. Reductions may be made whether indicated by analysis or not. Conversely, a political decision may be made to increase expenditure. The substantive merits of various policies have clearly been subordinated to their immediate financial implications.

Evaluation may be wielded as a weapon in the political wars. It may be used by one faction or party versus another. Of particular concern to the self-evaluating organization is a one-sided approach to evaluation that creates internal problems. It is not unusual, as was recently the case in Great Britain when the Conservative Party returned to office, for a government to view evaluation as a means of putting down the bureaucracy. A two-step decision rule may be followed: the recommendations of evaluation may be accepted when they lead to reduction and rejected when they suggest increases in expenditure. Before long the members of the organization become reluctant to provide information that will only be used in a biased way. The evaluative enterprise depends on common recognition that the activity is being carried out somehow in order to secure better policies, whatever these may be, and not in support of a predetermined position. If this understanding is violated, people down the line will refuse to cooperate. They will withhold their contribution by hiding information or by simply not volunteering to find it. The morale of the self-evaluating organization will be threatened because its members are being asked to pervert the essence of their calling.

It's the same the whole world over: the analytically virtuous are not necessarily rewarded nor are the wicked (who do not evaluate) punished. The leaders of the self-evaluating organization, therefore, must redouble their effort to obtain political help.

### Joining Knowledge with Power

To consider the requirements necessary for a self-evaluating organization is to understand why they are rarely met. The self-evaluating organization, it turns out, would be susceptible to much the same kinds of anti-evaluative tendencies as are existing organizations. It, too, must stabilize its environment. It, too, must secure internal loyalty and outside support. Evaluation must, at best, remain but one element in administrative organizations. Yet no one can say today that it is overemphasized. Flights of fancy should not lead anyone to believe that inordinate attention to evaluation is an imminent possibility. We have simply come back to asking how a little more rather than a little less might become part of public organizations. How might analytic integrity be combined with political efficacy?

Evaluative man seeks knowledge, but he also seeks power. His desire to do good is joined with his will to act powerfully. One is no good without the other. A critical incentive for pursuing evaluation is that the results become governmental policy. There is little point in making prescriptions for public policy for one's own private amusement. Without knowledge it would be wrong to seek power. But without power it becomes more difficult to obtain knowledge. Why should anyone supply valuable information to someone who can neither help nor harm him? Access to information may be given only on condition programmatic goals are altered. Evaluative man is well off when he can pyramid resources so that greater knowledge leads to enhanced power, which in turn increases his access to information. He is badly off when the pursuit of power leads to the sacrifice of evaluation. His own policy problem is how to do enough of both (and not too much of either) so that knowledge and power reinforce rather than

undermine one another.

The political process generates a conflict of interest within the evaluative enterprise. The evaluators view analysis as a means of deciding on better policies and selling them to others. Clients (elected officials, group leaders, top administrators) view analysis as a means of better understanding the available choices so they can control them. Talk of "better policies," as if it did not matter who determined them, only clouds the issues.

The evaluative group within an organization would hope that it could show political men the worth of its activities. The politicians, in turn, hope to learn about the desirability of the programs that are being evaluated. But their idea of desirability manifestly includes the support which programs generate for them and the organizations of which they are a part. Hence evaluation must be geared to producing programs that connect the interests of political leaders to the outcomes of governmental actions, otherwise, they will reject evaluation and with it the men who do it.

A proposed policy is partly a determinant of its own success; the support it gathers or loses in clientele is fed back into its future prospects. By its impact on the future environment of the organization, the proposed policy affects the kinds of work the organization is able to do. Pure evaluative man, however single-minded his concentration on the intrinsic merits of programs, must also consider their interaction effects on his future ability to pursue his craft. Just as he would insist on including the impact of one element in a system on another in his policy analysis, so must he consider how his present recommendations affect future ones. A proper evaluation includes the impact of a policy on the organizations responsible for it.

Consider in this organizational context the much-discussed problem of diverse governmental programs that may contribute to the same ends without anyone being able to control them. There may be unnecessary redundancy, where some programs overlap, side by side with large areas of inattention to which no programs are directed. More services of one kind and less of another are provided than might be strictly warranted. Without evaluation no one can really say whether there are too many or too few programs or whether their contents are appropriate. But an evaluation that did all this would get nowhere unless it resulted in different institutional processes for handling the same set of problems.

Even on its own terms, then, evaluation should not remain apart from the organizations on which it is dependent for implementation. Organizational design and policy analysis are part of the same governmental process. If an organization wishes to reduce its identification with programs (and the clients who support them), for example, so that it can afford to examine different types of policy, it must adopt a political strategy geared to that end.

The self-evaluating organization would be well advised not to depend too much on a single type of clientele. Diversification is its strategy. The more diverse its services, the more varied its clientele, the less the self-evaluating organization has to depend on any one of them, the more able it is to shift the basis of its support. Diversity creates political flexibility.

Any organization that produces a single product, so to speak, that engages in a limited range of activities is unlikely to abandon them willingly. Its survival, after all, is bound up in its program. If the program goes, the organization dies. One implication drawn from these considerations is that the traditional wisdom concerning governmental organization badly needs revision.[5] If the basic principle of organization is that similar programs should be grouped together, as is now believed to be the case, these organizations will refuse to change. On the contrary, agencies should be encouraged to differentiate their products and diversify their outputs. If they are not faced with declining demand for all their programs, they will be more willing to abandon or modify a single one. The more varied its programs, the less dependent the organization is on a single one, the greater its willingness to change.

No matter how good its internal analysis, or how persuasively an organization justifies its programs to itself, there is something unsatisfying about allowing it to judge its own case. The ability of organizations to please themselves must ultimately (at least in a democratic society) give way to judgment by outsiders. Critics of organizations must, therefore, recognize that their role is an essential one. Opposition is part and parcel of the evaluative process. The goal would be to secure a more intelligent and analytically sophisticated level of advocacy on all sides. Diverse analyses might become, as Harry Rowen has suggested, part of the mutual partisan adjustment through which creative use is made of conflicts among organized interests.

Competition, per se, however, need not lead to fundamental change. Organizations may go on the offensive by growing bigger instead of better, that is, by doing more of the same. The change in which they are interested is a change in magnitude. We are all familiar with the salesmanship involved in moving to new technologies or larger structures where internal dynamism and grandiose conceptions are mistaken for new ideas. Motion may be a protection against change.

Competition, if it is to lead to desirable consequences, must take place under appropriate rules specifying who can make what kind of transaction. No one would advocate unrestrained competition among economic units in the absence of a market that makes it socially advantageous for participants to pursue their private interests in expectation of mutual gain. Where parties are affected who are not directly represented in the market, for instance, the rules may be changed to accommodate a wider range of interests. Competition among rival policies and their proponents also takes place in an arena that specifies rules for exercising power in respect to particular decisions. Evaluators must, therefore, consider how their preferred criteria for decision will be affected by the rules for decision in political arenas within which they must operate.

We have, it appears, returned to politics. Unless building support for policies is an integral part of designing them, their proponents are setting themselves up for disappointment. To say that one will first think of a great idea and then worry about how it might be implemented is a formula for failure.[6] A good evaluation not only specifies desirable outcomes but suggests institutional mechanisms for achieving them.

If you don't know how to make an evaluation, it may be a problem for you but not for anyone else. If you do know how to evaluate, it becomes a problem for others. Evaluation is an organizational problem. While the occasional lone rider may be able to fire off an analysis now and then, he must eventually institutionalize his efforts if he is to produce a steady output. The overwhelming bulk of evaluation takes place within organizations. The rejection of evaluation is done largely by the organizations that ask for it. To create an organization that evaluates its own activities evidently requires an organizational response. If evaluation is not done at all, if it is done but not used, if used but twisted out of shape, the place to look first is not the technical apparatus but the organization.

Organization is first but not last. Always it is part of a larger society that conditions what it can do. Evaluation is also a social problem. So long as organizational opposition to evaluation is in the foreground, we are not likely to become aware of the social background. Should this initial resistance be overcome, and indiviudal organizations get to like evaluation, however, it would still face multiple defenses thrown up by social forces.

### Evaluation as Trust

For the self-evaluating organization all knowledge must be contingent. Improvement is always possible, change for the better is always in view though not necessarily yet attained. It is the organization *par excellence* that seeks knowledge. The ways in which it seeks to obtain knowledge, therefore, uniquely defines its character.

The self-evaluating organization would be skeptical rather than committed. It would continuously be challenging its own assumptions. Not dogma but scientific doubt would be its distinguishing feature. It would seek new truth instead of defending old errors. Testing hypotheses would be its main work.

Like the model community of scholars, the self-evaluating organization would be open, truthful, and explicit. It would state its conclusions in public, show how they were determined, and give others the opportunity to refute them. The costs and benefits of alternative programs for various groups in society would be indicated as precisely as available knowledge would permit. Everything would be above board. Nothing would be hidden.

Are there ways of securing the required information? Can the necessary knowledge be created? Will the truth make men free? Attempting to answer these profound queries would take me far beyond the confines of this exploratory article. But I would like to suggest by illustration that the answers to each of them depend critically on the existence of trust among social groups and within organizations. The acceptance of evaluation requires a community of men who share values.

An advantage of formal analysis, in which the self-evaluating organization specializes, is that it does not depend entirely on learning from experience. That can be done by ordinary organizations. By creating models abstracting relationships from the areas of the universe they wish to control, evaluators seek to substitute manipulation of their models for events in the world. By rejecting alternatives their models tell them will work out badly (or not as well as others), these analysts save scarce resources and protect the public against less

worthy actions. Ultimately, however, there must be an appeal to the world of experience. No one, not even the evaluators themselves, are willing to try their theoretical notions on large populations without more tangible reasons to believe that the recommended alternatives prove efficacious.[7]

Since the defect of ordinary organizations is that they do not learn well from experience, the self-evaluating organization seeks to order that experience so that knowledge will be gained from it. The proof that a policy is good is that it works when it is tried. But not everything can be tried everywhere. Hence experiments lie at the heart of evaluation. They are essential for connecting alleged causes with desired effects in the context of limited resources.

The ability of the self-evaluating organization to perform its functions depends critically upon a climate of opinion that favors experimentation. If resources are severely constrained, for example, leading to reluctance to try new ventures, the self-evaluating organization cannot function as advertised. Should there exist strong feeling that everyone must be treated alike, to choose another instance, experimentation would be ruled out. Take the case of the "More Effective Schools" movement in New York City. The idea was to run an experiment to determine whether putting more resources into schools would improve the performance of deprived children. In order to qualify as a proper experiment, More Effective Schools had to be established in some places but not in others, so that there would be control groups. The demand for equality of treatment was so intense, however, that mass picketing took place at the school sites. Favored treatment for these schools was taken as *prima facie* evidence of discrimination. It became apparent that More Effective Schools would have to be tried everywhere or nowhere. Clearly the social requisites of experimentation would have to exist for self-evaluating organizations to be effective. Unless groups trust each other, they will neither allow experiments to be conducted nor accept the results.

Although ways of learning without experimentation may be found, no evaluation is possible without adequate information. But how much is enough? Hierarchies in organizations exist in order to reduce information. If the men at the top were to consider all the bits of data available in the far-flung reaches of the organization, they would be overwhelmed.

As information is weeded and compressed on

its way through the hierarchy, however, important bits may be eliminated or distorted. One of the most frequently voiced criticisms of organizations is that the men at the top do not know what is going on. Information is being withheld from them or is inaccurate so that they make decisions on the basis of mistaken impressions. The desire to pass on only good news results in the elimination of information that might place the conveyer in a bad light. Top officials may, therefore, resort to such devices as securing overlapping sources of information or planting agents at lower levels. There are limits to these efforts, however, because the men at the top have only so much time to digest what they have been told. So they vacillate between fear of information loss and being unable to struggle out from under masses of data.

How might the self-evaluating organization deal with information bias? Organization members would have to be rewarded for passing on bad news. Those who are responsible for the flow of information must, at the least, not be punished for telling the truth. If they are also the ones in charge of administering the policy, it will not be possible to remove them for bad performance because once that is done their successors will be motivated to suppress such information. The top men must themselves be willing to accept the blame though they may not feel this is their responsibility and though their standing may be compromised. The very idea of a hierarchy may have to give way to shifting roles in which superior and subordinate positions are exchanged so that each member knows he will soon be in the other's position. The self-evaluating organization clearly requires an extraordinary degree of mutual trust.

The spread of self-evaluating organizations could enhance social trust by widening the area of agreement concerning the consequences of existing policies and the likely effects of change. Calculations concerning who benefited and to what degree would presumably aid in political cost-benefit analyses. The legitimacy of public institutions would be enhanced because they resulted from a more self-consciously analytical process that was increasingly recognized as such. Evaluation would be informative, meliorative, and stabilizing in the midst of change. It sounds idyllic.

More information, per se, need not lead to greater agreement, however, if the society is wracked by fundamental cleavages. As technology makes information more widely available, the need for interpretation will grow. Deluged by data,

distrustful of others, citizens may actually grow apart as group leaders collect more information about how badly off they are compared to what they ought to be. The more citizens trust group leaders rather than governmental officials, the greater the chance their differences will be magnified rather than reconciled. The clarification of objectives may make it easier to see the social conflicts implicit in the distribution of income or cultural preferences concerning the environment or the differing styles of life attached to opposing views of the ideal society. Evaluation need not create agreement; evaluation may presuppose agreement.

*Notes*

1. Dan Horowitz, "Flexible Responsiveness and Military Strategy: The Case of the Israeli Army," *Policy Sciences*, Vol. 1, No. 2 (Summer 1970), pp. 191-205.
2. Hans Thorelli, "Overall Planning and Management in Sweden," *International Social Science Bulletin*, Vol. VIII, No. 2 (1956).
3. The most dramatic and visible change can be found in the American presidency. Presidents have increasingly bureaucratized their operations. Within the Executive Office there now exist sizeable subunits, characterized by specialization and the division of labor, for dealing with the media of information and communication, Congress, foreign and domestic policy, and more. At the same time, Presidents seek the right to intervene at any level within the Executive Branch on a sporadic basis. The administrators are being prodded to change while the President stabilizes his environment. Thus we find President Nixon saying that he wants something done about that awful Bureau of Indian Affairs, as if it did not belong to him, or asking citizens to elect him again so he can save them from the compulsory busing fostered by his own bureaucracy. He wants to escape blame for bureaucratic errors but keep the credit for inspiring changes.
4. See Robert A. Levine, "Rethinking our Social Strategies," *The Public Interest*, No. 10 (Winter 1968).
5. William A. Niskanen, *Bureaucracy and Representative Government* (Chicago: Aldine-Atherton, 1971).
6. For further discussion along these lines see Jeffrey L. Pressman and Aaron Wildavsky, *Implementation: The Economic Development Administration in Oakland* (Berkeley and Los Angeles: University of California Press, forthcoming).
7. An exception of a kind is found in the area of defense policy where the purpose of the analytical exercises is to avoid testing critical hypotheses. Once the hypotheses concerning a nuclear war are tested, the evaluators may not be around to revise their analyses. See Aaron Wildavsky, "Practical Consequences of the Theoretical Study of Defense Policy," *Public Administration Review*, Vol. XXV, No. 1 (March 1965), pp. 90-103.

# 5

# The Influence of External Political Factors on the Role and Methodology of Evaluation

## Henry M. Brickell

I have never studied the influence of external political factors on educational evaluation, and thus I cannot speak as a scholar of political influence. I will speak instead as a bullseye—a well-riddled target of political factors. I am an object of these influences rather than an investigator of them. I have learned about political forces the way an iron filing learns about magnetic forces.

From among the different viewpoints from which I might choose to speak—teacher, administrator, evaluator, student of evaluation—I am going to speak from the viewpoint of a person who heads a non-profit educational evaluation business. Our business has to attract customers and win contracts in order to survive. We live on contracts.

Our customers are federal, state, and local governments. If **political** means **governmental,** then our business environment is 100% political. That is, the external factors that influence our evaluation work (apart from the professional factors that influence it) are 100% political. The government officials who employ us are engaged in winning and exercising power — power to decide who gets what. These officials administer educational programs — or the other government officials who are above, beside, or beneath them administer these programs — and their jobs, salaries, promotions and even their careers are intertwined with the programs they hire us to evaluate.

Their motives in hiring us are political; that is, governmental. They seek our help in deciding how to exercise their power over who gets what (and to exercise it more rationally, we would hope). Even if the government officials who hire us do so only because they are obligated by their funding agency to employ an evaluator, their motives in employing us nevertheless have to do with winning and allocating resources. At the simplest, if they do not hire an evaluator, they cannot keep their money coming in.

Moreover, the government—be it federal, state, or local—is a layered complex of people. We have to treat government as a complex rather than as a single entity. We have to recognize that government officials are as likely to use the art of politics in dealing with each other as in dealing with outsiders. The evaluative evidence we supply becomes a card in the political deck used in the game called government.

### Examples of Political Influence in Evaluation

Before preparing this article, I turned to a number of evaluation reports produced by my organization in the hope of finding an example of an evaluation study where external political factors had been at work. It happened that the first report I examined contained a good example, and so did the second, the third, and the fourth. In fact, I did not find any that did not yield an example; some could constitute full-fledged case studies.

[1]This paper and the related comments were published as part of the Research, Evaluation and Development Paper Series of the Northwest Regional Educational Laboratory (NWREL), and they are reprinted here with the permission of NWREL. The points of view or opinions expressed in this publication do not necessarily represent the official position or policy of NWREL.

Let me give you a few illustrations. The names of the individuals and the organizations in these examples have been changed so as to protect the guilty. If there is any recognizable resemblance between these descriptions and actual cases, blame it on my inability to erase the evidence. I hope you will not recognize any of these cases. As I said earlier, we still have to get more evaluation contracts from these same people.

## Example 1

Some time ago we evaluated the use of paraprofessionals in the schools of a major American city. In an earlier study of paraprofessionals in that same city, we had found that people were happy with their work. The paraprofessionals themselves, the school principals, the teachers, the kids, and even the parents were quite satisfied. But this second study of paraprofessionals was to deal with the actual impact they were having on pupil learning.

Shortly after receiving our contract from the city board of education, we learned that paraprofessionals were not hired or paid by the central administration. Instead, they were selected and paid by the several area superintendents who headed the geographical subdivisions of the school system. While meeting with area superintendents to explain the study, one of their spokesmen opened up with something like this:

*Okay, you evaluators. Let's get one thing straight from the start. We have these paraprofessionals here in these schools not only to help kids learn but to link us to the community. That's why we have them. That's why we're going to keep them. We're not looking for a report about test results that will cause any trouble with the board of education downtown. They've got their reasons for giving us the money to hire paraprofessionals; we've got our reasons for taking the money. So no matter what you find out about kids' achievement, we're going to keep our paraprofessionals. Don't make it difficult.*

Alerted thus, we made our study. And we were lucky that time. We found that the presence of paraprofessionals did in fact improve pupil achievement. Were we delighted! We never told anyone, of course, but the experimental groups became our home team and the control groups became the visitors from out of town. We sat at the edge of the field throughout the game, voicelessly cheering: "Make a significant difference!"

## Example 2

On another occasion we were employed to study a graduate training program. We arrived on the scene, as we so often do, a few months before the director was to submit his renewal request to his funding agency. The director himself was relatively new. Since taking the job, he had made a significant number of improvements in the program, as he explained to us in an early interview. He had also explained these improvements to his dean and to his funding agency. Now all he needed was the evidence. We searched in vain. Nothing in the data we gathered demonstrated the effect of these improvements, and that is what we wrote in our draft report. Like so many others with whom we have worked, the director offered to assist us by reviewing our draft before we put it into print. (We always seem to get this kind of help, even if we do not ask for it.) The dean then offered to help the director review our draft. Both of them called us in for a long and agonizing interview in which they challenged the accuracy of the data, our method of data gathering, the

competency of our interviewers, our interpretation of the data, the tone of our writing, and the overall quality of our draft report. They sent us back to rewrite it completely, then required us to turn over the basic data to them for re-analysis, and they did not re-employ us to continue evaluating the program as they had originally intended. I do not know what ever happened to our promises to transmit the findings to the graduate trainees who had supplied the data for the findings.

## Example 3

At another time we were serving as the external evaluator of a large-scale program for a federal agency. Our work included continuous reporting of progress in the program. The first submission we made was a formative evaluation report intended to help the program director and his staff get all activities properly launched. Our report was immediately returned to us (we had submitted it in draft, as usual) and we were told that 100 pages was too much help. The director could make do with a lot less. Besides, he and his staff felt that a fair amount of what we had to say was off target and not particularly useful. He asked us to shrink the length of the report, cut out some of the negative material, and try to write with a more balanced viewpoint. Then he could submit a copy of the report to his funding agency. We cut it in half, rethought the negative things we had said, eliminated some, and softened others.

Some time later, the entire program was transferred from one funding agency to another. The new agency found great fault with it and considered reducing its scope and its cost or terminating it altogether. Because we had not found that much fault with the program while serving as its external evaluator for the previous agency, we soon found ourselves siding with the program people against the new agency. Before many weeks had passed, we had become strong advocates of the program, thinking it was being unfairly treated by its new funders. You might say that we had begun to evaluate the behavior of the new agency. Moreover, we went to the top man in the agency, complained that his people were making a mistake, had them brought into his office, pointed out their errors, and appealed to him to stop them before they damaged the program. This was more awkward for us than you may realize; we had to win a new evaluation contract from the new agency in order to continue as the external evaluators. We worked our way through the situation by using the instinctive ability of every born evaluator: the ability to bite the hand that feeds you while seeming to be only licking it. Eventually, the funding agency decided to continue the program and to continue our services as external evaluator. Our relations have been only normally tense since that time.

## Example 4

Some time ago one of our staff turned in a draft evaluation report to the project director in a local school district. The local director wrote us a letter in response, noting a number of points at which he felt we had misjudged the project. We compared his letter to our evaluation report and found that the project director had turned in a perfect scorecard; his letter singled out 100% of our negative findings. Our staff member was then called before the entire local project staff and asked to defend and justify the findings. My telephone rang at about noon the day the staff member went out to see them, and he said: "The meeting just ended here in the school district, and I have agreed to make some changes, even though I honestly think the report is right as it stands. But I have a problem with one point. The director says that if the superintendent ever sees my recommendation saying that the superintendent himself ought to give the project more personal support, he will probably cancel our contract. What do you want me to tell him?" I was incensed! I said: "Tell him your comment stands. Let the superintendent go ahead and cancel the contract." You can see that I was in no mood to be pushed around by a project director. We always take strong stands like that on contracts of less than $10,000.

## Example 5

In another case a federal agency employed us to write an RFP calling for bids to evaluate more than $100 million worth of teacher training projects that had already been completed. The agency told us that it wanted the teacher training to be evaluated using pupil learning as the criterion. We said: "That's a terrible idea. Nobody can do that. Let's not put that in the RFP." The agency explained to us that pupil learning was the only criterion that really interested it. If teacher training didn't improve pupil learning, why should government spend money for it?

When we wrote the RFP, we were careful to work in a long section dealing with alternative criteria for evaluating teacher training: pupil learning, pupil behavior in immediate response to instruction, teacher learning, teacher behavior in immediate response to training, and so on. We tried to put enough clues in the RFP so that the bidders would be smart enough to reject pupil learning as a criterion, but they weren't.

After the government contracted with the winning bidder (a distinguished and nationally-known non-profit agency), the government hired us to monitor the contractor's work. Since we had written the RFP, we knew what the government expected of the contractor.

For six or eight months we watched the contractor attack the problem and shook our heads slowly, saying: "This isn't working; we knew it wouldn't work; he's not going to be able to solve the problem." But what should we report to the government? After all, we had written the RFP. Should we declare that nobody could do what we had called for? Or should we declare that this particular contractor could not do it? Our problem was worse than you might suspect. You see, our monitoring contract was of course conditional on the other agency's evaluation contract. Our PT boat was lashed to the side of its cruiser. If we fired a torpedo into his side, he would take us down with him. It took us some time to puzzle our way through the complex ethical considerations that occur to an evaluator at a time like this. Then, with mixed emotions, we fired the starboard tube. Down we went together. That did not make for good relationships between us and our professional colleagues in the other non-profit agency, and it wasn't good for our financial situation, either.

## Example 6

On another occasion we were retained by a state education department that was then financing a number of computer-based information systems. Each system was directed by a more or less aggressive director, and each one was competing for scarce funds within the department. All of the directors had been appointed to a committee to help decide which services should be supported, which ones consolidated with the others, which ones terminated, and what new ones started.

The committee had so much difficulty reaching agreement about these seemingly simple questions that it brought us in as outsiders to study the several systems and recommend what the department should do with them. We

conducted the study with energetic assistance from the various directors.

Our final report (reviewed beforehand by the director of each system) managed to jump over the question of hardware compatibility by concluding that the big new fourth-generation computers now becoming available made the question obsolete. All of the software being used could be run on any hardware configuration. And our report managed to finesse our way out of the question of conceptual compatibility.

As to which systems should be collapsed, continued, or expanded, we said that that depended on market demands. And so we recommended a field survey of users' interests to gather data about market demands. Of course, we offered to make that study if they would hire us again.

The committee examined our report and decided that they did not need any more help of that kind. So we turned elsewhere and rounded up 50-odd clients—the 50-odd intermediate service units that were wholesaling the systems to retail customers in local school districts. The service units hired us to make a users' study. When we completed the final report, the steering committee representing the 50-odd units asked us to make press-numbered copies of the reports to prevent any of the units from loaning its copy of the report to the special state investigator, who was just at that time examining the performance of the intermediate service units. They did not want the state investigator to do a hatchet job on them, using our report as a sharpening stone. We tried to tell the truth in the report yet not sharpen the state investigator's weapon. I don't think we made it. The 50-odd units haven't been back to see us.

## Example 7

In another case we were evaluating a 3-year-old project for a local school district. The innovation was being used in several schools at an extra cost of about $50,000 and was scheduled for expansion to the remaining schools if we found it successful or for termination if we did not. Don't take that too seriously. We have never yet made an evaluation study that the client permitted to decide the life or death of a project. Other factors, many of them more powerful than our findings, are always at work.

The innovation was expected to make a considerable improvement in cognitive as well as affective learning, according to what the superintendent, the assistant superintendent, and the principals had predicted to the board of education three years earlier. We designed a study, collected the data, made an analysis, and concluded that there was no significant difference between students in the experimental schools and comparable students in the other schools.

When we discussed the results informally with local personnel before writing the final report, we were offered good explanations of the findings. The principals explained that the board of education had not supplied full funding for the program. Rather, the board had cut the program back about half-way through, with the result that the principals could not buy the materials and hire the paraprofessionals needed to run the program full-scale. The central office administrators explained that the principals apparently had not given the teachers the necessary in-service training and classroom supervision needed to make the innovation work properly. The board of education explained that the administrators had for some reason not been able to deliver on their initial promises, despite the $50,000 extra for materials and paraprofessionals—a generous allocation that had caused parents in other schools to question the board's lopsided generousity. Each group suggested that we would be wise to reach its conclusions in our report.

In the final report. we said a combination of factors—some shortfall in performance by principals. central office administrators. and the board—had caused the disappointing results. We recommended that they run the program full-scale for three more years and. not surprisingly. that they hire us again so that we could give them the real answer as to whether the innovation was good enough to extend to the other schools.

### Example 8

In another state we had a contract to evaluate a large number of special education materials centers. When we first submitted a draft of the study questionnaire to our client. we got some helpful reactions. The review committee suggested to us that we eliminate some of the more negative items from the instrument; that we shorten the negative end of scales that ranged from **strongly agree** to **strongly disagree** or from **very good** to **very bad**; that we not name any service that was not already being rendered to teachers; and that we not administer the instrument to teachers who had not been receiving the services. The review committee made other helpful suggestions as to how we could improve our questionnaires so that our findings would be more useful in winning needed support for continuing the special education centers in the next year. which was their objective in having the evaluation made. We modified the questionnaire. of course—we want to stay in business—although we argued the committee out of some of the changes they wanted.

Later. when the findings were in. we telephoned the client to discuss the style in which the recommendations should be written. Should they be addressed to the local directors of the special education centers. to their advisory councils of classroom teachers. or to state officials responsible for the program? What was the target audience? We gave two or three sample recommendations written in several styles. They said the choice among the three styles was easy: they didn't want any of them. They said to eliminate all recommendations. The findings probably would not cause any trouble. but the recommendations certainly could. We complied.

### Example 9

At one time we worked for a state education department on the redesign of teacher education. It was in part an evaluation study. The design called for us to hold a series of meetings with the major parties at interest in teacher education: deans of schools of education. professors. school superintendents. school principals. classroom teachers. state department of education personnel. and citizens. We held 125 meetings with them to discuss what flaws existed in teacher education and how they ought to be corrected.

At the outset. the client asked us to begin the study of teacher education in October and file a final report complete with new institutional accreditation standards by December of the same year. I objected that three months was a little speedy: the client wanted a high participation study involving over 50 colleges and over 500 school districts and the topic was extremely complex. not to mention political. Besides. there were the Thanksgiving and Christmas holidays. The client said that the decision-making timetable in that particular state required action by January in order to affect teacher education two years later. Besides. he was under some pressure from teachers' groups and citizens' groups to get things moving. So we said we would try to finish by December. We failed. of course. By December we had not produced a convergence

of opinion among professors. teachers. school administrators. parents. and others on such questions as whether there should be performance-based standards for teacher education and certification. Issues like that take a little while to discuss.

When our client realized that we would not finish by December. he asked us at least to submit a progress report. So we drafted a 350-page (honestly!) progress report quoting verbatim from the minutes of the 125 meetings. taking care to represent all viewpoints. divergent as well as convergent. We dared not do anything except quote verbatim because we knew that otherwise the report would be rejected as inaccurate. When the participating groups received the progress report. they said two things: "This is way too long." and "You didn't include everything we said." So we wrote a second draft—396 pages. We submitted that one to our client. the state education department. which said. "This is way too long. Besides. where's the convergence you promised us when we gave you the contract in October?"

While our client wrestled with the second draft. the participating groups pored over it. They not only confirmed their thinking: the expanded it. That gave us the problem of taking their January-March thinking and working it into the draft as though it had occurred in December. We reworked the December draft to accommodate the corrections and the expanded thinking of our participants. By May we were still working on the December progress report. We had yet to satisfy our client and our review groups that we had produced an accurate progress report that captured the essence of everyone's thinking up to December—a progress report that would make the basis for further discussion in January. February. March. April. May. and so on.

You won't be surprised to learn that around the beginning of May the client called: "Look. I said December. You're taking too long." At that point. he took over the raw data. wrote a draft of the **final** report. and published it—doing something less than full justice to the promises he made to the participants about how their views would be used in shaping the redesign of teacher education.

But I had not been able to get universal agreement even on the December progress report. If my client didn't get a final report by May. he couldn't publish it in June; it couldn't go to the state board of education in September; the new regulations couldn't be put through public hearings in the fall: and the state legislature couldn't be notified in January that the new regulations would go into effect in September. 1976. So the client interrupted my orderly process. He took away the raw data. He wrote the final report.

Because I was advertised in the state for some months as Dr. Neutral from New York in as an honest broker between all the parties—promising. among other things. to defend the participants against unfair handling of their ideas by the state education department—my client still needed some kind of "final report" from me. We debated what it should say. I submitted a preface to his final report. saying that I worked on it from October through about March and had nothing to do with it after that. Following this disclaimer we spent considerable time discussing if I would later say what he wanted me to say. At the time of preparing this paper. these discussions were still going on.

### Example 10

I once made a study of alternative ways of financing non-public schools. The Catholic schools in a New England state were in considerable financial difficulty. A state legislative commission consisting of 25 members had been created to determine whether public funds should be used to help these schools. or whether they should be allowed to go under. Among other things. the commission wanted to know how much damage would be done to the public schools if the non-public schools collapsed and all their students suddenly transferred to public schools.

The commission was a cross-section of the state. Every viewpoint was represented. We had the advocates of Catholic schools and we had their opponents; we had the advocates of other private schools and their opponents; we had the parents who wanted financial aid and taxpayers who opposed it; we had public school people; we had the American Civil Liberties Union. Every voice had a place at the table.

With every politically significant interest represented. I found myself in the most neutral political environment I had ever worked in. The competing interests had to debate and come to terms with each other as to how the inquiry was to be made before the chairman could give me my marching orders. When I submitted plans for collecting data, turned in findings, or drafted recommendations. all of them had to be adjudicated among the commission members before the chairman could sign off on them. The effect of that, so far as I was concerned. was to neutralize various political factors and let me operate free of political considerations—free in the special sense that the competing forces were adjudicated before they could reach me and work their separate and conflicting influences on me.

## Summary

Are there external political factors that influence the role and methodology of evaluation? You bet there are. And they are powerful.

Because the seeking. the winning. and the exercising of power are a prominent part of life within an institution as well as between institutions. internal evaluation staffs are just as subject to political influences as external evaluation staffs. Perhaps you have noticed that.

Sometimes political forces control the populations we can sample. Sometimes they limit the data we can gather. Sometimes they shape our instruments. Sometimes they influence the designs we can use. Sometimes they guide our interpretations. Sometimes they shape our recommendations. Sometimes they touch the wording of our reports. And they always influence the impact of what we recommend.

I think I have never written an evaluation report without being conscious of the fact that what I say will be used in the winning and the exercising of power. that my findings are going to be lined up on one side or the other of a contest that somebody else has already set up. and that jobs are on the line—maybe my own job.

Once in a great while. I have had the privilege of sitting as a member—a nameless member—of a panel of judges and have been able to write a recommendation I thought the project director would never see. But much more often I have had to face him. his staff. his employer. and his funding agency and watch their faces as they hear. challenge. or attack my methodology. findings. conclusions. and recommendations.

Even if the subject of the evaluation is absent. I can never forget that the project monitor in the funding agency frequently identifies himself with the project and becomes its champion. So I have to think of the effect of my report on him. and on the larger program of which the project is a part. and on the agency sponsoring the program. Indeed. I even have to think about the overall fate and the future of research and development in education. I don't have to tell you that research. development. and evaluation are themselves enterprises for which somebody has to win and exercise power in the legislative and political arenas in order to decide who gets what. I often find myself wondering whether my evaluation reports. even as they help the profession win small battles against unsatisfactory projects. simul-taneously help it lose the war for research. development. and experimentation. But that is another matter

Let me finish by giving some rules for escaping the influence of external political factors. Let me offer five such rules:

- Do not work for anyone who has anything to do with the project you are evaluating.

- Employ exactly the same objectivity and the detachment you would use in undertaking a research study where **you** pick the problem. where **you** set up hypotheses of **your own** choosing. where **you** gather data without external restrictions. and where **you** draw **your own** conclusions.

- Report your findings in such a way that they have no implications whatsoever for the project you are evaluating.

- Do not work for the government—local. state. or federal—and try not to work for philanthropic foundations.

- Be independently wealthy.

If you can follow these rules. you can escape the influence of external political factors on your work as an evaluator.

As for myself. I am not going to follow any one of these rules. My organization would go out of business as evaluators if we tried it. We are going to have to struggle along with a few other rules. much spongier ones. and try to make the best of a political world. Here they are:

- Try to understand how the client thinks. Find out what he has to gain or lose from the evaluation. He may have the gains in mind before he awards the contract. but he will think about nothing but the possible losses once the evaluator sets to work. One client said to me just the other day—speaking. I thought. for all of his breed—"Studies just make trouble."

- Reassure the client at the outset that you can interpret the findings so as to give helpful suggestions for program improvement—no matter what the findings of the study are.

- Find out what the powerful decision makers—the client and those who surround him—will actually use as criteria for judging the success of the project. Gather and present evidence addressed to these criteria. You may. if you wish. also gather data on the official objectives of the project or even on objectives that happen to interest you. But never try to substitute these for data addressed to criteria the decision makers will use.

- Try to get a supervisory mechanism set up for the evaluation contract that contains a cross-section of all the powerful decision makers. Try to get it designed so that the members have to resolve the conflicts among themselves before giving you marching orders for the study or deciding whether to accept your final report.

- Write the report carefully. especially when describing shortcomings and placing blame. and do mention any extenuating circumstances. The client will appreciate that. Review the draft final report before submitting it to the client for his review. making sure in advance that you can defend any claim you make.

Following these rules will not help you escape political influences. The most they can do is help you cope with them.

# 6

# Comments on "The Influence of External Political Factors on the Role and Methodology of Evaluation"

## William J. Wright

In his paper Brickell provides a rich variety of explicit examples of the political influences that affect evaluation.[1] By doing so. he forces us to focus our attention on the boundary line between political realities and ethical values. and to see that the demarcation is not easily discernible. One can imagine two individuals arguing the merits of this paper. The first might argue that Brickell has identified reasonable and responsible strategies for dealing with the real world. He or she might suggest that Brickell has provided excellent advice on the way in which an enterprise dependent on "soft money" needs to operate in order to stay in business and provide evaluation services to those who seek such. The other reader might decry the expendiency underlying both Brickell's rules and the way in which some of the problem situations he faced were resolved. This reader might suggest that if evaluation is as devoid of ethical principles as this paper seems to suggest. then it is little wonder that its products are so unheeded.

The truth perhaps can be found between these extremes. One way to think of Brickell's paper is as a report from the front lines. Brickell has been a leader in the field of evaluation for quite some time. He has here provided a first-hand view of some of the forces that have assaulted his efforts. and alerted those who follow as to what awaits them. It is incumbent upon the latter to prepare themselves accordingly.

The primary issue raised by this paper is. then. the need to examine ways of solving the problems resulting from the inevitable intertwinement of politics and evaluation not merely as individuals. but as a profession. Evaluators are employed not just because people are obligated to employ an evaluator by their funding agency. Presumably it is because those who create or who direct the funding agency believe that evaluation will generate **credible** information on which decisions can in part be based. If evaluation is to grow as a profession. then we need to ensure that that belief is warranted. We need to help one another to examine our values and behavior in a way that will promote confidence in the worth of our efforts.

The first step in such a process ought to be an examination of whether there are commonly held. basic values among those who class themselves as evaluators.[2] If such exist. and I believe they do. then we ought to generate standards for evaluation which are consonant with these values. These standards could be akin to the *Standards for Educational and Psychological Tests*.[3] There are two general areas in which standards might be

generated—contracts and performance. Each area will be discussed briefly as will the possible benefits and the limitations of evaluation standards. Although a few examples of the kinds of standards envisioned are provided. their inclusion is simply illustrative. Whatever standards do emerge ought to represent the concensual judgment of a substantial number of prestigious evaluators.

### Contractual Standards

Most professions have general guidelines which assist their members in determining appropriate professional arrangements. Brickell's paper illustrates the need for similar standards in at least three areas.[4]

#### Respective responsibilities

About half of the cases cited by Brickell involved misunderstandings between the client and the evaluator about what the respective responsibilities were. Often. as this sample of cases makes clear. the evaluator is expected to answer questions which either cannot be answered at all in the current situation or which cannot be answered given the resources available. The contract should limit the scope of the inquiry by identifying those critical questions which will and those which will not be answered.

Sometimes the evaluator discovers that an important objective has been overlooked by the client in preparing the evaluation contract. Brickell's instance of the paraprofessional project evaluation is a good example. In this case the evaluator's charge was to investigate the impact of paraprofessionals on student learning. Yet the area superintendents had their own reasons for wanting paraprofessionals in the schools. namely. cementing community relations. When this situation occurs. the evaluator ought to identify the objective which is not part of the charge as an important. but unanswerable question given the current resources. Perhaps in addition. he or she ought to request more resources and a revised contract so as to permit an expanded investigation.

Contracts should also identify client responsibilities. For example. when a client restricts access to necessary information. the client thereby accepts responsibility for the inevitably flawed report. Given multiple client groups. there should be. as Brickell advises. a mechanism for resolving conflicts before the evaluator gets his marching orders.

#### Audience Restrictions

Contracts should also stipulate the restrictions to be placed on the use of the resulting report. The third case cited by Brickell illustrates this point particularly well. The evaluator. hired to conduct a formative evaluation. is asked to write a

---

[1] All too often these problems are ignored or dealt with on a sub-rosa basis. Notable exceptions are the contributions of House (1973). Cohen (1973). and Kearney and Huyser (1973).

[2] Value differences among evaluators do exist. If core values can be identified. or if dialogue among representatives of various points of view can produce agreement about core values. then the differences which exist need not negate the desirability or feasibility of establishing standards.

A precedent exists for this suggestion. George Madaus of the joint APA. AERA. NCME committee which prepared the 1974 revision argued the need for a companion volume on evaluation in a memorandum to his committee colleagues.

[4] A compilation by Robert Stake (1974) of the answers of prominent researchers to seven questions concerning evaluation contracts offers valuable insights into the process of preparing an evaluation contract. The responses of these individuals make it clear that even experienced evaluators and researchers perceive the need for contractual specificaions that are more clear about respective rights and responsibilities of client and evaluator than has been typical to date. Explicit standards in this area might prove very beneficial. especially for the new practitioner.

From William J. Wright, "Comments on 'The Influence of External Political Factors On the Role and Methodology of Evaluation,' " 5 (2) *Evaluation Comment* 8-10 (December 1976). Copyright 1976 by Center for the Study of Evaluation, University of California, Los Angeles.

report which can be used to justify continuation to the funding agency. If the evaluator is to help a program or project improve while it is in development, then the failings and flaws need to be carefully examined so that the client can determine what corrective actions are required. Yet, documenting one's inadequacies is seldom the best approach to use in soliciting funding. Indeed, if a funding agency wants an objective evaluation which meets their own criteria, then they should contract directly with an evaluator. Forcing a funded client to hire an evaluator whose reports go to the funding agency is rather like asking the infested country to provide a per diem for one's resident spies.

### Conflicts of interest

Sometimes one is faced with a situation which raises questions of conflict of interest. Brickell's fifth case involves the preparation of an RFP which was deemed "undoable." The preparer then agreed to evaluate the performance of the contractor and judged it inadequate. Given the role of the evaluator in the RFP preparation and the expectation of failure, it would seem that a conflict of interest existed.

The fifth case, and the third case as well, involved the employment of an external evaluator whose continued employment was contingent on some degree of success by the evaluated project. In such cases favorable evaluation promotes both project continuation and continuation of the evaluator's funding. The conflict of interest seems apparent.

The issue of whether someone who has been responsible for a formative evaluation, and thus presumably assisted the program to achieve its goals, should also conduct the summative evaluation, while not illustrated by Brickell, has also been an issue of concern in regard to conflict of interest.[5]

None of us is in a position to criticize the contractual arrangements of others. In the absence of standards one is forced to rely exclusively on personal judgment. And, indeed, one has to applaud the "firing of the torpedo" in Brickell's fifth case. It takes courage and a strong commitment to principle to act contrary to one's economic self-interest. The question of how to avoid such dilemmas, however, remains. The establishment of standards might provide a partial answer.

## Performance Standards

Reasonable contract standards can only go so far in solving the problems illustrated in Brickell's paper. Standards for performance would also seem to be indicated.

### Instrumentation and Sampling

In the eighth case cited by Brickell, the questionnaires developed for use in the evaluation were modified at the insistence of the client. Negative items were eliminated, and negative ends of the scales were apparently shortened. Moreover, the client urged that the sample to whom the questionnaire was to be given be altered. We don't know if the evaluator complied.

Not enough is known about what affect the client's suggestions had on the evaluation in question to address the cited case directly, but some general comments seem in order. If it is the responsibility of the evaluator to provide credible information, then he or she must insist on the right to collect evidence in which confidence can be placed. One simply cannot ignore the possibility of negative findings because the client would prefer it that way. To do so would be to ultimately destroy any confidence that one could place in positive findings—could place in evaluation.

### Interpretation and Reporting

In the case just cited, the client attempted to steer the evaluator onto a "positive results only" tack. The report was

then to be used to secure continued funding. The issue of the responsibility of the evaluator for the use which is made of his or her efforts is thus raised. The concern is a general one since even if a priori agreements are reached concerning how a report is to be used, that does not constitute an inviolable guarantee.

Hume's truism states that "Inference is never fully justified logically," and there are usually multiple interpretations one can arrive at from the same data set. Yet, one sometimes has to draw the line, to distinguish between differences in interpretation and misrepresentation, to reject the kind of "help" in report preparation to which Brickell frequently alludes. But the client is also clearly free to reject the evaluator's report. The question then becomes: what is the responsibility of the evaluator when the client, or someone else, reports the results of the evaluation and the evaluator disagrees with the report issued?

This question is not as easy to answer as one might suspect at first glance. Rebuttal, for example, could be quite costly in terms of the personal or corporate financial resources of the evaluator. The consequences in terms of future contracts could be disastrous. If the misrepresentation is perpetrated by the press or broadcast media, there may be no feasible recourse. In the development of standards one issue which could be addressed might be the establishment of some mechanism whereby the evaluator could turn to his or her colleagues, e.g., to an established panel on the ethics of evaluation. If they determine that a particular interpretation is indubitably in error, then more than a single voice would be raised in protest.

### Nonperformance

There are, however, pariahs among the paragons. A client ill-served by an evaluator should have some recourse. A mechanism for resolving critical disputes should perhaps be considered. The history of professional groups which attempt to judge nonperformance or malfeasance through appeal boards and similar means is not replete with success as the efforts of the American Medical Association and local police review boards bear witness. Yet, some arbitration models have proved fruitful in other areas, and might be useful in our field as well.

## Benefits and Limitations

There are several benefits that could emerge from the generation of evaluation standards. They would not be a substitute for the education of administrators and other clients in the purposes and methods of evaluation. Yet, their existence might facilitate that process and provide a useful reference tool for the client who is negotiating or monitoring an evaluation contract. Moreover, an informed clientele would perhaps be less likely to make unreasonable or unethical requests of evaluators.

A more general understanding of the limited role of evaluation might also be promoted by the generation of evaluation standards. In Brickell's first case, the paraprofessionals were viewed by the principals as being of great value because of their impact on community relations. The evaluation focused exclusively on student achievement outcomes. If there were no student learning gains, should the project have been scrapped? The principals would state that the evaluation was too limited. I, for one, would agree, and would argue further that such is inevitably the case. Evaluation can provide some of the data on which decisions ought to be based. It should not be viewed as a substitute for a reasonable decision-making process.

Finally, with the existence of standards, evaluation would move closer to becoming an identifiable profession. Those few who are unprincipled enough to use the cloak of evaluation to disguise unprincipled or shoddy information collection practices would be more easily recognized by their potential clients who would, in turn, have a clearer pic-

---

[5] The October 1974 issue of the newsletter of the AERA Special Interest Group: Educational Research and Development Evaluators, for example, focuses on this question.

ture of their own responsibilities and a more solid basis their expectations.

Of course. standards would not be a panacea. Circumstances will often occur that raise ethical and political difficulties for which there are no completely satisfactory solutions. Vigilance against the substitution of codified standards for a thoughtful. professional conscience will be necessary. There will no doubt be areas of fundamental disagreement among reasonable evaluators. and each of us will have to make our own decisions. hopefully. based on publicly communicated values.

The advantages of the testing standards have. however. outweighed any attendant disadvantages at least insofar as the membership of APA. AERA and NCME seem to be concerned. The same would probably hold true of standards for evaluation. Moreover. in a recent publication the National Council on Education Professions Development (1974) wrote:

> Despite the increasing expenditures. need. and significance for mustering the kind of evidence sought by evaluation research. both the quality and use of such evidence has been quite disappointing. Evaluation of Federal programs in education has proceeded on an ad hoc. improvisational basis with little provision for the conditions necessary to ensure adequate quality or valid use of the evidence produced by evaluation research. (p. 2)

The council recommends that the Congress require the executive branch to establish evaluation policy which "... should set forth the larger purposes of evaluation as a tool of government and should establish its metes and bounds." (p. 3)

Given this press. it would seem that steps ought to be taken to ensure that when evaluation standards do emerge. they represent the thinking of the members of the profession rather than some governmental bureaucracy. Insofar as Brickell's paper is a catalyst for serious consideration of ethical and political problems in evaluation. it makes a very valuable contribution to the field. If steps are taken to generate standards for evaluation. it will have served very well indeed.

### References

Cohen. D. K. Politics and research. In E. R. House (Ed.). *School evaluation: The politics and process.* Berkeley: McCutchan Publishing Corporation. 1973.

*Educational Research and Development Evaluators Newsletter.* 1974. 3. Southwest Educational Development Laboratory: Austin. Texas.

House. E. R. The conscience of educational evaluation. In E. R. House (Ed.). *School evaluation: The politics and process.* Berkeley: McCutchan Publishing Corporation. 1973.

Kearney. C. P.. & Huyser. R. J. The politics of reporting results. In E. R. House (Ed.). *School evaluation: The politics and process.* Berkeley: McCutchan Publishing Corporation. 1973.

Madaus. G. F. Need for a companion volume. A memorandum to the members of the Joint Committee on Test Standards Revision. May 7. 1973.

National Advisory Council on Education Profession.. Development. *Search for success: Toward policy on educational evaluation.* U.S. Department of Health. Education and Welfare. 1974.

Stake. R. E. How researchers have responded to seven key questions. Unpublished manuscript. Center for Instructional Research and Curriculum Evaluation. University of Illinois at Urbana-Champaign.

*Standards for educational and psychological tests.* Washington. D.C.: The American Psychological Association. 1974.

# PART II
# METHODOLOGY

The articles in this section do not exhaust the methodological papers in this volume, and the interested reader should consult the other sections, all of which contain some articles with an explicit methodological focus.

Few scholars and practitioners of evaluation deny the desirability of random assignment for making causal inferences, but considerable disagreement exists about the feasibility of randomization in many instances. The paper by Conner presents an analysis of 12 evaluations whose initial plans called for random assignment, and he explicates five factors that may facilitate the successful implementation of randomization. To assign at random does not guarantee that the "treatment" will be delivered and received in the planned manner, and Williams presents an interesting commentary on the difficulties of implementing planned changes.

In many evaluations, statistics play an important role in determining the degree of covariation between the planned change and outcome measures and in attempts to control statistically for sources of both random error and systematic bias. Berk and Brewer's paper deals with the power-broadly conceived— of statistics in helping draw inferences, while the debate between Crane and Schuerman deals with issues relating to rejection of the null hypothesis in conventional hypothesis testing.

More and more evaluations seem to be using administrative data banks. The article by Tabor highlights the role that accountants have played, and could play, in current evaluations since they have had many years of experience in using records to evaluate programs and projects. The paper of Roos et al. presents an interesting view on data banks derived from their many years of evaluation research using Canadian medical records.

# 7

## Selecting a Control Group: An Analysis of the Randomization Process in Twelve Social Reform Programs

### Ross F. Conner

*This study examines the randomization process in twelve different social reform projects in the fields of health, education, and law. All of the programs used the same type of evaluation plan: a true experimental design involving randomization of clients to treatment and control conditions. The implementation of this plan is discussed for each project. In addition, the projects are analyzed in terms of five aspects of the assignment process. The relationships between these aspects and the successful or unsuccessful implementations of the twelve evaluation designs are discussed. Finally, recommendations are made about issues which should be considered by program administrators and researchers before planning and implementing a true experimental evaluation.*

*T*n the last decade there has been a growing interest among social program administrators in valid methods and techniques for assessing the results of their programs. One method of obtaining meaningful results is a true experimental evaluation plan: program clients are randomly assigned either to receive the new program (the treatment group) or to receive the old program or no program at all (the control group). This method can provide outcome results which are more definitive than other techniques, because, at the outset of the program, a comparison is established between two groups of clients who are similar in all ways except the important one: only the treatment group is involved in the new program. This article analyzes the process of establishing treatment and control groups in twelve social reform projects. The comparative analysis reveals certain important components of the process which relate to successful or unsuccessful random assignment.[1]

From Ross F. Conner, "Selecting a Control Group: An Analysis of the Randomization Process in Twelve Social Reform Programs," 1 (2) *Evaluation Quarterly* 195-244 (May 1977). Copyright 1977 by Sage Publications, Inc.

## THE TRUE EXPERIMENTAL EVALUATION METHOD

The true experimental evaluation method is not new; it is basically the same model that scientists have used in laboratory research to determine cause and effect. This method was occasionally used to good effect in early field research (e.g., Chapin, 1940; Hill, 1944). In the late 1960s, when program administrators turned to social scientists for suggestions on social program evaluation methods, the scientists generally advocated a more scientific approach (e.g., Brim, 1969; Campbell, 1969; Freeman and Sherwood, 1969; Hyman and Wright, 1967; Rivlin, 1971; Rossi, 1969; Suchman, 1969). Evaluation researchers began to advocate various techniques for evaluating the effectiveness of social programs, including the true experimental design (Campbell, 1974; Guttentag, 1971; Hatry, Winnie, and Fisk, 1973; Riecken and Boruch, 1974; Weiss, 1972).

When these proposed methods actually were applied, program evaluators often had trouble implementing them. Although many evaluation researchers had written about the designs and methods that program administrators should consider, few had investigated the practical problems which arise in implementing an evaluation plan. At the present time, our knowledge of these problems is limited mainly to general discussions (Caro, 1971; Rossi and Williams, 1972; Struening and Guttentag, 1975); only occasionally are these problems presented in specific detail (Campbell and Erlebacher, 1970; Empey and Erickson, 1972; Gilbert, Light, and Mosteller, 1975; Gordon, 1973). This study is a systematic, comparative investigation of these problems for programs using a true experimental evaluation plan.

### THE USES OF RANDOMIZATION

The basic requirement for a true experimental evaluation design is a simple one: eligible clients must be assigned at random to the treatment group or the control group (cf. Campbell and Stanley, 1966). A researcher can accomplish this in different ways, depending on the type of project or the constraints of the setting. In the simplest case a researcher can list all eligible clients, then randomly select people for the treatment group or for the control group. By selecting clients in this way, a program researcher assures that the groups are equivalent before the treatment begins. This initial similarity of the two groups allows the researchers to conclude later whether it is the treatment that has caused changes.

Randomly selected client groups will usually have similar scores on outcome measures administered before any intervention program begins.[2] At the end of the program, clients' scores on the same outcome measures will have changed. It is likely that both treatment group and control group client scores will have changed from their preprogram levels. The difference in the changes between the control group and the treatment group is the effect attributable to the social program. Without the initial equivalency of the two groups which randomization provides, this kind of conclusion about causation would not be warranted.

In addition to its utility in determining causation, randomization has other advantages. This selection method can be a means for solving other problems. A large-scale social reform project usually has more clients than the project can adequately handle. Randomization provides a method which is not subject to favoritism or other biases in choosing clients. If the names of all eligible or interested clients are placed on a list which is then used for the random assignment of clients to the treatment group, the project administrators can be assured that everyone on the list had an equal chance of being selected.

Other selection systems usually are biased in some way. A first-come, first-served system is characterized by the selection of people who are part of the official communication network in an area and who learn about the program before others do. This system is subject to manipulation by the project managers, since they can notify people whom they would like to have in the program or to whom they owe a favor. This type of selection is also subject to manipulation by the clients. A client who learns about the program during the early stages of the sign-up can contact his friends and encourage them to enroll. If enough friends join the program, this process would produce a sample that was not representative. Moreover, the presence of a number of people who know each other and who probably share other experiences would complicate any explanation of program effects.

Another selection procedure which is sometimes used is that of the most needy (if the program is an ameliorative one) or the most deserving (in the case of a program that selects the best prepared or the most able). In the case of the most needy clients, there probably will be some improvement, even if the program itself really is having no effect. This occurs because these people are so needy; we would expect them to become less needy on their own. In the case of the most able, the opposite happens. We could expect a program to show negative effects if the program treatment itself really has no effect. Again, this occurs because the clients were selected on the basis of their extremity, but in this case this factor works against showing any program effects. Campbell and Stanley (1966) have discussed this problem of regression toward the mean and caution researchers against a most needy or most able selection procedure.

Apart from the issue of regression, there are other problems with selecting the most needy or most able clients. This procedure minimizes the heterogeneity of the treatment group. People who are most needy in one way are also likely to be similarly needy in other ways. This similarity could mean that the group of clients who receive the treatment may also be receiving other common ameliorative treatments. The presence or absence of program effects, then, could be due to these other common factors. In addition, there are no adequate statistical procedures which will adjust for preexisting differences between a needy or able treatment group and a less-needy or less-able control group. In at least one case where a needy treatment group was compared with a less-needy control group, the statistical adjustments made on pretest scores underadjusted and made the program appear to be harmful (Campbell and Erlebacher, 1970).

Since part of the reason for conducting a social reform project is to test an idea for continued or more general adoption, it follows that the sample of clients chosen for the project ought to be adequate to test the effects of the program. While the most needy or most able clients can still be the focus for a particular project, program administrators can get a better test of the program by expanding their criterion for entrance, then randomly selecting from among all the clients who meet the criterion. This will result in a more heterogeneous group which will improve the generalizability of any findings. In addition, program researchers will be better able to discover the kinds of clients who are affected most by the program, since the spectrum of clients experiencing the treatment is wider.

There is one other advantage of random assignment. Although social reforms usually involve special positive outcomes for clients (e.g., better education, better health care), there are large-scale social projects which involve negative outcomes (e.g., military service). In these cases randomization provides an easy, equitable method of dispensing the outcome. Such a selection procedure was used for a short time by the United States Army to fill draft quotas (Fienberg, 1971; Rosenblatt and Filliben, 1971). There are differing views on the advisability of random selection of participants in this case. Some writers view this use of randomization as a "denial of rationality, . . . a denial of man's humanity" (Wolfe, 1970: 1201). Others, however, see this as a selection method which is fair and nondiscriminatory (Fienberg, 1971: 260).

## METHOD

The studies reported here are a special set of projects drawn primarily from a bibliography of randomized field experiments (Boruch, 1974). The Boruch bibliography contains a large number of studies in a variety of different social program areas. The listing is not exhaustive of all randomized field studies and probably is somewhat biased toward the more successful studies, since unsuccessful projects are less likely to produce published reports. Consequently, the population of studies used in selecting the sample for the current research probably has this bias. Because the outcome of a study was less important for this research than was the process of randomization, the importance of the bias is questionable. The concern here was to make a first attempt at comparing the randomization process in a limited series of cases to uncover important variables for future study. In view of this goal, the possible bias in the sample toward more successful studies may be advantageous, since these studies are better documented, and project directors could be expected to be more thorough and candid in discussing their project.

The projects selected for intensive study met three criteria.

1. *Random Assignment Process.* Each project involved randomly assigning clients to study conditions. In general, individual clients were the units of randomization, and they typically were assigned either to a control condition or to a treatment condition. In several cases, groups of clients, rather than individuals, were the units of randomization, but the main interest remained the effects of different study conditions on individuals.

2. *Availability of Project Staff.* All of the projects discussed here are similar in a second way. The project administrators and researchers

were available and willing to discuss the implementation of their randomized evaluation designs. In many other cases, project staff either were unavailable or recalled very little about the randomization process. Discussions with project staff were essential to obtain the necessary information about randomization: project reports very rarely present anything but brief, superficial discussions of the process.

All project personnel contacted who had been involved in the randomization process agreed to talk with the researcher. They were honest about the problems they had faced in the random assignment process, and they were candid about the solutions they had tried or the compromises they had made in order to carry out the assignment. These issues were ignored or avoided in most of the program reports reviewed during the initial phase of this research.

3. *Heterogeneity of Project Type and Scale.* These twelve projects were selected for their dissimilarity on several dimensions. In order to increase the generalizability of the results of this study, projects of different types and sizes were chosen. These projects came from the fields of health, education, and law. They ranged in size from small programs which dealt with a select local population to large programs which extended nationwide. In spite of these differences, analysis of the programs revealed certain aspects of the randomization process which were consistently related to successful or unsuccessful assignment. Because these aspects were uncovered from a sample of dissimilar projects, we can be more confident that they are important considerations in general and not simply idiosyncratic aspects of these particular projects.

Once the projects were selected, all of the available reports from each project were read. In all cases project administrators and researchers wee contacted directly for additional information about the random assignment process. Generally, they provided special in-house reports and talked at length about their evaluation projects.

## DESCRIPTION OF PROGRAMS

The twelve projects analyzed here are summarized in Table 1. There are four health projects, two of which were confined to large cities: the Baltimore program in Alternative Ambulatory Care Delivery

Systems (Outpatient Care) and the Chicago Heart Association Nutrition Education Project (Nutrition). The other two projects are nationwide programs which are still in progress: the National Cooperative Multiple Risk Factor Intervention Trial (Heart Attack Prevention) and the American Heart Association Coronary Drug Project (Coronary Drug). In all four cases, individual subjects were randomly assigned to treatment or control groups.

Five of the twelve projects are educational programs. Three of these involved a large, nationwide population: the Follow Through Summer Effects Study (Summer Projects), the Emergency School Aid Act Programs (Desegregation), and the Emergency School Assistance Program (ESAP). All of these programs were sponsored by the U.S. Office of Education. The other two education projects were private, small-scale programs: the Metro High School Research Project (Metro High School) and the School-Based Program for Primary Prevention of Mental Disorders (Mental Illness Prevention). The Metro High School program randomly assigned individual students to study conditions; the other four projects assigned either classes or schools to treatment and control conditions.

The last three projects deal with legal reforms. Two of the projects occurred in Denver and had the same set of administrators and researchers: the program on the Effect of Legal Sanctions on Intoxicated Drivers (Drunk Drivers) and the program on the Effect of Court Appearance on Traffic Law Violators (Traffic Citations). The third program, known as the Volunteer in Parole Program (Parolee), was conducted in Illinois and involved random assignment of parolees to treatment or control conditions. In the Denver studies, ticketed drivers were distributed among different conditions according to the time period when they either committed a violation or appeared in court. Since these time periods were thought to be unrelated to both of these actions, the researchers felt that drivers were, in actuality, being "randomly" assigned to the conditions.

In the sections below, these twelve projects are briefly described. For each program several different aspects of the random assignment process are explored, including the control of the assignment, the location of the researchers, the outcome of the assignment procedure, and the outcome of the study. In several cases the programs are still in progress, so the results of some studies are not yet available.

# TABLE 1
Summary of Projects

| Project Type | Title, Location (Abbreviated Title) | Objective |
|---|---|---|
| Health | Alternative Ambulatory Care Delivery Systems, Baltimore (Outpatient Care) | Evaluated the effects of two types of clinic organizations for child outpatient care |
| Health | National Cooperative Multiple Risk Factor Intervention Trial, nationwide (Heart Attack Prevention) | Assessing the success of a three-treatment program to reduce the incidence of heart attacks in middle-aged men |
| Health | Heart Association Nutrition Education Project, Chicago (Nutrition) | Evaluated the effectiveness of four different ways of teaching clients to alter their diets |
| Health | American Heart Association Coronary Drug Project, nationwide (Coronary Drug) | Assessing the effectiveness of several drugs in reducing heart attacks among middle-aged men |
| Education | Follow Through Summer Effects Study, nationwide (Summer Projects) | Assessed the cognitive achievement gains of special summer programs for young children |
| Education | Emergency School Aid Act Programs, nationwide (Desegregation) | Evaluating the effectiveness of many different approaches to desegregation |
| Education | Metro High School Research Project, Chicago (Metro High School) | Assessed the establishment and outcome of an experimental "high school without walls" |
| Education | Emergency School Assistance Program, nationwide (ESAP) | Evaluated the effect on student achievement of many different integration programs |
| Education | School-Based Program for Primary Prevention of Mental Disorders, metropolitan Chicago (Mental Illness Prevention | Assessed the effects on students' attitudes of special units on different aspects of personality |

TABLE 1 (Continued)

| Project Type | Title, Location (Abbreviated Title) | Objective |
|---|---|---|
| Law | Effect of Legal Sanctions on Intoxicated Drivers, Denver (Drunk Drivers) | Assessed the effectiveness of three types of punishment for drunk drivers |
| Law | Effect of Court Appearance on Traffic Law Violators, Denver (Traffic Citations) | Assessed the effectiveness of four types of traffic citations for minor moving violations |
| Law | Volunteer in Parole Program, Illinois (Parolee) | Measured changes in parolee attitudes and behavior due to contact with a lawyer/advisor |

**HEALTH PROGRAMS**

*Outpatient Care.* Gelberd (1973) reports on a study which assessed the effects of two types of outpatient clinics on the efficiency and acceptability of medical services for a group of children from low-income urban families. The two clinics utilized different methods of organization. In one clinic, the multiphasic clinic, patients moved from station to station for various services administered by different personnel. In the "continuity-of-care" clinic, patients were treated in a manner similar to that used in private physicians' offices: patients were assigned to one of four medical teams for all services.

After several months of start-up time, patients as well as staff were randomly assigned to one of the two clinics. These assignments were carried out as planned, and a check of the pretest scores for the two groups confirmed their equivalency (Gelberd, 1973: 11). Parents of patients received a new clinic card indicating which clinic the patient was to visit. Random assignment was made by the research team after first grouping patient families by the number of children and by the number of visits to the clinic in the previous year. Within these blocks, families were randomly assigned to the multiphasic clinic or the continuity-of-care clinic; those assigned to the continuity-of-care clinic were then assigned to one of four staffs within that clinic. Families were unaware of these assignments.

The researchers also randomly assigned doctors, nurses, and other staff to one of the two clinics. There was no resistance to this process, even though the total staff was evenly divided on their opinions of the merits of the two clinics. Gelberd attributes their ready acceptance of random assignment to their youth and willingness to try new things, their familiarity with research, and their respect for the administrator of the two clinics, who was firmly committed to research.

The researchers used several different data sources, including questionnaires, interviews, and clinic records. These measures came from both patients and staff. In general, the continuity-of-care clinic was superior to the multiphasic clinic, especially from the viewpoint of the staff.

*Heart Attack Prevention.* The aim of this six-year program (the Multiple Risk Factor Intervention Trial, MRFIT) is to reduce the incidence of heart attacks among coronary-prone men by training them to stop smoking, to change their diets, and to take drugs to reduce hypertension.

The program is undertaking a true experimental evaluation of this intervention (Stamler et al., 1973). The program staff is now in the process of screening approximately 200,000 men at 20 sites to identify 12,000 who are coronary-prone. If a man is eligible, he must sign a form indicating his consent to participate in the study. The consent statement explains that men will be randomly allocated to two groups: half will be referred to their regular physicians, and the other half "will be offered an ongoing series of specific preventive measures, including intensive efforts to modify behavior with respect to diet and smoking."

Different randomization schedules were established for each site, then stored in a central computer. In order to determine a participant's assignment, a clerk or receptionist calls the Coordinating Center and obtains the assignment from the schedule for that particular site. Each site also has a set of sealed, ordered envelopes with the same assignments, but these are to be used only if the Coordinating Center cannot be reached after fifteen minutes of telephoning. Staff are instructed that the envelopes are to be used very infrequently; if certain centers use them too often, researchers at the Coordinating Center investigate the site. In the event an envelope is used, the open envelope and the enclosed assignment card are sent to the Coordinating Center along with other forms completed at the same time. In almost all cases assignments are determined by calling the Coordinating Center, in which case the unused envelopes are returned unopened with the forms. According to program researchers, this system has resulted in "flawless random assignment." At this point, the centers are still screening potential participants for the study.

*Nutrition.* The Chicago Heart Association instituted a program to determine whether eating habits can be effectively changed by teaching individuals to alter their consumption of fat and cholesterol, thereby lowering their serum cholesterol level. The Nutrition Education Project organized three centers in Chicago to recruit and teach participants who had high cholesterol levels (Mojonnier, 1973).

A total of 418 volunteers were assigned to one of five groups, consisting of regular care (a control group) or one of four special educational groups. The education groups taught the same new eating habits, but used four different approaches in teaching the material: self-teaching, individual teaching, group teaching, and a combination of all three methods. All participants were given thorough physical exams at the outset, as well as several nutrition tests. These measures were similar for the different study groups at the start of the program (Mojonnier, 1973: 3).

At the outset of the study, potential participants were told that they would be assigned randomly to different programs. Each of the three centers had a set of assignment envelopes, accompanied by a set of strict instructions about their use. Either the project nutritionist or the receptionist at a particular site made the envelope selection; this was not done by researchers. The project researchers did, however, closely monitor the assignment procedure.

Some of the participants were disappointed with their assignment to the control condition. The staff assured them that they would receive the program later, and this seems to have prevented dropout. After posttest measurements were taken, control clients were allowed to use the self-teaching material and were offered a special packet of nutrition information, but few controls took advantage of this.

In this project, the requirements for random assignment presented a special problem: because there were five treatment conditions, five times the number of participants were needed before one complete teaching group could be formed. During the first weeks of the study, recruitment was heavy, and there were enough participants to fill treatment groups quickly. As the study progressed, the number of participants decreased, and it would take two to three weeks before random assignment provided enough participants to fill a treatment group. Researchers reported that groups formed later in the program tended to be smaller and probably functioned differently than earlier groups.

*Coronary Drug.* This nationwide study is assessing the effectiveness of several drugs in reducing coronary heart disease. The main objective of the Coronary Drug Project is to evaluate the effects of the drugs on men of age 30 through 64 with a history of clinical evidence of previous heart attacks (Canner, Berge, and Klint, 1973).

There were five experimental groups which differed in the kind of drug used or the amount of a drug prescribed. An additional group received a lactose placebo and served as a control group. Qualified clients were given an orientation session on the purpose of the study, which included an explanation of the random assignment procedure and the use of the placebo condition. Each client signed a consent form in which he agreed to be in any one of the six study conditions. The clients were told that the study would last five years, with follow-up examinations given every four months.

The treatment assignments were made in a double-blind fashion: neither patients nor clinic personnel were informed of the drugs which were to be taken. This was accomplished by coding 30 bottles of drugs. More subjects were placed in the placebo condition so that the mortality rate of this group could be measured with greater precision, assuring that even small reductions in the mortality rates of drug groups would be detected. To guarantee that no one could differentiate the condition by identifying the drugs, all medications were placed in identical opaque gelatin capsules.

Assignments to conditions were made by researchers at a Coordinating Center, using different randomization schedules for each of 53 clinics. To make an assignment, a clinic worker would contact the Coodinating Center, where a researcher would enter the patient's name and identification number opposite the next available bottle number on the randomization schedule for that clinic. This bottle number was then sent to the clinic in a sealed envelope showing the patient's name and number. Once the patient had made his third visit and eligibility was assured, personnel at the clinic opened the sealed envelope and the patient was officially entered into the study. If a patient decided not to participate or was judged ineligible, his unopened envelope was returned to the Coordinating Center for later assignment to another patient in the same clinic.

Random assignment was successfully carried out by the researchers at the centralized Coordinating Center. Although program staff at each clinic notified the patients of their drug number, the role of these local staff in the assignment procedure was minimal. Because the program staff, like the patients, did not know which drugs were in which bottles, they did not know the conditions to which they were assigning patients. Consequently, they could not place certain patients in specific conditions even if they had wanted to do so.

Analysis of baseline data showed that the treatment groups were similar on a number of attributes, so the randomization was successful in equating groups. The primary outcome variable was total mortality in each of the treatment groups. Two treatment conditions were terminated early because patients in these conditions were having more heart attacks than patients in the control group (Coronary Drug Project Research Group, 1975). This outcome provides powerful evidence that treatments which are instituted in social programs are not always beneficial. In this case the presence of a control group was essential in making the judgment that two of the treatments were worse than no treatment at all. Because of the seriousness of the unsuccessful outcomes, these treatments were immediately terminated.

**EDUCATION PROGRAMS**

*Summer Projects.* In 1967 a national Follow Through program was established by the U.S. Office of Education and the Office of Economic Opportunity to sustain and supplement the educational and psycho-social gains made by economically disadvantaged children in Head Start or comparable preschool programs (McDaniels, 1973). The Summer Projects Study, a small component of the entire Follow Through project, was designed to investigate the achievement growth of poor children over the summer months (David, 1974).

To explore this idea, the researchers investigated the short- and long-term impact of several 1972 Follow Through summer programs by comparing students' achievement scores in the spring and fall of 1972, then again in the spring of 1973. The researchers selected ten sites and hoped to assign eligible children randomly to participate in the program. However, problems arose in six of the ten sites. Personnel at three of the sites decided to have a citywide summer program, so no control children were available in these places. At three other sites, there were too few children in the control groups that were formed. At the other four sites the assignment was more successful but still problematic. In these four cases, there were fewer control group children than treatment group children, although the groups should have been equal (David, 1974: 5).

Random assignment of clients to treatment groups was used, but the assignment was not under the control of the researchers. The assignment was twice-removed, in that the private research firm hired by the researchers did not control the assignment. Instead, the assignment to treatment and control conditions was made by different people at each site. The randomization procedure for this project was not successfully implemented, since only four of ten possible sites could be used at all. In addition, pretest data from two of the four remaining sites showed sizable differences between the treatment and control groups, which implies that assignment was not truly random at these two sites.

*Desegregation.* In 1972 the U.S. Congress enacted the Emergency School Aid Act (ESAA), which was designed to help schools achieve integration. The funds appropriated for the act were to be given directly to local school districts for innovative programs to end segregation. The evaluation plan for ESAA utilizes a sample of 99 representative ESAA-funded districts to make comparisons of the relative effectiveness of three different types of interventions: desegregation, desegregation in combination with compensatory education, and compensatory education without desegregation. Randomly selected experimental schools were compared with schools where no special intervention was taking place.

All districts selected for the study were asked to match all possible schools on the bases of socioeconomic status, type and percentage of minority students, and mean achievement. The list of paired schools was submitted to the Office of Education for the random selection of one matched pair, and the subsequent random selection of one school of the pair for the control condition. Although approximately a third of the district representatives complained when they were asked to submit the list of paired schools, none actually refused to participate.

Several months later the districts were notified which schools would be treatment and which control schools. The randomization was successfully accomplished, but only after a good deal of consultation between Office of Education personnel and local district representatives. (This is discussed in more detail below.) Washington personnel accepted a weak comparison group in only two of the 95 cases. Overall, then, the randomization was successfully implemented. The first-year progress report of the three-year study is available (Coulson et al., 1975), and the second-year report is forthcoming.

*Metro High School.* The Metro High School Research Project involved a one-year study of an experimental "high school without walls" operating within the public school system of a large city. The two most important aspects of the experimental program were the use of community resources for education and the development of closer, more personal teacher-student relations (Center for New Schools, 1971).

Several months prior to the experimental school's first term, the researchers publicized the new program in all 55 high schools in the system and interested students were asked to apply. The researchers assembled a pool of 2,000 applicants, from which they randomly selected four students from each school: two for admission to the program, and two to serve as controls. Although the researchers initially feared that their pool of interested students would include disproportionate numbers of very bright or troublesome students, pretest scores indicated that students in the study closely matched the general public high school system population on reading scores, previous tracking assignments, and ethnic and socioeconomic mix.

Random assignment of applicants to either the experimental or control group was easily accomplished. Students, teachers, and administrators all agreed that, with so many interested students and so few positions, random selection was the only fair selection method. The researchers themselves conducted the selection, so any subversion of the system could have occurred only in selective recruitment by teachers of certain students from a particular school. To avoid this, the researchers tried to publicize the open admission policy at the new high school. The school system's administrators had no objections to the random selection procedure; indeed, it was considered a boon since it provided an efficient, fair method of reducing the pool from 2,000 to 110. In this case, a requirement for true experimental evaluation provided the means for efficient program implementation. The researchers reported that the new school was generally effective.

*Emergency School Assistance Program.* In 1970 the U.S. Office of Education began to award small grants under the Emergency School Assistance Program (ESAP) to aid integrating school districts. An evaluation of ESAP's first year indicated that the racial climate in most of the schools improved during the year, but the study design did not permit any conclusive explanations for this improvement (RMC, Inc., 1971). For the second year of the program, the ESAP Washington staff, working with the Office of Planning, Budgeting, and Evaluation, a separate division of the U.S. Office of Education, designed a true experimental evaluation plan, the first ever used in a major Office of Education study (Crain and York, 1974: 5).

The experimental design involved several stages. The researchers drew a sample from all funded districts, then asked the superintendent of each district in the sample to select pairs of schools, matched by size, racial composition, and socioeconomic status. The pairs were randomly sampled, and one school of each pair was randomly designated as a control school (i.e., a nonfunded school). One to six pairs were selected from any one district, depending on its size. In all cases, the total number of control schools in a district was fewer than one-fourth of the eligible schools. The random assignment, then, was executed by the researchers in Washington.

The researchers originally selected 100 pairs of high schools and 200 pairs of elementary schools for the experimental analysis, plus a supplementary sample of 100 high schools and 200 elementary schools to combine with the other experimental schools for use in cross-sectional regression analyses. Forty percent of the districts refused to participate in the study when they first learned that they were selected for the evaluation. One staff member of the Office of Planning, Budgeting, and Evaluation met with the recalcitrant superintendents and principals to explain the reasons for the evaluation plan. Due largely to these efforts (which are described in more detail below), only 18 of the districts dropped out of the study. Unlike the ESAA study discussed above, ESAP researchers were not able to deny funds to districts which refused to cooperate.

The results of the study showed that ESAP had a significant impact on the achievement test scores of black high school boys. The regression analyses permitted the researchers to construct a model to explain this outcome: ESAP-funded projects and activities affected school racial policies and staff attitudes, which in turn affected the motivation of black male students and, subsequently, their achievement.

*Mental Illness Prevention.* The goal of this program is primary prevention of mental illness in children in grades four through eight (Schulmann, n.d.). The program consists of special units constructed for classroom presentation which deal with different aspects of personality (e.g., fear, friendship, communication with parents). The aim of the units is to increase a young person's awareness of his own behavior and feelings and of the universality of feelings, as well as to facilitate experimentation with new ways of behaving and reacting. Since its inception, the program staff has had a strong commitment to research on the effectiveness of its interventions. Previous study had indicated that certain units are most effective at certain ages (Schulmann, n.d.: 5).

The program's current research involves the assessment of the effect of teaching these different sets of units to students in the appropriate grade levels. The study design involves the use of randomly assigned experimental and control classrooms. To assemble the sample, the program researchers sent letters to all school principals in suburban school districts around Chicago. About 25 principals responded, including several from Chicago area schools who had not been contacted but had heard about the study and wanted to participate.

The researcher met with interested teachers at each school where there were at least two similar classrooms which could be in the study. This was necessary because experimental and control classrooms came from the same grade level within the same school. At each school the researcher explained the assignment procedure, then immediately selected the conditions for each classroom using a random number table. This selection procedure fascinated many of the teachers, and the researcher had to demonstrate the use of a random number table. The researcher had no difficulty in randomly assigning classes to experimental conditions. A preliminary report on the outcome of the study supports the differential effectiveness of certain units at certain ages (Meyers, 1974).

## LAW PROGRAMS

*Drunk Drivers.* Blumenthal and Ross (1973) conducted two studies on the Denver County Court's effectiveness in improving drivers charged either with driving while intoxicated or with routine moving violations. Each study utilized a study design that involved random assignment of drivers to various experimental conditions.

In their first study, Blumenthal and Ross wanted to compare the effectiveness of three types of sanctions on drivers who were found guilty of a first charge of driving while under the influence of alcohol (Drunk Drivers study). The three penalties were a fine, conventional probation, or rehabilitative probation (i.e., contingent on completion of an educational or clinical program). The researchers, with the help of the Presiding Judge of the Denver County Court, asked the court judges to assign these penalties on a fixed schedule. The researchers believed that the most feasible method for assignment was by months, rather than by cases. The researchers set up a schedule of five three-month cycles. During the first month of the cycle, all drunk driver cases were to receive fines; during the second month, all were to receive conventional probation; and all cases in the third month were to receive rehabilitative probation. The judges were allowed to vary the quantity of the penalty depending on the case, but were not to vary the type of penalty except in special cases. These exceptions were to be excluded from all analyses.

All convicted drunk drivers were to be assigned automatically to the treatment in effect that month. Since the drivers had no idea that they were in a study using different types of penalties, drivers could not place themselves into certain treatment groups. The use of five consecutive three-month cycles assured that any seasonal differences in type of drunken driver did not affect the study. Other than this seasonal variation, the researchers did not believe that drivers in any one month would be much different from drivers in either the previous or subsequent month. Consequently, this assignment process would result in three treatment conditions with the same types of drivers in each.

In theory, the judges were simply to implement the randomization schedule that the researchers had established. In practice, however, this did not occur. The researchers had included an exception clause in their instructions to the judges, and this concession turned out to an unfortunate one for the evaluation design. The researchers discovered early in the study that the number of cases granted special treatment was much higher than had been expected (this is discussed in more detail below). The researchers tried to get greater cooperation from the judges, but had little success.

In their data analyses, Ross and Blumenthal looked at differences among the original experimental groups and among the de facto groups. They found no evidence that the types of sanctions produce different effects on subsequent driver behavior. Their most powerful finding was that representation by a lawyer is very effective in obtaining more favorable treatment for the defendant.

*Traffic Citations.* Blumenthal and Ross's (1973, Vol. 2) second study was designed to test the effect of a required court appearance for drivers charged with routine moving violations (e.g., failing to signal a turn). Experimental traffic citations were developed for use by Denver patrolmen for moving violations. There were three experimental citations: (1) tickets requiring a court appearance, (2) warning tickets, and (3) tickets permitting payment of a standard $20 fine by mail. In addition, standard citations were also used as a control condition. These standard citations required the driver to appear at the clerk's office, where he had the option of paying a fine or appearing in court.

The researchers were unable to devise a practical way of randomly distributing the citations. They were afraid that, if all three citations were simultaneously available, patrolmen would be tempted to select citations which fit the crimes (in the patrolmen's judgments). Consequently, the four types of tickets available to the patrolmen were rotated on a weekly schedule. The researchers anticipated a sizable increase in the court load during the Required Court Appearance phase, so they rotated the Mail-In, Warning, and Standard Citation phases to mitigate this expected increase. All phases were to occur twice, with the exception of the Warning ticket, since this phase involved a sizable loss in municipal income.

The assignment of drivers to conditions was to have been under the strict control of the researchers, not under the control of the patrolmen. The patrolmen were issued only one type of ticket each week, so all drivers whom they stopped during any particular week had to be issued the same ticket. However, it was possible for a patrolman to decide not to stop certain motorists or to give them only a verbal warning if the patrolman did not want to issue a particular type of citation. In addition, patrolmen always carried standard citations to issue drivers whose violations were more serious than those under study. The assignment process, then, was actually controlled by many individual patrolmen, not the researchers. This permitted a subversion of the random assignment, and the researchers have evidence that this in fact occurred (details are presented below).

Other events occurred which also affected the original plan. The Denver area had bad floods during the week of the mandatory court appearance phase. This caused a one-week delay in the study and resulted in overwhelming numbers of people in court. Court personnel would not allow a second week of mandatory court appearance tickets. Consequently, the original plan was modified so that standard citations were used during that week, with court appearances required for half of the drivers. The court clerk was to assign an appearance only to those drivers whose tickets ended in an odd number, a procedure that ought to have resulted in two comparable groups. However, the clerk did not follow the researchers' directions (details below).

Blumenthal and Ross had to control for the initial differences in the experimental groups created by the subversion of the randomization. Once statistical controls were introduced, drivers who had appeared in court occasionally had better subsequent driving records, but the evidence was not consistent across different comparisons. Consequently, the researchers were not able to conclude that a driver who appears in court will have a better subsequent driver record.

*Parolee.* In 1971 the Young Lawyers Section of the American Bar Association developed the Volunteer in Parole Program to help young ex-offenders. The program brought together parolees and volunteer lawyers in order to provide each parolee with an interested counselor.

The program was instituted in several states, and the Illinois program staff decided to conduct a true experimental evaluation of its project (Berman, 1973). The parolees who participated in the program were selected by parole agents from the pool of Illinois ex-offenders. The agents were instructed to select five of their clients who they felt were most in need of the program. Two of the five selected by each Illinois agent were randomly picked to be in the program, and two others were assigned to the control group. The fifth parolee was not used except in a few cases where one of the other four parolees had to be dropped from the study after the time of selection but before the time of implementation.

Initially, the researcher had difficulty convincing program officials to assign parolees randomly (Berman, 1972: 122-127). The use of a control group seemed inefficient to the officials because twice as much work and time were required to obtain twice as many parolees as the program could accommodate. Once other evaluation methods were explained to the officials, they easily understood the need for a control group, although the need for random assignment was more difficult to comprehend.

Loss of parolees over the course of the study was a serious problem. Of 46 men originally assigned to the treatment condition and 44 assigned to the control condition, 16 were left in each group for the final analyses. The ability to find enough volunteer lawyers as well as the loss of those who had volunteered were also factors in the erosion of the randomly-assigned experimental and control groups.

In spite of these problems with dropout, the researcher was able to compare the groups on a number of outcome variables. The program succeeded in making the parolees more realistic about their job expectations and in increasing their belief that society was concerned about them. The program did not affect parolees' arrest rates, employment situation, use of community resources, feelings of happiness, or feelings of stigma. The results of the study indicated areas of the program which were in need of improvement, and some major changes were made in later versions of the program, notably the use of only newly released parolees.


## ASPECTS OF THE RANDOM ASSIGNMENT

Each of the twelve studies discussed above involved a true experimental evaluation design using randomization. In most cases the proposed design was successfully implemented. In other cases, the proposed evaluation design was not successfully implemented. Why did the outcomes differ? In the sections that follow, a number of aspects of the studies are explored to uncover reasons why the true experimental design was successfully implemented in some cases but not others. The aspects discussed are (1) the type of assignment plan, (2) the control of

## TABLE 2
### Aspects of the Random Assignment in the Twelve Projects

| ASPECTS | | Outpatient Care | Heart Attack Prev. | Nutrition Project | Coronary Drug | Summer Projects | Desegregation | Metro High | ESAP | Mental Illness Prev. | Drunk Drivers | Traffic Citations — Policemen | — Clerk | Parolee Project |
|---|---|---|---|---|---|---|---|---|---|---|---|---|---|---|
| Type of Assignment Plan | Fixed | X | X | X | X | X | X | X | X | X | | | X | X |
| | Flexible | | | | | | | | | | X | X | | |
| Control of Assignment | By researcher | X | X | X | X | | X | X | X | X | | | | X |
| | By others | | | | | X | | | | | X | X | X | |
| Location of Researcher | Outside program | X | X | X | X | X | X | | X | | X | X | X | X |
| | Within program | X | | | | | | X | | X | | | | |
| Number of Implementers | Few | X | | | | | X | X | X | X | | | X | X |
| | Many | | X | X | X | X | | | | | X | X | | |

TABLE 2 (Continued)

| PROJECTS | Explanation of Randomization to Clients | | Outcome of Random Assignment | |
|---|:---:|:---:|:---:|:---:|
| ASPECTS | Yes | No | Successful | Unsuccessful |
| Outpatient Care | | X | X | |
| Heart Attack Prev. | X | | X | |
| Nutrition Project | X | | X | |
| Coronary Drug | X | | X | |
| Summer Projects | | X[a] | | X |
| Desegregation | X | | X | |
| Metro High | X | | X | |
| ESAP | | X | X | |
| Mental Illness Prev. | X | | X | |
| Drunk Drivers | | X | | X |
| Traffic Citations — Policemen | | X | | X |
| — Clerk | | X | | X |
| Parolee Project | | X | X | |

a. Probably not explained at most sites.

[126]

the assignment, (3) the location of the researcher, (4) the number of implementers, and (5) the explanation of the randomization to the clients.

These aspects are listed in Table 2, and the twelve projects are characterized on each aspect. Each project is also rated on the outcome of the assignment process. A study had a successful assignment if clients were, in fact, randomly assigned to treatments, and if clients, for the most part, accepted their assignment. Some of the data on which these conclusions are based came from information in official program reports, in-house memos, and letters; some of this information has already been cited in the program description. In addition, a large amount of the data came from interviews with program administrators and researchers. Much of these data were cross-validated to assure their accuracy, either by talking with other project personnel or by using written reports. For example, a researcher's oral communication that clients had indeed been randomly assigned could be verified by analyzing pretest data from in-house reports. If assignment had, in fact, been random, the scores on a variety of pretest measures should be approximately the same for all treatment and control groups in the program.

Cross-validation provided a way to assess the tendency for program personnel to report only favorable information and to hide problems. Although this bias seems likely, it was not particularly apparent here. There are several possible reasons for this. The most important is that nearly all of the programs had successful evaluations. Because of this, program personnel were anxious to talk about their evaluation and about the problems they had faced and solved. Another reason is that program personnel were not threatened by academic researchers who had no power over them. If anything, the contrary was true: they were flattered that someone was interested in their program and their problems. In most cases, these people were anxious to learn about the problems of other program researchers and the solutions they had tried.

The aspects discussed here are not the only study components, but they were those judged most relevant to the success or failure of the random assignment procedure. Some of these aspects were suggested by program researchers or administrators themselves, because these were important considerations in their studies. Other aspects of the studies are discussed because previous evaluation researchers have suggested that these aspects might be important considerations (Weiss, 1972).

TYPE OF ASSIGNMENT PLAN

The studies presented here employed two types of random assignment: a fixed assignment plan with no exceptions, and a flexible assignment plan with exceptions permitted. Ten programs had fixed assignment plans, wherein clients were placed either in a treatment group or a control group according to a predetermined plan. Two programs, the Drunk Drivers study and the Traffic Citations study, used flexible assignment plans which permitted exceptions to the predetermined random assignment schedule. Although exceptions were to be allowed only under special circumstances, the assignment plans for these two programs did contain a provision for this, and this fact affected the implementation of the random assignment. Unlike nearly all of the other ten programs, these two programs were not successful in implementing the assignment. Although other factors are important in explaining this unsuccessful outcome (i.e., the lack of control by the researchers), the fact that exceptions to the random assignment plan were allowed is also a major one.

In the Drunk Drivers study, all ticketed drivers convicted in any given month were to be assigned to the same condition (Ross and Blumenthal, 1975: 153). The researchers decided to use this assignment method to increase judges' acceptance of the assignment plan. In addition, the researchers allowed the judges to disregard the assignment plan in "exceptional" cases. This option was used in an unexpectedly large number of cases (Blumenthal and Ross, 1973, Vol. 1: 6-7). During the months when the prescribed treatment was a fine, the judges assigned this treatment to nearly all convicted motorists (94% of the cases). When the prescribed treatment was conventional probation, only 68% of the convicted drivers received this treatment. The most serious disregard of the scheduled experimental treatment was during the educational-clinical rehabilitative probation periods: only 48% of the motorists were given this treatment (Ross and Blumenthal, 1975: 153). In these latter two conditions, then, judges made significant changes in the assignment plan, primarily by administering fines (32% were fined during the conventional probation months and 41% during the rehabilitative months).

A flexible random assignment plan was also used in the Traffic Citations study. Rather than have all four types of experimental citations available, the researchers gave officers books with only one kind of citation, then changed books each week (Ross and Blumenthal, 1975: 151). All drivers stopped for certain minor violations during a given week were to be given the same citation. Patrolmen also carried standard citations to use for more serious violations or for "exceptional" cases of minor violations. Although this was understandable and unavoidable, it undermined the research design. It was too easy for patrolmen to use their own judgment in awarding tickets.

When the researchers compared the mandatory court appearance group and the standard citation group on eight background variables, they found four significant differences (Ross and Blumenthal, 1975: 152). The mandatory court appearance group contained more young people, fewer minority-group members, more drivers with prior crash records, and more drivers who were involved in a crash. The researchers do not attribute these differences to time-linked changes in the type of violator or to random error. Instead, they feel that these differences reflect arbitrary decisions by patrolmen to change the assignment plan.

In these two programs, the random assignment procedure might have been improved by using a modified fixed assignment plan. That is, in the Drunk Drivers study, certain days of the week (ideally selected at random) could be designated for random assignment with no exceptions. On other days, the judges could assign drunk drivers as they saw fit. These judicially assigned groups would serve as quasi-experimental comparison groups for the randomly assigned groups. In the Traffic Citations study, a fixed assignment plan might have been used, with the patrolmen receiving assignments when they radioed headquarters. This process would be somewhat analogous to those used in the Heart Attack Prevention and Coronary Drug projects. This assignment method, or another like it, would prevent individual patrolmen from subverting the random assignment plan.

Based on this set of twelve studies, a fixed assignment plan appears to be a necessary but not a sufficient condition for successful random assignment. In two studies a fixed assignment plan was used, but randomization was not successfully implemented: the Summer Projects study, and the Traffic Citations substudy using the court clerk. In both cases, the fixed assignment plan broke down when it was controlled and implemented by people other than the researcher.

## CONTROL OF THE RANDOM ASSIGNMENT

Another important aspect of these evaluation projects concerns the control of the actual random assignment process. Does the researcher himself control the assignment, or do others do this? Although most people are familiar with the idea of a random drawing, they are usually unfamiliar with both the reasons why a valid random assignment is necessary and the methods required to implement random assignment. This lack of understanding could cause them to undermine the assignment process.

In all the studies the researchers were quite familiar with the theory and method of randomization. Consequently, we could expect that there would be a greater chance for successful random assignment in those programs where the researchers themselves controlled the randomization. This turned out to be the case. In the nine programs where the researcher was in control of the random assignment process, the randomization was successfully implemented in each case (Parolee, Outpatient Care, Heart Attack Prevention, Nutrition, Coronary Drug, Desegregation, Metro High School, ESAP, and Mental Illness Prevention programs). In programs where individuals other than the researcher controlled the random assignment, we could expect that chances for a successful assignment would be lower, because these individuals would not completely understand the need for randomization and, hence, would not be so concerned with maintaining the original assignment process. In the three programs where the researcher did not control the assignment (Drunk Drivers, Traffic Citations, and Summer Projects studies) the randomization was not successful, and the results obtained at the end of each study were not conclusive.

In the Drunk Drivers study and the Traffic Citations study, judges, policemen, or a clerk made the assignments. The judges and policemen had been given the option of varying the assignments in "exceptional cases," and they used this more often than the researchers had expected. These officials were probably less interested in undermining the assignment process than in avoiding pressure from drivers or from lawyers, which they could do by changing assignments. The pressure that the researchers were able to exercise over the judges or policemen was minimal. Hence, the officials understandably responded to the stronger pressure and used the "exceptional case" option. The problems were compounded because there were so many individuals who controlled the assignment process.

The researchers tried to influence the judges in the Drunk Drivers study to increase their adherence to the random assignment plan (Ross and Blumenthal, 1975: 153). The judges first responded by sincerely insisting that they were cooperating and that the departure was the fault of the other judges. When judges were subsequently confronted with details from cases in which they had not used random assignment, they had no difficulty in explaining why the case was an "exceptional one." Finally, the researchers tried some unusual enticements: later meetings with the judges "were held in a fine restaurant at government expense, but this factor did not appear to produce the sought-for feeling of obligation" (Ross and Blumenthal, 1975).

The researchers' influence declined even more when the Presiding Judge who had requested the study was replaced following a municipal election. The individual judge's commitment to the research had always been less than that of the Presiding Judge; consequently, there was little official support for the study left in the judicial system when he was replaced. In addition, there was a strong unofficial support for the use of fines in all cases. Defendants preferred fines and were especially successful in obtaining this penalty if they were represented by a lawyer. Lawyers were able to obtain continuances for their clients into months when the research schedule stipulated that fines were to be administered.

In the third program where the researcher did not control the randomization, the Summer Projects study, as well as in the Traffic Citations substudy where the court clerk assigned ticketed drivers, the reasons for the breakdown in the assignment plan were also related to the lack of influence. In the case of the Summer Projects, the researchers were twice removed from the process and so effectively had no influence. Different people controlled the process at each of the ten sites. At three of the sites, program officials simply decided to give the program to everyone, and the researchers could do nothing to stop them. At three other sites, there were only a few children in the control groups. At these sites the random assignment was probably abandoned, and most children were placed in the treatment group. At the four sites where assignment appeared more successful, the number of children in the control groups was still much smaller than it should have been. The individuals in charge of the random assignment at the sites did not understand the need for this type of assignment, and so did not execute it, or else saw no need to defend and maintain it if project personnel or parents of potential participants objected.

In the Traffic Citations substudy, the court clerk was to assign ticketed drivers to various study conditions according to the last number of the driver's citation (essentially a random assignment). This plan broke down when the clerk unilaterally decided to make exceptions to the plan. The researchers were removed from the assignment process and were powerless in securing compliance. The clerk's concern was not with intentionally subverting the assignment plan; instead, the clerk had firm ideas about the need for a court appearance for young drivers but not for drivers accused of serious violations. These ideas preempted the random assignment plan established by the researchers.

There were, then, four cases in this set of studies where the assignment process was not under the control of the researcher, and, in each of these cases, randomization was not successful. In the other nine cases randomization was under the researcher's control, and in all nine randomization was successfully implemented. This is strong evidence that in social program evaluation control of the randomization by the researchers is very important for the implementation of a true experimental evaluation plan. When other personnel undertake the randomization, the process seems to falter, either because these personnel are too busy with program implementation to be concerned with fine details of exact random assignment, or because they lack understanding of the process and so make changes in the plan that, to them, seem minor.

### LOCATION OF RESEARCHER

Some writers have suggested that the location of the researcher within the organizational structure of a social reform project is an important factor in the success or failure of the project's evaluation (e.g., Weiss, 1972). There are, of course, a number of different organizational structures, and, therefore, a number of locations for the researchers. In this analysis, we will group these locations into two general classes: inside and outside the project. A researcher is located inside the project if he plays a full-time part in the central program staff (i.e., he is located in the same general office as the program administrators, he is paid his total salary directly by the program, and so on). An outside researcher does not play a full-time part in the central staff. His primary loyalty and direct source of income is in an organization unrelated to the program (e.g., a university or a research consulting firm). In general, an outside researcher has been hired on contract specifically to develop and implement an evaluation. This dichotomy oversimplifies the situation; a better characterization of researchers' location would be in terms of degree along several continua (e.g., outside versus inside, no decision power versus considerable power). The small number of projects studied here did not permit such fine-grained divisions.

There are different ideas about the best location for the researcher (Weiss, 1972: 20). A researcher located within the program administration unit may be in a better position to conduct a good evaluation, because he will be aware of the program's components, knowledgeable about program changes, and familiar with the demands on the administrators. Because of these things, the researcher will have the trust and cooperation of the administrators. A major disadvantage of this arrangement is that the researcher may become so entrenched in the program organization that he loses his objectivity and hence cannot conduct a sound evaluation. This may occur unintentionally; the researchers may become so convinced that the project is effective that he cannot see its weaknesses. This may also occur intentionally if the researcher is afraid to confront the administrators with evidence of program weaknesses.

To help avoid this result, the researcher can be located outside the program administration unit. With this arrangement the researcher is less subject to direct and indirect pressures which could bias his evaluation. However, because the researcher is an outsider, he usually does not have the same degree of trust from administrators as a researcher located inside the program unit. The administrator may believe that the outside researcher does not understand the program as well, and that he does not understand the pressures on the administrator. Although these perceptions may be false, they will still affect the relationship between the administrator and the researcher.

There are, then, both advantages and liabilities to each organizational arrangement. In the programs studied here, both arrangements were used. Programs with researchers located within the project tended to have more success in implementing their evaluations. There were six programs where the researcher was within the project: the outpatient Care, Nutrition, Heart Attack Prevention, Coronary Drug, Metro High School, and Mental Illness Prevention programs. In all of these projects, the random assignment procedure was successfully implemented. It should be noted that the Metro High School study and the Mental Illness Prevention program are different from the other studies because the researchers and administrators within each project are the same people. Individuals in these projects are in an ideal position to implement true experimental evaluations, since their decision on a design is the final one. If they maintain their objectivity, they are also in an ideal position to maintain their design and obtain an honest outcome. However, if they cannot or do not maintain their objectivity, they can easily undermine their study.

In the other six projects—Drunk Drivers, Traffic Citations, Parolee, Summer Projects, Desegregation, and ESAP—the researcher was outside the program administration unit. In only half of these studies was the random assignment of clients successfully implemented (Parolee, Desegregation, and ESAP). In the other studies (Drunk Drivers, Traffic Citations, and Summer Projects) the design broke down at the outset when the assignment failed. Although the evaluations of these projects were completed, the results were equivocal at best.

Why were some of these projects with outside researchers successful in implementing randomization and others unsuccessful? Researcher inexperience does not seem to be a factor, since all of the researchers had both a good knowledge of research design and previous experience with field research. A more important variable is the degree of influence the researcher had over the program administrators. In the two projects with outside researchers and successful implementations (the Desegregation and ESAP studies), the researchers were part of the funding agency and, hence, had a great deal of power. In the Desegregation study, where the researchers had the power to withhold funds for noncompliance, implementation was even more successful. In the Parolee project, on the other hand, the outside researcher did not have a great deal of power, but did implement the randomization successfully. This project was a small-scale one, however, and entailed a fairly simple, researcher-controlled random assignment. Moreover, lawyer/advisers were scarce, so randomization provided a useful way to distribute resources fairly among parolees. In the Parolee project, these factors outweighed the researcher's lack of influence.

In the three unsuccessful studies (the Drunk Drivers, Traffic Citations, and Summer Projects studies), the outside researchers had little influence over the administrators. In all three studies, the researchers exerted what little power they had through intermediaries (a presiding judge in the Drunk Drivers study and the Traffic Citations study, a contracting firm in the Summer Projects study). The researchers did not control the assignment and could not withhold resources for noncompliance. The outcome of the assignment procedure in these studies suggests that, in a project with an outside researcher, the researcher should control the randomization and, if possible, be in a position to withhold or delay resources for noncompliance. For example, the release of some project funds could be made contingent upon the successful completion of the assignment process.

## NUMBER OF IMPLEMENTERS

In some of the first projects studied, the number of persons involved in implementing the random assignment seemed to be an important variable in the success or failure of an evaluation project. The more individuals involved in the assignment process, the easier it could be for each person to make small changes in the randomization plan. The small adjustments would be compounded and could result in a serious departure from the original plan. In the twelve projects analyzed here, there was a tendency for an unsuccessful assignment process to result from a project with many implementers, but only if the researcher did not closely control the assignment.

In two cases, the relationship between a large number of loosely controlled implementers and an unsuccessful assignment was clear. These studies were the Drunk Drivers study and the Traffic Citations study. The judges, who were to assign penalties randomly to drunk drivers, made small departures from this plan which undermined the random assignment. In the Traffic Citations study, the police officers who were to hand out only certain tickets at certain times did not do this; instead, they used their own judgment, allowing certain offenders to go free and punishing others with harsher citations. It should be noted that, in both cases, the researchers aided in the breakdown by giving the implementers this option, albeit only for exceptional cases. The researchers' tacit admission that the implementation process was flexible may inadvertently have communicated the wrong message to the judges and patrolmen.

In another case, the Summer Projects study, the idea that a large number of loosely controlled implementers results in unsuccessful random assignment was less clearly supported. It appears that the individuals who controlled the assignment at each site did not follow the assignment plan. At those sites where there were any control students at all, the number of students in the special treatment group was always larger than the number in the control group. However, this result could have occurred because of differential dropout rather than biased assignment. Unfortunately, data on dropout were not available, so it is not possible to determine which explanation is more plausible.

In several other studies (Heart Attack Prevention, Coronary Drug, and Nutrition projects) many implementers were again involved, but the outcomes were different. The Heart Attack Prevention and Coronary Drug studies each had many centers across the country where potential participants were screened, assigned to conditions, then followed for the duration of the study. Because the assignment process was very tightly controlled in both studies, the individual implementers were not able to undermine the assignment process. Each study had one center where the order of assignment for each site was generated and stored. In order to assign an individual in either study, personnel at each clinic would call the Coordinating Center to receive an assignment. In the Heart Attack Prevention study, clinic personnel knew the conditions to which participants were to be assigned, but they were not able to affect the assignment.

This type of subversion was almost impossible in the Coronary Drug study (Canner, Berge, and Klint, 1973: 1-13). This project involved a double-blind strategy: neither the clients nor the staff at a particular center knew which drugs were being administered to which clients. Consequently, even if a staff member wanted to assign a particular client to a certain condition, he was not able to do so because he could not differentiate the conditions. The procedure is not foolproof, however. Personnel at each clinic had access to all of the drugs which were being used. Although the drugs were in identical capsules, a staff member could have emptied representative capsules, assayed them, and broken the code for that particular site. Then, they could have deferred assignment for particular individuals until they thought that the probability of a certain assignment was high. Because this method of subversion is complex, it is unlikely that it occurred.

The Nutrition project also had several clinics, but they were located in the same city and were in close contact with the project researchers. Each clinic had a set of assignment envelopes which clinic personnel were to use in making the assignments. These envelopes were transparent, and it would have been easy for the different implementers to sort through the envelopes and to assign particular individuals to particular conditions. Project researchers believed that this did not occur, and a check on the comparability of pretest scores on several different indices among treatment and control groups supports this belief.

There are several reasons which may explain why the implementers did not subvert the assignment in this study. First, the different treatment conditions were in fact very similar, so there was little reason to change the prearranged order. Even those subjects selected for the control group were able to participate in one of the treatment conditions at the conclusion of the study, a delay of only a few months. A second reason relates to the importance of the goal of the treatment. The program officials hoped that alterations would occur in clients' diets which would make the clients somewhat healthier; they did not expect life-savings changes. In the Heart Attack Prevention study, by comparison, the program aims for just such effects. From the point of view of a clinic staff member who believes that the program will be an effective one, placing a client in a control group for the Heart Attack study involves a much greater deprivation than placing a client in a control group for the Nutrition study. Personnel in the Nutrition study, then, may not have felt as strongly about the consequences of assigning patients to the control group.

In seven of the projects under study here, there was only one person, or occasionally a few people, who implemented the random assignment plan. In all but one of these cases, the implementer was the researcher. These projects are the Parolee project, Outpatient Care project, Desegregation study, Metro High School study, ESAP study, and Mental Illness Prevention program. In all of these projects, randomization was successfully implemented. The one exceptional case where the implementer was not the researcher is the second part of the Traffic Citations study, where a single court clerk served as the implementer. In spite of the explicit instructions which the researchers gave to him, the clerk did not assign the cases according to plan.

The researchers involved in the Traffic Citations study strongly advise removing any control of the randomization from personnel involved in executing a program (Ross and Blumenthal, 1975). They are convinced that the control must remain with the researchers. Ross and Blumenthal may be overreacting to an understandably frustrating experience. Based on the experiences of several of the researchers in some of the other eleven projects under consideration here, we can conclude that the researcher does not have to be the person who actually implements the randomization if it is to be successful. However, it does appear that the researcher must have extremely tight control over the process if others implement it. Ross and Blumenthal's idea that program staff should not control randomization may be limited to the case where staff have definite ideas about the efficacy of certain treatments.

### EXPLANATION OF ASSIGNMENT PROCEDURE
### TO CLIENTS

Client assignment to treatment or control conditions in a true experimental design is rigidly arbitrary: no one has a greater likelihood of being in the treatment or control group. When they are placed in different treatments, clients do not receive special consideration because they are, for example, more needy or less needy, more deserving or less deprived. In addition, clients generally have no participation in the selection process. This process often seems too arbitrary to many administrators, who fear that clients will object to such a procedure. There is no clear evidence that clients object to the procedure per se. In spite of this absence of data, administrators sometimes use this argument as a reason not to randomize. Because of this fact, this aspect of the randomization process was explored in each of the twelve projects.

In half of the programs the randomization procedure was explained to the clients, and, in general, accepted. In the Heart Attack Prevention program clients signed a consent form which stated that all participants would be randomly allocated into two groups: one group would receive regular medical care and the other group would receive special "prevention measures." The words "control" and "experimental" were not used in the consent form. Later, clients were assigned to treatment groups. A clerk or receptionist at each center called the Coordinating Center for the assignment, then an Intervention Specialist informed the participant of his assignment. These specialists were staff personnel who were to work with clients to help them stop smoking, change their diets, and lower their blood pressure.

Several orientation speeches were suggested which intervention specialists could use at the time of randomization. The speech suggested for control clients emphasized that the participant had an above-average risk of developing heart disease and that he ought to consult his regular physician. The control clients were also told that they would be asked to return for testing in one year and that the results of these tests would be sent to the patient's physician. In closing, the intervention specialist emphasized that the patient's participation would help to cure heart disease. The speech which was suggested for the treatment group clients reiterated the program's three areas of intervention (i.e., smoking behavior, diet, and blood pressure) and the method to be used in the program (i.e., group counseling sessions). The researcher at the center for the Heart Attack Prevention program reported that both control and treatment group clients readily accepted these explanations, both at her center and at other centers.

Once their eligibility was determined, clients in the Nutrition project were told that they would be randomly assigned either to participate in the program or to be in a control, no-treatment group. Either a nutritionist or a receptionist at each of the three centers explained this to the clients, then selected an assignment envelope from her desk in the presence of the client. The envelopes were ordered, so the assignment was fixed. Although some control clients were initially disappointed with their assignment, all accepted the assignment once they were told that they could participate in the treatment in approximately a month. Although only a few actually returned to do this, this offer was successful in securing the continued participation of the control clients.

In the Coronary Drug project, clients were given an orientation session prior to enrollment in the study (Canner, Berge, and Klint, 1973: 1-13). During the session a clinic staff member told the client about the different drugs which were to be used and about the placebo control treatment. The random assignment procedure to be used in allocating clients to the different conditions was also discussed. Each client signed a consent form in which he agreed to participate in any of the conditions. The consent forms varied from clinic to clinic. The staff member then telephoned the Coordinating Center, where the actual random assignment was made. The assignment was sent to the clinic in a sealed envelope and opened when the patient came for his next visit. Neither the client nor the staff member knew what treatment the client had been given, only the bottle number of the drug that the client was to take. Because of this double-blind procedure, clients did not know if they were in a control or experimental group. Consequently, there was no problem with differential acceptance among the control and treatment group members.

The researchers in the Metro High School study found no resistance to a random assignment procedure for admission to their program. Applicants for the study were recruited from the pool of all Chicago high school ninth-graders. A letter was sent to the students from the

Chicago Schools explaining the objectives of the new high school and asking students to apply if they were interested. The letter also noted that enrollment was limited and that some students would be randomly chosen from each high school district. The researchers used this scarcity explanation to justify the admission procedure, not the scientific explanation (i.e., in terms of the need to determine program effects). This was readily accepted by students, teachers, and administrators as a fair method for selection. Although the random selection procedure for the purpose of admission was readily accepted in the Metro High School study, it is not possible to tell if the random selection procedure was also accepted for the purpose of evaluation. The letter to the students did not explain that some students would be randomly selected to participate in a control group. The students who were chosen as controls for the evaluation were asked to participate in an unidentified study and were offered a token payment ($5) for taking pretests and posttests. Because these students did not know that they were controls, it is not possible to conclude that they accepted their random assignment into the control group.

In two other projects, the random selection procedure was also explained and accepted in most cases, but in these studies some clients needed additional explanations before they agreed to the procedure. These projects are the Mental Illness Prevention program and the Desegregation project. In the Mental Illness Prevention project the researcher met with the interested teachers in the schools which were eligible for the study (i.e., the school had two classes at the same grade level which could be in the study). The researcher explained to the teachers of these classes that one class would be randomly selected to participate in the study and the other would be a control class. The teachers were told that this procedure was necessary in order to determine the effects of the program (i.e., the scientific explanation). Some teachers preferred one condition or the other, but in all cases the researcher convinced them to accept random assignment because of the need to determine program effects. The researcher then made the assignments in front of the teachers using a random numbers table. One experimental and one control condition teacher said, after the assignment, that she would not have participated if she had been chosen for the other condition. This may have been postselection justification, since in each case the teacher believed that she had been randomly selected into exactly the condition which she said she wanted.

The researchers in the Desegregation study had a more difficult task than those in the Mental Illness Prevention project. Local educational agencies which were interested in the Desegregation project were informed from the very beginning that they might be involved in an experimental evaluation. School districts which received grants were chosen from a pool of districts, all of which had agreed in writing to use randomly selected experimental and control schools. The Desegregation researchers worked hard to have a section included in the federal legislation which required school districts to agree to a true experimental evaluation.[3] When school districts were notified that they had received a grant, they also received a letter from the Assistant Commissioner for Program Planning and Evaluation which reiterated the evaluation requirement and explained that evaluation was necessary to determine "the causal relationship between ESAA funding and achievement." This letter only suggested that any particular school district might be part of the evaluation sample.

In preparation for the selection of the sample, school districts submitted a list of their schools, indicating for each school the socioeconomic level, the percentage and kind of minority students, and the mean achievement level. Following this, 30% to 40% of the districts complained to the researchers. Most of the district representatives argued that it would be unfair to deprive school children of the special program. The researchers again explained the need for this type of assignment and reminded the representatives that they had already agreed to the procedure. All of these districts remained in the program.

The Washington researchers selected districts which met several eligibility criteria (i.e., desegregation programs at grade levels 3, 4, 5, 10, 11, and 12; conditions conducive to good control). Then, the researchers paired schools within each of these districts on the basis of the figures which the districts had provided. The Washington researchers randomly selected pairs of schools, then randomly designated one as a treatment school and the other as a control school. School districts were notified of the assignments by telephone. This was followed by a letter to each district superintendent from the Assistant Commissioner of the Office of Planning, Budgeting, and Evaluation and the Associate Commissioner of the Bureau of Equal Educational Opportunity. The letter listed the proposed treatment and control schools. In addition, the letter detailed the focus, objectives, and methods of the evaluation, emphasizing that the evaluation was necessary to determine the impact of the program. For the first time, the district superintendents also learned that the control school would be ineligible for funds for a minimum of two years.

After this letter was sent, nearly all of the districts complained to Washington staff. Four to six districts had unique reasons why the control school ought to receive funds. One school system was under a court order to desegregate, and the control school had been designated by the judge as a target school. In another case, the control school had recently had a number of serious problems, including racial clashes, and the superintendent wanted at least some funds for the school. In these cases, the researchers agreed to the use of some funds. They did not, however, remove these districts from the sample. Instead, they included them, weakening the overall contrast between the control and treatment samples but maintaining the original design.

The complaints of other districts were more diffuse. When the Washington researchers asked the districts for specific objections, the local representatives usually had none. These district representatives were usually local research personnel for the school system. The Washington researchers believe that these local researchers did not adequately understand evaluation methodology and were somewhat threatened by the study design. Unable to explain to their superintendents why an entire school should lose funds, the local researchers were told to object to Washington. Many of the local researchers argued that parents of control group children would not accept the procedure. In several cases, the local representatives arranged open press conferences in the control school so that the Washington researchers would understand the degree of alleged parental dissatisfaction. In each case, the Washington researchers found that parents could understand the need for a control school to determine the effect of the special program. Much to the surprise of local researchers, parents in these districts accepted the scientific argument for control groups.

Several factors were operating here to cause local resistance to the evaluation plan. The least important of these factors was parent resistance, despite the arguments of local researchers. More important factors were local researchers' inability to explain the design to their supervisors and the consequent misunderstanding on the part of the administrators. In addition, administrators were upset that control schools would not be eligible for any funds for two to three years. The resistance, then, was not so much related to disagreement over a random assignment procedure as it was to a lack of communication between Washington and local school districts, and a particularly long treatment period. In 70% of the cases, local representatives stopped complaining after about three weeks of discussion between Washington and local districts. In the other cases, the Washington researchers arranged compromises which entailed using some funds in the control schools. Because these schools remained in the study, the researchers were able to maintain the true experimental design at the expense of reducing the contrast between treatment and control schools.

The ESAP study, unlike the six studies just discussed, did not involve an explanation of randomization to any of the clients. However, the study did entail an explanation to school administrators, who decided whether or not their schools would participate in the study. In this way, the ESAP study was similar to the Desegregation study and faced some of the same problems in convincing school administrators to implement randomization. In both cases local representatives felt that control schools should not be deprived of funds and that parents would object to the arrangement.

In their defense of the experimental plan, ESAP researchers, unlike the researchers in the Desegregation study, had not secured administrators' assurances that they would comply with an experimental evaluation and did not have the power to withhold funds if school districts did not comply. In spite of these differences, the ESAP researchers were able to convince most districts to accept the evaluation design, but only after prolonged discussions. One researcher was assigned the task of convincing the districts to remain in the study. He argued that the research design was necessary to determine whether the $1.5 billion program was justified. He emphasized the cost of the program and the Office of Education's accountability to Congress. Although districts could accept this, they were bothered by more practical issues, such as how to explain the loss of money to the principal of the control school. The researcher worked with local researchers to devise ways of explaining the need for controls to principals and superintendents. In some cases a scientific explanation was used, but in most cases explanations were used which did not address the issue of evaluation. One such explanation blamed the loss of money to a particular school on "the Washington bureaucracy." This explanation was usually accepted with a knowing smile. It is noteworthy that the ESAP researcher concentrated his efforts on local researchers, educating them about the need for control groups and benefiting from their knowledge about the school systems. By comparison, researchers in the Desegregation study did not deal with this group directly and felt that this was one of the main reasons why they faced resistance on the local level. The fact that the ESAP researchers were able to secure cooperation without threatening loss of funds would tend to support the idea of the Desegregation study personnel that local researchers must be consulted and educated about the proposed evaluation.

In four of the five remaining studies, randomization was not explained to the clients: Outpatient Care, Parolee, Drunk Drivers, and Traffic Citations. In the fifth study, Summer Projects, the assignment probably was not explained to the clients, although this is unclear since these data were not available for each of the separate sites. In two of these studies, the outpatient Care project and the Parolee project, the assignment was successful. In both of these projects, randomization occurred before the program began, and it was carried out using preexisting samples of clients. Client participation was not required as it was in some of the other studies. In addition, the control condition was present before the studies began and would have continued with or without the studies (i.e., multiphasic clinic care in the Outpatient Care study, or ordinary parole counseling in the Parolee project). Consequently, there was nothing highly unusual about assignment to the control condition, as there was in the ESAP study, for example. For these reasons, an explanation of the assignment process to the clients was not necessary.

Randomization was not explained in the Drunk Drivers study or the Traffic Citations study. Although the assignment procedures were unusual and complex, the reasons for them were not explained to clients or to implementers. These projects were not successful in their assignments, and part of the reason seems to be that program personnel did not understand the need for the procedure.

The Drunk Drivers study and the Traffic Citations study, like the Desegregation and ESAP studies, involved a large number of people who were neither clients nor researchers, but who intervened between these groups. In the legal studies the researchers dealt with judges and patrolmen who in turn dealt with drivers. Although these intervening actors did not understand the reasons for their actions, they had to confront clients and justify their actions. In the educational studies, an attempt was made to explain the assignment process to the intervening actors (i.e., school administrators) to good effect. In view of this fact, the researchers in the legal studies may have been more successful with their assignment plan if they had educated these personnel who were such a crucial link between the randomization plan and the clients.

## CONCLUSION

Evaluations have already become a standard part of many social reform projects, and the trend seems to be toward greater emphasis on this component. Federal and state agencies are beginning to require evaluations of their programs, in some cases true experimental evaluations. The experiences of the twelve studies reviewed here suggest that successful randomization is not as easy as drawing names out of a hat. There are a number of important issues involved in planning and implementing randomization which cannot be overlooked if the plan is to be successful.

The analysis of this set of twelve evaluation projects suggests several issues which program administrators and researchers about to begin planning an evaluation should consider. These issues are presented in Figure 1 and discussed in more detail below.

### THE RANDOMIZATION PLAN

The first consideration in planning the randomization is to decide who will control the assignment. The analysis of this factor in the twelve social projects revealed that researcher control of the process is quite important. Program administrators or other program staff are understandably preoccupied with many aspects of their program and do not have the time for careful attention to a seemingly minor aspect like randomization. The program researcher, on the other hand, has fewer tasks and can attend to the important details of the randomization process. Moreover, the researcher understands the requirements for a valid randomization and so knows which steps in the process can and cannot be modified.

The next consideration is to select the type of assignment: fixed or variable. Again, the analysis of the twelve projects supports one choice: fixed random assignment with no exceptions permitted. This is especially true when program staff are implementing the random assignment. When the researcher implements the random assignment, minor exceptions can sometimes be made (cf. the ESAP study and the

| The Randomization Plan | The Randomization Process |
|---|---|
| — decide who will control assignment | — centralize the random selection process |
| — decide type of assignment | — select one or a few implementers |
| — decide whether to block clients following intake, prior to assignment | — train the implementer(s) about the requirements for a valid randomization |
| — decide whether to inform clients | — devise a monitoring plan to check the assignment |

Figure 1: Issues in Planning and Implementing Random Assignment of Clients

Desegregation program), but these cases should continue to be included in the study. Generally, these exceptions weaken the comparison between the treatment and control groups which results in a less definitive study. Political realities may occasionally make these compromises necessary, but they should be undertaken only by the project researcher who fully understands their effects.

Once these issues are resolved, the program researcher must next decide whether to group or block clients on the basis of certain characteristics before they are randomly assigned. This was done for one of the projects analyzed here; in the Coronary Drug study, clients were blocked into low- and high-risk groups. This procedure can be very useful, as it would have been for another of the twelve projects discussed here. The researcher in the Parolee project, having finally convinced the program staff of the advantages of randomization, was placed in the awkward position of having to drop one important group of parolee clients (the narcotics offenders), because all of these men were assigned, by chance, to the control group. This illustrates the important fact that randomization is a means of obtaining equivalent groups—the best means available—but this procedure does not guarantee equivalence, especially with small samples. When there is a client characteristic which will affect the results, clients should be grouped according to this characteristic, then equally and randomly assigned to both treatment and control groups. In this way, clients with this important characteristic will be members of both groups, and thus differential effects of the treatment program can be assessed. However, blocking should be employed only when there is good reason to believe that the characteristic used to block clients interacts to a significant degree with the outcome variables.

A final consideration in planning the assignment is whether to inform clients about the random assignment procedure. This was done in many, but not all, of the projects analyzed here, and randomization was successful using both methods. Client consent, requiring disclosure of all study conditions, is becoming more common in human subject research; consequently, the decision for the social program researcher may not be *whether* to inform clients but instead *how* to inform clients.

The experiences of the projects studied here indicate that clients can understand and accept randomization as a necessary condition to determine program effectiveness. It is unclear whether an explanation in terms of scarce resources will be as readily accepted, since only one program used this explanation (the Metro High School study), and clients were given little choice in accepting the outcomes of the selection process.

The analysis of this aspect in the twelve social programs indicated that it is beneficial to develop a form of compensation for the control group members. In some cases clients were promised the same special treatment following the study (Nutrition project, Mental Illness Prevention project) or special consideration for other rewards (Desegregation study, ESAP study). In other cases, control clients were told that they would undergo testing in conjunction with the study which would benefit them (Heart Attack Prevention program, Coronary Drug project). These rewards helped to keep control clients in these studies and might be useful in other studies (cf. Hill, 1944).

## THE RANDOMIZATION PROCESS

Once randomization is planned, there are other considerations before the selection process is implemented. The studies analyzed here which had successful assignment procedures centralized their selection process. This was done by choosing one central location where actual assignments were made. In some cases individuals at many program centers across the country contacted the assignment center (e.g., Coronary Drug project); in most other cases, the assignment and the treatment occurred at only one center. When a project involves more than one treatment center, a plan for centralizing the assignment is necessary to assure proper implementation in all instances.

Whether there is one treatment center or there are many centers, as few staff as possible should be involved in the actual random selection of clients into study conditions. One person should be identified at each site to implement the procedure, and under no circumstance should other staff, who do not have this responsibility, make the assignments. The Traffic Citation study demonstrated how the sum of small deviations in the procedure on the part of many implementers can result in a major departure from the original plan.

Once staff have been identified to implement the randomization, these people should be trained about the requirements for a valid randomization. The researchers in the ESAP study did this to some extent, and this seems to have helped them implement their assignment plan successfully. The Desegregation study researchers did not conduct any orientation for program researchers at individual sites, and the researchers believe that this definitely hindered the assignment process. In the Heart Attack Prevention and Coronary Drug programs, the administrators hired personnel at each site with some prior research knowledge, even though this was not necessary since the assignment procedures were rigidly standardized and controlled. In general, the experiences of researchers from the twelve studies indicate that personnel are more likely to implement random assignment properly if they understand why the procedure is necessary.

The final consideration is to devise a monitoring plan to check the assignment procedure. In spite of perfect planning on each of the considerations just discussed, the random assignment may not occur exactly as planned due to unforeseen circumstances. Consequently, the researcher must carefully monitor the assignment as it progresses so that deviations will be noticed and corrections can be instituted before it is too late. The Traffic Citations study provides a good example of this. The researchers selected one court clerk to assign clients according to a fixed plan. The researchers did not explicitly train the clerk in randomization, but they believed he understood the assignment plan. The researchers did not monitor the process and discovered, too late, that the clerk had his own assignment plan.

If a researcher is to follow these recommendations about designing and implementing a true experimental evaluation plan, he or she must begin planning the evaluation at the outset of the project. These suggestions are best used in an evaluation which is instituted at the beginning of a program, not one added to an ongoing program. A good evaluation must be planned in conjunction with the implementation of the social reform program. A true experimental evaluation has certain requirements, such as the need for equivalent control groups, which must be recognized by program administrators in their decisions about program scope. It may be necessary, for example, to withhold treatment, at least temporarily, from part of the intended sample. These kinds of decisions cannot be made after the program is instituted. If the administrators and researchers agree on an evaluation plan which is part of the program implementation plan, the chances of a successful implementation are increased since the program and its evaluation are intertwined.

Useful evaluation also requires sufficient funding to implement the design. If control groups are used, these clients must usually be tested before the program begins, then followed so that a posttreatment test can be administered. This extra effort is costly and would not exist if treatment groups alone were followed. To plan and execute a true experimental evaluation design, additional researchers on the program staff usually are required, and this, too, adds to the cost of evaluation.

These investments in time and money are required for a good evaluation and can result in a large return. If program administrators successfully implement such a design, they have data on the effects of their programs which can be quite convincing to policy makers and clients alike. If the evaluation plan is such that it focuses on different aspects of the program or includes multiple treatment groups, administrators can prove that certain aspects of their programs should be expanded, other aspects should be modified, and some might even be discontinued. Administrators can then be more candid about the unsuccessful aspects of their programs, because they can provide convincing proof that other aspects were successful. In this way, good evaluations will help administrators abandon unsuccessful social reforms and expand productive ones. Rather than using evaluation to justify programs to which they are committed, program administrators and researchers can instead use the results of evaluation to refine programs so that they become more effective in dealing with our complex social problems.

## NOTES

1. This article is based on the author's doctoral thesis research conducted at Northwestern University; this research was funded in part by a Russell Sage Foundation grant. The author wishes to thank the members of his doctoral committee for their help and encouragement: Donald Campbell (chairperson), Robert Boruch, Andrew Gordon, and Camille Wortman. Special thanks go to the administrators and researchers from the projects analyzed here; their cooperation and interest was especially appreciated. The author is also grateful to Ronald Huff for his helpful comments on this paper, and to Carol Wyatt for her invaluable help in typing drafts of this manuscript.

Requests for reprints should be sent to the author at the Program in Social Ecology, University of California, Irvine, California 92717.

2. Although it is the best procedure available to produce similar groups, randomization does not *guarantee* equivalency between groups. This is particularly true for small groups, where it may be necessary to first block clients in important characteristics, then randomly assign similar kinds of clients to both the treatment and control groups.

3. From the *Federal Register* (February 6, 1973, Vol. 38: 3455):

Section 185.13(d). *Evaluation.* An assurance [is required] that the applicant will cooperate . . . in the evaluation . . . of specific plans, programs, projects or activities assisted under the Act. Such evaluations may require the establishment or maintenance of control groups or schools, and may include a reasonable number of interviews with, or questionnaires, achievement tests, and other evaluation instruments administered to, administrators, principals, teachers, students, program or project staff, and community members at reasonable times and places. Such evaluations may also require the applicant to provide reasonable assistance in the organization and administration of the evaluation.

## REFERENCES

BENNETT, C. A. and A. A. LUMSDAINE [eds.] (1975) Evaluation and Experiment: Some Critical Issues in Assessing Social Programs. New York: Academic Press.

BERMAN, J. (1973) "The volunteer in parole program: an evaluation." Lincoln: University of Nebraska. (unpublished)

——— (1972) "Parolees' problems, aspirations and attitudes." Ph.D. dissertation, Northwestern University. (unpublished)

BLUMENTHAL, M. and H. L. ROSS (1973) "Two experimental studies of traffic laws." Department of Transportation Reports HS-800 825 (Vol. 1) and HS-800 826 (Vol. 2). Washington, D.C.

BORUCH, R. F. (1974) "Bibliography: illustrative randomized field experiments for program planning and evaluation." Evaluation 2: 83-87.

BRIM, O. G. (1969) Knowledge into Action: Improving the Nation's Use of the Social Sciences. Report of the Special Commission on the Social Sciences. Washington, D.C.: National Science Foundation.

CAMPBELL, D. T. (1974) "Assessing the impact of planned social change." Lecture delivered at the Conference in Social Psychology, Budapest, May.
––––– (1969) "Reforms as experiments." American Psychologist 24: 409-429.
––––– and A. ERLEBACHER (1970) "How regression artifacts in quasi-experimental evaluations can mistakenly make compensatory education look harmful," pp. 185-210 in J. Hellmuth (ed.) Compensatory Education: A National Debate. Vol. 3 in The Disadvantaged Child. New York: Brunner/Mazel.
CAMPBELL, D. T. and J. C. STANLEY (1966) Experimental and Quasi-Experimental Designs for Research. Chicago: Rand McNally.
CANNER, P. L., K. G. BERGE, and C. R. KLINT (1973) "The Coronary Drug Project." American Heart Association Monograph 38.
CARO, F. G. [ed.] (1971) Readings in Evaluation Research. New York: Russell Sage Foundation.
Center for New Schools (1971) "A proposal for completion of research on the development of an alternative school." Chicago. (duplicated manuscript)
CHAPIN, F. S. (1940) "An experiment on the social effects of good housing." Amer. Soc. Rev. 5: 868-879.
COOK, T. D., H. APPLETON, R. F. CONNER, A. SHAFFER, G. TAMKIN, and S. J. WEBER (1975) Sesame Street Revisited. New York: Russell Sage Foundation.
Coronary Drug Project Research Group (1975) "Clofibrate and Niacin in coronary heart disease." J. of the Amer. Medical Assn. 231: 360-381.
COULSON, J. E., D. G. OZENNE, N. C. VAN GELDER, D. INUZURA, C. BRADFORD, and W. J. DOHERTY (1975) The First Year of Emergency School Aid Act (ESAA) Implementation: Preliminary Analysis. Santa Monica, CA: System Development Corporation.
CRAIN, R. L. and R. L. YORK (1974) "Evaluation with an experimental design: the Emergency School Assistance Program." To be published in a book of readings on evaluation by J. G. Albert, National Center for Resource Recovery.
DAVID, J. (1974) "Summer projects study." Cambridge, MA: Huron Institute. (unpublished)
––––– (1972) "Report on the design of the Follow Through Summer Effects Study." Cambridge, MA: Huron Institute. (Prepared for the Bureau of Elementary and Secondary Education, U.S. Office of Education, Washington, D.C.)
EMPEY, L. T. and M. L. ERICKSON (1972) The Provo Experiment. Lexington, MA: D. C. Heath.
FIENBERG, S. E. (1971) "Randomization and social affairs: the 1970 draft lottery." Science 171: 255-261.
FREEMAN, H. E. and C. C. SHERWOOD (1969) "Research in large-scale intervention programs," pp. 73-91 in H. C. Schulberg, A. Sheldon, and F. Baker (eds.) Program Evaluation in the Health Fields. New York: Behavioral Publications.
GELBERD, L. B. (1973) "Alternative ambulatory care delivery systems: an analysis of project evaluations." Washington, D.C.: National Center for Health Services Research and Development, Department of Health, Education and Welfare. (duplicated manuscript)
GILBERT, J. P., R. J. LIGHT, and F. MOSTELLER (1975) "Assessing social innovations: an empirical base for policy," pp. 39-193 in C. A. Bennett and A. A. Lumsdaine (eds.) Evaluation and Experiment: Some Critical Issues in Assessing Social Programs. New York: Academic Press.

GORDON, A. C. (1973) "University-community relations: problems and prospects," pp. 549-572 in J. Walton and D. E. Carnes (eds.) Cities in Change: Studies on the Urban Condition. Boston: Allyn & Bacon.

GUTTENTAG, M. (1973) "Subjectivity and its use in evaluation research." Evaluation 1: 60-65.

———— (1971) "Models and methods in evaluation research." J. for Theory of Social Behavior 1: 75-95.

HATRY, H. P., R. E. WINNIE, and D. M. FISK (1973) Practical Program Evaluation for State and Local Government Officials. Washington, D.C.: The Urban Institute.

HILL, R. (1944) "An experimental study of social adjustment." Amer. Soc. Rev. 9: 481-494.

HYMAN, H. H. and C. R. WRIGHT (1967) "Evaluating social action programs," in R. Lazarsfeld et al. (eds.) The Uses of Sociology. New York: Basic Books.

McDANIELS, G. L. (1973) "The current status of Follow Through as a social experiment." Washington, D.C.: National Institute of Education, Department of Health, Education and Welfare.

MEYERS, J. R. (1974) "A classroom preventive mental health program: preliminary progress report." Chicago: Children's Memorial Hospital.

MOJONNIER, L. (1973) "Preliminary report of the Chicago Heart Association Nutrition Education Project." Chicago: Chicago Heart Association.

RIECKEN, H. W. and R. F. BORUCH [eds.] (1974) Social Experimentation: A Method for Planning and Evaluating Social Intervention. New York: Seminar Press.

RIVLIN, A. (1971) Systematic Thinking for Social Action. Washington, D.C.: Brookings Institution.

RMC, Inc. (1971) Evaluation of the Emergency School Assistance Program. Final report. Bethesda, MD: Office of Planning, Budgeting, and Evaluation, U.S. Office of Education.

ROSENBLATT, J. R. and J. J. FILLIBEN (1971) "Randomization and the draft lottery." Science 171: 306-308.

ROSS, H. L. and M. BLUMENTHAL (1975) "Some problems in experimentation in a legal setting." Amer. Sociologist 10: 150-155.

ROSSI, P. H. (1969) "Practice, method and theory in evaluating social action programs," in J. L. Sundquist (ed.) On Fighting Poverty. New York: Basic Books.

———— and W. WILLIAMS [eds.] (1972) Evaluating Social Programs: Theory, Practice and Politics. New York: Seminar Press.

SCHULMANN, J. (n.d.) "Introduction to prevention project." Chicago: School-Based Program for Primary Prevention of Mental Disorders, Department of Child Psychiatry, Children's Memorial Hospital.

STAMLER, J. et al. (1973) "The new national cooperative multiple risk factor intervention trial (heart attack prevention program)." Chicago Medicine 76 (December 15).

STRUENING, E. L. and M. GUTTENTAG (1975) Handbook of Evaluation Research. Vols. I and II. Beverly Hills, CA: Sage.

SUCHMAN, E. (1969) Evaluation Research: Principles and Practice in Service and Social Action Programs. New York: Russell Sage Foundation.

U.S. Office of Education (1973) "Scope of work. Evaluation of the Emergency School Aid Act (ESAA). Basic LEA Program: A comparative evaluation of three types of educational intervention." Washington, D.C.: Department of Health, Education and Welfare.

WEISS, C. H. (1972) Evaluation Research: Methods of Assessing Program Effectiveness. Englewood Cliffs, NJ: Prentice-Hall.
WHOLEY, J. S., J. W. SCANLON, H. G. DUFFY, J. FUKUMOTO, and L. M. VOGT (1970) Federal Evaluation Policy. Washington, D.C.: The Urban Institute.
WOLFE, D. (1970) "Chance, or human judgment?" Science 167: 1201.

*Ross F. Conner is an Assistant Professor in the Program in Social Ecology and a research psychologist with the Public Policy Research Organization, both of the University of California, Irvine. He is coauthor of* Sesame Street Revisited *and is currently working on the nationwide evaluation of the American Bar Association's BASICS Project, a special correctional reform program.*

# 8

# Implementation Analysis and Assessment

## Walter Williams

T he underlying theme of this special issue of *Policy Analysis* is that the lack of concern for implementation is currently *the* crucial impediment to improving program operations, policy analysis, and experimentation in social policy areas. The three preceding papers have given sharp dimension to key elements of this theme. Two, those by Elmore and by Gramlich and Koshel, have explored the politics of implementation, showing the almost overwhelming complexity that arises from an implementation effort involving many actors at several different layers of government. Moreover, they have shown how political and bureaucratic factors interact with technique, often making it difficult to apply present methods and producing problems that our techniques cannot begin to handle.

Nothing comes across more strongly than the great naïveté about implementation. We have got to learn that the implementation period for complex social programs is not a brief interlude between a bright idea and opening the door for service. Because implementation was viewed that way in the performance contracting experiment, we still do not know whether performance contracting in education will or will not work. What we do know is that haste and a simplistic belief in the forces of the market are not compatible with a true test of the idea. Another point that emerges so strikingly from the papers

Work on this paper was supported by a grant from the National Science Foundation. A number of individuals commented on earlier drafts: Richard Elmore, Lucille Fuller, Eleanor Holmes, Laura Kemp, and Jeanette Veasey, all at the University of Washington; Robert Levine, New York City Rand Institute; and Arnold J. Meltsner, University of California, Berkeley. The author, however, is solely responsible for the views expressed.

From Walter Williams, "Implementation Analysis and Assessment," 1 (3) *Policy Analysis* 531-566 (Summer 1975). Copyright 1975 by the Regents of the University of California.

is the requirement for some specificity in the treatment packages to be implemented. We need more than just a catchy title reflecting a few hunches about how to educate disadvantaged children. And even where program details are put down on paper, the translation into useful field concepts often demands long, hard work.

The experience with experimental efforts puts into sharp focus the same implementation problems of politics and bureaucracy, timing and specification, that plague the regular programmatic activities of social agencies. Indeed, the problems for the agency are even more complicated, embedded as they are in the many layers of an organizational hierarchy. This paper looks at implementation primarily in the context of a large social agency and through the eyes of a policy analyst. My introductory paper pointed out that the major problem for policy analysis is not in developing relatively sound policy alternatives but in failing to consider the feasibility of implementing these alternatives. The aims of this paper are to provide a framework for investigating what the policy analyst must do to treat implementation issues more effectively, and then to develop some ideas about moving in that desired direction.

Figure 1 provides a basis for considering more fully the scope of this paper. Someone else, for expository purposes, might well have fewer or more stages than those depicted; however, the six stages shown do characterize what ought to occur when major social policy decisions are made or when a large and complex social experiment is undertaken. In either the policy or experimentation process there should be movement from speculation to a more orderly formulation of ideas, and then to some decision on what to do. Implementation, the stage between a decision and operations, starts with the development of program guidelines or design specifications; moves to what may be a quite lengthy stage of trying to work through a myriad of technical, administrative, staff, and institutional problems that confront a new activity; and ends when the experiment is deemed ready to test or when the nonexperimental activity is judged fully operational. At some point an assessment of the effectiveness of the operation may provide information that will start the process again.

Of particular importance are the analytic and assessment activities shown at the bottom of panels 2, 4, and 5 in figure 1:

> *Implementation Analysis*—Scrutiny of (1) the preliminary policy specifications, to determine their clarity, precision, and reasonableness; and

| | DECISION-MAKING | | | IMPLEMENTATION | | OPERATIONS |
|---|---|---|---|---|---|---|
| | 1 | 2 | 3 | 4 | 5 | 6 |
| **POLICY** | Search for information and theory; formulation of policy idea | Development of policy alternatives | Policy decisions | Policy specification | Field implementation | Operations |
| **EXPERIMENT** | Search for information and theory; theorizing | Development of alternative hypotheses | Decisions on experimental hypotheses | Experimental design and specification | Field implementation | Operations |
| | | IMPLEMENTATION ANALYSIS | | SPECIFICATION ASSESSMENT | INTERMEDIATE AND FINAL IMPLEMENTATION ASSESSMENT | OUTCOME ASSESSMENT |

Figure 1. Stages and Analytic/Assessment Activities in the Policy and Experimentation Processes

(2) staff, organizational, and managerial capabilities, to determine the degree to which the proposed policy alternative can be specified and implemented in its bureaucratic/political setting.

*Specification Assessment*—Assessment of the final policy or design specifications and measurement procedures, including interim feedback devices, to ascertain the degree to which the specifications correspond to decisions, are amenable to successful implementation, and are measurable.

*Intermediate Implementation Assessment*—Assessment of the degree to which a field activity is moving toward successful implementation and/or is providing useful feedback information to improve the implementation effort.

*Final Implementation Assessment*—Assessment of (1) the degree to which a field activity corresponds to the design specifications, and (2) the level of bureaucratic/political functioning, to determine whether or not there is a valid basis for testing a theory or for deeming a field activity fully operational.

Timing is crucial in these activities. Thus, if implementation analysis is to have any value, it must be performed *before* a decision is made, and its results must be available at the same time that the policy or experimental recommendations are. Surely policymakers at the time of choice ought to have reasonable estimates of the organizational capacity to carry out alternative proposals. But however obvious that may be, few people have ever thought in terms of analyzing implementation during the decision-making stages!

Experience shows that the field implementation period (stage 5 in figure 1) often stretches over several years, only to end in failure. Hence, early assessment can be critical. At the end of stage 4, even before the effort is made to move into the field, there should be a specification assessment to determine whether the final design corresponds to the decisions reached at the end of stage 3, provides sufficient program information and operational detail, and is amenable to measurement. Why is such an obviously necessary determination almost never made? Mainly because different organizational levels in an agency are responsible for a decision and its specification, and their efforts are not coordinated. Poor or improper specification is only discovered at the gloomy point of blaming someone for the failure or rationalizing it.

Before any program or project is deemed operational and its outcome ready to assess, there should be some opportunity to work out initial kinks and to make some adjustments for problems that could not be foreseen on the drawing board. But how much time should be taken for this? How long can one wait before getting an idea off the ground—or before deciding that it is never going to get off the ground? If a great deal of time is involved, intermediate implementation measures must be taken in stage 5 to provide feedback information for improvement or for an early decision either that the project will never become operational or that, even if it does, it looks in practice like a bad idea. At some later point, for the project that does get the go-ahead, there should be a final assessment to determine that the policy or experiment is actually in place and ready to move into operations and toward outcome assessment.

But a word of caution: The orderliness of the stages in figure 1 and the rigor of the definitions are heuristic devices used to facilitate exposition. Implementation is too complicated and too little is known about it to expect either orderliness or rigor when analysis and assessment are actually undertaken. Indeed, the study of implementation carries us into social science's weakest area—dynamics. The determination of whether or not a social program or policy can be implemented cannot be based on a static checklist. Rather, it must involve an analysis of whether technical, bureaucratic, staff, and institutional/political elements can be blended into a viable process. Implementation analysis must ask whether the organization can do what is desired in technical terms, whether it can function well in a bureaucratic sense (which involves micro-organizational issues), and whether it can operate successfully in its larger environment (macro-organizational/political issues). Questions of this type push into relatively uncharted research terrain. As Levine has observed, "much (probably most) public policy will continue to be carried out by public bureaucracies, and the manipulation of such bureaucracies is a vast unexplored area, resembling the continent of Africa during mid-nineteenth century."[1]

It would be nice if this paper could lay out strategies for analyzing and assessing implementation, not in the abstract but in terms of specific instruments and techniques that could now be applied with reasonable rigor; and it would be equally nice to be able to spell out

1. Robert A. Levine, *Public Planning: Failure and Redirection* (New York: Basic Books, 1972), p. 192.

the precise kinds of technical skills needed to carry out these strategies, and to pinpoint the organizational mechanisms that would be likely to move a decision effectively through the bureaucratic/political environment. Alas, this paper will be long on issues, short on solutions. Moreover, the implementation questions are so complex and subtle that one hardly knows where to begin; or, perhaps more accurately, one feels the need to do the impossible task of starting simultaneously down several paths.

All this makes organization of the paper difficult, but we must start somewhere and proceed in some sort of orderly sequence. The first section which follows considers briefly some key terms and distinctions and then discusses four overlapping sets of issues that cut across later discussion—the issues of (a) theory, specification, and implementation; (b) programmatic objectives; (c) detailed packaging of programs versus broad directional guides; and (d) implementation success. The second section discusses the implementation process, emphasizing especially the federal social agency and the role of the policy analyst there. The third section begins by considering past research on implementation and the potential contributions that several scholarly disciplines might make; it then proceeds to an overview of techniques and strategies for the analysis and assessment of implementation, and to a consideration of some of the problems that must be confronted, focusing on broad approaches that might be taken rather than on a detailed critique of any existing methodologies or stategies. Finally, a brief section presents some concluding observations.

Given the complexity of implementation and the paucity of knowledge about it, it is clear that we will not be able to solve most of the problems set forth in this paper at the present time. But surely we can move to more desirable ground, somewhere between ignoring implementation completely and achieving a level of sophistication that would permit us to treat most contingencies in a reasonable way. At the very least, simply recognizing the need to do something about the problem will have a salutary effect. In my previous experience with social programs for the disadvantaged, I have often wondered whether the programs would have been started quite differently, or in some cases not started at all, had there been systematic efforts by reasonable people to judge the capacity for implementation by considering the organization, techniques, and people in the field.

The weaknesses were often so obvious, had people only taken a look and asked a few simple questions. The first need in implementation is not for disciplinary giants to make breakthroughs in dynamic social theory, but for sensible persons with knowledge of program areas to ask if the people in the field can really do what is being proposed. We do have techniques for detecting gross defects in the implementation process, and this should be kept in mind as we struggle with the extraordinarily complex issues discussed below.

### KEY TERMS AND CROSSCUTTING ISSUES
#### Some Key Terms and Distinctions

Differences in the way some common words like "project," "program," and "inputs" are used necessitate a discussion of key terms. The usual distinction between a *program* and a *project* is that a project is a single operating activity while a program comprises many such activities bearing the same general title. For example, there may be a national Head Start program, a Head Start program in the city of Chicago, and many individual Head Start projects in these programs.

The term *input* is employed in this paper to describe an element or characteristic of a program, or of a project, or of the treatment package(s) that comprise a project or program. Inputs may include both nonhuman elements (such as a new reading curriculum's text and test material and scheduling routine) and the human elements involved in their use (e.g., reading specialists and teacher's aides). The term *output* is used to describe organizational change deriving from changes in inputs or other factors. Organizational change may be physical (for example, the rearranging of a classroom) or behavioral (less lecturing by the teacher). The term *outcome* describes change in the status and/or behavior of participants in a program or project. Outputs speak to the issue of whether or not an organization is doing things differently; outcomes have to do with whether or not participants are better off.[2]

Implementation has to do with inputs and outputs. Inputs are

2. A word of caution against becoming overly concerned with these definitions: I recognize that a discussion of terms is likely to be disruptive to the reader who disagrees with my definitions, but that a lack of discussion may mislead the reader who is unsure of my usage. So the discussion should be viewed as a means of laying out some ground rules about the jargon in an emerging area where terminology is still likely to be a problem.

basically static; outputs are more dynamic. In trying to determine whether or not an innovation has been implemented successfully, it makes sense to have a checklist that asks whether the project has certain specified elements. However, a far more important task is to determine whether or not implementation has taken place by assessing the degree of correspondence between expected and actual outputs.

Beyond drawing a sharp distinction between a decision and its implementation, as is done in figure 1, it is useful in discussing policymaking in a complex organization to distinguish between the decision-making process and the implementation process. For example, at the top of a federal agency there will be a group concerned mainly with major decisions, while at lower levels there will be others concerned mainly with putting programs in place. However, the decision-making and implementation processes each involve a series of points at which decisions must be made and subsequently implemented.

It will also be true that, from different organizational perspectives, an actor may be viewed by some as primarily a decision-maker and by others as primarily an implementer. An agency head will consider a bureau head responsible for implementing agency decisions. However, organizations in the field that are funded by the bureau will see the bureau generally and the bureau head in particular as a key decision-maker. These distinctions fit well with our commonsense image of the world, since we are talking about the quite general phenomenon of somebody deciding something and that something having to be carried out. When the situation involves a decision-maker and an implementer who are different persons or organizations, a *series* of decisions are likely to be made and implemented before the primary decision becomes implemented or fails to become implemented. Moreover, in the process of implementation it will almost always be necessary for the implementers to make decisions that may modify the primary decision and other decisions. In essence, there will be a number of decision-makers and implementers all along the way on a major decision/implementation path. Again, this notion is quite straightforward. Problems arise not in trying to appreciate it in some abstract conceptual way but in following the many trails that repeated decision/implementation points may produce.

### Crosscutting Concepts and Issues

*Theory, Specification, and Implementation*—Any new program or project may be thought of as representing a theory or hypothesis in that—to use experimental terminology—the decision-maker wants to put in place a treatment expected to *cause* certain predicted effects or outcomes. If the program or project is unsuccessful, the explanation may be that it "did not activate the 'causal process' that would have culminated in the intended goals (this is a failure of program), or it may have set the presumed 'causal process' in motion but the process did not 'cause' the desired effects (this is a failure of theory)."[3] That is, it is useful to distinguish between an idea that was put in place properly and did not work and an idea that was not tested because it was not actually implemented properly. However, whether the program was implemented can become an almost meaningless, or at least unmeasurable, notion when the underlying theory is little more than a catchy label with a few hunches attached. Besides looking out for theory and implementation failure, then, it is important to recognize the possibility of specification failure.

The concept of specification is quite broad. Specification may include what is to be done (the elements of the treatment); how it is to be done (guides for implementation and operation); what organizational changes (outputs) are expected; and what the specific, measurable objectives are. It is the key link between a theory and its implementation. In the policy process, specification determines whether a decision with imprecise operational language can be translated into a set of useful guidelines for action in the field.

*Program Objectives*—At the core of policy planning and policy analysis has been the notion that program objectives can be clearly defined in measurable terms, accepted by the various parties involved, and distinguished from input and environmental factors. But what we are finding over and over again is that program objectives are often so illusive as to be difficult to determine at all, much less define rigorously. Moreover, as we move from broad objectives that are subject to many interpretations to rigorous ones that are not, the likelihood of disagreement rapidly increases. For example, few would disagree with the goals of a program "intended to enhance learning and improve life opportunities," but this is hardly true of

3. Carol H. Weiss, *Evaluation Research* (Englewood Cliffs, N.J.: Prentice-Hall, Inc., 1972), p. 38.

objectives defined in terms of cognitive increments measured by specific standardized educational tests.

The tentativeness of program objectives and their potential interrelationship with inputs and environmental factors are gaining currency in recent discussions.[4] The points are well made by John Pincus in discussing educational research and development (R&D) policy:

> *If* [educational] *goals are in some sense undefinable, it is inappropriate to adopt the standard rationalist approach of first defining goals, then seeking means appropriate to achieve them efficiently. Instead, R&D strategy should be based at least in part on the converse approach.* If the present situation is unsatisfactory, then it may be wiser to try out systematic innovations and assess their consequences than to continue to pursue uncertain goals with unclear technologies.[5]

Separating objectives under actual field conditions from inputs and environmental factors is difficult. It is not that inputs, outputs, and outcomes cannot be distinguished conceptually, but that in the field the subtle interplay and feedback among inputs, the institutional environment, partial outputs, and partial outcomes are so complicated that they are likely to defy our ability to separate out independent effects. Hence, the path to developing more meaningful outcome measurement is through the study of inputs and outputs. Moreover, it is likely that the conceptualization of outcomes will change as we gain a better understanding of the subtle interrelationships among outcomes, program inputs, and the institutional/political environment.

*Detailed Packaging of Programs vs. Broad Directional Guides*— Thus far, at least implicitly, I have cast implementation in terms of a specific treatment package—e.g., a new classroom approach—that must move down a process from decision to field operations with a number of people in different layers of an organization or in different

4. For an important early discussion, see Robert S. Weiss and Martin Rein, "The Evaluation of Broad-Aim Programs: A Cautionary Case and a Moral," *Annals of the American Academy of Political and Social Science,* September 1969, pp. 133–42. A useful paper in thinking about program goals and with an extensive bibliography is Irwin Deutscher's "Toward Avoiding the Goal-Trap in Evaluation Research," mimeographed (Department of Sociology, Case Western Reserve University, May 1974).

5. John Pincus, "Incentives for Innovation in the Public Schools," *Review of Educational Research,* Winter 1974, p. 129.

organizations becoming involved. In this case the success of implementation depends heavily both on the clarity and specificity of the package and on the capability of the people taking part in the implementation process. There must be detailed instructions and a firm guiding hand throughout.

But there have been difficulties with the detailed-package, guiding-hand approach, and Robert Levine draws upon them to advance an alternative. He observes that

> we are forced willy-nilly to look for broad-brush programs, self-applied and incentive-guided, as exemplified by the market systems. . . .[6]

> . . . the contention here is that we need a new sort of planning. Rather than selecting desirable future states and laying out courses over deceptive terrain, both policy-making and policy planning should be directional. That is, policy-makers should decide what general sort of future would be better than an alternative, and policy planners should lay out steps that show a probability of moving in that general direction.[7]

The driving forces that will move people toward the broad directional goals set out by policymakers are competition, incentives, and self-interest—the forces of the marketplace, Adam Smith's unseen hand.

At their extremes the detailed-package, guiding-hand approach and the broad-direction, unseen-hand alternative seem to be 180 degrees apart. Yet these two approaches are much more similar than they appear: Assume, for purposes of exposition, a hierarchical organization such as a social agency. First, under both approaches decision-makers at the top of the organization will determine objectives and expect these objectives to be accomplished through the operation of some entity, such as a local school, that is not necessarily a part of their organization. Second, under both approaches higher echelons (such as policy planners) will seek means of moving the operators toward the desired objectives. Third, the two approaches do not necessarily differ in terms of the *final* specificity of the treatment package at the point of delivery—both may lead to individual projects of equally detailed specification.[8] What distin-

6. Levine, *Public Planning*, p. 135.

7. *Ibid.*, pp. 164–65.

8. The Levine quotation's mention of "broad-brush programs" may seem to contradict any notion of detailed specificity. But it is not unusual to find broadly conceived national programs embracing closely detailed projects. For

guishes one approach from the other are (1) the mechanics of determining the treatment and its degree of specificity, and (2) the bureaucratic levels at which decisions about specification are made.

The similarities become more striking with an examination of common problems. If the directional guides are so broad and nebulous that wide agreement is achieved simply because of their vagueness, we have the usual problems of poorly articulated goals and it is hard to see how incentives would work. If the goals are more specific, the problems of disagreement already discussed are likely to emerge. Further, these broad directions usually will have to pass through a bureaucratic structure, a factor which the incentive mechanism must take into account. Conversely, the more structured approach that has been used in the past has failed in part because it has not faced up to the complex issue of the kinds of incentives needed to motivate lower levels in the desired direction.

A fundamental assumption of the unseen-hand approach drawn from economics is that firms, in their self-interest, will seek and find efficient and effective means of production. The underlying model is one of a relatively homogeneous product for which the production process is well known. The big problem is to determine the appropriate incentives. But when the product is something like improved education or higher reading scores, where the means of production are not known and may be subject to much controversy, incentives may not lead to the desired outcome. The producer simply may not know how to get the desired outcome, as the recent performance contracting experience indicates so vividly. Even where the strategy calls for giving those in the field wide latitude in reaching a desired future state, it still may make sense to seek detailed packages so that there will be some options to choose from. Again, the overlapping nature of the issues is striking.

*Implementation Success*—At some point in time there should be a determination of the degree to which an innovation has been implemented successfully. What should the implemented activity be expected to look like in terms of the underlying decision? For a complex treatment package put in different local settings, decision-

---

example, while the national Head Start program is cast in terms of general educational objectives for preschool children, the *individual* Head Start projects may involve the detailed development of treatments.

makers usually will not expect—or more importantly, *not want*—a precise reproduction of every detail of the package. The objective is performance, not conformance. To enhance the probability of achieving the basic program or policy objectives, the implementation should consist of a realistic development of the underlying decision in terms of the local setting. In the ideal situation, those responsible for implementation would take the basic idea and modify it to meet special local conditions. There should be a reasonable resemblance to the basic idea, as measured by inputs and expected outputs, incorporating the best of the decision and the best of the local ideas.

Learning how to determine whether an implementation has been successful is not enough. We must also be concerned with the factors associated with implementation success and with the likelihood that such success will yield successful outcomes as well. Implementation success can be conceived of as an intermediate stage in a process moving toward improved outcomes. But organizational change—even if specified—does not necessarily bring positive outcomes. Events of the last several years in the social policy areas have made this painfully obvious. What is less obvious is that the factors which are most likely to lead to organizational change may not be the ones most likely to lead to better outcomes. For example, an educational program with broad objectives that says, in effect, "here's some money with which to move forward" is probably much more likely to produce organizational change than is a tightly specified treatment making the money conditional on numerous stipulations. In the latter case, many prospective innovators may simply reject the offer. Which approach will be more likely to yield positive outcomes is not clear. And certainly in terms of conditional probability, given that significant organizational change has occurred, the more detailed specification may yield a clear winner.

Both the detailed-packaging and broad-directional-guide approaches envision an effort to elicit different organizational outputs that will lead to improved outcomes for participants. In its most simplistic form, detailed packaging has stressed the optimum solution, a super technique for all seasons. *The* single best classroom approach for teaching disadvantaged preschool children can be found. At the other extreme, a focus on broad directional guides seems to imply that all you need to do to get people to find a means for producing positive outcomes for disadvantaged preschool children is to reward them for doing so. The detailed approach stresses the package; the other, the inducements. Both extremes may miss important elements of the truth.

These points are illustrated in an article by Silverman and Weikart that draws on their experience with preschool and regular school children.[9] Weikart had been successful in carrying out a series of carefully planned and executed preschool projects using Piagetian techniques. A later phase of the work compared the Piagetian approach with a Bereiter and Engelmann project and with a traditional approach that might be found in the usual classroom. Much to their surprise, Weikart and his colleagues found that all three approaches produced similar and significant learning gains. They had expected the traditional approach to be much like a control. These results have led them to abandon the notion that there is a single *best* approach and to push their own because they are comfortable with it.

It does now seem wrong to think in terms of a single best solution. At the same time, there is a need to seek methods that work better than those we have. For example, Weikart and his associates have searched for common elements in the several approaches they found successful. Silverman and Weikart observe:

> [We] find that each program had a consistent daily routine so that the children knew what was happening when; each had a strong commitment to its goals and methods on the part of the teaching team; each had paraprofessionals with teaching duties; and each demanded that a portion of the teacher's day be spent in planning and evaluation.[10]

Indeed, if there is a glimmer of hope in their work it is in the suggestion that a concern for details and structure may pay off; in education, such a concern would involve providing an articulated curriculum that lets teacher and pupil know what to do and what is expected, making relevant materials available, providing supervision, and so on.

The key point is that there may well be critical trade-offs between flexibility and conformance to specification. Detailed and inflexible specifications may stifle creativity or rule out an innovation when some elements are incompatible with local conditions. Yet a catchy

9. Charles Silverman and David P. Weikart, "Open Framework: Evolution of a Concept in Pre-School Education," in *High/Scope Foundation Report* (Ypsilanti, Mich., 1973), pp. 14–19.

10. *Ibid.*, p. 17.

program label with no concrete details may not be enough. There should be something to build upon and modify. As Weikart and Banet observe in this journal, "it is difficult to train teachers and supervisors to implement a model that consists only of some basic hunches about good education." Combining elements of both the detailed-packaging and broad-directional-guide approaches—specificity, flexibility, and incentives—may be the preferred implementation strategy.

### THE IMPLEMENTATION PROCESS

Implementation is first and foremost a bureaucratic and political problem. Bureaucratic and political factors—not conventional technical or methodological problems per se—represent the main near-term deterrents to more effective implementation. By this I certainly do not mean that powerful techniques exist in the implementation area, but rather that considerably better results could be achieved with our present limited tools if political and bureaucratic factors fostered rather than impeded implementation activities. Further, technical questions often seem almost trivial when compared to such issues as whether or not political jurisdictions will cooperate or whether a teachers' union will be in favor of implementing a new idea.

### Conceptualizing the Implementation Process

The general nature of the implementation process and the inter-relationship of technical factors with bureaucratic and political ones can be explored through a discussion of figure 2. Whether what is to be implemented is a detailed program package or a general directional guide, those who wish to get "it" into the field almost certainly will have to penetrate through bureaucratic/political layers in trying to reach the final set of actors—those who manage the treatment or service, those who deliver it, and those who receive it. Generally speaking, the higher the proposer/initiator/funder is in the hierarchical chain, the denser and more complex will be the bureaucratic/political layers that must be worked through. But things are not much simpler at the local level. Whether the impetus for a proposed educational innovation comes from the national level or out of a city school superintendent's office, the bureaucratic/political layers to be confronted will be relatively dense.

The most vexing problems in the implementation process are less

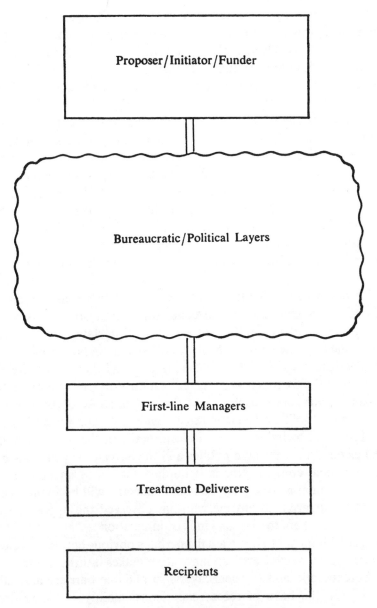

Figure 2. An Implementation Paradigm

likely to derive from big political or philosophical issues than they
are from more narrow problems arising from jurisdictional disputes.
The person trying to initiate changes—be he or she a federal pro-

gram director, or a governor, or a mayor—will often find specific directions blunted or subverted by lower-level bureaucrats trying to protect their turfs. These problems are the bane of any administrator, whether a U.S. commissioner of education or a local school superintendent, who must work with a hierarchical bureaucracy. As Pincus has observed in his work on factors associated with public school innovation, change is likely "when the innovation is perceived as favorable with respect to the current status and organization of the bureaucracy (because in a self-perpetuating nonmarket system, these bureaucratic values become socialized and tend to dominate other criteria; or in other words, the bureaucratic costs are the real costs of the system)."[11] This does not mean that the public school district is a Machiavellian jungle of bureaucratic intrigue (at least I hope it does not), but rather that it is a complex social phenomenon not comprehended without a detailed study of its institutional functioning.

The bureaucratic/political layers in figure 2 may contain a multitude of actors including, in an educational innovation, persons at different levels in a federal agency, personnel in state offices of education, the upper levels of a local school system, and a school principal. These actors stand between the initiator and those most directly involved in the treatment—in the education example, a supervisory teacher, a classroom teacher, and the students. By portraying the bureaucratic/political layers in this manner, I do not mean to imply the absence of technical issues. Indeed, many of the issues encountered as one works through politics and the bureaucracy may have a high technical content. Nor is it implied that once an innovation reaches the final actors, only technical concerns will be found. This should be apparent to anyone who has observed the opposition of classroom teachers to various kinds of innovation.

Figure 2 is meant to illustrate the perhaps obvious but nevertheless critical point that even after an innovation makes it through the various bureaucratic and political layers, formidable barriers may still remain. On the basis of recent experience, mainly in the field of education, I include in the figure a key element in implementation, labeled "first-line managers." These managers include administrators with direct responsibility for working with the treatment deliverers to see that the project is implemented and carried out. They may

11. Pincus, "Incentives for Innovation," p. 120.

play a crucial intermediary role, as Neal Gross and his associates observed after their study of a failure to implement a new teaching approach in a small school:

> Subordinates may be unable, or find it difficult, to make changes in their role performance unless management conforms to a set of expectations that subordinates "have a right to hold" for its performance. More specifically, subordinates have a right to expect management (1) to take the steps necessary to provide them with a clear picture of their new role requirements; (2) to adjust organizational arrangements to make them compatible with the innovation; (3) to provide subordinates with necessary retraining experiences, required if the capabilities for coping with the difficulties of implementing the innovation are to develop; (4) to provide the resources necessary to carry out the innovation; and (5) to provide the appropriate supports and rewards to maintain subordinates' willingness to make implementation efforts.[12]

Finally, figure 2 includes the recipients of the treatment, frequently a forgotten element when bureaucrats and treatment deliverers lock horns. Successful innovation requires a recipient who is both able to benefit from a treatment and willing to receive it—and knowing whether an intended recipient in fact has these qualities demands more than merely understanding his or her plight or deficiencies as perceived by professionals. This is vividly illustrated in recent efforts to "upgrade" children's television. As Tom Shales has observed: "A sad fact of children's TV reform is that while all the educational consulting and pro-socializing is going on, children still tend to prefer junk when they plop themselves down in front of a TV set. . . . Getting children to like what's good for them—or what some people think is good for them—could well be the hardest job ahead, then, for the children's TV reformers."[13] Shales cites some viewing statistics in which quality shows are pitted directly against the likes of a "Deputy Dawg" cartoon rerun. The outcome was 85 percent for junk and 15 percent for quality. One obvious explanation is that kids want to relax at home and do not want the busman's holiday of more schoollike offerings. The recipients whose welfare is ostensibly the main thrust of the innovation simply cannot be expected to accept passively what is offered.

12. N. Gross, J. Giacquinta, and M. Bernstein, *Implementing Organizational Innovations: A Sociological Analysis of Planned Educational Change* (New York: Basic Books, 1971), pp. 200–201.

13. Tom Shales, "Children's TV: Breaking the Snare," *Washington Post*, 19 May 1974.

*Responsibility for Implementation in the Federal Social Agency*

In the case of a major program in a large social agency, the multitude of layers and actors involved in the implementation process is striking, perhaps even appalling. With so many complex layers of power and authority, it is easy to lose the sense of direction that steers one toward the basic goals of the organization. What could be more obvious and fundamental than the fact that decisions need to be implemented, and that inattention to implementation will almost certainly be fatal? Yet a fantastic amount of bureaucratic foliage so obscures the way that social agencies can lose sight of this. *Responsibility for implementation tends to slip between the cracks.* Almost everyone assumes that specification and implementation are somebody else's task. Higher-ups see implementation as being a lower-level responsibility; but the lower levels look to higher echelons for specification and guidance.

Another reason why implementation slips between the cracks is that social agencies rarely deal directly with the building of implementation capability or see it as a separate activity. *The agency's program offices are concerned with operating what is in place, not with future large-scale implementation questions.* No separate staff is charged with *direct responsibility* for improving the capability to mount complex new programs. Instead, activities that may increase implementation capacity primarily *derive* from ongoing attempts to improve present operations. No one denies the importance of implementation, yet everyone has reasons why their office cannot or should not undertake it. When implementation responsibilities ever do get picked up, it is usually by a lower-echelon unit which cannot avoid them. Without an emphasis on implementation in general or a specific concern for capacity building, programs still get into the field —but through a process that is usually sloppy and poorly thought through.

*Top Management: The Key to Implementation Success*—Weaknesses in the agency implementation process may stem from more basic causes that relate to the fundamental issue of management responsibility. Recent work by the Urban Institute's program evaluation studies group highlights this point. On the basis of its earlier findings that the results of federal evaluation in the social areas have had a most limited impact on policy,[14] the group asks: "Why have

14. See: Joseph S. Wholey et al., *Federal Evaluation Policy* (Washington, D.C.: The Urban Institute, 1970); and Garth M. Buchanan and Joseph S. Wholey, "Federal Level Evaluation," *Evaluation*, Fall 1972, pp. 17–22.

those in charge of programs and those who evaluate them not been able to join their efforts in a way that leads more frequently to significant improvements in program performance?"[15] The group argues that the failure of evaluation results to have a material impact on policy derives from three prime causes:

*Lack of Definition*: the problem addressed, the program intervention being made, the expected direct outcome of that intervention, or the expected impact on the overall society or on the problem addressed are not sufficiently well defined to be measurable.

*Lack of Clear Logic*: the logic of assumptions linking expenditure of resources, the implementation of a program intervention, the immediate outcome to be caused by that intervention, and the resulting impact are not specified or understood clearly enough to permit testing them.

*Lack of Management*: those in charge of the program lack the motivation, understanding, ability, or authority to act on evaluation measurements and comparisons of *actual* intervention activity, *actual* outcomes, and *actual* impact.[16]

The first two causes flow from the basic failure to specify in terms that have clear operational meaning either the program objectives or the treatment and its relationship to the objectives. The Urban Institute group points to the vagueness of language in federal legislation and guidelines, where so much of what is said is cast in terms of "vaporous wishes" and almost meaningless phrases of guidance such as "improved local capacity" or "accessibility of services."[17] Just as with implementation, the process of evaluation runs into trouble because of specification failure. The parallel is hardly surprising. Both activities require a degree of concreteness—otherwise they become rather meaningless, futile exercises. Without a reasonable specification of objectives or of the treatment package, it is small wonder that evaluators flounder, struggling to create hard objectives out of vaporous wishes, or that implementers have developed massive regulations addressing mainly financial and administrative concerns.

15. Pamela Horst et al., "Program Management and the Federal Evaluator," *Public Administration Review*, August 1973, p. 300.

16. *Ibid.*, p. 301.

17. I note only a few terms; the reader may have other favorites. For additional Urban Institute choices, see Horst et al., "Program Management," p. 303.

Finding that clear specification is a necessary condition for sound outcome-oriented evaluation is hardly startling. What is less obvious is that the responsibility for determining definitions and the logic of treatment is not the responsibility of evaluators but of program management. The fundamental point, of course, is not that evaluators should be absolved of all blame for the shoddy work of the past. Rather, it is that evaluators can do little if program management either does not want evaluation or is not willing to exercise its responsibilities in developing specifications. Precisely the same thing is true for implementers. The attitude of management is the first and by far the most important factor in improving implementation. *Wanting better implementation will go a long way toward achieving it.* But "wanting it" does not mean that top-level management can simply mouth platitudes about the need for good implementation. Rhetoric is not enough. Management must make the hard choices required to institutionalize implementation as a critical part of programmatic activity.

Earlier experience with the Planning, Programming, Budgeting (PPB) System well illustrates the management issues involved. Separate surveys by the General Accounting Office and the Bureau of the Budget (now the Office of Management and Budget) were conducted three years after the start of the 1965 effort to implement PPB throughout the federal government. The surveys found that only three of sixteen domestic agencies had implemented a PPB system successfully, as measured by policy analysis becoming an important part of agency decision-making. In a summary article based on the findings of the two surveys, Marvin and Rouse observed: "The attitude of the agency head has been the single most important factor in the development of a PPB system and its integration with the agency decisionmaking system."[18] Agency heads who got relatively sound analysis accorded their central analytic offices (1) high status (generally assistant secretary rank or the equivalent), (2) direct responsibility and authority for carrying out analysis, and (3) sufficient personnel positions, in terms of both numbers and high civil

18. Keith E. Marvin and Andrew M. Rouse, "The Status of PPB in Federal Agencies: A Comparative Perspective," in U.S. Congress, Joint Economic Committee, *The Analysis and Evaluation of Public Expenditures: The PPB System*, vol. 3 (Washington, D.C.: U.S. Government Printing Office, 1969), p. 808.

service grades, to allow for the development of a viable analytic staff. The agency head was willing to make the basic changes in structure and status needed to get good analysis.

The changes needed for improved implementation may be even more difficult to make than those for policy analysis because the implementation process moves so widely and deeply in an organization. But if management has a hard task, it also has the power to start in the right direction. If it is willing to make basic structural changes, the biggest hurdle will have been passed. To say this does not deny that techniques are important or that developing technical capability in the implementation area is a critical prerequisite for improvement. Rather, the point is that the management commitment is more important. Not only that, but management's unwillingness to face up to the problems of implementation will so doom implementation efforts that technical improvements will probably have little or no effect. Finally, techniques are available for making real improvements in implementation—but, again, only in the presence of a strong commitment on the part of management.

*Policy Analysts and Implementation*—A central analytic office with responsibility for implementation analysis and assessment may be a key link between the agency's decision-making and implementation processes.[19] But if so, a lot of changes are needed. Elsewhere I have argued that the relatively good central analytic offices in the social agencies have both improved the basis of decision-making and had a significant influence on agency decisions.[20] The influence has generally been on people at the top of Washington's decision-making process—the agency head and the staffs of the Office of Management and Budget (OMB) or the White House. The analyst's *modus operandi* has been to produce a document, a policy analysis report, and to see that it moves up through the decision-making structure. In this milieu the big payoff is for good ideas and sound reasoning *without* a great deal of detail. Indeed, those at the top of the decision-making

19. This section will focus mainly on bureaucratic and political issues. In the following section I will address more technical issues concerning the policy analyst and implementation.

20. See my *Social Policy Research and Analysis* (New York: American Elsevier, 1971), p. 189, and "The Role of Social Scientists outside the Government in Social Policy," Public Policy Paper No. 7, mimeographed (Seattle: University of Washington, Institute of Governmental Research, August 1974), p. 10.

structure do not have time for programmatic detail—and they might not be comfortable with it even if they did. However, approval by the agency head and OMB does not magically convert a document's decisions into words that all will follow. Dollars and slot levels, of course, impel action, but action does not necessarily flow from a document's verbiage, however much lauded by the agency head and OMB. Implementation stands in the way. This simple truth has been very hard for analysts to comprehend.

To see how far removed central analysts have been from implementation—from both the agency's process itself and their own problems of getting action on approved decisions—let us speculate about some of the issues they would need to face in order to move toward a meaningful concern with implementation problems. It seems fair to generalize that analytic staffs in the past have been naive about the complexity of converting fairly abstract social policy concepts into terms useful for field operation. Policy analysis can include a step in which a decision document's relatively brief recommendations (e.g., more remedial education) are converted into detailed operational-type instructions. However, this detail is not a necessary condition for the high-level decision-making phase, so the step is best viewed as a separate activity beyond decision-making.

Reasonable specification is only one of the problems that a central analytic office must face if it is to have a marked effect on implementation. The analyst must address a number of other questions as well: How capable is the national office of developing guidelines or regulations for operating units and assisting the regional or local offices in carrying out these instructions? How capable are regional staffs of aiding in the implementation of a new policy? Is there clear responsibility for transmitting implementation information, and are there established lines of communication for such transmission? Basically, these are questions of linkages, from the top to the bottom of the implementation process, that concern capability, responsibility, and the analyst's own ties to the process.

Of critical importance for the central analyst in the implementation process may be his or her office's formal ties to the preparation of guidelines by the headquarter's staff. It is through these guidelines, not through the formal policy analysis report, that the field staff finds out about decisions. But what role should the analyst take here? One possibility is that the analyst should be responsible for judging whether what has been written in the guidelines is reasonable in terms of what was decided earlier. Such a determination is a straightforward matter, it would seem, until one confronts the reality of a large federal agency. Agency guidelines and regulations are often set out in massive documents or sets of documents prepared by many actors. A new program—especially if it has an established date set by law—may be in the field long before the final guidelines and regulations are issued. Does it really make sense to give an analyst the responsibility for passing judgment on these documents? If so, what is to be the process for changing those documents whose specifications are judged to be poor, and who is to be responsible for getting the new wording translated into action?

At the heart of the issue of implementation capability is the fundamental question of responsibility. Certainly it is reasonable to argue that the analysis of implementation capability should be carried out by an independent office, separate from the program bureaus *and* the central analyst, which reports directly to the agency head. *Yet the assessment of implementation capability seems to be so integral to any policy analysis underlying a decision that removing the responsibility from the central analyst would create a severe problem.* In making a set of programmatic recommendations, an analyst ought to answer for their implications, including the prospects for successful implementation. It seems almost frivolous to specify a set of complex programmatic actions without also considering in some detail the requirements for the implementation of those actions.

## RESEARCH, TECHNIQUE, AND STRATEGY
### Implementation as a Research Question

Little research has been done either on the implementation of social policies, programs, or projects or on the implementation process in a social policy organization such as a federal agency. The absence of studies is not explained by the nature of the topic itself. The question of implementation is one of the most fundamental of all the issues facing a large-scale organization. In its most general form, an inquiry about implementation seeks to determine whether an organization can bring together people and material in a cohesive organizational unit and motivate them in such a way as to carry out the organization's stated objectives. Implementation is such a basic issue that the failure to study it in the context of a social policy organization is most difficult to understand. This is especially true in light of the fact that the problem can be approached from several perspectives that cut across a number of academic disciplines.

The problem might be studied in terms of the development of a sound organizational structure by inquiring whether the organization has in place, or can be expected to develop quickly, the administrative and technical skills that will be required in operating a new program aimed at accomplishing specified objectives. It is the administrative science question of the soundness of a large bureaucracy's organizational structure and staff in terms of the administrative and technical demands of specific programs. Or, implementation could be looked at as a problem requiring the integration of a number of systems and subsystems, the kind of problem that might interest the sociologist with macro-type concerns or the systems analyst. Relatedly, the complex bureaucratic and political issues and their interface might pose questions of interest to political scientists.

The problem of implementing new programs might be looked at more from the perspective of interpersonal motivational factors. As Anthony observes: "The success or failure of the management control process depends on the personal characteristics of the manager: his judgment, his knowledge, and his ability to influence others."[21] In these terms the emphasis is on leadership—a blending of personal skill and experience that can get others to respond to direction in a dynamic situation. Viewed from this perspective, the implementation question is primarily one of the dynamics of interaction—the social psychological issue of how managers motivate others to carry out a program in line with stated objectives. One might cast this problem in terms of the individual manager or of an organizational unit with a focus on organizational development.

Another approach to the study of implementation might be in terms of incentives as discussed earlier. The incentive structure seems to be more the domain of the economist than of other social scientists. Finally, the social anthropologist might find observing the implementation process less crowded with other anthropologists and more rewarding than dropping in on still another exotic island.

21. R. N. Anthony, *Planning and Control Systems: A Framework for Analysis* (Cambridge, Mass.: Harvard University, Graduate School of Business Administration, 1965), p. 80.

A great deal might be gained from careful observation by a scientist trained to pick up the nuances of interpersonal relationships, say, or the effects of mores on behavior.

In response to my statement that there has been little research specifically on problems of implementation in social organizations, some might call attention to a missing reference or question how little is little. But the general claim of the paucity of research on efforts to implement social programs and policies surely is well justified. However, any claim concerning the actual or potential relevance of social science techniques or past research to the study of implementation in social organizations is likely to be controversial. Take the organizational area, for example. There is a vast literature from each of the disciplines of sociology, political science, public and business administration, economics, and the emerging area of organizational development. Who considers himself sufficiently in command of all this literature to judge its actual or potential relevance? Further, as just discussed, the organizational approach is only one of several that might be relevant to the study of social policy implementation. Given such a wide sweep of disciplinary areas and substantive approaches, it is clearly premature to claim that no relevant work will be discovered.

A few cautious statements seem warranted. First, just as with the lack of implementation concerns in social agencies, the lack of specific research on social policy implementation is baffling—a Kafkaesque situation of ignoring fundamental issues for which there seems to be no explanation. Second, search in other areas yields no obvious candidates for a ready mining of research techniques or studies directly relevant to social policy implementation.[22] Third, at this point not enough is known about implementation in social organizations to do more than determine the lack of obvious relevance of available research. Scholars simply have not yet done enough research, including theory building, on social policy implementation to be good appraisers of the more subtle relevance of past work in the social sciences—and in saying this I recognize full well

22. For an excellent effort to determine the relevance of past work to the study of implementing educational innovation, see Paul Berman and Milbrey McLaughlin, *Federal Programs Supporting Educational Change*, vol. 1, *A Model of Educational Change*, R–1589/1–HEW (Santa Monica, Calif.: The Rand Corporation, September 1974), pp. 3–11.

that more sophistication may show its irrelevance. Fourth, the biggest research need is to focus directly on social policy implementation, probably through careful case studies. At the same time, case material becomes more useful when ordered by a theoretical framework, but *probably* no single best theoretical framework will emerge. Rather, it is more likely that sound case material will be more valuable when approached by people with different disciplinary perspectives and frameworks that provide diverse interpretations. So let variety flower.

However, and this is the last proposition, a great deal should not be expected from research alone. Part of the reason is that it is most unlikely that social science breakthroughs in treating dynamics will be made in the near future. I am pessimistic about our present chances of developing the level of technical capability needed to make accurate *ex ante* predictions about which factors will bring about the acceptance of innovation and its successful implementation in a complex bureaucratic/political environment. In short, our research tools hardly seem likely to handle bureaucratic and political intrigue with great sophistication.

### Techniques of Implementation Analysis and Assessment

When considering major program innovations, decision-makers in social agencies should have available *ex ante* analyses addressing the likelihood that an innovation (1) will produce positive outcomes, (2) will be accepted by higher-level decision-makers, (3) can be put in place properly with available resources, and (4) will be accepted by those in the field who must either implement or operate the innovation. The first two are (or should be) the principal components of policy analysis; the second two, of implementation analysis. Asking *ex ante* whether a proposed policy alternative is likely to work has been fundamental to policy analysis. And now central analysts are getting more involved in determining whether the White House and the Congress will accept a new proposal and in developing an agency strategy for selling the idea.

It is important to realize not only that the two aspects of policy analysis are the counterparts of the two components of implementation analysis but also that the basic approaches to each set of questions are similar. Generally speaking, the big need in policy analysis has not been for overpowering techniques but rather for reasonableness, sensitivity, and the ability to order and synthesize diverse pieces of information that often are fragmentary and conflicting. The unfortunate tendency of early advocates of policy analysis to describe it in terms of such esoteric names as systems analysis (and worse) masked the truth that the better practitioners were seldom using much more than simple principles straight out of Paul Samuelson as a framework for formulating their inquiry. Nor in most cases were the analysts working with major research studies specifically performed to shed light on the main questions at issue; rather, they were usually trying to see if scattered research done for other purposes might provide a clue. Frequently the most useful information concerned existing programs and projects—some of it coming from formal reporting systems and some from discussions with people who had observed these activities. Over time, central analytic offices have supported relatively sophisticated research, such as the New Jersey negative income tax experiment, to develop information needed for decision-making. But it would be a great mistake not to recognize that the critical requirement in policy analysis continues to be for reasonable people asking sensible questions. The same can be said of implementation analysis. By this I do not mean to imply that implementation analysis is easy but rather that it involves activities which are much more familiar to us than might be thought.

Implementation analysis starts with a consideration of the clarity, precision, comprehensiveness, and reasonableness of the preliminary policy or design specifications. The analyst must ask if the proposal idea, rather than being merely a vaporous wish, addresses reasonable objectives cast in relatively specific terms, and if the treatment package is reasonably well specified. Specifications might include both physical and personnel inputs (equipment, skills) and expected outcomes in terms of physical and behavioral changes. Some sketchiness can be expected because the analysis concerns preliminary specifications that will go through additional rounds before reaching a final product. At the same time, it seems that the absence of any concreteness in terms of either objectives or the delivery system should be taken as a clear indicator of grave trouble at the beginning.

Implementation analysis, then, should investigate (1) the technical capacity to implement, (2) political feasibility, and (3) the technical and political strategies for implementation. The question of technical capacity is twofold. First, does the organization have sufficiently developed lines of communication (the means of communicating a decision to the field), a good enough administrative structure, and sufficient numbers of individuals with requisite administrative and technical skills in specific substantive areas to have a reasonable probability of moving the innovation into the field? Second, do the local operating entities have, or can they obtain, the staff skills needed to administer the treatment package? These questions certainly are not easy ones, but simply posing them may uncover such grave deficiencies that either action on the innovation will be postponed or major corrective measures will be seen as required. Much the same may be said for issues of political feasibility. One hardly needs a political crystal ball to know with some certainty that certain individuals and groups will oppose certain actions.

Just as important as the technical and political problems is the question of whether or not the organization can develop an implementation strategy to overcome potential blockages. For example, an effort to implement an innovation may seem feasible only after extensive efforts are undertaken to train people. It may make sense to try out a new idea on a small scale before making a full commitment to a national program. And even if a national program has already been decided upon, it still might be useful to carry out the implementation in stages, "starting small" to develop information on implementation problems. Alternatively, a special team could be created for the one-time effort to implement a new program. Such a team might be drawn from several different parts of an agency and would be disbanded after the implementation was completed. The team would have responsibility and authority to cut across the many layers involved in the implementation process.[23]

In devising a strategy for surmounting political barriers, scenarios might be developed to look at such factors as the principal actors, their motivations, and their beliefs.[24] Once the nature of the opposi-

23. Businesses sometimes use such an approach, usually labeled project management. A project manager and a small team of experts from various functional areas plan and coordinate a project that cuts across several departments. Once the project is deemed operational, the members of the project management team return to their regular jobs.

24. See: Arnold J. Meltsner, "Political Feasibility and Policy Analysis," *Public Administration Review*, November/December 1972, pp. 859–66. This article provides a useful summary of approaches to the analysis of political feasibility that are relevant to the following discussion.

tion is determined, the problem is to figure out how to get around it or eliminate it. A key question may concern the possible trade-offs between specification and flexibility that were discussed earlier. It is unrealistic to expect any implementation strategy to yield a surefire means of overcoming technical blockages and political opposition. But it makes little sense not to investigate the various potential blockages and then develop a strategy so that at least the obvious blunders might be avoided. So whether a reasonable strategy exists is a critical final question in implementation analysis.

Implementation assessment seeks to determine the extent to which the actual outputs of an organization have changed in the expected direction after the introduction of an innovation. How can it be determined whether or not the staff in an organization have changed their behavior, the way they interact with others, or their sentiments about the organization, other staff, or clients? Apparently it can be done. O'Connell, for example, in a study of an outside consultant's effort to initiate changes in a life insurance company's selling (branch) offices, made such an assessment through direct observation and the investigation of detailed records. In the study he recorded and measured the activities, interactions, and sentiments of staff in a small number of branch offices before and after the consultant's intervention.[25] O'Connell was able to determine significant output changes in the desired direction by applying the techniques of a trained nonparticipant observer armed mainly with a stopwatch (the branch manager spoke 11.35 minutes at a sales conference) and lots of recording materials. It seems to me, admittedly not an expert in doing this form of research, that people with substantive knowledge of the situation being studied, reasonable knowledge of organizational behavior, and some sensitivity can carry out this type of study to yield useful implementation information.

25. Jeremiah J. O'Connell, *Managing Organizational Innovations* (Homewood, Ill.: Richard D. Irwin, Inc., 1968). Even though direct applications from business to government are sometimes hazardous, the reader may find this volume useful for several reasons. First, it contains an extensive bibliography on earlier uses of the techniques employed. Second, it illustrates issues of implementation strategy through its description of the detailed planning of the implementation effort, which included the development of field instructions specifying both the physical and behavioral changes expected and the development of a multistage approach. Finally, O'Connell is able to obtain some outcome measures and presents an interesting discussion of output and outcome relationships.

As might be expected, however, implementation assessment presents a host of problems. There are technical and logistical difficulties in developing feedback mechanisms for intermediate implementation assessment. Seldom have organizations been able to construct reporting systems that provide useful information either for correcting or assessing a project. Equally difficult is the determination of appropriate points at which to assess implementation. One certainly can expect to hear the claim so frequently made in evaluations that it is much too early for an assessment. This claim should not necessarily be seen as an operator's rationalization for poor performances. The movement toward successful operations may not be along a straight path of improvement without setbacks. So even when the analyst knows how to assess implementation, he or she must still contend with judgmental issues concerning timing.

We can pursue issues of implementation analysis and assessment further by considering two techniques that may be used by social agencies to facilitate or carry out these activities—demonstration projects and monitoring. Historically, demonstration programs in the social agencies were often disguised operating efforts to meet political demands in a setting unencumbered by the restrictions of regular programs. Even when the demonstration effort did try to test new ideas, the programs often were administered by action-oriented people who were both impatient with and distrustful of relatively rigorous assessment procedures. Moreover, these projects in the best of circumstances focused on inputs and outputs, not on the project outcomes that are so dear to the hearts of policy analysts. For these reasons, research-oriented analysts have looked down on demonstration projects and on the action-oriented people who developed and funded them. Such projects might have been tolerated to keep bureaucratic peace in an agency but were considered to be of little value for purposes of developing information.

It is now becoming clear that such projects can serve a useful function in the development of information. This is especially true when decisions about new programs have been made or have a high probability of being made in the near future. Once a planning or budgeting process indicates that program changes will be made in the upcoming fiscal year, an elaborate experimental project taking several years is out of the question. The political decision has already been made. However, it may be appropriate to carry out one or more demonstration projects that will provide both a test of administrative and political feasibility and useful implementing experience. Indeed, a most reasonable proposition is that the administrative bugs ought to be worked out in a small-scale effort before any complex new program is launched full-scale.

This situation is different from the one in which a small-scale field testing program is undertaken in order to develop information concerning possible program alternatives *before* decisions are made. In the latter case, demonstration projects may be viewed in the same light as experiments. Time is available to develop and execute a research design, where it might not be in the case of demonstration projects for approved decisions.[26] While less severe than for experiments, the necessary conditions for a demonstration project to have a reasonable probability of yielding information useful for major program decisions are quite demanding. Moreover, the conditions are similar to those for experiments. This is hardly strange, as the reason for doing both kinds of projects is to generate information of sufficiently broad applicability to facilitate the *making* of major decisions. To provide such information, a demonstration project must be specified in operational terms and implemented in the field to meet these specifications. Further, the research design should support broad application and permit comparison with alternative concepts. If demonstration projects are to provide information for future major decisions, they must be carefully designed to yield information that can be generalized to many projects.

It is important to recognize the limits of the information derived even from well-designed demonstration projects. The information *can* show that the project adhered to its specifications and overcame political or administrative problems to become a viable activity, but *not* that the project benefited the participants. Yet even with no information on outcomes, sound information about the degree to which a well-defined program strategy can be implemented, *plus experience in the actual implementation,* is so much better than what we now have that the only debatable point is whether it *can* be gotten, not whether it *should* be.

Whether sound demonstration projects can be carried out is moot. First, the technical requirements noted above are formidable although generally significantly less severe than in an experiment for

26. If time does permit, the requirements presented below would also apply generally to field testing of approved decisions.

the same activity. Second, political and bureaucratic timing problems loom large. For example, will decision-makers take the time to allow for a good design and wait for its results? No one can say. However, the notion of sound demonstrations is so crucial to the improvement of implementation procedures in social policy organizations that it should be pushed. So while we must refrain from expecting too much, we must also see that some beginning efforts, even if halting, would be a great leap forward.

Agency monitoring generally involves site visits by teams composed of national and regional staffs, outside consultants, and/or local operators from other projects who consider such factors as administrative management practices, adherence to stated guidelines, and staff capability. In the past, monitoring efforts have focused far too much on inputs in a static sense, on relatively low-level administrative practices, or on issues of financial accountability. Yet monitoring has been the closest thing in the agency to an implementation assessment technique. A competent team of people with in-depth knowledge of both program substance and financial/administrative matters well may produce the kind of information needed to judge whether or not an activity is moving toward implementation success.

The main problems with monitoring have had less to do with techniques per se and more with a failure to ask the right questions. Again, perhaps the failure to specify substance has been a major culprit. The problem might be described as one of specification imbalance slanting concern toward financial and administrative practices. As Horst and her associates observe in discussing the development of social program guidelines,

> how-to-do-it rule making is the third kind of language that is commonly found. Here the terms are very concrete and specific. We find guidance on factors like the qualifications of project directors, the contents of affiliation agreements with other local agencies, reporting relationships, the use of consultants, and accounting practices. This guidance appears to be definite and all inclusive. Closer examination shows that it usually tells how to run the part of a project which does not deal directly with the intervention into society. Guidance for the part of the project which actually produces effects in society is not provided.[27]

27. Horst et al., "Program Management," p. 303.

However, if reasonable specifications about the program's operating elements exist, a monitoring team made up of relatively competent people who have in-depth knowledge about programs and bureaucracy, and who have not necessarily been trained as social scientists, should be able to assess both compliance with specifications and the viability of the project.

The issue of assessing viability needs further comment. Assessment in this case involves *ex post facto* judgments of whether an activity is running well in bureaucratic/political terms, not *ex ante* statements about which variables will yield smooth functioning. In the former situation, people with well-honed bureaucratic sensitivities should be able to assess within tolerable limits how well an activity is going and whether it is beginning to fit into its institutional environment. Surely it ought to be possible to spot the bad cases— but not necessarily to know what to do about them, since that step requires *ex ante* prediction.

The central role of reasoned judgment in assessing implementation should be clearly delineated. A static checklist of all the specified inputs (one teacher, two teacher aides, three talking typewriters, and so on) will not indicate the viability of the project. On the other hand, enough missing pieces may spell trouble. The exercise of judgment or of a composite of judgments of an activity in motion seems the only way to determine viability. At the same time, technique may facilitate judgment. A set of "dynamic" questions (e.g., does the principal support the project?), a common scaling system, or a sampling frame may keep those carrying out the assessment from missing important issues, provide a useful means of comparing judgments, and avoid selectivity biases. Good judgment, however, remains the key element. Methodology simply does not appear to be the big barrier. Nor do I see the need for highly trained social scientists to carry out the various tasks. The biggest need is not for hotshot methodology types but for competent, reasonable people with sound substantive knowledge of programs and of bureaucracy.

### CONCLUDING OBSERVATIONS

Implementation is a difficult topic, partly because it embraces a number of seemingly paradoxical notions. On the one hand, the underlying theme of this issue of *Policy Analysis* is the central importance of implementation for improving social program operations, policy analysis, and social experimentation. On the other hand, there is a mystifying neglect of implementation issues by social program people at all levels, by policy analysts, and by researchers. In the same vein, much discussion has focused on the great complexity of implementation, especially in a many-layered setting, with some of the problems apparently well beyond our present capabilities. Yet it is also argued that the immediate need is not for methodological breakthroughs but for the application of simple techniques with some common sense.

The first paradoxical pair—the importance of implementation versus its neglect—is something we shall have to live with, but hopefully not for too long. The second, the matter of methodology, bears further discussion and provides some suitable concluding observations for this paper.

How is the methodology issue to be reconciled? Both the systematic study of implementation and the development of better techniques for such study are needed. However, methodology may not be that much of a blockage during initial efforts to improve implementation in a social policy organization. This is so because the most basic descriptive information is in quite short supply. Under such circumstances, only the simplest methodological tools may be required to determine more precisely the structure of the implementation process (the level of technical competence, the degree of emphasis on administrative inputs, etc.) and the extent of communications between various levels and segments of an organization. Such studies often may produce mainly negative information showing deficiencies and misdirections. To recognize this fact, however, in no way negates the pressing need to fill these massive gaps in our knowledge. Moreover, the basic knowledge derived about implementation can help shape our understanding of what needs to be done if a social policy organization wants to improve implementation.

Beyond some point, progress will be difficult. Here the lack of techniques looms large. It is now beyond our ability in many cases to develop effective treatment packages through experimentation or other means and to determine effective means of implementation through the study of the dynamics of that process. Indeed, no one can be confident that research on the dynamics of implementation will yield major results in the near term. We must recognize both that implementation is where the research action ought to be and that progress is likely to be slow.

I would offer this as a single guiding rule: Always think about implementation problems, and always worry that others are not thinking about them, but do not expect major improvements to come quickly. This message—especially the stricture against expecting too much too fast—has particular relevance for the policy analyst. First, it has been argued that by far the most important step toward improvement is the strong commitment on the part of management (top decision-makers) to deal with implementation problems. Since this commitment will require significant organizational changes with high bureaucratic costs, matters seem certain to proceed slowly. Analysts may work for such changes, but the changes must occur before their own efforts in the implementation process will have any large payoff.

Policy analysts should be realistic not only about their organizations but also about their own skills and techniques. They have suffered from a naive overconfidence that has resulted in disappointment with and disparagement of limited success. Like sports fans, analysts dream of the big change that will take the team to first place. First it was PPB; then evaluation and experimentation. Now we analysts may be boarding the implementation bandwagon, seeking again the sure technological fix. This would be a grave mistake. Implementation analysis and assessment should not become the new hope for technical ascendance. If we listen to history, we should anticipate neither rapid technical advances nor smooth sailing for recommendations based on implementation analysis and assessment. This is not to counsel despair but to recognize both that progress is likely to be slow and that it is more likely to occur if we formulate reasonable notions of success.

# 9

# Feet of Clay in Hobnail Boots: An Assessment of Statistical Inference in Applied Research

*Richard A. Berk and Marilynn Brewer*

## INTRODUCTION

If there is one thing as certain as death and taxes, it is the routine application of statistical inference to quantitative evaluation research. Whether the probabilistic answer to a legitimate empirical question, the simple transcription of computer printout, or the ritual certification of scientific research, statistical inference is commonly attempted from virtually all manner of data. If broadly conceived as an effort to assess the role of random indeterminancy in research findings, these practices should be aplauded. However, admirable intention is insufficient. Too often statistical inference is either overused or misused with obfuscation and misunderstanding a typical result. In this paper, we will undertake a didactic review of some especially popular abuses and then try to provide clear rationales for the appropriate application of statistical inference in evaluation research.

## STATISTICAL INFERENCE AS HOBNAIL BOOTS

While we will later consider far more formally several legitimate models of statistical inference, it may prove useful at this point to remind some readers what, in general terms, statistical inference is intended to demonstrate. First, "Classical" statistical inference rests fundamentally on the idea of long run outcomes: the proportion of times over the long run that certain chance events will occur.[1] Thus, when we claim for example, that a particular difference between an experimental and control group is statistically significant at the .05 level, we are saying that, if there were actually no treatment effect, the given disparity could occur only five times out of a hundred were the identical study repeated over and over. In other words, we are claiming that the experimental result would occur so infrequently by chance alone that we rule out "luck of

AUTHORS' NOTE: George Borhnstedt and William Bielby provided a number of helpful suggestions and entertaining quips. We are grateful for both.

From Richard A. Berk and Marilynn Brewer, "Feet of clay in Hobnail Boots: An Assessment of Statistical Inference in Applied Research." Unpublished manuscript, 1977.

the draw" as an explanation for the effect; something else must be involved.[2] Alternatively, when we claim that a particular estimate of experimental effect has a .95 confidence interval of 20 units, for example, we are saying that if the identical study were repeated a very large number of times, 95 out of 100 such intervals around the sample statistic would include the "real" value of the effect we are trying to assess. Note, that the "real" value of the effect is taken as constant (though unknown), and what changes from replication to replication is *interval* (Barnett, 1973: 35). From this logic, it is generally agreed that the smaller the confidence interval for a given experiment and probability level, the more "accurate" one's estimate of treatment effects.[3] In short, whether one employs significance tests or confidence intervals, one is trying to assess the importance of random processes over the long run "contaminating" estimates of "real" processes.

While we would be among the first to acknowledge important ambiguities in current inferential procedures (see Morrison and Henkel, 1970; Barnett, 1973; Hollis and Nell, 1975), our initial purpose is to review common misapplications, not the more abstract issues debated by statisticians and philosophers of science. In other words, we will temporarily assume that classical approaches to statistical inference are essentially sound and within this framework address several practical matters.

Perhaps the most fundamental misunderstanding surrounding statistical inference involves a common assumption that once statistical significance has been achieved, the overall validity of one's findings is assured. In fact, statistical significance addresses only one of a large set of threats to validity (Campbell and Stanley, 1966; Cook and Campbell, 1975) and in many instances is the least of one's problem. In other words, research findings may be inaccurate for a host of reasons having *nothing* to do with random processes: poor measures, nonequivalent control groups, faulty summary statistics, subject reactivity, and so on. Yet, it is common to see claims for statistical significance trample over other considerations which in fact are far more important to any reasonable interpretation of treatment effects.

Derived in part from this rather general obsession with statistical significance, come a variety of more specific misunderstandings. For example, it is common to find researchers mistaking statistical significance for substantive significance. In fact, a social program may well produce effects which achieve the .05 level but which nevertheless have trivial practical implications. Put another way, by obtaining a very large sample one can almost guarantee statistical significance regardless of the real size of treatment effects. Similarly, it is common to find researchers interpreting significance levels (e.g., .05, .01, .001) as measures of the *size* of treatment effects. That is, an effect which achieves a smaller significance (alpha) level is presumed to be larger or more important. While it is true that ceteris paribus larger effects are more likely to be statistically significant, many other characteristics of the analysis are necessarily involved: the sample size, measurement reliability, the choice of test statistic (e.g., parametric versus nonparametric), the manner in which other variables besides the treatment effect are held constant, the location of the region of rejection (e.g., one-tail versus two-tail tests) and so on. In short, we have a large number of appropriate effect measures ranging from simple differences between means to nominal, ordinal, and interval coefficients, but alpha levels are not among them. Finally, it is incorrect to interpret alpha levels as indicators of one's subjective "confidence" in the results unless one is fully prepared to apply a Bayesian view of probability. A rejection of the null hypothesis at the .001 level does not make one more certain that a particular effect is "real" than a rejection at the .05 level. We will have a lot more to say about this later. Likewise, a more narrow confidence interval simply states that in numerous samples, the "real" effect will be included within a smaller range of possible values, it says nothing about how certain one is that for a given sample the population parameter falls within the interval. Again, we will consider this problem more carefully later.

Coupled with the misleading overemphasis on statistical significance are a number of related misunderstandings which only make interpretative errors more severe. Perhaps the most common problem involves confusion about what a failure to reject the null hypothesis means. It does *not* mean that the null hypothesis is actually correct. It only means that if it were correct, one could easily have obtained the sample statistic by chance alone. In fact, a very large number of null hypotheses similar to the one under consideration are almost certain to be consistent with the sample data. For example, a null hypothesis of no difference between experimentals and controls may be associated with an observed difference between experimental and control means of ¼ of a grade in reading skill. That disparity might be estimated to occur 20 times out of a hundred in numerous replications, sufficiently likely to retain the null hypothesis of no difference. However, if the null hypothesis were 1/10th of a grade level difference, the ¼ of a grade level disparity in observed reading skill between experimentals and controls might occur 25 times out of a hundred in numerous replications. Thus, this null hypothesis also would not be rejected. Indeed, it would seem more consistent with the data (i.e., in the maximum likelihood sense that it would produce the observed disparity more often)! In short, while we have developed research conventions which allow us to reject hypotheses when they are inconsistent with the data, we have no similar mechanisms for accepting null hypotheses as true. Rather, we "retain" the null hypothesis as a tentative *assumption* subject to further study.

The question of rejection of the null hypothesis raises an even more fundamental problem of why we conventionally assume a null hypothesis of "no effect." In other words, we begin our evaluation research with a premise that the intervention will fail; the burden of proof rests on the intervention to show a "real" effect. Clearly, this is inherently conservative. We retain the status quo unless strong evidence suggests the opposite. For many programs which on their face are at least benign, why not assume a treatment effect until the data proves otherwise? For example, in the case of Head Start, a popular program with parents, teachers, and students alike, why not initially assume an improvement of one grade level in reading skill until the data suggests differently?[4] That is, one would entertain the "null hypothesis" of a one grade level improvement and apply a one-tail test on improvements of *less* than one grade level.

However, in other instances one might *want* to favor a conservative position. For example, for programs which are controversial, dangerous or morally questionable, one would want to be very sure that only really large positive effects would be considered (Berk and Rossi, 1976). Thus, one might assume a "null hypothesis" of a 20 percent reduction in heroin traffic resulting from increased use of electronic surveillance and then apply one-tail tests for observed effects *larger* than a 20 percent reduction. The point is that researchers routinely begin with a null hypothesis of no difference when in fact that is not the most relevant or important premise.

In summary, statistical inference must not be interpreted as the dominant prerequisite of sound evaluation research. Statistical inference is designed to respond to one particular set of problems, and problems which are often both less important and less interesting than others. Moreover, far from the certification of "scientific validity," slavery to statistical inference reflects mindless, ritualistic research which too often diverts attention from more pressing matters. Given this tendency to rely so heavily on the trappings of rigor, the all too common additional interpretative errors would seem to turn mere tunnel vision into virtual blindness.

## STATISTICAL INFERENCE AS FEET OF CLAY

Classical statistical inference is designed to produce precise probability statements about the long run impact of stochastic factors on estimates of program (in the case of evaluation research) effects. However, as Hollis and Nell emphasize, "statistics does not become a calculus of probabilities either merely by being mathematically sound or merely by being christened a calculus of probabilities. . . . Statistics is a calculus of *probabilities* only insofar as some statement that known correlations[5] are likely to hold in unknown cases is true." (1975: 76, italics are the authors'.) In other words, one carefully specifies a particular model of the stochastic processes which is then usually *assumed* to hold in numerous independent replications. Or, as Malinvaud observes, "a [inferential] procedure will be approved to the extent that it would give good results if applied repeatedly to independent samples arising from the same process." (1970: 69). This means that one must specify a particular model of the stochastic process operating in the generation of observed data and then argue that the model remains invariant in repeated, independent "trials." Put more strongly, in the absence of numerous, independent (typically hypothetical) replications of a stochastic process, classical inference is meaningless. Clearly then, one critical task in any application of statistical inferences involves a precise description of the stochastic model and the circumstances in which it is applicable. We turn now to a review of such models, beginning with relatively simple ones.

## THE RANDOM SAMPLING MODEL

The mathematician Polya defines "generalization" as "passing from the consideration of a given set of objects to that of a larger set, containing the given set" (1954: 12). This process may be undertaken through accepted theory and prior studies or in combination with particular kinds of information derived from the manner in which the observed data were collected. The former approach is common in experimental studies when, for example, a researcher claims that characteristics of a work-release program in one state may well be similar to characteristics of work-release programs in other states (e.g., Waldo and Chiricos, 1977). Such generalizations are made with no reference to probability, but by arguing, at least implicitly, that particular programs and their subjects across different states are reasonably similar. In other words, stochastic processes are not formally addressed in such extrapolation. In the latter case, common in public opinion polls, to the degree that one can specify the stochastic processes by which the sample was chosen, statistical inference is directly relevant to the generalization effort. It is here that a random sampling model becomes appropriate.

The random sampling model begins by assuming that there exists some defined population of objects described by observations having fixed values; that is, nonstochastic values. Kish emphasizes this important point: "Imagine a file of N cards, each of which contains the desired measurement ($Y_i$) or measurements ($X_i$, $Y_i$, $Z_i$ ...) for one of the population elements. Computations on the entire file would produce the constant population value" (1965: 5). In other words, were one to compute the value of a univariate statistic such as the mean of $Y_i$ (or any other variable) for all of the N cards (e.g., the mean income for N individuals) over and over again, even spaced some time apart, one would always obtain the same result.

In many circumstances it is not feasible to obtain measures on the entire population of N potential cases. The costs in time and money may be prohibitive, or simply unnecessary. Therefore, one selects a subset of observations for study. In the case of N file cards, "sampling would consist of selecting a fraction of the cards" (Kish, 1965: 5). However, by sampling the potential observations, stochastic indeterminacy is usually built into one's data. Unless one chooses precisely the same observations in repeated samples, each sample will have a somewhat different composition. One consequence is that if one wanted to estimate the values of certain summary measures in the population (e.g., the population's mean income), different samples would generate different estimates. Obviously, this creates serious problems for the researcher since extrapolations to population characteristics will differ depending on the particular sample (or samples) on hand.

Fortunately, insofar as one chooses samples based on some clearly specified probability model, one can gauge the impact of the sampling procedures on one's population estimates.[6] The typical model requires that each observation (case) has a known probability of being selected which follows from the manner in which sampling is undertaken. Common techniques employ a table of random numbers or something approximating a "fair" lottery. Then, it is usually easy to estimate the sampling distribution of population estimates which describes the proportion of the time in numerous selection "trials" that various estimates would appear. From this information, confidence intervals and significance tests may be produced.

A bit more formally, Kmenta notes (1971: 104) that it is often instructive to consider a probability sample of size n ($x_1$, $x_2$, ... $x_n$) for a *given* variable as a particular instance or "realization" of n independent (assuming sampling with replacement), identically distributed random variables ($X_1$, $X_2$, ... $X_n$). They are random *solely because of the selection procedures*. For example, in the first sample, the first observation selected might be the income of the Jones family, in the second sample, the first observation might be the income of the Smith family, and so on. In other words, the probability sampling process takes a population of *fixed* values and generates observations which are now *stochastic,* and stochastic in predictable ways.

While the model assumes a very large number of independent probability samples drawn with identical procedures from a population of fixed values, in practice the researcher works with a single probability sample. This creates no serious problems as long as the actual sampling techniques closely approximate a single application of the underlying assumed model. In other words, the researcher is able to project what would happen *hypothetically* if many samples were in fact drawn in the specified manner.

The hypothetical sampling distribution of population estimates has at least three important applications. First, statisticians may use its properties to mathematically justify some estimators and estimation procedures over others. While this is usually of little immediate relevance to the applied researcher, it may be comforting to know that classical inference has a reasonably parsimonious foundation. Thus, that we typically estimate the variance by dividing the sum of squares of N-1 rather than N, for instance, is not based on whim or fancy but the desire for "unbiased" estimators.[7] Second, the hypothetical sampling distribution can be used to construct confidence intervals. These communicate the degree of precision that one might expect in estimates of population characteristics in repeated random samples. Finally, the hypothetical sampling distribution may be used in formal hypothesis testing in which case the inferential process is, in a sense, put in reverse. We start with assumed characteristics of an unobserved population and assess the probability that the sample characteristics would emerge in repeated drawings from that population. In other words, we are testing the "plausibility" of the assumption that random sampling from a specified population was the process by which the observed sample was generated.

To illustrate hypothesis testing, let us assume that based on prior research we know that the distribution of scores on a particular attitude scale for the population of U.S. college students in 1955 has a mean of 50 and a standard deviation of 10. A random sample of 500 U.S. college students in 1976 is found to have a mean of 52.5 on the same attitude measure. The question is whether the distribution of attitudes has changed during the intervening period.

One might begin with a null hypothesis of no change;[8] that is, the population of 1976 students has a mean of 50 and a standard deviation of 10. Then with information about the probability distribution of sample means, for example, (for samples of 500) randomly drawn from a population with the given parameters, the relative frequency of obtaining a sample mean at least as extreme as 52.5 may be used to determine the "plausibility" that this sample means would have occurred *if* the parent population had parameters identical to those of the 1955 population.[9] Note that this inferential process does not inform us what population values the sample actually reflects. If the null hypothesis is not rejected, it only means that such a sample *could* have been rather "easily" obtained by a random sampling of the specified population. If the null hypothesis is rejected (and because the random sampling has been actually observed), it is judged "unlikely" that the 1955 population mean is the same as the 1976 population mean. In this case, it might then be useful to estimate (with confidence intervals) the new mean.

Tests of the significance for difference between two or more sample means follow the same inferential logic. If a random sample is taken from one population and a second sample is drawn from a different population, the hypothesis testing model is usually applied to the null hypothesis that the two populations have identical means on the measure of interest. In this case, the obtained difference between sample means is compared to the probability distribution of the differences between means to be expected if pairs of independent samples were repeatedly drawn from the populations with a common mean. Again, the resulting probability estimate tells us nothing about the actual characteristics of the parent populations, only the extent to which the sample differences *could* have been generated by a process of random sampling from a single population.

It is important to understand that despite conventional practice, the underlying logic of classical statistical inference has been frequently challenged (e.g., Barnett, 1973). First, the hypothesis testing strategy rests fundamentally on the proportion of times in *repeated samples* that a particular estimate could occur (given a particular value of the population parameter). Yet, we make our decision to reject or not based on a *single sample* in which a *single* estimate has occurred. It is not at all clear what the probability over the long run of obtaining a given estimate communicates about the "probability" of obtaining the given estimate in a single sample. [10] In one telling sense, the probability of obtaining the estimates is 1.0 since it did in fact occur.

Second, the choice of a given level of significance (e.g., .01) while conventional, is still basically arbitrary. Decision theorists such as Ferguson (1967) have argued that the location and size of the rejection region should directly and formally reflect the *practical* consequences of rejecting the null hypothesis when it is true or not rejecting it when it is false. This requires in turn quantifying the actual costs of both kinds of errors and then choosing the region of rejection so that one's "losses" are minimized.

Third, it is all too easy to forget the underlying stochastic model and the relative frequency definition of probability in practical situations. As Lindley (1965: 68) explains,

> The probability quoted in the example of a significance test is a frequency probability derived from random sampling from a normal distribution: if one was to keep taking samples from the distribution, the histogram of the values of x̄ obtained would tend to $N(\theta, \sigma^2/N)$. But the interpretation of the prabability is in terms of degree of belief, because the 5%, or 1%, is a measure of how much belief is attached to the null hypothesis (H:$\theta = \bar{\theta}$). It is used as if 5% significance meant the posterior probability that $\theta$ is near $\theta$ is 0.05. This is not so: the distortion of the meaning is quite wrong in general.

Put another way, the random sampling model necessarily assumes that population values and therefore population parameters are fixed, while the sample composition and therefore sample statistics vary. The Bayesian model assumes that the population parameters vary while the given, single sample is fixed. For the former, one calculates how often in numerous independent samples, given particular population parameter values, one could have obtained the observed result. For the latter, one calculates how "likely" the assumed population parameters are, given the particular sample. Confusion often results from the fact that policy makers typically want to know how likely a particular value is when the researcher actually provides probability statements from the classical inferential model.

Finally, it is also easy to forget that while a decision about a null hypothesis is a firm binary decision (reject or not), it is possible to be wrong. This means that the potential for Type I and Type II errors [11] is often ignored and serious misunderstanding can result. Thus, if 20 independent significance tests were undertaken, on the average one will be statistically significant at the .05 level simply by chance alone: a Type I error. Yet, it is so very tempting to interpret such "findings" substantively, that otherwise sophisticated researchers are often seduced. We will have more to say about this later.

Similar problems plague confidence intervals. In particular, unless a policy maker wants to assess the consequences of stochastic sampling error in the context of what would happen *on the average* over numerous studies, the information provided is at best ambiguous. As Barnett (1973: 158) Notes:

> Suppose from data we obtain a 95% confidence interval for $\mu$ as $29.5 < \mu < 30.2$. It is suggested that it is of little value to someone needing to act in this situation to know that the '95% confidence' attaches not to the specific statement made, but to what proportion of such similarly based statements will be correct in the long run. This correct interpretation may justify the statistician in his professional activities at large (in the long run his advice is correct on 95 percent of occasions), but what of the present situation? A statistically naive client will almost inevitably attach the 95 percent to the statement $29.5 < \mu < 30.2$; the statistician himself can hardly avoid doing so implicitly when he puts the information to any practical use! Any probability interpretation of such an attitude must be interpreted in nonfrequency terms, for example, as a statement of the *subjective* probability. But with what justification? The Bayesian approach does not provide justification; although supporting such a statement in principle, it may lead to a quite different numerical result for the confidence interval.

In short, Barnett is arguing that the random sampling model is of somewhat limited value in many practical situations, and turning to a half-baked Bayesian interpretation does not really solve the problem. If inferences are to be drawn from a single sample in terms of the confidence one has about particular estimates, one best rely formally on Bayesian procedures.

## THE RANDOM ASSIGNMENT MODEL

The random assignment model addresses a different kind of problem: the degree to which chance is ruled out as an explanation for observed *associations* between the assignments of individuals to groups and their scores on an outcome measure of interest. However, like the random sampling model, chance factors formally enter not as a result of the social forces under study, but as a consequence of actions undertaken by the researcher.

In essence, the need for a probability model for random assignment emerges from a "solution" to another problem. In order to isolate the impact of a "treatment" on a group of subjects (or other units such as plots of land) from the impact of other factors, researchers often attempt to compare subjects receiving the treatment with subjects not receiving the treatment. However, insofar as such groups differ in important characteristics *before* the treatment is applied, the effects of these differences are confounded with any disparities resulting from the treatment. Therefore, it is desirable to shuffle subjects randomly such that a random subset are exposed to the treatment(s) and a random subset are not exposed to the treatment(s). Any systematic pre-existing differences between the two subsets are thus transformed into random group differences.

Unfortunately, the fact that subjects are randomly assigned to treatment and control conditions does not guarantee that even in the aggregate, the groups will actually be identical. The "luck of the draw" may generate nonequivalence (thus confounding treatment effects with "selection" effects), but the chances of this occurring can be ascertained; one *knows* the processes by which the assignment was undertaken. The random assignment model describes these processes and allows the researcher to gauge through statistical inference, the probability over the long run that what one takes for treatment effects actually results from initial chance differences between experimentals and controls (Fisher, 1971: 13-14; Lindquist, 1953: 11-12).

More formally, the assignment to either an experimental or control group can be viewed as a random event which each subject *individually* experiences (like the flip of a coin). If one were to arbitrarily define some variable "X" as equal to 1 should a *given* subject wind up in the experimental group and 0 should the same subject wind up in the control group, X becomes a random variable. With the number of people given 0s and the number of people given 1s predetermined (i.e., the group sizes), the marginals of the assignment process are known and fixed in repeated assignments of the subject pool.

Given N subjects, there would be N independent and identically distributed random variables. Then, just as in the random sampling model, each random variable would have a probability distribution (in this case binominal), and the set of random variables would have a joint probability distribution. Hence, one could speak about the pattern of 1s and 0s for a given "trial" as a "realization" of the underlying random assignment process.

Recall that the random sampling model was in part concerned with the impact of probability sampling on estimates of population parameters. In the random assignment case, this becomes a substantively trivial issue. While one could speak about "generalizations" to the population of all possible random assignment patterns for the given pool of subjects, proportions in the experimental and control groups are either fixed in advance or easily estimated a priori from knowledge of the random assignment process. Therefore, the thrust of the random assignment model is the assessment of chance *associations* between assignment to treatment and control groups and other characteristics of the subjects.

Though usually of secondary interest, subjects and their a priori *fixed* characteristics are seen as randomly shuffled between experimental and control groups so that any associations between assignment and confounding influences are a consequence of the luck of the draw. In other words, the expected value of any association between treatment and "biography" is zero. Of critical çoncern, however, the standard null hypothesis assumes that subjects have *already* attached a fixed[12] value(s) on the dependent variable(s) which is randomly associated with the treatment. In the absence of a "real" treatment effect, the expected association between treatment and outcome is zero.[13] Deviations from this expected outcome necessarily result from chance and can be assessed with statistical inference. If the observed association is so large that it would have occurred by chance very infrequently in a large number of independent replications of the assignment process, we conventionally reject as "implausible" the null hypothesis of no association. Alternatively, we can place confidence intervals around the association to reflect how precise our estimates of the treatment effect are likely to be.

While the details of the random assignment model are well accepted (Siegel, 1956) there remains considerable confusion about the inferential process underlying the use of statistical tests to assess the probability of chance associations. For most cases, the appropriate parametric techniques are *mathematically* equivalent to those appropriate under the random sampling model when samples are drawn from two (or more) separate populations and inferences are to be made about the equivalence of the parameters of the parent populations (e.g., comparisons between means). Because the mathematics are the same, researchers often fail to distinguish between the random sampling inferential model, where the question is whether different hypothetical populations have the same parameters, and the random assignment cases, where the question is whether different "samples" represent random splits of the same hypothetical population (see Lindquist, 1953: 49-50).[14]

In part because of such confusion, it has been suggested that the appropriate inferential statistics for the random assignment case should be based on non-parametric component randomization tests (see Edgington, 1966; Winch and Campbell, 1969). These tests rest on the *exact* probability distribution of all possible associations resulting from a random assignment process applied to the *given* data. For the null case (i.e., when the *actual* association between treatment and outcome is zero), these exact tests can be closely approximated by parametric tests, but when non-zero association is actually present, the probability distribution resulting from exact calculations will differ systematically (in a direction that induces a bias in favor of accepting the null hypothesis) from the distribution assumed by application of parametric tests (Alf and Abrahams, 1972).[15] Because of this, the appropriate use of the exact randomized component model is limited to very specialized cases (and then with qualifications) involving an inferential model somewhat different from that underlying the random assignment case.

The randomized component model applies to those situations in which neither random sampling nor randomization obtain, but where an observed research population is sorted into subgroups (based on *naturally occurring* processes), and the question is whether there is some "substantive" association between subgroup membership and scores on some other measure of interest.[16] It is substantively trivial to ask whether obtained differences among categories represent "real" differences between hypothetical populations since, in effect, the sample *is* the population of interest. What can be addressed, however, is whether an obtained non-zero association differs significantly from what might be expected by chance if observed values corresponding to subgroup membership and values on the outcome measure(s) had been distributed independently of one another among members of the observed population. In effect, the observed distribution is compared with all possible outcomes of a hypothetical "lottery," and the relative frequency with which the obtained association between category membership and values of the outcome measure could occur among this a priori distribution of all possible outcomes is used to assess the "plausibility" that such a random process *could* have generated the obtained differences.

To illustrate the randomized component model, suppose over the course of an academic year a particular 5th grade teacher has administered varying degrees of disciplines to the 35 children in his/her class, with discipline ratings ranging from 0 (no overt discipline across the year) to 5 (sent to the principal's office more than three times during the day). At the end of the year, the parents of one boy in the class register a complaint against the teacher, claiming that during the previous year he/she had systematically punished boys more frequently than girls. While investigating this complaint, the administration determines that for that year, the punishment rating for 17 boys in this teacher's class averaged 3.5. In contrast, the ratings for the 18 girls averaged only 2.5. These findings cannot be treated as a sample of the teacher's behavior since for purposes of evaluating the complaint, these results represent the universe of relevant behavior. Instead, the claim of "bias" can be evaluated against the null hypothesis that the obtained set of discipline scores were distributed among the 35 children of the class without regard to children's sex. This can be formally assessed with the distribution of outcomes for all possible partitionings of the 35 discipline scores into subsets of 17 and 18 (the obtained marginal frequencies of the two subgroups). The relative frequency with which these partitionings would produce outcomes (subset differences) as extreme as those obtained becomes the measure of the "plausibility" of the random generation model. Note that the inferential process is limited to the "plausibility" of chance as an explanatory model; no estimation of actual bias is possible within this framework. Nonetheless, even this limited type of inference has relevance to some evaluation settings and to the potential use of social science data in legal cases (Baldus and Cole, 1977).[17]

Both the random assignment and the randomized component models are vulnerable to all the standard abuses of the random sampling model. In particular, it is especially easy to be seduced by Type I errors. In evaluation research where one often examines a large number of possible treatment effects, the chance of getting one statistically significant effect at the .05 level in 20 independent outcomes is too often ignored. Instead of using adjustments for such multiple tests (e.g., Scheffe, 1959), the absence of any significant finding seems to encourage more searching. For example, at a recent conference on evaluation research, a director of a research division in a large federal agency explained his "winnowing" procedures approximately as follows. "When we evaluate a program, we are alert for a wide range of treatment effects. From the large number of possible effects, we emphasize the statistically significant ones in any policy recommendations." Or, as another researcher put it, "we often have as many as 50 programs in the field at any one time. The few showing statistically significant effects are selected for intensive follow-up."

On the other hand, the possibility of Type II errors can also be serious. Standard analyses of experimental designs sometimes neglect the existence of interaction effects: that the treatment may be differentially effective for subsets of subjects. Unfortunately, searching for such subject specific outcomes in an ad hoc manner is often a tricky business since if one tries a sufficient number of interaction effects, some will reach statistical significance through Type I error. Thus, the best procedure is to postulate a small set of possible interaction effects in advance and then discount one's probability levels as a consequence of independent multiple tests. Finally, there is really no substitute for replication. This cannot be overemphasized although formal replications are extremely rare in evaluation research. Whether this results from economic, political or practical constraints, our most powerful inferential tool is consequently neglected.

It is also critical to emphasize that all of the ambiguities involved in making inferences from a single "sample" in terms of long run outcomes apply to the random assignment model. In other words, all probability statements reflect the consequences of a very large number of random assignments of the same subjects of which the experimental groups are then exposed to the same treatments. Too often, however, policy makers want to make statements about the credibility of findings from a single experiment. This is only justified in instances where Bayesian inference is formally applied. The same point applies to the randomized component model.

## THE ECONOMETRIC MODEL[18]

The Ordinary Least Squares econometric model may be initially described as a more general formulation of the models described in the previous section. To translate freely from Malinvaud (1970: 82-85), the econometric models begins with a set of fixed, constant exogenous variables much like the "treatments" associated with experiments. That is, the values of the $X_i$'s are assumed to be subject to exact control and are held at some predetermined set of values. The endogenous variable is taken as a function of two forces, a linear deterministic relationship derived from the exogenous variables *and* random perturbations (i.e., it is *not* fixed).[19] The random "shocks" are assumed to have an expected value of zero, constant variance and zero covariance between shocks.

The following "sampling" process is therefore implied for the given set of X values; one observes the pattern of Y values at one moment in time. In other words, it is almost as if one has taken a snapshot of the Y values which freezes the stochastic Y values in some configuration. This process is then repeated a very large number of times so that a distribution of Y values is obtained for *each* given X value. The assumptions made about the stochastic component in Y requires that the mean (expected value) of each distribution of Y falls exactly on the regression line (representing the linear deterministic component), that each distribution has the same variance on the average in repeated "samples" and that the average covariance between any Y values in repeated "samples" is zero. Note that the X values are unchanged in repeated samples; what changes is the Y values.

Consider the following illustration. Suppose one were studying factors which affected the number of arrests made per day by each of the police precincts in Chicago. Moreover, for a given day on which data are collected, each and every precinct is covered. With the data in hand, a OLS model is built in which the number of police officers on patrol, the size of the precinct, the number of citizens in the precinct, and the proportion of citizens in the precinct with less than poverty level incomes. Assuming that the regression hyperplane does not fit perfectly (an $R^2$ less than 1.0), the residuals are interpreted as random perturbations. This means that one could return on the next day, gather data on the same variables, and the values on the exogenous variables would remain unchanged, while the values of the endogenous variable (number of arrests), would be a bit different. However, one would still be estimating the same "underlying" regression hyperplane since our assumptions about the stochastic processes leave it fundamentally unchanged. The deterministic component reflected in the hyperplane is assumed to be an "invariant causal law" which we must "estimate" because of random shocks which tend to obscure its real nature in a single "sample." We formally undertake this estimation (plus significance tests and confidence intervals) by assuming that we could observe the relationship between the endogenous and exogenous variables over and over on many different days (with the exogenous values fixed) with the only change a function of random forces having the convenient properties associated with OLS models.

The interpreting of statistical inference is more subtle. On the one hand, it is possible to view the data as a particular "realization" of the combined deterministic and stochastic components, just as one might view the results of a particular randomized experiment as a realization of the deterministic treatment effect and random forces introduced by the random assignment process. Then one's statistical inferences address the following: Could the observed deterministic component result solely from chance patterns? If in numerous realizations, the observed patterns attributed to deterministic factors could happen very infrequently were the null hypothesis true (e.g., all the regression coefficients equal zero), we reject the null hypothesis.

On the other hand, a kind of generalization can also be employed. The relevant population is all "samples" (i.e., realizations) of Y values for the *given* set of X values. In the police example, this population reflects all of the days for the full set of Chicago precincts for which we are prepared to *assume* that the deterministic component remains unchanged, and the stochastic disturbances have an expected value of zero, constant variance and zero covariance. Note, however, that this is a *theoretical* statement *not* derived from the sample data or empirical knowledge about how the data were actually generated. Recall that in the random sampling model, we knew the statistical population and the impact of the random sampling process because the researcher actually determined both. In contrast, here one's generalizations do not rest on statistical inference at all, but on theoretical arguments. One would have to claim in the Chicago illustration, that the data for the particular day on which the material was collected was a realization from a larger set of, for example, winter days. Should the exogenous variables be introduced to measure the impact of seasonal variation and days when school is not in session, one might be prepared to say that the model can be generalized over, for example, the years 1970-1974. However, these are still theoretical arguments.

The econometric model can easily be extended to situations in which the endogenous variables as well as the exogenous variables are stochastic. This is obviously critical since in many instances, the X values will vary from realization to realization. In the Chicago police example, one might have used weather as a predictor and quite clearly, that would change from day to day in a stochastic manner.

The econometric model with stochastic exogenous variables can be justified on two levels. First, one can treat the X values as fixed *once they are observed.* Then one would simply fall back on the model with fixed X values. For instance, the weather on the day arrest data were collected might be rainy. Consequently, one's population of realizations would include only rainy days/ that is, one's interpretations would be *conditional* on the given realizations of the X values (Malinvaud, 1970: 100).

Second, and more subtle, we can make the following new assumptions. We can assume that "the distribution of each of the explanatory variables is independent of the true regression parameters" and that "each of the explanatory variables is distributed independently of the errors in the model" (Pyndyck and Rubinfeld, 1976: 84). The former means that whatever X values are observed, we get unbiased estimates of the *same* population parameter values. In an important sense, we get "identical" results whichever X values happen to appear (i.e., the underlying deterministic component remains unchanged). The latter means that the stochastic component is also unaffected since it is independent of the stochastic X values (i.e., the stochastic component retains its OLS properties). In short, while the X values are stochastic, it does not make any important difference which values happen to be observed. In the context of our Chicago example, variations in, say, the number of officers on patrol from day to day in different precincts (perhaps as a consequence of illnesses) would in no significant manner affect our estimates of the underlying parameters. That is, the underlying relationship between the number of officers and number of arrests is unchanged.

Despite the introduction of stochastic exogenous variables, the "stability" of the observed relationships is still the critical *statistical* issue. As before, one can determine the probability of obtaining the observed coefficients given a particular null hypothesis of, for instance, random patterns. Alternatively, one could place confidence intervals around one's estimates. Generalizations, by contrast, once again rest on theoretical arguments. We claim that our assumptions hold for a particular set of circumstances and that therefore our coefficients (and the model) are meaningfully descriptive.

Additional issues are raised if our X values are stochastic as a result of random sampling. At the very least, random sampling is important because it supports our *assumption* that the particular X values observed do not fundamentally matter. If the X values and their paired Y values are selected at random, they are statistically "representative" of the population. Therefore, our claim that any set of realizations of X will provide estimates of the same regression parameters becomes more plausible. Yet, the fact of random sampling introduces again the possibility of statistical generalizations to a defined population. Thus, two kinds of generalizations become plausible. As in the random sampling model, we can speak about statistical inference to an actual population from which observations on exogenous and endogenous were selected *and* we can provide theoretical generalizations to other settings.

While we have emphasized the econometric model to this point (in part because of its statistical precision), there are analogous perspectives in sociology and psychology. For example, Winch and Campbell (1969) argue for the usefulness of statistical inference when the data do not derive from either random sampling or random assignment. Similar positions are advocated by Edgington (1966) and Siegel (1956). However, none provide any statistical assistance for generalizing despite differences in the details of the models suggested and the distributions applied. Siegel (1956: 104-111), for example, shows how the Chi-square distribution may be applied to contingency tables to test the assumption of independence between nominal variables. But, as in the general randomized component case, one's conclusions only involve the data on hand.[20]

No doubt many researchers will find aid and comfort in using statistical inference as justified by econometric traditions. We are nevertheless somewhat uneasy. First, statistical inference is subject to all of the abuses and ambiguities of earlier models. One must still consider Type I and Type II errors, the interpretative implications of classical probability, problems with backdoor Bayesian estimation, and the like.

Second, more than any of the models considered to this point, the econometric model rests on untested and often untestable assumptions. With our focus on statistical inference, we have provided only a taste of the range of simplifications one must be fully prepared to accept (see Malinvaud, 1970: 80-95). For example, in order for ordinary least squares to produce unbiased estimates of the regression coefficients, exogenous variables must typically be measured without error: both systematic error *and* random error (Malinvaud, 1970: 374-383). Since this is highly unlikely in most empirical contexts, one must be able to argue that the measurement error is random and practically small (compared to the variation in the "true" values of the exogenous variables). Alternatively, one may resort to other estimation procedures although this usually requires a great deal of information about the processes which generated the measurement error. Without such insight, one may simply replace an initial set of implausible assumptions with a second set of implausible assumptions. In summary, a high price is paid for the enormous flexibility of the econometric model. Accurate estimation requires a host of empirical assumptions whose links to reality are often suspect.

Third, especially when random sampling is not involved, the justifications for numerous hypothetical realizations from which the sampling distribution is necessarily derived, often requires dubious mental gymnastics. It is all too common to find statistical inference automatically applied when underlying justifications are either seriously flawed or simply ignored. In other words, the econometric approach seems to justify statistical inference almost regardless of the data's source. Thus, the model's potential for wide applicability is translated into unfettered license.

## TIME SERIES MODELS

Time series models as most commonly used in social science applications to date can be thought of as a variant of econometric models (see Hibbs, 1974). They, in essence, treat a particular sequence of observations over time as a representative realization of some underlying stochastic process. And once again, the central statistical concern is not generalization. Generalizations are approached through theoretical arguments.

Perhaps an illustration will be instructive. Consider a machine which produces a large number of ball-bearings one at a time. Even the best of machines in perfect working order will not produce ball-bearings of precisely the same diameter. There will always be slight fluctuations. However, a machine of high quality should produce ball-bearings which are on the average, the same diameter. Moreover, deviations from this diameter should be on the average about the same size and should follow no systematic pattern. That is, a ball-bearing that is too large will be followed by a ball-bearing which is as likely to be too small as too large. This implies that any sequence of ball-bearings will be pretty much the same as any other sequence of ball-bearings, and that therefore, any given sequence characterizes the production process as well as any other sequence. Put another way, we could sample a sequence of ball-bearings beginning at any arbitrary time and expect to find pretty much the same things as in any other sequence beginning at another arbitrary time.

This is the stochastic model of a "stationary" time series. The stochastic process is assumed to be invariant with respect to the *displacement* of time: the joint probability distribution of the sequence is constant.[21] Thus, one might say that for such models, time has no "historical" interpretation. Or, to quote Nelson (1973: 26), "in a probabilistic sense, history repeats itself in a stationary time series." In other words, the starting point of the series is irrelevant.

Suppose the ball-bearing machine is normally oiled once a day at noon but that on the particular day, the maintenance person responsible for this task is sick, and no one else oils the machine. Since the ball-bearing machine operates at high speed, generating a great deal of heat and friction, this is a serious oversight. By two p.m. several critical components of the machine are beginning to suffer from unusual wear with the result that some of the precision in the production process is lost. For example, ball-bearings are now coming out slightly larger in diameter and as time passes this problem becomes worse.

In statistical terms, the stochastic process is no longer stationary. A trend has been introduced: as time passes the ball-bearings are on the average increasingly large. The expected value of the series is no longer constant because the expected value of the "error" is increasingly positive. This means that the pattern will look quite different depending on when one examines it. At 2:15 p.m. ball-bearings will still be approximately the proper diameter. By 5 p.m. the machine may be turning out ball-bearings the size of golf balls. Therefore, it is no longer true that one could observe the series at any arbitrary point in time and obtain virtually the same picture of the stochastic process as at any other arbitrary time. Moreover, since "history" is not repeating itself, it is not at all clear of what a given series of 30 ball-bearings, for example, is representative.

In most social science applications, such nonstationarity (i.e., the joint probability distribution of the series is not constant) is treated as resulting from deterministic forces which must be "removed" before the stochastic forces are considered (Box and Jenkins, 1970). For example, if a linear trend exists, it may be removed either by regressing the time series on time itself (perhaps introduced as a sequence of integers), or through transforming the data into "change scores" through "differencing." (This involves using the simple difference between adjacent observations as the "new" series.) If either of these procedures removes the linear trend, one once again has a stationary series reflected either in the residuals (in the case of regression) or in the change scores (in the case of differencing). In other words, all of the convenient statistical properties of a stationary series can once again be assumed (e.g., "representativeness").   ·

It is critical to understand that most current applications of such models treat the deterministic component very differently from the stationary stochastic component. In regression language, any independent variables are viewed as having deterministic effects much as in the more general econometric perspective. For example, the effect of a change in the speed limit on a time series of automobile accidents (per month) is considered to have no stochastic component. Its impact might be assessed by introducing a dummy variable (0s before the speed limit was changed, 1s thereafter) into the regression analysis. The stochastic parts of the series reside in the residuals (which are stationary) and can be interpreted as a kind of uninteresing "noise" possessing OLS properties.[22] We do not care a great deal about its sources or nature as long as it is stationary noise. However, we do use statistical inference to separate its impact on the series from that of the deterministic part.[23] As in the econometric model one would want to determine if what is being viewed as a real (deterministic) association could be easily attributed to random patterns of noise. Generalizations are either trivial (since the series is stationary and therefore "history" has no real meaning) or must rest on theoretical generalizations.

Put most simply, typical time series models can be viewed as another kind of econometric model. The main difference is that the data are now arrayed over time instead of across space. One still treats the observation as random realizations from some underlying stochastic process and statistical inference may therefore be appropriate. However, all of the earlier caveats still apply. Moreover, one must be especially careful to make sure that the series under consideration is really stationary (or can be made stationary). Should the series not be stationary, statistical inferences are not only inappropriate, but very misleading (Berk, 1977).

## A CONCLUDING EXAMPLE

Perhaps the most important conclusion from our previous discussion is that the notion of "routine" statistical inference is a contradiction in terms. Classical statistical inference is a relatively fragile and limited research tool. It addresses a small subset of problems and then provides sensible answers solely in the context of long run outcomes. Moreover, in many instances, the policy maker cannot wait for the long run to arrive. He or she wants to know if the program "works" and should the evaluation be a randomized experiment, for example, the researcher can only say that if the same pool of subjects were just randomly assigned to treatment and control groups over and over, in but five cases out of a hundred on the average, would disparities as large or larger than those actually observed in fact occur. More important, there is no way of knowing whether or not this is one of those instances. The random sampling model, econometric model and time series model produce similar ambiguities.

However, when classical inference is appropriate and useful, it is critical to match the stochastic model to the question being addressed. This means deciding what the source or sources of stochastic error are and then selecting a model that best characterizes the random processes of concern. Consider the following examples in which the general research question is whether there is some substantively meaningful association between acquiring a high school diploma and the income of American males 30 years of age.

For the *random sampling model* to be formally appropriate, one must have drawn two probability samples from two defined populations. In this instance, the two populations might be all male high school graduates in the U.S. who reached the age of 30 during 1975 and all U.S. males of the same age who did not complete high school. Then, any differences between the samples in income levels could be tested against the null hypothesis that both samples were randomly drawn from populations with equivalent parameters. If this null hypothesis is rejected as improbable, it suggests that the income distribution for the population of high school graduates differs from that of nongraduates (i.e., that there *is* an association between acquiring a diploma and income) and estimations based on sample characteristics can be used to infer the respective population values. This inferential process does not indicate of course, whether income differences are directly attributable to high school education (as opposed to other population differences) nor can one rely on statistical inference to generalize to populations representing other times or places.

A somewhat different kind of stochastic process is assessed within the framework of the *randomization model*. In this case, the researcher begins with a pool of research subjects *homogeneous* with respect to the independent variable(s) of interest (e.g., all are without a high school diploma). Random assignment occurs *prior* to any variation in the independent (treatment) variable, and thus we can assume that any random split of the initial pool would generate samples with equal expected values (i.e., on the average) for income. One of these subsamples is then exposed to a brief educational treatment culminating in a high school diploma, while the other group is not given any opportunity to acquire a diploma. Some years later the annual income of all individuals in both groups is assessed. If the diploma treatment makes no difference, the income distributions of the two subgroups should not differ any more than expected for two random subdivisions of the same population. If this null hypothesis is rejected, it can be concluded that presence or absence of the specific diploma treatment contributes to group differences in income. These conclusions, however, apply only to the initial pool of subjects unless additional (nonstatistical) arguments are introduced.

The *randomized component model* would be appropriate if the relationship between high school diploma and income were being investigated for a specific group of employees at some point in time who already differ in the "treatment" of interest. For instance, if all male workers in a given industry were divided into those with and without diplomas, any association obtained between income and degree could be compared with the distribution of associations for all possible recombinations (pairings) of the values on the two variables holding the marginal distribution of the two constant. As a nonparametric procedure, the randomized component model makes no assumptions about the functional form of variable distributions. However, since the probability distribution is generated from the *obtained* income values, including any systematic differences based on diploma status, the impact of alleged stochastic processes may be inflated and resulting significance tests reduced in power (i.e., it is harder to reject the null hypothesis). And again, generalizations to other settings rest on theoretical arguments.

For the *econometric model* to be formally appropriate, differences in income between individuals would be viewed as a function of degree status and random perturbations. It matters little how subjects obtained a diploma (e.g., "naturally" or through some special program), how the data were collected (e.g., "sampled"), or whether the data reflect naturally occurring variation or an externally imposed research design. The "sample" is treated as a realization of an underlying process having both deterministic and stochastic components, and the issue is whether observed variation attributed to deterministic factors is really the product of random effects. Alternatively, one can estimate the impact of the deterministic component along with its instability. As the most general and flexible of the models discussed, the econometric model can be applied to virtually any data set as long as one clearly specifies the situations in which the model applies and the rationale for treating the data as one of many possible realizations. With this accomplished, statistical inference applies only to the defined settings. In this example, one might have data on adult males participating in an high school equivalency degree program in Chicago and be prepared to argue that the observed income patterns reflect an underlying process operating for similar programs and participants in Chicago during the 1970s.[24]

Finally, the *time series model* would be formally appropriate for situations in which one had observed the monthly earnings of adult males for several years and when (if at all) a high school equivalency diploma was awarded. Much like the econometric model, inferences rest on separating deterministic from stochastic effects, but in addition, special care must be taken to make sure that the error term is stationary and that adjustments are made for possible serial correlation among the residuals. Statistical inference formally applies only to that series although with proper justification, one might be prepared to generalize to other possible settings.

In summary, a reasonably informed policy maker may want to distinguish "real" effects from "chance" factors as one of the many criteria by which the plausibility and usefulness of findings are judged. However, we have tried to emphasize that under the ruberic of chance fall a variety of stochastic processes whose meaning and implications can be rather different. Chance can refer to such things as variation in univariate population estimates across a large number of probability samples, variation in estimated associations across a large number of random assignments of the same pool of subjects, or variation in estimated regression coefficients as a function of "real world" (i.e., not produced by the researcher) processes. Unless such differences are clearly articulated, misleading conclusions can result.

Building on our earlier example, a researcher may have gathered a probability sample of American males and applied ordinary least squares to determine the impact of having a high school diploma. Perhaps he or she estimates that having a high school diploma increases yearly income by an average of $1,000 per year, and that were there really no effect, the chance of obtaining a regression coefficient this large (or larger) is one out of one hundred; the coefficient is statistically significant. The researcher goes on to explain that "chance" refers to what would happen in a large number of probability samples drawn from the same population. In fact, this can be quite misleading. The kind of sample gathered is not formally addressed in the econometric model, and chance actually refers to what would happen in a very large number of *realizations* of the same underlying causal mechanism. Thus, statistical inference really involves the "stability" of the estimate in the context of random forces operating in the "real world" not in the context of variation produced by the investigator through probability sampling. In other words, the latter considers random error produced solely by the sampling process, the former considers random error inherent in the substantive phenomenon itself.

How might the policy maker be misled? First, ordinary least squares requires numerous assumptions which have little to do with probability sampling. Thus, a false sense of validity might be communicated if an econometric model is described as a random sampling model. Second, the policy maker might incorrectly conclude that the only source of stochastic error derives from the probability sampling process. The stochastic nature of the phenomenon in question would therefore be neglected. Put another way, he or she might believe that had there been no sampling (i.e., had the full population of interest been studied), stochastic processes would be irrelevant. Third, vital information about the ratio of deterministic to stochastic processes would be lost. Such insight could have critical implications for expectations about later replications and/or routinization of the "treatment." Finally, had the econometric model been properly described, additional possibilities for generalization might have surfaced. The underlying "invariant causal law" might have been viewed as appropriate to a range of contexts. Clearly, from a practical point of view at least, all of these errors could have serious consequences.

## NOTES

1. In this paper we will not consider Bayesian inference in any depth (see Box and Tiao, 1973). While we are sympathetic to this growing tradition, it is currently a far less common technique and beyond the scope of this paper in any case (cf. Wang et al., 1977).

2. There are some serious ambiguities here in the logic involved. These will be discussed in the next section.

3. For example, suppose that the estimated treatment effect for a manpower training program is a gain of $200.00 a month in future earnings, plus or minus $10.00: 95 percent of the time the "real" treatment effect lies within such an interval. (The $200.00 represents the difference between the posttest means for the experimental and control group.) This assumes that the study is repeated a very large number of times with the only change resulting from random assignment to treatment and control group; who winds up where. That is, membership in the treatment and control group will differ from study to study through the random assignment process. Then, each replication will almost certainly have its own estimated confidence interval varying in location because of differences in the estimated treatment and control group means (and thus their disparity) and in width because of differences in estimated standard errors (the standard deviation of the sampling distribution of the differences between the means). The first .95 confidence interval might be $202.00 plus or minus $7.00, the second .95 confidence interval might be $205.00 plus or minus $8.00, and so on. Ninety-five percent of such intervals will include the value of the population parameter (the "real" treatment effect). Finally, the smaller the confidence interval estimated for a given study at a particular probability level, the more "precise" our estimate of treatment effects.

4. Of course, a final assessment would have to consider such factors as cost-effectiveness.

5. Hollis and Nell are not referring literally to the Pearson Correlation Coefficient, but associations in general. Moreover, their point is meant to apply to estimates of univariate parameters as well and cannot be overemphasized.

6. Probability sampling actually has at least three important assets. First, since one knows from where the sample was drawn, one automatically knows one population to which generalizations may be reasonably made. Second, probability sampling is an excellent way of producing a "representative" sample of the population. Third, probability sampling provides the kind of sample for which sampling error can be formally addressed. In addition, none of these advantages prevents one from generalizing beyond the most immediate population (either in time or space) through theory or the results of prior research. Indeed, this is routine in survey research when, for example, attitudes among American adults about race relations which happen to be measured on March 15th, 1977, are taken as accurate indicators for all of 1977. Put another way, probability sampling interposes a statistically defined population between a set of observations and the theoretically relevant larger population of instances to which one may ultimately want to generalize.

7. By "unbiased" we denote that the mean of the estimator's sampling distribution equals the value of the population parameter. This is one of several desirable characteristics of estimators.

8. As discussed earlier, this is certainly not the only useful null hypothesis.

9. This particular test assumes that the standard deviation remains unchanged. Of course, one could test this as well.

10. Before the single sample is selected, the probability is either 1.0 or zero. The estimate either will occur or it will not occur.

11. Type I errors refer to falsely rejecting the null hypothesis, a false positive. Type II errors refers to falsely accepting (failing to reject) the null hypothesis, a false negative. The literature on these kinds of errors is large, but for a consideration of the "fishing" problems to be emphasized later, the papers by Ryan (1972) and Cook and Campbell (1975) are a good introduction.

12. We will see later that the assumption of fixed values is relaxed in the "Econometric" model.

13. The association involves the 1 and 0 indicating assignment and values on the dependent variable. This can be approached through regression using a dummy variable for the treatment (Kmenta, 1971: section 11-1), the point-biserial correlations (Kenny, 1972), or the more common difference between means on the dependent variable.

14. Both are hypothetical in the sense that they are not actually observed, but are abstractions based on idealized distributions having very specific and convenient properties. This is true even for the random assignment model for which the relevant inferential question is whether random

splits of a hypothetical population which is distributed normally, for example, and having parameters of certain values would infrequently produce differences between means as large or larger than those observed in the given random split.

15. When nonparametric tests (such as the Chi-square test of independence) are employed, random assignment and randomized component models coincide mathematically. Again, however, the research settings and the inference process involved must still be distinguished.

16. This is similar, but not identical, to the "econometric" model discussed later.

17. One can approximate inferences from the randomized component model with parametric tests. Thus, the choice of what inferential procedures to apply often reduces to what one is prepared to assume about the distribution of the dependent variable and resulting tradeoffs on such things as statistical power (Seigel, 1956).

18. As in the previous sections, we shall be stressing appropriate applications and their justifications. However, it is probably worth noting that in terms of formal *statistical* properties, the econometric model, the random sampling model and the random assignment model can all be derived from the general linear model. One can, for example, view analysis of variance or covariance applied to a randomized experiment as a special case of the general linear model.

19. Recall that all other models so far treated the observations as fixed. Stochastic error was introduced by random sampling, random assignment or random splits. Here, stochastic error is "inherent" in observations on the dependent variable.

20. Moreover, there is often a seriously misleading tendency to use such models as a blank check. In fact, they require the same careful consideration and justification as the econometric model and may often be inappropriate (Berk, 1977).

21. There are "weak" assumptions that one might make which also "work." However, such nuances have no real impact here.

22. Often the residuals are correlated with one another, and one must abandon OLS in favor of generalized least squares. However, this does not materially affect our discussion.

23. In the ball-bearing example, an OLS model would regress diameter on an interaction variable constructed by multiplying a dummy variable for the "treatment" (0s up to noon, and 1s thereafter) by time (1,2,3,... T). One could then apply statistical inference to determine whether the regression coefficient for the interaction term was larger than what could be expected from chance alone, if the lack of oil were really having no effect. Generalizing any findings to *other* machines raises additional questions. Here, one would have to argue from theory or other research that the machine on which the data was collected was or was not like other machines to which one might wish to generalize.

24. However, in practice, the substantive model posed here would probably be too simple.

# REFERENCES

ALF, E.F., and ABRAHAMS, N.M. (1972). "Comment on component-randomization tests." 77 Psychological Bulletin, 3:223-224.

BALDUS, D.C., and COLE, J.W.L. (1977). "Quantitative proof of intentional discrimination." Evaluation Quarterly, Volume 1,1.

BARNETT, V. (1973), Comparative statistical inference. New York: Wiley.

BARTLETT, M.S. (1975). Probability, statistics and time. New York: Wiley.

BERK, R.A. (1977). "Proof? No. Evidence? No. A skeptic's comment on Inverarity's use of statistical inference." ASR, Volume 42,3.

——— and ROSSI, P.H. (1977). "Doing good or worse, evaluation research politically re-examined." Social Problems, Volume 23,3.

BOX, G.E.P., and JENKINS, G.M. (1970). Time series analysis. San Francisco: Holden Day.

BOX, G.E.P., AND TIAO, G.C. (1973). Bayesian inference in statistical analysis. Menlo Park: Addison-Wesley.

CAMPBELL, D.T., and STANLEY, J.C. (1966). Experimental and quasi-experimental designs for research. Chicago: Rand McNally.

COOK, T.D., and CAMPBELL, D.T. (1975). "The design and conduct of quasi-experiments and true experiments in field settings." Chapter 7 in M.D. Dunette (ed.), Handbook of industrial and organizational research. Chicago: Rand McNally.

EDGINGTON, E.S. (1966). "Statistical inference and nonrandom samples." 66 Psychological Bulletin 6:485-487.

FISHER, Sir R.A. (1971). The design of experiments. New York: Hafner Press.

HIBBS, D.A., Jr. (1974). "Problems of statistical estimation and causal inference in time series regression models." In Herbert L. Costner (ed.), Sociological Methodology 1973-1974. San Francisco: Jossey-Bass.

HOLLIS, M., and NELL, E.J. (1975). Rational economic man: A philosophical critique of neo-classical economics. New York: Cambridge University Press.

KENNY, D.A. (1975). "A quasi-experimental approach to assessing treatment effects in non-equivalent control group designs." Psychological Bulletin, Volume 82,2.

KISH, L. (1965). Survey sampling. New York: Wiley.

KMENTA, J. (1971). Elements of econometrics. New York: MacMillian.

LINDLEY, D.V. (1965). Introduction to probability and statistics from a Bayesian viewpoint. Cambridge: Cambridge University Press.

LINDQUIST, E.F. (1953). Design analysis of experiments in psychology and education. Boston: Houghton Mifflin.

MALINVAUD, E. (1970). Statistical methods of econometrics. Amsterdam: North Holland Publishing Co.

MORRISON, D.E., and HENKEL, R.E. (1970). The significance test controversy. Chicago: Aldine.

NELSON, C.R. (1973). Applied time series analysis for managerial forecasting. San Francisco: Holden Day.

PINDYCK, R.S., AND RUBINFELD, D.L. (1976). Econometric models and economic forecasts. New York: McGraw-Hill.

POLYA, G. (1954). Induction and analogy in mathematics. Princeton: Princeton University Press.

SIEGEL, S. (1956). Nonparametric statistics for the behavioral sciences. New York: McGraw-Hill.

WALDO, G.P., and CHIRICOS, T.G. (1977). "Work release and recidivism: An empirical evaluation of a social policy." Evaluation Quarterly, Volume 1,1.

WANG, M.-M., NOVICK, M.R., ISAACS, G.L., and OZENNE, N. (1977). A Bayesian data analysis for the evaluation of social programs." Journal of the American Statistical Association, Vol. 72:711-722.

WINCH, R.F. and CAMPBELL, D.T. (1969). "Proof? No. Evidence? Yes. The significance of tests of significance." The American Sociologist 4:140-143.

# 10

## The Power of Social Intervention Experiments To Discriminate Differences Between Experimental and Control Groups

### John A. Crane

The discriminating power of a social experiment is defined as the probability that it will detect a specified difference in the population sampled. Analysis of twenty-five experimental tests of the effects of case services in social work shows that eighteen have a .95 probability of detecting differences only on the order of 25 percent or greater and that in most cases this must be increased by at least one-half as a result of measurement error. Most experiments thus have very large probabilities of type 2 errors, from eight to fifteen times as great as the probabilities of type 1 errors. This seriously weakens the policy relevance of the findings.

## The Problem of Assessing the Effectiveness of Case Services in Social Work

The problem of assessing the effectiveness of case services in social work continues to be of major importance to the field. This is demonstrated by the appearance in recent years of a number of compendia or critical appraisals of the existing body of research findings bearing on this problem.[1] A similar interest in effectiveness is evident in fields other than social work.[2] Typically, the approach to the research evidence has been to total up "statistically significant" and "statistically not significant" findings and to draw conclusions from the totals as to the general import of the evidence.[3]

This approach, while useful as a preliminary assay, overlooks several critically important design features of the research which bear heavily on its capacity to detect differences in outcomes between

From John A. Crane, "The Power of Social Intervention Experiments to Discriminate Differences between Experimental and Control Groups," 50 (2) *Social Science Review* 224-242 (June 1976). Copyright 1976 by the University of Chicago.

treatment and control groups.[4] In this article, these design features are identified and their effect on the discriminating capacity of evaluative research on case services in social work is demonstrated. It is shown that the research evidence available to date on the potency of social work treatment at the case level is not nearly as clear-cut as has often been assumed.

# Statistical Power Analysis and Its Uses in Social Experimentation

The findings of a social experiment are, as a rule, in the form of differences among samples from which inferences are to be drawn concerning differences among populations. The power of such an experiment is the probability that it will detect some specified difference in the populations from which its samples are taken. Because the power of an experiment varies markedly with the magnitude of the differences which are to be detected (as well as with other factors, referred to below), power analysis is a critically important, though neglected, topic in research on the effects of experimental social intervention. Ideally, its principal use in social experimentation is in the planning phase, where it provides a strong theoretical base for determining the feasibility and potential utility of any proposed experiment.[5] It can also be used to help clarify the findings of completed research. This article is devoted to the second of these uses, with a particular focus on the effects of case services under the auspices of social work, a problem with which nearly all experimentation to date in social work has been concerned.[6]

Both studies which employ a "no-treatment" control group and those which employ one or more "other-treated" control groups are within the scope of this article.[7]

# Determinants of the Power of an Experiment

If an experiment aims to detect differences in the proportion of success among different experimental groups, an upper limit to its power to detect any specified difference may readily be calculated from knowledge of the sample size, the estimated variation in the study populations of the characteristic being studied, and the level of statistical significance chosen by the experimenter.[8] The actual power of an experiment is equal to this upper limit if and only if the outcome measures employed in the experiment are free of error. If errors of measurement are made, they reduce the power of the experiment by reducing the observed magnitude of the differences between different experimental groups. This article, a preliminary report of a larger investigation,[9] is concerned mainly with assessment of the upper limits of power determined by variables other than measurement error. It includes a guide to the actual power of any particular study or proposed experiment in cases where estimates of measurement error are available. Because in many studies the amount of measurement error is itself subject only to relatively crude measurement, the actual power can often only be roughly estimated. For the experimental results evaluated in this paper, the upper limits of power to detect differences of less than 20 percent between experimental and control groups are frequently so low as to turn the estimation of actual power into an academic exercise.

## Selection of Studies for Power Analysis

Though the problem of determining the degree of difference between treated and control groups at which social intervention experiments in various fields should be aiming has not yet been fully explored, one can assume that different expectations of treatment impact may be appropriated for different outcome criteria. Therefore, if maximum advantage is to be taken of power analysis, the available research findings should be assembled by type of outcome criteria rather than by study or by author. The following classification of outcome criteria has proved to be useful for purposes of this article (though further efforts to refine and extend both the criteria and the list of relevant studies are under way):

1. *Economic functioning of the family*.—The following North American studies employed this criterion in one form or another: the Area Development Project (ADP) of Vancouver, the Chemung County Experiment, the Community Service Society of New York Project on Dependency, and the Mississippi AFDC Experiment.[10]

2. *Adequacy of parenting behavior*.—Two studies have employed, as outcome criteria, measures of the adequacy of parenting behavior: the Area Development Project of Vancouver and the Chemung County Experiment.[11]

3. *Children's problems*.—The following studies have employed as outcome criteria measures of children's problems and/or adaptive

behavior: the Study of the Effects of Treatment on the Behavior of Potentially Delinquent Boys Identified by the Glueck Prediction Scale, the Pursuit of Promise Study, the Girls at Vocational High Study, the Atlantic Street Center Delinquency Prevention Project in Seattle, and the Cambridge-Somerville Project.[12]

4. *Problems or patterns of adaptive behavior in family relationships.* —Measures of variables of this kind have served as outcome criteria in: the Area Development Project of Vancouver, the Chemung County Project, and the Planned Short-Term Treatment Project.[13]

In this paper the statistical power of each of twenty-five tests of the effects of social work intervention, taken from the above studies, is analyzed. Two studies could not be included because of lack of data needed for power analysis.[14]

# Method of Analysis

The method of power analysis employed in this paper is based on the dependence of the power of an experiment on the factors referred to above: sample size, magnitude of the differences to be detected, and level of statistical significance or "type 1 error" chosen by the experimenter. (In all cases, this last was found to be .05.) Specification of the exact relationships of these variables to statistical power as well as information about the transformations of the data which were employed to ensure comparability of differences in proportions at different points on a scale from 0 to 1 are provided in the Appendix, where the mathematical relationships between measurement error and the magnitude of observed differences are also given. In all cases, maximum discriminating power was determined over a range of percentage differences between pairs of different experimental groups of from 5 to 30 percent. Since large differences are easier to detect than small ones (which may, despite being small percentages, have important social consequences), the power of each experiment increases monotonically over the range employed.[15]

A useful measure of power, a mathematical function of the measure just described, is the magnitude of the difference in percentages or means between groups which can, in a given study, be detected with .95 probability. The usefulness of this measure derives from its being equal to the "level of statistical significance" chosen by all of the experimenters in the studies surveyed. The probability of committing a type 1 error is thus set equal to the probability of committing a type 2 error.[16] This appears to make good sense in evaluating case services, where the cost of the services is likely to be relatively modest compared with the cost of alternatives such as increased failure rate in school, increased admission of children to care, greater incidence of family relationship problems, and lowered economic functioning of families served. By the crudest of economic calculations, achieving relatively small differences in such variables is likely to be worth the cost of case services.

This second measure of power is also extremely important in assessing research on the effects of social interventions, since it provides evidence of the magnitude of the differences which have so far been rigorously tested by research and, on the other hand, of the magnitude of the differences on which the available evidence is relatively weak.

A further important use to which this measure can be put is to determine the implicit a priori weightings assigned, in any study, to type 1 and 2 errors. For example, in a study for which the experimenter has set type 1 error at .05 and has a .60 probability of detecting a difference between experimental and control groups of the order of 25 percent, type 2 error is $1 - .60 = .40$. This is eight times as large as type 1 error. Implicitly, the experimenter is treating type 1 error as eight times more important. The ratio between these two error probabilities is therefore an important datum in the assessment of the import of the results of any experiment.

# Discriminating Power of Experiments Concerned with Family Relationships and Parenting Behavior

Table 1 shows the power to discriminate the various degrees of difference of a set of findings taken from five projects in which measures of parent behavior and family relationships were used as outcome criteria. The findings are chosen for similarity of outcome criteria employed and as major rather than incidental findings of each of the research projects included. The data in this table provide a good deal of information on the maximum power of the experiments to discriminate differences of 30 percent or less between experimental and control groups. By taking into consideration the likely effects of measurement errors on the power of the experiment, one can, in addition, arrive at a set of plausible estimates of the actual as opposed to the maximum power of this group of experimental findings.

The data also throw a good deal of light on the implicit values placed by the experimenters on the relative importance of type 1 and 2 errors, expressed as a ratio of the two: researchers are much more

**Table 1**

MAXIMUM POWER OF EXPERIMENTS CONCERNED WITH FAMILY RELATIONSHIPS AND PARENTING
BEHAVIOR TO DETECT DIFFERENCES BETWEEN EXPERIMENTAL AND CONTROL GROUPS*

| STUDY | DATA SOURCE | CRITERION MEASURE | $D_{.95}$ | MAXIMUM POWER TO DETECT INDICATED PROPORTION DIFFERENCE | | | | | |
|---|---|---|---|---|---|---|---|---|---|
| | | | | .05 | .10 | .15 | .20 | .25 | .30 |
| Area Development Project | ADP, p. 66 | E-C on % showing no changes in family relationships | .25 | .11 | .30 | .58 | .82 | .95 | .99+ |
| Chemung County Project | Brown, p. 124 | Same as above | .35 | .07 | .17 | .32 | .52 | .71 | .86 |
| Chemung County Project | Brown, p. 124 | E-C on % showing no improved child care | .36 | .07 | .17 | .32 | .50 | .68 | .83 |
| Area Development Project | ADP, p. 66 | E-C on % showing improved child care | .25 | .11 | .30 | .58 | .82 | .95 | .99+ |
| Casework with Wives of Alcoholics | Cohen and Krause† | E-C on % of wives reporting decrease in husband's drinking | .32 | .07 | .17 | .32 | .51 | .70 | .86 |
| Pursuit of Promise Project | McCabe, p. 236 | E-C on % showing increase in level of functioning | .45 | .07 | .13 | .23 | .37 | .51 | .69 |
| Casework Methods Project | Reid and Shyne, p. 101 | C-E on % showing no change or aggravation in problems | .31 | .11 | .26 | .48 | .71 | .86 | .95 |
| Casework Methods Project | Reid and Shyne, p. 139 | % showing positive net change after 6 months (E-C) | .30 | .11 | .28 | .50 | .73 | .88 | .96 |

*Maximum power is achieved only if the data are free of measurement error. In this table, E = experimental group, C = control group, and $D_{.95}$ = the minimum proportion difference between E and C detectable with .95 probability, with type I error = .05. This difference is sharply increased by measurement error.

†Because the report of this study provides incomplete information on sample sizes, they were estimated for purposes of this analysis. See Pauline C. Cohen and Morton J. Krause, *Casework with Wives of Alcoholics* (New York: Family Service Association of America, 1971).

tolerant, implicitly, of type 2 than of type 1 errors. While determinants of these preferences cannot be fully analyzed within the scope of this paper, some of their consequences are considered below.

*Maximum power to discriminate differences as revealed in the data in table 1.*[17]—In four of the eight experimental tests in table 1 the maximum power to discriminate differences of 30 percent between experimental and controls is equal to or greater than .95, and in the other four the mean maximum power is approximately .81. For a difference between experimentals and controls of 25 percent, the number of comparisons in which a power of .95 is attained slips to two, and for differences of 20 percent or less, it drops to zero. For differences of 15 percent or less between experimental and controls, six of the eight studies clearly had the odds against them in that from the beginning their most optimistic (maximum) prospects for detecting such differences were less than 50:50. As shown in the column headed $D_{.95}$, six of the eight studies had a .95 (maximum) probability of rejecting differences only of .30 or greater.

*Actual power to discriminate differences: the effects of errors of measurement.*—The actual compared with the maximum discriminating power of an experiment depends on measurement errors, which in turn depend on the degree of development of the data collection instruments employed. As shown in the Appendix, the effect of measurement errors on the power of one experiment using the Geismar-Ayres Scale is to reduce a power of .95 to about .60 for differences of the order of 25 percent. This is not much better than 50:50. Data collection instruments employed in the sample of studies reviewed here vary from the ad hoc, which have had little systematic development, to structured disguised tests which have a considerable degree of standardization. For studies employing ad hoc measures of outcome, such as gross ratings of improvement in the client's overall problem, for which there has been no opportunity for the kind of careful testing and development to which the Geismar-Ayres Scale has been subjected, the effects of measurement error on power to discriminate differences can be expected to be greater than for the above example.[18] According to Nunally, even well-established and standardized tests of personality traits, attitudes, and sentiments contain very large measurement errors.[19] Thus, there appears to be a good deal of attenuation of power even in studies which employ such instruments. This suggests that, while there is clearly a need for more investigation of the effects of measurement error on statistical power, it seems safe to conclude that research on the effects of social work intervention on family relationships and adequacy of parenting behavior has so far been as conclusive as the researchers appear to have intended it only for very large differences between experimental and control groups. The policy implications of research which can detect only such large differences are at present unclear.

*Implicit values placed by researchers on type 1 and 2 errors.* —Some insight into decision making in research on the effects of social work intervention is afforded by an examination of the a priori values which are implicitly placed by researchers on avoiding the error of falsely rejecting a hypothesis of no difference between experimental and control groups, as opposed to falsely accepting such a hypothesis.[20] A measure of these value preferences of researchers is readily obtained from the data in table 1 by computing, for each comparison in the table, the probabilities of type 1 and 2 errors and taking their ratio. Type 1 errors, as already noted, have in all cases been set in advance by the experimenter as equal to .05. Type 2 errors are conveniently calculated if we remember that power equals 1 minus the probability of falsely accepting the null hypothesis (type 2 error). Using the example given in the Appendix, in which it was found that a reasonable estimate of the power of one experiment using the Geismar-Ayres Scale is .60 for a true difference of 25 percent between experimental and control groups, we find that the researcher's preference for the error of falsely accepting a hypothesis of no difference as against falsely rejecting it is

$$\frac{1 - .60}{.05} = \frac{.40}{.05} = 8.$$

That is, the researcher implicitly regards the error of falsely concluding that a difference of 25 percent exists as eight times more important than falsely concluding that such a difference does not exist. For a difference of 15 percent rather than 25 percent, the same preference is found to be 14.5:1. If all such preferences were calculated for the data of table 1, the majority would be at least as large as these two. One must inquire, therefore, whether there are reasonable grounds for the researchers' extreme preferences in errors. The decision as to the relative importance of these errors depends wholly on their consequences, not on any property of the errors themselves. In research concerned with family relationships and parenting behavior, for example, the consequences of failing to identify differences existing in a population (type 2 errors) might be to reduce efforts at family supportive services in favor of no treatment or some other alternative, when in fact the supportive services would have made an appreciable difference in the rate of admission of children to care, as well as other consequences of family malfunctioning. These consequences are clearly of major importance. A strong case can therefore be made that type 2 error is somewhat greater in importance than type 1 error. To tolerate type 2 errors of from eight to fifteen times the magnitude of type 1 errors is, under these circumstances, to put triple locks on the front door while leaving the back door ajar.

The practice of guarding against type 1 errors at all costs may stem partly from a scientific tradition in which an established body of theory is not lightly abandoned.[21] But this principle should not be unthinkingly applied in a field such as social work in which no firmly established body of theory exists and in which the consequences of error must be appraised in practical rather than scientific terms.

# Experiments Concerned with the Economic Functioning of the Family

Studies of the effects of social work services on family relationships and parenting behavior have absorbed only a relatively small fraction of evaluative research effort to date. A second important area has been the economic functioning of the family, a term which has generally been used to designate the amount and sources of family income as well as gains or losses in purchasing power resulting from more efficient management of income. Economic functioning has also been measured by changes in the allocation of family income to nutritious food and health care.

Table 2 shows, for six tests of experimental effects on these kinds of variables, maximum power to detect differences between experimental and control groups of from 0 to 30 percent. As a rule, data on the reliability and validity of the criterion measures employed in this set of comparisons are scarce. Generally, the criterion measures are based on self-report data obtained by interviews and/or questionnaires. From survey research it is known that data on family economic status and practices contain a good deal of error, of both unreliability and invalidity.[22] It is unlikely, therefore, that the validity of any of the measures listed in table 2 is greater than .75 or that their reliability is greater than .90.

The maximum differences detectable with a probability of .95, where the probability of type 1 error is set at .05, look very similar to, though somewhat less varied than, the differences in family relationships and parenting behavior. If validity approximates .75 and reliability .90, the true differences detectable at a .95 probability level are approximately 1.5 times as great as the differences indicated in the table. (For the method of calculation, see Appendix.) This suggests that in most cases the true $D_{.95}$ is 40 percent or greater. In the light of their probable consequences, differences much smaller than this appear to be of practical importance. Therefore, the policy implications of the outcome data in the area of family economic functioning appear to be about as weak as for the outcome data on family relationships and adequacy of parenting.

**Table**

MAXIMUM POWER OF EXPERIMENTS ON ECONOMIC FUNCTIONING OF THE FAMILY TO DETECT DIFFERENCES BETWEEN EXPERIMENTAL AND CONTROL GROUPS*

| STUDY | DATA SOURCE | CRITERION MEASURE | $D_{.95}$ | MAXIMUM POWER TO DETECT INDICATED PROPORTION DIFFERENCE | | | | | |
|---|---|---|---|---|---|---|---|---|---|
| | | | | .05 | .10 | .15 | .20 | .25 | .30 |
| Area Development Project | ADP, p. 66 | E-C on % no change in economic functioning, G-A Scale | .25 | .11 | .28 | .60 | .84 | .95 | .99+ |
| Chemung County Project | Brown, p. 124 | E-C on % showing improvement in economic functioning, G-A Scale | .36 | .07 | .17 | .32 | .52 | .71 | .86 |
| Community Service Society Project | Mullen et al., p. 314 | E-C on % not receiving welfare | .28 | .13 | .34 | .61 | .81 | .94 | .99 |
| Mississippi AFDC Project | Wilkinson and Ross, p. 370 | Special services sample and control group on % with increased income | .33 | .08 | .20 | .36 | .56 | .74 | .87 |
| Mississippi AFDC Project | Wilkinson and Ross, p. 370 | Same groups above on % with earnings last month | .30 | .21 | .28 | .51 | .72 | .87 | .94 |

*Maximum power is achieved only if the data are free of measurement error. In this table E = experimental group, C = control group, and $D_{.95}$ = the minimum proportion difference between E and C detectable with .95 probability, with type 1 error = .05. This difference is sharply increased by measurement error.

# Experiments in Which Measures of Children's Problems Are Used as Outcome Criteria

Table 3 shows, for eleven comparisons of experimental and control groups of outcome data on children's problems, the power of the findings for various levels of differences. While power is more varied than for comparisons analyzed in tables 1 and 2, in only four of eleven comparisons is the maximum power of detecting differences of the order of 20 percent equal to .95. The two most powerful comparisons are those taken from the Cambridge-Somerville Study, where $D_{.95}$ is equal to .14. But measurement error is once again a serious problem, since the data on which this comparison is based, official delinquency statistics, are notoriously poor measures of actual delinquency. The actual power of these comparisons is therefore likely to be very much less than the maximum power. If we assume the same level of validity and reliability as for the data on the economic functioning of families—which is probably to err on the generous side—the actual $D_{.95}$ is in the neighborhood of .21–.28 rather than .14.

If it is to be interpreted as an indicator of potential for future problems or of overall social adjustment, as seems to be the intention of the authors of the Girls at Vocational High Study, the data on percentage of high school graduations appear to be subject to substantial error, which would be reflected in very modest correlations with other measures of these complicated variables. Taken by themselves, data on percentage of graduations are probably quite reliable and "valid." The interpretation of the power of this kind of comparison depends, therefore, on the meanings to be assigned to the measure or on the use to which it is to be put. The majority of the measures employed in the Girls at Vocational High Study (attitude tests, personality inventories, or ratings) tend to have large measurement errors[23] and may therefore be expected to yield results which are less powerful than the ones analyzed here.

## Conclusions

The data presented in this paper show that the research evidence as to the effectiveness of case services in social work is much less clear-cut than has often been assumed. There is a need for caution in generalizing as to policy implications in areas such as the selection of one or another mode or theory of intervention. This creates a di-

**Table 3**

MAXIMUM POWER OF EXPERIMENTS ON TREATMENT OF CHILDREN'S PROBLEMS TO DETECT DIFFERENCES BETWEEN EXPERIMENTAL AND CONTROL GROUPS*

| STUDY | DATA SOURCE | CRITERION MEASURE | $D_{.95}$ | MAXIMUM POWER TO DETECT INDICATED PROPORTION DIFFERENCE | | | | | |
|---|---|---|---|---|---|---|---|---|---|
| | | | | .05 | .10 | .15 | .20 | .25 | .30 |
| Girls at Vocational High | Meyer et al., p. 161 | E-C on % graduation from high school | .15 | .25 | .68 | .95 | .99+ | .99+ | .99+ |
| Girls at Vocational High | Meyer et al., p. 161 | Same as above for 3-year cohort | .22 | .13 | .37 | .69 | .91 | .99 | .99+ |
| Girls at Vocational High | Meyer et al., p. 165 | Second year of cohort C-E on % "no failures" | .24 | .23 | .46 | .70 | .86 | .96 | .99 |
| Girls at Vocational High | Meyer et al., p. 165 | Year of cohort entry C-E on % "no failures" | .19 | .19 | .54 | .86 | .98 | .99+ | .99+ |
| Girls at Vocatonal High | Meyer et al., p. 162 | E-C on % "completed senior year" | .23 | .13 | .39 | .68 | .91 | .99+ | .99+ |
| Atlantic Street Project | Berleman and Steinburn, p. 421 | C-E on % having delinquency records, 5 months of service | .44 | .05 | .10 | .18 | .27 | .40 | .66 |

*Maximum power is achieved only if the data are free of measurement error. In this table E = experimental group, C = control group, and $D_{.95}$ the minimum proportion difference between E and C detectable with .95 probability, with type 1 error = .05. This difference is sharply increased by measurement error.

**Table 3** (*Continued*)

| Study | Data Source | Criterion Measure | $D_{.95}$ | Maximum Power to Detect Indicated Proportion Difference | | | | | |
|---|---|---|---|---|---|---|---|---|---|
| | | | | .05 | .10 | .15 | .20 | .25 | .30 |
| Atlantic Street Project | Berleman and Steinburn, p. 421 | Same after 4 months of service | .50 | .05 | .10 | .17 | .26 | .38 | .51 |
| Atlantic Street Project | Berleman and Steinburn, p. 421 | Same after 6 months of service | .62 | .04 | .08 | .22 | .33 | .46 | .60 |
| Casework with Female Probationers | Webb and Riley, p. 569 | C-E on % reporting "trouble with police" | .37 | .06 | .12 | .22 | .37 | .55 | .73 |
| Cambridge-Somerville Study | Power and Witmer, p. 335 | C-E on % of "serious" or "most serious" offenses | .14 | .25 | .68 | .97 | .99+ | .99+ | .99+ |
| Cambridge-Somerville Study | Power and Witmer, p. 324 | C-E on % having one or more appearances before Crime Prevention Bureau | .14 | .29 | .76 | .98 | .99+ | .99+ | .99+ |

lemma for those who would like to find in the results of evaluative research in social work a message to the effect that the potency of social work methods should be increased. Obviously, social work must always be in search of more potent methods. But in order to judge effectively the relative potency of different treatment methods, it is essential to apply research designs with adequate discriminatory power. Until this is done, there will be no clear-cut evidence favoring either of the following two alternatives: First, the intervention variables have been potent enough to produce socially important differences, but the research designs employed have not been powerful enough to detect such differences. Second, the intervention variables have been too weak to produce minimally adequate differences. At present, notwithstanding the success of behavior modification treatment of a number of problems, it appears necessary to keep an open mind about the relative effectiveness of different approaches to case services in social work.

To deal effectively with the need to increase the discriminatory power of evaluative research in social work, a first essential is to introduce power considerations into the planning of the research rather than after the findings are in. The practice of basing the selection of type 1 error levels merely on statistical conventions must be abandoned. It has long been known that the routine use of the .05 level has no scientific or logical justification.[24] Furthermore, error is error, and type 2 errors have no special claims to grace. In the initial planning phase of research, it would be wise to ignore statistical considerations altogether in favor of practical and theoretical ones. To put this another way, a set of explicit judgments must be made as to the degrees of difference between experimental and control groups which are of theoretical and/or practical importance. A further set of judgments must then be made, once again on substantive rather than statistical grounds, as to the relative importance of type 1 and 2 errors. In many cases, type 2 errors will be seen to be as important as type 1 errors. In this case, they should be set at the same level. It will also be frequently apparent that the experiment must be designed large enough to detect relatively small differences. Where this is unfeasible, either a nonexperimental method of evaluation must be resorted to or relatively low probabilities of finding a significant difference must be accepted. In this case, the experiment becomes an exploratory probe whose results are expected to be less than final. But a decision that this kind of result is all that may reasonably be aimed at must be made beforehand rather than after the fact.

The approach to planning experiments recommended here will make deliberate and conscious, and thereby bring under control, a process which often appears to be little more than a series of accidents.

Finally, it appears to be essential, in adding up the results of a collection of evaluative studies,[25] to take account of the wide variations in the conclusion-drawing power of the different studies in the collection. Otherwise, the aggregation of research results can be misleading.

# Appendix
# A Technical Note on Methods of Calculation

*Transformation of the data.*—In all cases, the data taken from studies were in the form of proportions or percentages. In order to render equal at any point on the scale from 0 to 1 the probability of detecting a specified difference between two proportions, the following transformation was employed:

$$\phi = 2 \sin^{-1} p ,$$

where $\phi$ = the transformed proportion and $p$ = the proportion to be transformed.[26]

*Calculation of statistical power.*—For this purpose, use was made of the relationship

$$Z_{B-1} = /\ \phi_1 - \phi_2/\sqrt{n/2} - Z_{\alpha/2},$$

where $Z_{B-1}$ = the normal deviate associated with the probability given by $1$ − the probability of type 2 error, and $\phi_1$ and $\phi_2$ are proportions transformed as above. The $\phi_1$ was determined from the proportion reported in the original study for either the control or experimental group, and $\phi_2$ was then calculated for raw score differences of .05, .10, .15, .20, .25, and .30; $Z_{\alpha/2}$ (the normal deviate associated with a two-tailed $\alpha$ error of .05) = 1.96. All power calculations are for two-tailed tests, since only two-tailed tests were employed in the twenty-five examples found in the literature. One-tailed hypotheses have greater power for differences in the direction of the hypothesis, but their use for evaluative research in social work is questionable, since they have zero power to detect deterioration effects (differences in the wrong direction). There appears to be enough cause for concern about the possibility of such effects that they should not be disregarded.

The quantity $n$ is the sample size where two equal-sized samples were employed, that is, $n_1 = n_2$. If $n_1 \neq n_2$, then $n^1$ was substituted for $n$, where $n^1$ = the harmonic mean of $n_1$ and $n_2$.

*Checking the findings for accuracy.*—The results shown in tables 1–3 were checked against the power tables provided by Cohen,[27] with which they closely agree. (In many instances, linear interpolations in Cohen's tables must be made.)

*Calculation of effect of measurement error on power.*[28]—Use was made of the relationship

$$\Delta_T = \frac{\Delta_y \sqrt{\rho_{xx'}}}{\rho_{xy}},$$

where $\Delta_T$ = true difference in the means of two populations, $\Delta_y$ = difference in means observed in the sample, $\rho_{xx'}$ = reliability of the criterion measure, and $\rho_{xy}$ = validity of the criterion measure.

*An example of the effects of measurement errors on the discriminating power of the experiments.* —Measurement error is itself difficult to measure, since it depends on the estimation of "reliability" and "criterion validity" of the outcome measure employed, quantities which are frequently unavailable or imprecise. Reliability, the proportion of true variation in a measure,[29] may also be taken as the correlation of the measure with its equivalent form. Criterion validity may be treated as the correlation of the outcome measure of the experiment with a theoretical completely valid measure.[30] The effect of unreliability and invalidity is to reduce the differences which an experiment is capable of detecting. As has been shown for the case of $F$ tests of differences among means,[31] the effect of unreliability and invalidity on the magnitude of the differences which may be detected by an experiment is given by the following relationship:

true differences which can be detected by a given experiment =

$$\frac{\text{square root of reliability}}{\text{validity}} \times \text{observed difference.}$$

Unless reliability and validity are perfect, the magnitude of the true detectable difference is always larger than the observed one.[32] Measures of family functioning and similar variables tend to have relatively low validity coefficients: when they are available at all, they are seldom greater than .5, with reliabilities in the range .6–.9.[33] The Geismar-Ayres Scale of Family Functioning is one of the more extensively used and carefully tested instruments employed in evaluative research in social work. Some data are available as to its internal consistency (reliability as defined above), showing that the range is apparently .58–.80 for different areas of family functioning.[34] This sets an upper limit to the overall criterion validity of the measure, as defined above, of roughly .80 (the square root of the mean). Geismar has provided some further data on the criterion validity of the Geismar-Ayres Scale in the form of the agreement of scores on this scale with scores on the Hunt-Kogan Movement Scale.[35] A more convincing estimate, however, of the criterion validity of the Geismar-Ayres Scale is to set it equal to that of the Hunt-Kogan Movement Scale, in view of the close agreement between the two measures.[36] The Hunt-Kogan Movement Scale showed, in a follow-up study, a correlation of .6 with adjustment level measured several years after treatment, the most stringent available evidence of criterion validity.[37]

Assuming then that the Geismar-Ayres Scale has a reliability in the neighborhood of .80 and a validity of about .6, the differences which it is capable of detecting are about one and a half times the differences which it would be capable of detecting, with given probability, if it were perfectly reliable and valid.

Thus, to detect true differences of .25, an experiment exploying the Geismar-Ayres Scale would have to have a large enough sample to detect differences of .17. The actual power of the Area Development Project to detect differences of the order of .25 is thus about .60, compared with the maximum figure of .95 shown in table 1. The odds, then, that this experiment will detect a true difference of 25 percent between experimental and control groups are 6 out of 10, not much better than 50:50.

# Notes

This paper is based on part of the work done in 1974–75 under a research fellowship from the Welfare Research Grants Directorate of Health and Welfare, Canada, grant 2562-C-2.

1. See, e.g., Ludwig L. Geismar, "Thirteen Evaluative Studies," in *Evaluation of Social Intervention*, ed. Edward J. Mullen, James R. Dumpson & Associates (San Francisco: Jossey-Bass, Inc., 1972), pp. 15–38; Maurice Kelly, "Casework in Jeopardy," *Social Worker* 40, no. 2 (May 1972): 66; and Joel Fischer, "Is Casework Effective? A Review," *Social Work* 18 ( July 1973): 5–21.

2. H. W. Riecken and R. F. Boruch, *Social Experimentation* (New York: Academic Press, 1974); and P. H. Rossi and W. Williams, *Evaluating Social Programs: Theory, Practice, and Politics* (New York: Seminar Press, 1972).

3. Fischer, p. 6; and Geismar, p. 17.

4. "Controls" or "control groups" are used in this paper with the same meaning commonly assigned to them in experimental research, i.e., to refer to groups exposed to a standard condition against which one or more experimental conditions will be compared (see B. J. Winer, *Statistical Principles in Experimental Design* [New York: McGraw-Hill Book Co., 1967], pp. 89–92). A discussion of the various forms of control groups appropriate for research in psychotherapy is given by Julian Meltzoff and Melvin Kornreich in *Research in Psychotherapy* (New York: Atherton Press, 1970), pp. 21–24. These authors distinguish untreated controls, other-treated controls, terminator controls, waiting-list controls, placebo-effect controls, and "patient as own control."

5. W. G. Cochran and G. M. Cox, *Experimental Designs*, 2d ed. (New York: John Wiley & Sons, 1957).

6. Power analysis is equally applicable (provided that the interest is in differences among random samples) to experimental services in disciplines other than social work, such as clinical psychology, and to most social experimentation and survey research at the so-called mezzo and macro levels.

7. Reviews by Fischer and Geismar include both types (see n. 4 above).

8. For the method of calculation of power used, see below. Power analysis is equally applicable where the interest is in differences among random samples in means or correlation coefficients. No such cases happen to be considered in this paper. In all cases, the judgment of the authors as to the appropriate statistic to use, whether means, proportions, or other statistics, was accepted for purposes of this paper.

9. John A. Crane, *Research on the Effects of Case Services in Social Work* (a report in preparation).

10. Area Development Project of Vancouver, British Columbia, *Research Monograph*, no. 3 (Vancouver: United Community Services of Vancouver, September 1969); Gordon E. Brown, *The Multi-Problem Dilemma* (Metuchen, N.J.: Scarecrow Press, 1968); E. J. Mullen, R. M. Chazin, and D. M. Feldstein, "Services for the Newly Dependent: An Assessment," *Social Service Review* 46, no. 3 (September 1972): 309–22; and Kenneth P.

Wilkinson and Peggy J. Ross, "Evaluation of the Mississippi AFDC Experiment," *Social Service Review* 46, no. 3 (September 1972): 363–77.

11. Area Development Project; and Brown.

12. W. C. Berleman and T. W. Steinburn, "The Execution and Evaluation of a Delinquency Prevention Program," *Social Problems* 14 (1967): 413–23; M. M. Craig and P. W. Furst, "What Happens after Treatment: A Study of Potentially Delinquent Boys," *Social Service Review* 29 (June 1965): 165–71: Alice McCabe, *The Pursuit of Promise* (New York: Community Service Society, 1967); H. J. Meyer, E. E. Borgatta, and W. C. Jones, *Girls at Vocational High: An Experiment in Social Work Intervention* (New York: Russell Sage Foundation, 1965); and E. Powers and H. Witmer, *An Experiment in the Prevention of Delinquency: The Cambridge-Somerville Youth Study* (New York: Columbia University Press, 1951).

13. Area Development Project; Brown; and W. J. Reid and A. W. Shyne, *Brief and Extended Casework* (New York: Columbia University Press, 1969).

14. Margaret Blenkner, Julius Jahn, and Edna Wasser, *Serving the Aging: An Experiment in Social Work and Public Health Nursing* (New York: Community Service Society, 1964); and L. L. Geismar and J. Krisberg, *The Forgotten Neighborhood: Site of an Early Skirmish in the War on Povery* (Metuchen, N.J.: Scarecrow Press, 1967).

15. Differences substantially larger than 30 percent are likely to be apparent without experimentation; experiments designed to detect these are aptly described as providing, in Tukey's phrase, "statistical sanctification" (quoted in J. Cohen, *Statistical Power Analysis for the Behavioral Sciences* [New York: Academic Press, 1969], p. 176).

16. To commit a type 1 error is to reject a hypothesis of no difference between experimental and control groups when it is true, whereas to commit a type 2 error is to accept this hypothesis when it is false. For a useful as well as readable discussion of these concepts, see Sidney Siegel, *Nonparametric Statistics for the Behavioral Sciences* (New York: McGraw-Hill Book Co., 1956), pp. 7–20.

17. For convenience, in discussing the data in tables 1–3, I have converted proportions to percentages.

18. In some of these studies, no meaningful estimate of validity may be available. This, of course, is all the more reason for caution in interpreting statistical findings from these studies.

19. Jum C. Nunally, *Psychometric Theory* (New York: McGraw-Hill Book Co., 1967).

20. It should be kept in mind that, after looking at his findings, the experimenter either accepts or rejects a hypothesis of no difference. If he accepts it he may make a type 2 error but obviously cannot make a type 1 error. Conversely, if he rejects the hypothesis of no difference he can make a type 1 error but not a type 2 error. The focus on this section of the paper is on the probabilities of each type of error prior to the analysis of the data. It is of interest that in twenty-two of the twenty-five examples cited in this paper the researchers accepted a hypothesis of no difference, and in the other three cases (the two findings from the Casework Methods Project and one from the Area Development Project) they rejected the hypothesis of no difference.

21. Karl R. Popper, *The Logic of Scientific Discovery* (London: Hutchinson, 1959).

22. P. M. Siegel and R. W. Hodge, "A Causal Approach to the Study of Measurement Error," in *Methodology in Social Research*, ed. H. M. Blalock and A. B. Blalock (New York: McGraw-Hill Book Co., 1968).

23. Nunally.

24. J. A. Crane, "The Insignificance of Statistical Significance," mimeographed (Vancouver: School of Social Work, University of British Columbia, 1969), p. 16; L. Kish, "Some Statistical Problems in Research Design," *American Sociological Review* 24 (1959): 328–38; H. Selvin, "A Critique of Tests of Significance in Survey Research," *American Sociological Review* 22 (1957): 519–27; J. K. Skipper, A. L. Guenther, and G. Maas, "The Sacredness of .05: A Note concerning the Uses of Statistical Levels of Significance in Social Science," *American Sociologist* 2 (February 1967): 16–18; Winer; and Cohen.

25. Fischer.

26. Cohen, p. 176.

27. Ibid., p. 189.

28. For further details, see A. T. Cleary, R. Linn, and G. W. Walster, "Effect of Reliability and Validity on Power of Statistical Tests," in *Sociological Methodology 1970*, ed. E. F. Borgatta and G. W. Bohrnstedt (San Francisco: Jossey-Bass, Inc., 1970); and F. M. Lord and M. R. Novick (with contributions by A. Birnbaum), *Statistical Theories of Mental Test Scores* (Reading, Mass.: Addison-Wesley Publishing Co., 1968).

29. J. P. Guilford, *Psychometric Methods* (New York: McGraw-Hill Book Co., 1954).

30. Lord and Novick.

31. Cleary et al., p. 136.

32. Ibid., p. 137.

33. Nunally; P. O. Johnson and R. W. B. Jackson, *Introduction to Statistical Methods* (New York: Prentice-Hall, Inc., 1953); L. S. Kogan, J. McV. Hunt, and P. Bartelme, *A Follow-up Study of the Results of Social Casework* (New York: Family Service Association of America, 1953); and Geismar, pp. 15–38. See also n. 18 above.

34. Ludwig Geismar, *Family and Community Functioning* (Metuchen, N.J.: Scarecrow Press, 1971).

35. Ibid., p. 140.

36. Brown, p. 139.

37. Kogan et al.

# 11

# Comments on Statistical Power in Evaluative Research Design

## John R. Schuerman

The article by John A. Crane entitled "The Power of Social Intervention Experiments to Discriminate Differences between Experimental and Control Groups" (*Social Service Review* 50 [June 1976]: 224–42) is an important contribution to our understanding of evaluative research design. The issue of statistical power is much neglected by evaluators of social programs. I wholeheartedly agree with Crane that, before the experiment is undertaken, it is essential to assess the power of the design to detect effects that the experimenter would consider important. However, in his discussion of the decisions the researcher must make when faced with low power, Crane does not discuss one possible outcome—namely, to abandon the experiment. If we undertake an experiment with little chance of detecting important differences, we will be likely to wind up only providing more fodder for the doomsayers of our profession. Trying to escape the consequences by labeling such fated research "exploratory," as Crane suggests, will not do.

I would like to make a number of other points in hopes of furthering the consideration of the important issues Crane raises.

1. Crane focuses primarily on two of the factors affecting the power of an experiment to detect a given difference, namely, the significance level and measurement error (by which he means both random errors of measurement and invalidity). Among other factors which affect power are the size of the sample, the nature of the particular statistical tests employed, and the variation of the criterion variable in the population being studied. The larger the sample, the higher the power; so researchers generally take as large a sample as is feasible within the limits of resources. However, faced with a dismal power analysis, researchers may want to find a way somehow to increase the sample size. In regard to variation in the criterion variable, it is sometimes possible to reduce that variation or control for it, either through the design or in the analysis of data.

2. The test of difference of proportions of successful cases is usually the least powerful of all statistical tests commonly employed in comparisons of two or more groups. Far more powerful are tests of differences in means of outcome variables or of correlations between treatment and outcome variables. Crane has ignored the fact that, in some of the studies he cites, the researchers did employ tests of differences in means. Such tests were far more powerful than

From John R. Schuerman, "Comments on Statistical Power in Evaluative Research Design," 51 (3) *Social Service Review* 524–526 (September 1977). Copyright 1977 by the University of Chicago.

those examined by Crane, but the results were usually similar to the tests of differences in proportions.

3. I agree with Crane that too much emphasis is placed on type 1 errors, at the expense of type 2 errors. The routine use of .05 as a decision level has little rational basis. However, Crane's suggestion that many times the probability of type 1 error might be set equal to that of type 2 error may be going too far. How high would Crane go with a decision level in, say, a study of the effectiveness of casework in which the researcher wants to detect a 15 percent difference? Would he raise it to .3 in order to have at least a 70 percent chance of finding such a difference? In some studies the experimental intervention represents a substantial investment of money and staff. Before adopting such experimental interventions widely, I would want to be fairly sure that they worked. In fact sometimes I would want to be surer than the surety provided by .05. A frequently suggested alternative to reporting acceptance or rejection at a predetermined decision level is to provide the obtained probability of the null hypothesis, thereby involving the reader in the decision.

4. Crane's power calculations are entirely for two-tailed tests. As he points out, one-tailed tests are considerably·more powerful. He asserts, however, that the use of one-tailed tests is questionable. At the risk of flying in the face of accepted statistical practice, I would disagree. Although the researchers often used two-tailed tests, their hypotheses were usually at least implicitly directional (the experimental group was expected to do better). I would argue that in such circumstances a one-tailed probability would be justified. As Crane notes, it is true that, should deterioration effects show up, the previous adoption of a one-tailed test would technically preclude the analysis of such effects (legally, you cannot find out if such deterioration effects are "significant"). However, there appear to be enough persons around eager to pounce on deterioration evidence that I do not fear such findings being lost to the field.

5. Finally, Crane implies that the attacks on casework that rest on the negative findings of a number of studies should be tempered by considering the power of each of those studies to find important effects. I agree that this is an important consideration so far lacking in such discussions. However, most studies of effectiveness examined several outcome measures. In such situations, the probability that one or more of the outcome measures will show significant differences is increased to the extent that the various measures are not perfectly correlated. Thus the power of a study as a whole (taken as the probability that one or more measures will show significance) is higher than that of any one statistical test. The actual estimation of this probability would be exceedingly difficult. The other edge of this sword is the familiar observation that the more tests you run, the more chance you will have of finding at least one significant, even if there is no difference between the groups (that is, probability of type 1 error is increased for the study as a whole).

More important, however, is the fact that many studies of effectiveness have been done, and if they are taken as a whole (an admittedly dubious procedure, given their diversity, but a procedure that appears to be the rage nonetheless) the "power" of the collection is far higher than that of any one study. That is, the probability that at least one study would find significant results will be fairly high. Taking a number of studies as a whole of course also increases the probability that one or more will show "significant" differences, even though there are no real effects.

# 12

# Author's Reply

## John A. Crane

I am very grateful for the questions raised by John R. Schuerman which provide me with a need and opportunity to expand on and in some cases extend several of the points made in my article.

In his first paragraph, Schuerman points out that sometimes an assessment of the power of a proposed experiment should lead to its abandonment. I quite agree. However, if Schuerman is also arguing that small-scale pilot or probe experiments have no place, then I disagree, since their use is often essential in order to find out how to make a larger-scale experiment more feasible and efficient. Moreover, exploratory, descriptive, and experimental objectives are being increasingly brought together in a single study,[1] a development which I applaud.

I shall now respond to each of Schuerman's other five points.

1. Schuerman is apparently accusing me of slighting three of the factors affecting the power of statistical tests—that is, the sample size, variation in the criterion variable, and the type of statistical test employed.

For the first he need only look at the equation used in my article to calculate statistical power: he will find that sample size entered into the calculation in each and every instance. The conclusion to the article emphasized the need to plan experiments large enough to meet predetermined criteria. This of course refers to sample size.

Variation in the criterion variable is also taken into account in the method I used to calculate statistical power. It is quite true, as Schuerman suggests, that the experimenter should always be alert to ways of reducing this variation.

The effect of differences in the power of different statistical tests employed was not directly relevant to my article, as all of the tests considered were of the same kind. I shall take up the general effect of this factor next.

2. Schuerman speaks of far more powerful tests of significance which researchers have employed and which my paper ignored. But "far more powerful" is extremely vague, and if Schuerman's argument is to be examined seriously, we must get down to specifics.

The problem posed by Schuerman is that a researcher with, say, fifty cases in his experimental and control groups may for some of the study hypotheses use parametric tests such as the $F$-test and for others use a test of differences of proportions. This choice will depend on the type of available data. According to Schuerman, the $F$-test will be "far more powerful."

In trying to make this assertion more specific, we encounter a formidable difficulty—namely, that where no parametric alternative to a test of differ-

From John A. Crane, "Author's Reply," 51 (3) *Social Service Review* 526-529 (September 1977). Copyright 1977 by the University of Chicago.

ences in proportions exists no meaningful comparison as to power is possible. This would be true, for example, of all, or nearly all, the cases in my article.

This problem should not be confused with the one in which the researcher's data permit him a choice of either a parametric test or a test of difference in proportions. In this case the parametric test will as a rule be far more powerful, simply because in reducing the interval-level data to a dichotomy the researcher throws away information.

In any event, it is inadvisable to make pat generalizations about the relative power of different types of statistical tests. One way around this problem is exemplified by Cohen,[2] who has designed power tables in which the probabilities of finding small, large, and medium differences are comparable for different types of tests. Thus a hypothetical researcher with experimental and control groups of fifty cases who has set type 1 error at .05 has power in his $F$-tests of .16, .71, and .98 to detect small, medium, and large differences, respectively.[3] For tests of proportions, the comparable figures are .17, .71, and .98.[4]

But another factor of major importance cannot be ignored: the assumptions underlying parametric tests are seldom as adequately met in research in social work as the assumptions underlying tests of differences in proportions. The effect of this is substantially to reduce still further the power of the parametric tests for this type of research.

Thus we can hardly pin our hopes on parametric tests to rescue experimental research in social work from the problem of low power.

3. A major conclusion of my paper was that in planning experiments we must use our heads instead of the formula. It is therefore a bit disconcerting to find Schuerman apparently looking for a formula as to how high we should go in setting type 1 error. In so doing he ignores the possible costs of type 2 errors and the possible benefits (including reduced costs) from, say, a 15 percent impact on a problem. Worst of all, he assumes that some "surety" of social significance is provided by some specified level of statistical significance (such as .05 or smaller). This assumption is so common in research in social work and so serious in its consequences that it merits further consideration.

But first to get a minor technical point out of the way: there is no reason to consider a type 1 error level of .20 or .30 to be statistically unorthodox and indicative of a "soft" study. B. J. Winer, past president of the American Statistical Association, suggests that, "when the power of tests is likely to be low, under (.05 and .01) levels of significance, and when Type I and Type II errors are of approximately equal importance, the .30 and .20 levels of significance may be more appropriate than the .05 and .01 levels."[5]

The social climate which has led to the identification of the .05 and .01 levels with scientific rigor is a problem for the sociology of social research, not a problem of research design.

But the most serious gap in information available to date on the results of social work interventions is the lack of any connection between statistical decisions and policy decisions. The implicit assumption in research to date has been generally that the statistical significance of a difference and its policy significance are equivalent. But it is entirely possible for a statistically insignificant difference, as determined by a particular study, to be nonetheless large enough to have important consequences for policy and, conversely, for a statistically significant difference to be too small to have any consequences for policy.

Statistical decision theory, in both its classical and modern version, provides for a linkage of statistical and policy decisions through the concepts of loss and risk functions and decision rules linking the two (the losses may be expressed in monetary or other kinds of units).[6] By one of these rules, for example, the risk of a maximum loss is minimized (this rule, it should be noted, assumes nature to be an adversary).[7] But in research in social work to date, the whole subject of loss functions seems so far to have been almost completely neglected. As a result, in few if any studies on the effects of social work intervention is there any real evidence that basing the policy decision —for example, whether or not to introduce a casework program—on the statistical decision made in the experiment will minimize expected losses or maximize expected gains. In these circumstances, tests of statistical significance have much the same scientific standing (and perhaps also serve much the same psychological purpose) as navigation magic once practiced by the Trobriand Islanders before putting out to sea in a canoe: they do no more than provide assurance that a required ritual has been performed.

As a rule, the researcher in social work is better off not using such tests. More useful procedures are available (see below).

4. Schuerman argues that researchers should, in order to increase the power of their experiments, relax their efforts to detect deterioration effects, leaving this problem to the vigilance of readers. In view of the extreme seriousness of deterioration effects, I cannot agree.

One effect of using one-tailed tests would be to increase the number of positive (i.e., statistically significant) findings. This would further complicate the problem, already a difficult one, of aggregating results over different studies (see below).

5. In regard to the issue of aggregating results, we again have a problem which requires us to use our heads rather than the formula. Unless we are able to resolve the ambiguities surrounding the use of statistical significance tests in social work research (see above), there is no point in attempting to aggregate the results of several such tests. Even if there were no ambiguity, there would still be the problem of how to aggregate significant and nonsignificant findings: these are simply not additive. Nor would we have any satisfactory method of taking account of the differential power of different studies (a problem I emphasized in my article).

A more useful reformulation of the problem of linking research decisions to policy decisions can be arrived at by reminding ourselves that policy decisions must nearly always rest on plausibilities, not on probabilities, and on the magnitude, not on the statistical significance, of experimental effects (to the extent that they can be based at all on research evidence). For the policymaker, the most useful experimental evidence would be information accumulated over a series of studies dealing with a specified criterion variable as to just how much difference is made by a given social program. For each study in the set, a maximum-likelihood estimate of this difference would be provided,[8] and the estimates from all studies in the set would be combined, after each had been weighted according to the power associated with its findings. Furthermore, around each such estimate a confidence interval could be supplied. This would provide a much more useful body of knowledge for policymaking than exists at present and would begin to make cumulative use of some of the expensively acquired information on the effects of social programs which now lies scattered in various research reports.

## Notes

1. Robert F. Boruch, "Coupling Randomized Experiments and Approximations to

Experiments in Social Program Evaluation," *Sociological Methods and Research* 4, no. 1 (August 1975): 31–53.

2. Jacob Cohen, *Statistical Power Analysis for the Behavioral Sciences* (New York: Academic Press, 1969), p. 278.

3. Ibid., p. 190.

4. Ibid., p. 305.

5. B. J. Winer, *Statistical Principles in Experimental Design* (New York: McGraw-Hill Book Co., 1962), p. 13.

6. John E. Freund, *Mathematical Statistics*, 2d ed. (Englewood Cliffs, N.J.: Prentice-Hall, Inc., 1971), p. 291.

7. Ibid., p. 247.

8. James G. Kalbfleisch, *Probability and Statistical Inference*, rev. ed. (Waterloo, Ont.: Department of Mathematics, University of Waterloo, 1975), 2:35–89.

# 13

## The Role of the Accountant in Preventing and Detecting Information Abuses in Social Program Evaluation

### *John G. Tabor*

America the beautiful has an ugly scar across her face.

Her cities are torn by violence and crime. Prejudice and racial hatred flare harshly. Her rivers and streams are polluted. Her hospitals are overcrowded and poorly staffed.

Despite much-publicized affluence, pockets of poverty throughout the nation swell with bitter and hopeless men and women in search of dignity, opportunity and self-respect.

Something has gone wrong in our society and something must be done to correct it. Not next year. Not tomorrow. But now. [1]

## THE CONTEXT OF SOCIAL PROGRAMS

The 1960s saw the birth of a great social consciousness movement. The problems in our society were cataloged, and attempts to solve these problems were made in many different spheres. The federal government launched numerous social programs to cure diverse social ills. Many of these programs were collectively titled the "Great Society" programs, or the "War on Poverty." Federal expenditures for social programs reached all-time highs. These outlays were supplemented by state and local government outlays. Private institutions contributed additional sums for grants aimed at researching and curing social ills.

Throughout this time, the business sector could not stand idle. Some firms, because of the personal conscience of managers and directors were voluntarily

From John G. Tabor, "The Role of the Accountant in Preventing and Detecting Information Abuses in Social Program Evaluation," pp. 77-99 in Howard W. Melton and David J.H. Watson (eds.), Interdisciplinary Dimensions of Accounting for Social Goals and Social Organizations, Grid, Inc., 1977. Copyright 1977 by Grid, Inc.

committed to active involvement in curing social ills. For many other firms, participation was much less voluntary. Various government agencies issued minimal performance standards for pollution control, job hiring practices, etc. Groups like Nader's Raiders would shame firms into efforts to cure social problems, especially those for which the firm was directly responsible. Investment funds were established that would trade only in the securities of firms that demonstrated social concern. Consumer groups would advocate purchasing only the products of firms which actively sought to improve the quality of life. In any case, firms could no longer strive to maximize profits while using up precious social resources which carried virtually no dollar cost to the firm itself. Firms would be held accountable for actions which debased the quality of life, and would be rewarded for their efforts to improve the social condition.

## THE PROBLEM OF MEASURING EFFECTS

Serious-minded attempts to cure social problems, whether sponsored by government institutions or private philanthropic organizations, or by businesses themselves, face a common problem: they need some means to measure the success of their efforts. Obviously, success can be considered only in relation to the goals of a program. The more clearly and concretely program objectives are stated, the more easily measures of success, of goal attainment, can be presented.

### LACK OF ADEQUATELY STATED PROGRAM GOALS

Unfortunately, a lack of adequately stated program objectives has been one of the biggest problems faced in evaluating program effectiveness. After examining the evaluations of fifteen programs in four federal agencies, Wholey concluded that most federal programs lack a clear statement of program goals or objectives.[2] As examples of the abuses in this area, consider the following: HEW's Maternal and Child Health programs included grants "for maternal and child health services."[3] A Department of Housing and Urban Development program's objectives are "to remedy the unsafe and unsanitary housing conditions ... (of) ... families of low income, in urban, rural, nonfarm and Indian areas, that are injurious to the health, safety, and morals of the citizens of the Nation."[4]

Obviously, if the objectives of any program are stated in such vague terms as the examples above indicate, it becomes difficult to determine any criteria for measuring program success, since success is left totally undefined. It is possible to observe programs in action and then infer what the objectives must be, but this is an acceptable procedure only if the program activities are geared toward meeting the true program objectives, rather than some personal motives of managers, who are using program funds for their own (perhaps equally philanthropic) purposes. A program may be quite effective in doing what it is doing, yet its activities may bear little relation to its mandated purpose.

Expressing program objectives adequately is no easy job. However, checklists, such as the one presented by Suchman,[5] which indicate the contents of a well defined set of program objectives, would go a long way in helping to remedy abuses in definition of program goals. With program objectives adequately stated, one at least has an idea of the basis on which program success is to be measured. However, the job of selecting or devising specific measurement devices, or indicators, remains.

## THE INDICATOR PROBLEM

### The Four Stage Measurement Process Defined

Sociometric and psychometric theory deals, at least in part, with the measurement problem. Cicourel quotes Lazarsfeld on the specification of the four steps in the measurement process: "'an initial imagery of the concept, the specification of dimensions, the selection of observable indicators, and the combination of indicators into indices.'"[6]

### Applying The Measurement Process To Social Programs: Initial Imagery & Specification Of Dimensions Of The Concept

In evaluating the success of a program, the imagery of the concept to be measured should come from an analysis of well-stated program objectives. For example, one purpose of an educational program might be to improve student achievement, which is defined as reading, mathematics, ability, etc. Alternatively a program may attempt to raise the self-esteem of pupils, in hopes that this will lead to longer periods of education. Some idea of what self-esteem means must be held before any measurement can take place.

The specification of the relevant dimensions of the concept expands upon the initial imagery conceptualization. The step is a crucial one, since omission of relevant dimensions of the concept can lead to greatly reduced usefulness of the entire measurements, if not total uselessness. Furthermore, failure to specify all the relevant dimensions of a complex concept can lead to undesirable behavioral consequences, namely, cases where the individual or program being evaluated attempts to beat the system.

Presumably the relevant dimensions of a concept being measured are derivable from the theory underlying the proposed effectiveness of a program. That is, there is some reason to believe, prior to actual implementation, that the program will reach its goals. Purported causal linkages between the program activities and the ultimate goal of the program usually exist. These linkages normally indicate what dimensions of the output (program effect) variables are expected to change and hence are relevant to the study. Similar analysis indicates what input variables (program activities) are expected to cause the change and the manner in which that change is to be brought about. Therefore, that analysis may help determine what dimensions of the input variables are relevant.

A much more difficult problem is one of anticipating possible side effects of a program—effects not intended and perhaps not wanted. Some experts in program evaluation advocate goal-free evaluation.[7] Rather than specify goals, one should simply measure all of the effects of a program, and evaluate the program on all of its effects.

But this sort of procedure has obvious weaknesses. Most apparently, one must somehow anticipate all that might happen as a result of the program. In complex programs, this is difficult, if not impossible, since the effects may be many and diverse. Failure to consider what may be the most important effects of the program may lead to evaluating the program on everything but its primary goal. Measuring anything and everything about the program may prove to be excessively cumbersome, and certainly wasteful of resources in that a great deal of ultimately irrelevant data might be gathered. Furthermore, without knowing why the program is suspected of causing particular changes, one may miss some relevant dimensions of the output variables.

## Applying The Measurement Process To Social Programs: Creation Of Specific Indicators

Creating indicators to measure the relevant dimensions of the concept of interest is limited only by the investigator's ingenuity. Many engineering measurements have proved useful in various pollution control projects. Standard medical tests may be useful to evaluate the worth of public health programs. Income is often used to measure the success of job training programs and other projects expected to have a very direct effect on poverty levels.

For many programs, personal characteristics of participants are the target of the change. Standardized and non-standardized tests of all sorts have been used to measure knowledge levels, achievement, aptitude, etc. Mental state of participants is often assessed through ratings by qualified psychologists. Attitudes, personality traits, and beliefs are often measured through interviews or questionnaires. Many off-the-shelf questionnaires are presented or at least described in such sources as Robinson and Shaver.[8] They have proved useful in the evaluation of some social programs.

In some areas, indicators which might prove useful in program evaluation have been cataloged. For example, Metfessel and Michael have extensively listed indicators which might prove useful in evaluating school programs.[9]

Some of the more ingenious indicators that have been used in the social sciences are reported by Webb, et. al. According to these authors:

> Today, the dominant mass of social science research is based upon interviews and questionnaires. We lament this overdependence upon a single, fallible method. Interviews and questionnaires intrude as a foreign element into the social setting they would describe, they create as well as measure attitudes, they elicit atypical roles and responses, they are limited to those who are accessible and will cooperate, and the responses obtained are produced in part by dimensions of individual differences irrelevant to the topic at hand.
>
> *But the principal objection is that they are used alone.* No research method is without bias. Interviews and questionnaires must be supplemented by methods testing the same social science variables but having *different* methodological weaknesses. (Emphasis in original.)[10]

After having reviewed numerous studies in which alternatives to interviews or questionnaires were used, these authors cataloged novel indicators into several basic groups. Examples of the type of indicators used follow. In most cases, subjects are unaware that any measurements are being made; hence, they can not react in atypical ways.

> The floor tiles around the hatching-chick exhibit at Chicago's Museum of Science and Industry must be replaced every six weeks. Tiles in other parts of the museum need not be replaced for years. The selective erosion of tiles, indexed by the replacement rate, is a measure of the relative popularity of exhibits.
>
> The accretion rate is another measure. One investigator wanted to learn the level of whisky consumption in a town which was officially "dry." He did so by counting empty bottles in ashcans.

The degree of fear induced by a ghost-story-telling session can be measured by noting the shrinking diameter of a circle of seated children.

Chinese jade dealers have used the pupil dilation of their customers as a measure of the client's interest in particular stones, and Darwin in 1872 noted this same variable as an index of fear.

Library withdrawals were used to demonstrate the effect of the introduction of television into a community. Fiction titles dropped, nonfiction titles were unaffected.

The role of rate of interaction in managerial recruitment is shown by the overrepresentation of baseball managers who were infielders or catchers (high-interaction positions) during their playing days.

Sir Francis Galton employed surveying hardware to estimate the bodily dimensions of African women whose language he did not speak.

The child's interest in Christmas was demonstrated by distortions in the size of Santa Claus drawings.

Racial attitudes in two colleges were compared by noting the degree of clustering of Negroes and whites in lecture halls. [11]

## Applying The Measurement Process To Social Programs: Combining Indicators Into Indices

When several indicators are used to measure the same program concept, the problem of combining these measures into a single, overall measure for the concept arises. For example, student achievement might be measured through three different achievement tests or a combination of test scores and psychologist ratings based on interviews. If a single decision or program effect on student achievement is to be made, some means of combining indicator scores into a single score must be found. The process may be purely judgmental, in that the evaluator may choose to ignore test scores in favor of sole reliance on ratings by psychologists. However, psychometric theory does have mathematical models for developing optimal weightings of the various separate indicators into a single score which are applicable in certain cases. The actual techniques need not concern us. In some manner the combination will be accomplished. In the discussion which follows, attention will be directed primarily to the separate indicators for a concept.

## THE NECESSARY CHARACTERISTICS OF INDICATORS: VALIDITY AND RELIABILITY

All indicators, no matter how creatively designed, should ideally possess two characteristics: validity and reliability. Without them, the usefulness of any indicator is severely limited. Briefly, validity is the extent to which an indicator measures all of the essential elements of the concept it set out to measure. Reliability is concerned with how consistently the indicator measures whatever it is that it measures.

Validity is obviously crucial. Unless the indicators measure what they are supposed to, namely the concepts derived from the program objectives, one will be evaluating the success of the program on the basis of irrelevant criteria. Decisions made on the basis of this data can be correct only by chance.

Validity is, however, related to reliability. Where certain mathematical expressions for validity and reliability exist, it can be proven that reliability sets an upper limit on the achievable validity. Intuitively, in order to measure the correct concept well, the indicator must measure consistently whatever it is that it measures. However, it is possible to have high reliability coupled with low validity.

Various facets of validity are discussed in the literature; predictive validity, content validity, construct validity, etc. are all different methods of viewing validity. Similarly, different forms of reliability measures are discussed in the psychometric literature. However, we need not be concerned about these alternative viewpoints. The simple ideas given above will suffice for our purposes. More important are the consequences of low validity and reliability, and what techniques are available to strengthen both the validity and reliability of indicators.

## Consequences Of Invalid Indicators

The greatest threat posed by invalid indicators is an incorrect decision on program effectiveness. The use of an invalid indicator means that the program is being evaluated upon some basis other than that suggested by the analysis of program goals. What that basis is can be determined only by careful analysis of the indicator actually used. Only if this invalid indicator correlates nearly perfectly with the actual concept which should have been used to evaluate the program will any decision on program effectiveness be correct, other than by chance.

The possibility of incorrect decisions is the most important threat posed by invalid indicators, but other problems do exist. Specifically, invalid indicators, when due to failure to capture all of the relevant dimensions of the concept used for evaluating the programs, often lead to cheating to "beat the system."

By now, Granick's work on Soviet productivity, and the dysfunctions caused by invalid indicators for productivity are renowned. When productivity was measured by weight of product produced, factory managers produced only the heaviest items in the product line, regardless of demand for them; badly-needed but lightweight products were not produced. When the measure of productivity was changed to the quantity of units produced, only the smallest, easiest to make items in the product line were produced. Defining productivity in terms of the dollar value of production has its problems since it ignores saleability of the products. Any of these three indicators leave open the possibility of maximizing current productivity by postponing routine repair and maintenance work, since it takes up valuable production time. Subsequent period production may be below normal in order to catch up on postponed maintenance, which may now be considerably more costly due to the aggravated condition of equipment.

Rivlin recounts similar dysfunctions in manpower training programs. Measuring success only in terms of job placement success would lead to quick placements ignoring "wage level, suitability, stability, or possibilities of advancement in employment. The result would be a lot of placements in low level, dead-end jobs, and little contribution to productivity." [12] Concentrating on increases in future earnings of people placed would lead to placing unemployed but already highly-skilled people or young people with a long life of potential earnings.

These examples could be continued. But in each case, the dysfunctions have been made possible through one form of indicator invalidity—fractional measurement. It means simply that all of the relevant dimensions of the concept for evaluation have not been captured in the indicator. Productivity is not simply the weight of units produced or the number of units produced. Nor can it be limited to effects on current output levels when activities designed to maximize current indicator values for productivity will adversely affect subsequent levels of the real productivity. The invalidity of the indicator makes such abuses possible, but it is undoubtedly the intense pressure caused by sole reliance on these indicators for evaluating performance which causes people to take advantage of the invalidity for their own ends.

### Curing Invalidity

What can be done to help create valid indicators and avoid the problems of invalid indicators? Unfortunately, little can be done, before the fact, to improve validity of indicators. Where the indicator is basically a rating by some person, personal biases can enter ratings if the rater has some prior knowledge about the individual being rated. Bias can be avoided if the rater is prevented from knowing any details about the person being rated. For example, membership in a particular group might signify that the person is supposed to score high or low on a particular rating scale.

Where an indicator is an interview or self-report questionnaire, these instruments can be pretested in situations similar to the one in which the instrument is to be used in practice. In-depth interviews with respondents can yield valuable information about how interviewees are interpreting questions and what they are responding to. Such interviews can help the interviewer learn the language nuances of the group to which measurements are to be applied. Utilizing these language nuances can improve the validity of questionnaires, since there is a better chance that the group are responding to the questions intended by the interviewer or questionnaire.

Various control scales can be administered to respondents to detect various response set biases. There is evidence to suggest that people tend to respond "Yes" more often than "No" to questions, regardless of content. Extreme responses are used as a matter of course by some people, instead of more moderate, middle-of-the-road responses. Where it appears that responses are following certain of these response sets, the substantive questionnaire data becomes suspect—people are simply not responding to the questions in a "valid" manner. The indicators are invalid in such situations. Identification of this fact at least puts one on guard about the suspect data. It may have to be eliminated from the evaluation or at least separated from other valid responses and analyzed separately.

But there are no ways to insure creation of valid indicators. The best that can be done is to use professional wisdom and ingenuity in designing instruments, and then pretest the instruments to determine whether the hoped-for validity actually exists. If it does not, the original instruments must be modified in attempts to increase validity. The process is a continuing one.

To avoid the abuses which invalid indicators permit, the use of multiple indicators to measure the same criterion is often helpful. Any one indicator is likely to measure only a few of the relevant dimensions of the criterion being used to evaluate a program. Using several different indicators increases the likelihood that more of these relevant dimensions will be tapped. As the combined, multiple indicator set approaches total validity, the possibility of beating the system is reduced, since too many separate indicators must be maximized simultaneously. In fact, when abuses occur, new standards for what constitutes a valid indicator in the particular situation are likely to arise. Specifically, means of avoiding abuses will be incorporated into the concept of a valid indicator in the particular situation.

Where indicators dependent on particular methodologies are subject to predictable biases, use of additional indicators, employing different methodologies with non-related biases can change a consistent bias in a single indicator into a random error term in a multiple-indicator set. It appears that this condition can then be attacked through methods to combat indicator unreliability. This is precisely the argument set forth by Webb, et. al., in the quotation from *Unobtrusive Measures* presented earlier.

## Consequences Of Unreliable Indicators

Reliability problems are also serious, but they are seldom fatal to the evaluation of program effectiveness. In terms of test score theory, an unreliable indicator measures both a constant, underlying trait, and a random, non-related, error factor. On repeated measurements during a period of no expected changes in the underlying trait, the measure of the underlying trait should remain constant, but the error term is expected to fluctuate randomly. The larger the error term in relation to the true score component, the more unreliable the indicator will be.

The effects of indicator unreliability are straightforward. The variance of measurements increases because of higher random components or error terms in the measurements. This means that there is more variability in measurements of the criterion variable throughout the population being sampled than there otherwise would be. When a social program is intended to cause a change in the criterion variable between two points in time, this increased variance can mask small, but real, changes in that variable. Larger real changes will be required before any statistical tests will conclude that the change is statistically significant. Estimates of program effects will have very wide confidence intervals surrounding them because the variability in measurements is so high.

The danger from unreliable indicators is that small program effects will be ignored as chance occurrences when they are, in fact, true effects.

## Curing Unreliability

What can be done to improve the reliability of indicators? Fortunately, procedures do exist to improve unreliable indicators. When the indicator is a questionnaire or interview, the addition of more items, each somewhat unreliable in itself, can improve the reliability of the combined measure, through cancelling the random fluctuations against each other. What is required is that the error terms be independent of each other for all items in the combined set.

When the indicator is a rating by an observer, two or more ratings by independent raters can be combined into an overall rating, with a higher reliability than that of any single rater. The requirement for these additional observations is that they be carried out under conditions substantially equivalent to those of the original rating.

It is even possible to measure the same variable under different methodologies, and then combine the separate scores into a single combined indicator score. As long as the errors of the separate methodological indicators are uncorrelated, the overall reliability will be higher than that of any single indicator.

Alternatively, attempts can be made to reduce the unreliability of any single indicator through the use of good "housekeeping" procedures which remove some of the random variation around the true criterion score. Reliabilities on speeded tests can be improved when automatic timing devices are used to replace a somewhat fallible person reading a watch and issuing stop and start instructions. Lighting in a testing location or across locations can be made uniform so that test score differences due to eyestrain are minimized or at least held relatively constant.

Raters can be given clear instructions on the use of the rating scale, with many illustrations of applications of the scale, and then be allowed several practice runs with the scale under the watchful supervision of the scale designer.

Just as careful wording of questionnaires can eliminate constant bias which would render the indicator invalid, it can also reduce random error due to fuzzy wording or to double-meaning of statements, which are dealt with in inconsistent ways by different individuals within the same target population or the same individual on two different occasions. It seems then that in some situations, methods exist for ameliorating the unreliability of indicators. The drawbacks are that the methods add to the cost of the measurement process. And it is probably cost considerations which limit the reliability actually achieved.

## THE ACCURACY OF MEASUREMENTS

Validity and reliability are important characteristics of indicators. It is important to note that these are characteristics inherent in the indicators themselves, not in measurements actually made with those indicators.

In order to reach rational decisions on program performance, another characteristic is necessary—accuracy. Accuracy pertains not to the indicators themselves, but to measurements made with indicators.

No formal definitions of data inaccuracy exist in the literature. Therefore, we will rely upon some intuitive definitions of the concept. The measures obtained from indicators can be biased, corrupted, altered, falsified, changed, etc. to display some wanted effect for the program. In the accounting tradition, this would probably be referred to as data manipulation. Errors are intentionally or unintentionally creeping into the measurement data obtained from the chosen indicators. Even if the chosen indicators are perfectly valid and reliable, the problem of data inaccuracy can still arise.

### MOTIVATIONS FOR DATA INACCURACY

Why do measurements on chosen indicators become inaccurate? A fair amount of data inaccuracy can be traced to deliberate attempts to falsify data. Unintentional errors also appear in the data. In this section, the motivations for inaccuracy are examined. In a later section, empirical evidence of this inaccuracy will be presented.

The classic work on data inaccuracy is Morgenstern's *On the Accuracy of Economic Observations.*[13] In that work, Morgenstern provides some of the reasons why data might be falsified on the firm, state, or federal government level. Relevant data might be suppressed or deliberately falsified because of misunderstandings about the data being requested, because of fear of taxing authorities, by a desire to avoid government interference in organization operations, or from a desire to mislead competitors. Self-preservation of the organization seems to be a prime motivating factor throughout these rationale. Hence, mono-polies and oligopolies are prompted to lie or hide data in order to preserve the profit advantages they enjoy. Income data derived from tax returns may be understated from a motivation by individuals or organizations to illegally mini-mize income taxes.

Governments are not beyond such actions, either. Government motivations might include a desire to maintain military security, which would lead to inac-curate data on defense budgets, CIA budgets, etc. Certain data might be falsi-fied to save face among other nations. Hence, data which demonstrates failure of a national plan might be falsified. Morgenstern contends this is a common act in Fascist and Communist totalitarian countries. This principle is also expounded by Campbell in *Reforms as Experiments :* "If the political and administrative system has committed itself in advance to the correctness and efficacy of its reforms, it cannot tolerate learning of failure." [14]

Data might be fabricated in an effort to bilk larger sums of money out of benevolent institutions or countries. Morgenstern reports that one of the promi-nent European administrators of the Marshall Plan stated his country would develop any statistics it needed to get as much as they possibly could out of the U.S.

Suicide statistics are largely unreliable because many countries regard sui-cides as disgraceful and they therefore try to keep suicides secret. This may be a form of boasting, or an attempt to hide failures in plans designed to prevent this self-destruction.

Finally, data may be falsified in attempts at bluffing, which Morgenstern points out is an "essential feature of rational strategies" in many gaming situa-tions.

While Morgenstern spoke solely of the inaccuracies in economic data, the motivations for falsifying data are not peculiar to economic data. Furthermore, it is quite possible that certain economic data might be used as an indicator to evaluate social programs. Unemployment data would certainly be useful in evalu-ating the effects of job training programs. The indicators to evaluate anti-poverty programs expected to have an immediate rather than delayed effect would certainly be income data. Hence, Morgenstern's work provides certain indications of why data to evaluate social welfare programs might be falsified.

Campbell provides a more personalistic concept of motivation for data falsi-fication or suppression. The underlying motivation again appears to be self-preservation but this is on an individual rather than organizational basis. The individual concerned is the program administrator.

In many cases, the program administrator is being evaluated at the same time and on the same basis as the program itself. Thus, an administrator may easily be motivated to show a successful outcome for a program in order to gain a favorable personal evaluation, thus saving his own job or future job prospects. This is particularly bothersome when one considers that the best administrators are likely to be assigned to programs with the least likelihood of success. Camp-bell feels that in these situations the pressures to corrupt the data are so intense that evaluation researchers should refuse to evaluate an administrator and, further, should make clear that the success or failure of a program may well be independent of the administrator's abilities. [15]

Even if his job is not at stake, the program administrator has typically in-vested a great deal of conviction, zeal, enthusiasm, and faith in the project, and this alone may motivate him to find some success in the program. The program designer, if different from the administrator, has similar investments in the program and may have similar motivations to show a success for the project. However, the opportunities for data corruption may not be as great for the designer as for the administrator.

Rivlin finds the same motivation to be a threat:

> Another reservation about the desirability of social experimentation concerns the honesty with which experimental results will be reported. No one likes to fail. Rightly or wrongly, the administrator of a successful program will receive more acclaim and greater opportunities for advancement than the administrator of an unsuccessful project. Under these circumstances will there not be a temptation to cheat a bit—to choose the most favorable measuring instruments, to "lose" the records of children who fail or patients who die, to coach participants on what to say to the evaluator or how to beat the test? . . .
>
> Even if experiments are honestly conducted, one might fear political interference in reporting results. Will government officials be willing to release results that show failure of a program to which an agency is already committed? Or, where the experimental results are mixed, might there not be a tendency to emphasize and publicize the positive results while deemphasizing, if not actually suppressing, the negative ones? [16]

Program administrators and designers are not the only ones who might be motivated to bias the data. Program personnel—those who administer the program treatment, may be just as likely to falsify data. They may view the evaluation as a drain on precious program resources: money, time, and administrator's attention. The evaluation is at best something to tolerate, at worst, something to sabotage. The program personnel may also feel that the program's success depends on how effectively they deliver the treatment, and hence will want to see some favorable effect to reinforce their self-image of personal competence. [17]

Program personnel may also see the new program as a challenge to concepts and methods they hold near and dear.

> If the program runs counter to traditional agency values (for example, if it stresses social factors in the rehabilitation of mental patients when the accepted emphasis has been on psychological factors), they may actively or passively undermine the program and—as a consequence— the evaluation. [18]

Besides the program designer, administrator, and treatment staff, two other groups are capable of contributing to data inaccuracy. First, the program participants, those receiving the supposed beneficial treatment, can falsify personal data or fake their performance which is to be the basis for program evaluation. The motivation to do so may be either gratitude for being given the supposed boon, or jealousy of others more fortunate, which may lead to personal vendetta against the program and its staff, as representatives of that part of society which has abused them.

Finally, the program record-keeping staff could be responsible for data inaccuracy. These individuals are probably not motivated to consciously tamper with the data for any reason. Rather, the errors would occur unintentionally in the process of handling the data. Some errors may be due to the inevitable fallibility of humans in clerical and computational routines.

Partners of several CPA firms have suggested that, at least in the financial bookkeeping departments of many social programs, the staff personnel are frequently underqualified. Furthermore, reporting regulations are either so vague that these staff people are classifying data arbitrarily, or so cumbersome—written in overly technical language—that staff just despair of making sense out of regulations and classify data as they please. For these reasons, the financial data for these programs tends to be in terrible shape. Great inaccuracies are generally found as part of the financial audit.

If social programs have the same people doing program evaluation record-keeping, or have equally competent help, the program data is likely to be in an equally sad state. One partner suggested that the same person often does keep both kinds of records. Hence, inaccuracies can become a significant problem.

In addition to intentional or unintentional human sources of inaccuracy, problems may arise from consistency errors. The indicator itself changes between measuring points, perhaps without the measuring or recording staff realizing a change has occurred. For example, data once reported on a calendar year basis could suddenly be collected on a fiscal year basis. Comparability is destroyed because the indicator itself has changed. Units of measure are sometimes confused and commingled—long and short tons, yards and feet, etc. may be inadvertently treated as though they are the same units, with no disclosure made of the change in units.[19] The items going into the computation of market or price indices change through time, so the yearly numbers are not strictly comparable. Record keeping systems are changed through time, making comparisons through time hazardous. Whenever indicators are changed, comparability is destroyed.

## SOME EMPIRICAL EVIDENCE OF DATA CORRUPTION AND SUPPRESSION

In the previous section, many possible causes, both intentional and unintentional, which might result in errors in the data used to evaluate social programs, have been discussed. It is hoped that that section has demonstrated good reason to suspect that errors will occur in the data, or that data will be suppressed. It has also shown some empirical evidence of these abuses. This section attempts to present additional evidence of abuses. Some of this evidence is at best anecdotal and inferential. Some is drawn from settings other than social programs, but in areas where the motivations for falsifications and suppression are much the same.

In the United States, the General Accounting Office (GAO) is empowered to make audits of various federal programs and deliver reports to the Congress. While much of the GAO work is aimed at examining the financial operations of agencies, or in determining whether federal funds have been used in accordance with the authorizing legislation, or whether the funds have been used efficiently, some audits have been geared toward assessing the effectiveness of a program in curing basic social ills.

In a *GAO Review* article on the evaluation of health programs, the following comment is made:

> Sufficient, accurate data is a major concern in evaluating the health system. In some areas, very little data exists or available data is deficient or is not fully used. ... Data must be studied with caution because of . . . the tendency on the part of some to make known only that data which backstops a program or makes a program look good.[20]

Glennan makes a similar comment about the data from federal manpower programs:

> Data produced routinely as a by-product of program operations suffer from two major flaws. They tend to be unreliable. Data for many projects are missing or contain numerous errors. [21]

Weiss makes the comment about program records in general:

> Unfortunately, experience has shown that organizational records are nowhere as useful as they should be. The organization's record keeping, the transfer of intake and service information to permanent records, tends to be haphazard. Records are inaccurate, out of date, months behind on entries. [22]

Corroborating evidence from federal decision-making based on the physical sciences is also available. In a report to Congress, William Magruder, director of the supersonic transport development project, claimed that "in the considered opinion of the scientific authorities who have counseled the government on these matters over the past five years" there was no evidence that the SST would cause any adverse effects on the atmosphere or the environment. This came in the face of a report by Nixon's ad hoc SST review committee which claimed that the noise level would be intolerable in many areas, the sonic booms would be intolerable to the vast majority of people affected, and that a fleet of SST's would release considerable water vapor into the stratosphere, with unknown effects. The ad hoc review committee report was one of several available to the administration, all of which reached similar conclusions.

Later in the SST debate, an advisory committee report stated that noise suppressors would reduce the noise problem to tolerable levels. It failed to state that the size and weight of the necessary equipment would so seriously reduce the load capacity as to make the vehicle totally uneconomical. [23]

In 1966, an independent laboratory report submitted to the Department of Health, Education, and Welfare, which showed the weed killer 2, 4, 5-T caused birth defects, was repeatedly sent back for further study and replication of results for 3½ years while the U.S. continued its use of the chemical to defoliate about 1/8 of the area of South Vietnam. The report became public as a by-product of a Nader investigation. [24]

A Nader investigation played a role in uncovering a change in decision based on facts in the cyclamate ban. In 1969, the Secretary of Health, Education and Welfare was required by law to ban the sale of foods containing cyclamates. However, he decided to permit the sale of these items as non-prescription drugs for treatment of diabetes and obesity. An advisory committee reported that this was a correct decision because the benefits from using these items far outweighed the possibility of harm. A Nader study prompted a congressional investigation. The same advisory committee, having received essentially no new evidence, issued a report that evidence does *not* show that cyclamate foods were of any use in controlling diabetes or obesity. Von Hippel and Primack conclude that the advisory committee appears to have adapted its evidence to the needs of the person it was advising. [25]

Another series of evidence of data corruption comes from the biological sciences. The Memorial Sloan-Kettering Cancer Center in New York City found one of its scientists falsified experiment data on skin transplants. Hailing a new method to eliminate transplant rejection, the researcher artificially colored patches of animals' own skin to make it appear it had been transplanted. [26] The director of the Institute for Parapsychology in North Carolina falsified his experimental data to show that animals were able to use their minds to physically influence material objects. [27] Finally, the fact that a research assistant forged his own recommendation letters to graduate school, and the failure to replicate original findings make it seem that this research assistant falsified data on the isolation of a "transfer factor" which could have led to a new cancer treatment. [28]

In a study of education programs, Wholey found that some states refused to send in data to evaluate programs under Title I of the Elementary and Secondary Education Act of 1965 because they "did not want to circulate information that they considered to be damaging to themselves in some way." [29]

An employee engaged in a methadone maintenance program reports that the program, faced with a funds cut-off because of insufficient program participants, created 60 fictitious or paper addicts in order to receive its grant renewal. Presumably, treatment data then had to be submitted for these people, which could not possibly be accurate. [30]

Campbell reports that during Orlando Wilson's Chicago Police Department reorganization, the record keeping system was reformed. This brought about a huge increase in the number of reported petty larceny offenses due almost totally to the fact that in the previous administration such complaints had not been recorded. Campbell also reports Etzioni's disclosure that a widely proclaimed 1965 crime wave in New York was caused by a change in record keeping. [31]

As a result of the last two sections, we see that significant motivation for rendering program data inaccurate exists for many groups connected with the program. The empirical evidence suggests the problem is actual, not merely potential.

## LEVELS ON WHICH PROGRAM DATA CAN BE MADE INACCURATE

The technique of corrupting program data can be an extremely powerful one since there are several different levels at which the data can be rendered inaccurate:

1. Participant characteristics or background data
2. Program treatment data
3. Program outcome data

The most obvious and direct way to bias program data is at the level of program outcome data, on the measures from the indicators chosen for evaluating the success of the program. Typically, those with a motivation to intentionally bias the program will know the direction that the data falsification should take in order to show the desired effect on program success. That is, they will know which test scores to inflate or deflate to make the program look successful. Hence they only require access to the data to realize their goals, if they so desire.

But the first two levels of data inaccuracy can achieve the same end result equally successfully. Programs are frequently instituted on a trial basis, since the resources necessary for treatment are in short supply, and the effectiveness of the program is still unconfirmed. One rational way to assess program effectiveness is through a two group experimental design. Two identical groups, ideally representative of the population ultimately to be serviced by the program, would be formed. One would be given the program treatment; one would not. If the program is successful, the group receiving the program treatment should fare better on the output or criterion measures to evaluate the program than does the control group.

However, judicious selection of participants for the treatment or the control group, participants not representative of the target population, can artificially make the program look good. Choosing individuals more highly skilled, more intelligent, more motivated, or healthier than the target population in general for the treatment group can favorably bias the program results. Creaming, choosing those most likely to change in the hoped-for direction, would provide a similar effect.

Selecting the control group from individuals more disadvantaged than the target population would also tend to make the treatment group look better. In order to make a program look unsuccessful, one need merely reverse the selection criteria for the treatment and control groups.

Alteration of program methodology could also be used to show favorable program results. Using more intensive or longer than specified sessions might bring more favorable program results. Replacing experimental treatments with proven effective treatments could do the same. Lengthening the actual time alloted on a speeded, timed test could improve test scores. Coaching experimental groups on the correct answers or expected performance would make a program look good. Alternatively, one could deprive the control group, again making the program look good. To make the program look bad, one reverses the above procedures.

Hence, alteration of data about program treatment characteristics or about program participant background traits, in order to conform with the program plans, can be used to bias the decision on program effectiveness, just as the more obvious alteration of program outcome data does directly. Even though all chosen indicators are all perfectly valid and reliable, data obtained from measurements with these indicators can be inaccurate. Throughout this discussion, the emphasis has been on intentional inaccuracy. But intentional or unintentional data inaccuracy can seriously affect the decision on program effectiveness. In the presence of substantial inaccuracy, decisions on program effectiveness will be correct only by chance.

## THE ROLE OF THE ACCOUNTANT
## IN SOCIAL MEASUREMENTS

Thus far, three basic methods of affecting social program data have been isolated: 1) invalid indicators can be employed; 2) unreliable indicators can be employed; and 3) measurements made from indicators of any degree of validity and reliability can be made inaccurate. What is the potential role for the accountant in helping detect or prevent these abuses? The accountant's primary help will be to detect or alleviate the last of the three problems, the inaccuracy problem. He has little to contribute towards curing the first two problems — invalidity and unreliability.

Indicators are obviously situation dependent; they will differ for health programs, educational programs, manpower training programs, etc. The development of indicators and assessment of validity are best done by experts in those program fields. These functions really require specialized knowledge in the particular subject area of the program. Consider the case of educational programs. One of the indicators which might be used for evaluating the success of such programs might be an intelligence test. But what intelligence test? The Terman and Merrill version of the Stanford-Binet? The Wechsler Intelligence scale for Children? The Thurstone Primary Mental Abilities test? There are several versions of each of these tests and other intelligence tests designed for children which have not been mentioned here. The fact that so many tests exist gives some indication of lack of agreement among experts in mental testing about the validity of various indicators. Furthermore, there still exists considerable debate in the test literature about the cultural biases of usual intelligence tests, which make them invalid for Black children, Spanish-speaking children, lower class white children, etc. Some efforts have been made at constructing tests free from cultural bias, but it appears they are not entirely acceptable as yet. Certainly accountants do not have the necessary training needed to decide which intelligence test to use for a particular program, or to assess the validity of any particular test chosen.

Consider another example. Self-esteem may be a useful criterion for evaluating various educational programs, or various other poverty-breaking activity programs. But what dimensions of self-esteem must one tap for evaluating a particular program? What specific indicator should be employed? Robinson and Shaver list over fourteen different off-the-shelf indicators which in some way measure self-esteem. [32] Again, the accountant is in no position to construct a new scale, or to decide which scale to employ in any particular evaluation project. Nor is he trained to assess the validity of any such scale chosen for a particular program. Accountants are not the professionals to solve validity abuses.

This conclusion appears applicable also to the assessment of reliability. Reliabilities are often computed on the results obtained from pretesting an indicator before it is used for its primary purpose in program evaluation. The decision about what kind of reliability measure to use requires a knowledge of psychometric theory, something accountants typically do not have. At best, they could compute a coefficient using a formula given to them, which is hardly a justifiable reason for suggesting they can serve a useful function in the process.

But it is in solving the problem of data inaccuracy that accountants come into their own world. Specifically, the auditing function is directed to the detection of data inaccuracy and to its prevention, through the system of internal control in use in the organization.

## INTERNAL CONTROL: DATA INACCURACY PREVENTION

Consider the concept of internal control. One facet of internal control is the insurance of data accuracy. Several basic concepts underlie the procedures for insuring the accuracy of data. These include the separation of duties, so that those doing the record keeping do not have any stake in the success of the program; redundancies in the record keeping system so that two separate persons provide a check on each other's work; hiring of qualified personnel so that unintentional errors due to inability or carelessness are minimized; and clear statements of operating procedures for record keeping personnel to follow in the performance of their duties so that inaccuracies due to confusion are reduced.

Accountants are the sole group to worry about building various controls into the business firm's information system. Data systems designed solely by data processing technicians have shown an appalling lack of controls, with the possibilities of theft and manipulation of the records readily apparent to anyone who carefully analyzes the system. Accountants, in their roles as internal control specialists, are now frequently requested to become members of the information system design committees in many firms.

It seems that accountants can apply their knowledge to designing internal control systems for social programs. For example, the concept of separation of duties can be extremely useful in trying to prevent data inaccuracy.

Earlier, various groups associated with a social program were seen to have some motivation to bias program data, usually in the direction of showing program success. Adequate separation of duties would demand that these groups be prevented access to program records to the greatest extent possible. Just as one would doubt the objectivity of any judgment of program success made by the program administrator, one should doubt the objectivity of data furnished by that individual or to which he or she has easy access. Obviously, the data might be perfectly accurate, but certainly there would be doubt regarding its accuracy in the minds of most rational observers.

The same principles apply to program designers and program treatment staffs. They certainly are not the ideal persons to ask for a judgment on program effectiveness. So, similarly, their access to program data used for the evaluation might cast doubt on the accuracy of that data.

The objective is to place the responsibility for record keeping in the hands of a group who have no interest in the outcome of the program, people with no ego involvement in the program. In some organizations, jobs are relatively secure in spite of an unsuccessful program outcome, as would be the case in a school system trying out a new educational program. Therefore, a record keeping department would have to keep records regardless of any new innovative programs being tried. Hence, as long as they are not associated with the initiation or implementation of the program itself, they should be objective in the process of measuring and in the collection and further processing of data. In other situations jobs are secure only as long as a particular program exists. Unsuccessful outcomes would probably lead to the demise of the program. Hence, anyone employed by the program itself might be motivated to find program success, and hence bias or corrupt data to show that success, if it does not actually exist, since their jobs are all dependent on program success. The most objective record keeper in a situation like that would be an outside group which contracts to do the measurement and data processing work. Although employment on a specific project may be contingent on project success, as long as the outside agency has a broad based clientele, continued employment is probably assured regardless of program outcome.

Where possible, these independent parties should have sole responsibility for taking measurements, collecting, and processing data, with various divisions of duties so that checks are provided on each person's work. Where program data is needed for the operation of the program, copies of the data can be given to the necessary individuals. The problem is that feedback may result in unauthorized changes in the program treatment, changes intentionally designed to generate program success. Therefore, part of the measurement process must include monitoring the content and intensity of the program treatment. While the record keeping staff will not be able to prevent these changes from occurring, at least they may be able to detect them, which in turn puts the evaluator on notice that any experimental design has been corrupted.

Where program staff are doing the actual data collection, other principles of internal control may help reduce the possibilities of data corruption. In education programs, the teaching staff, in addition to being the treatment delivery agents, are also often responsible for measurements on program output variables, usually in the form of tests. If the tests are not prepared by the individual teachers, the teachers should be denied access to the tests prior to the time of administration. Independent observers might visit classrooms on a random basis, without giving any prior notice, to determine that test conditions are not being corrupted—answers being given away, time limits being extended, etc. The tests would be taken from the teachers immediately after the testing period and sent to the data processing group without permitting access by principals, program designers, etc.

Obviously, the controls necessary or possible depend on the characteristics of individual projects and project locations. There is no single system of internal control which would be uniformly applicable to any class of social programs. But the same principles used in designing internal control systems in business firms appear useful in the social program environment. Furthermore, the same considerations which cause less than the best system to be used in business firms will limit the sophistication of the systems used in social programs. Internal control systems usually involve extra work than would otherwise be necessary, and this increases record keeping costs. Cost considerations may cause a firm or a social program to forgo certain methods of preventing inaccuracies. And even good systems of internal control may break down. Therefore, data inaccuracy may not be economically or totally preventable, but it may be detectable. This is the function of auditing per se.

## AUDITING: DATA INACCURACY DETECTION

The usual stated purpose of auditing is the independent expression of an opinion on the fairness of a firm's financial statements. Any proposed extensions of the audit function to data other than financial statements are always met with the criticism that one needs standards of fair presentation for the data in question. But it is possible to view the business auditing function as composed of two separate processes: first, a review to determine that the data collected on the indicators the firm has chosen to include in its financial statements is accurate, and secondly that the chosen indicators are those necessary for fair presentation of financial position, results of operations, and changes in financial position.

The first process is an attack on the accuracy problem; the second process is concerned with validity and reliability questions. Consider the concept of fair presentation in the financial statements. In the first place, the assumption is made that financial position, results of operations, and changes in financial position are the proper concepts to be reported. Presumably, the accountant, as accountant, has wrestled with the task of specifying the relevant dimensions of each of those concepts, as well as the task of designing specific indicators to measure each of the relevant dimensions. What are the specific indicators? They are the accounting principles, procedures, and techniques specified by generally accepted accounting principles. Generally accepted accounting principles represent a determination by the accounting profession, through its professional bodies, that certain indicators are valid for the purpose of presenting financial position, etc., and furthermore are reliable for those uses. (Note the traditional argument in financial accounting theory that historical cost data is reliable, while replacement cost data appears not to be.) But notice that it is accountants, using their professional wisdom as accountants who have made the determination of what indicators are valid and reliable enough for common use in financial statements.

Prior to *Statement on Auditing Standards No. 5*, the auditor determined whether the measurements made with indicators chosen by a particular firm were accurate, and then checked that the chosen indicators were acceptable under generally accepted accounting principles, which are cataloged by the accounting profession. The auditor as auditor did not himself determine whether the chosen indicators were valid and reliable.

Under *SAS 5*, the auditor's role is expanded, in that not only must he be satisfied that the chosen indicators are included within generally accepted accounting principles, but also satisfy himself that those generally accepted accounting principles are applicable in the particular situation facing the firm. But according to *SAS 5*:

> Specifying the circumstances in which one accounting principle should be selected from among alternative principles is the function of bodies having authority to establish accounting principles. When criteria for selection among alternative accounting principles have not been established to relate accounting methods to circumstances, the auditor may conclude that more than one accounting principle is appropriate in the circumstances. The auditor should recognize, however, that there may be unusual circumstances in which the selection and application of specific accounting principles from among alternative principles may make the financial statements taken as a whole misleading. [33]

But even under the new standard, the auditor must at best determine whether an indicator already acceptable under generally accepted accounting principles is valid in the particular circumstances. To do this, the auditor will use his knowledge and wisdom as a professional accountant. Auditing skills do not enter at this point. Hence, the basic part of auditing, even in the context of the business firm, is one of determining the accuracy of measurements with indicators which the accounting profession has declared to be valid and reliable.

This could therefore be the auditor's role in social programs: determining the accuracy of measurements on indicators which other professional bodies, having professional wisdom and knowledge in the subject matter of the social program, have declared to be valid and reliable in the circumstances. Where no such agreement about validity and reliability exist (as is often the case in social programs), the auditor could determine accuracy of measurements with indicators of unknown validity and reliability. The point is that validity and reliability considerations are not the responsibility of the auditor. He does not make any such determinations in financial statement audits in his role as auditor, and he cannot be expected to make these determinations in social programs. With responsibility limited to verifying the accuracy of measurements, the excuse that social program data cannot be audited because of lack of standards of fair presentation loses its power.

How will the auditor proceed in auditing the accuracy of social program data? The same techniques that apply in financial statement audits should carry over into the program evaluation setting. In *The Philosophy of Auditing*, [34] Mautz and Sharaf first showed that financial statements represent a series of assertions, and that these assertions were classifiable into several basic, general groups, groups which were not dependent on the financial statement setting. They then indicated the kinds of evidence which could be used to support the various generalized assertions. The matching between the assertions and the type of evidence possible are shown in Figure 5-1, which is adapted from Mautz and Sharaf. [35]

Specific auditing procedures will obviously depend upon the particular kind of social program—water pollution control, alcoholism reduction, educational enrichment, manpower training, etc. Furthermore, the detailed circumstances surrounding a particular site of a program may influence the evidence which is obtainable. But the Mautz and Sharaf framework should still provide a useful guide to the selection of audit procedures. All that can be given here is a hint about how that framework could apply.

In section IV, we noted that social program data could be corrupted on three different levels: the program participant characteristics, the program treatment administered, and the program outcome data. The auditor will have to be concerned with auditing all three levels of data.

Program participant characteristics are largely assertions about past events that have occurred to participants (the person completed high school, scored above the 75 percent percentile on a college entrance exam, worked in a particular kind of job, etc.) or about qualitative conditions (has a drug problem, comes from a home with a poverty level income, has an IQ of 120, etc.) The strongest evidence available about past events would be authoritative documents or statements by independent third parties. Evidence of completion of high school could come in the form of a high school diploma in the hands of the program applicant. Alternatively, a communication from the high school confirming graduation from high school would be useful evidence. Grades on standardized exams can often be confirmed with the testing services who maintain records. Grade reports from those agencies are acceptable when submitted by program participants as long as the report appears to be real and the data unaltered. Evidence that participants have worked at a given job can be obtained by contacting employers. Note, however, that auditing procedures will be easiest to apply when the participants are still in the program, rather than at some later date. Participants presumably are required to furnish some of the evidence to program staff in order to justify their admission to the program. The presence of the auditor on admission dates, when he could review documents brought by program participants can greatly simplify the auditing process. Plans must be made in advance, however, for these techniques to be used.

Assertions about treatment processes actually employed might involve assertions about the existence of physical things which may or may not be present (a particular kind of pollution control device is installed, a certain number of people are enrolled in the program) or about qualitative conditions (a particular type of educational enrichment technique is used, staff have particular skills and training, etc.). Again, the Mautz-Sharaf scheme indicates what evidence can be used to support particular kinds of assertions. Again, the point should be made that program treatment assertions become assertions about past events when the program is completed, and these kinds of assertions may be extremely difficult to verify. It is much easier to audit program treatment data

| Nature of Assertion | Type of Audit Evidence to Support the Assertion |
|---|---|
| Existence of physical things present<br>Simple quantitative conditions | Examination by auditor |
| Mathematical | Calculation by auditor |
| Existence of physical things not present<br>Past events | Statements by independent third parties<br>Authoritative documents<br>Statements by company personnel<br>Subsidiary or detail records |
| Existence of nonphysical things<br>Nonexistence of physical and nonphysical things<br>Qualitative conditions<br>Value-judgment quantities | Statements by independent third parties<br>Authoritative documents<br>Statements by company personnel<br>Subsidiary or detail records<br>Satisfactory internal control procedures<br>Subsequent actions by the company and others<br>Interrelationships within the data |

**FIGURE 5-1**

Source:  Adapted from R.K. Mautz and Hussin A. Sharaf, *The Philosophy of Auditing*, Evanston: American Accounting Association, 1961, p. 101.

during the course of operation, rather than after the fact. This suggests the usefulness of a continuing audit process.

The same Mautz and Sharaf guidelines would be used to select audit procedures for program outcome data also. However, we will not pursue the matter further at this point, since a discussion of audit procedures must be based on the actual program involved, with all the peculiarities of its specific environment.

## ENDNOTES

1. Robert Beyer, "The Modern Management Approach to a Program of Social Improvement," *The Journal of Accountancy* 127 (March 1968): 37.
2. Joseph S. Wholey, et. al., *Federal Evaluation Policy: Analyzing the Effects of Public Programs* (Washington, D.C.: The Urban Institute, 1970), pp. 28-9.
3. Ibid., p.29.
4. Section 1, U.S. Housing Act of 1937, amended, 42 U.S.C. 1401 et. seq., as cited in Wholey, op. cit., p. 30.
5. Edward A. Suchman, *Evaluative Research* (New York: Russell Sage Foundation, 1967), pp. 39-41.
6. Paul F. Lazarsfeld, "Evidence and Inference in Social Research," in D. Lerner, ed., *Evidence and Inference* (New York: The Free Press of Glencoe, 1959) as quoted in Aaron V. Cicourel, *Method and Measurement in Sociology* (New York: The Free Press of Glencoe, 1964), p. 15.
7. Michael Scriven, *Evaluation Bias and Its Control*, Occasional Paper Series, no. 4 (Kalamazoo: Evaluation Center, College of Education, Western Michigan University, 1975), pp. 32-3.
8. John P. Robinson and Phillip R. Shaver, *Measures of Social Psychological Attitudes* (Ann Arbor: Institute for Social Research, The University of Michigan, 1973).
9. Newton S. Metfessel and William B. Michael, "A Paradigm Involving Multiple Criterion Measures for the Evaluation of the Effectiveness of School Programs," *Educational and Psychological Measurement* 27: 941-43, reprinted in Blaine R. Worthen and James R. Sanders, eds., *Educational Evaluation: Theory and Practice* (Worthington, Ohio: Charles A. Jones Publishing Company, 1973), pp. 274-9.
10. Eugene J. Webb, Donald T. Campbell, Richard D. Schwartz, and Lee Sechrest, *Unobtrusive Measures: Nonreactive Research in the Social Sciences* (Chicago: Rand McNally College Publishing Company, 1966), p. 1.
11. Ibid., p. 2.
12. Alice M. Rivlin, *Systematic Thinking for Social Action* (Washington, D.C.: The Brookings Institution, 1971), p. 128.
13. Oskar Morgenstern, *On the Accuracy of Economic Observations*, 2nd edition (Princeton: Princeton University Press, 1963).
14. Donald T. Campbell, "Reforms as Experiments," *American Psychologist* 24 (April, 1969): 410.
15. Ibid.
16. Rivlin, op. cit., pp. 112-13.
17. John Mann, "Technical and Social Difficulties in the Conduct of Evaluative Research," *Changing Human Behavior* (Charles Scribner's Sons, 1965), reprinted in Francis G. Caro, *Readings in Evaluation Research* (New York: Russell Sage Foundation, 1971), p. 182.
18. Carol H. Weiss, *Evaluative Research: Methods for Assessing Program Effectiveness* (Englewood Cliffs: Prentice-Hall, Inc., 1972), p. 100.
19. Morgenstern, op. cit., p. 35.
20. "Evaluation of Federal Health Programs," *The GAO Review*, Summer, 1973, pp. 72-4.
21. Thomas Glennan, Jr., "Evaluating Federal Manpower Programs: Notes and Observations," Memorandum RM-5743-OEO. (Santa Monica, California: Rand Corporation, 1969) reprinted in Carol H. Weiss, ed., *Evaluating Action Programs: Readings in Social Action and Education* (Boston: Allyn and Bacon, Inc., 1972), p. 179.
22. Weiss, *Evaluative Research*, p. 54.

23. Frank von Hippel and Joel Primack, "Public Interest Science," *Science* 177 (September 29, 1972): 1167.
24. Ibid., pp. 1167-8.
25. Ibid., p. 1168.
26. Ronald Kotulak, "The Scientist [sic] Who Commit Professional Suicides," *The Chicago Tribune,* 29 December 1974, sec. 2, p. 8.
27. Ibid.
28. Ibid.
29. Wholey, op. cit., p. 34.
30. Personal communication from a student in Accounting D 50, Northwestern University, Summer, 1973.
31. Campbell, op. cit., p. 415.
32. Robinson and Shaver, op. cit., pp. 68-162.
33. Auditing Standards Executive Committee, *Statement on Auditing Standards No. 5* (New York: American Institute of Certified Public Accountants, 1975), as reprinted in *The Journal of Accountancy* 140 (September, 1975): 80-1.
34. R. K. Mautz and Hussein A. Sharaf, *The Philosophy of Auditing* (Evanston: American Accounting Association, 1961).
35. Ibid., p. 101.

# 14

# Using Administrative Data Banks for Research and Evaluation: A Case Study

*Leslie L. Roos, Jr., Noralou P. Roos, Patrick Nicol, and Cynthia Johnson*

## ABSTRACT

*This paper discusses methods of organizing and checking administrative data banks to increase their usefulness for research. Examples are drawn from the authors' studies using the Manitoba Health Services Commission data bank. The various uses of both manual and computerized checks are explained. A problem profile is developed for the Manitoba data bank; this profile summarizes different specific problems, incorporating threats to internal validity associated with the data. Techniques for operationalizing concepts are treated. The improvements in data collection represented by data banks are discussed in terms of the possibilities for developing multiple control group designs.*

## INTRODUCTION

Learning how to use a large data bank can be considered an effort at cost-effective, unobtrusive data collection. The importance of such efforts has been emphasized by Blalock, (1): "improvements in data-collection procedures will be far more important, in the long run, than the kinds of weak predictions that must be made whenever inadequate attention has been given to measurement problems at the data-collection stage."

Researchers using administrative data banks confront large amounts of substantive information, organized for particular operating purposes. Although the information may have been gathered with care, it certainly was not collected with an eye to satisfying tenets of measurement theory to surmount the limitations of the data bank.

This paper draws upon the authors' use of the Manitoba Health Services Commission (MHSC) data bank, which was designed primarily for paying physician's

AUTHORS' NOTE: This research has been supported by Grant Number 607-1075-43, Research Programs Directorate, Health and Welfare, Canada, by National Health Research Scholar Award 607-1114-48 to L. Roos, and by National Health Scientist Award 607-1001-22 to N. Roos. Preliminary work on this paper was supported by the Winnipeg Clinic Foundation. Early versions were presented at the 1977 ASAC meetings in Fredericton and the 1977 AIDS meeting in Chicago. The authors would like to gratefully acknowledge the help of Fred Toll, Steve Kavanagh, Hazel MacLeod, and Henry Shukier of the Manitoba Health Services Commission with this research.
From Leslie L. Roos, Jr., Noralou P. Roos, Patrick Nicol, and Cynthia Johnson, "Using Administrative Data Banks for Research and Evaluation: A Case Study." Unpublished manuscript, 1977.

claims, for such studies as compliance with medical standards, the efficiency of individual versus group practice, and the efficacy of particular surgical procedures. It focuses upon measuring data quality in large data banks. Although various analytical and statistical techniques are suggested, the main emphasis is upon the different "threats to validity" which complicate meaningful interpretation of the data.

## REORGANIZING A DATA BASE

The basic processes in using a data bank organized for administrative functions for research purposes include: taking the particular records needed out of the data bank; sorting them according to particular identifiers; aggregating records according to the researcher's particular purposes; and linking and/or merging of two or more files to assemble information stored in different places. The order in which these operations are performed will vary according to the purposes of the researcher and the structure of the data bank.

Checks of various types, both manual and computerized, help ascertain the reliability of the recorded information. Manual checks are analogous to the multiple measures suggested by Webb, (13) and involve obtaining information from other than the computerized record. They can be used to focus on possible errors at each stage in data collection and preparation.

First of all, manual checks may uncover information omitted from the data file or entered erroneously due to clerical or keypunching mistakes. Checks done at this stage are essential for understanding any coding procedures which may not be clearly explained in administrative code books. In the intermediate states of data processing, manual procedures can be used to uncover errors not found by computerized manipulation, which can not directly check all possible errors in information entered in the data file. They can also help ascertain the accuracy of computerized checks designed to sift through the information to pick up implausible, and possibly wrong combinations of codes. Finally, manual checks can be used to follow-up "deviant cases" initially identified in the computerized data analysis. Since observed scores toward either end of a statistical distribution are likely to include "significant measurement error, investigating such cases may well result in a better understanding of the conditions surrounding data collection and recording.

Successful computerized checks have several important advantages over manual checks. Complete manual checks are impossible for data banks involving several million individual records (such as MHSC's). Computers can perform with speed and accuracy many exhaustive checks just too time consuming to be done manually. Another advantage of the computerized checks is their relative unobtusiveness. Computer-readable information from the data bank may be processed at the researcher's home institution without additional demands upon the organization supplying the data. Even data processing done "in-house" by the supplying organization may be easier to implement than manual checks. Manual checks involve obtaining access to specific written records from various types of organizations and individuals; this may depend upon personal and institutional ties beyond those necessary for obtaining the administrative data.

Getting copies of desired information *before* it enters the data bank is a problem but the effort is worthwhile. Working manually with raw data can produce an important "feel" for the information in a data bank and allows researchers to explore various ideas before going to the computer analysis. It may be desirable to examine all entries for a sample of individuals. This approach seems particularly useful at the early, exploratory stages of a research project.

Getting some practice with the likely problems is critical when decisions must be made as to specifications for a long computer run. If at all possible, a subset of the information eventually needed should be analyzed by computer before the major, most complete pass through the data bank. The researcher can work back and forth between manual and computer-assisted checks to specify where more information is needed.

## CONSTRUCTING A PROBLEM PROFILE

The difficulties and checks involved in using a data bank can be summarized by a data quality problem profile, as presented in Table 1. Problem profiles will vary

**TABLE 1**
**Problem Profile for Manitoba Health Services Commission Data Bank**

| SPECIFIC PROBLEM | IMPORTANCE | HOW CHECKED |
|---|---|---|
| Coding Error (I) | Minor Importance | Manual Checks of Medical Records, Claims Forms, and Computer Records |
| Individuals Misidentified (I, EM) | Minor Importance | Computerized Check for Discrepancies |
| One Individual With Several Numbers (I, EM) | Minor Importance | Run Against Master Registration File |
| Individual Not Covered for Entire Period (I, EM) | Major Importance (From 16 to 22%) | Run Against Master Registration File |
| Reliability of Physician Diagnosis (I, Ins) | Potentially Important | "Pairing" of Claims for Reliability Checks |
| Operationalizing the "Episode of Illness" Concept | Potentially Important | Comparing Multiple Operationalizations of "Episode" Concept |

Threats to Validity are in Parentheses.
(I = Instability, Ins = Instrumentation, EM = Experimental Mortality)

from one data bank to another as well as from one study to another using the same data bank. But making such a profile is valuable early in the stages of a research project as various problems can threaten internal validity, what Cook and Campbell, (4) refer to as "the validity of any conclusions we can draw about whether a demonstrated statistical relationship implies cause." Incorporating these threats to internal validity into the problem profile highlights the general nature of the particular difficulties associated with the MHSC data. As listed by Campbell, (2) some of these threats are: (1) instability: "unreliability of measures, fluctuations in sampling persons or components, autonomous instability of repeated or equivalent measures." This has recently been characterized by Cook and Campbell, (3), as statistical conclusion validity; (2) experimental mortality: "the differential loss or respondents from comparison groups"; and (3) instrumentation: "in which changes in the calibration of a measuring instrument or changes in the observers or scores used may produce changes in the obtained measurements".

More recently, Cook and Campbell, (4) have expanded their discussion of validity to include threats to construct validity: "threats to the correct labeling of the cause and effect operations in abstract terms that come from common linguistic usage or from formal theory (p. 226)". Construct validity suggests a concern for rigorous operational definitions of causes and effects "so that manipulations or measures can be tailored to the construct they are meant to represent, (p. 239)". Cook and Campbell emphasize the desirability of multiple methods and measure to triangulate on a particular construct. This is often difficult, since information in a data bank may well be generated from one type of source, while relatively few measures will be available.

## MEASUREMENT RELIABILITY

In organizing the Manitoba Health Services Commission data to permit both checks on reliability and substantive analysis, a number of decisions had to be made. Since the focus of the research was upon tonsil/adenoid surgery, the diagnoses reported with each medical claim were organized according to their bearing upon such surgery. Respiratory diagnoses which were specific indications for tonsil/adenoid surgery were assigned to the first level, respiratory conditions in the same anatomical area were in the second level, and respiratory conditions in other areas were in the third level.

The psychometric theory literature discusses estimating the reliability of measures through the use of the same, or parallel, forms at two closely-related points in time, (3). Such formulations suggest specific questions relevant to the diagnoses in the Health Services Commission data bank: (1) would the same informed observer (such as a doctor) make the same judgment twice when observing the phenomenon? (2) would two different informed observers (such as two doctors) each make the same judgment when observing the phenomenon? The first question relates to test-retest reliability and the second, to interobserver reliability.

Another important problem in measurement theory is dealing with change which takes place between the time of the first and second measurement. For example, differences in respiratory diagnoses between two points in time may be due to unreliable measurement or to actual change in a patient's condition. In the MHSC research, a 14 day period was chosen as an appropriate maximum interval between two doctors' visits for specifying that the diagnoses were associated with the same episode of illness. This decision is justified in the following section and forms the basis for the checks on reliability.

For the data bank user, computerized checks on reliability are likely to be most important, although knowledge of data collection procedures may suggest additional manual checks. In the tonsillectomy/adenoidectomy study using the MHSC data, every 300th individual was selected for a reliability check. If two claims occured within a 14 day period, the first claim relating to respiratory diagnoses was "paired" with the claim immediately following. This permitted checking both intra— and interobserver reliability. The results were in genral accord with clinical trials, (6).

More advanced statistical techniques have been developed to estimate the reliability of measurement instruments using data collected at several (at least three) points in time, (15). Such techniques may have particular appeal to data bank researchers because, as noted earlier, standard checks using multiple methods and measures are likely to be unavailable in many situations. On the other hand, time-series information will probably be present. Such techniques presume interval or ratio scales; the ordinal nature of the respiratory data, coded according to the three levels mentioned above, does violate these assumptions. On the other hand, applying the Wiley and Wiley model to repeated diagnoses of the same individual by the same physician led to judgments of high reliability of measurement and high stability over the three time points which provided the data.

Computerized checks on reliability can be usefully supplemented by manual procedures; such checks may provide useful information about the conditions under which data were generated. In Manitoba, doctors often allow claims to accumulate for a few days; several claims for one individual might be entered together on a single claims form and automatically be assigned the same diagnosis. Obviously, this would lead to high agreement between diagnoses (high intra-observer reliability). A manual check of the 101 cases found only about eight percent of the claims forms to contain more than one visit; of these, almost all listed just two visits.

More generally, reliability checks using data banks have both certain limitations and intriguing possibilites. Koran, (6), has suggested improving studies of clinical reliability by using a large sample of patients (30 or more), physicians whose training is comparable, and several specific statistical conventions. These improvements could easily be incorporated into reliability studies based on the MHSC data.

## OPERATIONALIZING CONCEPTS

Designing constructs appropriately is a problem in all research. Our research needed a measure of "episode illness" which corresponded with medical knowledge and increased the study's face validity for physicians. Various researchers have stressed the inadequacy of usual measures (such as claims) and suggested the importance of appropriately defining an "episode" to better study ambulatory care, (12), (8). The measurement of "episode" was important for our ongoing studies of compliance to best medical standards (number of episodes before an operation) of the effects of surgery (number of episodes before and after surgery) and so forth. Since no single length of time is the consensus choice for defining tonsillitis episodes, (10), (7), the research question was: what are the consequences of different assumptions about the beginning and ending points of episodes?

Having claim forms for 101 individuals permitted carrying out an initial check manually. Several different algorithms were tried—defining an illness episode as being all respiratory claims: (a) within a 14 day period; (b) within a 21 day period; (c) within a 28 day period; and (d) within a month. A similar analysis carried out by computer led to a more formal operationalization of "episode." If the concept of an episode involves a number of closely-spaced physician encounters for a given problem with different episodes being more widely-spaced, an ideal cutting point might be relatively insensitive to *increasing* the time period between claims but considerably sensitive to *decreasing* this time period. The 14 day cutting point seemed to be appropriate for these respiratory diagnoses and to produce results most similar to those generated by the "examination month" definition of episode. The easier "examination month" operationalization appears to be almost identical to the more sophisticated one.

## DISCUSSION

Many data banks share one or more of the characteristics of the Manitoba Health Services Commission which makes our findings relevant beyond the scope of this particular study, (9): (1) wide coverage to facilitate generalizability; (2) a large enough N to permit a number of simultaneous controls in data analysis; (3) a long enough time series of data to permit analysis before and after a particular intervention; and (4) the potential for combining files so as to facilitate the analysis of interventions, the construction of comparison groups, and the generation of histories for individual respondents.

Data banks have unexplored potential for generating nonrandomized control groups, given the large population from which such groups can be drawn. A multiple control-group strategy has frequently been advocated, (14); complicated techniques for constructing different control groups can be employed with data banks, (11). Moreover, when large numbers of individuals are involved in both experimental and control groups, the data can be presented in much more detail.

## NOTES

1. The only systemic limitation on identifying individuals concerns two children in a family born in the same year, of the same sex, with the same initials. Claims for such individuals cannot be distinguished until one becomes nineteen or marries.

2. Westin and Baker (1975) have stressed that the introduction of computer procedures typically leads to the more explicit recognition of error rates and subsequent improvements in accuracy due to computerized checks.

## REFERENCES

(1)   BLALOCK, H.M. Jr. (1974). "Beyond Ordinal Measurement: Weak Tests of Stronger Theories" in H.M. Blalock, Jr., ed., *Measurement in the Social Science,* Chicago: Aldine.

(2)   CAMPBELL, D.T. (1969). "Reform as Experiments." *American Psychologist,* 24: 409-429.

(3)   CAMPBELL, J.P. (1976). "Psychometric Theory" in M.D. Dunetter, ed., *Handbook of Industrial and Organizational Psychology.* New York: Rand McNally.

(4)   COOK, T.D., and D.T. CAMPBELL (1976): "The Design and Conduct of Quasi-Experiments and True Experiments in Field Settings," in M.D. Dunette, ed., *Handbook of Industrial and Organizational Psychology.* New York: Rand McNally.

(5)   KENNY, D.A. (1975). "A Quasi-Experimental Approach to Assessing Treatment Effects in the Non-equivalent Control Group Design," *Psychological Bulletin,* 82:345-362.

(6)   KORAN, L.M. (1975). "The Reliability of Clinical Methods, Data and Judgements," *The New England Journal of Medicine,* 293:642-646, 695-701.

(7)   MOSCOVICE, I. (1976). "Development of a Method for the Analysis of the Utilization of Resources in an Ambulatory Care Setting," unpublished doctoral dissertation, School of Organization and Management, Yale University.

(8)   RICHARDSON, W.C. (1971). *Ambulatory Use of Physicians Services in Response to Illness Episodes in a Low-Income Neighborhood,* University of Chicago: Center for Health Administration Studies.

(9)   ROOS, N.P. (1975), "Contrasting Program Evaluation with Social Experimentation–A Health Care Perspective," *Public Policy* 23:241-257.

(10)  SCITOVSKY, A.A., and N. McCALL (1975). "Changes in the Costs of Treatment of Selected Illnesses 1951-1964-1971," discussion paper, Health Policy Program, School of Medicine, University of California, San Francisco.

(11)  SHERWOOD, C.D., J.N. MORRIS, and S. SHERWOOD (1975). "A Multivariate, Nonrandomized Matching Technique for Studying the Impact of Social Intervention," in

E.L. Struening and M. Guttentag, *Handbook of Evaluation Research,* Vol. 1, Beverly Hills: Sage.

(12)  SOLON, J.A., *et al.* (1967). "Delineating Episodes of Medical Care," *American Journal of Public Health,* 57:401-408.

(13)  WEBB, E.J., D.T. CAMPBELL, R.E. SCHWARTZ, and L.B. SECHREST (1966). *Unobtrusive Measure: Nonreactive Research in the Social Sciences,* Chicago: Rand McNally.

(14)  WEBB, E.J., and P.C. ELLSWORTH (1975). "On Nature and Knowing," in H.W. Sinaiko and L.A. Broedling eds., *Perspective on Attitude Measurement: Surveys and Their Alternatives,* Washington: Smithsonian Institution.

(15)  WILEY, D.E. and J.A.WILEY (1970). "The Estimation of Measurement Error in Panel Data," *American Sociological Review,* 35:112-117.

# PART III
# HEALTH

The articles in this section were chosen because they focus on issues that are believed to be relevant to evaluating the impact of a national health insurance program, whatever its eventual form. The first selection is a report from a task force of the American Psychological Association set up to propose recommendations for the continuing evaluation of a National Health Insurance Program. The next four articles deal with practices and concerns that observers believe will become more important and more prevalent should a national health insurance policy be adopted. One of the major forces behind the movement toward national mental health insurance has been the drive to contain rapidly increasing hospital costs. Feldstein's analysis of the reasons for the increase in costs and recommendations for what to do about it is quite instructive in this regard and suggests lessons for any advocates of a National Insurance Program. It is hoped that national health insurance will promote preventive over therapeutic medicine, and the article by Farquhar and his colleagues gives details about an apparently successful public education project aimed at changing behaviors that are believed to cause cardiovascular problems. If, as predicted, one of the results of national health insurance is to increase the demand for medical services, we might witness an expansion of the role of medical personnel other than M.D.'s. Hence, research comparing the quality of services provided by nurse practitioners and M.D.'s—as Spitzer and his associates have done—is of considerable importance. If, as also predicted, national health insurance increases the demand for ambulatory rather than in hospital services, then evaluations of ambulatory care will become increasingly important. Christoffel and Loewenthal's review highlights some of the innovations needed to responsibly evaluate the quality of ambulatory care.

The last two articles in this section were chosen because they address the thorny methodological and ethical problems that are particularly acute for the evaluation of health care services. Both Tukey and Gilbert et al. argue that more experimentation should take place because of the ethical implications of not rigorously testing medical innovations.

# 15

# Continuing Evaluation and Accountability Controls for a National Health Insurance Program

## APA Task Force on Continuing Evaluation in National Health Insurance

ABSTRACT: *In order to promote the evolution of an effective program of national health insurance, a system of continuing evaluation must be made an integral part of the development, delivery, and management of services. The objectives of an evaluation system would be to help (a) specify the goals of the national health insurance system in measurable terms so that progress toward those goals can be assessed, and effective components of programs can be identified; (b) provide a mechanism for effective cost management; (c) promote the provision of effective and safe services; (d) further the accountability of providers and system administration for the conduct of the insurance plan; (e) foster equal access to needed services by all segments of the population; (f) facilitate the development and efficient functioning of the service provision system; (g) promote the communication of information about the nature, extent, and costs of services to the public, to providers, and to Congress; and (h) assess the unintended or alternative outcomes of national health insurance. Sixteen characteristics that an evaluation and accountability system should possess in order to meet these goals are discussed, as are a number of practical difficulties in implementing such a system.*

Some form of comprehensive health insurance system will almost surely be legislated into existence within the next few years, whether as a national health insurance (NHI) system or as an extension and elaboration of the present system. As the legislation is written, Congress will be under great pressure to establish a system of organized health care accessible to all Americans. Public demand for accountability will require a clear sense of priorities, determination of program effectiveness, the containment of cost, and assurance of the availability of responsive, quality health services. Existing federal programs such as Medicare and Medicaid are thought to be inadequate in coverage for mental health services, and they exclude from participation a number of provider groups that could contribute substantially to the nation's health.

The probable advent of NHI provides psychology and the other health professions with a remarkable opportunity to display professional maturity and leadership in also urging Congress to build into the NHI provisions for systematic evaluation of covered services and reimbursement only for effective treatments and programs. In the vast majority of cases, the only really ethical position lies in providing the public with effective services or services whose effectiveness is under systematic evaluation. It is unlikely that any health profession would in the long run lose by affirming its confidence in its ability to provide effective services, and the public could only gain.

Evaluation is activity carried out to determine the consequences of implementing a treatment or program.[1] Applied to NHI, evaluation is activity carried out to help determine the worth of programs for improving health, preventing illness and disability, or providing necessary support. It pertains to a wide range of research activities extending from testing the effectiveness of a specific drug or medical procedure to examining a program of national scope. There are many ways in which evaluation could be accomplished, for example, reliance on expert opinion, obtaining of consensus judgments of consumers, logical analysis, etc.; but within the context of this paper, evaluation may be taken to refer to careful and systematic research for determining the extent to which a program is effective. The results of evaluation provide objective evidence of the effectiveness of a program for use by those who will decide what NHI should pay for. Good evaluation research is also directed toward considerations of cost, and cost control must be a powerful restraint within NHI if the system is to be viable. Evaluation research

The Task Force on Continuing Evaluation in National Health Insurance was established by the APA Board of Directors in May 1976. Members of the task force are Asher R. Pacht (Chair), Russell Bent, Thomas D. Cook, Lewis B. Klebanoff, David A. Rodgers, Lee Sechrest, Hans Strupp, and Milton Theaman. Gary D. Gottfredson and Stephen D. Nelson were the staff liaison members. This report represents the views of the task force, and is not necessarily policy of the American Psychological Association, which can only be made by the Council of Representatives.

[1] For the sake of simplicity, the term *program* will be used henceforth to refer generically to treatments, interventions, and other related concepts.

From APA Task Force on Continuing Evaluation in National Health Insurance, "Continuing Evaluation and Accountability Controls for a National Health Insurance Program," 33 (4) *American Psychologist* 305-313 (April 1978). Copyright 1978 by the American Psychological Association, Inc.

can be useful not only in the determination of whether a program works and in the provision of careful and reasonable measures of its benefits but also to provide comparative data on alternative programs so that cost-effectiveness may be judged. If NHI is to be economically sound and reasonably priced, all programs will have to be carefully evaluated to determine that their benefits are being achieved in a cost-effective way.

It is unrealistic to suppose that a national health insurance system would begin with coverage limited to those services with well-established effectiveness. Many of the health care procedures now considered standard have never been demonstrated in careful experimentation to be effective. Consequently, one realistic suggestion would be the convening of study groups to determine which treatments and other health services have been shown to be effective and then to set priorities for study among those that have not. Reimbursement under NHI might continue for all treatments and services currently judged reasonable; but on a gradual basis, currently accepted practices should be examined and dropped if proven ineffective. No new programs should be added without empirical test.

Decision making in most areas of human services is complex, and considerations other than the worth of a service often properly enter into the decisions. Regardless of the existence of evidence for or against a particular decision, political considerations will be especially likely to contribute heavily to decisions about what services are delivered and how. Nevertheless, in decisions about the delivery of health services within the context of NHI, those involved in the political process should be maximally informed about the effectiveness of the programs in question.

## Principles

There are many ways in which the problem of explicating a position about evaluation of and accountability for professional services might be approached. We have here elected to state some general principles that we strongly believe should guide the development of legislation when its time comes.

PRINCIPLE 1. *Legislation should provide for implementing programs in ways that facilitate rigorous evaluation.*

The history of social and health programs in this country is replete with instances of programs brought into being hastily and nationwide before any evidence of effectiveness could be accumulated. In many other instances, interventions have been introduced so haphazardly that no persuasive evidence of effectiveness could be gathered. It is of the greatest importance that the various features of NHI be introduced systematically, in such a way as to foster rather than re-

tard or frustrate evaluative efforts. The key to linking service delivery to evaluation is the dual recognition that no program or service can actually and effectively be implemented on a national basis instantaneously and that when we do not know precisely what to do about a problem, delay is not disastrous but prudent. What is needed is a set of deliberate strategies for introducing new programs in such ways that data can be collected to assess program effectiveness.

Ideally, evaluation should involve a true experiment, with sampling units, whether persons, hospitals, or HSAs (health services areas), being assigned randomly to various treatment and control conditions. For new interventions especially, such designs are often feasible, and where feasible they should be insisted upon as the most likely to produce high-quality, clear-cut findings. Many current interventions, however, cannot be evaluated against no-treatment control groups because of ethical considerations. Current programs will in most instances have to be tested against innovations that might replace them. Even so, data occasionally come to light that cast such serious doubts on the efficacy of currently accepted practices that a randomized experiment with an untreated control group is acceptable on ethical as well as scientific grounds.

Since the testing and demonstration of effectiveness of many programs is an iterative process, it is probable that the course of evaluating many programs will begin with small-scale demonstration projects and laboratory-type experiments, to be followed by larger scale tests. For many of the larger scale tests, true experiments may not be feasible. Nonetheless, services and programs can be implemented in ways that will facilitate their evaluation without needlessly depriving any group of services of known value.

By phasing in programs systematically at different places or at different times, data of an unusually valuable nature can often be obtained. Programs might, for example, be phased in by geographic regions or by political units so that one could determine whether there were systematic changes within regions or units associated uniquely with the implementation of the program. If a preponderance of the units changed after the intervention, and only after the intervention, and if the intervention began at different times for different units, the case for a causal effect of the program would be strong. Treatments might also be phased in by populations served or by naturally occurring units such as different military units, universities, hospitals, or service clubs.

Although there are limits on the interpretability of many natural variations in health programs because these variations are usually confounded with other variables such as the population served, opportunities to study normal variations should nevertheless be capitalized upon. For example, in the early days of tranquilizing drugs, the doses of chlorpromazine given in different institutions varied greatly, and only gradually did evidence become available that the very high doses were not needed and probably were harmful. The same conclusion would have been suggested earlier had easily available information about the practices and experiences of different institutions been used.

Program evaluation is still a new area of endeavor, and the expected development over the coming years of new research designs, better statistical techniques, and other methodological improvements will make the task of evaluating health care interventions easier and, in that respect, all the more mandatory.

PRINCIPLE 2. *The autonomy of the evaluation components should be guaranteed.*

Our definition of evaluation implies that evaluation should be objective—free of inappropriate political pressures, of the biases of narrow professional interests, of expectancies about what ought to be, and of any other prejudicial factors. In order to achieve that objectivity, it seems essential that any evaluation component established under NHI legislation should be autonomous in virtually every respect. Personnel should be recruited on the basis of scientific competence and personal integrity. The guarantee should be absolute that the evaluation component, although subject to oversight and review, control its own budget, plan its own studies, have authority to collect, analyze, and interpret its own data, and issue its own reports. The evaluation component should be established and operated in such a way that suspicions of either bias or insufficient courage would not be sustainable. There are unfortunate examples in the federal government of evaluative activities that lack credibility because of political and other influence.

There are three important points of contact between an evaluation component and the larger system of which it is a part. First, a variety of interest groups should have a role in the setting of priorities for study and in developing plans to accomplish research. Second, an evaluation component should enter into the decision-making process, but only to the extent of providing the best evidence possible. Third, provision should be made for review of the activities of the evaluation component to ensure that they contribute effectively and efficiently to the overall aims of the NHI system. Evaluation procedures and data should be open to public scrutiny by the time any reports using those data are issued.

PRINCIPLE 3. *The national health legislation should provide for adequate funding of evaluation.*

Evaluation of health care activities will entail costs of considerable magnitude. We propose that any NHI system have built into it a substantial and continuing mandate and capacity to fund research into the effec-

tiveness of all types of health care. Otherwise, evaluation is not likely to be funded adequately through alternative sources to achieve optimal cost-effectiveness, cost-containment, and health-enhancement goals. In recent decades, enormously costly federal programs have been funded and have proven disappointing in light of the original, perhaps overly idealistic, goals. We believe that the lack of provisions for evaluating these programs from the time of their origin contributed to their failure. The consequence of this failure was the unavailability of a rational basis for modifying the programs as evidence of their ineffectiveness began to appear. The belated addition, often under crisis conditions, of a research and evaluation component proved uniformly unsatisfactory as a way of salvaging programs showing clear signs of incipient failure. Billions of dollars have been wasted, the hopes and aspirations of large portions of the populace have been frustrated, and the federal government has suffered losses in public confidence and trust.

The financing of evaluation studies of the kind we are proposing will involve large sums of money and complex decisions. It is our opinion that research needed to support and improve the effectiveness of a national health insurance system should come from within the system itself, that is, should be paid for out of "premium dollars." Only in that way can the research enterprise be protected from the vagaries of funding decisions. Moreover, it seems only just that research meant to improve a system should be funded out of that system, but in a way that preserves autonomy. The level of funding that should be available cannot be specified in other than an arbitrary way, but it probably should be set at some percentage of the total NHI expenditures, should be a constant and dependable percentage over a period of years, and should be reviewed periodically to determine whether benefits being achieved from the research are outweighing costs. Annual health expenditures of a fairly direct nature amount to something over $150 billion per year and justify effort to develop empirical support for the efficacy of those expenditures. Even a small percentage increase in the efficiency of the system would justify a substantial research budget.

Although good evaluation research can sometimes be done with minimal financial outlay, it is often expensive; sometimes it is *very* expensive. Nevertheless, the justification for these costs is that the costs associated with not doing good evaluation research may be even greater. To begin with, there is a potentially great human cost, both individual and societal, in employing ineffective programs. Bloodletting, a primary medical procedure of the last century, and prolonged confinement in bed following surgery, a practice in the first half of this century, are two examples. Radical mastectomy for a single breast lesion may be a current example. Scarce resources are wasted when they are invested in ineffective programs. Moreover, there is danger in the belief that some condition is being treated when the treatment is in fact of little or no value. Attention is diverted from the problem, and it will persist and perhaps worsen. In addition, poor research is expensive. It is expensive because in the long run much money is spent on series of weak studies that even in the aggregate will rarely be persuasive. High-quality research is likely to be more persuasive and ultimately to involve a lower final dollar cost. Poor research may also be costly in a human sense because it can be misleading and either support the case for an ineffective treatment or steer decision makers away from a good one.

As with any other activity involving expenditure of public monies, evaluation research itself should be evaluated. The potential benefits should, however, be calculated from the proper base. It may well be a bargain to spend more on a good evaluation of an intervention than the intervention itself costs, if the intervention is likely to be regarded as a prototype for a national program. Account should also be taken of the likelihood that the benefits from many proven interventions will extend for years into the future, although the costs of the evaluation are incurred immediately. Determining whether an evaluation study is worth doing at the proposed cost will not always be simple, but the effort should be made.

Very often the best bargain in research is sound basic research on human processes and problems. Although the emphasis of research within NHI should, we believe, be on evaluating the effectiveness of programs, a strong case can be made for allocating at least some portion of the research dollar to more basic studies, particularly if areas can be identified which may have a high probability of later application.

PRINCIPLE 4. *The system should have articulated procedures for encouraging new and innovative programs with rigorous evaluation designs.*

The requirement that the effectiveness of a new program be demonstrated prior to its reimbursement under NHI might seem unduly to retard innovation or to make change almost tortuously slow. That need not be the case. Much of the slow pace of development that now exists comes from artificial barriers, professional jealousies, and lack of funds for research. None of these problems is inherent to an empirically based system. Some portion of NHI funds should be invested—perhaps through the National Institutes of Health, or an evaluation component within NHI—in demonstration projects, large-scale clinical trials, and other research activities. Undoubtedly, a large number of important health questions could be resolved within a very few years. Nevertheless, nothing should become routine in the system until tested and proven efficacious and safe. We have more than enough experience of the rapid acceptance of ineffective and even dangerous treatments to justify an insistence on the slightly more deliberate pace that an outcome-based system would follow.

The needs of an NHI system for information will require a type and level of research not now characteristic of that in most of the National Institutes of Health, although other federal agencies such as the National Center for Health Services Research and the National Institute of Mental Health do support some research of the sort envisioned here. With a fully operating NHI system, wide participation in health research will be required.

Nothing here should be taken as implying that development of new programs should be slighted. Special procedures should be established so that individual practitioners, clinics, or other provider units could be reimbursed for nonstandard but innovative services. Those procedures would probably involve prospective peer review focused on the prior research support for the innovation, the logic of the innovation, and the plan by which the innovation would be evaluated. The initial evaluation might be clinical and relatively informal, but with subsequent extension of the innovation, more rigorous evaluation designs could be demanded.

PRINCIPLE 5. *The system should provide for the evaluation of the relationship of program characteristics to outcomes, with primary focus on how programs affect recipients.*

Desired outcomes should be specified for every health service delivered or for every program to be implemented. Outcomes should be specified in ways that are conceptually clear and in forms that are measurable. It is also necessary to specify the time span during which outcomes should be detectable, for not every program will produce either immediate or permanent effects. Ideally, the set of outcomes expected from an intervention or a program should form a coherent body of related effects with clear linkages to the treatments employed. The outcomes to be assessed should be evident in the characteristics or behavior of the units to which services are delivered, so that, for example, when families are served, effects on families should be detectable, and when communities are served, community effects should be observable.

The focus of all programs under NHI, and thus of all evaluations of them too, should be on the recipient rather than on the provider or the system itself. Every effort should be expended to determine the actual health needs of persons insured by the system and how those health needs might best be met. The NHI and health care systems should then be structured so as to meet those needs. What providers might prefer to do, what might be easy or convenient, or what would be pleasant should be secondary considerations except when such factors pose obstacles to delivery of effective service. Nor should efficiency become such a preeminent criterion that it results in the impersonal or demeaning management of people.

At some point, the effectiveness of the entire health care delivery system must be examined. It will not suffice to evaluate health care treatment by treatment and service by service. The effectiveness of the system will be evident only in terms of system goals. Those goals will have to be stated objectively, and relevant data will have to be collected. The system will be judged deficient and will have to be corrected if system goals are not met. For example, one goal of the health care system might be that no more than .5% of pregnant women should go without prenatal care beyond the fourth month of pregnancy—the small allowance being for exceptional cases of women hiding their pregnancies or refusing care. If 10% of pregnant women are not receiving prenatal care, then the system is failing, no matter how good the care when it is given. Obviously, any single index or even any set of absolute goals must be applied with caution, and progress toward them must be viewed in context.

PRINCIPLE 6. *Guidelines on which accountability is based should be made explicit and generally understood in advance.*

The interests of the health care system, of providers of services, and of recipients of services coincide with respect to the need for mechanisms to control the delivery of services in such a way that quality and appropriateness are assured and that costs are minimized. Without doubt, a variety of control mechanisms will be required, because the problem is multifaceted and involves a number of different levels of analysis. At one level, provision must be made for determining what services will be covered under NHI, and that determination will involve complex issues having to do with costs to the system, needs of recipients, equity across social class lines, and national priorities. At another level, specifications for quality services will have to be devised and permissible variations stated. At still another level, some sort of review for compliance with specifications of quality will have to take place. It is important to all concerned that the process involved in control of health services delivery be open and comprehensible. Almost surely, mechanisms of control will have to include a system of peer review for providers of services.

Both providers and recipients of services will want the guidelines by which appropriateness, quality, and cost of services will be evaluated to be explicit and understood in advance of any interventions undertaken. Both providers and recipients should know at every step whether a specific treatment plan or procedure would be regarded as appropriate, of good quality, and

as a covered service for which reimbursement would be forthcoming from NHI. In general, guidelines should be as simple as is consonant with the assurance of quality of care. In particular, the guidelines for controlling costs should be straightforward, with as few special provisions as possible concerning such matters as proportion of costs covered, deductibles, co-payments, and the like.

PRINCIPLE 7. *Criteria examined via evaluation programs should be explicit and should represent the concerns of diverse constituencies.*

If the goals of accountability and quality of care are to be met, it will be necessary to specify treatment and case management criteria by which judgments can be made. The criteria must be stated in an explicit form; reliance on implicit judgments, even if made by peers, will not be sufficient. As with general guidelines, criteria should be available to all parties involved in the process. Patients and clients no less than peers should be aware of what is considered standard or quality treatment. Explicit criteria do not unnaturally limit decision making by provider and consumer, individually or jointly. Mechanisms for exception should be a part of the system. All that is required in most cases is that the reason for the exception be as explicit and reasonable as the criterion itself.

Consumer satisfaction with health services should be studied as carefully and routinely as with the most successful commercial products. If consumers are dissatisfied with the health services they receive, they may not continue to use those they need and may dissuade others from using them. Problems with consumer satisfaction are especially troublesome when health deficits are chronic and when consumer freedom to choose among services is limited. When health problems are chronic, dissatisfaction may lead to poor compliance with a treatment regimen that requires patient cooperation. A case in point is the poor compliance of some males with a hypotensive drug treatment that as a side effect produces impotence. When patients have little freedom of choice in selecting health services, dissatisfaction may lead to a failure to get treatment at all. Humane considerations demand that services be provided in ways that are satisfactory to clients if that is at all possible.

Ours is a large country with a diverse and pluralistic society. Consequently, any satisfactory health care system will have to be both complex and flexible. People of diverse backgrounds will require different types of services. Similarly, people living under some conditions will often require special services, although they will also have to recognize that they may incur some unusual risks by their choice of residence or way of life. Even within a given group or geographic area, people will have different needs or will respond differently to the same services. Neither the complexity of the task of providing diverse services nor the necessity of responding to complex needs should be underestimated. Flexibility and complexity in an adequate health care system will, of course, add to the problems involved in evaluating the system and its components, because a service may be differentially effective across geographic locations or ethnic and socioeconomic groups. Although demonstrating differential effectiveness and building provisions for different services into a national health program with effective quality-assurance mechanisms will be difficult, this effort will be required in an adequate overall health system.

Even though the focus of health program development and evaluation should be on the recipient, the needs of providers and of society more generally should not be ignored. Providers need a health care system within which they can work effectively and which will reward them financially and in other ways commensurate with their contributions to individual and societal welfare. To work effectively, providers need a health care system that not only sets forth clear expectations for behavior but also permits the exercise of individual judgment in the particular case. Providers need a system that is reasonably stable and predictable, and one that yields ample feedback about adequacy of performance. They also need a system that is not capricious but is forgiving of errors that will inevitably be made, without being at all tolerant of errors in the long run or of professional incompetence. In addition, providers should participate in the planning and development of the health care system, while at the same time sharing this responsibility with other interests so that they are not burdened with complete and final responsibility for everything that happens—or does not happen.

Other interests also have a legitimate stake in the way criteria are developed for accountability and assessing quality. Legislators need to be assured that their intentions in approving and funding a health insurance system are represented in the working of the system and in what it achieves. Administrators of the system need workable and efficient mechanisms so that they can perform the tasks with which they are entrusted, know that the system is functioning properly, and modify it appropriately. Taxpayers need to be confident that they are getting good value for their money and that the system is realistic and fair. All of these interests will benefit from an open, explicit system.

PRINCIPLE 8. *Evaluation and accountability mechanisms should make it possible to assess the degree to which the objectives of individualized treatment plans are achieved.*

Virtually every case seen within a health care system is in some respects unique and represents a fresh challenge to those involved in planning care. Because there are few health conditions that are not influenced by a wide variety of patient characteristics, specifications of treatment and outcomes by general prescriptions can serve only as general guidelines. In the individual case, it will often be necessary to tailor treatments or to modify expectations in light of the characteristics of that case. Since goals have to be set for the individual, some provision must be made for determining whether those individual goals are met.

A review system will have to be devised which will permit review of individual cases and determine the degree to which individual goals are met. The review process might well need the flexibility that would make possible a review of no more than a small percentage of some types of cases and a review of every single case of other types. It will be necessary for clinicians and case managers to be explicit about individualized treatment plans, how they will be evaluated, and procedures for reconciling any persistent differences between providers and those doing the review. It is to be expected that the assessment of the individual being treated will be an important part of the evaluation. Evaluation at the system level would then include aggregating data on outcomes across individual cases. A system might be judged effective if most treatment goals were being met in most cases, however diverse those goals.

PRINCIPLE 9. *Claims of special competency to perform services by any professional group should be evaluated.*

It is common for various professional groups to claim a special competency in service delivery achieved by special training or selection of members of those groups. Along with the claim of special competence very often goes pressure for licensure of the professional group as a certified, and often the only, provider of a type of service to the public. When any individual, profession, or institution claims special competence to perform some service on behalf of the public, the actuality of that competence should be demonstrated. In that demonstration lies much of what is meant by accountability. In some instances, a virtual monopoly may exist, and a potential client may have no basis for judging quality of service provided, nor have any choice in where to seek it. Under those conditions, a firm and dependable procedure for demonstrating exclusive competence is mandatory.

Through the existing system of statutory certification and licensure, a group of health service providers are identified whose members meet minimum levels of training and experience. This is a point from which systematic study of the various health professions can begin. Just as it seems reasonable to initiate health insurance coverage for currently accepted treatments and services, initial recognition should be accorded to present systems of licensure as entry levels for health service providers. The legal definition of practice under licensure laws will determine the professional's scope of practice. However, any claims made by professional groups that would result in an exclusive position in the health care system should be examined empirically, and status as a provider of a service should be based on evidence of the same nature as would be required for program effectiveness. As provider groups not now commonly recognized make claims on the health insurance system, evidence for effectiveness should be the basis for their inclusion as covered professions. The system should provide workable mechanisms for demonstrating such effectiveness.

PRINCIPLE 10. *The evaluation system should utilize the judgment and leadership of service providers to help promote both the functioning of service delivery and the cooperation of service providers throughout the evaluation process.*

Bringing about changes in our health care system will not be easy. Despite current efforts to require that the services offered be of demonstrated value, that idea is still considered radical by many. There are no ready and simple answers to questions about how changes of large magnitude might be brought about. Strong leadership exercised by the large and prestigious groups involved in the provision of health care service could be a powerful force for change if those groups displayed a unity of determination and commitment. Each of the individual health professions may have to take some degree of risk in order to demonstrate a persuasive level of unselfish interest. In the long run, none of the health professions stands to lose by insisting on empirical tests of its claims and services.

Every effort must be made to enlist the support of providers of services if evaluation efforts are to succeed. Providers should be prominently represented in those groups established to fix guidelines and define criteria for quality and appropriateness of services. The counsel of providers should be sought in developing review systems so that review will have a maximum effect on quality of care but will produce minimal administrative burden and disruption. Quality-assurance systems should be an integral part of the delivery of services. They should not and need not be onerous and limiting, but the help of providers in designing them will be required if their potentially undesirable features are to be avoided.

PRINCIPLE 11. *Provision should be made for the systematic collection of information compatible with the needs of program evaluation. Confidentiality must be protected, but at the same time, access to the information required for evaluation must be provided.*

No adequate and systematic program evaluation effort can succeed without an appropriate information system, and the existing health information system is not suited to the task. The need for evaluation of health services is so great that it justifies the development of an information system devised specifically to meet the requirements of evaluation of NHI programs. Such an information system would provide systematic, relevant, accurate, and timely information in a form that could be analyzed efficiently. An information system should be established which would provide for collection of comparable information across political units and geographical and time boundaries.

The problem of maintaining confidentiality of information cannot be ignored. Even apart from evaluation, absolute confidentiality of health records cannot exist under any feasible insurance system because some records must be reviewed by the payer. Currently, medical claims are reviewed in insurance companies by clerks at the very first level. A systematic evaluation plan would not represent a greater threat to confidentiality than the current forms of insurance review. For many evaluation purposes, however, individual-identifying information would be unnecessary because the research questions would require only data aggregated by categories, types of treatments, etc. For these research purposes, then, confidentiality concerning individual records would be preserved. Confidentiality might be more difficult to promise for individual providers, since there are often very few of them involved in any one study, particularly in the case of specialists. To a certain degree, those who exact the special and favorable position afforded by licensure probably forfeit any rights to absolute confidentiality involving their own behavior. Nonetheless, confidentiality is an important issue, and an evaluation system should not abuse it.

PRINCIPLE 12. *Special attention should be paid to changes in the functioning or effects of programs as they evolve. Both long- and short-term effects should be examined, and consideration should be given to the unintended as well as intended program consequences.*

Programs always change over time. Some of the changes may represent improvements, others may represent degradations. As programs come into being and reach operational stages, staff members may become more skillful, but they may also become blasé. Clients may become more faithful, but they may also come to take more for granted. Particularly when programs devised in one setting are copied elsewhere, some of the essential features that made the original program successful may be distorted or lost. It is essential that evaluation be regarded as a continuing process rather than as a discrete, point-in-time event.

Attending to the possibility of long-term program effects that are discrepant with more immediate effects is also important. It is possible that a program appearing to have little in the way of immediate effects might have long-term effects that would make the program worthwhile, ór that a program appearing immediately effective might have long-term effects of an undesirable nature. Naturally, health program decisions cannot be postponed until all the evidence is in, but provisions should be made for insuring that necessary evidence eventually becomes available.

Efforts should be expended to consider the broad ranges of possible consequences of a program in order to narrow the range of potentially surprising outcomes. During early planning stages for an evaluation, potential clients and experts from various fields relevant to the program might be asked to think about possible side effects. Once a program is in operation it should be monitored carefully to determine the unanticipated side effects. A time lag between the trial of a program and widespread program implementation may be necessary to detect delayed effects.

PRINCIPLE 13. *Procedures for controls on and reviews of the scientific quality of evaluation should be established.*

How is an evaluation to be evaluated? Some procedures and criteria will have to be established to review evaluations to determine whether they have been properly conducted and whether the conclusions are properly drawn. If the results of evaluation studies are really going to be the basis for policy setting within NHI, then it is essential that the evaluations be of the highest quality. The most efficient way to accomplish this review of evaluations will probably be to convene panels of experts. These panels would use such criteria as adequacy of problem definition, fidelity of adherence to program or treatment standards, appropriateness of the sample studied, soundness of the original research design and effects of any deviations from it, adequacy of data quality-control procedures, adequacy of statistical analysis, and overall legitimacy of the conclusions. Evaluation researchers within NHI must be held to exceptionally high standards. Ultimately, making the nonconfidential data, research design, evaluation, and results a part of the public record open to review by any interested citizen would probably be the most effective control on the process.

PRINCIPLE 14. *Procedures for disseminating the results of evaluation should be established.*

An overall strategy for disseminating the results of evaluation studies should be developed and implemented. Because of the diverse constituencies represented among those interested in health services and their delivery, no one mechanism for dissemination will be adequate. One tactic that might make research findings easier to disseminate would be, whenever possible, to make the existence of studies known from the beginning and to keep various interested groups informed of progress during the course of the work. The

final report on the work would then be anticipated with interest. The important thing, however, is that there be designated responsibility for disseminating the results of every study by all the appropriate channels. Those channels should be well established and provided for within the health insurance system and its evaluation component.

PRINCIPLE 15. *The national health insurance program should contain a formal mechanism for change incorporating the results of evaluation.*

Problems in achieving appropriate utilization of evaluation results can be anticipated. Findings may not be used and have the desired effect on policy even when they are available. One very important factor having to do with the utilization of research findings is centralized decision making; centralization facilitates the adoption of programs of demonstrated value. That NHI would be characterized by much centralized decision making seems beyond question, and many interventions can be implemented by the fairly simple expedient of announcing that reimbursement for them will begin at a certain time and that reimbursement for alternatives will have to be justified. Still, because the possibilities of nonutilization and misutilization will not be negligible, a panel will be needed to sift through research findings and evaluation studies in order to facilitate the appropriate utilization of results. One additional activity that could have considerable impact would be the conducting of regular, carefully planned workshops and other training activities to help administrators understand and use research findings. Scientists may also want to know more about how to conduct research that is persuasive and usable so that where decisions involving trade-offs must be made, they will be made in the direction of enhancing the impact of the research.

An effective plan for dissemination of information and support for its utilization would probably do much to promote the acceptance of evaluation efforts in the entire health field, including acceptance by providers, consumers, and legislators. One of the persistent criticisms of federally funded research is that so many of its results are never translated into practical programs.

PRINCIPLE 16. *A program should be developed to inform the public about the process of evaluation and its results.*

Acceptance of evaluation findings by the public, including those with direct or vested interests in health programs, will require general public understanding of evaluation as a process and of the links between evaluation and program decision making. If evaluation as an enterprise is not understood by any segment of the public, then there will probably continue to be resistance within that segment to the idea of evaluation and to conclusions stemming from it, particularly when those conclusions contravene popular beliefs or what many people would prefer to believe. The controversies about Laetrile and saccharin, for example, may be exacerbated by a general lack of understanding about the processes by which they have been evaluated and the reasoning that has gone into the conclusions about them. Some efforts have been made in the public media to explain the research on both substances. Such dissemination channels should be utilized routinely. It would also be desirable to devise longer term, systematic ways of increasing the general sophistication of the public about research on drugs and other substances. A continuing effort to inform the public about the process of health program evaluation, the results of evaluation activities, and the way it operates in the public interest is needed.

## Conclusion

Many of the evaluation and accountability principles outlined here will be difficult to implement. Naturally, no system of evaluation can instantly produce widespread improvements on current practice that has grown out of years of experience. Fully developing the potential of evaluation to contribute to the long-term improvement of the health system will require a recognition of the value of continuing evaluation, improvements in evaluation technology, development of a cadre of skilled personnel, and the cooperation and participation of health providers. Containing the cost of a national health insurance program will be extremely difficult without a first-rate accountability and evaluation system. Because evaluation and improved accountability have so much to contribute to the efficiency, safety, and effectiveness of our health system, we cannot afford to forgo their contribution.

# 16

## The High Cost of Hospitals—And What To Do About It

*Martin Feldstein*

T HE explosion of hospital costs is now the central problem of our national health-care policy. Congress and the Administration are actively considering plans to impose direct controls on the costs of more than 7,000 individual hospitals. More generally, now that Medicare and Medicaid provide benefits for the aged and the poor, it is the rapid increase of hospital costs that provides the primary impetus for national health insurance. Unfortunately, the current policy initiatives generally reflect a misunderstanding of why hospital costs have risen so rapidly and of how hospital-cost inflation is very different than the other types of inflation that trouble our economy.

The magnitude of the increase in hospital costs has been overwhelmingly greater than the general rise in prices. From 1950 to 1976, the overall consumer price index (which measures the cost of all goods and services bought by consumers) rose about 125 per cent. During the same period, medical-care costs as a whole rose nearly twice as much, 240 per cent. But the upsurge in the cost of hospital care was much more dramatic. Average cost per patient-day was only $16 in 1950. By 1976, it was about $175, an increase of more than 1,000 per cent.

While everyone is aware that hospital costs have risen rapidly, there is little understanding of why this has happened at such an unprecedented rate. Much has been written about the rise in hospital wage-rates and the supposedly low rate of increase in productivity among hospital staff. But such "explanations" miss the real nature of the problem. For there are two—and really only two—key ingredients to understanding the rise in hospital costs: *the changing nature of the hospital product,* and *the impact of insurance.* Of these, the second is the more crucial—and largely explains the first.

## The changing hospital product

The most obvious thing about hospital care today is that it is very different from what it was 25 years ago. Today's care is more complex, more sophisticated, and, it is to be hoped, more effective.

The rapid rise in hospital costs unquestionably reflects this rapidly changing product. The rate of hospital-cost inflation, therefore, cannot be compared without qualification to the rate of inflation of most other goods in the consumer price index. The consumer price index tries to measure the cost of buying an *unchanged* bundle of goods and services. But the meaning of cost inflation in hospital care is not that consumers are paying much more for the same old product, but that they are buying a different and much more expensive product today. Hospital-cost inflation is therefore quite different from the other types of inflation in our economy. To understand the nature of this problem, we must ask why hospital care has become much more sophisticated—and therefore much more expensive.

Higher incomes and greater education have undoubtedly played some role in increasing the demand for sophisticated hospital care, and scientific discoveries have obviously changed the technological possibilities in hospitals. *But the major reason, I believe, for hospital-cost inflation has been the very rapid growth in insurance.*

In addition to providing protection against unforeseen medical expenses, health insurance substantially lowers the net price of care that the patient pays out-of-pocket at the time he consumes services. There is now substantial evidence that patients, guided by their doctors, demand more services and more expensive services when a large part of the cost is offset by insurance.

Some simple but striking numbers will illustrate this point. In 1950, when average cost per patient-day was a little less than $16, private insurance and government programs paid 49 per cent of hospital bills. This meant that, on the average, the net cost to a patient of a day of care was just under $8. By 1975, average cost per patient-day had jumped to about $152—but private and public insurance were paying 88 per cent of the hospital bill, leaving a net cost to the patient of only $18. Thus, although the cost of providing a day of hospital care had increased more than ninefold (from $16 to $152), the *net* cost to patients had only just about doubled (from $8 to $18). Moreover, the general increase in the prices of all goods and services meant that $18 in 1975 could only buy as much as $8 in 1950! So in *real* terms, the net cost to the patient at the time of illness has not changed at all during the past 25 years.

Even if we disregard Medicare, Medicaid, and other government programs, the picture is not very different. In 1950, private insurance paid 37 per cent of private hospital bills. That meant that, on average, the net cost to a private patient for a day of hospital care was just under $10. By 1975, private insurance was paying for 79 per cent of privately financed hospital care. The average net cost to the patient at the time of illness, therefore, was only $32 per day— not the $152 incurred by the hospital. In the prices of 1950, this $32 is equivalent to $14. In *real* terms, the net cost per day to the patient had only increased by $4.

Looked at somewhat differently, with 79 per cent of private hospital bills now paid by insurance, an extra $10 of expensive care costs the patient only $2 out-of-pocket. It is not surprising, therefore, that patients and their doctors continue to encourage the growing sophistication (and expense) of hospital care.

I think this is the essence of the hospital-cost inflation problem: *Increased insurance has induced hospitals to improve their product and provide much more expensive and sophisticated care.*

### The usual explanations

Before considering the implications of this explanation, let me contrast it with the usual reasons offered for the rise in hospital costs. These traditionally boil down to four ideas: 1) Hospitals are inefficient; 2) labor costs have risen particularly rapidly; 3) hospitals have had a low rise in technical progress; and 4) hospital supply has not kept up with increasing demand. Each of these notions is basically incorrect.

Perhaps the most frequently heard explanation of rising hospital costs is that hospitals are technologically and managerially inefficient. But even if there are good reasons for criticizing the efficiency of hospitals, there is absolutely no reason to believe their inefficiency has been rapidly increasing over the past two decades. Inefficiency cannot possibly account for a 1,000-per-cent increase in hospital costs! It cannot begin to account for a significant fraction of that overwhelming increase.

Rising labor costs are also frequently cited as the primary cause of hospital-cost inflation. It is true that wages and salaries constitute a large share of hospital costs, and that hospital wages have risen more rapidly than wages in the general economy. Nevertheless, this does not begin to account for the rise in hospital costs. From 1955 to 1975, labor-cost per patient-day rose at a rate of nine per cent a year. But *as a fraction of the total hospital bill, labor costs actually decreased from 62 per cent in 1955 to 53 per cent in 1975.* In other words, non-labor costs rose faster than labor costs. Moreover, about one third of the increase in labor costs was due to a rise in the number of personnel per patient-day rather than an increase in hospital wage rates. I recently calculated that the earnings of hospital employees rose at 6.3 per cent a year from 1955 to 1975, while the average earnings of all private non-farm workers rose at 4.5 per cent. If the rate of increase of hospital wages had been held to this 4.5-per-cent national average, the overall rise in the average cost of a day of hospital care would have been reduced from 9.9 per cent a year to 8.8 per cent. In other words, *the rise of hospital wages in excess of the national average rate of wage increase can only account for about one tenth of the high rate of hospital-cost inflation.*

The third common explanation is that hospital-cost inflation is the result of a low rate of technical progress. I think this is clearly and obviously false. Hospitals have been the scene of extremely rapid technical changes. But these changes differ from those in other industries: They have not been cost-reducing. Technological progress in hospitals does not involve making the old product more cheaply, but making a new range of products that are more expensive.

Why have hospitals moved toward increasingly expensive ways of doing more things for patients, rather than toward providing old services more cheaply? Although some of this merely reflects the path of scientific progress, I believe it can be shown that it is our method of financing health services that primarily determines the pattern of technological change itself. Hospitals would not be buying the latest, expensive medical technology if they could not afford it. What permits them to afford it is our mode of insuring against hospital costs.

The final traditional explanation is that hospital costs have risen because supply has not kept up with demand. Usually, economic analysis of ordinary markets emphasizes that prices rise because supply does not increase as rapidly as demand. But in the case of hospitals, I think the opposite is true. *It is precisely because supply has kept pace with demand that hospital costs have gone up.* Hospitals have responded to the increased demand and increased willingness to pay for sophisticated services by providing them, and costs have gone up accordingly. The increase in demand has induced a rapid rise in the supply of a *more expensive* type of hospital care.

This brings me back to my original contention that the rise in hospital costs reflects a change in the product, largely induced by the growth of insurance. But this explanation of the rise in hospital costs raises an awkward question. Implicit in every discussion of hospital-cost inflation is the assumption that the rise in cost has been excessive and should not be allowed to continue at the same rate in the future. But if this rise reflects a change in product rather than an increase in inefficiency or a low rate of technological progress, why is it really a problem?

The answer in brief is that the current type of costly medical care does not really correspond to what consumers or their physicians would regard as appropriate if their choices were not distorted by insurance. The effect of prepaying health care through insurance, both private and public, is to encourage hospitals to provide a more expensive product than the consumers actually wish to pay for. And in the end, we do pay for it—in ever higher insurance premiums.

Although the consumer eventually pays the full cost of the expensive care through higher insurance premiums, *at the time of illness* the choice of the patient and his physician reflects the *net* out-of-pocket cost of the care. Because this net out-of-pocket cost appears so modest, the patient and physician choose to buy more expensive care than they would if the patient were not so well insured. In this way, our current method of financing hospital care denies patients and their physicians the opportunity to choose effectively between higher-cost and lower-cost hospital care.

### Why patients overinsure

If insurance is responsible for such an inappropriate expansion in the demand for expensive care, why has insurance grown so rapidly? In part, this growth reflects a family's rational demand for protection against unexpected illness. It is unfortunate but inevitable that this process tends to be self-perpetuating. *The high cost of care induces families to buy more complete insurance, and the growth of insurance induces the hospital to produce more expensive care.*

But this demand for protection cannot explain the comprehensive "first-dollar insurance"—i.e., insurance for all costs up to a specified limit—that now 'exists. Current insurance is often inadequate in protecting the family against the substantial bills that can cause real hardship. Why have Americans bought such complete coverage for relatively small bills? Why have they been willing to pay for insurance that provides little real protection against catastrophic illness but induces them to buy more expensive and sophisticated care for less serious illnesses?

Most insurance is now group insurance and, more specifically, insurance bought for employee groups. Decisions on the scope of coverage and on co-insurance rates and deductibles are generally made in collective bargaining by expert representatives of labor and management. Why would such experts forego higher wages in order to obtain excessive, shallow insurance? *The answer, I believe, lies in the tax treatment of premiums.*

Government policies encourage insurance by a tax deduction and exclusion that now cost the Treasury more than $6 billion a year. Individuals can deduct about half of the premiums they pay for health insurance. More important, employer payments for insurance are excluded from the taxable income of the employee as well as the employer. These premiums are also not subject to social-security taxes or state income taxes.

Thus, even for a relatively low-income family, the inducement to buy insurance can be quite substantial. Because of the income and payroll taxes, a married man who has two children and earns $8,000 a year will take home an additional $70 for each $100 the employer adds to his income. If the employer buys health insurance instead, the full $100 can be applied against the premium and there is no tax to be paid. In this case, the dollar buys nearly 50 per cent more in health-care services if paid through an insurance premium than if paid in wages to individuals who then buy the care directly. For workers in high tax brackets, the incentive is stronger.

I believe the subsidy is strong enough to induce employees and unions to choose higher insurance instead of higher wages. The primary effect of this insurance is to distort the pattern of medical care and to exacerbate the rising cost of hospital care. Moreover, this subsidy, which costs taxpayers several billion dollars a year, is quite regressive: The subsidy is greatest for middle- and upper-income employees in high-wage industries. In short, the current tax treatment of insurance premiums, particularly the exclusion of employer payments from the employees' taxable incomes, is a costly, regressive, and inefficient aspect of our tax system.

An important step in dealing with high hospital costs must be to change this aspect of our tax system, which now contributes significantly to the underlying problem of excess insurance. More generally, we must restructure the system of health insurance to correct the incentives faced by patients and their doctors. Other proposed "solutions" will only take us down a wrong road.

### Direct regulation of hospital costs

One such proposed "solution" is the direct regulation of hospital costs. At first glance it seems natural to apply the mechanism of public-utility regulation to hospitals. However, a more detailed examination of this proposal shows that controlling hospital costs differs fundamentally from public-utility regulation. And more important, the direct regulation of hospital costs would in the long run make the nature and quality of hospital services completely unresponsive to the preferences of patients and their physicians.

Consider the experience of hospital-cost regulation under the Economic Stabilization Program of 1971-1974. A special subcommittee of the Cost of Living Council continued to regulate hospital costs during the entire period of price controls. At first, controls were limited to hospital wages and to the prices charged for specific types of hospital service (e.g., an x-ray, a particular laboratory test, etc.). The controls were constantly being confounded by rapid increases in the quality or sophistication of services, which called for new (and higher) costs. During the final phase of the Economic Stabilization Program, the regulation of hospital costs was changed to a comprehensive limit on the overall increase in the cost per patient-day (with minor adjustments for changes in occupancy rates, etc.). The American Hospital Association then filed suit against the Cost of Living Council, charging that such control of the quality of hospital care went beyond the legislative mandate of the stabilization program. The issue became moot when the legislation expired in 1974.

The experience of the Economic Stabilization Program confirmed that the central issue in controlling hospital costs is limiting the quality of hospital care. The problem thus differs fundamentally from the usual issues of public-utility regulation. Such regulation is used to control the exercise of monopoly power, to set a fair rate of profit on invested capital, and to assure that *minimum* quality standards are maintained. In contrast to the typical public utility, most hospitals—being nonprofit institutions—earn no profits, and minimum standards are already regulated through annual accreditation by a professional association.

Direct regulation of hospital costs is inappropriate because there is no "technically correct" way for the regulators to set an appropriate *maximum* quality of hospital care. Determining the appropriate quality of care is totally different in this respect than fixing the appropriate rate of profit for a public utility. Controlling the quality of medical care is not a technical economic or legal question that can be solved by bureaucrats, by the political process, or by an administrative tribunal. Nor can it be assigned to the process of physician peer review: Although peer review can try to ensure the application of accepted standards of care, it cannot properly establish what those standards *should* be in each particular case. Here again we run up against the difference between setting a minimum standard and imposing a maximum standard on the quality of care. Neither patients nor doctors are likely to accept calmly any such bureaucratic imposition.

Deciding on the correct quality and style of medical care requires involving the individual family and its own physician in the decision of how much they want to spend for medical care and how much for other things. Although direct involvement of households is not possible in determining the appropriate level of spending on such things as public safety or national defense, it *is* possible for personal health services. Moreover, it is essential. The only limits on health care we can expect a patient to tolerate are those he sets for himself. Trying to impose them by administrative fiat will lead to particular scandals and general dissatisfaction.

Although imposing an arbitrary limit on the increase in hospital costs might be beneficial for a few years, in the long run it would make the quality of hospital care completely unresponsive to the preferences of the patients. How would a regulatory agency decide whether real hospital costs should rise at an annual rate of four per cent, or six per cent, or eight per cent? After adjusting for the increase in wages and in the prices of things that hospitals buy, should costs and therefore quality be allowed to increase at a rate of two per cent, or four per cent, or six per cent? An arbitrary choice would eventually mean that the quality of hospital care will be very different from the level that patients and their physicians would choose.

And what would regulation do about differences among hospitals in the cost and quality of care? Would current differences be "frozen in" by limiting all hospitals to the same rate of cost increase? On what basis would a hospital be granted permission to add new services that increase its quality? Or would regulation seek to make all hospitals have the same levels of quality and cost except for differences in the diagnostic mix of patients?

These questions show two adverse effects of direct regulation. First, to the extent that current differences are maintained by limiting all hospitals to approximately the same rate of cost increase, direct regulation would be unfair to those who now live in the areas served by lower-quality hospitals and who would prefer a more rapid increase in quality during the years ahead. And to the extent that all hospitals are required to have the same level of quality, direct regulation would force many lower- and middle-income families to pay for a more expensive style of care than they want, while denying many other middle- and upper-income families the opportunity to purchase the higher-quality care that they would prefer. In short, direct regulation of hospital costs is not compatible with allowing a variety of institutions to develop in response to differences in patients' preferences. Moreover, it is disturbing that the government is considering regulation of hospital costs at the very time that the public and the Congress have become sharply critical of the adverse effects of regulation in a number of other industries.

### The lesson for NHI

The nature of hospital-cost inflation and the weaknesses of direct regulation have important implications for national health insurance. Whatever form of insurance is developed must face squarely the problem of how the evolution of the quality and style of medical care will be determined.

It is crucial to recognize that the long-run problem is not to *reduce* or to *limit* the growth of medical spending but to achieve the *correct rate of growth* of that spending. This must ultimately come down to balancing additional spending on medical care against the alternative uses to which households might put their resources. And this requires comparing the expected gains from additional medical care—gains that are psychological as well as physical—with the satisfaction that households would enjoy from the alternative spending on food, housing, education, or recreation.

It is important that we develop an approach to national health insurance that is appropriate to the advanced technology of today's medical care and the ever-increasing affluence of the American people. Too much of the current debate relies on ideas about the delivery of medical care that have been inherited from a period with quite different technological and economic conditions. The challenge today is to find new methods of financing health care that protect families from financial hardship, while also making future health care more responsive to the preferences of the people.

Several years ago, I outlined an approach to national health insurance[1] that I still believe can serve these two objectives. The basic idea in this proposal is extremely simple: Provide every family with an insurance policy so that a family's spending on health care need never be more than a moderate fraction of its income—*but* use a system of co-payments to make most families conscious of the cost of their use of health-care services. In the next few pages I will summarize the form of such a national health insurance plan. But it will help to focus and clarify the discussion if I indicate at the outset the six objectives by which we should judge any proposed system of financing health care:

1. *It should prevent deprivation of care.* No one should go without medical care because of inability to pay.

2. *It should prevent financial hardship.* No family should suffer substantial financial hardship because of the expense of unforeseen illness or accident.

3. *It should keep costs down.* A financing system should both encourage efficient use of resources and discourage medical-care price inflation. Whenever possible, patients should use relatively low-cost ambulatory facilities rather than high-cost in-hospital care. Hospitals should be induced to moderate the forces that raise the cost of care: increased personnel, unnecessary pay raises, and a proliferation of technical facilities and services. Physicians should not be encouraged to increase their fees by the knowledge that, because of insurance, the cost to their own patients will rise little, if at all. In short, the financing method should encourage cost-consciousness in the decisions of patients, doctors, and hospital administrators.

4. *It should avoid a large tax increase.* A national health insurance program that raises substantial funds from taxpayers and returns it in the form of health insurance has a large hidden cost. By reducing the incentive to work, to invest, and to take economic risks, the increased tax rates would lower real national income. The magnitude of our total spending on health care makes this an important consideration. In fiscal year 1976, private health-care expenditures approached $78 billion; transferring this private spending to the public sector would require a very large increase in tax rates.

---

[1] "A New Approach to National Health Insurance," *The Public Interest,* No. 23 (Spring 1971).

5. *It should be easily administered.* The administration of a health-care system should not require complex procedures that are costly and inconvenient, or permit arbitrary decisions that will be resented.

6. *It should be generally acceptable.* Any new method of financing should be acceptable to physicians and hospitals, as well as the general public. A system that is disliked by any of these would encounter substantial political opposition and, if instituted, would be hampered by a lack of cooperation.

Before looking at the possible alternatives, let us examine the existing system. Although almost every American is now covered by some form of private or public insurance, the current coverage is still often surprisingly "shallow." That is, families incurring huge medical bills too often find that their insurance pays only a relatively small portion of them. A 1970 National Opinion Research Survey, updated to 1976 prices, found that more than 500,000 families had *out-of-pocket* expenditures of more than $3,000 for medical care. More than two million families spent over $1,500, and more than 10 per cent of all families spent over $1,200 out-of-pocket. Let me repeat: These expenses are out-of-pocket, i.e., *after* private and public insurance payments and reimbursements.

Although hospital insurance pays a high proportion of hospital bills, current policies generally impose a variety of ceilings on the use of benefits. The absence of "deep" coverage leaves a serious residue of financial hardship and also prevents some people from seeking potentially expensive care. We have already seen how the current system of financing medical care has contributed to the rapidly rising cost of care. In short, the current structure of health insurance fails by each of the first three criteria that I have suggested.

### Uniform comprehensive health insurance

The most widely debated proposals for national health insurance call for a program of universal, uniform, and comprehensive health insurance, something like an extension of Medicare to the entire population. The most comprehensive of these proposals, such as the Kennedy-Corman bill, would even abolish the small deductible and co-insurance provisions of Medicare, eliminate any limit on the length of covered hospitalization, and extend coverage to drugs, dental care, and even housekeeping services.

There is no doubt that under comprehensive insurance no one would be deprived of needed care because of inability to pay, or would suffer any financial hardship because of unforeseen illness. In terms of our other criteria, however, such plans must be judged unacceptable.

Although comprehensive insurance would remove the current incentive for patients to use in-patient rather than ambulatory care, it would not introduce any positive incentives for the efficient use of resources. Whatever cost consciousness still existing today among patients, doctors, and administrators would be removed. There would be no incentive to limit the rising cost of hospital care, to use paramedical personnel more widely, or to produce physicians' services more efficiently. With all bills paid by the government, nothing would limit the rise in hospital wage rates and physicians' income. In such a situation, the government would be forced to introduce direct controls in an attempt to contain costs.

Such detailed controls, fee schedules, and limits on hospital charges might prevent rising costs for a while, but the experience of Canada, Britain, and Sweden suggests that health costs rise very rapidly even under government health programs with extensive direct controls. Such controls could not achieve, and might actually work against, an efficient use of health resources. They would certainly require a large number of arbitrary policy decisions and engender the hostility of the basic providers. Such arbitrary decisions pose more serious questions than may be generally recognized. What is a "reasonable" level of daily hospital cost? At what rate should hospitals improve facilities, add staff, or raise the level of amenities? How many beds should there be per thousand population? How much should different medical specialists earn? These are not technical questions that could be answered "objectively" if only enough research were done—they involve tastes and value judgments about the relative desirability of different goods and services.

Finally, even if expenditures were not to rise, the provision of comprehensive insurance would require a substantial tax increase: over $44 billion to replace current private expenditures on physician and hospital services, and an additional $34 billion if drugs and other personal health care were to be included.

If such a $78 billion increase in government spending were financed by increasing the tax rate of the current social-security payroll tax, the rate would rise from its current level of 12 per cent to more than 20 per cent. If, instead, the $78 billion were financed by a general increase in the personal income tax, everyone's tax would have to rise by more than 50 per cent of its current level.

Comprehensive insurance would shift the problem of the health-care sector to a conflict between cost inflation and controls. No matter where the balance between these was struck, there would be no natural incentive to efficiency, and there would be a large government expenditure to be paid for by much higher taxes.

## The major-risk approach

I favor a different approach to national health insurance. My proposal is extremely simple: Every family would receive a comprehensive major-risk insurance (MRI) policy with an annual "direct-expense limit"—i.e., a limit on out-of-pocket payments—that increases with family income. A $500 direct-expense limit means that the family is responsible for up to $500 of out-of-pocket medical expenses per year but pays no more than $500—no matter how large the total annual medical bill. Different relations between family income and the direct-expense limit are possible. For example, the expense limit might start at $400 per year for a family with income below $4,000, be equal to 10 per cent of family income between $4,000 and $15,000, and be $1,500 for incomes above that level. The details of the schedule are unimportant at this point. The key feature is an expense limit that few families would normally exceed but that is low relative to family income.[2]

Major-risk insurance is the most important type of health insurance for the government to provide. It concentrates government effort on those families for whom medical expenses would create financial hardship or preclude adequate care. Because relatively few families have such large expenditures in any year, MRI need not be a very costly program. In terms of our six criteria, these are the advantages of MRI:

1. *It would prevent deprivation of care.* If the maximum annual expenditure on health were limited to 10 per cent or less of family income, no family would be deprived of care because of inability to 'pay. (If it is believed that certain types of preventive care and early diagnostic tests would not be undertaken as often as is desirable, the MRI policy could be supplemented by specific coverage for these services at relatively little additional cost.)

2. *It would prevent financial hardship.* MRI would also prevent financial hardship by limiting a family's financial risk to 10 per cent or less of annual income.

---

[2] The availability, in addition, of government-guaranteed loans for the post-payment of medical bills would allow families to spread expenditures below the expense limit over a period of a year or even more. I shall not discuss this "credit card" feature in more detail in order to concentrate on the principle of major-risk insurance.

3. *It would reduce cost inflation.* An increase in insurance coverage generally exacerbates the inflation of hospital costs. However, the universal provision of MRI should reduce hospital-cost inflation by eliminating (or at least decreasing) the current use of shallow-coverage insurance. This would be particularly true if, in introduc-ing national health insurance, the government eliminated the current tax subsidy for private health insurance. In any case, after MRI had removed the risk of major expense, families would then have little to gain from such insurance, for the cost of a policy would be high relative to the upper limit on expenses guaranteed by the MRI.

Of course, once a family had exceeded its direct-expense limit, MRI would be equivalent to comprehensive insurance, and the family would then have no incentive to limit its spending for medical care. To ensure that relatively few families do exceed their direct-expense limit, the MRI policy should make use of a co-insurance feature instead of a deductible. For example, the annual direct limit of $1,500 for families with incomes over $15,000 could be achieved by using a 50-per-cent co-insurance on the first $3,000 of medical bills. Fewer than one family in 15 had medical expenses of more than $3,000 in 1976 (including, of course, the expenses now paid by insurance). Therefore, fewer than one family in 15 would reach an expense limit that is based on $3,000 of spending. The co-insurance rates could be cut at lower income levels to keep the direct-expense limit to 10 per cent of income, e.g., a 33-per-cent co-insurance rate at an income of $10,000. At some income level it would probably be desirable to cut the $3,000 base so that the co-insurance rate did not have to fall too drastically. It is encouraging in this regard that fewer than one family in five had 1976 expenses exceeding $1,500; a 30-per-cent co-insurance rate would produce a direct-expense limit of $450.

More discussion of these details is clearly out of place here. What I want to emphasize is the general principle: The combination of a co-insurance rate and an expenditure base can be selected in a way that varies with income to make almost all families significantly sensitive to the costs of additional health spending, while still limiting each family's maximum out-of-pocket expenditure to 10 per cent of income or less.

Even for the small number of families who reach their limits, MRI would indirectly help to control expenditures. The basic cost per day in hospitals would not be determined by the willingness of those relatively few families to spend, but rather by the preferences of the far larger number of patients who would not be fully reimbursed.

MRI could prevent excesses in physicians' fees and hospital durations of stay by requiring that the same care be given and the same fees be charged to these patients as to those who are paying for their care. Because most medical services would be financed with substantial direct payments, the standards of "customary charge" and "customary care" would become meaningful reference standards, as they currently are not. In short, MRI would introduce a cost-consciousness and a basis for cost comparison that could improve efficiency and contain medical-care inflation.

4. *It would avoid a large tax burden.* The cost to taxpayers of an MRI program would not be large relative to the benefits conferred. The exact amount would depend on the particular schedule of co-insurance and the overall impact of the program on utilization and unit costs. I would estimate that an MRI form of national health insurance that covered *all* personal health care would raise government spending by no more than $19 billion at 1976 levels. Limiting the scope of coverage or introducing a small deductible per spell of illness could reduce this cost more than proportionately.

5. *It would be administratively simple.* MRI would be relatively simple and inexpensive to administer. Because MRI would act to contain cost inflation and to increase efficiency, there would be no need for detailed controls or essentially arbitrary policy decisions. Planning efforts could be concentrated on those problems that cannot be solved by the natural forces of supply and demand.

6. *It would be generally acceptable.* An MRI scheme should be acceptable to physicians, hospitals, and the general public. It would have the virtue of providing full protection against serious financial hardship without the controls or fee schedules that would accompany other forms of insurance. The current freedom of physicians and hospitals would be preserved. If MRI were administered by the same insurance companies that currently provide health insurance, the net effect would be a small increase in their total premium.

In conclusion, I want to reiterate that the problem of health care costs is not to *reduce* or to *limit* the growth of medical spending, but to achieve the *correct* rate of growth of that spending. In turn, this means that the form of national health insurance that the nation adopts should ensure that individual consumers play the central role in guiding the growth and form of their health services. I believe that MRI is the right way to protect families from the risk of financial hardship, while preserving individual freedom of choice and thereby making the future development of our health-care system responsive to the preferences of the people.

# 17

# Community Education for Cardiovascular Health

*John W. Farquhar, Nathan Maccoby, Peter D. Wood,
Janet K. Alexander, Henry Breitrose, Byron W. Brown, Jr.,
William L. Haskell, Alfred L. McAlister, Anthony J. Meyer,
Joyce D. Nash, and Michael P. Stern*

*Summary*  To determine whether community
health education can reduce the risk of
cardiovascular disease, a field experi-
ment was conducted in three northern California towns.
In two of these communities there were extensive mass-
media campaigns over a 2-year period, and in one of
these, face-to-face counselling was also provided for a
small subset of high-risk people. The third community
served as a control. People from each community were
interviewed and examined before the campaigns began
and one and two years afterwards to assess knowledge
and behaviour related to cardiovascular disease (e.g.,
diet and smoking) and also to measure physiological indicators of risk (e.g., blood-pressure, relative weight,
and plasma-cholesterol). In the control community the
risk of cardiovascular disease increased over the two
years but in the treatment communities there was a substantial and sustained decrease in risk. In the community in which there was some face-to-face counselling
the initial improvement was greater and health education was more successful in reducing cigarette smoking,
but at the end of the second year the decrease in risk was
similar in both treatment communities. These results
strongly suggest that mass-media educational campaigns
directed at entire communities may be very effective in
reducing the risk of cardiovascular disease.

## INTRODUCTION

CIGARETTE smoking, high plasma-cholesterol concentrations, and high blood-pressure are important risk factors for premature cardiovascular disease.[1][2] In 1972 we
began a field experiment in three northern California
communities to attempt to modify these risk factors by
community education.

The mass media, face-to-face instruction, or combinations of the two may be used in community education
campaigns. The habits influencing cardiovascular risk
factors are complex and longstanding ones, are often
reinforced by culture, custom, and continual commercial
advertising, and are unlikely to be strongly influenced
by mass media alone.[3-6] Face-to-face instruction and
exhortation also have a long history of failure, particularly when aimed at producing permanent changes in
diet[7] and smoking habits.[8] The disappointing results of
a very limited attempt to reduce cardiovascular risk with
a direct mail and lecture campaign reinforced pessimism
about the possibility of changing health behaviour
through public education.[9]

After considering the powerful cultural forces which
reinforce and maintain the health habits that we wished
to change, and in view of the failure of past health education campaigns, we decided to use an untested combination of an extensive mass-media campaign plus a
considerable amount of face-to-face instruction. We also
included three elements often ignored in health campaigns: (1) the mass-media materials were devised to
teach specific behavioural skills, as well as offering information and affecting attitude and motivation; (2) both
the mass-media approaches and, in particular, the face-
to-face instruction used established methods of achieving changes in behaviour and self-control training principles; and (3) the campaign was designed after analysis
of the knowledge deficits and the media-consumption
patterns of the intended audience. Our goal was to develop and evaluate methods for achieving changes in
smoking, exercise, and diet that would be both cost-
effective and applicable to large population groups.

### RESEARCH PROCEDURE

Three roughly comparable communities in northern California were selected for study. Tracy was selected as a control
because it was relatively distant and isolated from media in the
other communities. Gilroy and Watsonville, the other two
communities, share some media channels (television and
radio), but each town has its own newspaper. Watsonville and
Gilroy received fundamentally similar health education over
two years through a mass-media campaign. Additionally, in
Watsonville high-risk people received intensive face-to-face instruction. Two-thirds of this group was randomly assigned to
the intensive-instruction treatment group (W-I.I.) and one-
third which received health education through the media only,
was used as a control group (W-R.C.).

Data were gathered from a random (multi-stage probability)
sample of 35–59-year-old men and women through interviews
conducted in a survey centre set up in each of the three communities. These annual interviews were designed to measure
both knowledge about heart-disease and individual behaviour
related to cardiovascular risk. Knowledge was measured by a
25-item test of factors associated with coronary heart-disease.
Daily intake of cholesterol, saturated and polyunsaturated
fats, sugar, and alcohol were estimated,[10] and the daily rate of
cigarette, pipe, and cigar smoking was recorded. Plasma-thio-
cyanate assay[11] indicated that only about 4% of those reporting abstinence may have given inaccurate reports.

Coincident with each annual interview, we also measured
plasma total cholesterol and triglyceride concentrations, sys-

From John W. Farquhar, et al., "Community Education for Cardiovascular Health," *The Lancet*
1192–1195 (June 4, 1977). Copyright 1977 by *The Lancet*.
[296]

TABLE I—DEMOGRAPHIC CHARACTERISTICS AND
SURVEY-RESPONSE RATES IN EACH OF THREE COMMUNITIES

| Characteristics of community groups | Tracy | Gilroy | Watsonville |
|---|---|---|---|
| *Entire town (1970 census):* | | | |
| Population (total) | 14 724 | 12 665 | 14 569 |
| Population (35–59 yr) | 4 283 | 3 224 | 4 115 |
| Mean age of 35–59 yr olds | 47·0 | 46·2 | 47·6 |
| *Random sample (ages 35–59):* | | | |
| Original sample | 659 | 659 | 833 |
| Natural attrition (migration or death) | 74 | 79 | 107 |
| Potential participants for all 3 surveys | 585 | 580 | 726 |
| Participants completing 1st and 3rd survey | 418 | 427 | 449 |
| Percent of potential participants | 72 | 74 | 62 |
| Mean age at Oct., 1972 (yr) | 46·9 | 45·8 | 48·4 |
| Spanish speaking or bilingual (%) | 9·0 | 26·2 | 17·3 |

tolic and diastolic blood-pressure, and relative weight. Blood was collected into disodium E.D.T.A. 'Vacutainers' after a fast of 12–16 h. Plasma-total-cholesterol concentrations were determined by the procedures of the Lipid Research Clinics Program[12] and were adjusted for systematic variation in blood-sampling method.[13] Blood-pressure was determined by means of a standard mercury manometer with the cuff on the right arm and the patient sitting with the arm at heart level. Two measurements were recorded after the subject had been seated for several minutes and the second, taken approximately one minute after the first, was used for analysis. A different person measured blood-pressure in each community and all staff were trained in a standard manner. Other measurements made included plasma-renin and urinary sodium.[14 15] Results were sent to participants and their physicians.

The overall risk of coronary heart-disease developing within 12 years was estimated by a multiple logistic function incorporating the person's age, sex, plasma-cholesterol concentration, systolic blood-pressure, relative weight, smoking-rate, and electrocardiographic findings.[16]

The mass media and counselling campaigns were designed to produce awareness of the probable causes of coronary

TABLE II—COMPOSITION AND TREATMENT OF 9 PARTICIPANT
GROUPS IN COMMUNITIES

| Group | Treatment* | |
|---|---|---|
| Tracy total participants (n=384) | s | |
| Tracy high risk† (n=95) | s | |
| Gilroy total participants (n=397) | s+M.M. | |
| Gilroy high risk† (n=94) | s+M.M. | |
| Watsonville total participants (n=423) | s+M.M. | (for n=312 participants) |
| | s+M.M. +I.I. | (for 2/3 of high-risk participants and spouses n=111) |
| Watsonville intensive instruction (w-I.I.)† (n=77) | s+M.M. +I.I. | (2/3 of high-risk group randomly assigned to receive I.I.) |
| Watsonville randomised control (w-R.C.)† (n=40) | s+M.M. | (1/3 of high-risk group randomly assigned not to receive I.I.) |
| Watsonville reconstituted (wr)‡ (n=423) | s+M.M. | (weighted probability sample with I.I. group excluded) |

* s=Surveying and feedback of results (annual), M.M.=mass media, I.I.=intensive instruction programme.
† Participants in the initial survey at Watsonville, Gilroy, and Tracy whose examination results placed them in the top quartile of risk of coronary heart-disease according to a multiple logistic function of risk factors.
‡ To correct for bias resulting from exclusion of intensively instructed subjects—i.e., high-risk persons and their spouses—means for remaining subjects in high-risk and lower-risk groups were weighted to compensate for the differential numbers of excluded subjects in the two risk strata. Resulting weighted means were called means of the reconstituted sample—i.e., sample reconstituted after exclusion of intensively instructed subjects.

disease and of the specific measures which may reduce risk and to provide the knowledge and skills necessary to accomplish and maintain recommended behaviour changes. Dietary habits recommended for all participants were those which, if followed, would lead to substantial reduction of saturated fat, cholesterol, salt, sugar, and alcohol intake. We also urged reduction in body-weight through caloric reduction and increased physical activity. Cigarette smokers were educated on the need and methods for ceasing or at least reducing their daily rate of cigarette consumption.

The mass-media campaign in Gilroy and Watsonville consisted of about 50 television spots, three hours of television programming, over 100 radio spots, several hours of radio programming, weekly newspaper columns, newspaper advertisements and stories, billboards, posters, and printed material posted to participants. A campaign was also created for the sizeable population of Spanish speakers. The media campaign began two months after the initial survey and continued for nine months in 1973, was withheld for three months during the second survey, and then continued for nine more months in 1974.

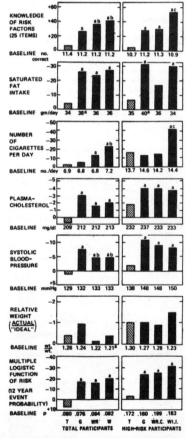

Fig. 1—Absolute baseline values and percentage change in selected variables after two years in control (shaded) or treatment (dark) groups.

See table II for definition of groups. a=P<0·05 for baseline or differences in percentage change of control versus treatment. b=P<0·05 for differences in percentage change within treatment G versus W (total) or WR. c=P<0·05 for differences in percentage change within treatment W-R.C. versus W-I.I.

Two-thirds (113) of the Watsonville participants whom we identified as being in the top quartile of risk of coronary heart-disease[16] were randomly selected for counselling. 107 attended counselling sessions and 77 high-risk individuals and 34 spouses completed all three interviews and examinations. These individuals, and their physicians, were informed by letter of their relatively high risk of coronary heart-disease (the letter was regarded as part of the "treatment"). They and their spouses were invited to participate in the instruction programme that was launched six months after the first baseline survey and was conducted intensively over a 10-week period through group classes and home counselling sessions. In the summer months of the second year, at a less intensive level, individuals were counselled about special problems (e.g., smoking and weight-loss) and were encouraged to maintain previous changes. The counsellors were graduate students in communication, physicians, and specialist health educators trained in behaviour modification techniques. Pre-tested protocols were used.[17]

The intensive instruction programme was designed[18-21] to achieve the same changes that were advocated in the media campaign. The strategy was to present information about the behaviour which influences risk of coronary heart-disease, to stimulate personal analysis of existing behaviour, to demonstrate desired skills (e.g., food selection and preparation), and to guide the individual through practice of those skills and gradually withdraw instructor participation.

### RESULTS

Baseline values were remarkably uniform. Both the media and media plus face-to-face instruction had significant positive effects on all variables except relative

#### TOTAL PARTICIPANTS

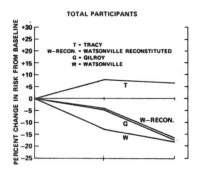

#### HIGH-RISK PARTICIPANTS

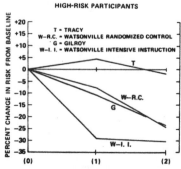

Fig. 2—Percentage change from baseline (0) in risk of coronary heart-disease after 1 and 2 years of health education among participants from three communities.

Groups are defined in table II. Cardiovascular risk is measured by a multiple logistic function of risk factors.

weight after the two years of campaigning (fig. 1). (However, relative weight was significantly lower among the Watsonville intensive-instruction group after one year.) Thus, for risk-factor knowledge, saturated-fat intake, cigarette use, plasma-cholesterol, and systolic blood-pressure there were slight-to-moderate changes in the expected direction. When the last three variables (and relative weight) were incorporated into the risk equation the net difference in estimated total risk between control and treatment samples was 23–28%. This difference is in part attributable to the fact that the greatest change occurred in individuals with the highest plasma-cholesterol and blood-pressure. Face-to-face intensive instruction (Watsonville I.I.) in high-risk subjects increased knowledge gain and the extent of reduction of smoking but not other variables. Reasons for the changes in blood-pressure are not yet clear but include a probable interaction between weight-loss and enhanced adherence to antihypertensive medications, the latter being an unintended consequence of exposure to health education.[22]

Changes in knowledge and risk factors produced in the first year in Watsonville and Gilroy were not only maintained, but improved further during the second year (fig. 2). Groups which received counselling show a greater decrease at the end of the first year than that in the media-only groups. But in the second year the groups exposed only to the media show further substantial gains and the apparent difference between the effects of media and media plus face-to-face instruction is reduced. The parallel relation of the two media-only groups (Gilroy and Watsonville reconstituted) indicates that the media campaigns had similar effects on risk in the two treatment communities.

### DISCUSSION

Unlike the subjects of previous studies of giving up smoking[6] and weight reduction,[7] our participants were randomly selected from open populations, thus providing a better basis for generalisations about future public-health education efforts. But since we were able to recruit only about two-thirds of the total samples of eligible participants selected in the three surveys, extrapolation of our results may be limited. Also we were not able to help participants learn to achieve sustained weight-loss.

In general the changes in knowledge, behaviour, and physiological endpoints that were observed in the first year of treatment were maintained, and even improved in the second year of study. Intensive face-to-face instruction and counselling seem important for changing refractory behaviour such as cigarette smoking and for inducing rapid change of dietary behaviour. But we must also learn how to use these methods to correct obesity, and to employ them effectively with limited resources (e.g., by training volunteer instructors). Mass media are potentially much more cost-effective than face-to-face education methods. Our results show that mass media can increase knowledge and change various health habits, but we believe that the power of this instrument could be considerably enhanced if we can find ways to use mass media to stimulate and coordinate programmes of interpersonal instruction in natural communities (such as towns and factories) and to deliver forms of specialised training and counselling about weight-loss and smoking avoidance.

Prevention of the premature cardiovascular disease epidemic of industrialised countries will require national purpose, planning, and action. It seems that part of this effort—i.e., persuading people to alter their life styles—can be achieved at reasonable cost.

This investigation was supported by grant HL 14174 (Stanford Specialised Center for Research in Arteriosclerosis) and contract NIH 71-2161-L (Stanford Lipid Research Clinic) from the National Heart, Lung and Blood Institute.

Requests for reprints should be addressed to J. W. F., Stanford Heart Disease Prevention Program, Stanford University, Stanford, California 94305, U.S.A.

#### REFERENCES

1. American Heart Association: Intersociety Commission for Heart Disease Resources, *Circulation*, 1970, **42**.
2. Blackburn, H. *in* Progress in Cardiology, (edited by P. Yu and J. Goodwin); vol. III, p. 1. Philadelphia, 1974.
3. Griffiths, W., Knutson, A. *Am. J. publ. Hlth*, 1960, **50**, 515.
4. Bauer, R. A. *Am. Psychol.* 1964, **19**, 319.
5. Cartwright, D. *Hum. Relat.* 1951, **4**, 381.
6. Robertson, L. S., Kelley, A. B., O'Neill, B., Wixom, C. W., Eisworth, R. S., Haddon, W. *Am. J. publ. Hlth*, 1974, **64**, 1071.
7. Stunkard, A. J. *Psychosom. Med.* 1975, **37**, 195.
8. Bernstein, D. A., McAlister, A. L. *Addict. Behav.* 1976, **1**, 89.
9. Aronow, W. S., Allen, W. H., De Cristofaro, D., Ungermann, S. *Circulation*, 1975, **51**, 1038.
10. Fetcher, E. S., Foster, N., Anderson, J. T., Grande, F., Keys, A. *Am. J. clin. Nutr.* 1967, **20**, 475.
11. Butts, W. C., Kuehneman, M., Widdowson, G. M. *Clin. Chem.* 1974, **20**, 1344.
12. Department of Health, Education and Welfare (N.I.H.) 75-628. Manual of Laboratory Operations, Lipid Research Clinics Program, Lipid and Lipoprotein Analysis, Bethesda, 1974.
13. Stern, M. P., Farquhar, J. W., Maccoby, N., Russell, S. H. *Circulation*, 1976, **54**, 826.
14. Lucas, C. P., Holzwarth, G. J., Ocobock, R. W., Sozen, T., Stern, M. P., Wood, P. D. S., Haskell, W. L., Farquhar. J. W. *Lancet*, 1974, ii, 1337.
15. Lucas, C. P., Holzwarth, G. J., Ocobock, R. W., Sozen, T., Stern, M. P., Wood, P. D. S., Haskell, W. L., Farquhar, J. W. *Angiology*, 1975, **26**, 31.
16. Truett, J., Cornfield, J., Kannel, W. *J. chron. Dis.* 1967, **20**, 511.
17. Meyer, A. J., Henderson, J. B. *Prev. Med.* 1974, **13**, 225.
18. McGuire, W. J. *in* Handbook of Social Psychology (edited by G. Lindzey and E. Aronson); p. 136, Menlo Park, California, 1969.
19. Bandura, A. Principles of Behaviour Modification; New York, 1969.
20. Thoreson, C., Mahoney, M. Behavioural Self-Control. New York, 1974.
21. McAlister, A. L., Farquhar, J. W., Thoreson, C. E., Maccoby, N. *Hlth Educ. Monogr.* 1976, **4**, 45.
22. Curry, P. J., Haskell, W., Stern, M. P., Farquhar, J. W. CVD Epidemiology Newsletter no. 20, p. 48. Council on Epidemiology, American Heart Association, January, 1976.

# 18

## The Burlington Randomized Trial
## of the Nurse Practitioner

*Walter O. Spitzer, David L. Sackett, John C. Sibley,
Robin S. Roberts, Michael Gent, Dorothy J. Kergin,
Brenda C. Hackett and Anthony Olynich*

**Abstract** From July, 1971, to July, 1972, in a large sub-urban Ontario practice of two family physicians, a randomized controlled trial was conducted to assess the effects of substituting nurse practitioners for physicians in primary-care practice.

Before and after the trial, the health status of patients who received conventional care from family physicians was compared with the status of those who received care mainly from nurse practitioners. Both groups of patients had a similar mortality experience, and no dif-ferences were found in physical functional capacity, social function or emotional function. The quality of care rendered to the two groups seemed similar, as assessed by a quantitative "indicator-condition" approach. Satisfaction was high among both patients and professional personnel. Although cost effective from society's point of view, the new method of primary care was not financially profitable to doctors because of current restrictions on reimbursement for the nurse-practitioner services. (N Engl J Med 290:251-256, 1974)

THE concept of using nonphysicians to provide primary health service has seldom been accompanied by quantitative clinical evidence that this new form of patient care is both safe and effective. Our interest in testing the primary-care performance of nurse practitioners was stimulated by three distinctive features of the medical situation in Ontario: the delivery of primary health care is still oriented toward family physicians, who constitute 48 per cent of all registered physicians in the Province; the total number of family physicians is adequate (with an average ratio of 1:1723 per total population), but they are unevenly distributed so that many rural and small-town family physicians are overburdened[1]; and a surplus of well trained,

From the schools of Medicine and Nursing, McMaster University (address reprint requests to Dr. Spitzer of the Department of Clinical Epidemiology and Biostatistics, McMaster University, 1200 Main St. West, Hamilton, Ontario, Canada, L8S 4J9).

Supported by a grant (DM34) from the Ontario Health Resources Development Plan, Ministry of Health of Ontario, and a National Health Grant (606-21-66) of Health and Welfare Canada (the latter for the quality-of-care component).

experienced nurses has existed in the Province for several years.[2,3]

An opportunity to perform the desired test was presented in 1970, when two family physicians in Burlington, a middle-class suburban town of 85,000 just east of Hamilton, approached the Faculty of Medicine of McMaster University for possible help in introducing this innovation into their practice. For at least two years, their practice had been "saturated" — accepting no new patients or families because of inability to manage an increased case load. The physicians believed that their office nurses, with appropriate additional training, could assume a substantial portion of the responsibilities for primary care.

With this opportunity and with the offered co-operation of these and other participants, a collaborative group was formed, and two complementary randomized trials were designed. In one of these trials, reported elsewhere,[4,5] the major emphasis was on the way in which physicians and nurses were affected by the new form of practice. In the second trial, which is reported here, the principal concerns were with the effects on patients and on the practice itself.

### PARTICIPATING PERSONNEL AND BACKGROUND

The two family practices under study had previously had no affiliation with a university or other institution. Patients in each practice were free to seek any desired source of primary care, and the costs of care, regardless of source, were completely covered by universal health insurance in Ontario.

One of the family physicians had received his medical degree in 1953 from the University of Durham and had practiced in Burlington for nine years; the other physician had graduated from McGill University in 1954 and had been practicing in Burlington for 14 years. One nurse had received her R.N. diploma in 1959, and the other nurse in 1948.

Before the study began, the nurses attended a special training program conducted by the schools of nursing and medicine at McMaster University. The emphasis of this program is on decision making and clinical judgment, rather than on procedural skills. The graduating nurse practitioners are qualified to become not physicians' assistants, but *co-practitioners*, sharing the family physician's responsibility for continuing care of patients. The nurse practitioner learns to evaluate each patient's presenting problems, and to choose from three possible courses of action: providing specific treatment; providing reassurance alone, without specific treatment; or referring the patient to the associated family physician, to another clinician or to an appropriate service agency.

### METHODS

The research contained at least three major methodologic challenges: the development of appropriate technics for assessing the outcome as direct effects on the patients' state of health; the development of quantitative methods for evaluating the process of medical care and the dynamics of an experimental practice; and the complex administrative logistics of preparing the patients, training interviewers and other data gatherers, maintaining the protocol and co-ordinating data reduction and analysis.

In this paper, we report the general design, logistics, and data of the trial, together with a summary of the results obtained for patients' health status and quality of care.

#### The Investigated Patients

Because many clinical problems in primary care involve an entire family, families were chosen as the unit for randomization. A "family," which was defined as a person or group sharing a common pro-

vincial health-insurance number, typically encompasses a breadwinner, the spouse, and the dependent children. From the business records or clinical records of all families using the two practices, 1801 families, representing approximately 4850 people, were enumerated.

To be eligible for the trial, a family had to be established as having an ongoing medical relation with the practices. This relation was demonstrated if one of the family members had either made contact with one of the practices in the prior 18-month period or (during later interviews) identified the doctor as the family physician. The eligible people comprised 1598 families, containing 4325 members.

#### Randomization

Because a case load half that of a family physician's was considered manageable for a nurse practitioner, the eligible families were stratified by practice of origin, and randomly allocated in a ratio of 2:1. They formed a randomized conventional group, assigned to continuing primary clinical services from a family physician and a conventional nurse, and a randomized nurse-practitioner group, whose first-contact primary clinical services were to be provided by a nurse practitioner. The resulting conventional group contained 1058 families (2796 members) equally divided between the two doctors, and the nurse-practitioner group comprised 540 families (1529 members), equally divided between the two nurse practitioners.

After these assignments were completed, adult patients were sent a letter explaining their clinical allocation and the plans of the study. For subsequent medical care, after July 1, 1971, patients in the nurse-practitioner group were asked to make appointments with the named nurse, instead of with their customary doctor. All the families were given the opportunity to refuse their assignment and opt out of the trial.

Figure 1 shows the timing of these procedures and of subsequent events in the performance of the study.

#### Selection of Patients for Surveys before and at the End of the Experimental Period

After the letters were distributed, a household survey was performed in a sample of the enumerated families, *the interview cohort*. This cohort received interviews to acquire the data needed for "paired comparisons" of change in health status and medical utilization. The patients for the interview cohort were chosen randomly as a single member from eligible families participating in the trial and living within 32 km of the doctor's office. To ensure sufficient numbers of children in the surveys, one third of the families were randomly designated as "child priority." The member for the interview cohort was then randomly chosen from any children contained in these families or otherwise, from the adults.

The resulting cohort that was successfully interviewed in both years included 817 patients, with 296 in the experimental group and 521 in the conventional control group. The refusal rates in the surveys were 11 per cent in 1971 and 5 per cent in 1972.

#### Data Obtained before the Experimental Period

*Measurements on patients.* Trained household interviewers administered pretested standardized questionnaires* to the interview cohort to obtain demographic information, information on prior use of clinical services and data satisfaction with health care. Special questionnaire instruments, described elsewhere, were used for assessing health status in physical function.

*Clinician activities.* Time-and-motion studies of the physicians and conventional nurses were used to indicate the mixture of clinical and nonclinical activities in a representative week of family practice.

*Activities of the practice:* A "day-sheet journal" was maintained for all clinical activities in the practices. For each visit or encounter with any medical or nursing practitioner, a separate entry was made in

---

*For 228 pages of questionnaire instruments used in this project order NAPS Document 02178 from National Auxiliary Publications Service, c/o Microfiche Publications, 305 E. 46th St., New York, N.Y. 10017; remitting $1.50 for microfiche-copy reproduction or $34.70 for photocopies. Checks or money orders should be made payable to Microfiche Publications.

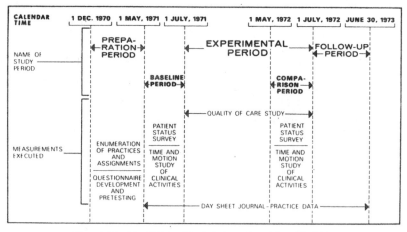

Figure 1. Schedule of Time and Events during Implementation of the Trial.

the journal, and included the following information: the patient's identification number; the date; the type of service; whether the patient was new to the practice; the presenting complaint (or complaints) or problems; diagnosis (or diagnoses); procedures (if any); the principal professional person who provided service at the particular visit; whether the doctor was involved in the visit or whether the nurse practitioner had provided the service alone without consultation; whether the patient was referred outside the practice; whether a prescription had been given to the patient; and the dollar value of service according to the provincial medical association's schedule of fees.[*]

In the eight-week base-line period, there were 2991 encounters for the groups who became the conventional and nurse-practitioner combined trial practice.

### Data Obtained during the Experimental Period

*Measurements on patients:* In addition to the cited data on health status, "dropouts" were identified, and all deaths were recorded.

*Clinician activities.* The quality of care in "clinical judgment" used by the co-practitioners was assessed with two quantitative methods. One of these was based on identifying and assessing the manner in which the practitioners managed a series of 10 indicator conditions. As suggested in Kessner's concept of "tracers,[2,*]" an indicator condition is a distinct clinical entity (such as a disease, symptom, state or injury) occurring frequently in primary care, with an outcome that can be affected favorably or adversely by the choice of treatment. The second method for assessing the quality of medical care was to evaluate the manner in which 13 common drugs were prescribed. Explicit criteria for adequacy in the management of indicator conditions and prescription of drugs were established before the trial by a peer group of nonuniversity family physicians practicing in the same area. The selected conditions and drugs were not known to the Burlington co-practitioners during the trial. These approaches received a preliminary report, with details presented elsewhere.[6]

*Practice activities.* All clinical activities were monitored throughout the entire experimental period and recorded in the day-sheet jour-

---

[*]A service ordinarily given by a physician, but now given by an unsupervised nurse practitioner, was rated at the same dollar value as a doctor's service for purposes of financial analysis, but could not be reimbursed by governmental health insurance.

nal. During the experimental year, data were obtained for 21,085 encounters.

### Data Obtained at the End of the Experimental Period

*Measurements on patients.* The household surveys of health status were repeated, with added questions on social and emotional function.

*Clinician activities.* The previous studies of clinical activities were repeated during the eight-week comparison period, one year after base line. Quality-of-care measurements were continued to the end of the trial.

*Practice activities.* The day-sheet journal surveillance was continued for a year after the trial to ascertain longer-term effects of this method of practice on profitability and cost effectiveness.

### RESULTS

### Base-line Survey and Encounter Data

*Measurements on patients (Fig. 2).* As determined in the 1971 household survey, the patients in the conventional and nurse-practitioner groups had highly similar values for physical function, ability to carry out usual daily activities and freedom from bed disability. The base-line health status of the two groups of patients showed only minor differences that were not statistically significant (at an $\alpha$ level of 0.05).

*Clinician activities.* Physicians had been involved in 86 per cent of all visits to the practices, and the conventional nurses alone had dealt with the remaining 14 per cent of encounters.

### Results during the Experimental Period

Of the 1598 families eligible for the trial, only seven families (two from the conventional group and five from the nurse-practitioner group) refused their assignments. Two families in the conventional group preferred care by nurse practitioners; two families in the

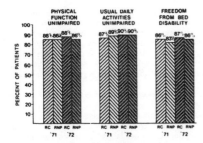

Figure 2. Physical Status of Patients in Surveys during Base-line ('71) and Comparison ('72) Periods.

These results are based on 521 subjects in the conventional (RC) group and 296 in the nurse-practitioner (RNP) group who were assessed in both 1971 and 1972.

nurse-practitioner group opposed the new concept, and three others had had a member under care by a doctor for a long-term problem.

*Measurements on patients.* During the year 0.9 per cent of families in the conventional and 0.7 per cent in the nurse-practitioner group left the practice because of dissatisfaction.

*Clinical activities (Fig. 3).* In 392 episodes of care for the 10 indicator conditions, the management was rated as adequate for 66 per cent of episodes in the conventional and for 69 per cent in the nurse-practitioner group. In 510 prescriptions similarly analyzed, an adequate rating was given to 75 per cent in the conventional group, and to 71 per cent in the nurse-practitioner group.*

*Practice activities.* The doctors in the conventional group continued to be involved in about 86 per cent of all patient visits throughout the trial. For visits of patients in the nurse-practitioner group, the doctors were involved in 45 per cent of visits during the first eight weeks. This proportion fell to 28 per cent by the 20th week, and rose from the 21st to the 44th week, when many new families were being seen for the first time. Starting with the final eight weeks of the trial the proportion of patient nurse-practitioner visits involving the doctor stabilized at 33 per cent. Subsequent follow-up study confirms that nurse practitioners handle two thirds of episodes without consulting a physician.

As noted from our enumerations and household interviews before the trial, the two original practices had provided care for an active roster of 1598 families who had an ongoing relation to the practitioners. Within eight weeks after the new form of practice was introduced, the physicians found that the demands on their own services had been reduced enough to allow new families to be accepted in the previously "saturated" practices. After one year, the practices had grown to 1952 active families, a net increase of 22 per cent.

### Results at the End of the Experimental Period

*Clinical outcomes.* As shown in Figure 2, the levels of physical status remained closely similar in the patients in the two groups. In measurements performed at the end of the trial in the 1972 survey, the index of emotional function was 58.3 per cent in 521 patients in the conventional and 57.9 per cent in 296 in the nurse-practitioner group. Corresponding values for the index of social function were 83.2 per cent and 83.9 per cent.[6a]

During the experimental period, there were 22 deaths — 18 in the conventional group and four in the nurse-practitioner group. The difference in crude death rates was not clinically or statistically significant.

In the follow-up survey, 97 per cent of patients in the conventional and 96 per cent in the nurse-practitioner group were found to be satisfied with health services received during the experimental period.

*Clinician activities.* Figure 4 shows the financial performance of the practices, as compared with the base-line-period level of 100 per cent. The drop of 5 per cent in actual gross practice revenue is explained by the absence of billing for clinical services provided by nurse practitioners. If reimbursement for these services had been permissible, the increased volume of services with a 22 per cent increase in number of families under care would have produced a 9 per cent rise in income. According to the dollar-weighting procedure for fees, services rendered by each nurse practitioner during the trial year were worth approximately $16,000, of which almost 50 per cent was for unsupervised service.

Together with other financial studies, these data indicate that the economic advantage that society attains

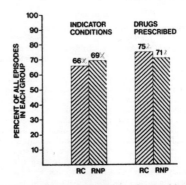

Figure 3. Percentage of Episodes of Care Rated as Adequate.

The denominators for these percentages were a total of 392 episodes for indicator conditions — 225 in the conventional (RC) and 167 in the nurse-practitioner (RNP) group — and 510 episodes for drugs (284 in the RC and 226 in the RNP group).

*The differences are not statistically significant at an α level of 0.05. Since demonstration of "no difference" or "no deterioration" is of greater concern in an experiment where we have compared a new form of practice with a standard practice, we also calculated β levels. Given the results, the probabilities of real deterioration of at least 5 per cent in physical function went from 0.02 to 0.01. The probabilities of real deterioration of at least 10 per cent were 0.004 for indicator conditions and 0.08 for drugs.

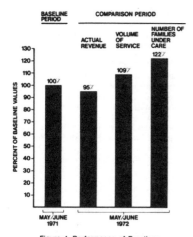

Figure 4. Performance of Practices.
The activities during the base-line period were given a value of 100 per cent for each of the three categories of performance assessed.

from the primary-care nurse practitioner is accompanied, under current Ontario regulations that prohibit billing for unsupervised nurse-practitioner services, by the physician's loss in net income of nearly $12,000 per year.

*Practice activities (follow-up observations).* One year after the experimental period had ended, the practitioners reported that they were at a new plateau of "saturation." As of June 30, 1973, 2256 registered families were under ongoing care, a 41 per cent increase from the 1598 families two years earlier.

### DISCUSSION

In recent years, a few health-care trials, some with an element of randomization, have been reported.[10-16] The current research adds further evidence that innovations in health care can be assessed with randomized controlled trials.

Neither the concept of the nurse practitioner nor the evaluation of this new concept is new. "Outpost nurses" have established an enviable record of clinical accomplishment in isolated areas in the Canadian North and Maritime provinces.[17] In the United States, Silver and his colleagues[18,19] pioneered many current concepts of the nurse practitioner's role in pediatrics. Yankauer et al.[20,21] dealt with other issues of education and the efficient deployment of nurses in pediatric ambulatory settings. Other investigators[22,23] have described the use of nurse practitioners in adult primary care.

Introduction of the nurse practitioner has often been accompanied by evaluative research, including descriptive studies,[18,24] surveys[25,26] and assessment of process.[23,27] Lewis and his colleagues[28] made a major contribution to the methods of assessing the effect of nurse practitioners by executing a randomized controlled study conducted in a hospital outpatient setting. Charney[29] later performed a similarly controlled trial of the nurse's work in well-child care, and Schlesinger et al.[30] used a matched design to test registered nurses in prenatal care.

The work reported here differs from earlier randomized controlled investigations of nurse practitioners, because of the following characteristics: to allow detection of small differences in the variables of interest, our study contained much larger numbers of patients than had previously been admitted to such trials; the role of "experimental subject," assumed by the collaborating physicians and nurses, was almost entirely divorced from the specially trained interviewers, abstractors and observers who acted as "data gatherers"; all the data, including base-line data, were gathered purposefully and prospectively; both traditional and new health-care measurements were incorporated into an experiment patterned after a clinical trial, with the attention directed primarily at changes in health status; the study was carried out in previously saturated practices that were non-university and non-institutional; and, finally, a unique characteristic of the setting was that patients, if dissatisfied, had complete freedom to seek care from another source. Not only were several family physicians in the community accepting new families, but Canadian universal insurance covers costs completely regardless of the chosen source of care.

The results demonstrate that a nurse practitioner can provide first-contact primary clinical care as safely and effectively, with as much satisfaction to patients, as a family physician. The successful ability of the nurse practitioners to function alone in 67 per cent of all patient visits and without demonstrable detriment to the patients has particularly important implications in planning of health-care delivery for regions where family physicians are in short supply.

The increased number of patients who could be added to the previously saturated practices is probably due mainly to the case load carried by the nurse practitioners, but cannot be attributed to their activities alone. The physicians involved in this trial believe that their own work became more efficient since they were forced to develop the rigor and clarity of thought needed to communicate with their co-practitioners.

The decreased gross revenue of the practices is attributable to current regulations that do not permit the governmental health-insurance plan to pay for services rendered by an unsupervised nurse. Since nurse practitioners can provide a major increase in total quantity of clinical service, without a reduction in quality, a suitable adjustment of these financial regulations would make the innovation more attractive to physicians, while allowing society to obtain the additional benefits in care at a net cost that is still less than that of conventional approaches. Several medical practitioners and officials of the provincial health-insurance plan are now collaborating in an effort to develop appropriate new formulas for these financial arrangements.

We are indebted to Dr. John R. Evans, formerly dean of the Faculty of Medicine of McMaster University (now president of the University of Toronto), for encouragement and support during the preliminary phase of this study (his leadership made possible the environment and the resources required for large-scale health-care trials in the Hamilton region) and to Dr. Alvan R. Feinstein, of Yale University, for counsel and critical review during preparation of the manuscript.

### REFERENCES

1. Spaulding WB, Spitzer WO: Implications of medical manpower trends in Ontario 1961-1971. Ont Med Rev 39:527-533, 1972
2. Ontario Ministry of Health, Research and Planning Branch: Mobility, Service and Attitudes of Active and Inactive Nurses. Toronto, Ontario Ministry of Health, 1968, p 13
3. Canadian Nurses' Association. Report of a Preliminary Survey to Explore the Nursing Employment Situation in Canada in Terms of the Number of 1971 Graduates of Canadian Schools of Nursing Registered/Licensed for the First Time in 1971 Who Were Able or Unable to Obtain Permanent Employment in Nursing as of September 30, 1971. Ottawa, Canadian Nurses' Association, 1972, p 18
4. Spitzer WO, Kergin DJ, Yoshida MA, et al: Nurse practitioners in primary care. III. The Southern Ontario randomized trial. Can Med Assoc J 108:1006-1016, 1973
5. Spitzer WO, Russell WAM, Hackett BC: Financial consequences of employing a nurse practitioner. Ont Med Rev 40:96-100, 1973
6. Spitzer WO, Kergin DJ: Nurse practitioners in primary care. I. The McMaster University educational program. Can Med Assoc J 108:991-995, 1973
7. Kessner DM, Kalk CE, Singer J: Assessing health quality — the case for tracers. N Engl J Med 288:189-194, 1973
8. Kessner DM, Kalk CE: A Strategy for Evaluating Health Services. Washington, DC, Institute of Medicine, National Academy of Sciences, 1973, p 219
9. Sibley JC, Rudnick KV, Bell JD, et al: A quantitative approach to quality of primary care. Clin Research 21:726, 1973
9a. Sackett DL, Spitzer WC, Gent M, et al: The Burlington randomized trial of the nurse practitioner: health outcomes outpatients. Ann Intern Med (in press)
10. Katz S, Vignos PJ Jr, Moskowitz RW, et al: Comprehensive outpatient care in rheumatoid arthritis: a controlled study. JAMA 206:1249-1254, 1968
11. McKee WJE: A controlled study of the effects of tonsillectomy adenoidectomy in children. Br J Prev Soc Med 17:49-69, 1963
12. Dawson JJY, Devadatta S, Fox W, et al: A 5-year study of patients with pulmonary tuberculosis in a concurrent comparison of home and sanatorium treatment for one year with isoniazid plus PAS. Bull WHO 34:533-551, 1966
13. Ford PA, Seacat MS, Silver GA: The relative roles of the public health nurse and the physician in prenatal and infant supervision. Am J Public Health 56:1097-1103, 1966
14. Mather HG, Pearson NG, Read KLQ, et al: Acute myocardial infarction: home and hospital treatment. Br Med J 3:334-338, 1971
15. Harpur JE, Kellett RJ, Conner WT, et al: Controlled trial of early mobilisation and discharge from hospital in uncomplicated myocardial infarction. Lancet 2:1331-1334, 1971
16. Hutter AM Jr, Sidel VW, Shine KI, et al: Early hospital discharge after myocardial infarction. N Engl J Med 288:1141-1144, 1973
17. Robertson HR: Health Care in Canada: A commentary (Science Council of Canada Background Study Series No 29). Ottawa, Information Canada, 1973, pp 99-100
18. Silver HK, Ford LC, Stearly SG: A program to increase health care for children: the pediatric nurse practitioner program. Pediatrics 39:756-760, 1967
19. Silver HK: The school nurse practitioner program: a new and expanded role for the school nurse. JAMA 216:1332-1334, 1971
20. Yankauer A, Connelly JP, Andrews P, et al: The practice of nursing in pediatric offices — challenge and opportunity. N Engl J Med 282:843-847, 1970
21. Andrews P, Yankauer A, Connelly JP: Changing the patterns of ambulatory pediatric caretaking: an action-oriented training program for nurses. Am J Public Health 60:870-879, 1970
22. Brunetto E, Birk P: The primary care nurse — the generalist in a structured health care team. Am J Public Health 62:785-794, 1972
23. Lewis CE, Resnik BA: Nurse clinics and progressive ambulatory patient care. N Engl J Med 277:1236-1241, 1967
24. Ford LC, Silver HK: The expanded role of the nurse in child care. Nurs Outlook 15:43-45, 1967
25. Day LR, Egli R, Silver HK: Acceptance of pediatric nurse practitioners: parent's opinion of combined care by a pediatrician and a pediatric nurse practitioner in a private practice. Am J Dis Child 119:204-208, 1970
26. Chenoy NC, Spitzer WO, Anderson GD: Nurse practitioners in primary care. II. Prior attitudes of a rural population. Can Med Assoc J 108:998-1002, 1973
27. Lees REM: Physician time-saving by employment of expanded-role nurses in family practice. Can Med Assoc J 108:871-875, 1973
28. Lewis CE, Resnik BA, Schmidt G, et al: Activities, events, and outcomes in ambulatory patient care. N Engl J Med 280:645-649, 1969
29. Charney E, Kitzman H: The child-health nurse (pediatric nurse practitioner) in private practice: a controlled study. N Engl J Med 285:1353-1358, 1971
30. Schlesinger ER, Lowery WD, Glaser DB, et al: A controlled test of the use of registered nurses for prenatal care. Health Serv Rep 88:400-404, 1973

# 19

# Evaluating the Quality of Ambulatory Health Care: A Review of Emerging Methods

## Tom Christoffel and Martha Loewenthal

While hospital quality evaluation activities have progressed dramatically in recent years, there has not been a comparable development and implementation of methods for the review and evaluation of ambulatory health care. Various technical problems regarding ambulatory records and the nature of ambulatory care itself have combined to retard the evolution of review methods. These problems are discussed, as are current efforts to overcome them. We have reviewed the relevant issues and literature and have attempted to provide a conceptual framework for better understanding the measurement of ambulatory health care quality. A selective bibliography of literature relating specifically to ambulatory care quality evaluation is presented as a guide to further study.

THE IDEA that effectiveness of medical care can and should be systematically tested is far from new. Almost a century and a half ago, Dr. Pierre Ch. A. Louis, a French statistician and physician, was challenging his medical colleagues to "demonstrate, rigorously, the influence and the degree of influence of any therapeutic agent, on the duration, progress, and termination of a particular disease." Over the years, Flor-ence Nightingale, E. A. Codman, and other insightful individuals returned to this idea, with special emphasis on hospital services. Nevertheless, evaluating the quality of patient care has yet to become an intrinsic part of health-care delivery.

In recent years, however, quality evaluation *within the hospital* has progressed dramatically, both quantitatively and qualitatively, and today the majority of hospital medical and nursing staffs are regularly evaluating the care that they provide.[†] But while advances in the inpatient setting have been impressive, there has not been a comparable development and implementation

* Assistant Professor of Health Resources Management at the University of Illinois School of Public Health. He was for four years a senior staff member in the Quality Review Center, Joint Commission on Accreditation of Hospitals.

† Research Associate with the Health Insurance Association of America.

Address reprint requests to: Mr. Christoffel at the School of Public Health, University of Illinois at the Medical Center, P.O. Box 6998, Chicago, IL 60680.

† A survey conducted in 1975 by the American Hospital Association found that 86 per cent of the hospitals responding (82 per cent response rate) had ongoing patient care audit programs. See S. Manley: Majority of Hospitals Conduct Medical Audit. Hospitals, J.A.H.A. 50:88, 1976.

of methods for the review and evaluation of ambulatory health care.[4] And while there was some justification for concentrating the early quality review efforts on inpatient care — the task is an easier one and the impact of suboptimal care is presumed to be greater for the hospitalized patient — continued emphasis solely on inpatient treatment is no longer valid.

Several features of the hospital setting facilitate quality review. The first of these relates to the advantages of focusing on outcomes of care when assessing quality.[†] Because hospitalization normally continues until the severe stage of illness and disability has passed, it is possible to pinpoint an intermediate patient outcome in the form of the discharge status. A second advantage in assessing quality in the hospital has to do with the necessity to convert the results of quality assessment into corrective action. Structures and mechanisms in the hospital, ranging from improved continuing medical education programs to restrictions in medical staff privileges, facilitate such action. A third advantage of the hospital relates to the novelty of quality assessment ideas and techniques to most physicians. Because it serves large numbers of practitioners, the hospital provides a locus for introducing quality review to physicians not easily reached in their offices and clinics.

Most medical care, however, is delivered in the ambulatory setting, not in hospitals. The National Center for Health Statistics reports that during the early 1970s there were close to 1 billion ambulatory visits annually, compared to fewer than 30 million annual short-stay hospital discharges — an average of five outpatient discharges per

person.[‡] Of this 1 billion total, 70 per cent were office visits and 10 per cent were hospital clinic visits. (Thirteen per cent of the "visits" were actually telephone consultations, and 7 per cent were physician–patient encounters at home, on the job, or elsewhere.)[§]

While hospital care generally represents more severe illness, many illnesses that do not result in hospitalization can and do cause morbidity. Furthermore, ineffective ambulatory treatment, even if not actually harmful, wastes limited resources. Thus, despite the numerous problems involved in ambulatory care evaluation, there is a pressing need for effective methods of reviewing the quality of ambulatory care.

A conceptual framework for the issues and problems involved in efforts to measure the quality of ambulatory care would make it easier to deal with the growing literature on this topic.[||] This article is an attempt to begin development of such a framework. The following pages will summarize the important literature on the subject. (The concern is almost exclusively with physician-delivered care, although some literature does exist on nurse practitioners and "physician extenders."[7, 38, 56, 77, 85, 128, 139, 141, 145] Major emphasis will be on methodological approaches; reports of applications of these methods will be discussed more briefly. In addition, a bibliography is included for additional reference.

---

† See Institute of Medicine: Advancing the Quality of Health Care: Key Issues and Fundamental Principles. Washington, D.C., National Academy of Sciences, 1974; and C. M. Jacobs, T. H. Christoffel, and N. Dixon: Measuring the Quality of Patient Care: The Rationale for Outcome Audit.. Cambridge, Ballinger Publishing Company, 1976.

‡ Reference 156 at page 3. Avedis Donabedian, M.D., M.P.H., points out (personal communication) that *episodes* of ambulatory care might better be compared to hospital discharges and that, since information on episodes is not available, the one billion ambulatory visits annually could be compared to 430 to 445 million *days* of hospital care annually during the early 1970s. The magnitude of the encounters involved should remain evident. Hospital care, of course, accounts for a much greater percentage of health resources than is reflected in these ratios.

§ See Danchik,[28] p. 9.

|| The closest to such a framework is Shortridge's[140] classification of ten research reports and the Primer prepared by Michnich, *et al.*[103]

The text is divided into three major sections: First, a delineation of the areas under discussion and an outline of evaluation problems, focusing on the complexities of ambulatory health care data, and including a discussion of classification and data considerations; next, an outline of concepts, the structural frameworks which facilitate understanding of both problems and solutions; and finally, a review of specific methods that have been proposed and/or tried as techniques for evaluating the quality of ambulatory care.

### Critical Characteristics of Ambulatory Care

Virtually all observers stress that an ambulatory setting, whether it be a hospital outpatient department,[14, 49, 71, 83, 119] a freestanding clinic,[11, 59, 60] an emergency room,[3, 19, 20, 64] or a physician's office,[5, 47, 87-89, 96] presents greater evaluation problems than does the inpatient setting. Several characteristics distinguish ambulatory care from inpatient care and present problems in terms of quality review.

1. *There Is No Easily Definable Episode of Illness in Ambulatory Care.* Unlike inpatient care, which is limited to the specific period between admission to and discharge from the hospital, ambulatory care is intermittent. It is thus difficult to assign a beginning and an endpoint to ambulatory illnesses, particularly chronic illnesses.[143] Yet assessment and comparison would be most meaningful if based on clearly delineated episodes of illness.

2. *Ambulatory Patients Are Less Likely Than Hospitalized Patients to Receive a Specific Diagnosis.* Most inpatient audit and data systems rely heavily on discharge diagnosis labels. But most ambulatory patients present with problems and do not go through a discharge diagnosis "labeling" process. This is reflected in the lack of a diagnostic coding system usable in the ambulatory setting.

3. *Ambulatory Medical Records Are Not Uniform and Are Seldom Complete.* Consistent, comprehensive records ideally follow the patient from history taking and physical examination, through laboratory tests to definitive diagnosis, appropriate management and subsequent course. Ambulatory records rarely reach this ideal, and the inconsistency and frequent weakness of individual record keeping systems plague the development of a uniform system of review.

4. *There Is No History of Quality-oriented Activities in Ambulatory Settings.* Hospitals have, for a long time, featured mortality and morbidity conferences, grand rounds, and the like, and the more recent and sophisticated quality review approaches have built on these traditions. Office practice, however, and even many clinic settings, do not have such traditions; nor do they, in most instances, provide an opportunity for simultaneous observation and exchange of ideas among physicians — a key feature of peer review activity. In fact, there is a significant lack of communications among care providers in the ambulatory setting.[50]

5. *The Physician Has Less Control over the Ambulatory Patient's Adherence to Instructions or Prescribed Regimen Than over the Hospitalized Patient.* The relationship between care and the course of an illness is complicated by a myriad of variables over which the physician has no control. One example is the follow-up visit: until treatment goals are reached, the hospitalized patient is at hand when the physician feels examination or treatment is called for; in an ambulatory setting, the patient must voluntarily present himself.

6. *There Is a Considerable Range in the Severity of Diseases and Conditions Treated on an Ambulatory Basis.* The patient population in most ambulatory settings will contain a few instances of serious morbidity amidst great numbers of minor problems.

Since minor problems are often self-limited, evaluating the quality of the care directed at such problems can be particularly difficult. Evaluating care provided for more serious problems must focus on groups of similar patients, as with inpatient quality review (but see Rubin[124, 125]). A meaningful quality review system either must evaluate very large numbers of patient encounters or must be able to select out the more serious diseases and conditions.

7. *There are Significant Differences Among Ambulatory Care Settings.* Emergency rooms and outpatient clinics both experience lack of continuity in care delivery, low follow-up rates and little likelihood that patients will come back to the same place for their next illness. Yet they both differ in many ways. And neither setting has a great deal in common with office practice. Such differences make it difficult, if not impossible, to apply one evaluation method to all outpatient settings.

Despite these major problems, if ambulatory care is indeed the application of systematic knowledge and consciously controlled skills, it should be possible to devise ways of measuring effectiveness. Patient records (or relatively detailed encounter forms) will be crucial to this measurement, since the alternatives — direct observation, patient interviews, and problem simulation — are limited in efficiency, practicality, and value.¶

## Classification Systems and Data

Meaningful quality review can be carried out systematically and on a large scale when based on routine collection of data that are retrievable, comparable, and specific. Ambulatory care data, however, have been — and continue to be — quite limited, and data on individual patient/provider encounters are recorded erratically

¶ R. Heather Palmer: Definitions and Data. *In* Richard Greene, Assuring Quality in Medical Care, Ballinger Publishing Company, 1976, pp. 48-50.

on numerous, unstandardized forms.[15] Since 1973, data in an aggregate form has been collected by the National Ambulatory Medical Care Survey; but the survey involves only a sample of private practitioners, so the national impact of its standardization has so far been minimal.[29, 110] Ambulatory data on regional and local areas are not available.

Information recorded by different physicians is often not comparable in definition and terminology. (The exception may be billing data, which some suggest can be put to nonfinancial uses.[101, 123]) The Conference on Ambulatory Medical Care Records, held in Chicago in 1972,[2, 14, 24, 39, 44, 48, 55, 62, 63, 99, 109, 157] urged that the basic core of data necessary to the functions of ambulatory care be identified, and that uniform terms, definitions and classifications be introduced for this basic core. The Consultants on Ambulatory Medical Care Records of the United States National Committee on Vital and Health Statistics, a new group which grew out of the Chicago Conference, recommended that ambulatory care records consist of three information components: 1) information that identifies and characterizes the patient, 2) information that identifies and characterizes the providers, and 3) information that identifies and characterizes each encounter between patient and provider.[75, 164]

The format developed by the Consultants matches, whenever possible, that used in the Uniform Hospital Discharge Data Set or the National Ambulatory Medical Care Survey. Each component item (e.g., sex, age, source of payment, diagnosis) has been defined and for most items the information to be recorded has been specified. Some items, including "reason for encounter," "diagnosis and/or problem," and "findings," were left unclassified, so that a classification scheme tailored to purposes of the data collection could be developed. But the open-endedness of these items seriously diminishes the data set's usefulness for evaluation purposes.[46]

With inpatient care, a discharge diagnosis identifies a patient's chart as part of a cohort for inclusion in an evaluation study, and diagnostic indexes utilizing ICDA and H-ICDA, as well as various data collection systems, serve to systematize the study process. Ambulatory records, however, are rarely comparable from place to place, are often unavailable, and usually cannot be identified by diagnosis. Little data are available that break down ambulatory visits according to presenting complaint, treatment modality, or discharge status. These deficiencies have seriously impeded the evolution of methods of quality review for ambulatory settings.[87]

Several developments have occurred recently, however, that promise to alter this situation. As part of the National Ambulatory Medical Care Survey, the National Center for Health Statistics has developed a symptom classification scheme composed of 13 classes, with a primary axis of principal anatomical sites, further divided into 197 subclasses or rubrics. The classification was specifically designed to code patients' description of their symptoms, complaints, and problems, with a four-digit numerical system that allows for expansion within each category.[111] According to Herr and Patrikas,[65] minor modifications would make this system compatible for use with the most commonly used ICDA-8 and H-ICDA coding systems. Further refining of this symptom code system is necessary if ambulatory care records are to be retrievable by diagnosis, operative procedure, and problem or presenting complaint.[120] Working under Federal contract, the American Medical Record Association has just completed such a revision (which incorporates the International Classification of Health Problems in Primary Care, a coding system published by the American Hospital Association.[45, 135, 168]

Sandlow[134] has developed a Categorical Problem Index that classifies presenting problems on three levels: 1) the organ system to which the problem belongs; 2) the pathological process of the problem (infectious, inflammatory, functional, neoplastic, degenerative, or other), and 3) the status of the problem (acute or chronic). The practitioner, using Sandlow's approach, classifies the type of management provided and records the dominant reason for the patient visit: diagnostic, therapeutic, maintenance, or patient-presented problem. Such an approach provides a meaningful way of organizing data for evaluation and comparison. Gonnella[53, 54] has suggested that optimal classification of outpatient visits requires a "staging concept," incorporating into the traditional diagnostic classification a dimension of disease severity. Patients with similar medical problems are classified into subcohorts based on the severity or "stage" of their health problem at different steps in the process of medical intervention. The patient groupings thus produced lend themselves more readily to evaluation of the results of ambulatory medical treatment.

Standardizing the information collected by the ambulatory record and developing classifications of the resulting data should go a long way toward improving medical data collection. But there will also have to be an improvement in provider completion of these records before routine data collection and effective quality review can be instituted. Two early studies of general office practice, Peterson[117] and Clute,[23] found that clinical records were minimal or nonexistent in 36 per cent of practices in North Carolina and in 35 per cent of practices in Ontario. In a 1973 study involving only 15 pediatricians, Starfield[149] found that records were a poor source of information about the sequence of activities performed and about the physicians' thought processes. And a recent study by the Joint Committee on Quality Assurance of Ambulatory Health

Care for Children and Youth[113, 153] found that records were often incomplete because of the physician's failure to report pertinent negatives and test results. These studies confirmed the findings of others that most records currently do not reveal the relationship of problems, diagnostic tests, diagnoses, responses and follow-up studies. Nonetheless, the researchers agreed that records can be useful for the retrospective analysis of such efforts as the performance of specific procedures.[170] (Much of the work pioneered by Morehead has been directed at the question, "Did the individual under care at a specific institution receive an adequate data base for adequate treatment?"[27, 104–108])

One unavoidable answer is simply better record keeping.[137] Perhaps the most important recent development is the growing use of the Problem Oriented Medical Record (POMR). Since its introduction by Weed in the mid-1960s,[159, 160] the POMR has been widely implemented. It seems particularly of value in ambulatory care settings, especially hospital outpatient departments. Weed, Hurst, and others have continually improved on the concept and have proposed audit of the POMR to evaluate clinical competence by means of an assessment of a "core of behavior," including thoroughness, reliability, analytic sense, and efficiency. POMR advocates suggest that the traditional, source-oriented record does not indicate enough about clinical behavior (assembling data, proposing hypotheses, etc.) to permit effective performance assessment. The Problem Oriented Medical Record is proposed as a means of better recording, better care, easier record evaluation, and as a system for quality of care evaluation itself.[72] Data supporting these claims are still inconclusive.

At least in the larger clinic settings, a major factor in the availability of records will be the move toward computerized record systems. Such systems make it possible to conduct concurrent quality and utilization monitoring.[26, 98, 167]

## Conceptual Issues

Earlier discussions of the issues involved in ambulatory quality review methods have been published. Shortridge[140] reviewed the research relating to the quality of care delivered in outpatient settings published through 1970. The studies are summarized and arranged according to conceptual emphasis, agent, source of standards, source of data, research design, and the unit of analysis. Michnich, et al.[103] recently provided a more extensive version of this type of categorization. Constanzo and Verlinsky[25] attempted to devise a framework for understanding the various methods used to assess health care, categorizing the different methodologies according to the aspects of care measured and the resources necessary for implementation, with the goal of identifying those areas in which no method of quality review exists, or in which review would be too costly to be practical. Palmer[114] described some of the problems of ambulatory evaluation as part of a general discussion of quality review strategies. Theoretical approaches have been outlined by Donabedian, Williamson, Brook, Starfield, and others.[17, 18, 25, 30, 32, 35, 40, 52, 66, 67, 121, 147, 163]

The general requirements of quality evaluation methodologies have been discussed by Gonnella, Louis, and McCord.[54] The essentials that the authors delineate are applicable to both ambulatory and inpatient settings. A good methodology should: 1) measure what happens to the patient, i.e., it should be directly or indirectly related to outcomes; 2) be relatively simple, timely, and inexpensive (in terms of both money and physician time) to apply, and it should not be disruptive of the medical system; 3) be consistent and objective, so that it can be applied repeatedly using the same set of ground rules, and 4) be widely accepted by the medical community. (These concerns also make clear that quality review is different than utilization review, although the two are clearly interrelated. The latter is concerned with appropriate allocation of resources and has data collection and administrative needs separate and distinct from those of quality review.)

In seeking to understand quality evaluation methods, it is perhaps most important to consider the answer to the question: What is being measured?

### What Is Being Measured?

The evaluation of medical care involves measurement, *i.e.*, comparison of an instance of care against a standard. This measurement can be considered from at least two different aspects: provider performance, *i.e.*, the performance of individual practitioners, groups of providers, an institution, or the health care system as a whole, or the impact of care, *i.e.*, on a patient, a group of patients, or an entire population.[35, 36] Opinion varies as to which approach is more important and which can be more accurately measured.

Barro[10] argues that the performance of the individual physician is of particular interest because (s)he is the major figure in the health care team and assumes the primary responsibility for delivering quality care. Any attempt to raise the quality of care, in her view, thus should be directed at improving the quality of the individual physician's performance. (The patient need not be involved in this type of approach, since physician performance can be measured through patient simulation tests.)

Impact can be measured in terms of outcomes of care for specific groups of patients or for a population. With the narrower focus, outcomes of care of patients treated in a specific setting are compared with expected outcomes and significant variations

traced back to contributing causes.[163] Outcome evaluation is discussed in considerable detail later in this article.

To measure the impact of medical care on an entire population, some way to measure the health status of that population is needed. A health status index would, ideally reflect change over time and could be used to compare the health of a single population at two different points in time or the health of two different populations. Considerable work has been done on the development of a single index of health status, incorporating mortality, morbidity and disability. Singly each of these components has limitations to its usefulness as a health indicator.[150]

Mortality was one of the earliest means of measuring health, or rather its absence, in a community. It is an easily definable, unambiguous event and statistics are easily available. When the compilation of mortality figures was first routinized, mortality was highly correlated with morbidity. Mortality rates reflected, at least crudely, the state of health of a population. Following a long period of declining mortality rates from 1900 to 1954, the crude and age adjusted death rates in the United States stabilized. Stability in the mortality rate cannot be equated with stability in health conditions. Mortality rates alone provide limited information about the health conditions of the living. Changing health conditions — an increase in life expectancy, chronic illnesses and impairments in the population — have led to the need for more sensitive and informative measures of health levels.

Health officials have attempted to assess the level of health in a community by measuring the morbidity of the population. Early efforts to measure morbidity were limited to recording the type and incidence of disease. More sophisticated measures have examined other dimensions, including intensity of the illness, duration of illness and the severity of any disability. These aspects of morbidity can be ambiguous and difficult to isolate, complicating both data collection and analysis.

Clinical indexes, reviewed by Balinsky and Berger,[8] are one means of measuring morbidity. Theoretical objections to the use of clinical diagnostic indexes are voiced by Lerner.[91] Is the measure of the health of a group simply the sum total of the measures of the health statuses of all individuals in the group, cumulated and averaged to derive a measure for the group as a whole, or is it an "emergent phenomenon," something greater than the mean to be measured in a different way?

There are several problems with the use of clinical indexes as health measures. All illness, although objectively defined and objectively measured, must be medically attended or it is not included in the total morbidity measure. There is a selection bias against those instances of morbidity that are not physician attended.

Research directed at the development of health status measures has more of a public health perspective than the currently quite separate efforts to develop measurements for the quality of care that are the subject of this article. Several studies suggest that these two areas of inquiry may merge. These studies tend to focus on disability as an indicator of the impact of illness. Disability is an element that can be abstracted from diverse illnesses, otherwise not comparable. Seminal work was done by Bush and Fanshel,[41] who developed a model of functional adequacy. With this model, a person is considered well "if he is able to carry on his usual daily activities. To the extent that he cannot he is in a state of dysfunction . . . [p. 1021]." This work was continued by Bush, Patrick and Chen[21] who developed a summary measure of well being involving 1) level of function at a point in time and 2) the probability of transition from one level to another.

Sullivan's[150, 151] two health indicators, expectation of a life free of disability and expectation of disability, correspond to Bush, Chen, and Patrick's function levels. Gilson's[13, 118] Sickness Impact Profile continues in this vein but explicitly includes aspects of physical, mental and social health for assessing the health status of groups. White and Kohn[84, 161, 162] have reported on the World Health Organization/International Collaborative Study, which begins the effort to relate health status to health care delivered.[169] Rutstein et al.[127] recently proposed a "sectional" indexing system to relate incidence of death, disease, and disability to quality of care. The considerable body of worthwhile health status literature is expanding rapidly.[8, 12, 22, 51] A still separate aspect of the evaluation of medical care involves measurement of the efficacy of diagnostic and treatment techniques, i.e., specific tests, treatment regimens, and drugs. The use of randomized controlled trials is critical to validating "appropriate" processes of care, i.e., to measure efficacy. Yet this method dates only from about World War II and is still largely underutilized. Full discussion lies outside the scope of this article.°°

(A literature has been developing regarding consumer evaluation of medical care, with particular focus on ambulatory care. A discussion of such material lies beyond the scope of this article, although some relevant items are included in the bibliography. [43, 70, 79, 82, 90, 158])

## Methods

Of the various conceptual issues just discussed, the one which has received the most attention is the conceptual distinction between structure, process, and outcome ap-

°° See A. L. Cochrane: Effectiveness and Efficiency. London, The Nuffield Provincial Hospitals Trust, 1972; and Byar, D. P., Simon, R. M., Friedwald, W. T., et al.: Randomized clinical trials: Perspectives on some recent ideas. N. Engl. J. Med. 295:74, 1976.

proaches — a paradigm developed by Donabedian[32-34] based on a classification used earlier by Sheps.[++]

### Structure (or Input) Studies

The *structural* approach to medical care evaluation focuses on the quality and quantity of resources, *i.e.*, the input of personnel, equipment, and facilities. The researcher is interested in such reasonably stable features as size of the facility and the physician's qualifications as indicated by class rank and board certification. Ambulatory care has been scrutinized in relatively few field studies of this type. Peterson[117] and Clute[23] were concerned mainly with physician performance, but also used scales for measuring the facilities, equipment, and training that were assumed to be requisites for "good" general practice. The structural variables measured included board certification, medical school class rank, and number of journals received. The authors could not document any meaningful and consistent correlations between input measures and the quality of care as assessed through direct observation, suggesting that such measures were not effective proxy measures of the quality of care. (The one exception was a correlation between "good performance" and time spent in postgraduate training in internal medicine in the Peterson study.)

### Process Studies

*Process* studies involve an assessment of how resources are used, including actual patient management or what is commonly known as the "practice of medicine," as evidenced in patient records, record abstracts, encounter forms, and direct observation. The rationale underlying process studies is that if the proper things are done, then the outcome will be the best attainable. This kind of review is most objective if standards of care are defined prior to review, *i.e.* explicit criteria. However, reviewers have also used "implicit criteria" to review both processes and outcomes of care in traditional one-to-one peer chart review.

Early descriptions of implicit process review include Makover,[100] Morehead,[27, 104-108] and Dreyfus.[37] A recent use of implicit review is found in the chart audit approach developed by Rubin.[6, 124, 125] Charts are selected for review by Rubin on the basis of time and date of appointment, rather than some medically significant basis such as disease category. Each member of an Audit Committee reviews several charts and notes what he feels to be deviations from "good" care. The criteria each reviewer follows are his own and implicit, except for instructions to note anything in the medical record (or missing from it) which reveals, or will lead to, such poor care that no one would be likely to defend it. The same charts are then turned over to other reviewers who follow the same procedure. Deficiencies (as determined by unanimous agreement of the Committee) may result in staff education and establishment, by staff consensus, of standards of patient care. No compulsory corrective action is directed at individual practitioners as the result of an audit, though such action might result from later failure to follow established standards.

The disadvantages of one-to-one chart review approaches are well known.[‡‡] They are subjective, time-consuming, episodic, and do not lead to systematic corrective action. They may detect some gross errors, but will not produce more generalized improvements.

A growing number of evaluation studies of ambulatory care have utilized more explicit process criteria.[11, 69, 80, 81, 112, 126, 130,]

---

++ M. C. Sheps: Approaches to the quality of hospital care. Public Health Rep. 70:877, 1955.

‡‡ Jacobs, Christoffel, and Dixon, pages 28-31; Palmer, page 67.

[142, 155] Lewis[92] suggests that the favoring of process criteria over outcome approaches may be due to an inventory mentality of medical accounting — an emphasis on developing checklists of procedures, rather than a concern with the efficacy of such procedures.

In studies such as those conducted by Payne and Lyons,[115, 116] the actual process of care, as reflected in the medical record, is compared to criteria established by a medical staff group or an external body of experts, such as a specialty society. In an early study of ambulatory care using the explicit process method,[71] Huntley reported on a procedure in which the charts of all patients seen in a hospital clinic were reviewed weekly to determine if they had met clinic criteria for history, physical examination, lab tests, and plans for the patient's continuing care. The study indicated that grossly abnormal findings were recorded in the charts of 64 of 480 patients (13 per cent) without being followed up or explained in any way. These deficiencies, it was concluded, indicated a need for provider education. It was assumed that if physicians knew the correct procedures they would follow them, but this assumption was not tested in practice. Williamson[§§] later found it not to be true.

The development of valid explicit criteria against which actual practice can be measured presents theoretical and practical problems. One possible approach is to use process and outcome criteria together, with the latter serving to justify inclusion of the former. Sandlow[134] has described an evaluation procedure for outpatient settings (modelled on one used for hospital inpatient review) using such an approach. Komaroff[77, 85, 139] has also linked process and outcome, using a protocol approach.

Other studies,[18, 95, 122, 148] however, have shown the tremendous difficulty inherent in determining which aspects of process correlate positively with desirable outcomes.

A more common approach is to seek wide peer agreement on criteria. But agreement is not easily arrived at, causing some to question the feasibility of generating meaningful criteria for quality review. This difficulty has led to several studies.[31, 61, 113, 149, 153, 154]

In a study conducted by Hare and Barnoon,[61] two groups of physicians were asked to generate criteria for the management and diagnosis of six common patient problems. One physician group consisted of practicing internists from different regions of the country, all members of the American Society of Internal Medicine; the other was made up of academic specialists. It had been hypothesized that the frequency of performance of specific criteria would correlate with the relative importance assigned to these criteria. But while a reasonably high level of agreement regarding criteria was found, both between the two groups of physicians and among physicians from different parts of the country, it was also found that physicians were not following their own criteria[|| ||] and that there was little or no correlation between the ranks assigned to the theoretical criteria and the frequency of actual performance.

Hare and Barnoon[61] reasoned that the criteria were developed for the ideal treatment of an average case, while in actual practice the physicians applied these criteria selectively to individual patients, rather than according to an ideal treatment developed for a hypothetical average patient. Donabedian[36] suggests that this dichotomy may also result from the fact that physicians

---

§§ J. W. Williamson, M. Alexander, and G. E. Miller: Continuing education and patient care research — physician response to screening test results. JAMA 201:938, 1967.

|| || Also see Novick et al.[112] It should be noted that doubts regarding the validity of the Hare and Barnoon results have prompted the Federal government, which funded the study, to commission Hulka to repeat it.

serve not only as medical advisors to their patients but often also as representatives of society, concerned with use of finite medical resources. Thus procedures may be ordered or not ordered for reasons other than strictly medical considerations.

A narrower but more detailed study of physician criteria was conducted by the American Academy of Pediatrics' Joint Committee on Quality Assurance.[113, 153, 154] This group also found that it was relatively easy to achieve a high level of agreement regarding the appropriateness (although not the necessity) of various processes of care according to diagnosis, but that adherence to the criteria was difficult to document, due to inconsistent recording of procedures performed. A high percentage of the physicians participating in the study indicated that they did not consider their records to be an accurate appraisal of the care they were actually delivering, since procedures often went unrecorded if no problems were uncovered.

A third study, conducted by Starfield,[149] involved 15 of 96 practicing pediatricians in Baltimore. The study measured the performance of several health maintenance procedures and the obtaining of cultures when certain infections were suspected. It was found that some procedures were uniformly well performed while others varied widely. No practitioner had a uniformly high rate of recording. The authors concluded that while the record can give evidence of procedures done, it is a poor source of information about the sequence of performance of activities, and about the physician's thought process.

Sanazaro suggests, as a partial answer to this documentation difficulty, that process criteria outline only the essential elements of diagnosis and treatment, since it is unrealistic to expect physicians to note the performance of every aspect of textbook treatment of a patient. Such essential elements would include:

1. Items in the history, physical examination, and laboratory and radiological procedures which confirm the diagnosis, influence the choice or application of treatment, and help establish prognosis.
2. Specific treatment which is known to be efficacious.
3. Procedures or treatments which are contraindicated [p. 272].[129]

For each diagnosis there are fewer essential criteria than optimal criteria. Sanazaro feels that there is a greater likelihood that physicians will record their performance of these essential criteria than of the much larger number of optimal criteria, and that failure to meet this smaller number of essential criteria, unless adequately justified, indicates clearly that corrective action is needed.

When rapid feedback is possible, as with a computerized medical records system, process criteria can be used as guidelines for the actual delivery of care. Thus, for example, the computer can be programmed to remind physicians of any patient for whom a strep-positive throat culture is recorded if no antibiotic has been prescribed. This is being done most notably at the Harvard Community Health Plan.[26] Such concurrent use of criteria is quality *assurance* in the proper sense of the term, while retrospective use of the same criteria is quality *assessment*.

A more extensive format for process criteria, developed specifically as guidelines for the delivery of care, are patient care protocols (clinical algorithms.[38, 56, 58, 77, 85, 86, 97, 128, 139, 141, 144, 145] These written, explicit standard procedures for commonly encountered patient problems are often quite intricate, with series of branching logic patterns to guide the provider through the various findings of history, physical, and tests. The protocols can be used to evaluate the quality of care retrospectively, after their use as care structurers or instead of such use.

Protocols have been developed for use by various providers, including physicians, nurse practitioners, and physician's assistants. An article by Grimm[58] describes a symptom-oriented protocol for acute pharyngitis, developed for use by all providers in a university health service clinic. The protocol has two major components — the collection of a standard data base and adherence to protocol decision logic. Protocol checklists are audited regularly within 72 hours of a patient visit. "These protocols, if followed, ensure a minimal standard of health care and create a medical-record format that is easily audited [p. 507]," the clinic staff found. After implementation of this protocol, the amount of data routinely obtained increased significantly, and use of laboratory tests became more effective. Appropriate use of antibiotics also increased. Physicians demonstrated significantly lower levels of acceptance and compliance with the protocols than did nonphysicians, though these protocols produced behavioral changes considered positive by the participants. There was no evidence, however, that the changes necessarily resulted in better health care or outcomes.

A frequent objection to the use of protocols is that the number needed, even to deal with the more common health complaints, would be staggering. A study begun at Beth Israel Hospital in Boston has refuted this objection.[135] It was found that a relatively small number of protocols was sufficient to provide significant practical utility. Multiple complaints contributed only 5 to 10 per cent of all cases seen.

Another difficulty with protocols is that in reality the measurement involved is of how closely a protocol has been followed, thus assuming the protocol as a model of optimal care and restricting practitioners to its options. Greenfield's[57] work, based on the UCLA Experimental Medical Care Review Organization experience, has attempted to solve this problem with a "criteria mapping" approach which uses the protocol-like specification of sequential judgments to evaluate care retrospectively. This technique would seem to be less restrictive than application of traditional process criteria of the "optimal" type.

Some work has been done to measure outcomes of care where protocols have been used.[56, 85, 139]

## Outcome Studies

Outcome studies involve an assessment of the end result of care — what actually happens to the patient. The outcomes of care most often used include mortality, disability, length of hospital stay, ill health and complications of disease or treatment. Other outcome measures are being developed that include satisfaction, adjustment, functional status,[76] and change in expected life span. Outcome is regarded by a growing number of researchers as the most accurate and important index of the quality of health care. Thus, for example, the Institute of Medicine's Committee to Develop a Policy Statement on Mechanisms for Advancing the Quality of Health Care reported:

> The committee believes strongly that the goal of quality assurance can only be achieved by relating assessments of quality to the measurement of results, recognizing that methods of measuring outcomes are not now well advanced, and that many factors other than health care affect health status [p. 2].[73]

Attempts to implement outcome evaluation in the ambulatory setting are not well enough established to provide real insight into feasibility and effectiveness. Most ambulatory evaluation projects are predominantly process oriented, while inpatient review is largely outcome oriented. Many of the initial outcome-oriented efforts — both inpatient and ambulatory — have been derived directly from Williamson's work,[132, 163–166] notably his classic 1971 JAMA article and his Health Accounting Project. In his approach, both diagnostic and therapeutic outcomes are assessed, the former representing "the data required to determine the need for care." Therapeutic outcomes are assessed by predicting the percentage of patients treated which will fall into each of several categories of functional impairment. When actual outcomes vary significantly from these estimates, more detailed process analysis can be undertaken.

One account of this approach describes the Health Accounting Project, as implemented at eight ambulatory care facilities in the East and Midwest.[1] A common audit topic for the clinics was urinary tract infections. The staff in each of the clinics estimated the percentage of patients with UTI whose outcomes would be 1) asymptomatic, 2) symptomatic, 3) restricted in activity, 4) dependent, or 5) dead. Using the physician-derived definitions of each of these outcomes, the actual patient outcomes were compared to the estimates. If the differences between them were significant, corrective action was instituted, or the criteria, *i.e.*, the estimated outcomes, re-examined.

Several difficulties were encountered. Physicians were not always consistent in their functional definitions. Some diagnosed urinary tract infections on the basis of two positive cultures, while others made the diagnosis on a purely symptomatic basis. Yet diagnoses must be standardized so that the outcomes being studied are outcomes of similar conditions. In addition, it was often difficult to determine what the therapeutic outcomes were. In some cases the patient was reached on the telephone and the outcome was determined from the conversation. In others, clinical testing of the patient was required to determine the outcome (creating obvious problems regarding fees for the testing).

An extensive application of the outcome approach to ambulatory care is being conducted at the George Washington University Health Plan.[136] Following Williamson's health accounting approach, physician participants identify key clinical conditions and

> . . . then estimate prevailing levels of impairment and define maximum acceptable standards for diagnostic accuracy and therapeutic outcomes for a given patient group with a common health problem. Outcomes are then measured and compared with standards. If unacceptable discrepancies exist, steps will be taken to improve outcomes by such strategies as educating physicians or altering patterns of patient flow. The outcome assessments are then repeated to measure the impact of these strategies [p. 50].[136]

Application of this approach was found to be considerably more difficult than anticipated. Its effectiveness in improving quality "remains to be seen," according to the authors of the study report.

Brook,[16] in a detailed critique of the Williamson outcomes approach, points out that:

> In addition to sharing some of the problems inherent in using process data to evaluate care, using outcome data presents other problems.
>
> 1. The success of this method depends upon knowledge of the natural history of the illness. Such information, if known, is usually reported in terms of death; information concerning other outcome parameters such as symptoms or activity level measured after a defined follow-up period is generally unavailable.
>
> 2. Physicians have not been trained to think in terms of group prognostic terms. . . .
>
> 3. Outcome data are not recorded routinely in a patient's chart; this information must usually be obtained from a patient interview.
>
> 4. [T]he major methods questions are encountered: the way symptoms affect a patient's life style depends upon social and economic factors as well as purely medical ones. . . . The expression of symptoms varies with ethnic origin and other factors;

this also makes comparison of data difficult.

5. Evaluation cannot depend upon long-term outcome measurements . . . because by the time one has finished collecting the long-term outcome data, the institution one is evaluating is likely either to have disappeared or to have changed remarkably and the purpose of the evaluation is no longer apparent [pp. 200-201].

As a final step in this "standard" outcome-evaluation approach, deficiencies in care are presumably corrected. Williamson's own early work suggests that correction does not always take place.¶¶ But Metcalfe and Mancini[102] document success in improving recognition of infected urine by a group of medical residents. The authors' description of "critical event outcome studies" is unfortunately rather vague, but suggests Greenfield's retrospective use of algorithms.

The emphasis on outcomes will become useful in ambulatory quality assessment only to the extent that actual outcomes of care can be defined objectively. There have been several attempts to do so. Shapiro's[138] study of the Health Insurance Program of Greater New York's group practice system compared the perinatal mortality rates among the infants of HIP subscribers with those of infants in the general population. Outcome was defined as "some measurable aspect of health status which is influenced by a particular element or array of those elements of medical care." Donabedian, Elinson, and others also developed outcome definitions and categories.[33]

An effort to develop what they termed "a taxonomy of end results" is the critical incident technique of Sanazaro and Williamson.[131–133] Two thousand physicians were asked to report episodes in which physician actions had had clearly beneficial or detrimental effects on patient outcomes. The incidents were then arranged into categories of physician-affected end results, including

¶¶ op. cit.

longevity, function, physical and psychologic abnormalities, and symptoms, and attitude toward, and understanding of, one's own condition. The classification was viewed as a first step in the development of more systematic objective criteria of effective physician performance. Lewis[93] also used this classification approach in comparing the quality of care in two nurse clinics.

Starfield has described the need for the conceptualization and measurement of outcomes,[146] and has proposed an approach[147] which involves seven categories — longevity, activity, comfort, satisfaction, disease, achievement, and resilience. Each category represents a continuum, into which indicators developed in other studies could be incorporated. The result is a "profile" of health status, rather than a single outcome index. Starfield presents a conceptualization of outcome, not a fully working model. If a workable scoring system could be developed, specific health care interventions could be evaluated according to their effect on the outcome profile over time.

An important subject for future research is the relationship between process and outcome. Fessel and van Brunt,[42] studying appendicitis and myocardial infarction, found that "Outcome, which would appear to reflect the quality of care much more accurately, may be unrelated to the recorded process of care [p. 134]." And, in pilot studies at UCLA, Lewis[92] found that "utilizing ambulatory problems, we have also failed to find significant associations between quality of the processes and outcomes of care [p. 804]." On the other hand, a small study by Starfield and Scheff [148] involving 53 children with low hemoglobins, found that "the prescription of therapy is one process that is related to good outcomes, and that follow-up of patients may also be."

It may be possible to apply Gonnella's classification of diseases into stages (described earlier) to quality assessment.[53, 54] He maintains that the seriousness of a patient's condition at any point in the treatment process is a good indicator of the outcome of the previous parts of the process. One could test whether a study population has a significantly higher incidence of advanced stage illness than a control norm. If it does, it could be inferred that something in the preceding steps of the care process needs improving. But Gonnella has not developed a way to relate this measure to specific inputs in the process of care. Ultimately, staging may prove most useful simply as an indicator of potential problem areas, rather than as an evaluatory instrument.

## Topic Selection

As Schroeder[136] and others have shown, evaluating the quality of care is neither simple nor easy. One important thing to note about both the process and outcome studies just reviewed — and the many like them — is that they have tended to look at relatively small numbers of patients and at only one or a few medical problems or conditions. Yet, effective evaluation presumably would need to focus on the great bulk of care. To deal with this problem, Kessner and his colleagues at the Institute of Medicine have explored the use of "tracers."

> In their simplest definition, tracers are specific health problems that, when combined in sets, allow health care evaluators to pinpoint the strengths and weaknesses of a particular medical practice setting or an entire health services network, by examining the interaction between providers, patients, and their environments [Footnote 80 at p. 6].[80, 81]

But it has not been shown that "tracer" diseases or problems are adequately representative of the overall quality of care being received by a population.

A second problem in the selection of audit topics concerns, in effect, overuse of the tracer technique. Criteria can be developed and applied most effectively in those conditions which can be diagnosed definitively and which can be prevented, cured, or objectively improved (ergo, the focus of quality assessment studies on urinary tract infections and similar favorites). But what of the more common ailments presented to the ambulatory care provider: depression, anxiety, obesity, and sore throats? The efficacy of standard treatments for these ailments will have significant cost implications, if nothing else. What of numerous fleeting or minor conditions? And what of those patients who are asymptomatic and never diagnosed? Kelly and Mamlin[78] describe a comparison of the true incidence or prevalence of a disease, as measured in an independently conducted multiphasic screening, and diagnostic outcomes as determined by treating-physician. Diagnostic outcomes were found generally unacceptable. Barr and Gaus[9] have suggested a population-based quality assessment approach, relating quality indicators to all members of a defined population, not just those who have made use of medical services. But this is clearly a difficult task, even with somewhat defined and limited populations.[94] Hulka[68] and her colleagues have undertaken a study which focuses both on general population and on patients actually treated, but results are just beginning to emerge.[69] Again, much work remains to be done.[74]

## Conclusion

The purpose of this essay has been to facilitate further study of ambulatory care quality review by providing an outline or framework of experiences to date. We have enumerated problems regarding ambulatory records and the nature of ambulatory care itself and have categorized the different conceptual approaches to the still elusive measurement of ambulatory care quality. The considerable amount of ongoing and new research on ambulatory care evaluation is encouraging for future progress.

## Acknowledgment

We are indebted to Drs. Katherine Christoffel, Avedis Donabedian, Steven Jonas, and Jeremiah Stamler for reviewing the manuscript and providing many helpful criticisms and suggestions.

## References

1. Accountants without ledgers. Group Pract. 22:32, 1973.

2. Akpom, C. A., Katz, S., and Densen, P. M.: Methods of classifying disability and severity of illness in ambulatory care patients. Med. Care (Suppl.) 11:125, 1973.

3. Albin, S. L., Wassertheil-Smoller, S., Jacobson, S., and Bell, B.: Evaluation of emergency room triage performed by nurses. Am. J. Public Health 65:1063, 1975.

4. American Society of Internal Medicine: Assessing Physician Performance in Ambulatory Care. Proceedings, San Francisco, American Society of Internal Medicine, 1976.

5. Andersen, N. A.: The objective measurement of quality in general practice. Ann. Gen. Pract. (Suppl.) 12:27, 1967.

6. Auditing ambulatory care. Hosp. Pract. 9(6): 155, 1974.

7. Bailit, H., Lewis, J., Hochheiser, L., and Bush, N.: Assessing the quality of care. Nurs. Outlook 23:153, 1975.

8. Balinsky, W., Berger, R.: A review of the research on general health status indexes. Med. Care 13:283, 1975.

9. Barr, D. M. and Gaus, C. R.: A population-based approach to quality assessment in health maintenance organizations. Med. Care 11:523, 1973

10. Barro, A. R.: Survey and evaluation of approaches to physician performance measurement. J. Med. Educ. (Suppl.) 48:1047, 1973.

11. Beaumont, G., Feigal, D., Magraw, R. M., et al.: Medical auditing in a comprehensive clinic program. J. Med. Educ. 42:359, 1967.

12. Berg, R. L.: Health Status Indexes. Chicago, Hospital Research and Educational Trust, 1973.

13. Bergner, M., Bobbitt, R., and Pollard, W. E.: The sickness impact profile: Validation of a health status measure. Med. Care 14:57, 1967.

14. Brenner, M. H., and Paris, H.: Record systems for hospital and outpatient clinics. Med. Care (Suppl.) 11:41, 1973.

15. Brenner, M. H., and Weinerman, E. R.: An ambulatory service data system. Am. J. Public Health 59:1154, 1969.

16. Brook, R. H.: Critical issues in the assessment of quality of care and their relationship to HMO's. J. Med. Educ. 48:114, 1973.

17. ———: Quality assurance: The state of the art. Hosp. Med. Staff 3:15, 1974.

18. ———, and Appel, F. A.: Quality-of-care assessment: Choosing a method for peer review. N. Engl. J. Med. 288:1323, 1973.

19. ———, Berg, M. H., and Schechter, P. A.: Effectiveness of nonemergency care via an emergency room. Ann. Intern. Med. 78:333, 1973.

20. ———, and Stevenson, R. L. Jr.: Effectiveness of patient care in an emergency room. N. Engl. J. Med. 283:904, 1970.

21. Bush, J. W., Chen, M.M., and Patrick, D. L.: Social indicators for health based on functional status and prognosis. In Proceedings of the Social Statistics Section. American Statistical Association, Washington, D. C., 1972, (pp. 89-92)

22. Chiang, C. L.: An Index of Health Mathematical Models. Vital and Health Statistics: Series 2, No. 5, Public Health Service Publication No. 1000, 1965.

23. Clute, K. F.: The General Practitioner: A Study of Medical Education and Medical Practice in Ontario and Nova Scotia. University of Toronto Press, 1963

24. Cooney, J. P. Jr.: The community hospital: Ambulatory services, statistics, and medical care record data. Med. Care (Suppl.) 11:158, 1973.

25. Costanzo, G. A., and Vertinsky, I: Measuring the quality of health care : A decision oriented typology. Med. Care 12:417, 1975

26. COSTAR, Research Digest Series, USDHEW Publication No. (HRA) 76-3145, National Center for Health Services Research, Rockville, Md. 208-52

27. Daily, E. I., and Morehead, M.: A method of evaluating and improving the quality of medical care. Am. J. Public Health 46:848, 1956.

28. Danchik, K. M.: Physician Visits, Volume and Interval Since Last Visit: United States - 1971. Vital and Health Statistics: Series 10, Data from the National Health Survey; no. 97. DHEW Publication No. (HRA) 75-1524, March, 1975.

29. Delozier, J. E.: The National Ambulatory Medical Care Survey: 1973 Summary, United States, May 1973-April 1974. Vital and Health Statistics: Series 13, Data from the National Health Survey; no. 21. DHEW Publication No. (HRA) 76-1772, October 1975.

30. Densen, P. M.: The quality of medical care. Yale J. Biol. Med. 37:523, 1965.

31. Dolan, T. F., Jr., and Meyers, A.: A survey of office management of urinary tract infections in childhood. Pediatrics 52:21, 1973.

32. Donabedian, A. : Evaluating the quality of medical care. Milbank Mem. Fund Q. (Part 2) 44:166, 1966.

33. ———: Promoting quality through evaluating the process of patient care. Med. Care 6:181, 1968.

34. ———: The quality of medical care. Chapter 7 In: Corey, L., Saltman, S. E., and Epstein, M. F.: Medicine in a changing Society. St Louis, C. V. Mosby Company, 1972.

35. ———: Measuring and evaluating hospital and medical care. Bull. N. Y. Acad. Med. (Second Series) 52:51, 1976.

36. ———: A frame of reference. Quality Rev. Bull. 2(6):5, 1976.

37. Dreyfus, E. G., Minson, R., Sbarbaro, J. A., et al.: Internal chart audits in a neighborhood health program: A problem-oriented approach. Med. Care 9:449, 1971.

38. Dutton, C. B., Hoffman, S., Ryan, L. K., et al.: Ambulatory health care—medical audit system. N.Y. State J. Med. 74:1545, 1974.

39. Eimerl, T. S.: The E Book system for record-keeping in general practice. Med. Care (Suppl.) 11:138, 1973.

40. Falk, I. S., Schonfeld, H. K., Harris, B. R., et al.: The development of standards for the audit and planning of medical care. Am. J. Public Health 57:1118, 1967.

41. Fanshel, S., and Bush, J. : A health status index and its application to health service outcomes. Operations Res. 18:1021, 1970.

42. Fessel, W. J., and Van Brunt, E. E.: Assessing the quality of care from the medical record. N. Engl. J. Med. 286:134, 1972.

43. Fisher, A. W.: Patients' evaluation of outpatient medical care. J. Med. Educ. 46:238, 1971.

44. Freeborn, D. K., and Greenlick, M. R.: Evaluation of the performance of ambulatory care systems : Research requirements and opportunities. Med. Care (Suppl.) 11:68, 1973.

45. Froom, J.: International Classification of health problems for primary care. Med. Care 14:450, 1976.

46. ———: Minimum basic data set. N.Y. State J. Med. 76:1541, 1976.

47. ———: Assessment of quality of care by profiles of physicians' morbidity data. J. Fam. Pract. 3:301, 1976.

48. Fry, J.: Information for patient care in office-based practice. Med. Care (Suppl.) 11:35, 1973.

49. Goetzl, E. J., Cohen, P., Downing, E., et al.: Quality of diagnostic examinations in the university hospital outpatient clinic. Ann. Intern. Med. 78:481, 1973.

50. Goldberg, G. A.: Implementing university hospital ambulatory care evaluation. J. Med Educ. 50:435, 1975.

51. Goldsmith, S. B.: The status of health status indicators. Health Serv. Rep. 87:212, 1972.

52. Gonnella, J. S., Goran, M. J., Williamson, J. W., et al.: Evaluation of patient care: An approach. JAMA 214:2040, 1970.

53. ———: Quality of patient care—a measurement of change: The staging concept. Med. Care 13:467, 1975.

54. ———, Louis, D. Z., and McCord, J. J.: The staging concept—an approach to the assessment of outcome of ambulatory care: Med. Care 14:13, 1976.

55. Gordon, B. L.: Terminology and coding of medical care data. Med. Care (Suppl.) 11:96, 1973.

56. Greenfield, S., Friedland, G., Scifers, S., et al.: Protocol management of dysuria, urinary frequency, and vaginal discharge. Ann. Intern. Med. 81:452, 1974.

57. ———, Lewis, C. E., Kaplan, S. H., et al.: Peer review by criteria mapping: Criteria for diabetes mellitus—the use of decision-making in chart audit. Ann. Intern. Med. 83:761, 1975.

58. Grimm, R. H. Jr., Shimoni, K., Harlan, W. R. Jr., et al.: Evaluation of patient-care protocol use by various providers. N. Engl. J. Med. 292:507, 1975.

59. Hagner, S. B., LoCicero, V. J., and Steiger, W. A.: Patient outcome in a comprehensive medicine clinic—its retrospective assessment and related variables. Med. Care 6:144, 1968.

60. Hanson, A. S., and Kraus, E. D.: An outpatient medical audit. Minn. Med. (Suppl. No. 2) 56:49, 1973.

61. Hare, R.L., and Barnoon, S. : Medical Care Appraisal and Quality Assurance in the Office Practice of Internal Medicine. National Center for Health Services Research and Development, Final Report, DHEW Publication No. (HSM) 110-70-420 (NTIS Publication No. PB-237-943/6GA), July 1973.

62. Harrington, D. C.: The San Joaquin foundation peer review system. Med. Care (Suppl.) 11:185, 1973.

63. Heasman, M. A.: Information for self-evaluation of patient care and feedback to physicians. Med. Care (Suppl.) 11:61, 1973.

64. Helfer, R. E.: Estimating the quality of patient care in a pediatric emergency room. J. Med. Educ. 42:244, 1967.

65. Herr, C. E. A., and Patrikas, E. O.: Keeping track of ambulatory care. Hospitals, J. A. H. A. 49:89, 1975.

66. Hetherington, R. W., Hopkins, C.E., and Roemer, M. I.: Health Insurance Plans: Promise and Performance. (Chapter IV—Quality of Care and Range of Services) , New York, John Wiley and Sons, 1975.

67. Howell, J. R., Osterweis, M., and Huntley, R. R.: Curing and caring—a proposed method

for self-assessment in primary care organizations. J. Community Health 1:256, Summer, 1976.

68. Hulka, B. S., and Cassel, J. C.: The AAFP-UNC study of the organization, utilization, and assessment of primary medical care. Am. J. Public Health 63:494, 1973.

69. Hulka, B. S., Kupper, L. L., and Cassel, J. C.: Physician management in primary care. Am. J. Public Health 66:1173, 1976.

70. Hulka, B., Zyzanski, S. J., Cassel, J. C., et al.: Scale for the measurement of attitudes towards physicians and primary medical care. Med. Care 8:429, 1970.

71. Huntley, R. R., Steinhauser, R., White, K. E., et al.: The quality of medical care: Techniques and investigation in the outpatient clinic. J. Chronic Dis. 14:630, 1961.

72. Hurst, J. W., and Walker, H. K. : The Problem-Oriented System. New York, MEDCOM, 1972.

73. Institute of Medicine: Advancing the Quality of Health Care: Key Issues and Fundamental Principles. Washington, D. C., National Academy of Sciences, August, 1974.

74. Institute of Medicine: Assessing Quality in Health Care: An Evaluation. Washington, D. C., National Academy of Sciences, 1976.

75. Jackson, C. B., Krueger, D. E., and Densen, P. M.: Ambulatory care medical records: Uniform minimum basic data set. JAMA 234:1245, 1975.

76. Kane, R. L., Woolley, F. R., Gardener, H. J., et al.: Measuring outcomes of care in an ambulatory primary care population: A pilot study. J. Community Health 1:233, 1976.

77. Kaufman, S. A., Komaroff, A. L., and Sherman, H.: Diagnostic protocols for physicians aids. Group Pract. 25(3):6, 1976.

78. Kelly, C. R., and Mamlin, J. J.: Ambulatory medical care quality. JAMA 227:1155, 1974.

79. Kelman, H. R.: Evaluation of health care quality by consumers. Int. J. Health Serv. 6:431, 1976.

80. Kessner, D. M., Kalk, C. E., and Singer J.: Assessing health care quality—the case for tracers. N. Engl. J. Med. 288:189, 1973.

81. ———: A Strategy for Evaluating Health Services. Washington, D. C., Institute of Medicine, National Academy of Sciences, 1973.

82. Kisch, A. I., and Reeder, L. G. L.: Client evaluation of physician performance. J. Health Soc. Behav. 10:51, 1969.

83. Klein, M. W., Malone, M. F., Bennis, W.G., et al.: Problems of measuring patient care in the out-patient department. J. Health Soc. Behav. 2:138, 1961.

84. Kohn, R., and White, K.: Health care: An International Study, New York, Oxford University Press, 1976.

85. Komaroff, A. L., Reiffen, B., and Sherman H.: Protocols for paramedics: A quality assurance tool. In Regional Medical Programs service Quality Assurance of Medical Care. USDHEW Publication No. (HSM) 73-7201, 1973, p.161.

86. ———, Sherman, H., and Kaufman, S.: Ambulatory care protocols improve efficiency and quality of care. Hosp. Med. Staff 3(7):1, 1974.

87. Kroeger, H. H., Altman, I., Clark, D. A., et al.: The office practice of internists: I. The feasibility of evaluating quality of care. JAMA 193: 371, 1965.

88. Last, J. M.: Quality of general practice. Med. J. Aust. 67:780, 1967.

89. ———: Objective measurement of quality in general practice. Ann. Gen. Pract. (Suppl.) 12 (6):5, 1967.

90. Lebow, J.: Evaluation of an outpatient pediatric practice through use of consumer questionnaires. Med. Care 13:250, 1975.

91. Lerner, M.: An approach to conceptualizing the level of community health. In: Proceedings of the Social Statistics Section, American Statistics Association, Washington, D. C., 1972, p. 81.

92. Lewis, C. E.: The state of the art of quality assessment—1973. Med. Care 12:799, 1974.

93. ———, Resnik, B. A., Schmidt, G., et al.: Activities, events and outcomes in ambulatory patient care. N. Engl. J. Med. 280:645, 1969.

94. Lieberman, H. M.: Evaluating the quality of ambulatory pediatric care in a neighborhood health center. Clin. Pediatr. 13:52, 1974.

95. Lindsay, M. I. Jr., Hermans, P. E., Nobrega, F. T., et al.: Quality of care assessment 1. Outpatient management of acute bacterial cystitis as the model. Mayo Clin. Proc. 51:307, 1976.

96. McDaniel, D. B., Patton, E. W., and Mather, J. A.: Immunization activities of private-practice physicians: A record audit. Pediatrics 56:504, 1975.

97. McDonald, C. J.: Protocol-based computer reminders, the quality of care and the non-perfectability of man. N. Engl. J. Med. 295:1351, 1976.

98. McFarlane, A. H., and Norman, G. R.: A medical care information system: Evaluation of changing patterns of primary care. Med. Care 10:481, 1972.

99. ———: Methods for classifying symptoms, complaints, and conditions. Med. Care (Suppl.) 11:101, 1973.

100. Makover, H. B.: The quality of medical care. Methodology of survey of the medical groups associated with the Health Insurance Plan of New York. Am. J. Public Health 41:824, 1951.

101. Mesel, E., and Wirtschafter, D. D.: Automation of patient medical profile from insurance claims data: A possible first step in automating ambulatory medical records on a national scale. Milbank Mem. Fund Q. (Health and Society) 54:29, Winter 1976.

102. Metcalfe, D. H. H., and Mancini, J. C.: Critical event outcome studies used as a teaching tool. J. Med. Educ. 47:869, 1972.

103. Michnich, M. E., Harris, L. J., Willis, R. A., et al.: Ambulatory Care Evaluation: A primer for Quality Review. Los Angeles, University of California, 1976.

104. Morehead, M. A.: Evaluating the quality of medical care in the neighborhood health center program of the Office of Economic Opportunity. Med. Care 8:118, 1970.

105. ———: Ambulatory care review: a neglected priority. Bull. N.Y. Acad. Med. 52:60, 1976.

106. ———: Donaldson, R., and Helmich, R.: The medical audit as an operational tool. Am. J. Public Health 57:1643, 1967.

107. ———, ———, and Seravilli, M. R.: Comparisons between OEO neighborhood health centers and other health care providers. Am. J. Public Health 61:1294, 1971.

108. ———, ———: Quality of clinical management in comprehensive neighborhood health centers. Med. Care 12:301, 1974.

109. Murnaghan, J. H.: Review of the conference proceedings (Report of the Conference on Ambulatory Medical Care Records) Med. Care (Suppl.) 11:13, 1973.

110. National Ambulatory Medical Care Survey: Background and Methodology. Vital and Health Statistics; Data Evaluation and Methods Research, Series 2, No. 61, DHEW Publication No. (HRA) 76-1335, (originally published April 1974).

111. National Ambulatory Medical Care Survey: Symptom Classification. Vital and Health Statistics; Data Evaluation and Methods Research, Series 2, No. 63, DHEW Publication No. (HRA) 75-1337, December 1974.

112. Novick, L. F., Dickinson, K., Asnes, R. et al.: Assessment of ambulatory care: Application of the tracer methodology. Med. Care 14:1, 1976.

113. Osborne, C. E., and Thompson, H. C.: Criteria for evaluation of ambulatory child health care by chart audit: Development and testing of a methodology. (Final report of the Joint Committee on Quality Assurance of Ambulatory Health Care for Children and Youth). Pediatrics (Suppl.) 56:625, 1975.

114. Palmer, R. H.: Choice of strategies. In: Greene, R.: Assuring Quality in Medical Care: The State of the Art. Cambridge, Ballinger Publishing Company, 1976.

115. Payne, B. C., and Lyons, T. F.: Method of Evaluating and Improving Personal Medical Care Quality: Episode of Illness Study. Chicago, American Hospital Association, 1973.

116. ———: Method of Evaluating and Improving Personal Medical Care Quality: Office Care Study. Chicago, American Hospital Association, 1973.

117. Peterson, O. L., Andrews, L. P., Spain, R. S., et al.: An analytic study of North Carolina general practice 1953-54. J. Med. Educ. 31:1, Part 2, 1956.

118. Pollard, W. E., Bobbitt, R., Berner, M., et al.: The Sickness Impact Profile: Reliability of a health status measure. Med. Care 14:146, 1976.

119. Pozen, M. W.: Effects of Physicians Education and Administrative Support on Hospital Ambulatory Care. Baltimore, The Johns Hopkins University, 1974.

120. Renner, J. H., and Banman, E. A.: Problem-specific coding systems. J. Fam. Pract. 2:279, 1975.

121. Roemer, M. I.: Evaluation of health service programs and levels of measurement. HSMHA Health Reports 86:839, 1971.

122. Romm, F. J., Hulka, B. S., and Mayo, F.: Correlates of outcomes in patients with congestive heart failure. Med. Care 14:765. 1976.

123. Rosenberg, S. N., Gunston, C., Berenson, L., et al.: An eclectic approach to quality control in fee-for-service health care: The New York City Medicaid experience. Am. J. Public Health 66:21, 1976.

124. Rubin, L.: Measuring the quality of care. Group Pract. 22:7, 1973.

125. ———: A Comprehensive Quality Assurance System, The Kaiser Permanente Approach. Alexandria, Va., American Group Practice Association, 1975.

126. Russo, R. M., Gururaj, V. J., Laude, T. A., et al.: A chart audit peer review system in an ambulatory service. Pediatrics 56:246, 1975.

127. Rutstein, D. D., Berenberg, W., Chalmers, T. C., et al.: Measuring the quality of medical care: A clinical method. N. Engl. J. Med. 294: 582, 1976.

128. Sackett, D. L., Spitzer, W. O., Gent, M., et al.: The Burlington randomized trial of the nurse practitioner: Health outcomes of patients. Ann. Intern. Med. 80:137, 1974.

129. Sanazaro, P. J.: Medical audit. Br. Med. J. 1:271, 1974.

130. ———, Goldstein, R. L., Roberts, J. S., et al.: Research and development in quality assurance: The EMCRO program. N. Engl. J. Med. 287: 1125, 1972.

131. ———, and Williamson, J. W.: Research in medical education: Classification of physician per-

formance in internal medicine. J. Med. Educ. **43:** 389, 1968.

132. ———, and Williamson, J. W.: End results of patient care: A provisional classification based on reports by internists. Med. Care **6:**123, 1968.

133. ———, and Williamson, J. W.: Physician performance and its effects on patients: A classification based on reports by internists, surgeons pediatricians, and obstetricians. Med. Care **8:**299, 1970.

134. Sandlow, L. J.: Quality for walking patients. Hospitals, J. A. H. A. **49**(5):95, 1975.

135. Schneider, D., and Appleton, L.: Reason for visit classification system for patient records in the ambulatory care setting. Q. R. B. **3**(1):20, 1977.

136. Schroeder, S. A., and Donaldson, M. S.: The feasibility of an outcome approach to quality assurance—a report from one HMO. Med. Care **14:**49, 1976.

137. Seawright, L. C., and Linden, C. R.: Record system ties patient data from hospital and private care. Hospitals, J. A. H. A. **50**(19):132, 1976.

138. Shapiro, S.: End result measurement of quality of medical care. Milbank Mem. Fund. Q. **45:**7, 1967.

139. Sherman, H., and Komaroff, A. L.: Ambulatory Care Project: Progress Report 1969—1974. Lexington, Mass., Lincoln Laboratory/Boston, Mass., Beth Israel Hospital, August 1, 1974.

140. Shortridge, H. M.: Quality of medical care in an outpatient setting. Med. Care **12:**283, 1974.

141. Sibley, J. C., Spitzer, W. O., Rudnick, K. V., et al.: Quality-of-care appraisal in primary care: A quantitative method. Ann. Intern. Med. **83:**46, 1975.

142. Smith, D. W., and Simmons, F. E.: Rational diagnostic evaluation of the child with mental deficiency. Am. J. Dis. Child. **129:**1285, 1975.

143. Solon, J. A., Feeney, J. J., Jones, S. H., et al.: Delineating episodes of medical care. Am. J. Public Health **57:**401, 1967.

144. Sox, H. C. Jr., Sox, C. H., and Tompkins, R. K.: The training of physician's assistants: The use of clinical algorithm system for patient care, audit of performance and education. N. Engl. J. Med. **288:**818, 1973.

145. Spitzer, W. O., Sackett, D. L., Sibley, J. C., et al.: The Burlington randomized trial of the nurse practitioner. N. Engl. J. Med. **290:**251, 1974.

146. Starfield, B.: Health services research: A working model. N. Engl. J. Med. **289:**132, 1973.

147. ———: Measurement of outcome: A proposed scheme Milbank Mem. Fund. Q. (Health and Society) **52:**39, Winter 1974.

148. ———, and Scheff, D.: The effectiveness of pediatric care: The relationship between process and outcome. Pediatrics **49:**547, 1972.

149. ———, Seidel, H., Carter, G., et al.: Private pediatric practice: Performance and problems. Pediatrics **52:**344, 1973.

150. Sullivan, D. F.: Conceptual Problems in Developing an Index of Health. Vital and Health Statistics, Series 2, No. 17, DHEW Publication No. (HRA) 74-1017 (first issued in the Public Health Service Publications Series No. 1000, May 1966).

151. ———: A single index of mortality and morbidity. Public Health Rep. **86:**347, 1971.

152. ———: Disability Components for an Index of Health. Vital and Health Statistics: Series 2, No. 42, Public Health Service Publication No. 1000, 1971.

153. Thompson, H. C., and Osborne, C. E.: Development of criteria for quality assurance of ambulatory child health care. Med. Care **12:**807, 1974.

154. ———: Quality assurance of ambulatory child health care—Opinions of practicing physicians about proposed criteria. Med. Care **14:**22, 1976.

155. Travis, L. W.: An audit of otitis media treated in the emergency room. QRB **2**(9):13, 1976.

156. United States National Committee on Vital and Health Statistics: Ambulatory Medical Care Records: Uniform Minimum Basic Data Set: Final Report. Vital and Health Statistics. Documents and Committee Reports, Series 4, No. 16, DHEW Publication No. (HRA) 75-1453, April 1975.

157. Vallbona, C., Quirch, J., Moffet, C. L., et al.: The health-illness profile: An essential component of the ambulatory medical record. Med. Care (Suppl.) **11:**117, 1973.

158. Ware, J. E., and Snyder, M. K.: Dimensions of patient attitudes regarding doctors and medical care services. Med. Care **13:**669, 1975.

159. Weed, L. L.: Medical records that guide and teach. N. Engl. J. Med. **278:**593, 652, 1968.

160. ———: Medical Records, Medical Education, and Patient Care. Cleveland, The Press of Case Western Reserve University, 1969.

161. White, K. L.: International comparisons of medical care. Sci. Am. **233:**17, 1975.

162. ———, Anderson, D. O., Bice, T. W., et al.: Health care: An international comparison of perceived morbidity, health services resources, and use. Int. J. Health Serv. **6:**199, 1976.

163. Williamson, J. W.: Evaluating the quality of patient care: A strategy relating outcome and process assessment. JAMA **218:**564, 1971.

164. ———: Evaluating the quality of medical care. N. Engl. J. Med. **288**:1352, 1973.

165. ———: Outcome assessment for implementing quality assurance systems. In: Quality Assurance of Medical Care USDHEW Publication No. (HSM) 73-7201, 1973, p. 313.

166. ———, Aronovitch, S., Simonson, L., et al.: Health accounting: An outcome-based system of quality assurance· Illustrative application to hypertension. Bull. NY Acad. Med. **51**:727, 1975.

167. Wirtschafter, D. D., and Mesel, E.: A strategy for redesigning the medical record for quality assurance. Med. Care **14**:68, 1976.

168. World Organization of National Colleges, Academies, and Academic Associations of General Practitioners/Family Physicians: International Classification of Health Problems in Primary Care. Chicago, American Hospital Association, 1975.

169. Zimmer, J. G., and Puskin, D.: Epidemiological model of the natural history of a disease within a multilevel care system. Int. J. Epidemiol. **4**:93, 1975.

170. Zuckerman, A. E., Starfield, B., Hochreiter, C., et al.: Validating the content of pediatric outpatient medical records by means of tape-recording doctor-patient encounters. Pediatrics **56**: 407, 1975.

---

## Publications Received

Stroman, Duane F.: *The Medical Establishment and Social Responsibility*. Port Washington, N. Y., Kennikat Press, 1976, 193 pp., $12.95.

Sloan, Frank A.: *The Geographic Distribution of Nurses and Public Policy*. Bethesda, Md., U. S. Department of Health, Education, and Welfare, 1975, 214 pp., $2.20.

White, P. A. F.: *Effective Management of Research and Development*. New York, Halsted Press, 1975, 295 pp., $24.95.

Monahan, John: *Community Mental Health and the Criminal Justice System*. Elmsford, N. Y., Pergamon Press, 1976, 332 pp., $15.00.

Srole, Leo, Langner, Thomas S., Michael, Stanley T., Kirkpatrick, Price, Opler, Marvin K., and Rennie, Thomas, A. C.: *Mental Health in the Metropolis*. New York, Harper & Row, 1975, 289 pp., $4.95.

Holahan, John: *Financing Health Care for the Poor*. Lexington, Mass., D. C. Heath and Company, 1975, 152 pp., $13.50.

Foley, Henry A.: *Community Mental Health Legislation*. Lexington, Mass., D. C. Heath and Company, 1975, 155 pp., $14.00.

Stepan, Nancy: *Beginnings of Brazilian Science*. New York, Neale Watson Academic Publications, Inc., 1976, 225 pp., $12.95.

Somers, Ann: *Health Promotion and Consumer Health Education*. New York, Neale Watson Academic Publications, Inc., 1976, 255 pp., $4.95.

Cassell, Eric J.: *The Healer's Art: A New Approach to the Doctor-Patient Relationship*. Philadelphia, J. B. Lippincott Company, 1976, 240 pp., $8.95.

Brooke, Paul A.: *Resistant Prices: A Study of Competitive Strains in the Antibiotic Markets*. Cambridge, Mass., Ballinger Publishing Company, 1975, 120 pp., $12.50.

Greene, Richard: *Assuring Quality in Medical Care: The State of the Art*. Cambridge, Mass., Ballinger Publishing Company, 1976, 293 pp., $17.50.

Stoupel, E.: *Forecasting in Cardiology*. New York, John Wiley & Sons, 1976, 141 pp., $18.00.

Mitchell, Bridger M., and Phelps, Charles E.: *Employer-Paid Group Health Insurance and the Costs of Mandated National Coverage*. Santa Monica, Calif. The Rand Corporation, 1975, 53 pp., $5.00.

Mitchell, Bridger M., and Schwartz, William B.: *The Financing of National Health Insurance*. Santa Monica, Calif., The Rand Corporation, 1976, 47 pp., $3.00.

*National Institutes of Health Guidelines for Research Involving Recombinant DNA Molecules*. Bethesda, Md., National Institutes of Health, Department of Health, Education and Welfare, 1976.

Egdahl, Richard H., and Gertman, Paul M., Eds.: *Quality Assurance in Health Care*. Germantown, Md., Aspen Systems Corporation, 1976, 355 pp.

# 20

# Some Thoughts on Clinical Trials, Especially Problems of Multiplicity

## John W. Tukey

*Summary.* Problems of statistical and conceptual design of experiments are exacerbated by ethical issues in many, if not most, clinical trials. Statutory requirements of demonstrated effectiveness are far from being clearly resolved—either qualitatively or quantitatively. Ethics, bolstered by informed consent, are likely to keep us from ever learning the answer to many questions. Unbalanced boundaries, focusing-down designs, historical controls, and not-very-sequential designs are among the possible consequences.

The pressures of ethics and equity on clinical trials have always been severe. Today they are more vigorous than ever before. Many of us are convinced, by what seems to me to be very strong evidence, that the only source of reliable evidence about the usefulness of almost any sort of therapy or surgical intervention is that obtained from well-planned and carefully conducted randomized, and, where possible, double-blind clinical trials [see the review papers of Byar *et al.* (*1*) and Peto *et al.* (*2*)]. Dare we prevent ourselves from obtaining reliable evidence?

### Surgical Intervention

The simplest, though not necessarily the easiest, special case is that of most surgical intervention, where all decisions rest with the patient and the patient's doctors. Consider then the case where we have something less than reliable evidence in favor of some form of surgical intervention. Some of the questions that arise are:

1) Ought a surgeon employ this plausible form of intervention?

2) Must he, under the penalties of malpractice?

3) Can a randomized study be ethically conducted in the hope of learning whether this form of intervention is better than its most favored competitor?

4) Can we fail to conduct such a randomized study in view of our responsibilities to future patients?

Clearly these are difficult questions.

It seems to me very obvious that we are obligated to do everything we can to make as clear as possible to the patients doctors the strengths and weaknesses of the incomplete evidence involved. This obligation falls most strongly upon statis-

ticians, but it must be shared by those of all professions who are in any way involved.

Once the strengths and weaknesses of the evidence have been made as clear as we know how to do, we have also to be very careful about how we interpret the evidence. At this point we may even, in particular, need to take into consideration the general experience of clinical trials. What fraction of what reputable experts thought was likely to be an improvement, and thus worthy of a clinical trial, does in fact prove to be an improvement? For further discussion of this point see Gilbert *et al.* (*3*).

### New Drugs

The next case in terms of difficulty is that of a new drug, which, until a favorable regulatory decision has been made, can only be used in controlled (and approved) experimental situations. If we have less than copper-riveted evidence that its use is an improvement, some of the crucial questions that arise are:

1) Should the regulatory body approve its general use?

2) If it does not, should or will use of the drug be subject to suit or prosecution for malfeasance?

3) Dare we fail to conduct a randomized double-blind trial to strengthen the evidence?

Again we have conflicting obligations, now falling mainly on the regulatory agency. The answer to the third question, given no favorable regulatory action, is relatively clear, at least as answers to such difficult questions go. For if we do believe that therapy with the new drug is an improvement, and the law forbids us to use it, except in an approved experimental situation, the best

we can do for individual patients is:

1) Offer each of as many patients as we can afford a probability of taking the new drug rather than the placebo.

2) Ensure that our patients do not know whether they are on drug or placebo, so that all will receive whatever psychological lift comes from a chance of receiving the possible improvement.

For the welfare of all future patients, we can

1) Assure that the "probability of taking" comes from a well-planned and well-conducted randomization.

2) Assure that the trial is fully "double-blind" so that we can be certain that knowledge by attending physicians of who was on drug and who was on placebo does not affect either unspoken messages to patients or general medical care.

3) Make the protocol of the study as responsive to medical knowledge and insight as possible.

By taking such precautions, and by being careful to wring as much out of the data as possible, we will have done what we can for future patients by getting evidence that is as strong as possible as soon as possible. This will tend both to decrease exposure to a real nonimprovement and to advance the date of regulatory approval for a real improvement, both of which are responses to an ethical obligation.

We may well wish to choose relative frequencies of administration of drug and placebo that are other than 50–50, either for statistical reasons or for ethical ones. We may also wish to plan for these probabilities to change as the study proceeds, perhaps along the lines suggested by Robbins (*4*) [but see also Byar *et al.* (*1*, pp. 76–78) and Peto *et al.* (*2*, p. 596)].

Again, the responsibility for making the evidence as clear as possible rests upon all those concerned, especially the statisticians. Beyond this, however, I would suggest that the regulatory agency has a continuing responsibility to make as clear as is reasonable, in advance,

The author is professor of statistics and Donner professor of science at Princeton University, Princeton, New Jersey 08540, and associate executive director, research, at Bell Laboratories, communication principles division, Murray Hill, New Jersey 07974.

how it will judge evidence for efficacy, so that the planning and conduct of clinical trials can be more effective, and hence more ethical.

## Old Drug, New Disease

The problem becomes still worse when we deal with a new use for an old drug. Our laws now prevent the advertising of the old drug for the new use, but they do not prevent any physician from prescribing it. The simple excuse for the ethics of the clinical trial is now lost.

It is no longer true that we can only give the drug to individual patients in an experimental situation. Any physician who believes the old drug to be an improvement for its new use can prescribe it for any patient. If he or she believes an improvement to be likely but not demonstrated, is there an ethical obligation to prescribe? Up to what level of "likeliness" can patients be asked to enter a randomized trial? Do the physicians who believe an improvement is likely have an ethical obligation to write vigorously in the medical literature to convince other physicians?

The difficulties with the "use, don't experiment" situation, which ordinarily arises only when the regulators have not approved the new use, include one interesting one, namely: *So long as drug house advertising is not permitted, use of an old drug for a new disease will tend to be confined to patients of more literature-reading and more literature-influenced physicians; thus, if the new use is an improvement, producing (or more likely, some would say, increasing) inequality of health care between two classes of patients.*

How is this to be balanced against the likely loss to individual patients randomly assigned to the placebo if a clinical trial is decided on?

## Safety and Relative Risk

Thus far, this discussion has bypassed safety, proceeding as if both surgical interventions and drug therapies were without risk. While this is often quite unreal, the only effect of safety on the issue that here concerns us is to make the problem more pressing. Not less.

## One Role for a Statistician

These are not easy questions. It is not my place to suggest answers. But I do have an obligation to do whatever I can

Table 1. Example of probabilities of not reaching significance.

| Situation considered | Probability of *not* reaching significance at 5% |
|---|---|
| First class alone | 95% |
| Second class alone | 95% |
| Two classes together | $(95\%)(95\%) =$ $(95\%)^2 = 90.2\%$ |
| Third class alone | 95% |
| Three classes together | $(95\%)(95\%)^2 =$ $(95\%)^3 = 85.7\%$ |
| Nine classes together | $(95\%)^9 = 63.0\%$ |
| Tenth class alone | 95% |
| Ten classes together | $(95\%)(95\%)^9 =$ $(95\%)^{10} = 59.9\%$ |

to reduce the frequency with which such questions arise—and the duration over which each difficult situation extends. What I can do as a statistician, I must. The largest feasible improvement I see my way to helping with at the moment is the sharpening of the understanding of the strength of the evidence. It is with this class of questions that we will now be concerned.

## Clinical Inquiries versus Focused Clinical Trials

The words "clinical trial" have a wide variety of meanings. Let us look at two extremes:

*The clinical inquiry.* This is where some intervention or therapy is hoped to be of help to some class of patients, not specified in advance, and where, consequently, we go in for massive data collection and for analysis of results for each of many classes of patients (by age, sex, previous medical history, prognosis, and symptoms, for example). (There also may be separate analyses for different end points.) The statistician must, I believe, call attention to the multiplicity of questions which any such inquiry poses, and he must, therefore, face up to the influence of this multiplicity on the strength of the evidence resulting from the inquiry.

*The focused clinical trial.* This is a trial in which both the class of patients and the end point to be considered are clearly specified in the initial protocol, and the only chance of multiplicity arises from analyses of the data at various cutoff dates during an ongoing study. (This kind of multiplicity also occurs in the clinical inquiry and its multiplicity has to be multiplied together with the other kinds of multiplicity there present.)

From a data analytic viewpoint, in particular in terms of the sort of statistical

formalisms that seem to help me, these two extremes are very different.

Indeed, I do not believe that a clinical inquiry, by itself, is likely to be an ethically satisfactory means of providing definitive evidence that an intervention or therapy is an improvement. (We will come to the more technical reasons for this later.) To say this is *not* to say there should be no clinical inquiries. Quite the contrary. Clinical inquiries may often play a very crucial and very useful role. However, at a time before such an inquiry has reached trustable conclusions, it will ordinarily be best to initiate, or to embody in the continuing clinical inquiry, a single focused clinical trial (or, possibly, a few such) from which one can come more rapidly to trustable conclusions.

It is right for each physician to *want* to know about the behavior to be expected from an intervention or therapy when applied to his particular individual patient (to whom the physician has the strongest ethical obligation). It is not right, however, for a physician to *expect* to know this—except, possibly, for the most dramatically effective and time-tested interventions or therapies. Most useful interventions or therapies change, for the better, the chance of a favorable outcome—change it from a smaller chance to a larger chance. Most physicians and surgeons recognize this and do not demand (though they may rightfully ask for) detailed and reliable forecasts for individual patients.

They feel that they have better reason, as indeed they do, to ask for differential forecasts of improvement by age, sex, symptoms, or the like. Again it is right for them to ask for such forecasts, but as we shall soon see, they are not likely to get them for newly tested innovations; that it would undoubtedly be good for their patients if they had them is not a reason for them to be possible.

This feeling, quite proper for all patient-treating physicians and surgeons, has undoubtedly helped in a rather widespread misinterpretation of the role of clinical inquiries, as opposed to focused clinical trials.

## Multiplicity and Significance

Let us emphasize one aspect of the analysis of clinical inquiries that is ethically necessary and is commonly observed: special attention is given to the results for whichever class or classes of patients for whom the results appear most favorable for the intervention or therapy under test.

Consider the simple arithmetic of asking multiple questions and concentrating on the most favorable answers. As just noted, once multiple questions are to be asked, there will be pressures, some ethical in nature, to concentrate upon those questions for which the results appear most favorable.

If we approach our data in terms of tests of significance (or in terms of confidence intervals) and neglect problems of multiplicity, we find ourselves in trouble. As another speaker has put it to me in private: "Even normal saline comes out significant 40 percent of the time." How can such things be?

Suppose that we are conducting a clinical inquiry about a single innovation which has no effect on any patient. Suppose we look at only ten classes of patients, defined by age, sex, and symptoms. For simplicity let us take these classes nonoverlapping, and let us suppose that the results for different classes are statistically independent. Then the probabilities of not reaching significance (wholly be chance) at 5% are as in Table 1, and the probability of finding at least one out of ten subgroups significant at 5% purely by chance, is

$$100\% - 59.9\% = 40.1\%$$

The moral seems to me to be abundantly clear: Knowing that, for one class of patient, a clinical inquiry has reached some specific level of significance, such as 4%, is not evidence of the same strength as knowing that a focused clinical trial, involving a single prechosen question, has reached exactly that level of significance, even if both the inquiry and the trial involved the same number of patients exposed to risk, and the same total number of end points, distributed in the same way. That ethics, and other reasonable motivations, ensure that we will look first at the results for whatever class was most promising is a vital fact, and cannot be neglected.

Once we admit that the best-appearing class will be examined first, we can see how to adjust our application of significance to the clinical inquiry. If there are $k$ classes of patients that *would have been looked at seriously if the results for them had seemed favorable*, it suffices (for one who would ask for about 5% significance in a focused clinical trial) to ask about significance at 5%/$k$ [that is (5/$k$) percent] for each of the classes that were indeed looked at seriously. Notice that it does not suffice for $k$ to be only as large as the number of classes actually looked at; we need to use the larger number of classes, each of which would

have been looked at seriously if the results for them had happened to look favorable.

If there are several end points, according to which we might have assessed improvements, then $k$ has to be further increased to become the product of the number of plausible end points multiplied by the number of plausible classes. It is easy for $k$ to become very large indeed.

I will turn later to the question of whether we can bear working to the 5%/$k$ standard, or even to one somewhere near this standard of rigor.

## Multiplicity and Bayes

In my judgment, Bayes's methods do not offer us any satisfactory way to deal with problems of multiplicity. I have yet to see a Bayesian account in which there is an explicit recognition that the numbers at which we are looking are the most favorable of $k$. Until I do, I doubt that I will accept a Bayesian approach to questions of this sort as satisfactory.

The type of solution to which some Bayesians are led, particularly those who are likely to say that they are practitioners of "empirical Bayes" seems also unsatisfactory. The reason why physicians and surgeons are willing to consider results for specified classes is simple: experience shows that some interventions and some therapies are much more favorable to some classes of patients than to others. A procedure that assumes

1) that the classes we have actually looked at are all those that we would have looked at, even if their results had appeared favorable, and

2) that it is a reasonable approximation to treat the true improvements for the classes concerned as a sample from a nicely behaved population (one that surely does not involve two more or less separate collections of true values or, in technical language, one that is much better behaved than just being unimodal), does not seem to me to be near enough the real world to be a satisfactory and trustworthy basis for the careful assessment of strength of evidence to which the ethical issues discussed above must dedicate us.

## Multiplicity and Decision Theory

Much the same remarks as those in the previous section seem to me to apply to any other "decision theory" approaches that I have seen.

## Multiplicity and Phased Experiment

The most extreme case of multiple questions arises in purposive breeding, in particular in those areas where it is easy to generate many strains. Trying to pick out, for high yield of kernels, a particular hybrid line of maize is much like trying to pick out, for high yield of antibiotic, a particular radiation-induced mutant strain of microorganism. In each case, it is easy to obtain many candidates to begin with. The practical constraint is on the total amount of experimentation—acres times years for maize, total volume of, or number of, cultures for microorganisms—that we can afford to devote to our search for improvement.

The statistics of this situation have been clear for a quarter of a century [see, for example, (5)]. The main points are:

1) The experiments should be divided into phases, with a selective reduction in the number of strains carried forward between each phase.

2) Provided equally plausible candidates can be easily obtained in unlimited numbers, the size of the trials for the individual candidates in the first phase should be so small, because there are so many candidates, that no significant differences among strains can be expected to be established.

The simplest analogy to this solution of the breeding problem is a clinical program that begins with a clinical inquiry and closes with a focused clinical trial.

In its simplest form the clinical inquiry is regarded only as the place where we spend the effort and the dollars required as a sensible entrance fee for the focused clinical trial (or perhaps the two or three focused clinical trials). It will undoubtedly be hard for anyone familiar with the effort and expense associated with large clinical inquiries to accept the idea that all of it was just to pay the entrance fee. Yet this is ordinarily the most efficient way to regard any clinical inquiry.

We have convinced ourselves that a regulator, physician, or surgeon who demands significance at 5% for a focused clinical trial should demand significance at 5%/$k$ for the best class of patients of a clinical inquiry. Suppose we are conducting a clinical inquiry and that our "best" class has at least reached significance at 5%, if analyzed as if, contrary to fact, it was the only class that might have been considered. If the innovation is indeed favorable, we have at least two strategies before us: (i) continue the clinical inquiry until what is then the best class reaches significance at 5%/$k$ and (ii) replace the clinical inquiry by a single focused clinical trial (or a few such) and carry out the focused clinical trial until it reaches significance at 5%.

Unless $k$ is noticeably less than 10, we can expect the second choice to take less time, to say nothing of less effort, thus meeting one of our ethical obligations to future patients, to say nothing of costing less.

The decision between these strategies will thus tend to favor the second choice, particularly as the decision-makers become better acquainted with the quantitative facts.

### What It Is Unethical to Learn

It is time for us to look at some consequences of the ethical issues that are somewhat more specific than the broad ones we have been considering.

We will never know, with any high relative precision, how much better a favorable innovation is than its current competitor. Once our clinical trial has accumulated favorable evidence for an innovation up to whatever level of significance regulators, physicians, or surgeons judge appropriate for action, we cannot, ethically, continue the trial (at least as we see the world today) *just to measure the improvement* with greater precision. Thus we will ordinarily be lucky indeed if we can distinguish among even three broad levels of improvement, say: small, medium, and large improvements.

This becomes painful whenever it is very expensive to put the innovation into practice. Those who are to pay for an expensive program are right to ask for a good idea of how much it will help; we are probably ethically right often to tell them that we cannot, in good conscience to our patients, find out.

Circumstances and costs may be such, however, as to limit the rate of introduction of the innovation, as severe limitations of foreign exchange limited British imports of streptomycin just after World War II. This limitation made a double-blind study of the efficacy of streptomycin in tuberculosis feasible, leading to the first adequate measurement of its helpful effects. I believe our ethical obligation to future patients should force us to consider randomized application during the period in which not all patients can receive the innovation.

### What Comes After a Focused

### Clinical Trial?

Suppose that we have had a focused clinical trial, and that it has established

Table 2. Half-octave number of end points, and the approximate corresponding chances of reaching significance at an individual (with no adjustment for repeated looking) two-sided 5% point (binomial comparison).

| Number of end points | Chance of reaching "5%" significance | |
|---|---|---|
| | 50% improvement | 20% improvement |
| 25 | 3/8 | |
| 35 | 1/2 | |
| 50 | 3/5 | |
| 70 | 4/5 | |
| 100 | 9/10 | |
| 150 | | 1/4 |
| 200 | | 1/3 |
| 300 | | 5/11 |
| 400 | | 4/7 |
| 600 | | 4/5 |
| 800 | | 7/8 |

the statistical significance of an improvement when the innovation is applied to certain other classes of patients, either to all patients or to those from a large class. Either at that time, or later, certain skilled physicians or surgeons may come to doubt the efficacy of the innovation when applied to certain classes of patients. What is their obligation to future patients, and how can they meet both this obligation and that to their individual patients?

In such a situation it should be possible to identify a class of patients for whom the doubters feel uncertain about the efficacy of the innovation (neither clearly for nor clearly against). Is it not now an ethical obligation of the doubters to join together, to plan an adequate randomized double-blind study of efficacy in this selected class, and to attempt to fund and carry out this study?

It would seem that only by such actions can we ethically learn more and more about the boundaries of efficacy of even the more important surgical interventions and medical therapies.

### And What of the Cost?

Any form of clinical trial is expensive. (Well-conducted ones are likely to seem more expensive before they are begun, though they may be less expensive before they are meaningfully concluded.) Who pays the cost is, in detail, a matter for legislative and public debate. In the main, however, the costs of clinical trials, like the cost of all collective undertakings, has to come out of everyone's pocket. As we think of new requirements concerning safety, as well as efficacy, we push these costs higher and higher. The

result of higher costs is, inevitably, fewer clinical trials. At what point do we lose instead of gain? I lack the information to take this question much further, but feel an obligation to raise it.

### Knowledge versus Opinion

When the law asks for proof of efficacy, or when the physician or surgeon asks for publications, carefully refereed and clearly written, that seem to deserve trust, the demand is for knowledge—knowledge of a restricted sort, coming with a $P$ value to indicate the size of residual doubt—not just for skilled professional opinion. Yet medical and surgical practice has always depended more on skilled professional opinion than on knowledge. I doubt that this will change within any of our lifetimes.

It would be wrong to focus on knowledge to the exclusion of opinion. When I seek medical or surgical care for someone near and dear to me, I want more than knowledge. Experts are usually experts by their opinion rather than their knowledge. I would hate to have had a hand in the leveling of medical practice to a uniformity based only on clearly recognized knowledge, something malpractice suits threaten us with to an unbearable degree.

It would be almost as bad, I believe, to disturb too deeply the practicing physician's or surgeon's belief in his or her own skill, much of which consists of informed professional opinion rather than knowledge.

In tightening the standards of knowledge from clinical trials, we need to do this without too greatly disturbing the dependence of practitioners, in the many areas not yet subjects of adequate clinical trials, on their own informed professional opinion. Indeed, we owe an ethical obligation to their future patients not to disturb them too greatly.

It is a difficult task to drive the nearly incompatible two-horse team: on the one hand, knowledge of a most carefully evaluated kind, where, in particular, questions of multiplicity are faced up to; and, on the other, informed professional opinion, where impressions gained from statistically inadequate numbers of cases often, and so far as we see, often should, control the treatment of individual patients. The same physician or surgeon must be concerned with both what is his knowledge and what is his informed professional opinion, often as part of treating a single patient. I wish I understood better how to help in this essentially ambivalent task.

## Large-Scale Decisions and Opinion

As the importance of health care becomes more engrossing for more people, we shall have to make more and more large-scale decisions. Dare we do this on the basis of informed opinion alone? Dare we face the ethical problems and costs involved in enough clinical trials to allow most such decisions to be made on the basis of knowledge?

It is time to turn to a few questions of a more specific character, questions which, like the relation of clinical inquiries to focused clinical trials, are more in line with the statistician's narrow responsibilities.

## Historical Controls

One of the most debated questions in clinical trials is that of "historical controls." It seems easy for some to argue that we know enough of how patients of variously specified ages, sexes, symptoms, and histories have responded to the old intervention or the old therapy, and that there is thus no need for a randomized trial. If our experience with the behavior of disease were different, this argument would be easy to accept. But phenomena such as the decline of tuberculosis mortality before any presumably efficacious treatments were widely used are not uncommon. [For disturbing examples more closely relevant to clinical trials, see Byar et al. (1, pp. 75–76) and Peto et al. (2, p. 592).]

How then should we reply to the cry that "historical controls are good enough"? Given both high expertise and a firm belief that the innovation will produce more than a 30% to 50% improvement, it can be hard to hold the line for randomized studies. Is there a possible compromise?

Perhaps there is, though it is not one that is likely to make those crying for historical controls entirely happy. If it is feasible to say, for example, that background changes in other aspects of intervention, therapy, or cure are certainly not going to make an improvement of more than 25% (or perhaps 50%) over the time from the historical controls to the new study (I wonder how often this is so?), then I could conceive:

1) starting a study without randomization;

2) analyzing the results of the new study by comparison with a 25% (or 50%) improvement over historical controls; and

3) planning, if this analysis seemed indecisive—and carrying out the plan—either to convert the study into a randomized study or to drop the trial of the innovation.

Beyond such an alternative, I have not seen an excuse for historical controls that seemed to me to be valid.

## Not-Very-Sequential Designs

On the one hand, the dangers of unfavorable response urge us to monitor quite frequently the results of a clinical trial as they accumulate. On the other, the costs of frequent analysis are still often underestimated.

The names associated with the basic papers on the impact of steady monitoring of a simple paired comparison are those of Armitage and McPherson [see Armitage et al. (6) and McPherson and Armitage (7)]. They showed just how far our assessment of significance can be displaced by indefinitely repeated testing.

The most qualitative result is easy to understand. If we continually test at $P\%$, stopping only when the innovation appears significantly better or significantly worse, we can think of looking and testing after 100, $100^2$, $100^3$, . . . patients have accumulated. At each such look, the data collected before the previous look are only 1/100th of that now at hand. The results would be much the same if we made repeated independent tests at $P\%$. Sooner or later the innovation will be significantly better or worse. So our chance of reaching significance is 100% not $P\%$.

The real question is not "do such things happen?" but rather "do they happen soon enough to matter in practice?" Armitage et al. (6) showed us that, regrettably, the answer is "yes."

What then ought our response to be? The pressure for repeated checking comes only from an appropriate desire to avoid unduly prolonging trials. This is especially important on the "innovation significantly bad" side (herein abbreviated as the "bad side"), since we are particularly conscious of the need to limit exposure to bad innovations. Since I see no need for the probability of stopping a trial of a neutral innovation, because it seems bad, to be as low as we need to have the probability of stopping because the neutral innovation seems good, I am quite willing to look at least somewhat more frequently on the bad side, thus raising the true value of $P$ on that side higher than for the good side.

What about the good side? Continuous looking is obviously wrong. If we allow for its effects, the trial will take longer to reach a conclusion because we have looked more often. Looking quite often is also ethically wrong because when we allow for how often we have looked, it will still take a longer time, on average, to reach a chosen level of significance, allowing for multiplicity, than if we looked less often. The only reasonable conclusion I can draw is that we ought to look only relatively infrequently.

Table 2 suggests some possible chosen values where our analysis is based on reaching a fixed end point, for instance, death. I believe I could bear to plan to look at three values from this half-octave sequence. (The table suggests that if I were to look at three values, perhaps I should space adjacent looks a full factor of 2 apart. But I fear the consequences of telling a trial manager he ought to get 100% more data before looking again.)

Since data will be coming in more or less steadily, how can we avoid looking more often? Especially since we expect to look more often on the bad side? Realistically, it is hard to believe that no one will look some, perhaps many, times more than prescribed. But we can hold down the amount of additional dilution this causes by fixing either the effective date or the actual number of end points as of which the "file is to be cut" and all records brought up to that date. Even if such dates are only several end points in the future at the time of decision, such precautions will greatly reduce the dilution that would arise if we stopped at exactly the point where things first looked good.

How much will three looks (at half-octave numbers of end points) cost us? About as much as $k = 2$ would! I have computed the effect for looking at 10, 20, and 30 end points, with one-sided tail areas of 1.07%, 2.07% and 2.14% (total 5.28%), and have found a combined level of 3.84%, corresponding to $k = 2.2$. Doing the same for 10, 20, and 40 end points gives 3.97% combined, which is in the same area. (Half-octave looks would correspond to 15, 20, 30 and thus, since 15 is closer to 20 and 30, to a $k$ a little smaller than 2.2.) More extensive calculations seem to have been carried out independently by Pocock (8).

## And Then?

Suppose that in Harold Jeffrey's words "all the allowed principles of witchcraft" have been used:

1) We have carefully randomized the patients.

2) It has been possible to do the study double-blind.

3) We are analyzing all of the patients who met the requirements of the protocol.

4) Even when seen from the viewpoint of the completed study, the protocol was well chosen and relevant.

5) Only one end point was contemplated in advance, and this is the one we are using.

6) We have only looked seriously at the data a few times, each of which was fixed well in advance.

What then?

Notice first that there may well be excellent reasons, often involving knowledge gained during the study, which can make any one or more of these desiderata either unwise to attempt or impossible to have. Real studies often have real problems, which we must meet as best we can.

If, however, we have a focused clinical trial with the characteristics just described, we have a study of the best sort anyone knows how to conduct, and our statements of significance are much more likely to mean what they say, espe-cially if we make some allowance for the number of looks, than most of those routinely found in the literature of any field, medico-surgical or not. As a result, we have, I assert, an ethical obligation to take the results of such a study most seriously.

*   *   *   *

I can hardly claim to have made any of our tasks easier by bringing forward the problems I have discussed. But it would not really have helped us to go ahead in ignorance of the problems that *are* there whether we like it or not.

The pressures of ethics *do* force us to sharpen our interpretation of the uncertainties of the data. The distinction between clinical inquiries and focused clinical trials *is* important. *Both* have important roles to play. There *are* questions we dare not try to answer. Both knowledge *and* opinion are important and must be managed by the same individuals. Historical controls are *not* an easy out. We *cannot*, ethically, either look only once or look very many times. Yet there is hope.

**References and Notes**

1. D. P. Byar, R. M. Simon, W. T. Friedewald, J. J. Schlesselman, D. L. DeMets, J. N. Ellenberg, M. H. Gail, J. H. Ware, "Randomized clinical trials: Perspectives on some recent ideas," *N. Engl. J. Med.* 295, 74 (1976).
2. R. Peto, M. C. Pike, P. Armitage, N. E. Breslow, D. R. Cox, S. V. Howard, N. Mantel, K. McPherson, J. Peto, P. G. Smith, "Design and analysis of randomized clinical trials requiring prolonged observation of each patient. I. Introduction and design," *Br. J. Cancer* 34, 585 (1977); for part II see *ibid.* 35, 1 (1977).
3. J. P. Gilbert, B. McPeek, F. Mosteller, *Science*, 198, 684 (1977).
4. H. Robbins, "A sequential test for two binomial populations," *Proc. Natl. Acad. Sci. U.S.A.* 71, 4435 (1974).
5. W. G. Cochran, "Improvement by means of selection," *Proceedings of the 2nd Berkeley Symposium on Mathematical Statistics and Probability* (Univ. of California Press, Berkeley, 1951), pp. 449–470.
6. P. Armitage, C. K. McPherson, B. C. Rowe, "Repeated significance tests on accumulating data," *J. R. Stat. Soc. A* 132, 235 (1969).
7. C. K. McPherson and P. Armitage, "Repeated significance tests on accumulating data when the null hypothesis is not true," *J. R. Stat. Soc. A* 134, 15 (1971).
8. MSC, paper on "Group sequential designs for clinical trials," by S. J. Pocock, *RSS News & Notes* (Royal Statistical Society) 3 (No. 9), 5 (1977).
9. The text of this article was prepared in part in connection with research at Princeton University, sponsored by the U.S. Energy Research and Development Administration, and was presented at the Birnbaum Memorial Symposium, 27 May 1977, at the Memorial Sloan-Kettering Cancer Center, New York.

# 21

# Statistics and Ethics in Surgery and Anesthesia

*John P. Gilbert, Bucknam McPeek, and Frederick Mosteller*

Ethical issues raised by human experimentation, especially in medicine, have been of increasing concern in the last half of the 20th century. Except for issues of consent and capacity to consent, ethical concerns raised by controlled trials center about the fact that individuals are being subjected, randomly, to different treatments. Two arguments are raised, and in each the patients are seen to be the losers. The first argument is an expression of the fear that the trial, by withholding a favorable new therapy, imposes a sacrifice on the part of some of the patients (the control group). The sec-

J. P. Gilbert is staff statistician at the Office of Information Technology, Harvard University, Cambridge, Massachusetts 02138 and assistant in biostatistics in the Department of Anesthesia, Massachusetts General Hospital, Boston 02114. B. McPeek is anesthetist to the Massachusetts General Hospital and assistant professor of anesthesia, Harvard University. F. Mosteller is professor of mathematical statistics in the Department of Statistics and chairman of the Department of Biostatistics, School of Public Health, Harvard University, 7th Floor, 677 Huntington Avenue, Boston, Massachusetts 02115.

ond argument raises the opposite concern that, by getting an untested new therapy, some patients (those in the experimental group) are exposed to additional risk. To a large extent, both arguments imply that investigators know in advance which is the favorable treatment.

Some empirical evidence on these issues can be obtained by examining how potential new therapies are evaluated and what the findings are. How often do new therapies turn out to be superior when they are tested, and how much better or worse is a new therapy likely to be than the standard treatment? We have investigated such questions for surgery and anesthesia.

## The Sample of Papers

For an objective sample we turned to the National Library of Medicine's MED-LARS (Medical Literature Analysis and

Retrieval System). For almost 15 years, this computerized bibliographic service has provided exhaustive coverage of the world's biomedical literature. Articles are classified under about 12,000 headings, and computer-assisted bibliographies are prepared by cross-tabulating all references appearing under one or more index subjects. For example, all articles indexed under prostatic neoplasms, prostatectomy, and postoperative complications might be sought.

We obtained our sample from the MEDLARS system by searching for prospective studies and a variety of surgical operations and anesthetic agents, such as cholecystectomy, hysterectomy, appendectomy, and halothane (*1*). The papers appeared from 1964 through 1973.

We found 46 papers that satisfied our four criteria: The study must include (i) a randomized trial with human subjects, (ii) with at least ten people in each group, (iii) it must compare surgical or anesthetic treatments, and (iv) the paper had to

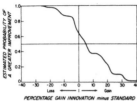

Fig. 1. Secondary therapies: estimated cumulative distribution of true gains (reduction in percentage with a particular complication).

be written in English because of our own language limitations. All the papers we found, by the MEDLARS search, that met these criteria are included in the sample. Although this sample is neither a strictly random sample nor a complete census of the literature of the period covered, the method does largely exclude personal biases in selection.

These papers evaluated two types of therapy. One type is designed to cure the patient's primary disease. An example is the trial of radiation therapy in addition to surgery for the treatment of cancer of the lung (2). The second type of therapy is used to prevent or decrease the rate of an undesirable side effect of the primary therapy. Examples are the various trials of anticoagulants to decrease the incidence of thromboembolism after operations on the hip. Because we felt that these two types of therapies might differ in the distributions of improvements we wished to study, as indeed they seemed to, we have recorded them separately using the terms primary and secondary therapies, respectively. While each of our sample papers has provided important information concerning the treatment of a specific disease or condition, prognosis, complications, and the like, we have concerned ourselves only with the comparison of effectiveness between competing therapies.

We have classified each therapy either as an innovation or as the standard treatment, to which the innovation was being compared. Although this distinction is usually clear, in a few instances some readers might disagree with our decisions. We took the position of the investigators, who usually indicated which therapies they regarded as the standards for comparison. Some papers report trials where several innovations were tested against one standard, or one innovation was sometimes tested against several standards, or the comparison was made for several distinct types of patients. To prevent one paper from hav-

ing an undue effect on the total picture, no more than two comparisons were taken from any one paper, the choice being based on the importance of the comparisons for the surgery. When two comparisons were used, each was weighted one-half. When several papers reported the same investigation, we used the most recent one.

## Comparisons of Innovations and Standards

To give a rough qualitative idea of how the innovations (I) compared with the standards (S), we have classified the outcomes by "highly preferred to" ($>>$), "preferred to" ($>$), and "about the same as" ($=$) in Table 1. In the first set designated $=$, the innovation was regarded as a success because it did as well as the standard and did not have other disadvantages, such as high cost, dangerous side effects, or the requirement of extra skill or training in its administration. Thus, it offers the surgeon an extra therapy when the standard may have drawbacks.

In the second set designated $=$, the investigators seemed indifferent to the equality; in the third set, the innovations were regarded as a disappointment because of undesirable features. The preferences reported reflect closely the views of the original investigators.

About 49 percent of the innovations were successful when compared to their matched standards, and 13 percent were highly preferred. Among pairs of primary therapies, the innovation was highly preferred in 5 percent, and among pairs of secondary therapies the innovation was highly preferred in 18 percent of the comparisons. Indeed, the totals of the two extreme categories were smaller in the primary comparisons than in the secondary—10.5 percent as compared to 27 percent.

The overall impact of the data in Table 1 is to suggest that, when assessed by randomized clinical trials, innovations in surgery and anesthesia are successful about half the time. Since innovations brought to the stage of randomized trials are usually expected by the innovators to be sure winners, we see that in the surgery and anesthesia area the evidence is strong that the value of the innovation needs empirical checking.

## Quantitative Comparisons

In addition to the qualitative comparisons of Table 1, we want to compare

Table 1. Qualitative comparisons between innovations (I) and standards (S) stratified by primary and secondary therapies. Where a paper had two comparisons, each was weighted one-half.

| Preference | Primary | Secondary | Total | Percent |
|---|---|---|---|---|
| I >> S | 1 | 5 | 6 | 13 |
| I > S | 4 | 4½ | 8½ | 18 |
| I = S (success) | 2½ | 6 | 8½ | 18 |
| I = S (indifferent) | 1½ | 1 | 2½ | 5 |
| I = S (disappointment) | 6 | 5 | 11 | 23 |
| S > I | 3 | 4 | 7 | 15 |
| S >> I | 1 | 2½ | 3½ | 7 |
| Total | 19 | 28 | 47* | (99) |

*One paper contributed to both the primary and the secondary column.

the performance of the innovation more quantitatively with the standard. For those primary therapies where survival gives a suitable measure of performance, we examine the distribution of the difference in survival percentages (I minus S). For the secondary therapies, we compare the percentages of patients not getting a specific complication such as abdominal infection or thrombosis. (Where we have used two complications in one study, each has been weighted one-half, as in Table 1.) If we merely take the observed differences, they are subject to variation over and above the true differences because of sampling error due to the finite samples used in the experiments. To adjust for these sampling errors, we use an empirical Bayes procedure, as described in the appendix. Efron and Morris (3) describe the general idea through an instructive sports example:

If we observed the batting averages for their first 50 times at bat for 200 major league batters, we might find them ranging from 0.080 to 0.450, yet we know that major league averages for a season ordinarily run from about 0.200 to 0.350 these days. The excess spread comes from the sampling error based on only 50 times at bat rather than the season's total experience. To adjust this, we can shrink the results toward the center of the distribution (roughly 0.275). How this is done is explained by Efron and Morris (3, 4) and more simply by them in (5); the explanation is given in detail for the present situation in (6).

After the shrinking is carried out, we can estimate the distribution of the true gains or losses associated with the innovation by methods discussed in the appendix and in (6). In Fig. 1, we give the estimated cumulative distribution for the true gains of secondary innovations. The graph suggests that about 80 percent of the innovations offer gains between $-10$ percent and $+30$ percent. In about 24 percent of the studies, gains of at least 20 percent occur. In about 10 percent of the studies, gains of more than 30 percent occur. About 12 percent of the time, losses of more than 10 percent occur. The sharp dip just to the right of zero improvement in Fig. 1 could, in a replication, move a few percent to the left or right of its present position. We have to emphasize that the cumulative is based essentially on a sample of 24 papers (not all secondary papers in Table 1 could be used here); but each paper is worth rather less than one whole observation of the difference because of the sample sizes in the investigations. If the sample sizes were infinite, we would not have the shrinking problem, and each paper would provide a full observation.

Gains or losses of modest size, such as 10 percent, while extremely valuable, are hard to detect on the basis of casual observation. We need careful experimentation and good records to identify such gains and losses. To get an idea of how hard it is to detect a difference of 10 percent, say that between 55 percent and 45 percent, it may help to know that two samples of size about 545 are required to be 95 percent sure of detecting the difference, by a one-sided test of significance at the 5 percent level. To be 50 percent sure requires samples of 136. Such large trials were rare in our samples.

### Nonrandomized Controlled Trials

In addition to the randomized clinical trials, 11 less well-controlled trials seemed appropriate for reporting. Results are shown in Table 2 in a manner similar to that used in the randomized trials. By and large, the distribution leans more favorably toward innovations than that seen in Table 1. A tendency for non-randomized trials to favor innovations is frequently noted. Although speculation is easy, the reasons for this are unclear. While in general a randomized trial provides stronger evidence than a corresponding nonrandomized trial, there are occasions where a nonrandomizing trial may be convincing. A nonrandomized study of abdominal stab wounds seems especially instructive because it provides strong evidence favoring a new policy. The hospital's standard policy had been to perform a laparotomy (surgical exploration of the abdominal cavity) on all patients with abdominal stab wounds. In

Table 2. Summary for controlled nonrandomized trials.

| Preference | Primary | Secondary | Total |
|---|---|---|---|
| I > > S | 2 | 3 | 5 |
| I > S | 1 | 1 | 2 |
| I = S (disappointment) | | 2 | 2 |
| S > I | | 1 | 1 |
| S > > I | | 1 | 1 |
| Total | 3 | 8 | 11 |

1967, the hospital instituted a change in policy, the results of which Nance and Cohn (7) report. The new policy demanded exploration only when the attending surgeon judged it necessary. (A patient might be observed for a period and then explored.)

The investigators give a record of (i) the substantial number of complications (25 percent) emerging from routine laparotomy when, in retrospect, the patient had not required surgical repair for the stab wound; (ii) the recovery without complications in the approximately 8 percent of patients who declined or otherwise passed by the former administrative rule of always performing a laparotomy; and (iii) evidence that delay before exploration under the old policy was not associated with an increase in the complication rate. These observations suggest that omitting the laparotomy for selected patients might be good practice.

Some might have said, on the basis of the data presented in (i), (ii), and (iii), that the proposed new policy of judgmental surgical decisions would be clearly preferable to routine laparotomy. Nevertheless, such inductive leaps have often failed in other attractive circumstances, sometimes because the new policy loses some advantages that the old one had, or falls prey to the fresh prob-

Table 3. Degree of control versus degree of investigator enthusiasm for portacaval shunt operation in 53 studies with at least ten patients. The table is revised from Grace, Muench, and Chalmers (8), table 2, p. 685 (©1966, Williams and Wilkins, Baltimore). Chalmers advised us of two additional studies to add to the well-controlled to moderate cell, raising the count from 1 to 3.

| Degree of control | Degree of enthusiasm | | | |
|---|---|---|---|---|
| | Marked | Moderate | None | Total |
| Well controlled | 0 | 3 | 3 | 6 |
| Poorly controlled | 10 | 3 | 2 | 15 |
| Uncontrolled | 24 | 7 | 1 | 32 |
| Total | 34 | 13 | 6 | 53 |

lems that may arise when any policy is totally changed. Changing from set policy to the regular use of judgmental surgical decisions plus keeping records provided an inexpensive type of quasi-experiment. The method has a grave weakness because the time period is not common to the differently treated groups; and, therefore, causes other than the change in treatment may produce at least part of the observed differences.

For the stab wounds, the need for a randomized clinical trial is not now compelling for the hospital partly because, in addition to the logic and data of (i), (ii), and (iii) above, the final quasi-experiment produced a large improvement. Although the percent requiring repair of the stab wound was about the same under the old and new policies (30 percent as compared to 28 percent), the overall complication rate dropped substantially from 27 to 12 percent. One fear would be that the unexplored group would produce a proportion of very severe complications. The evidence goes the other way. Among those not explored, the number without complications remained at zero even though the number not explored rose from 38 to 72 patients, and the percent explored fell from 92 to 40 percent. The average length of hospitalization over all patients dropped from 7.9 to 5.4 days. Had the effect been small, one might still be concerned whether possible biases and other changes could have given misleading results. All told, the evidence favoring the new policy seems persuasive for this hospital.

### Comparisons of Degrees of Control

Although randomized clinical trials are not the only strong form of evidence about therapies in humans, weakly controlled investigations may not give the same results as better controlled ones. Chalmers and his colleagues have compared (8, 9) views of many investigators who had make studies of a single therapy, with respect to the degree of control used in each investigation. We give the results of one example of such collections of investigations (8).

Table 3 shows the association between degree of enthusiasm and degree of control for the operation of portacaval shunt [slightly revised, by adding two cases, from Grace, Muench, and Chalmers (8)]. The counts in Table 3 are not of patients but of investigations. Table 3 shows that, among the 53 investigations, only six were classified as "well-controlled." Among the 34 associated with "marked enthusiasm," none were rated by the investigators as "well-controlled." The "poorly-controlled" and the "uncontrolled" investigations generated approximately the same distribution of enthusiasm: about 72 percent "marked," 21 percent "moderate," and 6 percent "none." The six "well-controlled" investigations split 50-50 between enthusiasm levels "moderate" and "none." Muench, who participated in collecting these data, has a set of statistical laws (10), one of which says essentially that nothing improves the performance of an innovation as much as the lack of controls. Because tables for other therapies have given similar results, one must be cautious in accepting results of weakly controlled investigations.

In Table 3, the rows for "poorly controlled" and "uncontrolled" studies suggest that repeated, weakly controlled trials are likely to agree and build up an illusion of strong evidence because of the large count of favorable studies.

Not only may this mislead us into adopting and maintaining an unproven therapy, but it may make proper studies more difficult to mount, as physicians become less and less inclined, for ethical reasons, to subject the issue to a carefully controlled trial lest the "benefits" of a seemingly proven useful therapy be withheld from some patients in the study.

## Strengths of Belief

A controlled trial of innovative therapy may sometimes impose a sacrifice on the part of some patients by withholding the more favorable of a pair of treatments. However, prior to the trial we do not know which is the favorable therapy. Only after the trial can the winner be identified. Some will say that the physician must have an initial guess, however ill-founded. It is unlikely that his view of the two competing treatments is exactly 50-50. The question then arises: If the physician fails to act on such a preference, is the patient getting responsible care? To help consider this question, let us review information obtained from experiments on incidental information.

Alpert and Raiffa (11) have performed a number of experiments on guessing behavior. Individuals were asked to estimate quantities about which they might have been expected to have some incidental information, such as the fraction of students in their class having a particular characteristic. Subjects were graduate students in the Faculty of Arts and Sciences and in the Graduate School of Business Administration at Harvard University. In addition to the basic estimate, the graduate students were asked to provide numbers below which various subjective probabilities would lie. If we think of the upper and lower 1 percent intervals as ones where a responder would be seriously surprised to find the true answer (that is to say, the responder felt 98 percent sure that the answer would lie between the chosen 1 percent and the 99 percent levels), then these responders were seriously surprised in 42.6 percent of the guesses or about 21 times as often as they should have been if the subjective estimates matched the true frequencies. Alpert and Raiffa's work (11) shows that experienced adults are likely to overrate the preciseness of their estimates. These people were too sure of their information. Although these people were not physicians in a patient relation, they were well educated and engaged in thoughtful work. Until we get contrary information from more relevant studies, such data suggest that strong initial preferences for therapies yet to be tested by controlled trials should be viewed with reserve. And, of course, the distribution shown in Fig. 1 and the results of Table 1 also show that, for therapies tested in trials, holding a view not far from 50-50 has some empirical foundation for surgery.

Shapiro (12) gives examples of wide variation among different physicians' estimates of probabilities in therapeutic situations, data pertinent to this discussion, but not the same as the Alpert-Raiffa point. Shapiro shows that physicians differ a great deal in their estimates; Alpert and Raiffa show that people are very frequently much further off than they expect to be.

## Do We Owe the Past or Future?

Let us consider the question of whether a present patient should give up something for future patients. We, or our insurance carriers, pay the monetary cost of our care. What we do not pay for is the contribution to the medical system by past patients. These patients, through their suffering and participation in studies, have contributed through their illness and treatments to the present state of evidence for all patients. Such contributions cannot be purchased by money but can be repaid in part by making, when appropriate, a contribution to the same system. One good way is through participation in well-designed clinical trials when the patient falls into the limbo of medical knowledge. Other nonmonetary ways are donating blood and organs. So one may feel an obligation to the system of medicine that has reached its present state without his or her assistance, and in addition each person has an interest in its general improvement as we next explain. [For a recent treatment of this point see Almy (13).]

In some circumstances, participation in the trial may turn out to be of help to the patient. Aside from the luck of getting the best therapy of several that are offered, this occurs, for example, when the patient has a disease for which treatments can be readily changed after the trial. Nevertheless, there are circumstances when the treatment is not reversible and when the chances are that the specific trial will be of little individual benefit—that is, when it has but slight chance of being a benefit to the patient, his family, or friends.

Under these circumstances, the patient may still be willing to participate in a trial. If the trial is recognized as part of a general system of trials in which patients participate only on such occasions as they qualify and when a trial seems necessary, then the patient may well benefit in the future not so much from the results of the particular trial he or she participates in but from the system that gives rise to it. Findings will come forward on many other diseases and the patient, or someone dear to him, will be likely to suffer from some of those diseases whose trials will have produced useful findings. It is not so much, then, the direct payoff of this present trial that we should have our eye on, but pooled benefits of the whole system. The longer the patient lives, the more likely it is that he or she will suffer from some other of the diseases being studied by careful trials. And insofar as they are not studied by careful trials, the appropriate conclusions may be slow in coming. By putting off the day when strong evidence is obtained, we reduce the patient's chances of benefiting most fully from modern medicine. Thus the patient has an interest not only in the trial he or she has the opportunity to engage in, but also a stake in a whole system that produces improved results that may well offer benefits in the future, if the patient survives the present difficulty. Thus, the social system will likely offer benefits through the larger system even when a particular component of the system may fail to pay off directly for a patient, his family, friends, or some other social group he belongs to.

A further statistical point that may not be much appreciated by potential participants in randomized trials is that the inferences apply primarily to the population sampled in the study. To the extent that individuals or groups decline to participate in studies, and to the extent that their responses may differ from those of the rest of the population (an interaction between participation and response to therapy), the treatments selected may not apply to them as well as to participants and people "like" them. For example, if those in the lower economic status were less likely to participate and if economic status related to the differential effectiveness of therapies, say, through additional lack of compliance, the study will not properly appreciate the value of the therapy for the nonparticipating group.

The lone individual may seem to have little incentive to participate because one seems so few among many. But the stake is not in any one person appearing in this study; it is in having people from segments of the population that represent that individual being properly represented in this and other studies so that the results of the whole system may be more assuredly applied to this patient when disease strikes. The idea is similar to that of being told not to complain of the system when one does not vote. But the extra feature here is that one gets to vote on certain special occasions, and then only a few are admitted to the booth, and so each opportunity to vote weighs much more heavily than usual.

If certain groups tend not to participate in the evaluative system, then they will not find medical evaluations of therapies as well pointed to their needs as if they did participate. Thus, each individual has a stake in wanting people like themselves represented. Since it is hard to say what "people like themselves" means, the good solution is to have the whole appropriate population volunteering in all the therapies tested. Participating presumably encourages others like me to participate too, and vice versa.

The main point of this discussion is that if participation seems to the patient to be a sacrifice, it should be noted that others are making similar sacrifices in aid of the patient's future illnesses. So even if the particular trial may not help the patient much, the whole system is being upgraded for his or her benefit. We have a special sort of statistical morality and exchange that needs appreciation.

### Responsibility for Research

Much of current popular discussion of the ethnical issue takes the position that physicians should use their best judg-

ment in prescribing for a patient. To what extent the physician is responsible for the quality of the judgment is not much discussed, except to say that he must keep abreast of the times. Some physicians will feel an obligation to find out that goes beyond the mere holding of an opinion. Such physicians will feel a responsibility to contribute to research. In similar fashion, some current patients may feel a responsibility to contribute to the better care of future patients. The current model of the passive patient and the active ongoing physician is not the most effective one for a society that not only wants cures rather than sympathy, but insists on them—a society that has been willing to pay both in patient cooperation and material resources for the necessary research.

### Quality of Life

In addition to a society willing to support medical research through responsible experimentation on human beings, in addition to physicians dedicated to acquiring knowledge on behalf of the sick, we must be certain that controlled trials are designed to seek answers to the appropriate questions. In our survey, we found most concern with near-term outcomes, both mortality and morbidity.

We need additional data about the quality of life of patients. Among our initial sample of 107 papers drawn through the MEDLARS search, quality of life seemed often to be a major consideration, although rarely did papers address more than a few features of that quality (14). Because much of medicine and surgery is intended to improve quality rather than to save life, measuring the improvement is important. As we have indicated above, different therapies frequently produce about the same mortality and morbidity, and so the ultimate quality of life achieved would bear heavily on the choice. Thus, for proper evaluation of alternatives, we need to assess the patient's residual symptoms, state of restored health, feeling of well-being, limitations, new or restored capabilities, and responses to these advantages or disadvantages.

For surgery, we need long-term follow-up and both objective and subjective appraisals of the patient's quality of life. Frequently, the long-term follow-up is carried out, but overall quality of life is rarely measured. For example, among 16 cancer papers in the initial sample of 107, follow-ups ranged from 2 months to 2 decades. With few exceptions, survival and recurrence data were the principal

information given, and because different treatments usually had similar rates, it would be fruitful to report contrasts among the treatments in the quality of life or death experienced by patients with the same disease but having different treatments. This might be especially appropriate because the therapies involved such features as castration, hormones, irradiation, chemotherapy, and various amounts of surgery. Developing and collecting suitable measures for quality of life after surgery requires leadership from surgeons and the cooperation of social scientists. We hope these developments will soon take place.

### Summary

Approximately half the surgical innovations tested by randomized clinical trials provide improvements. For those where reduction in percent of complications was a useful measure, we estimate that about 24 percent of the innovations gave at least a 20 percent reduction in complications. Unfortunately, about 12 percent of the innovations gave at least a 10 percent increase in complications.

Therefore, keeping gains and discarding losses requires careful trials. Gains of these magnitudes are important but are hard to recognize on the basis of incidental observations. When well-controlled trials have not been used, sometimes data have piled up in a direction contrary to that later found by well-controlled trials. This not only impedes progress but may make carefully controlled trials harder to organize. Most of the trials we studied did not have large sample groups. To dependably identify gains of the magnitude we found in the discussion on surgery and anesthesia, trials must be designed carefully with sufficient statistical power (large enough sample sizes) and appropriate controls, such as may be provided by randomization and blindness. As Rutstein (15) suggests:

It may be accepted as a maxim that a poorly or improperly designed study involving human subjects . . . is by definition unethical. Moreover, when a study is in itself scientifically invalid, all other ethical considerations become irrelevant. There is no point in obtaining "informed consent" to perform a useless study.

When we think of the costs of randomized trials, we may mistakenly compare these costs with those of basic research. A more relevant comparison is with the losses that will be sustained by a process that is more likely to choose a less desirable therapy and continue to administer it for years. The cost of trials is part of the development cost of therapy. Sometimes costs of trials are inflated by large factors by including the costs of the therapies that would in any case have been delivered rather than the marginal cost of the management of the trial. This mistake is especially likely to be made when a trial is embedded in a large national program, and this is also the place where trials are highly valuable because their findings can be extended to a whole program.

Surgical treatment frequently trades short-term risk and discomfort for an improved longer term quality of life. While long-term follow-up is frequently reported, a vigorous effort is needed to develop suitable measures of quality of life.

Table 1 gives empirical evidence that, when surgical trials are carried out, the preferable treatments are not known in advance. Although a common situation in a trial would be that the innovation was expected to be a clear winner, the outcome is in grave doubt. Empirical evidence from nonmedical fields suggests that educated "guesses" even by experienced, intelligent adults are way off about half the time. For these reasons we discount the pretrial expectations or hunches of physicians and other investigators.

Most innovations in surgery and anesthesia, when subjected to careful trial, show gains or losses close to zero when compared with standards, and the occasional marked gains are almost offset by clear losses. The experimental group is neither much better nor much worse off than the control group in most trials, and we have little basis for selecting between them prior to the trial.

The one sure loser in this system is a society whose patients and physicians fail to submit new therapies to careful, unbiased trial and thus fail to exploit the compounding effect over time of the systematic retention of gains and the avoidance of losses. Let us recall that our whole financial industry is based on a continuing return of a few percentage points.

All in all, the record in surgery and anesthesia is encouraging. We regard a finding of 50 percent or more successes for innovations in surgical and anesthetic experiments as a substantial gain and a clear opportunity for additional future gains. Well-conducted randomized clinical trials are being done. All of us, as po-

tential patients, can be grateful for a system in which new therapeutic ideas are subjected to careful systematic evaluation.

## Appendix

*Estimating the distribution of gains.* The model of the process is that of two-stage sampling. We regard the innovation and its paired standard as drawn from a population of pairs of competing therapies. Let $Z$ be the random variable corresponding to the improvement offered by the innovation (innovation minus standard), with mean $M$ and variance $A$. For the $i$th innovation with true gain $Z_i$, the experiment assesses the gain as $W_i$, and $W_i$ has mean $Z_i$ and variance $D_i$.

If we assume as an approximation that the distributions of $Z_i$ and $W_i$ are normal, then the posterior distribution of $Z_i$ has mean

$$Z_i^* = M^* + e_i(W_i - M^*)$$

where

$$e_i = A^*/(A^* + D_i)$$

$A^*$ is an estimate of $A$, and $M^*$ is an estimate of $M$. The posterior distribution of $Z_i$ is approximately normal with mean $Z_i^*$ and variance $(1 - B_i)W_i$, where

$$B_i = D_i/(A^* + D_i)$$

In the current problem the $D$'s are estimated from binomial theory because the $W$'s are the difference between two independent observed proportions. Details of obtaining $A^*$ and $M^*$ are given in (6).

To estimate the cumulative distribution of $Z$, we compute for each observation $W_i$

$$c_i = \frac{z - Z_i^*}{(1 - B_i)D_i}$$

then using normal theory we compute

$$\Phi(c_i) = P(X < c_i)$$

where $X$ is a standard normal random variable. Thus

$$\Phi(c_i) = [1/\sqrt{2\pi}\,] \int_{-\infty}^{c_i} \exp(-\tfrac{1}{2}x^2)\,dx$$

Finally

$$\sum_{i=1}^{k} \Phi(c_i)/k$$

estimates $P(Z < z)$ for each value of $z$. We thus release ourselves from the origi-

nal normal approximation for $Z$ and get a new distribution that is not normal but should be an improved approximation of the true distribution. When weights were used because one study gave two comparisons they modified both the estimation of $A$ and $W$ and the estimation of $P(Z < z)$.

### References and Notes

1. For a discussion of MEDLARS, see M. Day, *Fed. Proc. Fed. Am. Soc. Exp. Biol.* 33, 1717 (1974). Indexing is done by specially trained abstractors at the National Library of Medicine. The MEDLARS contents vary over time as additions are made to correct omissions. Our initial search turned up 36 randomized clinical trials. These are listed in (6), appendix 9–1, pp. 145–154. A repeat search, approximately 18 months later, done according to the same search instructions, revealed 13 additional randomized clinical trials as follows: R. B. Noone, P. Randall, S. E. Stool, R. Hamilton, R. A. Winchester, *Cleft Palate J.* 10, 23 (1973); R. Smith, *Trans. Ophthalmol. Soc. Aust.* 27, 17 (1968); B. Brehmer and P. O. Madsen, *J. Urol.* 108, 719 (1972); J. E. Rothermel, J. B. Wessinger, F. E. Stinchfield, *Arch. Surg.* 106, 135 (1973); R. K. Laros, G. I. Zatuchni, G. J. Andros, *Obstet. Gynecol.* 41, 397 (1973); W. H. Harris, E. W. Salzman, R. W. DeSanctis, R. D. Coutts, *J. Am. Med. Assoc.* 220, 1319 (1972); J. W. Roddick, Jr., and R. H. Greenelaw, *Am. J. Obstet. Gynecol.* 109, 754 (1971); I. L. Rosenberg, N. G. Graham, F. T. DeDombal, J. C. Goligher, *Br. J. Surg.* 58, 266 (1971); R. Brisman, L. C. Parks, J. A. Haller, Jr., *Ann. Surg.* 174, 137 (1971); J. M. Lambie, D. C. Barber, D. P. Dhall, N. A. Matheson, *Br. Med. J.* 2, 144 (1970); D. B. Haverstadt and G. W. Leadbetter, Jr., *J. Urol.* 100, 297 (1968); J. A. Haller, Jr., *et al.*, *Ann Surg.* 177, 595 (1973); D. J. Pinto, *East Afr. Med. J.* 49, 643 (1972).
2. A. B. Miller, W. Fox, R. Tall, *Lancet* 1969-II, 501 (1969).
3. B. Efron and C. Morris, *J. Am. Stat. Assoc.* 68, 117 (1973).
4. ———, *J. R. Stat. Soc. B* 35, 379 (1973).
5. ———, *Sci. Am.* 236, (No. 5) 119 (1977).
6. J. P. Gilbert, B. McPeek, F. Mosteller, in *Costs, Risks, and Benefits of Surgery*, J. P. Bunker, B. A. Barnes, F. Mosteller, Eds. (Oxford Univ. Press, New York, 1977), chap. 9, pp. 124–169. For formulas see pp. 156–161.
7. F. C. Nance and I. Cohn, Jr., *Ann. Surg.* 170, 569 (1969).
8. N. D. Grace, H. Muench, T. C. Chalmers, *Gastroenterology* 50, 684 (1966).
9. T. C. Chalmers, J. B. Block, S. Lee, *N. Engl. J. Med.* 287, 75 (1972).
10. J. E. Bearman, R. B. Loewenson, W. H. Gullen, "Muench's postulates, laws, and corollaries," *Biometrics Note 4* (National Eye Institute, Bethesda, Md. 1974).
11. M. Alpert and H. Raiffa, "A progress report on the training of probability assessors," unpublished paper, Harvard University (28 August 1969).
12. A. R. Shapiro, *N. Engl. J. Med.* 296, 1509 (1977).
13. T. P. Almy, *ibid.* 297, 165 (1977).
14. B. McPeek, J. P. Gilbert, F. Mosteller, in *Costs, Risks and Benefits of Surgery*, J. P. Bunker, B. A. Barnes, F. Mosteller, Eds. (Oxford Univ. Press, New York, 1977), chap. 10, pp. 170–175. The results of the initial sample of 107 are reported in (6). Of these, 36 were randomized and 34 could be used, 11 were nonrandomized controlled trials, 59 were series (study of one therapy). Our additional sample added 13 randomized trials for use in Table 1. Chapter 10 discusses quality of life.
15. D. Rutstein, *Daedalus* 98, 523 (1969).
16. This work was facilitated by NIH grant Gm 15904 to Harvard University, by the Miller Institute for Basic Research in Science, University of California, Berkeley, and by NSF grant SOC75-15702 A01. We appreciate the advice and assistance of A. Bigelow, M. Ettling, M. Gasko-Green, D. Hoaglin, V. Miké, A. Perunak, K. Soper, J. W. Tukey, and G. Wong.

# PART IV
# INCOME MAINTENANCE

Since 1964 there have been many attempts to decrease the number of Americans living in poverty. Many approaches were used, some stressing income supplements to the poor, others in-kind transfers, and others educational and vocational experiences for both adults and children. It is fair to say that the optimism which characterized the launching of President Johnson's "War on Poverty" has now waned, and that the stubbornness of the forces inducing poverty are now even more salient than they were previously.

The articles presented in this section deal with evaluations of current and prospective national programs designed to reduce poverty and to lower the cost of current attempts to alleviate its impact. The first paper is excerpted from a chapter by Lynn, and it details the global impact of the "War on Poverty." In a sense, therefore, it is less a program evaluation than the evaluation of a policy toward whose objectives many programs were directed. Lynn's verdict is interesting in that he finds both absolute and relative poverty diminished since 1964, though a new class of permanently poor persons may have been created whose needs cannot be met by present efforts designed to secure jobs.

The second paper is excerpted from a report by Goodwin that presents his own synthesis of the results and implications of both quantitative and qualitative evaluations of the Work Incentive Program (WIN). WIN is a program that originally stressed education and training for the jobless poor, but now puts more emphasis on direct job placement. Goodwin concludes that the evaluations show that poor persons do not differ significantly from others in their willingness to work but that WIN is not having much of an impact on job placement, largely because jobs for heads of households are not available.

The remaining papers from which we have taken excerpts are concerned with the four experimental tests of how a guaranteed minimum income affects participation in the labor force. The fear has been expressed that guaranteeing an income will decrease individuals' motivation to work, thereby seriously affecting the nature of the U.S. workforce and perhaps increasing the demand for social services that the guaranteed income is meant to decrease. The experiments reported here tested how various kinds of negative income tax influenced labor force participation among men and women with different characteristics: (a) those who were working but poor (the New Jersey study conducted by the Institute for Research on Poverty and Mathematica, Ind.); (b) those who lived in rural settings (the Rural Experiment conducted by the same contractors); and (c) those who were predominantly nonworking and female (the Gary Study conducted by the University of Indiana at Gary). The final study, conducted in Denver and Seattle by Stanford Research Institute with the help of the states of Colorado and Washington, was more comprehensive than the others, and had 5,000 respondents from one- and two-parent families who were black, white, or Hispanic.

The four reports are important from an evaluation perspective because they illustrate the use of several overlapping experiments to derive estimates of the magnitude of impact of a planned structural reform in the welfare system. The studies deserve close readings to learn how similar the results were, how much the designers of one experiment learned from their predecessors, how reasonably any differences between labor force results from each study could have been interpreted, and how comprehensive a picture of responses to a guaranteed income the studies present.

# 22

# A Decade of Policy Developments in the Income Maintenance System

## Laurence E. Lynn, Jr.

Summary: The Income-Maintenance System in 1974

Since 1935, the federal income-maintenance system has experienced virtually continuous evolution. The principal sources of this evolution have been, first, the pressures of program constituencies, including the program's congressional sponsors, for expansion and modification; second, the discovery or emergence of needs or problems that existing programs failed to meet; and, third, political competition: the search by both political parties and by individual legislators and committee or subcommittee chairmen for winning issues.

The outcome has been heavily influenced by the organization of the bureaucratic and political processes by which programs are initiated, designed, authorized, and financed. Because federal, state, and local agencies, congressional committees, and private interest groups are divided into numerous entities concerned with specific substantive or professional interests, the resulting programs are also fragmented. As the Joint Economic Committee's 1974 Report on its public welfare study pointed out, "11 committees of the House of Representatives, 10 of the Senate, and 9 executive departments or agencies have jurisdiction over the broad set of income security programs."[67] The term income-maintenance "system" is merely a handy euphemism.

Moreover, as the earlier description of program developments suggests, each component of the system moves more or less on its own trajectory. Programs differ in terms of the coalition of interest supporting them, the value contexts in which they are reviewed and modified, the frequency with which they are reviewed, the methods of financing, the competence of the administering agency, and the political stakes in continuing or changing

[66]See following section on housing allowances.

[67]U.S., Congress, Joint Economic Committee, *Report of the Public Welfare Study*, p. 1.

From Laurence E. Lynn, Jr., "A Decade of Policy Developments in the Income-Maintenance System." Pp. 55-117 in Robert H. Haveman (ed.), A Decade of Federal Antipoverty Programs: Achievements, Failures, and Lessons. Copyright 1977 by the Regents of the University of Wisconsin System on behalf of the Institute for Research on Poverty and reprinted by permission of Academic Press.

program objectives or design. Thus, they develop and change in different ways.

The process has been well summarized in the Joint Economic Committee's *Study of Public Welfare*: "In general, an incremental approach has been followed, but it is no longer possible—if, indeed, it ever was—to provide a convincing rationale for the programs as they exist in terms of who is covered and who is excluded, benefit amounts, and eligibility conditions. No coherent rationale binds them together as a system. Additionally, the programs are extraordinarily complex, and the eligibility conditions and entitlement provisions lack uniformity even among programs with similar objectives and structures. Public retirement programs, for example, differ widely in their generosity to covered workers. And, a number of income security programs reach the same part of the population but have been developed separately without apparent consistency of objectives, operational features, and equity."[68]

The product of these political and bureaucratic processes is summarized in Table 3.1. This table shows federal outlays and approximate numbers of beneficiaries for the various components of the income-maintenance system, together with total social welfare expenditures, for FY 1965, FY 1969, and FY 1974.[69]

Several interesting developments are summarized in Table 3.1: From FY 1965 through FY 1974, a period during which total social welfare expenditures by the federal government as measured by the Social Security Administration rose from 5.8 percent to 10.3 percent of gross national product, federal income-maintenance expenditures as defined in this paper grew from $27.7 billion to $102.1 billion annually. Most programs experienced significant growth in the number of beneficiaries. Thus, at the end of the period a much larger amount of income assistance was reaching much larger numbers of people.

Despite the incremental and nonsystematic nature of program developments, federal income-maintenance outlays were a virtually constant proportion, 73–74 percent of total federal social welfare outlays—which also includes programs such as compensatory education, community health services, and manpower training—especially if day care expenditures are considered.[70] Though this proportion dipped slightly during the Johnson years and rose again during the Nixon years, the variation is not notable. In other words, outlays for income assistance and human services were apparently growing at similar rates.

[68]U.S., Congress, Joint Economic Committee, *Studies in Public Welfare*, Paper No. 2, *Handbook of Public Income Transfer Programs*, 93rd Congress, 2d sess. (Washington, D.C.: U.S. Government Printing Office, 1972), p. 1.

[69]FY 1969 is chosen to permit comparative assessments of developments during the Johnson and Nixon presidencies.

[70]Federal social welfare expenditures accounted for nearly 60 percent of total social welfare expenditures—federal, state, and local—throughout the period.

TABLE 3.1
Federal Income-Maintenance and Social Welfare Programs: FY 1965, FY 1969, and FY 1974 Benefit Outlays and Numbers of Recipients

| Program, by type | Benefit outlays (in millions of dollars) | | | Recipients (in thousands) | | |
|---|---|---|---|---|---|---|
| | FY 1965 | FY 1969 | FY 1974 | FY 1965 | FY 1969 | FY 1974 |
| CASH ASSISTANCE | | | | | | |
| Social insurance | | | | | | |
| Old Age benefits | 15,226 | 17,317 | 34,600 | n/a | 16,300 | 19,100 |
| Survivors' benefits | | 6,415 | 13,200 | n/a | 6,000 | 7,200 |
| Disability benefits | 1,392 | 2,443 | 6,200 | n/a | 2,300 | 3,600 |
| Total OASDI | 16,618 | 26,175 | 54,000 | 20,870 | 24,600 | 29,900 |
| Unemployment insurance | 2,166[i] | 2,128[i] | 5,365[r] | 4,813[a] | 4,212[a] | 6,363[a] |
| Black Lung benefits | * | * | 975 | * | * | 503 |
| Railroad retirement | 1,118 | 1,536 | 2,670 | 911 | 971 | 994 |
| Total insurance | 19,902 | 29,959 | 63,010 | | | |
| Public assistance | | | | | | |
| AFDC | 959 | 1,704 | 4,009 | 4,323 | 6,076 | 10,845 |
| Old Age Assistance | 1,314 | 1,124 | * | 2,158 | 2,023 | |
| Aid to the Blind | 47 | 52 | * | 96 | 80 | |
| APTD | 292 | 417 | * | 530 | 710 | |
| Supplemental Security Income (SSI) | | | 1,839 | | | 3,600 |
| Total public assistance | 2,712 | 3,297 | 5,848 | | | |
| Veterans' benefits | | | | | | |
| Pensions | 1,740 | 2,167 | 2,569 | 2,039 | 2,236 | 2,310 |
| Compensation | 2,176 | 2,681 | 4,045 | 2,360 | 2,681 | 3,991 |
| Total veterans' benefits | 3,916 | 4,848 | 6,614 | | | |
| Total cash assistance | 26,530 | 38,104 | 75,472 | | | |

(Continued)

**TABLE 3.1** (*Continued*)

| Program, by type | Benefit outlays (in millions of dollars) | | | Recipients (in thousands) | | |
|---|---|---|---|---|---|---|
| | FY 1965 | FY 1969 | FY 1974 | FY 1965 | FY 1969 | FY 1974 |
| **IN-KIND ASSISTANCE** | | | | | | |
| *Food* | | | | | | |
| Food stamps | 36 | 251 | 2,865 | 633 | 3,224 | 13,536 |
| Food commodities | 213[j] | 272[j] | 281[j] | 2,238[b] | 2,544[b] | 233[b] |
| School lunch program | 130[a] | 162[a] | 412[a] | 17,024 | 20,100 | 23,800 |
| School breakfast program | * | 4 | 61 | * | 205 | 1,357 |
| Special milk program | 99 | 102 | 62 | 70[k] | 99[k] | 91[k] |
| Special assistance | * | 10 | 683 | * | 1,300 | 9,000 |
| Nonschool food[o] | * | 3 | 70 | * | 312 | 1,766 |
| Meals for the elderly | * | * | 200 | * | * | 20[f] |
| *Education[n]* | | | | | | |
| Basic grants | * | 146 | 51[g] | * | 281 | 220 |
| Supplementary grants | * | * | 204[g] | * | * | 304 |
| College work-study | 55 | 143 | 260[g] | 320[p] | 385 | 560 |
| NDEA loans | 100[c] | 186 | 417[g] | 317[c] | 429 | 674 |
| Insured loans | * | 60 | 382[g] | * | 787 | 938 |
| *Housing* | | | | | | |
| Low-rent public housing[q] | 236 | 352 | 1,207 | 30[l] | 35[l] | 1,109[l] |
| Homeowners' assistance (Section 235) | * | 1 | 401 | * | 4[l] | 419[l] |
| Rental housing assistance (Section 236) | * | * | 519 | * | * | 294[l] |
| Rent supplements | * | 5 | 249 | * | 13[d] | 148[l] |
| Direct rural loans | 132 | 9 | * | 16 | 7[m] | * |
| Insured rural loans | 1 | 498 | 1,779 | — | 48[m] | 106[l] |
| *Health* | | | | | | |
| Medicare, hospital insurance | * | 4,654 | 7,806 | * | 4,400 | 5,300 |

| | | | | | |
|---|---|---|---|---|---|
| Medicare, supplemental medical insurance | * | 1,645 | 2,874 | * | 9,000 | 11,600 |
| Medicaid | 296[h] | 2,275 | 5,833 | 1,294[c] | 9,500 | 24,279 |
| *Total in-kind assistance* | 1,198 | 10,821 | 26,616 | | | |
| *Total income maintenance* | 27,728 | 48,925 | 102,088 | | | |
| *Total social welfare* | 37,712[e] | 68,355[e] | 139,580[e] | | | |

*Source:* Robert Plotnick and Felicity Skidmore, *Progress Against Poverty* (New York: Academic Press, 1975), Table 6.9.

*Program did not exist.

[a]U.S. Department of Labor, Bureau of Employment Security, *Bulletin*, 1971; and U.S. Social Security Administration, *Social Security Bulletin*, July 1974. Figures given are total number of first recipients. Average weekly number of recipients were: FY 1965—1,327,000; FY 1969—1,101,000; FY 1974—1,965,000.

[b]Program Review and Analysis Office, U.S. Department of Agriculture, Division of Child Nutrition and Development.

[c]U.S. Department of Health, Education, and Welfare, Boston Office.

[d]U.S. Department of Housing and Urban Development.

[e]U.S. Social Security Administration, *Social Security Bulletin*, Social Welfare Series, various issues.

[f]Average number of meals per day.

[g]Includes all outlays under the School Nutrition program.

[h]Outlays under Title XIX of the Social Security Act. Total health care payments, including vendor medical payments under public assistance programs, were $555 million.

[i]Includes payments under (but not federal) temporary extended unemployment insurance provisions.

[j]Combined total of Section 6 Commodity Procurement and Surplus Commodity Distribution.

[k]Number of participating outlets.

[l]Number of housing units.

[m]Number of loans.

[n]An additional $618 million in payments to college students for FY 1974 is included under Social Security survivor benefits.

[o]Total of combined year-round and summer programs.

[p]Number of participating outlets.

[q]Excludes operating subsidies for LHA-owned projects.

[r]Data exclude state payments under temporary programs.

[s]Awards to students from federal funds (Office of Planning and Evaluation, U.S. Department of HEW).

[t]Less than 1000.

Only one new national social insurance or public assistance program was enacted: the Black Lung program, which serves a specific constituency. No new general assistance programs were enacted for people not well covered by existing programs—couples without children, new entrants to the labor force who are unemployed, single able-bodied adults who have exhausted unemployment benefits, families with children headed by an able-bodied male. The only major reform to occur was the substitution of the federally administered SSI program for the state-run OAA, AB, and APTD programs. Some significant structural changes occurred, however, including automatic cost-of-living adjustments in the OASDI program, extensions of unemployment insurance benefits,[71] and the reduced marginal tax rate on the earnings of the AFDC families.

Reflecting the general preference in Congress for enacting specific consumption subsidies, the major area of structural growth and diversification in the income-maintenance system was in-kind programs. A significant number of new programs were enacted: rent supplements, food stamps, higher education grants and subsidized loans, Medicare and Medicaid, and nutrition programs for the elderly. Within total federal social welfare outlays, however, the proportion accounted for by in-kind assistance rose sharply from 3 percent to nearly 20 percent. At the end of the decade, in-kind assistance accounted for 26 percent of income-maintenance outlays, as compared to 4 percent at the beginning. By 1974, expenditures on these programs amounted to $26.7 billion (plus $1.5 to $2.0 billion for day care), a 22-fold growth from FY 1965.

Ten years produced a much larger, more complex income-maintenance system transferring more resources to more people for diverse and often conflicting reasons. The question is, What, in fact, did these developments do for the poor?

## EVALUATING THE RESULTS

### The Effectiveness of Cash Transfer Programs

Is there less poverty now than in 1964? The answer is yes, using the indicator most widely used at the beginning of the decade: the proportion of the population with annual money incomes below the poverty level. This level is defined by the Social Security Administration as an amount equivalent to

---

[71] Also, by the end of 1974, the public services employment program was becoming a more important provider of income security for the temporarily unemployed. For background on public employment programs and an analysis of their role during the recent recession, see Mark Worthington, "Public Employment Programs," in *The Cyclical Behavior of Income Transfer Programs: A Case Study of the Current Recession*, Technical Analysis Paper No. 7, Office of Income Security Policy (Washington, D.C., Department of Health, Education, and Welfare, October 1975), pp. 103–122.

approximately three times the cost of a nutritionally adequate diet.[72] As Table 3.2 shows, whereas nearly 20 percent of the population were poor in 1964, only about 11.1 percent were poor in 1973. Moreover, the absolute number of people below the poverty threshold is smaller now than in 1964.

Improvements in the income-maintenance system played an important role in reducing the incidence of poverty during this period. The top portion of Table 3.3 shows that 44 percent of pretransfer poor households were taken out of poverty by cash transfer programs in 1972 as compared to only 33 percent in 1965. These programs reduced the official poverty gap by 64 percent in 1972, compared to a reduction of 53 percent in 1965.

There are wide variations in the antipoverty effectiveness of different cash transfer programs, however. Table 3.4 shows that Social Security benefits kept 32.3 percent of pretransfer poor families out of poverty in 1972, up from 23.3 percent in 1965. Thus Social Security accounts for two-thirds of the pretransfer poor families taken out of poverty by cash transfer programs. Needs-tested public assistance programs accounted for only 5.5 percent of the families lifted from poverty by cash transfers in 1972, given the existence of Social Security benefits. This proportion can be assumed to be somewhat higher now because of the Supplemental Security Income program, which raised average benefits for the adult categories of the needy starting in 1974.

If poverty is measured in relation to the standard of living enjoyed by the rest of the population rather than in absolute terms, however, the picture concerning poverty reduction appears different. The official poverty level of income is adjusted each year for increases in the cost of living but not for increases in the standard of living. Because of the uninterrupted growth that has taken place in per capita real income and per capita consumption, those who remain poor by the "official" definition are, in fact, falling farther behind the average standard of living enjoyed by the rest of the population.

As Table 3.5 shows, there has been only slight improvement in the share of money income received by the poorest fifth of the population in the last 10 years. The lowest 20 percent of American families received 5.2 percent of aggregate income in 1964, 5.4 percent in 1972. Viewing this conclusion in a different way, if poverty is defined as a level of money income that is less than one-half the median income, there has been virtually no change in poverty in the last decade.[73]

Estimates of improvements in the antipoverty effectiveness of cash transfer programs in relative terms mirror these data. The bottom portion of Table 3.3 shows that the proportion of pretransfer poor taken out of poverty in relative

[72]Molly Orshansky, "Counting the Poor: Another Look at the Poverty Profile," *Social Security Bulletin* 28 (1965): 3–29; and U.S. Bureau of the Census, *Current Population Reports*, Series P-23, No. 28, "Revision of Poverty Statistics, 1959 to 1968."

[73]Based upon the similar analysis by Robert Plotnick in Robert D. Plotnick and Felicity Skidmore, *Progress Against Poverty: A Review of the 1964–1974 Decade* (New York: Academic Press, 1975).

TABLE 3.2    Persons with Incomes below the Poverty Level, 1964-1973

| | 1964 | 1965 | 1966 | 1967 | 1968 | 1969 | 1970 | 1971 | 1972 | 1973 |
|---|---|---|---|---|---|---|---|---|---|---|
| Persons below poverty-level income (in thousands) | 36,055 | 33,185 | 28,510 | 27,769 | 25,389 | 24,147 | 25,420 | 25,559 | 24,460 | 22,973 |
| Percentage of total population | 19.0 | 17.3 | 14.7 | 14.2 | 12.8 | 12.1 | 12.6 | 12.5 | 11.9 | 11.1 |
| Poverty gap (in millions of current dollars)[a] | $11,000[b] | n/a | n/a | n/a | 9,800 | 10,100 | 11,447 | 12,034 | 12,032 | 11,975 |
| Poverty gap (in millions of 1973 dollars)[a] | n/a | n/a | n/a | n/a | $12,584 | 12,431 | 13,236 | 13,204 | 12,778 | 11,975 |

Source: U.S. Department of Commerce, Current Population Reports, Series P-60, No. 98, January 1975, Table 1.
[a]The poverty gap is defined as the difference between total income actually earned by the poor and their total income had each poor family and individual received income at the poverty threshold level.
[b]Economic Report of the President, 1964, p. 77.

TABLE 3.3    The Effect of Cash Transfers on the Poverty Population and Gap, 1965-1972 (in 1972 dollars)

| | Pretransfer poor households (in thousands) | Total pretransfer income gap (in millions of dollars) | Posttransfer poor (in thousands) | pretransfer poor taken out of poverty (in percentages) | Total posttransfer income gap (in millions of dollars) | Fall in income gap (in percentages) |
|---|---|---|---|---|---|---|
| *In absolute terms* | | | | | | |
| 1965 | 15,609 | 29,349 | 10,488 | 33 | 13,796 | 53 |
| 1968 | 14,933 | 28,590* | 9,750 | 35 | 12,235 | 57 |
| 1970 | 16,231 | 31,327 | 10,265 | 37 | 12,383 | 60 |
| 1972 | 17,640 | 34,294 | 9,958 | 44 | 12,484 | 64 |
| *In relative terms* | | | | | | |
| 1965 | 15,609 | 29,349 | 10,488 | 33 | 13,796 | 53 |
| 1968 | 15,738 | 32,259 | 10,913 | 31 | 14,850 | 54 |
| 1970 | 17,471 | 37,439 | 12,045 | 31 | 16,599 | 56 |
| 1972 | 19,557 | 44,689 | 12,898 | 34 | 19,265 | 57 |

Source: Robert Plotnick and Felicity Skidmore, Progress Against Poverty: A Review of the 1964-1974 Decade (New York: Academic Press, 1975), Table 6.1.

TABLE 3.4
Pretransfer Poor Households Kept out of Poverty by Cash Transfer Programs, 1965–1972
(in percentages)

|      | Social Security | Public assistance | Unemployment insurance | Veterans' benefits |
| ---- | --------------- | ----------------- | ---------------------- | ------------------ |
| 1965 | 23.3            | 2.9               | 0.9                    | 3.7                |
| 1968 | 26.0            | 4.1               | 0.4                    | 3.4                |
| 1970 | 26.7            | 5.0               | 0.8                    | 3.6                |
| 1972 | 32.3            | 5.5               | 1.1                    | 3.3                |

Source: Calculated from Robert Plotnick and Felicity Skidmore, *Progress Against Poverty* (New York: Academic Press, 1975), Table 6.5.

terms by cash transfers remained virtually unchanged, at approximately one-third between 1965 and 1972.

One recent study concluded on the basis of such evidence, "If poverty is defined as a relative state—deprivation of a level of living enjoyed by others—then no progress has been made in alleviating poverty in the United States in recent decades."[74]

## Correcting the Official Results

The official data on which such conclusions are based, however, understate the extent of both absolute and relative poverty reduction in recent years. For one thing, income is systematically underreported by the low-income population. For example, only three-fourths of the cash transfers known to be paid out by government are reported as income by the recipients.[75] Further, official data are reported in terms of "families" and "unrelated individuals," obscuring the extent to which there is income sharing or pooling by household units composed of more than one family or unrelated individual.

The most important shortcoming in the data, however, is that they exlude income in-kind. Indeed, no regular information is collected about the distribution of income in-kind by income class, though this form of income assistance is, as Table 3.1 showed, the fastest growing component of the income-maintenance system. Throughout the 1970s, the amount of transfers in-kind has exceeded the poverty gap estimates shown in Table 3.2, recently by very large amounts.

It is incorrect to conclude that poverty in an absolute sense, much less a relative sense, has been eliminated if in-kind assistance is taken into account. Not all of this aid goes to the poor. Recent analysis of FY 1972 federal programs suggests that the proportions going to the pretransfer poor range

[74]Benjamin A. Okner and Alice M. Rivlin, "Income Distribution Policy in the United States," processed, The Brookings Institution, Washington, D.C. (November 1974), p. 10.

[75]Ibid., p. 20.

**TABLE 3.5**
**Share of Aggregate Income Received by Families and Unrelated Individuals 1964–1972 (in percentages)**

| | 1964 | 1965 | 1966 | 1967 | 1968 | 1969 | 1970 | 1971 | 1972 |
|---|---|---|---|---|---|---|---|---|---|
| *Families* | | | | | | | | | |
| Lowest fifth | 5.2 | 5.3 | 5.4 | 5.4 | 5.7 | 5.6 | 5.5 | 5.5 | 5.4 |
| Second fifth | 12.0 | 12.1 | 12.4 | 12.2 | 12.4 | 12.3 | 12.0 | 11.9 | 11.9 |
| Middle fifth | 17.7 | 17.7 | 17.7 | 17.5 | 17.7 | 17.6 | 17.4 | 17.4 | 17.5 |
| Fourth fifth | 24.0 | 23.7 | 23.8 | 23.7 | 23.7 | 23.5 | 23.5 | 23.7 | 23.9 |
| Highest fifth | 41.1 | 41.3 | 40.7 | 41.2 | 40.6 | 41.0 | 41.6 | 41.6 | 41.4 |
| *Unrelated individuals* | | | | | | | | | |
| Lowest fifth | 2.4 | 2.6 | 2.9 | 3.0 | 3.2 | 3.2 | 3.3 | 3.4 | 3.3 |
| Second fifth | 7.1 | 7.6 | 7.6 | 7.5 | 7.8 | 7.8 | 7.9 | 8.1 | 8.2 |
| Middle fifth | 12.8 | 13.5 | 13.3 | 13.3 | 13.8 | 13.8 | 13.8 | 13.9 | 13.8 |
| Fourth fifth | 24.5 | 25.1 | 24.2 | 24.4 | 24.4 | 24.3 | 24.5 | 24.2 | 23.9 |
| Highest fifth | 53.1 | 51.2 | 52.0 | 51.8 | 50.8 | 51.0 | 50.5 | 50.4 | 50.9 |

*Source:* U.S. Bureau of the Census, *Current Population Reports*, Series P-60, various issues.

from 94 percent for surplus food commodities, 85 percent for food stamps, and about 75 percent for public housing, rent supplements, and Medicaid, to around 50 percent for Medicare and student aid programs, and to 25 percent for Section 235 and 236 housing assistance.[76] Further, the amount of in-kind aid may overstate its cash value to many recipients; if free to do so, they might well prefer to exchange their in-kind entitlement for a smaller amount of cash to purchase other desired goods or services. In other words, the cash value of the payments to such recipients exceeds the real value of the benefit.

However, the effects of considering all of these shortcomings in the official data on the size and rate of reduction in the poverty gap can be quite dramatic. Table 3.6, based on Timothy Smeeding's work, shows that the revised poverty gap was less than one-half of the official gap in 1972 if income in-kind, income misreporting, and redefinition of the accounting unit are taken into account. The table also shows that the overstatement of the poverty gap by the census procedures has increased sharply as income-maintenance benefits and, in particular, in-kind benefits, have grown in recent years.

Equivalent revised data are not available for relative income measurements. However, Table 3.7 summarizes a Brookings Institution analysis of the effect on 1973 income distribution of allocating in-kind benefits by income class. Because more than one-half of transfers in-kind—which include food, health, housing, higher education, and child care programs—were attributed in this analysis to those with 1973 incomes under $5000, their share of money income plus income in-kind was raised from 4.1 to 5.9 percent. The positive effect on the relative income share of the poor attributable to income in-kind can be assumed to have increased over the last 10 years as the importance of in-kind programs has increased.

Thus, a complete accounting for the income received by poor households—both cash and in-kind—during the past decade would show that income poverty in both absolute and relative terms has been steadily reduced, a development obscured by official poverty statistics.

Morton Paglin's recent critique of standard methods for assessing changes in the income distribution leads to the same conclusion.[77] He notes that even in an egalitarian economy, family incomes will be unequal at any point in time because families are at different points in their life cycles; both older and younger families can be expected to have relatively lower incomes. By defining perfect equality at any point in time as equal incomes for all families at the same stage of their life cycle, not equal incomes between different age groups, Paglin shows that "a considerable reduction of net inequality and a marked improvement in the share of the lowest quartile" occurred between

[76]Timothy Smeeding, "Measuring the Economic Welfare of Low Income Households, and the Anti-Poverty Effectiveness of Cash and Non-Cash Transfer Programs" (Ph.D. Dissertation, University of Wisconsin–Madison, 1975).

[77]Morton Paglin, "The Measurement and Trend of Inequality: A Basic Revision," *American Economic Review* 65 (September 1975): 598–609.

TABLE 3.6

The Census Poverty Gaps: Official and Revised (in millions of 1972 dollars)

|  | 1968 | 1970 | 1972 |
|---|---|---|---|
| Official census gap | 11,845 | 12,461 | 12,032 |
| Gap revised for income misreporting and misspecification of reporting unit | 9,590 | 9,917 | 8,893 |
| Gap revised for income in-kind | 8,330 | 8,184 | 5,353 |
| Revised gap as percentage of official gap | 70.3% | 65.7% | 44.5% |

Source: Timothy Smeeding, "Measuring the Economic Welfare of Low-Income Households, and the Anti-Poverty Effectiveness of Cash and Non-Cash Transfer Programs," (Ph.D. dissertation, University of Wisconsin–Madison, 1975).

TABLE 3.7

Distribution of Family Income before and after Income In-Kind, 1973 (in percentages)

| Income class | Money income | Income in-kind | Money income plus income in-kind |
|---|---|---|---|
| Under $5,000 | 4.1 | 55.3 | 5.9 |
| $5,000–$9,999 | 16.0 | 30.1 | 16.5 |
| $10,000–$14,999 | 25.3 | 8.8 | 24.8 |
| $15,000–$24,999 | 33.9 | 5.9 | 32.9 |
| $25,000–over | 20.7 | 0 | 19.9 |
| Total | 100.0 | 100.0 | 100.0 |

Source: Benjamin A. Okner and Alice M. Rivlin, "Income Distribution Policy in the United States," processed (The Brookings Institution, Washington, D.C., November 1974), Table 6.

1947 and 1972. Including income in-kind, he notes, would make the egalitarian trend even more marked. "[To] a large degree, the low percentage of the income pie going to [the poorest 20 percent] is a built-in result of the age-income profile coupled with the age distribution of the population, and is not purely related to the condition of a permanent class of people excluded from the average level of real income enjoyed by most families."[78]

## Transfers and Social Change

Income-maintenance programs might have had even more apparent success were it not for several potentially offsetting developments.[79]

First, the distribution of male earnings is becoming more unequal. A 1972 study of changes in the distribution of income earned by males before taxes

[78]Ibid., p. 606.
[79]Okner and Rivlin, "Income Distribution Policy," pp. 20–21.

between 1958 and 1970 concluded that "there has been a slow but persistent trend toward inequality in the distribution of earnings and in the distribution of wages and salaries. The trend is evident not only for the work force as a whole, but also for many occupational and industrial groups. If the effect of fringe benefits could have been included in the calculations, the trend would undoubtedly have been even more pronounced."[80] There are several explanations for this development: the increased number of part-time workers, an influx of young people into the labor force, and increases in highly paid occupations and their rates of pay. Whatever the reason, this trend cannot help but exacerbate the difficulties of achieving a more egalitarian income distribution.

Second, transfer payments may be inducing a kind of work withdrawal, especially among older workers. As Benjamin Okner and Alice Rivlin note, "In 1950, 46 percent of all men aged 65 and older were in the labor force; by 1960 the percentage had dropped to 33 percent and by 1972 to 24 percent. Thus much of the effect of the retirement programs has apparently been to replace the earnings of older workers with transfer payments without affecting their position in the income distribution."[81]

Third, data compiled by Okner and Rivlin show that "the proportion of people who are either family heads or primary individuals has increased markedly for both sexes and at all age levels."[82] Part of this increased household formation may be caused by increased transfer income, which permits people to live apart from their relatives. Whatever the reason, the increased rate of household formation may in part have offset the equalizing effects of transfer payments.

## Who Are the Poor Now?

During the past decade, economic growth and rising employment have benefited mainly the poor with work experience and job-related skills. In addition, the increased effectiveness of antipoverty programs has been unequal among different segments of the poverty population. The aged and the disabled have benefited the most from increased transfer payments, and households headed by a female of working age have benefited least.[83] Table 3.8 presents selected data concerning the effects of cash transfers in reducing poverty among different age–sex groups. Poverty reduction among the elderly, among white households, and among families with no or few children has been much more effective than for nonwhite, working age households with several children, especially families with a female head. Though inclu-

[80]Peter Henle, "Exploring the Distribution of Earned Income," *Monthly Labor Review* 95 (December 1972): 25.

[81]Okner and Rivlin, "Income Distribution Policy," pp. 20–21.

[82]Ibid., pp. 21–22.

[83]Barth, Carcagno, and Palmer, *Toward an Effective Income Support System*, Table 4, p. 25, and Table 7, p. 29. Plotnick and Skidmore, *Progress Against Poverty*, Tables 6.4 and 6.5.

TABLE 3.8
Poverty Reduction among Pretransfer Poor Due to Cash Transfers, by Age–Sex Group, Race and Sex of Household Head, and Family Size, 1965 and 1972 (in percentages)

| | Families | | | | | Race–sex of household head | | | | | Family size | | | |
|---|---|---|---|---|---|---|---|---|---|---|---|---|---|---|
| | All families | Male head 65 and older | Female head 65 and older | Male head under 65 | Female head under 65 | All households | White male | White female | Non-white male | Non-white female | 1 | 3 | 5 | 7+ |
| 1965 | 37 | 67 | 41 | 17 | 22 | 33 | 43 | 31 | 15 | 11 | 28 | 35 | 16 | 9 |
| 1972 | 47 | 79 | 63 | 30 | 25 | 44 | 55 | 41 | 30 | 19 | 39 | 40 | 26 | 15 |

Source: Robert Plotnick and Felicity Skidmore, Progress Against Poverty (New York: Academic Press, 1975), Table 6.9.

sion of in-kind income would narrow these differentials somewhat, it would not change the basic pattern.

As a result of these developments, the low-income population is becoming less and less similar to the population as a whole. For example:

Poverty reduction has been more successful for those with a strong attachment to the labor force.[84] In 1959, two-thirds of the heads of poor families had worked at least part of the time; the proportion has fallen to just over half in 1972. More than 31 percent of poor family heads had worked full time in 1959; in 1972, less than 20 percent had. Moreover, only 2 percent of nonworking family heads reported as a reason the inability to find work. "Thus," the Council of Economic Advisers concluded in 1974, "the vast majority of the poor who do not work seem to be in a situation where work is not a feasible alternative."[85]

Non-aged persons in families with female heads, and female unrelated individuals, were increasing both as a proportion of the poor population and in absolute terms between 1966 and 1973. Poverty among the aged and among male and male-headed families was dropping both absolutely and proportionately. "Among families with female head, 33 percent were classified as in poverty in 1972, compared to 6 percent for male-headed families. Among black female-headed families the proportion was 53 percent."[86]

In 1972, 31 percent of low-income families with a male head had three or more children, compared to 17 percent for nonpoor families. Only 22 percent of the wives in male-headed poor families worked in 1972 compared to 48 percent of wives in nonpoor families.

The implications of these data for public policy are sobering. Those who remained poor in the early 1970s were increasingly those for whom it has been most difficult to design and implement effective social programs.

The difficulty of designing and implementing effective antipoverty programs for the poor population is further underscored by the results of the Panel Study of Income Dynamics conducted by the University of Michigan Institute for Social Research.[87] Of the number of persons officially reported as poor by the Census Bureau, only 20–30 percent had incomes below the poverty level in all six years covered by the study. On the other hand, about 25 percent of the total population were below the poverty threshold in at least one of the six years, twice as many as were poor in any one year.[88] Thus, the number of *chronically poor* is significantly smaller than the official statistics imply, but the number of people who *experience poverty* is significantly larger.

---

[84]Okner and Rivlin, "Income Distribution Policy," p. 8: *Economic Report of the President*, 1974, pp. 162–163.

[85]*Economic Report of the President, 1974*, p. 163.

[86]Ibid., p. 165.

[87]For a useful summary of the study's findings, see U.S. Department of Health, Education, and Welfare, *The Changing Economic Status of 5000 American Families, Highlights from the Panel Study of Income Dynamics*, May 1974 (hereafter referred to as *The Panel Study*).

[88]Ibid., pp. ii–iii.

The main reasons for these changes in economic status are changes in the composition of the family and in the participation of family members in the labor force. Rather large changes in household income may result. While some of these changes could be considered as controllable by the household members, others were affected by external factors or even random events, and not all of the controllable changes—for example, separation and divorce—were related to economic considerations.[89]

Thus, though the level of poverty is related to age, race, sex of family head, and number of children, the determinants of who is poor at any one time are considerably more complex. Many of them are effectively beyond the reach of public policy.

## Is the War on Poverty Being Won?

During the first half of the past decade, a comparison of the rate of poverty reduction with unemployment statistics suggests that the increasingly tight labor markets during the period 1964–1968 removed many of the working poor from poverty. Since then, despite higher unemployment, the accelerated growth of income transfers, especially transfers in-kind, has insured continued reduction of the poverty gap and the poverty population. By the end of the period, well over 80 percent of pretransfer poor family units (including unrelated individuals) were receiving some kind of income assistance. There seems to be light at the end of the tunnel.

However, given that social welfare expenditures grew from $37 billion in FY 1965 to nearly $140 billion in FY 1974, compared to a 1964 poverty gap estimated at $11 billion, and given that the elimination of poverty has been a widely accepted national goal for a decade, it is reasonable to ask why poverty continues to exist at all. It certainly is not because the nation cannot afford to eliminate it. If increased annual outlays of little more than $5 billion could lead to a credible claim that income poverty has been eliminated, why not simply increase them and win the war?

### The Target Inefficiency of Transfer Programs

The answer is that income-maintenance policy has never aimed squarely at the target of eliminating poverty. At its inception, the war on poverty was not to be New Deal style of relief. It was to be a war on the causes of poverty. "Conquest of poverty is well within our power," the Council of Economic Advisers noted in 1964. "The majority of the Nation could simply tax themselves enough to provide the necessary income supplements to their less fortunate citizens. . . . But this 'solution' would leave untouched most of the roots of poverty. Americans want to *earn* the American standard of living by their own efforts and contributions."[90]

---

[89]Ibid., pp. vii–viii.
[90]*Economic Report of the President, 1964*, p. 77. Italics in original.

The emphasis throughout the Johnson years was on the variety of programs administered by OEO, on increased outlays for education and manpower training programs, and on other investments in human capital. In his last State of the Union Message, in January 1969, President Johnson stated that "the key to success [in breaking the back of poverty] is jobs. It is work for people who want to work." His only specific reference to antipoverty programs in this message was to the greatly increased outlays for manpower programs that had taken place.

Neither has Congress taken careful aim at the target of eliminating poverty. Instead, Congress has demonstrated a strong preference for aid to deserving vulnerable groups, not all of whom are poor—the elderly, the retired worker, the disabled, the temporarily unemployed, children—or aid to provide for specific and justifiable consumption needs—food, higher education, medical care, housing. In the case of in-kind assistance, a key factor underlying congressional support is often the interest of provider groups: suppliers of food commodities, builders, banks, colleges, and universities. Congress has steadily resisted aiding people simply because their incomes were low. The primary remedy for low income was to be work, not public charity, for the able-bodied poor.

Moreover, within its favored program categories, Congress has resisted or has retreated from measures that strongly favor the poor. Congressional resistance to income redistribution carefully targeted on the poor has become evident during the past decade and, perhaps ironically, especially during the past five years of the Nixon administration. The desirability of tightening eligibility and more carefully targeting resources on the poor was raised by the administration in a large number of income support or related programs—food stamps, the school lunch and special school milk programs, higher education student aid, social services, and rent supplements. In virtually every instance, Congress either liberalized the proposed new standards of eligibility or refused to approve standards that would have targeted federal assistance more directly on the poor.

There are several explanations for this behavior: the political difficulty, once a "need" is recognized, of restricting free or low-cost benefits to just poor people; middle-class resentment of excessive favoritism shown to the welfare population; the preference for broader eligibility by the program bureaucracies which, quite understandably, feel and look more successful if they are not limited to dealing with the most stubborn problems; the fact that the special interest groups supporting programs that benefit poor people represent broader constituencies.

The result is that the poor have been especially vulnerable to being whipsawed in the budget process. In the face of tight budgets, the administration will propose a more careful targeting of funds on the poor through devices such as fee schedules or more stringent income and assets tests. The inevitable protests from those who face reduced benefits and from provider groups cause Congress to compromise by retaining more liberal eligibility standards but limiting appropriations, leaving it to program administrators to ration the limited supply of appropriated resources without discriminating on the basis of income or assets.

The overall result of presidential and congressional efforts to shape income-maintenance programs is a high degree of "target inefficiency" as far as eliminating poverty is concerned. For example: Only 40 percent of federal cash transfer payments in 1972 went to the poor.[91] Only 16 percent of OASDI recipients, 24 percent of disability insurance beneficiaries, and 17 percent of Medicare recipients were in poverty in 1973.[92] Indeed, less than 75 percent of public assistance recipients were classified as poor.

OEO calculations showed that a total of $25.5 billion was spent on persons with low income in 1971 through both income-maintenance programs and human investment programs.[93] In contrast, total federal outlays on social welfare programs as estimated by the Social Security Administration amounted to $92.5 billion in 1971. The share going to the poor—slightly more than 25 percent—was strikingly stable from 1966 through 1971.[94]

In a recent study of unemployment compensation, Martin Feldstein shows that "15 percent of benefits in 1970 went to the 18 percent of families with incomes over $20,000. Only 17 percent of benefits went to families with incomes under $5,000." In general, "middle and upper income families receive most of the unemployment compensation."[95]

Thus, only a relatively small fraction of additional outlays on existing income-maintenance programs actually reaches the poor.

## Taxes and Redistribution

Nor does the federal tax system accomplish significant redistribution toward the poor. The combined effect of individual income and payroll taxes leaves the pretax and pretransfer distribution of income virtually unchanged.[96] The effects of progressivity in the individual income tax is offset, among other things, by the regressivity of the payroll tax used to finance social insurance benefits.[97] In 1974, the combined employer–employee payroll tax rate was 11.7 percent on the first $13,200 of annual earnings.

[91]Fried et al., *Setting National Priorities: The 1974 Budget*, Tables 3–5, p. 50.

[92]*Economic Report of the President, 1974*, p. 168.

[93]U.S. Department of Commerce, *Statistical Abstract of the United States, 1972*, p. 335.

[94]The different concepts of target efficiency should be noted. The extent of a program's target efficiency will depend on whether the target group is the pretransfer poor, the posttransfer, or, as has been suggested by Irwin Garfinkel and Robert Haveman, "Earnings Capacity and the Target Efficiency of Alternative Transfer Programs," *American Economic Review* 64 (May 1964): 196–204. Figures in the text are with respect to the posttransfer poor.

[95]Martin Feldstein, "Unemployment Compensation: Adverse Incentives and Distributional Anomalies," *National Tax Journal* 27 (June 1974): 237.

[96]Fried et al., *Setting National Priorities: The 1974 Budget*, pp. 49–50.

[97]For a good recent discussion of payroll tax issues, see Benjamin A. Okner, "The Social Security Payroll Tax: Some Alternatives for Reform," prepared for the Meetings of the American Finance Association, December 1974, and sources cited therein.

Thus, as earnings rise above $13,200, the payroll tax becomes a smaller proportion of earnings. The regressivity of the tax is compounded by the fact that earnings are a smaller proportion of income at higher levels of income. Moreover, there is serious horizontal inequity in the tax. Two-worker families pay more in payroll taxes than single-worker families with the same income.

Though Congress has eliminated or reduced individual income tax payments for low-income households in the last few years, it has simultaneously increased revenues from the relatively regressive payroll taxes both in absolute terms and as a proportion of total federal revenues. The net effect of these measures, even when account is taken of the distribution of the Social Security benefits they finance, is certainly not a pronounced redistribution of income in favor of the poor.

In summary, significant progress has been made in reducing poverty. The policymaking process that produces it, however, is probably more concerned with how it is reduced than with whether it is reduced. If a powerful special interest other than the poor supports the program, so much the better. Because several goals and constituencies are served simultaneously, it may take federal outlays of three or four dollars to produce a dollar of increased income to the poor. In view of the increasing number of competing demands for budgetary resources, further progress in reducing poverty through the existing income-maintenance system may be slower than it has been. The actual result, however, will depend on how the current agenda of issues with respect to poverty policy is resolved.


## DOES POVERTY HAVE A FUTURE?

The war on poverty began with a new President looking for a dramatic issue, some new data on the nature and causes of poverty in America, a set of existing programs providing cash, in-kind assistance, and services to the poor, and a relatively simple and appealing idea: Poverty in America could be ended if a determined attack were made on its causes.

Experience with the social interventions of the 1960s has taught "a new realism concerning social commitments."[98] The causes of poverty are more elusive than was realized, and public policies and programs to deal with them are less effective than had been hoped. Moreover, as growth in the complexity of the income-maintenance system convincingly demonstrates, centrifugal forces dominate policymaking, making the alleviation of poverty time-consuming and expensive.

On the other hand, a concern for the poor has become a permanent item on the nation's agenda. Ever larger amounts of resources are being channeled to the poor and near-poor through expanded income-maintenance and human services programs, and income poverty, in absolute and relative terms, is

[98]Lance Liebman, "Social Intervention in a Democracy," *The Public Interest*, No. 34 (Winter 1974): 29.

being reduced. New knowledge is being accumulated concerning who is poor and where the poor live, who moves into and out of poverty and why, the effects of different types of cash transfer systems on work behavior, and the costs and consequences of different policies and programs for dealing with poverty and poor people. Policy debates continue.

In short, the issue of poverty in America is still very much alive. The question is, What should be done now?

### The Side Effects of Success

Even though significant progress in alleviating poverty has been made through changes in the income-maintenance system, a set of new or exacerbated problems and issues has been created in the process.

The income-maintenance system was fragmented and complex at the beginning of the decade. It is more so now.[99] Once reason is that there are more individual programs. Another is that each program is more complex; not only may the law be complicated, the implementing regulations can be as thick as telephone books. It all adds up to fertile ground for inconsistencies, confusion, overlaps and gaps, unintended consequences, and countless issues that must be addressed somehow by a decisionmaking process that is already overloaded.

These problems of complexity have been documented and discussed in several recent studies.[100] For example, one analysis noted "the enormous inconsistencies in the primary elements of the existing transfer programs: the period for which income is counted in determining the transfer (the accounting period), who or what family group is the eligible party (the filing unit), the rate at which the benefits are reduced as income rises (the tax rate), and the definition of what income shall be counted. The four most important income-tested programs—SSI, AFDC, food stamps, and Medicaid—are inconsistent in all these dimensions. If one adds to this the fact that some beneficiaries of these programs are also taxpayers in the positive tax scheme (with its own inconsistencies), the problem is compounded."[101]

[99]Perhaps the only time when it was remotely appropriate to talk of an income-maintenance system was in the late 1930s, when there was unemployment insurance for the temporarily unemployed, old age insurance for the retired worker, and public assistance, which would wither away as old age insurance matured, all enacted in a single piece of legislation and all predicated on a simple idea: The causes of low income are the temporary unavailability of jobs and the physical inability to work.

[100]For example, see Barth, Carcagno, and Palmer, *Toward an Effective Income Support System*; Henry J. Aaron, *Why Is Welfare So Hard to Reform?* (Washington, D.C.: The Brookings Institution, 1973); Plotnick and Skidmore, *Progress against Poverty*; U.S., Congress, Joint Economic Committee, *Studies in Public Welfare*, a series of papers published in 1972–1975 and summarized in *Report of the Public Welfare Study*; and Barry M. Blechman, Edward M. Gramlich, and Robert W. Hartman, *Setting National Priorities: The 1975 Budget* (Washington, D.C.: The Brookings Institution, 1974), pp. 182–206.

[101]Barth, Carcagno, and Palmer, *Toward an Effective Income Support System*, p. 161.

The most detailed of the recent studies, that of the Subcommittee on Fiscal Policy of the Joint Economic Committee, included among its findings the following:[102]

*Work Incentives.* Because many families with children receive benefits from several programs—AFDC, food stamps, school lunches, Medicaid, housing assistance—they can receive benefit levels as high, for example, as $5900 in New York without working, and they can have total benefits reduced by 85 cents or more for each additional dollar of earned income.[103] In general, the study found, "working welfare mothers, on the average, could expect a net gain of only 20 to 36 cents per wage dollar if they were enrolled in the food stamp program (4–11 cents less if in public housing); and AFDC-UF fathers, if in the food stamp program, could expect a net gain of 33 cents per wage dollar."[104]

High benefit levels coupled with high implicit marginal tax rates on earned income act as a severe disincentive to work, the opposite of the result intended by the congressional architects of these welfare programs. For example, the University of Michigan Panel Study of Income Dynamics found a definite negative correlation between AFDC benefit levels and the work rates of women raising children alone.[105]

*Family Size and Stability.* In some cities and states, female-headed families receive more generous benefits than male-headed families; families headed by a male working full time for low wages can be worse off than a family headed by a woman with the same earnings; families with children receive more generous benefits than families without them; and men losing insured employment are treated less favorably than men losing uninsured employment. Such circumstances create incentives for fathers to desert their families or for women to choose against remarrying or have more children in order to increase family benefits.

The *Public Welfare Study* found that higher welfare payments are associated with a rising proportion of already broken families setting up separate households in order to receive welfare and a rising proportion of mothers raising children alone.[106] The study also found that for a single woman, having a baby would boost cash, food, and housing benefits by 57 percent and would bring eligibility for Medicaid as well. A couple headed by an unemployed man could expect to increase family income by 52 percent by having a child.

[102]U.S., Congress, Joint Economic Committee, *Studies in Public Welfare*, Paper No. 1 by R. Storey, "Public Income Transfer Programs: The Incidence of Multiple Benefits and the Issues Raised by Their Receipt" (Washington, D.C.: U.S. Government Printing Office, 1972).

[103]In some instances, extra earnings can actually lead to a reduction of family disposable income. See Barth, Carcagno, and Palmer, *Toward an Effective Income Support System*, p. 35.

[104]*Report of the Public Welfare Study*, p. 77.

[105]Ibid., pp. 77–78.

[106]Marjorie Honig, "The Impact of Welfare Payment Levels on Family Stability," *Studies in Public Welfare*, Paper No. 12 (Part I), "The Family, Poverty, and Welfare Programs: Factors Influencing Family Instability (Washington, D.C.: U.S. Government Printing Office, 1974), p. 37.

*Horizontal Equity.* Families with the same income and other characteristics receive different benefits depending on where they live. For example, a family with total benefits of $5900 in New York City could qualify for only half that amount in Atlanta. There are extreme variations from state to state in Medicaid benefits; per capita monthly Medicaid payments to the poverty population in 1973 ranged from over $100 in New York to less than $10 in the bottom 16 states.[107]

*Program Efficiency.* Because numerous income-tested programs exist side by side with a variety of non-income-tested programs, benefit increases in some programs will not be reflected in higher incomes for low-income beneficiaries.[108] For example:

- Increases in the OASI minimum benefit will be offset, at least partially, for some beneficiaries by reductions in Old Age Assistance benefits or in veterans' pensions. On the other hand, the increase will be received by some beneficiaries who also receive public or private pension income or veterans' cash benefits.

- Across-the-board increases in OASI benefits will not be received by beneficiaries of income-tested programs unless special "pass through" provisions are made. "Cases have been reported in which social security benefit increases led to losses not only of program benefits such as Old Age Assistance, Medicaid and food stamps, but also of special local advantages for the aged poor such as free garbage collection and property tax credits."

These types of problems are worse if account is taken of the variety of services and training programs for which welfare recipients are eligible. There is considerable inequity in the distribution of benefits from these programs and in the treatment of such questions as the definition of work-related expenses to be disregarded in computing program benefits. Problems of horizontal equity and perverse incentives are exacerbated if the combined effects of cash transfer and related service programs are considered.

There is another consequence of complexity and fragmentation worth noting. The greater the number of "parameters"—programs, eligibility criteria, regulations, administering agencies—in the system, the greater the number of issues to be resolved. Such issues are an increasing burden on the time of executive branch officials and of congressional committees and staffs. Inevitably, therefore, many apparently esoteric issues—for example, the filing unit, the accounting period, cost-sharing formulae, and assets and earnings tests—are left for lower-level staff experts to "work out," or are dealt with in regulations, or are decided without full awareness of their implications. Yet many of these issues can have effects on costs, eligibility, administrability, and equity far greater than the effects of more visible decisions relating to benefit levels and marginal tax rates. Further, there are

---

[107]*Report of the Public Welfare Study,* pp. 54, 56.
[108]*Studies in Public Welfare,* Paper No. 1, p. 21.

strong tendencies among congressional committees to tinker with the programs as problems arise. Often, however, such changes are made without full knowledge of their consequences or of their effects on the performance of the system as a whole.

The cumulative effects of handling complexity in a haphazard way or of turning it over to nonaccountable experts, aside from tangible ones relating to costs and benefits, can cause considerable erosion in public understanding of and confidence in the programs.

## Welfare Reform Yesterday and Today

An income-maintenance system that is highly inefficient, that is plagued with the types of problems documented in the *Public Welfare Study*, and yet does not eliminate poverty, might seem ripe for reform. However, a comprehensive overhaul of the system seemed far from the top of the nation's agenda after a decade of antipoverty efforts. In apparent contrast to 1964, when President Johnson declared war on poverty, and 1969, when President Nixon called for a fundamental change in the nation's approach to poverty, sentiment among public officials and many experts in 1974 was not particularly sympathetic to a new national debate over reforming the welfare system. Instead, "patching up" the present system in an incremental way seemed to many to be the better course of action. There were two main reasons for this general slackening of enthusiasm for welfare reform.

The first is the overall progress that has been made in reducing poverty through both increased income-maintenance outlays and improvements in the programs. The enactment of the SSI program, Medicare and Medicaid, the availability of food stamps to the working poor, and greatly increased Social Security benefits, for example, make the plight of the poor seem less urgent than before. "The growth of income support programs in recent years has made the case for welfare reform less compelling than it was five years ago," a Brookings Institution publication concluded in reviewing the President's FY 1975 budget proposal.[109]

The second is the discouraging record achieved by the advocates of major system overhaul. Even with forceful presidential support, policy initiatives that (a) call for the replacement of existing programs with new programs and approaches to social problems, (b) depend for their success on conscious coordination across different congressional and executive branch jurisdictions, or (c) primarily benefit a politically weak or unpopular constituency, stand a poor chance of success. Welfare reform—even a minimal form of it, the replacement of the AFDC program with a comprehensive program of cash assistance for the non-aged, able-bodied poor and coordination of the benefits and tax rates for different cash and in-kind programs—has all three strikes against it.

[109]Blechman, Gramlich, and Hartman. *Setting National Priorities: The 1975 Budget*, p. 182. See also Barth, Carcagno, and Palmer. *Toward an Effective Income Support System*, pp. 151–152.

The reception accorded President Nixon's Family Assistance Plan (FAP), as well as the recent controversy over the idea of housing allowances, are worth reviewing for the lessons they teach concerning the obstacles facing comprehensive reform.

## The Family Assistance Plan

In an 8 August 1969 speech, President Nixon proposed "a fundamental change in the nation's approach to one of its most pressing problems." The nation faces, he said,

> an urban crisis, a social crisis—and at the same time, a crisis of confidence in the capacity of government to do its job. . . . A third of a century of centralizing power and responsibility in Washington has produced a bureaucratic monstrosity, cumbersome, unresponsive, and ineffective. . . . Nowhere has the failure of government been more tragically apparent than in its efforts to help the poor, and especially in its system of public welfare.

He proposed reform of the adult categories of public welfare, but AFDC would be done away with altogether. "I propose that the federal government build a foundation under the income of every American family with dependent children that cannot care for itself—wherever in America that family may live." The foundation payment would be $1600 a year for a family of four. The first $60 per month of earnings would be disregarded in computing the family's benefit. Beyond that, a 50 percent marginal tax rate would apply. For the first time, therefore,

> The government would recognize that it has not less of an obligation to the working poor than to the non-working poor; and for the first time, benefits would be scaled in such a way that it would always pay to work. . . . But what of the others, those who can work but choose not to? The answer is very simple. Under this proposal, everyone who accepts benefits must also accept work or training provided suitable jobs are available, either locally or at some distance if transportation is available. The only exceptions would be those unable to work and mothers of pre-school children. Even mothers of pre-school children, however, would have the opportunity to work—because I am also proposing along with this a major expansion of day care centers to make it possible for mothers to take jobs by which they can support themselves and their children.[110]

In significant respects, the Family Assistance Plan was a legacy of President Johnson's war on poverty, a point worth noting.[111] As early as 1965, OEO's Office of Research, Plans, Programs, and Evaluation was sponsoring negative income tax approaches to the welfare dilemma. The momentum behind solving the problems of income deficiency was definitely building

[110]Nixon noted that "for the single adult who is not handicapped or aged, or for the married couple without children, the new system would not apply."

[111]For more detailed discussion of the origins of FAP, see Vincent J. Burke and Vee Burke, *Nixon's Good Deed* (New York: Columbia University Press, 1974); Daniel P. Moynihan, *The Politics of a Guaranteed Income* (New York: Random House, 1973); Walter Williams, *The Struggle for a Negative Income Tax: A Case Study 1965–1970*, Public Policy Monograph No. 1, Institute of Governmental Research, University of Washington, 1972.

throughout the Johnson years. Aside from OEO efforts inside the government, outside support for some type of guaranteed income was growing.

For example, a relatively new journal at that time, *The Public Interest*, sponsored a discussion of the desirability of a guaranteed annual minimum income in 1966. Professor James Tobin offered a concise statement of the problem; public assistance programs, he argued, were both inadequate and geared to need in a manner that provides perverse incentives to those dependent upon it. "Our governments administer a bewildering variety of welfare and social insurance programs. . . . *Yet half of the poor benefit from none of these; and most of the public money spent to supplement personal income goes to families above the poverty line.*"[112] Moreover, he pointed out, "Too often a father can provide for his children only by leaving both them and their mother."[113]

His sponsorship of a negative income tax[114] as a superior alternative to the existing programs drew a rejoinder from Alvin L. Schorr,[115] OEO's Deputy Director for Research, who pointed out difficulties with a negative income tax and argued instead for strengthening existing programs and adding to them a program of children's allowances. To most experts, however, reform seemed preferable to incrementalist tinkering, and by the end of 1968, a wide variety of guaranteed income and welfare reform schemes were being advocated by various authors and organizations.

President Johnson, though not embracing the cause of welfare reform, contributed to the developing momentum by promising, at the signing of the controversial 1967 Social Security amendments, that he would appoint a Commission on Income Maintenance with a broad charter to examine every aspect of our public welfare and income-maintenance programs and to propose necessary reforms. Though its report was published after Nixon announced his welfare reform proposals, the commission's views favoring a negative-income-tax approach to welfare reform began receiving publicity well before Nixon's August 1969 speech, and the papers prepared by the commission's staff were available to the designers of FAP.

The fate of FAP has become an often-told tale. To make a long story short, though approved twice by the House of Representatives, the Family Assistance Plan never passed the Senate, despite an epic struggle between the administration and the Senate Finance Committee. For one thing, extending welfare to the working poor provoked fears among conservatives of reduced work effort by the poor. More generally as Henry Aaron has noted, "Much of the controversy about the welfare system and welfare recipients [rested] on unresolvable ethical and philosophical differences, and some of it on persis-

---

[112]James Tobin, "The Case for an Income Guarantee," *The Public Interest*, No. 4 (Summer 1966): 33. Italics in original.

[113]Ibid., p. 34. He also criticized the 100 percent marginal tax rate on earnings.

[114]An idea for which Milton Friedman is generally regarded as the first sponsor.

[115]Alvin L. Schorr, "Against a Negative Income Tax," *The Public Interest*, No. 5 (Fall 1966): 110–117.

tent if unconscious racial prejudice."[116] By 1972, the Nixon administration itself had fallen into disarray over the issues of whether and how to bring about welfare reform.

However, President Nixon apparently did not give up on trying to reform the structure of public assistance for families. At his direction, HEW continued to develop welfare reform proposals during 1973 and 1974. The results of those efforts convinced HEW Secretary Caspar Weinberger, a relatively conservative Republican who had been director of OMB when FAP was defeated, that "patching up" the existing system was not a viable option. It would not cure extreme differences in benefits among people with the same needs, complex and unintelligible rules, inefficient targeting of benefits, disproportionately large bureaucracies, intrusions into the recipient's personal affairs, and severe work disincentives.[117] Weinberger supported, and urged President Gerald Ford to support, a welfare reform proposal akin to the Family Assistance Plan and based on a negative income tax.

As of late 1975 however, President Ford was uncommitted to welfare reform and was apparently still curious as to whether patching up the existing program would suffice.

## Housing Allowances

On 5 January 1973, in a move that provoked a storm of controversy, President Nixon halted all new commitments for the income-related housing assistance programs and for low-rent public housing construction. His message to Congress on 19 September 1973 announcing the administration's new housing plan made it clear that he favored an altogether different approach to assisting low-income families obtain housing. Though concerned with only one part of the income-maintenance system, the Nixon initiative constituted another attempt to promote serious thought about system reform.[118]

"Since 1937," Nixon said, "the federal government has tried to help low-income families by providing housing for them. Over the years, nearly $90 billion of the taxpayers' money has been spent or committed for public housing projects and other subsidized housing programs."

But the results had been dismal. "All across America, the federal government has become the biggest slumlord in history."

"But the quality of federally assisted housing is by no means the only problem. Our present approach is also highly inequitable. Rather than treating those in equal circumstances equally, it arbitrarily selects only a few low-income families to live in federally supported housing, while ignoring

---

[116]Aaron, *Shelter and Subsidies*, p. 1.

[117]*National Journal*, Vol. 6, No. 47, 23 November 1974, p. 1772.

[118]President Nixon had proposed major reforms in housing programs in 1970 that would have allowed public housing occupants to buy their homes, as individuals or as members of tenants organizations, and that would have lowered the rental payments of many public housing tenants to 20 percent of the first $3500 of income and 25 percent of income above that level. The bill, which also proposed drastic program consolidations, never cleared the legislative committees.

others. Moreover, the few often get a *new* home, while many other families—including those who pay the taxes to support these programs—must make do with inferior older housing. And since recipients often lose their eligibility for public housing when they exceed a certain income level, the present approach can actually reward dependence and discourage self-reliance."

His proposed solution suddenly brought a relatively unsung policy idea, the housing allowance, to the forefront.

"Our best information to date indicates that direct cash assistance will in the long run be the most equitable, least expensive approach to achieving our goal of a decent home for all Americans. . . ." Moreover, he went on, "the relationship between housing programs and welfare payments is particularly critical. We must carefully consider the ways in which our housing programs will relate to other programs which assist low income persons."

This housing message made it clear that President Nixon's concept for dealing with poverty was in a fundamental way the opposite of President Johnson's. "Instead of treating the root cause of the problem—the inability to pay for housing—the government has been attacking the symptom. We have been helping the building industry [substitute the welfare agency, the college, the hospital, the farm commodity producer] directly and the poor only indirectly, rather than providing assistance directly to low-income families."

His endorsement of direct cash assistance for housing was only tentative, however. (HUD had been ready to propose a national program, beginning with the elderly poor.) "In 1970, Congress authorized the housing allowance experiments. . . . This work should help us answer some important and difficult questions."

The idea of a housing allowance was not new.[119] In the 1930s and 1940s, the U.S. Chamber of Commerce and the National Association of Real Estate Boards urged the issuance of rent certificates to the poor to be redeemed by landlords. In 1968, President Johnson's Committee on Urban Housing urged experimental testing of the concept, and in 1969, HUD asked the Urban Institute to study the concept. In 1970, HUD tested housing allowances on a small scale in Kansas City, Missouri, and Wilmington, Delaware.

The experiments referred to by President Nixon had originated with a ploy by Senator Edward Brooke of Massachusetts. Though he wanted an operational housing allowance program to complement public housing, he settled for language in the authorizing legislation that described a sharply scaled-back housing allowance effort as an experiment. He felt that this approach would insure House–Senate conference approval of at least a beginning.[120]

---

[119]The background information is from *Congressional Quarterly Weekly Report*, Vol. XXXII. No. 18 (4 May 1974), p. 1110 ff.

[120]It is worth recounting a few of the details of the ploy, because they exemplify the differences between the two cultures inhabited by politicians and policy planners. "We were trying to use the guise of an experiment to make it (i.e., the housing allowance idea) operational," said Timothy D. Neagele, a Brooke aide. The senator added a restriction to the language of the bill that limited the experiment to areas where there was an adequate supply of standard housing.

The design of the experiment began in 1971, and payments began in 1973. By 1974, the project consisted of a series of three-year demand experiments, two-year administrative agency experiments, and five-year supply experiments.

Criticism of the Nixon approach centered around concerns that the supply of housing would continue to require direct subsidization lest the increased purchasing power of the poor be absorbed almost entirely by rent and price increases. Predictably, builders and developers were also opposed. Judging by the political opposition that greeted Nixon's speech and was evident in hearings held on the housing program moratorium, it is not clear that housing allowances will fare any better than FAP. However, as noted earlier Section 8 housing assistance may end up having effects similar to a housing allowance, though the assistance is paid to landlords rather than to tenants in the form of vouchers.

### New Welfare Reform Strategies

Despite the previous failures of comprehensive reform proposals, new proposals continue to flourish.[121] They include, among others, income supplementation plans such as the combined cash-grants—the negative-income-tax proposal of Congresswoman Martha Griffiths and the Joint Economic Committee's Subcommittee on Fiscal Policy,[122] and the Income Supplementation Program (ISP) of HEW;[123] proposals based on earnings supplements or wage rate subsidies;[124] and proposals placing major reliance on public employment programs.[125]

Income supplementation plans differ in detail but have in common the following structure: a minimum level of benefits to be guaranteed (subject to work requirements in some cases) to all eligible units with no income and a formula for reducing benefits as income increases. "The basic notion is to use income and family size as virtually the only criteria on which to base benefits, and to have universal coverage and national program uniformity."[126] This structure is consistent with the "cashing out," that is, the incorporation into

---

Brooke apparently added the restriction so that allowances would not merely drive up rents in tight housing markets. "We didn't want to subject it (the program) to a whole raft of criticism which might do it in," said Neagele. Recently, GAO accused HUD of, in effect, rigging the experiments by limiting them to localities with generally high vacancy rates.

[121]See *Report of the Public Welfare Study*, Chapter 7.

[122]See *Report of the Public Welfare Study*, Chapters 8–11.

[123]*National Journal Reports*, Vol. 6, No. 42 (19 October 1974), pp. 1559–1566; and *National Journal Reports*, Vol. 6, No. 47 (23 November 1974), p. 1772. .

[124]See Robert H. Haveman, Irene Lurie, and Thad Mirer, "Earnings Supplementation Plans for 'Working Poor' Families: An Evaluation of Alternatives," *Benefit Cost and Policy Analysis 1973* (Chicago: Aldine, 1974), pp. 291–318 and sources cited therein.

[125]See, for example, U.S., Congress, Joint Economic Committee, *Studies in Public Welfare*, Paper No. 19, "Public Employment and Wage Subsidies" (Washington, D.C.: U.S. Government Printing Office, 1974).

[126]*Report of the Public Welfare Study*, p. 154.

the basic benefit payment, of other income-tested, in-kind, and cash programs or the incorporation of such programs into revenue sharing or state supplementation programs. Thus, simplification of the entire system could result.

Earnings supplementation plans are founded on a distinction between the working poor and the nonworking poor. The working poor would have their earnings or their wages supplemented or subsidized so that their work effort yielded a higher income. Those without earnings would be aided through the public welfare system. Such plans are designed to target assistance on that category of poor people—the working poor—least benefited by existing programs and to achieve public acceptance, as well as a strong work incentive, through providing welfare assistance as a specific reward for work effort.

Public employment plans focus on increasing the number of jobs for those of the poor who are willing and able to work. Aid is channeled to the employable poor through the subsidized income they receive in government-created employment projects. Those who are without earnings or who are unable to work would be aided through the existing welfare system.

None of these reforms is built around a simple and understandable structure for channeling assistance to the poor and near-poor. Complexity to some degree is here to stay. For example, both the earnings supplementation and public employment plans require parallel welfare systems for the working and nonworking poor, and the latter approach requires separate treatment of the poor working in subsidized public jobs and those employed in private jobs. The income supplementation plans do not conclusively resolve questions concerning which in-kind programs should be cashed out. Few have proposed that day care, housing allowances, or Medicaid be cashed out, though Medicaid might be replaced by national health insurance. The continued existence of problems associated with cumulative benefits and tax rates is, therefore, a distinct possibility. Such plans have to address, as well, questions concerning the respective roles of social insurance and welfare, the role of state supplementation, and the relationship of the welfare system and the positive tax system, among other issues, though HEW's ISP addressed each of them. Moreover, each approach is subject to a variety of specific practical and philosophical objections, the effect of which is to create significant uncertainty concerning both their ultimate costs and effectiveness and their acceptability.

In contrast to these approaches, an incremental approach could consist of any of several different combinations of program changes. For example, an incrementalist strategy of welfare "revision" might consist of the following:[127]

(a) establishment of a federal minimum payment for AFDC with appro-

---

[127]See Barth, Carcagno, and Palmer, *Toward an Effective Income Support System*, p. 167, Note 1; and Blechman, Gramlich, and Hartman, *Setting National Priorities: The 1974 Budget*, pp. 189–198.

priate incentives for state supplementation, a requirement that all states adopt AFDC-UP, and the establishment of uniform definitions for eligibility, income and accounting periods;

(b) the addition of a housing allowance to existing in-kind programs;

(c) limited increases in the bonus value of food stamps without a concurrent liberalization in program eligibility;

(d) the enactment of a national health insurance scheme that insures uniform minimum access by the poor to basic health care;

(e) introduction of a flat dollar exemption plus a dependent's exemption into the payroll tax, with the revenue loss financed by an increase in the earnings base;[128]

(f) the enactment of an earnings supplement in the form of a refundable tax credit on earned income for low-income taxpayers (already enacted at least temporarily);

(g) incremental expansion of public service employment programs more carefully targeted on the poor.

Would it really be worth a difficult uphill battle to achieve basic reform in the income-maintenance system, or is incrementalism the better part of valor? There are strong arguments on both sides of the issue.

### Incrementalism versus Overhaul

#### The Case for Incrementalism

An incremental approach has several advantages. It has a proven record of success in reducing poverty. It can be counted on to improve further the adequacy of benefits and reduce or eliminate program inequities within and between jurisdictions. Depending on how the specific changes are designed, some improvements can also result in work incentives, the targeting of income-maintenance resources on the poor, and incentives for families to remain intact. Income poverty could be practically eliminated through a judicious combination of earnings subsidies, tax reforms, and incremental expansions in needs-tested programs.

Most important, incremental changes have a relatively good chance of being enacted within the framework of the fragmented and categorical policy process described in the earlier sections of this paper. Indeed, as with China, the existing income-maintenance system has shown a remarkable ability to absorb and assimilate its enemies; for example, Congress enacted an earnings supplement in 1975, adding it to the existing array of income-maintenance programs and tax expenditures, as an antirecession measure with no public debate and little public awareness. Incrementalism is not *an* approach, it is *the* approach to policymaking given existing institutions. To put the point differently, the only practical way to achieve the elimination of

[128]See Okner, "The Social Security Payoff Tax."

poverty and income redistribution in this country is to do it gradually, incrementally, and, to avoid a middle-class revolt, inefficiently.

There are other arguments for incrementalism. Major welfare reform proposals are seldom developed in the light of adequate knowledge about their consequences. The interrelationships among programs in the reformed system and their effects are hardly ever fully understood. Senator John Williams, not the designers of welfare reform, discovered the "notch" problem—the disincentive to work created by the possibility that reductions in welfare benefits would exceed earnings increases for some households—during Senate hearings on FAP.[129] The enactment of comprehensive reform risks unintended costs and consequences perhaps as unfortunate as those that occur with incrementalism.

Further, it is not practical to engage in elaborate controlled experiments to test every hypothesis concerning major societal effects of welfare reform. Incrementalism is the most practical way to learn how to solve social problems and how not to solve them.

## The Case for Overhaul

Unless they are enacted with unprecedented care, incremental changes are likely to leave largely unsolved or even make worse the problems created by the existing income-maintenance system: perverse incentives, horizontal inequity, inefficiency, program administration that is high in cost and low in quality, unaccountability, and stigmatization of those forced to deal with the system as it is. No one really wants such a system. Sooner or later, the cumulative effects of these problems will demand solution; the reemergence of "the welfare mess" as a national issue is inevitable. It is incumbent on those concerned with income maintenance to continue their efforts toward developing and discussing workable alternatives to the existing system and toward educating Congress and the public to the need for fundamental change.

The impulse for reform should extend beyond the income-maintenance system to the policy process itself. The report of the *Public Welfare Study* noted that "in contrast to the defense budget . . . there is no ongoing mechanism within the executive or legislative branch for assuring that income-maintenance programs function properly as a system. . . . Eleven committees in the House, ten in the Senate and nine executive department or agencies have jurisdiction over the broad set of income security programs."[130] It was this fragmentation of responsibility that both created the notch problem and inhibited its discovery.

More and more, social problems—for example, income maintenance, environmental protection and land use, caring for the elderly, housing and

[129]Burke and Burke, *Nixon's Good Deed*, pp. 153–156.
[130]*Report of the Public Welfare Study*, p. 1.

community development—cut across jurisdictional lines in the executive and legislative branches. Though both branches try to adjust to changing circumstances by reorganizing existing institutions and by creating new ones, fragmentation remains a serious obstacle to comprehensive thought and action.

Fragmentation, particularly when it is a costly obstacle to solving problems everyone can agree should be solved, should not simply be taken for granted. Congress partially recognized the need for cross-cutting institutions when it created the House and Senate Budget Committees and the Congressional Budget Office in 1974. Through these institutions Congress should pursue the issues raised by the *Public Welfare Study* and should examine the income-maintenance system as a whole in the light of their statutory responsibilities to examine priorities and to do future planning. In addition, Congress might consider creating a temporary joint committee on the income-maintenance system with respresentatives of each of the affected standing committees to consider omnibus income-maintenance legislation.

Welfare reform, in other words, should extend beyond substantive issues to the public processes for defining the problems, weighing the alternatives, and reaching decisions.

### A Verdict

In 1973. Secretary of Health, Education, and Welfare Elliot Richardson put this issue in the broadest possible perspective. "If we are to restore confidence in government, the first order of business must be action on welfare reform."[131] Though one may be sympathetic to incrementalism as a short-run expedient, it is hard to resist the conclusion that the eventual overhaul and simplification of the income-maintenance system is desirable in both programmatic and human terms. The existing, highly complex income-maintenance system is unfair, inefficient, and counterproductive. People do not understand it, nor do they have confidence in it.

A number of recent developments improve the chances for eventual enactment of welfare reform, especially some form of income supplementation plan or negative income tax.

The first is the light shed by recent research on the issue of whether aid to the working poor will cause them to work less.[132] The results of the New Jersey Graduated Work Incentive Experiment "clearly indicate that a negative tax type plan with a basic benefit as high as the official poverty line will not trigger large scale reductions in work effort among male heads of families."[133] Thus, there is now a respectable body of evidence laying to rest

---

[131]Elliot L. Richardson, *Responsibility and Responsiveness (II) A Report on the HEW Potential for the Seventies* (Washington, D.C.: U.S. Department of Health, Education, and Welfare, 1973), p. 24.

[132]See Irwin Garfinkel, "Income Transfer Programs and Work Effort: A Review," in *Studies in Public Welfare*, Paper No. 13 "How Income Supplements Can Affect Work Behavior" (Washington, D.C.: U.S. Government Printing Office, 1974), pp. 1–32.

[133]U.S. Department of Health, Education, and Welfare, *Summary Report: New Jersey Gradu-*

a fear that often seemed to dominate earlier welfare reform debates: that primary wage earners would significantly reduce work effort if they were generally eligible for cash assistance.

The experiment did suggest that "a national income-conditioned cash assistance plan would result in a rather substantial (percentage) reduction in the labor supply of the 15–20 percent of low-income wives who are employed."[134] However, it can be argued, as the HEW summary of the experiment's results points out, that society may be worse off when low-income mothers must work outside the home due to economic necessity.[135]

The *Panel Study of Income Dynamics* also has implications favorable to reform. For all but a small minority of those who experience poverty over a period of several years, having such a low income is a temporary phenomenon. Moreover, personal decisions based on economic considerations play only a limited role in causing household poverty. Thus, for the majority of welfare recipients, poverty is not "a way of life."[136] Welfare benefits are primarily a cushion against temporary adversity, not a subsidy for idleness, and as such are not in conflict with mainstream American values.

Second, the fact that eligibility for food stamps or some other type of income-maintenance program is now virtually universal means that future welfare reform debates will turn less on *whether* welfare benefits should be provided than on *how* they are provided. It is now possible to argue for welfare reform without proposing to make millions of people eligible for public welfare for the first time.

Third, many if not most approaches to requiring or encouraging greater work effort by the poor—manpower training, public service jobs, earnings supplements, vocational education—have been or are being tried. The evaluations of such programs to date suggest that they can have only a limited impact on poverty. For example, one recent study concluded that, though disadvantaged and low-income people have responded to training and have become more self-sustaining, the results were obtained on too small a scale to justify optimism concerning the results of a massive training program.[137] Further, the study found that "even those studies with the most optimistic results estimate average post-training annual earnings levels well below the poverty line . . . if child care and work expenses have to be financed from these earnings, there is not much left for the amenities of life. Training does reduce the poverty gap, but continued income supplementation is likely to be necessary for the graduates."[138] The argument that manpower and public

*ated Work Incentive Experiment* (Washington, D.C.: Department of Health, Education, and Welfare, 1973), p. vi.

[134]Ibid., p. vii.

[135]Ibid.

[136]*The Panel Study*, p. viii.

[137]U.S., Congress, Joint Economic Committee, *Studies in Public Welfare*, Paper No. 3 "The Effectiveness of Manpower Training Programs: A Review of Research on the Impact on the Poor" (Washington, D.C.: U.S. Government Printing Office, 1972), p. 13.

[138]Ibid., p. 14.

employment programs are a substitute for, rather than a complement to, an equitable and efficient income-maintenance system is likely to lose force over time.

The sum total of experience with the existing system and the results of research on poverty have irrevocably altered the content of the welfare reform debate in a manner that should be favorable to welfare reform.

Perhaps the most difficult obstacle facing welfare reform in the future will be budgetary. Welfare reform can win broad support only if most existing recipients, as well as the states that administer welfare programs, are not made worse off under the reformed system. The greater the amount of assistance that is channeled to the poor through the existing income-maintenance system, the more expensive it will be for the federal government to replace and simplify it without leaving anyone worse off.

For example, the Brookings Institution calculated the additional federal cost of a universal negative income tax that replaced the SSI, AFDC, and food stamp programs with a $4000 benefit level for a family of four and a 50 percent marginal tax rate on earnings, at $11 billion in FY 1977. The study noted that "even a program of this magnitude would lower the income of some beneficiaries."[139] Furthermore, the study was based on an annual accounting period. The extra cost could be significantly higher if shorter accounting periods were used to accommodate the temporary poor. Costs would be still higher if liberal filing rules and a less than 100 percent tax rate on unearned income were incorporated in the plan.

Thus, the most serious obstacle to significant welfare reform may turn out to be not the fear of its consequences but its cost. The apparent advantage of incrementalism is that it can be tailored to fit any budget in the short run. Though cost is not an insurmountable obstacle to significant reform, the momentum to overcome it is likely to be more easily generated during a change of administrations by a new President personally concerned about the issue. Though such a development cannot be predicted with high confidence, much stranger things have happened.

[139]Blechman, Gramlich, and Hartman, *Setting National Priorities: The 1975 Budget*, pp. 202–203.

# 23

# What Has Been Learned from the Work Incentive Program and Related Experiences: A Review of Research with Policy Implications

## *Leonard Goodwin*

## 1. INTRODUCTION AND SUMMARY

The Work Incentive (WIN) Program, authorized in 1967, has sought to put people on Aid to Families with Dependent Children (AFDC) to work. Initially, a variety of educational and training services were provided, with participants spending as much as a year in the program. More recently, education and training have been reduced in favor of immediate job placement. This document reviews selected research on WIN efforts, funded primarily by the Department of Labor, as well as related research on low-income families. The aim is to draw together empirical findings that illuminate the factors affecting WIN results and contribute to discussion of future welfare, work-training, and employment policies.

### Organizing the Research Studies

There are many ways to organize discussion of the research efforts. One way is chronological. A particularly illuminating way, however, is to examine them within a framework that shows the various systems affecting WIN and welfare operations.

Two systems immediately come to mind. The first is the donor system. It is made up of those who define and provide resources for WIN, namely, Congress and the executive branch (see chart 1). There is also the recipient system. It is composed of WIN participants who receive funds, training, or services and are subject to the requirements set by the donor system.

Two intermediary systems may be distinguished. The administrative system consists of those charged with overall responsibility for administering the various aspects of WIN, including the Departments of Labor and Health, Education, and Welfare (HEW). The delivery system includes the staff of local WIN offices. There is also the job market system to be considered and the constituency system, representing groups that influence the donor system.

Major interactions among systems are indicated by the crosshatched areas in chart 1. While recipients are also constituents of the donor system, their influence as constituents is relatively weak compared, for example, with the influence of social security recipients. The chart, in any case, is meant to provide only a rough and convenient approximation of reality.

Much of the research reviewed here has focused on characteristics of members of the recipient system and interactions among members of the recipient, delivery, and job market systems. Such a focus is eminently reasonable. When WIN was initiated 9 years ago, there were serious unresolved questions about the characteristics of welfare recipients in relation to their participation in the work force. It was not clear that recipients shared a strong work ethic or what other factors affected their trainability and work effort. Hence, much of the research focused on the labor force activity of welfare persons and the way in which the WIN effort affected that activity. That research is reviewed here, together with what is known about the results of offering jobs to welfare recipients.

### Research Conclusions

Listed below are the major conclusions that emerge from the research studies reviewed.

1. In general, welfare recipients and other low-income persons (along with most Americans) have a strong work ethic, want to work, and when feasible, do work. No study shows that a significant segment of the American population prefers indolence to work.

2. Substantial barriers stand in the way of welfare recipients' participating in the present job market system. They include lack of skills, poor health, need for child care, and lack of jobs at which they can earn enough to support their families.

From Leonard Goodwin, "The Work Incentive (WIN) Program and Related Experiences," R&D Monograph 49, U.S. Department of Labor, Employment and Training Administration.

CHART 1. Systems Involved in Operation of a National Public Program*

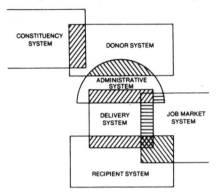

*Cross-hatched areas represent important interactions among systems.

SOURCE. Leonard Goodwin. "Bridging the Gap Between Social Research and Public Policy:Welfare, a Case in Point," *Journal of Applied Behavioral Science*, vol. 9, No. 1, 1973, pp. 85-114. Reproduced by special permission from the *Journal of Applied Behavioral Research*, copyright 1973 by the NIL Institute for Applied Behavioral Science.

3. Several researchers have sought to locate a group of persons similar to welfare recipients in most respects but not on welfare. All failed to locate such a group. Those on welfare have less education, less resources, and larger families than other low-income persons.

4. WIN is successful in helping some welfare recipients improve their earnings and length of time in jobs. Improvement occurs only when these persons obtain some kind of services from WIN and not when they are merely referred directly to jobs

5. Just what aspects of the WIN effort are responsible for helping trainees obtain and hold jobs has not been established. The formal categories of help, such as "education," "vocational training," or "on-the-job training" do not seem to signify the important events that help certain trainees improve their work effort over the longer run. A closer look at what happens in the WIN experience itself is needed.

6. In spite of the help WIN offers, it cannot of itself resolve the welfare issue. The training provided does not enable large numbers of welfare recipients to obtain work in the regular job market, allowing them to leave the welfare rolls. Moreover, those who enter WIN and fail to obtain jobs may be harmed by becoming more dependent upon welfare than they were when they entered the program.

7. Efforts to encourage employment of more welfare recipients by giving tax credits to businesses hiring recipients, by not deducting all the earnings of recipients from their welfare grants, and by imposing stiffer work requirements have had very limited impact. These efforts do little to change the job market situation faced by welfare recipients.

8. Work-for-relief efforts (merely working off one's relief payments in a makeshift job) are costly, inefficient, and resented by work supervisors as well as participants. On the other hand, provision of publicly supported jobs for welfare recipients has demonstrated that significant numbers of welfare recipients are willing to work and can perform competently in regular jobs over a period of time. However, providing jobs costs more than paying welfare, and relatively few persons who perform well in these jobs find equivalent employment in the regular work force, suggesting limitations in the job market system.

9. During any year, there is considerable movement of persons, not only on and off the welfare rolls, but above and below the poverty level. However, low-income families headed by women (and especially black women) are substantially less likely to leave poverty than are those headed by men.

10. Relatively little is known about the factors influencing low-income men to stay with or desert their families. There is reason to believe that desertion would be less likely if the men could earn enough to support their families adequately.

## Policy and Research Implications

A major implication of the research findings is that the locus of the welfare problem is not the welfare recipients as such. True enough, persons receive the welfare checks. But the evidence is that welfare recipients are willing to work and do work; they are, however, unable to command salaries at which they can support their families. The characteristics of the job market system are such that they cannot obtain work that leads to financial independence.

The WIN effort, as it involves training and supportive social services, helps some recipients. It improves their chances of obtaining and holding better jobs. But the effect is small in comparison with the total number of adult welfare recipients. By using a new research approach (discussed later in this chapter) to identify those aspects of WIN that are of greatest help to trainees, it should be possible to increase this effect. But improvement in the delivery system without change in the job market system can do little to change the welfare situation.

In keeping with this outlook, at least three policy options are open:

1. Stop trying to train welfare recipients at all, since the training has only small effects; cut back on benefits paid welfare recipients and raise eligibility standards so that more persons will take low-paid jobs in the current job market, even if the result is that they will be living below the poverty level.

2. Keep the status quo whereby welfare payments to 3 or 4 million families are accepted as normal, some training is offered some recipients, and supplementary benefits such as food stamps are continued; but no change is attempted in the job market system.

3. Attempt a major change in the job market by guaranteeing jobs to those who are willing and able to work but cannot find employment, while guaranteeing an income to those unable to work.

These different options reflect different value commitments. Research cannot determine which values are better, but it can help illuminate the consequences of choosing one rather than another option. A consequence of following either of the first two options is that a substantial number of persons are relegated to the bottom of the heap with little opportunity to rise through their own efforts. While research findings show a substantial yearly movement of persons above and below the poverty level in the current job market system, families headed by women, especially those headed by black women, show very little mobility. Members of these households will have little choice but to remain poor and disadvantaged under policies one and two.

Neither of those options, moreover, provides any additional incentive for low-income men to stay with their families.[1] Research indicates that the stability of a low-income family is significantly increased if the father has a job. When low-income families stay intact, there is a much greater chance of their moving out of poverty. Policy option three is explicitly aimed at providing jobs not only for welfare mothers but also for low-income men who might then be more inclined to stay with their families.

1. The current welfare program that makes payments to families where there is an employable father, AFDC-U, is ineffective in keeping families intact (see Wiseman, 1976 and ch. 6). It is a very small program, in any case, with benefits cut off as soon as the father works more than 100 hours per month.

# 2. WORK POTENTIAL AND WORK ORIENTATIONS OF WELFARE PERSONS

A number of research studies focus on the experiences of welfare recipients in the labor force—interactions between members of the recipient system and the job market system (as shown in chart 1 in ch. 1). While a major concern is with WIN participants, it is important to consider work experiences of welfare and low-income adults in general.

Welfare recipients clearly do not earn sufficient money on their own to raise their families above the poverty level. The question is whether they could earn more if they worked harder or if certain conditions were altered. Put another way, what potential do adult recipients have for earning enough money to support their families?

## The Earning Potential of Welfare Recipients

An early nationwide study of characteristics of 11,000 female welfare recipients and former recipients carried out for the Department of Health, Education, and Welfare indicated that the adults had relatively little education, low job skills, and numerous health problems (Levinson, 1970; Meyers and McIntyre, 1969[1]). Their potential for earning enough to support their families was seen as low. Even so, about one-third of the group that had received welfare continuously for the previous 3 years had worked at some time during that period (Meyers and McIntyre, p. 113).

These data were gathered through personal interviews with the sample of recipients. The question might be raised as to whether their responses, especially those on health status, could be taken at face value. Were these welfare recipients merely finding excuses for not working even more than they did? It is necessary to look at different approaches.

Another approach to the employment potential of welfare recipients was taken by Leonard Hausman (1969) in a doctoral dissertation sponsored by the Department of Labor. He used national data on the characteristics of men and women receiving Aid to Families with Dependent

Children (AFDC) and national data indicating the earnings of persons in the kinds of occupations that the welfare recipients had previously engaged in. The point was to determine how many welfare recipients, given their educational level and occupational category, could be expected to earn enough money to meet their level of need, based upon family size, and hence be able to leave welfare. Hausman found that about two-thirds of the female and one-third of the male recipients probably could not earn enough on their own to support their families (p. 5). (Male recipients make up less than 10 percent of AFDC recipients who are heads of households.)

There are limitations to the study. The calculations ignore individual differences among welfare recipients other than sex, education, and occupation. Also ignored are issues of health and psychological orientation. Hausman is aware that the estimates of need and income are based upon some questionable assumptions. The study does indicate, nevertheless, that the low education and low skill of welfare recipients lessen their chances of obtaining jobs at which they could earn enough to support their families.

Another source of evidence about the employability of welfare recipients is the judgments made by those registering and referring recipients for participation in WIN. Only about 10 percent of adult recipients are regarded as ready to participate in WIN. That is, 328,000 welfare recipients were certified as entering WIN in fiscal 1975, while there continued to be over 3 million heads of households receiving AFDC (U.S. Department of Labor and U.S. Department of Health, Education, and Welfare, 1976, p. 3).[2] It is not clear how many of those certified were among the 16 percent of AFDC recipients who work anyway. Even if none were included, the figures still indicate that about three-quarters of AFDC adults (100 percent - 16 percent employed - 10 percent in WIN) were regarded as unsuited for employment or training because of such problems as poor health and lack of child care arrangements.

The further question is whether those making the judgments were being "soft"—that is, were not realistically judging the work potential of welfare recipients. Or put another way, are there great numbers of welfare recipients

1. Citations in the text are to author, year, and page number where relevant. Full citations, arranged alphabetically by author, appear in the Bibliography.

2. Some increase in WIN participation would probably occur if the program was funded at a higher level —only $220 million was allocated in fiscal year 1975 for supported work and training.

who complain of illness and disabilities but are relatively healthy? Some light is shed on this issue by the physical examinations carried out by teams of experts in connection with the New York State effort to have welfare recipients work for their relief payments. Of 10,000 persons assessed for work in New York City, 65 percent were found to be medically disabled (Gupte, 1973). It is not altogether surprising that persons who live in conditions of poverty, with inadequate diets and health care, have medical difficulties.

All these difficulties are not necessarily irremediable, however. A pilot study sponsored by the Labor Department and headed by a medical doctor, Daphne Roe (1975), suggests that at least some persons can be helped. Detailed physical examinations and some psychological evaluations were carried out on 59 women and 12 men on welfare in upper New York State. Among the difficulties most frequently encountered were dental decay (including ill-fitting dentures), gross obesity, and emotional disturbances (p. 2). A wide variety of other physical difficulties were evident, ranging from anemia to the need for eyeglasses (pp. 89ff.). By providing medical treatment along with rehabilitation and work counseling, the project helped about 15 percent of these persons find jobs or stay on the job (p. 14). Since the pilot remedial effort lasted only 6 months, long-term results of health intervention are not available. An expanded effort is currently underway.

Conclusions regarding the potential of welfare mothers to work their way out of poverty and off welfare are given a firmer foundation by considering Frank Levy's (1976) analysis of a study of a national sample of 5,000 low-income families. The study, conducted from the University of Michigan, followed these families over a 5-year period, asking detailed questions about work and income. Levy's prime concern was to discover who rose above poverty during those 5 years and why. (He deducts welfare payments from income in calculating the poverty level.)

A striking finding is that significant numbers of people are moving out of poverty as well as into it. That is, there is a flow, rather than a stagnant pool of the same poor people over the years. Thus, 58 percent of the "target population"—nondisabled persons under 60 years old who were below the poverty level in 1967—were out of poverty in 1973 (p. 9). Among household heads, men have a much better chance of leaving poverty than do women. The proportions of family heads in the target population moving out of poverty between 1967 and 1973 were 54 percent for all men, only 37 percent for white women, and a mere 25 percent for nonwhite women (p. 107). The reason has to do with the lower earning power of women and, of course, the possibility that, in a household headed by a man, the wife also will work. Hence, intact households have a potential economic advantage.

A female head of household may escape from welfare because of increased child support money from the separated father, changes in family composition—e.g., children growing up and leaving—or improvement in health that allows for greater work effort.[3] But the woman's prospects of upward economic mobility are not bright, especially if she is black. Even when she works full time, her earnings are not generally sufficient to raise the living standard of her large family very high (pp. 35, 46).

This does not mean, of course, that no female head of household on welfare earns her way out of the situation. Wiseman (1976) examined a sample of about, 1,500 AFDC cases covering the years 1967 through 1972 in Alameda County, Calif. He used a multivariate analysis to determine the factors that affected the movement of mothers off welfare and out of poverty. He found that women who had recent job experience were much more likely to leave welfare and poverty than were those without such experience (pp. 39, 45). The absolute number here is small. Thus, Wiseman estimated that the prob-

ability of a welfare recipient's leaving the rolls during a 3-month period was about 2 in 100 if she had no previous work experience, but was about double that ratio if she had such experience (p. 42). Wiseman also found, in agreement with other studies, that movement of mothers off welfare is hindered if they have large families and are black (p. 44).

Friedman and Hausman (1975), using the same Michigan data as Levy, came up with additional findings. Their concern was with the variability in earnings. This is important because it is this variability that leads families into or out of welfare and poverty. Variability among men is related to the kind of industry in which they work. There is greater variability for white men in transportation, communication, and utilities jobs, for example, than there is for black men in such jobs (p. 172).

The variability in earnings of black men goes down the longer they are in the same household with their spouses, suggesting that greater family stability is associated with greater job stability (p. 172). These data also suggest the possibility that men with families are less likely to risk job loss in order to try for better jobs. Availability of a guaranteed income or job might increase such risk taking.

Among female heads of household, variability in earnings increases with job training, perhaps indicating that they found better jobs after training (p. 172). These results illuminate the recipient-job market interaction and suggest for further investigation approaches that could help low-income workers, especially female workers, move out of poverty.

The data just presented show clearly enough that a substantial number of heads of households are unable at given times to earn enough to support their families because of such factors as job market conditions, lack of skills, poor health, and need for child care. What still is at issue is whether these persons have contributed indirectly to their own conditions by perhaps having deviant psychological characteristics or values. For example, they may have failed to gain work skills because of an inappropriate time perspective (i.e., not planning ahead) or lack of work ethic.

It also is not clear whether some persons accept welfare in a given situation while others in the same position do not. Are welfare recipients the ones among the poor who prefer a handout, while others in the same social-economic situation prefer to make it on their own, as difficult as that might be?

# Characteristics of Welfare Recipients and Other Low-Income Persons

Miller and Ferman (1972) conducted a study in Detroit to compare the job experiences of AFDC recipients with the experiences of persons having similar characteristics who were not on AFDC. The adult (male and female) AFDC recipients sampled were between 22 and 55 years of age and earning $100 per month or more (p. 27). A total of 422 interviews were completed. The comparison group was chosen from census tracts in known low-income areas of Detroit. Eligible respondents were identified in

---

3. Escape from poverty is a better indicator than "escape from welfare" because welfare recipients can be dropped from the rolls for administrative reasons while still in poverty; e.g., men who work more than 100 hours per month are dropped from welfare regardless of earnings.

doorstep interviews by their heading a household and working at a job that was low paid—$2.50 per hour or less (p. 34). A total of 507 of these interviews were completed. Because the poor in Detroit, as chosen by census tracts, are predominantly black and because the sample was so predominantly black, no analysis by race is offered by the authors.

There typically are sampling problems in studies of low-income and welfare persons because of difficulties in gaining permission of welfare agencies and recipients for interviews and in locating poor persons. The authors are aware of limitations in their own efforts (p. 37) and, while the results cannot, in a strict sense, be generalized to all Detroit much less the country, they contribute to a pattern of findings that emerges from this and other studies.

Two general findings emerge from the data. First, wages and kinds of jobs, as well as job goals and previous family background (e.g., whether parents were divorced), do not differentiate welfare recipients from nonrecipients (pp. 111ff., 163ff.). Second, what do distinguish nonrecipients from those on welfare are higher levels of education, fewer children—only one-third of the nonrecipients (compared with over half of those on welfare) had two to four children—and greater resources to fall back on when laid off from work. (Only 5 percent of female recipients could fall back on savings, whereas 16 percent of nonrecipients could do so (pp. 65, 141).) Hence, the study fails to locate a group of persons not on welfare who are identical to welfare recipients.

About two-thirds of the welfare recipients and 80 percent of the nonrecipients were working at least 35 hours per week (p. 120). Any marked increase in income for most of these heads of households, therefore, would have to come from increased wages rather than increased hours of work. The Miller-Ferman findings confirm on the micro level what Levy found on the macro level: low-income heads of households are not too likely to leave poverty by increased hours of work because they already work regular hours (Levy, p. 44ff.).

Another study comparing female welfare recipients and low-income working mothers who were heads of households was carried out by Samuel Klausner (1972) in Camden, N. J., in 1969. Originally, the aim was to compare WIN participants with nonwelfare working mothers. AFDC respondents were chosen from official welfare records on the basis of their fulfilling WIN referral requirements. This restriction reduced the number of respondents available and necessitated the researcher's asking social workers for additional names, which compromised the representativeness of the sample (see vol. II, p. A-2ff.). Finally, only 45 of the 447 welfare recipients interviewed actually entered WIN, thereby voiding any meaningful study of WIN impact.

Selection of the nonwelfare comparison group was even more problematical with respect to representativeness than was choosing the welfare group. It was obtained by asking for names of low-income persons from organizations dealing with them; e.g., the Public Housing Authority. Eventually, the research project interviewed 102 low-income working mothers, most of them residing in public housing (vol. II, pp. A-2ff.).

Unlike the Miller and Ferman sample of welfare recipients, those in Camden were not necessarily employed. Only one-quarter had some earnings in 1969. In that sense, they are more typical of the welfare population at large. What emerges again in the Camden data is that the nonwelfare mothers have more resources than do the welfare mothers. Thus, 31 percent of the former received child support payments, as against 19 percent of the welfare mothers; and 14 percent of the former received social security payments, as against 5 percent of the welfare mothers (p. VI-4). These findings might seem obvious in that a family has to be especially deprived in order to receive welfare. The point, however, is that researchers are unable to find especially deprived families who reject welfare.

Overall, the mothers on welfare have about the same monthly income as the working mothers, but, as in the Detroit data, the size of the household is smaller among working mothers—3.5 versus 4.7 persons per household (p. VI-8). The per capita income of welfare families is only about 60 percent of that of working families. There were a few working mothers who, monetarily, could have done as well (or a little better) on welfare as they could by working (p. VI-11). They were probably influenced not to go on welfare by feelings of stigma associated with that program (p. VIII-7).

Measures of attitudes toward welfare, jobs, and family size were made during the study. No major differences were observed between the welfare and nonwelfare groups (p. VI-11). In addition, an effort was made to probe the underlying psychology of respondents. Projective measures were introduced, asking the subject to draw a picture of a person and tell stories about other pictures (vol. II, p. D7). Analysis of these kinds of responses (based upon standarized scoring procedures) enabled trained investigators to assess such characteristics as a person's ability to cope with difficulties and extent of future time perspective—concern with future consequences of present actions. Interestingly enough, the welfare recipients had more of a future time orientation than did the other group, a finding running counter to the speculation of Banfield and others that lack of future orientation causally leads to poverty (vol. II, p. D10). The project also administered a test of intelligence, on which AFDC mothers scored lower than the other mothers, but were in the normal range (vol. II, pp. D20, D32).

The attempt to discover whether welfare acceptance is associated with some gross psychological differences from others is certainly appropriate. The conclusion drawn from the results was that there was no evidence of gross psychological differences between recipients of welfare and others (vol. II, p. D32). Similarly, there were no significant relations between the psychological measures and work activity of the welfare mothers (vol. II, p. D32). These negative findings suggest that welfare recipients are like other people, but suffer from more difficulties and fewer resources than others. Moreover, there is no evidence from either the Klausner or the Miller and Ferman studies of the existence of a unique and large group of persons who are identical to welfare recipients in education, earnings potential, monetary resources, and family size and who choose to reject welfare.

Two other studies compare welfare and nonwelfare groups. One was directed by Harold Feldman (1972) in upstate New York. The other, which is discussed here, was conducted by Thompson and Miles. It involved interviews with about 6,000 persons who were supposed to represent low-income and welfare heads of households across the country. Concern was with the orientations of respondents towards jobs and family life. The difficulty of sampling welfare persons, which is great enough at one site, is increased many times when numerous States and locales are involved.

Thompson and Miles (1972) encountered difficulties in obtaining permission from welfare agencies to contact clients (vol. 4, p. 10ff.). Their aim was to survey women who had been AFDC recipients for 5 years or more as well as those who had left AFDC because of employment. Other groups to be interviewed included men and women on general assistance (welfare provided by local and State governments), those who had left assistance rolls, and low-income heads of households who had not been on welfare. Some States that failed to cooperate in providing access to welfare records had to be dropped from the study, lessening the representativeness of the sample.

If representativeness of the welfare and former welfare sample from 17 sites is open to question, the sample of nonwelfare, low-income heads of households is even more questionable. These were to be heads of families designated as poor by Department of Labor criteria at the same 17 sites (vol. 2, p. 6). Names of persons at the different sites were requested from such agencies as the employment service or public housing projects. When a respondent was unknown at the address provided by an agency, the interviewer might go to a nearby residence to see if the head of that household fit the criteria of the study (vol. 4, pp. 16ff.).

While the sample drawn is not respresentative of welfare and low-income persons in general, to the extent that findings are consistent with other data on poor people, they can be taken as supporting the validity of those data. Findings that are unusual would need to be checked in further research efforts.

Thompson and Miles attempted to determine if there were personality differences between welfare and nonwelfare adults, as well as personality factors that affected employment. They choose to use Cattell's Sixteen Personality Factor Questionnaire, which is a widely used instrument. Although data on its validity is not readily available (see Rorer, 1972) and there is no evidence relating scores on the questionnaire to work performance of welfare recipients, it is worthwhile to explore the usefulness of these kinds of measures. They administered the questionnaire to about half of their total sample and then stopped because of resistance to answering questions (vol. 2, p. 84). The representativeness of the results is thereby thrown into question. But in any case, the most striking finding is that welfare recipients fall within the average range of scores, as specified by the test authors, on 12 of the personality variables (vol. 5, pp. 56-57).

Deviations from the average occur with respect to feeling more suspicious of others and being more lacking in self-confidence. Such findings are readily explainable on the basis of AFDC recipients' negative social experiences, having to go on welfare in particular. Of greater significance is that welfare recipients are in the average range with respect to "undisciplined self-conflict," "tenseness," and "emotional stability." Welfare status is not directly connected with gross personality deviancy.

The authors do find some personality differences when a comparison is made among welfare recipients, former recipients who are now working, and low-income persons never on welfare. They report that, among white women, the welfare recipients are less confident and less secure than are former recipients who are working or those never on welfare (vol. 2, p. 85). Specific data on this matter, including numbers of respondents, are not provided. But again, it makes sense that those who have failed in the work world are not as secure as those who have had some success. There is no indication of psychological pathology in such results.

Thompson and Miles organized their data so as to answer the questions of whether welfare recipients differ from nonrecipients or whether workers differ from nonworkers with respect to certain attitudinal responses or demographic characteristics. Attitudinal responses, usually in a dichotomous, agree-disagree format, can provide some useful insights. Thus, among black women, 27 percent on welfare agreed that "I want to be a housewife, not a worker." Only 19 percent of the nonwelfare mothers agreed (vol. 3, p. 26). There is an important implication here; namely, that a substantial minority of welfare mothers are concerned about staying home and looking after their children.

Such a finding is consistent with that provided by Feldman. Sixty-three percent of the women in his sample indicated positive relations with their children as their greatest source of satisfaction; only 3 percent mentioned a job (p. 135). Klausner in his study found a portion of women who preferred to stay at home, whom he called "traditionalists." Goodwin (1972), in a study discussed later in this monograph, found that welfare women not in

WIN ranked the statement "getting along well with your family" higher than the statement "having a job that is well-paid" (p. 149). WIN women gave the reverse ranking. These scattered findings suggest the need for a better understanding of the family-work relationship among low-income women in designing more effective efforts to involve them in jobs.

Thompson and Miles find a positive relation between welfare status and delinquency of the children (vol. 3, p. ii). It is not possible to say from this analysis whether delinquency is associated with welfare acceptance as such or with the lower social-economic status of welfare families. Delinquency is unrelated to parents' work behavior. The work activities of welfare mothers did not interfere with their child-oriented activities, such as helping children with their homework (vol. 3, p. ii).

While the Thompson and Miles findings are of some interest, their efforts could have been much more productive if they had done two things: (1) Clustered the attitudinal items, rather than analyzing them one at a time and (2) conducted a multivariate analysis rather than merely presenting a large number of fourfold tables.

These two points will be examined briefly because the criticism applies to some degree to the Feldman and Klausner studies as well as some others to be mentioned. Moreover, the issues involved bear significantly on the design of future research that will move beyond the limitations of past studies. Information is lost by using dichotomus ratings (yes or no) for attitudinal items. It is better to use a rating scale of four or more steps. Responses to any individual item usually involve a great deal of error, which means that the responses have low reliability. That is, persons tend to be inconsistent in answers to single questions because of ambiguities in the wording, etc. In order to counter this, one prefers to be able to average the ratings of several items designed to measure the same general issue.

A statistical procedure for "clustering items" needs to be introduced in order to make sure that the items are, in fact, measuring the same topic. By having several items, moreover, the meaning of the topic being measured is more clearly recognizable. Thompson and Miles did not adopt this procedure. Hence there is no way of judging the reliability of any single item, such as, "I want to be a housewife, not a worker." In addition, this item might have clustered with others that would suggest a broad orientation toward life, family, and work. This broad orientation might have been labeled "family commitment."

The second point is that the way Thompson and Miles chose to present their data implies a multivariate analysis. That is, they wish to know what variables—including responses to attitudinal items and demographic characteristics such as educational level—distinguish welfare from nonwelfare persons. Welfare versus nonwelfare should be the dependent variable and the others the independent variables in a multiple regression equation. The solving of the equation would then reveal the extent to which a possible orientation, such as "family commitment," is directly related to welfare status, with other variables, such as level of education, being controlled. Without this kind of multivariable analysis, it is not possible to tell, for one thing, whether certain attitudinal differences between welfare and nonwelfare persons are merely the result of educational differences. What the Thompson and Miles study has to offer, therefore, is some interesting insights rather than substantial conclusions on which to base policy.

The Feldman study complements certain findings already mentioned. He conducted interviews with about 1,300 female heads of households in upstate New York, of whom about 400 previously had been on welfare and the others were at that time on welfare (1972, p.17). Each family had to contain at least one teenager, but the heads were to exhibit different employment and marital statuses. Rather than searching for a comparison group of low-income persons never on welfare, as in the Miller and Ferman study, Feldman compared those on welfare with those who had left welfare. (The fact that a family was able to leave welfare, however, almost automatically means that they are better off than those on welfare, so that comparability is limited.)

Sampling for the study involved use of county welfare lists of both welfare and former welfare recipients. By including enough counties in the study, Felman was able to obtain substantial numbers of respondents in the welfare-nonwelfare, work-nonwork, and husband-nonhusband categories (p. 17).

Feldman presents considerable demographic data about his sample, which Thompson and Miles unaccountably fail to do. And we see again, as in the Miller-Ferman and Klausner studies, that the employed have more resources to begin with. Thus Feldman found that the employed ex-welfare mothers had the highest level of education in the sample (10.7 years), while those presently on welfare and unemployed had the lowest (9.6 years) (p. 25). Non-employed mothers had more preschool children than employed ones, and those on welfare had more preschoolers than those formerly on welfare (p. 39).

The ex-welfare mothers who had married and were working had substantially higher per capita family incomes than the mothers on welfare (p. 37). Here again, as in the Levy analysis, it is clear that a major way out of poverty for a low-income mother is combining her earnings with those of a husband. Not all the ex-welfare mothers worked, and the per capita income for the families of these nonworking mothers was about the same as that of welfare families (p.37). Presumably these mothers preferred to look after their husband and children, rather than earn additional income. And there is evidence that these women found more positive relationships with their husbands than did employed women (p. 198). Whether a wife's staying at home increases accord or whether marital discord encourages women to go out and work cannot be determined from the data. The finding does suggest the need to develop a "family commitment" measure that would better elucidate the basis for labor force acitivity of mothers.

As mentioned earlier, all mothers in the study gained a great deal of satisfaction from their children (p. 136). The investigator asked the mothers a series of questions about specific parent-child relations to find out how highly the children think of their mothers and also inquired about how well the children get along with their peers and how happy they are. While these items are divided into subgroups and scores of individuals are averaged, there is no evidence that a statistical clustering of the items was undertaken. The clustering appears to have been done on the basis of the investigator's best judgment, not backed up by statistical analysis that would show that respondents really were answering the items in a similar fashion.

The responses do seem to be consistent and have face validity. They suggest that working mothers do not perceive their employment activities as having much negative effect on their children (p. 140). Nonworking mothers perceive a larger negative effect on their children if they worked. These perceptions did not seem to be influenced by whether there was a husband in the household (p. 176). (The study did not determine what the effects of working were from the child's viewpoint.)

When wives were asked about their relationships with their husbands, it was clear, as just indicated, that marital satisfaction was not enhanced by the wife's employment. The employed women tended to be more aggressive and less docile than nonemployed women, perhaps threatening the man's feeling of security (pp. 206ff.). These women saw their husbands as less effective than did the women

who were not employed. Feldman found that employed women gain considerable satisfaction from their jobs (as well as from their children) and have more confidence in their abilities than do nonworking mothers (p. 220).

A multivariate analysis would have more fully exploited the data Feldman gathered. For example, it could have been valuable to determine the extent to which the women's psychological characteristics (e.g., confidence in their own abilities) are related to work behavior when other factors such as education and number of children are controlled.

If the Feldman project was weak in its statistical analysis, it was the only one to look in depth at the life experiences of a group of women living in "Road Junction." As part of the project, Janet Fitchen (1972) entered this small, poor community in upper New York State, originally as a tutor for the children. She later used her acceptance in the community of 30 families as a basis for carrying out her detailed study of life activities and experiences there. Compared with the brief survey interviews, this kind of study provides more insight into the life style of poor persons living in a poor community.

Fitchen shows how family upheavals and lack of resources make it difficult for people to plan ahead and keep long-term jobs. Hence they tend to obtain low-skilled janitorial or factory jobs rather than get training for jobs that pay more but require continuing and punctual attendance. Fitchen found these people to be insecure and to think poorly of themselves. She goes on: "This low self-image is derived from their cumulative failures in so many aspects of their lives and is magnified and reinforced by their knowledge that society shuns them as 'trash' " (p. vi). The study does not deal directly with WIN or the experiences of WIN participants and so is not of direct value in setting WIN policy. It does suggest the need for a participant observation study bearing on WIN experiences.

Even with all this evidence that recipients of welfare have less resources and more family responsibilities than nonwelfare recipients, it nevertheless may be argued that the recipients lack adequate psychological orientations toward work (not part of the traditional personality measures used in the studies mentioned), which may cause them not to exert themselves educationally or to gain job skills. A study carried out by Leonard Goodwin (1972) was aimed explicitly at the issue of comparing work orientations among the poor with those among middle-class persons.

# Comparing Work Orientations

The study involved creation of nine clusters of items measuring various orientations toward work. One cluster was called the work ethic. It included 15 items rated on a 4-step agree-disagree ladder. Among the items were: Hard work makes you a better person; I like to work; you have to work hard in order to get ahead. Each cluster was developed through extensive pretesting with poor groups, including welfare recipients. And the final measures were found to be applicable to and reliable for middle-class as well as poor groups (p. 136ff.).

One set of respondents consisted of 250 long-term welfare mothers in Baltimore and their teenage sons. Another set consisted of almost 800 middle-class families in the city and suburbs of Baltimore, with separate interviews for mothers, fathers, and teenage sons or daughters. A third set consisted of about 1,400 WIN participants at six different sites around the country. And a fourth set was the WIN staff at those six sites. Each group rated the same items used to measure the several work orientations, while WIN staff and the suburban Baltimore respondents were asked in addition to give the ratings that they thought welfare persons in the WIN Program would give.

The work ethic score for each of these groups was high. No statistically significant differences were found among the mean values given by any of the adult groups (p. 112). Several ways of checking for respondent bias were introduced. One consisted of having interviewers of different race, class status, and sex carry out the personal interviews among the Baltimore welfare recipients. It was found that recipients tended to give higher work ethic responses to middle-class white interviewers than to black interviewers. Only the responses to the latter interviewers were used. There were still no significant differences between welfare respondents and others on the work ethic scale (p. 35).

Life goals, such as having a good job, having good family relations, and having good health were rated on a four-step ladder with best way of life at the top and worst way of life at the bottom. The same goal items clustered for poor as for more affluent persons, and the average ratings of all the items taken together showed no significant differences among groups. Thus the content of life goals and work ethic are shared across socioeconomic lines, and the strength of commitment to these values also is shared.

There were differences among groups with respect to other orientations. Welfare recipients had decidedly less confidence in their ability to succeed in the work world—they tended to agree more strongly with such items as, "Success in a job is mainly a matter of luck" (p. 83). They were strikingly more accepting of welfare—responding more positively to such questions as, "Would you go on welfare if you could not earn enough to support yourself and your family?" (p. 83) Goodwin explained these differences as the result of welfare recipients' experiencing failure in the work world and indeed having to accept welfare. He concluded that, while basic values such as the work ethic are shared across class lines, beliefs about one's abilities or choices of action depend upon the amount of success or failure one has experienced in the past.

While the Goodwin findings come from large numbers of individuals, his measures remain to be tested further on a national sample of welfare and WIN participants and middle-class respondents. Findings of low confidence of welfare people are consistent with those of Fitchen in her study of a small, poor community, of Thompson and Miles, and of Feldman.

# In Summary

Research has shown the following about the orientations and work experiences of welfare recipients:

1. Welfare recipients do not differ markedly from other Americans with respect to general personality characteristics or with respect to the work ethic and basic life goals. Where differences do occur—e.g., welfare recipients having lower self-confidence—they can be attributed to the recipients' continuing experience of failure.

2. There is no clearly differentiated group of poor persons who are just like welfare recipients but refuse to take welfare. Recipients generally have less education, less job potential, more medical difficulties, and more dependents than do those not on welfare.

3. While there is substantial movement in and out of poverty, the chances of a low-income (and especially black) family headed by a woman permanently moving out of poverty are much less than they are for a family with a male head. This is not because welfare mothers refuse to work. Many of them do work for varying periods of time, but they are not able to command a high enough salary in relation to the number of people in their families.

4. Some welfare mothers prefer to remain home to take care of their families rather than work. While low-income working mothers do not feel that they disadvantage their children by working, there is some evidence that working strains their relations with their husbands.

These results indicate that most persons are on welfare because they cannot earn enough in spite of their efforts to support their dependents. The next question is whether a work-training program can help.

# 3. IMPACT OF WIN: INPUT-OUTPUT EMPHASIS

Does WIN markedly help welfare recipients obtain jobs and leave welfare? This query moves the discussion from a concern only with the characteristics of the recipient and job market systems (chart 1, ch. 1) to a concern with how the components of the delivery system affect the characteristics of welfare recipients and their employability in the job market. Studies in this area are divided for convenience into two groups. The first, reviewed in this chapter, tends to emphasize how the characteristics of WIN participants and the WIN components (inputs) are related to subsequent work experiences (outputs) of those participants. The second group of studies tends to emphasize what happens in the WIN experience and how it affects the orientations of participants.

## WIN I Results

One of the early studies trying to relate WIN participants' characteristics to success in WIN and the work force was carried out by Thompson and Miles (vol. 5, 1972). It built upon their earlier effort, reviewed in the previous chapter, which delineated the characteristics of welfare recipients who obtained employment and left welfare, as compared with recipients who stayed on welfare. Their approach was to see whether the same characteristics that distinguished persons who had left welfare would also distinguish successful WIN participants, those who obtained jobs and left welfare (p. 1). This was a reasonable approach, and 1,200 black and white women entering WIN at 30 different sites became the initial subjects of the study.

The subjects were interviewed during a 2-month period in the summer of 1970, again 6 months later, and then 12 months after they had entered the program. By the time of the third interview, the number of respondents had shrunk to 920. Given the difficulties of maintaining a sample of this kind over time, this is a reasonable result.

The measure of success of WIN participants should have been related solely to their post-WIN experiences. But only half of the participants had left WIN by the end of 12 months. Hence, the measure of success included participation in WIN components. The highest success scores went to persons who had graduated from WIN and obtained well-paying jobs. Intermediate scores went to those enrolled in various WIN components. Lowest scores went to persons who had been back on welfare for "no good cause" (vol. 5, p. 12). The distribution of scores showed that only a quarter of the final sample were working, about half were still in WIN, and a quarter had dropped out and were on welfare.

The analysis consisted of determining what other variables were associated with the success measure. It suffered from the same limitations as the earlier study by these authors: A lack of clustering items to form reliable attitudinal measures; dependence on dichotomous responses to questions; and presentations of fourfold tables, looking at only two variables at a time rather than having a multivariable analysis.

The authors did offer a few correlations suggesting that the predictive ability of the variables under consideration was small. Thus, the self-confidence measure of the Sixteen Personality Factor Questionnaire was correlated only -0.12 with the success measure (p. 15). The attitudinal measures had little relation to success. There were two items that slightly distinguished black women who were successful from those who were not—strong belief about the importance of a steady job and rejection of the belief that luck is more important than hard work for success.

Demographic variables seemed to have some effect on success. The higher the education of the participant when she entered WIN, the more likely she was to be working afterward (pp. 25ff.). Similarly, the more work experience a participant had before entering WIN, the more likely she was to be working afterward (p. 28). These effects are not very strong, as seen in the fourfold tables, and they are hardly novel.

Thompson and Miles do present additional findings on the attitudes of participants toward WIN. They discover that taking part in WIN has some beneficial effect on participants' feelings about themselves and on their children. But this effect is independent of whether they obtain jobs (p. 62). Overall, little light is thrown on the reasons for success of WIN participants.

Another study, directed by Ann Richardson (1975), remedied the defect of short-range followup. It involved interviews with former WIN participants up to 2 years after they had left the program. The focus was on youth, because it was thought that young people provided a special problem. Thirteen sites around the country were selected on the basis of their having high or low dropout and placement rates for young participants. Each site was visited in 1973 in order to compile lists of names and addresses of persons 16 to 21 years old who had been in WIN during the period 1971 to 1973.

It was discovered at that point that the criteria for dropouts and, to some extent, placements were not consistent across sites—e.g., what was called a "dropout" at one site was classified as "other" at another site. Applying the same criteria across sites showed that youth were not dropping out at any greater rate than were others and, moreover, that there were very few participants under 18 years of age (p. 9). Hence the sites chosen for study did not constitute a meaningful sample. Technically, the results cannot be generalized. But when seen in the perspective of other studies, these results contribute to certain general patterns of findings.

The basic data consist of interviews with 518 persons under the age of 22 who had participated in WIN up to 2 years prior to the interview. One of the striking findings was the great program differences across sites. For example, at site B (41 respondents), more than one-third of the respondents had some vocational training. Only one-tenth from site E (24 respondents) had such training. Such a finding is specially pertinent in relation to what happened to participants after leaving WIN. Almost nine-tenths of those from site E entered laboring jobs, with none entering white-collar jobs. From site B, on the other hand, only about one-fifth entered laboring jobs, and almost half entered white-collar jobs (pp. 36, 192). These kinds of findings suggest that different WIN sites adopt different styles with respect to training and placing participants in jobs. Such styles may be based on such factors as judgments about the local labor market, requirements set by the WIN director's superiors, and resources available to the WIN site. This wide site variation is emphasized also in the Schiller studies, to be mentioned in a moment. The point is that, by pooling data from sites using very different approaches or operating in very different contexts, one may obscure positive relationships between training components and job achievements that are occurring at a few sites.

There is a complementary use of both tabular material and regression analysis in the Richardson study. The regression results show the extent to which WIN components, site, age, sex, etc., influence such matters as job placement and wages. A positive relationship was found between immediate job placement and having participated in on-the-job training (OJT). Participants across all sites who had taken OJT (N = 52) had a 15 percent greater chance of working following WIN termination than did those in the sample as a whole (p. 190). (Or put another way, according to Richardson, while 46 percent of the total group of 518 respondents reported that they were working following WIN termination, 61 percent of those who had participated in OJT reported that they were working.) Participation in vocational education while in WIN increased employment afterward by 5 percent (p. 190). Being white, male, and a high school graduate each added 5 percent to the probabilty of working immediately after WIN (p. 190).

A less sanguine picture emerges from consideration of labor force activity 30 months after leaving WIN. Participation in OJT increases the probability of longer term employment only 4 percent (pp. 121, 195). Participation in vocational education adds nothing to the probability of longer term employment (p. 195), and none of the other WIN components have any independent and positive effect (p. 195). However, small positive effects of being male, white, and a high school graduate continue.

One can interpret the very meager impact of WIN components on the longer term employment of participants as being the result of poor sampling, heterogeneity of sites, and the youth of the participants. All these factors probably contribute to the result. However, the author offers another explanation, which also probably has some validity. She proposes that the initial advantages provided by OJT and vocational education "are later swamped by the more immediate circumstances of day-to-day living—factors such as employers' attitudes toward young, relatively inexperienced workers, labor market conditions, and childbearing" (p. xiii).

There is one major effect on long-term employment that Richardson does not stress. Those who were working at the time of WIN termination were 20 percent more likely to be working over the long term than was the average member of the sample (p. 195). This difference occurs even while pre-WIN work experience has no bearing on subsequent employment. There is also a 5-percent increase in the probability of long-term work effort on the part of persons who spent 10 or more months in WIN (p. 195). Hence, WIN apparently has helped certain persons gain kinds of skills that enable them to obtain and hold onto jobs, even though it is not possible to identify those skills or trace the positive effects to participation in specific WIN components.

Before any hard conclusions about WIN are reached, it is necessary to consider the other studies that sought to relate participant characteristics and WIN training components to post-WIN labor force activity. One of these was conducted by Bradley Schiller (1972). Data were collected during 1971-72 from 36 sites around the country, chosen on the basis of differing unemployment rates, geographical location, and effectiveness of programs as measured by an index that combined measures of the extent of employment preparation, job placement, and quality of job placement among WIN participants. The precise method of site selection is not described in detail. In any case, Schiller and his colleagues spent about a week at each site in order to gather data about the site and interview a total of 635 WIN persons. Presumably, the latter represented a stratified, random sample of WIN current participants, graduates, and dropouts (p. C-3). How this kind of sampling was accomplished is not described. Given the small number of WIN interviews at any one site, it is difficult to see how one would obtain a representative sample of persons in these three categories. (For example, only 40 interviews were conducted at the Los Angeles site, where there were more than 6,000 enrollees.) As in the other studies, sampling difficulties would throw doubt on novel findings, if such were to be observed, but could help strengthen patterns of findings observed in other studies.

Schiller developed a means of measuring the effectiveness of WIN sites based on criteria set by administrators on the one hand and participants on the other. The measures were slightly different for these two groups, administrators giving greater emphasis to job placement and participants more to employment preparation. The two other criteria were quality of job placement and completion of the WIN Program (pp. 24-25). On the basis of interviews at the sites, Schiller created an effectiveness rating for each site and then tried to determine what factors were related to it. A wide range of effectiveness scores was obtained. And in the regression analysis, using first the administrators' view of effectiveness and then the participants', Schiller found that the significant predictors were characteristics of the participants themselves (sex, education, race) and the amount of community support for WIN (p. 36). WIN Program components did not significantly enter into the equations.

The other major consideration was what affected the job placement of individual participants. The only variable connected with the WIN effort that approaches statistical significance was interagency relations—i.e., relations between the WIN and welfare offices (p. 39). Measures of placement activity of WIN staff or supportive services did not significantly affect job placement. Another measure external to WIN that proved to be significant was the unemployment rate at each site (table B-3). Hence once again, the variables that have some impact on job placement appear to be those outside the WIN effort itself.

There is some uncertainty as to the adequacy of the measure of job placement. It was apparently a dichotomous variable (working or not working) based upon a report of WIN staff about each participant in the study.[1] There may have been instances in which WIN dropouts who got jobs on their own were later classified by WIN staff as "suc-

---

1. This information was provided by Bradley Schiller in a letter of Aug. 19, 1976.

cessfully" placed by WIN. Such an occurrence would dilute the possibly significant effects of WIN training in the regression analysis. In trying to account for the quality of job placement for WIN participants, Schiller came up with the same finding that no WIN activities were significant (table B-3) (and there is the same caveat about the accuracy of the data).

At the same time, Schiller reported that 76 percent of WIN participants who completed training obtained jobs at termination. Only 19 percent of those who dropped out of WIN prematurely had found jobs (p. 45). WIN, therefore, had a positive effect on those who stayed with it. The question arises as to why this kind of result did not appear in the regression equations. One reason is that the training variable in those equations was based upon respondents' subjective evaluation of how satisfied they felt with training, rather than on whether they had actually completed a training program.[2] Also, relatively few WIN participants completed training (29 percent) so that errors in measurement on a small number of persons could have a marked effect in the regression analysis.

This first Schiller study emphasized the importance of factors external to WIN—unemployment rates, interagency relations—influencing job placement of participants. It also showed, as did the Richardson study, that, overall, WIN was unable to connect that impact to participation in any of the WIN components. Do the subsequent more extensive studies establish this connection?

## WIN I Versus WIN II

A second Schiller (1974) project focused primarily on the job search and work activity of two sets of WIN participants; those who had left the program by 1972 and those who left afterward. The former were designated as WIN I participants, with 72 of the 349 interviewed having been in the first Schiller study. Those who left WIN after 1972 were designated as WIN II participants. The distinction rests upon the implementation in 1972 of the Talmadge amendments to the WIN legislation, which mandated greater emphasis on job placement and less emphasis on training.

A total of 571 persons were interviewed in 16 cities around the country between September 1973 and February 1974, covering a period of up to 3 years after WIN termination for some respondents (p. 2). No information was supplied on how the cities were chosen or the individuals selected for interviews, except that 72 respondents were part of the earlier study. Presumably, however, this was done on some reasonable basis.

A great deal of job search activity was found. The most frequently used sources for job leads were want ads, direct contact with employers, and friends (p. 21). But among those who got jobs, WIN was the most frequently used source of leads, accounting for one-third of the jobs obtained (p. 26). Friends, relatives, and direct contact with employers accounted for almost half of the jobs, while the employment service accounted for only 6 percent (p. 26).

In the course of examining job search, the labor force activities of the sample were explored. Regression analyses were conducted, using as the dependent variable employment status of respondents (presumably at time of interview). Men and the more educated showed significantly higher employment. But the effect was not of great magnitude. The variables of sex and education account for less than 6 percent of the total variance of employment scores (p. 32).

Vocational training did not significantly enter the equation. But this variable was measured only by asking respondents whether they had taken any vocational training since

leaving high school.[3] The actual training they received in WIN and whether they completed a program were not included. Hence the real impact of the variable is indeterminate in this study.

When a regression analysis was performed on the responses of 70 persons who had participated in the earlier Schiller study and on whom there was longitudinal data, only one variable was a significant predictor of current employment, and that was their employment status at the time of the previous interview in 1971 (p. 54). As in the Richardson findings, those WIN participants who obtain jobs immediately tend to continue in gainful employment. In some manner, the WIN experience encourages some participants to obtain and hold jobs.

The latter conclusion is reinforced by the second Schiller study's consideration of the overall employment impact of WIN I versus WIN II. Out of a total of 337 WIN I persons interviewed, 215 had completed their employability plan. Of that group, 83 percent were employed. However, only 34 percent of those who had dropped out of WIN were employed (p. 7). Among WIN II participants, no distinction was made between dropouts and completers of employability plans because Schiller found little in the way of employability plans in operation (p. 9). The fact that only 58 percent of the WIN II terminees were employed at time of interview (p. 7) suggests that WIN I training added something to the employment capability of welfare recipients which was lost in WIN II.

The earnings of the WIN I and WIN II respondents are not presented. Schiller probably found no significant differences, however, since in a subsequent section investigating the correlates of wages earned, he does not report membership in one or the other group as a significant variable. The variables that are significant in influencing wages among all respondents in full-time jobs are sex and education; yet they account for only about 17 percent of the variance in wages (p. 43). With respect to job tenure, the only significant predictor was the length of time since the person had left WIN (p. 49).

These findings add little new to an understanding of factors affecting employment of WIN participants. Schiller did point out that WIN staff had consistently emphasized the importance of "client motivation" in obtaining jobs (p. 34). This suggests that unmeasured variables are accounting for a large portion of the job success of WIN persons. It also is possible that, by looking across many WIN sites, one is "averaging out" significant results achieved at one or a few sites.

A study focusing on a single area, Ramsey County (St. Paul), Minn., was completed recently by Earl Hokenson and others (1976). Personal interviews were conducted in 1974 with 313 men and women who had terminated WIN during 1970-72. This group consituted the WIN I sample. The WIN II sample consisted of 508 men and women who had terminated the program since 1972.

The authors made an effort to measure attitudinal variables. The measures were intuitively reasonable. And one might expect the extent of WIN terminees' employment to be related to the degree to which they valued the work ethic, had confidence in their abilities, and experienced job satisfaction. The way in which the authors created these measures, however, appears inadequate. No evidence was offered, for example, on using statistical techniques to cluster the items assumed to be part of the "work ethic" (pp. 52ff.). The statistical reliability for that measure (the calculations of which are not presented) turned out to be so low as to make the measure meaningless (pp. 320ff.). The authors seemed unaware that Goodwin (1972) already had

---

2. Ibid.

3. Ibid.

developed reliable measures of work ethic and confidence in one's abilities.

The bulk of the authors' analysis consisted of tables relating one variable at a time to successful or unsuccessful employment. At the end, multiple regression results were presented. Two dependent variables were used—employment at WIN termination and, employment at the time of interview. Separate equations were computed for WIN I men and women and WIN II men and women, making eight equations altogether (pp. 324-25).

The equations showed very few significant predictors of employment status. The self-confidence measure had a significant, but small, effect only for WIN I men at termination. The health status of these men negatively affected their employment. Hokenson and others pointed out that many suffered from alcoholism, drug use, mental health problems, and police records (p. 35). The presence of a spouse in the home was positively related to employment of both men and women at WIN termination. Each of these effects was small. The authors did not present a stepwise multiple regression analysis to indicate the contribution of each variable to explaining the variance in employment scores. (The $R^2$ figures presented, around 0.25 for WIN I persons and 0.14 for WIN II persons, are not interpretable since they are based upon the contribution of all 17 variables when only a few are statistically significant.)

The major point here is that such variables as WIN basic education and vocational training and such demographic variables as education and family size do not affect employment at termination from WIN. Hokenson and others found, however, that 84 percent of the women who completed vocational training in WIN I obtained jobs at termination. Conversely, only 43 percent of the 35 women who started but failed to complete vocational training, and merely 33 percent of the 69 women who did not enter vocational training, got jobs at termination (p. 194). Similar results were observed for these women with respect to employment at followup (p. 195). Among the WIN I men, there was no marked effect from vocational training, but that may have been the result of relatively few (only one-quarter of 153 men) entering that component (p. 194).

The question arises as to why vocational education did not show up as a significant predictor of employment in the multiple regression equations for WIN I women. The authors did not address the issue. It is likely that they did not distinguish between those who entered and those who completed vocational training. Combining those categories would dilute the statistical impact of vocational training on employment. It is also possible that other variables included in the equation, such as level of education, are related to the effects of training. Those women who seemed to WIN staff better able to profit from vocational training, including perhaps the better educated and more job experienced, might have been assigned to that component. It could have been useful to explore the relationship of training to employment in a stepwise multiple regression analysis.

In any case, there is another indication here that WIN may have had a positive impact. Along this same line, there is a sharp difference in earnings between WIN I and WIN II participants. The average monthly gross earnings at followup were more than $100 greater for those women who terminated WIN I with a job than for those who terminated WIN II with a job. Even those who terminated WIN I without a job but had one at followup were earning an average of $80 more per month than their WIN II counterparts (p. 309). A similar finding is reported for the men There were no controls for education or other variables on these data. And the findings n.v. indicate only that WIN II participants were less job re·· than were those entering WIN I. On the other hand, der· .raphic data on the groups did not indicate marked differences (p. 170ff.). Hence again, as in the Schiller material, there is a hint of some-

thing positive happening in the WIN I effort, which emphasized training.

Returning to the multiple regression equations, one finds a really strong variable predicting employment at followup. This was employment status at the time of WIN termination. Those employed at termination—men and women from both WIN I and WIN II—were more likely to be employed later on (p. 325). This corroborates the findings of Richardson and Schiller on this point. And because prior work activity is unrelated to employment after the WIN experience (pp. 324-25), there is some suggestion that the experience facilitated work activity. While these kinds of results from any single study are suspect, one is able to have more confidence in them because they are corroborated by other studies.

Three other studies also add some evidence to the significance of the WIN effort as it involved some kind of training emphasis. The first was a followup of 121 former WIN I participants in the Chicago program. Under the direction of Audrey Smith and others (1975), they were interviewed an average of 18 months after termination. A major finding was that the female participants had upgraded the status of their pre-WIN jobs. The men had not done so (p.14). The authors attributed this result to the fact that the women had received training, whereas the men tended to get direct job placement (p. 12).

The second study is quite different, an econometric attempt by Ehrenberg and Hewlett (1975) to evaluate on a national basis the effect of WIN II in lowering AFDC payments. An advantage of this kind of effort, which views WIN results in relation to total AFDC costs, is that it takes into account displacement effects—the possibility that putting WIN participants to work merely displaces existing workers and sends them onto welfare. The authors carefully point out the limitations of the data (including possible reporting errors in the WIN II data) they use in coming to the tentative conclusion that WIN II lowers AFDC costs somewhat when some training is provided to the participants (p. 3). They question the advisability of focusing all effort on placement of WIN participants and cutting back on training (p. 9).

The third study was carried out by Michael Wiseman (1976), previously mentioned in chapter 2. It involved the collection of data from the cases of about 1,500 AFDC mothers and 1,500 fathers on AFDC-U during the period 1967 through 1972. Random samples were drawn each year, with information gained about these persons extending for the following 12 months (pp. 20-21). Using multiple regression techniques, Wiseman sought to account for the employment experienced by these persons. Among mothers, employment was hindered by the presence of young children (p. 45). Previous job experience significantly improved chances of subsequent employment (p. 45). But of most importance, he found a significant positive effect from previous employment training through WIN (p. 45). No breakdown of training components was possible from the data he had at hand.

The situation among the men was somewhat different. WIN training had no significant impact on subsequent employment (pp. 58-60). This consistent with the tendency for WIN men to be placed directly in jobs—e.g., see the A. Smith study just mentioned. A significant contribution was observed from the training the men received through programs other than WIN (pp. 58-60). Employment was significantly reduced as the number of hours AFDC-U men could work without losing welfare benefits was lowered to the present 100 hours per month.

Further hindrances were the experiences of being fired from or having to quit a previous job. Having other sources of income, on the other hand, increased employment possibilities. These findings suggest the possibility that, as men have negative experiences in the work force, they tend to lose confidence and withdraw from work activity. As they gain support—e.g., through having other sources of income—they are encouraged to risk further effort in trying to rise in the work force.

## Latest WIN II Results

In trying to draw together the findings reported in this chapter, it is appropriate to refer to the most extensive and sophisticated attempt to evaluate the impact of WIN that has just been reported by Schiller and others (1976).[4] The study uses a comparison group against which to view the impact of WIN II. Almost 2,500 participants and over 2,500 persons in the WIN registrant pool but not participating in the program were interviewed three ti: s at 78 sites across the country. The three waves of interviews were begun in March 1974 and ended in September 1975, providing a longitudinal perspective (pp. lff.). The basis for selecting the sites was not given, but presumably this was a representative sample of all WIN sites. Data were presented to show that the sample characteristics were similar to those of the national WIN population (pp. 50-56). The basic aim was to compare the subsequent job earnings (also weeks worked, weeks on welfare, and amount of the welfare grant) of those who participated in WIN with those who did not. A multiple regression technique was used to try to relate the dependent variables just mentioned to participation in prog. .n components and to demographic characteristics of the WIN groups. Measures were made in such a manner as to control for differences across sites (pp. 200ff.).

The importance of a comparison group becomes apparent in viewing pre-WIN earnings. One year prior to entering WIN, the comparison group and WIN participant group had similar earnings. Six months prior to entering WIN, the participant group, unlike the comparison group, suffered a sharp loss in earnings. The subsequent post-WIN earnings of the WIN participants were, therefore, partly the result of these participants' having come back to their normal earning power. This part of their earnings was controlled through use of the comparison group and was not attributed to WIN (pp. 4 lff. and 206ff.).

Schiller and others distinguished five levels of service provided by WIN, as follows: (1) No services, (2) advice and effort in job placement, (3) education, (4) vocational training, and (5) assignment to on-the-job training (OJT) or public service employment (PSE) (p. 117). Schiller and others argued reasonably that persons receiving different levels of training should be considered separately. They found that for men only the fifth level of training significantly distinguished the WIN participants from the comparison group (p. 120). That is, those men assigned to OJT or PSE were earning about $1,900 more per year than were their counterparts during the followup period.

Schiller and others correctly presented a caveat with respect to those findings. Because the followup period was only about 9 months, those 102 men (and 204 women) placed in OJT or PSE were still in subsidized employment (p. 119). There was no way to know whether their jobs would continue after the subsidy ran out or whether their earnings would remain the same. (Data from the previously mentioned Richardson (1975) study showed that the earnings impact of OJT tended to disappear after some 30 months.)

For women, the situation differed. There was a significant impact on earnings from vocational training (about $500 per year) and a smaller one from the job placement

effort (about $300 per year), as well as a major impact of about $1,400 per year from OJT or PSE (p. 120). (The last finding was subject to the same caveat as that for the men.) The overall results support evidence from other studies that WIN has a beneficial effect on job earnings.

There also was some indication that WIN lessened the welfare grant for women and perhaps for men (pp. 120, 222ff.). This finding complements that from the econometric study using macro data, mentioned earlier (Ehrenberg and Hewlitt, 1975), which concluded that WIN II was possibly responsible for some lessening of AFDC costs when some training was provided to participants.

These findings do not suggest that WIN is about to resolve the welfare issue. The possible reduction of $10 or $15 a month in a welfare grant or reduction of a few weeks in the time a small percentage of recipients are on welfare will not have major national impact. The fact that the program does have some positive effect, however, should not be ignored. The positive results could probably be increased if the variables affecting job success were better delineated. The study by Schiller and others is disappointing in this respect. In spite of three waves of interviews with some 2,500 WIN participants and two visits to each of the 78 sites to examine program operations, the researchers obtained little substantial data to indicate what was really happening at those sites that led to positive (and negative) impact on participants.

One might respond by pointing to the postive effects that have been shown at least for women through job placement advice and vocational training. Presumably, increased efforts in these areas would lead to increased earnings of welfare mothers. If this were so, then those sites in the study that offered more services should have WIN participants who showed higher job earnings. At this crucial point, the study came up with a blank. No significant relationship was found between the kind and amount of services offered at the sites and the subsequent earnings of WIN participants at those sites (pp. 259ff.).

This suggests that the positive impact of WIN on participants is not being identified adequately by the labels given the service efforts—e.g., "vocational training." If there was a standard and significant effect from "vocational training" as such, then the average earnings of graduates from sites with large programs should have been significantly greater than average earnings of graduates from sites where there were only small programs.

Under the label of "vocational training," different things probably are happening within the same site as well as among sites, especially with regard to the quality of staff-participant interactions. Certain staff persons may be better able than others to provide participants with a cumulative set of successful experiences that enhance their skills and self-esteem and lead them into regular, higher paid employment. Consideration of these possibilities fell outside the task that Schiller and others set for themselves. They did not conceptualize the quality of staff-participant interaction.

Complimenting the statistical analyses of WIN described above are a few studies which utilize participant observation.[1] While these studies provide novel insights into staff-trainee interactions, the generality of their results is left open to question. An evaluation design is needed which integrates quantitative and qualitative kinds of efforts.

---

4. The final report of this study was written by Bradley Schiller. The study, however, was carried out by three organizations, Pacific Consultants, of which Schiller is research director, CAMIL, and HETRON. Hence Schiller is not totally responsible for the results, and references are to the Schiller and others study.

1. Further information is provided in the original work from which this article is excerpted. Included is a discussion of the behavioral impact of providing job opportunities to welfare recipients and the little that is known about the relation of the work activity of these persons to their family structure and personal motivation.

## Bibliography

Ehrenberg, Ronald G., and Hewlett, James G.
    1975    *The Impact of the WIN 2 Program on Welfare Costs and Recipient Rates.*
           Technical Analysis Paper No. 15-C. U.S. Department of Labor, Office of the
           Assistant Secretary for Policy, Evaluation and Research, Office of Evalua-
           tion and Research. (pp. 17, 18)

Feldman, Harold.
    1972    *Effect of Welfare Women's Working on Their Family.* Ithaca, N.Y.: Cornell
           University. DOL No. 51-34-69-07-1. (pp. 8, 9, 21, 29)

           About 1,300 female heads of households were interviewed in upper New
           York State. Most of them were welfare mothers, while about 400 were for-
           merly on welfare. Orientations toward work and family were gathered. Work-
           ing mothers did not seem to affect their children negatively, although their
           working seemed to have a negative effect on marital relations.

Fitchen, Janet.
    1972    *The People of Road Junction.* Appearing as vol. III of Harold Feldman,
           *Effect of Welfare Women's Working on Their Family.* DOL No. 51-34-69-
           07-3. (p. 10)

Freidman, Barry L., and Hausman, Leonard J.
    1975    *Work and Welfare Patterns in Low Income Families.* Waltham, Mass.: Heller
           Graduate School, Brandeis University. DOL No. 51-25-73-03. (p. 6)

Goodwin, Leonard.
    1972    *Do the Poor Want to Work ? A Social-Psychological Study of Work Orienta-*
           *tions.* Washington : Brookings Institution. (pp. 9, 10, 21, 31)

Gupte, Pranay.
    1973    "65% of Relief Mothers Proving Disabled in Tests." *New York Times*, Sept.
           24, p. 1. (p. 6)

Hausman, Leonard J.
    1969    *The Potential for Work Among Welfare Parents.* Washington: U.S. Depart-
           ment of Labor, Manpower Administration, Manpower Research Monograph
           No. 12. (p. 5)

Hokenson, Earl, Reuther, Carol J., and Henke, Susan R.
    1976    *Incentives and Disincentives in the Work Incentive Program.* Minneapolis:
           Interstudy. DOL No. 51-27-73-09. (p. 16)

Klausner, Samuel Z. (with chapters contributed by others)
    1972    *The Work Incentive Program: Making Adults Economically Independent.*
           vols. I and II. Philadelphia: University of Pennsylvania. DOL No. 51-40-69-
           01. (p. 7)

Levinson, Perry.
    1970    "How Employable Are AFDC Women ?" *Welfare in Review,* July-August,
           pp. 12-16. (p. 5)

Levy, Frank.
    1976    *How Big Is the American Underclass ?* Berkeley: Graduate School of Public
           Policy, University of California. DOL No. 42-06-74-04. (pp. 6, 7, 25)

Meyers, Samuel M., and McIntyre, Jennie.
    1969    *Welfare Policy and Its Consequences for the Recipient Population: A Study of*
           *the AFDC Program.* Washington: U.S. Department of Health, Education, and
           Welfare, Social and Rehabilitation Service. (pp. 5, 35)

Miller, Joe A., and Ferman, Louis A.
    1972    *Welfare Careers and Low Wage Employment*. Ann Arbor : Institute of Labor and Industrial Relations, University of Michigan - Wayne State University DOL No. 51-24-69-05. (p. 7)

Richardson, Ann.
    1975    *Youth in the WIN Program: Report on a Survey of Client Backgrounds, Program Experience and Subsequent Labor Force Participation*. Washington: Bureau of Social Science Research. DOL No. 51-11-72-04. (pp. 14. 18)

Rorer, Leonard G.
    1972    "Review of Sixteen Personality Factor Questionnaire." *The Seventh Mental Measurements Yearbook*. ed. O.K. Buros. Highland Park, N.J.: Gryphon Press. vol. 1. pp. 332-33. (p. 8)

Schiller, Bradley.
    1972    *The Impact of Urban WIN Programs*. Washington: Pacific Training & Technical Assistance Corp. DOL No. 51-09-70-10. (p. 14)

    1974    *The Pay-Off to Job Search: The Experience of WIN Terminees*. Washington: Pacific Training & Technical Assistance Corp. (pp. 15, 31)

———, and others.
    1976    *The Impact of WIN II: A Longitudinal Evaluation*. Washington: Pacific Consultants. DOL No. 53-3-013-06. (p. 17 )

Smith, Audrey, Fortune, Ann, and Reid, William.
    1975    *After WIN: A Follow-Up Study of Participants in the Work Incentive Program*. Chicago: University of Chicago, School of Social Service Administration, Center for the Study of Welfare Policy. HEW No. 98-P-00500/ 5-03. (p. 17)

Thompson, David L., and Miles, Guy H.
    1972    *Self-Actuated Work Behavior Among Low-Income People*. vol. 2. Minneapolis: North Star Research and Development Institute. DOL No. 51-25-69-06-2. (p. 8)

    1972    *Factors Affecting the Stability of the Low-Income Family*. vol. 3. Minneapolis: North Star Research and Development Institute. DOL No. 51-25-69-06-3. (p. 8)

    1972    *A Study of Low-Income Families: Methodology*. vol. 4. Minneapolis: North Star Research and Development Institute. DOL No. 51-25-69-4. (p. 8)

    1972    *The Characteristics of the AFDC Population That Affect Their Success in WIN*. vol. 5. Minneapolis: North Star Research and Development Institute. DOL No. 51-25-69-06-5. (pp. 8, 13)

U.S. Department of Labor and U.S. Department of Health, Education, and Welfare.
    1976    *WIN at Work: The Work Incentive Program*, Sixth Annual Report to the Congress. Washington: U.S. Departments of Labor and Health, Education, and Welfare. (pp. 5, 35)

Wiseman, Michael.
    1976    *Change and Turnover in a Welfare Population*. Berkeley: University of California, Department of Economics. (pp. 6, 17, 24, 30)

# 24

# An Overview of the Labor-Supply Results

## Albert Rees

The purpose of this article is to provide a summary of the findings of the Graduated Work Incentive Experiment on labor supply, and to do so in a way that makes them accessible to readers who are not concerned with the finer points of methodology and technique. A more complete account of the methods of analysis will be found in the articles that follow. As a necessary preface to the summary of findings, we begin with a discussion of what we expected to find, and why.

### WHAT WE EXPECTED TO FIND

The sponsors of the experiment and the researchers all expected, from the outset, that the payment of substantial amounts of unearned income to poor families would reduce the amount of labor they supplied, though not by very large amounts. These expectations were based in part on theory and in part on the results of nonexperimental empirical research. We begin by reviewing what will be called here the static theory of labor-leisure choice.

### Static Theory

Figure 1 shows the labor-leisure choices of a hypothetical worker who is capable of earning $2.00 an hour. We assume that he is able to vary his weekly hours by such devices as voluntary overtime, part-time work, and multiple job holding; we also assume, for simplicity, that all hours worked are paid at the straight-time rate. In the initial situation, the worker is in equilibrium at point $X$ on indifference curve $I_0$, where he works 40 hours a week and receives a weekly income of $80. He is then offered a negative income tax plan that guarantees him $60 a week if he has no earned income and "taxes" earned income at 50 percent by reducing the guaranteed payment as earned income rises. This plan has a "breakeven" at point $C$ at an earned income of $120; to the left of this

From Albert Rees, "An Overview of the Labor-Supply Results," IX (2) *The Journal of Human Resources,"* 158-180 (Spring 1974). Copyright 1974 by the Regents of the University of Wisconsin System.

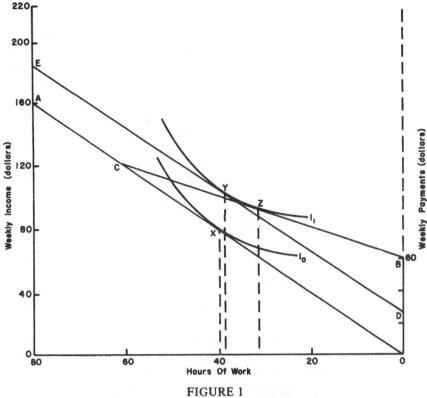

FIGURE 1

RESPONSE TO A NEGATIVE INCOME TAX

point he receives no payments. The opportunity set facing the worker is now
*BCA* rather than *OA*, and he chooses point *Z* on indifference curve $I_1$. His hours
and earned income have decreased and his total income has increased.

The reduction in hours from *X* to *Z* can be divided into an income effect
and a substitution effect by drawing line *DE* parallel to *AO*, which is tangent to
$I_1$ at *Y*. The distance *DO* shows the amount of payments that would yield as
much satisfaction as the original negative tax plan if the tax rate were zero. The
horizontal distance from *X* to *Y* is the pure income effect on hours, since the
wage rate, or the price of leisure, is the same at both points. The horizontal
distance from *Y* to *Z* is the pure substitution effect of the tax rate, since the
level of satisfaction is the same at both points. It should be noted that the
income effect refers to the combined effect on welfare or satisfaction of the
guarantee and the tax, and not that of the guarantee alone. A guarantee of $60 a
week with no tax would enable the worker to reach an indifference curve lying
above $I_1$.

As Figure 1 is drawn, both the income effect and the substitution effect of
the negative income tax reduce hours of work. The negative substitution effect

follows from the usual constraints of neoclassical utility theory on the shapes of indifference curves. If the curves are convex from the Southwest and $BC$ is flatter than $OA$, then $Z$ must lie to the right of $Y$. There is no such necessary relation between $X$ and $Y$. The expectation that $Y$ will lie to the right of $X$ rests on empirical evidence. This is the evidence that as real income has risen through time, hours of work have tended to fall and that, in cross-section, hours of work tend to be shorter in high-paid than in low-paid jobs. In other words, the empirical evidence all indicates that "leisure" (the term used, for convenience, to include all nonwork activity) is a normal good. That leisure is not an inferior good might be expected from the fact that most inferior goods have preferred close substitutes, and there is no close substitute for leisure.

In the case of wage increases, not only is the income effect negative, but it is sufficiently large to outweigh the positive substitution effect of a wage increase, which of course makes leisure more expensive. In the case of a negative income tax, both the income effect and the substitution effect will tend to reduce the amount of work supplied. The experiment enables us to observe points $X$ and $Z$ as the behavior of the control and experimental subjects, respectively. (It should be noted that point $Y$ is not observable.)

The preceding discussion has been cast in terms of the choice of hours of work by a single worker. If we think of the family as a single decision-making unit having a collective indifference map, the same analysis would apply to the. family. Moreover, it would apply to decisions about labor-force participation as well as to decisions about hours. Thus, a negative income tax might be expected to induce some members of the household to withdraw from the workforce, particularly those whose wage rate was low and who had good nonmarket uses for their time. Teenagers might withdraw to devote their full time to schooling, or wives to devote full time to keeping house.

Our expectations about labor-force participation rest more heavily on substitution effects than do those about hours of work. As real wages have risen through time, male labor-force participation rates have fallen, suggesting, as in the case of hours, that negative income effects outweigh the positive substitution effects of real wage increases. For married women, however, the evidence is mixed. In cross-section, holding education constant, the participation rate of wives falls as husbands' incomes rise. However, the participation rate of wives has risen through time as real wages have risen. Either the income effects are smaller than the substitution effects in this context, or they are offset by other changes in the opportunity set confronting wives—such as the availability of work-saving home appliances and prepared foods.

In the presentation above, we have assumed only one specification of the negative income tax plan. In the actual experiment there are eight, with four different guarantee levels and three different tax rates. (The eight plans are defined in Table 1, below.) The general expectation from the theory is that the plans with higher tax rates will have larger substitution effects and hence will produce greater reductions in labor supply, though, strictly speaking, this is true only as among plans that permit the family to achieve the same level of satisfaction. Similarly, one would expect from the empirical evidence on hours of work that, at the same tax rate, the plans with the most generous payments would cause the largest reduction in labor supply, whether generosity is measured in guarantee levels or in the average payments that would be made at the family's normal (preenrollment) income.

## Dynamic Considerations

The theory sketched above is too simple in at least three respects. (1) It assumes that the wage rate confronting each worker is exogenously given and that he can do nothing to affect it. (2) It implicitly assumes that the negative income tax is a permanent change in the opportunity set facing the worker. (3) It assumes that the negative income tax plan is introduced into a world without existing welfare plans. Relaxation of these assumptions gives rise to what can loosely be called dynamic modifications of the standard theory. Each will be discussed in turn.

*Endogenous Wage Change.* The worker could change his market wage in at least three different ways. First, he might withdraw from the labor force or reduce his hours in order to undertake training that would raise his wage at some future time. A permanent negative income tax would make it easier to do this by providing some income during the period of training. A temporary experiment provides an even stronger incentive in the short run, since in this case the training would have to be completed before the end of the experiment. These considerations suggest that there might be a greater reduction in labor supply early in the experiment than the static theory suggests, but that toward the end of the experiment this might no longer be true. If labor supply is measured in earnings rather than in man-hours, the effect toward the end of the experiment could even be to have a larger labor supply from the experimental group than from the control group. However, few of us gave sufficient weight to this line of argument at the beginning of the experiment to expect this result.

A second set of arguments suggests that earnings might fall more than hours throughout the experiment. The jobs open to a person of given skill and experience usually differ in the extent to which they are pleasant or unpleasant. Some involve heavy physical labor, disagreeable working conditions, inconvenient working hours, or inaccessible places of work. Others are lighter, more pleasant, and more convenient. Under conditions of sustained full employment, the less desirable jobs can be filled only at higher wages; the wage differentials thus called forth are known as compensating differentials.

The payment of a negative income tax could lead workers to shift toward pleasant jobs, sacrificing compensating differentials previously earned. Instead of substituting leisure for labor, they would substitute more agreeable work for disagreeable work. Such behavior would cause earnings to fall more than hours.

To the extent that average hours are reduced, there is another source of reduction in hourly earnings. By choosing not to work voluntary overtime, workers would reduce the hours paid at premium rates. In shifting from full-time to part-time jobs, workers might have to accept lower straight-time rates. It is not uncommon for part-time workers to receive less than full-time workers receive for similar work; for example, such differentials are often found in collective bargaining agreements for clerks in retail food stores.

Another possible influence of experimental payments on wages is through their effects on job search. One of the standard arguments in favor of unemployment insurance is that it permits the unemployed worker to search for a suitable job, rather than being forced by lack of income to accept one of the first job offers he receives, even if the wage offered is very low. More generally, any payments that are increased when a worker is not working will lower the cost of search and increase the expected wage of the job offer finally accepted. Negative income tax payments fall into this category, as supplements to unemployment insurance and even more strongly for those workers who are not eligible for unemployment insurance payments. Low-income workers are more likely than others not to receive unemployment insurance benefits. Some are in uncovered industries such as local government, domestic service, and agriculture. Some are new entrants to the labor force, or new residents in the state. Finally, some will have quit their last jobs or have been discharged for cause. Any difference between experimental and control families in the incidence and duration of unemployment should be considered as a change in labor supply, rather than as a result of deficient demand, because experimentals and controls were selected from the same population and face the same demand conditions.

*Limited Duration of Experiment.* We turn next to consideration of the effects on labor supply of the limited duration of the experiment. These, too, do not all work in the same direction. Consider first the male household head with a steady job involving hard work and long hours. If he knew that the negative tax payments were permanent, he might decide to take a job with lighter work and more normal hours. Yet, for a period of three years, such a shift might seem too risky. At the end of the experiment, he would need the higher earned income, but might be unable to get his old job back. For the steadily employed male head, the probability is that an experiment of limited duration will have smaller effects on labor supply than would a permanent program.

For other members of the household, whose attachment to the labor force is less secure, the effects of limited duration may be quite the opposite. Wives, teenagers, and other adults in the household are likely to be in and out of the labor force as family circumstances change. To the extent that periods of withdrawal from the labor force are planned in advance, a temporary experiment encourages the concentration of such periods during the experimental years, when the costs of not working are lower than normal. This may be particularly true toward the end of the experiment.

*Presence of Welfare.* The final consideration is the presence of preexisting welfare plans. At the beginning of the experiment, New Jersey did not give welfare to households with a male head—that is, it did not have a program known as Aid to Families of Dependent Children with Unemployed Parents (AFDC-U). This, indeed, was one of the important reasons for choosing New Jersey as the experimental site. Moreover, at the outset, we did not plan to include a site in Pennsylvania, but it became necessary to do so in order to enroll enough non-Spanish-speaking whites. In January 1969 (three months after the Trenton enrollment but before enrollment in the other sites), New Jersey introduced a welfare program for intact families. Until they were cut back in July 1971, benefits under this plan were more generous than those of most welfare programs in the country.

The presence of welfare complicates the comparison between control and experimental families. In the ninth experimental quarter, 25 percent of control families and 13 percent of experimental families were on welfare (these figures are the highest percentages for any quarter). Among experimental families, the percentage varied by plan, decreasing with plan generosity; ninth quarter figures show 23 percent on the 50-50 and 75-70 plans choosing welfare, compared with only 7 percent on the 125-50 plan. (These abbreviations for the plans are defined in Table 1, below.) It also varied by site, from 6 percent in Jersey City to 21 percent in Paterson-Passaic in the ninth quarter.

The general effect of welfare is to make the observed differences between experimental and control groups smaller than they would be in the absence of welfare. The underestimate occurs essentially because welfare may induce some withdrawal of work effort in the control group. On the other hand, the estimates derived from an experiment in the presence of welfare are perhaps more accurate estimates of the effect of a new national income maintenance program that is superimposed on existing programs.

A very careful analysis of the effects of welfare on the experiment is given in the full report.[1] This analysis suggests that the presence of welfare did not have a major effect on the estimated labor-supply differentials.

Taken as a group, these three arguments lead us to look for certain patterns in the experimental results. However, they do not modify substantially the overall expectations generated by the static theory because, for the household as a whole, they tend to be offsetting.

## The Nonexperimental Literature

In the postwar period, there has been a substantial empirical literature on labor supply, and this literature was important in forming our initial expectations. The

---

1 Irwin Garfinkel, "The Effects of Welfare on Experimental Response," in *Final Report of the Graduated Work Incentive Experiment in New Jersey and Pennsylvania,* Ch. C-II (Madison: Institute for Research on Poverty, University of Wisconsin, 1973).

studies fall into three general groups—studies of hours of work, studies of labor-force participation, and studies concentrating on the effects of nonlabor income.

*Hours of Work.* The studies of hours of work have already been mentioned. It is these studies that lead us to expect some reduction in labor supply for the experimental group, because they suggest that the income effect as well as the substitution effect of a negative income tax will be to diminish the amount of work supplied.

It should be noted, however, that the studies of hours of work have not been confined to low-income workers. They suggest that at or near the mean wage, increases in wage rates are associated with decreases in hours worked, but this need not be true at wages well below the mean, when the desire for added consumer goods may be stronger and the desire for additional leisure weaker. Low-income workers may have a stronger desire to reach the average level of living of their communities than middle-income workers have to rise above it. Indeed, this is exactly what is shown by the usual textbook diagrams of the backward-bending supply curve of labor, which show a forward-rising curve at very low wages, becoming vertical and then bending back as some higher level of wages is reached. Unfortunately, there is no empirical basis for the forward sloping portion of the curve. Moreover, even if substitution effects are stronger than income effects at low wages, the total effect of a negative income tax will still be to reduce hours, since the tax-induced reduction in net wage rates will not produce an income loss, as would a wage cut with no income transfer. The unique feature of a negative income tax plan is that income is increased at the same time as the net wage rate is reduced.

*Labor-Force Participation.* The portion of the labor-force participation literature that is relevant deals with the differences in strength of attachment to the labor force by age, sex, and marital status. The studies of such attachment show very high rates of participation by married men with wife present, only weakly affected by differences in education or the strength of demand. For teenagers, the elderly, and married women, average rates of participation are much lower, and such forces as differences in education or in the strength of demand induce much larger differences in participation rates.

Because of the previous studies of participation rates, we never expected any substantial fraction of the male heads of households to withdraw from the labor force when they received payments. It seemed much more likely that the response of male heads would be shorter hours or longer periods of search between jobs. For wives, teenagers, and the elderly, however, reductions in labor-force participation rates seemed a much more likely outcome.

We were aware, of course, of the popular view that large transfer payments can cause widespread idleness. There are experiences that support such a view, such as the experience with unemployment benefits for returning veterans after

World War II—payments that were sometimes called "rocking chair money." However, many of the veterans involved were single rather than household heads, and they lacked recent civilian work experience. Popular current views on the effect of welfare on work behavior are similarly based largely on experience other than that of male household heads—in this case, mothers without husbands—and, even here, they tend to be based on anecdotal information rather than on systematic evidence. If there were people who expected our experimental treatment to cause large declines in the participation rates of male heads, they were not in our research group.

*Nonlabor Income.* The last kind of research that is relevant consists of studies that have emphasized the effects of nonlabor income on labor supply. Several of them were designed explicitly to simulate from nonexperimental data the effects of a negative income tax program. Nevertheless, they were not influential in forming our expectations—in part, of course, because most of them have appeared since we began the experiment. The most striking thing about them is the very wide range of values of their results, and this lack of agreement weakens confidence in any of the findings.

First of all, these studies face a problem that may be insurmountable. Much of the nonlabor income reported in income surveys consists of transfer payments such as unemployment compensation; workmen's compensation; old age, survivors, and disability insurance; and temporary disability insurance. All of these payments except survivors insurance are totally or partially work conditioned—that is, they cannot legally be received by those who work, or by those who work or earn more than a stated amount. Work behavior determines whether nonlabor income is received and in what amount. If any of these types of work-conditioned transfers are included in the measure of nonlabor income used to simulate a negative income tax, the size of the negative effects on work effort will be overestimated, perhaps very greatly. There are, of course, types of nonlabor incomes that are not work conditioned—particularly dividends, interest, and certain types of pensions. However, the amount of dividend and interest income of the nonaged poor is negligible, and pensions tend to be received by those past prime working age. The nonlabor income of the working poor that is not work conditioned is hard to find in such existing data bases as the Census or the Survey of Economic Opportunity. Some investigators, searching for this needle in the haystack, seem to have seized in desperation at the handiest pitchfork instead. Even those who are clearly aware of the problem of work-conditioned transfers sometimes report amounts of nonlabor income (supposedly *not* work conditioned) that are so large as to call their definitions or procedures into question.

A second general difficulty with the simulation studies of negative income taxes is that they sometimes truncate their samples by current income, thus tending to include a disproportionate number of households that supply, perhaps temporarily, less than average amounts of labor—a selection which could bias the estimated coefficients toward large supply effects. Truncation on a measure such as hourly wages, which is uncorrelated or less highly correlated with the amount of labor currently supplied, would be far preferable. To be sure, the New Jersey—Pennsylvania sample is also truncated on family income, which may not have been the best variable to choose for this purpose. However, the problem is far less serious in a study that estimates labor-supply effects in a period subsequent to that used to select the sample and derives these estimates from a comparison of experimental and control groups where the experimental group receives an exogenous treatment.

It should also be pointed out that the nonexperimental studies estimate substitution effects from cross-sectional differences in average hourly earnings that may not be entirely independent of the effects of the amount of labor supplied. Those who work over 40 hours per week will receive premium pay for overtime; those who want to work only part time may have to accept lower hourly earnings. In an experiment, differential tax rates create a truly exogenous source of differences in net wages.

Despite these deficiencies, the studies that focus on the effects of nonlabor income reinforce the more general labor-supply studies in one important respect—they consistently find larger supply effects for women than for men; indeed, the estimated effects for men are sometimes very close to zero.

### A Summary of Expectations

The researchers involved in the experiment never agreed on and set down in advance a summary of what they felt was the most likely outcome for labor supply. In retrospect, this is unfortunate. Any attempt to do so now is bound to reflect to some extent our present knowledge of the results and thus to understate the degree to which we have been surprised. Despite this caveat, it still seems useful to attempt a summary in retrospect.

We never expected able-bodied male heads of households to withdraw from the labor force in response to temporary payments too small to support large families. We did expect some of them to reduce their hours of work, or to spend more time searching for new jobs when they lost or quit a job. We expected some teenagers to return to school or to stay in school longer as a result of the payments. We expected some working wives to leave the labor force to spend all their time in household work.

On the whole, the reduction in labor supply we expected to find in the experimental group was of the order of 10–15 percent. We did not expect to find any differential effects by ethnic group. However, we did expect to find that higher tax rates would produce greater reductions in labor supply, and so would higher guarantees.

## HOW WE ANALYZE THE DATA

The results presented in the following articles are more complex and somewhat more ambiguous than we anticipated they would be, and they are not easy to summarize. In attempting to do so, we must explain why we regard some of the results as more salient than others. This, in turn, requires some brief discussion of our methods of analysis, which will deal with dependent variables, the control variables, the treatment variables, and the time period.

### The Dependent Variables

There are at least four possible measures of the amount of labor supplied by the household: labor-force participation rates, employment rates, total hours of work, and total earnings. The total hours of work measure includes those not at work as supplying zero hours, and therefore the average level of this variable will be below the average weekly hours of those who are at work. With hours defined this way, the measures listed above are in order of increasing comprehensiveness. Employment includes changes in labor-force participation and in unemployment, which (as pointed out earlier) must be considered as a supply phenomenon in the context of differences between experimentals and controls. Hours includes variations in the two preceding variables and, in addition, variations in hours per week of those at work. Earnings reflects variations in all three preceding variables and, in addition, variation in earnings per hour worked.

It would therefore seem that earnings furnishes the best summary measure of the effects on labor supply. Unfortunately, however, there is a possible bias in the use of the earnings variable not present in the other measures. Experimental families filled out an income reporting form every four weeks; control families did not. The experimental families, therefore, may have learned more quickly than did the control families that what was to be furnished was gross rather than net earnings (that is, earnings before taxes and other deductions, *not* take-home pay). This differential learning process could have caused a spurious differential in earnings in favor of the experimental group, especially during the early part of the experiment.

The analysis of differences in hourly earnings between experimentals and controls supports the idea of this learning effect. For all three ethnic groups, reported average hourly earnings of male experimentals rise relative to those of controls early in the experimental period. For white and Spanish-speaking males, this differential is later reversed or disappears. For black males, it grows even larger toward the end of the experiment, a phenomenon that seems to result from an unusually small rise in hourly earnings in the black control group.

Because of the possible bias in the earnings measure, we shall emphasize the hours measure in summarizing the results. An exception is made in discussing the labor supply of the household as a *whole,* where the earnings measure, despite its defects, serves as an appropriate way of weighting the hours of different members of the household by the value of the labor they supply. It should also be recalled that family earnings are the basis on which payments were determined.

## Control Variables

In measuring supply effects, a large set of control variables was typically entered on the right-hand side of the regression equations. In part these were necessary to control for differences between the experimental and control groups resulting from the fact that families were not assigned to these groups by simple random assignment, but by a more complex stratified design. In part, however, their inclusion was in response to the fact that even in a simple random design, it is important to control for systematic differences that may survive the randomization process.

The control variables are used in two different ways. First, they are entered into the labor-supply equations as variables in their own right. Second, they are often interacted with the variables representing experimental treatments to see whether the treatment has differential effects in different subgroups of the treated population. A control variable that is highly significant in the first of these contexts may not be significant in the second.

One of the most important control variables is the preenrollment value of the dependent variable. Thus, if the dependent variable is hours, hours at preenrollment are usually entered on the right-hand side. This procedure captures the effect of many taste variables that cannot be specified individually, but will also reduce the significance of the control variables that are separately specified. It is worth noting that this kind of control variable cannot be used in a nonexperimental study based on a single body of cross-sectional data.

Some of these control variables, although they could have been expected to be very significant, in fact were not. Thus, after control for ethnicity, there was little systematic difference among experimental sites. On the other hand, health status and ethnicity turned out to be very important variables even when many other control variables were present. For this reason, most of the papers that follow run separate regressions for the three ethnic groups (white, black, and Spanish-speaking) and control for health status.

It is also important to control for potential earned income, since average income levels are not the same in experimental and control groups as a result of the complexities of the design model, and since there may be differential responses at different income levels. The income variable used for this purpose should be free of any influence from the experimental treatment. For this purpose we have used estimates of normal hourly earnings, either based entirely on observations from the control group or derived by methods that isolate and

## TABLE 1

### NUMBER OF EXPERIMENTAL FAMILIES BY PLAN

| Guarantee Level[b] (Percent) | Tax Rate[a] (Percent) | | |
|---|---|---|---|
| | 30 | 50 | 70 |
| 125 | no plan | 138 | no plan |
| 100 | no plan | 77 | 86 |
| 75 | 100 | 117 | 85 |
| 50 | 46 | 76 | no plan |

a  The tax rate, sometimes called the "offset rate," is defined as the rate at which the transfer payment is reduced as the family's income increases. All plans are linear and have the algebraic form: $P = G - tY$ for $Y < G/t$, where $P$ is the dollar amount of transfer payment; $G$ is the dollar amount of guarantee for a given family size; $t$ is the tax or offset rate; $Y$ is the family income; and $G/t$ defines the "breakeven" level of income.

b  Guarantee as a percent of the following basic support levels, referred to here as the "poverty levels": 2 persons, $2,000; 3 persons, $2,750; 4 persons, $3,300; 5 persons, $3,700; 6 persons, $4,050; 7 persons, $4,350; 8+ persons, $4,600. These differ slightly from the official poverty levels as of 1968. They were increased annually by the change in the Consumer Price Index.

abstract from treatment effects. Full descriptions of these normal wage variables are given in the papers that follow.

The foregoing brief account is by no means a complete listing of control variables. Some variables were important in some of the analyses and not in others, and further discussion is provided in the individual papers.

### Treatment Variables

In one sense, the experimental treatment in this experiment is very simple—it consists of giving families cash payments. These payments can be specified much more precisely than can the more amorphous treatments involved in experimental evaluation of counseling, training, or psychotherapy programs. In another sense, however, the treatment is complex. There were eight different payment plans, and within each plan there was variation in payments by family size. Table 1 shows the number of experimental families by payments plan.

In the design stages of the experiment, we all confidently expected significant overall effects of the treatment on labor supply, and attention was focused on measuring differential effects of the treatment plans. In retrospect, this emphasis may have been somewhat misplaced, since the overall treatment effect is not always unambiguous.

In general, two different methods of introducing treatment effects are used. The first is to include a dummy variable for any experimental treatment and two additional sets of variables that specify tax rates and guarantee levels. The second method uses the experimental dummy and a variable measuring average

TABLE 2

AVERAGE PAYMENTS PER FOUR-WEEK PERIOD,
CONTINUOUS HUSBAND-WIFE FAMILIES BY SITE

|  | All Sites | Trenton | Paterson-Passaic | Jersey City | Scranton |
|---|---|---|---|---|---|
| First year | $91.03 | $69.93 | $79.43 | $107.80 | $91.46 |
| Second year | 93.25 | 71.91 | 80.67 | 109.86 | 94.72 |
| Third year | 96.84 | 58.67 | 84.92 | 120.35 | 98.26 |
| Percent change, first to third year | 6.4% | −16.1% | 6.9% | 11.6% | 5.2% |
| Percentage increase in guarantee amount due to CPI |  | 11.7 | 16.6 | 16.6 | 10.5 |

payments levels. The payments reflect the guarantee level, the tax rate, family size, and earned income. To avoid introducing experimental response into the treatment variable, the preenrollment level of income is used in calculating payments. The payments calculation is useful in identifying families who are initially above the breakeven point of their plans, since, although they will be in the experimental group, they all will appear with zero payments.

In practice, two of our plans were dominated by New Jersey welfare during most of the period of the experiment, and attrition from these plans was very high. These were, of course, the two least generous plans—the 50 percent of poverty guarantee with a 50 percent tax rate (50–50 plan) and the 75 percent guarantee with a 70 percent tax rate (75–70 plan). In much of the analysis, these plans are omitted from the treatment group.

Before we discuss effects, it will be useful for the reader to have some idea of the size of the payments and their variation by plan. Table 2 gives, by experimental site, the average size of payments to continuous husband-wife families who received payments in a given four-week period for each of the three years of the experiment. The average payments per period can, of course, be converted to annual averages by multiplying by 13. Thus, the first-year annual average for all such families is $1,183. The average payments are slightly lower for all families than for continuous husband-wife families. We show the data for the latter here, since most of the labor-supply analysis is based on these families.

The data in Table 2 show a mildly rising trend through time, except in Trenton. This trend arises from two sources. First, guarantee levels were escalated annually during the course of the experiment according to the Consumer Price Index. The increase was based on July-to-July changes in the CPI and was implemented in all sites where payments were then being made in September

## TABLE 3

### AVERAGE PAYMENTS PER FOUR-WEEK PERIOD, CONTINUOUS HUSBAND-WIFE FAMILIES BY ETHNIC GROUP

|  | All | White | Black | Spanish-Speaking |
|---|---|---|---|---|
| First year | $91.03 | $87.65 | $ 97.65 | $ 86.96 |
| Second year | 93.25 | 91.03 | 96.59 | 92.23 |
| Third year | 96.84 | 90.11 | 102.83 | 100.32 |
| Percentage increase, first to third year | 6.4% | 2.8% | 5.3% | 15.4% |

1969 (5.5 percent), October 1970 (5.9 percent), and September or October 1971 (4.4 percent). Because of differences in the timing of the experimental period in different cities, Trenton received the first two cost-of-living adjustments, cumulating to 11.7 percent; Paterson-Passaic and Jersey City received all three, cumulating to 16.6 percent; and Scranton received the last two, cumulating to 10.5 percent. In Paterson-Passaic and Jersey City, the third increase in guarantees was in effect for less than a full year before the end of payments; in Scranton it was in effect less than two months, and in Jersey City about seven months. The average increase in guarantee levels for the final experimental year in the two sites that received all three increments thus lies between 11.7 and 16.6 percent, closer to the former figure in Paterson-Passaic, and slightly closer to the latter in Jersey City. When these increases are compared with the increases in average payments shown in Table 2, it can be seen that in every case the increase in payments is less than the increase in guarantees—and by substantial amounts in all sites but Jersey City.

The second factor tending to produce increasing average payments over time is rising unemployment rates. A weighted average unemployment rate for the four sites rose from 4.4 percent in 1969 to 7.1 percent in 1971, a factor that would also tend to produce rising payments as members of the experimental families who lost jobs experienced greater difficulty finding new ones.

In light of the increases in guarantees and the rise in unemployment, the smallness of the rise in average payments over the life of the experiment suggests that there was not an increasing withdrawal of labor supply or any growing falsification of income reports as experimental subjects learned to "beat the system." Either of these kinds of behavior would have produced more rapidly rising payments.

Table 3 gives, by ethnic group, the same kind of data as Table 2. The average payments rise most rapidly for Spanish-speaking families. Since these

TABLE 4

AVERAGE PAYMENTS IN DOLLARS PER FOUR-WEEK PERIOD,
CONTINUOUS HUSBAND-WIFE FAMILIES BY PLAN
(SECOND EXPERIMENT YEAR)

| | Tax Rate (Percent) | | |
|---|---|---|---|
| Guarantee Level (Percent) | 30 | 50 | 70 |
| 125 | no plan | 187.28 | no plan |
| 100 | no plan | 123.72 | 66.07 |
| 75 | 103.54 | 44.17 | 34.91 |
| 50 | 46.23 | 21.66 | no plan |

TABLE 5

PERCENTAGE CHANGE IN AVERAGE PAYMENTS PER PERIOD BY PLAN,
FIRST TO THIRD YEAR, CONTINUOUS HUSBAND-WIFE FAMILIES

| | Tax Rate (Percent) | | |
|---|---|---|---|
| Guarantee Level (Percent) | 30 | 50 | 70 |
| 125 | no plan | 8.9 | no plan |
| 100 | no plan | 9.1 | 13.9 |
| 75 | −4.5 | −10.3 | 15.1 |
| 50 | −2.6 | 3.2 | no plan |

payments rise more than those for all ethnic groups in any one site, something more than the distribution of ethnic groups by site must be at work.

Table 4 shows the average payments to continuous husband-wife families by experimental plan for the second experimental year. These payments vary from $187 per four-week period in the most generous plan to $22 in the least generous. In addition, of course, there is substantial variation within plans because of differences in family size and earned income.

Changes in payments from the first to the third year also vary by plan, as shown in Table 5. In the three plans with a guarantee equal to or above the poverty line, payments increase between 9 and 14 percent. The low guarantee plans vary more, but three of the five show decreases in payments. The decreases include both the plans with the lowest (30 percent) tax rate.

## Experimental Time

We had expected, before the experiment began, that the best results from the experiment would be obtained during the middle part of the experimental period. At the outset, participants might still be learning how to report income and how their payments would vary with changes in income. Toward the end of the experiment, anticipation of the termination of payments might also affect labor supply, producing unknown kinds of "end game" effects. When results are presented separately by years, results for the middle year generally should be the most reliable. Often we use the central two years—that is, quarters 3 through 10; for some purposes we average observations over the entire period.

It also should be recalled that experimental time does not have the same meaning in each site in terms of calendar time, because each site entered and left the experiment at a different date. To control for trends in the economy, calendar time is sometimes entered into the analysis in addition to experimental time.

## WHAT WE FOUND

The principal findings for three groups of participants—married men, married women, and the family as a whole—are presented in three separate articles in this *Journal,* and only a brief summary will be offered in this section.

A succinct summary of the findings is presented in Tables 6–8, which show a regression-estimated mean difference in several measures of labor supply for a selected subset of the sample observations—namely, 693 husband-wife families who met criteria for continuous reporting. This subset of families is selected because they are a reiatatively homogeneous group representing the modal family type among the working poor, for whom the analysis is not complicated by the problems of changes in family composition and missing data. (Other aspects of the sample selection, time period analyzed, and regression specifications are discussed in the articles which follow.) Negative differentials, both absolute and percentage, indicate smaller labor supply on the part of the experimental families compared with control families. Within each table, results are reported separately for each ethnic group. It should be noted that these groups showed important differences in responses.

## Male Heads

As brought out in Table 6 and in the paper by Watts and others [p. 195], the differences in work behavior between experimentals and controls for male heads of continuous husband-wife families were, as we expected, very small. Contrary to our expectations, all do not show a clear and significant pattern; indeed, they show a discernible pattern only after a great deal of refined analysis. Experi-

TABLE 6

HUSBAND TOTALS: REGRESSION ESTIMATES OF DIFFERENTIALS IN
LABOR-FORCE PARTICIPATION, EMPLOYMENT, HOURS, AND EARNINGS
FOR QUARTERS 3–10[a]

| | Labor-Force Participation Rate | Employment Rate | Hours Worked Per Week | Earnings Per Week |
|---|---|---|---|---|
| **White** | | | | |
| Control group mean | 94.3 | 87.8 | 34.8 | 100.4 |
| Absolute differential | −.3 | − 2.3 | − 1.9 | .1 |
| Treatment group mean | 94.0 | 85.5 | 32.9 | 100.5 |
| Percent differential | −.3 | − 2.6 | − 5.6 | .1 |
| **Black** | | | | |
| Control group mean | 95.6 | 85.6 | 31.9 | 93.4 |
| Absolute differential | 0 | .8 | .7 | 8.7 |
| Treatment group mean | 95.6 | 86.4 | 32.6 | 102.1 |
| Percent differential | 0 | .9 | 2.3 | 9.3 |
| **Spanish-speaking** | | | | |
| Control group mean | 95.2 | 89.5 | 34.3 | 92.2 |
| Absolute differential | 1.6 | − 2.4 | − .2 | 5.9 |
| Treatment group mean | 96.8 | 87.1 | 34.1 | 98.1 |
| Percent differential | 1.6 | − 2.7 | − .7 | 6.4 |

a The data for these tables consist of 693 husband-wife families who reported for at least 8 of the 13 quarters when interviews were obtained. The reported differentials in each measure of labor supply are the experimental treatment group mean minus the control group mean, as measured in a regression equation in which the following variables were controlled: age of husband, education of husband, number of adults, number of children, sites, preexperiment labor-supply variables of the husband. These means and the associated control-treatment differentials may therefore be interpreted as applicable to control and treatment groups with identical composition in terms of these variables. Percent differentials are computed using the mean of the control as base.

Official government labor-force concepts, used in the experiment, define someone as in the labor force if he is employed or unemployed. Someone is unemployed if he is actively seeking employment, waiting recall from layoff, or waiting to report to a new wage or salary job.

This and the following two tables appear as Tables 1, 2, and 3 in U.S. Department of Health, Education, and Welfare, *Summary Report: The New Jersey Graduated Work Incentive Experiment,* a Social Experiment in Negative Taxation sponsored by the Office of Economic Opportunity (December 1973), pp. 22–27.

mentals show a slightly higher participation rate than controls, a lower employment rate, and a correspondingly higher unemployment rate. The unemployment rate difference carries over into hours worked per week. However, on the

TABLE 7

WIFE TOTALS: REGRESSION ESTIMATES OF DIFFERENTIALS IN LABOR-FORCE
PARTICIPATION, EMPLOYMENT, HOURS, AND EARNINGS FOR QUARTERS 3–10[a]

| | Labor-Force Participation Rate | Employment Rate | Hours Worked Per Week | Earnings Per Week |
|---|---|---|---|---|
| **White** | | | | |
| Control group mean | 20.1 | 17.1 | 4.5 | 9.3 |
| Absolute differential | -6.7* | -5.9* | -1.4 | -3.1 |
| Treatment group mean | 13.4 | 11.2 | 3.1 | 6.2 |
| Percent differential | -33.2 | -34.7 | -30.6 | -33.2 |
| **Black** | | | | |
| Control group mean | 21.1 | 16.8 | 5.0 | 10.6 |
| Absolute differential | -.8 | -.3 | -.1 | .8 |
| Treatment group mean | 20.3 | 16.5 | 4.9 | 11.4 |
| Percent differential | -3.6 | -1.5 | -2.2 | 7.8 |
| **Spanish-speaking** | | | | |
| Control group mean | 11.8 | 10.7 | 3.4 | 7.4 |
| Absolute differential | -3.8 | -5.2 | -1.9 | -4.1 |
| Treatment group mean | 8.0 | 5.5 | 1.5 | 3.3 |
| Percent differential | -31.8 | -48.3 | -55.4 | -54.7 |

* Significant at the .95 level (two-tailed test).

a The data for these tables consist of 693 husband-wife families who reported for at least 8 of the 13 quarters when interviews were obtained. The reported differentials in each measure of labor supply are the experimental group mean minus the control group mean, as measured in a regression equation in which the following variables were controlled: age of wife, number of adults, number and ages of children, sites, preexperiment family earnings (other than wife's), and preexperiment labor-supply variables of the wife. These means and the associated control-treatment differentials may therefore be interpreted as applicable to control and treatment groups with identical composition in terms of these variables. Percent differentials are computed using the mean of the control as base.

See ft. a of Table 6 for the definition of labor-force participation.

two measures of earnings, experimentals do better than controls—a result that may reflect greater misreporting of earnings by controls. As a generalization, these differences are all quantitatively small and not statistically significant.

By far the most surprising result of the analysis for male heads is the complete failure to find any significant effect for black male heads in any of the analyses, despite the fact that black husband-wife families received larger average payments than did similar families in the other two ethnic groups. Indeed, the estimated supply response for blacks is not only insignificant, but preponderantly positive. This kind of finding for blacks is not limited to male heads; it recurs in the analysis of other components of the household.

TABLE 8

FAMILY TOTALS: REGRESSION ESTIMATES OF DIFFERENTIALS IN LABOR-FORCE PARTICIPATION, EMPLOYMENT, HOURS, AND EARNINGS FOR QUARTERS 3–10[a]

| | Number in Labor Force Per Family | Number Employed Per Family | Hours Worked Per Week | Earnings Per Week | Percent of Adults in the Labor Force Per Family | Percent of Adults Employed Per Family |
|---|---|---|---|---|---|---|
| **White** | | | | | | |
| Control group mean | 1.49 | 1.30 | 46.2 | 124.0 | 57.6 | 51.1 |
| Absolute differential | -.15** | -.18** | -6.2** | -10.1 | -5.3*** | -6.1** |
| Treatment group mean | 1.34 | 1.12 | 40.0 | 113.9 | 52.3 | 45.0 |
| Percent differential | -9.8 | -13.9 | -13.4 | -8.1 | -9.1 | -12.0 |
| **Black** | | | | | | |
| Control group mean | 1.38 | 1.17 | 41.7 | 114.0 | 54.3 | 46.9 |
| Absolute differential | -.07 | -.07 | -.2 | 4.1 | -1.6 | -1.6 |
| Treatment group mean | 1.31 | 1.10 | 39.5 | 118.1 | 52.7 | 45.3 |
| Percent differential | -5.4 | -6.1 | -5.2 | 3.6 | -2.9 | -3.3 |
| **Spanish-speaking** | | | | | | |
| Control group mean | 1.15 | 1.04 | 39.0 | 102.4 | 48.9 | 44.7 |
| Absolute differential | .08 | -.02 | -.4 | 5.0 | 2.4 | -1.0 |
| Treatment group mean | 1.23 | 1.02 | 38.6 | 107.4 | 51.3 | 43.7 |
| Percent differential | 6.7 | -1.5 | -.9 | 4.9 | 5.0 | -2.2 |

a The data for these tables consist of 693 husband-wife families who reported for at least 8 of the 13 quarters when interviews were obtained. The reported differentials in each measure of labor supply are the experimental treatment group minus the control group mean, as measured in a regression equation in which the following variables were controlled: age of husband, education of husband, education of wife, number of adults, number and ages of children, sites, and preexperiment labor-supply variables for the husband and wife. These means and associated control-experimental differentials may therefore be interpreted as applicable to control and experimental groups with identical composition in terms of these variables. Percent differentials are computed using the mean of the control group as base.

See fn. a of Table 6 for the definition of labor-force participation.

** Significant at the .99 level (two-tailed test).

We certainly did not anticipate this outcome; moreover, we have no plausible explanation for it after the fact. There is some indication in the earnings data that something peculiar happened to the black control group, but we don't know why. While there is always some possibility that the result arises from sampling variability, we should note that black continuous husband-wife families comprise more than a third of the total and are a larger group than the Spanish-speaking, for whom consistent and negative supply effects were found.

### Married Women, Husband Present

One of the first things to note about the labor supply of wives is that the participation rates are very low—around 16 percent, which is less than half the 1971 rates of all married women in the U.S. population as a whole (see Table 1 in the article by Cain and others, p. 202). This rate is low in part because the average family size in the experiment is very large, and we overrepresent families with small children. In part it is an unfortunate consequence of the decision to truncate the sample by family income, a decision that leads to an underrepresentation of working wives even among large families. In retrospect, it might have been preferable to truncate on the basis of husband's income or, better still, husband's wage rate. The same decision probably accounts in part for the rather sharp rise in participation rates of control wives over time, since at the outset we overrepresent families where the wife is temporarily out of the labor force.

The effect of the treatment is shown in Table 7 for the three ethnic groups separately. The measured work disincentives are seen to arise mainly from the behavior of white wives; the effects of the treatment on the labor-supply variables of black wives are close to zero and sometimes positive, and the effects on Spanish-speaking wives are negative in Table 7, sometimes positive in the results shown in the paper by Cain and others, but never statistically significant.

The results thus indicate that a temporary negative income tax program would cause a substantial percentage reduction in the proportion of working wives in large low-income families, at least among white wives. How such a result is evaluated in terms of social priorities will depend on one's views about the value of having mothers care for their own children. It should be remembered that these estimated effects are probably larger than those to be expected in an otherwise similar permanent income maintenance program. For the control families, no more than 19 percent of wives were in the labor force in any one quarter, but 41 percent were in the labor force in at least one of the 13 quarters (counting preenrollment). In other words, this is a group that enters and leaves the labor force frequently. The experimental treatment creates a strong incentive to concentrate periods out of the labor force during the life of the experiment. A permanent program, therefore, could be expected to have a somewhat smaller impact.

*The Labor Supply of the Family*

Hollister's analysis (p. 223) applies to the family as a whole, including male heads, wives, and all other members of the household 16 years of age and over, and it covers the full three years of the experiment. A summary of the results is shown in Table 8. The sample is still restricted to continuous husband-wife families. The hours and earnings effects for whites are consistently negative and range from 8 to 16 percent. For blacks, the earnings effects of the experimental treatment are large and positive. The hours effects are small and differ in sign. For Spanish-speaking families, all estimates are negative.

The results for the family as a whole for whites are thus consistent with those from the separate analyses of male heads and wives in showing appreciable and significant negative effects on labor supply. For blacks, the results again show predominantly anomalous positive responses, though not consistently so for hours. For Spanish-speaking families, the effects are negative, though they are generally smaller and less significant than those for whites.

## CONCLUSIONS

In general, the estimated effects of the experimental treatment on labor supply are in accord with our expectations. The major surprise is the absence of any negative effect on the labor supply of black households. For white and Spanish-speaking families, and for the group as a whole, the effects are negative, usually significant, but not very large. They consist of a reduction in hours of white male heads, an increase in the unemployment rate of Spanish-speaking male heads, and a large relative reduction in the labor-force participation rate of white wives.

If one calculates the cost of a negative income tax program on the assumption of no supply response, then these results strongly suggest that the estimated cost will be too low. However, the added cost produced by the supply response is a rather small portion of the total cost—not over 10 percent and probably closer to 5 percent. The estimates suggest that a substantial part of this will, in effect, represent added benefits for mothers whose withdrawal from paid employment is likely to be offset by increased "employment" at home. There is a further suggestion that tax rates higher than 50 percent may lead to a more pronounced supply response and, consequently, a larger increment to total cost. Whatever the percentage change in income, a higher tax rate requires that more of that change will be made up in benefits.

If the results we found by ethnic group were applied to the national low-income urban population using national ethnic weights, then the importance of our results for whites would rise and the importance of the results for the Spanish-speaking would fall. It is not at all clear that results for Puerto Ricans in New Jersey say anything at all about Mexican-Americans in the Southwest.

We place less weight on our results for blacks for a different reason. They are strange results that appear to arise from the unusual behavior of the black control group, whose labor supply and especially earnings fell relative to other control groups for reasons we do not understand. That the experimental treatment effects for blacks are often statistically significant is no assurance that they are not biased.

The patterns of labor-supply response that we have found are not as clear as we had expected. Yet in many ways they are clearer and more sensible than the results of much of the nonexperimental literature. Certainly they call into serious question the very large effects estimated in some of the nonexperimental studies. The burden of proof would now appear to be on those who assert that income maintenance programs for intact families will have very large effects on labor supply. Considering how little had been done in the experimental testing of economic policies when we began, we do not find our results disappointing.

# 25

# An Overview Evaluation of the NIT Experiment

*Peter H. Rossi and Katharine C. Lyall*

INTRODUCTION

The central purpose of this final chapter is to bring together the analyses made in the body of this volume to arrive at an overall evaluation of the NIT Experiment. We embark upon this enterprise with considerable ambivalence: As we noted in the opening chapter, there is much to admire in the boldness of the experimenters in venturing upon what history will undoubtedly regard as one of the major "firsts" in policy related empirical social research, in their unflagging devotion to carrying out a long-term research endeavor, and in the technical skills with which the resulting data were handled. Nothing we can say can detract from the considerable accomplishment that this experiment represents for social science research. Yet there is much to criticize as the preceding chapters have detailed. We trust that the very real admiration we hold for the accomplishments of the NIT experimenters will not be submerged in the minds of the readers by the equally real and important critical comments we have made in the body of this report.

It is easy enough to be a critic: All pieces of empirical research are more or less flawed. There are simply too many points at which mistakes can be made or unforeseen events intrude to permit perfection in either design or execution. We believe that critics have a responsibility to make two kinds of judgments about the criticisms they offer: First, it is necessary to make

From Peter H. Rossi and Katharine C. Lyall, "An Overview Evaluation of the NIT Experiment," pp. 175-191 in Reforming Public Welfare, Russell Sage Foundation, 1976. Copyright 1976 by Russell Sage Foundation.

distinctions, if possible, between those mistakes that constitute serious flaws and those that are less serious defects. Admittedly, this is a matter of judgment, yet we do believe that some sort of weighting ought to be suggested by responsible critics as a guide to those who have not digested the enormous volume of memoranda, working papers, analyses, and final reports produced by the experiment. Second, it is only fair to distinguish between defects that arise from incorrect planning and other errors of judgment and those that arise out of events or processes that could not have been anticipated in advance. This is essentially a distinction between "bad judgment" and "bad luck," the former being a legitimate criticism and the latter calling for sympathetic commiseration.

We will try to differentiate among the criticisms offered in these terms. Of course, the application of these distinctions is largely a matter of judgment, as the reader may discern in his pattern of agreement or disagreement with the observations that follow. We invite the reader to disagree and come to his own assessment of the NIT Experiment.

As we have indicated throughout the previous chapters, the experimenters attempted to narrow the scope of their research problem by carefully restricting the dimensions of their problem focusing on the limited objective of detecting labor supply response for a select group, the urban-industrial-working poor in intact families. There is no doubt that all research must be reduced to manageable proportions by some choices of the type discussed. It also must be recognized that these choices have a direct and important bearing on the usefulness of results of policy oriented research to policy-makers, not simply in terms of preserving the integrity of the research results themselves but also in terms of shedding light on the pivotal issues of the political questions raised by a policy. When it came down to the congressional debate on FAP, it was evident that while the labor supply question interested some congressmen in a general way, concerns were addressed more to the total costs of a national program, an issue to which the experiment could not offer an answer even when complete. Other congressmen—those who turned out to be the most vigorous opponents of FAP—were also preoccupied with the morality of giving support to non-working males/females at all. Such misgivings were not allayed by evidence that work dropped only modestly in a particular group or any sample. That is, the experimenters established their experimental objective with an eye to testing a piece of established microtheory rather than with a close eye to the hot political questions, apparently counting on OEO to make application of the results in the policy arena.

It has been stressed by the researchers and it is fair to recognize that the NIT Experiment was never conceived by its staff as a prototype negative income tax program but rather as a piece of behavioral research designed to get some information on the "raw materials" of income-conditioned transfer programs. Economic theory predicted that the two most important determinants of work response were the guarantee (or benefit level) and the marginal tax rate, so that an experiment was constructed to see what the "pure" response would be to policy manipulations of these parameters. The choice of an NIT program as a vehicle for these tests was a matter of timely convenience; the estimated responses to the component parameters in theory could be applied as well to the construction of other types of transfer programs. A number of the criticisms cited amount to arguing that although correct for theory testing this may have been an unnecessarily precise approach from the immediate policy standpoint and that to answer some of the most urgent political questions about NIT *as a program* would have required a different approach. Some critics have suggested that a "demonstration" project would have been more appropriate, a viewpoint to which we do not subscribe. A prospective NIT evaluation should have been a program of experiments with universes sampled of particular political relevance.

While an evaluation of the NIT Experiment should hold its principals to the quality of design and execution of research relative to the specific labor supply question posed, a full appreciation of the impact of the NIT on policy and experimentation requires it to be seen against the full sweep of the "welfare problem" to which it was addressed. It is one of the apparent ironies of the experiment that while its motivation sprang from a strong concern with poverty and a desire on the part of both the experimenters and OEO to affect national welfare reform, its most substantial contributions may well be of a more scholarly sort in the areas of experimental design and work behavioral response.

We divide the following comments into those concerning the design and execution of the experiment itself and those relating to the impact of the NIT on national welfare reform efforts and, more generally, on social experimentation as a policy research technique. We find this division useful, because, while there are obvious connections, the NIT was addressed to a very particular question of labor supply whereas many of the relevant and important issues raised by congressional policymakers concerned other questions that were not and could not have been addressed by this experiment. Whether this should be counted as a defect in the experimental design is less clear than the fact that it became a defect of the results for policy use.

## CONCERNING THE NIT DESIGN

As we noted in Chapter 2, the designers of the NIT were forced to make a number of decisions about the size, composition, and distribution of the sample, the geographic location of households, and the administrative procedures for carrying out the experiment, each of which necessarily had the effect of restricting the generality and usefulness of results. Given their time and budget constraints, there was no way to avoid making these choices, and the appropriate evaluation issue is the care and ingenuity with which these choices were analyzed as well as their impact on the final policy debate. As the previous chapters indicated, those design choices that lent themselves to formulation in terms of tradeoffs among alternative objectives and the efficient allocation of the budget were analyzed in the utmost detail and with great ingenuity; those that involved familiarity with survey technique and field procedures were settled more perfunctorily; and a few, such as the truncation of the sample by income and the ethnicity factor, simply escaped attention altogether.

First, the choice of the target population as work-eligible male-headed families was based on the logic that these units were likely to be most responsive to the disincentive effects of wage and tax rates and that the political resistance to an NIT focused primarily on the behavior of males rather than on female-headed families. We have found little evidence that either of these assumptions was questioned either at OEO or among the experimenters themselves despite the fact that by so restricting the sample they were eliminating the possibility of testing responses of a large percentage of the poor located in female-headed families. Rather, the intent was to try to identify the maximum work reduction effect of the most sensitive group and by this means to narrow the range of results that had been predicted from previous literature using cross-section data. It seems clear that the ultimate purpose for undertaking this effort in OEO's mind was to be able to make some rough estimates of national program costs for a variety of income-related transfer programs, but since this was not an explicit charge to the NIT itself, the damage done to this ultimate objective by intermediate design decisions aimed at a more restricted objective was not clearly perceived.[1] As it turned out during the debate on FAP many members of Congress showed an equal interest in female work patterns and insisted that female heads be included in work requirements of any reform bill. In all

---

[1] Note here particularly the point raised as part of the design controversy that those advocating the Watts-Conlisk model allocation had "shifted the objective to minimization of the national cost per family of the NIT due to reduced work effort." Watts has written that the national cost element was introduced "only as a means of inducing differential importance to precision in various parts of the response function" and not with the intent of being able to generate national program cost estimates. Our point is not that the NIT promised national cost estimates, which it did not, but that this was certainly the underlying interest that OEO had in the experiment, so that when the more important design problems flawed the results even for this "sensitivity sample," very little could be salvaged from the experiment to bolster the policy debate in the political arena where national impacts *were* the important question.

fairness, it should be pointed out that subsequent NIT experiments did cover more adequately such issues.

Second, the decision to plan the NIT as a series of "test bores" in a small number of urban sites rather than as a probability sample of some larger population of direct policy interest had the effect of exposing the results to site bias from special features of those particular labor markets.

The experimenters chose the test bore strategy for what they regarded as compelling administrative reasons[2] but having made this judgment apparently failed to follow through with further consideration of its implications for generalizability of results even to other portions of the national urban labor force. A careful analysis preceding this decision would have undoubtedly raised questions about how to sample households, so that inferences about urban poor families could be safely drawn. As it now stands, the four sites are a haphazard sample of convenience. Inter-site variances of some appreciable size raise questions whether this sample is a reasonable base from which to make estimates that would hold for the New York-New Jersey-Pennsylvania urban areas, let alone urban areas in the United States. To argue that the experiment was never intended to produce results generalizable to the nation is unconvincing, especially in light of the reasons given by OEO for funding the research, and it is at least implied in the choice of urban sites that information was sought that would be generalizable to major portions of the wage labor force employed in urban areas.[3]

No doubt this point is more problematical after the fact than it was when the experiment was being designed. This is because the final analyses revealed no substantial response to the two program parameters, the guarantee and the tax rates, around which the design had focused, so that there is a natural tendency to examine the sample for hints about the probable response of the national population to a NIT program. In asking what *can* be learned from the experiment one confronts directly the frustrations of an ungeneralizable sample representing no universe directly useful for the purposes with which the Congress, the administration, or those interested in welfare policy alternatives are concerned.

A third criticism hinges on an oversight, probably stemming from the

---

[2] A concern of accessibility and worry over relations with local welfare departments as well as the absence of an AFDC-UP plan in New Jersey were the main reasons for rejecting the alternative of a national or regional sampling frame. A check with any of the major sample survey organizations would have revealed that accessibility was not a serious problem. How serious were the problems of welfare department "permission" was a matter of judgment and hence may have been sufficient reason for making a decision to concentrate sampling in a few places.

[3] In the "bad luck" category is the fact that one of the major administrative reasons —absence of an AFDC-UP program—was eliminated during the experiment, so that little was gained in exchange for the "test bore" choice, not even freedom from welfare contamination.

casualness with which sites were chosen, that later turned out to be critical. No attention was paid in the initial design of the sample to the factor of ethnicity. If there had been no reason to suspect that there would be large ethnic differences, then such an omission might be viewed as "bad luck" rather than bad judgment. But there had been considerable attention given in previous literature to the question of whether the employment and earnings patterns of whites and blacks differed in some structurally determined ways or merely differed because of differences in employment-related characteristics, and certainly spoken and unspoken arguments in the political sphere made it plain that racial differences in work response would be an important part of the public policy debate.[4] Not as much attention had been paid to Puerto Ricans but there were sufficient and good a priori reasons to suspect that their work experiences might also differ from those of whites. When it became evident after some enrollment experience in the New Jersey sites that poor households found in the central parts of these cities were disproportionately black and Puerto Rican, a belated effort at increasing the number of white families in the sample by adding another site introduced a further uncontrolled factor of site-ethnicity confounding.[5]

A fourth observation centers on the sample allocation model and the considerations that went into the design controversy described in Chapter 2. It seems to us that the rejection of the ANOVA model was a correct strategy, especially since the secondary hypotheses to the testing of which such an allocation would have been crucial were so poorly formulated and so much more costly per observation than alternative allocations and since it seemed apparent that the Watts-Conlisk formulation could accommodate as complex relations as were likely to be detectable at the level of treatments being applied.

While some of the most interesting contributions to the technique of experimental design derive from this controversy, it appears that the controversy itself was costly to the NIT in terms of time delays and something of a case of misplaced emphasis in light of other more important design problems that emerged in the analysis and from the field experiences.

It also turned out that families in the control group and those in the experimental groups who were above the break-even point were not as in-

---

[4] For example, this question was taken up in considerable detail in Peter M. Blau and Otis D. Duncan, *The American Occupational Structure* (New York: John Wiley and Sons, 1967).

[5] There is some disagreement whether the confounding is large enough to render findings problematic in some way. Although multi-collinearity does not bias regression estimates, it does introduce larger error estimates. Hence, the confounding of site and ethnicity may not affect the sign of a response, but it may make a response of a given magnitude more difficult to detect with a given level of confidence. In short, site-ethnicity confounding reduces the efficiency of the sample.

expensive as projected since it became fairly expensive to motivate families to stay in the study so that the advantage of an allocation that stressed the differential costs of families eligible for payments as compared to those who were not was slighter than supposed.

A further oddity is the fact that despite the experiment's design as an explicit piece of NIT policy research, policy weights were assigned to specific plans within the policy space in a rather casual manner without any clear consultation with policymakers at OEO or in Congress. In consequence the allocation determined using the Watts-Conlisk model reflects primarily the researchers' a priori *notions* of the political importance of alternative plans. We regard this as a curiosity rather than a serious defect since it is not apparent that any consensus could have been elicited from the diffuse interests of congress and administration in any case, but the casualness with which these parameters were set stands in sharp contrast to the extended analysis and debate over other elements of the allocation model.

A fifth criticism of the NIT design is one in which "bad luck" is the real culprit. New Jersey was selected as a site partly because its welfare plan at that time did not cover intact families with able-bodied male breadwinners. The changes made to include such households, instituted by New Jersey within a few months of the start of the fieldwork in Trenton, could not have been anticipated easily. Such changes, however, did affect the nature of the experimental treatments, subjecting them to competition from welfare policy that changed the experiment to one that measured the effects of NIT on work response when added to generous AFDC-UP plans. As such, it was likely to underestimate the impact of NIT considered alone and also when used as a supplement to less generous AFDC-UP (or similar) plans. As we noted earlier, overlaying the experimental treatments with a competing AFDC-UP program made it much more difficult to determine in the final analyses whether the "treatment" was the nominal guarantee and tax rates, the difference between these and the competing AFDC rates, or some even more complex combination of rates with "kinks" at points where there occurred strong incentives to switch from one program to another.

A sixth observation is of an effect that escaped notice altogether until it became apparent from the final analyses. Defining the eligible population for the sample as intact families whose total income was less than 150 percent of the current poverty level resulted in a truncated sample, especially for whites, in which families tended to be larger than the poverty population in general, to have fewer wives in the labor force, to have lower than expected levels of homeownership, and so on.

Watts and his colleagues have suggested since that the sample might have been selected on the basis of the earnings of the major breadwinner with payments conditioned on total family income, a strategy that might well have rectified the low level of wives' labor force participation and some of the other sample peculiarities. Whatever the correct strategy might have been, it is clear that the implications of defining the target population were far-reaching and important. While the consequences of adopting standard poverty definitions established for another purpose were seriously debilitating to the results, the effect was so subtle that we doubt it would have been discerned before it emerged in the final analysis.

A final observation on the design centers on a neglect by the experimenters to think through a full conceptualization of what constitutes an experimental treatment. If we recognize an experimental treatment as *everything an experimenter does* to members of an experimental group that *he does not do* to members of a control group, we must recognize the possibility that part of the experimental response detected might in fact be attributable to different administrative experiences of the two groups. The experimenters attempted to minimize administrative contact with recipients by leaving the initiative to make contacts with field office personnel, and to seek explanations of the various treatments and plans or to raise reporting questions largely up to the families. Yet events occurred that made the administrative side of the experiment for those receiving payments grow larger and more intrusive than perhaps intended. The action of the Mercer County prosecutor led to a heightened concern with the possibility of fraud and the brief televised "exposé" by CBS may have raised anxieties in participating families that their responses were not as anonymous as they (and the researchers) would have wished. These are simply possibilities, and neither we nor the researchers have any evidence to establish or dismiss them as affecting, though unintended, facets of "treatment" in some sites. Clearly, such happenings were beyond the control of the experimenters but nevertheless may have had marginally differential effects on experimental and control groups in the New Jersey sites as well as differential effects between the New Jersey and the Pennsylvania sites. We have already noted one such administrative effect flowing from the relatively more experienced field staff that enrolled and administered the NIT in Scranton after nearly a year of learning by doing in New Jersey.

In a slightly different vein, we note that experimental payments should probably include the $260 per year in filing fees paid to retain experimental families in the sample. This sum represents the equivalent of a wage increase of about four dollars a week to an individual working a thirty-five to forty hour week or about a 4 percent boost in the average family's weekly income conditioned only on filing reports. While control families also received fees for mailing in monthly address cards and for participating in the quarterly interviews, the difference in payments for filing is considerable.

It seems possible that control families would have regarded these incentive payments quite differently from experimental families who received their filing fees as part of their payments checks and hence may have combined them in their minds with the work-conditioned transfer payments. Again. we have no evidence on this and do not regard it as a substantial problem in the NIT case. We merely note such possibilities here to draw the attention of future field experimenters to the fact that administrative features of the design can be as much a part of the experimental treatment as the formal design parameters and that in some cases it may prove to be as interesting to experiment with alternative administrative methods as with other program characteristics.

## CONCERNING THE IMPACT ON EXPERIMENTATION TECHNIQUE

In addition to information on the labor supply response of NIT recipients, the experiment yielded a number of lessons about the use and possible misuse of experimentation as a policy analysis technique.

First, the Watts-Conlisk model approach to the design of efficient sample allocations has been adopted by virtually all subsequent income maintenance experiments and has clearly contributed to sorting out the important determinants and assumptions of an optimal design. The value of obtaining efficient designs is apparent when the total cost of such large-scale survey work is considered.

Second, the NIT was undoubtedly a vehicle for training a rather large group of scholars and policy analysts in experimental techniques as well as producing a valuable pool of researchers with much empirical and analytical expertise in the field of poverty, welfare reform, and the construction of income-conditioned transfer programs. Alumni of the NIT are to be found in all major experiments mounted since 1968, as well as in the Office of Policy Analysis in HEW, HUD, and the new Congressional Budget Committee. In this respect the "level of policy debate" on welfare reform, at least among these individuals, was raised substantially.

Third, the relative expensiveness, in both time and money, of experimentation underscores the importance of reserving this technique for instances where there is a precisely defined hypothesis to be tested that cannot be examined satisfactorily with existing survey data. It follows that the behavioral response to be tested must be a complex function of several treatment parameters in which the *magnitude* and not just the direction of response is important to the policy decision.

Fourth, the NIT experience underlines the potential for experimentation with alternative *administrative* techniques as well as with responses to other dimensions of transfer programs. We have noted that one of the more persuasive results of the NIT to congressional opponents was the simple evidence that an NIT could, in fact, be administered without intruding excessively in recipients' lives or requiring an army of bureaucrats for the purpose. Robert Levine has suggested that "administrative experiments" related to existing programs may be more useful than tests of other characteristics of new programs.

Fifth, we can see in the policy history of the NIT the importance of *timing* experimentation to produce results before serious political debate begins and of having an interim product to sustain the interest of policymakers attempting to construct a defensible legislative position. This feature alone suggests that experimentation is not likely to be a promising technique for approaching short-term or cyclical issues; by the same token, the half-dozen areas likely to be of national policy concern three to five years ahead *are* generally distinguishable and can, with enough foresight, be amenable to experimental techniques.

Sixth, a corollary of the previous observation, is the potential for use of experimentation as a *delaying tactic* as one suspects was the case in Congress' "resolving" the FAP issue by authorizing an additional $400 million for further income maintenance experiments to run for at least five more years. This strategy appears destined to produce a repeat of the NIT experience in which the political issue becomes active well before experimental results are available or policymakers adopt some alternative transfer program under pressure to act more quickly.

Seventh, a notable effect of the NIT, especially among economists, has been to focus attention on the inadequacies of much non-experimental (secondary source) data in the fields of income, work, and wage statistics as well as other data series measuring consumption, assets, and savings necessary for the testing of microtheory hypotheses.[6] It is interesting to note that the adoption of poverty as an issue of national policy concern in the 1960s went far to elevate microeconomic issues to a status formerly reserved for the macro issues of unemployment and monetary policy. The care with which the NIT was formulated to test a well-specified aspect of microtheory and the attention it focused on gaps in panel data on individual and household behavior have made economists generally more sensitive to the need for improved survey techniques and primary data collection.

Finally, the NIT experience provides a valuable demonstration of the many and frequently subtle ways in which experimentation must be fitted

---

[6] For the first time, a panel devoted entirely to discussion of survey research techniques was on the program of the American Economic Association's Annual Meeting in December 1973.

to the political policy process on the one hand and to the scholarly process of research on the other in order to ensure the integrity of the research results themselves as well as their usefulness in policy debate. Further, the NIT confirms the suspicion that while experimentation can detect individuals' responses to changes in price and income incentives, these adjustments are much smaller and more complex than researchers are generally inclined to think, a finding which suggests that future experimental treatments will have to be much larger and, by implication, more costly to avoid being swamped by the great variety of exogenous influences on individual behavior.

## CONCERNING. WORK RESPONSE MEASUREMENT

A consistent theme running through earlier chapters has been a plaintive regret that the important variables relating to work response were not measured more adequately.[7] In designing an experiment as complex as an NIT it is tempting to want to use familiar measures and variables wherever possible, particularly measures that are well established and accepted in the research and policy communities. This saves time and intellectual energy needed for other aspects of the experiment and presumably forestalls any debate that might arise over the role of special measures in the final analyses.

The NIT researchers adopted, apparently without sufficient scrutiny, interviewing instruments of the Current Population Survey and the decennial Census as measures of initial labor force effort for the sample. The individual and household income measures generated by these sources have been extensively criticized in previous literature with general agreement that they are of proximate utility only when used in aggregated form. The researchers began to discover the inadequacy of these standard instruments for measuring the individual responses they were interested in as the data collection progressed and made some subsequent changes in the phrasing of questions on the report forms; in other instances the faultiness of a measure was not discovered until analytical work began on the data, too late to retrieve the entire series for use.

---

[7] This is one point at which the lack of survey experience on the part of the NIT staff shows up most strongly. Anyone with previous experience with household surveys in which income and/or expenditures were critical variables would have proceeded much more cautiously in arriving at operational measures. Certainly this would have been the point to call upon consultation with members of the psychological economics group at the Survey Research Center of the University of Michigan or the medical expenditures group at the Health Information Foundation at the University of Chicago.

In particular, more care and forethought should have gone into measurement of

1. *Pre-experimental earnings, income, wage rates, and hours worked.* It might have been worthwhile to postpone the payment of NIT benefits for a period of some months in order to get base line measures of these variables that would be consistent with those collected throughout the experiment.

2. *Earnings of household members.* The difficulties involved in this measure are not trivial. In addition to the confusion between gross and net income, more attention should have been paid to the problems of capturing earnings from casual labor, wages paid in cash, and other easily forgotten or ignored income in the respondents' reports. This problem of fugitive or forgotten income is important not simply to the NIT research results but also to the practicality of a national NIT administration if one does not wish to replace "armies of intrusive social workers" with armies of intrusive IRS agents.

3. *Wage rates of employed persons.* The labor supply model that lay behind the NIT Experiment is couched in terms of changes in the wage rates of persons subject to NIT payments. Wage rates do vary within the same job depending on differentials between shifts, overtime versus straight time, and so on. The wage rates calculable in the NIT Experiment are derivatives of earnings and reported hours of work and hence are some sort of weighted average of actual wage rates, the exact weighting being unrecoverable in the present series.

4. *Hours worked.* This became the main dependent variable used in tests of labor supply response largely by default and is also subject to reporting ambiguities. The fact that its reliability was not testable from the data collected does not guarantee that it was properly measured or that it contains no bias in experimental versus control comparisons.

5. *Other income.* It is clear from the tests of the NIT income series that this component of reported total family income is the most variable but least identifiable by source or type. It was the source of much of the trouble encountered in auditing monthly reports and the overlapping of NIT benefits with welfare payments. In many respects this is the most interesting source of differences among households since it says something about the ability of units to manipulate their incomes from non-wage sources, a major element in the creation of horizontal inequities in formula transfers.

This loss of information from poor measurement had several consequences: 1) It substantially reduced the amount of analysis and testing that could be done of various response hypotheses, including the main labor supply question, thereby raising the real cost of usable information after the fact well above the cost of designing and administering a single response survey in the first place. 2) In the case of earnings it is known to have biased the labor response of experimental families relative to control families, thereby creating a similar, though untestable, suspicion of the other measures. 3) It eliminated the possibility of cross-checking the labor response results obtained using hours with the alternate indices of earnings and wage rates, thereby also forfeiting a chance to see to what extent NIT payments are used as wage supplements by employers. 4) It made the data bank constructed from the NIT panel data much less useful for integration and use in other studies than originally intended. (The construction of a cross-section panel of micro unit data on the poverty population was an important planned by-product of the experiment, one for which OEO and HEW have supplied substantial funding.)

No doubt, a more careful construction and pretesting of dependent variable measures would have required a delay in getting the experiment into the field, but a delay that would have added significantly to the utility of the final results. Had as much effort gone into testing alternative ways of measuring these variables as into working out the design controversy the final analyses would have been much more convincing. In retrospect, the design controversy, itself the cause of considerable time delay, appears to be a mountain shrunk to mole hill size,[8] while the known and suspected deficiencies in the income, earnings, and hours worked series are defects that increasingly undermine the credibility of the research findings.

## CONCERNING OTHER TYPES OF MEASUREMENT

The inattention shown to the details of obtaining accurate measurements of the basic labor supply variables was surpassed by an even greater casualness in the specification of other series of interest. Housing costs, medical care, clothing, entertainment expenditures are particularly poorly measured to the extent that analyses of consumption effects attempted as part of the final analyses rest on faith in the analysts' abilities to patch things up with ingenuity and intuition.

At the least, benign neglect also characterizes the measurement of the non-economic variables. It is clear that the main method of developing measures exercised by the sociologists and social psychologists was the wholesale borrowing of instruments, good and bad, from previous studies that had enough notoriety to come to the attention of the researchers. We have previously noted the absence of any "intervening variables" hypothesis to guide the selection of non-economic measures; under these circumstances it would have been surprising to find detailed attention to the quality of the particular measures collected.

Because the interest in consumption patterns as affected by NIT pay-

---

[8] Especially since cost overruns make the payments to NIT families a minor rather than a major component in total NIT costs.

ments was undoubtedly larger than interest in social psychological effects, the defects in the measurement of the former are more serious than for the latter.

## CONCERNING FIELD OPERATIONS

A major achievement of the NIT Experiment was to demonstrate that it was possible to carry out a complicated field experiment over a moderately long period of time. This accomplishment excites admiration.

It is also clear that this accomplishment was one that was achieved by rapid learning in the field. The initial screening operation that located eligible households was less successful than later attempts to enroll families. Similarly, initial attrition rates in Trenton, the first site, were considerably higher than the attrition rates experienced by the last group of families recruited in Scranton. Language difficulties in the questionnaires for the Puerto Rican families were discovered and questionnaires revised accordingly. Field offices learned to check and follow up promptly omitted items on the respondents' reports, and cross-check procedures for welfare fraud were incorporated without serious disruption of the "minimum intrusion" strategy. After a disastrous start, final attrition proportions for the total sample were reduced below those for comparable samples used in other studies[9] demonstrating that by providing appropriate incentives it is ·possible to remain in relatively close and enduring contact with poor families for an extended period of time. In short, the field operations proved to be flexible, humane, and operable within the confines of budget and time allowances.

## CONCERNING THE ANALYSIS OF RESULTING DATA

Reading the volumes of the final report, one cannot avoid being impressed by the sophistication and skill with which the data of the NIT Experiment have been analyzed. The transformation of the basic data series into normal wages, income, and hours (as described in Chapter 5) was accomplished with great skill and the introduction of splines contributed to the advanced analytical education of policymakers and researchers alike. Indeed, the worst that can be said about the analyses performed is that

---

[9] For example, the 5,000 families studied in James Morgan, et al., *Five Thousand Families—Patterns of Economic Progress* (Ann Arbor: Institute for Social Research, 1974), apparently suffered an attrition rate in an annual survey extending over five years of around 67 percent, several magnitudes larger than the 23 percent experienced over a three-year period by the NIT families.

more talent and skill was devoted to this aspect of the study than was warranted by the quality of the basic data series. In addition, the separate analyses comprising the final report of the experiment were conducted in a variety of ways on a series of differently defined subsamples of the full data base, a situation that makes it difficult to get a consistent picture of the full findings. The latter is somewhat frustrating for the reader but not material to interpretation of the findings.

It should also be noted that it is the extremely high quality of the analyses that make this evaluation possible. The NIT researchers were extraordinarily clear and frank about the conduct of the experiment, carefully investigated (when they could) the quality of the data series, explored alternative interpretations, and so forth. The main task of the present authors was to gather together and evaluate findings that are presented in a very open fashion in the volumes of the *Final Report*. This candor and openness makes this study possible.

## DRAWING A BALANCE

It should be evident from the preceding that we are most critical of certain design features of the NIT Experiment and of the consequences for failures to feed into the political policy process. The design is flawed in ways that make it impossible to extrapolate from findings to any reasonable universe of the poor who might be the object of welfare reform. The basic variables measuring work response are defective in quality so that we cannot be sure that measurement defects have not swamped (or perhaps exaggerated) whatever NIT payment effects "really exist." And the findings themselves, ignoring the design defects, are frustratingly inconclusive, even for the restricted sample examined.

At the same time, it should be clear that we regard the experiment as a great success administratively and that the analyses were carried out in an excellent fashion. Virtually all the evidence the data can yield on the main labor supply question has been extracted.

What we *did* learn from the experiment was that for that small portion of the poverty population in male-headed, eastern, urban industrial families 1) there is no evidence of massive reductions in work effort attributable to an NIT although 2) the modest responses that do occur are differentiated in both direction and magnitude by race and sex, and 3) there appears to be no sensitivity to the program parameters, $g$ and $r$. Further, we learned that experimentation is an administratively feasible technique although we suspect that design of administrative features, such as the reporting period, means tests, fraud checks, and data processing arrangements, can have as much effect on the outcome and be of as much use to policymakers as the design and allocation of treatments and the sample itself.

The persuasiveness of these results and what they imply for the construction of a national welfare program have been the subject of knowledgeable debate. Boeckmann[10] has documented the mixed congressional reaction to the experimental results, both preliminary and final, noting that most participants in the FAP debate regarded the findings as "inconclusive," biased by the interests of the researchers, or failing to speak to the active issues of political concern about the FAP. Virtually no interest was shown in designing or fine-tuning a national program using the tax and guarantee rates examined by the NIT. By contrast, Barth et al.[11] have indicated that the results were extensively discussed within HEW and that a number of HEW officials "were willing to revise substantially this belief (in large disincentive effects) in the face of the experimental results and other relevant scientific evidence on labor supply." The academic community has been fascinated by the technical design contributions of the experiment and the demonstration that experimentation is an administratively feasible empirical research technique but has been correspondingly skeptical of the results in light of the kinds of design flaws discussed.

Particular disagreement has evolved around the meaning of non-response to the marginal tax rate with some arguing that this implies that an optimal national NIT program should incorporate very high tax rates in order to maximize the guarantee level for any specified welfare budget allotment while others argue that insensitivity to the tax rate merely means that policymakers are free to design transfer programs on the basis of other than strict efficiency and labor supply criteria.[12] Browning[13] has explored some of the redistributive effects between positive taxpayers and negative tax receivers, while Townsend and Lerman[14] have drawn attention to the politically potent fact that in-kind welfare programs are likely to survive in part because they embody greater inequities in benefits than could be either tolerated or afforded under a simple cash transfer program. The beneficiaries of current transfer programs constitute a client group with political

---

[10] Margaret Boeckmann, "Policy Impacts of the New Jersey Income Maintenance Experiment" (mimeo, n.d.).

[11] Michael C. Barth, Larry L. Orr, and John H. Palmer, "Policy Implications: A Positive View," in *Work Incentives and Income Guarantee,* eds. Joseph A. Pechman and P. Michael Timpane (Washington, D.C.: The Brookings Institution, 1975).

[12] Bette S. Mahoney and W. Michael Mahoney, "Policy Implications: A Skeptical View," ibid.

[13] Edgar K. Browning, "Income Redistribution and the Negative Income Tax: A Theoretical Analysis" (Ph.D. diss., Princeton University, 1971).

[14] Arthur A. Townsend and Robert I. Lerman, "Conflicting Objectives in Income Maintenance Programs," mimeo (Paper prepared for the Eighty-Sixth Annual Meeting of the American Economic Association, December 30, 1973).

influence that will be used to resist the replacement of current programs, and the NIT results are unable to tell us anything about the effects of pyramiding a cash transfer on top of in-kind programs.

In sum, then, we regard the New Jersey Experiment as setting an important precedent in illustrating the feasibility, and some of the pitfalls, of field experiments as research operations that can cast some light on important policy issues. In our view, however, it would be a mistake to regard the experiment as having provided definitive estimates of what work responses or other responses would be to a national NIT program. We have argued that experimentation is too complex, extended, and expensive a mode of research to be devoted solely to hypothesis-testing without equal weight being given to the evidence it can contribute to active policy issues and that sometimes apparently "technical" design decisions can have profound effects on the policy applicability of experimental findings.

# 26

# The Rural Income Maintenance Experiment

## U.S. Department of Health, Education, and Welfare

### EXECUTIVE SUMMARY

In the debate over alternatives to the current welfare system the effect of income maintenance programs on the work effort of low income people, particularly those who work and have family responsibilities, has proved a recurrent and politically significant question. Income support programs covering the so-called working poor have considerable appeal on equity grounds, but intuitive expectations and economic theory lead us to expect that they will cause recipients to decrease their work effort. To find out whether such a disincentive effect occurs, and the size of the effect, major social experiments have been conducted by the Office of Economic Opportunity and the Department of Health, Education, and Welfare.

In the recently completed New Jersey Graduated Work Incentive Experiment the work reduction for married men as a result of income maintenance payments of a type that might be enacted proved to be less than 10 percent. The reduction resulted solely from fewer hours worked; no evidence appeared of husbands quitting entirely to live on the experimental payments. The percentage of wives in the labor force fell sharply as a result of experimental payments, but since wives worked very few hours to begin with the effect on total family labor supply was small. The experiment appeared to have little effect on the attitudes and nonwork behavior of recipients.

The New Jersey Experiment dealt exclusively with urban families, and researchers doubted that the results, or the administrative techniques, could be applied to the rural poor. The poor appear to face very different labor market opportunities in rural areas than in urban areas, particularly since many are self-employed farmers, and attitudes toward work may differ between rural and

AUTHOR'S NOTE: The Rural Income Maintenance Experiment was conducted by the Institute for Research on Poverty, University of Wisconsin, for the Office of Economic Opportunity and the Department of Health, Education, and Welfare.

From the U.S. Department of Health, Education, and Welfare, "The Rural Income Maintenance Experiment." Unpublished manuscript, 1977.

urban settings. Many additional problems arise in the treatment of self-employment income and highly seasonal income in rural areas which do not often occur in urban low-income populations.

Since the results of the urban-based experiments might fail to apply to rural areas, and since an accurate estimate of incentive effects was necessary for estimates of program costs, the Rural Income Maintenance Experiment was carried out to measure labor supply responses and other effects of a negative income tax in rural areas. The results of this experiment are reported here.

The effects of the Rural Experiment, like those of other income maintenance experiments, were measured by comparing the behavior of members of an experimental group, who received cash payments according to one of several benefit formulas, with that of members of a control group who received no benefits. Thus what are described as changes in behavior as a result of the experiment are differences in behavior between the experimental group and the control group rather than changes over time in the behavior of the experimentals. A statistical technique was used which allowed the researchers to hold constant the effects of other characteristics such as the age or education of respondents and thus to isolate the effect of the experimental treatment.

The benefit formulas had a structure which appears in many current transfer programs and in many proposals for reform. They consisted of a basic benefit, a minimum level of income guaranteed to families with no other income; and an implicit tax rate, the rate at which the benefit was reduced as other income increased. Five different experimental treatments were used with basic benefit levels of from 50 to 100 percent of poverty level income and implicit tax rates ranging from 30 to 70 percent. Most of the results presented here are overall differences in response between controls and experimentals in all plans.

The experiment was carried out in two locations, one in Iowa and one in North Carolina. Families were selected randomly from within the experimental sites and, if eligible, were randomly assigned to a control group or to one of the five experimental treatments. Eligibility required a family income at the beginning of the experiment of less than one and one-half times the official poverty line. Of 809 original families, 729 remained in the program for the entire three years of the experiment.

Work and income responses to the experiment were examined separately for rural families whose income derived primarily from wages and for those whose main source of income was self-employed farming. On the basis of analyses which indicated significantly different response patterns by site and race, North Carolina whites, North Carolina blacks, and Iowa families (all white) were analyzed separately. In addition, effects of the experiment on attitudes and on nonwork behavior such as family stability, various forms of consumption, and school performance of children were examined for the whole group.

Table 1. Experimental Labor Supply Response of Families of Rural Wage Earners

| | Control/Experimental Differential as Percent of Control Mean[a] | | | |
| | N.C. Blacks | N.C. Whites | Iowa | Eight-State[b] Aggregate |
|---|---|---|---|---|
| All Family Members | | | | |
| Total hours worked for wages per quarter | −10 | −18 | − 5 | −13 |
| Husbands | | | | |
| Total hours worked for wages per quarter | − 8 | + 3 | − 1 | − 1 |
| Percent employed during qtr. | − 1 | − 1 | 0 | − 1 |
| Wives | | | | |
| Total hours worked for wages per quarter | −31 | −23 | −22 | −27 |
| Percent employed during qtr. | −25 | −28 | −38 | −28 |
| Dependents | | | | |
| Total hours worked for wages per quarter | −16 | −66 | −27 | −46 |

[a]Responses standardized to a 45 percent tax/80 percent basic benefit plan.

[b]The experimental sites were chosen to represent the low-income rural population of eight Midwestern and Southern states. See p. 37 for weighting procedure used to derive this estimate.

## Income and Work Response of Wage Earners

Experimental effects on several measures of income and work effort were examined for families whose main source of income was wages. The labor supply responses are shown in Table 1. The first three columns show responses for each of the geographic and racial groups; the fourth column shows an aggregate response weighted to represent the low-income rural nonfarm population of the eight Midwestern and Southern states which the experimental sites were chosen to represent. Responses are calculated on the basis of an average plan having a 45 percent implicit tax rate and an 80 percent basic benefit level.

For all family members combined, hours worked for wages were lower for experimental group members than for controls by a weighted average of 13 percent after holding constant nonexperimental differences. The differential was statistically significant for two of the three groups. The experiment had a similar negative effect on total family income and number of earners per family.

Labor supply responses varied greatly among family members. Hours worked by husbands moved in differing directions among the groups but on average remained essentially unchanged. No statistically significant evidence appeared in any of the groups of husbands withdrawing from the labor force in response to the experimental payments. For wives, large negative experimental effects, averaging 27 percent, appeared for hours worked, but they were statistically significant only for North Carolina blacks. Statistically significant negative effects on employment, averaging 28 percent, occurred for every group of wives. Among children living at home the experimentally induced differential in hours of work averaged a negative 46 percent, but the difference was statistically significant only for North Carolina white children.

Most of the experimental effects on work effort appeared to increase as implicit tax rates rose. The basic benefit level, however, appeared to have no significant effect on work effort.

### Income and Work Responses of Farmers

For farm operators and managers experimental effects on farm profit, labor supply on and off the farm, and farm efficiency and production were examined. Profit, defined as gross revenue less cash costs, was used as a measure of farm income. Both Iowa and North Carolina experimental groups showed declines in farm profit relative to controls, but the differentials were only marginally statistically significant.

Farm work by farm operators, however, showed a positive experimental effect of 11 percent in both states. The differential was significant in North Carolina but not in Iowa. Farm hours declined over time for all groups, but at a faster rate for controls than for experimentals. Experimental wives also tended to work more hours on the farm than controls. Implicit tax rates and benefit levels appeared to have no effect on the level of farm work.

In three-fourths of the North Carolina farm families and half of the Iowa farm families one of the spouses worked for wages. Experimentally-induced declines in hours of wage work occurred in every group, and for wives the effect was large. But the only statistically significant effect was that for North Carolina wives, which resulted from a large increase in wage work by the control group which was not matched by the experimental group. Because of the small sample sizes the results for wives must be treated with caution.

Total earnings and total hours worked, including both farm and wage work for operators and wage work for wives, fell for experimental farm families relative to controls in North Carolina but not in Iowa. But the relative decline in hours in North Carolina occurred mostly because of the estimated decline in the wage work of wives.

Efficiency of farm operations, measured by the amount of output produced with a given amount of inputs, declined for experimental farms relative to controls. In North Carolina efficiency decreased as implicit tax rates rose. Total output declined by a small amount on experimental farms relative to controls in both North Carolina and Iowa.

The decline in output appears inconsistent with the increase in farm hours. One plausible explanation is that the experiment provided an incentive either to defer sales of output until after the end of the experiment, or to engage in investment activities which have a payoff in the long run but not during the three years of the experiment. Alternatively, the implicit tax on money income might have encouraged a shift from production in the market to production for consumption at home, or to less productive activities which were more enjoyable, either of which would appear as a decline in measured efficiency. The experiment may also have caused a shift in methods of production, possibly to more risky techniques, which might have required higher labor inputs, at least during the transition period.

## Other Responses to the Experiment

In addition to labor supply and income responses, the study examined the effects of experimental payments on nutrition; various forms of consumption; health and health care; geographic mobility; debt and asset holdings; psychological well-being; marital dissolution and family interaction; and attitudes, delinquency, and school performance of children. Significant experimental effects were found in only a few cases, possibly because of the short duration of the experiment.

Increases in consumption of several kinds occurred as a result of the experiment. Interestingly, nutrition improved significantly as a result of the experiment among North Carolina families but not in Iowa, in part because the level of nutrition was initially much higher in Iowa. The probability of buying a house was slightly greater for experimentals than for controls, with most of the effect occurring in North Carolina, and houses were bought about three years earlier in the life cycle by experimentals than by controls. No difference was found in the price of homes bought. Expenditures on health care were unaffected by the experiment, and changes in health showed no consistent pattern.

The study examined holdings of durable goods and cars and acquisition of debt. Wage earners' stocks of consumer durables, cars, and liquid assets appeared to increase as a result of the experiment; effects on store debt and loan debt varied among the groups studied.

Experimental payments appeared not to increase the probability of leaving a job but did increase the amount of unemployment experienced by experimental group members. Members of the experimental group appeared more likely to change residence than control group members.

The experiment had very little effect on any of several measures of psychological well-being. Slight evidence appeared, however, that the level of the basic benefit, regardless of payments actually received, was positively related to psychological well-being, presumably through providing a greater sense of security to participants.

The experimental program appeared to have no important effect on the quality of family relationships. It had no effect on the number of marital dissolutions or on satisfaction with marriage or parent-child relationships as reported by wives and teen-agers. Division of labor in the household may have been affected slightly.

The aspirations, school attitudes, and school behavior of teen-agers were not affected by the experiment. Neither was self-reported delinquent behavior by teen-agers, nor their attitudes toward delinquency.

School performance did improve for grade school children in North Carolina, both black and white, as a result of the experiment. Children in grades 2 through 8 in the experimental group performed significantly better than the control group in attendance, comportment, academic grades, and standardized test scores. Similar improvements did not occur, however, for North Carolina children in grades 9 through 12 or for Iowa children. The lack of effect for Iowa children may be explained by the fact that they experienced richer home environments and performed better prior to the experiment than North Carolina children.

## Administration of a Negative Income Tax Program in Rural Areas

The experiment provided experience with the problems of administering an income-conditioned cash transfer program in a rural area. These included the treatment of income and assets for self-employed farmers and questions of comprehension of the program and accuracy of reporting by poorly educated participants.

The experiment established rules for the definition of self-employment and developed a method of calculating income for the purposes of a cash transfer program which differed from the IRS rules in disallowing accelerated depreciation and the investment tax credit, adding the value of rent-free housing to income, and imputing to income a percentage of assets above a given level. A one-month accounting period with a twelve-month carryover provision was developed to deal with the seasonal variability of farm income. Experience in administering the program led to additional recommendations to require the accrual method of accounting rather than the cash method and to treat both realized and unrealized capital gains as income.

Participants' understanding of the experimental rules proved very poor. Only about half of the families understood the basic benefit level, implicit tax rate, and breakeven level they faced, and the understanding of these program characteristics did not improve over time despite careful instruction of participants.

Benefits were calculated on the basis of family size, assets, and income as reported by the families. Data on family size, wage income, and transfer income were reported with acceptable accuracy, but assets and farm income were seriously underreported. On the basis of these results, in fact, underreporting by farmers could be expected to affect program costs far more than any likely response in their labor supply.

## SUMMARY OF RESPONSES

Many of the results of the Rural Income Maintenance Experiment resemble closely the results of the New Jersey Experiment. In wage earners' families, income of experimentals declined relative to that of controls somewhat more than in New Jersey, but still by a modest amount. In the Rural Experiment husbands' hours did not decline consistently as a result of the experiment, and those declines that were found tended to be even smaller, on average, than in New Jersey. As in New Jersey, husbands did not withdraw from the labor force, but the percentage of wives working fell considerably. A new result of the Rural Experiment was that wage work of dependents also fell. But since wives and dependents worked only a small number of hours initially the effect on total family work effort was small. As in New Jersey, the experiment had very little effect on various psychological and social variables.

The Rural Experiment provided considerable new information about the work response of farm families. Hours of wage work by experimental farm families declined relative to controls only for one group, and this differential appears to have been caused by large increases in hours by control wives. Hours worked in farming in North Carolina increased while profits and efficiency declined. The latter result may be explained by the incentive to shift work effort away from tasks yielding money income and toward investment or production of directly-consumable commodities.

Other interesting new results were the relative improvements in nutrition and in school performance of grade school children among North Carolina experimental families. A positive experimental effect also occurred for many forms of consumption, including purchase of cars, durable goods, and houses, and acquisition of loan debt.

The results of the experiment suggest, as did the New Jersey Experiment, that a universal income-conditioned cash assistance program would cause only a modest decline in the labor supply of families of wage workers. Husbands who worked primarily for wages would decrease their hours of work slightly or not at all and would not leave the labor force. Wives would be less likely to work than in the absence of payments, but the effect on the families' hours of work would be small since wives' hours of wage work in low-income families tend to be few. The desirability of wives' working less depends on one's view of the value of wives' time devoted to work in the market rather than work at home.

An income maintenance program would be unlikely to affect most social or psychological variables. It would be likely to have a positive effect on the school performance of elementary school children and on various forms of consumption, including adequacy of nutrition, at least in families where these variables are at low levels initially.

The results of the experiment also indicate that special care must be taken in defining administrative and reporting procedures for self-employed farmers in order to avoid serious problems of underreporting and misreporting of income and assets. Problems associated with accurate measurement of farm income and assets may be of greater importance among this population than any likely labor supply response.

# 27

# The Gary Income Maintenance Experiment: Summary of Initial Findings

## Kenneth C. Kehrer

### EXECUTIVE SUMMARY

The Gary Income Maintenance Experiment was one of a coordinated series of experiments supported by the U.S. Department of Health, Education, and Welfare and the Office of Economic Opportunity to test the work incentive effects and other consequences of alternative income support plans. The experiments were conducted with different population groups in different parts of the country. The income support plans tested in Gary were similar in structure to those of existing welfare and transfer programs, except that the benefit formulas were simplified and eligibility was universal, depending only on family income and family size, and the presence of a dependent child. Benefits were determined by the *support level,* that is, the basic benefit provided to a family with no other source of income, and an *implicit tax* or *benefit reduction rate,* that is, the rate at which the benefit is reduced as other sources of income increase. Some benefits were paid to all families with income below a *breakeven level,* with the largest benefits going to those families with the lowest incomes. Thus, under such a plan the size of the benefit decreases as family income rises, but total family income always increases as earnings from work increase.

Four different income support plans, combining two implicit tax rates and two support levels, were tested in Gary. The tax rate were 40 and 60 percent, and the support levels were equal to the poverty level and about three-fourths of the poverty level annual income for each family size. In 1972, for example, when the official poverty threshold for a four-person-nonfarm family was $4,275, the two Gary support levels were $4,300 and $3,300 for that family size. Benefit schedules were adjusted every six months to compensate for increases in the cost of living.

AUTHOR'S NOTE: This paper reports on research at Indiana University Northwest supported by the U.S. Department of Health, Education, and Welfare under contract SRS 70-63 with the Indiana State Department of Public Welfare.

From Kenneth C. Kehrer, "The Gary Income Maintenance Experiment: Summary of Initial Findings." Unpublished manuscript, 1977.

The income maintenance experiments were experiments in the sense that otherwise similar families were randomly assigned either to an experimental (payments-eligible) or control group. By comparing the behavior of the experimental and control families, it is possible to determine statistically the effects of the income support plans, because the only important difference between the two groups was the randomly assigned experimental status.

The experimental group families were eligible for the income support payments for three years. All participating families filed monthly reports of income and family composition changes, and were interviewed before the experiment, about three times a year during the experiment, and after the experiment. Selected families were eligible for child care subsidies at various subsidy rates, and for experimental information-referral services.

## Characteristics of the Participating Families

Each of the experiments studied the responses of different population groups. The Gary experiment focused on black families in an urban environment. Eligibility was also limited to families with at least one child under age 18. Of the 1,799 families who enrolled (voluntarily), 57 percent were assigned eligibility for experimental income support payments, while the remainder were control subjects. Almost 60 percent of the participating families were female-headed families (families without a male head of household present).

The families with a male head of household present (almost all of which were intact husband-wife families) usually had low incomes but generally were not extremely poor. The husbands were typically full-time workers who were able to earn enough to keep their families out of poverty—only 10 percent of these families had incomes below the poverty line. The wives, on the other hand, typically did not work outside the home—only 13 percent were employed at the start of the experiment. In the relatively few families where both the husband and the wife were employed, the wife's earnings usually raised family income so high that the family no longer qualified for the receipt of income support payments.

The husband-wife families studied in Gary would not be considered typical welfare families because of their attachment to the labor force and their income levels, and because public assistance payments were not generally available to husband-wife families in Indiana. But under the income support plans tested in Gary, many of these families were eligible to receive modest income supplements. The analysis of the Gary experiment can therefore provide insight into the consequences of extending an income supplement program to working, but low-income, families.

The families with female heads of household were generally much poorer than the husband-wife families studied. Over 80 percent were receiving welfare benefits from the Aid to Families with Dependent Children (AFDC) program immediately prior to the experiment. About three-fourths of the families that switched from AFDC to the experiment had incomes below the poverty line. The female heads on AFDC at enrollment were very dependent on welfare: 86 percent of their monthly income came from public transfers, with AFDC grants alone accounting for slightly more than half of their incomes. As with the wives studied, only 13 percent of the AFDC female heads were employed.

The female-headed families not on AFDC prior to the experiment were somewhat better off; only 38 percent had incomes below the poverty level. Approximately 60 percent of the income of the non-AFDC female-headed families came from earnings (40 percent of the female heads in these families were employed), while most of the rest of their income came from Food Stamps, Social Security, and other transfer programs.

The income support plans tested in Gary were considerably more generous than AFDC. Average experimental payments to female-headed families by the end of the second year of the experiment were $258 a month, as compared to $159 for AFDC payments. Thus, the Gary experiment can provide information about the effects of increasing the generosity of welfare payments to female-headed families and extending eligibility for income support to female heads who do not currently receive AFDC.

The research reported here is based on limited data from the first two years of the experiment. Because the analysis exploited only a small portion of the available data, these initial findings are still tentative. Once all of the data have been analyzed, the tentative conclusions summarized here may be revised. Nonetheless, several conclusions emerge from the data with strong statistical support.

## INITIAL FINDINGS ON WORK EFFORT RESPONSE

The initial analysis focused on the work effort of household heads who were of working age and capable of working. The work effort response at the end of the first and second years of the experiment was estimated using multiple regression analysis, a statistical technique that took into account the effects of major differences among families likely to influence work effort (e.g., age and education of household heads, family size, and labor market conditions). The available data have been subjected to numerous alternative specifications to test the sensitivity of the work effort response. While these sensitivity tests do not exhaust all possibilities, the narrow range of the response estimates do provide support for the tentative conclusions summarized here.

The initial analysis detected little difference in the work effort response among alternative income support plans. That is, the various support levels and implicit tax rates tested in Gary did not appear to result in greatly varying levels of work effort. Thus, the initial findings summarized in the following pages compare individuals eligible for the experimental support payments—regardless of the specific plan—with individuals who were control subjects.

Table 1. Summary of Initial Findings on Work Effort From the Gary Income Maintenance Experiment: Hours Worked at the End of the Second Year.

| | Effect of the Experiment on Total Hours Worked per Week | Mean Hours Worked by Control Group | Work Effort Response as a Percentage of Control Group Mean |
|---|---|---|---|
| Husbands | −2.5 | 36.0 | −7 |
| Wives | −1.0 | 5.7 | −17 |
| Female Heads | | | |
| On AFDC prior to the experiment | −.3 | 6.5 | −5 |
| Not on AFDC prior to the experiment | .3 | 14.7 | +2 |

Note: These estimates of the work effort response were obtained using statistical technique (regression analysis) that controlled for family composition, other family income, earnings of other family members, the individual's age, education, normal wage rate, and preexperiment work effort and AFDC status, and the unemployment rate and season at the time of the interview.

The initial findings indicate that the experiment had a modest disincentive effect on the work effort of household heads by the end of the second year (see Table 1). In intact families, husbands reduced their total hours worked by an average of 7 percent, and wives reduced their hours of work by 17 percent. These estimates are quite similar to those of the work effort response of husbands and wives in the New Jersey and Rural experiments. Female heads who switched from AFDC to the NIT reduced their hours of work by 5 percent. However, because both AFDC female heads and wives worked few hours prior to the experiment—about 6 hours a week on the average—their reductions in work effort had only a small impact on total family labor supply and earnings. Our findings indicated that female heads not on AFDC at enrollment actually increased their hours of work slightly relative to controls, but we have little confidence in this result.

## The Work Effort Response of Husband-Wife Families

A major focus of public debate over welfare reform has been the potential disincentive effects of extending coverage to all husband-wife families, or of increasing existing welfare benefits for these families. Currently only about half of the states provide benefits (under AFDC-UF) to intact, husband-wife families where the husband is unemployed.[1] The income support plans tested in the income maintenance experiments generally provide higher payments than existing AFDC benefits, and cover more husband-wife families than AFDC.

The work effort response of intact families to the support plans tested in Gary was centered among the husbands, who reduced their total hours worked by 2.5 hours a week in response to the experiment. This disincentive was largely the result of the complete withdrawal of a few individuals from the labor

Table 2. Comparison of Findings on Work Effort From Three Income Maintenance Experiments. (Percentage Changes in Hours Worked.)

|  | Husbands | Wives |
|---|---|---|
| New Jersey Experiment | –6 | –31 |
| Rural Experiment | –1 | –27 |
| Gary Experiment | –7 | –17 |

Note: These estimates are weighted averages of the response in hours worked of different population groups. Because there were some technical problems in estimating the response of black and Spanish-speaking groups, the estimates from the New Jersey experiment reported here are for whites only. Recent reanalysis of the New Jersey data for husbands provides evidence that the magnitude of the response for these groups is similar to the response of whites (see Kerachsky and Mallar, 1976).

force rather than of small reductions in work effort by most of the husbands. Those who were not well established in the labor market prior to the experiment were most likely to withdraw from the labor force.

The wives responded to the experiment by reducing their total hours worked by one hour a week. This decline in work effort consisted of both a disincentive effect on employment of a few wives and an across-board reduction in hours worked by those who continued to work. However, many of the wives who stopped working remained in the labor force since they continued to look for work. In general, the estimates of the work effort response of wives are statistically insignificant, partly due to the small number of working wives in our sample.

Earlier income maintenance experiments focusing on intact families were conducted in cities in New Jersey and Pennsylvania and rural areas of Iowa and North Carolina. These experiments tested income support plans with benefit levels set between 50 and 125 percent of the poverty line and tax rates of between 30 and 70 percent. However, most of the participating families were assigned to income support levels between 75 and 100 percent of the poverty level and tax (benefit reduction) rates around 50 percent, as in Gary. It is useful to compare the findings from these experiments which tested similar income support plans on different population groups.

For husbands, the estimated average experimental response of total hours worked from the completed experiments falls in the range between −1 and −7 percent (see Table 2). The average response of black husbands in Gary appears to have been about the same magnitude as the response of white husbands in cities in New Jersey and Pennsylvania. The Gary response was centered in a reduction in employment among a few husbands, while the response in the other experiments was characterized by a marginal reduction in hours worked by many husbands. One reason for this may be that, in the highly institutionalized labor market in Gary, husbands may not be able to make small adjustments to their work effort. The only way to reduce work effort may be to quit work altogether.

The results from the three experiments for wives indicate a large disincentive effect in percentage terms (the estimates range from −17 to −31 percent), although the response is more modest in absolute terms; the range of response for wives was between 1 and 5 hours a week. Black wives in Gary and in the New Jersey sites appear to have reduced their work effort less than the other wives studied in the experiments.

Thus, the evidence from quite different population groups suggests that the reduction in work effort by prime-age husbands in response to an income support plan with a support level of about 85 percent of the poverty level and a tax (benefit reduction) rate of around 50 percent would not be large. The work effort response of wives to such a plan would be larger in percentage terms, but would not be large in terms of actual hours. Further analysis of data from the Gary and Seattle-Denver experiments will examine the generalizability of these findings and the impact of alternative income support plans.

## The Work Effort Response of Female Heads

Switching female heads from AFDC to the experimental support plans resulted in only a modest reduction in work effort, .3 hours worked per week on the average (about 5 percent), despite the relative generosity of the experimental payments. The response consisted primarily of a few female heads who stopped working rather than an across-the-board reduction in hours worked. The modest disincentive effect—somewhat smaller than the negative experimental response of husbands in the sample—may reflect the work disincentive effects of the AFDC program, which enables mothers to reduce their work effort in order to care for their children. Switching from AFDC to a more adequate income support program may not lead to large reductions in work effort because many female heads may have already reduced their hours of work under AFDC. In any case, these estimates suggest that increasing the support levels of the AFDC program along the lines of the income support plans tested in Gary would result in a decline in the work effort of female heads by only a modest amount.

Female heads who were not on AFDC prior to the experiment appear to have increased their work effort slightly, by about .3 hours a week, in response to the experiment. However, the estimated responses for the group of female heads who were not on AFDC prior to the experiment are statistically insignificant and unstable over time. The sample size of this group is quite small and may not be large enough to permit us to estimate the effect of the experiment on their work effort with confidence.

## OTHER INITIAL FINDINGS

While work effort was the central focus of the initial analysis, it was not the only response of interest. Studies were also conducted on experimental responses in four other areas: the effects of income maintenance on family consumption; the demand for housing; the demand for social services; and the choices teenagers make among school, work and leisure. In addition, other studies investigated the utilization of the experiment's subsidized child care and social services information-referral programs, and the degree of participants' understanding of the rules of the experiment and the mechanics of the income support plans.

The effect of the experiment on family consumption was investigated by comparing differences between the experimental and control groups in debt, monthly purchases, and the acquisition of durable goods between mid-experiment and the period prior to enrollment. This preliminary analysis suggests that experimental families tended to use their additional income to increase their expenditures on clothing, medicine, and automobile repairs (but not to purchase automobiles), and to reduce their medical debt. In addition, families eligible for experimental payments spent 78 percent more on home production appliances and 64 percent more on furniture than control families. Initial examination of the housing consumption patterns of a subsample of families indicates that the experimental payments did not appear to induce families to move to different housing. On the other hand, among those families that did move during the experiment, public housing residents in the experimental group were about 50 percent more likely to move to private dwellings than similar control families, and experimental families were twice as likely to purchase homes. Thus, the experimental payments appear not to have influenced the decision of families to move but, among those families who would have moved anyway, the payments influenced their choice of residence.

Experimental families used social agencies less extensively than did the control families. Controlling for other factors, families eligible for experimental payments reduced their use of social service agencies about 13 percent. Thus, the evidence from the Gary experiment suggests that a universal income support program, available to more families and with higher benefits than AFDC in Indiana, may reduce the demand for social services to some extent.

The experimental payments appear to have had a positive effect on school attendance among male teenagers, who tended to reduce their labor force participation and continue their high school education. On the other hand, the experimental income support plans appear to have had no effect on high school continuation for female teenagers and no effect on college attendance for either sex. Of course, black female teenagers are already much more likely to finish high school than black males, so there exists less opportunity for a positive experimental response among females.

Child care subsidies were available to selected experimental participants at varying subsidy rates—100, 80, 60, and 35 percent. For most of these families, the availability of the subsidies was contingent on working (or engaging in a work-related activity). The number of families who used the child care program was much smaller than originally anticipated; less than 5 percent of eligible families used the program during the second year. The rate of utilization generally declined as the subsidy decreased, and utilization was higher among families with preschool children; for families with preschool children the rate of use in the 80 and 100 percent subsidy plans with a work requirement was 15 percent. These initial findings suggest that utilization of a child care subsidy program will depend on the rate of subsidy, and that utilization will be concentrated among families with preschool children.

The Gary experiment attempted to test the usefulness of "access workers" who provided information and referral services to a subgroup of the study sample. However, utilization of the access workers was much lower than expected and declined to an almost negligible level from the beginning of the program to the end of the first year of the study. About 25 percent of the eligible families contacted the access workers.

Household heads were highly knowledgeable about the rules that governed a family's eligibility for continued participation in the experiment. However, as had been anticipated, they were considerably less knowledgeable about the mechanics of the income support plans. These results are similar to findings from the New Jersey and Rural experiments.

## NOTES

1. However, eligibility for AFDC-UF benefits depends not only on income, but also on attachment to the labor force or on previous employment. All states provide benefits under AFDC to intact families where one of the parents is incapacitated.

# 28

## The Seattle-Denver Income Maintenance Experiment: Midexperimental Labor Supply Results and a Generalization to the National Population

*Stanford Research Institute and Mathematica Policy Research*

### SUMMARY

In the long-running debate over welfare policy, the effect of welfare programs on the work effort of recipients has been a central issue. Both economic theory and common sense suggest that cash payments based on income provide incentives to decrease work effort, but until recently little information has existed concerning the probable size of the effect. The disincentive to work is potentially a serious problem for several reasons. A decline in work will reduce both the national output and the income of low-income families, and will increase the cost of assistance programs; in addition, a policy that reduces the work attachment of the low-income population will run counter to strongly-held ethical beliefs and the goal of enabling recipients to become self-sufficient.

To provide information about the work incentive effects of income-conditioned cash transfers, the former Office of Economic Opportunity and the Department of Health, Education, and Welfare conducted a series of four social experiments. The last of these experiments, the Seattle-Denver Income Maintenance Experiment, has provided information about work effort responses that facilitates generalization to the national population and to a variety of possible programs.

The results from this experiment have now been used, as described in this report, to simulate the costs, distribution of benefits to different types of families and work incentive effects resulting from various programs, including the Carter Administration's proposed Program for Better Jobs and Income. A

From Stanford Research Institute and Mathematica Policy Research for the Department of Health, Education, and Welfare, "The Seattle-Denver Income Maintenance Experiment Midexperimental Labor Supply Results and a Generalization to the National Population." Unpublished manuscript, 1977.

number of different cash assistance programs—none with any jobs provision—were simulated to clarify the implications of choices among various benefit levels and benefit reduction rates. These simulations provided information useful in the development of the cash component of the Carter welfare reform proposal. In addition, the results of the Seattle-Denver Experiment were used in simulations of the Program for Better Jobs and Income to project the number of jobs needed for the program, and the costs and work incentive effects of combining a jobs program with a cash assistance program.

## Estimates of Work Incentive Effects

The Seattle-Denver Income Maintenance Experiment, conducted by Stanford Research Institute and Mathematica Policy Research, began in 1970 and will continue through 1978. It is the most comprehensive of the income maintenance experiments, covering nearly 5000 one- and two-parent black, white, and Hispanic-American families. The families were assigned either to one of several experimental groups receiving cash assistance payments or to a control group of families which received no experimental payments but continued to receive whatever benefits they were eligible for under current governmental programs. Comparison of the hours of work of experimental families with those of control group families during the course of the experiment enabled economists to measure the work disincentives of cash programs on the experimental group.

The programs studied in the experiment have a structure similar to that of most existing income-conditioned transfer programs, such as AFDC and SSI. They consist of a basic benefit, the amount of money a family receives when it has no other income; and a benefit reduction rate, the amount by which a family's benefit is reduced as its income from other sources increases. Programs of this form can be expected to reduce the incentives to work both because income received through such programs reduces the need to work and because benefits are reduced as earnings rise, thereby diminishing the reward from work. Under a 50 percent benefit reduction rate, for example, a recipient who earns $3.00 an hour will lose $1.50 in benefits for each hour of work, so that the net increase in income will be only $1.50 an hour.

Preliminary results based on the first two and one-half years of data closely resemble the results of earlier income maintenance experiments. Under various alternative cash assistance programs that contained no work requirement and were not combined with any provision for job search assistance, training, or public service employment, husbands in the experimental group worked only slightly less—6 percent fewer hours—than husbands in the control group. For wives and female family heads, the percentage decline in work effort was greater—17 percent and 12 percent, respectively—as compared with the relevant control group. But since most wives in low-income families and female family heads work relatively few hours, the absolute decline in their hours of work was small. These declines in hours of paid work were undoubtedly compensated in part by other useful activities, such as search for better jobs or work in the home.

In addition to comparing the experimental group with the control group, the Seattle-Denver researchers developed a method to measure how the work incentives that individuals face under the existing welfare system would be changed by introduction of a new program. It was found that individuals would adjust their work effort in response to changes in the amount of transfer payments they receive or in the size of the benefit reduction rate they face. Results implied, for example, that for a family with current income of $4000, a program that would increase the amount of their income by $1000 over their current total income, including cash assistance, would cause the husband to reduce his hours of work by a little less than an hour a week. If the new program also increased the benefit reduction rate the husband faced so that his returns from an hour of work were reduced by $1.00, he would reduce his average hours of work a week by an additional one and one half hours. Thus, such a program would cause him to reduce his work effort by a total of around two and one half hours a week. In the same situation, wives would work a total of five and a half hours less, and female heads would work almost four hours per week less.

## Simulations of Cash Programs

Estimates of work incentive effects from the Seattle-Denver Income Maintenance Experiment were used to conduct simulations of several income-conditioned cash assistance programs with no jobs component. These simulations were designed to permit direct comparisons of cash programs and to clarify the policy implications of different benefit levels and benefit reduction rates. Estimates were computed of costs, caseloads, and benefits received by various types of families under each of the simulated programs. The simulations were carried out by Mathematica Policy Research, using the Micro-Analysis of Transfers to Households (MATH) model and data from the March 1975 Current Population Survey.

The simulated programs had basic benefit levels of 50, 75, and 100 percent of the poverty line and benefit reduction rates of 50 and 70 percent. It was assumed that the simulated programs would replace the existing Food Stamp and Aid to Families with Dependent Children programs. All eligible families were assumed to participate.

These simulated cash programs differ greatly from the Program for Better Jobs and Income, and were not designed for comparison with that program. The results of these cash program simulations, however, provided considerable information about the policy implications of different benefit levels and benefit reduction rates, information that was useful in designing the Administration's welfare reform proposal.

The simulations indicate that in response to the relatively simple cash assistance programs described above, husband-wife families receiving benefits would reduce their hours of work between 13 and 20 percent, with the low end of this range associated with simulated programs with a 50 percent benefit reduction rate. The reduction in work effort would increase as the benefit reduction rates increased. While the percentage reduction for wives would be larger than that for husbands, their absolute decline in hours would be smaller because of the large number of wives who work few hours or not at all. The change in hours in single-parent families would be smaller than in husband-wife families—ranging from an increase of 1 percent to a decline of 16 percent—because most female heads receive transfer payments under the existing welfare system and have already adjusted their work effort to them. In fact, several of the simulated programs would decrease transfer benefits currently received by many female-headed families, thereby increasing the hours that such families work.

Even though the change in hours of work may be moderate, such changes in work effort were found to have important implications for program costs. For example, the simulations predicted that under a program with a basic benefit level of 75 percent of the poverty line and a benefit reduction rate of 50 percent, the reduction in work effort of husbands, wives, and female family heads receiving cash assistance would increase net program costs by 25 percent. In computing net costs, the costs of present AFDC and Food Stamp Programs, which are assumed to be abolished, were subtracted from total costs of the simulated programs.

Net program costs, numbers of families who would receive benefits, and costs attributable to program-induced changes in working hours are all sensitive to both program benefit levels and benefit reduction rates as shown in Table 1. For example, a relatively generous program, with benefit levels set at the poverty line and a benefit reduction rate of 50 percent, would have many more participants and higher program costs than a program that set benefit levels at 75 percent of the poverty line and benefit reduction rates at 70 percent. Total net costs attributable to reductions in work effort would be higher for such a program than for less generous, less costly programs, but the proportion of net cost caused by reduced work would be much lower. This is because the reduction in work effort per family is less under the plan with the lower benefit reduction rate and because the higher benefit reduction rate plan includes relatively more low-income families whose work effort response is greater.

As can be seen from Table 1, total net program costs were found to vary from a saving of $3.66 billion to a net cost of $27.61 billion. Savings occurred under the less generous simulated programs because benefits were smaller for many families than payments they currently receive under the AFDC and Food Stamp programs.[1] The fraction of net program costs resulting from decreases in work effort ranged from 58 percent of one of the less expensive programs to only 17 percent of the most generous program. The number of families covered ranged from 1.5 million to almost 18 million, with all but the two extreme plans falling between 4 and 10 million. Most of the difference lay in the number of husband-wife families covered; the number of female-headed families varied relatively little, since a large fraction of these families had such low incomes that they were covered under every program.

Table 1. Net program costs and numbers of participating families for alternative cash assistance programs: families receiving transfer payments or tax relief.

| Basic Benefit as Percent of Poverty line | Net Program Costs ($ Billion) | Net Program Costs Due to Changes in Work Effort ($ Billion) | (%) | Participating Families (Millions) |
|---|---|---|---|---|
| 50 PERCENT BENEFIT REDUCTION RATE | | | | |
| 50 | −2.54 | .53 | * | 4.4 |
| 75 | 7.44 | 1.88 | 25 | 9.7 |
| 100 | 27.61 | 4.58 | 17 | 17.9 |
| 70 PERCENT BENEFIT REDUCTION RATE | | | | |
| 50 | −3.66 | .41 | * | 1.5 |
| 75 | 2.36 | 1.36 | 58 | 5.1 |
| 100 | 12.20 | 3.07 | 25 | 8.0 |

* Percentage not computed when base is negative

Program costs were shown to increase as the basic benefit level increases, an effect which occurred both because more families became eligible and because benefits per family rose. However, costs decreased as the benefit reduction rate rose because benefits decreased for most families, especially higher-income ones, and fewer families were eligible. A high benefit reduction rate program would pay a relatively large share of its benefits to families with very low incomes, as compared with a low benefit reduction rate program. The percentage of net costs due to decreases in work effort, however, was higher in the high benefit reduction rate programs. This occurred both because the reward to work was lower and because only relatively low income families, whose work responses to changes in income are large, were eligible for benefits.

The way in which a cash assistance program is integrated with the income tax system was also found to have major implications for program costs, work effort, and the distribution of program benefits among the nation's families. Both the experimental programs and the simulated cash programs fully reimbursed taxes that were owed by persons eligible for transfer payments. In addition, taxes were partially reimbursed to families who were at income levels that were above those at which they qualified for a transfer payment, although the percentage of taxes that were reimbursed gradually fell as income increased, eventually falling to zero. This procedure was necessary to keep after-tax income from suddenly falling with an additional dollar of earnings. Two alternative reimbursement plans were simulated—one in which the rate of reimbursement fell relatively rapidly as earnings increased, and one in which the reimbursement rate decreased relatively gradually. Although the percentage of cost due to reductions in work effort was slightly greater under the first plan than the second, the cost of the tax relief was almost twice as high under the latter plan, and the number of families receiving tax relief was two and one-half times higher.

### Simulations of the Administration's Welfare Reform Program

The costs and work incentive effects of the Administration's Program for Better Jobs and Income were also simulated on the basis of the results of the Seattle-Denver Experiment. This welfare reform proposal includes both an income-conditioned cash assistance component which would replace the AFDC (and WIN), SSI, and Food Stamp programs, and various employment aids including a major public service jobs component. The program would provide a basic federal benefit floor for all persons and would encourage work by establishing different benefit structures for recipients who are expected to work and those who are not. States that presently pay benefits in excess of the proposed federal basic benefit would be encouraged to supplement these benefits by Federal subsidization of state payments that are fully consistent with the Federal incentive structure.[2]

The simulations estimated costs and caseloads for the Program for Better Jobs and Income and compared the work effort effects of adding public service jobs to a cash assistance component. Simulation results indicate that if jobs were not provided by the Administration's welfare reform proposal, total cash benefits would have been $19.5 billion in 1974. In the absence of a jobs provision, husbands, wives, and single parents participating in the Administration's proposed cash assistance component only would have decreased their hours of work—by 3, 9, and 2 percent, respectively. However, by increasing the earnings opportunities of low-income persons through the provision of the jobs component, simulations show that the Program for Better Jobs and Income would reduce cash transfer costs and also increase work effort, as compared to the work incentive effects of the cash component alone.

The simulations showed that, in 1974, an estimated 1.4 million full-time, full-year public service positions would have been required. The total wages for these jobs would have been $6.3 billion, and total cash benefits would have been $16 billion.[3] Hours of work for wives would have been reduced by about 4 percent, but for husbands they would have increased by about 2 percent and for single parents, 7 percent.

Work effort increases as a result of the jobs component for two reasons. First, the public service job will pay a higher wage than some persons can obtain in the regular labor market, and this tends to increase the number of hours these persons are willing to work. Second, the availability of public service jobs allows many persons to work during periods in which they would otherwise be unemployed.

Overall, the results of the simulations presented here make clear that while workers—particularly secondary earners—do respond to monetary incentives, cash assistance programs would not cause a massive withdrawal of workers from the labor force, as many have feared. When combined with jobs,as in the case of Administration's welfare reform proposal, they would result in increased work effort. Any reduction in work effort caused by cash assistance would be more than offset by the increased employment opportunities provided by public service jobs. The simulation results also suggest that changes in the basic benefit and benefit reduction rate of a cash assistance program may not only have major effects on costs and on work effort, but on the distribution of benefits among families of different types as well. They also show that the method of integration of the cash assistance program with the tax system can have major effects on costs and number of recipients and must be planned with care.

## NOTES

1. Net program costs were also calculated under a "hold-harmless" provision for AFDC participants, which ensured that their benefits under the simulated programs were at least as high as their current AFDC benefits. Although this resulted in only negligible increases in costs for the more generous of the simulated programs, net costs of the less generous programs increased by several billion dollars.

2. A description of the Administration's proposal is contained in Section IV of this report.

3. Transfer amounts from the Program for Better Jobs and Income are usually presented in fiscal year 1978 dollars. In order to be consistent with the remainder of the report, all dollar magnitudes have been adjusted to 1974 amounts. Thus, a direct comparison cannot be made between the estimates presented here for calendar year 1974 and those presented elsewhere for fiscal year 1978.

# PART V
# CRIMINAL JUSTICE

The papers in this section deal with the reduction of crime and criminal activity largely through attempts to increase deterrence. Reports based on two field experiments funded by the Police Foundation have been selected for inclusion because they deal with the effectiveness of forms of police patrolling. In the San Diego patrol car staffing excerpt a stratified sampling design was used to evaluate the consequences of putting one or two officers in a patrol car. Findings suggest that in terms of unit performance, efficiency, and police safety, one-officer units are at least equal to, or more advantageous than, two-officer units. The second study is an independent review of the Kansas City experiment sponsored by the Police Foundation, and it suggests that the absence of a deterrent effect in that study not be overgeneralized. This is largely because the highest level of police patrolling in the Kansas study was less than that found routinely elsewhere and because the achieved contrast between levels of patrolling may have been much less than planned.

Theories about the deterrent value of punishment are centuries old. A provocative paper by Ehrlich in 1975 suggested as a result of an econometric analysis of time series data that the death penalty may very significantly decrease the rate of murders. Ehrlich's analysis did not go unchallenged on methodological grounds and two critiques are particularly salient. The first critique by Passell and Taylor, which is reproduced here, questions Ehrlich's work on several grounds. Ehrlich's reply to Passell and Taylor is also included, and it gives preliminary results from Ehrlich's recent cross-sectional analysis of the deterrent effect of capital punishment which uses some of the same data from the longitudinal analysis. The complete study of the cross-sectional analysis can be found in the June 1977 *Journal of Political Economy.* The second, by Klein, Forst, and Filatov, which appeared in a volume edited by Alfred Blumstein et al. entitled *Deterrence and Incapacitation,* suggested that the data could not prove or disprove Ehrlich's conclusion. Ehrlich did not accept this criticism and responded in his article "Fear of Deterrence: A Critical Evaluation of the Report of the Panel on Deterrent and Incapacitative Effects," which appeared in the June 1977 issue of the *Journal of Legal Studies.* The last word has, we feel, not yet been said on this deterrence issue, but the debate is of great consequence for policy and, not incidentally, for the appropriateness of econometric methods for inferring cause from crime data.

The paper by Zimring argues that in deterrence studies nonexperimental methods cannot control for all the plausible alternative explanations of apparent causal relationships, and so he advocates the slower but surer methods of controlled experimentation. Zimring argues, in essence, that the tortoise should be preferred to the hare, for though the hare is faster, it is more likely to be wrong and to lead to policies that may be actively harmful because they are based on misinformation about causal connections.

The final study excerpted here contrasts two important policy options. The study suggests that providing temporary income to released prisoners reduces subsequent thefts more than job placement. Whether this superiority is maintained over longer time periods is not clear from the experiment, and is obviously an issue of some importance.

# 29

# Patrol Staffing in San Diego: One- or Two-Officer Units

*John E. Boydstun, Michael E. Sherry, and Nicholas P. Moelter*

## ABSTRACT

*This filed research project examined an issue which to date has been characterized by emotionally charged claims and counterclaims, but has generated little, if anything, in the way of testable proof that would advance rational policy-making. The issue is whether to staff police patrol cars with one or two officers. The importance if this issue can hardly be exaggerated, given the increasing budgetary problems in many of the nation's cities. Putting two officers in a patrol unit can cost almost twice as much as using one officer in a patrol unit. O.W. Wilson, in Police Administration, asserted his conviction that an officer patrolling alone is more efficient, effective, and safe than two officers in a patrol car. But until now, Wilson's view has remained an assertion.*

## BACKGROUND

Controversy and debate among police practitioners regarding the overall subject of police methods have persisted over the past 25 years. The issue of staffing a police car with one officer patrolling alone or with two officers working as a team has been a source of the controversy, but empirical research on these two methods of police patrol staffing has been lacking.[1]

For some time the Police Foundation has been interested in resolving some of the controversy surrounding one- or two-officer patrol car staffing. In the spring of 1974, the Foundation contacted the San Diego Police Department, which expressed an interest in obtaining funds for a comprehensive study of the issue.

As a result of preliminary meetings and discussions involving the San Diego Police Department, the Police Foundation, and System Development Corporation,

From John E. Boydstun, Michael E. Sherry, and Nicholas P. Moelter, "Patrol Staffing in San Diego: One- or Two-Officer Units." Report prepared by System Development Corporation for the Police Foundation, June 1977. Copyright 1977 by the Police Foundation.

the Foundation in October 1974 approved and provided funding for a cooperative planning and design effort involving joint participation of the San Diego Police Department staff and the evaluation staff of System Development Corporation. The purpose of this planning phase was to study the current patrol environment within the San Diego Police Department with the object of establishing an evaluation design and methodology. The ultimate goal was to resolve as many as possible of the issues in the controversy regarding unit performance, efficiency, and officer safety associated with using one- vs. two-officer patrol units.

## PATROL MANAGEMENT ISSUES ADDRESSED BY THE STUDY

The implications of the decision to use one officer instead of two in patrol units are not trivial. For example, the San Diego Police Department spends $112,045 more (an 83 percent increase) per unit per year to field a two-officer unit on a 24-hour basis than to field a one-officer unit. For a single eight-hour watch period, the difference in cost exceeds $100 per unit.

In deciding how to staff and use patrol units, managers need to be able to predict how many officers will be needed for any given situation, based on acceptable levels of unit performance, efficiency, and officer safety. Patrol units are expected to provide a variety of law enforcement and community services, in dissimilar areas, and under highly variable circumstances. Thus, managers must address the question of patrol unit staffing in terms of specific local expectations, areas, and circumstances—including specifically the time of day or watch period. Each unit assignment should meet acceptable levels of performance, efficiency, and safety, and requirements vary. If two officers actually are needed to perform the majority of tasks required of a particular patrol unit, it is clearly more economical to put them in the same car, rather than in two cars. But if one officer can acceptably handle most of the expected tasks, it is cheaper to put one officer in each car and send two or more cars when backup assistance is required.

Because it is difficult to predict the number of patrol officers required for an assignment, department administrators must allow themselves a margin for error. A second patrol officer in each car provides a built-in safeguard against underestimating the number of officers required, but it is an extremely expensive one.

Having enough units to ensure a reserve and operating an effective dispatch system for sending backup units from the reserve also are safeguards against error. The success of this approach depends on careful evaluation of each call-for-service so that the necessary number of units can be assigned initially, and also on making it possible for assigned units to request assistance when they need it. Because the frequency of calls-for-service and the number of officers needed per call are variable, the numbers of both assigned and available units vary. Systems for assigning priority to the calls-for-service are used to help dispatchers allocate the units according to both demand and availability. These dispatching policies, procedures, and actual experience influence unit performance. Department administrators must consider them in making unit staffing decisions, and in comparing unit performances on calls-for-service.

When units are not assigned to calls-for-service, the officers are expected to initiate patrol activities. The kinds of potentially valuable activities possible are many, and available opportunities for each type vary. Patrol officers generally have a great deal of discretion over the kinds of patrol duties they perform, and how much they do. Inasmuch as patrol unit staffing can be expected to influence unit performance on officer-initiated activities as well as on call-for-service assignments, patrol managers must consider the importance they wish to give to these activities, as well as to any differences in performance by one- and two-officer units.

For each kind of patrol activity a unit performs, whether assigned or self-initiated, there should, ideally, be some measure of performance quality as well as quantity. Few such measures have been developed. For this study, call-for-service results in terms of arrests made, formal (crime) reports filed, medical emergency transportation provided, and other (no formal report) dispositions served as measures of the quality of primary call-for-service assignments. Arrest subjects held to answer and arrest charges filed as requested were used to assess the quality of arrests. Citizen complaints were used as an overall measure of the public's satisfaction with services provided.

The efficiency issues involved in patrol unit staffing require determination of the time and resources expended for the types and qualities of patrol unit activities employed. The most direct approach, and the one used in this study, is to calculate unit cost for a standard interval of time and then measure the average amount of time units are spending on each activity. Subcategories of duties (such as call-for-service assignments to criminal calls resulting in arrests) can be used to include measures of unit time and money expended for a specified level of quality.

In addition to the type, quantity, quality, and cost of services performed by patrol units, patrol management must consider officer safety in making unit staffing decisions. Because of the variations in patrol unit activity, it is important to try to measure unit exposure to potential safety hazards as well as to tabulate the occurrences of assaults, injuries, and accidents. Both exposure itself and the results of exposure may be influenced by unit staffing decisions.

Finally, management must consider the preferences and opinions of patrol officers in making patrol unit staffing decisions. In some cities, contract negotiations already have established specific requirements for patrol unit staffing, but in most cases these decisions have not been based on a thorough, joint analysis of the performance, efficiency, and officer safety issues involved nor of the many contract options available for the same or lower cost.


## DESIGN OF THE STUDY

### Selection of Experimental Areas and Units

Financial considerations made it impossible to select a saturation sample that would include all the beats in San Diego. On the other hand, the study team concluded that a simple random selection of beats within the city would present potentially serious research problems because: (1) assignment of two-officer units, not only in San Diego, but in many other police departments as well, is based on the socioeconomic or ethnic characteristics of a patrol beat; (2) beats or areas of the city vary widely on such factors; and (3) all beats in San Diego have been staffed consistently with either one-officer or two-officer units for some years, making previous patrol staffing policy an important dimension (on the part of both the community and the police) to control.

Based on these conditions, the sample of units selected for this study was chosen through a stratified sampling procedure designed to control for the determinants outlined above. The first stratification is thus the previous staffing policy of the beats. This stratification assigns every beat in the Central Patrol Division to one of the areas described in Table 1.

TABLE 1

## EXPERIMENTAL SAMPLE GROUPS

Group I:   One-officer units in previously one-officer areas (the status quo)

Group II:  One-officer units in previously two-officer areas (an experimental control)

Group III: Two-officer units in previously one-officer areas (an experimental control)

Group IV:  Two-officer units in previously two-officer areas (the status quo)

The next problem was to choose, from within these four groups of beats, those beats to be staffed with either one- or two-officer experimental units. Beats were carefully evaluated on a variety of socioeconomic and demographic variables, using a Social Area Analysis of San Diego.[2] This analysis consisted of factor analyses of 126 census indicators. The three factors under this analysis which best predict all other factors are ethnicity (percentage of minority residents), socioeconomic status (a combination of housing value, income, and education), and family status (size of family units and percentage of families with children). Using beat rankings on these demographic dimensions, as well as on various measures of reported crimes on the beats, beats within "previously one-officer" and "previously two-officer" areas were matched to one another, and assigned equally to either the one-officer staffing condition or the two-officer staffing condition.

In summary, then, 44 patrol units were assigned equally in the one- and two-officer conditions, according to watch, area of city, and previous staffing policy as indicated in Tables 2, 3, and 4.

TABLE 2

## EXPERIMENTAL UNITS BY WATCH ASSIGNMENT

| PATROL WATCHES | EXPERIMENTAL UNITS N = 44 | |
| --- | --- | --- |
| | One-Officer Units | Two-Officer Units |
| First Watch (7 A.M.-3 P.M.) | 7 units | 7 units |
| Second Watch (3 P.M.-11 P.M.) | 8 units | 8 units |
| Third Watch (11 P.M.-7 A.M.) | 7 units | 7 units |
| TOTAL | 22 units | 22 units |

**Selection of Officers**

The Central Patrol Division of the San Diego Police Department had a total of 370 patrol officers operating a daily average (all watches combined) of 141 patrol

TABLE 3

## EXPERIMENTAL UNITS BY BEAT ASSIGNMENTS AND AREA OF THE CITY

| AREA OF THE CITY | EXPERIMENTAL UNITS N = 44 | |
| --- | --- | --- |
| | One-Officer Units | Two-Officer Units |
| Southeast San Diego | 6 beats 16 units | 6 beats 16 units |
| East San Diego | 2 beats 6 units | 2 beats 6 units |
| TOTAL | 8 beats 22 units | 8 beats 22 units |

units. Inasmuch as the study design called for controlling the staffing of 44 units, half of which would result in changes from previous staffing patterns, the impact on personnel assignments was potentially serious. Furthermore, the personnel policy then in effect allowed officer seniority and personal preference to determine changes in unit (beat and watch) assignments. To "freeze" assignments for the one-year experimental period would have been disruptive of staffing practices then in effect, and would have created an artificial condition during the observation of unit performance.

TABLE 4

## EXPERIMENTAL UNITS BY PREVIOUS PATROL STAFFING

| PREVIOUS PATROL STAFFING | EXPERIMENTAL UNITS N = 44 | |
|---|---|---|
| | One-Officer Units | Two-Officer Units |
| Previous One-Officer Staffing | 11 units | 11 units |
| Previous Two-Officer Staffing | 11 units | 11 units |
| TOTAL | 22 units | 22 units |

Based on these considerations, and on the fact that the design focused on units rather than on the officers themselves, the decision was made not to control individual officer assignments.

Table 5 compares the actual staffing with those that would have been expected if unit assignments had been frozen during the experimental period. Of the large number of officers involved, more than half worked in both types of study units, and the average officer assigned to a one-officer unit accounted for only 5.9 (6.7 percent) of the 84 watch periods studied for each unit, while the average officer assigned to a two-officer unit accounted for only 6.07 (7.2 percent) of the 84 watch periods studied for each unit. Thus, it does not appear that individual officer

TABLE 5

COMPARISONS OF ACTUAL AND EXPECTED[a] STUDY UNIT STAFFING

| STUDY UNITS | MEAN OFFICERS PER UNIT | | MEAN WATCH PERIODS PER OFFICER | | TOTAL INDIVIDUAL OFFICERS INVOLVED | |
|---|---|---|---|---|---|---|
| | EXPECTED | ACTUAL | EXPECTED | ACTUAL | EXPECTED | ACTUAL |
| One-Officer Units | 1.67 | 14.91 | 50.30 | 5.61 | 37 | 200[b] |
| Two-Officer Units | 3.34 | 27.68 | 50.30 | 6.07 | 74 | 280[c] |

[a] Expected if assignment had been frozen.
[b] Includes 26 who worked exclusively in one-officer units and 174 who worked in both types of study units.
[c] Includes 106 who worked exclusively in two-officer and 174 who worked in both types of study units.

differences could be expected to have had a major influence on unit performance as measured during this study.

Unit staffing (one or two officers) was controlled throughout the year of the study, and during that period the staff made a number of matched observations (both sampled and continuous) of the types of study units. The selected design permitted analysis of the overall difference between one- and two-officer units as well as more specific comparisons under particular conditions and circumstances.

A secondary analysis technique was also employed. The multi-variate analysis of variance (MANOVA) technique was used to examine various combinations of

## TABLE 6

COMPARISON OF DIFFERENCES IN PROPORTION OF CALL-FOR-SERVICE ASSIGNMENTS TO STUDY
UNITS BY CLASSIFICATION OF INCIDENTS AND SIGNIFICANCE
(Sample Data from Dispatch Records)

| INCIDENT CLASSIFICATION | PRIMARY ASSIGNMENTS | | | | $\chi^2$ VALUE (1 degree of freedom) | SIGNIFICANCE LEVEL |
|---|---|---|---|---|---|---|
| | One-Officer Units | | Two-Officer Units | | | |
| | N | % | N | % | | |
| Criminal | 908 | 19.5 | 1,193 | 19.3 | 0.07 | n.s. |
| Traffic | 476 | 10.2 | 577 | 9.3 | 2.41 | n.s. |
| Peacekeeping | 1,206 | 25.9 | 1,773 | 28.7 | 10.26 | p < .001 |
| Medical | 230 | 4.9 | 619 | 10.0 | 94.63 | p < .001 |
| Nuisance abatement | 11 | 0.2 | 9 | 0.1 | 1.18 | n.s. |
| Security checks | 393 | 8.4 | 589 | 9.5 | 3.79 | n.s. |
| Operational | 460 | 9.9 | 384 | 6.2 | 49.81 | p < .001 |
| Other (Special) | 88 | 1.9 | 97 | 1.6 | 1.62 | n.s. |
| Report-taking (All types) | 884 | 19.0 | 942 | 15.2 | 26.66 | p < .001 |
| TOTALS | 4,656 | | 6,183 | | | |
| Overall chi-square, 8 degrees of freedom | $\chi^2 = 171.22$ | | | | | p < .001 |
| Similarity of overall distribution Spearman rank-order correlation rho coefficient ($\rho$) | .850 | | | | | p < .05 |

information describing the units and their workloads. It attempted to identify and isolate the influence of factors including unit staffing on observed differences in unit performance, efficiency, and officer safety.

## FINDINGS

The overall performance of patrol units in terms of the type and frequency of call-for-service activities and officer-initiated activities proved to be about equal for units having one or two officers.

As shown in Table 6, dispatchers assigned significantly more peacekeeping and medical incidents and significantly fewer operational and report-taking incidents to two-officer units than to one-officer units. Although these differences were statistically significant, the actual percentage differences were minor. The largest percentage difference (5.1 percent) was for medical incidents and the reason for the difference is that six of the 22 two-officer units were combination police patrol and ambulance units. There were no ambulance units among the 22 one-officer units.

As another way to examine the relative mixes of primary assignments, each class was rank-ordered by frequency of occurrence, and a rank-order correlation test was made. This test (also shown in Table 6) revealed that one- and two-officer units had very similar (significantly correlated) mixes of assignments in terms of the rank-orders of types by frequency.

As shown in Table 7, two-officer units produced more traffic citations, and there were minor variations in the types of calls-for-service handled. Most of these latter variations were explained by the presence of patrol ambulances in the group of two-officer units.

TABLE 7
COMPARISON OF OFFICER-INITIATED PATROL ACTIVITY MEAN RATES FOR STUDY UNITS
(Sample Data from Officers' Journals)

| OFFICER ACTIVITY | UNIT TYPE | TOTALS | | PATROL WATCH | | | | | | AREA OF CITY | | | | PRIOR STAFFING | | | |
|---|---|---|---|---|---|---|---|---|---|---|---|---|---|---|---|---|---|
| | | | | FIRST | | SECOND | | THIRD | | ESD | | SESD | | FORMER 1-0 | | FORMER 2-0 | |
| | | X̄ | s.d. | X̄ | s.d. | X̄ | s.d. | X̄ | s.d. | X̄ | s.d. | X̄ | s.d. | X̄ | s.d. | X̄ | s.d. |
| ARRESTS (TOTAL) | 1-0 | 39.0 | 13.0 | 33.9 | 8.4 | 47.2 | 13.4 | 34.2 | 11.6 | 27.7 | 5.8 | 43.2 | 12.4 | 31.6 | 8.0 | 46.4 | 12.9 |
| [test] | | t=1.88 df=42 n.s. | | t=0.91 df=12 n.s. | | t=0.60 df=14 n.s. | | t=1.86 df=12 n.s. | | t=1.59 df=10 n.s. | | t=1.62 df=30 n.s. | | t=1.57 df=20 n.s. | | t=1.26 df=20 n.s. | |
| | 2-0 | 48.0 | 17.8 | 43.4 | 24.5 | 51.2 | 11.4 | 49.0 | 14.8 | 36.5 | 11.0 | 52.4 | 17.9 | 42.5 | 20.4 | 53.5 | 12.5 |
| Felony arrests (Adults) | 1-0 | 7.9 | 3.9 | 8.1 | 2.5 | 7.9 | 3.4 | 7.6 | 5.2 | 6.3 | 2.1 | 8.4 | 4.2 | 7.3 | 2.7 | 8.5 | 4.7 |
| [test] | | t=1.12 df=42 n.s. | | t=0.43 df=12 n.s. | | t=0.07 df=14 n.s. | | t=1.28 df=12 n.s. | | t=0.20 df=10 n.s. | | t=1.27 df=30 n.s. | | t=0.56 df=20 n.s. | | t=0.98 df=20 n.s. | |
| | 2-0 | 9.8 | 6.8 | 9.9 | 9.4 | 8.0 | 3.6 | 11.7 | 5.9 | 6.0 | 3.0 | 17.2 | 7.3 | 8.7 | 7.7 | 10.8 | 5.6 |
| Felony arrests (Juvenile) | 1-0 | 4.9 | 4.6 | 4.3 | 3.2 | 6.9 | 6.1 | 3.4 | 2.5 | 1.8 | 1.1 | 6.1 | 4.9 | 3.4 | 2.9 | 6.5 | 5.4 |
| [test] | | t=0.41 df=42 n.s. | | t=2.57 df=12 p<.05 | | t=0.79 df=14 n.s. | | t=0.13 df=12 n.s. | | t=2.14 df=10 n.s. | | t=0.12 df=30 n.s. | | t=2.13 df=20 p<.05 | | t=0.91 df=20 n.s. | |
| | 2-0 | 5.4 | 3.1 | 8.1 | 1.7 | 4.7 | 3.6 | 3.6 | 1.2 | 4.2 | 2.2 | 6.3 | 3.3 | 6.2 | 3.0 | 4.7 | 3.1 |
| Traffic citations[a] | 1-0 | 57.9 | 26.7 | 57.9 | 12.7 | 66.1 | 34.5 | 48.7 | 23.7 | 64.7 | 29.5 | 55.4 | 25.1 | 60.3 | 24.2 | 55.6 | 28.8 |
| [test] | | t=2.31 df=42 p<.05 | | t=2.65 df=12 p<.05 | | t=1.39 df=14 n.s. | | t=1.02 df=12 n.s. | | t=0.54 df=10 n.s. | | t=2.35 df=30 p<.05 | | t=1.44 df=20 n.s. | | t=1.75 df=20 n.s. | |
| | 2-0 | 77.2 | 27.3 | 76.9 | 12.2 | 92.1 | 35.4 | 60.4 | 15.0 | 74.0 | 24.6 | 78.4 | 28.2 | 74.5 | 19.7 | 79.8 | 33.0 |
| Traffic warnings | 1-0 | 52.6 | 17.5 | 43.9 | 12.1 | 58.5 | 20.2 | 54.7 | 15.3 | 62.3 | 13.3 | 49.0 | 17.6 | 52.2 | 17.0 | 53.1 | 18.0 |
| [test] | | t=0.59 df=42 n.s. | | t=0.72 df=12 n.s. | | t=0.36 df=14 n.s. | | t=0.05 df=12 n.s. | | t=1.50 df=10 n.s. | | t=1.24 df=30 n.s. | | t=0.45 df=20 n.s. | | t=1.07 df=20 n.s. | |
| | 2-0 | 56.2 | 21.3 | 50.1 | 17.6 | 63.1 | 26.9 | 54.3 | 13.8 | 50.3 | 11.8 | 58.4 | 23.5 | 49.0 | 14.5 | 63.4 | 24.3 |

COMPARISON OF OFFICER-INITIATED PATROL ACTIVITY MEAN RATES FOR STUDY UNITS
(Sample Data from Officers' Journals)

| OFFICER ACTIVITY | UNIT TYPE | TOTALS X̄ | TOTALS s.d. | FIRST X̄ | FIRST s.d. | SECOND X̄ | SECOND s.d. | THIRD X̄ | THIRD s.d. | ESD X̄ | ESD s.d. | SESD X̄ | SESD s.d. | FORMER 1-0 X̄ | FORMER 1-0 s.d. | FORMER 2-0 X̄ | FORMER 2-0 s.d. |
|---|---|---|---|---|---|---|---|---|---|---|---|---|---|---|---|---|---|
| | | | | | | PATROL WATCH | | | | AREA OF CITY | | | | PRIOR STAFFING | | | |
| Field interrogations | 1-0 | 51.5 | 24.5 | 67.6 | 26.9 | 51.5 | 21.2 | 35.6 | 11.3 | 45.3 | 16.9 | 53.9 | 26.4 | 60.4 | 26.4 | 42.6 | 18.4 |
| [test] | | t=1.91 df=42 n.s. | | t=0.06 df=12 n.s. | | t=1.98 df=14 n.s. | | t=1.88 df=12 n.s. | | t=1.48 df=10 n.s. | | t=1.52 df=30 n.s. | | t=0.35 df=20 n.s. | | t=2.06 df=20 n.s. | |
| | 2-0 | 69.7 | 36.2 | 66.7 | 20.9 | 90.5 | 47.4 | 49.0 | 13.3 | 61.2 | 16.9 | 72.9 | 40.7 | 64.1 | 19.3 | 75.4 | 46.7 |
| Open businesses | 1-0 | 2.5 | 3.5 | 0.7 | 0.9 | 0.9 | 1.2 | 6.1 | 4.2 | 4.8 | 5.2 | 1.6 | 2.0 | 2.8 | 4.5 | 2.2 | 2.1 |
| [test] | | t=0.82 df=42 n.s. | | t=0.55 df=12 n.s. | | t=0.08 df=14 n.s. | | t=1.31 df=12 n.s. | | t=0.75 df=10 n.s. | | t=0.40 df=30 n.s. | | t=0.51 df=20 n.s. | | t=0.78 df=20 n.s. | |
| | 2-0 | 1.8 | 2.0 | 1.0 | 0.9 | 0.9 | 0.8 | 3.6 | 2.3 | 2.8 | 2.8 | 1.4 | 1.4 | 2.0 | 2.4 | 1.5 | 4.7 |
| Citizen contacts | 1-0 | 92.9 | 32.9 | 87.1 | 13.3 | 113.1 | 40.4 | 75.2 | 23.7 | 123.6 | 49.2 | 84.7 | 18.5 | 99.7 | 40.5 | 86.2 | 20.8 |
| [test] | | t=1.85 df=42 n.s. | | t=2.30 df=12 p<.05 | | t=1.18 df=14 n.s. | | t=1.12 df=12 n.s. | | t=0.80 df=10 n.s. | | t=1.71 df=30 n.s. | | t=1.64 df=20 n.s. | | t=0.98 df=20 n.s. | |
| | 2-0 | 131.4 | 88.9 | 125.9 | 39.0 | 173.9 | 129.6 | 88.4 | 14.4 | 176.6 | 128.6 | 107.9 | 49.2 | 159.4 | 107.6 | 103.4 | 51.8 |
| Miles driven | 1-0 | 4856 | 603.9 | 4352 | 463.6 | 4949 | 624.3 | 4825 | 932.1 | 4701 | 489.2 | 4914 | 632.0 | 4542 | 544.4 | 5170 | 485.3 |
| [test] | | t=0.71 df=42 n.s. | | t=1.58 df=12 n.s. | | t=0.15 df=14 n.s. | | t=0.77 df=12 n.s. | | t=2.91 df=10 p<.02 | | t=0.61 df=30 n.s. | | t=2.24 df=20 p<.05 | | t=1.38 df=20 n.s. | |
| | 2-0 | 5026 | 913.3 | 4984 | 865.5 | 4886 | 955.8 | 5228 | 873.8 | 5753 | 644.3 | 4747 | 848.8 | 5298 | 921.0 | 4753 | 819.6 |

[a] Traffic citations include hazardous citations, non-hazardous citations, and parking citations.

## TABLE 8

CALL-FOR-SERVICE *PRIMARY* ASSIGNMENTS TO STUDY UNITS BY INCIDENT CLASSIFICATION AND DISPOSITION

| INCIDENT CLASSIFICATION | TYPE UNIT | ARREST MADE[a] N | % | FORMAL REPORT COMPLETED[a] N | % | MEDICAL TRANSPOR- TATION[a] N | % | OTHER DISPOSITION[a] N | % | TOTAL INCIDENTS[b] N |
|---|---|---|---|---|---|---|---|---|---|---|
| Criminal | 1–0 | 42 | 4.6 | 248 | 27.3 | 4 | 0.4 | 614 | 67.6 | 908 |
| [test] | | $x^2 = 0.15$ n.s. | | $x^2 = 12.11$ p<.001 | | $x^2 = 1.33$ n.s. | | $x^2 = 24.88$ p<.001 | | $x^2 = 73.99$ p<.001 |
| | 2–0 | 59 | 4.9 | 246 | 20.6 | 2 | 0.2 | 886 | 74.3 | 1193 |
| Traffic | 1–0 | 19 | 4.0 | 126 | 26.5 | 8 | 1.7 | 323 | 67.9 | 476 |
| [test] | | $x^2 = 0.60$ n.s. | | $x^2 = 0.00$ n.s. | | $x^2 = 25.34$ p<.001 | | $x^2 = 5.48$ p<.02 | | $x^2 = 26.12$ p<.001 |
| | 2–0 | 18 | 3.1 | 153 | 26.5 | 51 | 8.8 | 355 | 61.5 | 577 |
| Peacekeeping | 1–0 | 63 | 5.2 | 36 | 3.0 | 26 | 2.2 | 1081 | 89.6 | 1206 |
| [test] | | | | | | | | | | $x^2 = 3.59$ n.s. |
| | 2–0 | 81 | 4.6 | 46 | 2.6 | 24 | 1.3 | 1622 | 91.5 | 1773 |
| Medical | 1–0 | 11 | 4.8 | 9 | 3.9 | 85 | 37.0 | 125 | 54.3 | 230 |
| [test] | | $x^2 = 1.00$ n.s. | | $x^2 = .001$ n.s. | | $x^2 = 14.94$ p<.001 | | $x^2 = 12.33$ p<.001 | | $x^2 = 15.47$ p<.001 |
| | 2–0 | 21 | 3.4 | 24 | 3.9 | 321 | 51.9 | 253 | 40.9 | 619 |
| Nuisance abatement | 1–0 | 0 | 0.0 | 0 | 0.0 | 0 | 0.0 | 11 | 100.0 | 11 |
| [test] | | | | | | | | | | [n.a.] |
| | 2–0 | 0 | 0.0 | 0 | 0.0 | 0 | 0.0 | 9 | 100.0 | 9 |
| Security checks | 1–0 | 22 | 5.6 | 12 | 3.0 | 2 | 0.5 | 357 | 90.8 | 393 |
| [test] | | | | | | | | | | $x^2 = 1.21$ n.s. |
| | 2–0 | 33 | 5.6 | 22 | 3.7 | 1 | 0.2 | 533 | 90.5 | 589 |
| Operational | 1–0 | 126 | 27.4 | 31 | 6.7 | 5 | 1.1 | 298 | 64.8 | 460 |
| [test] | | | | | | | | | | $x^2 = 2.46$ n.s. |
| | 2–0 | 91 | 23.7 | 21 | 5.5 | 4 | 1.0 | 268 | 69.8 | 384 |
| Other | 1–0 | 0 | 0.0 | 7 | 7.9 | 0 | 0.0 | 81 | 92.0 | 88 |
| [test] | | | | | | | | | | $x^2 = 3.87$ n.s. |
| | 2–0 | 1 | 1.0 | 9 | 9.3 | 3 | 3.1 | 84 | 86.6 | 97 |
| Report-taking | 1–0 | 10 | 1.1 | 603 | 68.2 | 2 | 0.2 | 269 | 30.4 | 884 |
| [test] | | | | | | | | | | $x^2 = 4.31$ n.s. |
| | 2–0 | 11 | 1.2 | 641 | 68.0 | 1 | 0.1 | 289 | 30.7 | 942 |
| All classes | 1–0 | 293 | 6.3 | 1072 | 23.0 | 132 | 2.8 | 3159 | 67.8 | 4656 |
| [test] | | $x^2 = 30.60$ p<.001 | | $x^2 = 29.05$ p<.001 | | $x^2 = 78.88$ p<.001 | | $x^2 = 3.49$ n.s. | | $x^2 = 105.96$ p<.001 |
| | 2–0 | 315 | 5.1 | 1162 | 18.8 | 407 | 6.6 | 4299 | 69.5 | 6183 |

[a] Chi-square of frequencies compared to total incidents by incident classification, 1 degree of freedom.
[b] Chi-square of overall distribution of dispositions by incident classification, 3 degrees of freedom.

In terms of the quality of service provided, calls serviced by primary one-officer units were more likely to result in arrests and formal crime reports than were those serviced by two-officer units (see Table 8). Persons arrested by both types of units were equally likely to be held to answer. Also, as shown in Table 9, there were significantly fewer citizen complaints resulting from incidents handled by one-officer units. By these measures, the quality of service of one-officer units was at least as good as and perhaps better than that provided by two-officer units.

## TABLE 9

COMPARISON OF DISTRIBUTION OF COMPLAINTS AGAINST OFFICERS BY WATCH, AREA OF CITY, AND PREVIOUS STAFFING

| STUDY UNITS | TOTAL COMPLAINT INCIDENTS | | | WATCH 1 | | | WATCH 2 | | | WATCH 3 | | |
|---|---|---|---|---|---|---|---|---|---|---|---|---|
| | N | X̄ | s.d. | N | X̄ | s.d. | N | X̄ | s.d. | N | X̄ | s.d. |
| One-Officer Units | 52 | 2.36 | 1.52 | 18 | 2.57 | 1.76 | 21 | 2.62 | 1.21 | 13 | 1.86 | 1.55 |
| [test][a] | | t=2.16 df=42 p<.05 | | | t=0.54 df=12 n.s. | | | t=1.47 df=14 n.s. | | | t=2.83 df=12 p<.02 | |
| Two-Officer Units | 75 | 3.41 | 1.61 | 15 | 2.14 | 0.99 | 29 | 3.62 | 1.32 | 31 | 4.43 | 1.59 |

| STUDY UNITS | BY AREA OF CITY | | | | | | BY FORMER UNIT STAFFING | | | | | |
|---|---|---|---|---|---|---|---|---|---|---|---|---|
| | SOUTHEAST | | | EAST | | | FORMER 1/0 | | | FORMER 2/0 | | |
| | N | X̄ | s.d. | N | X̄ | s.d. | N | X̄ | s.d. | N | X̄ | s.d. |
| One-Officer Units | 43 | 2.69 | 1.57 | 9 | 1.50 | 0.96 | 24 | 2.18 | 1.58 | 28 | 2.54 | 1.44 |
| [test][a] | | t=1.39 df=30 n.s. | | | t=2.02 df=10 n.s. | | | t=0.69 df=20 n.s. | | | t=2.52 df=20 p<.05 | |
| Two-Officer Units | 56 | 3.50 | 1.62 | 19 | 3.17 | 1.57 | 29 | 2.64 | 1.37 | 46 | 4.18 | 1.47 |

[a] All tests were t-tests of unit means.

The overall efficiency of one-officer patrol units clearly exceeded that of units staffed with two officers even though one-officer units received more backup support, as shown in Table 10. The biggest difference in the use of backup between one- and two-officer units was that two-officer units received significantly more single-unit assignments than did one-officer units. The main reason for this situation, however, was that dispatchers had assigned two-officer units to 63.5 percent of all calls for which a *single* officer unit had been recommended, and had assigned one-officer units with backup to 52.8 percent of all calls recommended for *two* officers.

## TABLE 10

COMPARISON OF PRIMARY ASSIGNMENTS TO STUDY UNITS BY USE OF BACKUP
(Sample data from Dispatch Records)

| STUDY UNITS | PRIMARY ASSIGNMENTS | | | | | | TOTAL PRIMARY ASSIGNMENTS | | |
|---|---|---|---|---|---|---|---|---|---|
| | HANDLED ALONE | | | RECEIVED BACKUP | | | | | |
| | N | X̄ | % | N | X̄ | % | N | X̄ | % |
| One-Officer Units | 2147 | 97.6 | 46.1 | 2509[b] | 114.0 | 53.9 | 4656 | 211.6 | 100.0 |
| [test][a] | | t=6.22 df=42 p<.001 | | | t=0.54 df=42 n.s. | | | t=3.37 df=42 p<.01 | |
| Two-Officer Units | 3859 | 175.4 | 62.4 | 2324[c] | 105.6 | 37.6 | 6183 | 281.0 | 100.0 |

[a] t-test of differences between unit means.
[b] Includes 541 cases where backup was requested (10–87) by the assigned unit.
[c] Includes 299 cases where backup was requested (10–87) by the assigned unit.

As an indication that the level of backup provided in San Diego may have been excessive, study units reported that the backup support they received from other units was *not* needed in fully *50 percent* of the cases. In contrast, only 2.8 percent of all assigned calls were underdispatched, that is, resulting in a unit-initiated request for backup support. Even if only dispatches made as primary assignments to one-officer units are considered, the comparisons do not change much—56.5

TABLE 11

| MIX OF PATROL ACTIVITY | 2/0 VS 1/0 PRODUC- TIVITY/ DOLLAR | | REALLO- CATION OF TIME | | TIME- WEIGHTED EFFICIENCY |
|---|---|---|---|---|---|
| Calls requiring two officers | 1.4 | times | 60% | = | .84 |
| Calls requiring one officer | .6 | times | 20 | = | .12 |
| Officer- initiated activity | .4 | times | 20 | = | .08 |
| OVERALL EFFICIENCY OF 2/0 VS 1/0 UNITS | | | | = | 1.04 |

percent of the backup received was not needed, and 6.0 percent of the total assigned calls resulted in unit-initiated requests for backup. Although the absolute differences were small, significantly more of the total requests for backup support on call-for-service assignments came from one-officer units than from two-officer units.

The study found that both types of units responded equally fast to calls-for-service. Two-officer units required less time to service calls than did one-officer units, either singly or in pairs, but the relative time savings in minutes per call was not great enough overall to offset the cost-per-minute disadvantage of two-officer units, as shown in Table 11. The time and cost comparisons were even more unfavorable for two-officer units with regard to officer-initiated activities completed during the time when units were not involved in servicing calls. With the exception of traffic citations, one-officer units produced equivalent amounts of officer-initiated activity, and did so within a shorter period of available time and at substantially lower cost than did two-officer units.

One-officer units were shown to have overall safety advantages over two-officer units, as shown in Table 12. With an equivalent amount of estimated exposure, one-officer units had less involvement in resisting arrest, and only equal involvement in assaults on officers and in officer injuries. One- and two-officer units had equivalent safety records with regard to vehicle accidents and exposure (miles driven) to vehicle accidents. (See Table 13). Single one-officer units, which had a lower estimated exposure to potential hazards, also had significantly less involvement than single two-officer units in assaults on officers and in resisting arrest situations. Officer injuries were equivalent for both types of single units.

A multivariate analysis was performed to examine further the relationships between Area (of the city), Watch and Staffing and the outcome measures of resisting arrest, assaults on officers and officer injuries.[3]

## TABLE 12
### COMPARISON OF OFFICER SAFETY MEASURES

| OFFICER SAFETY MEASURE | TYPE UNIT | TOTALS | | BY WATCH | | | | | | BY AREA | | | | BY PREVIOUS STAFFING | | | |
| --- | --- | --- | --- | --- | --- | --- | --- | --- | --- | --- | --- | --- | --- | --- | --- | --- | --- |
| | | | | FIRST | | SECOND | | THIRD | | EAST | | SOUTHEAST | | ONE-OFFICER | | TWO-OFFICER | |
| | | $\bar{X}$ | s.d. | $\bar{X}$ | s.d. | $\bar{X}$ | s.d. | $\bar{X}$ | s.d. | $\bar{X}$ | s.d. | $\bar{X}$ | s.d. | $\bar{X}$ | s.d. | $\bar{X}$ | s.d. |
| Assaults | 1/0 | 1.54 | 1.50 | 1.00 | 0.92 | 2.50 | 1.87 | 1.00 | 0.76 | 0.67 | 0.74 | 1.94 | 1.52 | 0.82 | 0.83 | 2.36 | 1.55 |
| [test][a] | | t=1.53 df=42 n.s. | | t=0.31 df=12 n.s. | | t=1.36 df=14 n.s. | | t=1.71 df=12 n.s. | | t=0.67 df=10 n.s. | | t=1.46 df=30 n.s. | | t=0.52 df=20 n.s. | | t=1.84 df=20 n.s. | |
| | 2/0 | 2.36 | 1.92 | 0.86 | 0.64 | 3.86 | 1.90 | 2.14 | 1.46 | 1.00 | 0.81 | 2.86 | 1.96 | 1.00 | 0.77 | 3.72 | 1.78 |
| Resisting Arrests | 1/0 | 1.27 | 1.13 | 0.43 | 0.49 | 0.75 | 0.83 | 1.75 | 1.39 | 0.66 | 0.47 | 1.56 | 1.17 | 0.54 | 0.50 | 2.09 | 1.00 |
| [test][a] | | t=3.20 df=42 p<.01 | | t=2.11 df=12 n.s. | | t=2.29 df=14 p<.05 | | t=1.80 df=12 n.s. | | t=1.75 df=10 p<.01· | | t=3.03 df=30 p<.01· | | t=2.67 df=20 n.s. | | t=3.26 df=20 p<.01 | |
| | 2/0 | 2.95 | 2.12 | 1.43 | 1.05 | 3.86 | 2.31 | 3.50 | 1.98 | 1.50 | 0.96 | 3.50 | 2.18 | 1.54 | 1.08 | 4.36 | 1.97 |
| All Critical Incidents | 1/0 | 2.82 | 2.37 | 1.43 | 1.18 | 4.25 | 2.63 | 0.57 | 0.49 | 1.17 | 0.37 | 3.50 | 2.42 | 1.27 | 0.96 | 4.45 | 2.19 |
| [test][a] | | t=2.74 df=42 p<.01 | | t=1.21 df=12 n.s. | | t=2.34 df=14 p<.05 | | t=1.53 df=12 n.s. | | t=2.27 df=10 p<.05 | | t=2.74 df=30 p<.02 | | t=2.48 df=20 p<.05 | | t=3.64 df=20 p<.01 | |
| | 2/0 | 5.32 | 3.26 | 2.29 | 1.28 | 7.75 | 2.81 | 1.29 | 1.03 | 2.50 | 1.26 | 6.38 | 3.36 | 2.54 | 1.30 | 8.09 | 2.27 |
| Officer Injuries from Critical Incidents | 1/0 | 0.86 | 0.91 | 0.71 | 0.88 | 1.25 | 1.09 | 0.43 | 0.49 | 0.83 | 0.37 | 1.00 | 1.00 | 0.64 | 0.77 | 1.09 | 1.00 |
| [test][a] | | t=1.73 df=42 n.s. | | t=1.03 df=12 n.s. | | t=0.61 df=14 n.s. | | t=1.84 df=12 n.s. | | t=1.20 df=10 n.s. | | t=1.96 df=30 n.s. | | t=0.94 df=20 n.s. | | t=1.54 df=20 n.s. | |
| | 2/0 | 1.41 | 1.11 | 1.29 | 1.03 | 1.62 | 1.30 | 1.29 | 1.03 | 0.50 | 0.50 | 1.75 | 1.08 | 1.00 | 0.95 | 1.82 | 1.11 |

[a] All tests were t-tests of means.

## TABLE 13

### COMPARISON OF POLICE VEHICLE ACCIDENTS

| PATROL UNIT GROUPS | TOTAL POLICE VEHICLE ACCIDENTS | PATROL UNIT AT FAULT N | PATROL UNIT AT FAULT % | OFFICER(S) INJURED N | OFFICER(S) INJURED % | TOTAL COST OF EQUIPMENT DAMAGE |
|---|---|---|---|---|---|---|
| One-Officer Units [test][a] | 21 | 8 [n.s.] | 38.1 | 3 [n.s.] | 14.3 | $5119 [n.s.][b] |
| Two-Officer Units | 21 | 13 | 61.9 | 3 | 14.3 | 4457 |
| Total Study Units | 42 | 21 | 50.0 | 6 | 14.3 | 9576 |
| All Central Patrol Units | 133 | 70 | 52.6 | —na— | | 29,404 |

[a] All tests were chi-square with 1 degree of freedom.
[b] Median test based on chi-square. One-officer units had ten accidents above the combined median cost of $20 per accident, and two-officer units had seven accidents above the median cost.

In this analysis the outcome measures were expressed as percentages per unit of total occurrence rather than the raw number of occurrences. That is, the average one-officer unit experienced 1.85 percent of the total number of assaults on officers (Table 14).

## TABLE 14

### OFFICER SAFETY – MEANS AND CORRELATIONS

| Variable | Staffing 1-0 | Staffing 2-0 | Staffing Med | Watch 1 | Watch 2 | Watch 3 | Area 1 | Area 2 |
|---|---|---|---|---|---|---|---|---|
| Proportion of Total Assaults | 1.85 | 2.19 | 4.25 | 1.09 | 3.70 | 1.91 | .98 | 2.80 |
| Proportion of Resisting Arrests | 1.42 | 3.28 | 2.87 | 1.01 | 3.01 | 2.76 | 1.17 | 2.72 |
| Proportion of Officer Injury | 1.76 | 2.29 | 4.40 | 2.04 | 2.93 | 1.88 | 1.00 | 2.80 |

POOLED WITHIN-CELL CORRELATIONS (Standard Deviations or Diagonal)

| | Assaults | Resists | Injuries |
|---|---|---|---|
| Assaults | 1.37 | | |
| Resists | .06 | 1.55 | |
| Injuries | .73 | .25 | 2.01 |

The factors of Area, Watch and Staffing were each statistically significantly related to the set of outcome measures (at less than .01). None of the interactions of these factors was significant indicating that the effects of Area, Watch and Staffing combine additively. There are no specially dangerous (or safe) combinations of Area, Watch and Staff that need to be explained.

Southeast San Diego is more than twice as dangerous as East San Diego in terms of each safety measure. Watch 2 (3:00 PM to 11:00 PM) is about half again as dangerous as Watch 3 (11:00 PM to 7:00 AM) which is twice as dangerous as Watch 1 (7:00 AM to 3:00 PM) except for injuries where Watch 3 and Watch 1 are nearly equal.

The staffing factor was considered to have three categories in this analysis: one-officer, two-officer, and medical (patrol/ambulance—also two-officer). Medical units are twice as likely as others to be involved in assaults and injuries, while medical and two-officer units are equal in percentages of resisting arrest and are about twice as likely to be resisted as one-officer units.

The within-cell correlation matrix in Table 14 shows that the incidence of injury is strongly related to the incidence of assault or resisting arrest. When the frequencies of assault and resisting arrest are controlled statistically, the relationship of type of staffing to rate of injuries is no longer statistically significant. That is, the different rates of assault and resisting arrest account for the differences in the injury levels of the three types of units.

Both types of two-officer units (regular and medical) are clearly more dangerous than one-officer units, but medical units are especially dangerous. Medical units may be more dangerous because the attention of the officers is focused on medical rather than criminal problems, or because an incident which has already resulted in an injury to a citizen is inherently more dangerous than a non-injury incident.

Officer attitudes overall indicated a slight preference for two-officer units, although opinions appeared to be neutral on which staffing mode was more advantageous with regard to performance, efficiency, and safety. However, those patrol officers who were assigned to study units were stronger in their preference for two-officer units and saw them as providing advantages in performance, efficiency, and safety. Patrol experience in a two-officer unit and in Southeast San Diego (the patrol area considered to be most hazardous) was shown to be correlated with preferences for two-officer units and with opinions that they were more advantageous than one-officer units. Age and rank were also correlated with survey responses: Younger and lower-ranked officers showed more support for two-officer units. (See Table 15).

## CONCLUSIONS AND RECOMMENDATIONS

On the basis of this study, two-officer regular patrol units do not appear to be justified in San Diego. Separate comparisons of unit performance, efficiency, and officer safety under current conditions all suggest that one-officer units are at least equal to and often more advantageous than two-officer units. Given the cost differential, which enables 18 one-officer units to be fielded for less than the cost of 10 two-officer units, it seems clear that one-officer units should be the normal pattern in the city.

Police ambulance units are an exception to this general conclusion because the assumption is that frequently two officers are needed to handle and transport

## TABLE 15

### CONSISTENTLY SIGNIFICANT PEARSON CORRELATION COEFFICIENTS

| Independent Variables (Respondent Descriptors/Tests) | | COMPOSITE DEPENDENT VARIABLES (SIGNIFICANT LEVEL p<.05) | | | | | | |
|---|---|---|---|---|---|---|---|---|
| | | Patrol Unit Perform-ance r | Patrol Unit Efficiency r | Officer Safety r | Morale and Job Satis-faction r | Minimizing Use of Force r | Qualified Prefer-ence r | Relevance of Staffing Issue r |
| Age | $T_h$ | | -0.1400 | | | -0.1261 | -0.1250 | |
| | $T_i$ | | -0.2250 | | | -0.1837 | -0.1445 | |
| | $T_f$ | | -0.2451 | | | -0.1875 | -0.1689 | |
| Rank | $T_h$ | -0.1636 | -0.2446 | -0.1295 | -0.1259 | -0.1474 | -0.1505 | |
| | $T_i$ | -0.2453 | -0.3570 | -0.1580 | -0.2010 | -0.2402 | -0.2017 | |
| | $T_f$ | -0.2408 | -0.2997 | -0.1601 | -0.1611 | -0.3066 | -0.1655 | |
| Overall Patrol Experience | $T_h$ | | | | 0.1016 | | | |
| | $T_i$ | | | | 0.1180 | | | |
| | $T_f$ | | | | 0.1474 | | | |
| Patrol Experience (SESD) | $T_h$ | 0.2108 | 0.1758 | 0.2056 | 0.2467 | 0.1746 | 0.1980 | 0.2108 |
| | $T_i$ | 0.3372 | 0.1603 | 0.3007 | 0.3119 | 0.1830 | 0.2429 | 0.2458 |
| | $T_f$ | 0.2395 | 0.1395 | 0.2045 | 0.2543 | 0.1700 | 0.1753 | 0.2087 |
| Two-Officer Unit Experience | $T_h$ | 0.2069 | 0.1447 | 0.2089 | 0.2623 | 0.0916 | 0.2076 | 0.2215 |
| | $T_i$ | 0.2468 | 0.0902 | 0.2329 | 0.2119 | 0.1555 | 0.1623 | 0.1858 |
| | $T_f$ | 0.2731 | 0.0879 | 0.2016 | 0.2922 | 0.1324 | 0.1864 | 0.1864 |
| Education | $T_h$ | | -0.1029 | | | | | |
| | $T_i$ | | -0.1588 | | | | | |
| | $T_f$ | | -0.1565 | | | | | |

medical emergency patients. Special situations, tactical assignments, the need for field training, and other temporary conditions may justify temporarily staffing regular patrol units with two officers. However, in San Diego, current patrol conditions and unit performances would have to change markedly to justify continuing to assign two officers to the units studied, as a matter of routine.

Although one-officer staffing provides equal unit performance with fewer officer complaints, greater efficiency, and greater officer safety than does two-officer staffing, San Diego police officers in general have a slight personal preference for two-officer staffing. Among those officers assigned to study units, this personal preference for two-officer staffing is combined with a strong opinion that two-officer units are more advantageous in terms of performance, efficiency, and safety.

Thus it appears the findings from this study may not match the preferences of San Diego patrol officers—particularly those with experiences in two-officer units and in Southeast San Diego. When patrol officers were asked to identify changes that might be justified by a shift of current two-officer units to one-officer units, changes that presumably would make such a shift more acceptable to them, most frequently suggested responses were that additional personal protection in the form of shotguns or police dogs be made available. Either or both of these options could be implemented at lower cost than that of placing a second officer in a patrol unit. Improved backup was the second most frequent response. Backup requests (10-87s) averaged 1.2 minutes of dispatch delay and 6.0 minutes of unit response time—a total of 7.2 minutes to respond to a unit's request for backup support. The additional units made available by converting current two-officer units to single-officer units should help in efforts to reduce these delays.

The study also found indications that excessive numbers of backup units are dispatched without request, thus reducing the number of units available to respond to unit requests. One way to improve unit availability is to examine the current practice of dispatchers of assigning more officers to calls than the complaint operator recommends. Similarly, self-dispatching practices also should be reviewed.

To justify continuing to assign two officers to patrol units requires that performance, efficiency, and safety be made more competitive with that of one-officer units. There appears to be ample room for improvement in the productivity of two-officer units. On call-for-service assignments, dispatch operators should make more efficient use of two-officer units by assigning them more of the total of calls coming from outside their beat that require two officers, and fewer of the total of these calls that require only a single officer. Regarding officer-initiated activities, it would seem reasonable for patrol management to expect more from a two-officer unit than from a one-officer unit. This expectation should be independent of the specific nature of the officer-initiated activities. In this study, the available measures of officer-initiated activity levels were those traditionally associated with law enforcement: arrests, traffic citations, field interrogations, citizen contacts, and so forth. San Diego Police Department's Community Oriented Policing program suggests that other, or at least additional, measures of officer performance are needed to reflect the degree to which patrol officers focus their attention and efforts on the specific problems of their assigned beats. Whatever unit performance measures are eventually chosen, the unit staffing issue will remain. The justification for two-officer units will always depend in part on the department's ability to demonstrate that they are at least as cost-effective as one-officer units.

In order to reduce the involvement of two-officer patrol units in resisting arrest situations, it may be desirable to conduct unit-team training of pairs of officers in the handling of arrest subjects. A reduction in resisting arrest occurrences would not only reduce potential hazards to police officers but would increase the safety of arrest subjects.

For other police departments, the San Diego study should provide a new point of reference for considering patrol unit staffing. The commonly accepted assumption that two-officer units are safer, more efficient, and more productive than one-officer units can no longer go unchallenged—particularly in view of escalating labor costs. In San Diego these assumptions proved to be unfounded. Although no two cities nor police departments are exactly alike, most are sufficiently similar that the patrol unit comparison methods used in San Diego can be readily applied. It seems likely that other cities may find, as San Diego did, that one-officer patrol units can offer equal performance and increased officer safety as well as substantial cost saving over two-officer units.

## NOTES

1. Theodore H. Schell, et al., Traditional Preventative Patrol: National Evaluation Program, Phase I Summary Report (Washington, D.C.: NILECJ, June 1976).

2. Rosemary J. Erickson, *Social Profiles of San Diego: I. A Social Area Analysis* (La Jolla, California: Western Behavioral Sciences Institute, December 1973).

3. This analysis was prepared by Dr. J. Ward Keesling of the Studies and Evaluation Department of System Development Corporation.

# 30

# What Happened to Patrol Operations in Kansas City?

## Richard C. Larson

The Kansas City Preventive Patrol Experiment is by now well-known for its attempt to test the effectiveness of traditional preventive patrol, as practiced in the police department of Kansas City, Missouri.

Briefly reviewing the experiment: 15 patrol beats comprising a nearly rectangular area in the 24-beat South Patrol Division of Kansas City, Missouri, were selected for the experiment by the researchers and a task force of police officials. Of these 15 beats, five were selected as control beats; that is, preventive patrol was to continue as usual in those beats. At the core of the experiment, five were selected as "reactive beats," in which, according to the authors, ". . . there would be no 'routine preventive patrol' as such. Cars assigned those beats would enter them only in response to calls for service. Their noncommitted time . . . would be spent patrolling the perimeter of their beats or the adjacent proactive beats" (p. 28). According to the technical report, "perimeter" meant literally the streets comprising the beat boundaries.[1] The "proactive" beats, which were the remaining five beats, were to display, according to the authors, ". . . two to three times the usual level of police patrol visibility through the assignment to these beats of extra patrol cars and through the presence of cars from the reactive beats" (p. 28). It is important to note that the increase in patrol levels in the proactive beats was due to two causes: 1) the patrol in these beats (at least near certain borders) of one or more reactive units and 2) the assignment of a second full-time unit (in addition to the regular beat unit) to each proactive beat; thus, on average,

each proactive beat had two full-time proactive units assigned plus the limited patrol coverage of one reactive unit. By this experimental design, an attempt was made to vary police visibility from minimal (reactive) to same-as-usual (control) to "two-to-three" times same-as-usual (proactive).

In assigning the three different experimental treatments, the beats were matched together in groups of three to reduce disparities in ethnicity, income, crime incidents, residential permanence, and rates of calls for service. In addition, the judgment of task force members and other police officials was used to adjust the computer-derived optimal matching of beats in order to take into account idiosyncrasies of various beats, e.g., privately patrolled shopping centers. This judgment also resulted in a spatial dispersement of the reactive beats, a point that is very important when considering the results of the Kansas City Experiment; each reactive beat shared a beat boundary with at least one control beat. No two reactive beats shared any boundaries in common.[2]

The experiment was run for one year—from October 1, 1972, to September 30, 1973. Without delving into details here, the researchers found primarily negative results; that is, few of the many measured quantities, such as reported crime rates, victim-derived

[1] In the guidelines issued to personnel in the experimental area (October 2, 1972), "perimeter" was treated as follows: "Cars assigned to Reactive Districts may patrol the perimeter streets of their district or an adjoining portion of a proactive district." Here, "beat" and "district" were used interchangeably.

[2] As demonstrated in Figure C-1 of the report, the reactive beats occupied the four corner positions of the experimental area and the center position.

crime rates, citizens' perceptions of police presence and service, or response times, varied in a statistically significant way by experimental area. Because the focus of the experiment was on preventive patrol, and because the experiment yielded basically negative results, one is tempted to think that this result implies that patrol manning levels could be decreased (thereby reducing time available for preventive patrol) without incurring degradations in actual or perceived patrol performance. In this regard, it is important to note that the entire 15-beat experimental area in Kansas City did not incur a net decrease in patrol manning but, on the contrary, experienced an increase. The Kansas City Experiment focused on a spatial redistribution of patrol resources within a confined region (the 15-beat area); it did not examine the effect of a net reduction of patrol effort within the region. Thus the policy implications are likely to be constrained to questions relating to spatial redistributions of patrol resources, not to net increases or decreases in patrol resources.

Yet one might take the three experimental areas—reactive, proactive, and control—to represent three semi-isolated areas that can be treated independently. Then, if patrol performance in the depleted area is not noticeably degraded compared to the other areas, one might conclude that preventive patrol, per se, has little or no value. Far from being independent

Richard C. Larson is an Associate Professor at Massachusetts Institute of Technology and President of Public Systems Evaluation, Inc.

This review is condensed from a much longer critique that appeared in its entirety in the Journal of Criminal Justice, Vol. 3, January, 1976. Interested readers are referred to the longer version for details on many of the points raised here. All page citations refer to the original Kansas City Report documents.

From Richard C. Larson, "What Happened to Patrol Operations in Kansas City?" 3 (1-2) *Evaluation* 117-123 (1976). Copyright 1976 by the Russell Sage Foundation.

areas, the three types of beats comprise a closely intertwined, spatially distributed service system. The patrol force, as a service system, is a key component of the police emergency response system, which also consists of telephone complaint clerks, dispatchers, and strategies for their operation. Delays at the dispatcher's position due to all units being simultaneously busy are very dependent on the number of patrol units fielded. From the point of view of queuing theory, preventive patrol (or an equivalent activity that can be interrupted to respond to calls for service) provides required waiting time that keeps the probability of lengthy delay below some target value. Rates of calls for service, dispatching policies, on-scene service times, response and patrol speeds—all of these descriptors are required to understand the behavior of police emergency response systems. In this context, it is subsequently shown that the depleted areas can draw resources from nearby heavily manned areas to handle calls for service with nearly no increase in travel time. And the very act of responding to calls for service within the depleted areas retained a patrol visibility that was often close to that experienced previously. The examination of this issue is a major concern of this review.

Another aim is to demonstrate why one should not use the results of the Kansas City Experiment to extrapolate the general value of a visible patrol presence. The range of patrol coverages in the three experimental areas simply was not large enough to do this.

A third aim of this review is to describe the reviewer's opinion of the major positive policy implication of the Kansas City Experiment, namely, that patrol administrators in other cities, if they proceed with care, as in Kansas City, can be quite flexible in redistributing their resources spatially within a confined region. This conclusion, which seems to emerge as an unexpected by-product of the experiment, allows implementation of crime-directed patrols in high crime areas so that locations and strategies of such patrols can change on a day-by-day or even hour-by-hour basis. The need for such focusing of patrol efforts is amply demonstrated in the Kansas City Report, which revealed that aimless, purposeless patrol resulted in time spent on many nonpolice and trivial activities.

The researchers who designed the experiment and authored the final report are to be congratulated on a candid and frank discussion of the administrative, bureaucratic, and interpersonal problems that accompanied the experiment (and are likely to besiege any urban experiment of this magnitude and scope). These problems are discussed not only in Chapter IV of the technical report but also by one of the report's authors in a separate document.

The researchers are also to be credited for bringing an impressive array of surveys and analyses to bear on the evaluation of experimental outcomes. Included were surveys of community attitudes, analyses of police and citizen interactions ("encounters" and "transactions"), as reported by observers, analyses of crime rates (both reported to police and reported via a victimization survey), analyses of noncommitted police time (which have value independent of the experiment), analyses of traffic accident rates, and surveys of police officer attitudes regarding preventive patrol. Each should play an important role in evaluating other preventive patrol experiments; their testing in the Kansas City environment will enable others to build on this first experience in conducting related experiments in other cities.

In fact, the "seed" effect of the Kansas City Experiment may be its most important contribution. The experiment has sparked a lively debate in police circles and has prompted others to want to test their own hypotheses regarding preventive patrol in their own cities. These persons' acceptance of hypothesis generation, experimentation, and other aspects of the scientific method is surely a valuable contribution of the Kansas City Preventive Patrol Experiment.

## Critical Issues Affecting Experimental Results

### Lack of Description of Dispatch Procedures

Two primary activities of an urban police patrol force are 1) responding to calls for service and 2) performing preventive patrol.[3] The "call-for-service activity" is what ordinarily interrupts

preventive patrol.[4] In the Kansas City Experiment, it is the presence of cars responding to calls for service within the reactive beats that raises patrol visibility above zero.

Since call-for-service activity is such a crucial part of the total activity of a patrol force, it is surprising that the Kansas City researchers did not pay more attention to it. In particular, there is no description of the patrol dispatching procedures in Kansas City. It appears that if the 15-beat experimental area were to have remained isolated, dispatching procedures would have had to have been changed.[5]

With additional units in the proactive beats, and with reactive units patrolling beat perimeters, the dispatcher's "guesstimated" locations for units must change and therefore the order in which he contacts them for calls from each location will change (in general). Such changes affect travel times, patrol workloads (on calls for service), numbers of cross-beat dispatches, and other factors that bear on the Kansas City Experiment.

## Equal Manning Around the Clock

Unlike some departments that schedule manpower in accordance with call-for-service workloads and other anticipated police activities, Kansas City utilizes equal manning over 24-hour periods. This means that the majority of preventive patrol activity occurs during the early morning hours when citizens are asleep and therefore unable to perceive changes in preventive patrol levels. It also means that the least preventive patrol occurs during the high workload hours, typically from 1600 to 2400 hours, when citizens are not at work and best able to perceive changes in preventive patrol coverage.

In assessing the applicability of the Kansas City Experiment to their own

---

There are many other activities also, as aptly demonstrated in the technical report. These include patrol-initiated activities (e.g., car check, building check, car chase, assist motorist), transporting persons or papers, court appearances, errands, etc.

[4] Most of the minor miscellaneous activities can also interrupt routine preventive patrol, although most police departments consider many of these activities to be part of preventive patrol.

[5] According to the report, "... within the South Patrol Division's 24-beat area, nine beats were eliminated from consideration as unrepresentative of the city's socio-economic composition" (p. 27). No statement is made that suggests that the nine eliminated beats are isolated—in a dispatching sense—from the other 15.

situations, patrol administrators in cities that experience higher call-for-service workloads per car (which most likely occur as a result of patrol officers being scheduled in a way that reflects the 24-hour pattern of calls for service) must take into account these special attributes of the Kansas City Experiment.

## Non-Random Sampling by Participant Observers

The evaluation utilized participant observers who rode with police officers and gathered data on various aspects of the experiment. These observers were utilized heavily in obtaining the results of three chapters of the final report: VIII, "Police-Citizen Encounters"; X, "Police Response Time"; and XI, "Analysis of Police Noncommitted Time."

However, there is a subtle bias in the way in which the observers were assigned to cars: we are told that the participant observers scheduled their in-car hours for *high activity beats*. While it is unclear how this lack of randomness would affect police-citizen encounters,[8] it is clear that noncommitted police time would tend to be lower than region-wide averages and that response times could be affected. Response times would tend to be higher (due to heavier workloads and thereby greater numbers of cross-beat dispatches); this effect may be offset to some extent by the (presumably) smaller areas of the heavy workload beats. Whatever the net effect, it is clear that response times and cross-beat dispatches could be measurably biased compared with region-wide averages.

## Level of Preventive Patrol

The researchers claim that preventive patrol visibility was significantly curtailed in the reactive beats, stayed the same in the control beats, and increased two to three times in the proactive beats. There are several reasons why we should seriously question these claims. To do this, we must estimate quantitatively some measure of the level of preventive patrol.

*Police-citizen encounters could be affected negatively by the increased frequency of cross-beat dispatches in heavy workload areas. This increases the chance that the officers responding to a police incident in a particular beat are not normally assigned to the beat and so are not familiar with local situations requiring police service.*

**Preventive Patrol Equation.** It is not difficult to derive an equation that allows us to examine the level of preventive patrol by predicting the *frequency of patrol passings* (in number of passes per hour) in terms of simple quantities. Not only is the concept of preventive patrol frequency useful in itself, because it allows one to define precisely a level of preventive patrol, but once the preventive patrol frequencies are known, one can easily obtain estimates of other important per.ormance measures, such as the probability of a patrolling unit intercepting a randomly occurring crime in progress.

The key quantities that affect the level of preventive patrol in a beat are the following:

**N** = number of patrolling vehicles in the beat

**s** = effective speed (in mph) of the unit while patrolling

**b** = average fraction of time each unit is busy (*i.e.*, not performing preventive patrol)

**D** = total (unweighted) street mileage in a beat

The final concept we need is that of *effective patrollable street miles in the beat, L*. L represents the average number of miles driven between successive passings of a point in the maximum coverage area. Our equation for predicting patrol frequency in a beat is:

$$f = N s (1-b)/L.$$

**Patrol Frequencies in Kansas City.** Applying these concepts to the Kansas City Preventive Patrol Experiment, it would seem that any experiment focusing on the level of preventive patrol would attempt to measure, or at least to impute, the patrol frequencies (or correspondingly, the average time between patrol passings) in each of the three experiment zones (reactive, proactive, control). Yet this is not done in the technical report.

Regarding the parameters of the preventive patrol equation, we are given no information about L (the effective patrollable street miles) or s (the speed of patrol). The speed of patrol could easily have been estimated by using odometer readings recorded in most departments by the police officers at the beginning and end of each tour; in computing the estimate for s, one need

See the original paper for a slightly more complicated form incorporating differential levels of patrol.

only know these odometer readings, the time spent on non-preventive patrol activities, and the number of calls for service (all of which were data readily available to the Kansas City researchers).[8]

Using the following (not unreasonable) data estimates derived for Kansas City:[9]

**s** = 7.5 mph
**D** = 27.5 miles
**1 - b** = fraction of time on preventive patrol
= 0.60 *(liberal estimate)*
or
= 0.30 *(conservative estimate)*

The average frequency of preventive patrol passings *in the control beats* is found to be:

**f = 7.5 (1 - .40)/27.5**
**= 0.164 patrol passes/hour** *(liberal estimate)*

or about 6.1 hours between patrol passings. The conservative estimate would yield half as much patrol, or about 12.2 hours between patrol passings. Thus, even if the estimates giving rise to these figures are considerably in error (say ± 25 percent), we have the key result that preventive patrol "as usual" in the experimental zone is not very much preventive patrol. On a typical tour, using the liberal estimate, a citizen at a randomly chosen spot[10] in a control beat might see a patrolling vehicle pass him an average of once every six-or-so hours. If his eyes are directed toward the street only 10 percent of the time, he would see a patrol car about once every 60 hours.[11] Thus, removing patrol coverage to achieve minimal preventive patrol frequency might be difficult to perceive for the average citizen. It would be somewhat easier to perceive by persons in business in the experimental area who claimed to see police slightly more frequently than once a day prior to the experiment (p. 41).

In the proactive beats we are told

*Certain simple corrections have to be used in order to obtain a good estimate. Chief among these is the mileage traveled on calls for service.*

*For the derivation of the Kansas City parameters, see Journal of Criminal Justice, January, 1976.*

[10]*The random selection gives greater weights to the more heavily patrolled areas (in direct proportion to the relative coverages given those areas).*

[11]*Survey evidence in the report suggests that this is the approximate value for average time between sightings.*

that patrol coverage is increased to two to three times the usual levels. If this is true, the frequency of patrol passings increased to 0.33 - 0.49 passes per hour, using the liberal estimate. This level, it is suggested throughout the report, represents an unusually high amount of preventive patrol coverage. The associated times between patrol passings range from about three to about two hours. Thus, even at three times the usual preventive patrol coverage, the average point is passed by a patrolling vehicle only once each two hours. A major observation here is that this allegedly heavy level of preventive patrol is considerably less than the amount allocated in many cities on a typical day. For instance, the same formula applied to New York City, using much more precise data estimates, showed that 12 out of 20 representative precincts in 1969 experienced greater amounts of preventive patrol during the Saturday evening tour (a very heavy workload tour).

Thus, I am forced to reach the following conclusion:

"**The range of preventive patrol coverages experienced in the Kansas City Preventive Patrol Experiment is not broad enough to include the range experienced by other U.S. police departments.**"[12]

## Other Factors Affecting Patrol Visibility

At the crux of the experiment is the claim that patrol visibility was reduced to minimal levels in the reactive beats. The authors acknowledge that, inadvertently, reactive units would occasionally wander into these beats. Units were also authorized to enter the beats ". . . to apprehend a wanted suspect at a known location, for house checks (with house-to-watch slips), and for all warrant checks except traffic warrants or judgment orders."

**Patrol-Initiated Activities.** There is a very revealing analysis (pp. 45-59) of self-initiated patrol activities by experimental zone.[13] These activities are the following: 1) traffic violation, 2) assignment, 3) building check, 4) car check,

[12] R. C. Larson. Urban Police Patrol Analysis. (Cambridge, Mass.: MIT Press, 1972), pp. 159-162.

[13] Later in this review I question whether some of the reported results are specific to beats or cars. In the case of patrol-initiated activities, however, there is no ambiguity; the report emphasizes the fact that these data are beat-specific.

5) foot patrol, 6) warrant or subpoena, 7) car chase, 8) listing, 9) pedestrian check, 10) other, 11) residence check, 12) assist motorist. Of these twelve categories, it would seem that items 1, 3, 4, 9,11, and 12 would result from randomly patrolling an area and initiating activities to prevent or deter crime. However, these six activities comprise about 90 percent of all patrol-initiated activities, so we can use totals of patrol-initiated activities to get a valid indicator of patrol presence in each area. What is astonishing here is that the number of patrol-initiated activities in 1973 *in the reactive beats* did not decrease from 1972, but actually increased! The reactive beats accumulated 5,948 patrol-initiated activities in 1972 and 6,057 in 1973.[14] The authors make the following points about these data:

**A. Self-initiated incidents comprise only 30 percent of the total out-of-service incidents.**
**B. Those activities conducted on the perimeter of a beat are recorded as taking place within the beat.**
**C. Some activities may originate outside of a beat and, "due to their inherent mobility, terminate within a reactive beat."**

Point A does not diminish the importance of using self-initiated activities as a valid indicator of preventive patrol presence. Point B, regarding beat perimeters, is diminished in importance because only about six miles out of 27.5 (the approximate average street mileage per beat) is on the perimeter of a beat; this represents about 22 percent of the total street mileage of the beat. It would be difficult to justify an increased level of self-initiated activities on only 22 percent of the street mileage of the previous year. For those activities that actually did take place on the perimeter, it makes good sense to count them as having occurred within the beat; some people who live in the beat live at its perimeter, and the visible presence of, say, a car stop with red lights extends into the beat. Point C may be valid for a small minority of incidents, but it cannot explain such factors as a 9.4 percent increase in car checks in the reactive beats (car checks comprising 45 percent of all reactive beat patrol-initiated activities in 1973). Thus, the analysis of patrol-initiated activities leads me to question seriously the extent to which the experimental

[14] In 1973, the control beats experienced a 30 percent increase in patrol-initiated activities and the proactive beats a 44 percent increase.

conditions were maintained.

**Specialized Units.** More troublesome, other specialized units operated within the reactive beats, thereby maintaining police activity (and presumably, perceived police presence) considerably above zero. According to the report:

"**Since only the effectiveness of routine preventive patrol by the patrol unit was being tested, specialized units (i.e., traffic, helicopter, tactical, etc.) operated as usual. (Such units maintained city-wide mobility and continued to react to specific problems.) However, operation of these units was to remain at a level consistent with levels established for the preceding year**" (p. 29).

Given the experimental focus on regular beat cars, the concept of retaining the specialized units on an "operating-as-usual" mode is not unacceptable in itself. However, the impressive arsenal of evaluation tools that were brought to bear on other parts of the experiment were not at all directed toward the specialized units. In particular, we have no information about the activity levels of the traffic and tactical units, which could have been increased within the reactive beats due to perceived specific problems or simply to anxiety over the lack of routine police coverage within these beats. The lack of concern over the tactical units, in particular, concerns this reviewer because these units can be the most visible form of police presence.

In addition to the intrusions into the reactive beats by reactive units and the presence of other types of police units, there are other reasons for questioning the validity of the experimental design in its attempt to reduce patrol visibility to minimal levels. To obtain a simple estimate of the distance the unit will traverse *within the reactive beat* during an eight-hour tour as a result of responding to calls for service, I make the following simplifying, not unreasonable assumptions:

**1** When on patrol, the patrol position of the reactive unit is uniformly distributed over one or more sides of the perimeter.[15]

[15] The average travel distance predicted by the model does not depend on whether one, two, three, or four sides of the perimeter are patrolled. In fact, certain sides may be patrolled more heavily than others, and if the other model assumptions hold, the average travel distance remains unchanged.

**2** The location of the call for service is uniformly distributed over the reactive beat and is independent of the location of the service unit.

**3** The travel distance is the sum of the east-west distance and the north-south distance between the unit's location (at time of dispatch) and the call-for-service location.

**4** The beat is a square of dimension B (area = $B^2$).

Given these assumptions, one can show that the average E-W distance to the incident is $\frac{1}{2} B$ and that the average N-S distance is $\frac{1}{3} B$; in addition, the responding unit must leave the beat after servicing the incident, incurring an additional average travel distance of $\frac{1}{2} B$, assuming the unit travels in a straight line manner back to the side it was originally patrolling or to a random side. Thus, the average travel distance travelled within the reactive beat per dispatch is approximately:

$$\bar{d} = \underbrace{\frac{1}{2} B + \frac{1}{3} B}_{\text{travel to the incident}} + \underbrace{\frac{1}{2} B}_{\text{travel from the incident}}$$

This estimate is not dependent on which side of the beat the unit is patrolling at the time of dispatch. In fact, under a remarkable number of alternative assumptions regarding beat geometries and spatial distributions, it remains a very good approximation for the average distance travelled within the beat per dispatch.

If $N_{CFS}$ calls for service are answered per eight-hour tour, then the average mileage travelled within the reactive beat on calls for service per eight-hour tour is:

$$N_{MI} = \frac{4}{3} B \cdot N_{CFS}$$

Using data estimates of $B = 1.5$ and $N_{CFS} = 2.67$ for Kansas City, the average mileage travelled within the reactive beat on calls for service per eight-hour tour is:

$$N_{MI} = \frac{4}{3}(1.5)(2.67) = 5.34 \text{ miles}$$

In addition, the technical report shows that fully 1.58 cars (on the average) responded to each call for service in the reactive beats. This figure contrasts with 1.29 cars in the control beats and 1.15 cars in the proactive beats. A statistically significant result, the 1.58

figure suggests that police officers were anxious to provide back-up support for their fellow officers responding to calls in the reactive beats. Apparently, many, if not most, of the multiple responses were volunteer assignments rather than directives from the dispatcher.

However, the use of multiple responses forces us to modify estimated average mileage travelled within the reactive beat on calls for service per eight-hour tour to:

$$N_{MI} = \frac{4}{3}(1.5)(2.67)(1.58) \simeq 8.44 \text{ miles}$$

Thus, during an average eight-hour tour the typical 1.5 x 1.5-mile-square reactive beat is being traversed a total of 8.44 miles by marked police cars responding to calls for service. (It is interesting to note that this figure alone accounts for a patrol frequency of about once a day.)

**Use of Siren and Lights.** Apparently sirens and/or lights are not used very frequently on calls for service in the Kansas City Police Department. In a limited sample, sirens and/or red lights were used in only 1.2 percent of the responses in the control beats and 1.0 percent in the proactive beats. However, they were used in 4.9 percent of the responses in the reactive beats. This represents an increase in use of this emergency equipment of between 400 and 500 percent.

Because Kansas City residents were unaccustomed to hearing sirens or seeing lights on police cars responding to calls for service, such a five-fold increase in use almost certainly would increase citizens' perceptions of the level of police presence. Thus, the 8.44 miles driven per tour in the reactive beats (on calls for service) was not the typical slow-driven mileage associated with preventive patrol. At least half of that mileage was driven by cars responding hurriedly to calls for service and at least 1 in 20 calls (perhaps as many as 1 in 13) were responded to with siren and/or lights.

**Peak Period Activity.** All of these calculations have been based on averages that do not reflect variations in police workload by season, time of day, or day of week. One would expect citizens' perceptions of police presence to vary independently of police activity, according to these time factors. This is due to the fact that citizens are more likely to be out of doors during the summer months and on the streets after work hours. Thus, one would speculate that citizen opportunities for

judging police presence are most prevalent during the summer months and during the hours after work.

Assuming a workload scale factor of 2.1[16] and all else is constant, then the number of street miles traversed in the *reactive beats* per eight-hour *evening* tour during *summer months* in Kansas City is roughly:

$$N_{MI} = \frac{4}{3}(1.5)(2.67)(1.58)(2.1)$$

$$\simeq 17.7 \text{ miles}$$

In fact, due to dispatches that cause a responding unit to pass *through* a reactive beat, this figure could be even higher.[17] It is noteworthy that the particular experimental conditions in the reactive beats caused the usual number of miles travelled on calls for service, 9.5 to 12.2 miles, to increase to at least 17.7 miles, a percentage increase of 86 percent or 45 percent, depending on the base figure. This increase is due to two factors: 1) the necessity for the reactive unit to travel out of the beat after servicing the incident, and 2) the increased use of multiple units responding to calls for service. In terms of average frequency of passes of the unit, the calculated mileage corresponds to about two passes per day (while on calls for service) in a beat having 27.5 patrollable street miles.

It is well known that when the call-for-service workload is at its highest, routine preventive patrol is at its lowest. During the summer evening tour the typical Kansas City police unit is responding to calls for service approximately 39 percent of the time. Additional "committed time" would easily

---

[16] That is, that a patrol unit receives twice as many calls for service in the peak periods. The 2.1 figure is derived from hour-of-day records for the experimental year.

[17] When workloads are high, it is not unusual for units to be dispatched to beats that do not have any common boundaries with their own beats. This forces units to travel through one or more other beats to get to the beat of the incident. If a reactive beat is one of the "pass-through" beats, patrol visibility is increased there. Given the lack of details of the dispatching procedures in Kansas City, it is very difficult to estimate the frequency of occurrence of such dispatches. However, at workload levels of 56 percent or higher, one would expect that at least a few percent of dispatches (say 3-5 percent) were of this type.

increase this figure to 60 percent,[18] leaving, at most, 40 percent for non-committed time. Assuming that roughly half of that is spent on routine, mobile preventive patrol, this allows about 20 percent time (or 1.6 hours per eight-hour tour) for preventive patrol. Assuming a driving speed of 7.5 miles per hour, then roughly 7.5x1.6 = 12.0 miles could be driven by the unit in performing routine preventive patrol. This compares to at least 17.7 miles being driven within reactive beats responding to calls for service. Even if 70 percent (rather than 50 percent) of noncommitted time is spent on mobile preventive patrol, the mileage driven within the beat on such patrol is not likely to exceed the mileage traversed within the beat when it is made a reactive beat.

A typical beat (operating as usual) under these high workload conditions would experience 9.5 to 12.2 miles driven by units on calls for service plus the 12.0 miles driven on preventive patrol, or a total of 21.5 to 24.2 miles driven per tour (under heavy workload conditions).

The 17.7 miles calculated for the reactive beats represents little net reduction in miles travelled under these conditions. If one considers the increased visibility of units responding to these calls, rather than performing routine patrol, one would surmise that perceived patrol levels were not markedly decreased (and may actually have increased) within the reactive beats.

During evening summer-month tours, when citizens' opportunities for assessing police presence are maximized, the miles travelled by plainly marked police vehicles within the reactive beats to and from calls for service are greater than the miles that would have been travelled on routine preventive patrol by a police vehicle "operating as usual." Using reasonably conservative assumptions, the former figure is about 50 percent greater than the latter. Moreover, the mileage driven in a reactive beat by responding units is comparable (within about 20 percent) to the total mileage that would have occurred in that beat, if operations were as usual. Coupled with the facts that units on calls for service travel faster than units on preventive patrol

---

[*] A patrol unit fielded on an "average tour" (as sampled by the researchers) experienced a workload of 40 percent committed time (p. 501). It would appear to be conservative to increase this figure by only 50 percent (from 40 to 60 percent) during the heaviest workload hours.

and that units responding to calls within the reactive beats used sirens and/or lights at least five times as frequently as other units, we are led to conclude that the experimental design should not be expected in itself to reduce greatly citizen perception of police presence within the reactive beats.

## Response Time

The technical report emphasizes the fact that response time did not vary according to the measurement techniques used by type of beat (reactive, proactive, or control). It would be dangerous to draw the implication that patrol coverage could be removed from an arbitrarily selected region of a city and that region would suffer no degradation in response time. Obviously this is *not true* in most situations. The technical report states the following:

**"It was originally expected that response time to calls in the reactive beats would be greater in both time and distance when compared to proactive or control beats. This expected difference did not occur. The reasons for this lack of difference are unclear" (p. 496).**

However, using simple back-of-the-envelope models, we can show that for *this particular experimental design,* one would not expect travel time or distance to be significantly increased within the reactive beats.[19]

The participant observer data reveals that the reactive travel distance (however categorized) is just about 1 percent above the region-wide average, the control travel distance about 1.5 percent above, and the proactive travel distance about 2.5 percent below. The model described here suggests that, if these data were categorized by beat type rather than unit type,[20] the reactive beat travel distance would be about 10 percent above the control beat travel distance. Still, even a 10 percent difference is remarkably small, and is conditioned on the very particular design

---

[*] The reason is that the reactive beats were located to have at least two boundaries in common with proactive and control beats, giving patrol units in the latter beats easy access to reactive areas. For details of the travel time model used to establish this, see Journal of Criminal Justice, January, 1976.

[*] Evidence in the report suggests that travel times were incorrectly categorized by type of unit rather than type of beat. This would tend to understate any differences in travel time by type of beat.

of the Kansas City experiment. Other cities should not expect little or no change in travel distance if they arbitrarily remove units from areas.

An analysis of other components of response time is made difficult by scanty reporting in the technical report.

Average times from receipt of call until arrival at the scene hover around 6.4 minutes, according to the participant observers, with no statistically significant differences among experimental conditions. (The method of data categorization—by beat or by car—is not known.) For instance, the report states that proactive beat cars took the longest to arrive at the scene of the incident, about 6.55 minutes, and control beat cars took the shortest time, 6.26 minutes (p. 485). This reviewer finds it very unusual that the proactive condition has the largest time until arrival, of 6.55 minutes. If the categorization is by beat, one would expect the travel time to be least in proactive beats, due to the greater density of patrol units there. This would be especially noticeable if the closest car in the proactive beat "volunteered" to high priority calls within the beat.

As discussed earlier the participant observers who recorded the response time data selected their patrol units and beats to maximize the number of calls for service and other police activities manned during an eight-hour period. This calls into question virtually all the results of the response time analysis, which the reader is led to believe (until he scrutinizes the next chapter) are based on a strictly random sample. High activity beats typically have a greater fraction of cross-beat dispatches and, accordingly, a higher travel time. This effect of high workload is somewhat offset by the usually smaller size of high activity beats.

In addition, as the workloads of units become higher, the travel times, while increasing, become less and less dependent on the particular beat configuration or spatial allocation of the units; at the same time, the differences in travel times among the units tend to become smaller. Thus, there are apparent biasing trends whose net effects are complicated to predict, but the result of which is a serious contamination of the response time sample.

## Conclusions

Summarizing the key points of this review:

**1** The range of preventive patrol frequencies experienced in the Kansas City Preventive Patrol Experiment was not large enough to encompass the range experienced in many other cities. As shown by a simple mathematical model, even a doubling or tripling of patrol effort in the proactive beats does not adequately reflect routine levels of patrol experienced in other cities.

**2** The integrity of the experimental conditions is brought into serious question by the large number of patrol-initiated activities in the reactive beats. This number actually increased during the experimental year, thereby casting doubts on the lack of presence of patrol units in the reactive beats.

**3** The integrity of the experimental conditions is further damaged by the lack of control and accountability associated with the specialized units in reactive beats. Particularly troublesome is a lack of control on the activities of the tactical units.

**4** A significant visible presence in the reactive beats was provided by units responding to calls for service in those beats. This presence was created, in part, by much more frequent use of multiple units responding to calls in reactive beats and by a five-fold increase in the use of sirens and/or lights. The experimental design, by its very construct, resulted in a total mileage travelled in reactive beats during high workload periods comparable to that provided prior to the experiment (summing the totals of mileage associated with calls for service and preventive patrol). This fact, coupled with the higher visibility of a unit responding to a call for service (compared to one performing preventive patrol), leads to the conclusion that during high workload periods the experimental design should not have been expected in itself greatly to reduce citizen perception of police presence within the reactive beats.

**5** Although the researchers claim to be surprised at the lack of significant difference in travel distance or time (by experimental area), a simple model demonstrates that one should not expect a marked increase in travel distance in the reactive beats. However, this result pertains only to the particular experimental design utilized in Kansas City. An arbitrary removal of patrol officers from certain areas could in many instances increase travel distance to those areas by a significant amount.

Although the Kansas City Experiment may have fallen short in its attempt to prove or disprove the general value of preventive patrol, it offers an unexpected by-product that should be useful to patrol administrators. It implies that if conditions warrant a change in

the spatial deployment of units within a confined region (say a "precinct," "district," or "division"), then if procedures are followed that are similar to those used in Kansas City, such redeployments can be made without suffering marked degradations in either actual or perceived service in the depleted regions. In other words, a roll call sergeant or higher level police planner could on any given tour of duty assign two or more units to some beats (proactive), one unit to other beats (control), and no conventional units to the remaining beats (reactive). Changing crime patterns and other factors affecting public safety would seem to motivate the need for such flexible and focused deployments.

Following the Kansas City experience, the following would seem to be reasonable procedures to follow in implementing such flexible deployments:

**1. Sufficiency of Total Patrol Resources.** Based on analyses of the demands for patrol services throughout the region, a sufficient number of units should be fielded so as to keep delays at the dispatcher's position due to all units being simultaneously busy below some target value.

**2. Patrol Resources in Close Proximity.** Each depleted beat should share at least one boundary with a heavily manned beat, and perhaps one with a regular beat.

**3. Patrol of Common Boundaries.** At least one patrol unit in a heavily manned beat adjacent to a depleted beat should be directed to patrol near the common boundary between the two beats. The dispatcher should be made aware of the identity of this unit.

**4. Spatial Dispersement of Depleted Areas.** No two depleted areas should share boundaries in common.

**5. Patrol-Initiated Activities.** Units patrolling near the borders of the depleted areas should be encouraged to undertake patrol-initiated activities on the borders of (or even within) the depleted areas when, in the judgment of the officers, conditions justify such activity.

**6. Other Operations As Usual.** Traffic, tactical, and other special units should not be affected by the change in patrol deployments. In particular, they should not be discouraged from entering the depleted areas.

**7. Dispatch of Multiple Units.** Due to the lack of conventional patrolling in the depleted regions, the practice of dispatching multiple units into these regions may have to be increased in order to guarantee the safety of the

responding officers and the person(s) reporting the incident.

**8. Increased Use of Sirens and Lights.** To take maximum advantage of the limited time within the depleted areas, units should use sirens and lights more frequently than usual (in order to increase citizen awareness of police presence).

Many police departments perform limited, but unplanned versions of the Kansas City Experiment every day. This often occurs when too few officers report to roll call to field all of the cars in the district, and the roll call sergeant may decide to leave certain beats unpatrolled on that tour. If one beat has recently been reporting unusually high crime rates the sergeant may assign two or three cars to the same beat. Other beats, usually the majority, are assigned one car each. Thus, in a sense, reactive, proactive, and control beats are in use continually in many cities. It would be surprising if citizens or criminals, for that matter, could detect these changes from the one-car, one-beat principle, provided that the selection of beats for each condition changes frequently and is not publicized. However, following the Kansas City experience, in order to minimize any degradation in service in the depleted regions, it would seem necessary to follow most, if not all, of the eight suggestions above when implementing such deployments. ∎

Brown, C. E. "Discussion: Evaluative Research on Policing—the Kansas City Experience." *Police Chief* (XLII: 6, 1975).

Davis, E. M. and L. Knowles. "A Critique of the Report: An Evaluation of the Kansas City Preventive Patrol Experiment," and Kelling, G. L. and T. Pate. "Response to: The Davis-Knowles Critique of the Kansas City Preventive Patrol Experiment." *Police Chief* (XLII: 6, 1975).

Kansas City, Missouri, Police Department. "Annual Report," 1971, 1972, 1973, 1974.

Kelling, G. L., T. Pate, D. Dieckman, and C. E. Brown. "The Kansas City Preventive Patrol Experiment," published by the Police Foundation, Washington, D.C., 1974 (537 pp. plus appendices). Also see their "Summary Report" (60 pp.).

Larson, R. C. "Measuring the Response Patterns of New York City Police Patrol Cars." R-673-NYC, New York City-Rand Institute, 1971.

Larson, R. C. *Urban Police Patrol Analysis.* Cambridge, Massachusetts: MIT Press, 1972.

# 31

# The Deterrent Effect of Capital Punishment: Another View

## Peter Passell and John B. Taylor

In a recent paper in this *Review*, Isaac Ehrlich found a negative relationship between the use of the death penalty and homicide rates, over the three and a half decades from 1935–69 in the United States. This empirical finding, in apparent conflict with previous studies on the subject (see Thorsten Sellin, Robert Dann), takes on special meaning because (a) it is the first test of the capital punishment deterrence hypothesis to use econometric estimation techniques, and (b) its publication comes at a time when legislatures and the courts in both the United States and Canada are reshaping public policy on the use of the death penalty. Hence the importance of a second look at Ehrlich's results.

Such a reexamination, described below, suggests that the time-series model and data used by Ehrlich permit no inference about the deterrent effect of capital punishment on homicide. The data indicate that the parameters of Ehrlich's model are extremely sensitive to the choices of included explanatory variables and the functional form of the model; when recast in equally plausible alternative structures, the Ehrlich model fails to generate a deterrent effect for executions. Moreover, Ehrlich's methodological approach to the question, estimation of a single structural equation relating executions to murders, sharply limits the policy implications of the estimated coefficients.

Section I briefly describes Ehrlich's murder rate function and tests the model for parameter stability over the sample period.

*Columbia University. An early version of this paper was written before the Ehrlich appendix appeared; it uses an alternative data set, available on request from the authors. This paper was listed as a Columbia Workshop discussion paper; it was published in a modified and less technical version in 1976. The conclusion and findings are similar despite the different data set. We would like to thank Phoebus J. Dhrymes and David Kennett for their comments and assistance.

Section II considers his choice of explanatory variables and functional forms, and examines sensitivity of his estimate to these choices. Section III examines the pitfalls of inferring an execution-murder tradeoff from a single estimated equation.

### I

A representative sample of the empirical results reported by Ehrlich in support of the deterrence effect of capital punishment is his equation (1), Table 4, which is displayed as our equation (1) in Table 1. The logarithm of the *U.S.* annual murder rate $(Q/N)^0$ is explained by the logarithm of three deterrence variables (the clearance rate for murder $P_a^0$, the conviction rate for murder $P_{c/a}^0$, and the ratio of current executions to one-year lagged murder convictions $(PXQ_1)_{-1}$), as well as by the logarithm of five other explanatory variables (the labor force participation rate $L$, the fraction of the population between 14 and 24 years of age $A$, an estimate of permanent real per capita income $Y_p$, the unemployment rate $U$, and an exponential time trend $e^T$). The equation is estimated by a two-stage procedure in which $P_a^0$ and $P_{c/a}^0$ are treated as endogenous variables, and are first regressed on current and lagged values of the predetermined variables, lagged values of all the endogenous variables, and a group of otherwise excluded exogenous variables (real police expenditure per capita $XPOL$, real government expenditure per capita $XGOV$, and the fraction of nonwhites in the population $NW$). In the second stage an iterative procedure is used to estimate the first-order serial correlation coefficient along with the coefficients of the endogenous and predetermined variables.

Ehrlich presents several versions of this same model (Tables 3 and 4, p. 410), among which the major differences are the use of alternatives to $(PXQ_1)_{-1}$ as empirical sur-

From Peter Passell and John B. Taylor, "The Deterrent Effect of Capital Punishment: Another View," 67 (3) *The American Economic Review* 445-451 (June 1977). Copyright 1977 by the American Economic Association.

TABLE 1

| Equation | Constant | $P_a^0$ | $P_{c/a}^0$ | $(PxQ_1)_{-1}$ | $L$ | $A$ | $Y_p$ | $U$ | $T$ | $P_{63}$ | $C_{63}$ |
|---|---|---|---|---|---|---|---|---|---|---|---|
| (1) 1935-69 | −4.060 | −1.247 | −0.345 | −0.066 | −1.314 | 0.450 | 1.318 | 0.068 | −0.046 | | |
| $SSR = .048$ | (−1.00) | (−1.56) | (−3.07) | (−3.33) | (−1.49) | (2.20) | (4.81) | (2.60) | (−6.54) | | |
| $\hat{\rho} = .059$ | | | | | | | | | | | |
| (2) 1935-69 | −5.536 | −0.973 | −0.375 | −0.062 | −1.620 | 0.565 | 1.363 | 0.065 | −0.046 | | |
| $SSR = .049$ | (−1.40) | (−1.26) | (−3.10) | (−3.01) | (−1.87) | (2.33) | (4.52) | (2.34) | (−5.86) | | |
| $\hat{\rho} = .204$ | | | | | | | | | | | |
| (3) 1935-62 | −7.219 | 0.124 | 0.236 | −0.008 | −2.489 | 0.307 | 0.795 | 0.025 | −0.029 | | |
| $SSR = .019$ | (−2.67) | (−0.23) | (−3.04) | (−0.21) | (−3.71) | (1.65) | (3.47) | (1.16) | (−4.09) | | |
| $\hat{\rho} = .048$ | | | | | | | | | | | |
| (4) 1935-69 | −6.67 | −0.491 | −0.410 | 0.055 | −2.081 | 0.545 | 1.145 | 0.039 | −0.033 | −0.112 | |
| $SSR = .045$ | (−1.89) | (−0.69) | (−3.41) | (1.03) | (−2.60) | (2.00) | (3.02) | (1.26) | (−2.98) | (−2.00) | |
| $\hat{\rho} = .524$ | | | | | | | | | | | |
| (5) 1935-69 | −5.572 | −0.698 | −0.303 | −0.020 | −1.803 | 0.595 | 1.133 | 0.054 | −0.036 | −0.069 | −0.113 |
| $SSR = .036$ | (−1.70) | (−1.06) | (−3.01) | (−0.41) | (−2.27) | (2.93) | (4.38) | (2.21) | (−4.26) | (−1.36) | (−2.48) |
| $\hat{\rho} = .013$ | | | | | | | | | | | |
| (6) 1935-69 | −3.48 | −1.138 | −0.179 | −0.016 | −2.321 | 0.832 | 1.097 | −0.014 | −0.0262 | | |
| $SSR = .030$ | (−1.21) | (−2.35) | (−1.66) | (−0.94) | (−3.81) | (4.91) | (3.11) | (−0.56) | (−2.58) | | |
| $\hat{\rho} = .745$ | | | | | | | | | | | |
| (7) 1935-69 | −4.698 | 0.898 | −0.425 | 0.018 | −2.009 | 0.910 | 1.223 | 0.041 | −0.028 | | |
| $SSR = .060$ | (−1.10) | (−1.21) | (−2.95) | (0.73) | (−2.29) | (3.18) | (2.41) | (1.15) | (−1.91) | | |
| $\hat{\rho} = .604$ | | | | | | | | | | | |
| (8) 1935-69 | 0.178 | −0.00040 | −0.00054 | −0.00106 | −0.264 | 0.202 | 0.00012 | 0.00040 | −0.0034 | | |
| $SSR = .00015$ | (3.25) | (−0.88) | (−3.10) | (−1.26) | (−3.15) | (3.60) | (5.97) | (1.92) | (−6.01) | | |
| $\hat{\rho} = .214$ | | | | | | | | | | | |
| (9) 1938-69 | 0.188 | −0.00077 | −0.00075 | 0.0021 | −0.200 | 0.191 | 0.000091 | 0.00038 | −0.0023 | | |
| $SSR = .00014$ | (2.79) | (−1.38) | (−2.85) | (1.19) | (−2.20) | (2.82) | (3.22) | (1.41) | (2.80) | | |
| $\hat{\rho} = .216$ | | | | | | | | | | | |

Note:  $P_a^0$ = clearance rate for murder.
$P_{c/a}^0$ = conviction rate for murder.
$(PXQ_1)_{-1}$ = ratio of current executions to one-year lagged murder convictions.
$L$ = labor force participation rate.
$A$ = fraction of population between 14 and 24 (in equation (6) between 18 and 24 years old).
$Y_p$ = permanent income per capita.
$U$ = unemployment rate.
$T$ = time trend.
$P_{63}$ = zero from 1938-62; $(PXQ_1)_{-1}$ from 1963-69.
$C_{63}$ = zero from 1938-62, 1 from 1963-69.
$SSR$ = sum of squared residuals.
$\hat{\rho}$ = estimate of first-order serial correlation coefficient.

rogates for $P_{e/c}$, the subjective conditional probability of execution given conviction. Neither prior judgement nor the estimated coefficients provide much basis for choosing among variant equations. We chose to concentrate on equation (1) because it is the most common form in Ehrlich's tables and because it permits convenient comparisons with the tradeoffs computed by Ehrlich.

Equation (2), Table 1, shows our attempt to replicate equation (1), based on Ehrlich's (1975b) description of the data sources used. Note that the replication is not precise, though the differences are quantitatively small. The source of the differences probably lies either in minor data collection errors or in the use of different computer programs.[1] While these differences could be reconciled were we to use the same numbers and programs as Ehrlich, we feel that the data behind equation (2) are adequate to examine the validity of Ehrlich's conclusions.[2]

Behind the use of time-series estimation is the assumption that the structure and the coefficients to be estimated remain stable over the sample period. In Ehrlich's case it

[1] We used the instruction TSCORC of version 2.7 of TSP (Time-Series Processor).

[2] This opinion is based on the fact that our examination focuses on factors which dominate the minor differences between equations (1) and (2) such as the murder rate increase in the 1960's and the logarithmic transformation of the execution rate.

is assumed that the behavior of potential murderers is governed by the same variables with the same coefficients over the period 1935–69. If this assumption is in fact not correct, the estimated function would have little use either as an explanation of the causes of murder or of the policy implications of changing the value of an exogenous variable in the structure.

The assumption can be tested.[3] Consider for example the hypothesis that the murder rate function estimated in equation (2) has the same structure from 1935–62 as from 1963–69. Equation (3) with the time-series truncated at 1962 was estimated to test this hypothesis. The $F$-ratio, computed from the sums of squared residuals in equations (2) and (3) is 6.00, significant even at the 99 percent level. Thus, the hypothesis of structural homogeneity must be rejected. Further, there is nothing special about the shift point chosen for this test. Similar tests were computed[4] for the four possible structural shift points from 1961–64; the $F$-ratio indicates a significant shift for each of these periods. It is clear therefore that Ehrlich's equation has been estimated over different regimes, a fact which casts considerable doubt on the validity of his estimates.

Since our primary interest is in the deterrent effect of capital punishment, it is important to note that the coefficient of $(PXQ_1)_{-1}$ is very different in equations (2) and (3), turning from $-0.062$ and significant to $-0.008$ and insignificant when the sample period is changed. The $F$-test for the entire equation does not, however, exclude the possibility that changes other than changes in the coefficient of $(PXQ_1)_{-1}$ have generated the statistical significance.

Equations (4) and (5) provide a test of the hypothesis that the coefficient of $(PXQ_1)_{-1}$ is the same over two sample periods under two different sets of assumptions. In equa-

tion (4) we add a variable, $P_{63}$, equal to zero in the years 1938–62 and to $(PXQ_1)_{-1}$ in the years 1963–69. The $t$-ratio of this variable gives a test of this homogeneity hypothesis, given that all other coefficients are the same over the two periods. The value of the statistic indicates rejection of the hypothesis at the 90 percent level. In equation (5) we add another variable, $C_{63}$, equal to 0 from 1938–62 and to 1 from 1963–69. The $t$-ratio of $P_{63}$ in this equation gives a test of the hypothesis of homogeneity of the coefficient of $(PXQ_1)_{-1}$, given that all variables except the intercept are stable over the two periods. The value of this statistic also suggests rejection of homogeneity.

## II

Statistical tests for temporal homogeneity in Section I strongly suggest that the coefficients of relevant variables do not remain the same over the 1935–69 period; inclusion of the last few years is vital if one is to infer some deterrent effect for the conditional probability of execution. One casual explanation of this regression result is quite simple. During the 1963–69 period the logarithm of $(PXQ_1)_{-1}$ falls sharply and monotonically (from $-0.65$ to $-3.91$, the latter, 2.3 standard deviations below the sample mean) while the logarithm of $Q/N$ increases from its lowest sample value $-3.08$, to $-2.62$, the highest sample value. (See Figure 1.) It is possible, of course, that the rise in murder rates is causally linked to the fall

---

[3]All tests of significance in this paper and in Ehrlich's are based on asymptotic distribution assumptions. Thus what are conventionally called $t$-ratio or $F$-ratios in the classical linear regression model will only approximately have the appropriate $t$ or $F$ distribution in these models.

[4]These values are 5.92, 7.07, and 7.36 for the samples ending in 1961, 1963, and 1964, respectively.

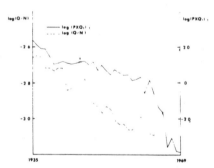

FIGURE 1. EXECUTION RATES AND MURDER RATES, 1935–69

in execution rates, as Ehrlich's theory would predict. However the regressions are not in themselves evidence for the existence of such a relationship.

For many observers, alternative explanations of the murder explosion of the 1960's are, a priori, more convincing. As large as increases in murder rates were, the growth rates of other crimes were greater. From 1963 to 1969, per capita reported murders increased 60 percent, robberies by 178 percent, auto theft by 104 percent (see *UCR*, Table 1). Yet few social scientists would choose to connect the increase in auto thefts to the fall in execution rates for murder. Possible nonexclusive explanations for murder rate increases include reduction in the opportunity cost of possessing deadly weapons, racial tension, increases in the difference between economic expectations and opportunities for poor people, reductions in the length of prison sentences. Some of these variables are not easily quantifiable (racial tension, economic frustration, real cost of weapons). Nonetheless their omission from multivariate models of murder rates may so seriously bias the estimated coefficients of included variables that the least squares exercise becomes meaningless. One variable, the expected length of prison sentences given conviction, is not available annually, but is obtainable by state for certain years. It is striking that when the average length of sentences served is included in 1950 and 1960 cross-section regressions, executions lose all explanatory power.[5]

The sensitivity of the estimated coefficient of $(PXQ_1)_{-1}$ to the choice of included variables is notable even for seemingly minor modifications. Ehrlich includes $A$, the fraction of residential population ages 14–24, to control for shifts in the size of the murder-prone population. Demographic statistics for this age group are easily found in standard reference sources, but the specific choice of the 14–24 year old age group meets no clear theoretical objective. One might plausibly argue on a priori grounds that this age group is unnecessarily broad, young teenagers not being more murder-

prone than adults older than 24. Note however that when a narrower target group variable $A^*$, the fraction of the residential population ages 18–24, excluding armed forces overseas, is substituted for $A$ in Ehrlich's basic equation, the regression results are qualitatively changed.[6] Equation (6) shows the estimated coefficient of $(PXQ_1)_{-1}$ reduced in absolute value and statistically not significantly different from zero.

We do not claim that the major cause of the increase in murders in the 1960's was age group shifts due to the baby boom. This demographic variable may simply be correlated with important omitted variables. What does seem clear, though, is that the data and model employed by Ehrlich do not permit discrimination among numerous plausible explanations of increased murder rates.

Further evidence of sensitivity comes from examining the mathematical transformations of the variables in Ehrlich's model. Theory suggests that an econometric structure should be specified in the mathematical form which conforms most closely to behavioral expectations. In practice, forms are usually chosen which are linear in the parameters to make it easier to interpret the statistical properties of the estimators. And commonly, the logarithmic transformation is chosen to facilitate interpretation of the linear parameter estimates as partial elasticities. In this latter case, the procedure is often justified *ex ante* on theoretical grounds and sometimes *ex post* on statistical grounds. But when the theoretical justification is weak, the results of the estimation are thrown into doubt if they are sensitive to the particular transformation chosen.

In the case of Ehrlich's choice of the logarithmic transformation, the theoretical justification is not convincing. While the elasticity of murder rates with respect to the

---

[5]See Passell, Tables 1 and 2.

[6]Our source for total residential population is the same as Ehrlich's. The source for the numerator of the fraction was U.S. Bureau of the Census, #114, Table 1 (1933–40), #98, Table 1 (1941–49), #441, #438, Table 4 (1950–69). It was assumed that one-half of all *U.S.* citizens abroad are 18–24, in order to calculate the remaining resident population for the years 1950–69.

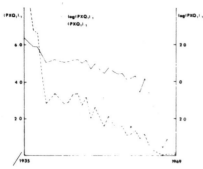

FIGURE 2. EXECUTION RATES, 1935 69: BEFORE AND AFTER *Log* TRANSFORMATION

conditional probability of execution might be approximately constant over some range of the variables, we see no reason why this constant elasticity should hold over the very large range in the observed time-series. However, Ehrlich's finding of significant deterrence effect using 1960's data does appear to be sensitive to the choice of this transformation. Equation (7) is identical to equation (2) with one exception: the data for the conditional probability of execution are employed without transformation to natural *log*s. Note that the coefficient of the execution variables turns positive and statistically insignificant. The intuitive reason for this sensitivity is suggested by the wide difference between the transformed and the untransformed series in Figure 2. Equation (8) uses data for all the variables in untransformed state; the coefficient of execution here is negative, but the *t*-statistic indicates that it is not significantly different from zero.[7]

Given the apparent sensitivity of the model to these transformations, one might be tempted to use statistical criteria to help one choose the correct transformation. But even if these criteria clearly suggested the

[7] Sensitivity to functional form is even more delineated when equation (8) is reestimated without the partially extrapolated deterrence data needed to include the years 1935-37. When equation (8) is estimated from 1938-69 the coefficient for $(PXQ_1)_{-1}$ is positive (.0021) and statistically insignificant with a *T*-value of 1.19 (see equation (9)).

choice of a particular transformation, one would still question estimation results which were extremely sensitive to this choice in light of the lack of a strong theoretical justification.[8]

### III

In this section we abstract from the criticism of Sections I and II to examine another aspect of the analysis. If one were to accept Ehrlich's estimated structure, would it be reasonable to infer a murder-execution tradeoff from the negative coefficient of $P_{e/c}^0$?

Ehrlich argues that this coefficient $(\hat{\alpha}_3)$ should be interpreted as an estimate of the partial elasticity of murder rates with respect to the risk of execution. Thus he is able to derive the estimated marginal tradeoff between executions and murders: $\Delta Q/\Delta E = \hat{\alpha}_3(Q/E)$. If one assumes $\hat{\alpha}_3 = -.065$ and $Q$ and $E$ equal to the time-series mean values, $\Delta Q/\Delta E = -7.7$. For $Q = 10,920$ and $E - 41$, $\Delta Q/\Delta E = -17.3$.

It is important to note, however, that behind this interpretation of $\hat{\alpha}_3$ lies an important assumption. The coefficient represents the murder-execution tradeoff only if it is possible to alter $PXQ_1$ without changing the value of any other independent variable in the equation.[9] Yet social scientists (including Ehrlich) interested in economic models of crime typically acknowledge the simultaneity of the system hence the logic

[8] One statistical procedure for choosing a transformation has been suggested by G. Box and D. Cox, where the choice is reduced to finding a single parameter $\alpha$ in the transformation $x_t = (x_t^\alpha - 1)/\alpha$, of all the variables in the model. As part of our sensitivity analysis we computed the correlation between the actual murder rates (untransformed) and the predicted murder rates (untransformed) as given by an equation fitted to the Box and Cox transformed variables for 100 values of $\alpha$ between 0 and 1. The highest correlation was at .19 which gave a negative and significant coefficient for the execution variable. However, since the model is not stable over the sample period these estimates provide little insight into the problem.

[9] This may not even be possible if one algebraically interprets the deterrent variables as ratios. If one formally differentiates murder rates with respect to executions in Ehrlich's equation (where $Q$ appears in the denominator of the arrest rate) one finds $\partial Q/\partial E > 0$. For further interpretation of this result see the authors.

of calling criminal behavior functions *supply* functions. For the purposes of estimation, Ehrlich explicitly argues that the probability of arrest and conditional probability of conviction are endogenously determined. Thus one must at the very least account for possible adjustment in these two variables before computing the policy implications of changing the probability of execution.

Traditional methodology offers two alternatives for generating an estimate of the tradeoff. One might estimate the rest of the structural equations in the simultaneous system, or one could estimate the reduced form equation for murder rates. The first alternative is beyond the empirical scope of Ehrlich's paper; no attempt is made to specify the other equation in the system. Ehrlich acknowledges the relevance of the second alternative and does produce negative and statistically significant estimates of the reduced form coefficients of the execution variable for certain specifications of $P_{e/c}$ over the period 1934–69. However our confidence in the value of these estimates is limited (a) by the possible sensitivity to functional form and time period of the estimates, and (b) by the untested assumption that the "modified reduced form" chosen by Ehrlich is not biased by omitted variables.

While it may not be possible to calculate the reduced form murder-execution tradeoff, it is interesting to note the potential sensitivity of the sign of that tradeoff to the elasticity of $P_{c/a}$ with respect to $P_{e/c}$. Many legal experts and social scientists believe that increases in $P_{e/c}$ will reduce $P_{c/a}$, since juries and judges will apply stricter standards for convictions when there is a greater prospect of execution.[10] This widely accepted hypothesis was used successfully as an argument by nineteenth and twentieth century legal reform movement leaders bent on abolishing whole categories of capital crimes and granting juries greater discretion in penalties imposed.[11] By Ehrlich's esti-

[10]See for example, Neil Vidmar; Hugo Bedau; James Bennett; Harry Kalven and Hans Zeisel; Zeisel; Robert Knowlton.

[11]See, for example, Maynard Shipley; John McCloskey.

mated equation (3) in Table 3, if the absolute value of the elasticity of $P_{c/a}$ with respect to $P_{e/c}$, $\epsilon_{ce}$, were greater than .174, the net impact of an increase in execution probabilities would, perversely, raise murder rates. More generally, the impact will be perverse if $| \epsilon_{ce} | > \alpha_3/\alpha_2$.

## IV. Conclusion

This examination of Ehrlich's estimates has limited focus. One might wish to examine further the theoretical basis for including or excluding variables in the model, the consistency between the data and alternative hypothetical models, the quality of the data (particularly for the deterrence variables $P_a^0$, $P_{c/a}^0$, $P_{e/c}^0$) used in the test, and the aggregation problems imposed by the use of national data.

We have essentially confined ourselves to a narrower analysis. First, we have shown that Ehrlich's model does not satisfy the statistical requirement of temporal homogeneity and that the results are sensitive to specification of the variables and transformation of the data. This sensitivity raises grave (and in our own opinion, overwhelming) doubt about the utility of Ehrlich's time-series estimates as partial elasticities. Second, we have argued that even if Ehrlich has captured the essence of the murder rate function in his regression, it is not possible to infer from it that a change in legal institutions which increased $P_{e/c}$ would reduce murder rates. In sum, on the basis of Ehrlich's research, it is prudent neither to accept nor reject the hypothesis that capital punishment deters murder.

## REFERENCES

**Hugo Bedau**, *The Death Penalty in America*, New York 1967.

**J. Bennett**, "A Historic Move: Delaware Abolishes Capital Punishment," *Amer. Bar Assn. J.*, Nov. 1958, *44*, 1053–54.

**G. Box and D. Cox**, "An Analysis of Transformations," *J. Royal Statist. Soc.*, Series B, Jan. 1964, *26*, 211–43.

**Robert Dann**, "The Deterrent Effect of Capital Punishment," *Friends Social Service*

*Series Bull. No. 29.* Philadelphia, Mar. 1935.

I. **Ehrlich,** (1975a) "The Deterrent Effect of Capital Punishment: A Question of Life and Death," *Amer. Econ. Rev.,* June 1975, *55,* 397-417.

———, (1975b) "The Deterrent Effect of Capital Punishment: A Question of Life and Death—Sources of Data," unpublished Appendix, May 1975.

**Harry Kalven and Hans Zeisel,** *The American Jury,* Boston 1966.

R. **Knowlton,** "Problems of Jury Discretion in Capital Cases," *Univ. Pennsylvania Law Rev.,* June 1953, *101,* 1099-1136

J. **McCloskey,** "A Review of the Literature Contrasting Mandatory and Discretionary Systems of Sentencing in Capital Cases," unpublished study for the Pennsylvania Governor's Study Commission on the Death Penalty, Harrisburg 1973.

P. **Passell,** "The Deterrent Effect of the Death Penalty: A Statistical Test," *Stanford Law Rev.,* Nov 1975, *28,* 61-80.

——— **and J. B. Taylor,** "The Deterrence Controversy: A Reconsideration of the Time Series Evidence," in Hugo Bedau and Chester Pierce, eds., *Capital Punishment in the United States,* New York 1976.

**Thorsten Sellin,** *The Death Penalty,* Philadelphia 1959.

M. **Shipley,** "Does Capital Punishment Prevent Convictions?," *Amer. Legal Rev.,* May-June 1909, *43,* 321-34.

N. **Vidmar,** "Effects of Decision Alternatives on the Verdicts and Social Perception of Simulated Jurors," *J. Personality Soc. Psychol.,* May 1972, *22,* 211-18.

H. **Zeisel,** "Some Data on Jury Attitudes Toward Capital Punishment," unpub. paper, Center for Studies in Criminal Justice, Univ. Chicago Law School 1968.

**U.S. Bureau of the Census,** *Current Population Reports,* Series P-25, No. 98, Aug. 13, 1954; 114, Apr. 27, 1955; 438, Jan. 21, 1970; 441, Mar. 19, 1970.

**U.S. Department of Justice,** Federal Bureau of Investigation, *Uniform Crime Report* (*UCR*), Washington.

# 32

## The Deterrent Effect of Capital Punishment: Reply

### Isaac Ehrlich

Despite its title, the comment by Peter Passell and John Taylor does not offer an alternative theory of criminal behavior or any coherent approach that can explain the data they have examined. Moreover, Passell and Taylor (hereafter called P-T) neither challenge the theory nor the statistical methodology I used in my (1975a) paper on the deterrent effect of capital punishment. Indeed, their work is not entirely novel since it duplicates in large measure an earlier published study by W. J. Bowers and G. L. Pierce, to which I have already responded elsewhere (1975b). Their main point lies in emphasizing some apparently negative results that they obtain upon shortening the sample period and altering the regression format. As I hope to show, however, Passell and Taylor have not adequately analyzed the data and their negative findings, and some of the inferences they draw are based on test statistics whose properties are not known. That they do not duplicate the results I reported in my (1975a) study with sufficient accuracy is bothersome in the context of their subsequent regression analysis, especially since others have reproduced my basic results to rounding errors.[1] Finally, Section III of their comment in which they argue for policy implications against reimposition of the death penalty on grounds of an automatic negative association between execution and conviction risks amounts only to speculation. In Sections I–III of this reply I shall address the technical aspects of their critique and their discussion of policy implications. In Section IV I shall report some additional findings concerning the issue of deterrence based upon indepen-dent bodies of data and briefly indicate their relation to the results obtained through the time-series analysis.

### I

The apparent sensitivity of some of the regression coefficients to deletions of observations relating to both the 1960's and the late 1930's has already been discussed in my own work (1973, n.28 and 1975b, part 3). But while Passell and Taylor have focused their attention on those subperiods in which specific regression results are relatively weak, they have not proceeded to analyze some of the inherent limitations of the data which account for these results.

In the first place, their main test of stability of the regression coefficients across the subperiods 1935–62 and 1963–69 is not defended. The reader may note that the estimation method I used, and which Passell and Taylor adopt, is the three-round non-linear estimation procedure proposed by Ray C. Fair. To my knowledge, the straightforward application of Chow's test by P-T to test the hypothesis of equality of regression coefficients[2] has not been established as a valid test procedure in the context of this non-linear simultaneous equation procedure. Thus, the properties of their test statistic are not known.

Second, the introduction of a dummy variable distinguishing the 1963–69 subperiod from the earlier period—the one dummy variable which appears to have a pronounced effect in their analysis—does not have an unambiguous effect on the coefficients associated with alternative risk measures. I have found, for example, that when a reduced form estimate of the conditional execution risk—$\overline{PXQ}_1$ in equation (6)

*University of Chicago and National Bureau of Economic Research. I would like to thank Ronald Gallant, Lawrence Fisher, Randall Mark, and William Wecker for useful suggestions and assistance.

[1] See Brian Forst, Victor Filatov, and Lawrence Klein.

[2] The reader may note that P-T apply the specific variant of Chow's test for the case where the number of degrees of freedom is inadequate for the regular test. They cannot estimate the regression parameters separately for the period 1963–69.

From Isaac Ehrlich, "The Deterrent Effect of Capital Punishment: Reply," 67 (3) *The American Economic Review* 452-458 (June 1977). Copyright 1977 by the American Economic Association.

of Table 3 in my (1975a) paper—is used as a regressor, the introduction of that dummy variable ($D_{6369}$) far from weakening the effect of $\widehat{PXQ}_1$ actually makes it stronger.[3]

What Passell and Taylor fail to note in their analysis are some important differences between subperiods ending in the early 1960's and the full observation set that can explain the apparent changes in coefficients associated with a few of the explanatory variables. Whereas the modified rates of change in the execution risk measures have been stable over the two decades preceding the 1960's, the objective risk of execution declined quite sharply starting about 1960. Variability in deterrence variables used as regressors is particularly small between the late 1930's and the early 1960's.[4] In addition, key variables in the analysis—the murder rate and the conditional risk of execution measures—are highly trended with time over subperiods ending in the early 1960's but much less so over the entire sample period.[5] Regressions based on samples ending in the early 1960's thus are unlikely to produce efficient estimates of the distinct partial association between the murder rate and execution risk.

As implied by the earlier discussion, however, it is not clear that the observed changes in regression estimates across a few subperiods are statistically meaningful. One factor that may contribute to some difference in the magnitude of residuals is that measures of execution risk in 1968 and 1969 are imprecise (see my 1975a paper, Table 2, note b). Indeed, estimates of the negative effect of execution risk based on regressions with 1967 and 1966 as ending dates, although virtually identical to results for the full period, are found to be associated with smaller standard errors.[6] Another such factor is that data concerning national murder statistics in earlier periods were reestimated by the FBI on the basis of the more complete censuses conducted in the 1960's. In addition, the variable $XPOL$ (real per capita expenditure on police) is measured for fiscal years since 1961, whereas in the previous years it is defined for calendar years.

But quite apart from the question of the validity of P-T's tests the relevant question is: Given the regressions based upon the full sample and all the various regressions obtained after deletions of specific subperiods, do the results lean in favor of the deterrence hypothesis or do they support the "alternative view" of P-T? I believe the answer is decisively in favor of the former proposition. The results I reported are consistent with sharp predictions concerning the signs as well as the relative ranking of deterrence and other variables. Moreover, the standard errors of the coefficients estimated from subperiods with earlier ending dates—even those reported by Passell and Taylor—are

[3]The following estimated regression equation relates to the effective sample period 1935–69. All variables are defined in my (1975a) paper. $\hat{\beta}/S_{\hat{\beta}}$ are in parentheses.

$$ln\,q^0 = -5.191 - 1.087\Delta^*\hat{P}^0a - 0.392\Delta^*\hat{P}^0c\mid a$$
$$(-1.30)\,(-1.50)\qquad(-3.36)$$
$$-0.155\Delta^*\widehat{PXQ}_1 - 2.016\Delta^*L + 0.343\Delta^*A$$
$$(-4.35)\qquad(-1.93)\qquad(1.29)$$
$$+\,1.344\Delta^*Y_p + 0.052\Delta^*U - 0.053\Delta^*T - 0.256D_{6369}$$
$$(4.83)\qquad(1.84)\qquad(-6.00)\qquad(-3.71)$$
$$\hat{\rho} = -0.26;\quad \hat{\sigma}_e = 0.054;\quad D.W. = 2.17$$

[4]For example, the variance of the modified rates of change of $PXQ_{1_{-1}}$ calculated for the value of $\hat{\rho} = 0.077$ for the period 1935–69 (2.331) is more than 10 times higher than the corresponding variance associated with this variable over the period 1938–62 (.192). At the same time the variances in corresponding values of the rates of change in $P^0a$ and $P^0c\mid a$ fall from .000899 to .000563 and from 0.0199 to 0.00432, respectively.

[5]For example, the zero-order correlation coefficients between these modified rates of change in $q^0$ and $PXQ_{1_{-1}}$ on the one hand, and the time trend variable on the other, are found to be $-.92$ and $-.92$ over the subperiod 1938–62. The corresponding correlations over the full sample period 1935–69 are $-.52$ and $-.86$, respectively.

[6]Compare the equation below, for the effective sample period 1935–67, with equation (3) in Table 3 of my (1975a) paper.

$$ln\,q^0 = -5.084 - 0.853\Delta^*P^0a - 0.295\Delta^*P^0c\mid a$$
$$(-1.73)\,(-1.48)\qquad(-3.35)$$
$$-0.0062\Delta^*PXQ_{1_{-1}} - 1.764\Delta^*L + 0.384\Delta^*A$$
$$(3.73)\qquad(-2.34)\qquad(2.01)$$
$$+\,1.105\Delta^*Y_p + 0.051\Delta^*U - 0.041\Delta^*T$$
$$(4.52)\qquad(2.21)\qquad(-6.47)$$
$$\hat{\rho} = -0.023;\quad \hat{\sigma}_e = 0.039;\quad D.W. = 1.88$$

considerably larger than the corresponding estimates based on the full observation set with 1969 or 1967 as ending dates.[7] The subperiod estimation involves loss of precious degrees of freedom already in short supply. With a sufficiently small number of degrees of freedom one is not likely to reject any particular hypothesis.

## II

As I argued in my article (1975b, pp. 218–19), and explained further in my subsequent paper (1977) on capital punishment and deterrence, there are both theoretical and statistical reasons for preferring a log-linear specification to a linear format in the variables' natural values. Passell and Taylor's analysis in this regard is inadequate. But the relative superiority of these two forms can be tested systematically via the Box and Cox procedure referred to in my (1975b) piece. Curiously, P-T did attempt to pursue this approach in their present paper and their application of the Box and Cox procedure, if valid, indicates that the optimal transformation they select is much closer to the logarithmic specification ($\lambda = 0$, where $\lambda$ denotes the coefficient of transformation) than to the linear specification ($\lambda = 1$). Moreover, their sketchy report in footnote 8 of their paper also indicates that at their selected optimal transformation the execution risk variable has a negative and "significant" effect. Their attempt to dismiss these results "since the model is [anyway] not stable over the sample period" is surprising in view of the importance they attribute to their experiments with the simple linear specification where they do not question their results on grounds of instability. More important, as my preceding analysis shows, they have not established the existence of instability.

The application of Box and Cox's analysis of transformations in the context of the estimation procedure used in my time-series

analysis is not straightforward. I have attempted to shed light on the issue of optimal transformations via independent cross-sectional regression analyses where data exigencies have dictated employment of classical least squares techniques. The results are decisive. With no exception, the tests conducted on the basis of data from 1940 and 1950 show that under the assumptions of the regression model the simple linear form must be rejected as an optimal transformation within alternative single parameter classes of "power transformations." In contrast, in all of the tests performed, the logarithmic specification cannot be rejected as an optimal transformation at conventional significance levels (see the author, 1977). The results of the statistical tests thus lend support to the emphasis I have placed on the log-linear specification in both my time-series analysis of murder and my previous research (1974).

But although the simple linear specification is found to be an inferior format, the qualitative deterrent effects of apprehension, conviction, and execution risks have been observed in my time-series analysis even upon the use of this specification. The results have already been illustrated in my article (1975b, p. 219). I might add that the ranking of the elasticities of the three deterrence variables that are inferred from those results is the same as the ranking predicted by the theory.

## III

In their Section III Passell and Taylor speculate that even if my results were valid, an increase in execution risk might raise the murder rate, if the risk of execution is sufficiently negatively related to the risk of conviction. Since their analysis in this regard is not directed against any of my own recommendations, I take it to be their independent contribution to the development of policy implications. Unfortunately, their discussion is not based on systematic theoretical or empirical analyses. P-T defend the proposition concerning a negative association between execution and conviction risks by reliance on "legal experts" and

---

[7]For example, I have estimated the standard error of the regression coefficient associated with $PXQ_2$ in the subperiod 1935–63 to be 0.041 as against 0.019 in the subperiod 1935–69 and 0.016 in the subperiod 1935–67.

"legal reform movement leaders" from the nineteenth and the twentieth centuries. We are not told, however, on what scientific grounds these opinions are based.

The "positive" analysis of optimal social defense against murder contained in my (1975a) paper does offer some implications in connection with the relationship between execution and conviction risks (see also the mathematical appendix to my 1977 article) but these implications hardly amount to any automatic rules. The theoretical analysis shows that execution and conviction risks may act as "substitutes," for example, in response to changes in exogenous factors such as *unwarranted* administrative or judicial edicts that affect the frequency of enforcement of the death penalty. But the risks of execution and conviction could also move in the same direction as a consequence of a change in the perceived risk of victimization from murder and related crime. For example, if there were universal agreement among all law enforcement agencies that the rate of crime exceeds what society should bear given its opportunities, then, with appropriate resource expenditures to produce socially optimal magnitudes of deterrence variables, there would be no reason to expect movements in execution risk to generate opposite movements in conviction risk.

I have provided some evidence bearing on the empirical significance of the association between execution and conviction risks for related movements in the rate of murder during the period of my time-series sample (see my 1975a paper, p. 415). It is inconsistent with P-T's predictions. Furthermore, the assertion that execution and conviction risks are negatively associated as a rule is clearly contradicted by the United States experience of the last 15 years. Although the probability of execution decreased dramatically between 1960 and 1968 or thereafter, compensatory movements in probabilities of conviction or arrest are not observed. On the contrary, the estimated unconditional risk of conviction actually decreased from 39 percent in 1960 to about 31 percent in 1969.

As I have repeatedly emphasized, even if effective as a deterrent, capital punishment may not be socially desirable. But the allegation that reintroduction of the punishment necessarily leads to a rise in murder cannot be defended.[8]

## IV

My paper (1975a, p. 416) cautioned that the empirical absence of a theoretically important variable—the severity of imprisonment for murder—may have affected the results obtained. Critics of my work also have speculated about potential biases due to absence of a wide gamut of additional factors ranging from latent effects of the baby boom to the collapse of societal values that allegedly account for the results. While the possibility of bias due to omitted variables never can be denied, some of the critics' arguments can be tested. Passell and Taylor, like Bowers and Pierce, argue that the observed negative association between the murder rate and the risk of execution is an artifact of the 1960's—a period in which the rates of other crimes increased even more sharply.[9] If the effect of $P^0e \mid c$ were an artifact of the 1960's however, it should have also affected the trends in other crimes—even crimes against property, which are not expected to be sensitive to

[8] Passell and Taylor carried this argument *ad absurdum* through an exercise (see their fn. 9) where they argue that if society fixed arrests at a constant level, then an increase in executions necessarily will increase murders even though the risk of execution restrains the murder rate. Their analysis is internally inconsistent and their inferences are erroneous. The point is elaborated in the author and Joel Gibbons.

[9] The mere fact that the rate of increase in robbery and other property crimes slightly exceeded that of murder between 1963–69 (68 percent as against 62 percent; Passell and Taylor's quoted numbers are inaccurate) but fell short of it between 1963–73, provides no systematic evidence for the position of the critics, contrary to their assertion, because movements in each crime reflect changes in arrest and conviction risks and other variables that are specific to that crime. Furthermore, P-T ignore the fact that from the late 1930's to 1963 the murder rate in the United States has been continuously on the *decline* while the opposite trend is observed in connection with other felonies. Against this background of conflicting long-term trends in murder and other crimes, the increase in the murder rate since 1964 is even more significant.

TABLE 1—MURDER SUPPLY FUNCTIONS, EXECUTING STATES *GLS* ESTIMATES[a]
($\hat{\beta}/S_{\hat{\beta}}$ in parentheses)

| | Sample | NOB | "$R^2$" | C (Constant) | T | $P^0c$ | $P^0e\,|\,c$ PX4Q | PX5 | NW | AGE | URB | $D_{40}$ |
|---|---|---|---|---|---|---|---|---|---|---|---|---|
| (1) | 1940 | 33 | .9529 | 8.93 | −0.206 | −0.709 | −0.382 | | 0.443 | −2.051 | −0.799 | |
| | | | | (2.96) | (−1.70) | (−4.90) | (−3.65) | | (6.29) | (−2.29) | (−4.68) | |
| (2) | 1940 | 33 | .9512 | 10.34 | −0.269 | −0.678 | | −0.339 | 0.485 | −2.372 | −0.814 | |
| | | | | (3.39) | (−2.17) | (−4.70) | | (−3.45) | (7.14) | (−2.57) | (−4.69) | |
| (3) | 1950 | 34 | .9281 | 3.85 | −0.501 | −0.765 | −0.303 | | 0.488 | −0.215 | −0.601 | |
| | | | | (1.42) | (−3.88) | (−5.18) | (−4.65) | | (6.57) | (−0.30) | (−2.76) | |
| (4) | 1950 | 35 | .9473 | 4.46 | −0.574 | −0.794 | | −0.353 | 0.436 | −0.071 | −0.769 | |
| | | | | (1.94) | (−5.27) | (−6.31) | | (−6.24) | (6.92) | (−0.12) | (−4.20) | |
| (5) | Pooled | 67 | .9279 | 3.85 | −0.394 | −0.700 | −0.311 | | 0.453 | −0.347 | −0.607 | 0.469 |
| | | | | (2.04) | (−4.31) | (−6.98) | (−5.94) | | (8.95) | (−0.64) | (−4.36) | (3.31) |
| (6) | Pooled | 68 | .9341 | 4.06 | −0.461 | −0.727 | | −0.334 | 0.432 | −0.216 | −0.674 | 0.446 |
| | | | | (2.26) | (−5.30) | (−7.55) | | (−6.59) | (8.89) | (−0.42) | (−5.11) | (3.32) |

[a] All variables except $D_{40}$ are measured in natural logarithms. All are weighted by the square root of the urban population (see fn. 12). See text for variable definitions. Computations performed via the Econometric Software Package. The "$R^2$" reported are for the transformed regression equations with the weighted variables.

changes in execution risk. Preliminary research into the trend of crime in the United States based on a similar econometric specification and time period shows that for all offenses as a group and for crimes against property, changes in the crime rate are insensitive to changes in the execution risk measures. The partial correlation between the murder rate and execution risk does not appear to be artifactual.

Moreover, an independent test of the basic propositions of the model and an investigation of the effect of additional variables are included in my 1977 study based on cross-state regression analyses for the years 1940 and 1950. These years are chosen because the level of enforcement of capital punishment in individual executing states appears to have been sufficiently high and variable to permit a meaningful test of the hypothesis of no deterrence. And the general uniformity in the reporting of urban crime rates (the dependent variable) in the FBI's *Uniform Crime Reports* permits some tests of temporal and cross-sectional homogeneity.

A full analysis of the data and the regression results is included in my 1977 article; Table 1 includes a few illustrations derived from available data on states that had executions. In the equations reported[10] explanatory variables are selected by the availability and compatibility of relevant data in 1940 and 1950. The term $P^0c$ is a measure of the unconditional probability of conviction of murder: the ratio of all commitments to state prisons for murder to an estimate of the total number of murders known in a given state. The term PX4Q is a measure of the conditional probability of execution given conviction, based on the average number of executions for murder in the four years preceding and including the sample year, and PX5 is an alternative measure based on the mean number of all executions over a five-year period. The T denotes the median time served in state prisons for murder by prisoners released in 1951. Because of data exigencies it is used as a measure of anticipated length of imprisonment in both 1940 and 1950. The terms NW, AGE, and URB denote, respectively, the percentages of nonwhites, the age group 15–24, and the urban population in the state population. They are introduced partly to serve as "correctors" for relevant variables. The term $D_{40}$ is a dummy variable distinguishing observa-

[10] The regressions are estimated via weighted ordinary least squares. Tests for homoscedasticity led to weighting by the square root of the urban population to generate generalized least squares estimates.

tions from 1940 (1) and 1950 (0) in the pooled regressions. It is introduced to account for potential data differences and the use of the variable $T$ in both 1940 and 1950, as well as for the effect of missing variables, such as the income distribution and changes in medical technology (see the author, 1975a, p. 407) which in the time-series analysis may have been accounted for by the trend variable.[11] The general investigation also has examined the impact of the level and distribution of income in the population, the effects of unemployment and labor force participation rates, the significance of alternative measures of the age distribution, and the effect of the risk of death through police intervention. The investigation has also dealt with interdependencies between murder and other related crimes. While many of these additional factors appear to be relevant, the reported effects of the basic set of deterrence and demographic variables introduced in Table 1 is found to be essentially unaffected by their exclusion.

The few reported results speak for themselves. The introduction of imprisonment severity aids in the estimation of deterrence effects. The impact of conviction risk is compatible with the one reported in the time-series analysis.[12] The fact that the

[11]The exclusion of $D_{40}$ from equations (5) and (6) in Table 1 here does not alter the effects of deterrence or any demographic variables other than $AGE$. Evidently, the latter is systematically higher in 1940 than in 1950.

[12]The regression results reported are not strictly comparable since they are obtained through different estimation procedures. In particular, the $GLS$ estimates may not be consistent. However, time-series results derived through application of $OLS$ techniques for serially correlated errors are quite consistent with the results derived through Fair's simultaneous equation procedure. The following equation has been estimated through the simple Cochrane-Orcutt iterative procedure for the effective period 1935–69. It is comparable to equation (3) of Table 3 in my (1975a) paper;

$$lnq^0 = -4.541 - 1.033\Delta^*P^0a - 0.292\Delta^*P^0c\,|\,a$$
$$\phantom{lnq^0 =} (-1.58)\ (-1.96) \qquad (-3.58)$$
$$-0.071\Delta^*PXQ_{1\,-1} - 1.203\Delta^*L + 0.513\Delta^*A$$
$$(-3.83) \qquad\quad (-1.52) \qquad (2.45)$$
$$+\,1.228\Delta^*Y_p + 0.068\Delta^*U - 0.045\Delta^*T$$
$$(4.91) \qquad\ (2.68) \qquad (-6.88)$$
$$\hat{\rho} = 0.023;\ \hat{\sigma}_e = 0.043;\ D.W. = 1.73$$

elasticity associated with the conditional execution risk measures appears to be higher in absolute magnitude is not incompatible with the proposition that the execution risk effect estimated from data for execution states *only* will be higher than that estimated from aggregate national data (see the author, 1975a, p. 408). As predicted by the theory, the estimated elasticity with respect to conviction risk exceeds that with respect to execution risk. The basic results are found to be stable over time and across regions.

Despite this evidence I do not claim that my general investigation has proven the validity of the general deterrence hypothesis definitively. Many difficulties in the theory's empirical implementation remain and these must be addressed in future work. However, the observed compatibility between the reported time-series and cross-section results, not always present in applications of economic theory, accords further support to the economic approach to criminal activity.

## REFERENCES

**W. J. Bowers and G. L. Pierce,** "The Illusion of Deterrence in Isaac Ehrlich's Research on Capital Punishment," *Yale Law J.,* Dec. 1975, *85,* 187–208.

**G. Box and D. Cox,** "An Analysis of Transformations," *J. Royal Statist. Soc.,* Series B, Jan. 1964, *26,* 211–43.

**I. Ehrlich,** "The Deterrent Effect of Capital Punishment: A Question of Life and Death," Nat. Bur. Econ. Res. working pap., series no. 18, 1973.

———, "Participation in Illegitimate Activities: An Economic Analysis," in Gary S. Becker and William M. Landes, eds., *Essays in the Economics of Crime and Punishment,* New York 1974, 68–134.

———, (1975a) "The Deterrent Effect of Capital Punishment: A Question of Life and Death," *Amer. Econ. Rev.,* June 1975, *65,* 397–417.

———, (1975b) "Deterrence: Evidence and Inference," *Yale Law J.,* Dec. 1975, *85,* 209–27.

———, "Capital Punishment and Deterrence: Some Further Thoughts and Additional Evidence," *J. Polit. Econ.*, forthcoming, Aug. 1977.

_____ and J. C. Gibbons, "On the Measurement of the Deterrent Effect of Capital Punishment and the Theory of Deterrence," *J. Legal Stud.*, Jan. 1977, 6.

B. Forst, V. Filatov, and L. R. Klein, "The Deterrent Effect of Capital Punishment:

An Assessment of the Estimates," unpub. paper, 1976.

R. C. Fair, "The Estimation of Simultaneous Equation Models with Lagged Endogenous Variables and First Order Serially Correlated Errors," *Econometrica*, May 1970, *38*, 507-16.

U.S. Department of Justice, Federal Bureau of Investigation, *Uniform Crime Report*, Washington, various years.

# 33

# Field Experiments in General Deterrence: Preferring the Tortoise to the Hare

## Franklin E. Zimring

"... an increase in the expenditure on police and courts in 1965 by $32 million could have reduced the loss from felonies by about $83 million."

Isaac Ehrlich, "Participation in Illegitimate Activities, An Economic Analysis," in Beeker and Landis, eds., *Essays in the Economics of Crime and Punishment* (1974), p. 110.

"One area ... received no preventive patrol. In the second area, police visibility was increased two to three times its usual level. In the third area ... normal patrol was maintained ...
[T]he three areas experienced no significant differences in ... crime."

Police Chief McNamara, *The Kansas City Preventive Patrol Experiment* (1974), p. iii.

The deterrent effect of criminal sanctions has long been a topic of lively debate, yet very little systematic research on the impact of law enforcement and sanctions existed until the relatively recent past. Over the past decade, however, empirical research on the deterrent impact of criminal sanctions has increased dramatically. Social psychologists, sociologists, economists, and statisticians have used a wide variety of methodologies to assess the nature and extent of deterrence variables. Within the literature emerging from this new generation of deterrence studies, there are two quite different strategies for producing data and insights on deterrence.

One approach is to gather aggregate data on crime and other social indicators and to study the variations in crime that occur between jurisdictions or over time. The concept is one of studying changes that occur naturally, attempting to control for all the other differences that occur in nature either between areas or over time to isolate

the contribution of general deterrence to differences in noted crime rates. Statistical tools, ranging from simple regression to complex simultaneous equations, are employed in the analysis of these data, and significant findings are frequently reported in the literature.[1]

The second approach attempts to assess the impact of changes in law enforcement or punishment policy by closely following what happens after particular policy shifts occur. Comparisons in reported crime rates are made before and after the policy change. In some studies, comparison or control areas are used to reduce the possibility that changes in the dependent variable (usually crime rates) are inaccurately attributed to the policy shift being examined. In general, the results reported in these "real change" studies have been less exciting than the estimates of

deterrent effectiveness derived from some of the cross-sectional and time studies.[2]

The Kansas City Preventive Patrol Experiment falls squarely within the tradition of this second approach to studying deterrence through attempts to induce and analyze "real" policy changes. The research reported is of special significance because the experiment utilized random assignment to produce control areas. The study is, in this regard, the most ambitious and most successful field experiment in law enforcement in the 1970s. For this reason, the patrol experiment is a suitable

---

*Franklin E. Zimring is Professor of Law and Director of the Center for Studies in Criminal Justice, University of Chicago Law School.*

---

[1] For a partial list of these studies, see Gordon Tullock, "Does Punishment Deter Crime?" The Public Interest (36, 1974), 103-11 (cited hereafter as Tullock). and Charles R. Tittle and Charles H. Logan, "Sanctions and Deviance: Evidence and Remaining Questions," Law & Society Review (Spring, 1973), 371.

---

[2] See, e.g., Barry Schwartz, "The Effect in Philadelphia of Pennsylvania's Increased Penalties for Rape and Attempted Rape," Journal of Criminal Law, Criminology and Penal Science (59, 1968), 509; H. Laurence Ross, "Law, Science, and Accidents: The British Safety Act of 1967," Journal of Legal Studies (2, 1973), 1; F. Zimring, "Firearms and Federal Law: The Gun Control Act of 1968," Journal of Legal Studies (4, 1975), 133 (a partial bibliography of intervention studies is in note 5 at p. 134); Mitre Corporation, High Impact Anticrime Program, National Level Evaluation Final Report, 1976.

---

From Franklin E. Zimring, "Field Experiments in General Deterrence: Preferring the Tortoise to the Hare," 3 (1-2) *Evaluation* 132-135 (1976). Copyright 1976 by the Russell Sage Foundation.

vehicle for discussing the uses and limits of experimentation in law enforcement, and for comparing the advantages of this approach with the quick and inexpensive insights of cross-sectional and time series approaches.

My own view is that policy experiments will gradually increase our modest knowledge of the impact of law enforcement on crime rates. In the long run, this contribution will be more important than the knowledge base supplied by even the most sophisticated attempts to study natural variations. To social scientists interested in rapid progress, this assessment will provide small comfort. Those who recall with affection the parable of the hare and the tortoise may be more favorably disposed.

## The Limits of Field Experimentation

Did the Kansas City Patrol Experiment prove that preventive patrol has no value in reducing crime? The obvious answer to this question is no, but a restatement of what the Kansas City findings teach us is a useful introduction to the problems and limits of field experimentation. My own version of the inference that can properly be drawn from the technical report of the study is this: "Increasing preventive patrol by a factor of two or more for twelve months in car-patrolled areas similar to those studied probably does not reduce the incidence of crime to a great extent." Each of the qualifications in this somewhat inelegant summary illustrates a limit on the utility of the method.

To begin, my assessment of the results speaks only of the comparison between the "proactive" (increased patrol) and "control" areas. The degree to which the "reactive" police beats conformed to the conditions the researchers meant to produce is in some dispute.[3] Without taking sides in that dispute, the problem can be used to illustrate a general principle of great significance: no field experiment in criminal justice will ever be executed in total conformity to its plan. Kansas City is an example of modest deviation.

Modest deviation is about the best we can expect from attempts to alter complex ongoing systems in predetermined ways.

My version of the Kansas City findings is limited to "car-patrolled areas similar to those studied" because there are great differences between areas and between car patrol and foot patrol that could lead to substantial differences in the impact of variations in patrol intensity. The problem of generalization is a persistent one in experimental science. Our capacity to generalize from particular experimental findings to broader behavioral conclusions depends on how much we know about the impact of other conditions. In law enforcement and crime control, we know very little. This knowledge gap hampers our capacity to generalize from experiments at the same time that it makes such experiments necessary.

There are a number of good reasons why any conclusion from this field experiment must be stated in probabilistic terms. When crime rates are used as a dependent variable, they must be measured imperfectly. Crimes reported by the police are a partial sample of all offenses and may be influenced by police desires to see the experiment work in desired directions. For different reasons, surveys of victims are imperfect measures of crime and also introduce problems of sampling error at the same time that they make the experimental design relatively insensitive: decreases in offenses must be fairly substantial before we can attribute any noted change to factors other than chance variation.[4]

All of these problems can be ameliorated, although the cures are neither quick nor inexpensive. Crime can be measured with both official and survey instruments, as was the case in Kansas City, and if both indicators perform consistently, confidence in the result can be increased. The experiment can and should be replicated. Experimental

shifts in foot patrol can be carefully measured.

But there are natural limits on the capacity to increase knowledge of crime control through experimentation, not the least of which are the time and cost of experimentation. There are also political and moral limits on the conditions that can be varied in the name of experimentation. The political limits are obvious and substantial. Imagine the fate of the brave researcher who would disarm some ghetto police to study the impact on injury and death rates. Putting police or citizens in potentially hazardous positions is also an obvious example of a moral constraint that limits the range of true experimentation. The moral problems with experiments that vary punishments are, to my mind, equally substantial. The answer to these problems, to the extent an answer exists, is to study those policy shifts that occur as a result of the political process. The rigor and reliability of such efforts are inferior to the controlled experiment; the degree of variance that can be observed will be limited by the political process. But if such evaluations are based on experimental logic and the results are reported with caution, such studies are probably the best technology available for issues not suited to true experiments.

The existing inventory of "intervention" studies displays a wide variation in both methodological rigor and substantive conclusion. Field experimentation in law enforcement has rarely been undertaken. Quasi-experimental evaluations of topics as diverse as variations in police patrol, punishment for rape, the introduction of portable breathalizer tests, drunk driving enforcement, and crackdown on speeders have produced decidedly mixed results.[5] In part, this may be due to the insensitivity of rigorous interrupted-time-series analysis to relatively small or relatively gradual declines in offenses or offense-related variables. It is clear, however, that if "intervention" evaluations are to be the primary building blocks for deterrence theory, progress will be slow and empirically justified generalizations difficult, a condition that is typical of social science.[6]

---

[3]See the article by Richard Larson in this issue and the dialogue on this topic between Richard Larson and the principal authors of the Kansas City report in the January, 1976, Journal of Criminal Justice.

[4]This problem is less serious in settings like Kansas City and the "high impact" program, where the amount of resources invested in prevention is great, than in cases where change occurs more gradually or is less costly. For a case study in which this issue is more troublesome, see H. Laurence Ross, "The Scandinavian Myth: The Effectiveness of Drinking-and-Driving Legislation in Sweden and Norway," Journal of Legal Studies (4, 1975), 285 ff (see especially pp. 309-10).

[5]Negative or inconclusive results are reported in all the analyses mentioned in note 2 except the Ross article.

[6]See Franklin E. Zimring and Gordon J. Hawkins, Deterrence: The Legal Threat in Crime Control (Chicago: University of Chicago, 1973), 339-367.

## Do We Need Experimentation?

From a social policy standpoint, it would be unwise to make a substantial investment of resources to prove the obvious. There are a number of scholars who believe the effectiveness of deterrent countermeasures is not only obvious, but has already been proved. Gordon Tullock, for one, finds "that punishment will indeed deter crime" because "if you increase the cost of something, less will be consumed."[1] Putting aside the issue of whether he is reasoning by analogy or by deduction, the simple statement of that theorem has few policy implications, because one does not know by how much one needs to increase "costs" to achieve palpable deterrent benefits. Tullock, I think, would agree that more than an axiom is needed to support major changes in punishment policy. But he argues that a large number of studies using multiple regression give substantial support to the deterrence hypothesis and that, since the economists and sociologists conducting these studies used "statistical tools that were somewhat different," the sociological studies "can be taken as an independent confirmation of the economists' approach."[8]

All of the studies Tullock refers to are statistical manipulations of the variations in crime and sanction rates that occur over time and between jurisdictions. Surprisingly, no study of a discrete attempt purposefully to manipulate deterrence variables is mentioned in his review article or in much of the rest of the emerging literature on deterrence.[9]

That does not mean Professor Tullock lacks for bibliography. Since 1970, the cross-sectional study of crime and punishment using multiple regression has become a cottage industry. Almost all studies of variations in rates of imprisonment per 100 crimes and rates of crime have noted a negative correlation between the two, and many (but not all) researchers reporting these results have attributed that relationship to the operation of the general deterrent effect of sanctions.[10] The relationship between the length of prison sentences and the crime rate is a more ambiguous matter. For most crimes, in most studies, there is no significant negative simple correlation between the average length of a prison sentence and the rate of crime. By the time additional control variables are added to the equation, weighted to the tastes of the researcher, and processed through the sophisticated machinery of statistical analysis, the published results are in disagreement, if not disarray.[11]

This is a relatively minor matter. The real problem is whether or not even the most sophisticated analyses of time-series and cross-sectional data can provide a scientifically rigorous test of the nature and extent of general deterrence. Putting aside such imposing tactical problems as the horrible quality of most crime statistics, my skepticism about the use of sophisticated statistical methods over time and between areas as a mechanism of measuring deterrence is based on three problems:

**1** Lack of information about, and capacity to control for, other factors that influence variations in crime rates over time and between areas.

**2** The problem of distinguishing between relatively high punishment rates as a cause of low crime rates and relatively low crime rates as a cause of relatively high punishment rates.

**3** The fact that such studies shed no light on the issue of how systems that differ in punishment policy come to be different.

The first problem is well phrased by Tullock: "Statistically testing deterrence is not easy because the prospect of punishment obviously is not the *only* thing that affects the frequency with which crimes are committed. The crime rate varies with the degree of urbanization, the demographic composition of the population, the distribution of wealth, and many other circumstances."[12] Tullock continues:

**"Some statistical technique is necessary to take care of these factors—and such techniques are now available. Using multiple regression . . . it is possible to put figures on each of these variables into the same equation and to see how much they influence the dependent variable, which, in this case, is the rate of a specific crime. Although there are difficulties, this procedure will give a set of numbers called coefficients that are measures of the effect of each of the purported causative factors on the rate of commission of the given crime. If punishment deters crime, it will show up in these figures as a coefficient that is both significant and negative."[13]**

The problem is that crime does indeed vary with "many circumstances." But we don't know what many of those circumstances are, or their predictive power under different social conditions. If one views a cross-sectional analysis as essentially a comparison of crime in South Dakota with crime in New Jersey, the question becomes whether or not it is possible to explain and measure all the differences other than criminal justice policy that account for differential crime propensities in those two states. If one views a time series analysis as essentially a comparison of the United States in 1970 with the United States in 1960, the problem becomes one of identifying all the crime-related differences that time has produced, measuring these with precision, and allocating any residual effects to changes in criminal justice policy. In an important sense, one must know everything about the non-deterrence factors that influence crime before one can find out anything about deterrence from uncontrolled time and area comparisons. Even then, it would be necessary to measure with some precision variables, such as the moral structure of a community, that only the bravest of the computer experts would ever attempt to quantify.

I do not believe our present knowledge of the factors that influence variations in crime permits us to control statistically for all differences between South Dakota and New Jersey other than criminal justice policy. Instead, it is presently possible to use a great variety of different cross-sectional statistical "controls," and it is beginning to appear that the results one obtains at the "residual" or deterrence end of the equation are heavily dependent on how the nondeterrent variables are selected, weighted, and measured.[14]

The second problem in interpreting studies of natural variation is that of separating causes from consequences. Assume that the total crime rate experienced by a society both influences and is influenced by criminal justice

---

Tullock, p. 105.

Tullock, p. 107.

See, e.g., Tullock, 110-11. See also Ernest van den Haag, Punishing Criminals (New York: Basic Books, 1975), 133-142. One intervention study, a classroom experiment, is mentioned.

Jack Gibbs, a scholar whom Professor Tullock credits with the first published cross-sectional research in this field, is skeptical of the implications for deterrence. See Gibbs, Crime, Punishment, and Deterrence (New York: Elsevier, 1975).

See Gibbs, cited above, pp. 145-188.

Tullock, p. 104.

Tullock, p. 104.

policy. Under such circumstances, a higher crime rate may reduce the rate of imprisonments per hundred crimes to a certain degree for reasons that have nothing to do with the weakening of general deterrence, while at the same time some increase in crime will occur that is attributable to less credible deterrent threats. Separating out that portion of the variation in the crime rate that is caused by changes in punishment policy does not seem possible using exclusively cross-sectional data. Whether or not some combination of cross-sectional and time series studies can successfully deal with this problem is a matter for debate. But whatever one's final theoretical position on this issue, the existing inventory of studies falls far short of providing a satisfactory solution to this problem.

The third problem of studies of natural variation in crime control policy

---

"Compare Isaac Ehrlich, "Participation in Illegitimate Activities: A Theoretical and Empirical Investigation," Journal of Political Economy (81), 521, with Brian E. Forst, "Participation in Illegitimate Activities: Some Further Empirical Evidence," Policy Analysis (Summer, 1976).

is that such studies shed no light on why punishment policy varies in real world settings and thus on how easy it would be to induce on a deliberate basis the kind of policy changes that occur naturally. Although the study of discrete attempts at intervention teach us the difficulties involved in changing policy, the studies of natural variation cannot investigate the causes of policy difference. One suspects that many of the characteristics of a society that influence its punishment policy also influence its crime rate. Unless all of these factors can be controlled for, the observed statistical relationship between punishment policy and crime may be spurious. Of equal importance is the fact that many readers of the literature that is emerging from multiple regression research may be tempted to think of punishment policy as an easily manipulable independent variable that can be shifted from "low" to "high" with a flip of the public-policy switch. Rarely is this the case in the real world.

## Conclusion

I am not arguing that studies of natural variation are without value. They are useful, in my view, more to generate

and refine hypotheses than to confirm them. And the use of comparative and time studies can be a useful complement to other methods of increasing knowledge. My fear is, however, that over-reliance on manipulations of secondary data are competing with experiments rather than complementing them. And my guess is that as the number of nonintervention studies increases, the apparent clarity of the results will diminish. We are already observing deviant "crime-generating" models leading to contradictory results. It is this guess about the econometric studies that leads me to the parable of the hare and the tortoise. The hare, we recall, got off to a fast start, but encountered problems related to overconfidence. The tortoise, slow but steady, prevailed.

Yet the parable is inappropriate in a deeper sense. Methodologies and disciplines should mesh rather than clash. Deterrence research should not become yet another example of what one observer called the "cross-sterilization of the social sciences." Our ignorance is vast. There is enough to go around. Humility in the use of a variety of imperfect methods is the real hope for sustained progress in learning more about the impact of law enforcement on crime.

# 34

# Transitional Aid for Released Prisoners: Evidence from the Life Experiment

## Charles D. Mallar and Craig V. D. Thornton

## ABSTRACT

Findings are presented from a controlled experiment designed to test the effectiveness of transitional aid programs for ex-prisoners in reducing theft crimes. Upon release from prison, a sample of men with high (ex ante) probabilities of committing theft crimes were enrolled in treatment and control groups. One year after release, a group receiving financial aid had significantly fewer arrests for theft crimes than did the controls. Calculations of the social benefit/cost ratio show that the benefits of transitional income maintenance substantially outweighed the costs. In contrast, the provision of job-placement assistance turned out to have no significant effect on post-release behavior.

## I. INTRODUCTION

Theft crimes have come to be analyzed by economists as utility/profit maximizing decisions made by rational people. In this framework, the conventional method of reducing crime is to change the rewards and costs associated with various activities. Attempts are made to make socially acceptable activities more desirable and criminal activities less desirable by increasing the costs associated with crime. This is done either by enhancing the rewards to legitimate activities or by increasing the expected punishment from crimi-

*Mallar is a Senior Research Economist at Mathematica Policy Research, on leave from Johns Hopkins University. Thornton is a Research Economist at Mathematica Policy Research.*

\* Financial support for this research paper was received from the American Bar Association, from the Employment and Training Administration of the U.S. Department of Labor (Grant 21-11-75-19), and from Mathematica Policy Research. Helpful comments on a previous draft were received from the editor and referees of this Journal. The conclusions drawn and any factual errors that remain are the sole responsibility of the authors. [Manuscript received March 1977; accepted September 1977].

From Charles D. Mallar and Craig V.D. Thornton, "Transitional Aid for Released Prisoners: Evidence from the Life Experiment," XIII (2) *The Journal of Human Resources* 208-236 (1978). Copyright 1978 by the University of Wisconsin Press.

nal actions (increasing the probability of being apprehended and convicted, making sentences more severe, etc.).

The recent Living Insurance for Ex-Offenders (LIFE) experiment conducted in the Baltimore area applied this concept to a particularly important class of criminals, the repeat theft offenders. The program's objective was to increase the choice set of released prisoners and thereby raise the opportunity cost of crime. Income-maintenance and job-placement services were provided to ex-prisoners for a short period after their release in an effort to allow them to engage in job-search activities and establish themselves in the labor market. It was hoped that this aid would give the men freedom to choose among a variety of activities so that they would not be forced by economic necessity to return to crime.

## II. THE EXPECTED IMPACT OF LIFE PROGRAMS

Recent studies of the financial condition of prisoners released from state institutions (see Lenihan [11], Witte [27], and Horowitz [8], for example) find that personal resources are low and public assistance generally unavailable. Most of these ex-prisoners are ineligible for unemployment insurance benefits due to their lack of recent employment and subsequent loss of entitlement while incarcerated. They are categorically ineligible for many welfare programs by virtue of their age, employability, family status, or other such factors. Socioeconomic studies have observed that ex-offenders in this type of environment fall into a cycle proceeding from prison release to unemployment to a return to crime and rearrest (see Pownall [17], for example). The LIFE program attempted to break this cycle by providing its participants with both the means and the opportunity to search for gainful employment.

Income maintenance should help to alleviate budget constraints and enable released prisoners to search for better jobs, to develop their human capital in other ways, to participate in more socially desirable leisure activities, and to live more normal life styles during their assimilation back into society. Economic approaches emphasizing income constraints, human capital, and the disutility from criminal activities all suggest that financial aid will lead to a reduction in the number of theft recidivists (see Becker [2], Ehrlich [4], and Block and Heineke [3] for a more detailed development of this general theory).[1] The provision of job counseling and placement services, since they facilitate the adjustment into the labor market, should also tend to reduce recidivism.

Expectations regarding the impact of the LIFE program were primarily derived from theoretical considerations, since prior to the fielding of this

---

[1] While the threat of loss of LIFE transfers and the relaxation of income constraints may reduce recidivism during the program, the expected effects on employment are less clear. The empirical results presented below suggest that the ex-prisoners receiving income maintenance had reduced employment during the program as they searched longer for higher paying jobs and enrolled in school or training courses.

experiment, there was no hard evidence on how released prisoners would respond to that type of assistance. Surveys of general populations and simulations of the effects of other post-release programs were only suggestive. In addition, the only previous research dealing with a system similar to LIFE consisted of internal evaluation reports of a stipend program for released prisoners in the state of Washington [26].

The findings from the evaluation reports on the Washington program are extremely difficult to interpret because the treatments vary due to the arbitrariness of the program's coverage and the high degree of administrative discretion allowed. In addition, the program does not include a control group, and researchers have not had a valid comparison group available. As a result, the empirical findings (specifically that there is a very small and insignificant decrease in aggregate recidivism after the program implementation) provide little evidence on the program's effectiveness. Comparisons of the current rate of recidivism to aggregate data for years just prior to the start of the program and comparisons of sample means for nonequivalent groups are not very helpful. The before vs. after comparison is so confounded by changing economic conditions and time trends in criminal behavior that the results must be discounted, and comparisons of sample means for nonequivalent groups are not relevant. Overall, the existing empirical literature cannot be the primary basis for expectations regarding LIFE.

## III. THE BALTIMORE LIFE PROGRAM

Using the expectations outlined in the previous section, the LIFE program was designed to reduce recidivism by providing both financial and job-placement assistance to released prisoners. The program was fielded in Baltimore during the fiscal years of 1972 through 1974 as a controlled experiment that was funded by the Employment and Training Administration of the U.S. Department of Labor. Since LIFE was viewed as a pilot experiment, only those prisoners with a high likelihood of responding to the treatment were included.[2] Eligibility for enrollment was limited to a highly selective subset of males, released from Maryland's state prisons, who planned to return to the Baltimore metropolitan area. The target population was limited to ex-offenders with a high probability of committing theft crimes and with no known history of alcohol or narcotic abuse. Prisoners who were first offenders, had never committed a property crime, were over 45 years old, had been on work release for more than three months, or had savings in excess of $400 were judged to have a relatively low probability of committing a theft crime and were excluded from the experiment.

---

2  A second set of experimental programs is currently under way in Georgia and Texas—the Transitional Aid Research Project (TARP).

TABLE 1
CHARACTERISTICS OF PARTICIPANTS
IN THE BALTIMORE LIFE EXPERIMENTS[a]

| Characteristics | All Partici- pants | Finan- cial Aid & Job Place- ment | Financial Aid Only | Job Place- ment Only | Control |
|---|---|---|---|---|---|
| Number of observations | 432 | 108 | 108 | 108 | 108 |
| Average age in years | 24.8 | 25.3 | 25.0 | 24.8 | 24.2 |
| Percent completed high school | 12% | 13% | 10% | 11% | 12% |
| Percent white | 12% | 12% | 8% | 8% | 20% |
| Percent having held job for over one year | 57% | 61% | 54% | 57% | 56% |
| Percent not arrested for over one year between incarcerations | 56% | 59% | 49% | 62% | 56% |
| Percent arrested *fewer* than three times | 9% | 8% | 7% | 14% | 7% |
| Percent arrested in the first year after release for any crimes | 53% | 50% | 49% | 58% | 56% |
| Percent arrested in the first year for theft crimes | 26.4% | 25% | 19.4% | 32.4% | 28.7% |

a   See Lenihan [12], App. B, for more detail.

For the trial program, the 432 prisoners who were enrolled in the pro-gram were randomly divided into four treatment groups. One group received financial aid of $60 a week for three months and job-placement services for up to one year after release. A second group received only the in-come-maintenance portion of the program, and a third received only the job-placement portion. A fourth group received no treatment and was followed as a comparison or "control" group (see [12] and [22] for more details on the sample strategy).

Table 1 presents some characteristics of the participants in the experiment. Not surprisingly, they come from extremely low socioeconomic backgrounds. Their educational attainments are minimal, their job attachments and work histories are weak, and the number of previous arrests is high. All these characteristics are strongly correlated with a higher incidence of recidivism (shown in the last two rows of Table 1).[4] Comparisons of the sample means in Table 1 support the hypothesis that the random assignments were successful in minimizing systematic differences among the treatment and control groups. All four groups are quite similar in terms of the pre-experiment variables observed. The only systematic differences in group means are found for those receiving financial aid who appear to be a slightly higher risk group (lower educational attainments, worse job histories, and more previous arrests).

As part of the experiment, detailed information was collected in order to describe and explain the socioeconomic status of participants. Baseline interviews were conducted prior to release in order to collect background information, including human capital variables such as age, education, vocational training, and criminal and employment histories. When the men returned to the Baltimore area upon release, they were interviewed again and the details of the program were explained. Follow-up interviews were subsequently administered once each month for a year following the person's release from prison in order to collect information concerning current activities and socioeconomic status (for example, employment status, earnings, arrests, welfare receipts, rents, etc.). However, in order to obtain more accurate data, court records rather than the interviews were used as the main source of arrest information.[5]

## IV. THE EFFECTIVENESS OF LIFE

Before any benefit/cost calculations can be made, it must be determined to what degree the program achieved what it set out to do, that is, reduce recidivism. In his initial study of the program, Lenihan [12] compared the mean rates of recidivism among experimental and control groups. He found that there was a sizable reduction in recidivism for those men receiving financial aid (27 percent fewer arrests for theft crimes other than auto theft). However, the provision for job-placement services did not appear to be effective in reducing recidivism. The sample mean differences in arrests for theft crimes between the financial-aid and control groups are given in the first five rows of Table 2, and the differences between the job-placement group and the controls are presented in Table 3.[7]

---

4  The rearrest rate after release from prison will be used throughout this paper as the measure of recidivism. It is the easiest measure to observe accurately and the least likely to be contaminated in a short-duration experiment.

5  In this case, as in Witte's study [27] of a sample of ex-prisoners in North Carolina, the participants in the experiment substantially underreported contacts with criminal justice authorities in personal interviews. However, estimates of the experimental effects derived from the interviews do not appear to be biased.

7  The control group used to calculate differences in sample means for the financial-aid program includes ex-offenders who received job-placement services only, as well as the zero treatment group.

TABLE 2

ESTIMATES OF REDUCED RECIDIVISM FOR THE FINANCIAL-AID GROUP REDUCTIONS IN ARRESTS

| Arrest Category | (1) All Respondents | (2) Financial-Aid Group | (3) Control Group | (4) Differential (2) – (3) | (5) Percent Differential $\frac{100 \times (4)}{(3)}$ |
|---|---|---|---|---|---|
| Robbery | 48 (11.1%) | 26 (12.0%) | 22 (10.2%) | 4 (1.9%) | 18.2% |
| Burglary | 40 (9.3%) | 13 (6.0%) | 27 (12.5%) | -14*** (-6.5%) | -51.9 |
| Auto theft[a] | 13 (3.0%) | 7 (3.2%) | 6 (2.8%) | 1 (0.5%) | 16.7 |
| Larceny (excluding auto) | 26 (6.0%) | 9 (4.2%) | 17 (7.9%) | -8* (-3.7%) | -47.1 |
| All theft crimes (excluding auto) | 114 (26.4%) | 48 (22.2%) | 66 (30.5%) | -18** (-8.3%) | -27.3 |
| All theft crimes, adjusted by regression[b] | 114.6 (26.5%) | 48.6 (22.5%) | 66 (30.5%) | -17.4** (-8.0%) | -26.3 |
| All theft crimes, adjusted in probit[c] | 111.5 (25.8%) | 45.5 (21.1%) | 66 (30.5%) | -20.5** (-9.5%) | -31.1 |
| All crimes | 230 (53.2%) | 107 (49.5%) | 123 (56.9%) | -16* (-7.4%) | -13.0 |

a   The auto-theft category in this table includes all arrests for "unauthorized use of an auto." All 13 of these arrests involved short-duration (possession for no more than an hour or two) "joy-riding" incidents (see Lenihan [12, p. 51]), and the cars were all abandoned intact. These crimes do not appear to be economically motivated, and the costs associated with them are much lower than the average for auto thefts. Therefore, the auto-theft category of crimes will be eliminated from most of the theft analysis in this paper. Since the financial-aid-group minus control-group differential is only one, the exclusion or inclusion of this crime type will have no appreciable effect on the absolute impact or benefit/cost estimates. Of course, the percent differential will be slightly smaller if the auto-theft category is included, since the base number of arrests is larger.

b   See Table 4 and the text for details on the regression equation used to adjust the sample means. The adjusted mean responses can can be interpreted as applicable to samples with identical composition in terms of the variables included in Table 4.

c   See Table 5 and the text for details on the probit equation used to adjust the sample means. The adjusted mean responses can be interpreted as applicable to samples with identical composition in terms of the variables in Table 5. The differential is computed for a probability of recidivism equal to the proportion of arrests in the control group (i.e., 30.5%).

*   Statistically significant at the 10 percent level.   **   Statistically significant at the 5 percent level.   ***   Statistically significant at the 1 percent level.

TABLE 3

ESTIMATES OF REDUCED RECIDIVISM FOR THE JOB-PLACEMENT GROUP REDUCTIONS IN ARRESTS[a]

| Arrest Category | (1) All Respondents | (2) Job-Placement Group | (3) Control Group | (4) Differential (2) − (3) | (5) Percent Differential $\frac{100 \times (4)}{(3)}$ |
|---|---|---|---|---|---|
| Robbery | 48 (11.1%) | 28 (13.0%) | 20 (9.3%) | 8 (3.7%) | 40.0% |
| Burglary | 40 (9.3%) | 22 (10.2%) | 18 (8.3%) | 4 (1.9%) | 22.0 |
| Auto theft[b] | 13 (3.0%) | 9 (4.2%) | 4 (1.9%) | 5 (2.3%) | 125.0 |
| Larceny (excluding auto) | 26 (6.0%) | 12 (5.6%) | 14 (6.5%) | −2 (−0.9%) | −14.3 |
| All theft crimes (excluding auto) | 114 (26.4%) | 62 (28.7%) | 52 (24.1%) | 10 (4.6%) | 19.2 |
| All theft crimes, adjusted by regression[c] | 115.4 (26.7%) | 63.4 (29.4%) | 52 (24.1%) | 11.4 (5.3%) | 21.9 |
| All theft crimes, adjusted by probit[d] | 115.4 (26.7%) | 63.4 (29.4%) | 52 (24.1%) | 11.4 (5.3%) | 21.9 |
| All crimes | 230 (53.2%) | 117 (54.2%) | 113 (52.3%) | 4 (1.9%) | 3.5 |

a  None of the differentials shown in this table is statistically significant.
b  See fn. a of Table 2.
c  See Table 4 and fn. b of Table 2.
d  See Table 5 and fn. c of Table 2.

TABLE 4
REGRESSION EQUATION USED TO ADJUST SAMPLE MEANS

| Variable | Definition | Coefficient | Standard Error |
|---|---|---|---|
| ARREST (dep. var.) | = 1 if the individual is arrested for robbery, burglary, or larceny in the first year; 0 otherwise | — | — |
| Constant | | 1.0433 | — |
| FINANCIAL | = 1 if the individual received financial aid from LIFE; 0 otherwise | −0.0804* | .0419 |
| JOBS | = 1 if the individual was offered job-placement assistance from LIFE; 0 otherwise | 0.0530 | .0418 |
| AGE | = the individual's age in years | −0.0449** | .0196 |
| AGESQ | = AGE squared | 0.0006** | .0003 |
| ED | = 1 if the individual completed high school; 0 otherwise | −0.0395 | .0612 |
| RACE | = 1 if the individual is white; 0 otherwise | −0.0505 | .0633 |

Number of observations = 432
$R^2 = .05219$
$\bar{R}^2 = .03881$
F statistic for the equation = 3.9007***
Equation:
$$ARREST = \beta_0 + \beta_1 FINANCIAL + \beta_2 JOBS + \beta_3 AGE + \beta_4 AGESQ + \beta_5 ED + \beta_6 RACE + \epsilon$$

\* Statistically significant at the 10 percent level. ** Statistically significant at the 5 percent level. *** Statistically significant at the 1 percent level.

When the sample mean differences are adjusted by regression techniques, the results are essentially unchanged (a representative equation is presented in Table 4).[8] The regression approach enables us to construct tests for hypothetical groups that are identical to each other with respect to the variables in the equation. The coefficient of the FINANCIAL variable (−0.0804) gives the percentage difference between the number of recidivists in the financial-aid and control groups. Thus, for a program involving

8 The similarity persists for models more complex than the one described in Table 4. Controlling for such factors as marital status, number of children, savings at release, housing status, number of previous arrests, vocational training experience, and previous work history did not alter the findings.

216 men (as in the experiment), the financial-aid group is expected to have 17.4 fewer arrests (.0804 × 216), or a 26 percent reduction in recidivism (17.4/66). Since the coefficient of *FINANCIAL* is significant at the 6 percent level (3 percent level for a one-tail test), the null hypothesis that the true difference is zero can be rejected with relative confidence.

The regression result for the job-placement variable, *JOBS*, indicates that this component of LIFE was ineffective. The coefficient is not only insignificant, but positive. The men who received job-placement assistance were more likely to recidivate than those who did not, and the hypothesis that this program had no effect on recidivism cannot be rejected.

The finding of a 26 percent reduction in recidivism for the income-maintenance program is only slightly smaller than the 27 percent difference in sample means. The fact that regression results correspond closely to those obtained by examining unadjusted differences in sample means should not be surprising. The explanatory power of the equations is very weak, and the groups have similar compositions (as seen in Table 1). Since there were no major differences in the personal characteristics of the experimental and control groups, controlling for such characteristics will not substantially change results.

The small differences in personal characteristics that were observed suggest that adjusting for them would probably lead to a slightly larger response estimate. Recall that the financial-aid group appears to be composed of men who would have higher probabilities of recidivism in the absence of the experimental program compared to those in the control group (see Table 1). Therefore, the regression findings of a slightly smaller response than that for the difference in sample means is somewhat surprising. In contrast, empirical results for a nonlinear probability model (see Table 5) are more in line with the expectation of a larger response estimate when we control for sample differences (a 31 percent reduction in recidivism vs. the 27 percent reduction for a difference in sample means estimate).

Nonlinear probability models are more appropriate specifications than least-squares regressions when the dependent variable is a dummy variable, as is the case here with *ARREST* (see Theil [20, pp. 628-35] or Finney [5]). Table 5 presents coefficients and marginal contributions estimated using a probit model. The variables included here are the same as those included in the OLS equation of Table 4. The slopes are evaluated at their maximums and at the mean proportion of arrests for the control group (30.5 percent). Probit estimates of treatment effects are shown in the last rows of Tables 2 and 3. For the financial-aid program, the probit estimate is slightly larger in magnitude than either the difference in sample means or the regression estimate. The 0.0951 reduction in the number of arrests at the mean translates into a 31 percent reduction in recidivism (vs. 27 percent and 26 percent for a difference in sample means and regression, respectively).[9] This suggests that

9  A 0.0951 reduction in the number of arrests is equivalent to 20.5 fewer arrests (0.0951 × 216) or a 31 percent reduction in recidivism (20.5/66).

TABLE 5
VARIABLES USED IN THE PROBIT EQUATION

| Variable | Coefficient | Standard Error | $\dfrac{dp}{dx_i}\bigg\|_{max}$ | $\dfrac{dp}{dx_i}\bigg\|_{mean}$ |
|----------|-------------|----------------|-------------|-------------|
| *ARREST* (dep. var.) | — | — | — | — |
| Constant | 1.7473 | — | 0.6970 | 0.6124 |
| *FINANCIAL* | −0.2712** | 0.1338 | −0.1082 | −0.0951 |
| *JOBS* | 0.1696 | 0.1335 | 0.0677 | 0.0594 |
| *AGE* | −0.0495*** | 0.0131 | −0.0198 | −0.0174 |
| *AGESQ* | −0.0049 | 0.0037 | −0.0020 | −0.0017 |
| *ED* | −0.1266 | 0.2029 | −0.0505 | −0.0444 |
| *RACE* | −0.1600 | 0.8095 | −0.0638 | −0.0560 |

Number of observations = 432
Chi-square statistics = 24.2589***
Equation:
$PROB = \phi(\beta_0 + \beta_1 FINANCIAL + \beta_2 JOBS + \beta_3 AGE + \beta_4 AGESQ$
$\quad + \beta_5 ED + \beta_6 RACE)$,
where *PROB* is the probability that *ARREST* equals 1 and $\phi$ is the standard normal distribution function.

** Statistically significant at the 5 percent level. *** Statistically significant at the 1 percent level.

the use of sample mean differences will slightly underestimate the reduction in recidivism. The coefficient for job-placement assistance is again insignificant, and the probit estimate is approximately equal to the regression estimate.

Additional evidence on the effects of financial aid can be found by examining the data on labor force activities and earnings of people in the experimental samples. Comparisons of the sample means for weekly activities and monthly earnings are presented in Table 6, separately for each of the four quarters during the first year following release from prison. As would be expected, the differential in terms of incarcerations was initially quite small and became larger as time passed. During the second half of the year, the men enrolled in the financial-aid program were 20 percent less likely to be in jail or prison than those in the control group. The proportion of each group engaged in legal activities (employed full or part time, or enrolled in school or a training program) follows a similar pattern. Initially, there was not much difference, but by the end of the first year the financial-aid group had a higher rate of participation in legitimate activities.

TABLE 6
SAMPLE MEANS FOR WEEKLY ACTIVITIES AND EARNINGS BY QUARTER[a]

| Dependent Variable[b] | Quarter 1 | | Quarter 2 | | Quarter 3 | | Quarter 4 | |
|---|---|---|---|---|---|---|---|---|
| | Financial-Aid Group | Control Group | Financial-Aid Group | Control Group | Financial-Aid Group | Control Group | Financial-Aid Group | Control Group |
| Incarcerated | .0355 | .0462 | .1294 | .1268 | .1480 | .1921 | .1987* | .2472* |
| Legal activity | .4476 | .4508 | .5509 | .5644 | .5760 | .5556 | .5973* | .5429* |
| Employed full time | .3711 | .4160 | .4822 | .5181 | .5351 | .5132 | .5469* | .4899* |
| School or training | .0370* | .0144* | .0422* | .0201* | .0280 | .0203 | .0336 | .0210 |
| Average earnings[c] | 42.47 | 45.37 | 54.08 | 52.50 | 55.31 | 48.42 | 50.46 | 43.84 |
| Average earnings per full-time worker[c] | 114.45 | 109.06 | 112.16 | 101.34 | 103.37 | 94.15 | 92.27 | 89.48 |

a   Adjusted means from regressions were computed and yielded essentially the same results as the comparisons of raw sample means in this table. The independent variable specifications used in the regressions were similar to the equation reported in Table 4.

b   Weekly data are available on employment, school or training, and incarceration, but only monthly aggregates are available for earnings.

c   Earnings are measured in dollars per week.

*   The differential is statistically significant at the 10 percent level.

Interestingly, the data on employment, school or training, and earnings also follow a consistent pattern that supports the findings for recidivism. While men in the financial-aid group were initially less likely to be employed full time (especially for the first quarter when they were receiving payments), they were more likely to be enrolled in a school or training program. Some men appeared to be using the transfer payments to augment their future earning abilities by attending school or training programs.

On average, men in the financial-aid group also had higher paying jobs when they were employed. The lower employment rates and higher earnings per employed worker during the initial period suggest that the financial-aid group was searching longer for jobs and finding higher paying positions. The higher rate of incarceration among controls during the last two quarters combined with the greater initial investments in human capital on the part of the financial-aid group appeared to have an impact on employment and overall earnings. By the last two quarters, those in the financial-aid group were more likely to be employed and had higher earnings, both overall and per employed worker. It is during this post-program period that employment and overall earnings become larger for the financial-aid group.

The empirical evidence of a substantial reduction in recidivism for the income-maintenance portion of the LIFE program is quite robust.[10] The question remains, however, as to what the long-run pattern for the differential in recidivism will be. On the one hand, the differential will widen if the income-maintenance group is able to obtain and keep better jobs because of human capital investment. Also, in later periods members of the control group who were arrested and incarcerated soon after release from prison will be released again and may continue to engage in theft activities (thereby increasing the likelihood of a widening differential in recidivism). On the other hand, men in the income-maintenance group may merely postpone theft activities until their eligibility for payment has expired. This, coupled with the fact that a larger proportion of the control group becomes incarcerated as time passes, could cause the arrest differential to narrow over time.

The evidence from LIFE suggests that any such tendencies for the arrest differential to change over time are relatively small. The data from the first year of the experiment show differentials that are growing over time. At the end of the first quarter after release, the differential for theft arrests was only two less for the financial-aid group (five fewer arrests for all crimes). This differential grew to 18 fewer theft arrests by the end of the first year (16 fewer arrests for all crimes). In addition, the differentials in incarcerations

---

10   In addition to the different estimation procedures for theft crimes, we experimented with changing the definition of economically motivated crimes. This also had little effect on the main results, even if we include all crime categories. The absolute differential for all arrests is just about equal to that for theft arrests other than auto (see the last row of Table 2). Also the number of incidents of multiple arrests is about the same for the financial-aid group as for the control group.

and legitimate activities grew substantially during the second half of the year following release (see Table 6).

The evidence from the second year after release shows that the arrest differential had stabilized and perhaps had begun to narrow. Lenihan [12] found that by the end of the second year the response differential had not declined appreciably. The differential in total theft arrests at that time was 16, as compared to 18 for the end of the first year. However, only data from court records were collected in the second year (interviews were not administered), and even the data from court records were of poor quality due to sample attrition (moves outside the covered jurisdictions) and related problems. Better follow-up data for a longer period of time would be useful for assessing the duration of reduced recidivism.

The analysis presented above supports Lenihan's preliminary results. The provision of financial aid led to a large and statistically significant reduction in theft rearrests, while the provision of job-placement services proved to be singularly ineffective in reducing recidivism. The question that remains is whether the reduction in recidivism is large enough to justify the costs of the program. Since the ratio of benefits to costs obviously will be less than one for the job-placement component of LIFE, it is unnecessary to examine it further. The comparisons of benefits and costs for the financial-aid component will be the subject of the following section.

## V. BENEFIT/COST ANALYSIS OF LIFE

The basic form of the benefit/cost approach that will be followed does not differ from that used in similar evaluations of other social programs. Therefore, a detailed review is unnecessary. Both benefits and costs are discounted to present value units. The present value of benefits is then compared to the present value of costs in order to decide if the program is worthwhile.[11]

The first step in constructing benefit/cost ratios is to enumerate and catalog the various benefits and costs. Table 7 summarizes the benefits and costs of the LIFE program from the various perspectives.

There are four basic types of social benefits from reduced recidivism in terms of reductions in resource costs associated directly with crime. First, there are savings in judicial costs associated with arrests, pretrial detention, court cases, incarceration, and post-release programs. Second, theft-related losses will decline; there will be fewer resource losses attributable to property damage, personal injuries inflicted during the commission of theft, and psychic costs to victims and potential victims. Third, fewer resources will need to be devoted to theft prevention (both public and private police

---

11   Benefits and costs will be based on sample differences in sample means between the experimental-treatment and control groups. Estimates based on more sophisticated empirical techniques do not substantially alter the findings.

and other protection expenses). Finally, the indirect social costs associated with criminal activity will be reduced.

A reduction in recidivism also probably will be accompanied by an increase in employment and hours worked. The discussion in Section II summarized the basis for this expectation. Those who receive financial aid are expected to spend less time in judicial proceedings and prison, and their overall employment rate should be significantly higher (it was observed to be approximately 16 percent higher during the first year after release for the LIFE program in Baltimore). Higher employment will in turn result in increased national output, as long as these released prisoners do not displace other workers in the labor market. If there is no displacement, the ex-offenders' earnings represent the value of increased output in competitive markets. However, the earnings differential for the first year after release may underestimate the benefits to society if the men receiving financial aid engage in more productive job search (information collection) while receiving transfers. In this case they will help to improve the functioning of the labor market, which will lead to a better match between their skills and industry's needs in the future even though their earnings are dampened initially.

Released prisoners receiving LIFE payments are less likely to participate in other public programs, such as public assistance, unemployment insurance, health care, drug treatment, etc. Similarly, the dependents of those receiving financial aid are less likely to participate in these programs because of the direct increases in income and reduced recidivism.[15] From a social perspective, only the reduction in resources devoted to administration represents savings. The transfers involved will be included (as benefits or costs) only from the perspectives of taxpayers and participants.

Administrative costs represent the primary social cost of the LIFE program. Another cost is the value of any forgone output of the program participants. It is important to include this, at least conceptually, since only the participant's net increase in productivity is a gain to society. There may be a potential for forgone output arising from the fact that the payments create incentives for participants to consume more leisure. For example, the reservation wage, the minimum wage necessary to induce a person to work, may rise while a participant is receiving payments. However, any reductions in labor supply attributable to LIFE will be included in our measure of net earnings differentials between experimentals and controls. Since the value of forgone output is subtracted from benefits, the only effective social costs are the costs of administering the program.

The social accounting excludes the value of all transfers: LIFE payments, welfare, and the value of the stolen property. The rationale for this is

---

15 From the *Survey of Inmates of State Correctional Facilities* [24], it appears that up to 40 percent of the LIFE sample are likely to have had dependents on welfare while they were incarcerated. We have not included the welfare differential attributable to incarcerations, since data are not available for LIFE. This will bias the estimates of welfare savings downward.

TABLE 10
SOCIAL BENEFIT/COST COMPARISONS

| Benefits | | Costs | |
|---|---|---|---|
| *Lower Bound* | | | |
| Averted costs of theft | | Administration of LIFE | $27,000 |
| Criminal justice system | $ 33,977 | | |
| Theft-related losses | 8,920 | | |
| Increased output | 60,583 | | |
| Fewer resources in welfare | 5,085 | | |
| Total | $108,565 | | $27,000 |
| Ratio of benefits to costs = 4.021 | | | |
| *Upper Bound* | | | |
| Averted costs of theft | | Administration of LIFE | $16,200 |
| Criminal justice system | $ 70,251 | | |
| Theft-related losses | 170,007 | | |
| Increased output | 604,791 | | |
| Fewer resources in welfare | 25,382 | | |
| Total | $870,431 | | $16,200 |
| Ratio of benefits to costs = 53.731 | | | |

that these are pecuniary costs and do not represent real resource costs of the program, but just the transfer of money (or goods) from one person to another. One difficulty with this assumption is that there may be a potential cost involving the LIFE transfer if the payments from a permanent program would reduce the penalties associated with future crime. This effect, however, is likely to be minimal since the present value of such payments is small.

A further difficulty with omitting transfers concerns the transaction costs associated with theft. The principal components of these costs are the costs of fencing stolen goods and administering compensation for insured property as well as the deadweight loss occurring whenever the criminal values the property less highly than does the victim. Since there is no accurate way to measure the change in these costs resulting from a reduction in theft transfers, the change in cost will not be included as a benefit. Thus, our estimates of the social benefits may be biased downward.

The major issue in evaluating social costs is how to derive an estimate for a permanent, large-scale program from a temporary small-scale experiment. First, there is the problem of separating administrative costs of the program from administrative costs of the research effort. Second, there are the initial fixed (start-up) costs and short-run inefficiencies that have to be worked out. Finally, there may be savings due to economies of scale. As an

TABLE 11
SUMMARY OF BENEFIT/COST FINDING
FOR THE LIFE FINANCIAL-AID PROGRAM

| Perspective | Lower Bound[a] | Upper Bound[a] |
|---|---|---|
| Society | 4.021 | 53.731 |
| Taxpayer I—Budgetary | 0.491 | 2.669 |
| Taxpayer II—Nonparticipant | 0.777 | 3.987 |
| Participant | 1.935 | 3.760 |

a  These bounds represent our best point estimates of the benefit/cost ratios calculated under widely different sets of assumptions (see Table 8). The differential between the upper and lower bounds would, of course, be larger if interval estimates were used in conjunction with the alternative assumptions in place of the best point estimates.

alternative to using the actual experience from the LIFE program, estimates can be derived from similar ongoing programs, such as unemployment insurance and public assistance. This alternative approach is used to estimate the administrative costs.

The results of the benefit/cost calculations are presented in Tables 10 and 11. The upper and lower bounds for the social benefit/cost ratio are derived in Table 10, while Table 11 presents a summary of the results for all the perspectives. While it is not clear that all segments of society benefited from the program, the results strongly indicate that overall the program is socially desirable. All crime-prevention savings, all reductions in the psychic costs of crime, all transaction cost reductions from fewer theft crimes (fencing costs, administrative costs of insurance, etc.), and all indirect social benefits have been omitted. In spite of all this downward bias, the estimates of the social benefit/cost ratio are overwhelmingly favorable. Even the lower bound estimate is significantly greater than one. Only administrative costs larger than $514 per case would yield a social benefit/cost ratio of less than one. Administrative costs of this magnitude are clearly beyond the range of any reasonable estimates. From an efficiency point of view, we can conclude that the program more than paid for itself.

## VI. CONCLUSION

The experimental evidence from LIFE shows that a program providing temporary income maintenance to released prisoners was quite successful in reducing recidivism, at least in the short run. The rearrest rates were significantly lower for men who were receiving financial aid, and the benefit/cost estimates indicate that the program was highly cost effective. In contrast, the job-placement program was a singular failure in terms of these same measures.

One limitation of the LIFE experiment was that it was designed to test transitional aid programs on a carefully selected, high-risk sample of released prisoners in a single city. It was argued that a reduction in recidivism would be larger, and consequently easier to estimate precisely, for such a group. Thus, the effect of this program on a more general population of ex-offenders released from state prisons would probably be less dramatic since a random sample would contain many individuals who already have low probabilities of recidivating. Further results on this point will have to wait until data from the follow-up TARP experiment with a more general population of state prisoners are available.[28]

Research in two other areas is also needed before a transitional-aid program like the income-maintenance component of LIFE can be conclusively recommended. First, it would be desirable to obtain better information concerning the long-run effects of the program. This is especially true with respect to data on the time paths of arrest, earnings, and welfare participation differentials.

Second, examining the program both under different economic conditions and in different labor markets would be helpful in determining what the effect of a nationwide program like LIFE would be. Some information on this second point will be available when the TARP experiment is completed. Since this other program includes a larger and more general sample of released prisoners in a wider variety of geographic locations, it will collect data from several labor markets and under a wider variety of general economic conditions. If the short-run effects of TARP are as favorable as those of LIFE, it would then be worthwhile to incur the added expense of a longer and more thorough follow-up analysis of the effects.

## REFERENCES

1. Orley Ashenfelter. "Estimating the Effects of Training Programs on Earnings with Longitudinal Data." Paper presented at the Conference on Evaluating Manpower Training Programs, Princeton University, May 1976.
2. Gary S. Becker. "Crime and Punishment: An Economic Approach." *Journal of Political Economy* 76 (March/April 1968): 169-217.
3. M. K. Block and J. M. Heineke. "A Labor Theoretic Analysis of the Criminal Choice." *American Economic Review* 65 (June 1975): 314-25.
4. Isaac Ehrlich. "Participation in Illegitimate Activities: A Theoretical and Empirical Investigation." *Journal of Political Economy* 81 (May/June 1973): 521-67.

---

28   See the discussion of this experiment in fn. 2.

5. D. J. Finney. *Probit Analysis*. 3rd ed. Cambridge, England: Cambridge University Press, 1971.
6. Irwin Garfinkel, Robinson G. Hollister, and others. "Design of the Benefit/ Cost Analysis of the Supported Work Demonstration." Princeton, N.J.: Mathematica Policy Research, 1976.
7. John Holahan. "Measuring Benefits from Prison Reform." Urban Institute Working Paper 963-14, 1973.
8. Robert Horowitz. *Back on the Street—From Prison to Poverty: The Financial Resources of Released Offenders*. Washington: American Bar Association, 1976.
9. George E. Johnson. "Labor Market Displacement Effects in the Analysis of Net Impact of Manpower Training Programs." Paper presented at the Conference on Evaluating Manpower Training Programs, Princeton University, May 1976.
10. J. V. Krutilla and O. Eckstein. *Multiple Purpose River Development: Studies in Applied Economic Analysis*. Baltimore: Johns Hopkins University Press, 1958.
11. Kenneth J. Lenihan. "Released Prisoners Financial Condition." *Crime and Delinquency* 21 (No. 3, 1975): 277.
12. ———. *When Money Counts: An Experimental Study of Providing Financial Aid and Job Placement Services to Released Prisoners*. Washington: Bureau of Social Science Research, Inc., 1976.
13. Michael A. Lettre and Anthony M. Syntax. "Applications of JUSSIM to the Maryland Criminal Justice Planning Process." Cockeysville, Md.: Governor's Commission on Law Enforcement and the Administration of Justice, 1976.
14. Charles D. Mallar. "A Comparative Evaluation of the Benefits and Costs from the Baltimore LIFE Program." Baltimore: Department of Political Economy, Johns Hopkins University, 1976 (mimeo).
15. Metropolitan Washington Council of Governments. *A Criminal Justice Planning Model for Prince Georges County*. Cockeysville, Md.: Governor's Commission on Law Enforcement and the Administration of Justice, 1975.
16. Joseph A. Pechman and Benjamin A. Okner. *Who Bears the Tax Burden?* Washington: Brookings Institution, 1974.
17. George A. Pownall. *Employment Problems of Released Prisoners*. U.S. Department of Labor. Washington: U.S. Government Printing Office, 1969.
18. President's Commission on Law Enforcement and the Administration of Justice. *Task Force Report. Crime and Its Impact: An Assessment*. Washington: U.S. Government Printing Office, 1967.
19. Jacob Stockfish. "The Investment Rate Applicable to Government Investment Projects." In *Program Budgeting and Benefit-Cost Analysis*, eds. Hinrichs and Taylor. Pacific Palisades, Calif.: Goodyear Publishing Co., 1969.
20. Henri Theil. *Principles of Econometrics*. New York: John Wiley & Son, Inc., 1971.
21. U.S. Congress, Joint Economic Committee. *Handbook of Public Income Transfer Programs: 1975*. Studies in Public Welfare, Paper No. 20. Washington: U.S. Government Printing Office, 1974.

22. U.S. Department of Labor, Employment and Training Administration. *Unlocking the Second Gate*. Washington: U.S. Government Printing Office, 1977.

23. U.S. Department of Justice, Federal Bureau of Investigation. *Crime in the United States: Uniform Crime Reports*. Washington: U.S. Government Printing Office, 1973.

24. U.S. Department of Justice. *Survey of Inmates of State Correctional Facilities*. National Prisoner Statistics Special Report. Washington: U.S. Government Printing Office, 1976.

25. Vera Institute of Justice. *Wildcat: The First Two Years, Second Annual Report on Supported Work*. New York: Vera Institute of Justice, 1974.

26. Washington State Department of Social and Health Services, Office of Research. *Adult Corrections Release Stipend Program: Evaluation Report No. 2*, 1973 (mimeo).

27. Anne Witte. "The Labor Market for Prison Inmates and Ex-Offenders." Chapel Hill: Department of Economics, University of North Carolina, 1975 (mimeo).

# PART VI

# EDUCATION

The articles in this section share a focus on programs designed to prevent or overcome deficits associated with educational or cultural "disadvantagement." The section begins with an excerpt from Levin's ambitious review of the effects of recent federal education and training programs for low-income populations. Levin concludes that these programs have achieved minimal success at best in their goal of reducing poverty, and he advances and examines several possible explanations for this limited success. Perhaps most important of all, Levin poses the crucial question of whether it is realistic to expect that education and training programs can solve the fundamental problems associated with poverty, particularly chronic poverty.

The Follow Through program, which is the subject of the next three papers, has been evaluated too recently to be included in Levin's review. Follow Through was created in response to early evidence suggesting that Head Start gains were not maintained in the schools, and it was originally implemented in the "planned variations" mode—i.e., different types of programs were introduced into the experimental primary schools throughout the country. The debate presented here is likely to play an important part in future decisions about early childhood education programs.

The paper by Stebbins et al. is edited from a much longer evaluation report submitted by Abt Associates. Many of the conclusions from the evaluation suggest that the so-called "basic skills" approach to early education is superior to alternative approaches. In the next excerpt House et al. dispute this conclusion, and criticize the Abt evaluation on several grounds—the classifications of Follow Through models and of outcome measures are called misleading, most of the measures are seen as inappropriate, and many of the analytic procedures are questioned. The Abt evaluations reply to these criticisms is contained in the papers by Anderson et al., who claim that the conclusions of the Abt evaluation have been misinterpreted and that the importance of certain methodological problems has been inflated. We invite readers to reach their own conclusions about Follow Through, since the evaluation by Stebbins et al. forms one important part of the argument for a return to the basics in primary schools.

The next two papers introduce a cross-cultural flavor, reminding us that overcoming educational deficits is a major issue in developing countries. Searle et al. describe their evaluations of a radio-broadcast mathematics program conducted in Nicaragua in 1976. The results of this randomized experiment indicate that an easily implemented radio instruction program can result in significant gains, both statistically and educationally. McKay et al. present an evaluation of a program combining nutritional, health, and educational care for disadvantaged preschool children in Cali, Columbia. Children were randomly assigned (by geographical units) to treatments of various lengths. The results lead the authors to conclude that the combined nutritional, health, and educational treatment can cause large gains in cognitive ability, that the effects are greater the longer the treatment lasts, but that one year of treatment is sufficient for gains. The policy significance and technical quality of these two studies make them exemplary in many ways.

# 35

# A Decade of Policy Developments in Improving Education and Training for Low-Income Populations

## Henry M. Levin

In modern societies, education and income are closely intertwined. Both census data and casual observation tell us that higher levels of education are associated with higher personal incomes. Sociologists have argued that education has a relatively powerful role in explaining social mobility among individuals, and economists have viewed education as an investment in human capital that raises the productivities and incomes of individuals.[1] Indeed, one of the basic philosophical tenets invoked by early advocates of universal schooling, such as Horace Mann, was the view that: "Education . . . prevents being poor."[2]

Henry M. Levin is Professor of Education, Stanford University, Stanford, California. The author wishes to acknowledge the assistance of Rita Duncan, Catherine Hackling, Esther Linan, Maureen McNulty, and Jean Rosaler in preparing the manuscript. He also wishes to express his appreciation to Dr. H. Thomas James and the Spencer Foundation for providing support for this work under the aegis of the project on "Education and Distribution of Income."

[1]Otis D. Duncan, David L. Featherman, and Beverly Duncan, *Socioeconomic Background and Achievement* (New York: Seminar Press, 1972); Gary Stanley Becker, *Human Capital* (Princeton: Princeton University Press, 1964); Theodore W. Schultz, "Investment in Human Capital," *American Economic Review* 51 (March 1961): 1–17; idem, "Investing in Poor People: An Economist's View," *American Economic Review* 55 (May 1965): 510–520.

[2]Arthur Mann, "A Historical Overview: The Lumpenproletariat, Education, and Compensatory Action," in *The Quality of Inequality: Urban and Suburban Public Schools*, ed. Charles U. Daly (Chicago: University of Chicago Press, 1968), p. 13.

Given the powerful role attributed to education by both intellectuals and layman in alleviating poverty and raising incomes, it is no surprise that the war on poverty relied heavily upon educational strategies to defeat the "enemy." In fact, the image of the first decade of the movement is easily characterized by such programs as Head Start, Job Corps, Upward Bound, Follow Through, and Title I of the Elementary and Secondary Education Act of 1965. In this paper, we will review the role that education played in the policy attempt to increase the opportunities and incomes of families and individuals who are characterized as fitting the low-income and disadvantaged criteria.

The approach that will be taken in this paper will be less a detailed description of the programs than a broader attempt to answer the following four questions: (1) Why was education considered to be such a crucial input for increasing the incomes and opportunities of the disadvantaged? (2) What were the particular educational strategies that were chosen, and why were they chosen? (3) Given both program evaluations and related research, how successful were these programs and approaches in alleviating poverty? (4) What have we learned that might enable us to reformulate the relationship between education and poverty? In large measure, these questions address themselves to the image, substance, and use of knowledge in a public policy context, subjects of investigations in the sociology of knowledge. Yet, there is little empirical analysis of social policy that uses such a framework for analysis. Accordingly, this exploration should be viewed as an attempt to understand a set of historic policy actions from an "image of knowledge" perspective.

In the next section we will review the major interpretations of the causes of poverty, and we will explore the focus of education within each interpretation. Next, we will present the actual programs that were implemented over the decade in order to show how they were consonant with a particular understanding of the educational tie to low income. Subsequently, we will review the success of the strategies that were chosen with respect to their educational outcomes and their probable effects in alleviating poverty. And, finally, we will use this feedback to reformulate the probable connections between education and poverty and to assess alternative strategies for the future.

## EDUCATION AND POVERTY

In order to understand the connection between education and poverty that undergirded the war on poverty, it is necessary to provide a brief review of the possible causes of poverty. Families in poverty fall essentially into two groups: those outside the labor force and those who have at least one potential

labor force participant.[3] The former include those who are not able to participate for reasons of age, family responsibilities (such as a single parent caring
for young children) and health. The latter include those who are capable of
working but are unemployed, underemployed, or are fully employed but
working at very low wages (the working poor). We will assume that educational programs and other types of public investments in human capital will
have little effect on the incomes of those who cannot participate in the labor
force, and income-maintenance policies represent a more appropriate response to the needs of this group.

But, we must now ask why those who are capable of working are poor. The
two major reasons that might be given are (1) that they are unwilling to work
enough, or that when they do work their productivity is so low that remuneration is necessarily small; and (2) that there is an inadequate employment
demand for workers to obtain productive employment, and that there is a
particularly low demand for workers from those groups whose incidence of
poverty is highest, such as minority individuals, teenagers, women, and rural
and ghetto residents. Capital investment is inadequate to create enough
employment in the areas where such workers are located; the productivity of
available capital is low; and there is pay and employment discrimination. The
latter explanation suggests that the demands for the services of the poor are
too low to provide adequate employment and/or remuneration to avoid poverty.

The difference between such explanations of poverty is important. It is the
choice between blaming poverty on inadequacies of the poor versus blaming
the poverty condition on the inadequacies of society.[4] For the former
explanation assumes that it is the low productivity of workers or their laziness
that determines their low incomes. The latter explanation assumes that the
size of the poverty population and its demographic composition will depend
on the adequacy, location, and productivity of capital investment as well as
employment discrimination. That is, there just are not enough jobs with
wages above the poverty level that are made available to such populations.

It is very clear which view provided the basis of the strategies selected for
the war on poverty. With its heavy emphasis on education, training, and other
programs of investment in human capital, more economic opportunity was
going to be given to the poor by reducing their inadequacies. As the *Economic
Report of the President* of 1964 stated without qualification: "If children of
poor families can be given skills and motivation, they will not become poor
adults."[5] The major programs of the Office of Economic Opportunity, the

---

[3]Lester C. Thurow, *Poverty and Discrimination* (Washington, D.C.: The Brookings Institution, 1969), Chapter II; Robert J. Lampman, "Approaches to the Reduction of Poverty,"
*American Economic Review* 55 (May 1965): 521–529.

[4]David M. Gordon, *Theories of Poverty and Underemployment* (Lexington, Mass.: Lexington
Books, 1972).

[5]U.S., President, *Economic Report of the President Together with the Annual Report of the*

Department of Health, Education, and Welfare, and the Departments of Labor and Agriculture all had this bias. Except for the employment-generating effects of the community action programs, and some of the training programs, and the relatively inconsequential Loans to Small Businesses, the possibilities of inadequate job demand for the poor was ignored. Indeed, the only major proposal in this direction, which would have created a public employment program (PEP) of a million or so jobs at the minimum wage of $1.25 an hour, was rejected.[6] Paradoxically, even had the program been adopted at the minimum wage, fully employed recipients would have still been in poverty.

Of course, it was assumed that full employment and prosperity were primarily matters of using correctly the tools of fiscal and monetary policy, so no direct labor market intervention in behalf of the poor was needed other than in the areas of reducing discrimination against minorities and of regional development. Under President Kennedy the disciples of the "new economics" were given free reign to formulate economic policy and to spread the gospel of Keynes. With the house revolution in economic counsel and commitment, it was expected that the intelligent use of countercyclical budgetary policies would provide full employment and high rates of economic growth at relatively stable price levels.[7] And, with the tax cut of 1964, the Keynesians were flushed with their early success.

Therefore it was assumed that the jobs would be there if only the poor had the skills and motivation to raise their productivity.[8] As Lester Thurow explains the more orthodox version of this view:

> Theoretically, labor income is determined by Labor's marginal productivity. Workers are paid according to how much they contribute to marginal increases in output . . . . If an individual's income is too low, his productivity is too low. His income can be increased only if his productivity can be raised. To raise a laborer's productivity requires knowledge of the factors that lead to changes in his marginal product.[9]

Of course, low educational attainments and inadequate training were prime suspects for explaining poverty status. First, education had long been viewed as a means of raising productivity and income. Second, empirical analyses of earnings functions appeared to confirm the contribution of education to earnings.[10] Finally, it was obvious that families headed by persons with low

---

*Council of Economic Advisers*, transmitted to the Congress, January 1964 (Washington, D.C.: U.S. Government Printing Office, 1964).

[6]Malcolm S. Cohen, "The Direct Effects of Federal Manpower Programs in Reducing Unemployment," *The Journal of Human Resources* 4 (Fall 1969): 491–507; Joseph A. Kershaw, *Government Against Poverty* (Washington, D.C.: The Brookings Institution, 1970), pp. 90–93.

[7]Arthur M. Okun, *The Political Economy of Prosperity* (Washington, D.C.: The Brookings Institution, 1970).

[8]Gordon, *Theories of Poverty and Unemployment*.

[9]Thurow, *Poverty and Discrimination*, p. 26.

[10]Schultz, "Investment in Human Capital"; Becker, *Human Capital*; W. Lee Hansen, "Total

educational attainments showed higher probabilities of being in poverty than those headed by more educated persons. For example, almost one-third of families whose head had less than eight years of schooling were found to be in poverty in 1967, while the comparable figure for families headed by high school graduates was less than 6 percent.[11]

We can summarize the tacit ideology behind the educational attack on poverty on the basis of the following assumptions. The existence of poverty among families with potential workers is due primarily to the low productivity of such workers; in turn, low productivity is attributable to low skills and initiative that result from the cultural and other disadvantages associated with these groups;[12] finally, government investments in education and in other areas of human capital would increase the opportunities and incomes of workers from such families by raising their productivities and resultant incomes.[13] It was thought that by increasing the job-related skills of the poor, education and training would provide an unusually promising vehicle for raising productivity and alleviating poverty.

### Educational Strategies to Defeat Poverty

But what kinds of educational strategies were to be used to fight poverty? The background for answering this question had already been established by the discovery of the disadvantaged or deprived child by educators.[14] While the traditional view of poverty saw this unenviable condition as a lack of wealth or income derived primarily from such malfortuitous factors as bad luck, low ability, and inadequate initiative, a different version of poverty was becoming more widely accepted in the early 1960s, the "culture of poverty." Based largely on the studies of such anthropologists as Oscar Lewis, it was argued that poverty is characterized by a number of class characteristics that tend to reinforce it and sustain it from generation to generation.[15] The main ingredients of the culture of poverty were the values and attitudes of the poor as well as the institutions that served them. That is, along with the substandard housing, inadequate nutritional and health services, and lack of other necessities experienced by the poor, they were also the victims of attitudes, language styles, work values, aspirations, and other types of behavior that represented important responses to and survival mechanisms for their present situations but did not provide the abilities to get out of poverty.

and Private Rates of Return to Investment in Schooling," *Journal of Political Economy* 71 (April 1963): 128–140; Giora Hanoch, "An Economic Analysis of Earnings and Schoolings," *Journal of Human Resources* 2 (Summer 1967): 310–329.

[11]Thurow, *Poverty and Discrimination*, p. 35.

[12]Lampman, "Approaches to the Reduction of Poverty," pp. 528–529.

[13]Kershaw, *Government Against Poverty*; Sar A. Levitan, *The Great Society's Poor Law: A New Approach to Poverty* (Baltimore: Johns Hopkins Press, 1968).

[14]Frank Riessman, *The Culturally Deprived Child* (New York: Harper and Row, 1962).

[15]Oscar Lewis, "The Culture of Poverty," *Scientific American* 215 (October 1966): 16–25.

Further, it was argued that the schools and other public services further reinforced these unenviable attributes.[16]

Perhaps the most important educational aspect of this concept is the view that poverty parents tend to pass on to their children the very characteristics with which they themselves are handicapped in their attempt to escape poverty. These disadvantages or deprivations include a lack of intellectual stimulation, lack of familiarity with and use of middle-class language and abstract problem solving, and those other behaviors that are considered necessary to do well in school and in the labor market. The result is that the disadvantaged child is less likely to do well in school than his more favored counterpart, and he is more likely to drop out of or "turn off" to school unless the school compensates for his "shortcomings." Accordingly, the school must provide compensatory education beyond its normal offerings in order to provide the child from a low-income family with an antidote to the "inadequacies" of his environment.

A second implication of this concept is that the culture of poverty is so pervasive that such deprivation must be countered when the child is very young. That is, adults who have experienced all of their development in poverty circumstances will at most be susceptible to specific training for jobs rather than to the more general educational intervention. But, if the schools are able to get poverty youngsters at a tender age—hopefully during the preschool period—the powerfully incapacitating effect of the culture of poverty might be successfully thwarted.[17] In effect, removal from the culture of poverty to a remedial environment that will inculcate middle-class skills and attitudes is viewed as the best foundation for providing social mobility out of the poverty setting.

In essence, the culture of poverty was thought to lead to disadvantages or deprivation with respect to what is needed to "make it" in the mainstream, and it is these deficits that compensatory education must eliminate.[18] The educational model corresponds very well with the concept of poverty embodied in the overall strategy of the war on poverty. While the poverty campaign assumed that low incomes were due primarily to low productivities, the educational palliative went considerably farther by identifying low productivity as a derivative of incompetence:

> Incompetence and poverty are interrelated. As a characteristic of individual persons, incompetence results in poverty. And, the poverty of one generation becomes, by virtue of the circumstances which hamper the development of abilities and motives, a basis for the incompetence of the next generation. As the burgeoning role of technology in our society calls for higher and higher levels of competence in larger and larger supply, those without at least

[16]Melvin L. Kohn, *Class and Conformity: A Study in Values* (Homewood, Ill.: Dorsey Press, 1969); Riessman, *The Culturally Deprived Child*.

[17]Benjamin Bloom, *Stability and Change in Human Characteristics* (New York: John Wiley and Sons, 1964).

[18]Harrow A. Passow, *Opening Opportunities for Disadvantaged Learners* (New York: Teachers College Press, 1972).

fairly high levels of competence find it harder and harder to earn their way in the marketplace and to participate in the affluence deriving from our technology.[19]

With all of the humanistic terminology used to describe cultural deprivation, disadvantage, or differences, it reduces to the view that children who are the product of such backgrounds will be incompetent students and adults.

> It is no longer tenable to regard the poor as just naturally inept, lazy, and untrustworthy. The poor, be they black or white, typically do an inadequate job of teaching their children the abilities and motives needed to cope with schooling even though they love their children as much as any parents do.[20]

Thus the job of compensatory education and training programs was to inculcate those characteristics that were associated with competence.[21] But exactly which characteristics these were and how to obtain them seemed much more open to question. Different educators defined the objectives differently, and the strategies that were proposed were just as diverse.[22] Perhaps the only area of agreement was that of teaching basic cognitive skills among young children and specific vocational skills among older ones and young adults.

The accord on improving IQ scores as well as reading and arithmetic proficiencies was reflected in much of the literature and in the evaluations of programs.[23] It was also evident in particular pronouncements on program expectations. For example, noted social psychologist Robert Havighurst, in heralding the beginning of aid given under Title I of the Elementary and Secondary Education Act of 1965 predicted that

> The next five years will see an all-out effort to:

[19]J. McVicker Hunt, *The Challenge of Incompetence and Poverty* (Urbana: University of Illinois Press, 1969), p. vii.

[20]Hunt, *The Challenge of Incompetence and Poverty*, pp. vii–viii.

[21]Alex Inkeles, "The Socialization of Competence," *Harvard Educational Review* 36 (Summer 1966): 265–283.

[22]Passow, *Opening Opportunities for Disadvantaged Learners*; Riessman, *The Culturally Deprived Child*; Helen E. Rees, *Deprivation and Compensatory Education* (Boston: Houghton Mifflin, 1968); Jerome Hellmuth, ed., *Disadvantaged Child: Compensatory Education, a National Debate* (New York: Bruner–Mazel, 1970); John M. Beck and Richard W. Saxe, eds., *Teaching the Culturally Disadvantaged Pupil* (Springfield, Ill.: Charles C Thomas, 1965); Edmund W. Gordon and Doxey A. Wilkerson, *Compensatory Education for the Disadvantaged: Programs and Practices, Preschool Through College* (New York: College Entrance Examination Board, 1966).

[23]Victor G. Cicirelli et al., *The Impact of Head Start: An Evaluation of the Effects of Head Start on Children's Cognitive and Affective Development*, Report presented to the Office of Economic Opportunity, contract B89-4530, Westinghouse Learning Corporation, Ohio University (June 1969); Sheldon H. White, "The National Impact Study of Head Start," in Hellmuth, *Disadvantaged Child*, pp. 163–184; Michael J. Wargo et al., "ESEA Title I: A Reanalysis and Synthesis of Evaluation Data from Fiscal Year 1965 through 1970" (Palo Alto, Cal.: American Institutes for Research, 1972); James S. Coleman, "Towards Open Schools," *The Public Interest* 9 (Fall 1967): 20–72.

(1) Raise the average IQ of children from low-income families by ten points;
(2) Eradicate that large segment of mental retardation which is due to environmental deprivation;
(3) Clear out 50 to 75 percent of the severe retardation in reading and arithmetic which now exists in elementary schools.[24]

At the secondary level the emphasis was also on the improvement of cognitive skills, with some focus on job training, particularly in light of a doubling of federal assistance for vocational education between 1965 and 1970. At the young adult level the concentration of programs was on encouraging further schooling as well as specific job training, while programs for adults focused primarily on job training.

To summarize, the educational strategies that were chosen were designed to compensate for the lack of competencies that were alleged to be associated with disadvantaged backgrounds. Because of the highly decentralized planning and implementation of most programs at the state and local levels of government, there was a great deal of diversity on the particular objectives and vehicles for inculcating competencies as well as the particular competencies that programs focused on. Yet, the attempt to improve cognitive skills seems to permeate most of the strategies at the preschool and elementary and secondary levels, perhaps because it was thought that these were closely related to productivity.[25] Beyond the elementary–secondary level the orientation of programs was on the provision of training for specific jobs as well as on financial and other assistance for obtaining postsecondary schooling.

## FEDERAL EDUCATION AND TRAINING PROGRAMS FOR LOW-INCOME POPULATIONS, 1964–1975

At least 30 separate federal educational and training programs for low-income populations were either initiated or expanded during the 10-year period 1965–1974. Of course such a list tends to be arbitrary in that a particular program might be included under noneducational classifications as well. For example, the School Lunch program might be included under nutritional programs as well as educational ones. In 1973, almost $6 billion was appropriated by the federal government for education and training of the poor. In this section we will review the most important of these programs.

Table 4.1 shows the major educational programs for low-income populations according to the particular group that the program was designed to serve. The classification of groups is done according to age and includes Preschool, Elementary–Secondary School, Young Adults, Higher Education, and Adults. The appropriations in millions of dollars are shown for the years 1965, 1969, and 1973, in order to give an indication of the magnitude and pattern of change in program support.

[24]Robert J. Havighurst, "The Elementary School and the Disadvantaged Pupil," in *Teaching the Culturally Disadvantaged Pupil*, eds. John M. Beck and Richard W. Saxe (Springfield, Ill.: Charles C Thomas, 1965).

[25]Richard Herrnstein, *IQ in the Meritocracy* (Boston: Atlantic Monthly Press, 1973).

TABLE 4.1

Major Educational and Training Programs for Low-Income Persons Funded at Federal Level, 1965–1974

| Program | Appropriations (in millions of dollars) | | |
|---|---|---|---|
| | 1965 | 1969 | 1973 |
| *Preschool* | | | |
| Head Start | 103 | 348 | 389[a] |
| *Elementary–secondary* | | | |
| ESEA of 1965 | | | |
|   Title I—educ. deprived | — | 1123 | 1810[a] |
|   Title VII—bilingual educ. | — | 7 | 50[a] |
|   Title VIII—dropouts | — | 5 | 8[a] |
| Upward Bound | (included in Talent Search) | | |
| School Lunch program | 146 | 162 | 226[a] |
| School Breakfast program | — | 3.5 | 18[a] |
| Emergency School Aid Act | — | — | 271[a] |
| Vocational Education | 156 | 248 | 434[a] |
| Teacher Corps | — | 21 | 38[a] |
| *Young adults* | | | |
| Neighborhood Youth Corps | 132 | 301 | 417[b] |
| Job Corps | 175 | 280 | 193[b] |
| *Higher education* | | | |
| Higher Education Act of 1965 | | | |
|   Title I—matching grants | — | 9.5 | 15[a] |
|   Title III—developing inst. | — | 30 | 52[a] |
|   Title IV | | | |
|     Educational Opportunity Grants | — | 134 | 274 |
|     Guaranteed Loans | — | 71 | 240[a] |
|     Work-Study | — | 146 | 274[a] |
|     Talent Search | — | 34 | 72[a] |
| *Adults* | | | |
| Adult Education Act of 1966 | 4.2 | 45 | 75[a] |
| Migrant Workers | 15 | 27 | 36 |
| Work Experience | 112 | 101[c] | 209[c] |
| Job Opportunities in the Business Sector | | | |
|   (JOBS) | — | 161[b] | 73[c] |
| Manpower Development Training Act | 397 | 404 | 381[b] |

*Sources:* Most of the data were taken from the Appendix, U.S. Budget, various years. Those programs that were administered by the Department of Health, Education, and Welfare were reviewed in the *Digest of Educational Statistics,* 1974; and those of the Department of Labor were reviewed in the *Manpower Report of the President, April 1974.* The figures drawn from different sources may not be similar because of changes in program definitions and in methods of reporting (e.g., appropriations, obligations, expenditures). Moreover, some of the earlier figures are revised in later documents. Accordingly, this listing is intended to provide a general pattern of the magnitude of the various programs, rather than a more rigorous classification for accounting purposes.

[a]Expenditures.

[b]Obligations.

[c]Work Incentive Program.

## EFFECTIVENESS OF EDUCATION AND TRAINING
## STRATEGIES IN REDUCING POVERTY

The fact that particular programs were marshaled to fight the war on poverty does not necessarily mean that the programs had that effect. That is, an evaluation of the education and training component of federal activities for low-income populations must not limit itself only to a description of the programs. Rather, it is important to know if the programs fulfilled their purported objectives, in this case, reducing the incidence of poverty in our society and improving the chances of young people from low-income backgrounds to escape the poverty of their parents. In this section we wish to review the various evaluations of programs, as well as related research based on similar programs, in order to see to what degree particular strategies were likely to have reduced poverty.

But this endeavor is not an easy one, for a large number of reasons. First, many of the programs were designed to assist children at the preschool and elementary school levels, and there is no dependable evaluation strategy for determining how changes in pupil attributes at those early ages will translate into economic benefits. Second, evaluations that do exist often deal with a specific local application of a federal program, and generalization beyond that program is risky. Third, even when positive effects on income are observed—and benefit–cost ratios are high—the effects might not be adequate to raise the recipient out of poverty. Fourth, it is often difficult to find poor nonrecipients of a program (as control populations) who are otherwise similar, in order to determine the effects of a program. This is a particular difficulty with the manpower training programs, where voluntary participation of trainees may result in selection biases that would tend to raise observed effects.

Nevertheless, the difficulties to which we have referred are not just unique to programs in education and training for the poor. These types of obstacles permeate virtually all evaluation research that is designed to assist public policy. The ignorance of the social sciences with respect to the complex set of genetic, psychological, social, cultural, political, educational, economic, and chance factors that affect a person's life chances do not augur well for any definitive answers about specific linkages between a particular educational or training strategy and the escape from poverty. Moreover, the amount of time that it would take to obtain life-cycle data on an experimental basis for a group of students or trainees as well as the cost of such experiments would seem to be an impractical luxury. Even if such experiments were feasible, it is not likely that they would provide definitive results for public policy, for reasons that have been discussed elsewhere.[53]

Yet, in the past decade a large volume of research and evaluations on

---

[53]Henry M. Levin, "Education, Life Chances, and the Courts: The Role of Social Science Evidence," *Law and Contemporary Problems* 39 (Spring 1975): 217–240.

various programs and types of educational strategies has accumulated. Certainly, we are the beneficiaries of much more empirical feedback than was Thomas Ribich in his very important early analysis of the use of education as an antipoverty investment,[54] and with a minimum of $40 billion to $50 billion invested by the federal government alone in training and educational programs, evaluations of these programs may provide a useful indicator of their effects. Accordingly, we will assume that the results of the evaluations should be taken seriously as guides to program performance, although in some cases we will argue that obvious biases exist in evaluation results, for reasons that will be noted.

Before proceeding, it is important to note two different criteria that evaluations of poverty programs might address. The first criterion is the total impact of the program on alleviating poverty, and the second one is the relative efficiency of the approach in contrast with other alternatives. According to the first guideline, we are concerned with the overall effect that the program had on removing people from poverty status. That is, we wish to focus on whether the programs worked, and the extent to which they worked. The second focus is one that asks whether the investment was worthwhile relative to other investments for doing the same thing. Typically, the latter issue represents the application of cost–benefit or cost–effectiveness criteria to the program to determine its relative efficiency.

But, questions of impact and those of efficiency do not necessarily obtain similar conclusions with respect to program assessment. That is, strategies that may have a large impact on poverty—because large expenditures were made and large populations were involved—may have low benefit–cost ratios because the effectiveness per dollar of expenditure was small. Conversely, strategies that may have had a small impact on poverty—because of low program expenditures and modest numbers of participants—may have shown a very high efficiency rating with respect to benefit–cost criteria. The overall impact of a program depends upon both its benefit–cost ratio as well as the expenditure and numbers of participants, and relatively inefficient programs may show much greater effects than efficient ones when there has been a far larger program effort in the former than in the latter.

Of course, this purview is based upon an historical analysis, and future policy might increasingly substitute more efficient programs for less efficient ones to obtain a higher total impact. But there are even situations in which benefit–cost ratios of educational or training investment on increasing income would give misleading implications with respect to impacts on poverty. First, there are some cases where there is a relatively large effect of investment on income according to benefit–cost criteria, but even after such increases the trainees were still found to be below the poverty level.[55] That is, when

[54]Thomas I. Ribich, *Education and Poverty* (Washington, D.C.: The Brookings Institution, 1968).
[55]David O. Sewell, *Training the Poor: A Benefit–Cost Analysis of Manpower Programs in the*

trainees who have experienced a relatively large increase in earnings are still below the poverty level, then it is difficult to argue that the high benefit–cost ratio is equivalent to a powerful antipoverty impact.

The second instance is that where a training program includes trainees drawn from both poverty and nonpoverty origins, and the calculations of increases in income includes gains for both groups. To the degree that the results are weighted heavily by larger gains between pretraining and post-training earnings for the nonpoverty trainees, the benefit–cost result may be misleading as a measure of effectiveness for fighting poverty. Yet, many training programs report results for both groups combined, and there is often some evidence that the major gains are made by those individuals who were not in poverty initially.

The final instance where benefit–cost ratios may be misleading with respect to evaluating antipoverty programs is in the case of educational programs for young children. In this case, the costs of education are incurred far in advance of the time that the individual will reach the labor market. Since additional earnings as a result of the investment in early childhood education will be discounted back to the time of the investment in order to compare them with costs, benefits will be heavily devalued relative to costs. While this procedure makes sense for calculating the relative efficiency of the program, it may rule against any program that would tend to assist the young out of poverty by building a sound educational foundation at an early age.

Accordingly, we will not assume necessarily that because an antipoverty educational program has a high benefit–cost ratio that it has had a powerful impact on alleviating poverty. Conversely, we will not assume that a program with a low benefit–cost ratio has had a low impact. In all cases we will attempt to view such aspects of the program as expenditure levels, numbers of participants, and the nature of the benefits, before making an assessment. In general, then, we will not rely on reported benefit–cost ratios in drawing our conclusions.

### Evaluation of Three Antipoverty Strategies

In the previous section, we noted that the education and training programs that characterized the federal attempts to reduce poverty can be divided into three strategies: those designed to improve basic cognitive skills, especially reading and mathematics; those designed to increase educational attainments; and those that focus on inculcating specific job skills. Table 4.2 shows these three approaches, the programs that were associated with each strategy, the measures of educational outcome for each one, and the nature of evidence that would indicate the impact of the strategy on reducing poverty.

---

*U.S. Antipoverty Program* (Kingston, Ontario: Industrial Relations Center, Queens University, 1971), p. 103.

**TABLE 4.2**
Antipoverty Strategies and Their Relations to Measures of Educational Outcome
and Evidence of Poverty Reduction

| | Antipoverty strategy | | |
|---|---|---|---|
| | Basic cognitive skills | Increased educational attainments | Specific job skills |
| Programs | Head Start<br>Title I, ESEA<br>Adult Educ. Act<br>Bilingual Educ. | Upward Bound<br>Neighborhood Youth<br>  Corps<br>Educational<br>  Opportunity Grants<br>Work Study<br>Talent Search<br>Dropout | Vocational Educ.<br>Job Corps<br>Work<br>MDTA<br>JOBS |
| Measure of educational outcome | High test scores | More schooling | Program completions and skills in job-related areas |
| Evidence of poverty reduction | Strong relation between test scores and earnings | Higher annual earnings without displacing other workers | Higher employment and , earnings, without displacing other workers |

Programs are grouped in Table 4.2 according to their principal focus. This does not mean that they were devoted exclusively to the particular strategy, since there is likely to be some overlap in objectives. Yet, the separation is especially useful for analytic purposes, and we do not believe that it will distort the overall assessment. Where the programs include other strategies as well, we will note their implications. Several programs that were presented in Table 4.1 and discussed in the previous section are not shown here because of the difficulties in evaluating their effects on poverty. Examples include the School Lunch and Breakfast programs, the Emergency School Aid Act, and Titles I and III of the Higher Education Act of 1965.

The first category includes those programs that would increase the basic cognitive skills of children and adults. These programs include Head Start, Title I of ESEA, the Adult Education Act, and Bilingual Education. It is expected that the success of these activities would be reflected in higher test scores and that the evidence of poverty reduction would be found in a strong impact of higher test scores on earnings. The second category reviews those programs that were designed to increase educational attainments. These include Upward Bound, Neighborhood Youth Corps, Educational Opportunity Grants, Work Study, Talent Search, and Dropout Prevention programs. The assumption is that the success of these approaches would be reflected in additional years of schooling acquired by persons in the programs relative to their nonparticipating counterparts. The evidence that these results would reduce poverty would be higher annual earnings associated with more schooling, without the displacement of other workers into the poverty category.

The third group of programs are those that are aimed at inculcating specific job skills. Programs that fit in this category include Vocational Education, Job Corps, Work Experience, Manpower Development Training Act (MDTA), and JOBS. The expectation is that these programs would show their educational outcomes on the basis of program completions and evidence of skills in job-related areas. These programs would indicate their impact on poverty by showing a strong positive impact on employment and earnings without displacing other workers.

Direct evaluations of results are not available for every program in each category, but there are enough findings on evaluations of similar strategies that we do not believe that the patterns would be contradicted by the inclusion of more evaluations. That is, it will be shown that there is a remarkable overall consistency in findings from program to program and among research studies that pertain to particular categories. In the case of each strategy, we will attempt to review first the available evaluations of the program with respect to its objectives. Second, we will summarize other research that evaluates similar types of programs and their educational effects. Finally, we will review the research that scrutinizes the tie between educational impacts and the reduction of poverty or increases in income. On this basis we will attempt to make a general assessment of the impact of the strategy on the reduction of poverty.

One concern that might be raised about the use of an antipoverty criterion alone as the basis of evaluation is the possibility that participants in programs received nonpecuniary benefits from compensatory education and training programs that are ignored in our analysis. While such a concern is valid in principle, we have chosen to ignore it for the following reasons: First, it is reasonable to limit one's focus to the antipoverty effects alone, because this claim is the primary basis for the existence of the programs. Accordingly, it is useful to ask if the programs were successful in terms of their own publicized *raison d'être* without considering secondary consequences. Second, nonpecuniary effects can be negative as well as positive. In essence, the question that must be posed is whether persons would have participated voluntarily in the programs if they knew *with certainty* that no pecuniary benefits would be forthcoming and if the costs to them of participating—including the cost of forgone income—were zero. The oppressive descriptions of many compensatory education programs,[56] as well as the chronic inability of many manpower training programs to obtain and retain enrollees (for example, Job Corps, Neighborhood Youth Corps, MDTA), suggests that even with the ostensible promise of economic gain the other aspects of the programs may not have been very appealing.

---

[56]Charles Silberman, *Crisis in the Classroom* (New York: Random House, 1970), Chapter 3; Annie Stein, "Strategies for Failure," *Harvard Educational Review* 41 (May 1971): 158–204.

## Basic Cognitive Skills

One of the most prominent educational approaches of the war on poverty was to increase the basic cognitive skills of disadvantaged youngsters and also adults. The basic emphasis of such programs was on reading and arithmetic proficiencies as well as other cognitive components, but programs objectives were often referred to with respect to increases in measured IQ at the preschool level and in reading and mathematics test scores at the primary and secondary levels. The presumption was that a person's productivity is largely determined by what he knows, and that poverty populations are often handicapped in improving their incomes by their lack of basic cognitive knowledge. Accordingly, about $2.3 billion dollars was spent by the federal government in 1973 on the four programs that we have included in this category. What were the ostensible effects of such efforts on improvements in cognitive skills?

In 1968, the OEO commissioned a National Impact Study of Head Start in order to ascertain how first, second, and third graders who had attended Head Start programs differed from comparable students who did not participate.[57] When the answers came in, it appeared that, while Head Start students approached the national norm on school readiness at grade one, they were considerably below the national norms on tests of language development and scholastic achievement in the three grades. Summer programs seemed to be ineffective in producing any gains in cognitive or affective development among children that could be discerned later when they were enrolled in the primary grades. And, even full-year Head Start programs were found to be only marginally effective in producing cognitive gains that persisted into the early elementary years.

These results were quickly attacked as being incomplete or biased in a number of ways.[58] Perhaps the most important of these criticisms was that the overall result masks underlying differences among programs, and that the evaluation should have discerned these differences in order to identify and delineate the ingredients of successful programs.[59] In addition, the groups of nonparticipants that were used for comparison purposes were slightly more advantaged than those in the Head Start programs.[60] But, since we are concerned primarily with the overall impact of Head Start in improving the

---

[57]Cicirelli et al., *The Impact of Head Start.*

[58]Walter Williams and John W. Evans, "The Politics of Evaluation: The Case of Head Start," *Annals* 385 (September 1969): 118–132; Sheldon H. White, "The National Impact Study of Head Start."

[59]Marshall S. Smith and Joan S. Bissell, "Report Analysis: The Impact of Head Start," *Harvard Educational Review* 40 (February 1970): 51–104; Joan S. Bissell, *The Cognitive Effects of Preschool Programs for Disadvantaged Children* (Washington, D.C.: National Institute of Child Health and Human Development, 1970).

[60]Donald T. Campbell and Albert Erlebacher, "How Regression Artifacts in Quasi-Experimental Evaluations Can Mistakenly Make Compensatory Education Look Harmful," in Hellmuth, *Disadvantaged Child,* pp. 185–210.

cognitive performances of students, the question of which programs succeeded and which ones failed is not of relevance if on the average they produced no change.[61]

Although the question of improper matching of comparison pupils and Head Start participants represents a more fundamental criticism, the actual impact on the overall results of the evaluation is problematic.[62] Not only do we not know whether there is a bias in the results as implied by Donald Campbell and Albert Erlebacher in their study of Head Start, but the mere existence of the bias would not necessarily change the rather consistent set of results that shows that in the primary grades former Head Start participants seemed to show almost no cognitive advantages over relatively similar nonparticipants.[63] Even the strongest critics of the National Impact Study of Head Start have not been able to show powerful effects of Head Start on cognitive test scores.

More recently, the Office of Child Development has reviewed longitudinal evaluations of particular preschool programs. These rather exemplary programs were directed by nationally known educators, and their results would be expected to be far better than those associated with a typical Head Start program. Even so, Bronfenbrenner found:

> Almost without exception, children showed substantial gains in IQ and other cognitive measures during the first year of the program, attaining or even exceeding the average for their age. . . . By the first or second year after completion of the program, sometimes while it was still in operation, the children began to show a progressive decline, and by the third or fourth year of follow-up had fallen back into the problem range of the lower 90's and below. Apparent exceptions to this general trend turned out to be faulted by methodological artifacts (e.g., self-selection of families in the experimental group). The period of sharpest decline occurred after the child's entry into regular school.[64]

This seems to be the present summary of the Head Start and preschool experience. Good programs are able to produce salutary increases in IQ for disadvantaged children, but these improvements are not maintained when the children enter the primary grades.

[61]Of course, information on which programs were successful and under what conditions is useful for reformulating Head Start in order to improve program performance, but that is a different issue.

[62]Campbell and Erlebacher, "Regression Artifacts"; Victor G. Cicirelli, "The Relevance of the Regression Artifact Problem to the Westinghouse–Ohio Evaluation of Head Start: A Reply to Campbell and Erlebacher," in Hellmuth, *Disadvantaged Child*, pp. 211–215; John W. Evans and Jeffrey Schiller, "How Preoccupation with Possible Regression Artifacts Can Lead to a Faulty Strategy for the Evaluation of Social Action Programs: A Reply to Campbell and Erlebacher," in Hellmuth, *Disadvantaged Child*, pp. 163–184; Donald T. Campbell and Albert Erlebacher, "Reply to the Replies," in Hellmuth, *Disadvantaged Child*, pp. 221–225.

[63]Campbell and Erlebacher, "Regression Artifacts."

[64]U.S., Department of Health, Education, and Welfare, Office of Human Development, *Longitudinal Evaluations: A Report on Longitudinal Evaluations of Preschool Programs*, ed. Sally Ryan, Vol. 1, (OHD) 74-24 (Washington, D.C.: Department of Health, Education, and Welfare, 1974).

Distinguished early childhood educator Susan Gray has responded to these results by suggesting:

> An effective early intervention program for a preschool child, be it ever so good, cannot possibly be viewed as a form of inoculation whereby the child is immunized forever afterward to the effects of an inadequate home and a school inappropriate to his needs.[65]

In recognition of the inability to maintain the earlier gains from preschool experience, the Office of Education began an experimental program in 1967, Follow-Through. The purpose of Follow-Through was to ascertain how to reinforce and increase the cognitive gains made in preschool during the first three years of elementary school.[66] Follow-Through has not been implemented widely during the decade, and at this date we still lack even the experimental results.

Over $12 billion was spent during the decade on the other major program for increasing the cognitive attainments of disadvantaged youngsters, Title I of the Elementary and Secondary Education Act of 1965. Finding that cognitive gains from preschool programs were not retained in the primary grades, it is useful to scrutinize Title I, which provided compensatory expenditures at both the elementary and secondary grades. The evaluation of Title I is especially important because it represents the largest single program in the education and training artillery of the war on poverty in both expenditures and numbers of pupils served. Fortunately, Title I required evaluations by both the local school districts and state education departments, and the U.S. Office of Education sponsored a number of national assessments as well.[67]

Since most of the Title I programs concentrated on reading skills, it is useful to examine the effect of the funds on those outcomes. The U.S. Office of Education carried out an extensive analysis of Title I reading programs for the 1966–1967 and 1967–1968 school years. On the basis of reading test scores, the study concluded:

> A child who participated in a Title I project had only a 19 percent change of a significant

[65]Department of Health, Education, and Welfare, *Longitudinal Evaluations*, p. 136.

[66]U.S., Department of Health, Education, and Welfare, Office of Child Development, *Implementation of Planned Variation in Head Start; I. Review and Summary of the Stanford Research Institute Interim Report: First Year of Evaluation*, by Joan S. Bissell (Washington, D.C.: Department of Health, Education, and Welfare, 1971) (HE21.2:H34/2/1); U.S., Department of Health, Education, and Welfare, Office of Education, *Longitudinal Evaluations of Selected Features of the National Follow-Through Program*, (OE) 72–98 (Washington, D.C.: Department of Health, Education, and Welfare, 1971).

[67]Harry Picariello, "Evaluation of Title I," U.S., Office of Education, Office of Program, Planning, and Evaluation (1969), mimeo; David G. Hawkridge, Albert B. Chalupsky, and Oscar H. Roberts, "A Study of Selected Exemplary Programs for the Education of Disadvantaged Children," Parts I and II, Final Report, Project No. 08 9013 for the U.S. Office of Education (Palo Alto, Cal.: American Institutes for Research, 1968), mimeo; Gene V. Glass et al., *Education of the Disadvantaged: An Evaluation Report on Title I, Elementary and Secondary Education Act of 1965, Fiscal Year 1969* (Boulder, Col.: University of Colorado, 1970); Michael J. Wargo et al., "ESEA Title I."

achievement gain, a 13 percent change of a significant achievement loss, and a 68 percent chance of no change at all [relative to the national norms].[68]

Further, the projects included in the investigation were

most likely to be representative of projects in which there was a higher than average investment in resources. Therefore, more significant gains should be found here than in a more representative sample of Title I projects.[69]

The ostensible inability of Title I programs to create even a nominal impact on student test scores in basic skills seems to be endemic to the program. Among many thousands of Title I project evaluations and a few compensatory programs, the Office of Education selected the 1000 most promising ones for examination by an independent research contractor. Of these, only 21 were found to have shown sufficient evidence of significant pupil achievement gains in language or numerical skills.[70] Not only are these results discouraging, but they also highlight the evaluation biases evident in local and state reports on compensatory education where the agencies that are responsible for the programs are expected to provide evaluations of their own activities. Only rarely are the evaluation claims supported by the evidence.

But, what of the other studies of Title I? In a national study of the results for 1969, it was found that Title I participants had a distinctly smaller improvement in reading than did nonparticipants.[71] The Office of Education also attempted a comprehensive review of all Title I projects through 1970. Based on these data, no evidence could be found that states were closing the achievement gap between advantaged and disadvantaged children.[72] Yet, because some individual projects had reported such successes, an attempt was made to scrutinize more closely the specific evaluations of those projects. Of some 1750 projects that were identified as appearing to meet the criteria of success in improving the cognitive functioning of disadvantaged children, only 41 (or 2.3 percent) were found to be successful when evaluated in a systematic way.[73] Of these programs, only half appeared to be supported by Title I funds.

Other summaries of Title I have been equally pessimistic. While a few projects of many thousands seem to have some positive impact on cognitive test scores, the vast majority do not show such evidence. Even among those projects that do show "statistically significant gains," the gains "may be educationally insignificant if one hopes that lower income children will completely catch up with middle class groups."[74] It has been argued that there is

[68]Picariello, "Evaluation of Title I."
[69]Ibid., p. 1.
[70]Hawkridge, Chalupsky, and Roberts, "A Study of Selected Exemplary Programs."
[71]Glass et al., *Education of the Disadvantaged*, p. 1.
[72]Wargo et al., "ESEA Title I," pp. 174–179.
[73]Ibid., Vol. 2, Chapter 7.
[74]U.S., Department of Health, Education, and Welfare, Office of the Assistant Secretary for

so much noncompliance with Title I regulations that this dereliction is a contributing factor to the results.[75] Yet, there is other evidence from research studies on school effectiveness that suggests that even large increases in resources will not improve substantially the cognitive outcomes for low-income children.

In 1966, the Office of Education published a massive research tome based on studying the statistical relationships between student and school characteristics on the one hand and student test scores on the other. This study—which is more popularly known as the Coleman Report, after its principal author James Coleman—found that school resources seemed to show a surprisingly weak relation with measured cognitive achievements of students.[76] The fact that the research was based upon a national sample of some three-quarters of a million students, 70,000 teachers, and several thousand schools as well as the relatively sophisticated analysis made this a landmark study. Critics argued that the statistical analysis tended to derogate school effects and inflate the impact of student backgrounds on test scores, and subsequent studies using Coleman data did find some resource effects.[77] But none of the observed effects of school variables on student test scores seemed to be of great enough magnitude to represent a useful policy device for raising substantially the cognitive performance of poor children.[78]

Other studies of the educational production relation have also found statis-

Planning and Evaluation, *Federal Programs for Young Children: Review and Recommendations; Volume II: Review of Evaluation Data for Federally Sponsored Projects for Children*, by Sheldon H. White et al., Huron Institute (OS) 74-102 (Washington, D.C.: Department of Health, Education, and Welfare, 1973), Chapter 2.

[75]Ruby Martin and Phyllis McClure, *Title I of ESEA: Is It Helping Poor Children?* (Washington, D.C.: Washington Research Project and NAACP Legal Defense and Educational Fund, Inc., 1969); Wargo et al., "ESEA Title I"; R. Stephen Browning and Jack Costello, Jr., "Title I: More of the Same?" *Inequality in Education*, no. 17 (June 1974): 23–45.

[76]U.S., Department of Health, Education, and Welfare, Office of Education, *Equality of Educational Opportunity*, James S. Coleman et al., (OE) 38001 (Washington, D.C.: Government Printing Office, 1966), Chapter 3.

[77]Samuel S. Bowles and Henry M. Levin, "The Determinants of Scholastic Achievement—A Critical Appraisal of Some Recent Evidence," *Journal of Human Resources* 3 (Winter 1968): 3–24; Glen G. Cain and Harold Watts, "Problems in Making Policy Inferences from the Coleman Report," *American Sociological Review* 35 (1970): 228–242; Eric Hanushek and John F. Kain, "On the Value of Equality of Educational Opportunity as a Guide to Public Policy," in *On Equality of Educational Opportunity*, ed. Frederick Mosteller and Daniel Moynihan (New York: Random House, 1972), pp. 116–145; Samuel S. Bowles, "Towards an Educational Production Function," in *Education, Income, and Human Capital*, ed. W. Lee Hansen (New York: National Bureau of Economic Research, 1970), pp. 11–60; Eric Hanushek, *Education and Race* (Lexington, Mass.: D. C. Heath, 1972); Henry M. Levin, "A New Model of School Effectiveness," in U.S., Department of Health, Education, and Welfare, Office of Education, Bureau of Educational Personnel Development, *Do Teachers Make a Difference? A Report on Recent Research on Pupil Achievement*, OE 58042 (Washington, D.C.: U.S. Government Printing Office, 1970), Chapter 3 (HE5.258:58042); Stephan Michelson, "The Association of Teacher Resourcefulness with Children's Characteristics," in *Do Teachers Make a Difference*, Chapter 6.

[78]Frederick Mosteller and Daniel P. Moynihan, eds., *On Equality of Educational Opportunity* (New York: Random House, 1972).

tically significant effects of particular variables on student test scores.[79] But, it appears that none of these results would provide for optimism in using the schools to close the cognitive achievement gap between disadvantaged and advantaged children. For example, Carnoy has simulated the effects of policies that might increase those inputs with statistically significant effects on achievement by at least one standard deviation for low-performance minority groups, raising the amount of resources for those groups considerably above what are available to the high performance students. These simulations of vast increases in compensatory resources indicated that typically only about one-half or less of the cognitive gap between the two groups of students would be closed for U.S. students with a somewhat larger gain for students in Puerto Rico.[80] The most comprehensive review of the literature on this subject concludes that comprehensive education programs—on the average—have not been successful in improving the relative performance of disadvantaged students, and studies of educational effectiveness offer little basis for optimism that the schools can be used to create such impacts.[81]

Up to this point, we have reviewed the evaluations of Head Start and Title I as well as research on school effectiveness with respect to increasing the cognitive skills of children from poverty families. While we do not have information on the success of bilingual programs, there is at least one study that has reviewed a program in Adult Basic Education. In a study of literacy training among hard-core unemployed blacks in Detroit, it was found that there were great difficulties in inculcating literacy skills as well as in increasing employment after literacy training among those who took instruction in the program.[82] These results are consistent with the compensatory education findings, and it should be noted that only a very small amount of funding was allocated to bilingual and adult literacy training in comparison with Head Start and Title I.

While we have shown that the impact of cognitive skills programs on

[79]Martin Katzman, *The Political Economy of Urban Schools* (Cambridge: Harvard University Press, 1971); Lewis J. Perl, "Family Background, Secondary School Expenditure, and Student Ability," *Journal of Human Resources* 8 (Spring 1973): 156–180; Donald R. Winkler, "The Production of Human Capital: A Study of Minority Achievement" (Ph.D. dissertation, Department of Economics, University of California at Berkeley, 1972); Jesse Burkhead et al., *Input and Output in Large City High Schools* (Syracuse: Syracuse University Press, 1967); Herbert J. Kiesling, "Measuring a Local Government Service: A Study of School Districts in New York State," *Review of Economics and Statistics* 49 (August 1967): 356–367; Richard Murnane, "The Impact of School Resources on the Learning of Inner City Children" (Ph.D. dissertation, Department of Economics, Yale University, 1974); Byron Brown, "Achievement, Costs, and the Demand for Public Education," *Western Economic Journal* 10 (1972): 198–219.

[80]Martin Carnoy, "Is Compensatory Education Possible?" in *Schooling in a Corporate Society*, ed. Martin Carnoy (New York: David McKay Co., 1972), pp. 174–185.

[81]Harvey A. Averch et al., *How Effective Is Schooling?* (Englewood Cliffs, N. J.: Educational Technology Publications, 1974).

[82]Thomas H. Patten, Jr., and Gerald E. Clark, Jr., "Literacy Training and Job Placement of Hard-Core Unemployed Negroes in Detroit," *Journal of Human Resources* 8 (Winter 1968): 25–46.

increasing the reading and arithmetic proficiencies of disadvantaged students was minimal, it is important to ask what effect higher cognitive performances might have on earnings. That is, if the programs had been successful in fulfilling their educational objectives how effective would such educational success be in alleviating poverty? The evidence suggests that the influence of cognitive skills on earnings is surprisingly small.

Almost invariably the measurable impact of educational attainment exceeds vastly the measurable impact of test scores on earnings in recursive and single equation explanatory models that use both variables as well as measures of socioeconomic status to determine earnings.[83] At most, about 10 percent of the variance in earnings on income can be explained by test scores for age-specific populations, suggesting that 90 percent or more of the variance is likely to be explained by other factors.[84]

Perhaps the best overall analysis of the possible impact that compensatory education for increasing reading skills might have on earnings is represented in a recent paper that addresses this issue.[85] A *National Reading Survey* was undertaken by the Educational Testing Service in 1973 under contract with the U.S. Department of Health, Education, and Welfare. It represented a national probability sample of men and women aged 16 and over in all geographic areas, and data were collected on socioeconomic and other background variables, educational level and reading proficiencies. Each respondent was asked to undertake a test of reading proficiency, which consisted of seventeen tasks, "carefully constructed to assess the respondent's capability to read the kind of material that appears frequently in day-to-day life in the contemporary United States."[86]

On the basis of single equation and recursive systems of equations for explaining wages, work hours, schooling, and annual earnings, the authors attempted to estimate the effects of reading scores and other influences on earnings and earning-related outcomes. Of particular relevance to this study

[83]William H. Sewell and Robert M. Hauser, "Causes and Consequences of Higher Education: Models of the Status Attainment Process," *American Journal of Agricultural Economics* 54 (December 1972): 851–861; Christopher Jencks et al., *Inequality: A Reassessment of the Effect of Family and Schooling in America* (New York: Basic Books, 1972); Zvi Griliches and William Mason, "Education, Income, and Ability," *Journal of Political Economy* 80 (Supplement, May–June 1972): S.74–S.103; Thomas Ribich and James Murphy, "The Economic Returns to Increased Educational Spending," *Journal of Human Resources* 10 (Winter 1975): 56–77; Samuel Bowles and Valerie Nelson, "The 'Genetic Inheritance of IQ' and the Intergenerational Reproduction of Economic Inequality," *Review of Economics and Statistics* 56 (February 1974): 39–51.

[84]Rarely is the simple correlation between test scores and earnings over .30. Even this value might be overstated, since some of the correlation is attributable to the covariance of socioeconomic status and education with test scores and earnings. Of course, measurement errors could bias the coefficient in the opposite direction, so on balance it is not clear that the value is either overstated or understated.

[85]Kan-Hua Young and Dean T. Jamison, "The Economic Benefits of Schooling and Compensatory Reading Education" (Princeton, N. J.: Educational Testing Service, December 1974), mimeo.

[86]Ibid., p. 2.

is the earnings equation and the earnings coefficient for the reading score variable. Only among white males was there evidence of a statistically significant effect of reading competence on earnings.[87] For white females and for blacks there was no apparent relation between reading proficiency and earnings. Even among the white males the effect was small. A one standard deviation increase in test score (equivalent to a rise from the fiftieth percentile to the eighty-fourth percentile) was associated with only $470 a year. This would have represented an increase of only about 3 percent in the earnings of the average white male in the sample, and there is no compensatory education program that has been shown to increase reading scores by such a large amount.

In contrast, a one standard deviation increase in schooling—about 2.85 years—was associated with about $2300 for the entire sample, $2800 for white males, $1600 for white females, $2000 for black males, and $1900 for black females. Thus, in contrast to the effect of test scores on earnings, the influence of the number of years of schooling is far more substantial. In summary, it appears that the cognitive skills strategy for raising people out of poverty was not very effective because there is little evidence of salient improvements in cognitive skills from the programs, and the evidence suggests that improvements in cognitive skills do not have very much impact on improving earnings.[88] Since there seems to be a stronger link between earnings and the number of years of schooling attained, it is useful to explore the second of the antipoverty educational strategies, the attempts to increase schooling attainments.

### Increased Educational Attainments

The evaluation of programs to increase the educational attainments of the disadvantaged is especially important because of the heavy emphasis on this strategy in the war on poverty and because the payoff to additional years of schooling is apparently rather sizable. Also, there is some evidence that compensatory education expenditures might have some effect on increasing the amount of schooling that is achieved. Ribich and Murphy analyzed a sample of persons who had been studied earlier in a national high school survey, Project Talent.[89] They found that students who had attended high

---

[87]Ibid., Tables 2 and 3.

[88]This is a particularly important finding when one considers the tacit assumption that underlies the IQ debate regarding the genetic versus environmental determinants of IQ: Jensen, "How Much Can We Boost IQ and Scholastic Achievement?" The major reason that the debate looms so large is the view that IQ is an especially crucial determinant of productivity and income. Herrnstein, *IQ in the Meritocracy.* If IQ is not an important determinant of productivity, the controversy is largely an academic one. For an overview of the use and interpretation of IQ in the U.S. class structure, see Samuel S. Bowles and Herbert Gintis, "IQ in the U.S. Class Structure," *Social Policy* 3 (November–December 1972, January–February 1973): 65–96; and Bowles and Nelson, "The 'Genetic Inheritance of IQ'."

[89]Ribich and Murphy, "The Economic Returns to Increased Educational Spending."

schools in school districts characterized by higher expenditures tended to obtain slightly more schooling than students from lower expenditure districts. While differences in expenditures among school districts are not exactly comparable with compensatory expenditures, we can infer from this study the possibility that compensatory education increases nominally the number of years that disadvantaged students might attend school.

Of the programs that we have listed under the increased educational attainments strategy, there exist evaluations of Upward Bound and Neighborhood Youth Corps. There are some analyses of the probable impacts of educational opportunity grants, but we know of no formal evaluation. Nor are we aware of formal evaluations of Work Study, those components of Talent Search besides Upward Bound, or the Dropout program.

The Upward Bound program attempted to identify able but needy youngsters at the secondary level who would not otherwise attend college, and to prepare and motivate them to continue their education beyond the secondary level. The estimated final educational attainments of Upward Bound students suggest that about 60–70 percent of them attended college, and almost one-third of them completed four years of college.[90]

In order to ascertain how much additional education was attained by Upward Bound students, it is necessary to know how many years of schooling they would have achieved in the absence of Upward Bound. OEO estimated that only about 8 percent of such disadvantaged students would have gone to college, but this figure was rejected because it was not derived from systematic research using control groups. A study of the siblings of Upward Bound participants estimated that about 43 percent of that group would enter college, a figure not very much less than the national average for all students of 47 percent. The main difference in favor of the Upward Bound students was that about 45 percent were expected to obtain a four-year degree in comparison with only about 32 percent of their siblings.[91] Nevertheless, it is clear that Upward Bound was somewhat selective in obtaining students from disadvantaged families where college attendance was already relatively high in comparison with disadvantaged students as a whole. That is, there was a tendency to select the "best" among the disadvantaged rather than a representative sample of students from low-income backgrounds.

In evaluating the social costs and benefits of the program, Garms found that the program was marginal in its performance. If such students simply replaced other students—particularly disadvantaged ones—there would be little or no net gain in reducing poverty. Also the fact that Upward Bound

[90]Garms, "A Benefit–Cost Analysis of the Upward Bound Program," p. 210.

[91]U.S., Congress, Senate, Committee on Labor and Public Welfare, Subcommittee on Employment, Manpower, and Poverty, *Examination of the War on Poverty: Staff and Consultants Reports on Family Planning, Neighborhood Service Centers, Organization and Coordination of Staff Reports*, Volume 3, Committee Print 80–325 (Washington, D.C.: U.S. Government Printing Office, 1967), p. 826. Garms, "A Benefit–Cost Analysis of the Upward Bound Program," pp. 208, 211.

tended to choose students who appeared highly likely to go to college anyway was considered to be a sign that the program as a whole had only a marginal impact on poverty reduction. Some of these assumptions have been criticized, but the criticism has not altered the substance of the analysis.[92]

The primary objective of the Neighborhood Youth Corps (NYC) was to increase the high school graduation rates of potential dropouts by providing paid work experience to high school students who are likely to drop out. A national evaluation of the in-school and summer Neighborhood Youth Corps found that the probability of graduating from high school did not increase as a function of participation in the program.[93] A study of NYC projects in Cincinnati and Detroit found similar results, including no reduction in dropouts, no increase in educational aspirations, and no improvement of scholastic achievement.[94]

While overall educational gains did not appear, participants in the NYC did seem to experience greater labor market success than did nonparticipants. Yet, even with such income gains, the NYC participants were still likely to be solidly entrenched in poverty. For example, NYC participants in five programs in Indiana were found to be earning about $950 annually in 1967 *after* having participated in the program. A somewhat comparable control group had about $675 in earnings for that year, and apparently only about $278 was attributable to program participation. The national sample of NYC participants earned about $552 more than their nonparticipating counterparts,[95] but even this amount was not attributable to higher wages but only higher voluntary participation in the labor force of about 2.3 months per year for NYC "graduates."[96]

It is very difficult to establish the impact of the Educational Opportunity Grants on increased educational participation of students from poverty backgrounds. According to Robert W. Hartman, about 7 percent of high school seniors from families with incomes of $3000 or less would attain one to three years of college and 8 percent would attain four years or more.[97] The compar-

[92]Pamela Christoffel and Mary Beth Celio, "A Benefit–Cost Analysis of the Upward Bound Program: A Comment," *Journal of Human Resources* 8 (Winter 1973): 110–114; Walter I. Garms, "Reply to 'A Benefit–Cost Analysis of the Upward Bound Program': A Comment," *Journal of Human Resources* 8 (Winter 1973): 115–118.

[93]Gerald G. Somers and Ernst W. Stromsdorfer, "A Cost–Effectiveness Analysis of In-School and Summer Neighborhood Youth Corps: A Nationwide Analysis," *Journal of Human Resources* 7 (Fall 1972): 446–459.

[94]Jon H. Goldstein, "The Effectiveness of Manpower Training Programs: A Review of Research on the Impact on the Poor," in *Benefit–Cost and Policy Analysis 1972* (Chicago: Aldine, 1973), p. 355.

[95]Michael E. Borus, John P. Breenan, and Sidney Rosen, "A Benefit–Cost Analysis of the Neighborhood Youth Corps: The Out-of-School Program in Indiana," *Journal of Human Resources* 5 (Spring 1970): 139–159; Somers and Stromsdorfer, "A Cost–Effectiveness Analysis," pp. 446–459.

[96]Goldstein, "The Effectiveness of Manpower Training Programs," p. 353.

[97]Robert W. Hartman, "Equity Implications of State Tuition Policy and Student Loans," *Journal of Political Economy* 80, Part II (May–June 1972): S147.

able national averages were 18 and 21 percent. Hartman has argued that grants to students from low-income families could have strong effects on increasing their participation in postsecondary education. But, for this change to take place would require that most poverty youngsters be able to take advantage of these grants, and the grants would need to be large enough to compensate for the relatively higher sacrifices required of poor families to obtain higher education for their children. Both of these assumptions might be questioned.[98]

For example, in 1970 about 70 percent of families that were in poverty were headed by persons with less than high school completion; and about two-thirds of unrelated individuals in poverty had less than a high school diploma.[99] These figures suggest that a large proportion of persons in the poverty category are not eligible to participate in substantial portions of postsecondary education. Further, the original Equal Opportunity Grants with their $200–$800 value in the freshman year and $200–$1000 amounts in later years were so modest relative to the total costs of participating in higher education, that only poverty students who were able to commute to low-cost public institutions while living at home or who had other scholarship assistance could take advantage of them.

An analysis of the Basic Educational Opportunity Grants suggests that their effects on improving the educational attainments of poverty youngsters may also be severely limited. First, the grants cannot be used to support room, board, and other expenses, which are more burdensome to poor families than to advantaged ones. Second, the fact that the grants will cover 50 percent of school costs up to $1400 means that the poor will have an incentive to choose cheaper schools than the advantaged because of the greater difficulty of matching the grant. In fact, Lee Hansen and Robert Lampman have suggested that the BEOG program is likely to provide relatively more aid to affluent families and less to impoverished ones than the description of the program implies because of certain regulations, including the possibilities that

> students from high-income families can qualify for maximum grants under the BEOG program if they want to go to the trouble of establishing independent status. Perversely, some students from low-income families may be forced out of dependent BEOG status. This could arise out of failure of parents to cooperate in supplying income or asset information.[100]

The effects of Work Study programs on increasing educational attainments

[98]For a pessimistic view generally of programs that would provide financial incentives for increasing educational attainments of the disadvantaged, see Eugene Smolensky, "Investment in the Education of the Poor: A Pessimistic Report," *American Economic Review* 56 (May 1966): 370–378.

[99]See Robert Plotnick and Felicity Skidmore, *Progress Against Poverty* (New York: Academic Press, 1975).

[100]W. Lee Hansen and Robert J. Lampman, "Basic Opportunity Grants for Higher Education," *Challenge* (November–December 1974): 46–51.

of the disadvantaged is not known, nor are the impacts of other activities of Talent Search beyond the Upward Bound component. Nor has there not been a systematic study of dropout prevention programs, although a careful study of one program in this area provides little grounds for optimism.[101] Even the effect of compensatory education programs generally on raising educational attainments is not encouraging. Although Ribich and Murphy found that students in school districts that were spending more money tended to achieve more years of schooling, the observed relation was small.[102] For each $100 of additional expenditure per year over the previous nine grades it was found that the average tenth grade child would attain about one-tenth of a year of additional schooling. An earlier analysis carried out by Ribich on disadvantaged males found that dropout rates among such students tended to be higher in districts that were spending *more* money.[103]

On the whole, it appears that programs designed to increase the educational attainments of disadvantaged youngsters were not overwhelmingly effective. The evidence of such programs suggests that they had little or no impact on increasing the educational attainments of disadvantaged youngsters, and those programs that appeared to be successful, such as Upward Bound, tended to concentrate on the least disadvantaged of the poverty group. But, again we must ask what impact would increases in educational attainments have on reducing poverty if the programs had been successful.

As we noted previously, there is a strong relationship between the amount of schooling that a person possesses and his income or earnings. For example, in the previous study which examined the effects of reading proficiencies, schooling, and other factors on earnings, it was found that each additional year of education was associated with about $932 in additional annual earnings for white males, $555 for white females, $689 for black males, and $658 for black females. Of course, the value of an additional year of schooling will vary according to the age, region, and other personal characteristics of the sample, so these incremental earnings should be considered as illustrative only. Other studies attempt to provide more detailed estimates of the returns to schooling.[104]

But, knowing that an individual who acquires more schooling will experience higher earnings—on the average—does not assure that providing more schooling for poverty groups will raise them above the poverty level. In order for that to happen it is necessary to show that the particular returns to more schooling for persons from poor backgrounds are high, and that when they achieve relatively more schooling they do not displace someone with relatively less schooling. That is, if a person who achieves more schooling is able

[101]Burton A. Weisbrod, "Preventing High School Dropouts," in *Measuring Benefits of Government Investments*, ed. Robert Dorfman (Washington, D.C.: The Brookings Institution, 1965), pp. 117–149.

[102]Ribich and Murphy, "The Economic Returns to Increased Educational Spending."

[103]Ribich, *Education and Poverty*, pp. 86–87.

[104]Hanoch, "An Economic Analysis of Earnings and Schoolings."

to improve his economic standing by bumping another person into the rolls of the unemployed or underemployed, then there may be no net impact on poverty reduction.

The evidence suggests that disadvantaged populations may not receive economic benefits from education to the degree that advantaged persons do. For example, Randall Weiss found that there was a much weaker relation between income and education among blacks than among whites.[105] Paul Wachtel found that the private rates of return to higher education were about 50 percent greater for higher socioeconomic status males than for lower status ones on the basis of his longitudinal data.[106] Bennett Harrison concluded that education had only a limited impact upon hourly earnings and virtually no effect on the probability of employment among predominantly nonwhite populations in 10 urban ghettos:

A number of different earnings models yielded estimated returns of from 3 to 9 cents per hour for each additional year of schooling, and over the interval of 9–12 years of schooling inclusive, an average return of 15 cents. Workers with at least some college received, on the average, only 20 cents more per hour than high school graduates who went directly to work and did not go to college.[107]

Thus, for these samples of workers, the average difference in earnings between high school graduates and junior high school graduates was only about $6 more per week, or about $300 per year if workers were fully employed. Harrison concludes that education "without a supply of jobs which utilize and reward the capabilities of ghetto workers is unlikely to have much impact."[108]

Some analysts have argued recently that labor markets are segmented so that persons from disadvantaged backgrounds, women, and minorities are likely to have access to jobs with lower earnings and employment stability than their more advantaged counterparts, males, and whites.[109] Institutional barriers prevent entry of the former groups into the primary labor market,

[105]Randall Weiss, "The Effects of Education on the Earnings of Blacks and Whites," *Review of Economics and Statistics* 52 (May 1970): 150–159.

[106]Paul Wachtel, "The Returns to Investment in Higher Education: Another View," in *Education, Income, and Human Behavior*, ed. F. Thomas Juster (New York: McGraw-Hill, 1975), p. 168.

[107]Bennett Harrison, "Education and Underemployment in the Urban Ghetto," *American Economic Review* 62 (December 1972): 809.

[108]Ibid., p. 811.

[109]Peter Doeringer and Michael Piore, *Internal Labor Markets and Manpower Training* (Lexington, Mass.: Heath Lexington Books, 1971); Gordon, *Theories of Poverty and Underemployment*; David Gordon, Michael Reich, and Richard Edwards, "A Theory of Labor Market Segmentation," *American Economic Review* 63 (May 1973): 359–365; Barry Bluestone, William Murphy, and Mary Stevenson, *Low Wages and the Working Poor* (Ann Arbor, Mich.: The Institute of Labor and Industrial Relations, 1973); Michael A. Carter and Martin Carnoy, "Theories of Labor Markets and Worker Productivity" (Menlo Park, Cal.: Portola Institute, 1974).

which is characterized by higher-paying jobs with greater employment stability and greater opportunities for promotion. Criticisms of these theories have argued less against the existence of the phenomenon than whether they can be explained by neoclassical analysis rather than requiring a new analytical framework.[110] In any event, the segmentation of labor markets provides a mechanism by which disadvantaged groups would receive lower payoffs to educational attainments than would other populations.

The relatively small effect of schooling on earnings of disadvantaged populations is also reflected in the findings of a study of low achievers who failed the Armed Forces Qualification Test.[111] The estimated total effect of a year of schooling on annual earnings was only about $44 for this sample, a difference of about $176 between grade school completers and high school completers. Even a one standard deviation increase in test scores for this sample would have provided additional annual earnings of about $168. Average annual earnings for this group of men was about $1800, and their average level of educational attainment was about nine years. It is highly doubtful that a policy of increased schooling or increased test scores would provide earnings above the poverty level for most of this group of men. Interestingly, a training variable was associated with about $300 of additional annual earnings, but even this would not come close to providing an escape from poverty, nor would high school graduation, a standard deviation increase in test scores, and training *combined*.

Not only is there some direct evidence that certain disadvantaged populations—especially nonwhites—do not obtain much additional income from more education, but there is also indirect evidence that suggests that education and training cannot be relied upon as the principal means to reduce or eliminate the poverty population.[112] Lester Thurow has stated very clearly

[110]Michael L. Wachter, "Primary and Secondary Labor Markets: A Critique of the Dual Approach," *Brookings Papers on Economic Activity*, No. 3 (1974): 637–693; Glen G. Cain, "The Challenge of Dual and Radical Theories of the Labor Market to Orthodox Theory," *American Economic Review* 65 (May 1975): 16–22.

[111]W. Lee Hansen, Burton A. Weisbrod, and William J. Scanlon, "Schooling and Earnings of Low Achievers," *American Economic Review* 60 (June 1970): 409–418.

[112]The existence and magnitude of differential returns to education for whites and nonwhites is a very controversial subject. Analysis of data for the 1960 Census found substantial differences in favor of whites: Weiss, "The Effects of Education on the Earnings of Blacks and Whites"; Hanoch, "An Economic Analysis of Earnings and Schooling." But scrutiny of later data, such as a special sample of households for 1967 and 1970 census data, have provided mixed conclusions. Finis Welch, "Black–White Differences in Returns to Schooling," *American Economic Review* 63 (December 1973): 893–907, sees a narrowing of returns to education between blacks and whites for younger as compared to older persons, and he attributes it to relatively greater improvements in the quality of education for blacks rather than decreases in discrimination. Stanley H. Masters, "The Effect of Educational Differences and Labor Market Discrimination on the Relative Earnings of Black Males," *Journal of Human Resources* 9 (Summer 1974): 342–360, using the same data set, finds that educational differences between black and white males explain only a relatively minor portion of income differences between the two groups, leaving the remainder to be explained by lower returns to education for blacks as well as other forms of

the assumptions that lead one to believe that education can improve the distribution of income and alleviate poverty:

> Any increase in the educational level of low-income workers will have three powerful—and beneficial—effects. First, an educational program that transforms a low-skill person into a high-skill person raises his productivity and therefore his earnings. Second, it reduces the total supply of low-skill workers, which leads in turn to an increase in their wages. Third, it increases the supply of high-skill workers, and this lowers their wages. The net result is that total output rises (because of the increase in productivity among formerly uneducated workers), the distribution of earnings becomes more equal, and each individual is still rewarded according to merit.[113]

If these assumptions are substantially correct, then a tendency toward equality in the distribution of schooling should be associated with greater equality in the distribution of income. Unfortunately, there seems to be no such consistent relationship. For example, between 1950 and 1970 the bottom fifth of the population increased its share of total education from 8.6 percent to 10.7 percent while the share of total education accounted for by the top fifth fell from 31.1 percent to 29.3 percent. Yet, between 1949 to 1969 the proportion of income received by the lowest fifth *declined* from 3.2 percent to 2.6 pecent, and the share received by the highest fifth *rose* from 44.8 percent to 46.3 percent.[114]

Other statistical analyses of the relationship between the distribution of education and the distribution of income have suggested a similar lack of correspondence between equality in education and income, and a study of changes in the income distribution for the period 1958–1970 shows a slight

discrimination and unmeasured influences. Leonard Weiss and Jeffery G. Williamson, "Black Education, Earnings, and Interregional Migration: Some Recent Evidence," *American Economic Review* 62 (June 1972): 372–382, also found a rise in returns to education for black males between 1960 and 1967, although they did not compare the 1967 returns for blacks with those of whites. The 1970 Census data show conflicting results, depending on whether one uses data grouped by educational attainment for the analysis or individual data from the public use sample: Charles R. Link, "Black Education, Earnings, and Interregional Migration: A Comment and Some New Evidence," *American Economic Review* 65 (March 1975): 236–240; Leonard Weiss and Jeffrey G. Williamson, "Black Education, Earnings, and Interregional Migration: Even Newer Evidence," *American Economic Review* 65 (March 1975): 241–244. The use of individual data suggests comparable returns to education for black and white males, while the use of grouped data persists in showing differences in favor of whites: Weiss and Williamson, "Even Newer Evidence." Of course, a black–white comparison is not the same as a comparison of the returns to education between persons who are drawn from poverty and nonpoverty backgrounds, although there is some overlap among the dichotomies. Harrison, "Education and Underemployment in the Urban Ghetto" and Bluestone, Murphy, and Stevenson, *Low Wages and the Working Poor*, represent studies of particular poor populations which provide a pessimistic outlook for the educational palliative for poverty.

[113]Lester Thurow, "Education and Economic Equality," *The Public Interest*, No. 28 (Summer 1972): 67.

[114]Thurow and Lucas, "The American Distribution of Income"; Lester C. Thurow, "Measuring the Economic Benefits of Education," in *Higher Education and the Labor Market*, ed. Margaret S. Gordon (New York: McGraw-Hill, 1974), p. 385.

but persistent trend toward greater inequality despite the tendency for education to be distributed more equally over the last three decades.[115] Perhaps the most sophisticated attempt to ascertain the determinants of changes in income inequality between 1939 and 1965 found that: "Most of the observed difference in inequality between 1939 and 1965 is explained by changes in employment conditions."[116] This finding tends to confirm the views of Thurow, Harrison, and others that changes in the level of education without an expansion of and improvement in job opportunities is not likely to improve the distribution of income.[117] With high levels of unemployment and underemployment at the lower educational levels, a gain for one worker through education may simply displace another worker who would have been employed in that job.

In a way we are describing a game of musical chairs. If there are fewer chairs than there are people, then even if a formerly chairless person obtains a seat he will displace someone who had previously occupied it. To the degree that more education assists him in getting that seat, we will observe a correlation between more education and the probability of obtaining a seat. What we might not observe is the person who is being displaced in the competition. That is, a private gainhold out of poverty for one person may simply be equivalent to relegating a different person to the poverty category. Certainly, this is consistent with the previously cited studies that find little relation between the distribution of education and the distribution of income under conditions of inadequate job demand. It might be noted that one estimate sets the total number of involuntary unemployed or underemployed at about 25 percent of a redefined labor force. This estimate includes the total numbers of official unemployed, underemployed and part-time workers seeking full-time work, housewives and students who would prefer to work if jobs were available, nonworking persons between 55 and 64, and several other categories which are not included in the official labor force and unemployment statistics.[118]

Thurow has characterized the "musical chair" situation as one of job competition where workers are placed in a queue based largely upon their education.[119] Education is seen as a measure of trainability by employers, for

[115]Peter Henle, "Exploring the Distribution of Earned Income," *Monthly Labor Review* 95 (December 1972): 16–27.

[116]Barry R. Chiswick and Jacob Mincer, "Time Series in Personal Income Inequality in the United States from 1939, with Projections to 1985," *Journal of Political Economy* 80, Part II (May–June 1972): S57.

[117]Thurow, "Education and Economic Equality"; idem "Measuring the Economic Benefits of Education"; idem, "Generating Inequality," draft manuscript, Department of Economics, Massachusetts Institute of Technology (January 1975); Harrison, "Education and Underemployment in the Urban Ghetto."

[118]Bertram Gross and Stanley Moses, "Measuring the Real Work Force: 25 Million Unemployed," *Social Policy* 3 (September–October 1972): 5–10.

[119]Thurow, "Education and Economic Equality"; idem, "Measuring the Economic Benefits of Education"; idem, *Generating Inequality*.

it is suggested that most actual job skills are acquired through experience and on-the-job training. In order to minimize training costs, employers select the "best" workers for the best jobs, where the worker's income will be determined primarily by the quality of capital that is available to him. Workers are then selected for jobs according to where they are in the job queue with the best jobs going to those at the head of the line and the poorer jobs going to those farther back. For those near or at the end of the line there are no jobs at all. In order to get a job they have to acquire some trait—for example, more education—that will place them further up in the queue, but having done this someone else will be deprived of a job who is farther back.

The job-competition metaphor seems to be one that is consistent with the data.[120] Persons who are farthest back in the job queue can only gain if they can improve their relative positions, but once they improve their relative positions they make others worse off. It is also consistent with the fact that educational requirements for jobs have been rising as the supply of educational persons increases.[121] Moreover, the job queue may be *much* longer than the number of available opportunities in urban ghettos and rural areas,

[120]That is, the model tends to provide a reasonable description of a process which would explain rising educational attainments for particular jobs; the positive association between an individual's education and his earnings; the preference of employers for persons with more education for more "productive" jobs; and the fact that the level of education of the unemployed and low productivity workers continues to rise without alleviating their condition. One challenge to the job competition model is the recent trend for the incomes of young college graduates to fall relative to young persons who have only high school completion: Richard B. Freeman, "The Declining Economic Value of Higher Education and the American Social System," paper prepared for the Aspen Institute for Humanistic Studies Conference on Education in a Changing Society (June 1975); idem, "Overinvestment in College Training?" *Journal of Human Resources* 10 (Summer 1975): 287–311. If job competition is determined strictly by one's educational credentials, then it would seem that the large recent influx of college-educated workers into the labor force relative to the meager set of traditional jobs that would normally be taken by such graduates would result in the college graduates replacing high school ones in the job queue. In such an event, the relative incomes of the two groups might have remained similar, as all persons were displaced in the queue. Of course, there are two reasons that the falling relative incomes of college graduates is not inconsistent with the job competition model. First, the adjustment of employers to the available labor supply is not likely to be instantaneous, so the upgrading of educational requirements for jobs might not have proceeded as rapidly as the appearance of the burgeoning surplus of college graduates. This may be particularly true in the short run, where college graduates who apply for existing high school graduate jobs are viewed as opportunists who are willing to take any job until a *real* career opportunity opens. In such a case, college graduates may be considered to be unworthy of hiring and training because of an anticipated high turnover. But, over the long run, the persistent surplus of college graduates will mean that they simply will not find those anticipated career opportunities that will take them away from lower-status work. The second reason that falling relative incomes of college graduates is not inconsistent with the job competition model is that there is no reason a priori to expect a constancy of wage differentials among educational groups as they change their positions on the job ladder. At the bottom, minimum wages and other institutions that create wage floors, such as union agreements, will prevent incomes from declining as rapidly for down-graded, employed persons in the lower portion of the job hierarchy in comparison with those in the middle.

[121]Ivar Berg, *Education and Jobs: The Great Training Robbery* (New York: Praeger, 1970).

so that even substantial increases in schooling will not place people high enough to obtain nonpoverty employment. Sex, race, and other personal characteristics may also be used by employers to rank people in the job queue, and additional education may not be adequate to compensate for low ranking due to other characteristics that are considered "undesirable."[122] Finally, even those persons who are able to obtain employment in the lower regions of the job queue will face subpoverty wages. For example, the existing minimum wage of $2 will relegate a family of four to poverty even if the family head is fortunate enough to be employed full-time, full-year at this wage. Thurow concludes that massive educational investments to alleviate poverty will be wasted without efforts to create more jobs and to reduce wage differentials.[123]

Even more ominous is the recent deterioration of the market for college-educated persons. Richard Freeman reports that starting salaries for college graduates in constant dollars fell some 11–25 percent between 1969 and 1974, and that this decline was greater than that for persons with less education. Further, his analysis has suggested that the result cannot be explained by economic conditions alone, and that it reflects what will apparently be a long-term malaise in the market for college graduates as the increase in supply of such persons exceeds available opportunities. Freeman has argued that this prognosis will tend to hold, even with rather drastic reductions in college participation. Accordingly, the hope that increased education will provide an efficient and effective cycle is seriously challenged by falling returns to higher education as well as the ostensible lack of effect of programs for increasing educational attainments and the lower returns to education of persons drawn from poverty backgrounds.[124]

To summarize, the strategy of alleviating poverty through programs that encourage disadvantaged persons to obtain more schooling seems to have been characterized by two shortcomings. First, it does not appear that the programs were very successful in raising educational attainments. Second, it does not seem likely that increasing educational attainments of the existing poor would have reduced substantially the poverty class in a society where there are simply an inadequate number of jobs at wages above the poverty level to absorb all job seekers. The result is that small increases in education relative to the population as a whole would have just nominal impacts on earnings, and large changes in the number of years of schooling obtained would likely secure nonpoverty status only at the expense of persons with less schooling who would have been filling those positions. As long as the job competition is composed of more job seekers than there are nonpoverty employment openings, the outcome will always be the same as that of the

[122]Michael Spence, "Job Market Signaling," *Quarterly Journal of Economics* 87 (August 1973): 355–374.

[123]Thurow, "Education and Economic Equality."

[124]Freeman, "The Declining Economic Value of Higher Education"; idem, "Overinvestment in College Training?"

musical chair game. While new people may find chairs, others will find that they have lost their seats in the competition. Accordingly, it does not seem likely that the "higher educational attainments" strategy represented a powerful antipoverty remedy.

### Specific Job Skills

The third education and training strategy utilized in the war on poverty for assisting the disadvantaged was that of inculcating specific job skills. These programs included the expansion of vocational education at the secondary level, Job Corps, Work Experience, and MDTA. The general purpose of these programs was to increase the job-specific skills possessed by the disadvantaged in order to increase their employment marketability. In one respect, this goal tends to reduce the complexity of the evaluation task since it may be possible to determine much more directly the success of these programs in reducing poverty by examining the associated gains in earnings. In contrast, the cognitive skills and increased educational strategies required that we review the educational success of those programs, and subsequently attempt to link educational success to impact on poverty reduction. With the programs that attempt to increase specific job skills, it is possible to evaluate poverty impacts more directly, although massive methodological problems persist.[125]

Evaluations of Job Corps refer to results obtained only during the second year of the program, 1966. The study by Glen Cain reports benefit to cost ratios that range between .60 and 1.89, but these were questioned as being optimistic by Levitan and Goldstein.[126] Cain used two sources of data to determine the income benefits for Job Corps participants. His first method entailed converting test score gains in mathematics and reading into assumed gains in educational attainments and the conversion of educational attainments, in turn, into Census-derived earnings. This procedure follows the approach developed by Ribich. It assumes that if a corpsman were able to raise his test scores by the amount associated with a movement from the fifth grade to the seventh grade, the additional earnings attributable to the Job Corps would be equivalent to those associated with two more years of schooling at the primary level. Based upon the poor relationship between test scores and earnings, we deem this method to be highly unreliable although an understandable early attempt at evaluation in light of the data deficiencies.

[125]Glen G. Cain and Robinson W. Hollister, "Evaluating Manpower Programs for the Disadvantaged," in *Cost–Benefit Analysis of Manpower Policies*, ed. Gerald C. Somers and W. Donald Wood (Kingston, Ontario: Industrial Relations Centre, Queen's University, 1970), pp. 119–151; Michael E. Borus, ed., *Evaluating the Impact of Manpower Programs* (Lexington, Mass.: Lexington Books, 1972); Daniel S. Hammermesh, *Economic Aspects of Manpower Training Programs* (Lexington, Mass.: Lexington Books, 1971).

[126]Glen G. Cain, "Benefit–Cost Estimates for Job Corps," Institute for Research on Poverty Discussion Paper No. 9–68 (Madison: University of Wisconsin, 1967), p. 5; Levitan, "Job Corps," pp. 21–22; Goldstein, "The Effectiveness of Manpower Training Programs," p. 358.

The second method used by Cain reviewed the earnings of a sample of ex-corpsmen and a sample of persons who were accepted for Job Corps but chose not to participate. One should bear in mind that while nine months was the normal term for graduation, the estimated average stay in the Job Corps was only about five months. The pre–Job Corps wage was estimated to be $1.17 an hour for both groups, and the average corpsman was making about 12 cents an hour more after six months in Job Corps. Unfortunately, it appeared that the "no-shows" kept pace with the higher wages of the corpsmen, and even with the gains and an expected unemployment rate of about 40 percent, the Job Corps graduates would have been making only about $1500 in annual earnings after leaving the program. Even the slight gain in wages observed in February 1967 for Job Corps trainees might have been affected by the fact that on 1 February 1967 minimum wage went from $1.25 to $1.40 an hour, and the comparison group of "no-shows" were interviewed prior to this rise.[127]

A later study, by Harry Woltman and William Walton, found that 18 months after leaving the Job Corps no statistically significant difference could be found between the wages of participants and "no-shows," and no impact could be discerned on employment rates either.[128] A study of a specific Job Corps Center found that six months after termination, the unemploymet rate was about one-third, and 70 percent of the former corpsmen were not working in jobs that were related to their training.[129] Further, the group that entered civilian employment was receiving a wage of less than $200 a month or $2400 a year if they were fully employed. When one discounts this amount by a 30 percent probability of unemployment, the approximate average expected wage after training was only about $1600 a year.

On the basis of both investment efficiency and poverty reduction, the Job Corps does not seem to have been very successful. The earnings received after training were still below the poverty level, and even the gains reported by Cain were considered to be suspect by Sar Levitan and by Jon Goldstein for a variety of reasons.[130]

Vocational education has two possible aspects that could reduce the probability of poverty status for participants. First, it may provide a curriculum that is well-suited to some disadvantaged students in maintaining their interest in school relative to other curricula. That is, disadvantaged students who pursue vocational curricula may obtain more schooling than comparable students in other curricula. This phenomenon may be particularly important, given the apparently high concentration of students from lower

[127]Cain, "Benefit–Cost Estimates for Job Corps," p. 26; Levitan, "Job Corps."

[128]Harry R. Woltman and William W. Walton, "Evaluation of the War on Poverty: The Feasibility of Benefit–Cost Analysis of Manpower Programs," a report prepared for the General Accounting Office (Washington, D.C.: Resource Management Corp., March 1968).

[129]Lane Rawlins, "Job Corps: The Urban Center as a Training Facility," *Journal of Human Resources* 6 (Spring 1971): 221-235.

[130]Cain, "Benefit–Cost Estimates of Job Corps"; Levitan, "Job Corps"; Goldstein, "The Effectiveness of Manpower Training Programs."

socioeconomic backgrounds in the vocational curriculum.[131] Second, the vocational curriculum may provide a greater contribution to employability and earnings for students who would end their formal schooling at the secondary level than would alternative courses of studies.

Unfortunately, there has been little analysis of the first of these possibilities except for the study of Arthur Corazzini. Corazzini estimated that about one-quarter of entering ninth graders in the vocational school of a medium-sized city could probably drop out in contrast to about 14 percent of the students entering the regular high school. He also observed that the students in the commercial studies in the regular high school had an even higher probability of dropping out, 39 percent. He then compared the costs and benefits of the reduction in dropouts between the vocational school and the commercial program, and concluded that the investment in "saving" dropouts through vocational education was more costly than the earnings benefits generated.[132] The problem with this analysis is that even the commercial curriculum is a vocational one, despite its presence in the regular high school. Accordingly, his comparison was that of the general vocational high school with a specific vocational curriculum. Further, the fact that the study lacked information on differences in student backgrounds means that we cannot be assured that the students were similar in the other factors that affect their propensities to continue or to drop out.

Although there is very limited information on the role of vocational education in producing higher educational attainments for the disadvantaged, there are a number of studies that review the employment and earnings benefits of vocational graduates in comparison with those of students in other curricula. Taussig found that the rates of unemployment of vocational graduates in New York City tended to be extremely high and did not seem to be better than for graduates of other curricula over the long run.[133] The fact that vocational schools put a heavy emphasis on placement would explain a superior performance in the short run. Moreover, even when the vocational graduates were employed, they were typically found in jobs that were unrelated to their training.

In his study for Worcester, Massachusetts, Corazzini found that recent

[131]Rupert N. Evans and Joel D. Galloway, "Verbal Ability and Socioeconomic Status of 9th and 12th Grade College Preparatory, General and Vocational Students," *Journal of Human Resources* 8 (Winter 1973): 24–36.

[132]Arthur J. Corazzini, "The Decision to Invest in Vocational Education: An Analysis of Costs and Benefits," *Journal of Human Resources* 3 (Summer 1968): 112, 114.

[133]Michael K. Taussig, "An Economic Analysis of Vocational Education in the New York City High Schools," *Journal of Human Resources* 3, *Supplement: Vocational Education* (Summer 1968): 59–87; Corazzini, "The Decision to Invest in Vocational Education"; Jacob J. Kaufman et al., *An Analysis of the Comparative Costs and Benefits of Vocational verus Academic Education in Secondary Schools*, Preliminary Report, Project No. O.E. 512, Grant No. OEG-1-6-000512-0817 (University Park, Pa.: Institute for Human Resources, Pennsylvania State University, October 1967); Teh-Wei Hu, Maw Lin Lee, and Ernst W. Stromsdorfer, "Economic Returns to Vocational and Comprehensive High School Graduates," *Journal of Human Resources* 6 (Winter 1971): 25–47.

vocational graduates were likely to be receiving 4 cents an hour to 25 cents an hour more than regular high school graduates.[134] This represented a difference of from $80 a year to $500 a year, with both groups making from $3300 to almost $4000 a year. But these are only the earnings of the employed, and no attempt was made to look at employment levels and differentials between the two groups. Without knowledge of the amount of unemployment and underemployment, it is not possible to determine the probable effect of vocational education in affecting poverty.

The most elaborate study is that of Teh-Wei Hu, Maw Lin Lee, and Ernst Stromsdorfer. They compared the employment and earnings levels of graduates of comprehensive secondary education programs and vocational education programs after adjusting for the socioeconomic status, IQ scores, and other personal factors that might have varied between the two groups. They found that in the first year after graduation the vocation graduates earned about $648 a year more than their nonvocational counterparts, but by the sixth year the annual earnings differential favoring the vocational graduates had been reduced to $192.[135] Apparently, the main effect on earnings was due to the higher initial levels of employment of the vocational graduates, who worked about seven and one-half weeks more than the nonvocational graduates during the first year after graduation, but only about two weeks more by the sixth year. This result supports the hypothesis that a principal advantage that vocational graduates have over nonvocational graduates is a much better job-placement service. While the average salaries of males after six years was almost $6000 and of females $2400, there is no discussion of the sampling bias. Typically, the nonresponses in a longitudinal survey of this sort are the "failures" who cannot be located or who do not respond to this type of survey. This is also reflected in the relatively high employment rates of the sample, and it suggests that the results cannot be used as reliable indicators of the status of the disadvantaged students who went through the programs.[136]

In summary, the two ways that vocational education programs might improve the plight of the disadvantaged are by providing higher education attainments and by increasing the marketable skills and thus the income and employment of high school graduates beyond what would be obtained through other educational routes. The evidence suggests that if such gains are associated with vocational education, they are marginal at best. More specific

---

[134]Corazzini, "The Decision to Invest in Vocational Education."

[135]Hu, Lee, and Stromsdorfer, "Economic Returns to Vocational and Comprehensive High School Graduates," p. 34.

[136]Typically, the measured IQ scores of the disadvantaged are in the 80–90 range, while the students in each of the curricula in this sample show IQ scores that average between 101 and 110. These data suggest that on the average these students are about one and one-half standard deviations in IQ above typical groups of disadvantaged students, and they throw doubt upon the applicability of findings of this study for the disadvantaged. See Kaufman et al., *An Analysis of the Comparative Costs*, Chapter 6.

evaluations of the experiences of disadvantaged students in different secondary curricula are needed to provide a better understanding of the effects of vocational education on the future earnings of students from low-income backgrounds. None of these studies isolate that group from the more general student populations that undertake vocational training.

The Work Experience program was designed to take heads of families receiving assistance under the Aid for Dependent Children (AFDC) and train them for employment. The job placement rates for trainees who terminated their participation between the middle of 1966 and the end of February 1967 was about one-third. Completers had a 50 percent rate of placement and noncompleters had a 22 percent rate of placement, and the respective salaries were $248 and $239 a month.[137] In 1968, the program was subsumed under the Work Incentive Program (WIN). On the basis of the first 18 months of operation of WIN, about 2.3 million AFDC recipients were assessed, and some 400,000 were referred to the program. About 229,000 enrolled over this period, and about 120,000 terminated their training. About 24,000 "successful completions" were established, meaning that they were on the job 3 to 6 months after placement—a ratio of one successful completion for each five terminations. By the end of April 1972 the number of cumulative enrollments had reached 385,000, the number of cumulative terminations had grown to 257,000, and the number of successful completions was 61,500.[138]

Persons with the highest placement rates were those with the strongest educational attainments and those with the longer employment histories, so the most disadvantaged were least likely to benefit from enrolling in the program. Moreover, there is some evidence that WIN selected the "best" of the available crop, as reflected in the observation that while only about 16 percent of AFDC mothers were high school graduates in 1969, about 41 percent of those AFDC mothers enrolled in WIN were high school graduates. Indeed, one of the evaluations found that: "Those WIN enrollees who achieve placement status . . . are a heterogeneous group that exhibits few of the characteristic problems associated with disadvantaged persons."[139] Accordingly, it would seem that WIN successes were those persons who were only marginally out of the labor market or out of employment. Goldstein has noted that: "After 2 years of operation only 1 percent of the assessed AFDC recipients had completed training and been employed for a minimum of 3 months," and ". . . since there is evidence that WIN authorities 'creamed' in selecting enrollees, the prospects for improved placement rates and for subsequent reductions in the welfare rolls by expanding a structurally unaltered program are not encouraging."[140]

[137]Levitan, "Work Experience and Training," p. 79.

[138]Goldstein, "The Effectiveness of Manpower Training Programs," p. 361.·

[139]J. David Roessner, Employment Contexts and Disadvantaged Workers (Washington, D.C.: Bureau of Social Science, November 1971), p. 192, as cited by Goldstein, "The Effectiveness of Manpower Training Programs," p. 364.

[140]Goldstein, "The Effectiveness of Manpower Training Programs," pp. 364–365.

The purpose of the program on Job Opportunities in the Business Sector (JOBS) was to place disadvantaged persons who required training and other types of employment-related services in jobs in the private sector. The hope was that such an approach would minimize the cost to the public sector of increasing employment and training of this group. Unfortunately, the great expectations that were heralded for the program by both business and government far exceeded its performance. Placements, training, and long-term unemployment under the JOBS aegis appeared to fall far short of pledges by the business community, and the evidence gathered in a government study by the General Accounting Office suggests that even those data that are available overstate the success of JOBS.[141]

Firms failed to provide many of the services that they were paid for under government contract; significant portions of the "trainees" were hired for jobs that required no skills and for which no training was normally required; and nondisadvantaged persons were also hired in sizable numbers under the program. While no systematic evaluation of the entire program was conducted, virtually all of the partial evaluations yield the conclusion that the program had little or no impact on training and no apparent long-term effect on reducing poverty except for its immediate employment effects.[142] Even the employment effects are suspect, since it is likely that a substantial portion of job placements under JOBS would have been undertaken without government subsidies and do not represent net increases in employment of the disadvantaged.

The Manpower Development Training Act was the largest training program over the decade, with about 2.2 million enrollees between 1964 and 1973 and federal obligations of almost $3.2 billion. While many studies have been made of the earnings and employment benefits of the MDTA,[143] few have concentrated on the contribution of such programs to the economic status of the disadvantaged. Some studies have suggested that the disadvantaged benefit

[141]U.S., General Accounting Office, *Evaluation of Results and Administration of the Job Opportunities in the Business Sector (JOBS) Program in Five Cities* (Washington, D.C.: General Accounting Office, 1971).

[142]Goldstein, "The Effectiveness of Manpower Training Programs," pp. 365–369; General Accounting Office, *Evaluation of Results*; Greenleigh Associates, *The Job Opportunities in the Business Sector Program: An Evaluation of Impact in Ten Standard Metropolitan Statistical Areas* (New York: Greenleigh, June 1970); Levitan, Magnum, and Marshall, *Human Resources and Labor Markets*, pp. 353–359.

[143]Garth L. Mangum and John Walsh, *A Decade of Manpower Development and Training* (Salt Lake City: Olympus Publishing Co., 1973); Ralph E. Smith, "An Analysis of the Efficiency and Equity of Manpower Programs" (Ph.D. dissertation, Georgetown University, 1970); Einar Hardin and Michael Borus, *The Economic Benefits and Costs of Retraining* (Lexington, Mass.: D. C. Heath and Co., 1971); David A. Page, "Retraining under the Manpower Development Act: A Cost–Benefit Analysis," Reprint No. 86 (Washington, D.C.: The Brookings Institution, 1964); Gerald G. Somers, ed., *Retraining the Unemployed* (Madison, Wisconsin: University of Wisconsin Press, 1968); Sewell, *Training the Poor*; Ribich, *Education and Poverty*; Ernst W. Stromsdorfer, "Determinants of Economic Success in Retraining the Unemployed: The West Virginia Experience," *Journal of Human Resources* 3 (Spring 1968): 139–158.

more from MDTA programs than do the nondisadvantaged, while other studies show that whites and the nondisadvantaged received the largest earnings and employment benefits in comparison with blacks and the disadvantaged.[144] Ralph Smith found that among the disadvantaged persons who completed MDTA training in 1967, the annual increase in earnings was only about $269 and did not compensate for the cost of training.[145]

A more optimistic picture of gains for the disadvantaged is reflected in a report prepared for the Department of Labor that is cited by Mangum and Walsh. Disadvantaged trainees who had enrolled in institutional training programs had posttraining annual earnings of about $3363, or about $1210 more than their pretraining earnings; and disadvantaged trainees who had received OJT had almost $3900 in posttraining annual earnings, for a gain of about $1400 over earnings in the pretraining period. These gains were about twice those of the nondisadvantaged participants, although the nondisadvantaged still ended up in the posttraining period with considerably higher earnings than the disadvantaged, since they had higher earnings before training. But these data may not reflect an accurate picture because they were based only on those trainees who had at least one job during the pretraining and posttraining periods. That is, trainees who were unemployed in either period are not reflected in the data, and one-third of the institutional enrollees and 10 percent of the OJT trainees had not obtained employment during the 16-month posttraining period. Since blacks, the less educated, and welfare recipients were more heavily represented in institutional training programs, there is some inferential evidence that the disadvantaged were more likely to be among the unemployed, even though a specific breakdown of unemployment is not shown according to the advantaged and disadvantaged distinction.[146]

The question of whether MDTA was responsible for the gains is also raised by the methodology that was used. A comparison of pretraining earnings to posttraining ones ignores the possibility that persons comparable to the trainees might have experienced similar results. For example, if persons who were out of employment or who were dissatisfied with the present employment volunteered for training under MDTA while otherwise identical counterparts searched for new jobs or continued to move up the training or mobility ladder on their jobs, then nontrainees would also have shown earnings gains. The study that we cited did not have any such "control group." Yet, previous experience with a comparison of earnngs gains using the pretraining to posttraining differences versus the comparison of earnings with a control group of nontrainees found MDTA related gains of about $1524

---

[144]Sewell, *Training the Poor*; Stromsdorfer, "Determinants of Economic Success"; Smith, *An Analysis of the Efficiency and Equity of Manpower Programs*; Hardin and Borus, *The Economic Benefits and Costs of Retraining*.

[145]Smith, *An Analysis of the Efficiency and Equity of Manpower Training*.

[146]Mangum and Walsh, *A Decade of Manpower Development and Training*, pp. 24–25, 27, and 35.

when using the previous methodology but only $216 when the changes were compared with those of a comparable group of nontrainees.[147]

Using Social Security earnings records, trainees were matched to non-trainees on the basis of previous earnings histories as well as age, sex, and race, and the gains in earnings were compared. According to this methodology, it was found that the gains of the Social Security "controls" were greater than those of the MDTA trainees. While this method of comparison is probably more reliable than the simple pretraining to posttraining differences in earnings for trainees, there are still problems in using it.[148] The differences in results, however, do point out the shaky nature of effectiveness claims when the study does not use control groups as a basis for comparison.

From the studies that have been reviewed, it appears that the disadvantaged are likely to experience some increase in earnings from MDTA participation, but the increases may be quite small and inadequate to remove them from poverty status.[149] As an example, David Sewell found that a predominantly black group of trainees in North Carolina received posttraining gains in annual earnings of about $433 over nontrainees, but the posttraining earnings of $2406 were still considerably below the poverty level for the group.[150] Thus, one might ask how effective MDTA has been in alleviating poverty. It would seem that the only reasonable answer would be to argue that it has had a slight impact, but not a profound one. Moreover, it can hardly be viewed as representing a future hope, in itself, for the following reasons. First, trainees were volunteers, suggesting that they were somewhat more highly informed, motivated, and able than nontrainees. Accordingly, they probably represented the "best" of the disadvantaged with respect to employment and earnings possibilities, and it is not likely that a random sample of the disadvantaged would have received equally high benefits from training. Second, in the absence of job expansion or upgrading, it is likely that much of the increase in employment and earnings came at the expense of other workers who were displaced. None of these evaluations have considered the "musical chairs" impact, and their calculations of the cost–benefit ratios surely overstate the social returns to manpower training.[151]

[147]Hardin and Borus, *The Economic Benefits and Costs of Retraining.*

[148]Mangum and Walsh, *A Decade of Manpower Development and Training*, pp. 37–41; Assembly of Behavioral and Social Sciences, National Research Council, National Academy of Sciences, *Final Report of the Panel on Manpower Training Evaluation: The Use of Social Security Earnings Data for Assessing the Impact of Manpower Training Programs* (Washington, D.C.: January 1974).

[149]Goldstein, "The Effectiveness of Manpower Training Programs," pp. 340–350.

[150]Sewell, *Training the Poor.*

[151]That the choice of methodology can have a powerful impact on the statistical findings and their policy interpretations is reflected in recent controversies. Compare Coleman et al., *Equality of Educational Opportunity*, Chapter 3, with Bowles and Levin, "The Determinants of Scholastic Achievement"; Cain and Watts, "Problems in Making Policy Inferences"; and Hanushek and Kain, "On the Value of Equality." Also compare David J. Armer, "The Evidence on Busing," *The Public Interest*, No. 28 (Summer 1972): 90–126, with Thomas F. Pettigrew et al., "Busing: A

In summary, the improvement of job skills strategy does seem to have a slight effect on removing persons from poverty, particularly at the margin. MDTA and perhaps WIN or Work Experience programs seemed to have some impact in this direction, especially for those individuals who were very close to the poverty line and had previous employment experience and relatively higher levels of education than the average disadvantaged person. The available evidence on Job Corps shows no such effect nor do the existing evaluations of Vocational Education.

## RETROSPECTION AND REFORMULATION

In the previous section, we reviewed the rationale for the inclusion of education and training programs in the war on poverty as well as the descriptions of the programs and their apparent impact on reducing poverty. We suggested that the overall thrust of such programs was predicated on the view that the poor are poor because of their low productivities resulting from personal incompetencies.[152] By providing more education and training it was hoped to raise competencies, productivities, and earnings of the impoverished. A wide variety of programs were either initiated or expanded during the poverty decade, and the evaluations and relevant research suggest that their effect on the reduction of poverty was minimal. In this section, we wish to ask why the failures were so great and what alternatives might be considered.

While there are many different answers to the question of what went wrong, there are few who would deny the basic failure of existing approaches toward education and training for alleviating poverty. It is instructive to compare the radical critique of David Gordon with the following statement by Arthur Jensen in the introduction to his well-known paper: "How Much Can We Boost IQ and Scholastic Achievement?"

> Why has there been such uniform failure of compensatory programs where ever they have been tried? What has gone wrong? In other fields, when bridges do not stand, when aircraft do not fly, when machines do not work, when treatments do not cure, despite all conscientious efforts on the part of many persons to make them do so, one begins to question the basic assumptions, principles, theories, and hypotheses that guide one's efforts. Is it time to follow suit in education.[153]

Of course, the question is a rhetorical one, in that it is an invitation for Jensen to provide his own conclusions on the subject just as Gordon as well as Bowles and Gintis provide theirs.[154] In fact, there are many answers to this question,

Review of 'The Evidence'," *The Public Interest*, No. 30 (Winter 1973): 88–131, and David J. Armer, "The Double Standard: A Reply," *The Public Interest*, No. 30 (Winter 1973): 119–131.

[152]Hunt, *The Challenge of Incompetence and Poverty.*

[153]Gordon, *Theories of Poverty and Underemployment*; Arthur R. Jensen, "How Much Can We Boost IQ and Scholastic Achievement?" *Harvard Educational Review* 39 (1969): 1–123.

[154]Gordon, *Theories of Poverty and Underemployment*; Bowles and Gintis, "IQ in the U.S. Class Structure."

and they will vary according to the worldviews of the analysts. Such views are based upon deeply, ingrained social, educational, and political experiences that affect their understanding of how the world works. The result of these experiences is that the policy analyst, social scientist, and layman alike will interpret the evidence in the context of their beliefs about the fundamental social, political, and economic workings of society.[155]

These views on the nature of social reality are the contexts that mold the interpretation of observed phenomena on the causes and alleviation of poverty. On the subject of the appropriate role of education and training in reducing poverty and the particular experiences of the past decade, there are at least five identifiable views: (1) the genetics perspective; (2) the professional perspective; (3) the technocratic reform perspective; (4) the welfare capitalism perspective; and (5) the socialist perspective. Each of these provides a different understanding of the apparent failures of the educational and training programs to make substantial inroads against poverty, and each suggests a different palliative.

### The Genetic Perspective

This view suggests that compensatory education and presumably other training programs have failed because the poor simply do not have the ability to improve their skills. This thesis is most closely associated with a reasonable interpretation of the work of Arthur Jensen, even though Jensen himself has been relatively cautious in giving a specific policy interpretation.[156] The core of the argument is that IQ is the primary basis for learning skills in life, and IQ is primarily inherited through the genotype passed on from parents to children rather than being inculcated through environmental influences. As elaborated by Richard Herrnstein on a theme borrowed from Michael Young, productivity in modern society is closely related to IQ.[157] Accordingly, a person with a high IQ is relatively more productive than one with a low IQ, and in a society where rewards such as income and social status are distributed according to merit, the ranking of income and IQ will be similar. Moreover, such a meritocracy will be based largely on inheritance, since the main determinant of the hierarchy will be IQ, which is passed on from generation to generation.

[155]Peter L. Berger and Thomas Luckman, *The Social Construction of Reality* (New York: Doubleday and Co., 1966); Karl Mannheim, *Ideology and Utopia* (New York: Harcourt Brace and Co., 1936); Robert K. Merton, *Social Theory and Social Structure* (Glencoe, Ill.: The Free Press, 1949); idem, *The Sociology of Science*, ed. Norman W. Storer (Chicago: University of Chicago Press, 1973); Michael Polanyi, *Personal Knowledge*, Harper Torchbook Edition (New York: Harper and Row, 1964); Thomas S. Kuhn, *The Structure of Scientific Revolutions* (Chicago: University of Chicago Press, 1962); Karl R. Pepper, *Objective Knowledge: An Evolutionary Approach* (Oxford: The Clarendon Press, 1972); Levin, "Education, Life Chances, and the Courts."

[156]Jensen, "How Much Can We Boost IQ and Scholastic Achievement?"

[157]Herrnstein, *IQ in the Meritocracy*; Michael Young, *The Rise of the Meritocracy* (London: Thames and Hudson, 1958).

The consequences of this explanation are straightforward. The poor are impoverished for the same reasons that their children cannot learn. They simply have limited potential as reflected in their low IQ scores. The solution is equally straightforward. Do not expect too much from the poor in the areas of either educational development or economic development since they are limited by their genetic code, which has doomed them to incompetence on both counts. This theme would seem to explain the persistence both of poverty and of the failures of educational and training programs for the disadvantaged. From a policy perspective, it would appear that, at best, the poor must be the wards of a benevolent society that would provide them with the amounts of and types of education that might make them minimally functional while relying on income-maintenance programs to alleviate poverty.

But our previous presentation suggests that the genetic view is flawed on two counts. First, the assumption of fixed intelligence is challenged by the educational programs that have experienced sharp increases in IQ scores during the duration of the programs, even though when the environments were changed the IQ scores reverted back to the lower levels.[158] Second, and more important, IQ and IQ-related test measures are poor predictors of economic success, and differences in cognitive scores generally do not seem to be associated with any substantial differences in earnings.[159]

### The Professional Perspective

The professional perspective seems to be based upon the premise that we have not yet begun to *try* compensatory education and training programs with any degree of seriousness. The assumption that underlies this interpretation is that schooling and many training programs are basically sound, but they are starved for resources. This is reflected in the words of an anonymous school administrator who characterized the billion dollars or so of annual expenditures on Title I as the Black River described by Mark Twain: "It's one mile wide and one inch deep." Educational professionals when faced with the great dilemma of having to solve this major issue through schooling see the problem as one where the available resources are not enough. They seek smaller class sizes, more remedial specialists, more teacher aides, additional instructional materials, more teacher time to prepare classes and to plan curricula, more consultants and administrators, and more of virtually all school inputs.

Accordingly, the professionals see the failures being resolved by increased spending on the various compensatory and training programs. But, the weakness in this view is that the available evidence suggests that increases in these resources are not likely to have a salient effect on educational out-

---

[158]Bronfenbrenner, *Is Early Intervention Effective?* Ryan, *Longitudinal Evaluations.*

[159]Bowles and Gintis, "IQ in the U.S. Class Structure"; Bowles and Nelson, "The 'Genetic Inheritance of IQ'."

comes, and the schools do not seem to be organized so that additional resources will improve the educational plights of the disadvantaged.[160] Additionally, there is little support for the view that increased cognitive outputs will have a strong impact on the economic status of the disadvantaged.

## The Reform Perspective

The reform perspective is not dissimilar to the professional one, in the sense that it is based upon the view that education and training institutions can contribute substantially to increasing economic equality. The difference is that the reformers view the schools and programs as requiring various kinds of technical adjustments in order to succeed. These technical reforms vary all the way from teacher retraining and the adoption of new curricula and educational technology to the restructuring of educational organizations to improve the incentives for serving the poor. The latter innovations include educational vouchers and political decentralization that would alter drastically the governance of the schools with respect to professionals, parents, students, and the community. Greater equity in financing of the schools is also part of the reform agenda.[161]

The reform posture is also the one that is held by those who look to evaluation and social experimentation to come up with successes in place of the previous failures.[162] That is, some reformers believe that the answers for improving the education of the disadvantaged already exist,[163] while others believe that existing solutions are inadequate and that we must search for more effective approaches. Finally, others yet see the problem as one of finding ways of constructing more incentives for the education and training enterprises to address the needs of the disadvantaged as well as other clientele.[164]

These approaches are characterized by two difficulties. First, there exists little evidence that any particular strategy is superior to any other, and evaluations have not tended to settle the controversies among adherents of different reforms. Indeed, the existing evaluations have been more a source of controversy than of enlightenment.[165] Second, the very educational and training objectives that are the focus of the evaluations and the reforms do not seem to be closely related to economic outcomes. That is, the evidence that

---

[160]Averch et al., *How Effective Is Schooling?*

[161]Pincus, *School Finance in Transition*; John E. Coons, William H. Clune III, and Stephan D. Sugarman, *Private Wealth and Public Education* (Cambridge, Mass.: Belknap Press, Harvard University Press, 1970); Arthur Wise, *Rich School, Poor School* (Chicago: University of Chicago Press, 1968); Robert Hartman and Robert Reischauer, *Reforming School Finance* (Washington, D.C.: The Brookings Institution, 1973).

[162]Alice Rivlin, *Systematic Thinking for Social Action* (Washington, D.C.: The Brookings Institution, 1971).

[163]Silberman, *Crisis in the Classroom.*

[164]Pincus, "Incentives for Innovation in the Public Schools."

[165]Rivlin, *Systematic Thinking for Social Action.*

we presented suggests that while these educational reforms may be valuable in themselves, they do not seem to show a strong impact on the alleviation of poverty. Finally, there is the issue of whether educational reforms that violate the major tenets of our society are even possible.[166]

## The Welfare Capitalism Perspective

In our previous analysis, it was suggested that education and training programs alone cannot make serious inroads into poverty without increases in jobs to absorb the more highly trained and educated. But, the historical evidence suggests that U.S. capitalism has been unable to sustain a high enough level of job demand at nonpoverty wages to employ all who want to work at incomes above the poverty level. Without an adequate number of jobs that can employ the existing human resources, there is little hope that a more highly trained disadvantaged group will find the placements and earnings to take them out of poverty. Indeed, to the degree that improvements in economic status of one group will be made, they will likely be made at the expense of some other group, as long as the supply of educated and trained workers exceeds the demand for them.

This condition suggests that if our society with its heavy domination of monopolistic elements is going to be able to eliminate poverty, it can only be done by state-generated employment and reduction of wage differentials. Where monetary and fiscal policies as well as education and training have failed to achieve this goal, then the government must generate employment directly through public employment programs. This solution is based on the welfare capitalism perspective, since it accepts the basic framework of monopoly capitalism while requiring the state to compensate for the failure of capitalism to equitably fill such human needs as employment, health care, education, and income maintenance.

The kinds of interventions that would be made by government in such a system in order to alleviate poverty have been suggested by Thurow in his call for a deliberate attempt to increase employment and reduce wage differentials. Among the solutions that he suggested were:

> In addition to a frontal attack on wage differentials, programs to alter the demands for different types of employees would include research and development efforts to alter the skill-mix generated by technical progress; guaranteed government jobs; fiscal and monetary policies designed to create labor shortages; public wage scales designed to pressure low-wage employers; and incentives to encourage private employers to compress their wage differentials. If quick results are desired, quotas must seriously be considered since they are the only technique for quickly altering the types of laborers demanded.[167]

Christopher Jencks et al., too, have called for similar types of solutions as

---

[166]Henry M. Levin, "Educational Reform and Social Change," *Journal of Applied Behavioral Science* 10 (August 1974): 304–320.
[167]Thurow, "Education and Economic Equality."

well as a greater attempt to redistribute income directly through increasing taxation of the rich while at the same time raising the guaranteed income of the present group of poor. While Jencks et al. refer to this as socialism, it is welfare state capitalism of the Scandinavian variety.[168]

What would be the role of education and training under such a program? Education and training would still take place, but the specific approaches would represent direct responses to job demands rather than preparation for jobs that may not exist.[169] Probably an increasing amount of training would take place on the job or in institutions in direct conjunction with job needs. There would be a greater trend toward continuous use of retraining programs both in institutions and on the job, as technological change and other dynamic conditions altered training and educational needs. It would also be necessary to construct a better system of job information and educational planning to match the dynamic changes in employment with changes in educational preparation.

### The Socialist Perspective

The socialist perspective is based upon the view that poverty is an integral part of the capitalist system, having its basis in the capitalist mode of production, with its property relations, productive hierarchy, and need for a reserve army of unemployed and underemployed.[170] That is, a poverty class is the direct outgrowth of the social relations of production and the quest for capital accumulation reflected under capitalism. The fundamental contradic-

---

[168]Jencks et al., *Inequality: A Reassessment*; Gosta Rehn and Erik Lundberg, "Employment and Welfare: Some Swedish Issues," *Industrial Relations* 2 (February 1963): 1–4; Rudolf Meidner and Rolf Anderson, "The Overall Impact of an Active Labor Market Policy in Sweden," in *Manpower Programs in the Policy Mix*, ed. Lloyd Ulman (Baltimore: Johns Hopkins University Press, 1973); Margaret H. Simeral, "On the Feasibility of a Counter-Cyclical Manpower Program," unpublished paper (Eugene, Oregon: Department of Economics, University of Oregon, April 1975).

[169]A recent study of community colleges, technical schools, and proprietary institutes found that even over a three- to four-year period after graduation the vast majority of graduates who had taken professional or technical-level training were unable to get training-related jobs. Among graduates or lower-level clerical or service worker programs the job placement was higher, but with the exception of secretaries almost all were at the federal minimum wage. The study concluded that the very extension of postsecondary education to the disadvantaged through community colleges and other technical schools and institutes tended to maintain class and income inequalities rather than overcoming them: Wellford W. Wilms, "The Effectiveness of Public and Proprietary Occupational Training," a technical report submitted to the National Institute of Education (Berkeley, Cal.: Center for Research and Development in Higher Education, University of California, October 1974). Also see Jerome Karabel, "Community Colleges and Social Stratification," *Harvard Educational Review* 42 (November 1972): 521–562.

[170]Paul Baran and Paul Sweezy, *Monopoly Capital* (New York: Monthly Review Press, 1966); Thomas Weisskopf, "Capitalism and Inequality," in *The Capitalist System*, ed. Richard C. Edwards, Michael Reich, and Thomas E. Weisskopf (Englewood Cliffs, N. J.: Prentice-Hall, 1972), pp. 125–133; Steve Marglin, "What Do Bosses Do?" *Review of Radical Political Economics* (Summer 1974): 60–112.

tion between capital and labor, the alienation of the worker from the process and product of his work and from his fellow worker, underemployment, unemployment, inequality, and poverty are considered to be built in to the structure of capitalist society.[171] Accordingly, the socialist view of the welfare-capitalist approach is that it is merely an attempt to address the symptoms of the problem rather than its cause, and any permanent, stable, and democratic solution must go beyond welfare capitalism to a democratic socialist state.[172] In such a state, the capital would be socially owned and managed with goals of equity in participation, employment, and social welfare replacing the motive of profit maximizing and private capital accumulation.

The failure of educational and training policies to increase employment is seen in the socialist framework as the domination of capital over the needs of workers rather than as a failure of education *per se*. In fact, education and training programs are seen as preparing the young for the highly unequal occupational and earnings positions that characterize the workplace by reinforcing the class differences in student backgrounds that already exist. Differences in the resources available to schools as well as the class orientations of educational institutions and internal tracking have the effect of assisting in the reproduction of class differences from generation to generation.[173] Discontinuous and segmented labor markets and discrimination represent mechanisms by which additional education and training for the disadvantaged will fail to be translated into substantial economic gains.[174] And the personality traits that are inculcated according to social class by the schools to fill out the work hierarchy—or the ranks of the unemployed—are the same characteristics that supervisors seem to use in rating workers and selecting them for various positions in work organizations or not hiring them at all.[175]

Since the socialist perspective sees the existence of a poverty class as an organic part of capitalist society and views the educational and training programs as reinforcing initial class distinctions among children, the only solution is to eliminate capitalist institutions and replace them with socialist

[171]Charles H. Anderson, *The Political Economy of Social Class* (Englewood Cliffs, N. J.: Prentice-Hall, 1974).

[172]Michael Harrington, "Welfare Capitalism in Crisis," *The Nation* 219 (28 December 1974): 686–693.

[173]Bowles, "Unequal Education and the Reproduction of the Social Division of Labor"; Bowles and Gintis, "IQ in the U.S. Class Structure"; Samuel S. Bowles, "Understanding Unequal Economic Opportunity," *American Economic Review* 63 (May 1973): 346–356; Herbert Gintis, "Education, Technology, and the Characteristics of Worker Productivity," *American Economic Review* 61 (May 1971): 266–279; William Behn et al., "School Is Bad; Work Is Worse," *School Review* 82 (November 1974): 49–68.

[174]Gordon, *Theories of Poverty and Underemployment*; Carter and Carnoy, "Theories of Labor Markets and Worker Productivity."

[175]Gintis, "Education, Technology, and the Characteristics of Worker Productivity"; Richard C. Edwards, "Alienation and Inequality: Capitalist Relations of Production in a Bureaucratic Enterprise" (Ph.D. dissertation, Department of Economics, Harvard University, 1972); Bowles and Gintis, "IQ in the U.S. Class Structure."

ones. That is, schools and training programs are viewed as mirrors of the larger society, and the faithfulness of this correspondence both functionally and historically means that they cannot be used for structural social changes.[176] The socialist agenda is necessarily that of a radical transformation of the social institutions of our society that would begin with democracy in the workplace and social ownership of capital.[177] Changes in education and training would correspond to changes in other institutions, rather than being relied upon to create that change. The strategy of how capitalist societies will be transformed is a subject of great controversy on which there are a large variety of viewpoints.[178]

## The Future Role of Education and Training in the War on Poverty

While we have presented five different perspectives on the failure of the educational and training programs of the 1965–1974 decade to make a large impact on poverty reduction, the choice of explanations and attendant solutions will depend more on one's political and social values than upon the "evidence." That is, much of the evidence supports more than one perspective, and there simply is little unambiguous evidence that points in a particular direction. While we have argued that the evidence is in conflict with some views, we should be cognizant of the caveat of Campbell:

> Non-laboratory social science is precariously scientific at best. But even for the strongest sciences, the theories believed to be true are radically under justified and have, at most, the status of "better than" rather than the status of "proven."[179]

It has been argued that persons who select a particular interpretation of the relationship between education and poverty do so on the basis of factors other than the social science evidence supporting that view.[180] If this is true, it is doubtful that the next decade of educational and training programs for reducing poverty will be heavily influenced, directly, by many of the social science findings that were set out, such as the apparently weak relationship between cognitive test scores and earnings. When social science evidence conflicts with a deeply rooted commitment to a view of social reality, it is likely to be

[176]Bowles, "Unequal Education"; Levin, "Educational Reform and Social Change."

[177]The socialist perspective is the one that I believe represents the best descriptive analysis of the persistence of poverty. Yet, my efforts to change these outcomes are concentrated on activities within the reform and welfare capitalist arena. In essence, my professional work tends to be dominated by the reform perspective; my political activity is focused on welfare capitalist changes of the Swedish variety; and my vision of a fairer and more productive society is embodied in a utopian version of democratic socialism.

[178]Andre Gorz, *Socialism and Revolution* (Garden City, N. J.: Anchor Books, Doubleday and Co., 1973).

[179]Campbell, "Qualitative Knowing in Action Research," p. 2.

[180]Levin, "Education, Life Changes, and the Courts."

rejected. When it conforms with that view, it is likely to be accepted. In this sense, contact with the findings of a research article simply represents one additional experience that must be balanced among the many factors that create our images of knowledge and our beliefs.

Accordingly, the best indicators of reformulation over the next decade would seem to be the trends that were evident in the latter part of the first poverty decade rather than the social science summaries. There is no reason to look for any sharp discontinuity in policy in the absence of cataclysmal changes in the social and political institutions for social decisionmaking. Though Vietnam, Watergate, the energy crisis, inflation, and unemployment may be viewed as cataclysmal events, I do not see them as events that will drastically alter poverty policies over the next decade. Rather, they may just further reinforce the shifts that we have been witnessing already.[181]

What are these shifts? In my view, there is a long-term and gradual movement away from the professional viewpoint toward the perspective of reform and welfare capitalism. While the decade of poverty began with the view that more education and training resources would make great inroads on poverty, that view has received less and less acceptance as money itself has not seemed to make a difference. In response, there has been a search for various reforms and mechanisms that can make the education and training mechanism more productive. In fact, the OEO posture in the late 1960s represented a salutary move in that direction by sponsoring demonstrations and experiments with educational vouchers and educational performance contracting. At all levels of government, there are increasing emphases on program evaluation and research to determine what works.[182]

But, the recent recession has tended to move us beyond reform to a direct intervention in the workplace through the enactment of a public employment program, even though such a program could not muster political support back in 1964. The Emergency Employment Act of 1971 authorized a $2.25 billion Public Employment program (PEP) with $1 billion to be spent in the first year and $1.25 billion to be spent in the second year. The lack of preparedness for administering the program meant that some of the allocations were not spent during the appropriate fiscal years. Nevertheless, PEP employed more than 400,000 persons from its beginning in the summer of 1971 through the end of June 1973. Of those, about 37 percent were Vietnam veterans, nearly three-fourths were male, about two-fifths were minority-group members, about 18 percent were economically disadvantaged, and 14 percent were former welfare recipients.[183] It must be pointed out that the program was designed to

[181]Levin, "Educational Reform and Social Change."

[182]Daniel Weiler et al., *A Public School Voucher Demonstration: The First Year at Alum Rock* (Santa Monica, Cal.: The Rand Corporation, June 1974); Irwin Garfinkel and Edward M. Gramlich, "A Statistical Analysis of the OEO Experiment in Educational Performance Contracting," *Journal of Human Resources* 8 (Summer 1973): 275–305; Rivlin, *Systematic Thinking for Social Action*.

[183]Sar A. Levitan and Robert Taggart, eds., *Emergency Employment Act: The PEP Genera-*

serve the long-term unemployed rather than the disadvantaged *per se,* and during recession the unemployed may have large segments of persons who are not included in the disadvantaged category. In fact, about three-quarters of PEP participants had at least a high school education, a higher proportion than that of the civilian labor force generally. As unemployment rates continue to rise, several billion dollars more will be allocated to PEP.[184]

This movement toward the more direct solution of inequalities created by monopoly capitalism is reflected not just in the Public Employment program. It is also mirrored in other income security programs such as Food Stamps. Between 1973 and 1975, the Food Stamp program was expected to increase from $2.2 billion to $3.9 billion, according to the 1975 proposed budget. Increasingly, it is being recognized that education and training can only be a part of the solution of the poverty problem, rather than the principal engine for poverty reduction. This movement toward welfare capitalism is an important reflection of the increasing acceptance by the American people that poverty is not an accident or a function of incompetence, but that it is a manifestation of the values and institutions of the overall social system. Whether this decade will experience the official recognition of the welfare state is unclear, but it will surely witness a decreasing emphasis on the view that education and training will solve the fundamental problems of equity, justice, and human well-being.

---

*tion* (Salt Lake City, Utah: Olympus Publishing Co., 1974); U.S., Department of Labor, *Manpower Report of the President; A Report on Manpower Requirements, Resources, Utilization, and Training* (Washington, D.C.: U.S. Government Printing Office, 1974), pp. 153–154.

[184]U.S., Department of Labor, *Manpower Report of the President.* The fact that PEP has been recognized as a necessary program for the nondisadvantaged may also tend to increase its acceptability for addressing the economic problems of the disadvantaged as well.

# 36

## An Evaluation of Follow Through

*Linda B. Stebbins, Robert G. St. Pierre, Elizabeth C. Proper,
Richard B. Anderson, and Thomas R. Cerva*

Poor children tend to do poorly in school. By means of Head Start and Follow Through, the federal government set out in the 1960s to learn what compensatory education, applied early, could do to reduce this tendency.

In Follow Through, a number of prominent educators, advocating various educational theories and strategies (models), were funded to become "sponsors" and to apply their insights in selected school districts (sites). The Follow Through national evaluation was assigned to document the experience. As part of this evaluation, the U.S. Office of Education commissioned Abt Associates in 1972 to analyze the data generated by the extensive program of testing and interviewing which was part of Follow Through and to draw from them appropriate conclusions about the effectiveness of the various models' approaches to compensatory education.

### EVALUATION OF PLANNED VARIATION

The Follow Through planners did not fully appreciate at the outset the difficulty of alleviating the complex problems of lower achievement among disadvantaged children. The general assumption was that the program impact

Excerpted from *Education as Experimentation: A Planned Variation Model, Volume IV-A: An Evaluation of Follow Through* by L. B. Stebbins, R. G. St. Pierre, E. C. Proper, R. B. Anderson, and T. R. Cerva. Report to the U.S. Office of Education pursuant to Contract No. 300-75-0134, Cambridge, Mass.: Abt Associates Inc., 1977. This report is part of the fourth volume in a series of annual reports prepared by Abt Associates Inc. for the U.S. Office of Education. In this article we refer to these reports by their volume numbers rather than by author. The authors of each report are as follows and the full citation for each report is included in the list of references: Volume I-A: Early Effects of Follow Through (Cline, 1974); Volume I-B: Monographs (Cline, 1974); Volume II-A: Two Year Effects of Follow Through (Cline, 1975); Volume II-B: Appendices and Monographs (Cline, 1975); Volume III-A: Findings: Cohort II, Interim Findings: Cohort III (Stebbins, 1976); Volume III-B: Appendices (Stebbins, 1976); Volume IV-A: An Evaluation of Follow Through (Stebbins, St.Pierre, Proper, Anderson, and Cerva, 1977); Volume IV-B: Effects of Follow Through Models would be so great that the evaluation design, no matter what its level of sophistication, would easily demonstrate the Follow Through effect. As Egbert (1973: 25) says:

> Its design stemmed from the conviction that sufficient improvement could be affected in the institutions serving children that children's development would be so markedly superior as to be readily demonstrated on measures of achievement, cognition, self-concept, social maturation, and capacity to function independently. Follow Through's design was born also from the conviction that unless such substantial differences were manifest, the really massive increases in spending that would be required could not be justified. In view of the results reported by Miller, Engelmann, Gordon and others in the January, 1968, meetings of prospective sponsors, this conviction did not seem unrealistic, assuming that programs developed in small scale settings could be implemented on a larger scale in a number of communities.

The national evaluation was designed to address the following questions:

- Does Follow Through have a greater impact on disadvantaged children than do regular school programs?[1]

- Do the various education strategies being tested in Follow Through have different impacts?

- Do differences in impact have any relationship to the characteristics of children, e.g., socioeconomic status and preschool experience?

- Do differences in implementation of an educational strategy bear any relationship to the differences in impact?

- Do some educational strategies consistently show better results than others over time, or does the impact vary from year to year?

The early evaluation planners foresaw the advantages of collecting vast amounts of longitudinal information about the Follow Through (FT) children and non-Follow Through (NFT) comparison children, their families, and their teachers, for the research. As shown on Table 1, the massive data base encompasses three cohorts of children.[2] These cohorts are divided into six specific groups, otherwise known as streams (three streams entering kindergarten [K] and three streams entering first grade [EF]). This table shows the progression of children in each of the cohorts and streams through the grade levels during each successive school year, beginning in 1969. Although some sponsors imple-

---

(Bock, Stebbins, and Proper, 1977); Volume IV-C;: Appendices (Abt Associates, 1977); Volume IV-D: A Longitudinal Study of Follow Through (Ferb, Larson, and Napior, 1977); Volume IV-E: Supplementary Analyses: Reanalysis of Selected Data Sets (Proper, St.Pierre, and Cerva, 1978); Volume IV-F: Supplementary Analyses: Appendix (Proper, St.Pierre, and Cerva, 1978); NFT Study: A Non Follow Through Study (Monitor, Watkins, and Napior, 1977).

TABLE 1

Grade Level of Follow Through Children in  Each Cohort and Stream, by Year

| | 1969–70 | 1970–71 | 1971–72 | 1972–73 | 1973–74 | 1974–75 | 1975–76 |
|---|---|---|---|---|---|---|---|
| Cohort I | | | | | | | |
| K† | K | 1 | 2 | 3 | | | |
| EF†† | 1 | 2 | 3 | | | | |
| Cohort II | | | | | | | |
| K | | K | 1 | 2 | 3 | | |
| EF | | 1 | 2 | 3 | | | |
| Cohort III | | | | | | | |
| K | | | K | 1 | 2 | 3 | |
| EF | | | 1 | 2 | 3 | | |

† Entering kindergarten stream.
†† Entering first grade stream.

mented programs in certain sites in 1968, very little of the data collected during that year was ever evaluated.[3]

From the beginning, a number of research projects have investigated the impacts of Follow Through. Some projects described programs; others investigated parent attitudes and characteristics; still others studied institutional change and instrument development. This report contributes to the total evaluation by concentrating on assessments of the child, parent, and teacher data.

Beginning with the Cohort I group and continuing through Cohort III, each cohort was to be subjected to more or less intensive evaluation. In 1969, Stanford Research Institute (SRI) was the contractor responsible for designing both the data collection and evaluation, in conjunction with the USOE program staff. Change in the national evaluation strategy, however, was recommended by various reviewers. To accomplish this change, the data collection and data analysis functions were separated, and "USOE, assisted by a consulting group, assumed full responsibility for specifying the experimental design, tests, and projects where testing would be done" (GAO, 1975: 9). In 1972, competitive procurements were issued. SRI was awarded the contract for data collection and Abt Associates Inc. was awarded the contract for data analysis.

The national Follow Through evaluation is subject to many of the problems inherent in field social research (i.e., nonrandom assignment, unclear definition of treatment, problems of assessing implementation, less than ideal instrumentation) and careful judgment must be used in drawing conclusions. Evaluation of these planned variations provides us with an opportunity to examine the educational strategies under real life conditions as opposed to contrived and tightly controlled laboratory conditions. This evaluation, which has been structured to alleviate the problems likely to be found in evaluation of large-scale, innovative, education programs, reveals some meaningful patterns and provides empirical information on program impacts.

## EDUCATIONAL STRATEGIES
## AND MEASURES OF EFFECTIVENESS

The Follow Through sponsors espouse a wide range of approaches to the education of children from low socioeconomic background, as the research strategy of planned variations requires. The objectives of the sponsor approaches vary accordingly, as do the suggested measures of the goal attainment. Some sponsor goals relate directly to the dimensions that standardized tests aim to measure; others do not lend themselves to any well-developed or economical means of assessment. To evaluate each model's performance on every measure of interest to any sponsor would impose unreasonable costs and burdens on the evaluation and on the people involved; the measures actually administered therefore represent a compromise between the demands of diversity and the practical constraints of resources and available instruments. Unfortunately, we have no data on the adequacy or costs of this compromise so it remains a topic of conjecture and controversy.

### Educational Strategies

At one time Follow Through program embraced 22 sponsors working with 178 sites. These sponsors represented the spectrum of approaches to early childhood education existing in 1968-1971. This evaluation report includes evidence on the progress of children served by the 17 models listed in Table 2 (counting the five Self-Sponsored sites as a single model or group).[4] These sponsors share the perception that some children in our society, particularly those from families with low socioeconomic status have special educational needs.

The Follow Through programs reflect a broad spectrum of strategies for implementing these goals. Examination of each sponsor's goals and objectives reveals that the philosophical bases underlying the sponsor approaches vary widely. Some are more oriented toward basic skills achievement, while others are more concerned with developing a desire to learn and yet still others are oriented to learning how to learn.

### Classification of Models by Goals and Objectives[5]

For the purpose of this evaluation, we judgmentally classify models along two dimensions according to their stated goals and objectives for classroom learning environments; emphasis on the learning domain and degree of structure.[6] Three major classifications in the learning domain are found in the spon-

TABLE 2
Follow Through Models Included in the Analyses

| Full Model Name | Name Used in Report | Sponsoring Institution or Agency |
|---|---|---|
| Bank Street College of Education Approach | Bank Street | Bank Street College of Education |
| Behavior Analysis Approach | BA | Support and Development Center for Follow Through–University of Kansas |
| California Process Model | Cal Process | California State Department of Education–Division of Compensatory Education |
| Cognitively Oriented Curriculum Model | Cognitive Curriculum | High/Scope Educational Research Foundation |
| Cultural Linguistic Approach | CLA | Northeastern Illinois State College |
| Direct Instruction Model | Direct Instruction | University of Oregon–College of Education |
| EDC Open Education Follow Through Program | EDC | Education Development Center |
| Florida Parent Education Model | Parent Education | University of Florida |
| Home-School Partnership Model | Home-School Partnership | Clark College |
| Individualized Early Learning Program | IELP | University of Pittsburgh–Learning Research and Development Center |
| Interdependent Learning Model | ILM | City University of New York–Institute for Developmental Studies |
| Language Development (Bilingual) Education Approach | SEDL | Southwest Educational Development Laboratory |
| Mathemagenic Activities Program | MAP | University of Georgia |
| The New School Approach to Follow Through | NSA | University of North Dakota |
| Responsive Education Model | Responsive Education | Far West Laboratory for Educational Research and Development |
| Self-Sponsored | Self-Sponsored | – – – |
| Tucson Early Education Model | TEEM | Arizona Center for Early Childhood Education |

sors' descriptions: emphasis on basic skills, emphasis on cognitive conceptual skills and emphasis on self-esteem and sense-of-control (affective measures). These learning domain emphases are based, to some degree, on the philosophical orientation of the model. In Volume III-A we classified sponsors' models according to their major philosophical basis: reinforcement learning theory, cognitive conceptual theory, and psychodynamic theory. Some models did not fit into this scheme, and so we have used another classification in this volume. Based on the sponsors' statements of goals and objectives, we have tried to identify the emphasis of each model on one or two domains of learning. The classification of models by philosophical orientation is not totally congruent with the classification of models by learning domain; we find that both are useful in understanding the intent and approach of each model.

White et al. (1973: 121-122) have defined the three major theoretical orientations to Follow Through as follows:

> The behavioristic approach maintains that all behaviors are learned, it implies that educational disadvantage exists because specific pre-academic and/or social skills necessary to success in school have not been acquired. These skills must be taught to the child using appropriate instructional techniques to attain specified behavioral objectives. The contingencies between environmental stimulus and child response are carefully planned in advance, with reinforcement (or reward) being used to encourage the desired behaviors.

> The cognitive development approach emphasizes the process of cognitive growth more than the learning of specific content. It is assumed that the disadvantaged child has not had sufficient experience with his world in a manner that is conducive to cognitive growth. He needs appropriate interactions with people and materials to learn how to process information and solve problems in a logical and efficient manner. Often, in addition, his verbal skills as they relate to thought processes are inadequate. Instructional techniques vary, but the child's self-guided activity and experimentation with various aspects of the environment are seen as important. Learning is facilitated when there is a "match" between the child's level of cognitive development and the experiences encountered.

> The psychodynamic approach considers socioemotional goals to be essential for optimal development of the "whole" child. Learning presupposes the development of a "healthy" individual. A positive self-image, trust, emotional stability, constructive peer relationships, etc., are essential to successful learning. Instructional technique emphasizes the quality of interpersonal relationships and an environment which supports self-actualization. Free choice and self-determination are important. It is usually assumed that the child "knows what is best" for his personal growth.

The trichotomy of philosophical orientations defined by White et al. (1973) is based on the sponsors' preschool programs. The psychodynamic orientation has been modified for the Follow Through program in kindergarten through third grade. The educational strategies used by the Follow Through sponsors who emphasize this approach also include a cognitive component of encouragement of exploration and discovery in academic areas.

The second dimension which is useful in our classification is the degree of structure of the model. White et al. (1973: 123-124) also classified the structure dimension, as follows:

> High structure involves the predetermination of both teacher and child behaviors by the curriculum. In this case the teacher follows a specifically defined role prescription developed by the project planners. The child's behavior is directly dependent upon the teacher's and also fits the prescribed role. Neither teacher nor child behavior should vary greatly among classrooms implementing the same curriculum.
>
> The middle of the structure continuum included both projects with a mixture of high and low structure situations which offer broad guidelines for teacher and child. Many projects use highly structured instructional periods and periods of free play. Also, many projects delineate long-term goals that do not provide step-by-step curriculum for obtaining behavioral objectives. For example, it may be specified that every child should learn math, reading, and spelling without specifying how the child is to be taught.
>
> In low structure models . . . teachers are free to act on the basis of their own feelings, intuitions, educational philosophy, etc., as long as they are congruent with the overall goals of the project. Both teacher and child are free to choose curricular activities and to act spontaneously according to their needs. Individual behaviors vary widely from classroom to classroom since there are not specified behavioral objectives.

The low structure models are highly dependent upon the teachers' ability to "plan structure" which moves the individual student toward program goals.

Table 3 shows our classification of the Follow Through models based upon stated goals and objectives for the classroom learning environment, particularly in terms of the learning skills the model desires to instill. A detailed description of each model is included in Volume IV-B.

The models unclassified on the degree of structure (Self-Sponsored, California Process, Parent Education, and Home-School Partnership) place greater emphasis on parent/community involvement than on the classroom environment in improving the education of children. Although we know very little about the classroom learning environment for these models, the sponsors' stated goals and objectives do permit a classification on the model's emphasis on the learning domain.

Two of the models expressing a specific basic skills emphasis (Behavior Analysis and Direct Instruction) have adopted a highly structured approach which is compatible with their behaviorist educational strategy. Two other models (Self Sponsored and California Process) also appear to place primary emphasis on the development of basic skills, particularly reading and math.

TABLE 3

Typology of Models with Respect to the Classroom Learning Environment

| Degree of Structure | Emphasis on Learning Domain | | |
| --- | --- | --- | --- |
| | Basic Skills | Cognitive/ Conceptual | Cognitive/ Affective |
| High | Behavior Analysis <br><br> Direct Instruction     IELP | | |
| Medium | | Cognitive Curriculum <br><br><br> TEEM <br> CLA <br> SEDL | Responsive Education <br><br> ILM <br> MAP |
| Low | | | Bank Street <br> EDC |
| Unknown | Self Sponsored <br><br> California Process | NSA <br> Parent Education <br> Home-School Partnership | |

Most of the models emphasizing cognitive conceptual skills (Cognitive Curriculum and TEEM) use a moderately structured approach. Other models with a cognitive emphasis (NSA and Parent Education) use an unknown degree of structure. Four model descriptions (IELP, CLA, SEDL and Home-School Partnership)[7] suggest varying degrees of structure to develop *both* basic and cognitive skills. The psychodynamic approaches (Responsive Education, Bank Street, EDC, ILM, and MAP) tend to have medium to low structure and place emphasis on *both* the acquisition of self-esteem and cognitive thinking processes.

## Measures of Effects on Children

A battery of existing standardized tests was chosen to comprise national evaluation outcome measures.[8] This battery was selected, after careful consideration, as a "best compromise" between the need for accountability and the difficulty of measuring sponsors' diverse goals and objectives. The measures selected provide a basis for comparisons between a model's Follow Through groups and comparison non-Follow Through groups in attainment of basic skills, cognitive and conceptual skills, and affective outcomes including both self-esteem and attitude toward school and learning.

We agree with those who urge that caution be exercised in drawing conclusions from the matching of a model's goals with the measures included in battery of tests for children. Whereas the basic skills measures are probably a reasonable battery for examining achievement which might be expected in that learning domain, the measures on the cognitive and affective domains are much less appropriate. We describe the measures thoroughly so that the reader may judge their adequacy for evaluating Follow Through success. Needless to say, we report results only with respect to the outcomes that were measured. We estimate affects for each model in all domains, emphasizing in each case the domain where the greatest impact might be expected. And we caution the reader that *outcome measures other than the ones available might have been able to demonstrate effectiveness in the domains which go untapped in this evaluation.*

Table 4 shows the specific instruments (and subtests) used in the analysis of the Follow Through and non-Follow Through children at the various grade levels. We have grouped the instruments/subtests according to our interpretation of the model's goals (see Table 3). For example, models which advocate a behaviorist educational strategy and place the greatest emphasis on basic skills might be expected to demonstrate success on the measures we have labelled "basic skills." Some Metropolitan Achievement Test (MAT) subtests measure acquisition of basic skills which are taught directly. Other MAT subtests and the Raven's Coloured Progressive Matrices measure acquisition of cognitive skills and processes which may or may not be directly taught, but which the child may apprehend indirectly through various experiences. Models which advocate cognitive and psychodynamic educational strategies include these kinds of outcomes in their stated goals and objectives for children and might be expected to demonstrate success on these measures. Affective measures include the Coopersmith, a measure of self-esteem; the Intellectual Achievement Responsibility Scale positive (IARS (+)), a measure of the child's tendency to accept personal responsibility for positive happenings; and the IARS (–), a measure of the child's tendency to accept personal responsibility for negative happenings. Psychodynamic *models* might be expected to demonstrate success on these measures.

TABLE 4
Instruments Used in Evaluation, by Time of Administration and Type of Measure*

| When Administered | Type of Measure | | |
| | Basic Skills | Cognitive-Conceptual Skills | Affective Skills |
| --- | --- | --- | --- |
| Entering Kindergarten or Entering First | Wide Range Achievement Test (WRAT) | | |
| | Peabody Picture Vocabulary Test (PPVT) | | |
| | Caldwell Preschool Inventory (PSI) | | |
| Leaving Kindergarten** | PPVT | | |
| | Metropolitan Achievement Test (MAT) – Primer | MAT – Primer | Intellectual Achievement Responsibility Scale (IARS) |
| | ● Listening for Sounds | ● Reading ● Mathematics Concepts | ● Locus of Control-positive ● Locus of Control-negative Absence from School |
| Leaving First Grade** | MAT – Primary I | MAT – Primary I | Absence from School |
| | ● Word Knowledge ● Word Analysis ● Mathematics Computation | ● Reading ● Mathematics Concepts | |
| Leaving Second Grade** | MAT – Primary II | MAT – Primary II | |
| | ● Word Knowledge ● Spelling ● Mathematics Computation | ● Reading ● Mathematics Concepts ● Mathematics Problem Solving | |
| Leaving Third Grade | MAT – Elementary | MAT – Elementary | IARS |
| | ● Word Knowledge ● Spelling ● Language (Parts A & B) ● Mathematics Computation | ● Reading ● Mathematics Concepts ● Mathematics Problem Solving Raven's Coloured Progressive Matrics (Raven's) | ● Locus of Control-positive ● Locus of Control-negative Coopersmith Self-Esteem inventory (Coopersmith) |

*Table includes only measures used in evaluation. For example, the WRAT was also administered at the end of kindergarten.

**Measures used in evaluation of Cohort III-K only.

## Quality of Data

The reliability of WRAT and MAT Follow Through data collected with the battery of instruments administred to the children is as high as the publisher's estimates. Reliability coefficients (coefficients of internal consistency) calculated on the responses of the local analytic sample, range from the high 80s through middle 90s (except the IARS (+) and IARS(–)). Since the reliabilities are approximately equal to the publisher's estimates, the data associated with these outcomes are measured with an acceptable degree of internal consistency. This high degree of reliability prevails in the coefficients calculated for the FT and NFT samples within each model as well.

The validity of the instrument battery is more difficult to assess. Due to the diversity of models' goals and objectives, selecting a valid set of measures of effectiveness required some "best compromise" choices from among instruments which were fully developed and commonly used as of 1971-1972. Probably no choice of a single instrument battery could ever be acceptable to all sponsors, and certainly this one was not. No instrument has escaped criticism, especially the MAT and the Coopersmith. Whatever the criticism, however, the battery does provide a wide range of measures of achievement in basic skills, cognitive conceptual skills, and affective development.

## ANALYSIS STRATEGY[9]

Assessing Follow Through impact is not as simple or straightforward as might appear at first glance. It is an axiom of evaluation that in order to attribute differences in observed outcomes to a program, children who participate in the program must be compared to similar children who do not. In a traditional research paradigm, "similarity" is achieved by random assignment of children to treatment and control groups, with such assignment occurring before treatment begins. The circumstances surrounding the inception of Follow Through did not permit random assignment. In fact, systematic attempts were made to attract into the treatment groups those children most in need of the program; i.e., the most disadvantaged children in the community. This has meant that the comparison groups are often less disadvantaged than the treatment groups (Egbert, 1973).

The problem of nonrandom subject assignment to treatment and comparison groups has plagued the evaluation of compensatory programs from the beginning and has weakened many attempts at assessment. This might suggest that "true experiments" are the only appropriate vehicle for measuring the impact of social programs. Evans and Schiller (1970: 219-220) point out the practical unacceptability and danger of such a choice. As Evans and Schiller state,

[This is] a position which is untenable practically. . . . [We] must arrive at some judgment using the best information we have at hand. . . . The problem is that in the absence of formal, objective studies, programs will be evaluated [and decisions made by Contress] by the most arbitrary, anecdotal, partisan, and subjective means. . . . Compared with the weakness of this method for making decisions, the problems of [the lack of a true experiment] pale to a most minor flaw indeed.

Given the need to provide information to decision makers, the essential problem becomes the development of an evaluation approach that will provide the most valid and comprehensive information possible. To this end, the Follow Through evaluation planners (United States Office of Education and Stanford Research Institute) adopted a quasi-experimental design, judgmentally selecting at each site a comparison group as similar to the treatment group as possible. Since this design does not suggest a single "appropriate" analysis, we have subjected the data to a variety of analytic procedures, so as to compensate for the drawbacks of the quasi-experimental design. The multiple strategies approach anticipates the common and valuable practice of performing secondary analyses such as those performed on the Equality of Educational Opportunity data.[10] Any single analytic treatment of quasi-experimental data is inevitably subject to well-founded methodological criticism, especially when the data are being used to assess the impact of major educational programs. Subsequent reanalyses using other techniques and approaches help to assess the validity of the original results. Ideally, after several reanalyses have been accomplished and a body of literature accumulated, all available information is integrated to refine and clarify understanding of the problem (or program). Our analytic cross-validation anticipates some of the more obvious alternative analyses and should provide other researchers with a broader basis for designing further thoughtful approaches to the Follow Through data.

The remainder of this chapter is divided into four sections. In the first section (Constraints on the Development of Analytic Strategies), we discuss issues which constrained the development of the analyses in order to make clear why we chose certain strategies. The outcomes of these discussions are that we have chosen three different types of comparisons: local, pooled, and norm referenced. In both local and pooled comparisons, we have contrasted the performance of the sample of NFT children within the same site. We base these comparisons on our predictions of children's performance, given what we know about their background characteristics and how those background characteristics relate to performance in a larger group of children.

In local comparisons, we base our predictions of all FT and NFT sample children within a given sponsor.[11] This means that our predictions are based on children from a varying number of sites for each sponsor. It also means that our predictions are based on a different set of children for each sponsor. In pooled comparisons, we base our predictions on the performance of all sample NFT children across all sponsors. This means that our predictions are based on the performance of the same set of children for each sponsor. Thus, in a sense, pooled comparisons provide a common yardstick against which we compare the performance of each and every site's FT and NFT children across all sponsors. On the other hand, local comparisons provide a series of sponsor-specific yardsticks. By using both common and model-specific yardsticks, we hope to provide two different but appropriate ways to examine sponsor performance. In norm referenced comparisons we have provided the reader with a third yardstick. This one is probably the most difficult to be measured against. Here we compare the performance of a given site's FT children with the performance of children in the MAT publisher's norm sample; children who, on the average, were not disadvantaged. Thus, with this comparison, we are asking if FT children are performing as well as nondisadvantaged children.

In the second section of this chapter (Analytic Strategies) we specify the analytic strategies we selected. All of our analyses (except norm referenced) make statistical adjustments to outcome scores of FT and NFT children based on background variables. Most of the analyses are based on data collected about children at entry to kindergarten and exit from third grade and are thus termed the "Entry-Exit" analyses. A subset of children included in the Entry-Exit analyses were also tested at an interim time point and thus are included in the "Longitudinal Analysis." In this analysis we compute results at the sponsor level for two separate time periods—fall kindergarten to spring first grade and fall second grade to spring third grade.

While each of our analyses adjusts for children's background characteristics, one background characteristic needing special attention is preschool experience. Children who have attended some form of preschool before entering the public school system may perform differently at entry to school from children who have not been previously exposed to some form of schooling. However, preschool experience may vary widely. Some children have had fairly formalized instruction at the nursery level while others have had a more informal child care experience.

Trying to categorize type of preschool experience from the data available has been particularly troublesome. However, this year we have developed working definitions and applied them to the set of children where the most complete information about preschool is available—Cohort III-K. Analyses of Cohort III-EF, Cohort II-K, and Cohort II-EF children do not take preschool experience into account.

As part of the Entry-Exit analyses we have developed three methods to assess differences between FT groups and the local and pooled NFT comparisons while taking preschool into account. Each method adjusts for a common set of background variables but handles preschool experience in a different manner. The first ignores the potential for preschool differences in deriving two sets of results at the site level (Local and Pooled Analyses). We have performed these analyses with each of the four cohort streams (Cohort III-K, Cohort III-EF, Cohort II-K, Cohort II-EF). The second method statistically adjusts for preschool differences at the site level (Preschool Adjusted Local and Preschool Adjusted Pooled Analyses). Finally, the third method examines effects separately for each preschool group (blocks on preschool experience) at the sponsor level (Preschool Blocked Local and Preschool Blocked Pooled Analyses. See Volumes IV-A and IV-B). The last two methods have been performed on only the Cohort III-K stream. The Longitudinal Analysis mentioned above also blocks on preschool experience (Longitudinal Analysis. See Volume IV-D).

In the third section of this chapter (Supplementary Analyses and Their Consequences) we present a series of auxiliary analyses which add to qualify, and help us interpret our primary and secondary analyses. Included in this section are discussions of attrition, the adequacy of our set of background variables for the statistical adjustment of outcome scores, the degree to which our data meet the assumptions required by our analyses, and the comparability between and relationships among effects which are derived from different types of analyses. In general, these auxiliary analyses uphold our confidence in the appropriateness of our primary and secondary analyses.

In the final section of the chapter (Definition and Consequences of Initial Mismatch) we discuss the degree to which the various groups we compare are poorly matched on background variables. Those results which are based on groups which are poorly matched have been displayed in Summary of Effects[12] tables along with all other results. However, in an effort to inform the reader as to the existence of this "mismatch" problem we have pointed out those effects which are questionable due to mismatch by "shading" the appropriate sections of relevant tables. By shading we mean that a grey mask has been placed over the section of each table containing the effects that we consider to be possibly misleading. The mask allows the reader to see the effects and interpret them if desired, but serves as an effective warning that something may be amiss. We do not discuss any shaded effects, nor do these effects enter into any aggregations presented in the following section. Thus, the sponsor and site discussions are based solely on effect estimates which we believe to be valid.

## PATTERNS OF EFFECTS

Recent evaluations of Project Follow Through emanate from a variety of sources and perspectives. Reports from the model sponsors, the participating communities, the national evaluation contractors, and the U.S. Office of Education suggest that the pattern of effects is a complicated mixture of success and failure with respect to the educational and social service objectives of the program.

By design, one portion of the national evaluation of Follow Through Planned Variation models focused on the results of tests administered to Follow Through (FT) and non-Follow Through (NFT) comparison children, questionnaires administered to their teachers, and interview data collected from their parents. These data are the basis of our evaluation. The patterns of effects which are reported provide one perspective on the effectiveness of the various alternative instructional strategies with respect to one set of objectives: improving the school performance of low-income children in kindergarten through grade three. In pursuit of its general purpose, the improvement of children's life chances, Follow Through has provided a broad range of services. We report here only on the instructional component of Follow Through, and within that only on a restricted set of educational outcomes.

We have addressed three essential questions with the national evaluation data:

- Do the various education strategies being tested in Follow Through have different impacts?

FIGURE 1

DOMAINS OF THIRD GRADE TESTING IN FOLLOW THROUGH

| Outcome Domains | Tests | |
|---|---|---|
| BASIC SKILLS | Word Knowledge <br> Spelling <br> Language <br> Math Computations | Metropolitan Achievement Test (MAT) |
| COGNITIVE CONCEPTUAL SKILLS | Reading <br> Math Concepts <br> Math Problems <br><br> Raven's Progressive Matrices | |
| AFFECTIVE OUTCOMES | Coopersmith Self-Esteem <br><br> Achievement Responsibility, Positive <br> Achievement Responsibility, Negative | Intellectual Achievement Responsibility Scale (IARS) |

- Do differences in impact have any relationship to such characteristics of the children as socioeconomic status and preschool exeprience?

- Do some educational strategies consistently show better results from others over time, or does the impact vary from year to year?

We present our responses to these questions in varying detail throughout Volumes IV-A through D. Volumes IV-B and D, for example, devote discrete sections to detailed presentations of each model's patterns of effects. In this chapter, however, we have attempted to average the data in meaningful ways which permit us to demonstrate the consistencies that we have discerned in the patterns of effects.

Our evaluation of Follow Through Planned Variation models focuses on the progress of FT children relative to NFT comparison children in three learning domains as measured by the Follow Through test battery.[13] For convenience in summarizing the results, we have grouped the eleven outcome tests as indicated in Figure 1. The "basic skills" are the simplest objectives of traditional elementary schooling: vocabulary, spelling, the conventions of written language, and simple arithmetic computation. "Cognitive conceptual skills"— comprehension, reading, mathematical concepts, mathematical problems, and abstract problem solving—are also traditional academic goals, but are more complex and tend to require application of some basic skills. "Affective outcomes," finally, are approximate measures of the children's self-concept and of their tendency to attribute success or failure to themselves rather than to others.

In order to capture some of the important aspects of model diversity and to permit us to draw conclusions about types of models, we have divided the models into three broad categories, according to their areas of primary emphasis:[14]

- *Basic Skills Models.* These models focus first on the elementary skills of vocabulary, arithmetic computation, spelling, and language.

- *Cognitive Conceptual Skills Models.* These models emphasize the more complex "learning-to-learn" and problem solving skills.

- *Affective/Cognitive Models.* These models focus primarily on self concept and attitudes toward learning, and secondarily on "learning-to-learn" skills.

The patterns that we have discerned are based on data gathered on children in Follow Through Cohorts II and III, entering-kindergarten (K) and entering-first (EF) streams. The children in Cohorts II and III entered Follow Through in 1970 and 1971, respectively. For each Follow Through group [15] in each project, and with respect to each of eleven test scores, our analyses asked, in effect, the question: "How much better did the Follow Through group perform than it would have performed if it had been outside Follow Through?" Where it seems to have performed substantially better, we have indicated a *positive* effect; where less well, a *negative* effect. Where the difference was too small to seem educationally important, or where it was statistically insignificant and thus could easily be explained by differences among children within the group, we declared it to be a *null* effect.[16] Where the character of the Follow Through group cast serious doubt on the validity of an estimate of untreated performance, we omitted the associated comparison from the summaries.[17]

As Chapter Four of Volume IV-A explains, we have estimated the performance of similarly-disadvantaged groups outside Follow Through by combining in several ways the available information on the NFT comparison groups. The averages that make up these summaries include two estimates of each effect: The "adjusted local effect," which in essence compares the Follow Through group with its own local comparison group, and the "adjusted pooled effect," which compares it against the total NFT sample. We performed similar analyses on all four cohort streams (with one important exception, the local and pooled adjusted effects for the Cohort III kindergarten stream are adjusted for pre-school experience), taking the fullest possible account in each case of all the measured characteristics of both the Follow Through and comparison populations.[18] Except as noted all model averages and model type averages combine the local and pooled estimates of effects across all four cohort streams.

The patterns of effects are complex. Almost every model has at least one site in which the FT children performed better on some test than did NFT children. The evidence indicates that some models have improved the test performance of children in some sites to national norm levels, but none has managed to achieve this high level of success consistently in all sites. In this chapter, we summarize the patterns of effects in several ways that make evaluative sense, but we do not pretend to have exhausted the information to be found in our results. The reader who wishes to impose other criteria of successful performance will find in Volume IV-B all detailed information necessary to any further summaries.

We should not be surprised, of course, to discern variable results in a planned variation experiment: the model sponsors differ widely in their educational goals and emphases. Some believe, for example, that affective progress must precede academic progress: that until children come to feel good about themselves and to accept responsibility for what happens to them, it is unreasonable to expect them to learn the basic and cognitive conceptual skills that school success requires. Under these models children are expected to make better academic progress after they develop a positive self-image. Other models—the more behavioristic and/or academically oriented ones—hold that acquisition of basic and conceptual skills will provide success experiences which will improve the child's self-image and sense of control.

Although no model explicitly ignores any of the three outcome domains, each places primary emphasis on improving performance in one or two of them. When Follow Through began, each model confidently expected to have laid by third grade, in its own way, the foundation for continuing balanced progress in school performance. We now have the means to assess how well these diverse paths actually have led to the kinds of successes that the tests measure. We are in no position, of course, to extrapolate our findings to the children's future performance, particularly in terms of increased "life's chances."

The next section of this chapter discusses the answer to the questions raised at the beginning of this chapter and presents the various patterns of "effects" that the Follow Through models have achieved in their respective sites; the details of these effects are set forth model in Volume IV-B.

### Do the Various Educational Strategies Being Tested in Follow Through Have Different Impacts?

Overall, Follow Through intervention has succeeded in raising some scores for some children, while apparently not doing so for others: merely to intervene is not to guarantee that test scores will rise. But nobody today seriously expects disadvantage, in all its variety, to yield tamely to any known panacea or set of panaceas. One important motivation for the planned variation approach was the hope that by trying many kinds of intervention in many settings we might be able to learn what works under what circumstances. Do some models or types of models have importantly better effects than others? Five major findings bear on the answer to this questions.

### Finding 1: The effectiveness of each Follow Through model varied substantially from site group to site group; overall model averages varied little in comparison.

No model has shown itself to be powerful enough to succeed everywhere it has been tried. Figure 2 indicates that eleven models had at least one group with a positive average effect on basic skills. That is, all but two models appear to provide a net benefit to some groups of disadvantaged children relative to other similarly disadvantaged groups. The same finding obtains in the other domains. Every model, on the other hand, had groups with negative average effects. In each model with more than three groups, the range of group average effects was wider than the total range of the thirteen model averages. Each model might have performed very differently in other sites: if each had been judged by its results in one site only, and that site had been diabolically chosen, the rank order of model averages could have been almost reversed. For this reason, we have taken care not to overinterpret small difference. in averages or rankings among models. It is well that the Follow Through planned variation design called for each model to be implemented in a wide variety of places; without this diversity, we would not have been able to demonstrate so clearly the importance of local conditions.

Since each model discussed in this chapter has only a few groups (from 3 to 16), and since group averages vary widely within each model, each model's average depends heavily on the precise set of groups considered. Since, furthermore, most of the model averages for all groups are very close to zero and to each other, especially for the affective outcomes and, to a lesser extent, for the cognitive conceptual, one would expect the rank order of model averages to be substantially different in the total set of groups and in various subsets of it. Table 5 shows the rank order of the mean scores of eleven models[19] in each domain as computed for all groups, and separately, for the groups in Cohort III-K only.[20]

To single out this subset of groups for special attention is, in an important sense, to give the models the best possible legitimate chance to show a positive effect, since Cohort III-K was the largest and best-documented cohort stream and also the latest, so that the sponsors had had the greatest opportunity to develop their models and implementation strategies.

With a few notable exceptions, the rankings for the Cohort III-K sites are fairly similar to those for all sites, but their similarity varies by model type and outcome domain. The basic skills rankings are substantially more similar (Spearman's $P = .87$) than those for cognitive conceptual skills ($P = .61$), which in turn are more similar than those for affective outcomes ($P = .46$). Much of the instability arises among the models that give primary emphasis to the affective outcomes, as Table 5 indicates. It is clear from Table 5 that EDC's effects, especially in the affective domain, were much more favorable in Cohort III-K than in the other cohort streams. On the other hand, Bank Street, another affective/cognitive model, had less favorable effects in Cohort III-K, especially in the cognitive domain.

Across all outcome domains and model types, the average model's rank in Cohort III-K differed from that in all groups by slightly less than two ranks, as Table 6 shows. As will be evident from more detailed summaries later in this chapter, the absolute values of the model averages are also very sensitive to changes in the set of groups being averaged. It would therefore be inappropriate to set a criterion level for model averages and to declare all models "successful" whose average effect over all groups exceeds the criterion: adding or substracting very few groups could create whole new lists of "successful" models.

FIGURE 2
SITE AND MODEL AVERAGE EFFECTS IN THREE OUTCOME DOMAINS
FOR THIRTEEN FOLLOW THROUGH MODELS ACROSS ALL COHORT STREAMS

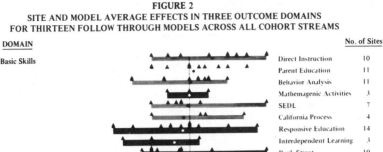

Somewhat more stable comparative patterns emerge at a more aggregated level:

- *Direct Instruction* and *SEDL* are consistently in the top half (five ranks) of the rankings in all domains, both overall and in Cohort III-K. *TEEM* and *Cognitive Curriculum* consistently fall in the bottom half.

- *Behavior Analysis* and *Parent Education* are always in the top half in basic skills and affective outcomes, and *Responsive Education* in cognitive conceptual skills.

TABLE 5

Ranks of Mean Scores in Three Outcome Domains for Eleven Models,
for All Groups, and for Cohort III-K Groups Only

| Model | Domain of Primary Emphasis | Outcome Domain | | | | | | Number of Groups | |
|---|---|---|---|---|---|---|---|---|---|
| | | Basic Skills | | Cognitive Conceptual Skills | | Affective Outcomes | | | |
| | | All Groups | C3K Groups | All Groups | C3K Groups | All Groups | C3K Groups | All | C3K |
| Direct Instruction | | 1 | 1 | 1 | 2.5 | 1 | 5.5 | 16 | 5 |
| Behavior Analysis | Basic | 3 | 2 | 10 | 7.5 | 2 | 4 | 13 | 7 |
| SEDL | Skills | 4 | 3 | 2 | 2.5 | 3 | 3 | 8 | 5 |
| California Process | | 5 | 6 | 8 | 10 | 5 | 7.5 | 8 | 4 |
| TEEM | | 8 | 9 | 7 | 7.5 | 11 | 11 | 15 | 6 |
| Cognitive Curriculum | Cognitive Conceptual | 9 | 8 | 11 | 9 | 8 | 7.5 | 9 | 5 |
| Parent Education | Skills | 2 | 4 | 4 | 6 | 4 | 2 | 12 | 5 |
| IELP | | 11 | 11 | 6 | 5 | 6 | 5.5 | 3 | 3 |
| Responsive Education | Affective | 6 | 5 | 3 | 1 | 7 | 9.5 | 16 | 6 |
| Bank Street | Outcomes | 7 | 10 | 5 | 11 | 9 | 9.5 | 12 | 5 |
| EDC | | 10 | 7 | 9 | 4 | 10 | 1 | 10 | 5 |
| Group totals, Means of rank by domain of primary emphasis | Basic Skills | 3.3 | 3.0 | 5.2 | 5.6 | 2.8 | 5.0 | 45 | 21 |
| | Cognitive Conceptual Skills | 7.5 | 8.0 | 7.0 | 6.9 | 7.2 | 6.5 | 39 | 19 |
| | Affective Outcomes | 7.7 | 7.3 | 5.7 | 5.3 | 8.7 | 6.7 | 38 | 16 |
| Spearman's $\rho$ | | .87 | | .61 | | .46 | | | |

- *California Process, Bank Street,* and *IELP* vary near and below the middle of the rankings.

- *EDC,* as noted above, ranges from the top to near the bottom of the rankings, depending mainly on the cohort.

- *Mathemagenic Activities* and *ILM,* with only three site groups each, are inadequately represented for this sort of comparison.

But the main lesson of site variability is that the models are not powerful enough to countervail unmeasured site-specific determinants of outcomes. Any model can "fail" by having a group perform lower on a test than it would have without Follow Through. Nearly every model has shown that it can "succeed" in the sense of showing mor positive than negative effects in some group.

Community size also appears to be a factor in the site variability we observe. As shown in Table 7, the Cohort III-K site groups are pretty well distributed over the matrix. But since there are only 58 sites in the Cohort III-K, hardly any cell of the model by community size (12 x 5) portion of the matrix has

TABLE 6

Instability of Model Outcome Rankings,* by Model Type and Outcome Domain

| Model Type (Domain of Primary Emphasis) | Outcome Domain | | | All Outcomes |
| --- | --- | --- | --- | --- |
| | Basic Skills | Cognitive Conceptual Skills | Affective Outcomes | |
| Basic Skills | 0.75 | 1.50 | 2.00 | 1.42 |
| Cognitive Conceptual Skills | 1.00 | 1.25 | 0.50 | 0.92 |
| Affective/Cognitive Outcomes | 2.33 | 4.33 | 4.00 | 3.56 |
| All Models | 1.27 | 2.18 | 2.00 | 1.82 |

*The tabulated index of ranking instability is the mean absolute rank difference per model between the rankings in all groups and those in Cohort III-K groups only (cf Table 5).

enough replications to lend any generalizability to the average effect by model. The only empty cell in the model type by community size breakdown, however, is in rural areas for affective sponsors. In general, there are few rural sistes in this cohort stream. Each of the other 14 cells in the model type section of Table 7 has from one to seven sites. Figure 3 displays what there seems to be in the way of a community size effect. We have selected the model type by community size and all models by community size average effects for this display, combining the medium and small cities. There is a fairly strong tendency for the middle-sized communities to have better Follow Through performance from that experienced by either the very large or very small ones. The strongest exception to that pattern appears in the affective performance of cognitive sponsors, but that cell includes only two sites.

This pattern is probably real, although hardly commanding. And given the reasonable distribution of community size across model types, even a much stronger pattern would not have much impact on the overall evaluation. A model that specialized in New York, Philadelphia, and the rural areas might indeed suffer relatively to other models that hewed to the middle ground. SEDL, for example, approaches such a distribution, and indeed its middle-sized sites generally had positive results whereas its big and little ones had negative results.

These examples strongly suggest that it is only when we aggregate even beyond the model level to that of the model type that really consistent patterns appear. Table 5 displays these patterns as means of ranks by domain of primary emphasis; they are more qualitatively apparent in Figure 2 as groupings of model types. We rest our principal conclusions, Findings 2 through 5 below, upon these patterns; Figure 4 displays them graphically.

The stability of the model type patterns is even more apparent in Table 8. Here we contrast the rankings shown in Figure 2 (which are based on our broad-

TABLE 7

**Number of Groups for Each Community Size in the Cohort III Kindergarten Stream**

| Model | Domain of Primary Emphasis | Community Size | | | | | |
|---|---|---|---|---|---|---|---|
| | | New York & Philadelphia | Other Big Cities | Medium Cities | Small Cities | Rural Areas | All Sites |
| Direct Instruction | Basic Skills | 1 | | 3 | | 1 | 5 |
| Behavior Analysis | | 2 | 2 | 2 | | 1 | 7 |
| SEDL | | 1 | 1 | | 1 | 2 | 5 |
| California Process | | | 3 | | 1 | | 4 |
| TEEM | Cognitive Conceptual Skills | | 3 | 1 | 2 | | 6 |
| Cognitive Curriculum | | 1 | 2 | | 2 | | 5 |
| Parent Education | | 1 | 2 | | 1 | i | 5 |
| IELP | | | 1 | | 1 | 1 | 3 |
| ILM | | 1 | 1 | | | | 2 |
| Responsive Education | Affective/ Cognitive Skills | | 2 | 4 | | | 6 |
| Bank Street | | 2 | | 2 | 1 | | 5 |
| EDC | | 1 | 1 | 2 | 1 | | 5 |
| Model Type | Basic Skills | 4 | 6 | 5 | 2 | 4 | 21 |
| | Cognitive Skills | 3 | 9 | 1 | 6 | 2 | 21 |
| | Affective/ Cognitive Outcomes | 3 | 3 | 8 | 2 | | 16 |
| All Models | | 10 | 18 | 14 | 10 | 6 | 58 |

est set of results, incorporating two estimates of the Follow Through effect on each outcome in each group) with those which appear when we consider only the "more appropriate" of the two estimates of each effect.[21] The "more appropriate" rankings, although based on only half as many estimates and therefore presumably subject to more instability, correlate very highly with the overall rankings and actually sharpen somewhat the contrasts among the model types.

*Finding 2: Models that emphasize basic skills succeeded better than other models in helping children gain these skills.*

TABLE 8

Ranks of Mean Scores in Three Outcome Domains for Eleven Models: All Estimates, and the "More Appropriate" Estimate for Each Group

| Model | Domain of Primary Emphasis | Basic Skills | | Cognitive Conceptual Skills | | Affective Outcomes | |
|---|---|---|---|---|---|---|---|
| | | All Estimates | "More Appropriate" | All Estimates | "More Appropriate" | All Estimates | "More Appropriate" |
| Direct Instruction | | 1 | 1 | 1 | 2 | 1 | 1 |
| Behavior Analysis | Basic | 3 | 4 | 10 | 10 | 2 | 3 |
| SEDL | Skills | 4 | 3 | 2 | 1 | 3 | 5.5 |
| California Process | | 5 | 5 | 8 | 4 | 5 | 5.5 |
| TEEM | | 8 | 8 | 7 | 8 | 11 | 11 |
| Cognitive Curriculum | Cognitive | 9 | 10 | 11 | 11 | 8 | 5.5 |
| Parent Education | Conceptual | 2 | 2 | 4 | 7 | 4 | 2 |
| IELP | Skills | 11 | 11 | 6 | 6 | 6 | 5.5 |
| Responsive Education | | 6 | 6.5 | 3 | 5 | 7 | 8 |
| Bank Street | Affective | 7 | 6.5 | 5 | 3 | 9 | 9 |
| EDC | Outcomes | 10 | 9 | 9 | 10 | 10 | 10 |
| Means of ranks by domain of primary emphasis | Basic Skills | 3.3 | 3.2 | 5.2 | 4.2 | 2.8 | 3.2 |
| | Cognitive Conceptual Skills | 7.5 | 7.8 | 7.0 | 8.0 | 7.2 | 6.0 |
| | Affective Outcomes | 7.7 | 7.3 | 5.7 | 5.7 | 8.7 | 9.0 |
| Spearman's $\rho$ | | .98 | | .84 | | .91 | |

[593]

FIGURE 3
AVERAGE EFFECTS FOR COMMUNITY SIZE BY MODEL TYPE
AND FOR COMMUNITY SIZE BY ALL MODELS
FOR THE COHORT III KINDERGARTEN GROUPS

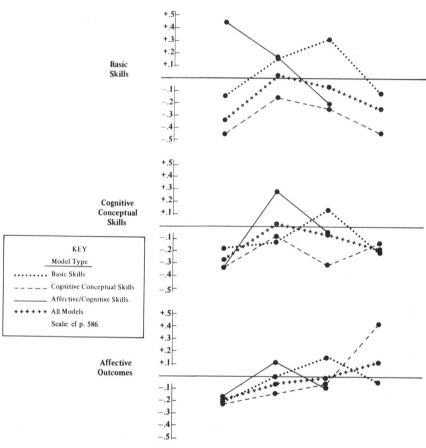

The four basic skills models ranked, on the average, substantially higher than did those of either of the other types with respect to their effects on basic skills test scores, as Figure 4 indicates. The groups of disadvantaged children served by these models have tended, moreover, to perform better on the basic skills tests than have similarly disadvantaged groups outside Follow Through, as evidenced by the positive overall average effect for this model type: the excess of positive over negative effects amounted to 8.6% of all trustworthy effects estimates for these models. Figure 2 indicates also that the Direct Instruction

FIGURE 4
AVERAGE EFFECTS AND PROFILES OF MEAN RANKS
FOR THOSE EFFECTS IN THREE OUTCOME DOMAINS
FOR THREE MODEL TYPES IN ALL COHORT STREAMS

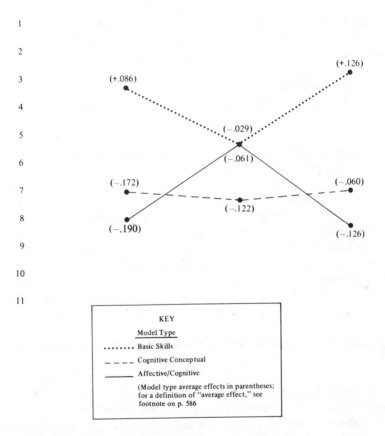

| Mean of Model Ranks | DOMAIN | | |
|---|---|---|---|
| | Basic Skills | Cognitive Conceptual Skills | Affective Outcomes |

KEY

Model Type

........ Basic Skills

_ _ _ _ Cognitive Conceptual

_____ Affective/Cognitive

(Model type average effects in parentheses; for a definition of "average effect," see footnote on p. 586

Model of the University of Oregon, a basic skills emphasis model, had a distinctly higher average effect on basic skills scores than did any other model, of whatever type.

On the other hand, only two of the four basic skills models achieved a positive balance of basic skills effects, although all four were among the top six in the ranking. Also in the top six were one cognitive conceptual model, Parent Education, with a positive average effect, and one affective/cognitive model, Mathemagenic Activities, whose positive and negative effects just balanced each other out.

It is reasonably clear from these results that if an educator is aiming primarily at enhancing spelling, vocabulary, and arithmetic computation skills, one of the basic skills models would be a better bet than the others. Our earlier finding of wide site variability still holds, however: even the model with the best track record had more than one site in which the Follow Through children did less well, on the average, than we estimate they would have done if they had been outside Follow Through. Unmeasured local circumstances, including those associated with implementation, still have had more influence on results than have the philosophies of the models' sponsors.

*Finding 3: Where models have put their primary emphasis elsewhere than on the basic skills, the children they served have tended to score lower on tests of these skills than they would have done without Follow Through.*

Except for Parent Education and Mathemagenic Activities, mentioned above, all models other than the basic skills models showed more negative than positive effects on basic skills scores. For the cognitive conceptual models, the excess of negative over positive effects was 17.2% of all trustworthy effects; for the affective/cognitive models, it was 19.0%. It appears that the NFT children are receiving educational experiences that teach them the basic skills by third grade more effectively than would the compensatory programs offered by Follow Through. The educational theories of some of the Follow Through sponsors predict, to be sure, that the traditional academic benefits of their interventions should become evident over the long term, not necessarily by third grade; some, indeed, doubt that the kinds of educational outcomes measured by the basic skills tests will ever be important to the "life chances" of children. Be that as it may, instruction in the cognitive conceptual and affective domains does not seem to have transferred to improved basic skills test scores; the reader's value system will govern his judgment of the seriousness of this finding.

*Finding 4: No type of model was notably more successful than the others in raising scores on cognitive conceptual skills.*

As Figure 2 shows, each of the three model types is well distributed over the range of model average effects on cognitive conceptual scores; if any of the three is less effective than the others, it is the type that aims primarily at enhancing these skills. Only three models (two basic skills and one affective/cognitive) show more positive than negative effects in this domain. The basic skills models, relatively successful in their "own" domain, cluster near both extremes of the cognitive conceptual ranking. No model type has an overall average positive effect. Since our measures of this domain include tests of such important and complex skills as reading comprehension and problem solving, the relative infrequency of positive results is a serious matter. Direct Instruction's basic skills emphasis, and that of SEDL as well, seem to have transferred to a relatively respectable showing on the more advanced cognitive conceptual outcomes, as has the affective/cognitive approach of Mathemagenic Activities. If the cognitive conceptual models are to enhance test scores in their domain of principal emphasis, the results have not shown up by the end of third grade.

*Finding 5: Models that emphasize basic skills produced better results on tests of self-concept than did other models.*

On the average, children served by basic skills models have performed substantially better on the Follow Through tests of self-esteem and achievement responsibility than have the children in the models that aim directly to develop these outcomes, as Figure 4 indicates. Improved basic skills scores, where they have been achieved, do not seem to have been bought at the price of reduced scores in the domain of feelings and motivation. It appears that those models which provide children with success and non-threatening failure experiences in the course of achieving small, "bite-sized" goals have demonstrated that, consistently with the theory espoused by some of these models, the success experience transfers into a demonstrably improved self-concept, in terms of the measures in the Follow Through outcome battery.

The foregoing findings reflect very clear general patterns in the Follow Through data. An additional observation of some substantive interest also bears on the question of site variability and permits us to control for much of that variability. This observation, and the rest which follow in answer to the two remaining questions, seem to hold, but with less certainty and generality.

*Finding 6: Model comparisons in New York and Philadelphia yield results which are similar to those found in overall comparisons.*

The performance of models in "big cities" (New York and Philadelphia) permits us to compare models with less concern with the confounding of site variability. While the patterns of model effects in big cities are similar to overallodel effects, the absolute level of effectiveness differs. Most models were less effective in New York and Philadelphia than in other sites. This holds for basic and cognitive-conceptual skills, but not as strongly for affective outcomes.

**Do Differences in Impact Have Any
Relationship to the Characteristics of Children,
e.g., Socioeconomic Status and Preschool Experience?**

Our data suggest two tentative answers to this question.

*Finding 7: Some models are more successful in their most disadvantaged sites.*[22]

The Follow Through planned variation models were designed to improve the performance of low income children. However, one might expect that the children from the lowest socioeconomic backgrounds would present the models with their severest tests of effectiveness. Our analyses do not permit us to address the question as it pertains to types of children; i.e., very disadvantaged versus less disadvantaged. We can, however, address it in terms of the groups of Follow Through children found in each site. Six models (Direct Instruction, Parent Education, Behavior Analysis, Responsive Education, Bank Street, and EDC) have higher average effects in the low-income sites than in the high-income sites for both the basic skills and cognitive conceptual domain.[23] On the affective measures, six models (Direct Instruction, Parent Education, Behavior Analysis, California Process, Bank Street) have higher average effects in their most disadvantaged sites. That is, approximately half of the Follow Through models (with more than three sites) are most effective when helping the children in the most disadvantaged communities, demonstrating that some models can be effective with groups of children from very low income families.[24]

*Finding 8: Two models are consistently more effective with Head Start children.*

Follow Through was designed originally to follow through on children's Head Start or other comparable preschool experience. In general, Follow Through and non-Follow Through children who attended Head Start are more disadvantaged than the children who attended other preschool or who did not attend any preschool. Thus, we want to ascertain if Follow Through has been particularly effective with Head Start children, both because of Follow Through's original purpose and because it provides us with another opportunity to explore Follow Through's effectiveness with the most disadvantaged.

We explored Follow Through's effectiveness with different preschool groups only in the Cohort III-K stream. Only a few models produced differential effects across preschool groups.[25] Direct Instruction and Bank Street are consistently more effective with the Head Start children than with other preschool groups across all three domains. Behavior Analysis appears to be more effective with the No Preschool group in basic skills. TEEM and Cognitive Curriculum appear to be more effective with their No Preschool groups in the Cognitive Conceptual domain.

## Do Some Educational Strategies Consistently Show Better Results than Others Over Time, or Does the Impact Vary from Year to Year?

We have examined this question from two perspectives, longitudinally and across Cohorts II and III, reaching two conclusions:

*Finding 9: Most models are more effective during kindergarten and first grade than during second and third grade.*

The Follow Through models place varying degrees of emphasis on the acquisition of basic skills, cognitive conceptual skills, and affective development. Although all sponsors expected to demonstrate effectiveness in all domains by the end of third grade, we can expect the models to produce various time sequences of progress in achieving this goal. We have divided the progress of these children during the course of the program into two parts: progress during kindergarten and first grade (early) and progress during second and third grade (late). A study of the progress of FT children during these two intervals shows that most programs produce substantial progress early on math measures.[26] However, only a few of the programs are able to maintain these early benefits in math during the later period of the program.

The reading area appears to be much less tractable. Direct Instruction, Behavior Analysis, and Bank Street models produce predominantly nonnegative effects, that is, progress in readint which ie either greater than or equal to the progress of comparison children. Only the children associated with the Direct Instruction Model appear to perform above the expectation determined by the progress of the non-Follow Through children. Moreover, the Direct Instruction children are the only group which appears to make more progress in reading, both early and late. In general, most models appear to be more effective during kindergarten and first grade than during second and third grade. The Direct Instruction Model is the only program which consistently produces substantial progress.

*Finding 10: Some Follow Through sponsors grew in effectiveness over time.*

Although we have not been able to determine the degree of treatment implementation, we might surmise that implementation should improve over time, and that a model's effectiveness should be related to the length of time a sponsor has spent in a site. Models encounter many problems in the development and implementation of an educational approach.

We have the opportunity to study model effects over time by examining data on twelve models which implemented their programs in a total of thirty-six sites in both Cohort II-K and Cohort III-K.[27] One would expect the adverse effects of model development problems and model-specific implementation problems to diminish from one cohort to the next, as the sponsors gained experience. We therefore expect to find greater model effectiveness in Cohort III-K than in Cohort II-K.

We can see a tendency to improve across time for those models which performed differently across the two cohorts on basic and cognitive conceptual skills. On the other hand, most models did not do as well in Cohort III-K as in Cohort II-K on affective outcomes. Two other patterns in the data are apparent. First, the strongest performers on basic skills in Cohort II-K (Direct Instruction, Parent Education, California Process) showed little change in Cohort III-K. This pattern is not evident in the cognitive conceptual and affective areas. Second, the weakest performers in Cohort II-K (EDC, Home-School Partnership,

Cognitive Curriculum, and Responsive Education) improved substantially in Cohort III-K on both basic and cognitive conceptual skills.

These findings suggest that the length of time that a model is active in a site was moderately related to its effectiveness as assessed by basic and cognitive conceptual skills measures. Those models which appeared weaker in Cohort II-K were most easily able to improve their effectiveness, while the models which performed relatively well early in Cohort II-K did not improve as much.

### What Follows from These Results?

Let us finally reiterate that this report is by no means a comprehensive evaluation of the national Follow Through endeavor. To be sure, we have examined a sizable number and variety of outcomes, and we have done just about all that the data and the state of the analytic art allow in order to find out why the results turned out as they did. We should be most surprised if further analysis of these data were to yield qualitatively different conclusions to anybody in the future.

But our report has really more the character of a report card than that of a complete catalogue of all that is good and bad, successful and unsuccessful about Follow Through. Sponsors, project leaders, parents, teachers, and children have other valuable insights to provide. Those who have to make practical decisions about Follow Through would be mistaken to base their actions on only a part of the available evidence, whether our part or another. They would be equally mistaken to ignore our results: seen in the proper context and interpreted judiciously, they embody a unique part of the history from which we must learn if we are to build upon our collective experience.

From time to time we are asked questions which bear upon the believability and generalizability of the patterns we have presented here. Perhaps we can best put our findings into context and delimit the range of their applicability by discussing here some of these questions and our best answers to them. We find, for example, across all models, all groups, and all measures, there are fewer positive effects (12.8%) than negative (19.6%) and a preponderance (67.6%) of null effects. This distribution immediately raises three questions:

1. *Why are there so few positive effects?* Apparently, it is genuinely hard to raise the test scores of disadvantaged children, even in comparison to those of other disadvantaged children, by means of the kinds of compensatory interventions that Follow Through has tried. Why? Several possible answers, more or less consistent with each other, suggest themselves.

   a. *Disadvantaged children are different from the general population.* Much of the philosophy of some models is based on the proposition that different children should have different educational experiences directed at different objectives which imply in turn different criteria for evaluation. Disadvantaged children, some argue, are not defective children but merely *different* children who should not be judged by the same standards as other children. In our view, this argument amounts to a concession that compensatory education might not have the power to enable its clients to compete successfully with their peers in the nation at large. Be that as it may, our evaluation has undertaken to apply a uniform standard to all the diverse manifestations of Follow Through.

b. *It is difficult to implement change* in the functioning of institutions by means of intervention from the outside. Efforts to innovate in schools, even spearheaded by well-placed insiders, are often frustrated by the overt or covert unwillingness of teachers, parents, pupils, administrators and others to change accustomed ways of carrying out the business of education. Abundant anecdotal evidence attests to the wide variety of problems that the sponsors have faced in trying to implement their models in the sites. Any extensions of Follow Through to other districts, however, would probably encounter analogous circumstances, and so we are confident that our findings reflect the outcomes one might expect from a broader Follow Through program, even though the available evidence on the particular implementation difficulties to date was too unsystematic to contribute directly to the findings.

c. *In some Following Through models, children get very little practice in test-taking.* Several models make it a point to shield children from evaluative testing. Other models, however, provide ample opportunities for children to develop test-taking skills and to develop familiarity with items similar to those found on standardized tests. Therefore, one would not be surprised to find many FT children doing less well on the tests in the outcome battery, relative to an NFT standard, than do the FT children more accustomed to test-taking.

d. *Disadvantage is resilient.* Implicit in much of the early thinking which led to Head Start and Follow Through was the idea that disadvantaged children were like a compressed spring: if an educator could merely remove whatever obstacles prevented children from realizing their potential, then they would in the normal course of events expand and stay expanded, barring further negative intervention from outside. When it was alleged that Head Start gains tended to decrease over time, two possible explanations arose: (a) public schooling destroys the benefits of Head Start, recompressing the spring, as it were; or (b) disadvantaged children are not like compressed springs, but rather like shorter springs that are already at their equilibrium state: if intervention expands them, they tend to return to their normal position in the absence of continuing effort to keep them stretched. Follow Through was designed to cover both of these possibilities, by improving the performance of the public schools and by extending the compensatory effort in time. The results of the present Follow Through evaluation effort are consistent with the idea that whatever the forces may be which cause and maintain low test performance among children from families of low socioeconomic status, many of the compensatory interventions that have been tried to date are not strong enough to countervail them. That is, the models appear to be less effective in raising test scores than originally expected.

2. *Why are there so many negative effects?* The advocates of Follow Through did not enter upon the program with the expectation that compensatory services with firm theoretical foundations, implemented by concerned professionals over a considerable period of time, at substantial cost, and with the active co-operation of the parents of the children being served, could be detrimental to children. How, then, do we explain the fact that we find half again as many negative effects as positive? The question is worth asking, if only to provide another opportunity to make clear what the results really say.

The outcome tests were designed to assess performance with respect to the traditional objectives of schooling, pursued in the usual ways. They are not necessarily the best possible tests of performance with respect to the more innovative objectives of some Follow Through models. In many cases, the measured objectives do not match the objectives of these models. For example, there are models which place little emphasis on mathematical skills, choosing instead to focus on the development of higher-order conceptual skills and expecting math proficiency to follow later, once the child has "learned to learn." Such a program would tend to divert the child's attention from the basics and thus confer a relative advantage in that field upon the comparison group; our evaluation would detect a "negative effect." To interpret such a negative effect in a positive light, one would have to show that (a) the FT children gain more of the higher-order skills than do the NFT, and (b) the higher skills actually do transfer eventually to the basic proficiencies. Up to third grade, and judging by the measures in the Follow Through battery, we have found little evidence of such a process.

One's interpretation of our findings will therefore depend on one's educational values and objectives: if one believes that the primary function of schooling is to enhance the kinds of skills that the tests in this outcome battery measure, then the results justify a conclusion that Follow Through has been, in a minority of cases, a less productive experience than traditional schooling would have been. If, on the other hand, one believes that other broader objectives are more appropriate, and that our instruments do not measure those objectives, then one could speculate—or adduce independent evidence—that these negative results may be offset by progress on other unmeasured outcomes. Our results cannot confirm or deny that possibility they bear only on the evaluation of Follow Through with respect to traditional criteria.

3. *Why are there so many null effects?* To balance the picture, let us also note that most of the effects are null. That is, as determined by the analyses, most Follow Through groups have performed neither better nor worse than expected of similarly disadvantaged non-Follow Through groups on the tests administered at the end of third grade. There are at least three possible explanations for the null effects.

a. *FT and NFT may not be very different in practice:*

- NFT children generally receive assistance from Title I and other programs, and so we have clearly not compared Follow Through to "the absence of compensatory education."

- In some locations, there is evidence that NFT classrooms have picked up FT techniques and materials from enthusiastic FT participants, thus muddying the practical distinction between treatment and control.

- Finally, implementation difficulties may have kept the Follow Through models from making as much difference as they would have wished.

To the extent that any of these arguments explain the preponderance of null effects, however, the evaluative implications for Follow Through seem rather negative. If Follow Through is worth what it costs, it should be more productive than other, generally less expensive, compensatory programs. If technology transfer in the teachers' lounge is all it takes to wipe out the difference between FT and NFT, then simpler and less expensive dissemination procedures than sponsorship ought to suffice to spread the benefits of Follow Through throughout the nation. And if a program cannot be put into practice, what real value does it have?

b. *FT and NFT may be very different, but both ineffective.* Our best evidence of the ineffectiveness of NFT is the oft-cited tendency of disadvantaged children to fall farther and farther behind their more advantaged peers. If this pattern holds for the NFT groups—and we have made no direct test of the hypothesis—then our comparative results suggest that it also holds, and slightly more often, for the FT groups. Our best interpretation of the large number of nulls is the same as for the small number of positive effects: it seems to be hard to make a difference.

c. *The tests of differences may not have been powerful enough.* By reason of small sample sizes within some sites, in fact, our analyses were sometimes not sensitive enough to detect all of the effects which may actually exist; the footnote on page 132 discusses the extent of this problem.

4. *Did we study the right outcomes?* Our results comprise evidence on the effectiveness of Follow Through intervention of various kinds in helping disadvantaged children to score better on tests of several academic skills, self-concept, and achievement responsibility than they would have done without Follow Through. Some of the models' sponsors place high priority on the skills tested, and some do not. To the extent that the tests overlap the models' objectives, our results provide evidence on the models' success in attaining those objectives. But whether or not we have anything to say about the models' achievement of their own goals, we do have some important findings about their performance with respect to some rather widely accepted (if controversial) criteria. We have simply laid several uniform measuring sticks up against each member of a very diverse set of educational situations. Our report describes

such apparent program effects as we have discerned in each measured domain; the reader must decide whether there was any reason to expect effects and what judgments about the programs properly follow.

We should also point out that, as in all social science—or in any other kind of science, for that matter—the designers of Follow Through had to live with a pervasive trade-off between relevance and measurability. The characteristics one would most like to know can usually be measured only indirectly, approximately, and at great cost. Anything the evaluator can actually get at will always find somebody to call it the "wrong measure." In our judgment, the Follow Through design and instrumentation represent as good a resolution of this trade-off as the political and methodological climate of the 1960s would give one any rason to expect. Even with the experience of the intervening decade, it is not obvious that anybody is in a position to do importantly better.

5. *Were the outcomes measured adequately?* Again, the measures in the Follow Through battery were the best available at the time that instrumentation decisions had to be made. Some mid-stream instrument changes were made, at some cost to the longitudinal integrity of the evaluation. As in any large-scale data collection effort, especially a long-term one in a mobile population beset here and there with serious social unrest, the testing and interviewing process encountered many practical difficulties. Abt Associates was not a party to the data gathering, but the quality of the data we have received over the years from the Stanford Research Institute bespeaks a high level of care and ingenuity devoted to overcoming those difficulties.

Here and there throughout the report, we have remarked that the basic skills test scores have tended to correlate more highly with other measured characteristics than have the scores on cognitive conceptual skills, and both more highly than the affective scores. It is not surprising that the simplest and most concrete outcomes, such as spelling, computation, and vocabuilary, would be more reliably measured than would more abstract, reactive outcomes such as self-esteem or achievement responsibility. If a child completes several arithmetic computations correctly, he has the skill being measured. If he says he feels good about himself, the response may have any of a number of meanings. Because of such considerations, the prudent reader will place more confidence in the reported effects on the simpler outcomes, but even the patterns in the more complex outcomes are anything but random.

6. *Did our analyses set too high a standard of success?* Before we would declare an apparent effect "real," whether positive or negative, we required it to be statistically significant (at the conventional pL .05 level and also to exceed a quarter of a standard deviation of the outcome measure. The first requirement merely obliged us to base each finding on a large enough number of cases that it would be unlikely to result from the differences among members of the groups being compared, rather than from differences among the groups;

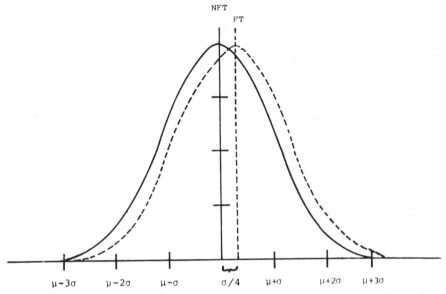

NFT

FT

μ−3σ    μ−2σ    μ−σ    σ/4    μ+σ    μ+2σ    μ+3σ

Figure 5: Two normal distributions with the same variance and means separated by 0.25 standard deviation, illustrating the minimum "educationally-significant" FT/NFT difference.

this criterion has nothing to do with high or low standards of accomplishment. Overall, 30% of the effects were "significant."

The second criterion, which we have called "materiality" or "educational significance," arose from a consensus early in the project that mean test score differences that amounted to less than a quarter of a standard deviation might well be "significant," thanks to large samples, but that they would not be educationally interesting. Figure 5 displays a somewhat idealized picture of a difference of this magnitude. We decided, in effect, that if the FT and NFT distributions coincided even more closely than Figure 5 shows, we were willing to ignore the differences among them. Overall, 49% of the effects were "material."

As further evidence of the reasonableness of this judgmental standard, we note that a quarter of a standard deviation corresponds roughly to about two months' progress in terms of grade equivalents.[28] Over a three-year or four-year period of intervention, a program really ought to generate a couple of months' relative progress; if not, it has not made much of a dent in the problem that the outcome measure is intended to document. A year would be too much to ask; a week, too little. In our judgment, two months is a comfortable criterion. The reader who wishes to impose a more or less stringent standard can do so by reference to the detailed results of our computations of effects, presented in Volumes IV-B and IV-C.

7. *Could attrition have led us to mistaken conclusions?* As Chapter Four of Volume IV-A points out in some detail, our analytic sample comprises only a minority of the children who were pretested and to whom the Follow Through "treatments" were applied. What of the others? Did they leave because they were in some relevant sense different from those who stayed? Had they all stayed, how would they have performed on the outcome tests, and would our measure of program effectiveness turned out differently? The pluperfect subjunctive is, unfortunately notoriously unresearchable. Our closest approach to answers to such questions derives from a series of studies of the attrition question which we performed when the extent of developing attrition become apparent. From the results of these studies, we conclude, to our relief, that the same kinds of children left the FT and NFT groups, site by site, at least with respect to income and pretest scores. We therefore feel reasonably confident that attrition has not done serious damage to our comparisons of FT with NFT. Our results apply less well, it is true, to the more mobile segment of the disadvantaged population than to those who tend to stay in one place. But then the Follow Through world was not sampled probabilistically from any larger population: it is simply an availability sample, clustered by more or less relevant political criteria, of variably disadvantaged children and the adults associated with them. All anybody can do to generalize from such a "sample" is to describe it thoroughly, as we have done in Chapter Three, and then to surmise cautiously that "this is the kind of thing that happens when these treatments are applied to these sorts of children." We claim neither more nor less generality for our findings.

8. *But what if some of the models were not adequately implemented?* Is it fair, after all, to judge the effectiveness of an educational strategy by its poor performance in a school system that bungled the model in practice, dramatically altered it, or simply ignored it? Do we really know how powerful the models are before we have at least ensured that they have been implemented?

Perhaps our clearest finding is that each model's performance varies widely from site to site. An unknown proportion of this variation results from implementation problems, of which we have no analytically useful record. In comparison with the site variations, those of the overall model averages were not very large. As this pattern began to be clear in the early years of the evaluation, we turned our primary attention from the study of model average effects to that of site effects, so as not to obscure the results of good implementations by averaging them with those of bad ones. Most of the models were tried out in enough sites that one might reasonably expect at least one good implementation: if a model did not make its point in any of its sites, however powerful it might be in principle, one might legitimately wonder about its practical value.

In a practical sense, we can be fairly confident that a model *can* produce at least as much progress as it showed in its best site. On the other side of the coin, the same model can clearly do at least as badly as it did in its worst site. Lacking information about implementation (what if a model did best in a site that had not implemented it well?), we can only give the models the benefit of the doubt in this matter. If future evaluations of externally-guided compensatory interventions wish to be able to attribute outcomes more confidently to the specific kinds of intervention applied, they will have to take steps to find out, systematically, what local people did with the models and other associated program resources. Model labels have turned out to carry only a small fraction of the relevant information.

## NOTES

1. This early objective was later eliminated, reflecting the intention to examine the impacts of each of the planned variation strategies rather than the impact of Follow Through as a program.

2. There is a fourth cohort consisting of children in three big cities: New York, Philadelphia, and Chicago. These data were used peripherally in the Head Start Planned Variation evaluation reported in Volume IIB of *Education as Experimentation: A Planned Variation Model,* pp. IV-3, IV-6.

3. See Haney, 1976 for details of other Follow Through evaluations.

4. A few models are not included in this evaluation because we do not have data. See sample selection criteria in Chapter Three of Volume IV-A.

5. Many researchers have attempted to categorize the Follow Through models according to various dimensions specified in the models. The programs are usually classified along two dimensions: the *theoretical orientation* and *educational philosophy* underlying the programs (Maccoby and Zellner, 1970; White et al., 1973, or the curriculum or *educational goals* (Bissell, 1973; Cline et al., 1974; Egbert, 1973).

6. Sponsor's goals and objectives are stated in several sources, i.e., USOE, 1973, Judd and Wood, 1973, and sponsor descriptions from 1975 proposals.

7. In our presentation of the patterns of effects, SEDL is grouped with the basic skills models while the other three sponsors are grouped with the cognitive conceptual models.

8. Certain instruments (the PPVT, the WRAT, the IARS and the Ravens's described in this section) were modified to make their administration more appropriate for the Follow Through and non-Follow Through children.

9. This section is the introduction to a much lengthier discussion of the technical approach used in the evaluation. Additional details are presented in Chapter Four of Volume IV-A.

10. A multiple strategies approach was also used in the analysis of the Head Start Planned Variation data (Smith, 1973).

11. Within this chapter "sponsor" refers to the program implemented by a sponsor while "model" refers to a type of analysis, i.e., "analytic model."

12. See Chapter One, Volume IV-B for an explanation of Summary of Effects tables.

13. We point out in Chapter Two of Volume IV-A that tests of basic skills achievement provide a more appropriate estimate of the children's performance in that domain than do tests of cognitive conceptual and affective development in their respective domains. The relative performance of FT and NFT children on each of the tests in Figure 1 is discussed in Volume IV-B along with detailed descriptions of the samples of children, the perceptions of the parents and teachers, and a description of each planned variation model. The tests leave much to be desired as indices of performance in the outcome domains, but they were the best available at the time of selection and they do provide

insights we would not otherwise have. It behooves the reader to keep in mind precisely which tests generated the evidence we present.

14. As indicated earlier, we arrived at this classification judgmentally, based on the stated goals and objectives of the models. Other classifications are possible, and the reader may wish to examine the patterns of effects achieved by other grouping of models; the necessary detailed information is presented in Volumes IV-B and IV-C. We follow this scheme because it yields some revealing and relatively stable patterns that illuminate the performance of Follow Through.

15. A "group" in these discussions comprises all the FT children in a model's local project in one of the four cohort streams (Cohorts II and III, each with entering kindergarten (K) and entering first (EF) streams). Responsive Education's Cohort III-K children in Duluth, for example, constitute a "group." The groups are the units of the effect averages reported in this chapter.

16. Our criterion of "educational importance" or "material significance" was set at one-fourth of a standard deviation of the outcome variable. For those outcomes that possess national grade-equivalent norms, in the ranges of scores actually achieved by Follow Through children, this criterion corresponds to a difference on the order of two months of achievement. We also required "statistical significance" at the $p < .05$ level, in order to ensure that we did not draw undue conclusions from groups of inadequate size. In general, the most particularly in the entering kindergarten streams, the statistical criterion turned out to be the more stringent of the two; fully 25% of the null effects were "material" but not "significant," whereas only 5% were "significant" but not "material." We surmise that an extra year's attrition in the kindergarten streams may have diminished the numbers of children in the various groups sufficiently to reduce the power of our statistical tests in some cases and to create some tendency toward Type II error.

17. We have omitted from these summaries all effects whose covariance adjustment was larger than one-half an outcome standard deviation.

18. Average effects are computed by assigning a value of +1 to each positive effect, −1 to each negative, and zero to each null, and then computing the simple mean of these values. The average effect is thus the number of positive effects, less the number of negative effects, divided by the total number of effects; in other words, it is the proportion of net positive effects. Average effects in the basic skills and cognitive conceptual skills domains are computed on a maximum of eight effect estimates per site/cohort stream group: two estimates of the effect on each of four test scores in each group. In the affective domain, we have only three scores, and so the averages are computed on a maximum of six estimates per group.

19. These eleven models are the ones that had at least three groups in Cohort III-K.

20. These are, more precisely, those Cohort III-K groups on which we had the information necessary to carry out the preschool-adjusted analyses reported in detail in Volumes IV-B and IV-C and discussed from a methdological point of view in Chapter Four of Volume IV-A.

21. Chapter Four of Volume IV-A discusses the criteria by which we selected the "more appropriate" analysis for the estimation of each effect.

22. With a few exceptions, most of the New York and Philadelphia FT samples are classified as high income sites. Incomes for all sites, however, are unadjusted for potential differences in cost of living.

23. We have not attempted to determine whether the difference between the means for the high and low income sites is statistically significant.

24. The question of a "regression artifact" applies to the site-level effects. This discussion, however, is based upon aggregations of trustworthy site effects, thereby eliminating most of the potential for a regression artifact.

25. The number of effects entering into each average is very small (8 for Basic Skills and Cognitive Conceptual, 6 for Affective). We only discuss instances where the groups differ on at least two effects. (On the figures a differential of two effects is shown by a difference between groups of .25.)

26. Details of the analysis and results are presented in Volume IV-D.

27. We have compared the effects from analyses of Cohort II and Cohort III which were *not* adjusted for preschool.

28. Chapter Four of Volume IV-A discusses this conversion and its pitfalls.

# REFERENCES

BISSELL, J. S. Planned variation in Head Start and Follow Through. In J. C. Stanley (ed.), Compensatory education for children, ages 2 to 8. Baltimore: Johns Hopkins University Press, 1973.

BOCK, G., L. B. STEBBINS, and E. C. PROPER. Education as experimentation: A planned variation model, Volume IV-B, Effects of Follow Through models. Report to the U.S. Office of Education pursuant to Contract No. 300-75-0134. Cambridge, MA: Abt Associates Inc., 1977.

CLINE, M. G. (ed.). Education as experimentation: A planned variation model, U.S. Office of Education pursuant to Contract No. OEC-0-72-5221. Cambridge, MA: Abt Associates Inc., 1974.

——— (ed.). Education as experimentation: A planned variation model, Volumes II-A and II-B, Two year effects of Follow Through. Report to the U.S. Office of Education pursuant to Contract No. OEC-0-72-5221. Cambridge, MA: Abt Associates Inc., 1975.

Education as experimentation: A planned variation model, Volume IV-C, Appendices. Report to the U.S. Office of Education pursuant to Contract No. 300-75-0134. Cambridge, MA: Abt Associates Inc., 1977.

EGBERT, R. L. Planned variation in Follow Through. Unpublished manuscript, 1973.

EVANS, J. W., and J. SCHILLER. How preoccupation with possible regression artifacts can lead to a faulty strategy for the evaluation of social action programs: A reply to Campbell and Erlebacher. In J. Hellmuth (ed.), Disadvantaged child. Compensatory education: A national debate (Vol. 3). New York: Brunner, Mazel, 1970.

FERB, T., J. LARSON, and D. NAPIOR. Education as experimentation: A planned variation model, Volume IV-D, A longitudinal study of Follow Through. Report to the U.S. Office of Education pursuant to Contract No. 300-75-0134. Cambridge, MA: Abt Associates Inc., 1977.

General Accounting Office. Follow Through: Lessons learned from its evaluation and need to improve its administration (Report to Congress, MWD-75-34). Washington, D.C.: General Accounting Office, 1975.

HANEY, W. Analysis of interim Follow Through evaluation reports (unpublished first draft). Cambridge, MA: Huron Institute, 1976.

JUDD, D. E., and S. E. WOOD, et al. Follow Through materials review (Research report to the U.S. Office of Education pursuant to Contract No. SB0208(a)-73-C-007, Prime Contract No. OEC-0-72-5249). Portland, OR: Nero and Associates, 1973.

MACCOBY, E. E., and M. ZELLNER. Experiments in primary education: Aspects of Project Follow Through. New York: Harcourt Brace, 1970.

MOLITOR, J., M. WATKINS, and D. NAPIOR. Education as experimentation: A planned variation model, A non Follow Through study. Report to the U.S. Office of Education pursuant to Contract No. 300-75-0134. Cambridge, MA: Abt Associates Inc., 1977.

PROPER, E. C., R. G. ST.PIERRE, and T. R. CERVA. Education as experimentation: A planned variation model, Volume IV-E, Supplementary analysis: Reanalysis of selected data sets. Report to the U.S. Office of Education pursuant to Contract No. 300-75-0134. Cambridge, MA: Abt Associates Inc., 1978.

——— Education as experimentation: A planned variation model, Volume IV-F, Supplementary analyses: Appendix. Report to the U.S. Office of Education pursuant to Contract No. 300-75-0134. Cambridge, MA: Abt Associates Inc., 1978.

SMITH, M. S. Evaluation findings in Head Start planned variation. In A. Rivlin and P. M. Timpane (eds.), Planned variation in education. Washington, D.C.: Brookings Institute, 1975.

———, and J. S. BISSELL. Report analysis: The impact of Head Start. Harvard Educational Review, 1970, 40(1), 51-104.

STEBBINS, L. B. (ed.). Education as experimentation: A planned variation model, Volumes III-A and III-B, Findings: Cohort II, Interim findings: Cohort III. Report to the U.S. Office of Education pursuant to Contract No. 300-75-0134. Cambridge, MA: Abt Associates Inc., 1977.

———, R. G. ST.PIERRE, E. C. PROPER, R. B. ANDERSON, and T. R. CERVA. Education as experimentation: A planned variation model, Volume IV-A, An evaluation of Follow Through. Report to the U.S. Office of Education pursuant to Contract No. 300-75-0134. Cambridge, MA: Abt Associates Inc., 1977.

U.S. Office of Education. A guide to Follow Through. Washington, D.C.: DHEW, U.S. Office of Education, 1973.

WHITE, S. H., et al. Federal programs for young children: Review and recommendations (HEW Service Publication No. (OS) 74-101). Washington, D.C.: U.S. Government Printing Office, 1973.

# 37

## No Simple Answer: Critique of the Follow Through Evaluation

### Ernest R. House, Gene V Glass, Leslie D. McLean, and Decker F. Walker

Follow Through has been the largest and most expensive federal educational experiment in this country's history. Conceived in 1967 as an extension of Head Start, Follow Through was designed as a service program to improve the schooling of disadvantaged children in the early elementary grades. Before it was under way, however, an expected $120 million appropriation was slashed to only $15 million for the first year. A decision was then made by the U.S. Office of Education to convert the program into a planned variation experiment, which systematically would compare pupils enrolled in different models of early-childhood education—the Follow Through models—to each other and to pupils from non-Follow Through classes.

Follow Through was organized in such a way that the developers, or sponsors, of innovative educational programs worked with local school districts, or sites, from around the country. The sites volunteered to implement a particular sponsor's model of early-childhood education. Designed for children in kindergarten through third grade, the sponsors' models have been quite varied, ranging from highly structured to open-education approaches. Both sponsors and sites received federal funding. Over the past ten years more than twenty sponsors have worked with over 180 sites at a cost of over $500 million.

This study was supported by a grant from the Ford Foundation to the Center for Instructional Research and Curriculum Evaluation, University of Illinois at Urbana. We wish to acknowledge the valuable assistance of Elizabeth J. Hutchins, research assistant at the University of Illinois.

From Ernest R. House et al., "No Simple Answer: Critique of the Follow Through Evaluation," 48 (2) *Harvard Educational Review* 128-160 (May 1978). Copyright 1978 by President and Fellows of Harvard College.

Although Stanford Research Institute was originally responsible for both data collection and analysis, the major data analysis was eventually conducted by Abt Associates, Inc. The analysis compared thirteen of the models of early-childhood education, using data based on a sample of over twenty-thousand students enrolled in Follow Through models for a four-year period. The total evaluation of Follow Through cost between $30 and $50 million.

*An Unfair Evaluation*

While the Office of Education saw the program as an experiment to determine which model worked best, the sponsors saw the purpose as program development, and the parents saw the program as providing services to their children. This meant conflicting expectations for the evaluation, and many sponsors and parents have felt unfairly treated by evaluators.

The sponsors complained repeatedly that the standardized instruments employed in the evaluation could not properly measure the outcomes of their models. In 1969, at a meeting in California, Krulee (1973) reports:

> Dissatisfaction with certain aspects of the evaluation effort had been developing for some time. . . . Some sponsors viewed the evaluation effort as seriously biased in a particular direction and as being unfair to certain sponsor approaches. Specifically there was the impression that the cards were stacked, through reliance on measures of cognitive change, for those sponsors that were behaviorally (i.e., cognitively) oriented and against all other sponsors. This issue had been building up for some time. Moreover, there were some judgments expressed that the criticisms had previously been made and that SRI [Stanford Research Institute] was failing to respond to them. The sponsors were reasonably unified on this issue. One might have expected the behaviorists—the favored sponsors—to rise to the defense of SRI, but that was certainly not the case. (p. 129)

Early in the evaluation, the sponsors were promised by Stanford Research Institute and the Office of Education that special instruments would be used to measure the diverse effects of their models. Although such measuring devices did not then exist, the Stanford group was confident that they could be developed. However, the evaluators eventually decided that the special measures could not be created. After the drastic curtailment of data in 1972 by the Office of Education, only a few standardized instruments were included in the evaluation. The sponsors' complaints, in turn, grew more vociferous. They had been led to believe that certain kinds of outcomes would be used to judge their models, and the evaluators were unable to deliver. In this sense, the evaluation was unfair to the sponsors. Moreover, many of the actions deviating from the original agreement were taken by the Office of Education or its contractors without approval of the sponsors.

Although treated unfairly, the sponsors were not blameless. In spite of dissatisfaction with the evaluation, they continued to cooperate and to receive large sums of money from the government. Admittedly, they were under some pressure to continue in the program because of their previous heavy investment in it, but their continued cooperation was a tacit acceptance of the changed situation.

Parent groups, especially in Black communities, were also unhappy with the evaluation. The organized parents were suspicious of both evaluators and sponsors and, in 1972, strongly attacked the evaluation. The parents felt excluded from decision making in the program and from input into the evaluation. They saw their children as being at the mercy of the experts.

In conclusion, many of the problems we will discuss in the following pages have their roots in the history of the Follow Through program and its evaluation. The lack of strong results and the push to determine "what works best" has resulted in many errors in measurement, analysis, and interpretation. Furthermore, the overall evaluation has been unbelievably expensive. One must doubt whether "what works best" was the proper question to pursue and whether a quasi-experimental design was the appropriate evaluation approach to answering this question. Moreover, the evaluation was not responsive to the concerns of sponsors and the needs of parents.

## Measurement Problems

### Model and Outcome Typologies

In the main part of the evaluation, the effects of thirteen different Follow Through models are compared.[2] Four instruments are used as the basis of comparison: a standardized achievement test of reading, language, and mathematics

2 However, during the ten-year evaluation effort, twenty-two models were evaluated. The first part of the Abt Associates report gives information for thirteen models (Stebbins et al., 1977) and the second part includes information for seventeen models (Bock et al., 1977). The full names of the models and their sponsors are as follows (the names or acronyms used for the models in text and in the Abt Associates report are given in italics):

Bank Street College of Education Approach
    Bank Street College of Education
Behavior Analysis Approach
    University of Kansas, Support and Development Center for Follow Through
California Process Model
    California State Department of Education, Division of Compensatory Education
Cognitively Oriented Curriculum Model
    High/Scope Educational Research Foundation
Cultural Linguistic Approach [CLA]
    Northeastern Illinois State College
Direct Instructional Model
    University of Oregon, College of Education
EDC Open Education Follow Through Program
    Education Development Center
Florida Parent Education Model
    University of Florida

Home-School Partnership Model
    Clark College
Individualized Early Learning Program [IELP]
    University of Pittsburgh, Learning Research and Development Center
Interdependent Learning Model [ILM]
    City University of New York, Institute for Developmental Studies
Language Development (Bilingual) Education Approach [SEDL]
    Southwest Educational Development Laboratory
Mathemagenic Activities Program [MAP]
    University of Georgia
The New School Approach to Follow Through [NSA]
    University of North Dakota

(Metropolitan Achievement Test); a test of nonverbal problem-solving ability (Raven's Coloured Progressive Matrices); a measure of self-esteem (Cooper-smith's Self-Esteem Inventory); and a measure of children's tendency to assign responsibility for their academic success or failure to their own efforts rather than to external agents or conditions (Intellectual Achievement Responsibility Scale). All instruments were administered to children included in the Follow Through evaluation sample and to matched control groups.

To compare the performance of the various models, students' scores on each instrument are computed and corrected in a rather complex way. (This procedure is taken up in another section and so will not be discussed here.) These corrected scores are then used to compute an "average effect"—the mean difference between Follow Through and non-Follow Through pupils—for each site. These effects are, in turn, averaged across all sites where a given model was in use to determine the average effect for that model. In this way, the thirteen models are compared on each of the eleven subtest scores generated from the four outcome measures.

Unfortunately, neither these simple direct comparisons nor the data that would permit them are reported. Instead, the evaluators choose to group the individual models and the outcome measures into three parallel categories—that is, each model and each outcome measure are classified as being representative of or assessing, respectively, basic skills, cognitive-conceptual skills, or affective skills. The evaluators then compare the different types of models on each of the outcome domains.

The models are classified on the following basis (Stebbins et al., 1977, pp. 131–132):

| | |
|---|---|
| Basic Skills | These models focus first on the elementary skills of vocabulary, arithmetic computation, spelling, and language. |
| Cognitive-Conceptual | These models emphasize the more complex "learning-to-learn" and problem solving skills. |
| Affective-Cognitive | These models focus primarily on self-concept and attitudes toward learning, and secondarily on "learning-to-learn" skills. |

This grouping is intended "to capture some of the important aspects of model diversity and to permit us to draw conclusions about types of models." The evaluators state that "we arrived at this classification judgmentally, based on the stated goals and objectives of the models." They admit that other classifications are possible but maintain that their scheme "yields some revealing and rela-

---

*Responsive Education* Model
  Far West Laboratory for Educational Research and Development
*Self-Sponsored*
  These programs were organized at the local level without outside sponsorship.

Tucson Early Education Model [*TEEM*]
  Arizona Center for Early Childhood Education

tively stable patterns that illuminate the performance of Follow Through" (Stebbins et al., 1977, p. 131).

The evaluators group the outcome measures into the same three categories: measures of basic skills (word-knowledge, spelling, language, and math-computation subtests of the Metropolitan Achievement Test), measures of cognitive-conceptual skills (reading-comprehension, math-concepts, and math-problems subtests of the Metropolitan together with Raven's Coloured Progressive Matrices), and measures of affective outcomes (Coopersmith Self-Esteem Inventory and Intellectual Achievement Responsibility Scale). This battery was considered by the Office of Education to be "a 'best' compromise between the need for accountability and the difficulty of measuring sponsors' diverse goals and objectives" (Stebbins et al., 1977, p. 35).

These two parallel sets of groupings—the models and the measures—are critical to the interpretation of the evaluation findings. Of the ten numbered findings highlighted in the report, four of the first five depend directly on these groupings (Stebbins et al., 1977, Digest, pp. xxv–xxvii, and chap. 5):

Finding 2:  Models that emphasize basic skills succeeded better than other models in helping children gain these skills.

Finding 3:  Where models have put their primary emphasis elsewhere than on the basic skills, the children they have served tended to score lower on tests of these skills than they would have done without Follow Through.

Finding 4:  No type of model was notably more successful than the others in raising scores on cognitive conceptual skills.

Finding 5:  Models that emphasize basic skills produced better results on tests of self-concept than did other models.

Whenever any advantage of one model type over another is indicated, the findings favor the models labeled "basic skills." Thus, a strong message of the evaluation is that basic-skills models did better than the other types. We are justified, then, in asking: What exactly is a basic-skills model? What do basic-skills models have in common? How do they differ from others? In short, what is the basis for the three-fold distinction among both models and measures, and is the distinction justified?

Table 1, reprinted from the Abt Associates report, shows that four programs are judged to be basic-skills models, four cognitive-conceptual, and five affective-cognitive. Four others are judged to be borderline cases. Apparently the evaluators are in some doubt about the differences between basic-skills and cognitive-conceptual models, since they place as many models on the boundary between the categories as in either of the two classifications. Strangely, nothing is reported about how the final decision was made on these borderline cases. Two of these models (CLA and Home-School Partnership) do not appear in any of the tables or charts used to support the numbered findings. Presumably, complete data for sites within these models are not available.[3] Of the remaining two

[3] The number of models presented in these tables varies from a maximum of thirteen (Stebbins

TABLE 1

*Typology of Models with Respect to the Classroom Learning Environment*

| DEGREE OF STRUCTURE | EMPHASIS ON LEARNING DOMAIN | | |
| --- | --- | --- | --- |
| | *Basic Skills* | *Cognitive-Conceptual* | *Affective-Cognitive* |
| *High* | Behavior Analysis IELP Direct Instruction | | |
| *Medium* | CLA SEDL | Cognitive Curriculum TEEM | Responsive Education ILM MAP |
| *Low* | | | Bank Street EDC |
| *Unknown* | Self Sponsored California Process Home-School Partnership | NSA Parent Education | |

*Source:* Stebbins et al., 1977, p. 25.

models, one (IELP) is classified as a cognitive-conceptual and the other (SEDL) as a basic-skills model. Why, the report does not say.

In addition to these internal evidences of uncertainty about the classification scheme, several other questionable decisions can be noted. First, individual models are classified into one of the three model types on the basis of a sponsor's *"stated* goals and objectives" (Stebbins et al., 1977, p. 22, emphasis added). As anyone familiar with innovative educational programs knows, some distance frequently exists between a project's stated aims and those it actually pursues. In describing an innovation to those not familiar with it, one emphasizes as many good points as possible and ordinarily does not say much about the priorities among these points. In any event, to read self-descriptions of program goals and make a judgment about the model type is an exceedingly complex matter, one where reasonable people are likely to disagree. Furthermore, the judgments apparently were made intuitively. Nowhere are any procedures or criteria specified. The report does not describe the individuals who read the statements of goals and objectives, their training, the time they took, or the directions given to them. Overall, the three-fold classification system for Follow Through models does not meet the criteria that such schemes are normally expected to meet in social-science research. Serious questions must be asked about a classification derived under such conditions.

et al., 1977, Figure 5–2 and others) to a minimum of eight models (Stebbins et al., 1977, Figure 5–7). Footnotes suggest that acceptable data sets were not available for all sites on all measures and that this accounts for the models not presented.

The model typology, furthermore, may be biased toward the so-called basic-skills programs. To see why this is a possibility, one must examine how the outcome measures are classified. This classification is as puzzling as that of the models. The measures are divided into three groups to parallel the typology adopted for the models. Thus, the categorization of measures reflects a complex judgment that is dependent on the clarity of the prior judgments about model categories: "We have grouped the instruments/subtests according to our interpretation of the model's goals. For example, models which advocate a behaviorist educational strategy and place the greatest emphasis on basic skills might be expected to demonstrate success on the measures we have labeled 'basic skills' " (Stebbins et al., 1977, p. 35).

Because of this procedure some of the subtests of the Metropolitan Achievement Test are classified as basic-skills measures (word knowledge, word analysis, spelling, and mathematical computation), while other subtests are classified as cognitive-conceptual measures (reading, mathematics concepts, mathematics problem solving). The report states that this division was made because "some . . . subtests measure acquisition of basic skills which are taught directly" while others "measure acquisition of cognitive skills and processes which may or may not be directly taught" (Stebbins et al., 1977, p. 37).

There appears to be some basis for such a distinction. The subjects listed under the basic-skills domain can be taught by rote: to spell, to associate a word with a relevant picture, to identify the written form of a word spoken by the teacher, and to do simple arithmetic problems. The subtests labeled "cognitive-conceptual" require something more than simple memory: picking the sentence that best describes a picture, reading a paragraph and answering questions on it, and solving everyday problems that require translation into mathematical form. It seems reasonable to say that these latter skills "may or may not be directly taught" but may be "apprehended indirectly through various experiences."

It is decidedly misleading, however, to label the first set "basic skills" and thus imply that the second set is not basic. Such a classification favors models that emphasize rote learning. It implies that skills taught directly by rote methods are basic while skills taught in other ways are not. It also implies that the ability to read paragraphs and answer simple multiple-choice questions about their contents is not a basic skill. All of the subtests of the Metropolitan Achievement Test measure skills that both the public and professionals generally consider to be basic to mathematical ability and literacy. It would have been fairer to label the first set "mechanics of reading, writing, and arithmetic," noting that mechanics can be taught by rote methods, and to label the second set, "reading comprehension and arithmetic word problems," reserving the term "basic skills" for the complete combined set. These revised labels would better conform to the ordinary usage of the terms. As it is, labeling mechanics as "basic skills" gives them an importance in relation to the others that they do not deserve.

In conclusion, the typologies used to group models and measures for purposes of interpretation are technically and conceptually faulty. The faults are such as to favor positive results for the models misleadingly called "basic skills."

*Selection of Outcome Measures*

A major part of the Follow Through evaluation design was a comparative field experiment (actually, a quasi-experiment). As noted previously, Stanford Research Institute had promised to develop instruments especially designed for the evaluation but was unable to accomplish this. The Office of Education eventually decided that the outcome measures should be selected from existing standardized tests and had an outside panel of educators make this selection. The Abt Associates report does not say why this decision was made, but the reasons are likely to have been the low cost, easy use, and widespread acceptability of standardized measures, in comparison with unstandardized ones, especially the kinds of measures that would have to be created for this evaluation. We will consider in detail each of the standardized tests included in the Follow Through outcome battery.

The Metropolitan Achievement Test (MAT) is composed of items testing word knowledge (test booklet presents a written word; pupils choose the correct written definition from written alternatives), spelling (examiner reads a word aloud; pupils choose correct spelling from written alternatives), language (test booklet presents sentences with errors; pupils choose the correct form for the sentence from written alternatives), reading (test booklet presents a paragraph; pupils answer multiple-choice questions), mathematics computation (test booklet presents numbers to be added, subtracted, multiplied, or divided; pupils answer multiple-choice questions), mathematics concepts (booklet presents problems on elementary math concepts such as inequality or time measurement; pupils answer multiple-choice questions), and mathematics problem solving (booklet presents everyday problems in consumer economics, practical measurement, and other common situations; pupils answer multiple-choice alternatives).

The material included in these subtests is generally considered important for early-elementary school pupils to learn. Furthermore, available data indicate that the MAT is a technically sound instrument—highly reliable, well-normed, largely free of practical or conceptual flaws. Other good measures exist, but the MAT is certainly a reasonable choice for the material it covers.

The Raven's Coloured Progressive Matrices is a completely different type of test. It is generally considered to be a measure of nonverbal problem-solving ability. Each item presents a geometric pattern with a piece missing, and children are asked to choose the missing one from four alternatives. The raw score can be translated into an IQ score (although for the Follow Through evaluation, the Raven's test was altered slightly, which would preclude direct conversion of raw scores to intelligence quotients). Buros's *Sixth Mental Measurement Yearbook*, a standard reference in the testing field, lists the Raven's test as "an intelligence test—group" rather than as an achievement test. The reviewer of the test in this reference work claims that the Raven's Matrices "should be quite helpful as screening devices for groups where estimates of intelligence need to be determined" and notes also that they have "already been found helpful in comparing various . . . socioeconomic and ethnic groups" (Bortner, 1965, p. 764).

The critical question is whether the Raven's test is an appropriate outcome measure for the Follow Through evaluation. Unlike achievement tests, intelligence tests are generally designed in such a way as to make it very difficult to improve scores by explicit instruction. Experiences of the type normally provided in schools do not often affect intelligence scores. If, during test construction, an item is discovered that can be taught and learned in school, the item is replaced by another one that does not favor children with specific types of schooling. In practice, individuals' scores do sometimes improve slightly after intensive instruction, particularly for individuals who have limited experience with tasks similar to those on the test.

Obviously, one would not ordinarily use an intelligence test to measure the effect of any instructional program, because the test would likely favor finding no improvement with instruction—the null hypothesis. In fact, "no effect" was what the Follow Through evaluation found. Moreover, inclusion of the Raven's test would especially tend to discredit those Follow Through models labeled "cognitive-conceptual," since the test is presented as measuring skills in that domain. The Raven's test, then, appears to have been an inappropriate outcome measure, and its use may have placed an unfair burden on the cognitive-conceptual Follow Through models.

The Coopersmith Self-Esteem Inventory is designed to measure how children feel about themselves and about school, and how they think other people feel about them. Children are asked to indicate whether each of fifty-eight statements is "like me" or "unlike me" (e.g., "I often wish I were someone else"). These self-evaluations would probably be considered important for school children, and most people would be concerned if a school program lowered students' self-evaluations.

Questions can be raised, however, about the adequacy of the Coopersmith Inventory for the Follow Through evaluation. The instrument requires youngsters to make complex judgments about their feelings toward themselves, but children in the third grade may not be able to form stable judgments. In addition, an inspection of the items shows that considerable verbal skill is required to comprehend them. Third-grade children must listen to and read a statement as well as keep it in mind long and well enough to judge the extent to which it is "like" or "unlike" them. The scores of Follow Through children on the Coopersmith correlated significantly ($r \sim .3$) with such measures of general academic ability as the MAT subtests (Stebbins et al., 1977, pp. 178–185), indicating a modest contribution of verbal ability to Coopersmith scores.

The Intellectual Achievement Responsibility Scale (IARS) presents accounts of a child's experience of success or failure. Children are asked to choose which of two given explanations of an event best explains that event. One of the explanations assigns responsibility to an external agent or circumstance (e.g., "teachers usually say that"), while the other assigns responsibility to the child (e.g., "your work was good"). Each account is presented in a positive and negative form. High scores on the IARS indicate that a child attributes success to internal rather than external causes, an explicit objective of programs such as the Bank Street model.

The authors of IARS have found that children below the third grade "could not keep an item and its two alternatives in mind long enough to make meaningful responses," and noted that "some children in even the third, fourth and fifth grades were not able to read well enough to take the test in written form. It was decided, therefore, that individual oral presentation of the scale was desirable for children below the sixth grade" (Crandall, Katkovsky, & Crandall, 1965, p. 98). In a summary statement they note that "from the inconsistencies and small magnitude of many of the relations found that the scale is in need of further refinement" (p. 108).

Responding to some of these points, staff at Stanford Research Institute rewrote the items in simpler terms so that the test could be administered in written form to third-grade children. Since the Abt Associates report gives no details or references to these revisions, the exact form of the IARS used in the Follow Through evaluation is unknown, and no assessment can be made of the items.

In addition to the points raised above, there are a number of other problems with the Coopersmith and IARS. The tests had lower correlations with the covariates and the other outcome measures than did the subtests of the MAT (see Stebbins et al., 1977, Appendix Table A4-1). The achievement tests show the typical pattern of moderately high intercorrelations (average $r$ about .60 to .70), while the intercorrelations (averaged across several cohorts) of the Coopersmith and the two IARS scales are rather low (see Table 2).

Thus, the composite measure on which the evaluators based their assessment of affective outcomes of the Follow Through program is the sum of three scales that have low correlations with one another. High intercorrelation, or internal consistency, of subscales is usually regarded as a necessary condition for a valid measure. Because the measures of affective outcomes have low intercorrelations, their validity is doubtful.

Information on the stability reliability of the Coopersmith and the IARS is extremely limited. In a lengthy book giving correlations between self-esteem and demographic characteristics, Coopersmith (1967) presents no evidence for the stability of his self-esteem inventory scores, and we could find only two studies relevant to this question. Dyer (1964) assessed the stability reliability of Coopersmith results over a five-week interval on a sample of thirty fifth-grade pupils; a correla-

TABLE 2

*Correlations among the Coopersmith Inventory and the Intellectual Achievement Responsibility Scales (IARS)*

|  | Coopersmith | IARS (−) | IARS (+) |
|---|---|---|---|
| Coopersmith | 1.00 | .15 | .30 |
| IARS (−) | .15 | 1.00 | .35 |
| IARS (+) | .30 | .35 | 1.00 |

*Note:* This table has been constructed on the basis of data in Stebbins et al., 1977, pp. 178-185.

TABLE 3

*Five-Month Stability Reliability Coefficients of the Coopersmith Inventory in the Elementary Grades*

|  | Grade | | | |
|---|---|---|---|---|
|  | 2 & 3 | 4 | 5 | 6 |
| Reliability | .69 | .39 | .71 | .40 |
| 95% confidence interval | .54 – .79 | 0.9 – .62 | .42 – .85 | .10 – .57 |
| Sample size | 75 | 39 | 27 | 89 |

*Source*: Drummond, McIntire, & Ryan, 1977, p. 945.

tion coefficient of .88 was obtained. Drummond, McIntire, and Ryan (1977) studied this question over a five-month period for pupils in grades two through twelve (see Table 3). The stability reliability coefficients for the total score varied erratically across the elementary grades, making any categorical judgment of the reliability of the instrument impossible.

Although the Abt Associates report presents reliability data for both the Coopersmith Inventory and the IARS (Stebbins et al., 1977, Table 2–7 and Appendix Tables A2–7 to A2–9), the coefficients assess the consistency of the items internal to the tests and give no assurance of stability of the total test scores across time. The internal consistency reliability coefficients, which are typically high for all manner of tests provided they are sufficiently long, are unusually low for the IARS ($r = .55$ and .56).[4]

The data from the comparison between Follow Through and non-Follow Through groups add a further reason to question the validity of the two affective tests. The evaluators' findings for achievement tests show a predominance of negative effects—that is, the pupils enrolled in Follow Through models did worse than the control groups on twenty of twenty-six comparisons (Stebbins et al., Figure 5–2). Most evaluators would regard these findings as evidence of an initial nonequivalence, not fully corrected by analysis of covariance, of Follow Through and non-Follow Through groups rather than evidence of the detrimental effects of Follow Through. But in the assessment of affective outcomes, six models show Follow Through above non-Follow Through and seven show the reverse—what one would expect from low reliability tests.

More circumstantial evidence on the validity of the IARS can be gleaned from a study by Wang and Stiles (1976). The IARS and a Self-Responsibility for School Learning (SRIS) inventory, which is a similar instrument, were administered as outcome measures in an evaluation of the University of Pittsburgh Learning, Research, and Development Center's model of instruction (which is related to the IELP model in the Follow Through study). The IARS, unlike the SRIS, failed

4 These values of the internal consistency coefficients correspond to average correlations below 0.10 between items on the IARS.

to successfully discriminate between treatment and comparison groups when administered after instruction. Such failure is a consequence of invalidity, not a proof of it, but the presumption of poor validity grows when the IARS fails to discriminate in a situation where a nominally equivalent instrument (SRIS) discriminates successfully.

The results of the significance tests from the analyses of covariance likewise raise doubts about the validity of the Coopersmith as well as the IARS. Of 243 local analyses of covariance (eighty-one sites anl three affective scales), 11 percent (twenty-six) were statistically significant at the .05 level. Of these twenty-six significant results, eight showed Follow Through groups above non-Follow Through ones and eighteen showed the opposite. The findings look little different from a handful of chance differences.

Overall, the affective outcome measures selected for the Follow Through evaluation seem far less appropriate and technically far more questionable than the MAT. The concerns expressed here about the reliability and validity of the Coopersmith and IARS would clearly indicate that no basis exists for the assertion made by the Abt Associates analysts in their evaluation that "models that emphasize basic skills produced better results on tests of self-concept than did other models" (Stebbins et al., 1977, p. xxvi).

*Coverage of Outcome Domains*

One more question about the outcome measures remains to be raised: How well and how fairly do these instruments measure the outcome domains indicated by the sponsors? Does the one viable instrument, the MAT, adequately cover the outcomes of all the models? The outcomes the evaluators designate as "basic skills," which we have relabeled "mechanics of reading and arithmetic," are covered quite thoroughly by the MAT. The items on the MAT subtests used to measure basic skills have been systematically selected from their content areas, and these areas themselves—vocabulary, spelling, simple arithmetic—are well enough understood that we can accept the subtests as both adequate and fair.

By contrast, the analysts' cognitive-conceptual domain, which we have called "reading comprehension and arithmetic word problems," is poorly defined. The evaluators judge simple reading comprehension to belong to this domain, as well as the ability to solve simple everyday math problems and highly abstract visual puzzles. The report, however, does not indicate what else might belong to this domain. Moreover, no analysis is offered of cognitive-conceptual skills except that they are ones which "may or may not be directly taught, but which the child may apprehend indirectly through various experiences" (Stebbins et al., 1977, p. 37). The subtests of the MAT included under cognitive-conceptual measures would seem to meet this loose and somewhat inadequate criterion, but the Raven's does not, since no evidence exists that the skills it measures may be "apprehend[ed] indirectly."

Even if we accept the Abt Associates definition of the cognitive-conceptual domain, the question still remains as to how thoroughly and fairly the outcome measures test this area. One way to judge would be to list skills mentioned as goals by the sponsors of the cognitive-conceptual models (the procedure Abt Associates follows in classifying the models), and to determine the extent to which the outcome measures sample these skills. The second part of the Abt final report (Bock, Stebbins, & Proper, 1977) includes brief synopses of the goals of seventeen models. The four models classified unequivocally in the Abt Associates report as cognitive-conceptual mention the following goals:

Cognitive Curriculum
[Designed to] focus . . . on developing children's ability to reason. . . . development of skills in initiating and sustaining independent activity, defining and solving problems . . . assuming responsibility for decisions and actions, and working cooperatively with others to make decisions. . . . focus on math, science, reading, social studies, art, and on interests such as housekeeping, construction, or puzzles. . . . developing logical thinking skills in four major cognitive areas (classification, seriation, spatial relations, and temporal relations). (Bock et al., 1977, pp. 89–90)

TEEM
Designed to support the use of language in relating experiences and in learning how to learn. . . . children will learn from peers. . . . the child learns language, intellectual skills, attitudes, and societal arts and skills in a single activity. (pp. 41–42)

Parent Education
Does not enunciate specific achievement goals for children. . . . focuses exclusively on involving parents as equal partners in the educational process. (p. 101)

NSA
Designed to focus on integration of knowledge and understanding. . . . Children are encouraged to initiate their own activities and take responsibility for their own learning, either individually or in small groups. . . . stresses a child-centered approach to learning how to learn. (p. 185)

In the face of such a list, it is easy to understand and sympathize with the evaluator's admission that "no common battery could be developed that would encompass all the various sponsors' goals and objectives" (Stebbins et al., 1977, p. 10). Clearly, the measures of cognitive-conceptual skills the evaluation uses cover only a small selection of these goals, a selection that is biased toward reading and mathematics. Indeed, once the Raven's test is excluded, only reading and math skills are measured in this domain.

With the affective measures employed in the evaluation one finds the same situation, only more so. The synopses of the five models labeled affective-cognitive mention the following goals:

Responsive Education
The goals . . . are for learners to develop problem solving abilities, healthy self-concepts, and culturally pluralistic attitudes and behaviors. . . . The child . . . engages in . . . raising questions, planning, making choices and setting goals. The child discovers individual self-strengths, preferences, and liabilities. Each child develops a repertoire of abilities for building a broad and varied experiential base as well as self-confidence. . . . the child may take on the role of leader, follower, or evaluator. . . . the child grows [in the ability to] . . . address personal and social

issues . . . [and] takes greater responsibility for learning. ( Bock et al., 1977, p. 30)

ILM

The model's goal . . . is learning how to learn. . . . children are taught positive attitudes toward each other, cooperative and responsive behavior, and self-evaluation. . . . designed to further children's cognitive and language skills, and their ethnic identity. . . . children develop skills in verbal fluency . . . and in . . . specific academic areas (language, reading, arithmetic). (pp. 139–140)

MAP

[The goal is] the development of cognitive and affective skills. . . . encourage children to involve themselves physically, socially, and mentally. . . . children . . . develop a personal sense of what is an appropriate next task. . . . [and] a sense of . . . self-regulation. . . . Academic skills are taught. . . . [as well as] art, health and physical education, [and] music. (p. 193)

Bank Street

[The model has] the immediate goal of stimulating children's cognitive and affective development, and. . . . it emphasizes personal growth. . . . Academic skills and emotional social development . . . are emphasized equally. . . . adults help [children] to expand their world and sensitize them to the meaning of their experiences. . . . [The program] provides appropriate ways of organizing and extending . . . children's expressed interests. Math, reading, and language are taught as tools to carry out an investigation of these interests. . . . Children write creative stories, write their own books, read for pleasure, engage in dramatic plan [sic], music . . . art . . . [and] social studies. . . . aims [to] . . . enhance children's capacity to probe, reason, solve problems, and express their feelings freely and constructively. (p. 53)

EDC

[Does not list goals.] The . . . model is more a philosophy than a technique. . . . the sponsor does not prescribe a detailed instructional program. (p. 114)

From what was previously noted about the Coopersmith and the IARS instruments, one sees that very few of the objectives of the affective models were tapped in the Follow Through evaluation.

To their credit, the Abt Associates analysts recognize that the cognitive-conceptual and affective domains are less adequately sampled than the basic skills domain: "Whereas the basic skills measures are probably a reasonable battery for examining achievement which might be expected in that learning domain, the measures on the cognitive and affective domains are much less appropriate" (Stebbins et al., 1977, p. 35). The evaluators excuse themselves for this imbalance by blaming the state of the art of measurement. They claim that the measures selected are a "best compromise" between the need for accountability and the difficulty of measuring sponsors' diverse goals and objectives (p. 35). Having seen the compromise they then switch the grounds of argument, retreating to the position of neutral reporters: "We describe the measures thoroughly so that the reader may judge their adequacy for evaluating Follow Through success. Needless to say, we report results only with respect to the outcomes that were measured" (p. 35).

In spite of sensitivity to the problem and laudable efforts to make the reader aware of all the difficulties, the Abt Associates evaluators do compare the models on the three different outcome domains. They do this even though they admit that their basic-skills measures are a much better sample of model goals than the other types of measures. This is not good evaluation practice. Suppose one were to compare automobiles on the basis of three criteria—economy, comfort, and safety. Would the comparison be fair if the indices of economy were much more complete and accurate than the indices of comfort or safety? Would the bias be eliminated if readers were warned of the relative inadequacies of the latter two measures? No.

In summary, the classification of models and outcomes and the selection of measures favor models that emphasize rote learning of the mechanics of reading, writing, and arithmetic. The analysts admit as much in their report. Yet they continued to compare programs in ways they knew were unfair. It should again be noted that Abt Associates did not choose the measures; these were selected at an earlier point in the evaluation. Nonetheless, the Abt findings depend upon assumptions about the adequacy of measures that the evaluators admit are not defensible. The critical reader will do well to ignore completely their fourth finding—"No model was notably more successful than any other in raising scores on cognitive conceptual skills" (Stebbins et al., 1977, p. xxvi)—and to assume that the national evaluation amounts essentially to a comparative study of the effects of Follow Through models on the mechanics of reading, writing, and arithmetic.

## Problems in Data Analysis

The comparisons between the Follow Through and non-Follow Through groups represent the core of the Abt Associates analysis. Unfortunately, a serious methodological problem is involved in the definition the evaluators adopt for the effect of a Follow Through model. The measure of effect is a conjunctive definition involving the size of the average difference between Follow Through and non-Follow Through groups at a particular site and the statistical significance of the difference. The differences between covariance-adjusted mean scores of Follow Through and non-Follow Through groups on variables such as reading or math achievement are classified according to the definitions in Table 4.

As an example of how the definition of an effect is applied, consider the Bank Street site in Brattleboro, Vermont. An analysis of covariance comparing seventeen Follow Through pupils with twenty-four comparison pupils in Brattleboro shows an adjusted mean difference on the Coopersmith Inventory favoring the control group by 2.68 points. This difference is not statistically significant at the .05 level, even though it is educationally significant, since the difference exceeds one-quarter standard deviation.[5] Hence the effect is scored 0. Abt Associates reduces all findings in this way in order to measure the effect of Follow Through

---

[5] *Viz.*, $.25\sigma = .25 \times 7.22 = 1.80$.

TABLE 4

*The Abt Associates Report Definition and Scoring of Program Effect*

| COVARIANCE-ADJUSTED DIFFERENCE BETWEEN FOLLOW THROUGH AND NON–FOLLOW THROUGH: | COVARIANCE-ADJUSTED DIFFERENCE BETWEEN FOLLOW THROUGH AND NON–FOLLOW THROUGH | |
| --- | --- | --- |
| | *Significant at .05 level* | *Not significant at .05 level* |
| *Less than a quarter of a standard deviation* | Difference is statistically significant but *not* educationally significant.<br><br>Effect = 0 | Difference is neither statistically nor educationally significant.<br><br>Effect = 0 |
| *More than a quarter of a standard deviation and favors Follow Through* | Difference is statistically and educationally significant.<br><br>Effect = +1 | Difference is educationally but *not* statistically significant.<br><br>Effect = 0 |
| *More than a quarter of a standard deviation and favors non–Follow Through* | Difference is statistically and educationally significant.<br><br>Effect = −1 | Difference is educationally but *not* educationally significant.<br><br>Effect = 0 |

*Note:* This table has been constructed on the basis of the Abt Associates criteria for defining model effect (see Stebbins et al., 1977, pp. 132–133).

and summarizes these in the three principal figures of their report (Stebbins et al., 1977, Digest, Figures 1–3).

The reasons the Abt evaluators give for their definition of effect (Stebbins et al., 1977, pp. 132–133) are only superficially convincing. The definition of an effect is inadequate, for the findings are clouded by matters involving three highly technical factors of data analysis: the statistical description of a model's effect on an outcome measure, the selection of a proper unit for inferential analysis (pupil, classroom, school, or site), and the uses of the analysis of covariance in quasi-experimental research. Each of these concerns is dealt with, and some are partially resolved, in the following section.

### Confounding of Program Effect with Number of Pupils

Essentially the Abt Associates definition of an effect confounds the effectiveness of a program with its number of pupils. In general, small sample size will reduce statistical power and obscure differences between groups; large samples should produce many statistically significant differences, favoring either the experimental or control group. *Ceteris paribus,* larger programs could appear to be more effective. No convincing reasons exist to warrant confounding the size of the mean differences with their inferential reliability. It is not possible to predict in general how Abt's confounding of sample size and effectiveness distorts the results in the

Follow Through evaluation. The net distortion will depend on whether the null hypothesis is true or false, which in turn depends on such factors as "true" program effects and degree of experimental control over extraneous conditions.

The confounding, however, probably had implications such as the following. Suppose that Follow Through model A is implemented in fifty cities and in each instance an experimental group of twenty pupils shows a covariance-adjusted mean one-quarter standard deviation above the mean of the twenty control pupils at the same sites. Suppose further that Follow Through model B is implemented in ten cities, and in each instance an experimental group of 100 pupils shows a covariance-adjusted mean one-quarter standard deviation above the mean of the 100 control pupils at the same sites. At each model A site, the difference between groups is not statistically significant, but at each model B site, it is. Following Abt's definition of effect, model B scores a perfect +1 score, and model A scores 0. However, for both models, there are 1000 Follow Through scores averaging one-quarter standard deviation larger than 1000 non-Follow Through scores. The only difference between the models is that A is implemented with smaller groups and in more cities than B—an irrelevant difference for nearly any purpose.

To reiterate, the effect of a given model as defined by the analysts is potentially confounded with the number of pupils at each site. Whether such confounding obtained in practice and therefore renders suspect the evaluators' ranking of the models' effectiveness is an empirical question that can be illuminated by the reported data. A graph of the relationship between the average size of the pupil samples for each model and the effectiveness as measured by Abt Associate appears in Figure 1. Each of thirteen models is ranked on basic-skills, cognitive, and affective outcome measures. The horizontal axis ranks the models with respect to the average square root of their sample size across all sites.[6]

The data in Figure 1 show some of the predictable consequences of confounding sample size with measured effectiveness. For example, as sample size decreases, the variance of effects as indicated by ranks diminishes (from 16.74 in roughly the top third in terms of average sample size to 14.37 in the middle third to 7.72 in the bottom third). Hypothetically, then, a "large sample" model (such as ILM) suffering from bad experimental conditions favoring the non-Follow Through group would show up poorly, whereas a "small sample" model (such as California Process) could have its true effectiveness masked by a statistically nonsignificant finding due to its sample size.[7]

Clearly what is required is a definition of model impact that reflects only the magnitude of the difference in performance between Follow Through and non-Follow Through groups. No model should benefit or suffer from the conse-

---

[6] For example, the average sample size across sites for the SEDL model was 200 pupils and for the California Process model was about seventy pupils. The average square root of sample size is used to rank the models because it is the quantity used in judging statistical significance.

[7] The curvilinear correlation of $avg \sqrt{N}$ is $\eta_{xy} = .31$ (the $avg \sqrt{N}$ variable being arbitrarily divided into rough thirds).

FIGURE 1

*Scatter Diagram of the Relationship between the Average Site Size
for Models and the Rank Measure of Model Effectiveness*

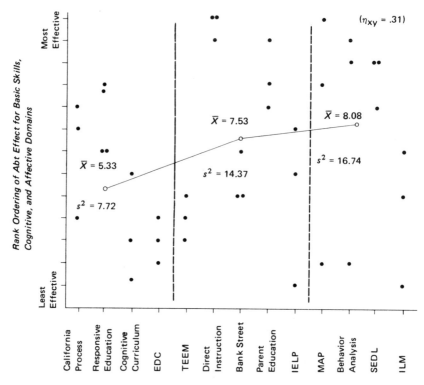

*Rank of Models by Average $\sqrt{N}$ of Model Sites from Smallest (left) to Largest (right)*

quences of an arbitrary decision to try it out on 200 instead of 100 pupils. While no data are available in Parts A (Stebbins et al., 1977) and B (Bock et al., 1977) of the Abt Associates report which permit the calculation of the average difference between Follow Through and non-Follow Through groups on the outcome measures, such data are available in the appendices (*Education as Experimentation*, 1977). There one can find for each model the covariance-adjusted mean differences and standard deviations for each outcome measure at all sites included in Cohorts III-K, III-EF, and II-EF.[8] We have measured the effect for

---

[8] The cohorts refer to the year and entry level of Follow Through pupils. Cohorts II and III began in 1970 and 1971 respectively. Cohorts designated with a *K* entered Follow Through as kindergarten students and those designated with *EF* entered in the first grade (Stebbins et al., 1977, p. 7).

each model at each site by calculating the average difference between Follow Through and non-Follow Through covariance-adjusted means from the "local" analyses (i.e., analyses in which only Follow Through and non-Follow Through pupils in the same city or town are compared) and dividing by the standard deviation of the outcome measure. The results for MAT Total Reading, Total Math, Spelling, and Language scores appear in Tables 5 and 6.

The model effects given in Tables 5 and 6 are different from those in the Abt Associates report (Stebbins et al., 1977, Digest) in at least three respects, two of which are defensible and the third arbitrary: firstly, the effect-size measures in Tables 5 and 6 are not confounded by sample size and so are preferable to those in the Abt report; secondly, the size measures are based only on local-analysis results and thus should better control for historical sources of invalidity; and, finally, data on Cohort II-K are missing from Tables 5 and 6, because they are not reported in the appendices (*Education as Experimentation*, 1977). Also, we used data not adjusted for pupils' preschool experience.

The average effects for the subtests of the MAT have themselves been averaged to create the composite ranking of the models that appears in Table 6. This new

TABLE 5
*Model Effects[a] on MAT Scores*

| Model | Number of sites | TOTAL READING Mean effect | S.D. | TOTAL MATH Mean effect | S.D. | SPELLING Mean effect | S.D. | LANGUAGE Mean effect | S.D. |
|---|---|---|---|---|---|---|---|---|---|
| Parent Education | 8 | −.003 | .253 | −.027 | .301 | −.026 | .298 | −.163 | .241 |
| Direct Instruction | 11 | −.058 | .643 | .288 | .798 | .007 | .560 | .850 | .811 |
| Bank Street | 6 | −.059 | .580 | −.333 | .575 | −.283 | .557 | −.108 | .457 |
| Behavioral Analysis | 7 | −.081 | .228 | .070 | .311 | −.073 | .294 | .003 | .292 |
| SEDL | 5 | −.153 | .441 | .039 | .303 | −.324 | .490 | .044 | .222 |
| Responsive Education | 9 | −.159 | .375 | −.124 | .454 | −.308 | .354 | −.214 | .387 |
| MAP | 3 | −.203 | .323 | .200 | .131 | .050 | .171 | .105 | .326 |
| ILM | 2 | −.210 | .373 | −.209 | .332 | −.247 | .521 | −.172 | .600 |
| IELP | 3 | −.242 | .411 | −.258 | .348 | −.139 | .300 | −.640 | .151 |
| Cognitive Curriculum | 6 | −.248 | .467 | −.131 | .410 | −.113 | .573 | −.320 | .494 |
| EDC | 7 | −.305 | .183 | −.116 | .408 | −.216 | .118 | −.211 | .236 |
| California Process | 3 | −.336 | .301 | −.263 | .326 | −.103 | .274 | −.239 | .258 |
| TEEM | 11 | −.344 | .397 | −.092 | .256 | −.317 | .330 | −.182 | .301 |

*Note.* These effects were calculated for Cohorts III-K, II-EF, and III-EF on the basis of data available in the appendices of the Abt Associates report (*Education as experimentation*, 1977).
[a]Effect = $(\bar{X}_{FT} - \bar{X}_{NFT})/\sigma_x$, where means are from the local analysis of covariance.

TABLE 6

*Model Effects Averaged Across MAT Reading, Math, Spelling, and Language Effects*

| Model | Type of model[a] | Mean effect | Ranking by Abt effect[b] | Recalculated ranking | Change in ranks |
|---|---|---|---|---|---|
| Direct Instruction | Basic | .272[c] | 1 | 1 | 0 |
| MAP | Aff. | .038 | 2 | 2 | 0 |
| Parent Education | Cog. | −.055 | 3 | 4 | −1 |
| SEDL | Basic | −.099 | 4 | 5 | −1 |
| Responsive Education | Aff. | −.201 | 5 | 7 | −2 |
| ILM | Aff. | −.210 | 6 | 9 | −3 |
| Behavior Analysis | Basic | −.020 | 7 | 3 | +4 |
| Bank Street | Aff. | −.196 | 8 | 6 | +2 |
| California Process | Basic | −.235 | 8 | 12 | −4 |
| TEEM | Cog. | −.234 | 10 | 11 | −1 |
| IELP | Cog. | −.320 | 11 | 13 | −2 |
| EDC | Aff. | −.212 | 12 | 10 | +2 |
| Cognitive Curriculum | Cog. | −.203 | 13 | 8 | +5 |

[a] Basic = Basic-Skills models; Aff. = Affective-Cognitive models; and Cog. = Cognitive-Conceptual models.

[b] This ranking was derived from scores on basic skills and cognitive-conceptual outcome measures.

[c] This average includes a mean effect of +.850 on the MAT Language subtest and is much larger than other effects. If this unusually large effect is removed, the mean for Direct Instruction sites is +.079.

ranking is compared with the Abt Associates ranking of model effect on both basic-skills and cognitive-conceptual tests, since the latter two categories include all of the MAT subtests. The two sets of ranks are largely comparable, although some shifts occurred, as would be expected. Using Table 6, we find an overall net decline of one ranking point from the Abt analysts' ranking to our recalculated one for both the basic-skills and affective-cognitive model types and a net increase of one ranking point for the cognitive-conceptual models. When the models are classified under the three model types employed by Abt Associates, the averages of the effects are as follows: *basic-skills,* −.021; *cognitive-conceptual,* −.203; and *affective-cognitive,* −.156. These differences are small and insignificant. They are based on a logic and a methodology that have many shortcomings, not the least of which is the typology of the models. In the Abt Associates report, the SEDL and IELP models were considered borderline cases (see Table 1); for purposes of data analysis the former is arbitrarily considered basic-skills and the latter cognitive-conceptual. If that decision is reversed, the average recalculated effects for the three model types would be as follows: *basic-skills,* −.076; *cognitive-conceptual,* −.148; and *affective-cognitive,* −.156. Trivial differences have become even more so.

*The Aggregation Problem—Pupil, Class, or School*

The report of the Abt Associates offers a thorough discussion in support of their decision to base all results on data with individual pupils as the unit of analysis (Stebbins et al., 1977, pp. 67–69). The mathematics of the unit-of-analysis problem can become abstruse (Glass & Stanley, 1970, pp. 501–508; Haney, Note 2), and the proper unit of statistical analysis in such circumstances is a point on which methodologists disagree. The report acknowledges as much: "Within each site, the Follow Through data present the opportunity for selection among three units of analysis; school, class, and child. Arguments can be made for the selection of each unit" (Stebbins et al., 1977, p. 67). Indeed they can. But the argument advanced by the Abt analysts to justify using the pupil as the unit of analysis is not compelling and may be *ad hoc*. It confuses the fundamental notion of statistical independence with one of its loosely associated phenomena, "intact groups." From this shaky basis the report leaps to an unsound conclusion:

> Coupling these considerations with the need to develop an analysis that can respond to the large variability among sites, it becomes evident that few, if any, sites have enough schools or classrooms to support a site-level analysis. It is on this practical consideration that any attempt at analyzing aggregates of children flounders. Consequently, the unit of analysis selected in this evaluation is the child. (Stebbins et al., 1977, p. 67)

The perception of a "need to develop an analysis that can respond to the large variability among sites" would appear to stem from a sense of foreboding that anything short of using the pupil as the unit of analysis would result in statistically nonsignificant results.

The Abt Associates resolution of the unit-of-analysis issue runs counter to the conventional logic of data analysis that they adhere to elsewhere. When a case cannot be made convincingly for the appropriateness of one method of analysis over another, both analyses should be performed and the results compared. If the results agree, the dispute over method is irrelevant. If results disagree, then the findings can be seen to depend on fine distinctions among methods about which there are unresolved differences of opinion. The analysts wisely follow this practice in performing analysis of covariance, a method about which there is considerable controversy. Several different analyses of covariance are performed (e.g., "local," "matched," "true score," "pooled"), and the results can be easily compared. However, on the unit-of-analysis question, the Abt evaluators argue unconvincingly for a method of analysis known in advance to be more likely than other methods to yield statistically significant differences. Inevitably someone would have to perform the alternative analyses and compare the results with the Abt Associates report, as we have done below.

The effects depicted in Table 5 are calculated for each model at each of eighty-one sites for, as we previously noted, three cohorts. These findings constitute the raw data for an analysis of variance using site as the unit of analysis. One-factor analyses of variance were performed on MAT Total Reading, Total Math, Spelling, and Language scores. The F-ratios for the reading, math, and spelling subtests are all less than one, indicating no statistically significant differences. A significant $F$-ratio was obtained only for the language subtest,[9] and this finding was due entirely to the deviation of the Direct Instruction mean results from those of other models. When Scheffé contrasts were performed comparing the four basic skills models with the five affective ones, none of the four contrast-estimate ratios to their standard errors was greater than one, again indicating no statistically significant differences.

Clearly, then, none of the findings accepted by the Abt Associates evaluators as statistically significant hold up as significant when reanalyzed with a different unit of analysis. And no cogent arguments are made that the results based on one unit of analysis are valid while those based on another are not. Indeed, different units are probably relevant to different substantive questions.

The argument against relying on the individual child as the unit of analysis in the Follow Through evaluation is well put by Cronbach (Note 3) in a paper widely available in mid-1976. Cronbach says his work was influenced by a monograph by Haney. The title of Haney's paper? "Units of Analysis Issues in the Evaluation of Project Follow Through" (Haney, Note 2). Furthermore, Gilbert, Mosteller, and Tukey (1976) recommend conducting multiple analyses in circumstances such as the Follow Through evaluation:

> Any attempt to infer what will be caused by an active intervention from data involving either no intervention ("natural experiments") or unrandomized intervention has to be subject to possibilities of error that are hard to evaluate. Any attempt to assert that the statistical significance or confidence associated with such an analysis allows us to conclude reliably what active intervention will do is dangerous and unsound.
>
> The best we know how to do in such a situation is to seek out alternative methods of fallible inference, use up to several of them, and then, recognizing their fallibility, trust moderately in their combined message. (pp. 155–156)

*Analysis of Covariance*

Abt Associates performed a variety of analyses on the Follow Through data, but the evaluators have used just one basic technique, analysis of covariance (ANCOV). Because the experimental and control groups differed on background variables, the analysts used ANCOV to adjust the average test scores at the end of third grade so that the averages were more like what one would obtain if the children in the Follow Through and non-Follow Through groups had been similar in background when they entered the evaluation. Since the Follow Through children generally scored lower than non-Follow Through children in kindergarten, the Follow Through third-grade scores were raised and the non-Follow Through scores lowered by this statistical adjustment.

Any analyst faced with these initial differences between Follow Through and non-Follow Through would consider using ANCOV for their data analysis, in spite of its flaws. Our complaint is that Abt Associates provide no other analyses

---

[9] $F_{12, 69} = 5.6$.

to give an indication of the effect of the flaws. In situations such as in Follow Through, where one group is more disadvantaged than the other, ANCOV may underestimate the differences between the groups (Campbell & Erlebacher, 1975). The error gets larger as ANCOV becomes more effective, but the size of the error and its direction may be impossible to determine (Cronbach, Rogosa, Floden, & Price, Note 4). This error could especially damage the Follow Through analysis, since one of the criteria for an effect is that the difference between average test scores exceed a fixed quantity. This dilemma is another reason for our recalculations, and our different results give us even more cause for concern.

The unit-of-analysis, or aggregation, problem reappears in considering the analysis-of-covariance procedures that Abt Associates employs. Although the choice of a proper unit of analysis—pupil, classroom, or city—is often considered only in connection with inferential analyses, Cronbach (Note 3) shows that it has important implications for covariance adjustment in nonrandomized experiments. To simplify a complex argument, the correlation of variables can vary radically when calculated on individual scores or classroom means. Thus, when used with one unit of analysis—for example, the pupil—ANCOV gives no clue as to what adjusted means might be when used with another unit of analysis—e.g., the classroom. Cronbach (Note 3) persuasively argues that, for the sake of both inferential validity and proper covariance adjustment, the classroom is the appropriate unit of analysis. Thus, the Abt Associates analysts commit a serious oversight in failing to consider the classroom as the unit for covariance adjustment.

Another problem with the use of ANCOV in the Follow Through evaluation is that it requires almost every child to have both a kindergarten and a third-grade score on many tests, although allowance was made for some missing pretest scores. As a result, many children with two or more but less than four years of exposure to Follow Through could not be considered part of the experiment.

The Abt Associates analysts give some attention to this problem of attrition and present evidence indicating that no differential attrition occurred between Follow Through and non-Follow Through groups. Though many pupils left the school during the experiment and many others were not present for the pre- or posttest sessions, these losses did not seem to alter the composition of either the Follow Through or non-Follow Through groups. For once fate was evenhanded.

We are not, however, concerned only with the evenhandedness of the attrition. At least half of the potential students were lost: "Approximately 70 percent of the FT [Follow Through] and NFT [non-Follow Through] children who were tested in the kindergarten year of Cohort III-K are *not* present in the analytic sample (The analagous attrition rate for Cohort II-K was about 50 percent.)" (Stebbins et al., 1977, p. 82). As we noted earlier, the site-level analysis allows only weak inferences because of the small number of model sites with valid data. (A site was dropped from the analysis if the number of children with valid data dropped below twelve.) A more lenient analytic strategy would no doubt have allowed retention of many more children and, therefore, sites. Another problem is that of differential attrition across models. The report gives no indication for any model of how many children dropped out or, equally interesting, dropped in. Furthermore, while one criterion for including a child in the evaluation is that the child did not move from a Follow Through to a non-Follow Through class or vice versa (Stebbins et al., 1977, p. 46), the report gives no figures by model for how often this occurred. There is no analysis of attrition bias by models or by sites, although such comparisons would be of value.

## Interpretation

### *Variation among Sites*

The Abt Associates report's primary finding, which is justifiably its first finding, is that there is great variation from site to site in the results of each model. The variation of the means within each model (from site to site) is greater than the variation of the means among the models. For example, the effects of the Direct Instruction model on basic skills varied dramatically. In seven of the ten Direct Instruction sites the experimental classes did better than the comparison ones, but in the other three sites the reverse was true (Stebbins et al., 1977, p. 136). Although the Direct Instruction model had some of the best sites, it had at least one site that performed worse than every other model. The Bank Street model had several sites in which the experimental groups were below the comparison classes in basic skills, but one of its sites was rated as equal to the best Direct Instruction site. This variation in effect from site to site was strong for every model in every domain.

Despite difficulties in design, scope of measurement, and analysis, the Abt Associates finding of the predominance of intersite variation remains valid. This finding is an important confirmation of contentions that the success of any educational innovation is dependent on contextual factors that can neither be implanted in the local scene nor controlled by outside parties. "Unmeasured local circumstances, including those associated with implementation, still have had more influence on results than have the philosophies of the sponsors" (Stebbins et al., 1977, p. 146).

If the concentrated effort of highly competent and well-funded sponsors working with a few sites cannot produce uniform results from locality to locality, it seems doubtful that any model program could do so. This does not mean that model programs are worthless but only that their effects will vary substantially, depending on interaction with local circumstances. Abt Associates is to be strongly congratulated for discovering the intersite variation. This finding is truly a significant contribution to educational research, one that could lead to different evaluation designs and different dissemination policies.

### *Comparisons among the Follow Through Models*

Because of the intersite variation within each model, the Abt Associates analysts finally abandoned attempts to compare models directly, and the major conclusions do not discuss the individual models. However, the summary charts show results for individual models side-by-side and ranked from best to worst. This is an explicit comparison. We believe such comparisons are misleading, since they cannot be supported by the evaluation and lead the reader to draw inappropriate conclusions. Apparently to skirt the intersite-variation problem, yet still draw conclusions about models, the analysts grouped the models into three types and drew conclusions about the types. But the typology does not correct the flaws in the evaluation and is itself of doubtful validity.

*Comparisons between Follow Through*
*and Non-Follow Through Groups*

An important finding by the Abt Associates analysts is mentioned only inconspicuously in the report. Not listed as a major conclusion but rather inserted in the last paragraph of the Digest is a striking statement: "In general Follow Through's externally-stimulated compensatory interventions do not seem to have been reliable tools for raising the average test scores of groups of disadvantaged children" (Stebbins et al., 1977, p. xxix). If one compares the Follow Through groups as a whole with the non-Follow Through groups as a whole, the former did no better on the outcome measures than did the comparison classes. After the enormous effort and funding put into developing the Follow Through models, this finding defies common sense and raises as many questions about the overall evaluation as it does about the Follow Through models. Can it be that so much effort had no measurable outcome?

There are many possible reasons why the Follow Through groups did not do better on the outcome measures. Perhaps the Follow Through models were no more effective than normal instruction; the measuring instruments may not have been sensitive to the varied effects of the Follow Through models; the comparison classes may themselves have been strengthened considerably by outside aid; and the nonequivalence of the Follow Through and non-Follow Through groups may not have been fully corrected by analysis of covariance. Although the analysts discuss why there were so few differences favoring the Follow Through models (Stebbins et al., 1977, pp. 158–167), the report does not provide a definitive explanation. Thus, we think the analysts were justified in not emphasizing the Follow Through versus non-Follow Through differences too heavily.

Pupils were selected for the Follow Through program if they scored low on a variety of measures, including school aptitude and family income. Comparing programs that enroll such extreme groups with programs that enroll slightly more advantaged groups presents difficult design and analysis problems that are capable of introducing error into the results. In the case of Follow Through, as in so many other compensatory programs, the experimental groups score no higher and even lower than comparison groups by the end of the program, but they usually scored lower when they began school. Whether to attribute the general finding of no significant differences to the new programs themselves or to their evaluation is a debatable point. The differences in performances between Follow Through and non-Follow Through students are small and well within the range attributable to various artifacts of the study.

## Conclusions

The Follow Through evaluation was defective in a number of ways. The classification of models and outcome measures is misleading and perhaps untenable. The outcome measures assess very few of the models' goals and strongly favor models that concentrate on teaching mechanical skills. The definition of model effectiveness and the statistical procedure, analysis of covariance, employed to assess effectiveness are questionable. And the unit of analysis, the individual pupil, apparently favors the basic-skills models.

We therefore conclude that the Follow Through evaluation does not demonstrate that models emphasizing basic skills are superior to other models. In the face of the conflicting claims being made, our argument is worth repeating. The coverage of outcome domains is so poor that no judgment of best model can legitimately be made, no matter how large the difference in test scores. Even within the narrow domain measured by the Metropolitan Achievement Test (whether one calls it "mechanics," "basic skills," or whatever), no model can dependably claim superior results. Some argue that the MAT measures the fundamental outcomes for judging the quality of an early childhood curriculum. Many disagree, but few would argue that these outcomes are unimportant. With one exception the point is moot, since overall intersite variation among models is so much larger than between-model differences.[10]

Even if dependable differences were found on the MAT, such differences would be inadequate evidence of which model is best. Follow Through was to be an investigation of models of comprehensive early childhood education—not just reading, not just arithmetic, not just language usage. An attempt was made to measure more than a few narrow scholastic outcomes but that attempt was not successful. It serves no one well to proceed as if it had been. Although who did best on the MAT might be a valid question, it would be wrong to confuse that question with the one that was actually asked.

The truth about Follow Through is complex. No simple answer to the problem of educating disadvantaged students has been found. Even with the narrow outcome measures employed, models that worked well in one town worked poorly in another. Unique features of the local settings had more effect on test scores than did the models. This does not mean that federal programs are useless or inappropriate for pursuing national objectives; however, many of the most significant factors affecting educational achievement lie outside the control of federal officials. Educational policy makers should expect that the same program may have quite different effects in different settings.

## Recommendations

*Evaluations Must Be Sensitive to a Wide Range of Outcomes*
Follow Through began as a program designed to improve the life chances of

---

[10] The exception is a higher average for pupils at Direct Instruction sites on the language

disadvantaged children. But it is questionable that any battery of standardized tests can be successfully used to evaluate a large-scale social program, and tests have particular drawbacks when used with young children. The evaluation was marked by a faith on the part of many, particularly in government, that test scores are the ultimate good. There was a faith on the part of the evaluators that they could develop new tests to measure the less tangible outcomes. There was a faith on the part of many sponsors that their programs could raise test scores, no matter how inappropriate the tests were. Less faith all around will be warranted in future studies.

### Evaluations Should Be Sensitive to Local Conditions

One of the positive features of the Follow Through evaluation is that each model was implemented at several sites. Otherwise, it would have been impossible to detect the strong outcome differences between sites. Future evaluations should assume that such differences will occur. Evaluations should also systematically describe programs as well as their conditions of implementation. If not, many of the results will be uninterpretable, as was the case in the Follow Through evaluation. A strong qualitative component should be included even in quantitative evaluations.

### Field Experiments Should Be Randomized and Small in Scope

In Follow Through the complexities of the covariance adjustments ultimately proved to be impossible to sort out. Nonrandomized quasi-experiments seem unable to avoid equivocality because of this problem. To avoid the insurmountable problems associated with statistical adjustment of scores, field experiments should be randomized.

Field experiments should also be small in scope. The massive nature of the Follow Through program and evaluation caused many problems, including the eventual reduction of outcome measures. Rather than undertaking such national experiments and attempting to draw global conclusions, we suggest decentralized experiments. If one must persist in using the experimental procedure, a few models could be compared to each other at local sites.

### Multiple Data Analysis Techniques Should Be Employed

No one data analysis technique, however elaborate, adequately handles the complexities inherent in educational research. The advice of Gilbert, Mosteller, and Tukey (1974) should be taken seriously and followed to the extent economically possible. Moreover, any important data set should be analyzed by at least two independent teams using different analytic approaches. It is better to have two teams with modest budgets than one team with the whole amount.

---

subtest of the MAT (see Tables 5 and 6). The difference can be traced to Part B of the subtest, in which the items are very similar to exercises in the Direct Instruction materials.

### Government Control of Programs and Evaluation Should Be Reduced

Many of the difficulties of the Follow Through evaluation can be traced to frequent government interference. Government guidance was often heavy-handed and misdirected and shifted unexpectedly from month to month. Certainly the government has a duty to ensure that an evaluation proceeds properly; once an evaluation contract is negotiated, however, the evaluation should be conducted at some distance and with considerable freedom. Ideally, evaluators should not stand to gain or lose from the results of the evaluation.

An even broader question is whether the federal government should be advocating particular models of instruction at all. On the basis of previous experience and this evaluation, we think not. Government advocacy of particular instructional models assumes both the feasibility of wide implementation and the similarity of effects in different locales. However flawed, this evaluation does suggest these assumptions are contrary to fact. When combined with the experience of other government programs, the evidence is strong that educational improvement strategies that acknowledge local circumstances will be far more effective in the long run.

### Fairness Should Be a Major Criterion for Judging Evaluations

Every evaluation revolves around an understanding, often tacit, as to what the evaluators will do. In Follow Through, evaluators secured the cooperation of the sponsors on the basis of certain promises, but as the evaluation evolved, the evaluators were unable to fulfill some of these. Promising to assess less tangible outcomes and then reneging on that promise is unfair. If evaluators find their task impossible, at the very least they should renegotiate the agreement.

Fairness also implies treating all parties equitably, achieving a balance of claims. Unfortunately, there is only the semblance of fairness in the Follow Through evaluation. The outcome measures are closer to the goals of some models than others, and the understanding among the sponsors, the evaluators, and the Office of Education was not fulfilled. If the sponsors had understood clearly that they would be evaluated primarily on the basis of standardized test scores, then the evaluation would have been fair in at least one sense.

### Evaluations Like This Are No Longer Needed

Enough experience exists to suggest that these massive experiments with narrow outcome measures are bad investments. The results are highly equivocal, and groups such as sponsors and parents feel excluded, even abused, because their goals and interests are not represented in the evaluation. A pluralistic society requires a variety of evaluation criteria and approaches. Groups that are significantly affected by an evaluation must have their interests reflected in the evaluative criteria or they will perceive the results as illegitimate.

### Important Evaluations Should Be Examined in Depth

It often appears to outsiders that evaluators agree about nothing, but it is through serious criticism and counterargument that we can develop a consensus about appropriate evaluation practice. It is also the only way of ensuring evaluations of high quality and of protecting the public from poor studies. We have no desire or expectation that our critique will be the last word on the Follow Through evaluation, but we hope it will lead to a dialogue in which the merits and demerits of the evaluation will emerge. Such enlightenment is perhaps the most that the process of evaluation itself can offer. We would encourage foundations and government agencies to regard critiques and counterarguments as friendly acts that build the evaluation profession.

## Reference Notes

1. Egbert, R. Personal communication, April 28, 1977.
2. Haney, W. *Units of analysis issues in the evaluation of Project Follow Through* (Report submitted to the U.S. Office of Education). Cambridge, Mass.: Huron Institute, 1974.
3. Cronbach, L. J. *Research on classrooms and schools: Formulation of questions, design and analysis* (Stanford Evaluation Consortium, Occasional Paper). Unpublished paper, Stanford University, 1976.
4. Cronbach, L. J., Rogosa, D. R., Floden, R. E., & Price, G. G. *Analysis of covariance in nonrandomized experiments: Parameters affecting bias* (Stanford Evaluation Consortium, Occasional Paper). Unpublished paper, Stanford University, 1977.

## References

Bock, G., Stebbins, L. B., & Proper, E. C. *Education as experimentation: A planned variation model, Volume IV–B, Effects of Follow Through models.* Cambridge, Mass.: Abt Associates, Inc., 1977. (Also issued by the U.S. Office of Education as *National evaluation: Detailed effects,* Volume II–B of The Follow Through Planned Variation Experiment series.)

Bortner, M. Review of Raven's Coloured Progressive Matrices. In Buros, O. K. (Ed.), *The sixth mental measurements yearbook.* Highland Park, N.J.: The Gryphon Press, 1965.

Campbell, D. T., & Erlebacher, A. How regression artifacts in quasi-experimental evaluations in compensatory education tend to underestimate effects. In C. A. Bennett & A. A. Lumsdaine (Eds.), *Evaluation and experiment.* New York: Academic Press, 1975.

Coopersmith, S. *Coopersmith self-esteem inventory.* San Francisco, Calif.: W. H. Freeman and Company, 1968.

Crandall, V. C., Katkovsky, W., & Crandall, V. J. Children's beliefs in their own control of reinforcements in intellectual-academic achievement situations. *Child Development,* 1965, 36, 91–109.

Drummond, R. J., McIntire, W. G., & Ryan, C. W. Stability and sex differences on the Coopersmith self-esteem inventory for students in grades two to twelve. *Psychological Reports,* 1977, 40, 943–946.

Dyer, C. O. Construct validity of self-concept by a multi-trait–multi-method analysis. (Doctoral dissertation, University of Michigan, 1963). *Dissertation Abstracts International,* 1964, 25, 8154. (No. 64–8154)

*Education as experimentation: A planned variation model, Volume IV–C, Appendices, Parts 1 and 2.* Cambridge, Mass.: Abt Associates, Inc., 1977.

Elmore, R. F. *Follow Through: Decisionmaking in a large scale social experiment.* Unpublished doctoral dissertation, Harvard University, 1976.

Gilbert, J. P., Mosteller, F., & Tukey, J. W. Steady social progress requires quantitative evaluation to be searching. In C. C. Abt (Ed.), *The evaluation of social programs.* Beverly Hills, Calif.: Sage Publications, 1974.

Glass, G. V, & Stanley, J. C. *Statistical methods in education and psychology.* Englewood Cliffs, N.J.: Prentice-Hall, 1970.

Haney, W. *A technical history of the national Follow Through evaluation.* Cambridge, Mass.: Huron Institute, 1977. (Also issued by the U.S. Office of Education as *The Follow Through evaluation: A technical history,* Volume V of The Follow Through Planned Variation Experiment series.)

Krulee, G. K. *An organizational analysis of project Follow Through, final report.* Evanston, Ill.: Northwestern University, 1973. (ERIC Document Reproduction Service No. 093 446).

Stebbins, L. B., St. Pierre, R. G., Proper, E. C., Anderson, R. B., & Cerva, T. R. *Education as experimentation: A planned variation model, Volume IV-A, An evaluation of Follow Through.* Cambridge, Mass.: Abt Associates, Inc., 1977. (Also issued by the U.S. Office of Education as *National evaluation: Patterns of effects,* Volume II-A of The Follow Through Planned Variation Experiment series.)

Wang, M. C., & Stiles, B. An investigation of children's concept of self-responsibility for their school learning. *American Educational Research Journal,* 1976, 13, 159–179.

# 38

## Pardon Us, But What Was the Question Again? A Response to the Critique of the Follow Through Evaluation

*Richard B. Anderson, Robert G. St. Pierre, Elizabeth C. Proper and Linda B. Stebbins*

Abt Associates' five-year analysis of the national Follow Through data has reached several conclusions about the performance of this bold and costly educational experiment. These conclusions have important implications for government, for educators, and for researchers. A Ford Foundation–funded and widely disseminated critique written by House, Glass, McLean, and Walker (1978), which appears in this volume, does not take issue with any of these conclusions. The House group gives prominent mention, in fact, to only one of them, and while it comments favorably on that conclusion, it does so in a context of such shrill negativism that the reader of the critique must carry away the impression that we have said nothing that is either valid or important. We do not concur. People who care about education should care about what we have learned.

Our report to the U.S. Office of Education (Stebbins, St. Pierre, Proper, Anderson, & Cerva, 1977) presents three principal conclusions interspersed with a number of secondary findings that provide a context for them. At the same time, the secondary findings must be understood in light of the principal ones, or they are bound to be misunderstood. The press and our critics have unfortunately chosen to wrench some of these out of context, to draw from them some illogical and irresponsible inferences ("simple answers"), and then to try to attribute these inferences to us. Since this journal has far more readers than our very long report

From Richard B. Anderson et al., "Pardon Us, But What Was the Question Again?: A Response to the Critique of the Follow Through Evaluation," 48 (2) *Harvard Educational Review* 161-170 (May 1978). Copyright 1978 by President and Fellows of Harvard College.

will have, we appreciate this opportunity to make clear what we actually found and what these findings seem to imply.

## Main Findings

Any careful reader of our report will come away convinced of the validity of the following three principal findings. To the extent that the critique by House and associates deters people from receiving and acting on these findings, we feel that it has done a disservice to the public, to education, and to evaluation.

### *Variability of Effects*

Each Follow Through model had very different effects on test scores in the various communities in which it was implemented. Differences in effectiveness between sites within each model were greater than overall differences in effectiveness between models. None of the seventeen models in the evaluation demonstrated that it could compensate consistently for the academic consequences of poverty. From this finding (Stebbins et al., 1977, pp. 135–136), with which the House group (1978, p. 154) agrees, we conclude that the Follow Through strategy of externally sponsored curricular change is not a *reliable* tool for raising the test scores of poor children; the strategy is sensitive to too many influences over which it has no control. Local circumstances and behavior clearly have more to do with children's test performance than do the intentions, theories, and rhetoric of outside interveners. Taken as a whole, the evidence presented in our report (Stebbins et al., 1977) suggests that if a local school system has the potential for effective compensatory education, then outside resources of the Follow Through kind can sometimes catalyze this potential. But if not, intervention seems likely to be somewhat disruptive and counterproductive. Since the variables customarily measured in evaluation research have not turned out to explain the distribution of Follow Through effects, researchers must make up their minds to look beyond those variables to the characteristics that distinguish localities; they must learn not to treat programs as black boxes, with money and theories as inputs and achievement changes as outputs.

### *Small Differences between Follow Through and Non–Follow Through Performance*

In most cases, the Follow Through groups scored about as one would expect similarly disadvantaged groups to score without Follow Through. Where differences were apparent, Follow Through groups scored lower more frequently than they scored higher (Stebbins et al., 1977, p. 158). It appears clear, then, that the Follow Through strategy is not an effective tool for raising poor children's test scores. Not only are the effects unstable, but they are small, on the average, and a disquietingly large minority of them are in the wrong direction. The critique by House and associates mentions this finding only in passing.

*Poor Performance Relative to Grade-Level Norms*

With few exceptions, Follow Through groups were still scoring substantially below grade level at the end of three or four years' intervention (Bock, Stebbins, & Proper, 1977, passim). Poor children still tend to perform poorly in school even after the best and the brightest theorists—with the help of parents, local educators, and federal funds, and supported by the full range of supplementary services associated with community-action programs—have done their best to change the situation. The critique ignores this finding, which, by the way, is subject to none of the uncertainties that analytic complexities may have introduced elsewhere.

## Responses to the Main Points of the Critique

With all due respect to our distinguished colleagues who prepared the critique, we take strong exception to its content. In responding point by point, we shall endeavor to avoid the journalistic tone that we deplore in the critique, but we hope that our restraint will not be mistaken for acquiescence.

*Fairness in Evaluations and Critiques*

We do not agree that Follow Through has been the victim of "an unfair evaluation" (House et al., 1978, p. 132). To our way of thinking, an evaluation is valuable to the extent that it uncovers useful and important information about program performance and presents that information in a way that helps decision makers to take appropriate action. By the same token, an evaluation is "fair" to the extent that it treats alike any components it may compare and to the extent that its recommendations are qualified to distinguish direct inference from interpretation.

Before declaring an evaluation "fair," our colleagues seem to require that it address with uniform precision every objective of the activity being evaluated (House et al., 1978, pp. 132–133). This, it seems to us, is a suicidal criterion for evaluators to espouse. By its light, any program that wishes to rid itself forever of the discomforts of evaluation need only add to its list of objectives one metaphysical, obscure, or otherwise unmeasurable purpose (say, the improvement of "life chances," a phrase of great importance in compensatory-education legislation). Since such an outcome can be assessed only obliquely and imprecisely, if at all, any evaluation of that program must thenceforth be an "unfair evaluation."

Faced with a program having many goals of varying degrees of measurability and emphasized differently in its various organizational components, it seems appropriate to apply a common measuring stick to each component and then to say, as we have done, "This is how you performed on these tests; if you can show that you have done better in other ways, please do." It would have been wrong to claim that our results represent a comprehensive evaluation of each Follow Through project. We have been careful not to make any such claim, although our critics seem to want to give the impression that we have.

If, by the way, we were wrong to attend to only a portion of the range of objectives espoused at one point or another in the vast Follow Through terrain, how do our colleagues justify limiting their critique to a narrow view of our subsidiary findings? They have chosen, as James Kilpatrick (1977) did before them, to blow entirely out of proportion our secondary findings about differential performance of models by category and to treat them as if they were our primary results, rather than merely the most transparently newsworthy ones. Kilpatrick can be excused, perhaps. He is a journalist, and his only source material was a prior article from the *Washington Post* (Feinberg, 1977). Kilpatrick put forth simple answers—"in education, basics are better"—to questions that, as we were careful to point out, our data could not answer. We provided the House panel with a complete set of our report documents, and we spent a good deal of time helping its chairman understand the context of our findings. Since our colleagues have chosen to adopt Kilpatrick's strange distortions of emphasis, we can only conclude that they are really criticizing *his* findings, not ours. If that is indeed what they are doing, we would have been grateful if they had done it much more explicitly.

### The Location and Character of Our Principal Analysis

Comparisons between models and comparisons between model types, the validity of which is questioned by the critique, in no way constitute our principal analysis. In fact, our principal analysis consists of more than two thousand separate answers to questions of the kind, "In this specific site, and with respect to this specific outcome subtest, how much better or worse did the Follow Through group score than one would expect a similarly disadvantaged group outside the program to score?" The results of this analysis are detailed in the second part (Bock, Stebbins, & Proper, 1977) and third part (*Education as experimentation,* 1977) of our 1977 report. The summaries in the first part (Stebbins et al., 1977), which are those being criticized by House and his colleagues, represent one attempt to bring that mass of local results down to a manageable volume for purposes of interpretation. We point out very carefully (Stebbins et al., 1977, p. 131) that we do not wish to argue that those summaries are the only possible ones, or even the best ones; we have therefore made available all necessary details so that interested readers can make their own aggregations—as House and associates did—or eschew aggregation altogether.

### The Model Contrasts and Fallacies in the Critique's Reanalysis

Our colleagues have argued that the model patterns we reported are not really there. We remain unpersuaded. Consider what we actually say: models that emphasize the kinds of skills tested by certain subtests of the Metropolitan Achievement Test have tended—very irregularly—to produce groups that score better on those subtests than do groups served by models that emphasize those skills to a lesser degree (Stebbins et al., 1977, pp. 135–148). This is hardly an astonishing finding; to have discovered the contrary would have been much more surprising.

In their eagerness to prove the patterns spurious, our colleagues conducted two forms of reanalysis: a site-level analysis of variance (House et al., 1978, pp. 151–152) that we had considered doing and then rejected because the power of the associated significance test would be so low as to predetermine the (null) result; and a weighted aggregation of the numerical site mean effects (House et al., 1978, pp. 147–150), paralleling our aggregation of the qualitative effects. The first showed what it had to show: no "significant" differences from model to model—consistent with our main findings, but foredoomed to come out that way simply by inadequate sample size and not by any patterns in the data.

Their second reanalysis differed from its analogue in our report in a number of important respects. First, they computed their average model effects differently, and they based them on only one of our two parallel analyses for each site. They also took into account only two of the four cohort streams in the data base, whereas we averaged all four together. While the critique acknowledges these differences, it neglects to mention two others. They included four tests in their averages; we included eight. Moreover, we omitted from the averages certain estimates whose validity we doubted on methodological grounds; they restored them.

Considering that their parallel analysis differs from ours in so many ways, we consider that the very substantial similarity between the results of the two approaches (we calculate that Spearman's $rho = .78$ between the two sets of model ranks) supports our contentions very much more strongly than theirs. The qualitative shape of our findings is evident in theirs; in fact, they confess that "the two sets of ranks are largely comparable" (House et al., 1978, p. 150). Some individual models change ranks, and some of the patterns are weaker, but we had explicitly declined to draw contrasts between models (Stebbins et al., 1977, p. 135), precisely because of the variability within the models that is our clearest and most significant finding. Their aim, after all, is to show that our findings are mere flukes, meaningless wiggles in a random walk through noisy data. We think that they have not made their point with this reanalysis.

We take strong exception to the accusation that "the Abt evaluators apparently tried to accentuate the differences [among models]" (House et al., 1978, p. 131). Such a statement is an affront to our professional integrity, and we deny it. Yes, the expectation at the beginning of Follow Through was that there would be large differences between models. No, we did not create differences where they did not exist. Let us repeat once more: the major finding of our report is that differences between sites within a model were larger than differences between models.

By the same token, the critique argues long and hard that problems with the measures, analysis strategy, and methods of summarizing the data invalidate most of our conclusions. If so, it seems hardly consistent on our colleagues' part to accept our finding about the variability of results from site to site (House et al., 1978, p. 154). This conclusion is based on the same data, analyzed with the same methods, and summarized in the same way as all our other conclusions. We do not understand how those criticizing our methods so severely can single out one of our conclusions and declare it believable while choosing to reject all the others. At the very least, our critics have to show how it alone managed to escape the taint of our alleged errors.

Our colleagues point out, furthermore, that we chose to combine two factors, statistical significance and educational significance, to determine the effectiveness of each model at each site.[1] They then argue that "the Abt Associates definition of an effect confounds the effectiveness of a program with its number of pupils" (House et al., 1978, p. 146). Rather than make a determination of the effectiveness of each model at each site using tests of statistical significance, they suggest that "what is required is a definition of model impact that reflects only the magnitude of the difference in performance between Follow Through and non–Follow Through groups" (House et al., 1978, p. 147). We prefer the traditional method of demanding statistical significance as a minimal criterion for accepting a difference between two groups as real. We concede to our critics the right to define the success of a Follow Through model in any way they like, but we are certain that had we not used statistical significance as a criterion, they would have complained about the lack of reliability of the effects at small sites. It seems rather curious to us that in their reanalysis of some of our data, using the site rather than the child as the unit of analysis, they change their position on the use of tests of statistical significance and use an analysis of variance to support their (superfluous) contention of no differences between models.

Although House and his colleagues correctly point out the possible bias associated with incorporating sample size into estimates of effect, they fail to inform the reader that a similar bias, operating in exactly the opposite direction, would arise if one were to accept their proposed alternative of using the adjusted difference between treatment and comparison groups as a measure of effect. The argument is simple. The absolute value of the difference between the means (on some measure) of two samples drawn at random from the same population will tend to be larger for small samples than for large samples. Thus, while the critique argues that our analysis is biased in favor of finding a larger number of significant differences for large-sample models, we must point out that their proposed alternative is also biased—in favor of finding large differences for small-sample models.

*Mismatch between Treatment and Comparison Groups*

The mismatch was both more and less of a problem than the critique suggests. The critique deals harshly with our report on the matters of pretreatment comparability and use of covariance adjustment to equate groups statistically. In fact, the treatment and comparison groups were not perfectly matched. However, a careful look at the data belies the assertion that "control groups were grossly mismatched with the Follow Through groups" (House et al., 1978, p. 131). In 47 percent of the 138 sites included in the evaluation, the treatment-group and comparison-group pretest means were within one-quarter standard deviation of each other. In 77 percent of the sites, they were within one-half standard deviation. More importantly, the differences were not particularly biased toward either group. Treatment-group means were above comparison-group means

---

[1] Their Table 4 (House et al., 1978, p. 146) displays this composite definition in a gratuitously unfavorable fashion. The symmetry of the definition would be more apparent if the first two rows of this matrix were interchanged, thus preserving ordinal sequence in the three rows.

in 44 percent of the sites, while the opposite was true in 56 percent of the sites. These facts, based on data available in our report, contradict the critique's unsupported assertion that gross and lopsided mismatch between treatment groups and comparison groups runs rampant in the Follow Through evaluation, as it did in the Westinghouse-Ohio (1969) evaluation of Head Start. In this respect, as in many others, the Follow Through design, with all its flaws, represented a giant step forward in the state of the art in the 1960s.

The second point to be made with regard to mismatch concerns the qualification of our results. Notwithstanding the evidence presented above, there were cases where noncomparability of groups was a problem. As the critique correctly states, the error introduced by the analysis of covariance "gets larger as ANCOV becomes more effective" (House et al., 1978, p. 153)—that is, large covariance adjustments are prone to reflect large errors in adjustment. Being cognizant of this fact, we omitted from our summaries of the data any site-level effect whose covariance-adjusted posttest difference exceeded a specified criterion. Although the details of the criterion and its development are not important for the purposes of this discussion, it is important to note that we did what we could to rid our summaries of any site-level comparisons that we judged to be in danger of serious bias. Despite our critics' claim to be nervous about covariance adjustment, their site-level reanalysis is not only based on our covariance-adjusted results (their complaints notwithstanding, they did not reanalyze the raw data but accepted our site-level results and resummarized them), but it also completely ignores the warnings we placed on results from mismatched sites. After cautioning us about the possible errors arising from large covariance adjustments (which we recognized and therefore excluded from our summaries of the results), they decided to include, as discussed above, just such large adjustments in their summaries.

*Attrition*

The critique takes us to task on two counts with regard to attrition of children from the evaluation. We plead not guilty. House and associates state, for example, that "there is no analysis of attrition bias by models or by sites" (House et al., 1978, p. 154). They must have misunderstood our report, for this statement simply is not true. We report analyses designed to yield information on possible bias due to differential attrition from treatment and comparison groups within each site and each model (Stebbins et al., 1977, p. 83).

House and his colleagues further criticize us for dropping sites from the evaluation if the number of children with valid data fell below twelve. According to them, "A more lenient analytic strategy would no doubt have allowed retention of many more children and, therefore, sites" (House et al., 1978, p. 153). Since our analysis strategy was consciously set up to enable us to make statements about the effectiveness of each model within each of its sites, we wanted to be certain that each site had at least a minimum number of children. Even without this argument, a quick look at the data presented in our report (Stebbins et al., 1977, p. 46) reveals that the requirement of at least twelve children in each treatment and comparison group resulted in the loss of a total of forty-eight out of the thousands of children included in the four cohorts and seventeen models taking part in the evaluation. Again our critics have made an assertion that is contradicted by data readily available in our report.

### Practical Implication of Our Results

Whether or not differences between models are real, it does not follow that all future Follow Through funds should be diverted to models that emphasize rote learning. We never said it did. Kilpatrick (1977) said so, but as far as we know, he still has not seen our report. Once again our colleagues' eagerness to prove the obvious makes us suspect that they have really criticized Kilpatrick's column, not our report. Let us just reiterate that each of the models that we labeled "basic skills" had highly inconsistent results like all the others. Even the model with the best overall showing had several sites with net negative results. Such wide variability within each model implies that the "model" is not a useful organizing concept for the Follow Through test data.

Some of those involved in the Follow Through evaluation had hoped to identify at least one or two models that could be packaged and disseminated in full confidence that the model would then work wherever a school system might adopt it. Perhaps the greatest single payoff from the nation's investment of more than half a billion dollars in Follow Through may well be the realization that such strategies, while plausible ten years ago, are misguided now. This result would have been more palatable if it had emerged in a more positive form. But the investment will truly be lost if we permit ourselves to be distracted from the main issues by such off-the-subject offerings as the critique by House and colleagues.

## Conclusion: An Unfair Critique

From the foregoing comments, the reader must not conclude that we share no area of agreement with our colleagues. In fact, we agree with them in a number of important respects, although the reader of the critique alone would get the clear impression that we wrongheadedly persist in disagreeing with some very elementary truths that the critics therefore feel obliged to defend.[2] No canon of professional behavior forbids a critic from taking issue where none is offered, but the indirect effect of doing so is akin to that of calumny and plagiary, both proscribed by all conventions. Feeling keenly the unfairness of this pervasive aspect of the critique, we must protest it in the strongest terms. Our only defense, ultimately, is to urge the reader to take the trouble to read our report before accepting either the critique's claims or its innuendos.

We agree, however, with House and his colleagues that the Follow Through evaluation design suffers from many logical and methodological deficiencies. Few have better reason than we to know of these design problems, inasmuch as we have spent the past five years working through the exceedingly complex analytic

---

[2] An analogously insidious strategy takes the well-known form of asserting, "There is surely nothing to the rumor that...."

issues that they imply. The reader of our report (though not the reader of the critique) knows that we devoted a great deal of care and attention to identifying these problems, determining their likely consequences, conducting auxiliary analyses to estimate and minimize those consequences, and formulating and reporting appropriate qualifications to delimit the range of applicability of our findings.

We appreciate our critics' acknowledgment that Abt Associates was not to blame for the well-known faults of the design—it was complete before we arrived on the scene—but we wish that they had displayed equal candor in their discussion of the analysis. They have left the reader of their critique to gather that they are the first to have discovered the extent of mismatch between treatment and comparison groups, the weakness of the measurement battery, the dangers of covariance underadjustment, and so forth. Since our colleagues have not seen fit to acknowledge our earlier attention to these matters, we wish merely to note for the record that we were neither so naive nor so irresponsible as to ignore them. They address only one logical or methodological issue that we neglected: the "confounding of effect with sample size," which we have discussed above and which we are inclined to dismiss as a red herring in view of its lack of substantial consequence.

Let us note in closing that *Webster's Collegiate Dictionary* offers two definitions for the word "criticize": to consider the merits and demerits of and judge accordingly; and to stress the faults of. We think it is clear that our critics adopted only the second definition in their paper on the Follow Through evaluation and that they made a mistake in doing so. Yes, our report should be the subject of intensive scrutiny by respected professionals. Yes, there is room for debate about our findings and interpretations. However, we believe that the needs of educators, policy makers, and evaluation researchers would be better served by a critique in which the authors consider the demerits *and* merits of the evaluation and judge it accordingly.

Although the critique does acknowledge a few things we did right (and even attributes some of them to us), their article is on balance so overwhelmingly negative that it does a disservice to the Follow Through evaluation. As we argued earlier, the interpretations presented in our report have value for the educational community. However, the reader of the critique might be dissuaded from reading our report where, in addition to the topics discussed in this paper, we comment on such diverse issues as the effectiveness of Follow Through models with children in large cities; with children who have had Head Start experience; with particularly disadvantaged children; with children in kindergarten and the first grade as opposed to the second and third grades; and the change over time in effectiveness of Follow Through models.

The reader of our report would also discover one of the first large-scale studies to use a strategy of multiple parallel analyses, incorporating several methodological innovations and addressing many problems that are usually ignored in evaluation research. We have achieved some success, for example, in obtaining answers to the following questions. Did differential attrition of pupils from treatment and comparison groups bias the evaluation results? Were the results dependent on the particular covariate set used? Did violation of the assumptions of the primary analyses bias the evaluation results? Would a nonparametric analysis yield results leading to the same conclusions as the results of the primary analyses? Did using the child as the unit of analysis invalidate our statistical-significance tests? Did the inclusion of pupils with particularly low pretest scores bias the results? Finally, did the use of a fallible covariate bias the results? We therefore venture two recommendations. First, we ask interested readers to take the time to read at least the first part of our report (Stebbins et al., 1977), and not to let the critique and our response to it be the last word on the subject. Second, we urge that future critical reviews of important evaluations be more even handed. After all, even evaluators like to be evaluated fairly.

# References

Bock, G., Stebbins, L. B., & Proper, E. C. *Education as experimentation: A planned varia- tion model, Volume IV–B, Effects of Follow Through models.* Cambridge, Mass.: Abt Associates, Inc., 1977. (Also issued by the U.S. Office of Education as *National evalua- tion: Detailed effects,* Volume II–B of The Follow Through Planned Variation Experi- ment series.)

*Education as experimentation: A planned variation model, Volume IV–C, Appendices, Parts 1 and 2.* Cambridge, Mass.: Abt Associates, Inc., 1977.

Feinberg, L. "Basic" teaching methods more effective, study says. *Washington Post,* 20 June 1977, pp. 1; 8.

House, E. R., Glass, G. V, McLean, L. D., & Walker, D. F. No simple answer: Critique of the Follow Through evaluation. *Harvard Educational Review,* 1978, 48, 128–160.

Kilpatrick, J. J. Basics better in education, Cambridge group finds. *Boston Evening Globe,* 1 July 1977, p. 19.

Stebbins, L. B., St. Pierre, R. G., Proper, E. C., Anderson, R. B., & Cerva, T. R. *Education as experimentation: A planned variation model, Volume IV–A, An evaluation of Follow Through.* Cambridge, Mass.: Abt Associates, Inc., 1977. (Also issued by the U.S. Office of Education as *National evaluation: Patterns of effects,* Volume II–A of The Follow Through Planned Variation Experiment series.)

Westinghouse Learning Corporation & Ohio University. *The impact of Head Start: An evaluation of the effects of Head Start on children's cognitive and affective develop- ment.* Washington, D.C.: Office of Economic Opportunity, 1969. (Distributed by De- partment of Commerce, Clearinghouse for Federal Scientific and Technical Informa- tion, Springfield, Va.)

# 39

# Formal Evaluation of the Radio Mathematics Instructional Program, Nicaragua—Grade 1, 1976

*Barbara Searle, Paul Matthews, Patrick Suppes, and Jamesine Friend*

## 1. INTRODUCTION[1]

THE Radio Mathematics Project was established in July, 1973 to investigate the teaching of primary-school mathematics by radio in a developing country. The project is funded through the Institute for Mathematical Studies in the Social Sciences at Stanford University and is jointly sponsored by the Ministry of Public Education of Nicaragua and the United States Agency for International Development (AID).

In early 1975 the project initiated daily mathematics lessons in 16 experimental classrooms in the department of Masaya in rural Nicaragua. The project lessons were based on the official Nicaraguan mathematics curriculum. They were composed of a recorded portion, and a postbroadcast portion designed by the project staff and taught by the classroom teacher.

In 1976, the first-grade lessons, with some revisions, were broadcast by the national radio station and were used in approximately 50 classrooms, some of which served as experimental classrooms for the evaluation reported here. The experimental program is fully described in Searle, Friend, and Suppes (1976); we present here brief characterizations of both the experimental and traditional instructional programs and then describe the experimental design, sampling

---

This work is supported by the United States Agency for International Development Contract AID/CM−TA−C−73−40.

[1] The Grade 1 Instructional Program, the subject of this report, was designed, written, and produced in Nicaragua under the direction of Project Director Jamesine E. Friend and Co-Director Vitalia R. Vrooman. Among the many staff members who contributed to the work are: David Cardoza Solis, Irmina Cuadra de Venegas, Norma Guadamuz de Velarde, Francisco Herrera Perez, Inez del R. Larios, Julia Ledee, Gladys Gutierrez Lopez de Gamez, Juan Jose Montenegro Pineda, Mirna Osorio Ruiz, Alicia de Quintanilla, Emigdio Quintero Casco, Luis Ramirez Aubert, and Thomas Tilson. We are indebted to William Wagner and Mario Zanotti for helping in various aspects of the analysis.

---

From Barbara Searle et al., "Formal Evaluation of the Radio Mathematics Instructional Program, Nicaragua−Grade 1, 1976." Unpublished manuscript, 1977.

procedures, and testing instruments used to assess the effectiveness of the programs. Finally, we present the results. Anticipating this final section, we remark that the first-grade radio instructional program has produced levels of student achievement in mathematics that are higher than those of similar students in traditional classrooms, and that these gains are statistically significant as well as educationally substantive.

## 2. THE RADIO INSTRUCTIONAL PROGRAM

The 1976 first-grade instructional program consisted of 150 30-minute radio lessons for children and teacher's guides that provided directions to teachers for postbroadcast activities. Most lessons were accompanied by student worksheets.

During project radio lessons the students participated in a variety of instructional activities, responding to oral exercises as well as using the student worksheets. Other activities such as games, songs, and riddles were used to change the pace of lessons. The radio lessons were characterized by a high rate of student responses—four responses per minute on the average.

The instructional segments of the radio lesson were drawn from different mathematical topics and required different types of student responses. Instructional material took the form of exercises supported by minimal amounts of explanation and during each program the children worked from 40 to 50 mathematics exercises.

The topics of the first-grade curriculum were allocated to five major *strands*—number concepts, addition, subtraction, applications, and measurement. Within each strand the topics were further subdivided into exercise classes, which in turn were used to construct the lesson segments that comprised both the radio and postbroadcast portions of the mathematics lessons. The full curriculum consisted of 563 exercise classes, from which 1,314 lesson segments were constructed.

Fifty-four classrooms in the Nicaraguan departments of Masaya, Granada, and Carazo were used in the evaluation of the radio instructional program—30 experimental (radio) classes and 24 control (traditional) classes. (The selection of these classes is described in a later section.)

First-grade radio lessons (in Spanish) were broadcast each schoolday morning at 9:00 a.m. through the facilities of the national radio system, Radiodifusora Nacional. Each lesson occupied approximately 25 minutes of the 30-minute time slot. The remaining time was filled with an introductory announcement, a closing announcement, a countdown immediately preceding the lesson, music, and occasional short announcements for teachers. The project purchased and distributed the radios but schools without electricity were expected to supply their own batteries.

Two major broadcasting difficulties occurred during the year: power failures at the radio station and preemption of radio time by political events. In addition, errors made by radio engineers resulted in the loss of some lesson time.

Student worksheets and teacher's guides were distributed monthly through the office of the School Inspector in each department. Teachers obtained their monthly paychecks at these offices and the materials were delivered to the office prior to their scheduled visits.

Each teacher participating in the program attended two 3-hour teacher training sessions held before school started in February. These sessions were used to discuss the teacher's role during radio lessons, the mechanics of material distribution and use, and the relationship of the radio lessons' content to the official mathematics curriculum. Teachers were also given the opportunity to listen to lessons and to learn more about the goals of the project.

For most experimental classes, contact between project personnel and teachers of the experimental classes was strictly regulated and kept to a minimum. After the teacher training sessions, all information flow between the project and these teachers occurred through two channels—the radio and the office of the School Inspector in each department. An exception to this procedure was made for eight classes that were included in a weekly testing program. These classes were visited about every two weeks, at a time other than the mathematics period, for the administration of a 20-minute mathematics test.

Supervision of experimental classes was not undertaken by the project. Teachers of experimental classes were supervised by the regular school inspectors in the same way as teachers of traditional classes. However, departmental school inspectors do not have cars and they rarely visit schools. Project personnel made occasional unannounced visits to schools during broadcast time to observe whether the radio lessons were being used by the teachers in experimental classes. On the average, three such visits were made to each school during the year.

The project employed one procedure that was meant to be an indirect means of supervision. (We do not know if it was perceived by teachers in this way.) Each month, one segment of a radio lesson was identified as a test, and the teachers were asked to return the students' worksheets for this lesson to the office of the School Inspector. These worksheets were packaged separately and teachers were reminded of the tests by radio for several days before they occurred. A record was kept of the number of worksheets returned each month by each teacher; the returned worksheets were examined to determine if teachers had graded the papers to evaluate student performance as was suggested in the teacher's guide.

We can summarize the description of the radio instructional program by listing the components of the experimental treatment.

1. Radio mathematics lessons, approximately 25 minutes long, broadcast once each school day at a fixed time.

2. Teacher's guides, containing (a) specific tasks for teachers before, during, and after the broadcast, and (b) a general description of the material to be taught by the radio lessons and the material that should be taught by the classroom teacher.

3. Individual student worksheets for most lessons.

4. Several sets of supplementary materials for use during or after the radio lessons (e.g. posters, cardboard rulers).

5. Tests administered to all students once a month by the radio, with answer keys provided to teachers in the teacher's guide.

6. Two 3-hour teacher training sessions at the beginning of the school year.

7. Occasional and irregular visits of project personnel to schools.

## 3. THE TRADITIONAL INSTRUCTIONAL PROGRAM

The traditional mathematics program in Nicaragua cannot be described in as much detail as the experimental program. The official curriculum is described in a guide prepared by the Ministry of Education. The guide is not supplied free for teachers but it can be purchased at bookstores in the capital city of Managua. It presents a week-by-week outline of the topics that teachers are expected to cover with many suggested exercises and practice procedures. No textbooks or supplementary materials are provided by school authorities; many teachers make or buy their own supplies. About five years ago an AID program financed the distribution of mathematics textbooks to schools. These books were intended to be used as student workbooks but some teachers did not allow students to write in them in order to preserve them for later use. They were seen occasionally in classrooms by project personnel.

Information was obtained about the traditional instructional program by systematic observations of traditional classrooms in June, 1974 before radio lessons were instituted. Twenty-eight mathematics classes were observed—15 in urban schools and 13 in rural schools.

All the classrooms had blackboards, but other teaching aids were generally absent. Students were using textbooks in only one classroom. Class size ranged from 18 to 46 with a mean of 31 and a median of 30. However, this was the fourth month of school and the number of children attending classes when the observations were made was approximately two-thirds of the number matriculated.

In half the classes observed the students were separated into ability groups. Eleven of these classes were in rural schools and three were in urban schools. The majority were at the first-grade level. Most classes had two ability groups, but several had either three or four. The observers noted that in most of the classrooms with ability groups the teachers spent more time with the highest groups than with the others. During one particular classroom observation the high ability group received 40 minutes of teacher direction, whereas the low ability group received only 5 minutes.

The content being taught in first grade ranged from counting to 10 to division. In many of the classrooms the major activity was copying computation exercises from the blackboard and solving them in student notebooks. There was little work with concrete materials; although eight classes used materials during the lesson, in three of the classes the materials were used by only a few children and in most cases they were used for only a short part of the lesson.

The classroom observations were summarized here to give the reader a sense of what happens in traditional classrooms. These observations did not form the basis for our characterization of the traditional instructional program; the objectives of that program were taken to be those published by the Ministry of Public Education.

## 4. DESIGN AND SAMPLING PROCEDURES

The effectiveness of project lessons was assessed using a randomized field experiment (Riecken & Boruch, 1974). Because the experimental treatment (the radio instructional program) was administered to intact classrooms, the sampling procedures assigned classrooms to treatments.

The population of first-grade classrooms was stratified by department and by school location (rural or urban) and equal numbers of classes were chosen from each stratum. In each of the three departments, eight classes were designated as control—four each in urban and rural schools; ten classes were designated as experimental—five each in urban and rural schools. The three departments—Masaya, Granada, and Carazo—are roughly equal in size; in 1971 the number of primary-school students was, respectively, 17,600, 13,500, and

15,400. In each department approximately 30% of the students are in rural schools.

The strategy was to designate *schools* randomly as experimental or control and then to select classrooms at random within these designations. This was done to prevent the occurrence of a control and an experimental class in the same school with the attendant problems of contamination. The initial pool contained all public primary schools except those with a 1975 first-grade matriculation of less than 15 students, those that had previously used the project radio lessons, and two schools in Carazo affiliated with a teacher training school.

The first step in selecting classes was to prepare a list of schools with eligible classrooms for each of the six subpopulations formed by stratifying by department and location. Then lists of experimental and control schools were prepared by random assignment from the master list for each subpopulation. Schools were used in the order in which they appeared on the prepared list. One school refused to participate and was replaced by the next on the list. If a school had more than one first-grade section, one section was selected at random and assigned to the appropriate treatment. The result was a set of 30 experimental classrooms and 24 control classrooms. None of the teachers of these classes had prior experience with the project lessons and it is unlikely, although not absolutely certain, that any of the students did.

Because the difficulty of randomly assigning units (i.e. subjects, classrooms, or other groups) to treatments is often cited as an obstacle to using experimental techniques in the field (Boruch & Riecken, 1975) it seems important to discuss our use of this technique. At the outset of our work in Nicaragua we alerted all of the education officials with whom we worked of our intention to choose experimental and control classes at random and very early obtained the permission of the Minister of Education to use this procedure. To assure the success of the experiment we required that all usage of the experimental lessons be with our permission, even in classrooms that were not part of the research design. We refused requests to participate from all teachers in schools that had been designated as control, even if there were no classes from that school in the present control group. Thus, the ease with which we were able to impose random assignment can probably be attributed to three factors: (1) We made our intention known from the outset; (2) we received official approval and support for the policy; and (3) we established clear and consistent procedures, implemented from the beginning of our work, for use of the program.

## 5. MATHEMATICS ACHIEVEMENT TESTS

Students in control and experimental classes were administered both a pretest and a posttest. The results of these tests were used to compare the effectiveness of the radio instructional program with that of the mathematics program found in traditional classrooms.

*PRi Il ,1*

The pretest was a modified version of the mathematics section of the kindergarten-level *Test of Basic Experiences* (TOBE), published by CTB/McGraw Hill in both English and Spanish. The Spanish version of the test was developed for Spanish-speaking students in the United States; the modifications made to adapt the test for use in Nicaragua are described in Searle et al. (1976). The content of the 28-item test includes numeration, fractions, ordinal numbers, geometry, telling time, weight, length, size, and other basic concepts. Each item is presented orally and the student responds by marking one of four pictures displayed in a printed test booklet with one item per page.

It is not possible to compare performance of Nicaraguan and American children on the TOBE test because the test was altered for the Nicaraguan administration (and the publisher did not standardize the test on a Spanish-speaking population). However, results from administration of the test in 1975 indicate that several properties of the test were similar for the English and Nicaraguan versions. The reliabilities were comparable—the KR-20 reliability coefficients were 0.82 and 0.83 for the Nicaraguan and English versions respectively. The standard error of measurement for the Nicaraguan version was 1.91, compared with 2.10 for the English version.

*I'( I'1EST*

All project tests, except the TOBE test just described, were developed by the project, for several reasons. First, there are no standardized tests in use in Nicaragua and we were unable to find suitable versions of achievement tests in Spanish for which data were available and which would be appropriate for the Nicaraguan setting. Furthermore, it seemed important to have a test designed to assess achievement of the objectives of the Nicaraguan curriculum. Such a strategy would increase the likelihood of detecting performance differences attributable to the teaching method adopted—traditional or radio. Finally, it seemed important to adopt a test design that would provide information about achievement on each topic in the curriculum in order to investigate not only the overall effectiveness of the program, but its impact on different portions of the curriculum. A multiple matrix-sampling design satisfied this requirement (Shoemaker, 1973).

The evolution of the design for the first-grade posttest is described in Searle et al. (1976). The test used two types of items, **G** items that were read aloud to an entire class and **I** items that varied among individuals in a classroom. (**G** is an abbreviation for group, **I** for individual.) The distinction between the item types will be clarified by some examples.

Oral component      Written component

G items

"What is 2 plus 2?"      ____
"Circle the number 84."      48   84   74   47

I items

"Find the sum."      $\begin{array}{r} 12 \\ + \ 3 \\ \hline \end{array}$    or

$2+2 =$ ____    or
$21+14 =$ ____

"Circle the largest number."    2   5   9    or
21   12   32    or
79   77   81

The matrix-sampling structure of the test, which had four **I**-item forms (**I** forms) and four **G**-item forms (**G** forms), is shown in Figure 1. All **I** items were tested in every classroom; one-fourth of all **G** items were tested in each classroom. Sixteen different types of test papers were assembled—each **G** form paired with each **I** form. **G** forms were assigned at random to classrooms, and test papers containing the correct **G** form and one of the **I** forms were distributed at random to students within the classroom.

The test contained 40 **I** items and 44 **G** items. These 84 items were used to assess student achievement on approximately 30 instructional objectives of the radio curriculum. In addition, they provided information about a few topics that were part of the official curriculum but were not taught in experimental classrooms. The topics covered by the test will be discussed in the Results section of this report.

## TEST ADMINISTRATION

Both the pretest and the posttest were administered by the project staff, rather than by the classroom teachers. For greater uniformity of

TEST ITEMS

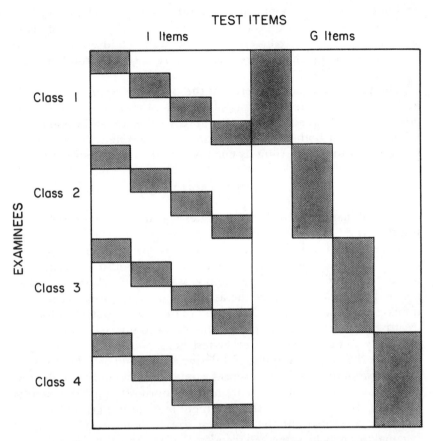

Figure 1. Matrix-sampling design of first-grade achievement test.

administration, the posttest had tape-recorded instructions. All in-structions for both tests had been pilot tested and modified on the basis of classroom trials (in classrooms not otherwise involved with the project). Results from earlier administrations of the tests showed that students were able to follow the directions for responding.

At the beginning of the year first-grade classrooms were quite crowded, and the seating arrangements would have made it easy to copy. Therefore, test administrators were instructed first to excuse all children 6 years and under. (These students are not fully matricu-lated; the official school admission age is 7 years.) Then, children were removed at random (by referring to the teacher's class list) until the number of students was reduced to the number of seats available, leaving an empty space between children who sat on benches. At the end of the year, if a room could accommodate all the children in the above manner, all were posttested. If not, then the names of those who had been pretested were read and those children were given priority for taking the posttest; others were chosen at random until the room was filled.

The pretest was administered in the period between February 23 and March 29, at the beginning of the school year. The posttest was administered between October 10 and November 15, at the end of the school year. In both cases, the testing of experimental and control classes was distributed roughly equally over the entire testing period.

## 6. DATA ANALYSIS

A combination of analysis strategies was used to understand the test data fully. The matrix sampling procedure described above aims to achieve inferential validity by randomly assigning units—in this case by randomly assigning urban and rural schools to experimental or control conditions, and randomly assigning test forms to classrooms and students. Under the assumptions of random assignment unbiased estimates of population test scores can be obtained for the treatment and control groups and the scores compared, even though not every student answered every test item.

While the matrix sampling test design was not intended to provide an analysis of individual differences, some assessment of the influence of variables such as pretest score and sex on posttest achievement is desirable. If, for example, the treatment and control groups did not have the same distributions of pretest scores, then the matrix sampling analyses may be subject to dispute. Because characteristics such as pretest score and sex were not factors in the random assignment of individuals for the matrix sampling design, the effects of such characteristics must be taken into account statistically after the data are collected.

Multiple regression was used as the statistical method for analysing individual differences, with posttest achievement being expressed as a linear combination of observed factors. At the present time the project's data base can be used to identify the following factors:

1. pretest score
2. urban or rural
3. sex
4. experimental or control

It would also be desirable to consider additional factors such as age, parental income and number of times previously enrolled in the same grade. As more data are received from Nicaragua these and other factors will be considered.

Finally, posttest scores were also analysed by item content to determine whether the effects of the experimental program varied with content area. It was expected that the score differences between the experimental and traditional students would be greater on those topics  covered more thoroughly by the radio instructional program.

## 7.  RESULTS

### Sample Sizes for Pretest and Posttest

The numbers of students taking the pretest and the posttest are shown in Table 1. Of those students taking the pretest, only about half also took the posttest. Of the children who took the posttest, about two-thirds had also taken the pretest. Of those students who did not take the pretest, some were present at the beginning of the school year but were not pretested because of overcrowded conditions. The remainder entered school after the beginning of the year. Unless otherwise noted, the analyses reported here use only those students with both pretest and posttest scores.

### Pretest Results

Average pretest scores are presented in Table 2, which compares the experimental and control groups. It also compares the pretest-only groups with the groups that took both the pretest and the

TABLE 1

Number of Students in Different Testing Conditions
in 1976 First-grade Testing Program

| Test Period | Condition | Experimental | | Control | |
|---|---|---|---|---|---|
| | | N | % of total | N | % of total |
| Pretest | Pretest only | 342 | 49.1 | 260 | 46.1 |
| | Both pretest and posttest | 354 | 50.9 | 304 | 53.9 |
| | Total | 696 | 100.0 | 564 | 100.0 |
| Posttest | Posttest only | 217 | 37.8 | 134 | 30.4 |
| | Both pretest and posttest | 354 | 62.2 | 304 | 69.6 |
| | Total | 571 | 100.0 | 438 | 100.0 |

TABLE 2

Comparison of Pretest Scores for Groups in Different
Test Conditions for 1976 First-grade

| | Score[a] | | | | | |
|---|---|---|---|---|---|---|
| | Experimental | | | Control | | |
| Condition | N | Mean | SD | N | Mean | SD |
| All students | 696 | 20.92 | 4.63 | 564 | 20.28 | 5.20 |
| Pretest only | 342 | 20.44 | 5.61 | 260 | 19.99 | 5.74 |
| Both pretest and posttest | 354 | 21.38 | 4.18 | 304 | 20.53 | 4.67 |

[a] Maximum score = 28.

*Note.* Difference between pretest only and pretest & posttest $f = 6.78$ df = 1, 1256 p < .01. Difference between experimental and control groups $f = 4.96$ df = 1, 1256 p < .01.

posttest. Approximate $F$-ratio statistics for a two-way analysis of variance were calculated for these comparisons by multiplying the variance of the means by the harmonic mean number of observations and dividing by a weighted average of within-cell variances. These $F$ statistics indicate that students who were not posttested had significantly lower (p < .01) pretest scores than students who were present for the posttest, and that the experimental group had significantly higher (p < .01) pretest scores than the control group. The former difference, while not large, is in the direction expected if students with lower ability as measured by pretest are more likely to drop out or be absent from school as the school year progresses. The difference between the experimental and control groups, while statistically significant, is small.

*Matrix-sampling Analysis of Posttest*

As discussed earlier, the posttest contains two types of items—those given to all students in a classroom (**G** items) and those given to subsets of students within a classroom (**I** items). For purposes of the first analysis reported here we consider **G** and **I** forms as two separate tests, each with a matrix-sampling design. Methods described by Sirotnik (1974), and discussed fully in Suppes, Searle, and Friend (1978), were used to estimate means and standard errors for each test. The mean posttest scores for the experimental and control groups are obtained by adding the average scores for each test form, while the standard errors are calculated using a weighted average of items-by-students interaction variances (i.e., the residual variance after main effects of items and students have been removed) across the blocks of the matrix sampling design.

The estimates in Table 3 show a superiority of the experimental group on both tests. For the **G** test, with 44 items, the means are 33.1 and 20.7 for experimental and control groups respectively. For the **I** test, with 40 items, the means are 22.1 and 13.5.

TABLE 3

Matrix Sampling Estimates of
Posttest Means and Standard Errors

| Test Forms | Experimental[a] | | Control[b] | |
|:---:|:---:|:---:|:---:|:---:|
| | Mean | SE | Mean | SE |
| G | 33.1 | 1.0 | 20.7 | 1.4 |
| I | 22.1 | 1.2 | 13.5 | 1.2 |
| G & I | 55.2 | 1.6 | 34.2 | 1.8 |

[a] N = 571
[b] N = 438

The assumptions of this analysis are that both items and students have been assigned at random to forms. Neither of these conditions is exactly met in the present case. In particular, students are assigned to **G** forms under the obvious restriction of their class membership. Thus, the assumption of randomness is relatively weak in the case of the **G** forms, in which all students in the class received the same form. (A reanalysis of the data using the class as the unit of analysis is described in Suppes, Searle, and Friend [1978], the results support the conclusions reached here.) Despite the deviations from the assumptions of randomness, the matrix sampling analysis is useful in providing an estimate of the average test scores that would be obtained if every student responded to all test forms. The precision of an estimated mean can be evaluated by considering the estimated mean plus or minus twice its standard error. For the estimates of Table 3 the experimental group scores on the order of 11 standard errors higher than the control group for the combined **G** and **I** forms indicating a robust favorable effect of the experimental treatment on posttest achievement. However, formal tests of statistical significance are reserved for the more detailed analyses presented below.

*Regression Analyses of Posttest*

Table 4 gives the distribution of students who took both pretest and posttest, classified by test form, urban/rural classroom and sex. Recall that each student takes a subtest consisting of one **G** form and one **I** form, and that there are about twice as many urban as rural

TABLE 4

Distribution of Students With
Both Pretest and Posttest

| Posttest form | Control | | Experimental | |
|---|---|---|---|---|
| | Rural | Urban | Rural | Urban |
| G–1 | | | | |
| Male | 26 | 11 | 17 | 40 |
| Female | 30 | 13 | 17 | 28 |
| G–2 | | | | |
| Male | 2 | 45 | 10 | 37 |
| Female | 0 | 43 | 19 | 38 |
| G–3 | | | | |
| Male | 21 | 19 | 14 | 44 |
| Female | 14 | 16 | 14 | 25 |
| G–4 | | | | |
| Male | 16 | 10 | 19 | 10 |
| Female | 18 | 20 | 12 | 10 |
| I–1 | | | | |
| Male | 16 | 20 | 16 | 29 |
| Female | 16 | 28 | 15 | 23 |
| I–2 | | | | |
| Male | 17 | 28 | 16 | 34 |
| Female | 21 | 20 | 14 | 24 |
| I–3 | | | | |
| Male | 16 | 12 | 11 | 35 |
| Female | 14 | 26 | 18 | 24 |
| I–4 | | | | |
| Male | 16 | 25 | 17 | 33 |
| Female | 11 | 18 | 15 | 30 |

students. The random assignment of schools, classrooms and test forms should give approximately equal numbers of students in the "rural" cells and also in the "urban" cells. The notable exception to this desired result is test form **G–2** where there are too few rural students in the control group.

Within the matrix sampling design it is difficult to obtain individual posttest scores that permit comparison of all individuals, since the distribution of scores for various test forms may vary and no individual takes every test form. For the present data the sample sizes and number of test forms allow the option of performing separate regression analyses for each test form, and then comparing regression results across test forms to observe consistent effects.

An alternative approach would be to add dichotomous (i.e., 0 or 1) variables to the regression corresponding to the effects of each test form. The multiple regression would then use the full data set and estimate test form effects apart from the effects of other factors. However, this regression would assume that the distributions of scores for the posttest forms differ only in mean and that the effects of regression variables are the same for each test form. Because we were unwilling to make this assumption a single regression analysis was not undertaken.

The multiple $R$'s for each test form regression indicated a significant degree of relationship ($p < .001$) between posttest achievement and a linear combination of the identified factors. Multiple $R$'s and standard errors of estimation are presented in Table 5. These

TABLE 5

Regression Multiple $R$'s
for each Test Form

| Posttest Form | $R$ | SE |
|:---:|:---:|:---:|
| G–1 | .706 | 2.02 |
| G–2 | .610 | 2.31 |
| G–3 | .704 | 2.24 |
| G–4 | .651 | 2.21 |
| I–1 | .656 | 2.25 |
| I–2 | .552 | 2.41 |
| I–3 | .564 | 2.64 |
| I–4 | .714 | 2.32 |

suggest that the separate regressions are comparable, in terms of variance accounted for and goodness of fit of the regression plane. Regression coefficients and beta weights (i.e. coefficients divided by their standard errors of estimation) are given in Tables 6 and 7, and beta weights are plotted across test forms in Figure 2. Beta weight values greater than 1.65 may be considered "large" and values greater than 2.00 "strong." These results indicate that both treatment and pretest scores have strong effects on posttest scores for every test form, while the urban/rural variable has a weaker but consistent effect, and sex has no large or consistent effect. Note that although significance tests are reported for each test form regression, the regression results are evaluated primarily with regard to the consistency of results across regressions.

TABLE 6

Regression Coefficients for G Test Forms

| Form | Independent variables | Coefficient | Beta weight |
|------|----------------------|-------------|-------------|
| | Constant | 0.993 | |
| | Pretest | 0.232 | 6.51[a] |
| G–1 | Urban/rural | –0.036 | –0.11 |
| | Sex | –0.050 | –0.16 |
| | Treatment | 3.061 | 9.21[a] |
| | Constant | –1.648 | |
| | Pretest | 0.273 | 6.84[a] |
| G–2 | Urban/rural | 1.796 | 3.65[a] |
| | Sex | –0.353 | –1.05 |
| | Treatment | 3.037 | 8.51[a] |
| | Constant | –1.154 | |
| | Pretest | 0.283 | 7.01[a] |
| G–3 | Urban/rural | 0.533 | 1.40 |
| | Sex | –0.375 | –1.06 |
| | Treatment | 3.002 | 8.33[a] |
| | Constant | 1.135 | |
| | Pretest | 0.191 | 4.09[a] |
| G–4 | Urban/rural | 0.658 | 1.56 |
| | Sex | 0.259 | 0.59 |
| | Treatment | 3.192 | 7.57[a] |

[a] $p < .001$

To summarize, the following conclusions can be drawn from the basic regression analyses:

1. Students participating in the experimental program score higher on all posttest forms than control students.

2. Students with higher initial ability (as measured by pretest scores) score higher on all posttest forms.

3. Students in urban classrooms generally score higher on posttest than students in rural classrooms.

4. There are no appreciable sex differences in posttest achievement.

The actual magnitudes of effects can be judged from the values of the regression coefficients in Tables 6 and 7. For example, the effect of the radio program is to raise posttest scores roughly 3 items for **G** forms and form **I–4**, almost 2 items for forms **I–1** and **I–3**, and about 1 item for form **I–2**.

The multiple regressions estimate only linear effects of the factors; additional questions concerning possible nonlinear and interactive effects were answered by an examination of regression residuals, defined as the differences between predicted and observed posttest scores. Evidence was sought for nonlinear effects of both pretest scores and interactions of treatment with pretest and urban/rural.

**Treatment-by-urban/rural interaction.** Table 8 presents an analysis of treatment-by-urban/rural interactions for **G** and **I** test forms. If there is no interaction, then the expected values of the mean residuals are zero and the variance of the mean residuals should be predicted by the within-cell variances. An approximate $F$-ratio statistic can be obtained for each table of residuals by calculating the variance of the means, multiplying by the harmonic mean number of residuals

TABLE 7

Regression Coefficients for I Test Forms

| Form | Independent variable | Coefficient | Beta weight |
|------|---------------------|-------------|-------------|
| I–1 | Constant | –3.685 | |
| | Pretest | 0.337 | 8.75[a] |
| | Urban/rural | 0.307 | 0.84 |
| | Sex | –0.351 | –0.99 |
| | Treatment | 1.858 | 5.23[a] |
| I–2 | Constant | –4.265 | |
| | Pretest | 0.349 | 7.82[a] |
| | Urban/rural | 0.247 | 0.65 |
| | Sex | 0.302 | 0.78 |
| | Treatment | 1.078 | 2.93[b] |
| I–3 | Constant | –2.860 | |
| | Pretest | 0.312 | 6.52[a] |
| | Urban/rural | 0.524 | 1.19 |
| | Sex | 0.207 | 0.48 |
| | Treatment | 1.726 | 3.97[a] |
| I–4 | Constant | –2.885 | |
| | Pretest | 0.288 | 6.58[a] |
| | Urban/rural | 0.770 | 2.02[c] |
| | Sex | –0.205 | –0.56 |
| | Treatment | 3.491 | |

[a] $p < .001$
[b] $p < .01$
[c] $p < .05$

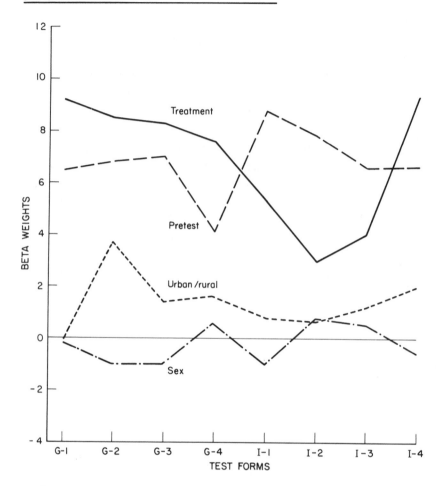

Figure 2. Regression beta weights plotted across **G** and **I** test forms.

in each cell, and dividing by a weighted average of within-cell variances. This $F$ statistic can be used to judge the magnitude of any interactive effect; for the numbers of observations and interaction degrees of freedom in Table 8, values of $F$ greater than 3.84 should be considered significantly large ($p < .05$).

Table 8 shows that the interactions for **G** and **I** forms are in opposite directions and neither $F$ statistic is large. These results indicate that the experimental program affects posttest achievement equally for both urban and rural students.

**Differences within the experimental group.** Within the experimental group classrooms differed with respect to the degree of participation in the experimental program. Some classrooms were judged by project staff to have used the radio broadcasts less frequently than others. Furthermore, some classrooms were used in the weekly testing program. Taking these factors into account three groups were identified as follows:

1. Low use—irregular use of radio broadcasts and supplementary project materials (11 classrooms);
2. Regular use—use of radio broadcasts as intended by the project (11 classrooms);
3. Weekly testing—regular use with supplementary testing (8 classrooms).

Since the effect of the experimental program was to raise posttest scores, it would be expected that regular use would raise scores more than irregular use. Also, test-taking experience would be expected to improve posttest scores, so that the weekly testing group would be expected to do better than the regular use group.

Table 9 presents mean residuals and approximate $F$-ratio statistics for **G** and **I** test forms. For **I** test forms the mean residuals indicate effects in the expected direction, with the weekly testing group doing better than predicted by the regression, the low use group doing worse than predicted, with the regular use group in between. The $F$ statistic for the **I** test forms is significant ($p < .05$). For **G** test forms the weekly testing group does better than predicted, while both the low use and regular use groups perform about as predicted. The magnitude of the $F$ statistic is not significant here. Note that the magnitudes of the mean residuals range from .028 to .446 compared with a main effect of treatment on the order of from 1.0 to 3.0 items, so that conclusions about the impact of the experimental program are not substantially modified by consideration of variations within the experimental group.

TABLE 8

Mean Regression Residuals for
Treatment by Urban/rural Interaction

| Test forms | | Control | Experimental | $F$ | df | p |
|---|---|---|---|---|---|---|
| G | | | | 0.283 | 1, 654 | ns |
| | Urban | .0949 | −.0989 | | | |
| | Rural | −.0682 | .0520 | | | |
| I | | | | 0.263 | 1, 654 | ns |
| | Urban | −.1000 | .1040 | | | |
| | Rural | .0719 | −.0549 | | | |
| G & I | | | | | | |
| | Urban | −.0027 | .0027 | | | |
| | Rural | .0019 | −.0015 | | | |

TABLE 9

Mean Regression Residuals for Treatment Subgroups

| Test forms | Mean residual | N | F | df | p |
|---|---|---|---|---|---|
| **G** | | | | | |
| Low use | .089 | 120 | | | |
| Regular use | .093 | 132 | 1.04 | 2, 351 | ns |
| Weekly testing | −.224 | 102 | | | |
| **I** | | | | | |
| Low use | .446 | 120 | | | |
| Regular use | −.149 | 132 | 3.48 | 2, 351 | < .05 |
| Weekly testing | −.332 | 102 | | | |
| **G & I** | | | | | |
| Low use | .267 | 240 | | | |
| Regular use | −.028 | 264 | | | |
| Weekly testing | −.278 | 204 | | | |

*Item Analysis of Posttest*

We turn now to an examination of performance on the topics that comprise the first-grade curriculum. The results of the posttest item scores for experimental and control students are summarized in Table 10. The mean item score for the experimental group (65.6%) is approximately 25 percentage points higher than the mean score for the control group. These results are for all children who were post-tested.

The comparison of scores by topic for experimental and control students, presented in Table 11, indicates that the experimental students score consistently higher on all topics except for geometry. The

TABLE 10

Descriptive Statistics for 1976 First-grade Posttest

| Descriptor | Experimental | Control |
|---|---|---|
| Number of classes | 30 | 23 |
| Number of students | 571 | 438 |
| Number of test items | 84 | 84 |
| Mean item score (% correct) | 65.6 | 40.6 |
| Standard deviation | 19.9 | 18.9 |
| 95% confidence interval about mean | 61.3–70.0 | 36.5–44.7 |

TABLE 11

Comparison of 1976 First-grade Posttest Scores of
Experimental and Control Students by Topic

| Topic | Number of items | Mean percentage correct | | |
|---|---|---|---|---|
| | | Experimental | Control | Difference |
| Numeration | 22 | 63.2 | 46.5 | 16.7 |
| Fractions | 4 | 78.5 | 32.5 | 46.0 |
| Oral addition | 6 | 73.4 | 35.8 | 37.6 |
| Vertical addition | 9 | 61.4 | 42.8 | 18.6 |
| Horizontal addition | 6 | 62.1 | 32.5 | 29.6 |
| Oral subtraction | 4 | 67.4 | 28.8 | 38.6 |
| Vertical subtraction | 9 | 47.0 | 22.6 | 24.4 |
| Horizontal subtraction | 3 | 48.8 | 22.5 | 26.3 |
| Money | 7 | 71.6 | 51.2 | 20.4 |
| Time | 1 | 68.1 | 14.7 | 53.4 |
| Length | 1 | 85.4 | 56.4 | 29.0 |
| Oral problems | 6 | 83.7 | 52.7 | 31.0 |
| Basic concepts | 3 | 86.6 | 64.6 | 22.0 |
| Geometry | 1 | 66.5 | 79.1 | –12.6 |
| Multiplication | 2 | 29.6 | 27.8 | 1.8 |

results for three topics require special mention. These three—basic concepts, geometry, and multiplication—were not taught by the radio lessons. The "basic concepts" topic includes comparisons of size (which is taller, shorter, wider, narrower), weight (which is heavier, lighter), and so on. The pretest results indicated that entering first-grade students knew these concepts quite well and therefore further practice was not included in the instructional program. Multiplication was not taught because the project staff thought the topic too difficult for first-grade students. The small amount of geometry required for first grade was difficult to teach by radio and was left to the teachers.

The radio lessons seem to be especially successful with oral topics—oral addition, oral subtraction, and oral word problems. For these three topics the difference between experimental and control groups is greater than 30 percentage points. This result is not surprising, since the radio instructional program gives such heavy emphasis to oral presentations, but we feel it is of particular importance in a setting, such as rural Nicaragua, where most transactions are oral.

## 8. CONCLUSION

We summarize here some of the more salient aspects of this study. (a) The experimental program was implemented without support from project staff in Nicaragua beyond the preparation and distribution of materials. Teachers were unsupervised, although they probably felt an obligation to use the radio lessons because they had been directed to do so by their School Inspectors. (b) The mean posttest item score for the experimental group was approximately 25 percentage points higher than the mean item score for the control group. This difference was highly significant ($p < .001$) both before and after adjusting the means of the two groups for effects of pretest and urban/rural classrooms. (c) Regressions of posttest scores on several independent variables indicated highly significant effects of the treatment variable and pretest score, a significant effect of urban/rural classrooms, but no significant effect of the sex of the student.

In summary, it seems reasonable to conclude that the Radio Mathematics Program provides effective instruction in the experimental schools in Nicaragua.

## REFERENCES

Boruch, R. F. On common contentions about randomized field experiments. In R. F. Boruch & H. W. Riecken (Eds.), *Experimental testing of public policy.* Boulder, Colorado: Westview Press, 1975.

Riecken, H. W., & Boruch, R. F. (Eds.). *Social experimentation: A method for planning and evaluating social intervention.* New York: Academic Press, 1974.

Searle, B., Friend, J., & Suppes, P. *The radio mathematics project: Nicaragua 1974–1975.* Stanford, California: Stanford University, Institute for Mathematical Studies in the Social Sciences, 1976.

Shoemaker, D. *Principles and procedures of multiple matrix sampling.* Cambridge, Mass.: Ballinger, 1973.

Sirotnik, K. Introduction to matrix sampling for the practitioner. In W. J. Popham, (Ed.), *Evaluation in Education.* Berkeley, California: McCutchan, 1974.

Suppes, P., Searle, B., & Friend, J. *The radio mathematics project: Nicaragua 1976.* Stanford, California: Stanford University, Institute for Mathematical Studies in the Social Sciences, in preparation.

# 40

# Improving Cognitive Ability in Chronically Deprived Children

*Harrison McKay, Leonardo Sinisterra, Arlene McKay,*
*Hernando Gomez, and Pascuala Lloreda*

In recent years, social and economic planning in developing countries has included closer attention than before to the nutrition, health, and education of children of preschool age in low-income families. One basis for this, in addition to mortality and morbidity studies indi-

produce some degree of malnutrition (3); failure to act could result in irretrievable loss of future human capacity on a massive scale.

Although this argument finds widespread agreement among scientists and planners, there is uncertainty about the

In conferences and publications emphasis was increasingly placed upon the inextricable relation of malnutrition to other environmental factors inhibiting full mental development of preschool age children in poverty environments (5). It was becoming clear that, at least after the period of rapid brain growth in the first 2 years of life, when protein-calorie malnutrition could have its maximum deleterious physiological effects (6), nutritional rehabilitation and health care programs should be accompanied by some form of environmental modification for children at risk. The largest amount of available information about the potential effects of environmental modification among children from poor families pertained to the United States, where poverty was not of such severity as to make malnutrition a health issue of marked proportions. Here a large literature showed that the low intellectual performance found among disadvantaged children was environmentally based and probably was largely fixed during the preschool years (7). This information gave impetus to the belief that direct treatments, carefully designed and properly delivered to children during early critical periods, could produce large and lasting increases in intellectual ability. As a consequence, during the 1960's a wide variety of individual, research-based preschool programs as well as a national program were developed in the United States for children from low-income families (8). Several showed positive results but in the aggregate they were not as great or as lasting as had been hoped, and there followed a widespread questioning of the effectiveness

*Summary.* Beginning at different ages in their preschool years, groups of chronically undernourished children from Colombian families of low socioeconomic status participated in a program of treatment combining nutritional, health care, and educational features. By school age the gap in cognitive ability between the treated children and a group of privileged children in the same city had narrowed, the effect being greater the younger the children were when they entered the treatment program. The gains were still evident at the end of the first grade in primary school, a year after the experiment had ended.

cating high vulnerability at that age (1), is information suggesting that obstacles to normal development in the first years of life, found in environments of such poverty that physical growth is retarded through malnutrition, are likely also to retard intellectual development permanently if early remedial action is not taken (2). The loss of intellectual capability, broadly defined, is viewed as especially serious because the technological character of contemporary civilization makes individual productivity and personal fulfillment increasingly contingent upon such capability. In tropical and subtropical zones of the world between 220 and 250 million children below 6 years of age live in conditions of environmental deprivation extreme enough to

effectiveness of specific remedial actions. Doubts have been growing for the past decade about whether providing food, education, or health care directly to young children in poverty environments can counteract the myriad social, economic, and biological limitations to their intellectual growth. Up to 1970, when the study reported here was formulated, no definitive evidence was available to show that food and health care provided to malnourished or "at risk" infants and young children could produce lasting increases in intellectual functioning. This was so in spite of the ample experience of medical specialists throughout the tropical world that malnourished children typically responded to nutritional recuperation by being more active physically, more able to assimilate environmental events, happier, and more verbal, all of which would be hypothesized to create a more favorable outlook for their capacity to learn (4).

The authors are members of the multidisciplinary research group of the Human Ecology Research Foundation, Apartado Aereo 7308, Cali, Colombia; the first three are scientific directors of the foundation. H. McKay is a senior research associate in the School of Education, and A. McKay and H. Gomez are doctoral candidates in the Department of Psychology, at Northwestern University, Evanston, Illinois.

of early childhood education as a means of permanently improving intellectual ability among disadvantaged children on a large scale (9).

From pilot work leading up to the study reported here, we concluded that there was an essential issue that had not received adequate attention and the clarification of which might have tempered the pessimism: the relation of gains in intellectual ability to the intensity and duration of meliorative treatment received during different periods in the preschool years. In addition to the qualitative question of what kinds of preschool intervention, if any, are effective, attention should have been given to the question of what amount of treatment yields what amount of gain. We hypothesized that the increments in intellectual ability produced in preschool programs for disadvantaged children were subsequently lost at least in part because the programs were too brief. Although there was a consensus that longer and more intensive preschool experience could produce larger and more lasting increases, in only one study was there to be found a direct attempt to test this, and in that one sampling problems caused difficulties in interpretation (10).

As a consequence, the study reported here was designed to examine the quantitative question, with chronically undernourished children, by systematically increasing the duration of multidisciplinary treatments to levels not previously reported and evaluating results with measures directly comparable across all levels (11). This was done not only to test the hypothesis that greater amounts of treatment could produce greater and more enduring intellectual gains but also to develop for the first time an appraisal of what results could be expected at different points along a continuum of action. This second objective, in addition to its intrinsic scientific interest, was projected to have another benefit, that of being useful in the practical application of early childhood services. Also unique in the study design was the simultaneous combination of health, nutrition, and educational components in the treatment program. With the exception of our own pilot work (12), prior studies of preschool nutritional recuperation programs had not included educational activities. Likewise, preschool education studies had not included nutritional recuperation activities, because malnutrition of the degree found in the developing countries was not characteristic of disadvantaged groups studied in the United States (13), where most of the modern early-education research had been done.

## Experimental Design and Subjects

The study was carried out in Cali, Colombia, a city of nearly a million people with many problems characteristic of rapidly expanding cities in developing countries, including large numbers of families living in marginal economic conditions. Table 1 summarizes the experimental design employed. The total time available for the experiment was 3½ years, from February 1971 to August 1974. This was divided into four treatment periods of 9 months each plus interperiod recesses. Our decision to begin the study with children as close as possible to 3 years of age was based upon the 2 years of pilot studies in which treatment and measurement systems were developed for children starting at that age (14). The projected 180 to 200 days of possible attendance at treatment made each projected treatment period similar in length to a school year in Colombia, and the end of the fourth period was scheduled to coincide with the beginning of the year in which the children were of eligible age to enter first grade.

With the object of having 60 children initially available for each treatment group (in case many should be lost to the study during the 3½ year period), approximately 7500 families living in two of the city's lowest-income areas were visited to locate and identify all children with birth dates between 1 June and 30 November 1967, birth dates that would satisfy primary school entry requirements in 1974. In a second visit to the 733 families with such children, invitations were extended to have the chil-

dren medically examined. The families of 518 accepted, and each child received a clinical examination, anthropometric measurement, and screening for serious neurological dysfunctions. During a third visit to these families, interviews and observations were conducted to determine living conditions, economic resources, and age, education, and occupations of family members. At this stage the number of potential subjects was reduced by 69 (to 449), because of errors in birth date, serious neurological or sensory dysfunctions, refusal to participate further, or removal from the area.

Because the subject loss due to emigration during the 4 months of preliminary data gathering was substantial, 333 children were selected to assure the participation of 300 at the beginning of treatment; 301 were still available at that time, 53 percent of them male. Children selected for the experiment from among the 449 candidates were those having, first, the lowest height and weight for age; second, the highest number of clinical signs of malnutrition (15); and third, the lowest per capita family income. The second and third criteria were employed only in those regions of the frequency distributions where differences among the children in height and weight for age were judged by the medical staff to lack biological significance. Figure 1 shows these frequency distributions and includes scales corresponding to percentiles in a normal population (16).

The 116 children not selected were left untreated and were not measured again until 4 years later, at which point the 72 still living in the area and willing once

Table 1. Basic selection and treatment variables of the groups of children in the study. SES is family socioeconomic status.

| Group | N | | Characteristics |
|---|---|---|---|
| | In 1971 | In 1975 | |
| T1(a) | 57 | 49 | Low SES, subnormal weight and height. One treatment period, between November 1973 and August 1974 (75 to 84 months of age) |
| T1(b) | 56 | 47 | Low SES, subnormal weight and height. One treatment period, between November 1973 and August 1974 (75 to 84 months of age), with prior nutritional supplementation and health care |
| T2 | 64 | 51 | Low SES, subnormal weight and height. Two treatment periods, between November 1972 and August 1974 (63 to 84 months of age) |
| T3 | 62 | 50 | Low SES, subnormal weight and height. Three treatment periods, between December 1971 and August 1974 (52 to 84 months of age) |
| T4 | 62 | 51 | Low SES, subnormal weight and height. Four treatment periods, between February 1971 and August 1974 (42 to 84 months of age) |
| HS | 38 | 30 | High SES. Untreated, but measured at the same points as groups T1–T4 |
| T0 | 116 | 72 | Low SES, normal weight and height. Untreated |

again to collaborate were reincorporated into the longitudinal study and measured on physical growth and cognitive development at the same time as the selected children, beginning at 7 years of age. At 3 years of age these children did not show abnormally low weight for age or weight for height.

In order to have available a set of local reference standards for "normal" physical and psychological development, and not depend solely upon foreign standards, a group of children (group HS) from families with high socioeconomic status, living in the same city and having the same range of birth dates as the experimental group, was included in the study. Our assumption was that, in regard to available economic resources, housing, food, health care, and educational opportunities, these children had the highest probability of full intellectual and physical development of any group in the society. In relation to the research program they remained untreated, re-

ceiving only medical and psychological assessment at the same intervals as the treated children, but the majority were attending the best private preschools during the study. Eventually 63 children were recruited for group HS, but only the 38 noted in Table 1 were available at the first psychological testing session in 1971.

Nearly all the 333 children selected for treatment lived in homes distributed throughout an area of approximately 2 square kilometers. This area was subdivided into 20 sectors in such a way that between 13 and 19 children were included in each sector. The sectors were ranked in order of a standardized combination of average height and weight for age and per capita family income of the children. Each of the first five sectors in the ranking was assigned randomly to one of five groups. This procedure was followed for the next three sets of five sectors, yielding four sectors for each group, one from each of four strata. At

this point the groups remained unnamed; only as each new treatment period was to begin was a group assigned to it and families in the sectors chosen so informed. The children were assigned by sectors instead of individually in order to minimize social interaction between families in different treatment groups and to make daily transportation more efficient (17). Because this "lottery" system was geographically based, all selected children who were living in a sector immediately prior to its assignment were included in the assignment and remained in the same treatment group regardless of further moves. In view of this process, it must be noted that the 1971 N's reported for the treatment groups in Table 1 are retrospective figures, based upon a count of children then living in sectors assigned later to treatment groups. Table 1 also shows the subject loss, by group, between 1971 and 1975. The loss of 53 children—18 percent—from the treatment groups over 4 years was considerably less than expected. Two of these children died and 51 emigrated from Cali with their families; on selection variables they did not differ to a statistically significant degree from the 248 remaining.

A longitudinal study was begun, then, with groups representing extreme points on continua of many factors related to intellectual development, and with an experimental plan to measure the degree to which children at the lower extreme could be moved closer to those of the upper extreme as a result of combined treatments of varying durations. Table 2 compares selected (T1-T4), not selected (T0), and reference (HS) groups on some of the related factors, including those used for selecting children for participation in treatment.

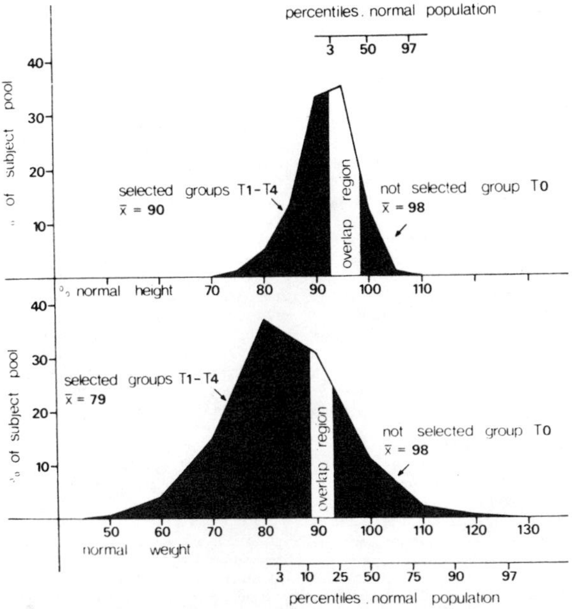

### Treatments

The total number of treatment days per period varied as follows: period 1, 180 days; period 2, 185; period 3, 190; period 4, 172. A fire early in period 4 reduced the time available owing to the necessity of terminating the study before the opening of primary school. The original objective was to have each succeeding period at least as long as the preceding one in order to avoid reduction in intensity of treatment. The programs occupied 6 hours a day 5 days a week, and attendance was above 95 percent for all groups; hence there were approximately 1040, 1060, 1080, and 990 hours of treatment per child per period from period 1 to period 4, respectively. The total number of hours of treatment per group,

Fig. 1. Frequency distributions of height and weight (as percent of normal for age) of the subject pool of 449 children available in 1970, from among whom 333 were selected for treatment groups. A combination of height and weight was the first criterion; the second and third criteria, applied to children in the overlap regions, were clinical signs of malnutrition and family income. Two classification systems for childhood malnutrition yield the following description of the selected children: 90 percent nutritionally "stunted" at 3 years of age and 35 percent with evidence of "wasting"; 26 percent with "second degree" malnutrition, 54 percent with "first degree," and 16 percent "low normal" (16).

then, were as follows: T4, 4170 hours; T3, 3130 hours; T2, 2070 hours; T1 (a and b), 990 hours.

In as many respects as possible, treatments were made equivalent between groups within each period. New people, selected and trained as child-care workers to accommodate the periodic increases in numbers of children, were combined with existing personnel and distributed in such a way that experience, skill, and familiarity with children already treated were equalized for all groups, as was the adult-child ratio. Similarly, as new program sites were added, children rotated among them so that all groups occupied all sites equal lengths of time. Except for special care given to the health and nutritional adaptation of each newly entering group during the initial weeks, the same systems in these treatments were applied to all children within periods.

An average treatment day consisted of 6 hours of integrated health, nutritional, and educational activities, in which approximately 4 hours were devoted to education and 2 hours to health, nutrition, and hygiene. In practice, the nutrition and health care provided opportunities to reinforce many aspects of the education curriculum, and time in the education program was used to reinforce recommended hygienic and food consumption practices.

The nutritional supplementation program was designed to provide a minimum of 75 percent of recommended daily protein and calorie allowances, by means of low-cost foods available commercially, supplemented with vitamins and minerals, and offered ad libitum three times a day. In the vitamin and mineral supplementation, special attention was given to vitamin A, thiamin, riboflavin, niacin, and iron, of which at least 100 percent of recommended dietary allowance was provided (18).

The health care program included daily observation of all children attending the treatment center, with immediate pediatric attention to those with symptoms reported by the parents or noted by the health and education personnel. Children suspected of an infectious condition were not brought into contact with their classmates until the danger of contagion had passed. Severe health problems occurring during weekends or holidays were attended on an emergency basis in the local university hospital.

The educational treatment was designed to develop cognitive processes and language, social abilities, and psychomotor skills, by means of an integrated curriculum model. It was a combi-

Table 2. Selection variables and family characteristics of study groups in 1970 (means). All differences between group HS and groups T1-T4 are statistically significant ($P < .01$) except age of parents. There are no statistically significant differences among groups T1-T4. There are statistically significant differences between group T0 and combined groups T1-T4 in height and weight (as percent of normal), per capita income and food expenditure, number of family members and children, and rooms per child; and between group T0 and group HS on all variables except age of parents and weight.

| Variable | Group | | |
|---|---|---|---|
| | T1-T4 | T0 | HS |
| Height as percent of normal for age | 90 | 98 | 101 |
| Weight as percent of normal for age | 79 | 98 | 102 |
| Per capita family income as percent of group HS | 5 | 7 | 100 |
| Per capita food expenditure in family as percent of group HS | 15 | 22 | 100 |
| Number of family members | 7.4 | 6.4 | 4.7 |
| Number in family under 15 years of age | 4.8 | 3.8 | 2.4 |
| Number of play/sleep rooms per child | .3 | .5 | 1.6 |
| Age of father | 37 | 37 | 37 |
| Age of mother | 31 | 32 | 31 |
| Years of schooling, father | 3.6 | 3.7 | 14.5 |
| Years of schooling, mother | 3.5 | 3.3 | 10.0 |

nation of elements developed in pilot studies and adapted from other programs known to have demonstrated positive effects upon cognitive development (19). Adapting to developmental changes in the children, its form progressed from a structured day divided among six to eight different directed activities, to one with more time available for individual projects. This latter form, while including activities planned to introduce new concepts, stimulate verbal expression, and develop motor skills, stressed increasing experimentation and decision taking by the children. As with the nutrition and health treatments during the first weeks of each new period, the newly entering children received special care in order to facilitate their adaptation and to teach the basic skills necessary for them to participate in the program. Each new period was conceptually more complex than the preceding one, the last ones incorporating more formal reading, writing, and number work.

**Measures of Cognitive Development**

There were five measurement points in the course of the study: (i) at the beginning of the first treatment period; (ii) at the end of the first treatment period; (iii) after the end of the second period, carrying over into the beginning of the third; (iv) after the end of the third period, extending into the fourth; and (v) following the fourth treatment period. For the purpose of measuring the impact of treatment upon separate components of cognitive development, several short tests were employed at each measurement point, rather than a single intelligence

test. The tests varied from point to point, as those only applicable at younger ages were replaced by others that could be continued into primary school years. At all points the plan was to have tests that theoretically measured adequacy of language usage, immediate memory, manual dexterity and motor control, information and vocabulary, quantitative concepts, spatial relations, and logical thinking, with a balance between verbal and nonverbal production. Table 3 is a list of tests applied at each measurement point. More were applied than are listed; only those employed at two or more measurement points and having items that fulfilled the criteria for the analysis described below are included.

Testing was done by laypersons trained and supervised by professional psychologists. Each new test underwent a 4 to 8 month developmental sequence which included an initial practice phase to familiarize the examiners with the format of the test and possible difficulties in application. Thereafter, a series of pilot studies were conducted to permit the modification of items in order to attain acceptable levels of difficulty, reliability, and ease of application. Before each measurement point, all tests were applied to children not in the study until adequate inter-tester reliability and standardization of application were obtained. After definitive application at each measurement point, all tests were repeated on a 10 percent sample to evaluate test-retest reliability. To protect against examiner biases, the children were assigned to examiners randomly and no information was provided regarding treatment group or nutritional or socioeconomic level. (The identification of group

HS children was. however. unavoidable even in the earliest years. not only because of their dress and speech but also because of the differences in their interpersonal behavior.) Finally. in order to prevent children from being trained specifically to perform well on test items. the two functions of intervention and evaluation were separated as far as possible. We intentionally avoided. in the education programs. the use of materials or objects from the psychological tests. Also. the intervention personnel had no knowledge of test content or format. and neither they nor the testing personnel were provided with information about group performance at any of the measurement points.

## Data Analysis

The data matrix of cognitive measures generated during the 44-month interval between the first and last measurement points entailed evaluation across several occasions by means of a multivariate vector of observations. A major problem in the evaluation procedure. as seen in Table 3. is that the tests of cognitive development were not the same at every measurement point. Thus the response vector was not the same along the time dimension. Initially a principal component approach was used. with factor scores representing the latent variables (20). Although this was eventually discarded because there was no guarantee of factor invariance across occasions. the results were very similar to those yielded by the analyses finally adopted for this article. An important consequence of these analyses was the finding that nearly all of the variation could be explained by the first component (21). and under the assumption of unidimensionality cognitive test items were pooled and calibrated according to the psychometric model proposed by Rasch (22) and implemented computationally by Wright (23). The technique employed to obtain the ability estimates in Table 4 guarantees that the same latent trait is being reflected in these estimates (24). Consequently. the growth curves in Fig. 2 are interpreted as representing "general cognitive ability" (25).

Table 5 shows correlations between pairs of measurement points of the ability estimates of all children included in the two points. The correspondence is substantial. and the matrix exhibits the "simplex" pattern expected in psychometric data of this sort (26). As the correlations are not homogeneous. a test for diagonality in the transformed error co-

Table 3. Tests of cognitive ability applied at different measurement points (see text) between 43 and 87 months of age. Only tests that were applied at two adjacent points and that provided items for the analysis in Table 4 are included. The unreferenced tests were constructed locally.

| Test | Measurement points |
|---|---|
| Understanding complex commands | 1, 2 |
| Figure tracing | 1, 2, 3 |
| Picture vocabulary | 1, 2, 3 |
| Intersensory perception (33) | 1, 2, 3 |
| Colors, numbers, letters | 1, 2, 3 |
| Use of prepositions | 1, 2, 3 |
| Block construction | 1, 2, 3 |
| Cognitive maturity (34) | 1, 2, 3, 4 |
| Sentence completion (35) | 1, 2, 3, 4 |
| Memory for sentences (34) | 1, 2, 3, 4, 5 |
| Knox cubes (36) | 1, 2, 3, 4, 5 |
| Geometric drawings (37) | 3, 4 |
| Arithmetic (38, 39) | 3, 4, 5 |
| Mazes (40) | 3, 4, 5 |
| Information (41) | 3, 4, 5 |
| Vocabulary (39) | 3, 4, 5 |
| Block design (42) | 4, 5 |
| Digit memory (43) | 4, 5 |
| Analogies and similarities (44) | 4, 5 |
| Matrices (45) | 4, 5 |
| Visual classification | 4, 5 |

variance matrix was carried out. and the resulting chi-square value led to rejection of a mixed model assumption. In view of this. Bock's multivariate procedure (27). which does not require constant correlations. was employed to analyze the differences among groups across measurement points. The results showed a significant groups-by-occasions effect. permitting rejection of the hypothesis of parallel profiles among groups. A single degree-of-freedom decomposition of this effect showed that there were significant differences in every possible Helmert contrast. Stepdown tests indicated that all components were required in describing profile differences.

The data in Table 4. plotted in Fig. 2 with the addition of dates and duration of treatment periods. are based upon the same children at all measurement points. These are children having complete medical. socioeconomic. and psychological test records. The discrepancies between the 1975 N's in Table 1 and the N's in Table 4 are due to the fact that 14 children who were still participating in the study in 1975 were excluded from the analysis because at least one piece of information was missing. a move made to facilitate correlational analyses. Between 2 percent (T4) and 7 percent (HS) were excluded for this reason.

For all analyses. groups T1(a) and T1(b) were combined into group T1 because the prior nutritional supplementa-

tion and health care provided group T1(b) had not been found to produce any difference between the two groups. Finally. analysis by sex is not included because a statistically significant difference was found at only one of the five measurement points.

## Relation of Gains to Treatment

The most important data in Table 4 and Fig. 2 are those pertaining to cognitive ability scores at the fifth testing point. The upward progression of mean scores from T1 to T4 and the nonoverlapping standard errors. except between T2 and T3. generally confirm that the sooner the treatment was begun the higher the level of general cognitive ability reached by age 87 months. Another interpretation of the data could be that the age at which treatment began was a determining factor independent of amount of time in treatment.

It can be argued that the level of cognitive development which the children reached at 7 years of age depended upon the magnitude of gains achieved during the first treatment period in which they participated. perhaps within the first 6 months. although the confounding of age and treatment duration in the experimental design prohibits conclusive testing of the hypothesis. The data supporting this are in the declining magnitude of gain. during the first period of treatment attended. at progressively higher ages of entry into the program. Using group T1 as an untreated baseline until it first entered treatment. and calculating the difference in gains (28) between it and groups T4. T3. and T2 during their respective first periods of treatment. we obtain the following values: group T4. 1.31; group T3. 1.26; and group T2. .57. When calculated as gains per month between testing periods. the data are the following: T4. .22; T3. .09; and T2. .04. This suggests an exponential relationship. Although. because of unequal intervals between testing points and the overlapping of testing durations with treatment periods. this latter relationship must be viewed with caution. it is clear that the older the children were upon entry into the treatment programs the less was their gain in cognitive development in the first 9 months of participation relative to an untreated baseline.

The lack of a randomly assigned. untreated control group prevents similar quantification of the response of group T1 to its one treatment period. If group HS is taken as the baseline. the observed gain of T1 is very small. The proportion of the gap between group HS and group T1 that was closed during the fourth treatment period was 2 percent, whereas in the initial treatment period of each of the other groups the percentages were group T4, 89; group T3, 55; and group T2, 16. That the progressively declining responsiveness at later ages extends to group T1 can be seen additionally in the percentages of gap closed between group T4 and the other groups during the first treatment period of each of the latter: group T3, 87; group T2, 51; and group T1, 27.

### Durability of Gains

Analysis of items common to testing points five and beyond has yet to be done, but the data contained in Fig. 3, Stanford-Binet intelligence quotients at 8 years of age, show that the relative positions of the groups at age 7 appear to have been maintained to the end of the first year of primary school. Although the treated groups all differ from each other in the expected direction, generally the differences are not statistically significant unless one group has had two treatment periods more than another. A surprising result of the Stanford-Binet testing was that group T0 children, the seemingly more favored among the low-income community (see Table 2), showed such low intelligence quotients; the highest score in group T0 (IQ = 100) was below the mean of group HS, and the lowest group HS score (IQ = 84) was above the mean of group T0. This further confirms that the obstacles to normal intellectual growth found in conditions of poverty in which live large segments of the population are very strong. It is possible that this result is due partly to differential testing histories, despite the fact that group T0 had participated in the full testing program at the preceding fifth measurement point, and that this was the first Stanford-Binet testing for the entire group of subject children.

The difference between groups T0 and T1 is in the direction of superiority of group T1 ($t = 1.507$, $P < .10$). What the IQ of group T1 would have been without its one treatment period is not possible to determine except indirectly through regression analyses with other variables, but we would expect it to have been lower than T0's, because T0 was significantly above T1 on socioeconomic and anthropometric correlates of IQ (Table 2). Also, T1 was approximately .30 standard deviation below T0 at 38 months of age on a cognitive development factor of

a preliminary neurological screening test applied in 1970, prior to selection. Given these data and the fact that at 96 months of age there is a difference favoring group T1 that approaches statistical sig-

nificance, we conclude not only that group T1 children increased in cognitive ability as a result of their one treatment period (although very little compared to the other groups) but also that they re-

Table 4. Scaled scores on general cognitive ability, means and estimated standard errors, of the four treatment groups and group HS at five testing points.

| Group | N | Average age at testing (months) | | | | |
|---|---|---|---|---|---|---|
| | | 43 | 49 | 63 | 77 | 87 |
| | | *Mean score* | | | | |
| HS | 28 | − .11 | .39 | 2.28 | 4.27 | 4.89 |
| T4 | 50 | −1.82* | .21 | 1.80 | 3.35 | 3.66 |
| T3 | 47 | −1.72 | −1.06 | 1.64 | 3.06 | 3.35 |
| T2 | 49 | −1.94 | −1.22 | .30† | 2.61 | 3.15 |
| T1 | 90 | −1.83 | −1.11 | .33 | 2.07 | 2.73 |
| | | *Estimated standard error* | | | | |
| HS | 28 | .192 | .196 | .166 | .191 | .198 |
| T4 | 50 | .225 | .148 | .138 | .164 | .152 |
| T3 | 47 | .161 | .136 | .103 | .123 | .120 |
| T2 | 49 | .131 | .132 | .115 | .133 | .125 |
| T1 | 90 | .110 | .097 | .098 | .124 | .108 |
| | | *Standard deviation* | | | | |
| All groups | | 1.161 | 1.153 | 1.169 | 1.263 | 1.164 |

*Calculated from 42 percent sample tested prior to beginning of treatment.  †Calculated from 50 percent sample tested prior to beginning of treatment.

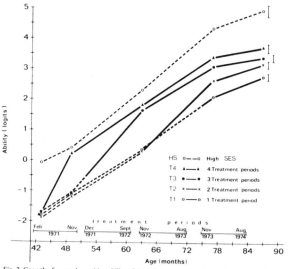

Fig. 2. Growth of general cognitive ability of the children from age 43 months to 87 months, the age at the beginning of primary school. Ability scores are scaled sums of test items correct among items common to proximate testing points. The solid lines represent periods of participation in a treatment sequence, and brackets to the right of the curves indicate ±1 standard error of the corresponding group means at the fifth measurement point. At the fourth measurement point there are no overlapping standard errors; at earlier measurement points there is overlap only among obviously adjacent groups (see Table 4). Group T0 was tested at the fifth measurement point but is not represented in this figure, or in Table 2, because its observed low level of performance could have been attributed to the fact that this was the first testing experience of the group T0 children since the neurological screening 4 years earlier.

tained the increase through the first year of primary school.

An interesting and potentially important characteristic of the curves in Fig. 3 is the apparent increasing bimodality of the distribution of the groups with increasing length of treatment, in addition to higher means and upward movement of both extremes. The relatively small sample sizes and the fact that these results were found only once make it hazardous to look upon them as definitive. However, the progression across groups is quite uniform and suggests that the issue of individual differential response to equivalent treatment should be studied more carefully.

### Social Significance of Gains

Group HS was included in the study for the purpose of establishing a baseline indicating what could be expected of children when conditions for growth and development were optimal. In this way the effectiveness of the treatment could

Table 5. Correlation of ability scores across measurement points.

| Measurement points | 1 | 2 | 3 | 4 | 5 |
|---|---|---|---|---|---|
| 1 | – | .78 | .68 | .54 | .48 |
| 2 | | – | .80 | .66 | .59 |
| 3 | | | – | .71 | .69 |
| 4 | | | | – | .76 |
| 5 | | | | | – |

be evaluated from a frame of reference of the social ideal. It can be seen in Table 4 that group HS increased in cognitive ability at a rate greater than the baseline group T1 during the 34 months before T1 entered treatment. This is equivalent to, and confirms, the previously reported relative decline in intelligence among disadvantaged children (29, p. 258). Between the ages of 4 and 6 years, group HS children passed through a period of accelerated development that greatly increased the distance between them and all the treatment groups. The result, at age 77 months, was that group T4 arrived

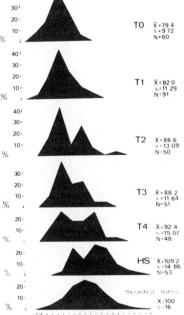

Fig. 3. Mean scores on the Stanford-Binet Intelligence Test at 8 years of age. Groups T0-T4 had had 1 year of primary school. Group HS children had attended preschool and primary schools for up to five consecutive years prior to this testing point. Mental age minus chronological age is as follows:

| Group T0 | – 18 months |
|---|---|
| Group T1 | – 15 months |
| Group T2 | – 11 months |
| Group T3 | – 9 months |
| Group T4 | – 5 months |
| Group HS | + 10 months |

at a point approximately 58 percent of the distance between group HS and the untreated baseline group T1, group T3 arrived at 45 percent, and group T2 at 24 percent. Between 77 and 87 months, however, these differences appear to have diminished, even taking into account that group T1 entered treatment during this period. In order for these percentages to have been maintained, the baseline would have had to remain essentially unchanged. With respect to overall gains from 43 months to 87 months, the data show that reduction of the 1.5 standard deviation gap found at 43 months of age between group HS and the treated children required a duration and intensity of treatment at least equal to that of group T2; the group HS overall growth of 5.00 units of ability is less than that of all groups except T1.

As noted, group HS was not representative of the general population, but was a sample of children intentionally chosen from a subgroup above average in the society in characteristics favorable to general cognitive development. For the population under study, normative data do not exist; the "theoretical normal" distribution shown in Fig. 3 represents the U.S. standardization group of 1937 (30). As a consequence, the degree to which the treatments were effective in closing the gap between the disadvantaged children and what could be described as an acceptable level cannot be judged. It is conceivable that group HS children were developing at a rate superior to that of this hypothetical normal. If that was the case, the gains of the treated children could be viewed even more positively.

Recent studies of preschool programs have raised the question whether differences between standard intellectual performance and that encountered in disadvantaged children represent real deficits or whether they reflect cultural or ethnic uniquenesses. This is a particularly relevant issue where disadvantaged groups are ethnically and linguistically distinct from the dominant culture (29, pp. 262-272; 31). The historical evolution of differences in intellectual ability found between groups throughout the world is doubtless multidimensional, with circumstances unique to each society or region, in which have entered religious, economic, ethnic, biological, and other factors in different epochs, and thus the simple dichotomy of culture uniqueness versus deprivation is only a first approximation to a sorely needed, thorough analysis of antecedents and correlates of the variations. Within the limits of the dichotomy, however, the evidence with regard to the children in our study suggests that the large differences in cognitive ability found between the reference group and the treated groups in 1971 should be considered as reflecting deficits rather than divergent ethnic identities. Spanish was the language spoken in all the homes, with the addition of a second language in some group HS families. All the children were born in the same city sharing the same communication media and popular culture and for the most part the same religion. Additionally, on tests designed to maximize the performance of the children from low-income families by the use of objects, words, and events typical in their neighborhoods (for example, a horse-drawn cart in the picture vocabulary test), the difference between them and group HS was still approximately 1.50 standard deviations at 43 months of age. Thus it is possible to conclude that the treated children's increases in cognitive ability are relevant to them in their immediate community as well as to the ideal represented by the high-status reference group. This will be more precisely assessed in future analyses of the relation of cognitive gains to achievement in primary school.

## Conclusions

The results leave little doubt that environmental deprivation of a degree severe enough to produce chronic undernutrition manifested primarily by stunting strongly retards general cognitive development, and that the retardation is less amenable to modification with increasing age. The study shows that combined nutritional, health, and educational treatments between 3½ and 7 years of age can prevent large losses of potential cognitive ability, with significantly greater effect the earlier the treatments begin. As little as 9 months of treatment prior to primary school entry appears to produce significant increases in ability, although small compared to the gains of children receiving treatment lasting two, three, and four times as long. Continued study will be necessary to ascertain the long-range durability of the treatment effects, but the present data show that they persist at 8 years of age.

The increases in general cognitive ability produced by the multiform preschool interventions are socially significant in that they reduce the large intelligence gap between children from severely deprived environments and those from favored environments, although the extent to which any given amount of intervention might be beneficial to wider so-

cietal development is uncertain (32). Extrapolated to the large number of children throughout the world who spend their first years in poverty and hunger, however, even the smallest increment resulting from one 9-month treatment period could constitute an important improvement in the pool of human capabilities available to a given society.

### References and Notes

1. D. B. Jelliffe, *Infant Nutrition in the Tropics and Subtropics* (World Health Organization, Geneva, 1968); C. D. Williams, in *Preschool Child Malnutrition* (National Academy of Sciences, Washington, D.C., 1966), pp. 3–8; N. S. Scrimshaw, in *ibid.*, pp. 63–73.
2. N. S. Scrimshaw and J. E. Gordon, Eds., *Malnutrition, Learning and Behavior* (MIT Press, Boston, 1968), especially the articles by J. Cravioto and E. R. DeLicardie, F. Monckeberg, and M. B. Stoch and P. M. Smythe; J. Cravioto, in *Preschool Child Malnutrition* (National Academy of Sciences, Washington, D.C., 1966), pp. 74–84; M. Winick and P. Rosso, *Pediat. Res.* 3, 181 (1969); L. M. Brockman and H. N. Ricciuti, *Dev. Psychol.* 4, 312 (1971). As significant as the human studies was the animal research of R. Barnes, J. Cowley, and S. Franková, all of whom summarize their work in *Malnutrition, Learning and Behavior*.
3. A. Berg, *The Nutrition Factor* (Brookings Institution, Washington, D.C., 1973), p. 5.
4. In addition to the authors' own experience, that of pediatricians and nutrition specialists in Latin America, Africa, and Asia is highly uniform in this respect. In fact, a generally accepted rule in medical care of malnourished children is that improvement in psychological response is the first sign of recovery.
5. D. Kallen, Ed., *Nutrition, Development and Social Behavior*, DHEW Publication No. (NIH) 73-242 (National Institutes of Health, Washington, D.C., 1973); S. L. Manocha, *Malnutrition and Retarded Human Development* (Thomas, Springfield, Ill., 1972), pp. 132–165.
6. J. Dobbing, in *Malnutrition, Learning and Behavior*, N. S. Scrimshaw and J. E. Gordon, Eds. (MIT Press, Boston, 1968), p. 181.
7. B. S. Bloom, *Stability and Change in Human Characteristics* (Wiley, New York, 1964); J. McV. Hunt, *Intelligence and Experience* (Ronald, New York, 1961); M. Deutsch *et al.*, *The Disadvantaged Child* (Basic Books, New York, 1967). As with nutrition studies, there was also a large amount of animal research as that of J. Denenberg and G. Karas [*Science* 130, 629 (1959)] showing the vulnerability of the young organism and that early environmental effects could last into adulthood.
8. M. Pines, *Revolution in Learning* (Harper & Row, New York, 1966); R. O. Hess and R. M. Bear, Eds., *Early Education* (Aldine, Chicago, 1968).
9. The 1969–1970 debate over the effectiveness of early education can be found in M. S. Smith and J. S. Bissel, *Harv. Educ. Rev.* 40, 51 (1970); V. G. Cicirelli, J. W. Evans, J. S. Schiller, *ibid.* p. 105; D. T. Campbell and A. Erlebacher, in *Disadvantaged Child*, J. Hellmuth, Ed. (Brunner/Mazel, New York, 1970), vol. 3; *Environment, Heredity and Intelligence* (Harvard Educational Review, vol. 3, *Child Development Research*, vol. 3, and *Child Development and Social Policy*, B. M. Caldwell and H. N. Ricciuti, Eds. (Univ. of Chicago Press, Chicago, 1973), pp. 331–402; T. Kellaghan, *The Evaluation of a Preschool Programme for Disadvantaged Children* (Educational Research Centre, St. Patrick's College, Dublin, 1975), pp. 21–33; U. Bronfenbrenner, *Is Early Intervention Effective?*, DHEW Publication No. (OHD) 74-25 (Office of Human Development, Department of Health, Education, and Welfare, Washington, D.C., 1974).
10. S. Gray and R. Klaus, in *Intelligence: Some Recurring Issues*, L. E. Tyler, Ed. (Van Nostrand Reinhold, New York, 1969), pp. 187–188.
11. This study sprang from prior work attempting to clarify the relationship of moderate malnutrition to mental retardation, in which it became evident that malnutrition of first and second degree might be only one of many correlated environmental factors found in poverty contributing to deficit in cognitive performance. We selected children for treatment with undernutrition as the

first criterion not to imply that this was the major critical factor in cognitive development, but to be assured that we were dealing with children found typically in the extreme of poverty in the developing world, permitting generalization of our results to a population that is reasonably well-defined in pediatric practice universally. Figure 1 allows scientists anywhere to directly compare their population with ours on criteria that, in our experience, more reliably reflect the sum total of chronic environmental deprivation than any other measure available.
12. H. McKay, A. McKay, L. Sinisterra, in *Nutrition, Development and Social Behavior*, D. Kallen, Ed., DHEW Publ. No. (NIH) 73-242 (National Institutes of Health, Washington, D.C., 1973); S. Franková, in *Malnutrition, Learning and Behavior*, N. S. Scrimshaw and J. E. Gordon, Eds. (MIT Press, Cambridge, Mass., 1968). Franková, in addition to showing in her studies with rats that malnutrition caused behavioral abnormalities, also was the first to suggest that the effects of malnutrition could be modified through stimulation.
13. *First Health and Nutrition Examination Survey, United States, 1971–72*, DHEW Publication No. (HRA) 75-1223 (Health Resources Administration, Department of Health, Education, and Welfare, Rockville, Md., 1975).
14. H. McKay, A. McKay, L. Sinisterra, *Stimulation of Cognitive and Social Competence in Preschool Age Children Affected by the Multiple Deprivations of Depressed Urban Environments* (Human Ecology Research Foundation, Cali, Colombia, 1970).
15. D. B. Jelliffe, *The Assessment of the Nutritional Status of the Community* (World Health Organization, Geneva, 1966), pp. 10–96.
16. In programs that assess community nutritional conditions around the world, standards widely used for normal growth of preschool age children have been those from the Harvard School of Public Health found in *Textbook of Pediatrics*, W. E. Nelson, V. C. Vaughan, R. J. McKay, Eds. (Saunders, Philadelphia, ed. 9, 1969), pp. 15–57. That these were appropriate for use with the children studied here is confirmed by data showing that the "normal" comparison children (group HS) were slightly above the median values of the standards at 3 years of age. Height for age, weight for age, and weight for height of all the study children were compared with this set of standards. The results, in turn, were the basis for the Fig. 1 data, including the "stunting" (indication of chronic, or past, undernutrition) and "wasting" (indication of acute, or present, malnutrition) classifications of J. C. Waterlow and A. Rutishauser [in *Early Malnutrition and Mental Development*, J. Cravioto, L. Hambraeus, B. Vahlquist, Eds. (Almqvist & Wiksell, Uppsala, Sweden, 1974), pp. 13–26]. The classification "stunted" included the children found in the range from 75 to 95 percent of weight for age. The "wasting" classification included children falling between 75 and 90 percent of weight for height. The cutoff points of 95 percent height for age and the 90 percent weight for height were, respectively, 1.8 and 1.2 standard deviations (S.D.) below the means of group HS, while the selected children's means were 3 S.D. and 1 S.D. below group HS. The degree of malnutrition, in accordance with F. Gomez, R. Ramos-Galvan, S. Frenk, J. M. Cravioto, J. M. Chavez, and J. Vasquez [*J. Trop. Pediat.* 2, 77 (1956)] was calculated with weight for age less than 75 percent as "second degree" and 75 to 85 percent as "first degree." We are calling low normal a weight for age between 85 and 90 percent. The 75, 85, and 90 percent cutoff points were 2.6, 1.7, and 1.3 S.D. below the mean of group HS, respectively, while the selected children's mean was 2.3 S.D. below that of group HS children. Examination of combinations of both height and weight to assess nutritional status follows the recommendations of the World Health Organization expert committee on nutrition, found in *FAO/WHO Technical Report Series No. 477* (World Health Organization, Geneva, 1972), pp. 36–48 (Spanish language edition). In summary, from the point of view of both the mean values and the severity of deficit in the lower extreme of the distributions, it appears that the group of selected children, at 3 years of age, can be characterized as having had a history of chronic undernutrition rather than suffering from acute malnutrition at the time of initial examination.
17. The data analyses in this article used individuals as the randomization unit rather than sectors. To justify this, in view of the fact that random assignment of children was actually done by sectors, a nested analysis of variance was performed on psychological data at the last data

point, at age 7, to examine the difference between mean-square for variation (MS) between sectors within treatment and MS between subjects within treatments within sectors. The resulting insignificant F-statistic (F = 1.432, d.f. 15,216) permits such analyses.

18. Food and Nutrition Board, National Research Council, *Recommended Dietary Allowances*, (National Academy of Sciences, Washington, D.C., 1968).

19. D. B. Weikart acted as a principal consultant on several aspects of the education program; D. B. Weikart, L. Rogers, C. Adcock, D. McClelland [*The Cognitively Oriented Curriculum* (Eric/National Association for the Education of Young Children, Washington, 1971)] provided some of the conceptual framework. The content of the educational curriculum included elements described in the works of C. S. Lavatelli, *Piaget's Theory Applied to an Early Childhood Curriculum* (Center for Media Development, Boston, 1970); S. Smilansky, *The Effects of Sociodramatic Play on Disadvantaged Preschool Children* (Wiley, New York, 1968); C. Bereiter and S. Englemann, *Teaching Disadvantaged Children in the Preschool* (Prentice-Hall, Englewood Cliffs, N.J., 1969); R. G. Stauffer, *The Language-Experience Approach to the Teaching of Reading* (Harper & Row, New York, 1970); R. Van Allen and C. Allen, *Language Experiences in Early Childhood* (Encyclopaedia Britannica Press, Chicago, 1969); S. Ashton-Warner, *Teacher* (Bantam, New York, 1963); R. C. Orem, *Montessori for the Disadvantaged Children in the Preschool* (Capricorn, New York, 1968); and M. Montessori, *The Discovery of the Child* (Ballantine, New York, 1967).

20. H. McKay, L. Sinisterra, A. McKay, H. Gomez, P. Lloreda, J. Korgi, A. Dow, in *Proceedings of the Tenth International Congress of Nutrition* (International Congress of Nutrition, Kyoto, 1975), chap. 7.

21. Although the "Scree" test of R. B. Cattell [*Multivar. Behav. Res.* 1, 245 (1966)] conducted on the factor analyses at each measurement point clearly indicated a single factor model, there does exist the possibility of a change in factorial content that might have affected the differences between group HS children and the children at later measurement periods. New analysis procedures based upon a linear structural relationship such as suggested by K. G. Jöreskog and D. Sörbom [in *Research Report 76-1* (Univ. of Uppsala, Sweden, 1976)] could provide better definition of between-occasion factor composition, but the number of variables and occasions in this study still surpass the limits of software available.

22. G. Rasch, *Probabilistic Models for Some Intelligence and Attainment Tests* (Danmarks Paedagogiske Institut, Copenhagen, 1960) in *Proceedings of the Fourth Berkeley Symposium on Mathematical Statistics* (Univ. of California Press, Berkeley, 1961), vol. 4, pp. 321–33; *Br. J. Math. Stat. Psychol.* 19, 49 (1966).

23. B. Wright and N. Panchapakesan, *Educ. Psychol. Meas.* 29, 23 (1969); B. Wright and R. Mead, *CALFIT: Sample-Free Item Calibration with a Rasch Measurement Model* (Res. Memo. No. 18, Department of Education, Univ. of Chicago, 1975). In using this method, analyses included four blocks of two adjacent measurement points (1 and 2, 2 and 3, 3 and 4, 4 and 5). All test items applied to all children that were common to the two proximate measurement points were included for analysis. Those items that did not fit the theoretical (Rasch) model were not included for further analysis at either measurement point, and those that remained were exactly the same items at both points. Between measurement points 1 and 2 there were 126 common

items included for analysis; between 2 and 3, 105 items; between 3 and 4, 82 items; and between 4 and 5, 79 items. In no case were there any perfect scores or zero scores.

24. Let $M_w$ = total items after calibration at measurement occasion W; $C_{w,1,+1}$ = items common to both occasion W and occasion W + 1; $C_{w,1,-1}$ = items common to both occasion W and occasion W − 1. Since $C_{w,1,+1}$ and $C_{w,1,-1}$ are subsets of $M_w$ they estimate the same ability. However, a change in origin is necessary to equate the estimates because the computational program centers the scale in an arbitrary origin. Let $X_{w,1,+1}$ and $X_{w,1,-1}$ be the abilities estimated by using tests of length $C_{w,1,+1}$ and $C_{w,1,-1}$ respectively. Then:

$$X_{w,1,-1} = \beta 0 + \beta X_{w,1,+1} \qquad (1)$$

Since the abilities estimated are assumed to be item-free, then the slope in the regression will be equal to 1, and $\beta 0$ is the factor by which one ability is shifted to equate with the other. $X_{w,1,-1}$ and $X_{w,1,+1}$ are abilities estimated with one test at two different occasions (note that $C_{w,1,-1} = C_{w,1,+1}$); then by Eq. 1 it is seen that $X_{w,1,-1}$ and $X_{w,1,+1}$ are measuring the same latent trait. Because the scales have different origins, $X_{w,1,-1}$ is shifted by an amount $\beta 0$ to make them comparable.

25. It must be acknowledged here that with this method the interpretability of the data depends upon the comparability of units (ability scores) throughout the range of scores resulting from the Rasch analysis. Although difficult to prove, the argument for equal intervals in the data is strengthened by the fact that the increase in group means prior to treatment is essentially linear. Further discussion of this point may be found in H. Gomez, paper presented at the annual meeting of the American Educational Research Association, New York, 1977.

26. T. W. Anderson, in *Mathematical Methods in the Social Sciences*, K. J. Arrow, S. Karlin, P. Suppes, Eds. (Stanford Univ. Press, Stanford, Calif., 1960).

27. R. D. Bock, *Multivariate Statistical Methods in Behavioral Research* (McGraw-Hill, New York, 1975); in *Problems in Measuring Change*, C. W. Harris, Ed. (Univ. of Wisconsin Press, Madison, 1963), pp. 85–103.

28. Gain during treatment period is defined here as the mean value of a group at a measurement occasion minus the mean value of that group on the previous occasion. Thus the group T1 gains that form the baseline for this analysis are the following: treatment period 1 = .72; period 2 = 1.44; period 3 = 1.74.

29. C. Deutsch, in *Review of Child Development Research*, vol. 3, *Child Development and Social Policy*, B. M. Caldwell and H. N. Ricciuti, Eds. (Univ. of Chicago Press, Chicago, 1973).

30. L. M. Terman and M. A. Merrill, *Stanford-Binet Intelligence Scale, Form L-M* (Houghton, Mifflin, Boston, 1960), adapted for local use.

31. F. Horowitz and L. Paden, in *Review of Child Development Research*, B. M. Caldwell and H. N. Ricciuti, Eds. (Univ. of Chicago Press, Chicago, 1973), vol. 3, pp. 331–335; S. S. Baratz and J. C. Baratz, *Harv. Edu. Rev.* 40, 29 (1970); C. B. Cazden, *Merrill-Palmer Q.* 12, 185 (1966); *Curriculum in Early Childhood Education* (Bernard van Leer Foundation, The Hague, 1974).

32. Colombia has now begun to apply this concept of multiform, integrated attention to its preschool age children in a nationwide government program in both rural and urban areas. This is, among developing countries, a rarely encountered confluence of science and political decision, and the law creating this social action must be viewed as a very progressive one for Latin America. Careful documentation of the results

of the program could give additional evidence of the social validity of the scientific findings presented in this article, and could demonstrate the potential value of such programs in the other regions of the world.

33. Adapted from a procedure described by H. G. Birch and A. Lefford, in *Brain Damage in Children: The Biological and Social Aspects*, H. G. Birch, Ed. (Williams & Wilkins, Baltimore, 1964). Only the visual-haptic modality was measured.

34. The measure was constructed locally using some of the items and format found in C. Bereiter and S. Englemann, *Teaching Disadvantaged Children in the Preschool* (Prentice-Hall, Englewood Cliffs, N.J., 1969), pp. 74–75.

35. This is a locally modified version of an experimental scale designed by the Growth and Development Unit of the Instituto de Nutrición de Centro America y Panama, Guatemala.

36. G. Arthur, *A Point Scale of Performance* (Psychological Corp., New York, 1930). Verbal instructions were developed for the scale and the blocks were enlarged.

37. D. Wechsler, *WPPSI: Wechsler Preschool and Primary Scale of Intelligence* (Psychological Corp., New York, 1963).

38. At measurement points 3 and 4, this test is a combination of an adapted version of the arithmetic subscale of the WPPSI and items developed locally. At measurement point 5, the arithmetic test included locally constructed items and an adaptation of the subscale of the WISC-R (39).

39. D. Wechsler, *WISC-R: Wechsler Intelligence Scale for Children-Revised* (Psychological Corp., New York, 1974).

40. At measurement points 3 and 4 the mazes test was taken from the WPPSI and at point 5 from the WISC-R.

41. Taken from (39). The information items in some instances were rewritten because the content was unfamiliar and the order had to be changed when pilot work demonstrated item difficulty levels at variance with the original scale.

42. At measurement point 4 the test came from the WPPSI, at point 5 from the WISC-R.

43. At measurement point 4 this was from *WISC: Wechsler Intelligence Scale for Children* (Psychological Corp., New York, 1949); at point 5 the format used was that of the WISC-R.

44. At measurement point 4 this test was an adaptation from the similarities subscale of the WPPSI. At point 5 it was adapted from the WISC-R. Modifications had to be made similar to those described in (38).

45. B. Inhelder and J. Piaget, *The Early Growth of Logic in the Child* (Norton, New York, 1964), pp. 151–165. The development of a standardized format for application and scoring was done locally.

46. This research was supported by grants 700-0634 and 720-0418 of the Ford Foundation and grant 5R01HD07716-02 of the National Institute for Child Health and Human Development. Additional analyses were done under contract No. C-74-0115 of the National Institute of Education. Early financial support was also received from the Medical School of the Universidad del Valle in Cali and the former Council for Intersocietal Studies of Northwestern University, whose members, Lee Sechrest, Donald Campbell, and B. J. Chandler, have provided continual encouragement. Additional financial support from Colombian resources was provided by the Ministerio de Salud, the Ministerio de Educación, and the following private industries: Miles Laboratories de Colombia, Carvajal & Cia., Cementos del Valle, Cartón de Colombia, Colgate-Palmolive de Colombia, La Garantía, and Molinos Pampa Rita.

# PART VII
# MENTAL HEALTH

The articles in this section address different concerns in the evaluation of mental health services. Many evaluations have suggested that most forms of psychotherapy are not demonstrably effective with most kinds of clients under most conditions, and some studies have even indicated that some forms of psychotherapy might even be harmful to some clients. In the first paper presented here, Smith and Glass attempt to reverse the conventional wisdom. To do this, they present a statistical integration of nearly 400 evaluations of psychotherapy and counseling. Their reanalysis suggests to them that "the typical therapy client is better off than 75% of untreated individuals," and that no difference in effectiveness exists between various types of psychotherapy. The Smith and Glass article is important for its methodology and for substantive content. Not surprisingly, the critiques of the article suggest difficulties in both, and we have included here some of the rejoinders to Smith and Glass which appeared in the *American Psychologist*.

The final article in this section addresses a much different concern. Calsyn and Davidson examined the growing use of Goal Attainment Scaling (GAS) in the evaluation of mental health programs. Briefly, they conclude that while GAS can be a useful component in research design as part of the structure of dependent variables, it is unsuited as an evaluative device that substitutes for traditional sampling, experimental design, and measurement concerns. It is not clear whether the developers of GAS were interested in seeing their tool used as the sole means of evaluation. It is clear, however, that some evaluators have simply measured shifts in where clients stand on a GAS scale and have overinterpreted any resulting shifts.

# 41

# Meta-Analysis of Psychotherapy Outcome Studies

## Mary Lee Smith and Gene V Glass

ABSTRACT: *Results of nearly 400 controlled evaluations of psychotherapy and counseling were coded and integrated statistically. The findings provide convincing evidence of the efficacy of psychotherapy. On the average, the typical therapy client is better off than 75% of untreated individuals. Few important differences in effectiveness could be established among many quite different types of psychotherapy. More generally, virtually no difference in effectiveness was observed between the class of all behavioral therapies (systematic desensitization, behavior modification) and the nonbehavioral therapies (Rogerian, psychodynamic, rational-emotive, transactional analysis, etc.).*

Scholars and clinicians have argued bitterly for decades about the efficacy of psychotherapy and counseling. Michael Scriven proposed to the American Psychological Association's Ethics Committee that APA-member clinicians be required to present a card to prospective clients on which it would be explained that the procedure they were about to undergo had never been proven superior to a placebo ("Psychotherapy Caveat," 1974). Most academics have read little more than Eysenck's (1952, 1965) tendentious diatribes in which he claimed to prove that 75% of neurotics got better regardless of whether or not they were in therapy—a conclusion based on the interpretation of six controlled studies. The perception that research shows the inefficacy of psychotherapy has become part of conventional wisdom even within the profession. The following testimony was recently presented before the Colorado State Legislature:

Are they [the legislators] also aware of the relatively primitive state of the art of treatment outcome evaluation which is still, after fifty years, in kind of a virginal state? About all we've been able to prove is that a third of the people get better, a third of the people stay the same, and a third of the people get worse, irregardless of the treatment to which they are subjected. (Quoted by Ellis, 1977, p. 3)

Only close followers of the issue have read Bergin's (1971) astute dismantling of the Eysenck myth in his review of the findings of 23 controlled evaluations of therapy. Bergin found evidence that therapy is effective. Emrick (1975) reviewed 72 studies of the psychological and psychopharmacological treatment of alcoholism and concluded that evidence existed for the efficacy of therapy. Luborsky, Singer, and Luborsky (1975) reviewed about 40 controlled studies and found more evidence. Although these reviews were reassuring, two sources of doubt remained. First, the number of studies in which the effects of counseling and psychotherapy have been tested is closer to 400 than to 40. How representative the 40 are of the 400 is unknown. Second, in these reviews, the "voting method" was used; that is, the number of studies with statistically significant results in favor of one treatment or another was tallied. This method is too weak to answer many important questions and is biased in favor of large-sample studies.

The purpose of the present research has three parts: (1) to identify and collect all studies that tested the effects of counseling and psychotherapy; (2) to determine the magnitude of effect of the therapy in each study; and (3) to compare the effects of different types of therapy and relate the size of effect to the characteristics of the therapy (e.g., diagnosis of patient, training of therapist) and of the study. Meta-analysis, the integration of research through statistical analysis of the analyses of individual studies (Glass, 1976), was used to investigate the problem.

## Procedures

Standard search procedures were used to identify 1,000 documents: *Psychological Abstracts, Dissertation Abstracts*, and branching off of bibliographies of the documents themselves. Of those documents located, approximately 500 were selected for inclusion in the study, and 375 were fully analyzed. To be selected, a study had to have at least one ther-

From Mary Lee Smith and Gene V Glass, "Meta-Analysis of Psychotherapy Outcome Studies," 32 (9) *American Psychologist* 752-760 (September 1977). Copyright 1977 by the American Psychological Association.

apy treatment group compared to an untreated group or to a different therapy group. The rigor of the research design was not a selection criterion but was one of several features of the individual study to be related to the effect of the treatment in that study. The definition of psychotherapy used to select the studies was presented by Meltzoff and Kornreich (1970):

Psychotherapy is taken to mean the informed and planful application of techniques derived from established psychological principles, by persons qualified through training and experience to understand these principles and to apply these techniques with the intention of assisting individuals to modify such personal characteristics as feelings, values, attitudes, and behaviors which are judged by the therapist to be maladaptive or maladjustive. (p. 6)

Those studies in which the treatment was labeled "counseling" but whose methods fit the above definition were included. Drug therapies, hypnotherapy, bibliotherapy, occupational therapy, milieu therapy, and peer counseling were excluded. Sensitivity training, marathon encounter groups, consciousness-raising groups, and psychodrama were also excluded. Those studies that Bergin and Luborsky eliminated because they used "analogue" therapy were retained for the present research. Such studies have been designated analogue studies because therapy lasted only a few hours or the therapists were relatively untrained. Rather than arbitrarily eliminating large numbers of studies and losing potentially valuable information, it was deemed preferable to retain these studies and investigate the relationship between length of therapy, training of therapists, and other characteristics of the study and their measured effects. The arbitrary elimination of such analogue studies was based on an implicit assumption that they differ not only in their methods but also in their effects and how those effects are achieved. Considering methods, analogue studies fade imperceptibly into "real" therapy, since the latter is often short term, or practiced by relative novices, etc. Furthermore, the magnitude of effects and their relationships with other variables are empirical questions, not to be assumed out of existence. Dissertations and fugitive documents were likewise retained, and the

The research reported here was supported by a grant from the Spencer Foundation, Chicago, Illinois. This paper draws in part from the presidential address of the second author to the American Educational Research Association, San Francisco, April 21, 1976.

Requests for reprints should be sent to Gene V Glass, Laboratory of Educational Research, University of Colorado, Boulder, Colorado 80302.

measured effects of the studies compared according to the source of the studies.

The most important feature of an outcome study was the magnitude of the effect of therapy. The definition of the magnitude of effect—or "*effect size*"—was the *mean difference between the treated and control subjects divided by the standard deviation of the control group*, that is, $ES = (\bar{X}_T - \bar{X}_C)/s_C$. Thus, an "effect size" of $+1$ indicates that a person at the mean of the control group would be expected to rise to the 84th percentile of the control group after treatment.

The effect size was calculated on any outcome variable the researcher chose to measure. In many cases, one study yielded more than one effect size, since effects might be measured at more than one time after treatment or on more than one different type of outcome variable. The effect-size measures represent different types of outcomes: self-esteem, anxiety, work/school achievement, physiological stress, etc. Mixing different outcomes together is defensible. First, it is clear that all outcome measures are more or less related to "well-being" and so at a general level are comparable. Second, it is easy to imagine a Senator conducting hearings on the NIMH appropriations or a college president deciding whether to continue funding the counseling center asking, "What kind of effect does therapy produce—on anything?" Third, each primary researcher made value judgments concerning the definition and direction of positive therapeutic effects for the particular clients he or she studied. It is reasonable to adopt these value judgments and aggregate them in the present study. Fourth, since all effect sizes are identified by type of outcome, the magnitude of effect can be compared across type of outcome to determine whether therapy has greater effect on anxiety, for example, than it does on self-esteem.

Calculating effect sizes was straightforward when means and standard deviations were reported. Although this information is thought to be fundamental in reporting research, it was often overlooked by authors and editors. When means and standard deviations were not reported, effect sizes were obtained by the solution of equations from $t$ and $F$ ratios or other inferential test statistics. Probit transformations were used to convert to effect sizes the percentages of patients who improved (Glass, in press). Original data were requested from several authors when effect sizes could not be derived from any reported information. In two instances, effect sizes were impossible to reconstruct: (a) nonparametric statistics irretrievably disguise effect sizes, and (b) the reporting of no data except the alpha level at which a mean difference was significant gives no clue other than that the standardized mean difference must exceed some known value.

Eight hundred thirty-three effect sizes were computed from 375 studies, several studies yielding effects on more than one type of outcome or at more than one time after therapy. Including more than one effect size for each study perhaps introduces dependence in the errors and violates some assumptions of inferential statistics. However, the loss of information that would have resulted from averaging effects across types of outcome or at different follow-up points was too great a price to pay for statistical purity.

The effect sizes of the separate studies became the "dependent variable" in the meta-analysis. The "independent variables" were 16 features of the study described or measured in the following ways:

1. The type of therapy employed, for example, psychodynamic, client centered, rational-emotive, behavior modification, etc. There were 10 types in all; each will be mentioned in the Results section.
2. The duration of therapy in hours.
3. Whether it was group or individual therapy.
4. The number of years' experience of the therapist.
5. Whether clients were neurotics or psychotics.
6. The age of the clients.
7. The IQ of the clients.
8. The source of the subjects—whether solicited for the study, committed to an institution, or sought treatment themselves.
9. Whether the therapists were trained in education, psychology, or psychiatry.
10. The social and ethnic similarity of therapists and clients.
11. The type of outcome measure taken.
12. The number of months after therapy that the outcomes were measured.
13. The reactivity or "fakeability" of the outcome measure.
14. The date of publication of the study.
15. The form of publication.
16. The internal validity of the research design.

Definitions and conventions were developed to increase the reliability of measurement of the features of the studies and to assist the authors in estimating the data when they were not reported. The more important conventions appear in Table 1. Variables not mentioned in Table 1 were measured in fairly obvious ways. The reliability of measurement was determined by comparing the codings of 20 studies by the two authors and four assistants. Agreement exceeded 90% across all categories.[1]

---

[1] The values assigned to the features of the studies, the effect sizes, and all procedures are available in Glass, Smith, and Miller (Note 1).

Analysis of the data comprised four parts: (1) descriptive statistics for the body of data as a whole; (2) descriptive statistics for the comparison of therapy types and outcome types; (3) descriptive statistics for a subset of studies in which behavioral and nonbehavioral therapies were compared *in the same study;* and (4) regression analyses in which effect sizes were regressed onto variables descriptive of the study.

## Findings

### DATA FROM ALL EXPERIMENTS

Figure 1 contains the findings at the highest level of aggregation. The two curves depict the average treated and untreated groups of clients across 375 studies, 833 effect-size measures, representing an evaluation of approximately 25,000 control and experimental subjects each. On the average, clients 22 years of age received 17 hours of therapy from therapists with about $3\frac{1}{2}$ years of experience and were measured on the outcome variables about $3\frac{3}{4}$ months after the therapy.

For ease of representation, the figure is drawn in the form of two normal distributions. No conclusion about the distributions of the scores within studies is intended. In most studies, no information was given about the shape of an individual's scores within treated and untreated groups. We suspect that normality has as much justification as any other form.

The average study showed a .68 standard deviation superiority of the treated group over the control group. Thus, the average client receiving therapy was better off than 75% of the untreated controls. Ironically, the 75% figure that Eysenck used repeatedly to embarrass psychotherapy ap-

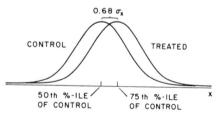

AVE. EFFECT SIZE: $0.68\ \sigma_x$
STD. DEV. OF EFFECT SIZE: $0.67\ \sigma_x$

Figure 1. Effect of therapy on any outcome. (Data based on 375 studies; 833 data points.)

TABLE 1: *Conventions for Measurement of the Features of Studies*

| Study feature | Value | Study feature | Value |
|---|---|---|---|
| Experience of therapist (when not given) | Lay counselor (0 years) MA candidate (1 year) MA counselor (2 years) PhD candidate or psychiatric resident (3 years) PhD therapist (4 years) Well-known PhD or psychiatrist (5 years) | Type of outcome measure (*continued*) | Work/school achievement: grade point average, job supervisor ratings, promotions. Personality traits: MMPI or other trait inventories, projective test results. Social behavior: dating, classroom discipline, public speaking, information-seeking behavior, sociometrics. Emotional-somatic disorder: frigidity, impotence. Physiological stress: galvanic skin response, Palmer Sweat Index, blood pressure, heart rate. |
| Diagnosis of client (neurotic or psychotic) | Neurotic unless symptoms or labels clearly indicate otherwise. | | |
| IQ of client (low, average, high) | Average unless identified as otherwise by diagnostic labels (e.g., mentally retarded) or institutional affiliation (college attendance). | Reactivity of measurement | 1 (low): Physiological measures; grade point average |
| | | | 2  Projective device (blind); discharge from hospital (blind) |
| Source of subjects | Clients solicited for purpose of the study. Clients committed to institution, hence to therapy. Clients recognized existence of problem and sought treatment. | | 3  Standardized measures of traits (MMPI, Rotter) |
| | | | 4  Experimenter-constructed questionnaires; client's self-report to experimenter; discharge (nonblind); behavior in presence of therapist |
| Similarity of therapist and client ("very similar" to "very dissimilar") | College students: very similar Neurotic adults: moderately similar Juveniles, minorities: moderately dissimilar Hospitalized, chronic adults, disturbed children, prisoners: very dissimilar | | 5 (high): Therapist rating; projective device (nonblind) |
| | | Form of publication | Journal Book Thesis Unpublished document |
| Type of outcome measure | Fear, anxiety: Spielberger & Cattell anxiety measures, behavioral approach tests. Self-esteem: inventories, self-ideal correlations, ratings by self and others. Adjustment: adjustment scales, improvement ratings, rehospitalization, time out of hospital, sobriety, symptomatic complaints, disruptive behavior. | Internal validity (high, medium, low) | High: Randomization, low mortality Medium: More than one threat to internal validity Low: No matching of pretest information to equate groups |

pears in a slightly different context as the most defensible figure on the efficacy of therapy: The therapies represented by the available outcome evaluations move the average client from the 50th to the 75th percentile.

The standard deviation of the effect sizes is .67. Their skewness is +.99. Only 12% of the 833

effect-size measures from the 375 studies were negative. If therapies of any type were ineffective and design and measurement flaws were immaterial, one would expect half the effect-size measures to be negative.

The 833 effect-size measures were classified into 10 categories descriptive of the type of outcome being assessed, for example, fear and anxiety reduction, self-esteem, adjustment (freedom from debilitating symptoms), achievement in school or on the job, social relations, emotional-somatic problems, physiological stress measures, etc. Effect-size measures for four outcome categories are presented in Table 2.

Two hundred sixty-one effect sizes from over 100 studies average about 1 standard deviation on measures of fear and anxiety reduction. Thus, the average treated client is better off than 83% of those untreated with respect to the alleviation of fear and anxiety. The improvement in self-esteem is nearly as large. The effect sizes average .9 of a standard deviation. Improvement on variables in the "adjustment" outcome class averages considerably less, roughly .6 of a standard deviation. These outcome variables are measures of personal functioning and frequently involve indices of hospitalization or incarceration for psychotic, alcoholic, or criminal episodes. The average effect size for school or work achievement—most frequently "grade point average"—is smallest of the four outcome classes.

The studies in the four outcome measure categories are not comparable in terms of type of therapy, duration, experience of therapists, number of months posttherapy at which outcomes were measured, etc. Nonetheless, the findings in Table 2 are fairly consistent with expectations and give the credible impression that fear and self-esteem are more susceptible to change in therapy than are the relatively more serious behaviors grouped under the categories "adjustment" and "achievement."

TABLE 2: *Effects of Therapy on Four Types of Outcome Measure*

| Type of outcome | Average effect size | No. of effect sizes | Standard error of mean effect size | Mdn treated person's percentile status in control group |
|---|---|---|---|---|
| Fear-anxiety reduction | .97 | 261 | .15 | 83 |
| Self-esteem | .90 | 53 | .13 | 82 |
| Adjustment | .56 | 229 | .05 | 71 |
| School/work achievement | .31 | 145 | .03 | 62 |

* The standard errors of the mean are calculated by dividing the standard deviation of the effect sizes (not reported) by the square root of the number of them. This method, based on the assumption of independence known to be false, gives a lower bound to the standard errors (Tukey, Note 2). Inferential techniques employing Tukey's jackknife method which take the nonindependence into account are examined in Glass (in press).

TABLE 3: *Effects of Ten Types of Therapy on Any Outcome Measure*

| Type of therapy | Average effect size | No. of effect sizes | Standard error of mean effect size | Mdn treated person's percentile status in control group |
|---|---|---|---|---|
| Psychodynamic | .59 | 96 | .05 | 72 |
| Adlerian | .71 | 16 | .19 | 76 |
| Eclectic | .48 | 70 | .07 | 68 |
| Transactional analysis | .58 | 25 | .19 | 72 |
| Rational-emotive | .77 | 35 | .13 | 78 |
| Gestalt | .26 | 8 | .09 | 60 |
| Client-centered | .63 | 94 | .08 | 74 |
| Systematic desensitization | .91 | 223 | .05 | 82 |
| Implosion | .64 | 45 | .09 | 74 |
| Behavior modification | .76 | 132 | .06 | 78 |

Table 3 presents the average effect sizes for 10 types of therapy. Nearly 100 effect-size measures arising from evaluations of psychodynamic therapy, that is, Freudianlike therapy but *not* psychoanalysis, average approximately .6 of a standard deviation. Studies of Adlerian therapy show an average of .7 sigma, but only 16 effect sizes were found. Eclectic therapies, that is, verbal, cognitive, nonbehavioral therapies more similar to psychodynamic therapies than any other type, gave a mean effect size of about .5 of a standard deviation. Although the number of controlled evaluations of Berne's transactional analysis was rather small, it gave a respectable average effect size of .6 sigma, the same as psychodynamic therapies. Albert Ellis's rational-emotive therapy, with a mean effect size of nearly .8 of a standard deviation, finished second among all 10 therapy types. The Gestalt therapies were relatively untested, but 8 studies showed 16 effect sizes averaging only .25 of a standard deviation. Rogerian client-centered therapy showed a .6 sigma effect size averaged across about 60 studies. The average of over 200 effect-size measures from approximately 100 studies of systematic desensitization therapy was .9 sigma, the largest average effect size of all therapy types. Implosive therapy showed a mean effect size of .64 of a standard deviation, about equal to that for Rogerian and psychodynamic therapies. Significantly, the average effect size for implosive therapy is markedly lower than that for systematic desensitization, which was usually evaluated in studies using similar kinds of clients with similar problems—principally, simple phobias. The final therapy depicted in Table 3 is Skinnerian behavior modification, which showed a .75 sigma effect size.

Hay's $\omega^2$, which relates the categorical variable "type of therapy" to the quantitative variable "effect size," has the value of .10 for the data in Table 3. Thus, these 10 therapy types account for 10% of the variance in the effect size that studies produce.

The types of therapy depicted in Table 3 were clearly not equated for duration, severity of problem, type of outcome, etc. Nonetheless, the differences in average effect sizes are interesting and interpretable. There is probably a tendency for researchers to evaluate the therapy they like best and to pick clients, circumstances, and outcome measures which show that therapy in the best light. Even so, major differences among the therapies appear. Implosive therapy is demonstrably inferior to systematic desensitization. Behavior modification shows the same mean effect size as rational-emotive therapy.

EFFECTS OF CLASSES OF THERAPY

To compare the effect of therapy type after equating for duration of therapy, diagnosis of client, type of outcome, etc., it was necessary to move to a coarser level of analysis in which data could be grouped into more stable composites. The problem was to group the 10 types of therapy into classes, so that effect sizes could be compared among more general types of therapy. Methods of multidimensional scaling were used to derive a structure from the perceptions of similarities among the 10 therapies by a group of 25 clinicians and counselors. All of the judges in this scaling study were enrolled in a graduate-level seminar. For five weeks, the theory and techniques of the 10 therapies were studied and discussed. Then, each judge performed a multidimensional rank ordering of the therapies, judging similarity among them on whatever basis he or she chose, articulated or unarticulated, conscious or unconscious. The results of the Shepard-Kruskal multidimensional scaling analysis appear as Figure 2.

In Figure 2 one clearly sees four classes of therapies: the ego therapies (transactional analysis and rational-emotive therapy) in front; the three dynamic therapies low, in the background; the behavioral triad, upper right; and the pair of "humanistic" therapies, Gestalt and Rogerian. The average effect sizes among the four classes of

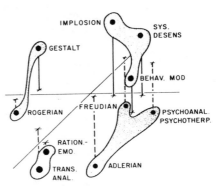

Figure 2. Multidimensional scaling of 10 therapies by 25 clinicians and counselors.

therapies have been compared, but the findings are not reported here. Instead, a higher level of aggregation of the therapies, called "superclasses," was studied. The first superclass was formed from those therapies above the horizontal plane in Figure 2, with the exception of Gestalt therapy for which there was an inadequate number of studies. This superclass was then identical with the group of behavioral therapies: implosion, systematic desensitization, and behavior modification. The second superclass comprises the six therapies below the horizontal plane in Figure 2 and is termed the *nonbehavioral superclass*, a composite of psychoanalytic psychotherapy, Adlerian, Rogerian, rational-emotive, eclectic therapy, and transactional analysis.

Figure 3 represents the mean effect sizes for studies classified by the two superclasses. On the average, approximately 200 evaluations of behavioral therapies showed a mean effect of about $.8\sigma_x$, standard error of .03, over the control group. Approximately 170 evaluations of nonbehavioral studies gave a mean effect size of $.6\sigma_x$, standard error of .04. This small difference ($.2\sigma_x$) between the outcomes of behavioral and nonbehavioral therapies must be considered in light of the circumstances under which these studies were conducted. The evaluators of behavioral superclass therapies waited an average of 2 months after the therapy to measure its effects, whereas the postassessment of the nonbehavioral therapies was made in the vicinity of 5 months, on the average. Furthermore, the reactivity or susceptibility to bias of the outcome measures was higher for the behavioral super-

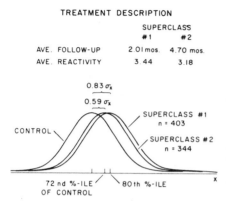

Figure 3. Effect of Superclass #1 (behavioral) and Superclass #2 (nonbehavioral).

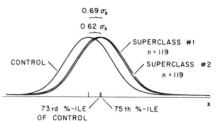

Figure 4. Effect of Superclass #1 (behavioral) and Superclass #2 (nonbehavioral). (Data drawn only from experiments in which Superclass #1 and Superclass #2 were simultaneously compared with control.)

class than for the nonbehavioral superclass; that is, the behavioral researchers showed a slightly greater tendency to rely on more subjective outcome measures. These differences lead one to suspect that the $.2\sigma_x$ difference between the behavioral and nonbehavioral superclasses is somewhat exaggerated in favor of the behavioral superclass. Exactly how much the difference ought to be reduced is a question that can be approached in at least two ways: (a) examine the behavioral versus nonbehavioral difference for only those studies in which one therapy from each superclass was represented, since for those studies the experimental circumstances will be equivalent; (2) regress "effect size" onto variables descriptive of the study and correct statistically for differences in circumstances between behavioral and nonbehavioral studies.

Figure 4 represents 120 effect-size measures derived from those studies, approximately 50 in number, in which a behavioral therapy and nonbehavioral therapy were compared simultaneously with an untreated control. Hence, for these studies, the collective behavioral and nonbehavioral therapies are equivalent with respect to all important features of the experimental setting, namely, experience of the therapists, nature of the clients' problems, duration of therapy, type of outcome measure, months after therapy for measuring the outcomes, etc.

The results are provocative. The $.2\sigma_x$ "uncontrolled" difference in Figure 3 has shrunk to a $.07\sigma_x$ difference in average effect size. The standard error of the mean of the 119 different scores (behavioral effect size minus nonbehavioral effect size

in each study) is $.66/\sqrt{119} = .06$. The behavioral and nonbehavioral therapies show about the same average effect.

The second approach to correcting for measurable differences between behavioral and nonbehavioral therapies is statistical adjustment by regression analysis. By this method, it is possible to quantify and study the natural covariation among the principal outcome variable of studies and the many variables descriptive of the context of the studies.

Eleven features of each study were correlated with the effect size the study produced (Table 4). For example, the correlation between the duration

TABLE 4: *Correlations of Several Descriptive Variables with Effect Size*

| Variable | Correlation with effect size |
|---|---|
| Organization (1 = individual; 2 = group) | −.07 |
| Duration of therapy (in hours) | −.02 |
| Years' experience of therapists | −.01 |
| Diagnosis of clients (1 = psychotic; 2 = neurotic) | .02 |
| IQ of clients (1 = low; 2 = medium; 3 = high) | .15** |
| Age of clients | .02 |
| Similarity of therapists and clients (1 = very similar; ... ; 4 = very dissimilar) | −.19** |
| Internal validity of study (1 = high; 2 = medium; 3 = low) | −.09* |
| Date of publication | .09* |
| "Reactivity" of outcome measure (1 = low; ... ; 5 = high) | .30** |
| No. of months posttherapy for follow-up | −.10* |

\* $p < .05$.
\*\* $p < .01$.

TABLE 5: *Regression Analyses Within Therapies*

| | Unstandardized regression coefficients | | |
|---|---|---|---|
| Independent variable | Psychodynamic ($n = 94$) | Systematic desensitization ($n = 212$) | Behavior modification ($n = 129$) |
| Diagnosis (1 = psychotic; 2 = neurotic) | .174 | −.193 | .041 |
| Intelligence (1 = low; ... ; 3 = high) | −.114 | .201 | .201 |
| Transformed age[a] | .002 | −.002 | .002 |
| Experience of Therapist × Neurotic | −.011 | −.034 | −.018 |
| Experience of Therapist × Psychotic | −.015 | .004 | −.033 |
| Clients self-presented | −.111 | .287 | −.015 |
| Clients solicited | .182 | .088 | −.163 |
| Organization (1 = individual; 2 = group) | .108 | −.086 | −.276 |
| Transformed months posttherapy[b] | −.031 | −.047 | .007 |
| Transformed reactivity of measure[c] | .003 | .025 | .021 |
| Additive constant | .757 | .489 | .453 |
| Multiple $R$ | .423 | .512 | .509 |
| $\sigma_e$ | .173 | .386 | .340 |

[a] Transformed age = $(Age - 25)(|Age - 25|)^{\frac{1}{2}}$.
[b] Transformed months posttherapy = $(No. months)^{\frac{1}{2}}$.
[c] Transformed reactivity of measure = $(Reactivity)^{2.75}$.

of the therapy in hours and the effect size of the study is nearly zero, −.02. The correlations are generally low, although several are reliably nonzero. Some of the more interesting correlations show a positive relationship between an estimate of the intelligence of the group of clients and the effect of therapy, and a somewhat larger correlation indicating that therapists who resemble their clients in ethnic group, age, and social level get better results. The effect sizes diminish across time after therapy as shown by the last correlation in Table 4, a correlation of −.10 which is closer to −.20 when the curvilinearity of the relationship is taken into account. The largest correlation is with the "reactivity" or subjectivity of the outcome measure.

The multiple correlation of these variables with effect size is about .50. Thus, 25% of the variance in the results of studies can be reduced by specification of independent variable values. In several important subsets of the data not reported here, the multiple correlations are over .70, which indicates that in some instances it is possible to reduce more than half of the variability in study findings by regressing the outcome effect onto contextual variables of the study.

The results of three separate multiple regression analyses appear in Table 5. Multiple regressions were performed within each of three types of therapy: psychodynamic, systematic desensitization, and behavior modification. Relatively complex forms of the independent variables were used to account for interactions and nonlinear relationships.

For example, years' experience of the therapist bore a slight curvilinear relationship with outcome, probably because more experienced therapists worked with more seriously ill clients. This situation was accommodated by entering, as an independent variable, "therapist experience" in interaction with "diagnosis of the client." Age of client and follow-up date were slightly curvilinearly related to outcome in ways most directly handled by changing exponents. These regression equations allow estimation of the effect size a study shows when undertaken with a certain type of client, with a therapist of a certain level of experience, etc. By setting the independent variables at a particular set of values, one can estimate what a study of that type would reveal under each of the three types of therapy. Thus, a statistically controlled comparison of the effects of psychodynamic, systematic desensitization, and behavior modification therapies can be obtained in this case. The three regression equations are clearly not homogeneous; hence, one therapy might be superior under one set of circumstances and a different therapy superior under others. A full description of the nature of this interaction is elusive, though one can illustrate it at various particularly interesting points.

In Figure 5, estimates are made of the effect sizes that would be shown for studies in which simple phobias of high-intelligence subjects, 20 years of age, are treated by a therapist with 2 years' experience and evaluated immediately after therapy with highly subjective outcome measures.

ESTIMATED EFFECT SIZES

| | |
|---|---|
| PSYCHODYNAMIC | 0.919 |
| SYSTEMATIC DESENSITIZATION | 1.049 |
| BEHAVIORAL MODIFICATION | 1.119 |

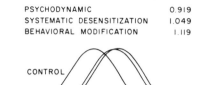

x

Figure 5. Three within-therapy regression equations set to describe a prototypic therapy client (phobic) and therapy situation.

This verbal description of circumstances can be translated into quantitative values for the independent variables in Table 5 and substituted into each of the three regression equations. In this instance, the two behavioral therapies show effects superior to the psychodynamic therapy.

In Figure 6, a second prototypical psychotherapy client and situation are captured in the independent variable values, and the effects of the three types of therapy are estimated. For the typical 30-year-old neurotic of average IQ seen in circumstances like those that prevail in mental health clinics (individual therapy by a therapist with 5 years' experience), behavior modification is estimated to be superior to psychodynamic therapy, which is in turn superior to systematic desensitization at the 6-month follow-up point.

Besides illuminating the relationships in the data, the quantitative techniques described here can give direction to future research. By fitting regression equations to the relationship between effect size and the independent variables descriptive of the studies

ESTIMATED EFFECT SIZES

| | |
|---|---|
| PSYCHODYNAMIC | 0.643 |
| SYSTEMATIC DESENSITIZATION | 0.516 |
| BEHAVIORAL MODIFICATION | 0.847 |

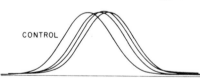

x

Figure 6. Three within-therapy regression equations set to describe a prototypic therapy client (neurotic) and therapy situation.

and then by placing confidence regions around these hyperplanes, the regions where the input–output relationships are most poorly determined can be identified. By concentrating new studies in these regions, one can avoid the accumulation of redundant studies of convenience that overelaborate small areas.

## Conclusions

The results of research demonstrate the beneficial effects of counseling and psychotherapy. Despite volumes devoted to the theoretical differences among different schools of psychotherapy, the results of research demonstrate negligible differences in the effects produced by different therapy types. Unconditional judgments of superiority of one type or another of psychotherapy, and all that these claims imply about treatment and training policy, are unjustified. Scholars and clinicians are in the rather embarrassing position of knowing less than has been proven, because knowledge, atomized and sprayed across a vast landscape of journals, books, and reports, has not been accessible. Extracting knowledge from accumulated studies is a complex and important methodological problem which deserves further attention.

### REFERENCE NOTES

1. Glass, G. V, Smith, M. L., & Miller, T. I. *The benefits of psychotherapy.* Book in preparation, 1977.
2. Tukey, J. W. Personal communication, November 15, 1976.

### REFERENCES

Bergin, A. E. The evaluation of therapeutic outcomes. In A. E. Bergin & S. L. Garfield (Eds.), *Handbook of psychotherapy and behavior change.* New York: Wiley, 1971.

Ellis, R. H. Letters. *Colorado Psychological Association Newsletter,* April 1977, p. 3.

Emrick, C. D. A review of psychologically oriented treatment of alcoholism. *Journal of Studies on Alcohol,* 1975, *36*, 88–108.

Eysenck, H. J. The effects of psychotherapy: An evaluation. *Journal of Consulting Psychology,* 1952, *16*, 319–324.

Eysenck, H. J. The effects of psychotherapy. *Journal of Psychology,* 1965, *1*, 97–118.

Glass, G. V. Primary, secondary, and meta-analysis of research. *The Educational Researcher,* 1976, *10*, 3–8.

Glass, G. V. Integrating findings: The meta-analysis of research. *Review of Research in Education,* in press.

Luborsky, L., Singer, B., & Luborsky, L. Comparative studies of psychotherapies. *Archives of General Psychiatry,* 1975, *32*, 995–1008.

Meltzoff, J., & Kornreich, M. *Research in psychotherapy.* New York: Atherton, 1970.

Psychotherapy caveat. *APA Monitor,* December 1974, p. 7.

# 42

# Overly Broad Categories Obscure Important Differences Between Therapies

## *Susan Presby*

The methodological and statistical approach taken by Smith and Glass (September 1977) in doing a meta-analysis of psychotherapy outcome studies is impressive in that it enables the researcher to extract information not available through the analysis of individual studies. I would like to note, however, the distortions that emerge when the types of therapy under study are organized into two "superclasses" of behavioral and nonbehavioral therapies. These "superclasses" ignore important differences among the nonbehavioral therapies, for example, the superior effects of rational-emotive therapy (RET) as compared to the others in that class. These differences are cancelled in the use of very broad categories, which leads to the erroneous conclusion that research results indicate negligible differences among outcomes of different therapies.

Smith and Glass refer to an analysis using four classes of therapies rather than two, but they do not report results. Knowledge of these results would be useful in determining whether four classes, as opposed to two, maintain the essential findings based on the original data.

Of interest, too, would be an articulation of the criteria used by the judges who assessed similarities among therapies for the purpose of categorizing them. The placement of RET closer to psychodynamic than to behavioral therapies indicates that the behavioral aspects of RET were given small consideration. Yet these behavioral aspects are an important component (Ellis & Harper, 1975) and merit attention when the theory and techniques of RET are delineated.

Due to the recent emergence of the theory and practice of cognitive-behavior therapy, of which RET was a forerunner and is an example (Beck, 1976; Ellis, 1977; Lazarus, 1976; Mahoney, 1974; Mahoney, 1977; Meichenbaum, 1977), one can expect that future analyses of outcome studies will include more studies of this therapeutic approach. In view of the distortions that occur with imprecise categorization, as noted above, it would seem important for psychologists to clearly delineate cognitive-behavior therapies and to begin to focus on them as a distinct category to be compared to such other traditional categories as psychodynamic, client-centered, and behavior therapies.

In sum, it is hoped that the approach taken by Smith and Glass will receive further attention and that, in addition, greater attention will be paid to the delineation of the characteristics of specific therapies and to the effects of the categorization of these therapies into broader classes for the purposes of analysis.

## REFERENCES

Beck, A. T. *Cognitive therapy and the emotional disorders.* New York: International Universities Press, 1976.

Ellis, A. Rational-emotive therapy: Research data that supports the clinical and personality hypotheses of RET and other modes of cognitive-behavior therapy. *The Counseling Psychologist,* 1977, *7*, 2–42.

Ellis, A., & Harper, R. A. *A new guide to rational living.* North Hollywood, Calif.: Wilshire, 1975.

Lazarus, A. A. *Multimodal therapy.* New York: Springer, 1976.

Mahoney, M. J. *Cognition and behavior modification.* Cambridge, Mass.: Ballinger, 1974.

Mahoney, M. J. Reflections on the cognitive-learning trend in psychotherapy. *American Psychologist,* 1977, *32,* 5–13.

Meichenbaum, D. *Cognitive behavior modification.* New York: Plenum, 1977.

Smith, M. L., & Glass, G. V. Meta-analysis of psychotherapy outcome studies. *American Psychologist,* 1977, *32,* 752–760.

# 43

# Meta-Analysis—A Mixed Meta-Phor?

## Philip S. Gallo, Jr.

Smith and Glass (September 1977) have presented some conclusions to readers of the *American Psychologist,* which, if justified, have great import for the field of clinical psychology. Utilizing some unique and interesting data-analysis techniques, the authors conclude, "The results of research demonstrate the beneficial effects of therapy" (p. 760). They further conclude, "Despite volumes devoted to the theoretical differences among different schools of psychotherapy, the results of research demonstrate negligible differences in the effects produced by different therapy types" (p. 760). These conclusions must have been met with mixed emotions on the part of clinical psychologists, who would certainly be pleased to find evidence of the effectiveness of therapy while being dismayed to find that their particular type of therapy was no more effective than competing types. However, they can emit a collective sigh of relief, or regret, as the case may be, since it can rather easily be shown that neither conclusion is necessarily warranted from the data presented.

It is possible to attack the conclusions on methodological grounds, pointing out that many of the cited studies did not use appropriate control groups to rule out placebo effects, that "shrinkage" effects can occur in the estimation of population means, that the underlying assumptions of their "meta-analysis" technique are not justified, etc. No matter how plausible such arguments may be, they are never wholly convincing, and it is my opinion that a much more damaging case can be made from a much simpler line of argument. Essentially, that argu-

ment has to do with the fact that somewhat different analysis techniques were used to draw the two different conclusions, and that if the same analysis technique were used, one might come up with very different conclusions.

The conclusion that therapy is beneficial is based on the technique that the authors dub "meta-analysis." Essentially, this technique consists of deriving a $Z$ score for the effect of some treatment by subtracting the mean score of a control group from the mean score of a treated group, and dividing the resulting difference by the standard deviation of the control group. Applying this method to 833 comparisons of psychotherapy and control groups, the authors generate a psychotherapy group mean of .68. Since the technique automatically sets the control group mean equal to zero, and the control group standard deviation equal to one, it can be seen that the typical (mean) therapy patient exceeds the control group mean by .68 standard-deviation units. The authors conclude that the typical psychotherapy patient would fall at the 75th percentile of untreated control group patients, and hence would exceed the adjustment score (on whatever dependent measure was being used) of 75% of control group patients.

The conclusion that differences among therapies are negligible is based upon a number of different types of analyses, including an overall analysis of all 10 identified analysis techniques, combining analysis techniques into "superclasses," and regressing effect sizes over various descriptive variables that characterized the therapy setting. Of par-

ticular interest is the analysis of all 10 therapy types, which was performed by calculating $\omega^2$ for the effect of the different types. The obtained value of $\omega^2$ is .10, indicating that 10% of the variance in the treated patients' level of adjustment could be attributed to the differential effects of different therapies.

Given that the differential effects of different therapies account for only 10% of the variance in the adjustment scores of treated patients, it would be instructive to know how much of the variance in the total subject population can be attributed to the effects of psychotherapy in general. Fortunately, Smith and Glass have provided us with sufficient information to perform such an analysis. The control group has a mean of zero and a standard deviation of one. The experimental group has a mean of $+.68$ and an unknown standard deviation. For the sake of calculational simplicity, we shall set the standard deviation of the experimental group also equal to one and assume that each distribution contains 833 data points.[1] We would thus have an estimate of $MS_e$ that would be equal to one.

Working backwards from $MS_e$, an entire $F$ table can be reconstructed

---

[1] Neither of these assumptions is in any way critical to the eventual outcome of the procedure to be described. Assuming that there are only 833 data points total will change the obtained outcome by $-.0057$. Assuming the variance of the treatment group is twice that of the control group will change the outcome by $-.0319$. Assuming the variance of the treatment group is half that of the control group will change the outcome by $+.0298$.

From Philip S. Gallo, Jr., "Meta-Analysis—A Mixed Meta-Phor?" 33 (5) *American Psychologist* 515-517 (May 1978). Copyright 1978 by the American Psychological Association.

from the data. The obtained $F$ ratio would have a value of 192.59, with $df$ of 1 and 1,664, certainly significant beyond any level one would care to name. Having obtained an $F$ ratio, the appropriate terms could be plugged in to the formula for $\omega^2$. The resulting value of $\omega^2$ would be .1031, which if rounded would reduce to .10. Thus, 10% of the total variance in the adjustment scores of both treated and control patients could be accounted for by the effects of psychotherapy.

When put into the same units of analysis, namely, the percentage of variance in the dependent variable that can be accounted for by the independent variable, we can see that the size of the effect of psychotherapy in general is of *exactly* the same size as is the differential effect of different therapies, at least when they are not combined or equated on the different descriptive variables. Unfortunately for Smith and Glass's argument, the same 10% of variance accounted for cannot be adduced as evidence for the beneficial effect of psychotherapy on the one hand and as evidence for the lack of a differential effect on the other hand.

Given the reanalysis of the data that I have presented, the appropriate conclusions are as follows: (a) Psychotherapy has a real, measurable, and quite weak effect upon the adjustment scores that constitute the dependent measure, and (b) different types of psychotherapy have a real, measurable, and quite weak effect upon the adjustment scores that constitute the dependent measure, and this effect becomes even weaker when therapy types are aggregated into superclasses and relevant variables are equated.

Although accurate, those conclusions beg the real issue. As Smith and Glass themselves tend to imply, the real issue is one of cost-efficiency. Their examples cite senators pondering NIMH appropriations and college presidents deciding whether to continue funding for counseling centers. They are certainly to be commended for attempting to make their case on the basis of the size of the effects obtained, rather than merely lining up hundreds of significant studies for and against, or, as they have so aptly put it, using the "voting method." Once one abandons a knee-jerk reliance on "significance" as the pivotal

tool for decision making, one is drawn inexorably into a cost-efficiency analysis. Smith and Glass inform us that their average patient was involved in 17 hours of psychotherapy. Assuming a $30/hour average rate, the typical patient paid $510 for therapy. It might be argued that at least a portion of patients received their therapy "free," but there is really no such thing as "free" psychotherapy. If the patient doesn't pay for it, then we all do, with tax dollars, contributions to charitable organizations, etc. The real question becomes, did these patients receive value for their 17-hour, $510 investment?

Before I attempt to answer that question, let us examine two hypothetical situations that have the same effect size as that of psychotherapy, that is, an effect that accounts for 10% of the variance and hence raises the average treated individual .68 of a standard deviation above the mean of the untreated population.

In Example 1, assume that 40-year-olds alive today can look forward to a mean life expectancy of 70 years, with a standard deviation of 10 years. Assume furthermore, that a treatment has been developed which, after 17 one-hour visits and an investment of $510, will raise the average person's life expectancy by .68 standard deviations over untreated individuals—in other words, it would increase life expectancy by 6.8 years. Would you pay $510 and give up 17 hours of your time to increase your life expectancy by an average of 6.8 years? Frankly, I wouldn't want to be standing in front of that clinic when it opened its doors—the odds are that I would be trampled to death.

In Example 2, assume that the particular make and model car that you drive has a mean gas mileage of 16 miles per gallon (mpg) with a standard deviation of 1 mpg. Assume furthermore, that you can purchase a gadget for $510 that requires 17 hours of your time to install, that will raise the gas mileage of your car .68 of a standard deviation above that of untreated cars—that is, by .68 mpg. Would you buy the gadget and install it on your vehicle? I wouldn't. A little arithmetic shows that if I drive an average of 15,000 miles per year and pay an average of 60¢ a gallon for gasoline, it will take me over

22 years just to pay back the price of the gadget alone.

The two examples above are admittedly extreme, but they illustrate the point that the same size effect can be incredibly important, or almost totally unimportant, depending upon the context. They also illustrate that I cannot answer the question that I have raised, namely, is psychotherapy worth the effort and expense? In order to do a cost-efficiency analysis, three types of information are necessary: first, the cost, in meaningful terms, of the course of action; second, the benefits to be expected, in meaningful terms; and third, the benefits to be expected, in meaningful terms, of alternative courses of action. Unfortunately, all we know in this case is the cost. We certainly do not know how the patients' adjustment would have been affected had they chosen to spend their $510 on a trip to Hawaii, dancing lessons, a new wardrobe, plastic surgery, or a sail boat. There is no data on alternative courses of action.

Of more critical importance, what does an improvement of .68 of a standard deviation mean to a patient? Smith and Glass have aggregated dozens of different dependent measures together, ranging from elaborate clinical judgments to scores on pencil-and-paper tests. Any attempt to extricate meaningful information from such a hodgepodge is impossible. Moreover, even if we could extricate it, we would not know what it meant in most cases. How important is it to score .68 of a standard deviation above a control group on a pencil-and-paper test of self-esteem or manifest anxiety?

It is not Smith and Glass who are at fault here, but rather the studies that were available to them. Too many studies of psychotherapy outcomes, or any other area of psychology for that matter, are conducted in a matter of a few short weeks or months, use dependent measures chosen for convenience and simplicity of measurement, and are undertaken in the prevailing "publish or perish" atmosphere that hangs over us all. As long as the philosophy of our institutions encourages the massive production of quick and easy studies, neither meta-analysis nor any other type of "analysis" will enable us to answer our profession's most pressing questions. Until such time as we collectively realize that good research will often take years to complete, that dependent measures must be chosen because they are meaningful, and that the purpose of research is to obtain knowledge, the case for psychotherapy will remain unproven.

REFERENCE

Smith, M. L., & Glass, G. V. Meta-analysis of psychotherapy outcome studies. *American Psychologist*, 1977 *32*, 752–760.

# 44

## An Exercise in Mega-Silliness

### H. J. Eysenck

The article by Smith and Glass (September 1977) begins promisingly by referring to my "tendentious diatribes" (p. 752) on the outcome problem in psychotherapy, inviting the reader to study two papers of mine, one of which I have no recollection of writing, and which the reader will look in vain for in the journal appearing in the list of references—indeed, the year and volume number given in the reference do not agree! The authors go on to the "astute dismantling of the Eysenck myth" (p. 752) by Bergin, not mentioning that the Bergin myth has in turn been astutely dismantled by Rachman (1971). No discussion of the issue can be regarded as meaningful which accepts the quite erroneous and—indeed, in places—absurd arguments of Bergin and pays no attention to the serious criticisms brought forward by Rachman. Indeed, the latter is not even mentioned in the bibliography, although his book *The Effects of Psychotherapy* is a classic in the literature. Smith and Glass have a somewhat arbitrary method of reference selection that does not augur well for their major opus.

This major opus disregards completely some of the major findings of Rachman's book, for example, that there are large differences in recovery (spontaneous remission) between different types of patients; the analysis takes no account of this effect. The analysis accepts without a word of warning subjective reports of therapists as a major source of information on outcome, although it is well known that such assessments are extremely unreliable even when made by well-qualified psychiatrists who have no personal involvement in the patient's recovery (Block, Bond, Qualls, Yalom, & Zimmerman, 1977); the distortion which is likely to arise when a therapist assesses his own patients' progress can well be imagined. It is noted that "subjectivity of the outcome measure" has much the highest correlation with effect size; this alone would invalidate all the complex statistics offered. Smith and Glass also do not mention the problem of selection, so well discussed by Rachman; patients for psychoanalysis are much more highly selected (for high intelligence, emotional resources, ego strength, etc.) than are patients for behavior therapy, and hence much more likely to improve spontaneously.

The most surprising feature of Smith and Glass's (1977) exercise in mega-silliness is their advocacy of low standards of judgment. More, they advocate and practice the abandonment of critical judgments of any kind. A mass of reports—good, bad, and indifferent—are fed into the computer in the hope that people will cease caring about the quality of the material on which the conclusions are based. If their abandonment of scholarship were to be taken seriously, a daunting but improbable likelihood, it would mark the beginning of a passage into the dark age of scientific psychology.

The notion that one can distill scientific knowledge from a compilation of studies mostly of poor design, relying on subjective, unvalidated, and certainly unreliable clinical judgments, and dissimilar with respect to nearly all the vital parameters, dies hard. This article, it is to be hoped, is the final death rattle of such hopes. "Garbage in—garbage out" is a well-known axiom of computer specialists; it applies here with equal force. There is only one sentence in the article with which one can wholeheartedly agree: "Extracting knowledge from accumulated studies is a complex and important methodological problem which deserves further attention" (p. 760). Until it has received such further attention, it would be highly dangerous to take seriously the "results" reported by Smith and Glass. Only better-designed experiments than those in the literature can bring us a better understanding on the points raised; in particular, placebo groups must be included in all designs which aim to study therapy-specific effects, and several therapists must be included for each method in order to obtain evidence on the therapist variance. I would suggest that there is no single study in existence which does not show serious weaknesses, and until these are overcome I must regretfully restate my conclusion of 1952, namely that there still is no acceptable evidence for the efficacy of psychotherapy.

#### REFERENCES

Block, S., Bond, G., Qualls, B., Yalom, I., & Zimmerman, E. Outcome in psychotherapy evaluated by independent judges. *British Journal of Psychiatry*, 1977, *131*, 410–414.
Rachman, S. *The effects of psychotherapy*. London: Pergamon Press, 1971.
Smith, M. L., & Glass, G. V. Meta-analysis of psychotherapy outcome studies. *American Psychologist*, 1977, *32*, 752–760.

# 45

# Reply to Eysenck

## Gene V Glass and Mary Lee Smith

We have numbered our responses to correspond to the successive paragraphs in Eysenck's (this issue) rejoinder:

1. Of our two citations of Eysenck's work, the 1952 reference is correct. The 1965 reference should have been to the *International Journal of Psychiatry*, not the *Journal of Psychology*. We read Rachman (1971) when it appeared and again when we began the project on which we recently reported. On the substantive issues involved, we continue to stand with Bergin (1971).

2. "Spontaneous remission" was not ignored. We chose to consider only studies that used control groups. The purpose of using a control group is to render consideration of "spontaneous remission" immaterial.

Our concern for the "subjectivity" of outcome measurement was exercised in the most impartial and sensible way we could imagine. "Subjectivity"—we called it "reactivity" —was quantified and included in regression analyses of outcomes. The effects of "reactivity" can be assessed and controlled by use of the regression equations in Table 5 in Smith and Glass (1977). Likewise, other aspects of "the problem of selection" (e.g., intelligence and diagnosis of clients) can be assessed and corrected statistically by reference to the regression equations in our Table 5. Again, the putative more likely "spontaneous remission" of "patients for psychoanalysis" is irrelevant; we considered only studies that used control groups. (If, incidentally, Eysenck's speculation were true, it would work *against* psychodynamic therapies' showing large effects; aspirin would show no superiority to a pla-

cebo among patients, all of whom recovered from headaches for extraneous reasons.)

Not only did we control ex post facto with regression analysis against the points Eysenck nonetheless raised, but the results in our Figure 4 are based only on those studies in which Eysenck's concerns are controlled experimentally. We regard these data as particularly persuasive.

3. Eysenck's points in his third paragraph are largely ad hominem and rhetorical; and one might not readily suspect that an important methodological issue lies buried here; but it does. One of us has addressed the point recently (Glass, in-press-a, in-press-b). We will attempt to put forward the issue briefly, aware that there is too little space here to elaborate upon it satisfactorily. Designing future experiments and appraising the results of completed experiments are quite different endeavors. **There are** many prudent safeguards that should be incorporated into the next experiment to be performed; but once completed, it is an empirical question whether the presence of that safeguard is systematically related to the findings of many experiments. In our analysis of psychotherapy outcome studies, such features as use of randomization versus matching and double versus single versus no-blinding had virtually no correlation with study findings. The mass of "good, bad, and indifferent" reports show almost exactly the same results. Connoisseurs' distinctions about which studies are "best" and which ought to be discarded would lead, in this instance, to a profligate dismissal of hundreds of findings. We and our students have studied the covariance

of many properties of designs and analyses with experimental findings (Glass, Smith, & Miller, in press; Hartley, 1977; Hearold, 1978; Miller, 1978).

It is one thing to say that questions of "good design" are insignificant in evaluating the impact of this particular collection of 400 experiments, and another matter to say that the next experiment I propose to conduct needn't have a "good design." The former may very well be true, the latter virtually never. The two circumstances are quite analogous to two uses of a test and the related issue of test reliability. There is no contradiction in maintaining that a test must have high reliability if one wishes to make correct decisions about individuals, but far lower reliability is tolerable if only certain group characteristics are of interest (since measurement errors will average out in groups). One wants one's next study to be well designed because one wants to believe its findings and plan subsequent studies on the basis of them. But once the study is completed and its findings join those of dozens of other studies on the same topic, the sophistication and validity of the study design become an entirely different matter, and conceivably a minor one.

4. We disagree with Eysenck's opinion of the psychotherapy outcome literature, namely, that "there is no single study in existence which does not show serious weaknesses." The effects of psychotherapy could hardly have been so treacherous and elusive as to have tricked hundreds of investigators over the past 40 years (disguised as spontaneous remission in Jones's study, masquerad-

ing as the placebo effect in Brown's study, hiding cleverly behind a bad statistical analysis in White's study, etc.). As arduous as were the reading and reanalysis of the nearly 400 studies we included, we were often pleased to find excellent experiments, well executed and well reported. Probably, the best of them was the comparison of psychodynamic psychotherapy and behavioral therapy reported recently by Sloane, Staples, Cristol, Yorkston, and Whipple (1975). It satisfied many more criteria than Eysenck specified in his fourth paragraph. We were gratified to see that Sloane et al.'s results nearly exactly matched our compilation of effects across the 400 studies: essentially no difference between behavioral and nonbehavioral therapies and an average effect of about two thirds of a standard deviation above control groups for each.

## REFERENCES

Bergin, A. E. The evaluation of therapeutic outcomes. In A. E. Bergin & S. L. Garfield (Eds.), *Handbook of psychotherapy and behavior change.* New York: Wiley, 1971.

Glass, G. V. Integrating findings: The meta-analysis of research. *Review of Research in Education,* in press. (a)

Glass, G. V. Reply to Mansfield and Busse. *Educational Researcher,* in press. (b)

Glass, G. V, Smith, M. L., & Miller, T. I. *The benefits of psychotherapy.* Baltimore, Md.: Johns Hopkins University Press, in press.

Hartley, S. S. *Meta-analysis of the effects of individually paced instruction in mathematics.* Unpublished doctoral dissertation, University of Colorado, 1977.

Hearold, S. L. *Meta-analysis of the effects of television on social behavior.* Unpublished doctoral dissertation, University of Colorado, 1978.

Miller, T. I. *The effects of drug therapy in psychological disorders: A meta-analysis.* Unpublished doctoral dissertation, University of Colorado, 1978.

Rachman, S. *The effects of psychotherapy.* London: Pergamon Press, 1971.

Sloane, R. B., Staples, R. F., Cristol, A. H., Yorkston, N. J., & Whipple, K. *Psychotherapy versus behavior therapy.* Cambridge, Mass.: Harvard University Press, 1975.

Smith, M. L., & Glass, G. V. Meta-analysis of psychotherapy outcome studies. *American Psychologist,* 1977, *32,* 752–760.

# 46

## Do We Really Want a Program Evaluation Strategy Based Solely on Individualized Goals? A Critique of Goal Attainment Scaling

*Robert J. Calsyn and William S. Davidson*

A recurring area of debate among practitioners, policy makers, and researchers has focused on how program success should be measured. These discussions have been concerned with the adequacy of evaluations of therapeutic and social programs. On the one hand, clinicians and program administrators have complained that highly standardized or experimental evaluations of programmatic or therapeutic effectiveness are insensitive to the richness of therapeutic interaction and often ignore the idiosyncratic goals which are established for each client and/or program. Consequently, practitioners view such evaluations as irrelevant to their day-to-day activities. Conversely, policy makers have continued to search for a common measurement device which would allow for meaningful comparisons across social groups and programs.

One innovative response to this apparent dilemma was suggested by Kiresuk and Sherman (1968). They proposed the use of an individualized goal attainment scaling (GAS) as a procedure that would allow for individualized clients goals but at the same time provide data that would be used in evaluating

From Robert J. Calsyn and William S. Davidson, "Do We Really Want a Program Evaluation Strategy Based Solely on Individualized Goals?: A Critique of Goal Attainment Scaling," *Community Mental Health Journal* (forthcoming). Copyright 1978 by Behavioral Publications.

an entire program. Since publication of their initial article on GAS methodology, GAS in some form or another has been adopted in hundreds of human service agencies.

Although GAS was initially proposed as an evaluation technique, a recent survey by Calsyn, Tornatzky, and Dittmar (1976) indicates that many programs have adopted GAS because of its therapeutic potential. The Program Evaluation Resource Center (PERC), which has been largely responsible for disseminating GAS, has expanded its diffusion effort to include workshops and articles on the possible therapeutic benefits of GAS in addition to advocating the use of GAS as a program evaluation technique.

The aim of this article is to examine how successfully the GAS methodology has met this dual objective. In short, it appears that Kiresuk and Sherman should be commended for their attempt to make program evaluation more relevant to direct service providers. Yet, it will be argued that GAS has considerable limitations with respect to fulfilling the original purpose of being a universal program evaluation technique.

After presenting an overview of the GAS methodology, research on the therapeutic benefits of GAS is summarized. Then a detailed examination is made of GAS as an evaluation technique. Data on the reliability and validity of GAS scales is reviewed. Considerable attention is given to the relative merits of GAS versus uniform assessment devices for program evaluation purposes when clients are not randomly assigned to treatment or program. Potential difficulties decision makers may face in interpreting GAS scores are also highlighted. Finally, suggestions are offered for improving the quality of program evaluation efforts.

## OVERVIEW OF GAS METHODOLOGY

The basic approach of GAS calls for defining a unique set of goals for each client and/or program rather than defining more general program goals to be measured across all clients or programs. Within the GAS framework, the criterion of program success becomes the extent to which individual goals are achieved rather than achievement of uniform criteria which are assessed of all clients going through the program (e.g., recidivism, reduction in anxiety, gain in achievement test scores). The basic three steps in the GAS methodology usually include the following sequence:

1. *Assignment of clients to designated intervention.* The initial step in the evaluation of any social intervention program involves the assignment of target group individuals to one of several intervention programs or therapeutic techniques. This phase can actually involve several alternatives ranging from assignment of individuals to the only program available through random assignment of individuals to one of several programs in a comparative framework. As will be seen later, the alternative chosen at this step has implications for the use and interpretability of GAS results.

Table 1.
Example of a Goal-Attainment Scale

| Column 1 | Column 2 | Column 3 |
|---|---|---|
| Worst outcome expected | Unemployed and not in job training | −2 |
| Less than expected outcome | Unemployed but in job training | −1 |
| Expected outcome | Part-time employment and in job training | 0 |
| More than expected outcome | Full-time employment and earning less than $125/wk | 1 |
| Best outcome expected | Full-time employment and earning more than $125/wk | 2 |

*2. Selection of goals and the creation of the GAS scales.* The next step recommended for the use of GAS methodology is the selection of the idiosyncratic goals for each particular case. After a particular goal is decided upon, a scale is formed which details the relative positive and negative outcomes which could reasonably be expected of this client. For example, if enhancing job performance were the goal, the scale might resemble Table 1 (column 2). In order to make the individualized scales as comparable as possible across clients or programs, anchor points from worst anticipated outcome to most positive outcome are used as a template in specifiying individualized GAS scale points (see column 1 in Table 1). As indicated in column 2 of Table 1 the goal settor writes down specific values (usually behavioral) which would be considered measures of the various levels of outcome for a particular client on a particular goal. Although five scale points are usually recommended, only two points are absolutely necessary for construction of a GAS scale. Finally to do statistical analyses some numerical value must be assigned to each of the scale points. Column 3 depicts five values which are often used. It is also possible to give more importance to certain scales by multiplying the scales by different weights.

Several types of individuals have been used to establish the individualized GAS scales. Kiresuk and Sherman had an independent intake committee establish the client's GAS goals and scales, so that the goal setting process was independent of the therapy process. Since Kiresuk and Sherman's initial presentation of GAS, a number of other procedures for establishing GAS scales have been introduced. These include: having the client choose his own goals and scale points, having the therapist establish the scales, and having the therapist and client mutually establish the GAS scales. Again the choice of goal setting effects the interpretability of the GAS results.

*3. Follow-up assessment of the client's standing on the goals after termination from the program.* The final step in the GAS methodology involves the rating of the client on the GAS scales at some point following the client's termination from the intervention program. In the original Kiresuk and Sherman article the rating was done by an independent rater who had no previous contact with the client. However, since that time, other raters have been used including the clients themselves, the client's therapist, or the client and therapist mutually. The choice of raters also affects the quality of the evaluation using GAS.

It can be seen from the above description that the GAS methodology allows for highly idiosyncratic specification of desired intervention outcomes. Since these individualized goals are converted to common metric of best anticipated to worst anticipated outcome, the social researcher can tabulate program outcomes through an average GAS score and compare programs or groups of individuals within any particular program using parametric statistical procedures (e.g., analysis of variance and $t$).Thus, a program with a mean GAS score of one (1) is considered to be more effective than a program with a mean GAS score of minus 1 ($-1$).

## THERAPEUTIC IMPACT OF GAS

Sixty-seven percent of the 71 past and present users of GAS surveyed by Calsyn, Tornatzky and Dittmar indicated that they used GAS for therapeutic purposes. Two research studies provide some evidence that GAS, when used in certain ways, may in fact have some therapeutic value. Jones and Garwick (1973) found in a true experiment that Day Treatment clients who constructed their own GAS scales achieved higher GAS scores than clients who were not involved in the goal setting. Unfortunately a confound exists in Jones and Garwick's study which may render the results artifactual. When evaluated by a follow-up interviewer, sixty-four percent of the client constructed scales were thought to underestimate the client's expected level of performance. In comparison, only 47% of the scales constructed by the intake interviewer were thought to be underestimates. This difference of course could account for the observed group difference in goal attainment.

LaFerriere and Calsyn (1976) avoided this confound by assessing outcome independent of the goal setting process. In their study they compared the efficacy of mutual goal setting by clients and therapist using GAS to the usual short-term outpatient treatment. Clients were randomly assigned to conditions. GAS clients had significantly more positive outcomes as measured by standardized measures of anxiety (Welsh Anxiety Scale, Anxiety Scale of the Multiple Affect Adjective Checklist), self-esteem (Rosenberg's Self-Esteem Scale), and depression (Depression Scale on the Multiple Affect Adjective

Checklist). Clients in the Goal Attainment Scaling condition also rated themselves higher than clients in the control condition on motivation to change and actual change. Therapists did not perceive the Goal Attainment Scaling clients to be more motivated to change, but therapists did perceive the Goal Attainment Scaling clients to have actually changed more as a result of therapy than the clients in the control condition.

Several ancillary pieces of data suggested that the goal-setting process had greater impact on the client than the therapist. Goal Attainment Scaling clients were able to list more specific goals than control clients. Similarly, Goal Attainment Scaling clients also reported using these goals in therapy more than control clients. Therapists, on the other hand, did not report discussing specific therapy goals more often with Goal Attainment Scaling clients than control clients. Future research should include content analysis of therapy tapes to better determine the nature of any differences in the therapy process caused by goal-setting. In addition, future research should compare mutual goal-setting between therapist and client against goal-setting by the client without therapist involvement.

In summary, although these two studies suggest that GAS can be an effective therapeutic tool, more research needs to be done to determine more precisely under what conditions GAS has its greatest therapeutic impact. Finally, it is important to remind future researchers that in evaluating the therapeutic effectiveness of GAS, it is essential that outcome criteria be used that are independent of the goal-setting process itself. Thus, GAS scales which are constructed as part of the therapy should not be used to evaluate the therapeutic benefits of GAS.

## PSYCHOMETRIC QUALITY OF GAS SCALES

To have any value for comparative evaluation purposes, an assessment device must be both reliable and valid. Below are summarized various GAS reliability and validity studies conducted by PERC.

### Reliability

The first reliability issue for GAS might be labeled *content* reliability, i.e., to what extent do different raters agree on the application of a given pre-defined content category to any particular client. In a study by Grygelko, Garwick, and Lampan (1973) of 44 clients, correlation coefficients of agreement between intake interviewers and therapists ranged from a low of $-.27$ to a high of .64 with a mean of .24. The content categories of alcohol use (.64), suicide (.58), and family marital problems (.55) produced the highest correlations of agreement, while interpersonal ($-.27$), physical complaints ($-.06$), and financial ($-.05$) produced the least amount of agreement. Thus, there is generally only slight agreement between different raters concerning the "content" of a given client's goals.

A second reliability issue concerns the extent to which different raters agree on the relative amount of goal attainment on specified goals. Research to date indicates moderate reliability across raters for GAS scales. Correlations ranging from .51 to .85 are reported in studies on the agreement between interventionists (therapists) and follow-up interviewer's ratings of client goal attainment (Baxter, 1973). Similarly, client's assessment of their goal attainment correlated .73 with a follow-up worker's assessment (Jones & Garwick, 1973).

A related set of issues is the extent to which there will be agreement between goal-attainment assessed by different modalities. More specifically, does it matter if GAS follow-up assessment is done in person versus by phone or mailing, etc. Audette (1974) examined the extent to which similar ratings resulted from in person versus telephone ratings. This study reports a correlation of .66 between the ratings accomplished by these two approaches. In summary, it can be seen that GAS has shown a fair amount of agreement between clients, therapists, and follow-up workers and some indication that GAS ratings may be generalizable across different modalities of GAS ratings. Another issue which has *not* been addressed independent of reliability across raters is the extent of reliability observed across the dimension of time (i.e., temporal stability of GAS ratings).

## Validity Criteria

A final set of issues concerns the extent to which GAS ratings in fact measure or tap the dimension or constructs they are purported to measure. In other words, to what extent do GAS ratings reflect individualized improvement in mutually agreed upon problem areas. One common approach in addressing this issue has been to examine the relationship of a particular measure to other measures which supposedly assess the same dimension.

Examination of GAS validity have been primarily accomplished by means of comparing GAS ratings with other assessment devices. In the studies conducted thus far, GAS scores have not been highly correlated with treatment outcomes measured by more standard measuring instruments (Garwick, 1974). Most correlations fall below .30. However, since GAS scales are individually tailored to the client, a fairer assessment of validity of GAS scores would be to compare GAS scores with some other assessment of client change. Mauger (1974) found a correlation of .30 between MMPI change scores and GAS ratings. Baxter reports correlation ranging from .19 to .50 between GAS scores rated by a follow-up worker and therapist's global assessment of the client's progress in therapy. If the therapists' rating of GAS scores are used, the correlations with global ratings range from .58 to .85. However, it must be pointed out here that since the therapist scores both the GAS ratings and the global ratings, it is questionable whether these latter correlations should be considered true indicants of the validity of GAS across measurement modalities. Finally, Baxter reports that GAS scores correlate .23 with an index of consumer satisfaction. This result is surprisingly low considering that GAS ratings are supposed to reflect goals chosen specifically to meet individual client needs. In brief, GAS methodology has not demonstrated an impressive pattern of relationships to similar variables assessed through other assessment techniques. While it may be argued that the highly idiosyncratic nature of GAS methods would preclude the necessity for such comparisons, it appears imperative that future work with GAS ratings continue to explore the relationship of GAS ratings to other assessment techniques.

In summary GAS is deficient on a number of psychometric dimensions. First of all there is little agreement among raters concerning the "content" of a given client's goals. Although moderate reliability between raters has been demonstrated with regard to level of goal-attainment on a specified goal, little support exists for the validity of GAS scales.

## LIMITATIONS OF GAS WITH RESPECT TO RESEARCH DESIGN

Since GAS methodology was originally offered as a measurement tool, Kiresuk and his associates have concerned themselves primarily with studying the reliability and validity of GAS as outlined above. However, certain research design problems must be approached differently when the outcome of treatment programs is measured solely by the GAS method. The central concern to be addressed here, critical to all evaluation research and program planning, is to what extent are the results which have been observed attributable to the program intervention or therapy technique in question. In other words, to what extent can clients, program planners and interested consumer groups be confident that the high level of goal attainment displayed by program A is directly attributable to program A per se.

One crucial element in determining the quality of the evaluation is knowing how the participants were assigned to the group being served or the several groups being compared. This was the initial step of the GAS methodology as originally proposed by Kiresuk and Sherman and outlined previously. Random assignment of participants to groups is the most preferred way to maximize the interpretability of observed differences between clients after treatment. Given random assignment to groups, there exists a specified probability value that initial differences between program participants will be evenly distributed across the various groups being compared. With this paradigm, significant differences observed between groups at post or follow-up assessment can be attributed to the intervention program. If clients are not randomly assigned to treatment groups, then an alternative explanation can be offered for why clients in one program were "superior" at the follow-up assessment, namely that the clients in the superior program were in some way special, e.g., more intelligent, more motivated for treatment, etc. This is a particularly salient issue for new programs who are often accused of taking only the "easy" cases.

Although the random assignment procedures was followed by Kiresuk and Sherman in their initial GAS project, data collected by Calsyn, Tornatzky, and Dittmar (1976) indicated that only 18.3% of current and past users of GAS methodology randomly assigned participants to intervention approaches.[2] Unfortunately, it would appear that most program evaluations using the GAS methodology have resorted to less sophisticated evaluation designs. Participants have often been assigned to different treatment programs on the basis of clinical judgments concerning preferred treatment modality, availability of beds or therapists, or participant preference. In a large number of cases no comparison group exists because there is only a single treatment program. All of these latter research designs are open to criticisms which have been described by Campbell and Stanley (1966) as selection biases and/or interactions with selection biases. In other words, it is plausible that differences between groups or improvement in the single group under examination are just as attributable to the initial characteristics of the program participants or the interaction of the client's initial characteristics with other variables rather than the efficacy of the particular program.

### Controlling for Selection Biases Using GAS versus Uniform Measuring Instruments

There are some potential checks on the problems outlined here which have not been followed by those evaluators using the GAS methodology to date. Regardless of whether GAS or uniform measuring instruments are used, the program evaluator should use demographic information available on the program participants to determine the characteristics of the group or groups being evaluated. While this check provides little help in the case of a single group being evaluated, when two groups are compared the participants in the two programs can be compared on the initial distribution of age, sex, race, marital status, educational level, occupation, previous interventions, concommitant interventions, etc. If the clients in the two programs were highly similar on such demographic characteristics, the program evaluator has gained some minimal counterargument to the selection bias issue. However, nothing can be said concerning dimensions which are not assessed.

In situations where the program evaluator is using uniform assessment devices (with or without GAS) additional strategies are available. If the program evaluator has administered particular assessment devices to all participants upon program entry in a prepost format, pretest scores can be examined for differences in the participants prior to entry to the program(s). Again, finding highly similar patterns of scores between programs provides an additional counterargument to the selection bias issue. Even if significant differences occurred between groups at the pretest on the outcome measures, a number of options are opened to the evaluator for statistically controlling these initial differences (Porter, 1973; Kenny, 1975). While it must be stressed that none of these techniques are foolproof (Cronbach and Furby, 1970; Campbell and Erlebacher, 1970), the evaluator at least has some information with respect to the potential bias and a statistical strategy for dealing with the potential bias.

The evaluator who is relying solely on GAS methodology cannot use statistical technique (e.g., covariance analysis) to adjust for any potential selection bias, since in the standard GAS methodology there is no pretreatment GAS score for clients. The goal settor determines scale points which are expected outcomes after treatment, but the goal settor does not establish the client's standing on his desired goal at intake.[3] Thus, the evaluator using only GAS must trust the clinical judgment of the workers setting the goals and the raters determining goal attainment. The evaluator must assume that any pretreatment client differences between programs have been adjusted for, because the GAS scale points have been individually chosen with respect to what is "reasonably expected" of each program participant. In other words the program evaluator using GAS must assume that if none of the clients assigned to the two program received treatment, the same percentage in each of the groups would achieve a rating of a $+2$ on the scale, the same percentage would achieve $+1$, etc. Only with this highly tenuous assumption is it safe to suggest there are any observed differences in the effectiveness of the two programs under investigation. It is not necessary to assume that the goal settors are perfect in their judgments about what is "expected" of each participant, only that the extent of their errors in judgment are the same for both groups.

The relevant question becomes under what circumstances can the assumption be made that the errors in judgment made by goal settors and follow-up raters are equally distributed across clients in all treatment programs being compared. This assumption will have some validity if the following conditions are present:

(1) Evidence exists that indicates that goal attainment is not related to initial client characteristics.

(2) The same people are setting the goals for clients in all programs. These raters should be unaware of what treatment program the client is to receive, or at the very least they should not have a prior investment in seeing one treatment program produce more positive results than those with which it is being compared.

(3) The same people should make the GAS follow-up ratings in all treatment programs. These raters need not be the same people who set the initial individualized goals. However, these raters should not be aware of the treatment received by the client, or at least they should not have any investment in seeing one program found more effective than other programs being evaluated.

Some evidence has been forthcoming that indicates that GAS scales can be specifically adapted to each participant so that initial participant characteristics are not related to eventual goal attainment. Baxter and Tripp, (1972) found all of the correlations between eight demographic variables and the partici-pants GAS score at follow-up to be less than .20. Similarly, severity of problem ($r = .10$), thought of suicide ($r = .15$) and current medication ($r = .14$) were not significantly correlated with GAS score. In another study, Meade (1971) found a low correlation between the Shipley-Hartford Intelligence Scale scores and GAS ratings. (Cited but not referenced in Garwick, 1974).

Although the evidence is fairly impressive that GAS scores are not systematically related to initial participant characteristics, the issue is hardly resolved. Future work will need to examine the relationship between GAS ratings and previous program involvement, motivation for program involve-ment, extraneous life events, and other variables which have been shown to be related to measures of successful outcome.

Again, each program evaluator should engage in the necessary checks to determine the presence of such relationships in the particular program being investigated. While in previous research GAS scores have not been related to initial client characteristics, the program evaluator using GAS ratings should first determine if any initial differences on demographic variables exist between clients and in the programs being compared. If differences do exist, the next step should be to calculate the correlations between goal attainment ratings and those demographic variables. If the correlations are not significant, the program evaluator can place some credibility in the argument that even though there was apparently an initial selection problem, it did not appear to be related to the construction of the individual GAS scales and the ultimate goal attainment score. If the correlations are found to be significant, any significant differences between programs on GAS scores may possibly be due to an interaction between client differences and the GAS methodology rather than differences in the effectiveness of the programs being compared. Campbell and Stanley have described this problem more formally as a selection-instrumenta-tion interaction. The authors are unaware of any statistical procedures available to manage this problem. It should also be pessimistically noted that evaluators using only a single group are left with no safeguards for such concerns.

Knowing that initial client characteristics are unrelated to goal attainment is not sufficient evidence for assuming that goal setter errors regarding what is "reasonably expected" of each client are equivalent in the programs being compared. Evidence must also be presented that the goal setters for the various programs are not systematically different in the kinds of GAS scales they construct. The best procedure for ensuring that goal setters in the various programs are equivalent is to use the same goal setters in all the programs being evaluated. If different goal setters are used for each program, the evaluator runs the risk that the goal setter for program A might use different types of scales than the goal setter in program B uses. Since, as indicated previously, GAS scales have shown very poor content reliability, this should be a major concern of any program evaluator. In addition, if different goal setters are used for the two programs, the evaluator runs the risk that the program evaluator for program A might consistently overestimate what is reasonably expected of clients, while the goal settor in program B might consistently underestimate what is reasonably expected of clients. This, of course, will result in a situation where program B has a much better chance of appearing to be the superior program. Obviously the goal settors should either be unaware of what treatment program the client will be assigned to, or at least they should not have any investment in seeing one program found more effective than another. Similar arguments can be advanced for having the same people determine goal attainment at follow-up for clients across all programs being evaluated.

Unfortunately, the requirement that the same person set the goals for clients in all programs being compared results in a conflict with good treatment practice. As indicated earlier, research by LaFerriere and Calsyn (1976) and Jones and Garwick (1973) indicates that having the client involved in the goal setting process produces better therapy outcomes. However, since the client typically only goes through one treatment program, having clients set the goals will conflict with the requirements for a good evaluation (i.e., that the same people set the goals for clients in all programs being compared). Additional innovation will be required to resolve this conflict between good therapy practice and the needs of the program evaluator when GAS is the only program evaluation measure.

In summary, when clients are not randomly assigned to treatment, the program evaluator using GAS must trust the judgment of those setting the goals to adjust away any initial client differences. As we have pointed out, this may be a reasonable assumption under certain circumstances. While the GAS program evaluator can gather some information with respect to meeting the assumptions, he has no statistical means of adjustment if the assumptions are not met. On the other hand, the program evaluator using uniform measuring instruments can adopt a different strategy and use information on all demographic variables and pretest measures of the outcome variable to determine equivalence between the programs. If equivalence is lacking, he can use statistical techniques to try to correct for pretreatment differences in clients. In addition when the evaluator relies solely on GAS, the requirements of good evaluation are in direct conflict with good therapeutic procedures.

## LIMITATIONS OF GAS FOR DECISION MAKING

To be a good program evaluation technique, the information provided decision-makers must be clear, unambiguous, and congruent with policy-making needs (Suchman, 1967). However, without considerable study of individual client GAS forms, it is nearly impossible to know the significance of a program's mean GAS score. The first issue concerns what goals were achieved by a given program. Since program success is measured in "goals achieved," rather than specific criteria, like days of hospitalization, recidivism, employment, etc., two programs can have the same mean GAS score and have accomplished radically different objectives. Knowing only that a certain percentage of clients goals were achieved may not be problematic for privately funded programs who treat voluntary clients. However, "goals achieved" may not be a satisfactory criterion of success for most publicly funded programs which are accountable to public officials and the general public as well as clients and service providers. Most funding sources will want outcome data on specific criteria (e.g., hospitalization rates, arrests, drug usage, etc.). This will be particularly true if there is some disagreement between the funding source and the service provider as to what the goals of the program should be. For example, a drug education program may define its role in terms of clarifying the values of youth with respect to drugs, whereas the funding sources are interested only in a reduction in drug usage. In such situations it is highly unlikely that a funding source will find acceptable an evaluation based exclusively on goals set by clients or therapists. Similarly, in situations where clients have been ordered by the judicial system or other authority to receive treatment for a specific behavior (e.g., drunkeness, child abuse), goals individually defined by therapists or clients will be marginally acceptable.

## SUMMARY AND RECOMMENDATIONS

Although GAS appears to have some therapeutic value, GAS has been found wanting as an evaluation technique. First of all there is considerable variability in the content of scales constructed by different goal settors. Although the reliability of the GAS scales is adequate, the validity of the scales is questionable. It addition, unlike uniform measuring instruments, the technique does not have any way to statistically adjust for potential selection biases. More importantly policy implications of GAS scores are not always clear. Goals set by therapists and/or clients may not always be consistent with the goals set by funding sources or other representatives of the larger society.

One solution to this apparent conflict between therapy and evaluation is to use both individualized GAS goals and uniform assessment devices. For example, the authors are aware of a methadone maintenance program which gets periodic urine samples from all of its clients but allows clients and therapists to set individualized goals. In this way the requirements of the funding source that their evaluation include a measure of drug reduction are met, while at the same time allowing for client and therapist input into the goal setting and evaluation process. Other programs have followed these procedures with a variety of target populations (Seidman and Rappaport, 1974). This strategy can avoid many of the shortcomings without completely sacrificing the idea of individualized client goals. This strategy would allow for the continued and expanded use of GAS methodology as part of the intervention process leading to increased participant involvement in the treatment planning process as well as involving the participants directly in the accountability process. To maximize the probability that the standardized assessment devices are tapping the most salient dimensions program directors might convene a planning group consisting of interventionists, citizens, clients, and public officials to outline the multiple objectives and outcome criteria for those participants going through the programs. Since no one criteria will apply to every participant who goes through the program and since there is usually considerable disagreement over what the objectives of a program should be, a multivariate model of assessment is necessary. For most programs, some of the outcome measures will be obvious (e.g., reduced arrest rates and clean urines for convicted heroin addicts). If specific criteria are not obvious for a program (e.g., an outpatient psychotherapy program), the authors recommend using what might be called trans-situational quality of life measures (e.g., self-esteem, depression, anxiety, social skills). These are goals which would be considered desirable in a variety of situations. In addition, all programs should employ a measure of consumer satisfaction.

In conclusion, it appears that the GAS methodology has been differentially effective in meeting its two aims. On the one hand, there is some evidence to suggest that GAS is highly useful as a therapeutic and/or program management tool. However, the apparent lack of necessary psychometric properties inherent in the GAS procedure suggest that it should not be used as a solitary program evaluation tool. Rather GAS should be included as part of a multivariate assessment strategy which would also include uniform measuring instruments that would be administered to all clients.

## NOTES

1. The authors wish to thank JoAnn Ohm and Lynn Honaker for typing the many drafts of this manuscript. Reprint requests should be sent to Robert J. Calsyn, Psychology Department, University of Missouri - St. Louis, 8001 Natural Bridge Road, St. Louis, MO, 63121.

2. If systematic rotation (e.g., where therapist A sees every fifth client) is considered an unbiased method of client assignment, the percentage of programs assigning clients to treatment in an unbiased manner increases to 28.2%. This percentage increases to 38.6% if only programs who reported using GAS for program evaluation purposes are included in the sample. Nevertheless the conclusion stated in the text that most programs using GAS have not followed the research design procedures suggested by Kiresuk and Sherman remains unchanged.

3. The authors are aware of only one procedure for establishing pretreatment GAS scores without totally abandoning the idea of individualized treatment goals. This procedure would first have the GAS goal settor establish a standard number of scale points from most positive outcome desired to most negative outcome feared. Some numerical value would, of course, be attached to each of the scale points. A variation in the standard GAS procedure where the goal settor indicated the clients' standing in his desired goal at intake would result in clients' having a pretreatment GAS score. Thus, the original GAS template of expected outcome would be replaced with a scale of most desired outcome to worst outcome feared and clients would be allowed to vary in how close they were to their desired goal at intake. Since this technique would have the same potential

clinical judgment problems as the standard GAS procedure, the authors would not endorse using this technique as the sole evaluation tool.

# REFERENCES

AUDETTE, D.M. Activities of the follow-up unit. Chapter 2 of Program Evaluation Project Report, 1969-1973. Minneapolis: Program Evaluation Project, 1974.

BAXTER, J. Combination Validity/Reliability Study. Unpublished data report from the Program Evaluation Project Report, 1973.

_____, and TRIPP, R. Unpublished data report from the Program Evaluation Project, 1972.

CALSYN, R., TORNATZKY, L.,and DITTMAR, S. Incomplete adoption of an innovation: The case of goal attainment scaling. Evaluation (in press).

CAMPBELL, D., and ERLEBACHER, A. E. How regression artifacts in quasi-experimental evaluations can mistakenly make compensatory education look harmful. In J. Hellmuth (ed.), Disadvantaged Child Vol. 3. Compensatory Education: A National Debate. New York: Bruner/Mazel, 1970.

CAMPBELL, D., and STANLEY, J. Experimental and quasi-experimental designs for research. Chicago: Rand McNally, 1966.

CRONBACH, L., and Furby, L. How we should measure "change" – or should we? *Psychological Bulletin,* 1970 (74), 68-80.

GARWICK, G. A construct validity overview of goal attainment scaling. Chapter Five of Program Evaluation Project Report 1969-1973. Minneapolis: Program Evaluation Project, 1974.

GRYGELKO, M., GARWICK, G., and ZAMPMAN, S. Findings of content analysis. *Program Evaluation Project Newsletter,* 1973, 4(7), 1-3.

JONES, S., and GARWICK, G. Guide to goals study: Goal Attainment Scaling as a therapy adjunct? *Program Evaluation Project Newsletter,* 1973, 4(6), 1-3.

KENNY, D. A. A quasi-experimental approach to assessing treatment effects in the non-equivalent control group design. *Psychological Bulletin,* 1975 (82), 345-362.

KIRESUK, T., and SHERMAN, R. Goal-attainment scaling: A general method for evaluating comprehensive community mental health programs. *Community Mental Health Journal,* 1968 (4), 443-453.

LAFERRIERE, L., and CALSYN, R. Goal-attainment scaling: An effective treatment technique in short-term therapy. *American Journal of Community Psychology.* In press.

MAUGER, P. A study of the construct validity of Goal-Attainment Scaling. Chapter Six of Program Evaluation Project Report 1969-1973. Minneapolis: Program Evaluation Project, 1974.

PORTER, A. Analysis strategies for some common evaluation paradigms. Occasional paper No. 21, Michigan State University, College of Education, 1973.

SEIDMAN, E., and RAPPAPORT, J. The educational pyramid. *American Journal of Community Psychology,* 1974 (2), 119-130.

SUCHMAN, E. Evaluative Research. New York: Russell Sage Foundation, 1967.

# PART VIII
# EVALUATIONS IN THE "PUBLIC INTEREST"

Most evaluation research is commissioned by public officials and is conducted by professional evaluators using textbook-like methods. The articles in this next section are grouped under the loose heading of "Evaluations in the 'Public Interest'" to illustrate that they were (or easily could have been) conducted by nonprofessionals seeking to evaluate services that they wanted to see evaluated. Evaluations conducted under such auspices can often be particularly successful in prompting utilization, because they are linked to the assessment of specific practices and are conducted by groups that are prepared to link the evaluation results to public calls for a change in how things are done.

The rise of consumerism and the increased awareness of the power of public opinion in correcting grievances has led to a greater effort to use evaluative methods to define areas of perceived injustice and to delineate and publicize their scope. The first article describes the Chicago Tribune Task Force Study of overcharging for simple auto repairs. The study demonstrates how experimental methods can be used by journalists to define and highlight a problem and to cause change. The Bridges and Oppenheim study refines a method often used by journalists and citizen action groups which the authors employed in order to test whether there was racial discrimination in charging for banking services. This report and others have resulted in bringing the issue to public attention and initiating attempts to pass corrective legislation. The article by Mladenka illustrates how surveys of citizens can be used to assess the effectiveness of a wide range of local services. Studies of this type can be easily conducted by nonprofessionals, and serve both to evaluate current conditions and to draw attention to local needs that are not being met by local authorities. In the final paper, Bush and Gordon argue for the desirability of using clients in evaluations of social service programs as potent sources of information about effects rather than as passive respondents.

# 47

## Auto Repairs: Proceed with Caution

### The Chicago Tribune Task Force

The garage mechanic dipped his fingers into the oil dripping from the under-side of the car, rubbed them together, and said ominously, "Metal filings. Your transmission is shot!"

You know the feeling. It's the same one you would have when the doctor says, "I have some bad news . . ."

You had feared the worst as you stood beside your disabled car, your stomach in a knot as you strained to read the diagnosis in the mechanic's eyes.

Then he said it. And you *knew* it was going to cost!

Almost everyone drives a car, but few are in the driver's seat when it comes to diagnosing a problem. A Tribune Task Force investigation found the average motorist has less than a 50-50 chance of getting a good repair job at a fair price.

Auto repair is a $30-billion-a-year business in the United States and a third of it is unnecessary, according to Sen. Philip Hart [D., Mich.], who presided over a 1974 Senate investigation of monopoly in the auto industry.

And Virginia Knauer, consumer adviser to President Ford, has said problems with auto repair shops top the list of U.S. consumer complaints.

Some states allow prosecution of a mechanic who cheats a customer. Illinois, however, has no laws whatsoever for the car owner's protection. In fact, if you are unsatisfied and refuse to pay a mechanic's bill, he can take you to court and even have your car towed away.

To determine how the average motorist fares with a car problem in Chicago, the Task Force conducted a three-month experiment to evaluate area auto mechanics and find whether there is a system for diagnosis and repair.

The verdict:

A simple transmission difficulty—cost of diagnosing and repairing it estimated at under $10—can cost anywhere from nothing to $394.

The same pattern emerged with brake and ignition repairs.
Of 52 garages, dealerships, and repair shops tested:

- Twenty-two did the proper work at, or below, the estimated fair price.

For the experiment the Task Force used four American-built cars representing the major auto makers—American Motors, Chrysler, Ford, and General Motors—each car with a predetermined malfunction.

Each of the cars—a 1974 Chevrolet Nova, a 1973 Ford Maverick, a 1973 Plymouth Suburban, and a 1974 AMC Gremlin—was thoroughly checked by William Cecil Armstrong, instructor of automotive service technology at Waubonsee Community College in Sugar Grove, near Aurora.

After pronouncing each car in good mechanical condition, he deliberately caused a minor malfunction a good mechanic should be able to spot immediately.

A typical test went like this:

*March 3, 9 a.m.* Nova arrives at Waubonsee College. Armstrong and associates spend two hours checking car. Mileage logged at 28,477.

*11 a.m.* Armstrong punctures vacuum hose to transmission so car will not shift gears smoothly. Estimate cost of diagnosis and repair at "under $10."

*12:45 p.m.* Car arrives at Aamco Transmissions, 2902 N. Clark St. Mileage logged at 28,535. Car left overnight for examination.

*March 4, 11:30 a.m.* Aamco advises car will need rebuilt transmission. Aamco told to "go ahead with the cheapest repairs. Only what it needs."

*March 5, 4 p.m.* Car picked up at Aamco. Reporter billed $340. Car returned to Waubonsee College for examination. Armstrong reports repair job totally unnecessary.

Reporters found other garages that would remedy the same transmission problem for $5, $287, $8.43, $394, $16, $91.97, $33.34, $100, $6, $61.91, and free.

The initial test with the Nova caused optimism when a Chevrolet dealer, City Auto Sales, 2301 S. Michigan Av., quickly spotted the punctured hose and replaced it for $8.43.

The next stop, after Armstrong had reexamined the car and again punctured the hose, was the Aamco shop on Clark Street that charged $340.

"This transmission is going to have to come out of here. It's an internal problem," explained Tom Kartholl, the service writer.

Dipping his fingertips into some oil in the transmission pan, which had been lowered by a mechanic, he added, "Look at this! Those are metal filings. This transmission is being eaten away inside."

"Is that serious?" the reporter asked.

"It could be very serious," Kartholl said. "It cut a hole in your vacuum line. We can fix that, but this transmission is being eaten away. Something in there is rubbing, and causing these metal filings."

Cost of the diagnosis was $45, to be refunded if repairs were made—$340 for an "absolutely necessary" job, or $486 for a rebuilt transmission "guaranteed for life."

"You know, General Motors wants you to buy a new car every two years," Kartholl said. "The transmissions on these are notorious."

The reporter reluctantly agreed to Aamco's minimum repair job, picked up the car two days later, paid $385 less $45 for "inspection service" and returned the vehicle to Waubonsee College.

Armstrong, on learning Aamco's diagnosis, said, "That's one of the oldest tricks in the business. There are always going to be metal filings in the fluid, but when they show them to people, they get hysterical. There was nothing wrong with the transmission."

With the reconditioned transmission, and the hose once again punctured by Armstrong, the Nova was driven straight to another Aamco transmission shop, at 7800 S. Stony Island Av.

"It keeps losing power . . . and it goes whusssh," the reporter explained.

"Your transmission is going to have to be rebuilt," Percy Jackson, the Aamco manager, reported after his mechanic checked it.

"It'll cost you $394, plus tax, with a six-month guarantee. Or, if you want it custom rebuilt, it's $489, guaranteed for as long as you own the car."

"Oh, wow!" gasped the reporter. "What caused it to give out?"

"It's just from wear and tear," the Aamco man said, "That's all."

That's all. Except the very same transmission, with a bright, shiny blue paint job to prove it, had just come from another Aamco shop, checked by an expert mechanic, and found to be in top condition.

Jackson listed the parts he said the car would need on a piece of paper, and charged $31.50 for his diagnosis.

With the same car, and the same hose punctured, reporters got the car repaired for $18 at AA Auto & Truck Service, 610 W. 35th St.; $5 at Gem Motor Service, 520 Madison St., Maywood; and $19.75 at Transmission Exchange, 2007 S. Marshall Blvd.

The Task Force investigation showed chances of getting a fair deal were about the same, whether at certified auto dealers, specialty repair shops, or nameless back-alley garages.

Waubonsee was selected as the control center for the experiment because its modern automotive department and instructors were recommended by the National Institute for Automotive Service Excellence, a nonprofit organization in Washington, funded by the auto industry.

Armstrong, 56, designated by Waubonsee officials to oversee and coordinate the project, is certified by the National Institute, and has taken courses at Ford, Chrysler, and General Motors factories and dealerships.

The transmission experiment was basically the same with each car. Allowances were made only for differences in manufacture. While the Nova's hose was punctured, a vacuum hose on the Maverick was disconnected, so the car would not shift smoothly.

Detecting the trouble should have been as simple, for a mechanic, as finding a loose wire for an electrical appliance repairman, Armstrong said.

A cotter pin, which held a linkage rod to the Plymouth's transmission, was removed.

On the Gremlin, with its standard transmission, a rod on the underside of the clutch was turned, so that gears could not be shifted without depressing the clutch pedal all the way to the floor.

Garages and repair shops were carefully selected to be representative of the North, South, and West sides, and all suburban areas.

After each garage visit, the cars were returned to the college for an assessment of whether the work was done properly, and at a fair price.

Results of the transmission tests ranged as follows:

- Nova: $5 hose to $394 for rebuilt transmission.

- Maverick: Free adjustment to $391 for rebuilt transmission.

- Plymouth: $19.22 for linkage repair to $100 for reconditioned valve body.

- Gremlin: $6 adjustment to $147.87 for new clutch.

A third Aamco shop was selected during the Maverick test to see whether another make of auto made a difference.

After Armstrong certified the car to be in top condition, he pulled loose a vacuum hose, and the Maverick, air hissing from the opening, was driven to Aamco at 2164 N. California Av.

A mechanic drove the car, after which Jim McGrath, manager, reported, "It's an internal problem. You can't drive it any more, or it'll get worse. We'll have to tear it down to find the problem."

He charged $46 for the examination, which he said disclosed "the clutch plates are no good, the pump is bad—it doesn't circulate the fluid.

"We can rebuild the old transmission for $391, give you a six-month guarantee," he said. "Or we can custom rebuild it for $489 . . ."

When the reporter balked at Aamco's rock-bottom $391 to fix a problem the reporter knew was caused by a disconnected hose, a man who said he was Bill Mutz moved in to negotiate.

"He quoted you the retail price. I do a lot of work for companies on their fleets. The price for companies is $235," Mutz said.

Chicago Police Department vehicles were being serviced in the shop, which is near the Shakespeare District station.

A day later, after an inspection by Armstrong, a reporter took the same car, with the same malfunction, to Great Western Auto, 3550 N. Southport Av., where a mechanic determined, "It's nothing but a loose hose." He fixed it for $5.

The Shell Service Station, 24 E. 18th St., found the trouble for $6. Jerry Lee, the mechanic, said $2 of that was for a new hose.

United Transmission Center, 7460 N. Milwaukee Av., Niles, diagnosed the same problem as a $287.75 repair job. Santo "Sonny" Cerami, general manager, said it was "definitely" necessary.

"There's metal particles dropping into the pan," he said. "It might be the pump, clutches, the plates, anything."

While Armstrong had said $10 would have been a reasonable fee to repair the Nova or Maverick, he suggested it would be worth up to $20 to locate and replace the missing cotter pin and disconnected rod on the Plymouth transmission.

Pestka-Atra Transmission Center, 2735 W. Lawrence Av., charged an even $100, saying it was necessary to "overhaul the valve body."

"But the car has only 16,000 miles on it," the reporter protested.

"Mileage don't mean a damn thing," explained Valentine "Bud" Fallucca, owner of the shop. "The shift pattern was way out of adjustment. Sometimes it's no good for a car to sit too much. The fluid doesn't flow and it causes trouble."

Hillside Standard Service, 4804 Butterfield Rd., Hillside, had the next look at the Plymouth, and completely misdiagnosed the problem, charging $61.91 for a rebuilt distributor, part of the car's electrical system.

Lee and Frank's Transmission, 5347 S. Kedzie Av., found the problem but charged $35 to replace fluid and filters—the third time it was done on the Plymouth.

The Gremlin, with its stickshift, was used to test mechanics' proficiency in repairing manual transmissions. Armstrong estimated a reasonable charge to adjust the trouble at "no more than $10."

South Commons Amoco [Standard] Service Station, 2800 S. Michigan Av., did the job for $9.25. Maday Brothers, 1019 Davis St., Evanston, found the problem for $6.

"My policy is to try to explain to the customer what he needs and not sell him what he doesn't need," Maday owner Rudy Stein said. "People who don't know anything about a clutch, you can sell them anything."

Action Automatic Transmission Co, 4300 W. 63rd St., not knowing a new throwout bearing [part of the clutch] had just been installed, said the bearing had "burned itself out" and charged $64.75 to replace it.

Whenever possible, reporters asked for the old parts that were taken off a car, which had been marked for identification at the college. Some garages refused to surrender them. Others pleaded they were lost in the trash or "ground up."

United Transmissions, which charged $287.75 to repair the Maverick's transmission, did return the "old" parts as requested.

However, the Waubonsee staff determined the parts could not have been those from the test car because the car would not have been driveable with them.

The test cars fared little better at auto dealers that sell and service Fords, Plymouths, Chevrolets, and AMC cars.

One new car dealer, Bennett [AMC] Motor Sales, 6440 W. Roosevelt Rd., Oak Park, confronted with evidence he had charged $147 to replace a perfectly good clutch, called the reporters "underhanded."

Abe Zelmar, 59, owner of Transmission Exchange, where the Nova was correctly repaired for a $19.75 "minimum fee," said, "Everybody I know has been ripped off by a transmission shop at one time or another.

"That's what's wrong. It's a blind business—same as going to a doctor."

## HOW EXPERT MECHANIC SET UP OUR REPAIR TEST

The name plate on the office desk reads: Cecil Armstrong, Top Wrench.

"Top wrench" is not a title, but it is an apt description. William Cecil Armstrong, who set up the control system for the Tribune Task Force investigation of auto repair shops, is one of the top automotive experts in the Chicago area.

Armstrong, 56, is an instructor in automotive technology at Waubonsee Community College in suburban Sugar Grove. In the last six years, he has taught every automotive course the school has offered.

Armstrong said he always stresses morality. "My philosophy is this: There is no substitute for honesty. If you tell a man the truth, you don't have to try to remember what you told him."

Armstrong is certified by the National Institute for Automotive Service Excellence, a nonprofit organization in Washington, D.C., funded by the auto industry, as a general auto mechanic with competence in repair of engines, front ends, brakes, automatic transmissions, manual transmissions and rear axles, heating and air conditioning, electrical systems, and engine tuneups.

The National Institute also certifies him as a general truck mechanic with competence in gasoline engines, diesel engines, drive trains, brakes, suspension and steering, and electrical systems.

He holds a doctor of motors degree on diesel engines, given by the Dana Corp., and has a diploma in tractor and equipment training.

Armstrong began tinkering with cars when he was 6 years old, was licensed to drive in Dallas at 10, and completely overhauled his own Model T Ford when he was 12.

He got his first formal automotive training as a teen-ager in the Civilian Conservation Corps during the 1930s, and during World War II helped build Boeing aircraft engines. He subsequently worked as a mechanic, shop foreman, and service representative for Ford and Chrysler, and taught automotive technology at Area Vocational-Technical School in Wichita, Kansas.

He has attended training schools for mechanics offered by Ford, Chrysler, and General Motors plants and dealerships. And he recently was recruited by the city of Elgin to find a better way to test truck and auto mechanics who apply for work with the city.

Once The Tribune decided to investigate auto repair shops, it enlisted the aid of Waubonsee Community College because the automotive department there was recommended by the national institute for its modern service laboratory, and its top instructors. Ken Ronzheimer, director of the automotive department there, agreed to participate and appointed Armstrong to coordinate the project.

Armstrong volunteered his time for the investigation because "this kind of thing will be beneficial to the entire automotive industry."

The plan called for four cars, one made by each of the nation's major auto manufacturers—General Motors, Ford, Chrysler, and American Motors Corp.

Armstrong, after certifying that each car was in good mechanical condition, devised a simple mechanical problem that, without trickery, tested the skills of an auto mechanic.

He made sure the mechanical problems on each car were as similar as possible, without unfair variation. And, he assessed the quality of the repair work that was done.

In three months, he and his associates received more than 50 visits from Tribune Task Force reporters, each time examining the test cars to ensure sound mechanical condition, then arranging each car so it would malfunction.

To test the mechanics' proficiency with automatic transmissions, for example, Armstrong punctured or disconnected a vacuum line so gears would not shift properly. On a car with a manual transmission, he accomplished this by loosening a rod to the clutch.

Before and after every visit to a repair shop, each car was checked at the college, and its condition recorded there.

## $78.35 CAR REPAIR BILL—HOW'S THAT FOR STARTERS

Envision yourself in the shoes of this unfortunate driver.

His disabled 1971 Dodge was being pushed in to Milex Precision Auto Tune-up Center ["Coast to Coast Tune-up Specialists"], 3055 W. Devon Av.

The engine was dead.

"Give me your phone number and we'll give you a call back as soon as we can get to it," said Larry Sievert, who identified himself as the shop owner. Milex advertises use of sophisticated machines to diagnose such problems.

But Sievert was talking to a Tribune Task Force reporter investigating the auto repair industry. Unlike the average motorist, the Tribune reporter knew what was wrong with his car—an ignition wire was loose. The question was—would the mechanic know it?

The phone rang several hours later: "This is Larry at Milex. The engine is basically sound. But . . ."

"What's it going to cost me?"

"$95."

"I just want to get the car running. How much will it cost me to get the car running?"

"You got a lot of open wires. The spark plugs are worn down."

"How much will it cost to just get it running?"

"$75."

"You can't get it running for any less than that?"

"No. The timing is off, and the plugs are fouled. It needs adjusting."

"Well, it that's what it takes to make it start. I need the car for my job."

"This will make it run good."

The Tribune Task Force stopped at 51 other repair shops, and found that motorists stand less than a 50-50 chance of getting a good repair at a fair price in the Chicago area. Before the Dodge was pushed to the Milex garage, a nationally certified mechanic, participating in this controlled investigation, had pulled loose a wire attached to a relay box under the hood.

The day before, the car, with the same loose wire, had been fixed for free at South Western Dodge, 7340 S. Western Ave.

When the reporter picked up the car at Milex he was given a bill for $78.35, itemized as follows:

Custom [tuneup], $19.95; spark plugs, $14.85; points and condenser, $6.50; rotor and distributor cap, $8.45; ignition wires, $18.80; pollution control valve, $3; emission hose, $2.80; oil, $1.25; plus $2.75 sales tax.

The '71 Dodge, which earlier had been certified in good running condition, was one of five cars used in a three-month investigation, under the supervision of William Cecil Armstrong, an instructor of automotive service technology at Waubonsee Community Collee in west-suburban Sugar Grove.

The ultra-modern facilities at Waubonsee were selected as a control center for the experiment after the school was recommended highly by the National Institute for Automotive Service Excellence, a Washington-based, nonprofit organization funded by the auto industry.

The American public spends $30 billion every year on automotive repairs—$10 billion of it unnecessarily, according to a Senate investigation. The Task Force wanted to see how a motorist would fare in Chicago.

The cars used to test mechanics' skills in diagnosing and repairing minor malfunctions of brakes and transmissions were a 1974 Chevrolet Nova, a 1973 Ford Maverick, a 1973 Plymouth Suburban station wagon, and a 1974 American Motors Gremlin. The Dodge was added to the original four in the electrical system experiment to test more garages.

The autos, chosen to represent the major car manufacturers, were taken to 52 garages and repair shops throughout Chicago and the suburbs, with these results:

- Only 22 of the 52 performed the proper repair job, at or below the suggested fair price.

- Nine overcharged or were unable to diagnose the trouble.

- Twenty-one made repairs Armstrong found unnecessary, did inadequate work, or quoted estimates far in excess of what the job should have cost.

Every car used in the experiment was thoroughly checked over by Armstrong and his associates at Waubonsee before the test.

Armstrong caused a minor malfunction on each car. After every garage visit, the cars were again checked at Waubonsee.

Armstrong estimated that a fair price for detecting and repairing the ignition malfunction on the Maverick, Gremlin, Dodge, and Plymouth would be $5. He said $15 would have been a fair price for finding the trouble on the Nova.

April 9 was a typical test day:

*9 a.m.*—The Maverick was driven to Waubonsee, checked out, and the ignition system certified in top condition. After the car is started, a wire to the solenoid, a switch that activates the car's starter when the ignition key is turned on, is loosened so it will not make contact. The car will run but it won't start again once turned off.

*10:50 a.m.*—The Maverick leaves the test center.

*11:55 a.m.*—The Maverick arrives at 127th Street and Ashland Avenue, Calumet Park. The ignition key is turned off. The car will not start again.

*12:05 p.m.*—The Maverick is pushed by another auto one-half block to Rakowski Bros., Inc., Auto Service Center, 1549 W. 127th St. The mechanic is told the car won't start. The car is left for examination.

*1:20*—The reporter phones Rakowski and is told the car needs a new starter.

*4 p.m.*—Rakowski advises the reporter the car is ready. A new starter had been installed. Cost: $62.75.

*8 p.m.*—The car is picked up and returned to Waubonsee.

Before leaving, however, the reporter asked for the old starter that Rakowski took off the car.

"That will cost $15," the Rakowski representative said. "We return those to have them rebuilt."

The reporter said he did not have the additional $15 but would return with the money the following day. When he did, he was met by another man, who only identified himself as "Tom." He raised the price of the old starter by $10.

"It will cost you $25," he said.

The reporter asked why the old starter had to be replaced.

"A starter is like a light bulb," the Rakowski man said. "It just burns out."

Three days later the reporter, driving the Maverick with the same wire disconnected, drove to the Brandywine Union 76 service station at Ardmore and Roosevelt roads, Villa Park.

"I had a breakdown on the tollway," he said. "A service truck got me started, but the driver said not to turn off the engine."

The station attendant looked under the hood, found the loose wire, and squeezed it with a pair of pliers.

"The guy who put this on didn't tighten the wire," he said.

"What do I owe you?" asked the reporter.

The mechanic waves his hand, turned, and walked away.

On a return visit to Brandywine, the mechanic, who identified himself as Elmer Jakubek, station owner, was asked why he fixed the car free of charge.

"We're like doctors. We can do what we want. We can make a big job out of a little one," he said. "You can hook people once, but if you get caught, you're dead."

The 52 garages' fees for repairing the loose wire on the test cars were in the following ranges:

- Dodge and Plymouth—From free to $78.35 for a tuneup.
- Gremlin—From $2 to $10.80.
- Nova—From $18 to $67.75 for a new starter.
- Maverick—From free to $62.70 for a new starter.

The Nova was fixed by Keystone Chevrolet Co., 4501 W. Irving Park Rd., for $18, including a battery charge, which Armstrong said was unnecessary.

Sun Auto Electric, 4810 W. 87th St., Burbank, charged $37.14 to fix the Nova. The bill included $8.40 to disconnect the seat belt buzzer ["That may be your problem"], and another $8.40 for a solenoid, the switch that activates the starter.

Several days later, Peterson-Western Shell, Inc., 6000 N. Western Av., replaced the solenoid with another. A new starter also was installed for a total cost of $67.75.

When the reporter said he wanted the old parts back, he was charged $10 for them.

Peterson-Western Shell is operated by Steve Pearlman, 33, who received widespread publicity earlier this year for a free course in auto mechanics he teaches to the public in his station every Monday night, "so they won't get ripped off."

Pearlman said he was in Hawaii on April 29, the day the Nova was brought in for repairs, but said he would "stand by the judgment" of his mechanic.

"When we run a car through a test on our equipment—the latest in design, incidentally—the test would show a drain on the starter," he explained.

"The mechanic put on a new starter, and the car was working."

A spokesman for the Chicago-based Sun Electric Co., manufacturer of the electrical diagnostic machine used by Pearlman, said this is impossible.

Rather than showing a drain on the starter, he said, the auto diagnostic machine would have shown a "zero reading" if the car had a disconnected wire indicating no electrical drain.

Pearlman said the solenoid was put on the car though it already had a new one because the solenoid and starter "come as a unit."

The previous garage, however, put a solenoid on without disturbing the starter.

TABLE 1
WHAT EACH GARAGE CHARGED TO FIX IGNITION

| Garage | Car used | What we did | Our expert's cost estimate | Garage cost or estimate | Garage response |
|---|---|---|---|---|---|
| Keystone Chevrolet 4501 Irving Park Rd. | 1974 Chevrolet Nova | Disconnected starter circuit at solenoid | $15 | $18.00 | One hour labor to check ignition system. |
| Sun Auto Electric 4810 W. 87th St. Burbank | 1974 Chevrolet Nova | Disconnected starter circuit at solenoid | $15 | $37.14 | Replaced solenoid, by-passed seat belt system; "was needed." |
| Peterson-Western Shell, Inc. 6000 N. Western Av. | 1974 Chevrolet Nova | Disconnected starter circuit at solenoid | $15 | $67.75 | Installed rebuilt starter; "diagnostic machine showed starter needed." |
| Joe Falore Ford, Inc. 9205 S. Western Av. | 1973 Ford Maverick | Disconnected starter circuit at relay box | $5 | $13.16 | Replaced relay and checked ignition system. "The starter was okay; we wouldn't replace it." |
| Rakowski Bros. Inc. 1549 N. 127th St. Calumet Park, Ill. | 1973 Ford Maverick | Disconnected starter circuit at relay box | $5 | $62.70 | Installed rebuilt starter; "must have been defective." |
| Brandywine, Union 76 Ardmore and Roosevelt Rds. Villa Park | 1974 Chevrolet Nova | Disconnected starter circuit at relay box | $5 | Free | "It's awful tempting. I'm afraid to be dishonest. You can hook people once but if you get caught, you're dead." |

**TABLE 1 (Continued)**

| Garage | Car used | What we did | Our expert's cost estimate | Garage cost or estimate | Garage response |
|---|---|---|---|---|---|
| South Western Dodge 7340 S. Western Av. | 1971 Dodge Dart | Disconnected starter circuit at relay box | $5 | Free | "We get all the work we can handle. We don't have to do more than needs to be done." |
| Milex Precision Auto Tune-up Center 3055 W. Devon Av. | 1971 Dodge Dart | Disconnected starter circuit at relay box | $5 | $78.35 | Tuned engine; denied they said it was the cause of the problem. |
| Montgomery Ward Auto Service Center Dixie Sq. Shpg. Ctr. Harvey | 1974 AMC Gremlin | Disconnected starter circuit at relay box | $5 | $8.00 | Checked system, replaced wire. "If they need it we put it on; if they don't, we don't." |
| Northwest AMC, Inc. 6333 Northwest Hwy. | 1974 AMC Gremlin | Disconnected starter circuit at relay box | $5 | $10.80 | Checked and cleaned ignition circuit. |
| Charley & Eddie Svr. 26 E. Burlington Av. La Grange | 1974 AMC Gremlin | Disconnected starter circuit at relay box | $5 | $2.00 | "I never make a practice of selling people things they don't need." |
| Sears Auto Center Harlem & North Avs. | 1973 Plymouth Station Wagon | Disconnected starter circuit at relay box | $5 | $3.00 | "There's no sense in selling a starter when its not needed." |
| Hydro-Motive 1851 E. 95th St. Chicago | 1973 Plymouth Station Wagon | Disconnected starter circuit at relay box | $5 | $2.00 | "I hate to put stuff on a car when it doesn't need it. I hate to work dirty." |

Pearlman also said it would have been impossible to test the old starter once it had been removed from the car, because "we have no way of bench-testing a starter."

Armstrong disproved this by taking the starter Pearlman had removed, setting it on the radiator of the car, and operating it with a battery charger.

In ignition tests involving other cars:

Joe Falore Ford, Inc., 9205 S. Western Av., charged $13.16 to remedy the same problem on the Maverick that Rakowski did for $62.70. Brandywine had done it free of charge.

Northwest AMC., Inc., 6333 Northwest Hwy., charged $10.80 to repair the Gremlin and clean electrical wires. The Montgomery Ward Auto Service Center in the Dixie Square Shopping Center, Harvey, charged $8. Charley & Eddie Service Station, 26 E. Burlington Av., La Grange, did it for $2.

Hydro-Motive, 1851 E. 95th St., got the Plymouth back on the road for $2. Sears, Roebuck and Co. auto center at Harlem and North Avenues did it for $2.

After the ignition portion of the Task Force investigation was completed, reporters returned to the Milex Precision Auto Tune-Up Center on Devon Avenue and asked Larry Sievert why his shop charged $78.35 for the problem that another garage fixed free.

"You must take into account that you have all new parts in the car now," Sievert said.

## BRAKE REPAIRS—GOOD BREAKS AND BAD FOR DRIVERS

You slam on the brakes just when you need them most. But your car keeps moving.

This is, perhaps, your greatest fear as a driver. Every motorist knows that brakes are supposed to stop an automobile and most don't hesitate to tell the mechanic, "Get them fixed," when they act up.

But Tribune Task Force reporters, using cars they knew had only a minor brake problem, learned that "fix the brakes" in Chicago can mean anywhere from $4.50 to $131.12 out of the average motorist's pocket.

The brake problem was simple—estimated to cost no more than $30 to fix— but many garages tested by the Task Force unnecessarily installed expensive parts.

The $131.12 bill was presented by Clark-Maple Chevrolet, Inc., 1038 N. Clark St., for two new brake master cylinders. The car has only one.

"With brakes, you don't fool around," a Clark-Maple service writer said.

What the Clark-Maple serviceman did not know was that the brakes on the 1974 Chevrolet Nova were newly installed, had been thoroughly checked by a nationally certified auto mechanic at Waubonsee College, near Aurora, and everything—including the master cylinder—had been found to be in good condition.

Then, before the car was taken to Clark-Maple, the fluid was drained from one compartment of the master cylinder so the brakes would be defective.

The problem could have been corrected by replacing the fluid and bleeding the brake lines to remove air bubbles.

While none of the garages visited tried to sell the reporters complete brake jobs, several ordered the replacement of perfectly good parts without testing them.

One garage, asked to remedy the same minor problem on another car, repaired the brakes but also disconnected a wire leading to the brake warning light on the instrument panel. If the brakes were to fail again, the driver would have no indication of trouble without the warning light.

The tests were part of a rigidly controlled, three-month investigation in which automobiles were taken to 52 garages, dealerships, and repair shops to evaluate the skills of mechanics in detecting minor malfunctions of the brakes, transmissions, or ignition systems.

Waubonsee College, in west-suburban Sugar Grove, was selected as the control center for the experiment after being highly recommended by the National Institute for Automotive Service Excellence, a nonprofit, Washington-based organization funded by the auto industry.

The school designated William Cecil Armstrong, 56, an instructor in the college's automotive service technology department, to oversee the tests. Armstrong is certified by the National Institute and has taken courses offered by Ford, Chrysler, and General Motors.

The tests Armstrong engineered were designed to see how the average motorist with a mechanical problem would fare in Chicago.

The verdict: Anyone driving a car stands less than a 50-50 chance of getting the correct repair job at a fair price.

The cars used for the experiment and the price range for brake repairs on each were:

1974 American Motors Gremlin—$12 adjustment to $71.21 for new master cylinder.

1973 Ford Maverick—$17.25 adjustment to $65.55 for new master cylinder.

1973 Plymouth Suburban—$4.50 to $19.95 to refill old cylinder.

1974 Chevrolet Nova—Two garages suggested returning to the mechanic who had installed the master cylinder; the third charged $131.12 for 2 new ones.

A typical test went like this:

*April 26, 9 a.m.*—Nova, with new set of brakes, thoroughly checked over at Waubonsee and found to be in perfect mechanical condition.

*10:30 a.m.*—Armstrong siphons brake fluid from one of the dual compartments on the master cylinder so a warning light on the dash will indicate brakes need attention.

The proper repair would be to add fluid and bleed air from the brake line. He estimated a fair repair cost at $30.

*1:30 p.m.*—Nova delivered to Clark-Maple Chevrolet with explanation that "the brakes are soft and the light comes on when I hit them." Reporter told to leave car and check by phone next day.

*April 27, 11:30 a.m.*—Clark-Maple reports car not ready. Waiting for small part.

*4 p.m.*—Car still not ready. Waiting for master cylinder, garage reports.

*April 28, 2:30 p.m.*—Clark-Maple reports car ready but bill not prepared.

*5 p.m.*—Reporter picks up car. Charge is $131.12. Reporter told to come back next day if he wants itemized bill.

*April 29, 9 a.m.*—Reporter returns to Clark-Maple and is given itemized bill, including cost of two master cylinders. Reporter requests old master cylinder. Takes old cylinder back to Waubonsee, where Armstrong pronounces it "in perfect shape."

After being charged $131.12 at Clark-Maple Chevrolet for what should have been a simple brake adjustment, reporters confronted Herbert Schrecke, service writer, with the bill.

"You assume that when the master cylinder is down, there's got to be a leak," he said. "When the master cylinder's down, it's a matter of safety. You just don't fiddle around and take a chance."

When the invoice charge for two master cylinders was questioned, Schrecke said: "There's something wrong there. There should be only one master cylinder there."

Schrecke blamed "the [office] girls—they don't know what they're doing." He referred the reporters to Thomas Ceglarek, a Clark-Maple vice president.

Ceglarek said the billing for two cylinders must have been a clerical error. "It's rare," he said. "It's really rare that should happen. It's a mistake."

He called in George Peltier, parts manager, who said: "It's an oversight. My men get in a hurry. We're shorthanded."

Both the Goodyear Service Store, 11442 S. Michigan Av., and Milex Auto Center, 1000 E. 162nd St., South Holland, checked the same malfunction on the Nova but made no attempt to rectify it.

Both said it was a problem with the master cylinder and urged the driver to take the car back to whoever had installed the cylinder.

On the Maverick, Armstrong—after draining some brake fluid—loosened a nut of the master cylinder to make it appear the cylinder was leaking, thus making it easier for a mechanic to spot the source of the problem.

At the Midas Muffler Shop, 510 W. Roosevelt Rd., the reporter was told, "You need a master cylinder on your car."

"I do? What's a master cylinder?"

"It's a part that goes to the brakes."

"How much is it going to cost me?"

"The bill would be somewhere around $60."

"There's no way you can repair that thing, is there?"

"There's no other way."

The bill was $65.55—$38.95 for a new master cylinder, $26 for labor, plus tax. When the reporter asked for the old part, he was told that would be another $15.

The master cylinder will be rebuilt," the Midas mechanic said. "We get a price in exchange for the original part. If you want to pay the $15 . . . then you can have the part."

When reporters returned to question Melvin Shapiro, owner of the Midas shop, he said there should have been no charge on an old part if it was replaced by a new part; charges were only made on parts replaced by rebuilt parts.

The same car with the same minor problem was repaired for $17.25 at Al's Standard Service, Butterfield and Midwest roads, Oakbrook Terrace, and for $30.70 at Al Piemonte Ford, Inc., 2500 North Av., Melrose Park. Piemonte included the cost of a new gasket to make sure the replaced oil would not leak out of the cylinder.

The Montgomery Ward service center, in the Evergreen Shopping Center, Evergreen Park, charged $71.24 for the Gremlin—$43.16 for a new master cylinder, $27 for labor, plus tax. The shop promised to return the old cylinder after the reporter said, "I drive my car on the job, and I think I can get reimbursed . . . but I'll need the part."

When he called for his car, however, the old part was nowhere to be found. The mechanic said he had thrown it away.

Ed-N-Sam Motors, Inc., 8484 South Chicago Av., correctly diagnosed and corrected the Gremlin's problem for $27.58.

After the same car was repaired for $12 at the Sears shop in the Woodfield Shopping Center, Schaumburg, it was returned, according to schedule, to Waubonsee for examination.

"Whoever repaired this car unplugged the wire to your brake warning light," Armstrong said, pointing to the disconnected wire. "This could be fairly dangerous because the light is designed to warn you before the brakes go out."

The Sears mechanic who worked on the car subsequently denied disconnecting the wire to the light, which was working properly when the car was brought in.

Kenneth O'Toole, service manager at Sears' Woodfield shop, acknowledged that the disconnected brake light could be dangerous and added, "It's making a unit not function as designed."

"I certainly hope it is not a common occurrence here," he added.

"It sounds as though we corrected the problem to a safe degree, but we didn't do the final thing," O'Toole said.

"Apparently he [the mechanic] didn't know how to do it," added Henry Lorch, auto center manager.

In all, The Tribune visited 52 Chicago-area garages to test mechanics' skills at fixing minor problems with transmissions, ignition systems, and brakes.

Twenty-two of the 52 garages did the proper work at or below a suggested fair price; another nine were unable to diagnose the trouble or charged more than necessary to remedy it; and 21 garages performed unnecessary repairs, did sloppy work, or quoted prices in the hundreds of dollars for a minor repair.

Those prices ranged from free to $394 for correcting a transmission problem caused by a disconnected vacuum hose, and free to $78.35 for an ignition problem caused by a disconnected starter wire.

The lowest price for fixing the brakes on any of the cars was $4.50, charged by the Venture Car center at River Oaks West, in Calumet City, for the Plymouth.

"It's a common problem," explained Steve Schmiedl, service manager. "I wouldn't put on any parts that weren't absolutely necessary."

Jeffrey Czach, 25, who repaired the Plymouth for $18.44 at Czach Automotive, 6935 W. Irving Park Rd., said, "When people trust you, it makes your job a lot easier."

At Elmhurst Chrysler-Plymouth, 200 W. Grand Av., Elmhurst, where the Plymouth was put back on the road for $19.75, Michael Helmer, service writer, explained: "It was not an especially difficult problem. A customer leaves himself wide open if he does not exactly specify what he wants done to a car."

TABLE 2

What Each Garage Charged to Fix Brakes

| Garage | Car used | What we did | Our expert's cost estimate | Garage cost | Garage response |
|---|---|---|---|---|---|
| Clark-Maple Chevrolet 1038 N. Clark St. | 1974 Chevrolet Nova | Fluid drained from one compartment of master cylinder | $30 | $131.12 | Replaced master cylinder: "safety precaution"; charged for two master cylinders; "mistake." |
| Goodyear Service Store 11442 S. Michigan Av. | 1974 Chevrolet Nova | Fluid drained from one compartment of master cylinder | $30 | Free | No work done, told to return to dealer who put on master cylinder. |
| Milex Auto Center 1000 E. 162nd St. South Holland | 1974 Chevrolet Nova | Fluid drained from one compartment of master cylinder | $30 | Free | No work done, referred to dealer who put on master cylinder. |
| Al Piemonte Ford 2500 North Avenue Melrose Park | 1973 Ford Maverick | Fluid drained from one compartment of master cylinder | $30 | $30.70 | Thorough inspection of brake system; replace fluid and gaskets. |
| Midas 510 W. Roosevelt Rd. | 1973 Ford Maverick | Fluid drained from one compartment of master cylinder | $30 | $65.55 | New master cylinder. "When you see a master cylinder is wet underneath you don't get careless, you assume it leaks." |
| Al's Standard Service Butterfield & Midwest Rds. Oakbrook Terrace | 1973 Ford Maverick | Fluid drained from one compartment of master cylinder | $30 | $17.25 | "'I emphasize sales a lot but I only sell what a guy needs." |

**TABLE 2 (Continued)**

| Garage | Car used | What we did | Our expert's cost estimate | Garage cost | Garage response |
|---|---|---|---|---|---|
| Wards Auto Ser. Ctr. Evergreen Shpg. Plaza Evergreen Park | 1974 AMC Gremlin | Fluid drained from one compartment of master cylinder | $30 | $71.24 | New master cylinder; replaced as safety precaution. |
| Ed-N-Sam Motors 8484 S. Chicago Av. | 1974 AMC Gremlin | Fluid drained from one compartment of master cylinder | $30 | $27.58 | "I come here at six in the morning and I don't want anyone to blow my head off for cheating." |
| Sears Auto. Ctr. Woodfield Shpg. Mall Schaumburg | 1974 AMC Gremlin | Fluid drained from one compartment of master cylinder | $30 | $12.00 | Brakes repaired but wire to dashboard brake light disconnected. "Somebody dropped the ball." |
| Elmhurst Chrysler-Plymouth 200 W. Grand Av. Elmhurst | 1973 Plymouth station wagon | Fluid drained from one compartment of master cylinder | $30 | $19.75 | "It was not an especially difficult problem." |
| Czach Automotive 6935 W. Irving Park Rd. | 1973 Plymouth station wagon | Fluid drained from one compartment of master cylinder | $30 | $18.44 | "When people trust you it makes your job a lot easier." |
| Venture Car Center River Oaks West Calumet City | 1973 Plymouth station wagon | Fluid drained from one compartment of master cylinder | $30 | $4.50 | "A master cylinder costs a lot. I wouldn't put on any parts that weren't absolutely necessary." |

# 48

# Racial Discrimination in Chicago's Storefront Banks

## William Bridges and Jerrold Oppenheim

**Research Brief**

*A multiple regression analysis of survey data was carried out to evaluate the extent and form of price differentials in Chicago currency exchanges. These institutions, which are partially regulated by the state, cash checks, write money orders, and remit utility payments in return for small service fees. The results showed that there were price differentials for obtaining financial services of small value (under $200), with higher prices being charged in Latino and Black neighborhoods. The inclusion of interaction terms for ethnic composition, however, demonstrated that the form of the pricing function was relatively constant across neighborhoods.*

*I*n this note, we report the results of a pilot study that was undertaken to answer the following question: is there sufficient evidence of racial discrimination by Chicago currency exchanges to warrant the instigation of legal proceedings under the federal Civil Rights Act? Currency exchanges, which are almost unique to Chicago, where branch banking is not allowed, serve residents in areas of the city so poor that they cannot attract a bank. Here exchanges serve as the only institutions that will cash welfare checks, sell food stamps and money orders, and remit utility payments. (Some places, especially grocery stores, will perform some of these functions. But currency

AUTHORS' NOTE: *The assistance of Jay Rosen, David McDowell, and Richard Berk in the collection and analysis of data is gratefully acknowledged.*

exchanges have exclusive contracts with the state for distribution of food stamps and, surprisingly, distribution of most welfare checks.)

Of course, currency exchanges charge for these services. For the most part, they charge 1 to 2% of the amount to cash checks and write money orders and $.20 to $.30 to remit utility payments. They get $.575 from the state for each food stamp transaction, and they handle public assistance checks without charge. Customers of several currency exchanges report that there are sometimes additional, unposted, and illegal charges—most commonly, for check-cashing and food stamp purchases. Our study was undertaken in the belief that differential prices might occur in a more systematic pattern, according to the racial or ethnic composition of the areas they serve.

The federal Civil Rights Act mandates that "All persons within the jurisdiction of the United States shall have the same right . . . to make and enforce contracts . . . as is enjoyed by white persons, and shall be subject to like . . . exactions of every kind, and to no other" (42 U.S.C. 1981). Private businesses are thus forbidden to discriminate racially or even to take advantage of or merely exploit a pattern of residential racial segregation (see Clark v. Universal Builders). Of course, states are also forbidden from race discrimination (42 U.S.C. 1983).

If a chain of currency exchanges is charging higher prices and making more net profits from its business with blacks than from its business with whites, it is clearly in violation of the law. Similarly, if an individual business serving virtually only blacks (very common in tightly segregated Chicago) makes relatively high profits from relatively high prices, it too can be accused of exploiting Chicago's race segregation by which a third of the city's population is forced to live in neighborhoods that usually lack banks and, due to state licensing restrictions that apply everywhere, also have few currency exchanges. Since Chicago is so segregated, it is not difficult to find businesses that service only blacks and others that serve only whites.

Thus, this initial look at pricing data resembles previous social science research insofar as it attempts to document the existence of special consumer costs for the disadvantaged (Caplovitz, 1976; Wise, 1974; Marcus, 1969; Groom, 1966). To fulfill the definition of exploitation given in the case cited above, it is necessary that we examine data relevant to the costs of doing business in various locations. However, because cost data have not yet been obtained, sources of price differentials that are cited in earlier literature cannot be examined here. Thus, higher prices may result from differential size or volume of business and any concomitant lack of efficiency (Harrison, 1974: 14; Sturdivant, 1968; Federal Trade Commission, 1968). However, a pattern of high prices in black or Spanish-speaking neighborhoods is a signal to lawyers and, one hopes, to judges that further investigation is necessary. Another hypothesis that we have not yet tested is whether differential prices reflect a pattern of discrimination against the poor generally, rather than specific racial or ethnic exploitation (Sturdivant and Wilhelm, 1968). However, our investigation is unique insofar as currency exchanges are partially regulated by the state.

Illinois does not regulate currency exchange *rates,* so it cannot be easily accused of taking part in any discriminatory pricing pattern that is found. For present purposes at least, we are assuming that its licensing restrictions are uniformly applied across the city (although that itself injures black communities, most of which lack other financial institutions aside from grocery stores). However, Illinois law does require the posting of all rates charged, and it turns out that this regulation is widely honored only in part—some posted rates are understated, others are simply left out. If this practice occurs more frequently in black neighborhoods than others, the state regulatory agency may be enforcing its rules in a racially discriminatory way.

To test whether any of these widely suspected forms of race discrimination were occurring, we decided to do a pilot survey. If those results were promising, we would do a more thorough and systematic analysis.

## DATA

This report is of that first test and thus represents highly tentative, albeit suggestive, results based on flawed data. A 1975 Yellow Pages telephone directory of every currency exchange in Chicago was used; every tenth exchange was chosen. These were plotted on a 1970 map that showed the race, based on census data, of 15 arbitrarily drawn sections of the city. Ten exchanges were added to the original group to be certain all areas of the city were represented. This brought the total to 58 exchanges, although 15 were later lost due to survey errors (mostly failure to collect all data). (A later survey has been completed, but not analyzed, of all 480 currency exchanges in Chicago.) The racial composition of the clientele of each exchange was taken to be that of the 1970 census tract in which the exchange was located. Where an exchange sat on the boundary of two or more tracts, the mean proportion of the various census tracts was computed, and that average score was assigned.

Data collected for each exchange included posted check-cashing and money order fees for increments of $5 face value and charges for utility payments and license plates.

## FINDINGS

Tables 1 and 2 provide a general introduction to the results in showing the mean cost (dollars) of cashing checks in exchanges that are classified according to the race or ethnic status of their census tracts. Thus, the figure of $.66, which appears in the third row and second column of Table 1, is an average of 84 different prices: the costs of cashing $15, $20, $25, and $30 checks in each of 21 different currency exchanges that are in census tracts that are 7% black or higher. The bimodal distribution of the racial composition variable permitted

TABLE 1
Check-Cashing Service Charge (mean $) for Sub-Populations
Defined by Racial Composition of Census Tract

|  | Customer Composition | |
| Amount of check | 3% Black or Less | 7% Black or More |
| --- | --- | --- |
| Less than $5 | .336 | .40 |
| $5 - 14 | .442 | .55 |
| $15 - 34 | .546 | .66 |
| $35 - 64 | .669 | .809 |
| $65 - 99 | .784 | .935 |
| $100 - 144 | .866 | 1.006 |
| $145 - 249 | .912 | 1.060 |
| $250 - 499 | 2.186 | 2.099 |
| $500 and over | 4.318 | 5.002 |
| N | (22) | (21) |

## TABLE 2
Check-Cashing Service Charge (mean $) for Sub-Populations
Defined by Spanish-Speaking Composition of Census Tract

| | Customer Composition | | |
|---|---|---|---|
| Amount of check | Less than 1% Spanish | 1-5% Spanish | 5-100% Spanish |
| Less than $5 | .357 | .370 | .318 |
| $5 - 14 | .508 | .467 | .531 |
| $15 - 34 | .613 | .577 | .636 |
| $35 - 64 | .763 | .703 | .776 |
| $65 - 99 | .878 | .824 | .895 |
| $100 - 144 | .942 | .872 | 1.013 |
| $145 - 249 | 1.007 | .912 | 1.10 |
| $250 - 499 | 2.31 | 1.93 | 2.308 |
| $500 and up | 4.713 | 4.082 | 5.75 |
| N | (15) | (19) | (9) |

dichotomizing the census tracts into two groups, "3% or less" and
"7% or more," of approximately equal size.

Applying simple arithmetic to the values in these tables, it is apparent
that while service charges rise monotonically with the face value of
the checks, the increase does not appear to be a simple linear function.
In Figures 1 and 2, these check-cashing costs have been plotted against
the natural logs of the checks' face values; and for checks for less than
$200 ($e^{5.3}$), the service charge increases in a linear fashion with the
*log* of the amount. In the $200 range, there is a sharp bend that is
followed by a rather steep increase in the service charges. While it is
not presented here, data for money order purchase charges reflect the
same underlying pattern. Figure 1 also shows, as we expected, that
check-cashing costs are generally higher in exchanges that are located
in areas with higher proportions of blacks. However, it seems to be the
case that the amount of the "surcharge" associated with race does not
itself vary with the size of the check. Thus, the gap between the two
lines is nearly as wide at the lower end of the range as it is at the higher.

In comparing service charges across areas with differing concentrations of Spanish-speaking people, there is an interesting anomaly.
According to Figure 2, the least expensive places to cash checks are
those areas with some, but at least a few, Latinos. The most costly

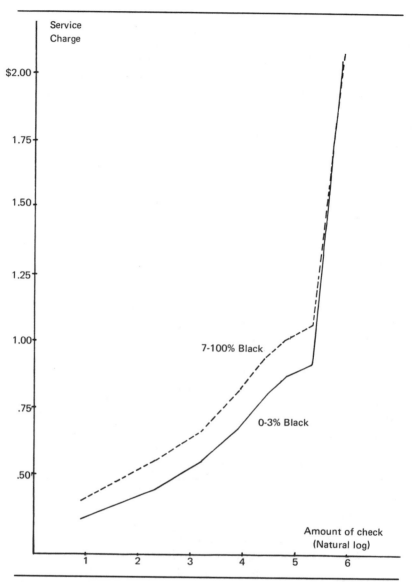

**Figure 1: Check-Cashing Costs by Amount of Check by Black Census Tract Composition**

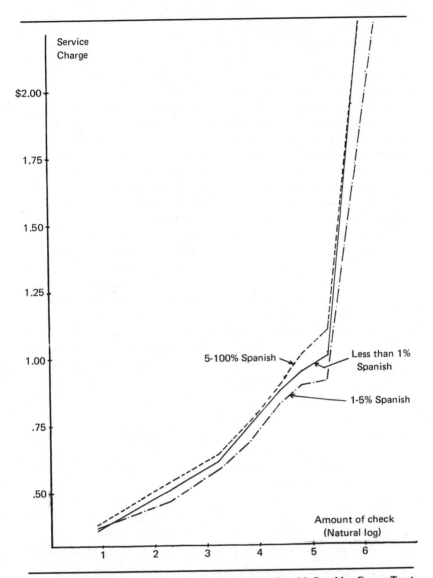

**Figure 2: Check-Cashing Costs by Amount of Check by Spanish-Speaking Census Tract Composition**

exchanges are those with the highest concentrations of Spanish-speaking, but the least Spanish areas are not the least expensive—they charge more than exchanges in the 1 to 5% Spanish-speaking tracts. The probable explanation for this is that there is a negative correlation between percentage black and percentage Spanish (−.29), so that the least Spanish areas in the sample are likely to be those that are the most black and, hence, those with abnormally high rates.

In order to introduce adequate controls for neighborhood composition, to evaluate the linearity of the underlying relationship, to allow for the presence of interaction effects, and to provide estimates of the relative size of various effects, the data were analyzed using multiple regression techniques. Because of the dissimilarity of the relationships over and under the $200-dollar threshold, separate models were constructed for these two situations. In addition, data for money order service charges and check-cashing charges were analyzed separately. The final result was a total of four different models.

In each case, we attempted to fit the data with several different explanatory equations. To the basic model (equation 1), we added terms in two steps. First, terms of percentage black and percentage Spanish-speaking were included and, in the next step, we introduced terms for interaction by race, for interaction by Spanish neighborhood composition, and for quadratic effects for percentage Spanish-speaking. These models are presented in equations 2 and 3, respectively.

$$Y = a + b_1 X_1 + e \qquad\qquad [1]$$

$$Y = a + b_1 X_1 + b_2 X_2 + b_3 X_3 + e \qquad\qquad [2]$$

$$Y = a + b_1 X_1 + b_2 X_2 + (b_3 X_3 + b_4 X_4) + b_5 X_1 X_2 + b_6 X_1 X_3 + e \quad [3]$$

Where:

$Y$ = service charge

$X_1$ = amount of service (i.e., value of check or money order)

$X_2$ = percentage of black in census tract

$X_3$ = percentage Spanish-speaking in census tract

$X_4$ = percentage Spanish-speaking squared

$X_1 X_2$ = interaction of percentage black and amount of service

$X_1 X_3$ = interaction of percentage Spanish and amount of service

An additional consideration was whether the relationship between the service charge and the value of the service would best be described in linear or nonlinear terms. Consequently, in each of the four analysis groups, i.e., checks and money orders that are over or under $200, equations 1 and 2 are fit where the independent variable, "amount of service," was entered in raw score form, natural log form, or reciprocal form (see Johnston, 1972: 50-52). The major distinction between the latter two curvilinear forms is that the reciprocal effect model posits a ceiling price that the regression line asymptotically approaches, while the natural log form allows for a decreasing rate of increase but does not establish an upper bound on the maximum charge.

In the top half of Tables 3 and 4, the best-fitting regression models for each of the four analytic groups are presented. By comparing the proportion of variance explained with and without terms for percentage black and percentage Spanish-speaking, one is able to assess whether the notion of a "surcharge" or price differential plays an important role in regard to total price. Because the sample was not a probability sample, no significance tests were used. However, for checks and money orders below the $200 dollar cutoff, including terms for the race and ethnic composition of the exchange location added about 8 and 4% to explained variance, respectively. Over the $200 dollar boundary, the addition of race and ethnic terms to the equation had virtually no effect. There is no ready explanation for this disappearance of the ethnic surcharge at this level. One possibility is that the exchanges claim to honor a voluntary agreement to price services at 1% of face value on large transactions. If so, the presence of this simplistic rule of thumb may provide some protection for disadvantaged consumers.

The bottom panels of Tables 3 and 4 include data that allow us to evaluate the suitability of different functional relationships between transaction value and price to evaluate the relative contribution of interaction and quadratic effects. As we expected, for transactions under $200, the best-fitting models were those that related price to the logarithms of the face values of instruments. For both checks and money orders, the linear form had slightly less explanatory power than did the semi-log form, but the worst-fitting by far was the reciprocal

## TABLE 3
### Regression Model for Predicting Service Charges
### for Checks and Money Orders Less than $200

| | Service | | | |
| | Check Cashing | | Money Order | |
| | Step 1 | Step 2 | Step 1 | Step 2 |
|---|---|---|---|---|
| Variable | b | b | b | b |
| Face value (natural log) | .1350 | .1350 | .0953 | .0953 |
| % Black | -- | .0016 | -- | .0009 |
| % Spanish-speaking | -- | .0036 | -- | .0008 |
| Constant | .263 | .180 | .311 | .271 |
| R² (adj) | .411 | .519 | .404 | .448 |
| R² (adj) with linear face value | .382 | .461 | .321 | .364 |
| R² (adj) with reciprocal vace value | .115 | .192 | .106 | .174 |
| R² (adj) with log of face value and interaction terms and quadratic effect of % Spanish-speaking | -- | .521 | -- | .451 |

transformation. Substantively, this implies that the variable costs that an operator encounters, such as increased risk with larger transactions, are passed on at a diminishing rate to his or her customers. It is also interesting that the functional form that assumes a ceiling price, i.e., the reciprocal form, does the worst in accounting for prices charged. For transactions of $200 or over, the best-fitting model is now linear, both curvilinear transformations now decrease the explanatory power of the equations.

The final row of both tables presents the $R^2$ obtained when the data are analyzed with equations resembling equation 3. These permit us to resolve the issue of interaction effects and the curvilinear pattern that was noted earlier for percentage Spanish-speaking. When interaction terms for race and ethnicity are added along with the quadratic effect of percentage Spanish, we find only a slight increment to the proportion of variance explained. This increment ranges between .2 and 1.7% of variance in the four subpopulations and was therefore judged to be

## TABLE 4
Regression Model for Predicting Service Charges for
Checks and Money Orders of $200 or More

| | Service | | | |
| | Check Cashing | | Money Orders | |
| | Step 1 | Step 2 | Step 1 | Step 2 |
|---|---|---|---|---|
| Variable | b | b | b | b |
| Face value (raw form) | .0122 | .0122 | .003 | .003 |
| % Black | -- | .0013 | -- | .0021 |
| % Spanish-speaking | -- | .0089 | -- | .0035 |
| Constant | -1.50 | -1.62 | .21 | .162 |
| R² (adj) | .495 | .495 | .062 | .061 |
| R² (adj) with log of face value | .479 | .479 | .057 | .056 |
| R² (adj) with reciprocal of face value | .443 | .443 | .049 | .048 |
| R² (adj) with linear face value, interaction terms and quadratic effect of % Spanish-speaking | -- | .512 | -- | .066 |

substantively trivial. Thus, the nature of the price differential, where it exists, is that of a constant "surcharge" rather than a change in the basic "rules of the game."

In the subpopulations where substantial discriminatory effects were found, it is appropriate to examine the relative size of the race and ethnic terms and the transaction value term. Restricting our attention to checks, we find that each percentage point change in the racial composition of the location (white to black) is associated with an increase in service charge of $.0016. While this seems minuscule at first glance, it translates to $.145 increase in service charge when one goes from a 95% white to a 95% black location—a not impossible shift in Chicago. Thus, if our equation were used to predict the service charge for cashing a $25 check in the two racial locations, we would predict a $.61 charge in the mostly white locale and a $.75 charge in the mostly black locale. Stated somewhat differently, the individual cashing this check in the mostly black area pays a service fee of which 20% is an added surcharge. A slightly less invidious result obtains for money orders. With regard to differential pricing between Spanish and non-Spanish locations, there is an even larger coefficient of differential prices. This occurs in part because we are observing a partial measure and there is a negative correlation of percentage black and percentage Spanish-speaking. Another explanation is that the range in Spanish composition is also narrower than the range of black composition, and the empirically incurred surcharges are perhaps closer together than are the idealized ones of the regression model.

Before stating conclusions, we would permit to one other problematic aspect of the findings: in three of our subpopulations, we are able to account for only 50% of the variance in service charges and in the fourth, expensive money orders, for only about 6%. This lack of fit probably stems from three distinct sources. Because the results are not linear, we cannot be sure of having hit upon the most satisfactory functional relationship. The procedures of classifying exchanges according to the percentage of the population of their census tracts who are minorities certainly introduce some measurement error into those variables. Finally, there are important variables that we have not been able to include in this initial survey. Thus, some exchanges are chain operations and others are not; the socioeconomic character of the location is probably important. And we might also discover an impact stemming from the presence of additional sources of financial services in the location, i.e., supply.

## CONCLUSIONS

Since the analysis suggests a $.14 surcharge for blacks cashing checks, it seems to support the conclusion that any Southside black with the $1 for round-trip carfare and more than seven checks to cash ought to do his business on the white Northside.

On a more practical level, the results encourage more systematic research. Extrapolating these results for a moment, it would appear that at least some individual exchanges are "exploiting" Chicago's residential race segregation by charging higher prices to blacks and thus (presumably) reaping extraordinarily high profits. (Financial data will ultimately be necessary to prove this, of course. But as a practical matter, that can only be obtained by legal process, after a law suit has commenced and a judge is persuaded that there is a substantial legal and factual controversy requiring for its resolution the disclosure of such sensitive information.)

It also appears worthwhile to check within each chain of exchanges for similar patterns. And, since the data are readily available to do it, we will also see if there is a pattern of exchange failure to post all rates.

Ultimately, we hope for court or agency supervision of currency exchanges to ensure that profit levels do not correlate with race of clientele. A happy, though unlikely, byproduct would be supervision to ensure that profits, and thus prices, are at "reasonable" levels.

## REFERENCES

CAPLOVITZ, D. (1976) The Poor Pay More. New York: Free Press.

Federal Trade Commission (1968) Economic Report on Installment Credit and Retail Sales Practices of District of Columbia Retailers. Washington, D.C.: Government Printing Office.

GROOM, P. (1966) "Prices in poor neighborhoods." Monthly Labor Rev. (October): 1085-1090.

HARRISON, B. (1974) "Ghetto economic development: a survey." J. of Econ. Literature 12 (March): 1-37.

JOHNSTON, J. (1972) Econometric Methods (second ed.). New York: McGraw-Hill.

MARCUS, B. H. (1969) "Similarity of ghetto and non-ghetto food costs." J. of Marketing Research 6 (August): 365-368.

STURDIVANT, F. (1968) "Better deal for ghetto shoppers." Harvard Business Rev. (March): 130-139.

——— and W. WILHELM (1968) "Poverty, minorities and consumer exploitation." Social Science Q. (December): 643-650.

WISE, G. L. (1974) "Differential pricing and treatment by new car salesman: the effect of the prospect's race, sex and dress." J. of Business 47 (April): 218-230.

## CASE

Clark v. Universal Builders (1974) 501 F. 2d (7th Cir.), cert. den. 95 S. Ct. 657, 419 U.S. 1070, 42 L. Ed. 2d 666.

*William Bridges is an Assistant Professor of Sociology at the University of Illinois at Chicago Circle. His research interests are in the study of institutional discrimination and other topics related to social inequality. Currently he is engaged in a secondary analysis of the role of industrial and organizational factors as causes of women's inferior labor market status.*

*Jerrold Oppenheim is Director of Consumer Litigation at the Legal Assistance Foundation of Chicago. His work currently includes the economics of electric power rate structure, the economic relationship between Blue Cross plans and hospitals, and the legal standing of consumers before state administrative agencies.*

# 49

# Citizen Demand and Bureaucratic Response: Direct Dialing Democracy in a Major American City

*Kenneth R. Mladenka*

**Verba and Nie** (1972: 54) observe that most analyses of participation "have focused on the citizen as voter."

> At the other extreme is the citizen-initiated contact, in which the citizen contacts an official on some problem. The problem may be very narrow, a situation made possible by the fact that the citizen "chooses the agenda" of the participatory act. Though the outcome may have little measurable impact on the overall system, the outcome may be very important for him. And, unlike the situation in relation to voting, his own activity may make a major difference. Furthermore, the set of these dispersed contacts may represent a major allocative mechanism in society.

However, we know very little about that mode of participation wherein the citizen contacts government in regard to a public matter. The available evidence does suggest that many citizens never engage in this form of participation. Aberbach and Walker (1970) reported that only a third of the respondents in a survey of citizen attitudes in Detroit had ever contacted city government in regard to municipal services, while Levy et al. (1974) found that the streets department in Oakland received about three complaints daily. In addition, blacks are less likely to contact government than whites. Relying on survey data, Eisenger (1972)

AUTHOR'S NOTE: *The author wishes to thank several anonymous reviewers for this journal for their helpful and detailed comments. An earlier version of this paper was presented at the 1976 annual Urban South Conference, Norfolk, Virginia.*

discovered that only 33% of whites and 11% of blacks had ever initiated a contact at any level of government, while Verba and Nie (1972) concluded that even when socioeconomic status was controlled blacks were less likely to communicate their grievances directly to public officials. Although more blacks than whites perceived government as relevant to their personal problems, only 25% of those black respondents acknowledging government's relevance had ever contacted it. However, in their analysis of actual citizen-initiated contacts in Detroit, Jones et al. (forthcoming) discovered that "neighborhoods with a high proportion of black residents are more likely to initiate contacts, when the influence of the social well-being of the neighborhood is held constant."

Even less evidence is available in regard to how well government responds to these individual citizen demands and whether responsiveness varies on the basis of race and income.[1] A number of writers have observed that the bureaucracy is less responsive to lower-class individuals (Fox, 1974; Lipsky, 1970; Parenti, 1970; Sjoberg et al., 1966). In general, it is alleged that poor persons lack the resources and organizational skills necessary to insure bureaucratic responsiveness. Despite these assumptions, we have little idea whether governments systematically discriminate against black and other low income individuals in regard to their requests for assistance.

## RESEARCH DESIGN

How well does the municipal bureaucracy respond to the citizen who contacts government in regard to a chughole in the street, debris on a vacant lot, an obstructed drainage ditch, a missed garbage pick-up, or a variety of other service-related grievances that are directly communicated on a daily basis to public officials? Further, how does the subsequent response vary on the basis of the socioeconomic characteristics of the contactors? Social scientists are unaccustomed to analyzing these individual transactions between citizen and government. However, we agree with Eisenger (1972: 43) that this form of participation taps an important dimension of the representative relationship since citizen contacting "is a demand for representation in that the contactor asks in effect that an official act on behalf of his concerns." On the basis of the evidence, it is hypothesized that black and other low-income neighborhoods will be less likely to contact government about a public matter. In addition, government will provide a more satisfactory response to contacts from wealthier areas.

In order to test these hypotheses, data on individual contacts were gathered through an examination of bureaucratic records in the city of Houston.[2] Initially, an effort was made to analyze those citizen contacts with both a "broad" and a "particularized referent."[3] A systematic sampling technique was employed to generate 538 cases from all *recorded* contacts with city government in 1973 (Blalock, 1960: 397-399). The address of each contactor was then located by census tract and the demographic characteristics of these units were employed as predictor variables.[4] In addition to the demographic indicators, variables include the nature of the demand,[5] the municipal bureaucracy responsible for processing the citizen grievance, and the action taken by the appropriate department in response to the demand.[6] In order to verify the governmental response contained in municipal records, a random sample of contactors (N = 35) was interviewed by telephone. The interview results indicate that these recorded responses are an accurate reflection of the action taken by the bureaucracy.[7]

Before proceeding to the findings, several points should be noted. First, the analysis does not include *all* of those contacts communicated directly to the mayor and city councilmen. Although investigation revealed that most citizen contacts with elected officials which deal with a particularized request are automatically referred to the bureaucracy for action and processed in a normal manner, there was no way to determine how many requests were ignored. For example, contacts which express a general policy preference are unlikely to be forwarded through bureaucratic channels. Second, it should be emphasized that the Verba and Nie study relied on respondent recall of individual experiences with government and analyzed a much wider range of citizen contacts with public officials. The data presented here are limited to *recorded* contacts with the municipal bureaucracy in a single city. Third, there was no way to determine how many individual requests for service failed to be recorded by the central agency and forwarded to the appropriate municipal department for action. However, several days of participant-observation revealed no instance in which a citizen contact did not at least receive initial consideration by government.

## INITIAL FINDINGS

Preliminary analysis revealed that 45 (9.3%) of the contactors made more than one request and accounted for 100 (18.6%) of the 538 demands. It should be noted that all of these individuals were concerned with different service delivery problems in each of their contacts. Consequently, it cannot be assumed that these additional requests indicated dissatisfaction with the bureaucratic response to the initial contact. Therefore, each subsequent request was treated separately in the coding scheme. In addition, 519 (96.5%) of the contacts were made in regard to a personal residence while only 19 (3.5%) were related to a business activity. The distribution of citizen demands by issue area is presented in Table 1.

An examination of the table reveals that citizen contacting at the local level is dominated by a concern with those municipal services that directly and immediately impinge on the life of the individual and his family. For example, the citizen is much more apt to contact government about a missed garbage pick-up or the overgrown lot adjacent to his home than he is to complain about inadequate facilities at the neighborhood park. Consequently, most contacts have a narrow focus. In a number of instances it was impossible to distinguish between those contacts where the subsequent decision of government would have relevance only for the individual initiating the contact and those citizen-government transactions

**TABLE 1**
**Distribution of Citizen-Initiated**
**Contacts by Service Area**

| Service Area | N | Percent of Total | Rank Order |
|---|---|---|---|
| Drainage | 121 | 22.5 | 1 |
| Water Maintenance | 113 | 21.0 | 2 |
| Overgrowth | 63 | 11.7 | 3 |
| Debris | 57 | 10.6 | 4 |
| Sewer | 56 | 10.4 | 5 |
| Street Maintenance | 47 | 8.7 | 6 |
| Stray Animals | 26 | 4.8 | 7 |
| Garbage | 20 | 3.7 | 8 |
| Other | 19 | 3.6 | 9 |
| Traffic | 16 | 3.0 | 10 |

where any benefits conferred would have a wider impact. However, a careful analysis of each contact and interviews with a sample of contactors strongly *suggest* that in most cases the decision to engage in this form of participation was made on the basis of strictly personal considerations. In only a few instances did a citizen demand that government address those problems and issues with apparent relevance for large numbers of people in the community. For example, most street and drainage related complaints specifically refer to the inadequacy of these services in the immediate vicinity of the contactor's residence.[8] However, this finding does not refute the conclusion that only one-third of all citizen initiated contacts are about "particularized" matters (Verba and Nie, 1972: 67). Since a tendency probably exists for government officials to record only those requests which they can do something about, the data analyzed here may be skewed in the direction of particularized contacts. For example, the citizen who insists that a chughole in a neighborhood street be repaired has made a specific demand that can be processed through normal bureaucratic channels. However, the individual who expresses his preference on a general policy question to an elected official or communicates his opinion on a service delivery issue with a broad referent ("the city needs better police protection") is unlikely to find that the contact is handled in the same fashion as a particularized request. The small number of contacts encountered during the data collection stage with a general policy focus or broad referent indicates that many of these contacts may not be recorded by municipal officials. Consequently, comparisons with the wider range of contacts analyzed by Verba and Nie are not appropriate.

An examination of the distribution of contacts in Table 1 also indicates a fairly close correspondence between the issue concerns of the contacting population and the priorities of the larger community. The available survey evidence for Houston suggests that many of the issues salient to the sample of contactors are the same issues that concern other citizens as well (Southwest Center for Urban Research, 1972). Consequently, the contacting population is not a deviant group in terms of the nature of its demands on government.[9]

The relationships between citizen-initiated contacts and the subsequent bureaucratic response are presented in Table 2.[10] Only one out of every three citizens who contacts city government can expect a substantive response to his demand for service. Eighty-one percent of the stray animal, 44% of the overgrowth and debris, 56% of the water maintenance, and one-half of the garbage related problems were satisfactorily resolved through bureaucratic action. However, a similar response was forthcoming for only one out of every three sewer and one out of every ten drainage and street related complaints. Although drainage and street repair requests comprise one-third of all citizen-initiated contacts, these demands account for only one-tenth of the responses. Similarly, stray animal, overgrowth, debris, water maintenance, and garbage complaints constitute one-half of all contacts and account for three-fourths of the substantive responses.

Governmental responsiveness to citizen-initiated contacts appears to be a function of the effort and resources required for compliance with the demand. When the municipal bureaucracy is contacted in regard to stray

TABLE 2
Association (Theta) Between Demand and Response

| Type of Contact | Satisfactory Response | No Response | Total |
|---|---|---|---|
| Drainage | 10.0% (N=12) | 90.0% (N=108) | 22.3 (N=120) |
| Sewer | 33.9 (19) | 66.1 (37) | 10.4 (56) |
| Stray Animals | 81.0 (21) | 19.0 (5) | 4.8 (26) |
| Overgrowth | 44.4 (28) | 55.6 (35) | 11.7 (63) |
| Debris | 43.9 (25) | 56.1 (32) | 10.6 (57) |
| Water | 55.8 (63) | 44.2 (50) | 21.0 (113) |
| Streets | 12.8 (6) | 87.2 (41) | 8.8 (47) |
| Traffic | 37.5 (6) | 62.5 (10) | 3.0 (16) |
| Garbage | 50.0 (10) | 50.0 (10) | 3.7 (20) |
| Other | 57.9 (11) | 42.1 (8) | 3.5 (19) |
| Percent | 37.4 | 62.6 | 100.0 |
| Total N | 201 | 336 | 537 |

Theta = .27, p < .01

animals or a missed garbage pick-up the subsequent decision of government is responsive to the citizen in a majority of cases. However, demands for service that would entail a considerable expenditure of resources are generally ignored. No action is taken in regard to most drainage and street maintenance contacts. Similarly, demands requiring an intermediate level of effort are accorded an intermediate level of response.[11] This pattern of differential response does not appear to be a function of citizen priorities. For example, water maintenance complaints account for one-fourth of all citizen contacts and receive a high level of response. However, drainage complaints also constitute one-fourth of all service requests but experience a low probability of favorable governmental action.

This pattern of bureaucratic action is further supported by an examination of the relationship between the various municipal bureaucracies responsible for decisions in regard to citizen contacts and the subsequent response.[12] The association (Theta) between municipal department and responsiveness is .42. Some city bureaucracies do a considerably better job than others in responding to citizen-initiated contacts. For example, Public Works receives 45% of all service contacts but provides only 14% of the substantive responses. By comparison, the Rabies Control and Water departments are responsible for less than one-fourth of all citizen contacts but account for over one-third of the total responses.

## SUMMARY

Several significant findings have emerged so far. First, the evidence does not support the conclusion that a majority of all citizen contacts are directed toward "collective" rather than "particularized" benefits (Verba and Nie, 1972). In fact, the great majority of citizen-initiated contacts in this study were aimed at very narrow benefits. It should be emphasized, however, that the Verba and Nie investigation relied on respondent recall of individual experiences with government rather than on an analysis of recorded citizen-government transactions. Therefore, it may be that the respondents would be more likely to recall those contacts directed toward the important social issues of the day and less likely to remember those participatory efforts intended to secure narrow personal benefits. Also, Verba and Nie analyzed a much wider range of citizen contacts with government. Second, the evidence suggests a fairly close correspondence between the concerns of the sample of contactors and the issue priorities of the larger community. Although the contacting population is unique in terms of its decision to participate, it appears to accurately reflect the service priorities of the general public.

Third, the absolute level of governmental responsiveness to citizen contacts is very low. A large majority of all demands for service are ignored by the municipal bureaucracy. Fourth, the recorded frequency of citizen contacting is also very low. Apparently, most citizens never avail themselves of the opportunity to communicate their grievances directly to public officials. In fact, the municipal government processes an average of only 35-50 citizen-initiated contacts daily. Although a number of studies have documented the low incidence of citizen contacting (Verba and Nie, 1972; Eisenger, 1972; Aberbach and Walker, 1970), the extent of nonparticipation is still surprising.[13] This absence of widespread participation may be related to the discovery that the municipal bureaucracy chooses to ignore most citizen demands. Does the bureaucracy react with a minimum of substantive action to expressed citizen grievances because it experiences minimal pressure from the low volume of individual demands, or is the depressed level of participation related to an awareness on the part of the citizen that the typical contact will meet with a low probability of response?

In order to determine the attitude of municipal administrators toward citizen complaints, interviews were conducted with approximately 25 bureaucrats in Public Works, Parks and Recreation, Libraries, and Public Health. An effort was made to identify and interview those agency personnel responsible for setting and implementing departmental policy in regard to citizen contacts. Although the evidence is limited, the interviews did suggest that the importance of citizen contacting varies from agency to agency. For example, Streets and Drainage maintain that considerations of equity and efficiency require a routinized maintenance system that is insensitive to sporadic and isolated instances of demand-making. Since maintenance decisions are allegedly made on the basis of technical-rational criteria, these agency personnel believe that a lack of responsiveness to citizen contacts contributes to an equitable distribution of resources across neighborhoods. By comparison, the Water and Rabies Control departments partially rely on citizens complaints for the identification of problem areas and maintenance needs. In both cases, however, the low level of demand-making precludes the possibility of any sanctions for unresponsiveness. If it chooses, the municipal bureaucracy may disregard citizen contacts with impunity. None of the bureaucrats interviewed perceived this form of participation as a source of pressure. Consequently, citizen-initiated contacts play an insignificant role in the decision-making and resource allocation process. At best, individual grievances are utilized as a secondary source of information. At worst, they are considered a nuisance and ignored.

In general, it can be concluded that citizen contacts do not play a vital role in the administrative feedback process. The complexity and routine of day-to-day operations in most municipal agencies is little affected by an occasional complaint about service inadequacies. Unfortunately, elected officials were not interviewed. Consequently, we have little idea whether these officals are more sensitive to citizen contacts than administrators. It should be noted, however, that in most instances elected officials are forced to rely on the bureaucracy for the resolution of constituent problems. Since many of the contacts with the mayor and city councilmen are about particularized matters, and since most of these complaints are forwarded to the service delivery bureaucracies for action, the citizen is largely dependent on the administrative apparatus for the redress of service-related grievances.

## THE DISTRIBUTION OF RESPONSIVENESS

It should be emphasized, however, that the absolute level of demand-making is irrelevant for those thousands of persons who do contact government in regard to a myriad of service related matters. The citizen who complains that the debris and overgrowth in a vacant lot is an eyesore and health hazard, the individual who argues that the potholes in a residential street make for dangerous driving conditions, and the irate housewife who insists that an obstructed drainage ditch be cleaned before the next downpour are concerned only that government take some action to correct the situation. The question that we now ask is whether those contacts that originate in white and upper-income neighborhoods receive a more favorable response than requests from poorer parts of the city.

The census tracts in the city were divided into three groups on the basis of the percentage of blacks and Chicanos in each.[14] The relationship between ethnicity and demand type is expressed in Table 3. The types of demands transmitted to the urban bureaucracy are similar across tracts with varying degrees of racial concentration. For example, drainage and water related contacts are the first or second service priority in all three groups, while overgrowth complaints rank third or fourth. Although significant neighborhood differences are noted in regard to such concerns as the repair of residential streets, the evidence does suggest that the service priorities of the contacting population are fairly constant across racial groupings. In addition, predominately white neighborhoods do not account for the bulk of citizen-initiated contacts.[15] In fact, when the number of demands is standardized in terms of population one discovers that less than a third of all contacts originate in white tracts. Tracts with medium and high concentrations of blacks and Chicanos account for 38% and 35%, respectively, of the total contacts.[16]

Further analysis reveals that responsiveness to citizen contacts does not vary on the basis of the racial composition of neighborhoods. An

**TABLE 3**
**Association (Theta) Between Racial**
**Concentration and Type of Contact**

| Type of Contact | Low Concentration | Medium Concentration | High Concentration | Total |
|---|---|---|---|---|
| Drainage | 24.1% (N=41) | 18.7% (N=29) | 21.5 (N=37) | 21.5 (N=107) |
| Sewer | 10.6 (18) | 11.0 (17) | 7.0 (12) | 9.5 (47) |
| Stray Animals | 3.5 (6) | 7.7 (12) | 3.5 (6) | 4.8 (24) |
| Overgrowth | 10.6 (18) | 16.1 (25) | 10.5 (18) | 12.3 (61) |
| Debris | 6.5 (11) | 11.0 (17) | 14.5 (25) | 10.7 (53) |
| Water | 21.8 (37) | 18.7 (29) | 24.4 (42) | 21.7 (108) |
| Streets | 11.8 (20) | 6.5 (10) | 8.7 (15) | 9.1 (45) |
| Traffic | 3.5 (6) | 2.6 (4) | 2.9 (5) | 3.0 (15) |
| Garbage | 4.1 (7) | 3.9 (6) | 4.1 (7) | 4.0 (20) |
| Other | 3.5 (6) | 3.9 (6) | 2.9 (5) | 3.4 (17) |
| Percent | 34.2 | 31.2 | 34.6 | 100.0 |
| Total N | 170 | 155 | 172 | 497 |

Theta = .04, p > .05

examination of Table 4 suggests that there is only a slight tendency for contacts originating in those areas of the city with medium concentrations of blacks and Chicanos to experience a greater probability of favorable governmental action. This finding is best explained by the fact that the residents of these tracts tend to emphasize stray animal complaints in their contacting activity. Since a majority of contacts in regard to this service issue are satisfactorily resolved through bureaucratic action, citizen demands from tracts with large numbers of blacks and Chicanos tend to receive a slightly higher level of responsiveness. An examination of Table 5 suggests that this discovery of little variation in responsiveness on the basis of the racial characteristics of neighborhoods holds when the type of contact is held constant.[17]

The relationships between tract characteristics, service priorities, and governmental responsiveness were further explored through the use of discriminant function analysis. The objective of this multivariate technique is to "statistically distinguish between two or more groups of cases" (Nie et al., 1975: 435).

> To distinguish between the groups the researcher selects a collection of *discriminating variables* that measure characteristics on which the groups are expected to differ. . . . The mathematical objective of discriminant analysis is to weigh and linearly combine the discriminating variables in some fashion so that the groups are forced to be as statistically distinct as possible. In other words, we want to be able to "discriminate" between the groups in the sense of being able to tell them apart.

**TABLE 4**
**Association (Gamma) Between Racial**
**Concentration and Response (all contacts)**

| Response | Low Concentration | Medium Concentration | High Concentration | Total |
|---|---|---|---|---|
| Satisfactory Response | 37.6% (N=64) | 41.9% (N=65) | 36.6% (N=63) | 38.6% (N=192) |
| No Response | 62.4 (106) | 58.1 (90) | 63.4 (109) | 61.4 (305) |
| Percent | 34.2 | 31.2 | 34.6 | 100.0 |
| Total N | 170 | 155 | 172 | 497 |

Gamma = .01, p > .05

Percent Black, percent Chicano, and average value of owner-occupied housing units were employed as the independent variables in an effort to classify citizen contacts on the basis of the racial and socioeconomic characteristics of tracts. The ability of these predictors to distinguish among types of demands is low. Only 25% of citizen contacts were correctly classified on the basis of the selected predictor variables. It can be inferred, therefore, that the issue concerns of the contacting population do not vary on the basis of the demographic characteristics of neighborhoods. The relationship between the predictor variables and bureaucratic responsiveness was also explored through discriminant analysis. Again, the results suggest no variation in responsiveness to citizen contacts on the basis of race and wealth. Only a small percentage of all substantive responses were correctly classified by the discriminating variables.

## CONCLUSION

Verba and Nie (1972: 113) observe that

if one wants to maximize popular control over governmental activities that affect the lives of citizens, both types of mechanisms—the contacting and the electoral—are needed. Because governmental policies are almost always quite general, their application to a specific individual in a specific situation involves particular adjustments or decisions made by low-level government officials. Insofar as this is the case, the ability of the citizen to make himself heard on such a matter—by contacting the official—represents an important aspect of citizen control.

TABLE 5
Association (Gamma Between Racial
Concentration and Response (water-related contacts)

| Response | Low Concentration | Medium Concentration | High Concentration | Total |
|---|---|---|---|---|
| Satisfactory Response | 59.0% (N=22) | 59.0% (N=17) | 55.0% (N=23) | 57.0% (62) |
| No Response | 41.0 (15) | 41.0 (12) | 45.0 (19) | 43.0 (46) |
| Percent | 34.0 | 27.0 | 39.0 | 100.0 |
| Total N | 37 | 29 | 42 | 108 |

Gamma = .07, p $>$ .05

There are at least two reasons why citizen-initiated contacts in Houston are unsuccessful in terms of providing a degree of control over government and obtaining benefits from political authorities. First, the absolute level of recorded contacting is very low. Few citizens are sufficiently motivated to communicate their grievances directly to public officials. This finding supports the results of previous research. Consequently, individual citizen demands are not perceived as a source of pressure. It should be emphasized, however, that this study is limited to an analysis of recorded contacts. It may be that many citizen contacts with a general policy focus are not processed through normal bureaucratic channels. Therefore, the level of contacting activity may be higher than reflected in agency records. Second, a majority of all contacts are simply ignored by government. Although our data did not allow us to address directly the issue of citizen accessibility to government, the evidence suggests that the *level* of contacting does not vary on the basis of socioeconomic status and race. In addition, the analysis revealed little variation in governmental responsiveness to citizen contacts on the basis of neighborhood characteristics. However, accessibility to public officials has little meaning if the political authorities systematically ignore a majority of all contacts. Citizen-initiated contacts can affect government policy only if public decision makers are constrained to pay more than passing attention to this mode of participatory activity.

These findings, however, should not be allowed to diminish the potential significance of citizen contacting. Although the research reported here strongly *suggests* that the opportunities for affecting and adjusting the policy decisions of government through individual contacting are seldom if ever explored by most citizens in Houston, it cannot be assumed that this pattern is typical of most American cities. Intercity variations in contacting activity may be a function of the racial and socioeconomic characteristics of the population, the level and quality of municipal services, citizen satisfaction with these services, the attitudes of urban bureaucrats toward the legitimacy of contacting, and the availability of such alternative modes of participation as "cooperative" activity (Verba and Nie, 1972). Nor can it be assumed that municipal administrators will always choose to ignore most citizen-initiated contacts. In fact, Jones et al. (forthcoming) reported that the Environmental Enforcement Division in Detroit *always* investigated citizen complaints.

And, finally, contacting activity deserves further study because of the potential involved for affecting the direct policy decisions of government. Citizen-initiated contacts with government may have a policy significance beyond the absolute numbers involved. For example, Levy et al. (1974) found that expenditures for the resurfacing of residential streets in Oakland were allocated on the basis of citizen complaints, traffic volume, and an agreement with the utility company whereby improvements were deferred if the company anticipated work on underground lines within five years. It is significant, however, that the Oakland streets department received an average of only *three* complaints daily. In addition, upper-income individuals were more likely to complain about the quality of local streets. Therefore, the allocation of street expenditures in Oakland favored wealthier neighborhoods. Because of the instrumental nature of contacting activity, citizen contacts with government may play an important role in the distribution of urban public services. A growing body of literature on the distribution of municipal services (Lineberry, 1974, 1975; Levy et al., 1974; Jones et al., 1975; Mladenka and Hill, 1975a, 1975b) suggests the importance of bureaucratic "decision rules" in the service delivery process. The findings reported by these researchers indicate that in addition to relying on strictly technical-rational criteria in the allocation of services (traffic volume as a guide to street construction and improvement, circulation rates as a rule for allocating library services, reported crime rates in determining the allocation of police resources), municipal bureaucrats may heed citizen contacts as well. If such contacting activity is skewed in the direction of a particular socioeconomic group, the equitable delivery of services across neighborhoods may be affected.[18] In fact, citizen contacting may represent one of the few distinctly political influences on the generally apolitical process of municipal service delivery. Therefore, future research might profitably explore the relationship between instrumental, nonelectoral modes of participation (citizen-initiated contacts as well as communal/cooperative activity) and the allocation of resources in urban environments.

## NOTES

1. David Easton (1965: 38-39) defines a demand "as an expression of opinion that an authoritative allocation with regard to a particular subject matter should or should not be made by those responsible for doing so. As such, a demand may be quite narrow, specific, and simple in nature as when grievances and discontents, relevant to a given experience, are directly expressed." It is in this narrow sense that the concept of demand is employed in this study.

2. The City of Houston maintains a central office responsible for the processing of all individual citizen requests for service. All citizen contacts, including those initially transmitted to elected officials and individual city departments, are eventually routed through and processed by this agency before forwarding to the appropriate municipal department for action. A record of the subsequent bureaucratic response is then returned to the central office. The data analyzed in this study were gathered from these agency files.

3. Verba and Nie (1972: 66) define contacts with particularized referents as those "in which the issue refers only to the respondent or his immediate family, and in which a government decision responsive to that contact would presumably have little or no direct impact on others in the society." Contacts with broad referents "refer to issues or problems that are more public in nature in which government actions would affect a significant segment of the population, if not the entire community or society."

4. The fallacy of the ecological correlation is unlikely to apply since municipal bureaucrats have no way of ascertaining the racial and socioeconomic characteristics of individual contactors. Therefore, if bureaucratic responsiveness to citizen-initiated contacts varies on the basis of race and wealth, such variation is apt to be a function of bureaucratic perceptions of specific neighborhoods rather than individuals. Consequently, aggregate level data on neighborhood characteristics are appropriate in this instance.

5. Each contact was coded into one of ten categories: Drainage, Water Maintenance, Overgrowth, Debris, Sewer, Street Maintenance, Stray Animals, Garbage, Traffic, and "other." Practically every drainage related contact referred to an obstructed drainage ditch in a residential neighborhood, while water related contacts include broken and leaking mains and lines and defective household meters. Debris contacts include complaints about debris in the streets, trash in a neighbor's yard, and abandoned vehicles, while Traffic related contacts refer to traffic congestion, parking in a prohibited area, and heavy vehicles damaging residential streets. The "other" category includes contacts in regard to dangerous buildings, libraries, parks, and police.

6. The various bureaucratic responses were coded into one of five categories. The first category consists of those replies where the contactor is informed by government that some indefinite action will be taken in the future. The typical response in this category is that needed repairs will be performed according to scheduled maintenance procedures. A Category II response means that the citizen contact was never acknowledged by the bureaucracy, while the third category consists of those instances where an alleged investigation of the reported problem by the appropriate agency revealed no unsatisfactory conditions. A Category IV response indicates that preliminary action had been taken and that a follow-up inspection will be conducted, while Category V implies that the problem described in the contact has been satisfactorily resolved through bureaucratic action.

7. The interview data suggest that those citizens receiving a Category IV (preliminary action has been taken) or Category V response (problem has been satisfactorily resolved) were at least somewhat satisfied with the bureaucratic action taken to address the service grievance described in the contact.

8. The differences between contacts with "particularized" as opposed to "broad" referents tend to dissolve if an effort is made to distinguish between them

on the basis of the impact of the subsequent governmental response. For example, the failure on the part of government to repair a chughole in a residential street has relevance for those drivers who do not live in the immediate neighborhood. Therefore, it is more appropriate to classify contacts (as to their narrow or societal referent) on the basis of the *intent* of the citizen in initiating the contact.

9. The major difference between the issue concerns of the sample of contactors and the service priorities of the respondents in a Houston Model Cities survey occurred in regard to streets. In the latter survey, streets were mentioned as a top priority by 39% of the respondents. However, this service area accounts for only 9% of the total contacts in the sample analyzed here.

10. A "satisfactory response" consists of Categories IV and V, while a "no response" includes Categories I, II, and III. It should be noted that a Category IV reaction may be interpreted as only a partial response. Sixty-five percent of these responses occurred in regard to stray animal and overgrowth complaints. Since many stray animal and overgrowth contacts refer to a private responsibility, the customary procedure is for the appropriate municipal agency to communicate with the person in violation and inform him that the situation must be corrected within a specified time limit. Since the interview data suggest that this action on the part of government was generally sufficient to resolve a problem described in a particular contact, Category IV responses were assumed to represent a satisfactory response.

11. For example, 44% of overgrowth and 44% of debris related contacts receive a satisfactory response.

12. These municipal departments are Public Works, Public Health, Water, Parks and Recreation, Traffic and Transportation, Sewer, Solid Waste, and Rabies Control.

13. It should be noted, however, that this absence of widespread citizen contacting in Houston may not be atypical. Levy et al. (1974) discovered that the streets department in Oakland received only three citizen complaints daily.

14. The percentage of blacks and Chicanos in "low" tracts ranged from 0 to 10%, from 10.1% to 60% in "medium" tracts, and from 60.1% to 100% in "high" tracts.

15. Again, it should be emphasized that caution must be exercised in inferring individual level behavior from aggregate level data. The possibility exists that wealthier whites account for most of the contacts with government in even predominately black neighborhoods. However, the telephone interviews conducted with a number of contactors suggest that the individual attributes of contactors are representative of the demographic characteristics of the tracts in which they reside. Also, it may be that the comparatively low level of contacting in white neighborhoods is directly related to the delivery of superior services in these areas. However, analyses of service delivery patterns across neighborhoods in Houston do not support this assumption (Mladenka and Hill, 1975a, 1975b).

16. Tracts were also classified on the basis of mean per capita income. The association between income and contacting was almost identical to that reported between ethnicity and contacting.

17. The relationships between ethnicity and responsiveness for each category of contacts were highly similar to the one reported in Table 5. For example, the association between race and response (Gamma) for overgrowth contacts was .08. In addition, the associations between *income* and responsiveness, for all citizen contacts as well as for each category of contacts, were highly similar to those reported between ethnicity and responsiveness.

18. In fact, the data presented here for Houston suggest that citizen-initiated contacts *do* affect the delivery of services for some bureaucracies. For example, it will be recalled that the Water and Rabies Control departments partially rely on individual contacts for the identification and resolution of service related problems. However, contacts in regard to these service areas are also equally distributed across neighborhoods. Therefore, the equitable delivery of services is not affected. Although contacting activity in some areas *is* skewed in the direction of particular socioeconomic groups (streets, for instance), the absolute level of bureaucratic responsiveness to these grievances is very low. Consequently, the possibility of inequity in resource allocation on the basis of contacting activity is not realized.

## REFERENCES

ABERBACH, J. D. and J. L. WALKER (1970) "The attitudes of blacks and whites toward city services: implications for public policy," pp. 519-537 in J. P. Crecine (ed.) Financing the Metropolis. Beverly Hills, Calif.: Sage.

BLALOCK, H. M. (1960) Social Statistics. New York: McGraw-Hill.

EASTON, D. (1965) A Systems Analysis of Political Life. New York: John Wiley.

EISINGER, P. K. (1972) "The pattern of citizen contacts with urban officials," pp. 43-69 in H. Hahn (ed.) People and Politics in Urban Society. Beverly Hills, Calif.: Sage.

FOX, D. M. (1974) The Politics of City and State Bureaucracy. Pacific Palisades, Calif.: Goodyear.

JONES, B. D., S. R. GREENBERG, C. KAUFMAN, and J. DREW (forthcoming) "Bureaucratic response to citizen initiated contacts: environmental enforcement in Detroit." Amer. Pol. Sci. Rev.

——— (1975) "Service delivery rules and the distribution of local government services: three Detroit bureaucracies." Paper delivered at the annual meeting of the American Political Science Association.

LEVY, F. S., A. J. MELTSNER, and A. WILDAVSKY (1974) Urban Outcomes. Berkeley: Univ. of California Press.

LINEBERRY, R. L. (1975) "Equality, public policy and public services: the underclass hypothesis and the limits to equality." Paper delivered at the annual meeting of the American Political Science Association.

——— (1974) "Mandating urban equality: the distribution of municipal public services." Texas Law Rev. 53 (December): 26-59.

LIPSKY, M. (1970) Protest in City Politics: Rent Strikes, Housing, and the Power of the Poor. Chicago: Rand McNally.

MLADENKA, K. R. and K. Q. HILL (1975a) "The distribution of urban police services." Paper delivered at the annual meeting of the Midwestern Political Science Association.

——— (1975b) "The distribution of benefits in an urban environment: parks and libraries in Houston." Paper delivered at the annual meeting of the Southwestern Social Science Association.

NIE, N. H., C. H. HALL, J. G. JENKINS, K. STEINBRENNER, and D. H. BENT (1975) Statistical Package for the Social Sciences. New York: McGraw-Hill.

PARENTI, N. (1970) "Power and pluralism: a view from the bottom." J. of Politics 32 (August).

SJOBERG, G. (1966) "Bureaucracy and the lower class." Sociology and Social Research 50 (April).

Southwest Center for Urban Research (1972) Second Annual Model Neighborhood Survey Report I–Resident Priorities. Houston: Southwest Center for Urban Research.

VERBA, S. and N. H. NIE (1972) Participation in America: Political Democracy and Social Equality. New York: Harper & Row.

*Kenneth R. Mladenka is an Assistant Professor of Government, Institute of Government and Department of Government, University of Virginia. He is currently studying (with William Lucy) the conceptual issues associated with equity and urban service distribution under a grant from the Department of Housing and Urban Development and the National Training and Development Service.*

# 50

## The Advantages of Client Involvement
## in Evaluation Research

### Malcolm Bush and Andrew C. Gordon

### PART 1: CLIENT EVALUATION

We were asked recently by an agency of the federal government to evaluate the impact of moving child wards of the state from residential child-care institutions to other less institutional placements. The funding agency cautioned us about the problems of particularly difficult children and parents, of whom pyromaniacs were their primary example. No sooner had we begun our research than we discovered a pyromaniac.

According to the agency records, a mother had set fire to her rented apartment. The mother was consequently declared unfit and the child removed to a child-care institution. We talked to the child about his life as a ward, and his account cast that initial incident in an entirely different perspective: One winter the furnace had broken down in their rented inner-city apartment, and the landlord made no attempt to repair it. During one particularly bitter cold spell the mother, in desperation, lit a fire in a wastebasket. The wastebasket tipped over and the apartment caught fire. This was apparently not a criminal act but an attempt to deal with a difficult, even life-threatening situation. The child's description of the event bore little resemblance to that in the case record.

The information we gathered from interviewing this child and many like him contributed a great deal to our understanding of the problem we were studying. It has caused us to consider more systematically how client perspectives can be useful in evaluation research.

The purpose of this paper is to illustrate the ways in which client participation in the process of assessment can help us to understand both the impact of the programs being evaluated and the problems which the programs were designed to alleviate. We shall discuss some perennial problems in evaluation research, construct validity, access to information, and the subjectivity of personal accounts, in the light of the possibility of client involvement in

From Malcolm Bush and Andrew C. Gordon, "The Advantages of Client Involvement in Evaluation Research." Unpublished manuscript, 1977.

the process of research. We shall illustrate our arguments with examples from our own research in child welfare—research which has studied programs and options for children who were forced to leave home to live with surrogate parents—and from other areas which are currently the objects of evaluation research.

## Clients as Sources of Information

*The Subjectivity of Client Information.* The first task for advocates of client involvement in evaluation research is to consider the common charge that client information is subjective and unverifiable. We were warned by some child welfare officials that children and their parents were biased in the judgments they made about social welfare programs, immature, dishonest, blinded by vested interests, and fickle in their wants and desires. We were occasionally accused of bias ourselves for wanting to elicit information from the children in the first place. That latter charge, incidentally, is commonplace in situations where researchers listen to subordinates in hierarchical systems, even when they listen to superordinates as well (Becker, 1966).

The problem of subjectivity in social science research has been addressed by a comparatively recent school of epistemology, an epistemology which has implications for the social scientist who uses client descriptions to measure the effects of ameliorative programs. This post-behaviorist epistemology suggests a model of man as an agent who has the power to initiate change and to control the manner and the goal of his performances, who can perceive things, can be aware of things other than himself, and is aware of that awareness (Hampshire, 1965; Harre and Secord, 1972). The important implication of this epistemology for our purposes is that clients' accounts of the impact of programs and services on their lives can be regarded as phenomena and not epi-phenomena, and hence as useful descriptions of events. Thus, to use an example from our research, if a child, in talking about child welfare institutions, mentions the amount of discomfort he felt there, or the lack of care and attention he received, those comments are prime sources of data for the evaluation of outcomes.

Furthermore, such information is not as suspect by virtue of being unverifiable as is sometimes thought. First, other people have some access to children's thoughts—in this example, their fellow wards, school friends, and house parents; and second, the language of those thoughts is a common language and hence comprehensible and open to examination by others. Moreover, the information can be verified by other kinds of information, namely, the children's behavior at times when they are not describing to the researcher their view of the care they are receiving. If that behavior is discordant with the children's accounts, the situation calls for further investigation. Thus, clients' accounts of events are authentic, revisable, and subject to empirical criticism just like other accounts (Harre and Secord, 1973: 101).

In our research, client data withstood the validation process. Since it matters a great deal to a child where he or she lives, there are compelling reasons for the child to give the researcher a straightforward account of various surrogate homes. Children constantly assumed—this was one of the hazards of the research—that we could help remove them from homes they disliked or help to guarantee their tenure in homes they found supportive. There is no reason to assume that a child would risk lengthening his stay in an uncomfortable home or shortening it in a supportive home in order to fool a researcher. (Children seemed to assume that we would communicate with state officials about their plight and would not communicate with their surrogate parents, despite our disclaimer that we would not, except in extreme conditions, communicate with anyone about them individually.)

Clients, in addition, were very willing to explain in detail, and to allow us to question them in detail, about their lives as clients, simply because few other people listened to them on the subject. They were not, therefore, prone to brush us off with quick answers, and they gave us time to check their accounts by asking them a variety of questions about important details. Clients turned out to be thoughtful witnesses of social service programs partly because they had a great deal of time and reason to think about the effects of those services. When asked about the benefits and problems of particular programs, clients avoided trivial complaints and satisfactions, and mainly discussed fundamental strengths and weaknesses.

Finally, we could ensure that clients turned out to be good witnesses by interviewing them in groups and thus soliciting "the stubborn reality of group opinion" (Campbell, 1974: 28). Sometimes there was consensus about a particular service, sometimes there was disagreement, but the view of the dissenters was respected by the rest of the group, and sometimes dissenters' opinions were treated with guffaws. Within a single group, then, one could begin to evaluate the trustworthiness of specific pieces of information.

*The Subjectivity of Official Records and the Need for Client Validation.* Validation of client information will occasionally turn up systematic biases in clients' account. We discovered, for example, that compared with the accounts of a variety of adults connected with the children's lives, children who are removed from their homes tend to exaggerate the degree to which they are personally responsible for the break-up of their families. We also discovered, however, that there are systematic biases in the accounts officials give of social welfare services. We found the official case records, the most common source of data about clients, prone to error and bias; these accounts can frequently benefit from being checked against clients' statements.

The case records of clients in the child welfare system were voluminous. But as we discovered, they did not uniformly serve the purpose of recording information about clients' problems and the progress being made to solve or alleviate those problems. They were more likely to demonstrate social workers' grasp of the specialized language of neo-Freudian analysis and to show that services which attracted matching federal funds had been delivered. Case records do not always reflect the client's true condition. There is indeed evidence from the fields of mental health and geriatrics that new case workers are instructed never to write anything positive about their clients in the case records. The reason is that federal inspectors of residential facilities are rumored to insist on the deinstitutionalization of clients supported by Medicare and Medicaid payments once positive remarks begin to appear in their case records. Thus workers are instructed not to write that clients "had a good," but they were "slightly less disturbed today than yesterday" (Chow, 1977; Springer, 1977).

There is another pressure to exaggerate the degree of disability the clients suffer which is just as disasterous for the evaluation researcher seeking good data. State and federal funds for institutional care of many kinds are greater for more severe categories of disablement. This clearly reasonable funding policy has the consequence of persuading some administrators to classify patients into more severe categories than their conditions warrant. If evaluation researchers accept those classifications as baseline data, their conclusions about the effects of the program on those patients will reflect that bias.

One last pressure which encourages the exaggeration of disabilities is the growing national trend toward the coding of specific diagnostic assessments. For monitoring purposes and to meet mounting demands for accountability, various forms of computerizable data bases for services to children are being developed. There are important advantages in these attempts to computerize child welfare information systems, for example, the opportunity to make data comparable across jurisdictions. But computerized coding of cases also carries the deficiency bias to its extreme. For the purposes of quantitative processing, in most of these systems only numerical codes are available; one or more of these must be filled in, and all of them are deficiency labels. Reimbursement categories are also limited to categories of deficiency. Such systems tend only to make biases explicit, not to counter them. Alternative perspectives, including that of the client, are not incorporated.

Even in situations where case records are written for the purpose of describing a client's reaction to particular programs, the records might not, in fact, reflect that reaction but rather the personal relationship between the case worker and the client, and this reaction might be dictated by the issue of how easy the client is to handle. There is obviously a difference between a client's reaction to a program and the client's reaction to administrators and officials, but this difference is often confused in case records. (For an extended discussion of the priorities some service bureaucracies set on controlling rather than benefiting their clients, see Cloward and Piven, 1965.) If case records are characterized by an exaggeration of the clients' condition and a concentration on the clients' acquiescence to instructions rather than on their progress, official documents about clients have to be balanced and checked against clients' own accounts of their condition and progress.

*Clients as Prime Witnesses.* This argument so far has contended for the parity of clients' accounts with the accounts of other actors. There are, however, occasions when clients can be regarded as prime witnesses, as the most effective reporters of the impact of programs. This is true, for example, when the question at issue is whether clients are satisfied with services rendered. The terms "soft" as opposed to "hard" and "attitudinal" as opposed to "behavioral" are used to describe such client measures. Both these terms, however, carry some degree of stigma, and it might be more accurate to talk about satisfaction measures as private as opposed to public criteria. This terminology has the advantage of pointing to the reason why clients' assessments of satisfaction are likely to be more important than others people's assessments. Clients are the only first-hand witnesses to the impact of a program as judged by these private criteria (Harre and Secord, 1972: 121). While their testimony should still be subject to validation by people who have some, though less direct, access to those private criteria, their testimony remains the central testimony, and as witnesses they are primi inter pares.

*Client Data and the Reinterpretation of Events.* There are occasions when a client's view of the world can drastically alter one's interpretation of seemingly straightforward data. We have an example from child welfare of an event which has several commonplace and accepted explanations but which has a very different explanation when seen from the children's perspective. Stealing is endemic in child welfare institutions. Some observers attribute that to the children's delinquent or predelinquent tendencies, despite the fact that most dependent or neglected children do not come into care because of their own bad behavior (Jenkins and Norman, 1972; Geiser, 1973). Other observers attribute the stealing to "acting out," a phrase derived from Freudian theory which suggests that certain abnormal behaviors occur as the result of the suppression of some conflict or trauma. But the view from the children is very different. Personal possessions are uncommon in institutions. Most of the children are from poor families, and institutions generally do not have much money to spare in their budgets for gifts. Furthermore, institutional dress codes, rules, shared living and sleeping areas, and tight daily schedules leave very little opportunity for the expression of individual tastes and personalities. For these reasons, what few personal possessions do exist take on exorbitant importance, and the abnormal tensions of group living are taken out on other people's possessions. This explanation, which incidentally transforms the source of the problem from the children to the ameliorative intervention, could not have emerged from a statistical analysis of the determinants of delinquent behavior or indeed from the reports of adults who were not privy to the children's accounts.

*Client Data and the Prediction of Client Behavior.* Client information may sometimes provide the best predictions of clients' own behavior. Transportation researchers are currently battling with the problem of how to attract confirmed motorists back to public transportation. The experimental assessment of various changes designed to increase ridership would take years and be very costly; by the time the data were analyzed, real-world conditions might well change sufficiently to invalidate the findings. Client surveys, on the other hand, are comparatively cheap and quick, and the results suggest that there is wide agreement between people about what changes in public transportation— and these have to do with quite subtle components of total travel time—would encourage them to switch to public transportation (Wachs, 1976). These particular results have been validated to some degree by the strong agreement among long-time users of public transportation, new users, and nonusers.

There is another example of clients' prediction of their own behavior in a very different field. In the mid-1960s, a number of colleges used a variety of sophisticated measures to determine which of their incoming freshmen would be likely to join political groups and take part in demonstrations. No measure or group of measures turned out to be useful until the researchers decided to ask the incoming students themselves whether they would be likely to become involved in this kind of political activity. That measure turned out to be a more useful predictor of the students' later behavior (Astin, 1969).

*Quantification of Client Data.* Client data, like other data, can be quantitative or qualitative. The quantification of data sometimes enables theorists and policy makers to see patterns of responses which would not otherwise be visible. Our experience suggests, however, that it is especially important with client data to quantify the information as late as possible in the research process. While we learned a great deal about child welfare before we planned our interviews with clients, we learned a lot more about the nature of clients' concerns after those interviews; a premature structuring of response categories before the final survey was conducted would have obscured many of the clients' most important concerns.

The use of standard tests of personality to the exclusion of other measures is an even more premature structuring of responses and runs the risk of completely obscuring the client's reaction to services in cases where there is no strong reason to expect that the services rendered will have any impact on the personality characteristics measured by the tests. The quantification of clients' self-report data results, of course, in measures neither more nor less subjective than those produced by quantification of other people's reports on clients. "Indeed, much of what we think of as experimental measures, recorded on the occasion of pretest and posttest for both experimental and control groups, are in fact quantifications of subjective judgments" (Campbell, 1974: 17).

*Client Information: Some More Advantages.* Clients are in a particularly effective position to observe a program. They witness every aspect of the program that affects them and are full-time witnesses of the effects of the program for as long as they are clients. Staff, on the other hand, witness only some of the program, some of the time. Clients also have experience of preprogram conditions, which means that their personal accounts of the changes wrought by the program can be compared with the results of a more formal comparison of pretest and posttest measures (Campbell, 1974: 26). It also means that clients can act as unofficial historians, pointing out how pre-existing programs, rules, attitudes, and priorities modified the impact of the program. Indeed, some programs are transformed during the evaluation period, and such changes may account for changes observed in the outcome measures; clients are also in a position to observe these events.

Clients' abilities to understand bureaucratic behavior may provide them with a tool for obtaining the services they require. The interaction between programs or agencies and clients is a two-way street. If the only view a researcher has of this interaction is the organization's official view, he is likely to miss those techniques and devices employed by the organization, ostensibly for the purpose of doing the organization's business, but in fact serving the organization's need to be able to live with its clients. Clients are often aware of these devices and can exploit them. Sometimes, when there are fiscal, political, or bureaucratic constraints on the actual delivery of services an agency is supposed to provide, clients have learned how to persuade reluctant officials to deliver those services; they, rather than the officials, are the best informants on how this can be done. Indeed, since clients differ on their competency in extracting services from bureaucracies (Gordon, 1973), one way to improve the success of some programs may be to experiment, not with new versions of the program, but with strategies to teach clients how to obtain or even exploit mandated services.

There is one last practical reason for seeking out client information. Clients may cooperate fully and give the researcher full access to other essential information only when they perceive that their participation and understanding of the situation are taken seriously.

## Clients and the Definitions of Problems

As evaluation researchers, we are often asked to accept the definitions of problems that are presented to us by people who are administering or funding the ameliorative programs. Since, however, there is never a perfect correlation between program and problem, where programs are successful we only discover that they are successful in terms of the program director's definition of the problem. Where they fail our knowledge of the underlying problem is often so rudimentary that we cannot begin to work out the causes of the failure.

It is our experience that clients of social welfare systems define their problems in ways that are sometimes very different from the ways in which they are described by social welfare and funding agencies, and that those different definitions add immensely to our understanding of the underlying problems.

In the field of the welfare of dependent and neglected children, research has concentrated on the ameliorative effects of therapeutic interventions by social workers trained to deal with emotional problems. There is a vast social work literature which describes the problems of these children as primarily emotional and which describes the task of intervention as one of easing the trauma consequent on the children's removal from their natural home. (See Kadushin, 1974: 3; Perlman, 1972: 204.)

Since the early 1960s, a number of research projects have been completed on the effectiveness of therapeutic interventions. (See, for example, Mullen, Chazin and Feldstein, 1970.) Some of the studies are methodologically quite adequate with random assignment of clients to experimental and control conditions. They have, however, one thing in common: the researchers are rarely able to conclude that a program had even modest success in achieving its major goals (Mullen and Dumpson, 1972; Segal, 1972). These findings have triggered reproaches from social-action social workers that therapeutic intervention is so inadequate as to be worthless, and responses from more traditional caseworkers that the methods of evaluation research are too crude to pick out subtle but important changes in people's lives.

Those reactions are interesting, but in the light of our research they miss some important points. We discovered from talking to children and their natural and surrogate parents that the vast majority of dependent and neglected children came into care for reasons connected with the parents'—not the children's—problems, that in a substantial number of cases the parents' difficulty had to do with physical illness or poverty, and that the acute emotional upset which characterized a minority of the children occurred not only when the children were removed from home but also when they entered their fourth or fifth surrogate home (Bush, 1976; Gordon, Gordon, McKnight, Bush, 1976). In other words, since the aim of the years of evaluation research on child welfare was to seek knowledge which would allow policy makers to improve the lot of children and families in trouble, some of that research should have been focused on ways to maintain homes threatened by ill health and acute poverty, and on ways to reduce the number of surrogate homes that dependent and neglected children move through after they leave their own homes. Evaluation researchers should have tested the definitions of the problems by funding agencies and social welfare organizations against definitions by people experiencing the problem.

A question that this argument raises is why clients' definitions of a problem should be trusted more than official definitions. We are not suggesting that, a priori, they should be, but that the logic of all of the participants' definitions should be examined before the researchers determine the direction of their work.

There are, moreover, some reasons for distrusting official definitions. The first is that in the usual situation where social problems have multiple long-term causes, a social welfare organization is often unable for fiscal, legal, and political reasons to intervene in the problem at the stage where intervention would be most effective. Child welfare departments can do nothing about the level of payments mandated by Aid to Families with Dependent Children programs. Physicians do not customarily involve themselves in nutrition programs for poor populations, and promoters of educational excellence for the purpose of promoting equal opportunity have no control over rates of unemployment or discrimination in hiring practices. Evaluation researchers should not be bound by the constraints that sometimes bind the helping professions. Indeed, if evaluation researchers are able to demonstrate where intervention is most effective, they might be able to give the helping professions reason, incentive, and support for changing the direction of their efforts.

The second bias we observed is that social welfare agencies feel bound to use the resources at their disposal even when there is a disparity between the nature of the resources and the nature of the problems the agencies are required to address. The disparity is then obscured when an agency re-describes the problem in terms which make it consonant with its resources. Thus, social welfare agencies with a staff well trained in handling emotional problems tend to define problems, including very practical ones, in terms of emotional deficits, and agencies with federal matching funds for particular categories of people in need may define some of their clients' needs so as to include them in the federal definitions. The trap for evaluation researchers is that they might be unaware of this switching of definitions, accepting at face value definitions presented by agencies eager to retain special funding or to utilize highly trained staff, even though the agencies may be aware of the gap between resource and problem. Clients, however, can be quite resistant to agencies misinterpreting their needs, and when asked about the relationship between what they need and what they are given, can set the record straight. (For examples from the field of public welfare and mental health, see Handler and Hollingsworth, 1969, and Bodgan, 1974.)

The third bias, which in child welfare has the same effect as the second but springs from a different cause, is one familiar to social psychologists under the heading of blaming the victim (Ryan, 1971) or of attributing cause to behavior (Jones and Nisbett, 1972). We noticed a strong tendency in case records of a state social welfare department to re-define practical problems in terms of personal deficiencies. Clients who were initially described as being in care for reasons of family health or inadequate housing were, over a short period, re-described as being in care for reasons of personal failings. This process has two consequences: it ensures that the program instituted to attack the re-defined problem will have no impact on the real problem, and it prohibits the use of the client's strengths and resources to combat the original problem. Hence, "cure" or "amelioration" is seen in terms of doing something to, rather than doing something with, clients.

There is research evidence to suggest that some part of the variance for success in ameliorative programs rests with clients and their families: the classic example is Christopher Jencks's analysis of the part families play in the educational achievement of their children (Jencks, 1972). Programs which ignore that possibility may well end up in the large pile of research projects with no demonstrable effects.

## Clients and Outcome Measures

The clients' role in the choice of outcome measures will obviously depend on the extent to which their definitions of the problems are taken into account, and there will be at least as many competitors for outcome measures as there are versions of the problem. It will often be necessary for researchers to choose among many outcome measures those measures which they think will in fact be affected by the ameliorative program. This is a process in which clients are well equipped to help.

Although ameliorative programs are often designed to cope with fairly narrowly defined problems, the political need to justify the expenditure of program funds and to demonstrate that a whole host of somewhat related problems will be settled at the same time resulted in a broad range of politically important outcome measures being tacked on to the smaller list of outcomes actually relevant to the program. (For a discussion of the "over-advocacy trap in evaluation research," see Campbell, 1969.) The child welfare services we investigated had as their goal the provision of decent homes for children who could no longer live in their own homes. Yet there was a strong political demand to show as well that the effects of placing dependent and neglected children in such homes included dramatic decreases in the rate of juvenile delinquency, teenage pregnancies, and poor scholastic achievement. These effects could not be demonstrated, since it was unrealistic to expect that even an exceptionally supportive home would quickly countermand the influences of a lifetime of chaotic living arrangements and the large number of extra-domestic influences affecting the children's lives. Moreover, some of the homes that clients found very supportive might have appeared inadequate by these standards.

There is more to this problem, however, than realistic versus inflated expectations. The problem raises the issue of the comparative usefulness and respectability of attitudinal and behavioral outcomes, and the part client satisfaction should play in the evaluation of social programs.

*Satisfaction Measures as Outcome Measures.* An ameliorative program can have beneficial or negative effects on a person's life without those effects manifesting themselves in physical behavior. An old person or a ward of the state can feel sustained by good care, a dying person comforted by skillful nursing, and an unemployed worker vastly relieved by income supplements, without those effects having a dramatic effect on traditional outcome measures. There is, of course, a range of programs where such results as better health, testing scores, or work performance, are amenable to behavioral measures, but social services are becoming more involved in "soft services" where such measures are not the most appropriate.

There still remain several problems with the notion that indications of client satisfaction can be adequate measures of the success of social programs. There is some evidence that the question "Are you satisfied with the service you are getting?" invites the response, "Yes," more frequently than expected. A number of studies concerned with the quality of social services report very high degrees of satisfaction as measured by satisfaction scales and find that questions about satisfaction have virtually no power of discrimination (Jacob, 1972; Katz, Gutek, Kahn, Barton, 1975; Moch, 1975). Our research suggests that these results should be treated with caution. First, while we also found that general questions of satisfaction did not discriminate, questions about specific aspects of service delivered, couched in more concrete terms than satisfaction, did discriminate. Children rated different surrogate homes very differently on the amount of time, understanding, attention, care, and affection they received. Second, although most of the scores on these dissatisfaction/satisfaction scales were in the satisfaction part of the scale, there were large differences between mean ratings of different kinds of placements, as much as two points on a five-point scale. Third, children expressed strong preferences among the different placements thay had experienced themselves, that is, when they anchored the comparison in their own experience.

While there is a tendency for clients to resist criticizing social services on quantitative scales of global satisfaction, comparative questions will show that some services are much less satisfactory than others. Furthermore, conversations we had with children in our research indicated an extreme dissatisfaction with placements they had actually rated in the middle of the satisfaction scales. For whatever reason, the inhibition which prevents strong criticism on scaled ratings of services does not carry over to ordinary conversations about services.

The other problem with the use of the term "satisfaction" is that is may confuse the real purpose of services in the same way that process measures do when used to evaluate programs. The term "satisfaction with services" may well cue clients to consider the manner in which the services were delivered rather than the effects the service had on the problems which brought clients to the agency. The same strategy of making satisfaction questions specific, in this case specific to outcomes related to the clients' definition of the problem, would solve the difficulty.

## PART 2: THE BROADER CONSEQUENCES OF CLIENT PARTICIPATION FOR EVALUATION RESEARCH

In Part 1 of this paper we explored the ways in which client participation can improve evaluation researchers' understanding of ameliorative programs. In the process of thinking about the ways in which client information fits into scientific inquiry, we began to consider the premises on which that inquiry is based, and the purposes for which the inquiry is undertaken.

## Patterns or Particles: The Tyranny of the Mean

Evaluation researchers are interested in determining patterns of outcomes of ameliorative programs, and social welfare administrators have similar concerns as they make decisions about the allocation of resources. We discovered such patterns in our research. Dependent and neglected children who could not live at home preferred foster homes to institutions, a finding which, incidentally, contributes to a debate which has been going on for more than 100 years. These differences, we discovered, were highly significant by the customary standards of probability testing. However, while those results help policymakers with some very broad-brush decisions, they are less useful in decisions about the precise allocation of resources to various programs and they do not help social workers make decisions in the cases of individual children.

Under close scrutiny, such findings become less and less clear cut. First, while the average differences between types of care (for example, between foster homes and institutions) were great, there were also differences within each type of placement and the range within each type was so large that the decision which institution to place a child in was as important as the decision whether to place the child in an institution at all. Moreover, certain groups of children went against the norm and preferred institutions. Older children who had been in a large number of surrogate homes were one such group. But even within such a group there were differences of an unpredictable nature. In short, each particular surrogate home and each particular child had to be examined individually before a proper decision could be made about where to place the child. And that entailed ignoring average outcomes to ask individuals what they required. In many sciences a minority, particularly a small minority, is unimportant, but such minorities are the stuff of social welfare.

One response of administrators to dilemmas of this kind is to accept the need for individual decisions but to request personality inventories of individuals so that routine decisions can still be made without the necessity to examine each case on its complex merits. But here again, there is a difficulty which has to do with the connection between average outcomes for individuals and one particular outcome. "Propositions about traits are actuarial statements, valid over situations in the aggregate. . . . The trait measure, however, has negligible power to forecast what the higher scorer is likely to do in any one situation" (Cronbach, 1976: 20).

When even the most exciting patterns occur in data analysis, evaluation researchers need to go beyond them to discover the exceptions to the rule and the wishes of the minority. That finally means consulting each client individually on each individual decision.

We now turn from the question of the usefulness of these patterns to the question of their validity and the possibility of discovering average outcomes and shared understandings of events.

## The Limits of Shared Understanding and the Nature of Evaluation Research

Practitioners of evaluation research are accustomed to long discussions about the validity of their results. Quite often, however, what is logically the first issue in a research project, the issue of whether the chosen dependent and independent variables really represent the situation being studied, is the most ignored in practice. If the translation of real-world events to measures has not been performed well, sophistication in data collection and analysis is a wasted exercise.

But there is a more important problem. Construct validity may not be simply a matter of the accuracy of the symbolic representation of real-world events because the assumption that a unitary representation of those events is possible may itself be invalid. A number of social scientists working in very different contexts have doubted that assumption. Howard Becker, drawing from a variety of research on the sociology of deviance, suggests that in studying complex problems one must always look at the matter from a single actor's perspective because the participants do not have a common point of view, and that means making the decision about whose side the researcher wishes to represent (Becker, 1966). Ricardo Zuniga, reflecting on the usefulness of North American social science for understanding the Allende government in Chile and the revolt against it, asks whether there is a universal common social reality, since that commonality presupposes that people share similar interpretive definitions of situations (Zuniga, 1975). Becker's example is particularly relevant to our discussion of client evaluation; the discordance he describes is caused by people being at different points of what he calls the hierarchy of credibility, a hierarchy where doctors and professors rank highly and patients and students rank poorly. In Zuniga's example, there are two sets of discordant views. The first is between a North American vision of human behavior based on studies conducted in a normal, stable, evolving political climate, and a Chilean vision set in an abnormal, unstable, revolutionary political climate. The second set he observes within Chile, where the right and the left during the Allende government were so divided that the majority of the topics talked about in right-wing newspapers were not even mentioned in the communist press and vice-versa. It was not that right and left-wing papers had different reactions to the same events; they did not have a common reality.

One can imagine a number of characteristics of groups studied by the evaluators of social programs which would divide people in such a way as to forbid a common reality. The denial of a common reality does not, of course, mean that the only alternative is an entirely individualistic, relativistic view of human experience. While some understandings may not be common between groups, they may be common within groups.

The relevance of this discussion for client evaluation is clear. If clients and professionals differ not only in the way they interpret events but also because they have different perceptions of the course of the same event, we are faced with the task not merely of validating opinions by a comparison of different actors' accounts but of choosing between different realities.

A prime example of different realities occurred in our research over the issue of why particular children were obliged to leave home in the first place. The question is critical because the answers to the question should suggest which children should be removed from home and which children might be able to stay at home with the help of supporting services. We return to the example we used at the beginning of the paper. Each of our respondents in that story was asked precisely the same question about the circumstances which led to the break up of the home. The child told us that he left home because one cold night his mother lit a fire in a bucket to warm an unheated apartment, set the place on fire, and was charged with arson. The mother talked about her lost battle with illness, unemployment and consequent poverty; and the social worker talked about the family's social and behavioral inadequacies.

These are not all parts of a single account. They cannot be completely reduced (as a historian might escape the issue) to a mixture of short, intermediate, and long-term causes. And they certainly suggest different remedies. The child's view suggests that the removal of the family to a warm apartment or from the prosecution of a noncomplying landlord might have kept him out of care. The mother might have considered that she could have coped more adequately if she had better medical care or a job. And the social work record would suggest a therapeutic remedy. If evaluation researchers are not to be reduced to the role of conducting studies other people think up, but are interested in understanding as fully as possible the problems in question, on some occasions they will have to choose among such disparate descriptions of key events.

The problem we have set out has been described by others not as one of different realities but as one of different values, a problem which does not hinder, or even make difficult, scientific inquiry. "No one denies, social scientists, unlike mathematicians, deal with topics about which different people do indeed hold incompatible moral and political values," but "wholly irreconcilable values are compatible with the acceptance of the same set of facts" (Runciman, 1975: 57). "As Weber puts it, 'the validity of a prescription as a norm on the one hand and the truth value of an empirical statement on the other hand, lie at absolutely heterogenous levels'" (Runciman, 1975: 54).

Runciman recognizes, however, that there is another class of intellectual activity besides scientific inquiry: the transmission of the sense of an event, behavior, or even culture, which has to do with meaning and which cannot escape individual values. Frequently anthropologists undertake this sort of activity; the exercise will come out differently depending on who is doing the observing and the writing. "Since there cannot be a meaning neutral language in which to talk about meaning, in a way that logic furnishes a topic neutral language in which to talk about validity, the ethnographer's task can never be straightforwardly or exclusively an empirical one" (Runciman, 1975: 91)

Now there might be a variety of ways to square or explain the difference between the view that there are different realities and the view that there are merely different values. For evaluation research, however we settle this problem, there remains the fact that different people's different meanings may result in different definitions of problems and different opinions as to whether differing solutions have worked. If, as policymakers and politicians must be, we are interested not just in whether "A" causes "B" but whether "C" satisfies the needs of "D" perceives he has, we are perforce in the area of meaning as well as explanation, with all the attendant difficulties, and to return to the central topic of this paper, in the area where client views are essential to our understanding.

## CONCLUSION

As evaluation researchers, we may legitimately adopt one of several roles. We might concern ourselves with prediction, while recognizing the limitations of our power to predict in a science which like biology and unlike mechanics is historical and open-ended. Or we might be interested in building theories of human behavior, theories which while containing testable hypotheses go beyond such testing to deal with intellectual constructs that cannot be tested as wholes because they are more than predictions of physical events (Bronowski, 1977). Then there is a more modest option, the proponents of which maintain the view that finally the most realistic task of the "social scientist in each generation is to pin down the contemporary facts" (Cronbach, 1976: 26).

Whichever role we adopt, statistician, theoretician, or historian, the importance of actors' or clients' views of things being done to them and for them remains constant. We shall neither construct useful theories of human behavior or demonstrate recurrent patterns of human behavior in areas where behavior includes private events without the information and perspective of the actors. Nor, at the more practical level of social policy, shall we understand what programs and events alleviate problems unless we consult clients of those programs. Client participation is not a luxury in evaluation research. It is a necessity for the various kinds of understanding we seek from the endeavor.

## REFERENCES

ASTIN, A. W., "Personal and Environmental Determinants of Student Activism," Measurement and Evaluation in Guidance, 1969, 1, 153-162.
BECKER, H. S., "Whose Side Are We On?" Social Problems, 1966, 14, 239-247.
BOGDAN, R., Being Different: The Autobiography of Jane Fry, New York: Wiley, 1974.
BRONOWSKI, J., "Humanism and the Growth of Knowledge," in J. Bronowski, A Sense of the Future, P. E. Ariotti (ed.), Cambridge Mass.: MIT Press, 1977, 74-104.
BUSH, M., A Client Evaluation of Foster Care, Unpublished dissertation, Northwestern University, Evanston, Ill., 1976.

CAMPBELL, D. T., "Reforms as Experiments," American Psychologist, 1969, 24, (4), 409-429.

——————, "Qualitative Knowing in Action Research," Kurt Lewin Address, Society for the Psychological Study of Social Issues, Meeting with the American Psychological Association, New Orleans, September 1, 1974.

CHOW, S., Evaluation and Accountability in Care for the Elderly, Unpublished paper, School of Education, Northwestern University, Evanston, Ill., 1977.

CLOWARD, R. A., and PIVEN, F. F., "The Professional Bureaucracies as Influence Systems," in M. Silberman, (ed.) The Role of Government in Promoting Social Change, New York: Columbia University School of Social Work, 1965.

CRONBACH, L. J., "Between the Two Disciplines of Scientific Psychology," American Psychologist, 1975, 30, (2), 116-127.

GEISER, R. L., The Illusion of Caring: Children in Foster Care, Boston: Beason Press, 1973.

GEISMAR, R. L., "Thirteen Evaluative Studies," in E. J. Mullen and J. R. Dumpson (eds.), Evaluation of Social Intervention, San Francisco: Jossey-Bass, 1972, 15-39.

GORDON, A. C., GORDON, M., MCKNIGHT, J. L., and BUSH, M., "Experiences of Wardship: Interim Report No. 2," Center for Urban Affairs, Northwestern University, Evanston, Ill., 1976.

GORDON, L. K., "Bureaucratic Competence and Success in Dealing with Public Bureaucracies," Social Problems, 1975, 23 (2), 197-208.

HAMPSHIRE, S., Thought and Action, London: Chatto and Windus, 1965.

HANDLER, J. F., and HOLLINGSWORTH, E. J., "The Administration of Social Services and the Structure of Dependency: The Views of AFDC Recipients," Social Service Review, 1969, 43, (4), 406-421.

HARRE, R., and SECORD, P. F., The Explanation of Social Behavior, Oxford: Basil Blackwell, 1972.

JENCKS, C., et al., Inequality: A Reassessment of the Effect of Family and Schooling in America, New York: Basic Books, 1972.

JENKINS, S., and NORMAN, E., Filial Deprivation and Foster Care, New York: Columbia University Press, 1972.

JONES, E. E., and NISBETT, E., "The Actor and the Observer: Divergent Perceptions of the Causes of Behavior," in E. E. Jones et al., (eds.) Attribution: Perceiving the Causes of Behavior, Morristown, N. J., General Learning Press, 1972.

KADUSHIN, A., Child Welfare Services, New York: Macmillan, 1974.

KATZ, D., GUTEK, B. A., KAHN, R. L., and BARTON, E., Bureaucratic Encounters: A Pilot Study in the Evaluation of Government Services, Ann Arbor: University of Michigan, Institute for Social Research, 1975.

MISCHEL, T., (ed.) Human Action: Conceptual and Empirical Issues, New York: Academic Press, 1969.

MOCH, M., "Quality of Service Measurement, Program and Instrumentation," Social Security Administration Contract, No. 600-75-0141, Nov. 24, 1975.

MULLEN, E. J. and DUMPSON, J. R., Evaluation of Social Intervention, San Francisco: Jossey-Bass, 1972.

MULLEN, E. J., CHAZIN, R. M., and FELDSTEIN, D. M., Preventing Chronic Dependency, New York: Community Service Society of New York, 1970.

PERLMAN, H. H., "Once More with Feeling," in E. J. Mullen and J. R. Dumpson (eds.), Evaluation of Social Intervention, San Francisco: Jossey-Bass, 1972, 191-210.

RUNCIMAN, W. G., A Critique of Max Weber's Philosophy of Social Science, Cambridge: Cambridge University Press, 1972.

RYAN, W., Blaming the Victim, New York: Vintage Books, 1972.

SEGAL, S. P., "Research on the Outcome of Social Work Therapeutic Interventions: A Review of the Literature," Journal of Health and Social Behavior, 1972, 13, 3-17.

SPRINGER, M., The Future of Mental Hospitals, Unpublished paper, School of Education, Northwestern University, Evanston, Ill., 1977.

WACKS, M., "Consumer Attitudes toward Transit Service: An Interpretive Review," American Institute of Planners Journal, January, 1976, 96-104.

ZUNIGA, R., "The Experimenting Society and Radical Social Reform: The Role of the Social Scientist in Chile's Unidad Popular Experience," American Psychologist, 1975, 30 (2), 99-115.